A PRIDE OF
EAGLES

A PRIDE OF
EAGLES

A HISTORY OF THE RHODESIAN AIR FORCE

BERYL SALT

30° South Publishers (Pty) Ltd

Helion & Company Ltd

Also by Beryl Salt:
The Valiant Years
A History of Rhodesia
Encyclopaedia of Rhodesia (co-authored)

First published in 2000 by Covos Day Books (ISBN 0-620-23759-7)
Second edition co-published in 2015 by:

HELION & COMPANY LTD
26 Willow Road
Solihull
West Midlands
B91 1UE
England
Tel. 0121 705 3393
Fax 0121 711 4075
email: info@helion.co.uk
website: www.helion.co.uk

and

30° SOUTH PUBLISHERS (PTY) LTD.
16 Ivy Road
Pinetown
Durban 3610
South Africa
www.30degreessouth.co.za

Designed & typeset by SA Publishing Services (kerrincocks@gmail.com)
Cover design by SA Publishing Services, South Africa
Maps and diagrams by Genevieve Edwards

Printed in UK by Lightning Source, Milton Keynes, Buckinghamshire
Printed in South Africa by Pinetown Printers, Durban, KwaZulu-Natal

ISBN (UK) 978-1-908916-26-6
ISBN (South Africa) 978-1-920143-73-2

British Library Cataloguing-in-Publication Data
A catalogue record for this book is available from the British Library

The publishers would like to express their special thanks to John Reid-Rowland for his mammoth effort with the indexing and proof-reading of this book. His immeasurable contribution, coupled with his encylopedic knowledge of the subject, has ensured a book that is vastly improved on the original edition.

To Dickie,
who painstakingly edited the earlier chapters and was always there to help and encourage me.
Thank you so very much. I am only sorry you were not here to see the end of the story.
Beryl

Table of Contents

List of maps and charts

Glossary

A/A	Anti-aircraft
AK	Kalashnikov or AK-47. This was a Russian-designed weapon manufactured in Europe and China. It became a standard weapon for guerrilla movements world-wide. It was also used by the Rhodesian Security Forces. It was easy to use and could withstand bad treatment.
Ammo	Ammunition.
ANC	African National Congress (South Africa).
ANC	African National Council (Rhodesia).
AP	Anti-personnel land-mine.
ASP/ASAP	As soon as possible.
Avgas	Aviation fuel.
Bailiff	Member of the BSAP.
Blues	Army term for the air force.
Bok-bok	A game in which two teams compete. One team lines up, one behind the other. The first man in line holds onto a tree or other solid object; the rest bend down and hold the thighs of the man in front. The second team, one after the other, leap onto the backs of the first team, landing as far up the line as possible until all the members of the second team are sitting on the backs of the first team. The feet of the leapers must not touch the ground once they have landed. The object of the second team is to bring the first team to the ground.
Browns	Air force term for the army.
BSAP	British South Africa Police.
Bundu	Bush.
CAA	Central African Airways.
Call sign	A group of operators, each group with its own radio identification numbe.
Camo	Camouflage.
CAOS	Combined Air Observers' School and Airgunners' School.
casevac/ed	Casualty evacuation.
Chaminuka	A famous Shona spirit medium.
Chimurenga	A Shona word for the War of Liberation
CID	Criminal Investigation Department of the BSAP
CIO	Central Intelligence Organization.
CO	Commanding Officer
COIN	Counter Insurgency.
ComOps	Combined Operations, central planning and coordinating organization.
CT	Acronym for communist terrorist
DA	District Assistant–– the black assistants who worked with district commissioners to administer black rural areas.
Dak	Dakota.
DFC	Distinguished Flying Cross.
DFM	Distinguished Flying Medal.

DR	Dead Reckoning.
DSO	Distinguished Service Order.
DZ	Dropping Zone.
EFTS	Elementary Flying Training School.
ETA	Estimated Time of Arrival.
FACP	Forward Air Force Command Post.
FAF	Forward Air Field.
Fireforce	Highly mobile group of troops ferried by helicopter direct to a contact with the enemy. Each flight of troop-carrying G-Cars was escorted by a K-Car, helicopter gunship.
Flak	Anti-aircraft fire.
FN	(Fabrique Nationale) Belgian-designed 7.62 semi-automatic and automatic NATO weapon on general issue to Rhodesia Security Forces.
Fred/Freddie	Nickname for Frelimo.
Frelimo	The Front for the Liberation of Mozambique.
G-Car	Troop-carrying Alouette helicopter.
Gee	Radar aid to navigation and target identification.
Gomo	Hill or mountain (Shona).
Gook	A term used for insurgents—originally used by Americans fighting in the Far East.
Hooterville	Air Force slang for Gwelo. Later used for Mabalauto, an airfield on the south-western border of the Gonarezhou game reserve.
Hot extraction	A lift out by helicopter under dangerous circumstances. A special winch and harness could be used so that the helicopter did not have to land.
Hot pursuit	Cross-border pursuit of the enemy.
IFF	Identification—friend or foe.
Indaba	Traditional meeting of African chiefs.
ITW	Initial Training Wing.
Jesse	Thick thorn bush.
JOC	Joint Operational Centre. A local military HQ where police, the army, the air force and special branch cooperated and pooled their intelligence.
K-Car	(Killing Car) A heavily armed Alouette.
Koppie	Hill.
Kraals	Groups of African huts.
Lemon	An operation that came to nothing.
Loc	Location.
Lynx	Cessna 337.
LZ	Landing Zone.
M/T	Motor transport.
MAP	Ministry of Aircraft Production.
Mayday	International distress call.
ME	Middle East.
MFC	Military Forces Commendation.
MNR	Mozambique National Resistance, an anti-Frelimo organization.
MP	Member of Parliament.

NATO	North Atlantic Treaty Organization.
NCO	Non-commissioned Officer.
NS	National Service/Serviceman.
OAU	Organization of African Unity.
OCTU	Operational Conversion Training Unit.
Op	Operation.
OP	Observation Post.
OTU	Operational Training Unit.
Pan	International emergency call.
ParaDak	Dakota-carrying paratroopers.
PATU	Police Anti-Terrorist Unit.
PF	Patriotic Front, an alliance between Robert Mugabe's ZANU and Joshua Nkomo's ZAPU.
PJI	Parachute Jumping Instructor.
POW	Prisoner of War.
Prang	Aircraft crash or attack, depending on context.
PRAW	Police Reserve Air Wing
PV	Protected Village. A fenced and heavily guarded area where villagers were resettled to prevent their giving aid to the insurgents.
R&R	Rest and recuperation.
R/T	Radio telephone.
RAAC	Rhodesian Air Askari Corp.
RAAF	Royal Australian Air Force.
RAF	Royal Air Force.
Rams	Radio Activated Marker System.
RANA	Rhodesian and Nyasaland Airways.
RAR	Rhodesian African Rifles.
Rat pack	Ration pack.
Recce	Reconnaissance.
RF	Rhodesian Front, a political party.
RLI	Rhodesian Light Infantry.
RPD	Portable light machine gun.
RPG-7	Rocket-propelled grenade
RR	Rhodesia Regiment (territorials).
RWS	Rhodesian Women's Service.
Sam	Surface-to-air missile, guided by infra-red. SA-7 was shoulder-launched.
SAP	South African Police.
SAS	Special Air Service (Rhodesian).
SB	Special Branch.
SCR	Silver Cross of Rhodesia.
SF	Security Forces.
Sidewinder	Air-to-air missile.
Sitrep	Situation report.
SKS	(Simonov) 7.62-millimetre semi-automatic carbine.
Sneb	White phosphorus air-to-ground rocket.

SOP	Standard Operational Procedure.
SS	Selous Scouts.
Strela/SAM-7	Soviet-manufactured heat-seeking missile.
Sunray	Leader.
Swapo	South West African People's Organization.
TA/TF	Territorial Army, Territorial Force.
Terr	Nickname for a terrorist, insurgent.
Troopie	A Rhodesian soldier.
TTL	Tribal Trust Land.
U/S	Unserviceable.
UANC	United African National Council (formerly ANC) of Bishop Abel Muzorewa.
UDI	Unilateral Declaration of Independence.
UN	United Nations.
Unimog	2.5-tonne Mercedes 4×4 truck.
VC	Victoria Cross.
VE Day	Victory in Europe.
Vlei	Marshy low-lying area.
WO	Warrant Officer.
WOP	Wireless Operator.
WVS	Women's Voluntary Service.
ZANLA	Zimbabwe African National Liberation Army, ZANU's military wing. Trained mainly by the Chinese.
ZANU	Zimbabwe African National Union of Robert Mugabe, the political wing.
ZAPU	Zimbabwe African People's Union of Joshua Nkomo, political wing.
ZIPRA	Zimbabwe People's Revolutionary Army, ZAPU's military wing. Trained mainly by Russians.

Author's notes and acknowledgments

The book which follows covers the proud history of an elite force from the time in 1920 when the idea of flying was an impossible dream for most people, until that day in 1980 when the Rhodesian Air Force ceased to be and became the Air Force of Zimbabwe.

The time period is 60 years. The idea of having a history of the force came into being in the early 1970s when the Rhodesian Air Force was considering celebrations for the 25th anniversary of its re-formation following World War II. Alan Cockle was then PRO and he suggested that a book covering the period would be an appropriate form of recognition. I was asked by Wing Commander Len Pink, to write this official history. As the project developed, there were long discussions about where we should begin. Obviously, the early history needed telling. The pre- World War II work to create an air force and the war-time exploits of the Rhodesian squadrons must be included. Finally, an appropriate date seemed to be that on which the first heavier-than-air machine landed on Rhodesian soil—1920—and the arrival of the *Silver Queen*.

So we had a starting date, and a closing date—November 1972—with a publication date set for 1975. However, by early 1973 the Bush War had escalated. The closing date of November 1972 was no longer the correct one. Every day new drama was being lived. My brief changed. Keep what you have—keep writing. I did.

The years passed and the battles raged. Then came the end. It soon became obvious that this book could not be published in Zimbabwe at that time in the way it had been written. In 1982, I left for Johannesburg carrying the book in various forms with me. In a new country, earning a living became the number one priority, and the years passed. Still I gathered information. It was beginning to look as though the book was destined to remain a manuscript. Then on a visit to Zimbabwe, I met Peter Cooke, who introduced me to Chris Cocks, and the rest—as they say—is history.

This is not the story of seven years of Bush War. It is the narrative of a fighting force, which grew from an ambitious idea in the minds of a few far-sighted men, through the crawling and toddling stages into a self-contained air force unique for its size. And more especially, it is the story of the men and women who dedicated themselves to that force and in some cases gave their lives.

So many people helped me in so many different ways that it is impossible to name you all and specify your particular contributions. Please accept my deepest thanks to all of you who gave so freely of your time and your memories to create this book, and know that it could not have been written without your help. My particular thanks go to Anne and Peter Cooke for their detailed work on the Roll of Honour and to Bill Sykes for tirelessly 'editing' and chasing up all the personal stories. Also particular thanks to Eric Smith, Archie Wilson, John Deall, Peter Petter-Bowyer, Chris Dams, Len Pink, Paul Hill, Charles Buchan, Tol Janeke and William Hunter Johnson.

Beryl Salt

Foreword

A wide range of authoritative books is in print regarding the contribution and sacrifice made by Rhodesian servicemen and women in support of king and country, and subsequently in the defence of their homeland. However, apart from that excellent narrative *Bush Horizons*, which portrays the progression of aviation in Rhodesia from 1896 to 1940, there exists no recognized publication that focuses specifically on the air force from its inception in October 1940 to 30th September 1980 when, with the advent of Zimbabwe, its name, purpose and direction changed, so ending a chapter of magnificence in the saga of a unique, highly motivated and cost-effective service.

This book, *A Pride of Eagles*, written by Beryl Salt, will go a long way to filling a void in the life and times of the Rhodesian Air Force. This story is a blend of historical facts and personal narratives, which combine to give an insight into the unsurpassed contribution, in proportion to the population, made by our airmen to the ultimate victory in the air battles of World War II. In addition to manning the three designated Rhodesian squadrons, a considerable number of our airmen served with distinction in Royal Air Force squadrons, operating in all the theatres of war in which these formations were engaged. Many never returned. I take the opportunity here to mention that this valuable manuscript would never have surfaced had it not been for the dedicated research, and collation of data, carried out by those two outstanding Rhodesians, Wing Commander Peter Cooke and his wife Anne. These two, together with their team of willing helpers and the enthusiasm of Beryl Salt, combined to bring this project to fruition. We owe them a debt of gratitude. I therefore feel honoured to have been invited to write the foreword to *A Pride of Eagles* and have great pleasure in doing so.

As I was a foundation member of the Southern Rhodesian Air Force from its inception in October 1939, and served through all its stages until my retirement in April 1973, there are two factors that I especially recall with pride. One such memory is that of the wonderful bond of comradeship and selfless cooperation that prevailed among our splendid security forces, whether operationally or in friendly inter-service rivalry on the sportsfield. This quality and hallmark of the Rhodesian psyche stems, no doubt, from that momentous day, 11th July 1890, when the Pioneer Column and their escort, a contingent of the British South Africa Company Police, each inspired by the all-pervading spirit of Cecil John Rhodes, the founder, crossed the Shashi River into Matabeleland. The other factor is the magnificent response of air force personnel, regular and reserve, in their determination to combat and overcome all facets of the repressive onset of international sanctions, imposed over 15 years following the Unilateral Declaration of Independence.

It had been predicted that our air force would be rendered ineffective in a matter of months. The assumption was that this would result from the absence of necessary spares and ordnance for our aircraft, with particular reference to the non-availability of starter cartridges, considered essential items for starting the engines of our jet aircraft. But how wrong they were! Thanks to the irrepressible spirit and expertise of all ranks, these hurdles were overcome by one means or another. Not only did the air force remain cost effective, but also actually expanded its operational capability, including an improved radius of action in strike potential. Thus the redesign of the aircraft roundels, to include a centrepiece depicting our traditional military lion holding aloft a tusk in a gesture of defiance can be said, in retrospect, to have been singularly appropriate.

With Rhodesia facing, virtually alone, the unimpeded incursion of guerrilla factions on a large scale, the new generation of ground and aircrews was ready and professionally more than able to fulfil both its tactical and strategic roles with consummate success. *A Pride of Eagles* will perpetuate in print a tribute to Rhodesia's airmen who served their country gallantly on the ground and in the air, in war and in peace, and will remain a memorial to those who laid down their lives for a cause they believed in. I am proud to have been associated with such men.

Air Marshal A.O.G. Wilson, ICD, OBE, DFC (US), RhAF (Retd)
Queensland
Australia
14th May 2000

CHAPTER 1

First flights

It had been arranged that the day of the arrival of the first aeroplane should be a general holiday as from the time the warning guns were fired. When at 10 am on Friday the reports echoed through the town, all work stopped automatically and there was a general rush to the racecourse. The evacuation of the town was amazingly rapid and complete. Within half an hour of the signal, every shop and office and even banks and the post office were silent as on a Sunday. Not merely did the Europeans make haste to the aerodrome but the whole native population streamed there. (Bulawayo Chronicle)

It was 5th March 1920 when the first heavier-than-air machine made its appearance in the skies north of Bulawayo. In no time the grandstand at the racecourse was packed to overflowing while the Southern Rhodesia Volunteers band stood ready to provide a musical welcome, and mounted police under Major Tomlinson and Lieutenant MacLean endeavoured to keep the crowd clear of the actual landing area.

Among the crowds of natives there were numerous individuals who rejoiced at the prospect of proving that they were indeed the tellers of truth. These were boys who saw service in the East Africa Campaign and therefore had seen the wonderful 'great birds' in action. It appears that such tales as they had to tell were firmly rejected by the mass of the natives. Hence the satisfied expressions on the faces of the veterans.

The watchers were divided between admiration and apprehension as the machine began to descend in graceful spirals, its engines shut off. It lightly touched the ground and ran over the grass daintily; then swung round until it stopped in the centre of the ground facing the grandstands. (Bulawayo Chronicle)

The cheering crowd surged forward to greet the heroes of the moment—Pierre van Ryneveld and Christopher Quintin Brand as they stepped down from the oily *Silver Queen*.

Three other men vital to the enterprise, whose names are hardly ever mentioned, were the aircraft mechanics: Mr Burton from Rolls-Royce, Flight Sergeant Newman (who took over from Burton at Cairo) and Sergeant Sherratt. They flew in the *Silver Queen* to Bulawayo, then finished the trip to Cape Town by rail.

As so often happens, these backroom boys received little glory but it was their hard work and expertise that made this first London to South Africa flight possible. In fact the expedition had been plagued with mechanical problems and during one forced landing at Korosko, near Wadi Halfa, the aircraft ran into a pile of large boulders and the fuselage was irreparably damaged. A second Vimy was supplied by the Royal Air Force, Middle East at the request of the South African government.

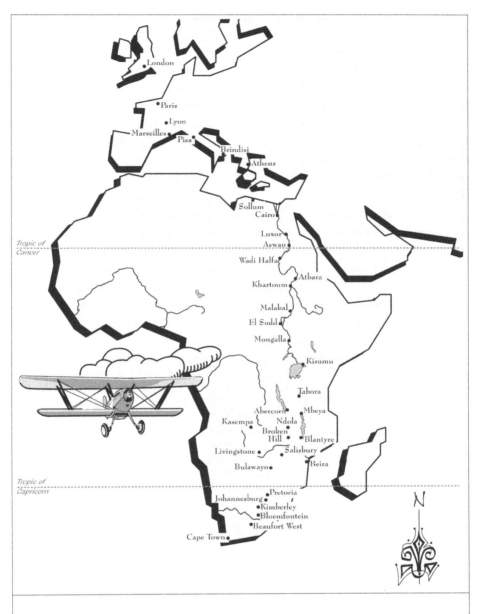

ROUTE FOLLOWED BY MOST
EARLY FLIGHTS DOWN AFRICA

Mr Burton was replaced by Flight Sergeant Newman and so it was the *Silver Queen II* that landed at Bulawayo. This plane had a new Vickers Vimy airframe but was powered by the two, still serviceable, 350 hp Rolls-Royce Eagle engines, and carried the long-range fuel tanks that came from the original aircraft.

Early on the morning of the following day, 6th March, spectators eager to witness the *Silver Queen's* take-off once more flocked to the racecourse. The aircraft's engines were tested for a full 30 minutes and at 07h55 the *Silver Queen* taxied out to the downwind extremity of her take-off path; the engines roared and the aircraft lumbered across the field. Her speed was agonizingly slow. The spectators held their breath as she laboured toward the tree line. There was a faint cheer as she lifted from the ground, her wheels brushing the bushes as she scrabbled for height. For what seemed an eternity her wheels dragged across the treetops and then she sank from sight and there came the horrifying sound of a grinding crash. The epic journey was over. Aston Redrup, a civil aviation pioneer, who was among the crowd that day, says that he believed her fuel load was too heavy. He remembers that after the crash the ground was awash with petrol and that numerous bystanders were happily lighting cigarettes and throwing their matches down. The aircraft was a total write-off but, fortunately, the crew escaped with only cuts and bruises.

The *Bulawayo Chronicle* spoke for everyone:

> *It is difficult to realize that the pitiful wreck is the remains of that thing of wondrous beauty that shot out of the northern sky on Friday and circled down to earth before the enraptured gaze of thousands.*

That might have been the end of the first flight down Africa had it not been for the generosity of General Smuts, Prime Minister of the Union of South Africa. He had stepped in when the first crash occurred and organized the gift of *Silver Queen II* and now once more he came to the rescue, telegraphing that another aircraft would be made available. The replacement was a DH 9, named Voortrekker and it was this aircraft in which Van Ryneveld and Quintin Brand finally reached Cape Town on 20th March 45 days after leaving England. Many years later one of Van Ryneveld's sons and a nephew of Quintin Brand were both destined to serve with the Royal Air Force and continue a great tradition.

Forty-five days and three aircraft to cover the distance between London and Cape Town! The flight proved that such a journey was possible but it also demonstrated that air travel was unreliable, difficult and even downright dangerous; not to be undertaken lightly. However, despite all the obvious problems there were men in Rhodesia far-seeing enough to realize that the aeroplane was here to stay and that it had much to offer in a country of vast distances and bad roads. After all, in the 1920s it was a hazardous enough undertaking to stray outside the main centres in a car. Roads were little more than tracks through the bush, and tended to be sand traps or muddy bogs, while bridges were non-existent. One traveller writing during this period, complained in a letter to the newspaper about the number of farm gates that had to be opened and closed on the main road from Rhodesia to South Africa.

Pioneers in the air
However, long before the arrival of the *Silver Queen*, there were those who had an ambition to take to the skies. Among them Arthur Harris, late air marshal, who was living in Rhodesia at the outbreak of World War I in 1914. He joined the 1st Rhodesia Regiment but a year later transferred to the Royal Flying Corps. Another young man who once worked on a gold mine at Gatooma, Hazelton Nicholl, also rose to the rank of Air Vice-Marshal. While G.H. Hackwill, later to serve as member of parliament for the constituency of Lomagundi, earned

a place in the record books for the first unqualified victory at night in a combat between two aircraft. On the night of 28th/29th January 1918, he and Lieutenant Banks were on patrol in a pair of Sopwith Camels of No 44 Squadron, when they encountered a German raiding force heading towards London. Captain Hackwill succeeded in shooting one of the enemy Gotha aircraft down in flames. Quintin Brand also shot down a Gotha over Kent in 1918, the propeller of which is in his daughter-in-law's house in Harare.

Major Robert Hudson MC, Rhodesia's first minister of defence and later chief justice, commanded a squadron in France as did his brother Major Frank Hudson MC. During the war the idea of raising money to buy aircraft caught the public imagination. Five hundred pounds was donated in two weeks during July 1915. In all, Rhodesians donated enough to buy four aircraft at £1,500 each. Lieutenant A.R. Browne of Umvuma was killed in a dogfight in December 1915 while flying Gatooma No 1, an aircraft that had been purchased with money raised by the people of the Midlands town.

In all, Rhodesia contributed over £200,000 and nearly 6,000 men to the Allied war effort between 1914 and 1918 at a time when the total European population numbered fewer than 24,000. She could ill afford the 700 dead.

The first commercial flights

A little more than a month after the *Silver Queen*'s arrival in Bulawayo the first flying company was registered in Rhodesia. It was titled Air Road Motors Ltd and did not actually own any vehicles or aircraft, but it was a beginning. The company acted as local agents for South African Aerial Transport Ltd and it was not long before the first appeared in the *Bulawayo Chronicle*.

> *Air-Road Motors have pleasure in announcing that they are booking flights per the 'Rhodesian Queen' during show week. Apply Aviation Manager, corner of Main Street and Fifth Avenue.*

The aircraft, a Le Rhône Avro flown by Captain C.R.Thompson and Earle Rutherford, arrived in Bulawayo on Sunday 23rd May 1920. It was named the Rhodesia, and it was in this aircraft that hundreds of air-minded Bulawayo residents had their first flight. It moved on to become the first aircraft to land at Gwelo on 29th May and continued via Que Que and Gatooma to Salisbury, where it arrived on June 11th. For thousands of Rhodesians it was their first sight of a flying machine and hundreds took the opportunity of a flip, the cost being £3 per passenger per flight of ten minutes or £5 for 20 minutes.

One of the most active and enthusiastic pioneers of aviation in southern Africa was Major Allister Miller DSO who had served with the Royal Flying Corps in France during World War I. He had been the founder of South African Aerial Transports Ltd which unfortunately was dissolved soon after the Rhodesian tour, but he had obviously seen enough to believe that flying had a future because during the winter of 1922 he launched a new company: Rhodesian Aerial Tours. His plan was to establish regular flights between the larger centres and his aircraft was the main attraction at the Bulawayo Show in June that year. When two European prisoners escaped from a hard labour gang at the show ground, Major Miller joined the search. The prisoners finding there was nowhere much to go, eventually returned of their own accord, but Major Miller had made history, having undertaken the first aerial search in Rhodesia.

On July 5th, Major Miller took off from Bulawayo in Matabele with his first fare-paying passenger, Mr M.J. O'Donnell of P D Whisky fame. They flew via several towns in the Midlands to Salisbury for Show Week in August. All seemed to be going well until 13th August.

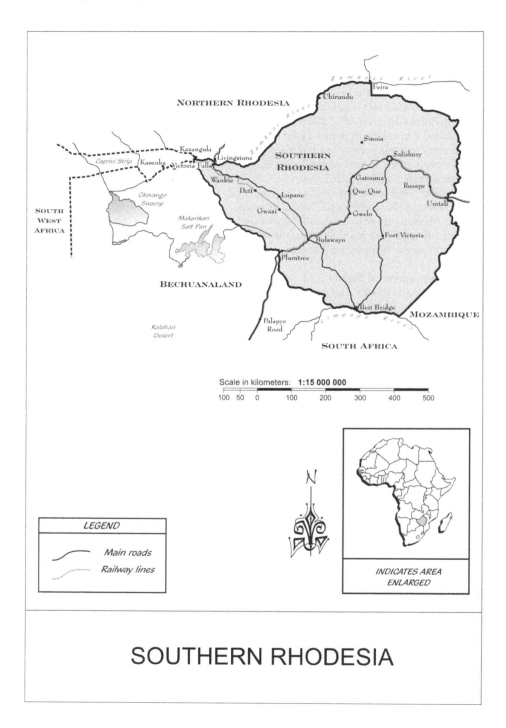

SOUTHERN RHODESIA

Major Miller left Salisbury on Sunday morning...with Mr Walker (mechanic) and Mr R. Markel, president of Rhodesian Maize Breeders Association as passengers. The plane made an excellent flight and rose to 11,000 feet before sighting Rusape.

Apparently they made an excellent landing but the pilot had to:

...take off on sandy ground, slightly uphill. The wind caused the plane to swerve into some small trees that caught the right wing and caused considerable damage. (Bulawayo Chronicle)

The Matabele never flew again, the company that had lost its only aircraft closed, and Major Miller returned to South Africa. Although it may have seemed at the time that the whole project was a complete waste of time and money, Major Miller had found time to lecture the cadets while he was in Bulawayo. These lectures and the thrill of seeing a flying machine and even of being able to ride in one must surely have stirred some young imaginations and that undoubtedly paid dividends later.

It was to be three years before any further air activity occurred; then in July 1925, two DH 9 aircraft flew from South Africa via Bulawayo to Livingstone. The pilots, members of the Union of South Africa Defence Force, were Lieutenant Tasker and Captain Charles Meredith (later to become Air Vice-Marshal Sir Charles Meredith), prime mover of the Empire Training Scheme and the establishment of the Rhodesian Air Training Group (RATG) during World War II.

Early in 1926, Sir Alan Cobham flying a DH 50 visited Bulawayo to survey a possible air route for Imperial Airways Ltd. The same year saw the first military flight through Rhodesia. Four Royal Air Force Fairey IIIDs under the command of Wing Commander C.W.H. Pulford OBE AFC, flew from Cairo to Cape Town and back calling at Bulawayo on the outward and return journeys. In later years this became an annual event and led to the establishment of close ties between Rhodesia and the Royal Air Force.

Another event of even greater significance occurred that same year. It was arranged with the Air Council in Britain that the Royal Air Force would accept two candidates each half year from Southern Rhodesia as apprentices and one candidate nominated by the governor for a cadetship at the Royal Air Force College at Cranwell. These men, trained by the Royal Air Force together with Royal Air Force personnel seconded to Rhodesia, were to provide the basis for Rhodesia's own air force.

The Rhodesian Aviation Syndicate Bulawayo Flying Scheme was the headline in *The Chronicle* on 9th August 1927.

Commercial aviation should be established in Bulawayo in definite form in a few days from now. A firm with the attractive title of The Rhodesian Aviation Syndicate has been formed. A de Havilland aeroplane is all but ready for flight; and Captain J.D. Mail AFC, a pilot with an excellent war record and 3,000 flying hours to his credit will make an experimental trip in a day or so. The venture has been chiefly financed by Mr Harry C. Stewart, a mine owner and rancher at Filabusi. The aeroplane, which is a three-seater, was at one time the property of Captain Mail. Messrs Stewart, A.G. Hay, Mail and Redrup are the members of the syndicate and Mr John Coghlan is acting in a legal capacity. (Bulawayo Chronicle)

Captain Mail had come from Natal, early in 1927, to join Cairns Motor and Cycle Supply Company, bringing his aeroplane, Baby Tank, with him. It was a World War I surplus DH 6 and it made the journey from Natal, somewhat ignominiously, by rail. With the assistance of Aston Redrup, the aircraft was unpacked, reassembled and by the middle of August was ready for flight. The *Bulawayo Chronicle* carried a vivid description:

> *With a spluttering roar 'Baby Tank' left the racecourse and soared into the air on Sunday 14th afternoon for its first flight in Rhodesia. During the past year or two Bulawayo has welcomed quite a number of aeroplanes and airmen. But this, the first flight of the first machine of the Rhodesian Aviation Syndicate was something different, for it spoke of the initiative and determination of Rhodesians.*

Captain Mail cabled the news to the manufacturers, de Havilland, in England. They were suitably impressed and cabled back:

> *We are very pleased and interested to receive your long cable of August 18th. We congratulate you heartily upon your enterprise in getting the old DH 6 into the air again. There must be very few DH 6s left in the world.* (Bulawayo Chronicle)

Six weeks later came the first charter. The Duc de Nemours who had been invited to dine with the headmaster of Plumtree School, wished to travel the 60 miles (96km) from Bulawayo to Plumtree by air! At 16h30 on 20th September Baby Tank took to the air, watched by an enthusiastic crowd. To think that one could, in just a few minutes make a journey of so many miles! Sadly, on this occasion it was not to be. Just about eleven miles out Baby Tank developed engine trouble and her pilot was forced to make an emergency landing in a clearing.

The pilot and his passenger pushed the aircraft into a nearby ploughed field and a take-off was attempted but one of the wheels struck a tree stump, the aircraft slewed round and smashed into a tree. There was nothing to do but walk the five miles back to Bellevue and hitch a lift into town, which must have been more than a little humiliating. The aircraft was towed back to the Drill Hall for repairs but it was never to fly again.

It may seem that flying in Rhodesia was particularly hazardous but it must be remembered that the frames were little more than wood and canvas and the engines far from reliable. True, the first Atlantic crossing had been completed in 1919 but it was a feat not repeated until Charles Lindbergh achieved the impossible in this very year, 1927. Everyone said he was mad. This same month Great Britain won the Schneider Trophy and the event was reported in *The Chronicle* complete with the news that one competitor completed one lap at 299 mph—the highest speed ever reached by man!

At the time of Baby Tank's crash, Mr Hay was in London. In reply to urgent messages, he visited de Havilland and not only arranged the purchase of a Cirrus Moth Mark II, but also negotiated a franchise with the company, obtaining the agencies in Northern and Southern Rhodesia for de Havilland aircraft and Cirrus engines. These were the first such franchises obtained in southern Africa.

These negotiations took some time and the new aircraft, later named Bulawayo, did not arrive until 30th December 1927. By this time the people of Bulawayo had already seen a Cirrus Moth, piloted by Lieutenant R.R. Bentley of the SAAF on his record-breaking flight from England. He completed the journey in 26 days and still took time to thrill the citizens with a display of aerobatics during his stopover in November.

The first Moths were manufactured in 1925 and were powered by Cirrus engines developed on de Havilland's suggestion from war surplus Renault 8-cylinder engines then available for 25 shillings. The task of adapting these engines was undertaken by Major Frank B. Halford. Later de Havilland engineers designed their own engines for the famous Gipsy Moth. A further variation was the Leopard Moth, a luxury three-seater monoplane with a high wing, with which de Havilland won the King's Cup Air Race in 1933.

On January 11th 1928, Bulawayo undertook its first private charter flight to Nantwich Ranch near Wankie and in February, Captain Mail delighted the crowds at Salisbury Racecourse with a display of aerobatics and took numerous passengers on flips. At the end of February, Douglas Mail left the Aviation Syndicate and his place was taken by Mr Wright. Only four days later, Wright with Major Newman as passenger, crashed close to Milton School in Bulawayo. The aircraft was a complete wreck.

So much, for the moment, for civil aviation but what about the military side? Well, things were stirring but painfully slowly. In 1928, Colonel Watson CMG DSO, the commandant of the Southern Rhodesia Defence Force, reported that one member of the territorial force was available with a Moth machine for use in emergencies. He hoped that more young men showing an interest in aviation would become available to the territorial force.

What they were to do once they became available is unclear, as there was no one on the staff of the defence force with any special interest in, or knowledge of, aviation matters. The defence force owned no aircraft and so far landing fields only existed at Bulawayo, Salisbury and Gwelo, although sites had been selected at Umtali, Gatooma and Que Que.

Horses, it appears from the records, were considered much more useful and reliable than the new-fangled flying machines! Horses, in fact, were taken on strength and struck off the roll with as much ceremony as territorial force officers with flying experience. The Permanent Staff Corps' orders for as late as 1935 still listed the names of riding horses, though their appointments were not promulgated.

What with the demise of the Aviation Syndicate's only aircraft, and a singular lack of interest from the Defence Department, 1928 was a year of no progress. However, interest in aviation was sustained by a series of visitors. Sir Alan Cobham returned in a borrowed Moth with the object of organizing a flying-boat service from England to the Cape via Livingstone. Lady Heath flew an Avro Avian solo from Cape Town to London, and the Honourable Lady Mary Bailey flew both ways, also solo, in a de Havilland Moth.

The third Royal Air Force flight from Cairo to Cape Town took place and the SAAF carried out its annual flight north. While in August, Lieutenant Pat Murdoch set up a new record of 13 days for the England to Cape Town flight using an Avro Avian powered by a Cirrus engine.

So 1928 came to a close and 1929 dawned. Perhaps this would prove a luckier year for Rhodesian aviation. Certainly it began on a more hopeful note. On 24th January a letter signed by Aston Redrup, then secretary of the Rhodesian Aviation Syndicate appeared in the *Bulawayo Chronicle*.

The Rhodesian Aviation Syndicate will shortly be absorbed by the Rhodesian Aviation Company, which will be affiliated with the Cobham Blackburn Airlines. Real credit is due to Mr Issels who in London recently attained the close cooperation of Cobham Blackburn Airlines, who have a large interest in the Rhodesian Aviation Company. Cobham Blackburn Airlines advise that an aeroplane and pilot will leave the U.K. next month. (Bulawayo Chronicle)

This pilot was Captain Benjamin Roxburgh-Smith DFC, who had farmed for a short time near Bulawayo, after a flying career during World War I. The aircraft was a Bluebird, single-engine, two-seater, open cockpit biplane. A second-hand Avro was to be purchased in South Africa and the company was scheduled to begin operations in June.

In February 1929, the Royal Air Force carried out its annual flight from Egypt to the Cape landing at Bulawayo on the way south. It so happened that Rhodesia Railways was on strike at the time and it was arranged that the RAF planes should carry mail from Victoria Falls to

Bulawayo at the normal rates. This must have been the first occasion on which letters were carried by air within Rhodesia.

On the return journey the RAF flight was accompanied by a South African Air Force flight. Both flights landed in Gwelo en route to Salisbury on 18th March and the people of Gwelo were thrilled by their first air force visit. Their delight turned to dismay, when during take-off one of the RAF machines crashed killing the pilot, Flying Officer Burnett and his passenger, Sergeant Turner. There was a further mishap at Salisbury when a South African Air Force machine suffered engine failure on take-off and finished up among the motor cars and spectators. Fortunately only a few spectators suffered minor injuries.

In April 1929, Colonel Watson relinquished command of the Southern Rhodesia Defence Force and was replaced by Colonel George Parson DSO, who appears to have taken more interest in air matters. His report for the year states that in his view the future of aviation depended largely on aerodrome facility development, which was in part a community enterprise. There seem to have been two officers on the reserve who held pilot's licences but there is no mention of their qualifications or whether they engaged in any kind of flying practice.

The most hopeful note for the future of military aviation in Rhodesia was the entry into Cranwell on 1st September 1929 of the first Southern Rhodesia governor's nominee, N.H. Jackson, who had been educated at Plumtree School.

The entry for 1930 was R.G. Watson. Then there seems to have been a break before the Northern Rhodesian nomination of A.M. Bentley (later Air Vice-Marshal) in 1934. Bentley was to return to Rhodesia in 1938 as a flying officer in command of a Wellesley Squadron. With his father as a passenger he flew down to Plumtree School to lecture the boys and so became the first old Prunitian to arrive there by air. In 1935, the nominee was A.D. Jackson who died in the Sudan as a result of malaria contracted while trying to recover his aircraft from a swamp.

Late in 1937 and early in 1938 the nominees were J.B. Holderness and E.M.C. Guest, both of whom would gain prominence later.

In 1933, Stanley Wilson was nominated by the governor for an apprenticeship at Halton. When he qualified as a fitter in 1938 he applied for secondment to the Southern Rhodesia Air Unit but unfortunately there were no vacancies.

Only a very few boys were fortunate enough to be accepted for training with the Royal Air Force; most young men interested in flying had no option but to turn to civil aviation.

In recognition of this fact, and in order to help the various flying clubs, the government offered grants to any club prepared to train pilots. Fifty pounds was payable for each ab initio pilot trained, up to a maximum of five per club per year. On reaching 'A' licence standard the club received a further £100 per pilot. Pilots trained under this scheme became members of the Defence Force Reserve. Up to the end of 1929, no claims had been submitted but things were to change in the very near future.

At the time of Sir Alan Cobham's flight in 1929, Imperial Airways and the Air Ministry were carrying out a joint survey beginning in South Africa and working north. This resulted in an agreement between the British government and Imperial Airways for a weekly service between Egypt and Cape Town. The route covered 5,600 miles (8,960km) with 27 aerodromes and 30 intermediate landing grounds. Many of the landing strips were unserviceable during the rainy season, the section between Khartoum and Nairobi being particularly difficult.

Early in November 1929, Captain Roxburgh-Smith returned from South Africa with a second Avro Avian. Aboard the aircraft was Daniel Sievewright Judson, known as Pat. He was the son of Dan Judson, famous in Rhodesia for his part in the rescue of a group of Europeans from the Mazoe Mine during the 1896 Mashona Rebellion. Pat had recently obtained his 'B'

Commercial Flying Licence and was to join the Rhodesian Aviation Company as an assistant pilot. Everyone connected with the company had great hopes, though its first year of activity showed a loss of £935, which was covered by grants from the Beit Railway Trustees and the Rhodesian government.

The first director of civil aviation

Even though flying in Rhodesia was still attempting to get airborne the government saw the need to introduce legislation that would control the creation and day-to-day running of airfields and provide standards for air navigation. The Aviation Act was promulgated in June 1929 and came into force in January 1930. In the main, this act was a copy of the United Kingdom legislation on the subject but there were two additional and interesting clauses. The first stated:

> *In time of war all aircraft, aerodromes and landing grounds etc. could be taken over, subject to payment of compensation.*

and the second:

> *The government may out of moneys to be appropriated by parliament for the purpose, establish and maintain roads and aerodromes, and provide and maintain roads and approaches thereto and apparatus and equipment therefor, and may for the purpose acquire land and interests in and rights to and over land.*

There was no mention of setting up a department of civil aviation as such, but in May the Government Gazette carried the following announcement:

> *It is hereby notified that His Excellency the Governor in Council has been pleased to approve the appointment of Lt Col George Parson DSO, as director of civil aviation with effect from 1st April 1930.*

Colonel Parson was still commandant of the territorial forces and the only other paid official of the Department of Civil Aviation was the supervisor of aerodrome construction. The vote for Civil Aviation in the 1930/31 Budget was £5,660 out of a predicted national income of £2,371.500. No special allocation was made for military flying and it was clearly intended that use should be made of the few civil aircraft in case of emergency.

1931 saw the flight time from London to the Cape cut to six days eleven hours, this feat was performed by Lieutenant Commander Glen Kidston in a Lockheed Vega. Speed was becoming the most sought after attribute of an aircraft and Flight Lieutenant G.H. Stainforth exceeded the highest hopes of the manufacturers when he reached the (at that time) unbelievable speed of 407 mph in his Supermarine S 6B at Calshot. In February the first half of the London to Cape Town air route was opened with a service from Croydon Aerodrome to Mwanza on Lake Victoria.

A fatal accident

Flying was becoming, if not exactly commonplace, at least not quite such a headline affair. Among Pat Judson's pupils were Rhodesia's first woman pilot, Mrs F. Fiander and her one-armed husband. Pat was carrying out the dual tasks of pilot instructor and airman officer of the Territorial Force Reserve. He was doing a wonderful job pioneering flying throughout the Rhodesias and Nyasaland but sadly it was soon to end.

The Adjutant of the 1st Battalion Rhodesia Regiment was Lieutenant A.E. 'Jock' Speight. He was well known in sporting circles having played rugby for Rhodesia against the New Zealand All Blacks in 1928 and captained Rhodesia's cricket team against Percy Chapman's first official MCC touring team. Jock had learned to fly with the Salisbury Light Plane Club and held an 'A' licence but he had not flown for some time so it was decided that he needed a refresher flight before going solo again.

On 20th November 1931, Pat Judson and Jock Speight took off in the Rhodesian Aviation Company's Gipsy Moth VP-YAB. Speight was to perform some circuits and bumps but at a height of about 100 feet something went wrong. The aircraft, overshot, wobbled, rocked and then spun into a dive, crashing at the end of the runway. Pat Judson died instantly; Jock Speight died later in the afternoon.

Although the Board of Inquiry concluded that the aircraft had stalled, the opinion of the flying club members was that there had probably been a misunderstanding in the cockpit as to who 'had control' and in that split second things went wrong.

The official investigation of this crash was one of the first tasks of Major Dirk Cloete MC AFC, who had been engaged as inspector of aircraft with effect from April 1st 1931. Dirk Cloete had had a distinguished career during World War I and the years that followed. When the South African Air Force was formed, he was seconded from the RAF and made responsible for the layout of the first aerodromes in the Union and also for the training of the first SAAF pilots. From April 1st 1932 he was appointed technical adviser to the Department of Civil Aviation.

This accident appears to have been due to pilot error but two Puss Moths had also crashed in the Union of South Africa and as a result all Moths were grounded pending an inquiry. It was established later that the South African accidents were due to structural failure in the wing when the aircraft was flying in conditions of severe turbulence. A total of nine such accidents occurred worldwide before the problem was diagnosed and the defect rectified.

The grounding of their Puss Moths was yet another burden for the Aviation Company that had suffered a bad year. First, Imperial Airways had taken over the African interests of Cobham Blackburn Airlines and early in 1931 it was announced that they were withdrawing their support from the Rhodesian company. As a result Captain Roxburgh-Smith resigned in May. His place had been taken by Pat Judson until his tragic death in November.

On 9th December 1931, the second half of the London to Cape Town air route started experimentally when the de Havilland Hercules, City of Karachi, piloted by Captain H.W.C. Alger and Major H.G. Brackley—took Christmas mail through Rhodesia and Nyasaland arriving at Cape Town on 21st December. One of the ambitions of Imperial Airways was to run a regular airmail service between London and Cape Town. As with every endeavour there were teething troubles. On the first flight north the mail had to be carried by African porters for part of the way...but in true Royal Mail tradition they did get through. Each subsequent flight proved a little more reliable, until by the end of the year Imperial Airways mail service was running with 99% efficiency.

Sir Alfred Beit, whose money had until now been used mainly for the provision of railways in southern Africa was quick to see the value of air travel. On 10th February, in Bulawayo, he said: The principle duty of the Beit Trust is to improve all communications in Rhodesia and in Africa generally. Two weeks later it was announced that the Trust had made a grant of £50,000 for the facilitating of air transport in Southern Rhodesia and Northern Rhodesia on the imperial route. Facilities at Salisbury Aerodrome were to be improved and a hangar and runways were to be constructed at Broken Hill. The route ran Mbeya, Mpika, Broken Hill, Salisbury, Bulawayo, Pietersburg. For the peace of mind of the pilots flying the airmail route, two new landing-grounds were to be built and three already in existence were to be enlarged. Along the route, wireless facilities were to be improved and it was suggested that work on the tarred strip road should be pushed ahead to offer another way out in case of an emergency. The aerodrome and landing-ground work was made the responsibility of the newly established Department of Aviation.

The beginning of the fight for an air unit

During this period, news carried in the local papers mostly concerned overseas events and for some time this information had been anything but cheerful. Periodically during 1932 there had been reports of a German rabble-rouser by the name of Adolf Hitler who seemed to spend his time swaggering around at the head of a motley army of thugs making impossible speeches. At least they seemed impossible to the rest of the world—but suddenly in January 1933, the world woke to the shock realization that Hitler had become Chancellor of the German Reich. In March 1933 he was granted dictatorial powers, ostensibly only until April 1937, but a few far-sighted people even in far-away Rhodesia began to realize that another world war was imminent.

However, to fight a war or even prepare for one, takes money and a great deal of it. During the Budget debate in May 1933, the Rhodesian government appeared hesitant about trying to form even a very small air force, believing that the cost would be prohibitive for a country the size of Southern Rhodesia.

In view of these financial constraints the Honourable R.A. Fletcher, member for Matopo, suggested that an increased subsidy should be given to the Rhodesian Aviation Company, which was in financial trouble as always, in return for their help in training pilots. Jack Keller, popular Labour member for Raylton and constant critic of the government, added his share to the debate.

Lawrence John Walter Keller* had a quick brain and an equally quick tongue, which he was not afraid to use. He believed in modern methods, particularly in the use of the aeroplane, which, as he pointed out, could also be used for riot control. Later in the debate, R.A. Fletcher also spoke out in favour of an air force as an integral part of the defence force.

So the year 1933 passed with no concrete moves being made towards the establishment of an air unit. In the civilian field, however, there was progress. The Honourable St V. Norman was appointed technical adviser to the Beit Trustees and resulting from his report, a new company was formed in October. It was called Rhodesia and Nyasaland Airways Ltd (RANA) and had an authorized capital of £25,000. The principal shareholders were Imperial Airways (Africa) Ltd and the Beit Railway Trustees Ltd who took over the assets of both the Rhodesian Aviation Co. Ltd and Christowitz Air Services, which had operated between Salisbury and Nyasaland since 1932. At this time RANA owned four DH Puss Moths and a DH Fox Moth. The company's first main commercial air route joined Blantyre, Salisbury, Bulawayo, Victoria Falls, Lusaka, Broken Hill and Ndola. The total number of aircraft then registered in Southern Rhodesia was 12. Early in the following year 1934, the de Havilland Aircraft Company (Rhodesia) Ltd was formed in Salisbury, its main purpose being to service aircraft and train pilots.

On 25th April 1934, nearly a year after his last speech on the subject, Jack Keller, once again pushed for an air unit. Knowing there was to be an offer of aid for imperial defence, he rose to his feet during the introduction of a motion on the Compulsory Defence System. His suggestion, based on notes supplied by Douglas Mail, called for the creation of one flight consisting of four aircraft. The planes, which could be obtained at a cost of £1,500 each, were to be flown by volunteers who would come from the defence force and from the civilian

---

* Every effort has been made to establish the first names of Rhodesians mentioned in the book.

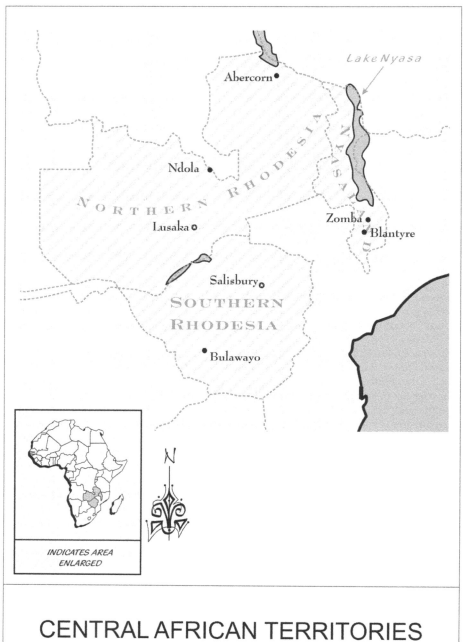

INDICATES AREA
ENLARGED

CENTRAL AFRICAN TERRITORIES

population. His estimate of the cost of purchasing the aircraft and running the Air Arm for one year, was £12,850.

Today this sum sounds ludicrously small but Jack Keller's figures were very close to the amount finally agreed on for setting up the air unit.

The member for Raylton went on to detail the uses that could be made of this air unit: aiding training at the annual defence force camps, locust extermination, riot control, rescue, showing the flag and transport for government officials. Finally, he gave a brief description of the method of training reserve pilots used by the Royal Air Force and then went on to say:

We have something better than that in Southern Rhodesia—this gentleman (Captain Mail) has received an invitation from the military authorities in Bulawayo to give a series of lectures on the technical and flying side of aviation. He tells me that there are a number of officers, attached to the defence force today, who, for the purpose of attaining that technical and flying knowledge which they desire, are perfectly willing to pay their own expenses week in and week out if the government will provide the plane.

Lieutenant Colonel Guest answered, and supported by Colonel Brady, staunchly (but perhaps blimpishly) maintained that for defence there must be men on the ground, and that an air arm would be purely complementary, the gilt on the gingerbread so to speak. Jack Keller listened glumly. In fact the resolution which was finally adopted stated that:

This house respectfully requests the government to make an annual contribution to the Royal Navy and that such annual contribution be not less than one penny in the pound calculated on the revenue of the Colony.

In 1934 this worked out to about £10,000—very nearly the amount needed to set up the air scheme. Colonel Nangle made one final appeal for the air arm:

It is impossible to have a training ship on the Makabusi* but we would like to see a wing of the Royal Air Force established here, or brought here once a year on an extended visit.

He closed by moving an amendment:

That this House respectfully requests the government to consider an annual contribution to the Royal Navy or other branch of imperial defence, in consultation with the British government.

This motion was accepted. It was not what Jack Keller had hoped for but it was a move in the right direction. Some progress had been made but it was pitifully small when measured against Hitler's creation in October 1934 of a German air force and his urgent expansion of the German army and navy.

Few people seemed to realize the menace—but in November of the same year Winston Churchill, speaking in the House of Commons, warned of the threat created by Germany's rearmament policy—particularly by his armament in the air.

★ The Makabusi, the butt of many jokes, is a very small stream that runs through Salisbury.

CHAPTER 2

Small beginnings

In March 1935 the disarmament clauses of the Versailles treaty were repudiated by Germany and conscription was reintroduced in that country. The European powers took the hint and in April, Britain, France and Italy held a conference aimed at establishing a common front against possible German aggression.

In the face of a worsening world situation, with Japan also rearming and in possession of considerable tracts of China, the Rhodesian parliament met on 2nd May to discuss the estimates of expenditure for the coming year. Almost unbelievably, before considering the estimates for defence, Lieutenant Colonel Guest suggested that the House consider the establishment of a defence force brass band, at the approximate cost of £6,000 (half the amount required to form an air unit!)

Predictably, Jack Keller sailed into battle. He repeated his report of the previous year and added:

> *I have always said in the House and I maintain it, that the first thing the government will do, in the case of serious trouble, will be to send frantic wires to Pretoria to send up their aeroplanes, because that will be the only adequate defence...*

Jack Keller's impassioned plea for more modern thinking on defence was opposed by Major, the Honourable, R.J. Hudson, Lieutenant Colonel Guest (who was later to give so dearly for the air force and who was to become the first minister for the Air) and Colonel Brady. The debate concluded without any resolution being passed either on the formation of an air unit or to what use the £10,000 offered the previous year was to be put. It seemed that once more little or nothing had been achieved.

Meanwhile civil aviation continued to expand. Southern Rhodesia now boasted three aerodromes and 27 landing grounds in addition to 20 private landing fields. Colonel Parson still acted as commandant of the territorial forces as well as director of civil aviation. RANA was receiving a subsidy of £1,500 a year and provision had been made to pay the Air Ministry £300 for ground engineering services.

Royal Air Force visits continued and in 1935 the visit coincided with a period of rioting on the Copperbelt in Northern Rhodesia (now Zambia), so the Royal Air Force pilots were able to give a convincing demonstration of their ability to deploy police reinforcements speedily into a problem area.

Meanwhile, despite the fact that nothing had apparently been decided regarding the air unit, official inquiries were made in June as to the possibility of using the municipal airport in Salisbury for training military pilots. Negotiations were begun for hangar accommodation etc. but when the municipality requested a reasonable contribution from the government towards the upkeep of the aerodrome, it was decided that a separate military aerodrome was a necessity. It was stated that pilots under instruction might prove a danger to commercial flying.

The air section is established

Then came the bombshell. In November, Government Notice No 765 established the air section of the territorial force and on November 1st, flying training began under the supervision of de Havilland's instructors at Belvedere Airport. The air unit had beaten the brass band, but how?

There was no financial provision for the undertaking so presumably the money came from the territorial force and cadet vote. There was no question of buying aircraft as yet—therefore the amount required was small and it would appear that the 1st Battalion Rhodesia Regiment went ahead on its own. Sir Ernest Lucas Guest said later that the air unit was begun as a force complementary to the ground forces, simply to be the eyes of the army and was primarily for local use as part of the 1st Battalion. The officers and men taking part in the flying training were to come under the officer commanding 1st Battalion for administration and discipline. In later years, Colonel N.S. Ferris who was their commanding officer, liked to say that he could claim the distinction of being the first air officer commanding.

So after all the argument the air section came into being almost unnoticed. The pupil pilots used Belvedere, Salisbury's civil airport and were trained by de Havilland instructors on Tiger Moth aircraft. Scott Robertson was the first instructor and one of the first six pupil pilots was John Holderness whose log-book shows that he actually began flying on Friday 13th November 1935. Training continued into the new year 1936.

In March, a young group captain was sent out from the Air Ministry in London to advise on the development of the air unit. He was born in England but emigrated to Rhodesia when he was 18 and at the outbreak of World War I in 1914 enlisted in the 1st Rhodesia Regiment and served in South West Africa. His name was Arthur Harris, later to become commander in chief of Bomber Command. One of the suggestions he made was to cause great furore in the Legislative Assembly but at the time he came and went with little publicity.

On the world scene the last months of 1935 and the first part of 1936 presented a picture of mounting chaos. Vicious anti-Jewish laws had been passed in Germany and the swastika had become the official flag. Italy had invaded Abyssinia in October 1935 and little had been done by the League of Nations, except to impose half-hearted sanctions. In January, Japan walked out of a naval conference in London having previously rejected all naval agreements. Early in March, German troops entered the Rhineland showing blatant disregard for all previous agreements and later in that same month the Nazis won 99% of the vote in the German elections.

In July, army units in Spanish Morocco revolted and proclaimed General Franco head of the Spanish State. A civil war resulted, which lasted two years and led to Spain becoming an ideological battleground. Russia sent advisers to the socialist government; opponents of fascism organized an international brigade, while Germany provided air power for General Franco, using the opportunity to perfect techniques of dive-bombing.

Against this background of gathering gloom, the Governor of Southern Rhodesia, His Excellency Sir Herbert Stanley opened a new parliament on 16th March 1936. He told members that a Council of Defence was being set up to advise on matters concerning the Colony's system of defence. Deep sorrow was expressed in the House at the death of His Majesty King George V, and the Colony's loyalty to His Majesty King Edward VIII was affirmed.

Once again, Budget time had come round. Expenditure for the year 1936/7 was, for the first time in the Colony's history expected to top the £3,000,000 mark, but only just. The European population was then just over 50,000.

The Minister of Finance, the Honourable H. Smit, in his estimates of expenditure, allowed £58,000 for defence, a net increase of £18,500 over that of the previous year. This amount, he said was to be expended on the establishment of an air unit, at a cost of £13,724 and to provide for more intensive training of the territorial active force.

This news stirred a violent attack from the anti-air force brigade. Major G.H. Walker (Salisbury South, Labour Member) said that the country could not afford the force, that the aircraft being obtained from the United Kingdom were reconditioned and would be obsolete in no time, and anyway, Against whom are these aircraft to fight!

On the following day, Prime Minister Godfrey Huggins, replied. He said that the air unit had been started as the Colony's contribution to imperial defence. He emphatically denied the suggestion that it would be inefficient and he pointed out that Germany was requesting the return of her ex-colony Tanganyika. He concluded, If that happens we might very well have an enemy only too close!

One interesting point is that in this budget there is a cut in the amount to be spent on civil aviation of £3,000. The decrease is due, the minister reported, to the non-repetition of the provision of £5,000 made last year for the imperial defence scheme provision for the Military Air Unit now being made under Vote 21. In other words the government had got round the money situation in the previous year by voting extra funds to civil aviation. At any rate, now everything was out in the open and the way was clear for the foundation of an air unit with its own aircraft.

On 1st April 1936, Dirk Cloete became staff officer Air Services and director of Civil Aviation replacing Colonel Parson who had retired.

So far so good—but on 9th April flying training, which had been in operation since the previous November, came to an abrupt halt. Five of the six men involved were returned to battalion duties. This news stirred a hornets' nest in the House. The explanation, when it came, revolved around the visit of Group Captain Harris. It seemed that until his arrival in the Colony it was believed that almost anyone could learn to fly. In March, Harris had disabused the military authorities in no uncertain terms. He made it emphatically clear that military pilots needed at least matriculation or a near equivalent.

The point was confirmed by the acting director of Education, when he saw the RAF standard syllabus. As a result, an air selection board was set up on April 20th to inquire into the qualifications of all candidates for the air unit. Only John Holderness and Roger Cazalet had the necessary educational standard so, rather than incur further expense, all training was stopped. It was, however, suggested that the other pilots, who had been training for five months and had reached the solo flying stage, should be allowed to qualify for the Civil Pilots' 'A' licence without further expense to themselves.

The next attack by the anti-air brigade was led, once again, by Major Walker. In a speech at a meeting of the ratepayers held at the Grand Hotel on 26th May, he deplored the choice of site for the new military aerodrome. It was, he said, a large and beautiful area of woodland that was a favourite picnic spot. In fact the land at Hillside was commonage, which the government had repossessed from Salisbury Council. Despite the major's efforts, work began on the clearing of trees and the construction of the military airfield that was later to be called Cranborne.

On 17th July 1936, the Government Gazette announced the official formation of an air unit, which was to be titled Air Section, Southern Rhodesia Defence Force.

The first six apprentices

Just four days later, on 21st July 1936, six boys set out on a great adventure. They were 16 years old and had been chosen from a large number of applicants to be inducted into the Permanent

Staff Corps of the Royal Air Force at Halton for a three-year course of training as mechanics. They looked very young as they said their goodbyes to family and friends and boarded the train at Salisbury Station for the start of their journey to Cape Town and the great overseas! One of the boys, Ralph Parry, remembered coming from Bulawayo to Salisbury where he was met at the station by members of the BSAP and taken in a mule cart to the police camp for his interview and medical. The other five boys in this intake were R.G. (Ron) Boswell, B. (Mick) Gibbon, S.R. (Stan) Young,* F.J. (Otto) Gericke and R.A. (Ron) Cashel. An item in the *Rhodesia Herald* on July 20th reports the boys' departure and goes on to say:

> *Several Rhodesians are at present in the RAF and others have been through training courses and are now in civil aviation in the Union. Mr A.M. Bentley is at Cranwell College and Mr R.N. Stidolph holds a short service commission in the RAF; both these men attended Plumtree School, Bulawayo.*

Even though the air section was now an established fact, Major Cloete was taking an extremely depressed view of matters. On 23rd July, writing to the officer commanding Southern Rhodesia Forces, he complained of the attitude adopted by those in authority in the 1st Battalion Rhodesia Regiment who he alleged had attempted to frustrate the organization of the air section on proper lines. He complained that a very large majority of the youths of the Colony were not physically fit and suggested that because of these difficulties no contract should be signed with the de Havilland Company for flying training until the selection of suitable persons for training as pilots is completed. He was being overly pessimistic, both in the short and the long term, as 21 men with the necessary qualifications applied for the first entry and during five years of war, Rhodesia would supply over a thousand young men of aircrew standard.

A meeting was held at defence headquarters to agree the contract with de Havilland. A minimum of six pilots per year were to be put through a three year training course and brought to RAF pilot specifications. Nobody at that meeting realized that before the first course was complete Rhodesian pilots would be asked to move to battle stations.

Southern Rhodesia's first full-scale air rally was staged on 13th August 1936. It was organized by the Bulawayo Light Plane Club with flying under the control of Major Cloete, and Captain Rod Douglas as announcer. Two days earlier Major Cloete and Lieutenant J.B. Holderness had flown to Wankie to welcome the Royal Air Force flight, which had come from Heliopolis in Egypt to take part in the air display. Between 3,000 and 4,000 people watched the formation flying and aerobatics of the 25 aircraft that included local machines as well as the planes from South Africa and Britain. Two days later the show was repeated at Salisbury Airport in front of an estimated crowd of 20,000, which must have included just about the entire population of Salisbury.

A *Rhodesia Herald* report commented, Never before in the history of the Colony have so many people been brought together in one area by one event.

Perhaps it was the excitement of the rally or the pressure of the worsening world situation but on the Monday following the rally the *Rhodesia Herald*, in its leader, offered a £60 scholarship for the training of a pilot under the direction of de Havilland and Company at Salisbury. The paper received 200 applications.

No 1 Pilots' Course
Meanwhile the search was on for the six men who would have the honour of being the

---

* Stan Young later took a pilot's course and was killed in November 1942.

first pilots to be trained under the government scheme. Entry was open to citizens between the ages of 18 and 25. The education standard required for flying duties was matric or its equivalent. (Junior Cambridge being considered sufficient for ground duties!) Candidates had to be British subjects and were required to serve for five years on the active list and five years on the reserve. The uniform of the force was to be the same as that of 1st Battalion Rhodesia Regiment.

Eventually a choice was made: J.B. Holderness and A.B.T. Cazalet (the two men who had been members of the ill-fated course of the previous year); R.M. Marshall; G.A. (Graham) Smith;* E.T. (Eric) Smith (all members of the 1st Battalion Rhodesia Regiment) and M.C. Barber who had been a detective sergeant in the British South Africa Police and was transferred to the Permanent Staff Corps on six months' probation for duties as a staff officer with Air Services Staff. He had attested for 12 years and was appointed acting sergeant!

According to Eric Smith's log-book, he began flying on October 6th 1936. The training was organized by de Havilland at Belvedere, and because all the pupil pilots were in full-time employment, it had to take place early in the morning, late in the afternoon and at the weekends.

The air section had no aircraft of its own and the pilots were trained on de Havilland machines. A report carried in *The Herald* at the end of November states that de Havilland had four training machines then, two Tiger Moths and two Major Moths. One of the Tiger Moths, however, had to be stationed at Bulawayo for pilot training there. The Tiger Moth was the standard trainer used by the RAF and was satisfactory from that point of view but obviously an air section had to have aircraft of its own. First official mention of this happy event came from the Prime Minister, Sir Godfrey Huggins, at the St Andrew's Night Banquet on 30th November: "We have started a small air force in this Colony and before the end of the year with the assistance of the Imperial Government, we shall have six Hawker Hart machines for training our air unit." The prime minister was being optimistic; it was to be almost a year before the Harts flew in Rhodesia.

On a more cheerful note, Salisbury was in holiday mood that Christmas and a popular place to visit was the aerodrome where,

Joy-flippers are now allowed to handle the controls themselves under reliable supervision. Yesterday large numbers of people went for flips or stayed earthbound to watch a stunting aeroplane. (Rhodesia Herald)

This mixture of joy-flippers and military pupil pilots worried the aerodrome superintendent who tabled a somewhat acid report at the end of the year:

It would appear that the danger has been overlooked as the de Havilland School has contracted with the government to train the cadets of the air unit at the municipal airport. I beg you to submit that the instruction work should be carried out at the military aerodrome.†

By new year 1937 Germany and Italy had recognized General Franco's government in Spain and were giving his rebel army their open support. Even in Rhodesia, the newspapers were full of accounts of the aerial bombardment of Spanish cities complete with harrowing details of the dead and wounded. Air warfare had assumed horrifying proportions in the

---

* Graham Smith, who actually came in as a replacement for Mike Curry who had to drop out because of law examinations, had done some flying at university and so came in with previous experience.

† This of course was not ready yet.

imagination. To some strategists it appeared that no city could withstand heavy attack from the air, a belief that was to influence military tactics throughout the coming war.

On 9th March 1937, the governor of Southern Rhodesia opened the 8th Parliament, saying:

> *In the difficult and dangerous times through which the world is passing, there rests upon each part of the Empire an obligation to take such measures as its circumstances allow, to defend itself and thus to contribute to the defence of the whole. My ministers are not unmindful of the obligation. Arrangements have been made to increase the number of men in training in the active force with effect from October 1st.*

Following the governor's speech the *Rhodesia Herald* suggested in a leading article, that more pupils should be trained, even if the standard was considerably lower.

On 23rd March came the Budget and a provision of £22,358 for the air unit. This was to cover salaries and allowances for five instructors and ground staff and the purchase of six Hawker Harts at £700 each as well as the running and maintenance costs and payment to de Havilland for pilot training. Provision was also made for the employment of two corporal clerks and the secondment from the Royal Air Force of five personnel (one flight lieutenant, one flying officer, one flight sergeant and two sergeants). These men were to start arriving in the Colony in August. Incidentally during the budget debate the subject of the brass band was raised again. A promise was made that the Colony would have its brass band within 12 months!

Meanwhile Mr D. de Waal had arrived from Pretoria to join the staff at de Havilland as a pilot instructor and during March he indulged in some formation flying over Salisbury in company with Graham Smith and C.S. Style, who was chairman of Salisbury's newly formed flying club. The *Rhodesia Herald* reported the event:

> *Considering the fact that Mr Style and Mr Smith have not had much opportunity of practising formation flying for some considerable time, the attempt was highly successful and it aroused a great deal of curiosity amongst those below who were disturbed by the unusual drone of three aeroplanes overhead.*

To some extent the air unit was now marking time, waiting firstly for the new aircraft to arrive and then for expert help in unpacking and assembling them.

On 24th August, there stepped from the Bulawayo train, four men who were (with one other) to be the midwives, instructors and moulders of Southern Rhodesia's air force. They were: Flight Lieutenant J.A. (Jimmy) Powell, Flight Sergeant A. Greenwood and Sergeants V.J. Royce and C.P. Horton. They had been seconded from the Royal Air Force and their first task was to unpack and assemble the Hawker Hart aircraft, which had arrived in packing cases and were being stored at the BSAP depot.

The Hawker Harts take to the air

To the people of Salisbury, who were anxious to see the new aircraft flying, this task seemed to take an unconscionable time. Towards the middle of September, the Honourable R.C. Tredgold, Minister of Justice and Defence, was asked about the non-appearance of the aircraft. He replied:

> *We hope to have the first of the SR force machines ready to take to the air by the end of October or early November. This machine will be dual controlled. While the other machines are being assembled and tested, instruction will be carried out in this one. The machines have been packed*

for two years and have to be thoroughly inspected. Even the fabric covering the wings is being taken off and examined for flaws. Meanwhile, additional accommodation for the machines has to be provided. The military aerodrome at Salisbury is usable at the moment but needs to have a good deal of work done on it.

He also mentioned the possibility that in future, mechanics might be trained in Rhodesia but said that he hoped that members of the Royal Air Force would always be available. He also referred to the possibility that Rhodesians serving with the RAF might return to work with the air unit and said that Acting Pilot Officer H.G. McDonald, who had been killed in an accident the previous weekend had been considered.

Towards the end of September the first Hawker Hart made its maiden appearance lumbering ignominiously behind a mule team as it was towed in a partially assembled state from police headquarters to the military airfield at Cranborne.

Early in the following month, the fifth member of the RAF team arrived. He was Flying Officer V.E. Maxwell, who was later to become the first officer commanding of No 237 Squadron. And in the same month the second course of six pupil pilots was commissioned as second lieutenants in the air section. They were R.J.D. Christie, A.T.R. Hutchinson, E.W.S. Jacklin, H.C. Peyton, E.E. Spence and N.S.F. Tyas. Two men from this group were to win particular places in Rhodesian Air Force history. Peyton, tragically was one of the first two Rhodesian Air Force casualties in the Second World War, and Ted Jacklin was to be the first Rhodesian chief of Air Staff and founder of Rhodesia's postwar air force.

During the previous six months, newspapers had been regularly reporting Italian and German bombing attacks on Spanish cities and so it was no surprise that Britain should consider an Air Raid Precaution Bill, but the timing, 5th November, Guy Fawkes Day, displayed a certain macabre humour. On the following day, Italy joined Germany and Japan in an anti-communist pact. Lord Halifax, who was the British government's appointee with special responsibility for foreign affairs, visited Hitler in an attempt to settle European problems but merely set a pattern of appeasement, which was to send the world staggering from crisis to crisis.

In Rhodesia two runways, hangars, workshops and offices were nearing completion at the Cranborne Aerodrome and two Hawker Harts, SR 1 and SR 2 had been assembled; so by the middle of December 1937, everything was ready for an official inspection by Colonel J.S. Morris, Officer Commanding the Southern Rhodesia Forces.

The parade of members of the air unit, was drawn up by the new hangar and offices and in front of two of the Hawker Hart machines numbered SR 1 and SR 2. The parade was under the command of Flight Lieutenant J.A. Powell of the RAF. With him was Flight Lieutenant V.E. Maxwell also of the RAF. The new aircraft were taken up by the two RAF pilots, Colonel Morris accompanying Flight Lieutenant Powell. (Rhodesia Herald)

These Hawker Harts together with the later Audax were to be in use by the air unit for the next three years including the campaign against the Italians in Abyssinia.

According to Squadron Leader N.V. Phillips writing in *Bush Horizons*:

The flying students of the air unit soon came to admire the skill, and hang upon the utterances, of the two RAF flying instructors Powell and Maxwell. Powell was in command of the military aerodrome. He was an excellent squadron man and a brilliant pilot, slightly built but very wiry; about five foot ten inches in height, he carried himself as a typical regular officer. Off duty he loved a good party, but he was strict and tough on duty. He got the respect he demanded. He referred to the students as 'bograts' to their faces, but he did not spare himself in the furthering of their air force education or the standard of flying. Had it not been for Jimmie Powell the pilots of the air unit would not have achieved the meticulous standard he demanded, and which they in turn were to pass on until the reputation of Rhodesians as airmen was rarely doubted. Jimmie's forte was aerobatics. Maxwell was more of the solid, quietly spoken and staid type. He was responsible for the ground training of the students and Maxie, as he later became known, acted as their adviser and father confessor. On many occasions he made peace between Jimmie and the bograts when discipline became too tough or had been breached. Maxie delighted in a rough and tumble at times, and on the rugby field this short, stocky man was an excellent hooker. Maxie was a steady pilot. Among other skills required by a pilot he excelled in instrument flying and picking up messages. Both these men were masters of improvisation and did the best job possible with the limited equipment but, what is more important, they maintained the tremendous enthusiasm of the air unit throughout their stay in Rhodesia.

Maxie was later to marry a Rhodesian girl but, unfortunately, he was killed by a German flying bomb in London on 23rd February 1944. Squadron Leader Powell was to do an extremely fine job on operations, until his death on a long-range bombing mission in northern Italy while holding the rank of group captain, with the DSO and OBE.

On 14th January 1938, the *Rhodesia Herald* took a look at the new military aerodrome:

The hangar is complete and includes a lecture room, an operations room, workshops and complete office accommodation. An area 1,000 yards square has been cleared and two runways 1,000 by 15,000 yards at right angles to each other are in use. The first year is to be spent in ab initio training in de Havilland Tiger Moths and it is only when they have completed 80 hours in these machines that they are to be taught to fly the Hawker Harts. (Rhodesia Herald)

On completing 20 hours solo in Harts and passing various examinations, the pupil pilots were to qualify for their wings. *The Herald* noted that training could be given in bombing and gunnery as the aircraft were equipped with one camera gun and moving target bombsights. The Harts also carried two wireless sets, one of which is a two-way telephonic and telegraphic radio. The pupil pilots, who were on the verge of going solo were still only part-time airmen. Their flying was done between 06h00 and 08h00 and between 16h30 and 18h00, added to which they had to find time for four lectures a week.

Early in the New Year 1938, a suggestion was made that the air unit should be used to carry out photographic survey work in the Sabi River area. This was agreed provided that it did not interfere with the training and these surveys became a regular part of the unit's activities during 1938.

A highlight of February was a visit by Lord Trenchard, the grand old man of the RAF and in the same month the first contingent of Rhodesians to be selected for short service commissions with the RAF left Rhodesia. They were Arthur Macdonald Imrie, Keith D'Alroy Taute, C.A.J. MacNamara, Robert Duncan S. Olver, Jack Elliot Thomas, Spencer Ritchie Peacock-Edwards, William John Alexander (Susie) Wilson, N.G. MacFarlane, G.R. Gunner, Duncan Frank Hyland Smith and Thomas Cedric Cundill. These men were to complete four years' active service and seven years in reserve and they were all destined to see a great deal of active service, with the exception of Thomas who was unfortunately killed in an air crash on 30th January 1939. Robert Duncan Olver was one of the crew of the only all-Rhodesian-manned Lancaster which was shot down on May 8th 1942.

With the world situation growing daily more tense, the *Rhodesia Herald* again put forward the suggestion that a greater number of pilots should be trained to a lower standard. At the same time, Sir James MacDonald (president of the Bulawayo Light Plane Club), appealed for government subsidies to pilots with 'A' licence, so that they could increase their proficiency. Neither suggestion was taken up but on February 21st 1938, the Southern Rhodesia Air Unit received another precious aircraft, a Tiger Moth bearing RAF markings, which was flown from Johannesburg by Mr J. Finnis, the de Havilland instructor in Salisbury. The machine was fitted out for night-flying and for instruction in blind-flying.

On the safety side, Sergeant Maurice Barber was sent on a parachute-packing course to the South African Air Force at Roberts Heights. On his return he became responsible for parachute safety. During this period, no one—pilot, observer or casual passenger—was allowed to fly without one.

CHAPTER 3

A time to prepare

The 1st April 1938 was a special day for the air unit. This was the date on which the baby began to grow up, separating from the territorial force, and taking the official title of the Southern Rhodesia Air Unit. The commanding officer was Jimmie Powell and the staff officer of Air Services was Major Dirk Cloete, who also held the post of director of civil aviation.

For Umtali the real celebration came ten days later when at 16h00 the three Hawker Harts appeared skimming low over the tops of the Vumba Range, descending in a formation dive and then soaring away up into the clouds. The occasion was Umtali's Air Display, which marked the official opening of the gliding club. The Prime Minister, Sir Godfrey Huggins, flew down in a Hornet Moth piloted by Dirk Cloete. The Minister of Justice and Defence, R.C. Tredgold and Colonel J.S. Morris, commanding Southern Rhodesia Forces travelled in two air unit machines, piloted by Powell and Maxwell, while Lieutenant J.B. Holderness piloted the third air unit machine.

Saturday afternoon featured a gliding display with a civic dinner in the evening, and then on Sunday morning it was the turn of the members of the air unit to show their paces. According to reports, Powell and Maxwell gave an outstanding display.

1937 had been a good year for Rhodesia. Transport and communications had improved and the economy had received a boost with the arrival of more than 300 immigrants. Unfortunately events in the rest of the world were not so happy. In February 1938, the dictator Adolf Hitler had assumed supreme military command in Germany. In Austria the majority of German-speaking people wished to unite with Germany. This union had been forbidden under the terms of the Treaty of Versailles. Demands for union or anschluss, as it was known, had increased following Hitler's rise to power in Germany. In March 1938 Hitler demanded and received the resignation of the Austrian Chancellor. A Nazi supporter, Seyss-Inquart became the new Chancellor and he invited the German army to occupy Austria on 12th March, and on the following day Austria's union with Germany was officially proclaimed.

Not unnaturally with these disturbing developments occurring in Europe, the 1938 Rhodesian Budget showed an increased spending on defence; £38,700 in an overall budget of three and a half million. The opposition in the Southern Rhodesian Assembly suggested a greater defence expenditure but the resources of the Colony with its population of only 50,000 Europeans, precluded over-generosity. The problem was where the available manpower could be used to the greatest effect.

The minister of defence, replying to the Budget debate was forced to appeal to members to keep their emotions in check. While the position in Europe was serious it did not justify becoming hysterical and making impossible gestures, however magnificent. He reminded the assembly that Rhodesia had limited resources and was obliged to make the best possible use of what she had. With reference to the air unit he said:

The time may come when campaigns are fought out in the air but at the present time we must recognize the fact that, despite its great power of inflicting casualties and its enormous range, the air arm is only one arm of the military machine. If we over-develop that arm at the expense of our ground forces we are developing a machine that is unsound and one-sided.

Continuing, the minister said that training pilots to a point where they were fully qualified military pilots was a long term process but he believed that this was the way to make a valuable contribution to imperial defence. It had been suggested that Rhodesia could train 5,000 pilots, but to produce 5,000 military pilots would cost somewhere between £5,000,000 and £8,000,000, at an estimated cost of between £1,000 and £1,400 for each pilot. To send half-trained pilots into battle would be a tragedy. He concluded by saying that it was intended to increase the number of pupil pilots from six to 12 a year.

Pilots of the first course receive their Wings

12th May 1938 was the proudest day to date for the air unit. The members of the first course of six pilots (plus Captain Style) received their flying badges (Wings) from the Governor, Sir Herbert Stanley. They were granted commissions in equivalent ranks in the RAF Reserve. These were the men who had commenced their training in October 1936—Holderness, Cazalet, Marshall, Barber and the two Smiths, Eric and Graham. The flying badge was similar to the RAF badge but in place of the letters RAF was a miniature of the coat of arms of Southern Rhodesia. This later became the badge of the RRAF except that the King's Crown (Tudor) was replaced by the Queen's Crown (Edwardian).

The Travelling Flying School

Just over a week later the Midlands Flying Club held an air rally, which was attended by members of the air unit. During an informal meeting on Sunday morning 22nd May, Dirk Cloete made the first official mention of a new scheme: a Travelling Flying School to be sponsored by the government. The plan was that the school would visit centres where there were sufficient pupils for a month, during which time the trainees would be put through their air licence. The school would return after about six months so that new pupils could take their licence and the pilots already qualified could do a refresher course.

In Umtali a few days later, Major Cloete gave more details:

What is aimed at is to give an equal opportunity to all who are willing to learn to fly. They (the government) will supply the instructors and the ground engineers and will help the local organizing committee to keep down overhead expenses, trying to work the schools at a cost of £2 per flying hour.

The scheme, aimed at improving civil aviation in Southern Rhodesia, was to be financed by the government and Sir Abe Bailey's Trust, a coronation gift of £3,500. On May 30th 1938, the RAF boxing team arrived in Salisbury, flying from Durban in a SAAF Airspeed Envoy. The boxers were seen in action on June 1st with a convincing win against the Rhodesians who lost four bouts out of seven. Just a week later came the news that the SAAF aircraft carrying four members of the team between Bulawayo and Pietersburg was missing.

The search for the missing machine began early this morning (Tuesday 7th) and two Rhodesian Air Force Hawker Harts, piloted by Flight Lieutenant J.A. Powell and Flight Lieutenant V.E. Maxwell left Salisbury shortly after sun up, arriving at Bulawayo about 08h20.
(Rhodesia Herald)

One interesting point here is that this is the first use of the term Rhodesian Air Force. Powell and Maxwell began their search after arranging refuelling facilities near the Transvaal border. The missing plane was eventually sighted by the South African Air Force 25 miles north of Pont Drift on the Limpopo River just south-west of its junction with the Shashi. A land party was sent out from Pretoria but did not reach the scene of the crash until Wednesday 8th June. All those aboard had died in the crash. The *Rhodesia Herald* commented:

> *A surprising feature of the disaster has been the time needed to reach the scene once the plane had been located. The rescue party were engaged two days in making their way through the thick bush in rough country over a distance that is covered in a few minutes by air.*

This episode demonstrated in a dramatic way the fact that Rhodesia had large tracts of wild country where the only means of fast travel was by air.

In July 1938, Maxwell and Powell took time to carry out photographic surveys of the eastern border area and of the Gwai, Mangwe and Ingwezi river systems in the south-western areas of the country. These surveys were invaluable for planning water supplies and for map-making.

The air unit was now a well-knit group. The message picking-up team was led by Maxwell. John Holderness excelled at aerobatics and the formation flying team consisted of Powell, the leader, Holderness and Graham Smith. The unit's first jolly in July was to take part in an air rally at Gatooma. One of the most popular parts of these displays was the feat of picking up messages. These messages were suspended on a rope between two posts about five feet (1,5 metres) above the ground. The aim was to catch the message with a hook, which was let down from underneath the aircraft. The air unit team became so polished at this operation that they could perform it without a hitch—even flying in formation!

During the year, members of the unit had built themselves a mess at Cranborne using the packing cases in which the Harts had arrived. Apparently as the last nail went home, a party started that was to set the tone for later festivities…continuing as it did well into the early hours. Graham Smith (then Flying Adjutant) described the mess as just the job. It consisted of a large room about 24 feet (eight metres) by 16 feet (five metres) with a small partitioned area that acted as a bar. One of the first items of furniture presented to the mess was a beautiful table. It received its blooding at the hands of some of the members of the MCC team that visited Rhodesia at the end of 1938. The cricketers autographed the table and the signatures were then carved into the wood, most noticeable being that of Tom Goddard. This table was later to stand proudly in the officers' mess at New Sarum. Along with the table, the mess began collecting silver under the direction of Jimmie Powell, who had been promoted substantive squadron leader in August 1938.

The 11th August saw the commencement of night flying, an activity that was remembered with nostalgia by all who took part:

> *In those days (night flying) had a tang to the occasion, which the electrically-illuminated, air-conditioned airman of today misses. The black smoke from paraffin-filled gooseneck flares wafting across the landing path, the dust, and, my dear, the ghastly smell of petrol! All savoured from an open cockpit; heaven on earth, and at most times closer to the former than you really should be.* (Bush Horizons)

Sometime earlier, Dirk Cloete had left for the United Kingdom to collect a Dragon Rapide for the Southern Rhodesian government. While he was in England he consulted with the Air Council on the best ways of developing Rhodesia's air strength, and it was recommended that a complete front-line squadron be formed. To this end, the Air Ministry agreed to sell Rhodesia six Hawker Audaxes and three Gloster Gauntlets at a nominal cost.

Returning to Rhodesia in the Rapide, irreverently known as the Gin Palace because it had VIP fittings that included a cocktail cabinet, Cloete had as passengers two new RAF airmen on secondment. They were leading aircraftmen A. Higham and Martin Madders (who was to retain his contact with aviation in Rhodesia for the rest of his career, eventually becoming director of civil aviation). The DH Dragon Rapide was a twin-engine, six-seater development of the Moth and shared with the Dakota the distinction of being the most reliable, useful and easily maintained aeroplane of its class. When in production the Rapide sold for just under £4,000.

The Harts go round Rhodesia

On 1st September 1938, a flight of five Hawker Harts set out on the first round Rhodesia trip. This jaunt was partly to show off the new aircraft and partly to give the young pilots experience in cross-country flying. The Harts left Salisbury at 08h30 arriving at Bulawayo in midmorning. From there they flew to the Victoria Falls for lunch. After a night's rest they continued to Wankie where they gave an exhibition of flying on the Friday afternoon; then back to Bulawayo on Saturday morning to prepare for a display on Sunday. Always the most popular events were the aerobatics and the demonstration of message collection.

In fact, during the message picking-up display at Bulawayo Airport on the Sunday, messages were collected without fault on three successive occasions, a feat that had not even been seen at the Hendon Air Display during the previous nine years!

On the following weekend it was the turn of Fort Victoria to host the air unit.

> *This visit was eagerly welcomed, as few people in Fort Victoria have seen the air unit before. After circling the aerodrome, the machines broke formation with Squadron Leader Powell leading, and landed. The other members who arrived were Captain Style, Flight Lieutenant Maxwell and Lieutenants Barber and Smith.* (Rhodesia Herald)

There were the usual aerobatics and picking-up of messages, which thrilled the crowd, but the highlight of the afternoon was probably when Graham Smith buzzed the VIP tent where the prime minister was having tea and collected festoons of bunting. Graham's comment on the subject was: Well, Jimmie Powell always said, "If you're going to fly low...fly low!"

The air unit does its first training with territorials

During the following week came the camp for territorial troops at Gwelo. At the end of August 1938, members of the Bulawayo Light Plane Club had taken part in military manœuvres staged by the 2nd Battalion, Rhodesia Regiment in the Umzingwane area. However, the camp in Gwelo was the first time that the air unit had taken part in a training session with the territorials.

> *The troops marched to Gum Tree Drift, about three miles from the camp. There a mobile loudspeaker outfit enabled Squadron Leader Powell of the air unit to tell the troops exactly what manœuvres an air unit Hawker Hart, flown by Flight Lieutenant Maxwell was performing. First the aeroplane demonstrated a dive attack coming from a height of 1,000 feet or more above the heads of the troops, who deployed over the open veld. Then the machine disappeared and Squadron Leader Powell explained that it would demonstrate a low-flying attack on a transport train composed of army lorries. Cleverly making use of cover to conceal his approach and drown the noise of his engines, Flight Lieutenant Maxwell came suddenly over the tops of the trees 100 yards from the troops who were taken completely by surprise.* (Rhodesia Herald)

The troops were given a lecture on signalling aircraft by means of white strips laid on the ground and Maxwell gave a demonstration of message dropping and collection. According to the *Rhodesia Herald*:

> *It is understood unofficially that one of the messages gathered by the plane...was concerned with lunchtime beer! Marching back to camp with the band playing...the column had just passed over the now notorious Gum Tree Drift, when with a roar of engines and the shriek of the wind through the rigging, the two aeroplanes suddenly appeared flying low over the trees and swooped down on the column. Not sure whether this was business or exhibition flying, the troops were a trifle slow in seeking cover.*

While the Gwelo Camp may have seemed like play-acting, events in Europe had taken on a deadly serious quality. Czechoslovakia, a republic created in 1918 from the western provinces of Austria-Hungary including Sudetenland, had a large German-speaking population. Sudeten Germans had been agitating since 1935 to join Germany. Following Austria's union with Germany in March, their demands grew more insistent.

It was in the middle of September 1938—in fact the very day that Rhodesian troops were receiving their first lecture on aerial tactics—that Neville Chamberlain, the British Prime Minister, and the French and Italian premiers met Hitler in Munich to discuss the problem of Czechoslovakia. The first meeting took place in September and the Munich Agreement was signed on 29th September. Under this settlement 10,000 square miles of Czechoslovakia were to be ceded to Germany and another 6,000 square miles to Poland and Hungary. In effect this transferred one third of the Czech population to German rule. In return the four powers represented at Munich guaranteed what was left of Czechoslovakia against unprovoked aggression.

Many people in Britain and France welcomed this agreement because they believed it had prevented a European war. Chamberlain himself said, I believe that it is peace in our time. Few of the men involved with imperial defence shared his optimism. On the day following the signing of the Munich Agreement, Sir Robert Brooke-Popham, Air Chief Marshal and Governor of Kenya wrote to the governor of Southern Rhodesia:

> *Sir, I have the honour to inform you that I received information from the Colonial Office to the effect that in the event of war it is probable that the squadron from Southern Rhodesia would be sent to Kenya and be placed under my orders for operations. I should be glad to know whether this information is correct. In the event of your reply being in the affirmative I should be glad if I could be supplied with the following information:*
>
> *a)   The time that would probably elapse between the declaration of the precautionary stage or of the opening of hostilities and the arrival of the squadron in Kenya.*
> *b)   The number of aeroplanes that will be sent and the strength of personnel, officers and men.*
> *c)   The type of aeroplanes and engines and the nature of petrol and oil required. As regards petrol, the particular information required is whether the engines require leaded fuel or whether they can use only unleaded petrol.*
> *d)   The type of bombs that the aeroplanes can carry.*
> *e)   The general position regarding spare parts.*
> *f)   The number of reserve pilots, aeroplanes and engines.*
> *In the event of the squadron being sent I presume that part of the personnel would be sent up by air using civil aircraft and that the remainder would travel with the heavy kit by sea. The duties for which the squadron would be required depend upon our enemies. Should we be engaged with Germany alone and Italy definitely neutral, the proposed duties of the squadron would be*

mainly coast reconnaissance from Mombasa and the possible attack on commerce, destroyers or submarines. Should Italy be hostile or a doubtful neutral, part or the whole squadron would be employed on the reconnaissance for the KAR (Kings African Rifles) on the northern and eastern frontiers of Kenya. (Signed R. Brooke-Popham)

Rhodesia's delay in beginning pilot training made it impossible for her to accept this challenge. To date only seven pilots had their wings, although another six were nearing the end of their first year's training and only six aircraft were available. So the reply had to be: This government is not in a position to give an assurance that the Southern Rhodesia Air Unit will be available for service in Kenya on the outbreak of war. One more year was to make all the difference.

No 3 Pilots' Course
With October came the new intake: Course No 3 of the Air Unit Pilot Training Scheme. In 1938 the scheme was extended: six pilots were taken on in Salisbury and six in Bulawayo. The six selected in Salisbury were Peter Fletcher, Stan Flett, Sandy MacIntyre, Les Olver, Colin Palmer and Cyril Sindall. The six pilots taken on in Bulawayo were H. Baron, Paul Holdengarde, E.P. Kleynhans, Geoff Robinson, J. Wrathall and Brian White.

As the size of the air unit increased so, inevitably, did the work and Hugh Peyton, later to die in tragic circumstances, was seconded to the permanent staff to help out. Hugh did not get on too well with income tax returns and such like and he was returned to his own department at the end of the year when his place was taken by Ted Jacklin. Ted was to prove the best possible man for this and almost any other job to do with the young air force. He had already made his mark on the rugby field representing Rhodesia against Sam Walker's British Isles XV, which toured Rhodesia and South Africa.

The Flying Circus
October also saw the start of the unique Travelling Flying School known off the record as the Flying Circus. The schedule for 1938/39 was Que Que from 23rd October to 18th December, Shabani for six weeks, followed by Gatooma from 29th January to 12th March, Umtali from 18th March to 13th May, Fort Victoria from 8th July and Wankie starting on 19th August.

The first team on the Flying Circus circuit comprised Charles Prince as the flying instructor and Hugh Gundry as ground engineer. Unit equipment consisted of a Tiger Moth, a personal motor car and Hugh's box of tools. Later D.D. Longmore took over from Charles Prince and Chummy Page from Hugh Gundry. Flying was done mainly in the early morning and late afternoon to meet climatic conditions and the demands of the students' normal employment. If there was a shed on the airfield, it became the office of the chief flying instructor and chief engineer. In the move from one town to another, one of the team would pilot the car and the other the aircraft.

Back at Belvedere, Jack Finnis was tutoring the students of the second course, who were by this time well advanced in the elementary flying stage. The only mishap of the year occurred in December while the air unit was on a visit to Rusape. A cog on the magneto of Graham Smith's machine stripped and the pilot made a forced landing. No damage was done.

Just before Christmas 1938 a conference of military representatives from the African colonies was held in Nairobi. Squadron Leader Powell attended on behalf of Southern Rhodesia.

Obviously, the subject of the possibility of moving Rhodesia's air unit to Kenya in the event of hostilities was still being considered because the inspector general in his year-end report to the secretary of State for the Colonies remarked:

In view of the constitutional position of Southern Rhodesia I do not think it is practicable for this flight to be dispatched during the precautionary stage. I am informed by the staff officer Air Services that if it is constitutionally possible it is essential that this move would take place during the stage referred to above. It is understood the Nairobi squadron will move at this stage and Kenya will be left without any aircraft for reconnaissance purposes. In the Southern Rhodesia Air Section are a number of territorials. Difficulties arise if they are to be called up for service before the war stage. These difficulties could however be overcome providing the personnel consent in advance to serve when called on to do so at any time before the outbreak of hostilities. I anticipate they will be agreeable to do this.

From future events it seems that they all were quite willing.

At the end of the year, Dirk Cloete resigned as director of civil aviation and officer in charge of the air section leaving to take a high position in South Africa. The air unit lost a good but somewhat austere commander who always displayed sound judgement in air matters.

Strength of the air unit at the close of 1938

Under Major Dirk Cloete—43 men.

One squadron leader: J.A. Powell

One flight lieutenant: V.E. Maxwell

One captain: C.S. Style

Six lieutenants: M.C.H. Barber, A.B.T. Cazalet, J. Holderness, R.M. Marshall, E. Smith, G. Smith

Eighteen second lieutenants: R.J.D. Christie, E.W.S. Jacklin, A.T.R. Hutchinson, H.C. Peyton, E.E. Spence, N.S.F. Tyas, P. Fletcher, S. Flett, A. MacIntyre, L.R. Olver, C. Palmer, C. Sindall, J. Wrathall, H. Baron, P. Holdengarde, E.P. Kleynhans, G. Robinson, B. White

Five airmen ground staff—seconded from RAF:

Flight Sergeant A. Greenwood, Sergeant C.P. Horton, Sergeant V.J. Royce, Corporal A. Higham, Leading Aircraftman M. Madders

Southern Rhodesia Permanent Force:

NCO Corporal A.B.P. Simpson

Four photographers: Aircraftmen S.L. Wilson, R.C. Palgrave, R.H. Krahner, D.R. Allen

Captain C.W. Robertson was appointed to the air unit as honorary medical officer.

There were also six apprentices at RAF Halton.

CHAPTER 4

The first in the field

The first ferry

It was in February 1939 that welcome news was received. The Audax aircraft were ready to be collected and so Jimmie Powell, Captain Claude Style, John Holderness and Eric Smith together with Sergeant Charles Horton set out for Cairo. The journey was made in the Rhodesian government Rapide and took a week, including two days in Nairobi.

However, on arrival at the RAF base in Heliopolis, it was found that the Audaxes were still in their crates, so with Jimmie Powell in the lead, the five men set off on a tour of the Holy Land. Eric Smith remembers: Jimmie Powell had £500 that he thought would cover expenses but travelling and subsistence came to only about one pound a day and the use of all the money took a deal of explaining! The Rhodesians had a good time seeing the sights of the Middle East, quite an eye-opener to young men who had never been out of Rhodesia.

In Cairo the members of the flight met Air Vice-Marshal H.R. Nicoll, Air Officer Commanding Middle East, and in Palestine they met Air Commodore A.T. (Bomber) Harris. Both these men had lived in Rhodesia and gave the visitors a warm welcome. All too soon the aircraft had been assembled and the members of the air unit left Heliopolis for Luxor on 11th March 1939.

The flight back gave the Rhodesian pilots their first taste of flying in open cockpits under desert conditions with heat and poor visibility owing to sandstorms. The first real problem occurred at Malakal on the Nile when Captain Style's aircraft suffered damage while landing. The Audax was left at Malakal.

It was at Mpika, in Northern Rhodesia that the flight began to experience typical tropical summer weather. Eric Smith recalls:

> There was also a heavy storm at Mpika. Flying with no navigational aids, we were forced right down near Lusaka, but luckily came out of the low cloud where the ground was comparatively flat. We took off from Lusaka the first time on 17th (March) climbed to 20,000 feet to try to fly above the storm but couldn't so landed and took off again the following day, the 18th. This time we flew under the storm and literally round the Matusadonna Mountains to reach Salisbury. Jimmie was ok in the covered Rapide. The rest of us were in open cockpits. Flying through hail over the Umvukwes was not funny!

Assessing the value of the flight Jimmie Powell said:

> Contact was made with the RAF at a number of stations, including Nairobi, Khartoum and Cairo, while experience of flying over as diversified territory as the 10,000 foot mountains of Kenya and the flat desert country of the Sudan and Egypt was of particular value.

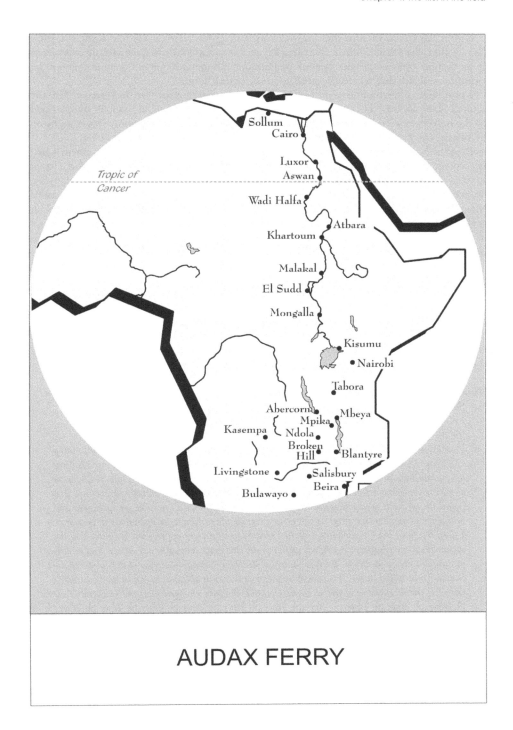

AUDAX FERRY

Within Rhodesia, air unit training was continuing. Aircraftmen Freddie Kimpton, John Gray, John Oliver Ross Collins, Griffiths, Payne, Lucas and Johnson were gaining experience as mechanics while some members of 1st Battalion Rhodesia Regiment were learning to be airgunners, a skill that was to be put to good use before long.

World wide, governments were talking peace but preparing for war. In January 1939 the United States increased her defence budget. On 26th January, General Franco's troops aided by the Italians entered Barcelona and the following day Franco's rebel regime was recognized by Britain and France. To all intents and purposes the Spanish Civil War was over.

On 15th March, Hitler showed exactly what he thought of the Munich Agreement when he ordered the German army into Prague and declared that Czechoslovakia had ceased to exist. Two days later, Chamberlain accused Hitler of breaking his word but otherwise no action was taken. On 22nd March, German troops occupied the old German city of Memel in Lithuania. Danzig in Poland had also once been part of Germany and the Polish government recognizing the parallel, announced, on March 28th that any German attempt to alter Danzig's status without Polish consent would result in war. On March 31st Britain unilaterally guaranteed Poland's sovereignty.

For some time, British, French and Soviet discussions about a possible alliance had been in progress. Russia believed, quite rightly, that Poland could not be defended without Russian cooperation and on 18th April the Russian foreign minister proposed a ten-year alliance with Britain and France. Meanwhile Germany was also having secret talks with Russia and on 28th April Hitler cancelled the non-aggression agreement that had been signed with Poland in 1934.

On 5th April Italy invaded Albania. War clouds were gathering and Africa would not remain uninvolved. Should Italy be drawn into a European war on the side of the Germans there would be a major threat in East Africa.

Rhodesia commits to East African defence

5th April 1939

From: Air Marshal W.G.S. Mitchell, Air Officer Commanding, Middle East

To: the Governor, SR Salisbury

Your Excellency, I have the honour to inform Your Excellency that in my capacity as coordinating authority for air operations in the Middle East I have received instructions from the Air Ministry to communicate directly with you regarding the cooperation of the SR Air Unit in the event of war. I understand from the Air Ministry that Your Excellency is already aware that it is hoped in the event of war that the SR government will provide all possible air assistance and will agree to move such aircraft as can be made available to Kenya for operations in that area. I should inform Your Excellency that the situation as at present appreciated indicates that the major threat from Italian East Africa would in the first place develop in the Sudan and on this account our plan provides for the withdrawal of the RAF Squadron at present at Nairobi to the Sudan in the initial stages. It is important therefore that such air forces as can be made available from SR should move to Kenya as soon as possible after the emergency arises. Subject to Your Excellency's approval I propose that the SR Air Unit should come under the Royal Air Force station commander, Nairobi and be employed in cooperation with the KAR. The primary role of the Hart and Audax aircraft would be reconnaissance designed to give early information of enemy advance into Kenya and to take such action as circumstances permitted.

This letter goes on to say that all RAF personnel might have to be removed. Southern Rhodesia would, therefore, have to provide technical personnel who were to be civilian volunteers if necessary. Spare parts for the aircraft would also be a problem but a suggestion from Southern Rhodesia offered a solution:

...the best solution from our point of view would be for the RAF Middle East to hold the necessary technical stores at Nairobi for the use of the SR flight as the supply held in this colony is extremely small and insufficient to be split up. Arrangements have been made with Rhodesian and Nyasaland Airways Ltd, to provide aircraft at 24 hours' notice within the limits of their fleet for the conveyance of personnel and aircraft spare parts from Salisbury or elsewhere to such destinations as may be decided on at the time in the event of war.
(From Acting Sec Dept Justice to P.M. 18th April 1939)

Second ferry

Now that the air unit was committed there were two major priorities, one was to get as many pilots trained as possible; the other was to have more aircraft available. Four Audaxes had been flown to Rhodesia in March but two were still with the RAF in Heliopolis. Graham Smith, who was holidaying in England, received a request to return via Heliopolis and collect one of them. The other was to be flown out by Jimmie Powell who would fly up in the Rapide with Eric Smith.

On this second flight it was Graham Smith who suffered a mishap. The brakes of his aircraft began giving trouble at Kisumu. When he landed at Lusaka, the tail wheel swivelled causing the aircraft to flip. Graham Smith released his harness and promptly fell out on his head; his fellow pilots remarked afterwards that he never fully recovered from the incident!

This flight was scheduled to bring back three aircraft: two from Cairo, and the Audax that had been left at Malakal on the previous trip. However, only two reached Salisbury because Graham Smith's machine had to be left in Lusaka.

Two further Audax planes arrived at Salisbury shortly before five o'clock yesterday evening (26th April) for the Southern Rhodesia Air Section. They were accompanied by the Dragon Rapide plane that had taken the personnel of the flight to Cairo to take over the machines. The three planes were met on nearing Salisbury by a flight of five Harts and escorted by them to the military aerodrome, the eight planes flying over the city in formation...The pilots were accompanied by Lieutenant W.J. James of the BSAP. (Rhodesia Herald, 27th April 1939)

Meanwhile the country was catching war fever. A course of lectures on air raid precautions began on 24th April. This was arranged by Colonel W.H. Ralston who had been designated ARP officer for the Colony. It may seem laughable, when we look back, but at least it showed a spirit of preparedness.

With all due pomp and ceremony, parliament was opened on 3rd May. The governor announced that a commission which had been appointed to consider closer cooperation among Southern Rhodesia, Northern Rhodesia (Zambia) and Nyasaland (Malawi) had reported back favourably. Unfortunately, the idea was to be placed on hold and by the time it was re-examined the political climate had changed out of all recognition. An expansion of the air unit was announced and the following day came the Budget, estimated expenditure being £3,779.210— about £100,000 more than the estimated income. But this amount was to be met out of the previous year's surplus with no rise in the level of taxation, which showed that Rhodesia's finances were healthy. Defence and police votes were to be increased to a total of £600,000.

Members of No 2 Pilots' Course receive their Wings

Ten days later, on 13th May, the second intake of pilots received their Wings. These were Ted Jacklin, Eric Spence, Tickey Tyas, Hugh Peyton, R.J.D. Christie and A.T.R. Hutchinson. A description of the ceremony was carried in the *Rhodesia Herald*:

The parade of pilots and other ranks was drawn up in front of the line of Audax, Hart and other machines and on the arrival of His Excellency, gave the Royal salute that was sounded by the trumpeters of the BSAP. Following the ceremony, the governor received tea in the officers' mess and inspected the recent additions to the facilities, which included a large new hangar. Meanwhile five of the machines had taken to the air and carried out formation flying.

Suddenly the need for pilots seemed to catch the Colony's imagination. A correspondent to the letters page of *The Herald* suggested that more flying scholarships should be made available. The writer offered to provide two himself and a third when 12 others were given.

During the last weekend in May, 31 aeroplanes from all over the country gathered in Umtali for an Air Rally. Once again there were polished displays by the air unit of message picking-up, formation-flying and aerobatics.

Unfortunately, flying training carries risks and on June 2nd came the news that Hugh Salisbury James had been killed in a flying accident near Lincoln, in England. Hugh James had taken up a short service commission with the RAF in February 1938. Pallbearers at the funeral were Pilot Officers Kane, N.G. MacFarlane, Thomas C. Cundill and Arthur M. Imrie, Rhodesians from among the 13 who had joined the RAF the previous year.

Two weeks later, a new director of civil aviation and officer commanding the air section was appointed. He was Lieutenant Colonel Charles Warburton Meredith AFC who had been commanding officer of the Aircraft and Artillery Depot at Roberts Heights, now known as Voortrekkerhoogte in South Africa. Shortly after taking up his new position he made his strong feelings known: there was to be no more talk of air sections and air units, the thrust would be towards the establishment of an autonomous air force!

Towards the end of June, almost casually during an address by the Secretary of State for Air to the Empire Press Union in London, came mention of a plan that was to lead to Rhodesia's greatest single contribution to the war effort. This plan that was already under way was to set up training facilities in territories such as the Middle East, Far East, Ceylon, Hong Kong, Southern Rhodesia, Kenya, West Africa and Malta. This was the first mention of what was to become The Empire Air Training Scheme in which The Rhodesia Air Training Group was to play such a prominent role.

The air unit's first 'cruise' outside the Colony

July 1939 proved an exciting month. First, *The Herald* was able to announce that owing to public support eleven more flying scholarships were now available. Secondly, six more RAF ground instructors arrived: Sergeant F.G. Tipping (armament), Sergeant F. Moss (photographic section), Sergeant H. Clark (radio), Corporal J.T. Jones, Leading Aircraftmen, D.M. Hutchinson, V.A. Frost, and J.F. Ridgeway. But most exciting of all was the occasion of the air unit's first cruise outside the borders of the Colony.

At 06h15 on 14th July, five aircraft of the unit left Salisbury to take part in the Royal Air Force Day at Nairobi. Their route took them via Lusaka, Mpika, Mbeya, Dodoma, Dar es Salaam, Zanzibar and Mombasa to Nairobi. The flight was led by V.E. Maxwell, who was accompanied by Charles Meredith. The pilots were Lieutenants John Holderness, Graham Smith, Hugh Peyton and Eric Spence. The RAF lent a helping hand in the shape of Sergeant Vic Royce and Corporal Alec Higham, Aircraftman Freddie Kimpton and Corporal Ivor de B.C. Fynn who went along to man the radio.

The unit made quite an impression with its aerobatics and ability to pick up messages. The display was, however, marred by a tragic accident when a RAF Vickers Wellesley piloted by Lieutenant C.F. Camp of the South African Air Force crashed killing the pilot.

John Holderness had the dubious honour of flying Charles Meredith back to Salisbury and he later confirmed the following story. Apparently, the engine developed a fault and the aircraft began to lose height. John decided that he could reach base. The engine became rougher and more height was lost. John, have you got the situation under control? asked the colonel. Yes, sir, came the reply. Meredith sat back and never touched the controls, even though he had vastly more experience than the man at the controls, and by virtue of his command, was empowered to take over. He relaxed and seemed quite happy as John Holderness battled on losing more and more height, eventually dragging the aircraft over the trees onto the airfield. Holderness remarked later how much he appreciated the colonel's restraint.

All in all, everybody seemed very satisfied with the air unit's first official showing outside the Colony. The other members of the air unit were keeping busy surveying the country. By August the Shabani district from Fort Victoria to Filabusi had been photographed ready for map-making.

That same month the flying circus arrived in Fort Victoria but its fame had spread much further afield as an article in the Newsletter of British Aircraft Constructors showed:

> *Southern Rhodesia has the world's First Travelling Flying school. Faced with the difficulty of providing air instruction in several different centres, not one of which appeared large enough to support a local unit, the progressive Colony decided to establish a school that could move from town to town. Since last October the unit has trained more than one dozen pilots at Que Que and Gatooma to the stage of qualifying as 'A' pilots. The equipment used consists of a Tiger Moth, a tent, a box of tools, some spares, six helmets, earphones and goggles.*

(Newsletter of British Aircraft Constructors)

Probably owing to the influence of Charles Meredith, increasing reference was being made at this time to the Southern Rhodesia Air Force. Maxie Maxwell was even signing pilots' log-books as commanding officer No 1 Squadron, SR Air Force, though there had as yet been no official notification of a change in title.

Winter 1939, war clouds might be looming heavy on the horizon but the Salisbury Agricultural Show must go on. The opening day, Wednesday 16th August, and one of the first points to visit, for the small boys in the crowd, was the air unit Hawker Hart and Audax, which had been flown to the civilian aerodrome at Belvedere and towed into position in the showground. Perhaps it was the interest caused by this exhibit that caused a *Rhodesia Herald* reporter to visit the military aerodrome:

> *There has been a fair amount of building activity at the military aerodrome during the past two or three months. A new hangar and a storehouse for technical equipment have been added to the accommodation available as well as workshops for wireless, photographic and armament sections. Quarters for non-commissioned officers and airmen are now in the course of erection. The area of the aerodrome has also been increased to approximately 200 acres.*

Back in May, Italy and Germany had signed the Pact of Steel. This had been expected. But then came startling news. Russia and Germany had signed a non-aggression pact. What was even worse but was unknown at the time was a secret annexure, which divided Eastern Europe between Germany and the Soviet Union. The British government, which had also been negotiating with the Soviet Union, replied by warning Germany that Britain would fulfil her guarantees to Poland. Hitler, believing that Britain would back down again, as it had done the year before over Czechoslovakia, scheduled his attack on Poland for 26th August, only to have his plans thwarted by Mussolini who said Italy was not ready for war. Hitler delayed his attack for a few days.

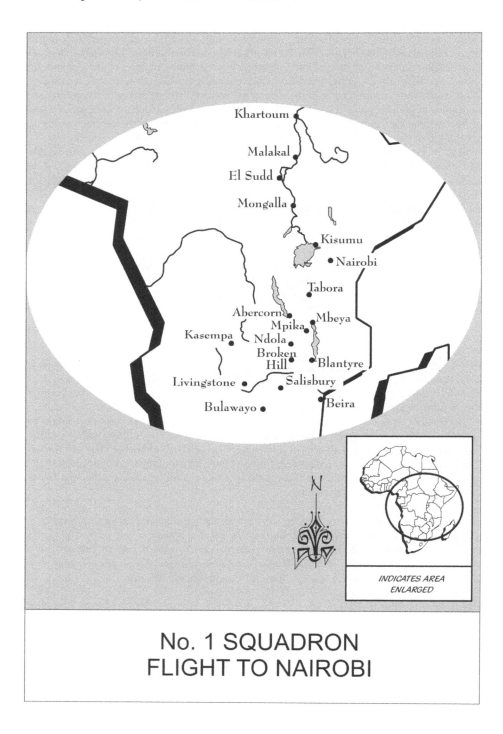

No. 1 SQUADRON
FLIGHT TO NAIROBI

The air unit moves north

Meanwhile on 23rd August, the secretary of state in London telegraphed the government in Salisbury:

In view of movement of RAF squadron to war stations in Sudan, SR asked to take any preliminary steps desirable to facilitate expeditious movements SR Troops and air unit to Kenya in accordance with co-ordination scheme.

On the following day the War Diary, Southern Rhodesia reads:

It was decided that arrangements should be made for the move of a contingent of SRAF to Nairobi.

The secretary of state in London was informed that the SR Air Unit could move within 24 hours from the receipt of a request to do so. Next day the request arrived:

We should be glad if the SR Air Unit could move to Kenya at earliest possible moment.

Jimmie Powell was in London where he had gone with the Prime Minister, Sir Godfrey Huggins, so Maxwell was in command in Salisbury. Accordingly it was Maxwell who received the historic order to move north:

August 26th 1939
To: Squadron Leader V.E. Maxwell
From: Colonel H.M. Watson
You are to leave for Nairobi at 06h00 on 27th August 1939 with personnel and aircraft as shown in Annexures A & B.★

Eric Smith remembers:

It all began on Saturday morning 26th August 1939 when we were summoned to headquarters, kept hanging around till 3 pm and curtly told we were leaving for Kenya at 6 am next morning. We were then packed off, lunchless, to Cranborne to overload our Audax and Harts with essential spares and equipment. Our first experience of the proverbial 'flap' kept us going until about 7 pm that evening. As there was no hope of settling any of our private and civilian affairs we did the next best thing and assembled at Meikles Hotel, attending a hilarious ball and finishing at the Ace of Spades just in time to discard evening dress, don uniforms and present ourselves for take-off. Our ragged kangaroo-like departures went unnoticed by the small group of emotional misty-eyed and uncritical spectators.

Martin Madders who was ground crew ex RAF, says that it was a rush job to get the aircraft ready, particularly SR 6 which had been cannibalized to repair other aircraft. Ground crew were divided, some accompanying the flight to Nairobi, some, unlucky ones, remaining in Salisbury. Arthur Greenwood, Vic Royce and Martin Madders were among those left behind to help with future training. Madders remembers that there was such a shortage of ground crew that all garage mechanics and private aircraft workers—in fact anyone who knew anything about machinery and engines—were recruited.

So the air unit took to the air on their way to battle stations. Eric Smith was flying in Audax SR 12 and Graham Smith was in SR 3. Eric, reporting on the flight, said:

At Mpika Graham Smith's aircraft gave trouble with the carburettor. The Rolls-Royce carburettor was fastened in with scores of bolts. The ground crew worked in the dark most of the night, lost bolts and eventually gave it up till the morning. Nobby Clark was in Graham's plane, so a case of tools was left for him to work with and the rest took off leaving me to keep Graham company. They got the plane going in the morning and took off from Mpika. Now we were on our own. I didn't have any maps but I had flown the route twice before and knew the general direction. Graham took off first. His compass was giving trouble and he took off on a course 30 degrees from the correct one. I tried but I couldn't catch him. I was too heavily loaded with tools. Luckily Graham spotted a river that was where it should not have been and realizing he was off course circled to allow me to catch up. From then on we didn't have too much trouble. Incidentally, Sergeant Charles (Darky) Horton who was flying with me, grew so attached to the Rhodesian squadron that he refused a commission in order to stay with us and eventually was commissioned in the squadron.

Owing to the problems experienced by Graham, the squadron had to make an extra night stop at Moshi, and arrived in Nairobi at 08h30 on 29th August. Their arrival made headline news in the newspapers and on the radio. There was no strict security blackout—but then the war had not started yet. It was a matter of days!

While the air unit was on its way north, the Southern Rhodesia Parliament, at a special sitting, which lasted only 80 minutes, passed the Emergency Powers (Defence) Bill through all its stages. This bill gave the government power to govern by regulation in the event of war. As Sir Godfrey Huggins had not yet returned from Britain the Honourable Percy Finn acted as prime minister.

Within 24 hours of its arrival in Nairobi, the air unit was at work patrolling the Somaliland border from forward bases with scratch RAF ground crews. Eric Smith remembered:

'A' flight under the command of Flight Lieutenant Graham Smith patrolled the northern sector as far as the Abyssinian border and 'B' flight under my command, patrolled the southern sector down to the coast. Immediately an intense if friendly rivalry sprang up between the flights and continued throughout the whole of the East African Campaign.

The Rhodesian press published a report that was calculated to lay fears to rest:

It should be made clear that it is a section of the Colony's air force that has gone to Kenya. The rest of the unit remains in the Colony.

That sounds encouraging but Meredith was to write later:

The aircraft and equipment required for the unit left only four Harts and about eight light aircraft in Rhodesia and war having been declared, the absolute maximum war effort that could have been expected would have been the replacement of aircrew wastage in the unit in Kenya. Even this would have been on a partially trained basis and wholly contingent on the availability of replacement aircraft, spares and equipment. For this contingency no provision had been made and no planning was in existence.

A few days later than he had originally planned, Hitler ordered his attack on Poland. It was September 1st. The time was 04h45 hours. Without any declaration of war, the German army swept across the Polish border. This ended any hope of peace but the French still clung to the vain hope that war could be avoided. While the bombs rained down on Warsaw and the panzer divisions rolled forward, Chamberlain delayed issuing an ultimatum. At last on September 2nd he told Hitler that unless German troops were withdrawn, Germany must consider herself at war with Britain. Hitler ignored the ultimatum. Britain and Germany were at war.

Budget 1939

The air unit was to receive an estimated £33,177; additional aircraft were to be purchased for £3,900 and the establishment of manpower was to be increased. Provision was made for the inclusion of a sergeant armourer, a wireless operator, five more aircraftmen and a storeman.

★ Orders for the move to Kenya

26th August 1939
To: Squadron Leader V.E. Maxwell
From: Colonel H.M. Watson

1) *You are to leave for Nairobi at 06h00 on 27th August 1939 with personnel and aircraft as shown in annexures A and B and on arriving you are to report to the officer commanding Royal Air Force Station Nairobi. Should there be no station commander at that point you are to report to the general officer commanding in chief, East African Forces, and request that officer to notify the air officer commanding in chief Middle East of your arrival, and thereafter you are to await instructions as to whose command you will fall under.*

2) *Personnel*

a) *Officers. Lieutenants Martin Pearce, Arthur Downing and Reg Bourlay have been commissioned in the territorial forces and called up for duty for the purpose of flying Rapide aircraft. Their expenses are to be met by you from your imprest fund in the same manner as for your remaining personnel.*

b) *Other ranks. On arrival at Dodoma, wireless operators shown in annexure A are to be deplaned and instructed to report to the officer commanding Kings African Rifles at that centre or if there is no such officer then the provincial commissioner. Deputy assistant adjutant general is preparing instructions for transmission by these personnel. Corporal Alec Higham at present in Nairobi should be taken on your strength.*

3) *Aircraft*

a) *The two Rapides shown in annexure B with civil registration marks have been chartered from RANA and other than in exceptional circumstances are not to be flown by other than RANA pilots. Lieutenant Pearce is the senior of these pilots attached for duty and the allocation of aircraft should be delegated to him.*

b) *On arrival at Nairobi, arrangements are to be made to send the three Rapides back to Salisbury. Lieutenant Pearce should be detailed to fly SR 8; that officer should be instructed to detail pilots for the RANA aircraft.*

4) *Route and times*

a) *The route to be followed and the estimated times of departure are set out in annexure C.*

b) *Return: The three Rapides SR 8, VP-YBJ and VP-YBT are to return by the same route as on the forward journey unless in your discretion circumstances necessitate alteration. They should be dispatched from Nairobi after allowing one clear day after arrival and if you adhere to your itinerary this will be Wednesday 30th August 1939. Should there be any delay in forward itinerary or in preparing the Rapides for the return flight they should be dispatched as early as possible. You are to place Lieutenant Pearce in charge of the flight and provide him with adequate written instructions in regards to the return journey.*

You are also to provide him from your imprest account with sufficient money to meet the expenses of the crews on the return journey and include in your instructions details of the method of accounting for the money on his arrival in Salisbury.

5) *Safety at aerodrome*

As it is possible that landing grounds at Mbeya, Dodoma and Mushi may be unsafe for landing, signals have been made requesting that you be informed before commencing any one leg that the aerodrome at which you intend to land is safe. In case of a breakdown in these arrangements and in any event you are to exercise caution before landing and to institute a system whereby if any aerodrome appears unsafe one aircraft only is to land and the pilot having satisfied himself by inspection that the control of the aerodrome is in safe hands is to make a pre-arranged permissive signal for the remainder of the flight to land. Should the pilot of the first aircraft to land make a negative signal, or be attacked or captured you are to use your discretion as to whether to institute an air attack and also as to the point at which you will land the remainder of the aircraft.

6) *Intercommunications*

All arrivals and departures signals are to be addressed to Aviation Salisbury. The administrations of the territories through which you pass have been informed that the flight will be operating on 900 metres with a call sign SR 9 and have been requested to keep watch for the flight.

7) *Administration arrangements for arms and ammunition equipment*

Harts and Audaxes are to be fitted with front and rear guns and to carry 250 rounds of ammunition each for the front gun, three drums for the rear gun. In addition, each aircraft will be provided with one rifle and 20 rounds of ammunition.

8) *Fuel and oil*

Arrangements have been made with Shell Company for sufficient supplies of fuel and oil to be available at all landing points for both forward and return journeys and in this connection it should be noted that the chartered Rapides are to draw supplies on both journeys on government account.

9) *Stores, equipment etc.*

In accordance with discussions you have included in these loads to be carried by air such items as you can conveniently stow and will require.

10) *Imprest account*

An imprest account of £50 has been arranged by the paymaster and is to be accounted for in terms of instructions issued by that officer.

11) *Discipline*

For disciplinary purposes, all Royal Air Force personnel have been granted local ranks in SR Air Force equal to Royal Air Force ranks held. The extent of disciplinary powers thus conferred on the Royal Air Force personnel and SR personnel is under consideration but generally will be in terms of the SR Defence Act.

12) *Guard*

A request for the provision of a guard at Mbeya has been transmitted to the officer commanding 7 Brigade Kings African Rifles. Personnel records with which you are provided are to be handed to the officer to whom you report at Nairobi.

Nominal roll of persons accompanying SR flight

Officers

Flying Personnel

 Squadron Leader Maxie Maxwell (RAF)

 Lieutenant Ron Marshall

    Lieutenant Graham Smith
    Lieutenant Eric Smith
    Second Lieutenant Hugh Peyton
    Second Lieutenant Eric Spence
    Second Lieutenant Alec Hutchinson
    Second Lieutenant Ron Christie
    Second Lieutenant Ted Jacklin
    Second Lieutenant Tickey Tyas
    Lieutenant Martin Pearce   RANA
    Lieutenant Reg Bourlay   RANA
    Lieutenant Arthur Downing   RANA

Medical personnel

One medical officer
    Captain C.W. Robertson MO

Other ranks

Fitters
    Sergeant C.P. Horton   RAF
    Corporal Alec Higham   RAF Nairobi
    Corporal V.A. Frost   RAF
    Aircraftman Walter Pollard

Riggers (Aero)
    Corporal J.F. Ridgeway   RAF
    Aircraftman W.J. Lucas

Armourer
    Sergeant G. Tipping   RAF

Wireless operator/mechanic
    Sergeant H. Clark   RAF

Wireless operators
    Sergeant Ken Murrell
    Corporal H.L. (Mollie) Maltas
    T.J. MacDonald

Posts and telegraphs
    B. Coulson
    C.F. Lindeque (to be deplaned at Dodoma seconded from KAR)

Four airgunners
    Aircraftman Alan Burl
    Aircraftman Oliver Ross Collins
    Aircraftman John Gray
    Aircraftman Freddie Kimpton

One clerk
    Corporal Alan Simpson (ex army and police stores)

Aircraft
    Audax   SR 10, SR 11, SR 12, SR 13
    Harts   SR 3, SR 6
    Rapides   SR 8, VP-YBJ, VP-YBT (The last two are on charter from RANA)

CHAPTER 5

The phoney war

Britain declared war on Germany on 3rd September 1939. On the following day this notice appeared in the *Rhodesia Herald*:

> *Southern Rhodesia Defence Force*
> *Recruits are urgently required*
> *Reserve called to report*
> *Recruiting offices opened.*

And on another page:

> *Warning: Prohibition of transactions in respect of Southern Rhodesia aircraft and parts of aircraft. All owners and possessors of Southern Rhodesia aircraft are hereby notified that under legislation to become effective from the outbreak of war, the sanction of the minister of defence is required for the sale, transfer, letting or hire and changing of an aircraft registered in the Colony.*

According to a *Rhodesia Herald* report:

> *In Salisbury the young men rushed to the state lotteries hall to enlist. There was a lottery draw on that afternoon and a number of ladies hopeful of winning the jackpot were in attendance; but the menfolk stripped to the waist and not heeding the revolving wheels and dancing balls, went past for their medical examinations. There was such a rush at the recruiting station that some men waited all day in queues for examination.* (Rhodesia Herald)

The air unit becomes No 1 Squadron

On 6th September a discussion was held with the minister of defence. It was agreed that Middle East should be informed that the name of the Southern Rhodesia Air Unit was to be changed to No 1 Squadron, Southern Rhodesia Air Force and that the Colony was prepared to build the squadron to full strength. It was also agreed that RANA would be taken over and converted into a Communications Squadron.

The Prime Minister, Sir Godfrey Huggins, was in London when war broke out and so was the Minister of Defence, the Honourable R.C. Tredgold who gave a statement on the Colony's defence position on 11th September.

> *The training section of the air unit has been greatly expanded to meet war conditions and it will soon be possible to train a large number of recruits in Salisbury...Recruits who are prepared to serve either in the Rhodesian Air Section or the RAF will be accepted on the same general basis.*

Their medical, educational and general fitness will be examined and then they will be called up as and when required. Again each case will be considered by the local tribunal.

Three days later, the Southern Rhodesia Air Force recruiting drive went into full gear with a front page centre advertisement in the *Rhodesia Herald*:

Air Force
Applications are invited from citizens who are desirous of being considered for service in the air force on flying and ground duties.
The following basic conditions are essential:
a)   Male, British, European
b)   Over 18 and under 25 years of age
c)   Willing to:
*   1)   Train and/or serve beyond the borders of the Colony as may be required*
*   2)   Attend interview if required and medical examination*
Personnel already serving, NO MATTER IN WHAT UNIT, must without exception submit applications through their commanding officers.

With reference to this last stipulation, the number of men wishing to transfer from other units was to be a major bone of contention.

The response to the recruiting campaign was overwhelming: 499 applications were received in 12 days. One of the first organizations to be hit by this rush to join the air force was RANA that lost nearly all their technical staff. RANA, therefore, appealed through the pages of the newspaper for women and men who were too old or not fit enough for military service to help the company out by taking positions such as bookkeeping, storekeeping and office work. They also needed people who were prepared to clean plugs, spray paint, stitch fabric and carry out any other of the many tasks needed to keep aircraft in the air. They also appealed for any women who had even an elementary knowledge of the internal combustion engine to come forward.

On 25th September, defence headquarters issued a memorandum confirming that Lieutenant Colonel Meredith was to continue as both officer commanding the air force and director of civil aviation, stating that in future the military aerodrome would be known as Cranborne Air Station. Obviously more office accommodation was required for headquarters and a house in Montagu Avenue was acquired. Squadron Leader Powell now back in the Colony was soon busy speeding up the training of ground and aircrew. Martin Madders talking about this time says:

When Powell returned from the UK he ordered every aircraft to be got ready to fly by the following day. Crews were named. They took off at the crack of dawn, armed with toilet rolls and scientifically 'bombed' the drill hall. The army was not amused.

Sir Godfrey Huggins had also returned to the Colony and on 2nd October in a broadcast to the country reported:

More than two thirds of what was considered to be the Colony's available manpower for military service has already volunteered, in spite of the fact that those engaged in mining, farming and transportation have been warned that they should not enlist at present...In regard to the Rhodesia Air Force, the recruitment campaign which was only started on September 15th indicates that our ability to help in the air and with the necessary ground staff is much greater than was expected. This, of course, will be one of our most valuable contributions.

Accommodation problems

There were some enormous problems, however, one of the greatest being a shortage of accommodation. Public Works were doing their best but in the meantime tents and other temporary housing were being utilized.

Madders remarks that there was no accommodation for the sudden influx that occurred with the outbreak of war. A hangar was cleared of aircraft and filled with beds. Mrs Madders (as she was later to become) cooked the first meal in the sergeants' mess. One of the men was unfortunate enough to have his bed under the hoist. The boys came back late one night, fixed the four corners of the bed to the hoist and lifted him off the ground complete with bed.

A further problem was the shortage of equipment. By the 2nd October there were 30 pilots, ten airgunners and 15 mechanics under training. Appeals had been made to the Air Ministry for aircraft but no action had been taken as yet. The control of de Havilland had been taken over and without exception the personnel joined the air force. Certain problems had come up as far as the takeover of RANA was concerned and that had been postponed until 1st November 1939.

Discussions with the third civil flying company, Flights Ltd were still in progress. It was estimated that the Rhodesian Government Flying School would have a full capacity of 100 trainees with an output of 30 every six weeks. In his letter to Commandant Southern Rhodesia Forces, Colonel Meredith remarks that No 1 Squadron in Kenya still required 19 aircrew to bring it up to strength and that these men would be ready by 6th November. As far as ground personnel were concerned, it was hoped to send 90 men north in batches of 30 from the middle of December.

Apprentices arrive back

As for ground crew instructors, the six men who had trained with the Royal Air Force: Ron Boswell, Ron Cashel, F.G. (Otto) Gericke, Brynmor Hyla (Mick) Gibbons, Ralph Mays Parry and Stanley Ryder Young had arrived back in the Colony and started duty with the Southern Rhodesia Air Force on 5th October. These men had come back by sea, sailing across the Atlantic to the American coast and then back to the Cape, presumably to dodge the powerfully armed, German pocket battleship, the Graf Spee, which was reported to be in the South Atlantic. More would be heard of this craft in the near future. Parry remembers being taken straight to Cranborne on his arrival, shown a big box and told: There's an aircraft. Build it. These were the Gloster Gladiators that had been purchased from the RAF.

Meanwhile the situation at Cranborne Air Station had become chaotic. There were inadequate cooking facilities and off duty rooms. It was decided that no further men would be called up until proper messing arrangements could be made. On 20th October 1939, the *Rhodesia Herald* printed a long article about the air force reporting that six weeks' initial flying in DH Tiger Moths was to be followed by training on Hawker Harts and Audaxes that would include night flying. The pilots would then be awarded their wings, which would be the equivalent of a 'B' licence. There was also a description of Cranborne Air Station:

> *Cut from the bush is a great flying field, bounded on the west by the hangars and living quarters. At present the recruits are housed in tents but shortly they will have moved into new barrack huts, which are being built among the trees to the north. To the north-west are the NCO's quarters built of brick. These were started before the war; and to the north-east is the CO's house. South of this are the officers' quarters. Provision has been made for extension of all these new quarters.* (Rhodesia Herald)

Which was just as well as it turned out!

Pilot training continued, with the men and equipment available until the end of March 1940, when Southern Rhodesia's air force training ceased. By that time the school had trained 15 pilots through intermediate and advanced stages, passed 62 pilots through elementary stage, trained nine airgunners and three flying instructors, together with a number of fitters, riggers and photographers. (Archives s800 Notes prepared for visit of Inspector General Oct 1942)

At the end of October 1939, Meredith travelled to London by way of Broken Hill in Northern Rhodesia. His aim was to obtain supplies of aircraft and equipment in order to extend Rhodesia's air training facilities. His ideas were received with enthusiasm in London because the Air Ministry realized that there was a necessity to get initial air training out of Britain where it was vulnerable to both air attack and the possibility of a German invasion. So it was that the discussions developed along the lines of a much larger scheme than Meredith had envisaged. It was to involve not only Rhodesians but also men from Britain, the Empire and its allies. Meanwhile many young Rhodesians were not waiting for the scheme to get off the ground. Those that were in Britain at the outbreak of war had already volunteered straight away; many others made their way by the fastest route to the United Kingdom. According to the *Rhodesia Herald*'s correspondent in the United Kingdom:

> *During a second special tour organized by the Air Ministry, I witnessed youthful Rhodesians and South Africans undergoing training as officer pilots at one of the numerous stations 'somewhere in England'...Of the 50 pupils undergoing advanced squadron training, there are 16 South Africans and Rhodesians, who were highly praised to me by their instructors.*
> (Rhodesia Herald)

On the world front, the various parts of the British Empire had followed Britain's lead and declared war on Germany. Australia and New Zealand on September 3rd, South Africa on the 6th, and Canada on the 10th, the day on which the British Expeditionary Force began crossing the Channel to reinforce the French army.

In Poland the Germans were giving the world its first taste of the blitzkrieg, with its tactics of speed and shock. It was a fresh approach to war and its overwhelming success surprised not only the Poles but also the Germans themselves. Never before had a nation's military capacity been so utterly annihilated in so short a time with so little loss to the attacking force. The basic principle, which had been developed by a British First World War officer, Liddell Hart, was to attack where it was least expected and to move fast, using armoured vehicles to cut supply lines and disrupt communications. Hitler's forces conquered Poland in 18 days.

Seeing the way things were going and wanting her share of the plunder, the Soviet Union joined in on 17th September 1939, attacking from the east. Warsaw surrendered officially on 27th September and a Polish government in exile was established in Paris, while Poland was divided between the victors.

For Britain, the war at sea was going as badly as the war on land. The aircraft carrier, HMS *Courageous* had been torpedoed in September, and on October 14th *The Royal Oak* was sunk while at anchor in Scapa Flow with the loss of 833 lives.

The Italians had so far shown no signs of entering the war and so life for No 1 Squadron at first consisted of rather monotonous patrol work. Then in the middle of November came a report that a small tanker had been sunk off Ponta Zavora, 180 miles (288km) north-east of Lourenço Marques. It appeared that this ship had fallen prey to the German raider *Graf Spee*, which had rounded the Cape and was now operating in the Indian Ocean. Eric Smith remembered:

> *I was asked to report with one pilot to Nairobi. We were given sealed orders to report to the naval commander, Mombasa. The commander was named Blunt. Orders were to seek and destroy the*

'Graf Spee'. Patrols immediately set out. Blunt reported that an oil slick had been spotted north of Mombasa near Malindi. "Go and seek and clobber" we were told. We hunted all over the place but couldn't find it. We reported back to Blunt who remarked, "It was a good job you didn't. It was His Majesty's submarine 'Cyclops'!" Our long range reconnaissance aircraft, Puss Moths and Rapides of the Civilian East African Airways were frantically searching the Indian Ocean and we were equally frantically practising our strike under the personal direction of the officer commanding, East Africa Air Force, Wing Commandeer Shaw. This was to approach at sea level, pushing with both feet on the dash board, go into a steep climb, stalling off at the top and neatly dropping the single 500 pounder down the 'Graf Spee's' funnel. When we had acquired some precision in the manœuvre, we timidly inquired about the break away. Curtly he replied, "Don't worry about that," and softened the remark by adding, "but you will put Rhodesia on the map." Praise be the 'Graf Spee' was by then half way across the Atlantic. (Eric Smith)

In fact, immediately after sinking the *Africa Shell*, Captain Hans Langsdorff had taken the *Graf Spee* back round the Cape. For the moment the excitement was over.

In Kenya, Colonel W.H.A. Bishop GSO at HQ East Africa Force had only praise for the instant response with which Southern Rhodesia met the war situation:

We had expected that there would be a little delay between the outbreak of war and the dispatch of the air force but there was no delay at all. The response was immediate.

Reinforcements go north overland
Arrangements were meanwhile being made to reinforce No 1 Squadron of the Southern Rhodesia Air Force. The 90 men were to make the move north by train and road. The logistics involved were a nightmare. Below is an example of the rations involved for five days:

Quantities in pounds:
Biscuits, ship 340
Preserved meat 340
Tinned vegetables 115, or dried vegetables 60
Meat extract 15 or MB ration in tins 450 tins
Tinned bacon 70 or tinned ham 70 or meat loaf 85 or pork and beans 225
Tinned cheese 30
Fresh fruit 115
Coffee 55
Dried fruit 15
Sugar 100
Margarine 345, marmalade 30
Tinned milk 60
Mustard 5, Pepper 5, Salt 10
Rice or oatmeal 15
Curry powder 5
Cooking fat 30
Tinned salmon or herring 160
Also 147 cases of petrol and 49 gallons of lubricating oil.

The basic number of men was later raised to 20 officers and 90 other ranks, all Europeans, and it was arranged that eight ambulances should accompany the force.*

The platform at Salisbury railway station was packed with wives, parents, friends and

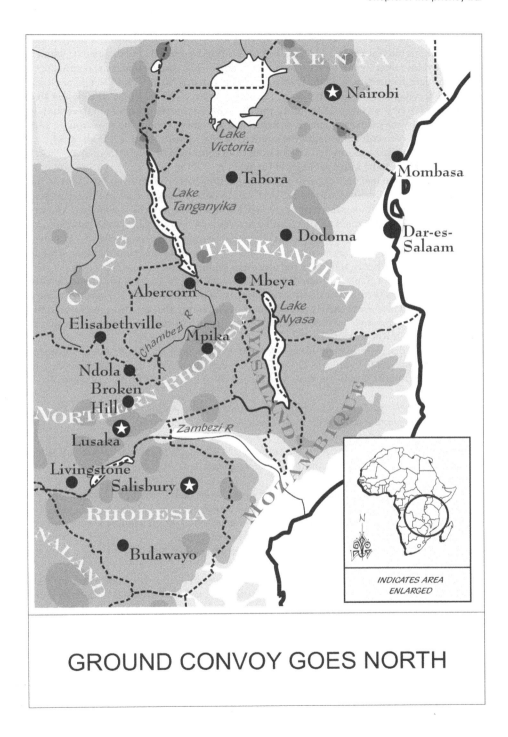

GROUND CONVOY GOES NORTH

relations on 19th November as the train carrying the airmen puffed out. The detachment arrived without hitch at Broken Hill at 05h15 on 22nd November. There the men de-trained and climbed into their lorries for the long journey north. The convoy under the command of Adjutant Flight Lieutenant William Francis Bryanton reached Nairobi 3rd December eleven days after leaving Broken Hill. It was in fact a masterpiece of efficiency, considering that the distance covered was over 1,000 miles and the conditions were primitive in the extreme. Incredibly, only one casualty occurred and this man was able to rejoin the squadron on 14th December. This detachment brought the strength of No 1 squadron up to 133 all ranks.

It was now possible to form a 'C' flight under the command of Flight Lieutenant Tickey Tyas who was later to be killed at Keren in Eritrea.

The squadron still had only the seven aircraft that they had brought from Rhodesia so the aircraft situation was critical. However, RAF headquarters Middle East promised to help with eight Hind aircraft together with spares sufficient for nine months' operations. Another problem was uniforms. Stocks of SRAF uniforms were not held in Nairobi and this led to all kinds of difficulties. Eric Smith says that at one stage the squadron personnel got so browned off with the situation that they turned up on parade for the air officer commanding, Middle East wearing hockey boots, red socks and any other oddments they could find.

Early in November, Colonel Meredith travelled via Cairo to London to discuss defence matters. There were three major discussion points as far as the Southern Rhodesia Air Force was concerned. These were the costs involved in maintaining the squadron in Nairobi, the possibility of creating two further Rhodesian squadrons and the establishment of an air-training scheme in Rhodesia itself.

Obviously as discussions went ahead, Meredith was keeping the Rhodesian government informed through Mr Lannigan O'Keefe, Southern Rhodesia's high commissioner in London. The points of discussion were then passed on to the prime minister in Salisbury:

It is a principle that a squadron will be granted full national designation only if total cost including equipment is borne by the country concerned.

It was financially out of the question for Southern Rhodesia to provide aircraft for three complete squadrons so the high commissioner suggested that:

Personnel for the three squadrons should be posted to the RAF carrying the designation 'Rhodesia' in the Royal Air Force title. The effect will be that personnel and aircraft will be paid by the Air Ministry and therefore saving will accrue to us, which the Air Ministry will suggest should be added to our proposed contribution to the training scheme.
(Letter from High Commissioner to P.M., 18th December 1939)

It was finally agreed that the squadron already serving in Kenya should be given an RAF number but should carry the name Rhodesia in the title and that it should undertake army cooperation duties. It was further agreed that Rhodesia would provide personnel for this and two other squadrons. Rhodesians serving in other RAF squadrons would be allowed to transfer if they wished.

The air-training scheme

It was also decided that training in Rhodesia should begin with one initial training wing through which pupils would pass to three elementary flying training schools and three service flying training schools. This programme was quite beyond the technical and manpower resources of the Southern Rhodesia government and would require provision by Air Ministry in London, of aircraft, equipment and personnel. It also required the establishment of six air stations, which would have to be built using local resources. On the matter of who was to finance the scheme, the Air Ministry's attitude was one of indifference. The matter was one of top priority and Meredith was told, to buzz off and get air training going because the Canadian scheme is bogged down in apples! The Canadian Treasury Department wanted to set apple exports against their share of the expenses, hence the reference to apples!

Colonel Meredith had no authority to commit Rhodesia financially although he did have the authority to agree to the establishment of the schools on Rhodesian soil. In reply to his query about finances, Meredith was told to get whatever you want from the Southern Rhodesian government and we will settle up later. So Colonel Meredith left London on 26th December 1939 with a blank cheque which, to the delight of the Southern Rhodesian Treasury, was honoured immediately and without question.*

At this point, the Rhodesian government had already agreed to far-reaching building plans at a cost of £12,000 for Cranborne alone. However, accommodation was still a major problem at Cranborne with aircraft packed into one end of a hangar, the rest of the space being used for sleeping quarters. During December, one further Hornet Moth had been acquired making a total of 16 aircraft available for training purposes and one aircraft for transport. The strength of officers and other ranks at the Air Station was 137. A further six men were taken on in the aircraft and engine repair depot raising the strength to 13, excluding the officer commanding.†

One interesting point is that the Rapide used for transport retained its civil markings throughout the war as it was used for trips to Mozambique, which of course remained neutral.

On the war front, British shipping was increasingly falling prey to German submarines and magnetic mines. On the last day of November, Russia invaded Finland and towards the middle of December came the Battle of the River Plate. The Graf Spee had been responsible for the sinking of nine British ships when she was cornered by three British destroyers off the coast of the River Plate. A running fight developed. The British vessels were outgunned but kept attacking until they drove the German ship to take shelter in Montevideo harbour. The Uruguayan authorities denied permission for the German battleship to remain in this neutral harbour and on 18th December 1939, the German crew cleared harbour and scuttled their ship. The effect on British morale, starved of victories, was out of all proportion to the size of the achievement, but it did bring a little peace of mind to the authorities in southern and East Africa.

* **Officers with the Nairobi draft—22nd November 1939**
William Francis Bryanton, squadron adjutant
A.E. Stringer, camp commandant
H.A.O. Wootton
Pilots
Stan Edward Flett
Paul Holdengarde
Evert Phillip (Boop) Kleynhans
A.S. (Sandy) MacIntyre—later commander No 266 Rhodesia Squadron
L.P. (Les) Olver
Colin Murray (Fatty) Palmer
Graham Michael Robinson

---

* Memo on RATG Rhodesiana No 28.

† Monthly report, Defence HQ Archives

Cyril Leonard Sindall
Brian Domley White
John William James (Jack) Taylor—KIA
Miles Andrew Johnson—KIA
C.P. (Cyril) Chilvers
Herbert Spencer (Farmer) Hales—later commander No 208 Rhodesia Squadron
J. (John) Walmisley—later commander No 237 Rhodesia Squadron

The rest were all aircraftmen except Leading Aircraftman Roderick Henneded Trollope
Coates-Palgrave (photographer)
Sergeant W.A.B. Maxwell—medical orderly
Corporal R.G. Keeling—medical orderly

Eighteen officers and 87 other ranks with Southern Rhodesia Air Force
One officer and four other ranks with Southern Rhodesia Medical Corps
One officer Permanent Staff Corps. (Archives S 730/51 1–24)

CHAPTER 6
First loss in the desert

New year 1940 dawned with nothing much happening. Hitler was consolidating his gains in eastern Europe and Italy was still sitting on the fence. This inactivity in the land war meant that the Southern Rhodesia Air Force squadron stationed in Kenya could prepare for its new role of army cooperation. The training, which was carried out with 22 Mountain Battery, Royal Artillery and the 2nd Battalion Kings African Rifles, provided the Rhodesian airmen with experience in air gunnery and low-level bombing. The squadron also took part in operations with 1st East African Light Battery and tactical reconnaissance exercises with 1st and 2nd East African Brigades. Two-way wireless telegraphy training, low-level flying and dive-bombing with 2nd Battalion Kings African Rifles was followed by practice target spotting for ack-ack batteries. All of which would prove highly useful in time to come.

By the end of January the strength of the squadron was 27 officers and 110 other ranks. One hundred and ninety flying hours were logged for the month of January. During February a ground party went on detachment to Isiolo for division exercises while two groups of pilots left for the Middle East to collect some very welcome Hawker Hardys from 102 Maintenance Unit.

Alec Hutchinson remembers:

> *Left in a Valencia from Nairobi on 11th February. Flew to Khartoum. Then on a river boat to Wadi Halfa. Brought back eight Hardys. Arrived back in Nairobi on 7th March. Then because there was not much doing went off on 14 days' leave.*

The monotony was broken in the middle of February when a draft of 20 pupil pilots passed through Nairobi on their way to the Middle East for training. They were given a warm welcome and shown the sights. Meanwhile the men of the large December draft were nearing the end of their training and were ready to pass out.

On 7th March eight new Hardys arrived and on the same day the ground detachment arrived back from Isiolo. The training had been extremely useful and there had only been one mishap when Audax SR 11 piloted by Hugh Chinnery Peyton crashed. The pilot and his passenger, Corporal J.F. Ridgeway, (RAF) had only minor cuts and bruises but the aircraft was extensively damaged. Apparently, Hugh Peyton had attempted a forced-landing on rough ground and the aircraft cartwheeled. The way in which the squadron dealt with this aircraft set a pattern, waste not want not being the motto. The Audax was dismantled and transported back to Nairobi from Isiolo so that the engine and airframe could be salvaged. The SRAF technicians were already proving themselves past masters at making do and mending.

One of the first official ceremonies staged by the squadron was a flypast for General Wavell, General Officer Commanding Chief Middle East when he visited Nairobi on 14th

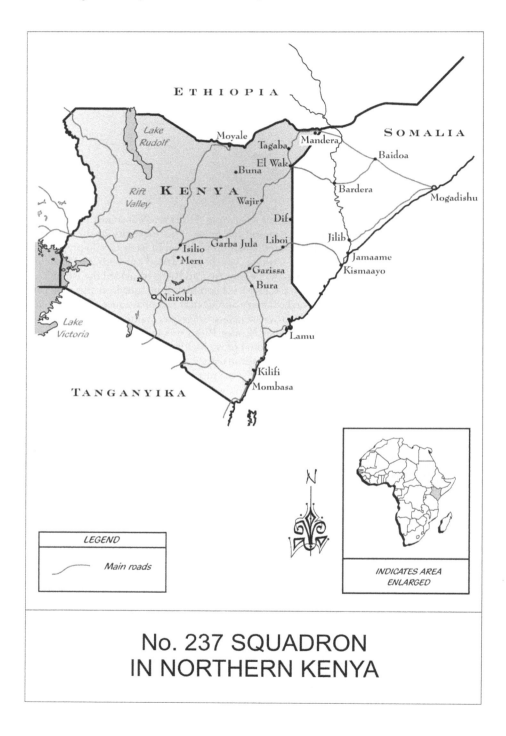

No. 237 SQUADRON
IN NORTHERN KENYA

March. This was the first occasion on which the squadron had been able to put nine aircraft in the air. A week later squadron numbers were swelled by the arrival of Flying Officer Theodosiou and a further 96 airmen. They had travelled the long way round, Salisbury to Durban by rail, Durban to Mombasa by sea and Mombasa to Nairobi by rail. They were accompanied by Flying Officer Greenslade, a grand old man who had served in the Royal Flying Corps during the First World War, and did not want to be left out of this one. So by the end of March, the strength of No 1 Squadron SRAF had risen to 28 officers and 209 other ranks, while flying time was now in the region of 250 hours a month.

A name change for the squadron

April 1st 1940 brought a change that was not popular with the squadron. No 1 Squadron Southern Rhodesia Air Force was officially redesignated No 237 (Rhodesia) Squadron Royal Air Force. It was a title of which the members were to become very proud but at first there was deep resentment about dropping the old name. At the same time the motto Primum Agmen in Caelo—The First Force in the Sky or First in the Field was adopted. There were changes in administration as well. By arrangement with the secretary of state in London, the squadron became a RAF responsibility as far as maintenance costs and pay were concerned.

In Europe the so-called phoney war ended abruptly with Germany's invasion of Denmark and Norway on 9th April. Hitler had been preparing his attack for some time and Britain had in fact dispatched troops and air support to Norway two days before the invasion began but the British forces arrived too late to be of much help. One Rhodesian airman who fought in this campaign was Caesar Barrand Hull. Born in Shangani he enlisted with the RAF in September 1935. He was wounded during the defence of Norway but recovered in time to take part in the Battle of Britain, during which he was killed while commanding No 43 Squadron RAF. The Norwegians resisted gallantly, holding out until 10th June but once again the German blitzkrieg proved invincible. The lull was over. Hitler had begun his move west.

Up to this point, Italy had shown a great reluctance to become involved but at any moment that might change. No 237 Squadron was placed on stand-by, all personnel on leave were recalled and further leave was cancelled. 'B' flight prepared to proceed on detachment to Malindi while on 2nd May 'A' flight ground party left for Isiolo. Despite the stand-by, time was found for a rugby match in Nairobi during which Graham Smith, who was captaining the side, slipped a cartilage and had to leave the field while Ted Jacklin showed brilliant form and was an inspiration to his side. (*Rhodesia Herald*)

'B' flight left for Malindi on 12th May by which time 'A' flight was carrying out reconnaissance flights along the Garissa/Liboi road.

Peyton and Kimpton go missing

Early on the morning of 16th May, Hardy K5914, with Flying Officer Hugh Peyton as pilot and Corporal Freddie Kimpton as gunner took off on a routine reconnaissance of the Garissa/Liboi road. They did not return. Aircraft carrying out sorties in the area were requested to search for the missing aircraft. At dusk the search was suspended but on the following day 'A' flight again flew search and rescue missions. Eric Smith says:

> *The area we were working was almost without landmarks. Even the roads were mere tracks winding through featureless scrub. At this stage there were instructions that military aircraft must not fly within 20 miles of the Italian border.* Peyton may have gone further north than he*

⋆ This order had been given because Italy was still officially neutral and the British authorities did not wish to give the Italians any excuse to join on the German side.

should and missed the track he was looking for. It would seem that he reached the border and for some reason turned south and followed the boundary until he ran out of petrol. The plane was eventually found just inside the Italian border. Apparently Hugh broke his arm at the time of landing. They stayed with the plane for three days; then they began to walk. Kimpton refused to leave his pilot, staying with the injured man until he died six or seven days later. Kimpton then continued alone for another three miles, chewing bark to help his thirst, until he collapsed. Their bodies were eventually found by the South Africans when they advanced a year later. Had the aerial search been pushed closer to the border they might have been found but Maxwell obeying orders refused to allow his pilots to search within 20 miles [32km] of the border. (Eric Smith)

It is possible that some of the bad feeling towards Maxwell, which came to a head later, dated from this episode. It was to be a year before the truth was known—meanwhile the search continued. A total of seven aircraft took part and the hunt went on for five days. Hope was abandoned on 22nd May by which time 125 flying hours had been expended and an area of 21,000 square miles covered. Obviously, this first loss depressed the whole squadron.

The month of May ended with Operations Records reporting day after day:

Normal routine patrols by aircraft from Wajir, Garissa and Malindi.

The squadron strength was now 27 officers and 208 other ranks. Flying time for May had been 378 hours 10 minutes.

Italy enters the war
On 3rd June 'C' flight ground party left for Garissa and on the following day 'C' flight air party joined them. This allowed the two aircraft that had been at Garissa on detachment from 'B' flight to return to Malindi. During the first weeks of June routine patrols were flown by 'A' flight from Wajir, 'C' flight from Garissa and 'B' flight from Malindi.

Operations Record June 10th 1940:
Italy declares war on the Allies. All flights warned to stand by for war sorties.
The disposition of the squadron:
'A' flight—four aircraft at Wajir
'B' flight—four aircraft at Malindi
'C' flight—four aircraft at Garissa
Headquarters and seven reserve aircraft at Nairobi. Task in general allocated to squadron by East Africa Force headquarters is to report enemy movements into Kenya from Italian East Africa.

Each flight was allotted a specific area as listed below with the requirement that all pilots should report any enemy movement along the roads in the particular area allocated.

'A' Flight—Wajir—Area ZZ1
Wajir—Buna—Moyale—halfway Buna-Tagaba—Wajir
Z2 Wajir—El Wak plus 45 miles and return
Z3 Wajir—Bor-Gerile road—junction roads Gerile to Bardera and El Wak to Bardera and return Wajir direct
Z4 Wajir—Dif to within 20 miles of Afmadu. Return
Z5 Wajir—Dif to a point 20 miles along the Afmadu road. Gerile to a point 20 miles along the road. Gerile to Bardera and return Wajir direct

'B' Flight—Malindi—Area X
X1—Malindi—Hindi Ijara—Malindi
'C' Flight—Garissa—Area Y
Y1—Garissa—Liboi—Geldeza and return
Y2—Garissa—Liboi—Dif—Wajir and return
Y3—Garissa—Garba Jula—Liboi—Garissa
Y4—Garissa—Galma Galla—Kolbio and return.

A typical day's flying would be:

Operations Record 11th June:
Dawn sorties as under were carried out:
Hardy K4055   Pilot Fg Off Spence—A/C Stowe
Audax K7548   Pilot Fg Off Miles Johnson—A/C Burl
Audax K7540   Pilot Fg Off Holdengarde—A/C Bell
Audax K7546   Pilot Fg Off Christie—A/C Marshal
Audax K7545   Pilot Fg Off White—Sergeant Murrell
Audax K7534   Pilot Fg Off Olver—A/C Horobin
Areas patrolled   X1, Y1, Y3, Y4, Z1, Z2, Z5   No movement seen.
Afternoon sorties:
Hardy K4319   Pilot Fg Off Spence—A/C Hall
Audax K7546   Pilot Fg Off John Walmisley—A/C Strickland
Hardy K4055   Pilot F/Lt Smith—LAC Morton
Areas patrolled   X1, Y1, Y3, Y4, Z2, Z2, Z5, Z5   No Movement seen.

On 13th June movement was seen and felt. The story as told in the *Rhodesia Herald* went like this:

> *First contact was made with the enemy in a most undignified manner. A number of men were sleeping, because of the heat, on the roofs of native shops in Wajir and that morning they were awakened by three Italian bombers roaring down on them. The men jumped the15 feet to the ground and, clad in pyjamas and one of them in a sarong that he lost in the rush, dived into trenches. The place was pasted up pretty badly and the squadron lost its petrol dump.*
> (Rhodesia Herald)

The squadron Operations Record tells the story in less dramatic terms:

> *Wajir attacked by three Caproni 133s. Approximately 30 high explosive and incendiary bombs dropped and aircraft and personnel machine-gunned. Fg Off R.J.D. Christie and Cpl J.H. Killner slightly injured by bomb splinters. All petrol and oil stocks destroyed. Audax 7531 holed in the radiator by machine gun bullet. Fresh supplies of petrol and oil conveyed to Wajir by air from Nairobi and by road from Nanyuki and sorties not interrupted. Dawn sorties were X1, Y1 and Z1. During last sortie the Italian police post at El Wak was bombed and machine-gunned by Audax K7546—Pilot Fg Off Sindall—A/C Ron Marshall. Approximately 50 native police observed at Italian El Wak. Police station attacked by dropping 2 x 20-lb bombs and machine-gunned. Visibility poor. Weather fair.*

So at last No 237 (Rhodesia) Squadron had tasted battle. The 14th June was quiet but on the 15th the Italians struck again:

Wajir attacked by two Caproni 133s. Bombs were dropped from 5,000 feet and no damage done.

The greatest problem facing the men guarding the northern frontier of Kenya was one of supply. The countryside was covered with bush and small thorn trees with few roads. It was hot and unfriendly and waterless, except for those months when it rained and then movement became almost impossible as the countryside became a quagmire. All supplies had to be carried nearly 400 miles (640km) from the nearest railhead and transport, which was acutely scarce, sustained severe punishment on what passed for roads.

By the middle of June a pattern had developed of daily sorties at dawn and in the early afternoon. Most of these flights drew a blank but there was the excitement of the odd tip-and-run raid on Italian transport.

A column of four armoured cars, eight lorries and about 150 troops was located eight miles north of Moyale. The column was attacked with bombs, and machine-gunned. Two armoured cars, one lorry and one machine gun were destroyed and the troops dispersed. In addition to the above sortie, two aircraft of 'A' flight carried out a search at El Wak and Osman Dille for two of the South African Air Force Hartebees that had failed to return to Wajir on the evening of June 15th after carrying out a bombing raid on Bardera. (Operations Record June 16)

One of these aircraft was in fact located by Flying Officer Miles Johnson who made a supply drop. At dawn on Tuesday 18th June the Kings African Rifles, supported by No 237 Squadron mounted an attack across the Italian Somaliland frontier on the post at El Wak. The enemy, taken by surprise, withdrew but soon regrouped and counter-attacked forcing the British troops to pull back across the border, leaving the Italian fort in flames. During this operation an aircraft K7546 of 'A' flight flying low to deliver a message was holed in the radiator and the pilot was forced to land when the engine seized. Fortunately Flying Officer John Walmisley managed to bring the aircraft down on the British side of the border and neither he nor his gunner, Aircraftman Marshal was injured.

A strong force of Italians had pursued the retreating British troops across the border and the army commander told Walmisley that his forces were pulling out. The Rhodesians were not about to allow a repairable aircraft to fall into enemy hands so the wings were removed and an attempt was made to tow the disabled plane to safety. However, the undercarriage collapsed after the plane had been towed over the rough terrain for about ten miles. The army commander agreed to allow the Rhodesians one hour to strip what they could from the now immobile aircraft after which it was set on fire.

The rest of the month passed with sorties and attacks by No 237 Squadron on Italian forts, troops and transport while in return the Italian air force carried out raids on Garissa, Moyale and Wajir.

The Italian ground forces continued their advance and by the beginning of July Moyale was under siege. The Rhodesians supported the ground forces by bombing and machine-gunning the artillery positions round the town. Flying Officer Alec Hutchinson, with Aircraftman Rhodes William Horobin as gunner, was piloting Audax SR 109. He was returning from one of these sorties when he spotted a European with two Somalis and a camel walking along the road towards Garissa. Hutchinson says:

I came down low and dropped a message, 'Signal if you need help'. The white man, the Somalis and the camel all lay down and waved their arms and legs at me. It turned out that it was Major Preller of the SAAF. He had crash-landed in a Fairey Battle after taking part in a raid on

Afmadu. I dropped a message in a military encampment at Shaya Nuna asking for a lorry to be sent to collect him. A ground force was also sent out to collect his crew who had stayed with the aircraft.

Again and again, the Harts and Audax of the Rhodesian squadron flew sorties in support of Moyale's hard-pressed garrison. In return the Italians had a couple of goes at Wajir without doing much damage but the odds were too high and eventually the British were forced to withdraw leaving some wounded behind.

'A' flight came under attack again at their advanced landing ground at Bura where they had moved to cooperate with 2nd East African Infantry Brigade. Some equipment was destroyed but there were no casualties. During the attack Italian aircraft dived to within 50 feet of the ground to machine-gun British positions. Audax K7549 was damaged during these attacks and rendered unserviceable. This aircraft was subsequently transported by road to Nairobi for repair. It was calculated that about 120 bombs were dropped on Bura that day. The remaining two serviceable aircraft were flown out to Wajir at dusk.

Following this attack, there was a general reorganization. 'A' flight withdrew to Nairobi. 'B' flight, which had been helping out at Wajir, returned to Bura and 'C' flight reassembled at Garissa. The East African ground forces were also regrouped and a second Infantry Division was formed. No 237 Squadron was allocated to 1st African Infantry Division, which had its headquarters at Mitubiri.

Operations Record July 27:

A nomadic Somali arrived at Garissa with news of Hardy K5914 that failed to return from a sortie on May 16th 1940. (This was Hugh Peyton's machine). He, the Somali, was closely interrogated by army and police intelligence officers, and the location of the aircraft roughly established from his statements. The Somali brought into Garissa the flying helmet of the crew of the aircraft and a pad of forms 790 that had been found underneath a tree near the aircraft. The following message written and signed by the airgunner of the aircraft was on the form 790. 'This was our camp from 16/5/40 – 18/5/40. When we set out on foot for places unknown'. The remains tell the story.

Hutchinson says:

We went out to look for the aircraft and bombed the track with flour bombs to mark the spot. They sent out a recce unit and Gold Coast engineers who salvaged the engine, which they brought back on a three-ton truck. The plane was actually just on the wrong side of the Italian border.

The Operations Record places the aircraft at a spot two miles (3.2km) east of the border and five miles (8km) north-east of Jara Jila.

During the month of July, the squadron received four more precious aircraft and a reinforcing draft of 53 airmen who arrived by road in five three-ton trucks and a light van. These vehicles were taken over by the squadron as part of its initial mechanical transport. The minister of defence visited the squadron on August 25th and on the same day six Hardy aircraft arrived from 102 Maintenance Unit. Almost as though the Italians had scented the new aircraft, Garissa was attacked on 27th and 28th August. Neither raid did any real damage and August ended on a quiet note with cloudy weather and bad visibility.

At the beginning of September, the squadron received instructions to prepare for a move to the Sudan. With this end in view 'A' flight returned to Nairobi on 3rd September and on 7th

September 'B' flight came in from Bura. Almost as though they were bidding the squadron farewell, three Italian CA 133s attacked Garissa at 18h15 on 8th September, diving from 4,000 feet to drop seven salvos of bombs, which hit a short distance from the south edge of the landing ground. They followed this attack by machine-gunning the landing field but no damage was done. Two days later 'C' flight left Garissa without too much regret and on that same day, two Harts and one Audax aircraft that had flown up a year before, left Nairobi to return to Salisbury.

The next three days were spent packing in readiness for the move to the Sudan and on 17th September, the first convoy of six vehicles rolled out towards Khartoum, carrying three officers and 37 other ranks. For No 237 Squadron the first phase was over. They had tasted battle and were ready for whatever lay ahead.

CHAPTER 7

The home front

On 12th January 1940, the Government Gazette announced that a separate Department of Air would come into being and that uniformed personnel would carry air force ranks:

> *The Department of Air is now completely separate from that of Defence. All administration and command of the air force will eventually be undertaken by RAF and SRAF personnel.*
> (Government Gazette)

Colonel, the Honourable E. Lucas Guest was appointed minister for Air. Lieutenant Colonel Meredith, with the rank of group captain was to form and command the Rhodesian Air Training Group (RATG) as well as being secretary for Air. This was an economy measure as there was no point in having a civilian secretary for Air who would merely duplicate paper work already performed by RATG headquarters, particularly as RATG controlled its own finances both capital and recurrent.

At this stage, in early January 1940, the staff consisted of, in addition to Group Captain Meredith, two territorial officers and a typist. With a heavy building programme ahead, the priority was to obtain staff that could handle layouts, design and construction, organize supplies of building materials and control finance and accounting.

Major C.W. Glass, an architect by profession who had been released from his civilian employment with the Public Works Department to join the army, agreed to transfer to the air force with the rank of squadron leader, later wing commander with the title: Director of Works and Buildings. His section was responsible for the layout of air stations and the design and construction of buildings. His staff consisted of architects, quantity surveyors and draughtsmen as well as non-professional staff. The actual building was done by civilian contractors and at one stage, virtually every builder in the Salisbury, Bulawayo and Gwelo areas was employed on RATG work. The finance and accounts section was handled by Mr C.E.M. (later Sir) Cornelius who was attached to the air force as treasury representative and he was joined by an accountant, A. James, who held the rank of flight lieutenant. James was killed in an aircraft accident quite early on and his place was taken by Flying Officer G. Ellman-Brown, also an accountant in civilian life, who had been recruited by Flight Lieutenant James. Ellman-Brown was the principal finance officer (RATG) and his final rank was that of group captain. The finance section had complete control of all funds, which came from the Air Ministry in London and from the Southern Rhodesia government.

The position of Director of Supplies whose department was responsible for the location and purchase of all building materials and equipment, was taken by a Bulawayo businessman, Squadron Leader W.H. Eastwood.

These three sections formed the nucleus of the RATG headquarters and their urgent task was to establish the air sections. A timetable, giving opening dates was drawn up, based on units of six weeks so that pupil pilots would be able to pass from one phase to the next without delay. Meredith writing in 1970 commented: It is to the credit of all concerned—both local and overseas––that opening dates were adhered to and the pupil unit phase of six weeks was not disrupted.

The Stables
Obviously more accommodation was required for headquarters and The Stables was offered to Charles Meredith by the prime minister. Meredith, not realizing what the buildings were, replied that he needed something larger than a stable! But he followed Sir Godfrey Huggins's advice and took a look. The Stables had been erected in 1911 on Jameson Avenue between Third and Fourth Streets, and had been due for demolition long before but no one had got around to it. The building was now empty except for one or two civil servants tucked away at the south-western end. The fabric was in a bad state of repair and there were no water or sewerage facilities. The only good thing about the area was that there was plenty of space. RATG took over the buildings, whitewashed, repaired, renovated, added bits and handed them back in 1945 in shipshape condition; in fact, sections of the old Stables were still in use in 2000.

The training scheme gets underway
The official beginning of the training scheme was 23rd January 1940. Two days after this, the monthly Defence Report stated that Cranborne Air Station had four serviceable Harts, one Audax awaiting rebuilding, eight training aircraft (Tiger Moths and others), one Tiger Moth undergoing repair and two Hornet Moths available for transport and training. The Communications Squadron had six Dragon Rapides serviceable, one DH Dragon undergoing overhaul and three Leopard Moths serviceable. Not much but it was an infinitely better situation than that of three months earlier.

Recruiting for ground forces had been temporarily suspended so that reorganization could take place. Despite some bad feeling among the army types, it was agreed that applications for transfer from ground to air forces would be considered, though increasingly the army felt that a man should make up his mind at the beginning which service he wished to join.

It was 5th February when construction began on the first RATG Flying School and it was ready for occupation on May 24th, an incredible achievement only made possible by the hard work and cooperation of everyone involved. The building operations were carried out on a labour plus 20% basis with one buyer for all materials. This may not have been the cheapest method but it was the easiest and fastest. Lucas Guest announced on 21st February that three complete air training schools were to be established in Rhodesia. Bulawayo and Salisbury were the obvious choices for two––the site of the third was still to be officially announced. This created argument among the other centres as each pushed its special claims. Gwelo and Umtali were particularly insistent, with Gwelo representatives even visiting Salisbury to ensure that their views were known. By the middle of March, the number of flying schools to be established in the Colony had risen to six.

And before the end of March the invasion had begun as reported in the *Rhodesia Herald*:

> *About 100 officers, pilots and technicians of the RAF, who will lay the foundations of Southern Rhodesia's part in the Empire Air Training Scheme passed through Bulawayo by special train this afternoon (24th March) and will arrive in Salisbury tomorrow morning. They brought their wives and children with them.* (Rhodesia Herald)

The first party led by Squadron Leader T.W.G. Eady, started their duties on Tuesday 26th

March. Temporary billets were found for their wives and families in Salisbury. The question of accommodation was to become a trying one and, during the following years, there was to be a constant stream of letters to the paper complaining about the lack of suitable homes, particularly for families with young children. A further source of friction was the effort made by the RAF officers to get the local men to sign on again with the RAF. The six SRAF men who had been trained at Halton stood firm, maintaining that they had signed on for 15 years with the Rhodesia Staff Corps and did not wish to re-sign with the RAF. They were called in to the commanding officer's office and told they must sign. They still refused even though threats were made. They approached a lawyer who took up their case with the authorities and nothing further was heard about the matter. (Ralph Parry)

The men were beginning to arrive, the airfields were being prepared but what of the aircraft? These were to be of three types: de Havilland Tiger Moths for elementary training and North American Harvard and Airspeed Oxford machines for intermediate and advanced training. The Harvard was an American single-engined high-speed trainer, while the Oxford was a twin-engined training aircraft.

The final flying course of the SRAF was completed at Cranborne on 6th April 1940, leaving a gap before the opening of the RAF schools. During this period, Rhodesian pupil pilots were sent either to England or to Habbaniya in Iraq for training. The first contingent to go to Britain left early in March and travelled via Durban.

Meanwhile work on the new buildings was proceeding with speed and on 12th April, Lucas Guest was present at a roof-wetting ceremony for a new hangar at Belvedere. In this same week, the first of the new Harvards arrived. They had been assembled in South Africa and were flown to Salisbury via Bulawayo by Rhodesian pilots.

One side effect of the arrival of so many RAF personnel was the fillip it gave to local sport. In the middle of April, there was a soccer match between the Royal Air Force and the Postal Sports Club, which Postals won by eight goals to one but according to the *Rhodesia Herald* the visitors were not disgraced!

During the war years not only was the Rhodesian government to make enormous contributions to the war effort but individual citizens were to collect amazing amounts of money for the purchase of aircraft. The first such gift of enough money to purchase a training aircraft, came in mid-April from Mr J. MacAllister Smith and the Inez Mine, Gatooma. There were many others and one Spitfire was actually paid for with money raised entirely by Rhodesia's African population.

30th April 1940 was Budget day. Obviously, money would have to be raised to pay for the war effort and an amount of £1,339.249 was set aside for war expenditure from a total revenue of almost £5,000,000. In other words, a quarter of the total revenue was to be spent on the war effort. The Rhodesian government offered to meet the full cost of the air force headquarters establishment and the cost of barrack equipment. Thereafter Southern Rhodesia would contribute £80,000 a year towards the cost of maintenance and operation of the training schools. The government also offered to bear the full capital cost of fixed assets required in connection with the scheme. (See end of chapter)

On 2nd May, much to the annoyance of the people of Umtali, the government announced that Gwelo had been chosen as the site for the third flying school. It was possibly felt that Umtali with its surrounding mountains might prove too dangerous for pilot training.

In Europe the war had been going all Germany's way. Norway and Denmark had fallen with lightning speed and on 10th May 1940, Hitler's armies attacked Holland, Belgium and Luxembourg. The British Prime Minister, Neville Chamberlain, resigned and Winston Churchill took over. Nothing, it seemed could halt or even hinder the German advance. Once again, the Blitzkrieg ran like clockwork. With vicious precision the Luftwaffe screamed down on The Hague and Rotterdam, while German land forces cut through Belgium and rounded the end of the Maginot line into north-eastern France. The Dutch capitulated on 15th May. Rommel's tanks broke through the French lines at Sedan and raced for the Channel reaching the coast on 20th May, cutting the Allied armies in two. The Belgian army capitulated on 27th May.

Then almost inexplicably the German advance slowed, allowing Operation Dynamo, the evacuation of the Allied troops from the Dunkirk beaches to be completed successfully. Between 27th May and 4th June, over 200,000 British and 120,000 French troops were evacuated from the beaches at Dunkirk. More than 850 vessels took part in the evacuation, half of them small craft that braved the miraculously benign waters of the Channel to bring the men home. All the heavy equipment had to be abandoned.

With the battles in western Europe came news of Rhodesian casualties. Anthony Booth, attached to Coastal Command, was shot down into the sea during the Dunkirk evacuation but though reported missing at the time, turned up in a prisoner of war camp. Leading Aircraftman W. Palmer was not so fortunate, as he was killed in action during the retreat.

The first school opens
Back in Rhodesia a further contingent of 260 RAF ground staff consisting of wireless operators, mechanics and recruits arrived in the middle of May. The first school, No 25 Elementary Flying Training School at Belvedere Air Station was officially opened, on 24th May, by Air Chief Marshal Sir Robert Brooke-Popham. Writing after the war Meredith said:

> This was a notable achievement in a matter of fewer than five months starting with nothing. It was also notable in that the opening preceded by some weeks the opening of the first of the schools in the Empire Air Training Scheme in Canada, which had been planned before the war began. Although the Canadian scheme had been planned weeks before the war and much earlier than Rhodesia's, because of the enthusiasm and support generated in Rhodesia, the first of the RATG stations, Belvedere, was opened on 24th May 1940 several weeks before the first Canadian station became operative. The RATG was not only Southern Rhodesia's main contribution to World War II, but was also one of the most important happenings in Rhodesian history... It led to development during a period that otherwise might have been a depression. The total local amount* spent on the scheme greatly exceeded the annual Southern Rhodesian budget at the time and there were 150 separate non-public accounts (messes, canteens etc.) with an annual turn over of £350,000. But, most important, the RATG proved in the long term to be a most successful immigration scheme since many of the staff and trainees returned to settle in Rhodesia after the war, some of them becoming leading citizens in the land. (Meredith memo)

With a scheme the size of the RATG, accidents were bound to occur and on 20th June RATG recorded its first casualty when a pupil pilot, Sergeant Ivan Campbell, crashed a few miles outside Salisbury close to the Gatooma road. He was buried with full military honours in Salisbury cemetery. The second flying training school, at Cranborne, opened on 10th July and in August the first Link Trainers were installed at No 25 Elementary Flying Training School (EFTS) and No 20 Service Flying Training School.

On 16th August came the opening of the first school at Guinea Fowl (Gwelo), No 26 EFTS. This was a notable achievement, taking only 12 weeks from bare veld to the commencement of flying training. The construction included special sole-use arrangements for water supplies,

---

* The total amount is a little exaggerated, though expenditure on the scheme did rise to over £4,000,000 by 1943.

water-borne sewerage and a rail siding for the train that conveyed personnel from Cape Town. The speed with which everything was completed far outstripped Belvedere. As an instance of slick timing, Sir Charles relates that early in the morning of the very day that Guinea Fowl was due to open, the special train from Cape Town drew into the siding with 500 or more future trainees. Without a hitch they were given a breakfast of bacon, eggs and sausages.

Meanwhile further agreements had been completed between the governments of Southern Rhodesia and Britain, covering the opening of a fourth elementary flying training school and a fourth service flying training school. Work went ahead immediately, the sites chosen being Mount Hampden near Salisbury and Heany in Bulawayo.

At the same time, the general public was contributing generously to the Speed the Planes fund, which now stood at the almost unbelievable amount of £37,000. On the war front, the evacuation of Allied troops from France had been unbelievably successful, and the battered remains of two armies had landed safely in the United Kingdom. Mussolini, who had delayed his entry into the war, saw the ease with which western Europe had fallen to the Germans and decided that Italy should join the winning side. On 10th June, Italy declared war on the Allies. Four days later German troops entered Paris, and, ten days after that, hostilities ceased in France. General De Gaulle flew to London. He was recognized as the leader of the Free French Forces and set up a government in exile in West Africa. On the last day of June, the Germans occupied the Channel Islands. Heavy aerial attacks on the British Isles began on 10th July when 70 German aircraft carried out a raid on dockyards in South Wales. Six days later Hitler ordered preparations to begin for the invasion of the United Kingdom, with the provisional date set for the middle of August 1940.

Rhodesians in Britain
Britain had become an embattled island and reports from the capital were appearing regularly in the *Rhodesia Herald*:

> *The first Empire troops to come to this country from Africa—a contingent of Southern Rhodesian airmen—have arrived. The contingent represents part of the technical and maintenance personnel of a Rhodesian bomber and fighter squadron to be established in Britain, and is the first to come under the British government scheme to form squadrons composed entirely of men from the Empire. It was learned tonight that from Southern Rhodesia already about 40 men have joined the RAF at their own expense and five of those have been awarded the DFC, one of them being credited with bringing down six Messerschmitts.*
> (Rhodesia Herald, 7th Aug. 1940)

A report from *The Herald*'s UK correspondent describes the arrival of this first contingent:

> *I travelled to a Scottish port to see the first contingent of these enthusiastic young men arrive. It was, I thought, a pleasant unexpected ceremony that was staged for them. Their drably painted ship emerged from a rainsquall to find herself in an anchorage patterned with craft of all kinds and sizes, from British warships to Norwegian tramp steamers. "I didn't think there were so many ships in the world," one of the Rhodesians said to me. Cruising among them was an admiral's barge with high officers of the Royal Navy and the RAF, the mayor of the port city and Mr Lanigan O'Keeffe, Rhodesia's High Commissioner, waiting to greet the first official contingent of airmen from Southern Rhodesia. Following the barge was a pilot's launch filled with journalists and photographers from all parts of Britain. The Rhodesians, who will provide ground staff for the Rhodesian bomber and fighter squadron now forming in Britain, crowded the shoreward side of the vessel to respond to our first wave and cheer of welcome. Hundreds of*

Rhodesians who had mustered in rank on a ferry also waved and cheered the newcomers, as did the residents ashore, who left their dining tables to crowd the windows of their houses. Crews and passengers on nearby ships joined in the spontaneous welcome. The Rhodesians, many of whom were getting their first sight of Britain in the grey twilight of a cloud-smothered sky, were greatly heartened by the warmth of this welcome. The rainsquall passed as we climbed aboard to take part in the official welcome of the Rhodesians, who had mustered in rank on the well deck. Their bronzed faces were turned eagerly to the upper deck where an admiral and a RAF group captain gave them messages from the Dominion secretary and the Air Ministry. Then Mr O'Keeffe spoke to them in friendly, fatherly terms and they cheered mightily when he told them that of the 40 flying Rhodesian volunteers serving in the RAF, five had already won the DFC––a remarkable proportion. The mayor too, was informal and amusing and he called forth a great laugh of pleasure when he pulled a pouch out of his pocket and told them that it contained the only tobacco he ever smoked––Rhodesian! Some in smasher hats and khaki shorts, the Rhodesians buttoned up their greatcoats as the chilly evening breezes blew across the bay. (Rhodesia Herald, 16th Sept. 1940)

Before long, the Rhodesians had settled down in their new homes and were decorating their doorsteps with Rhodesian crests, Zimbabwe birds and Matabele elephants. Meanwhile the second contingent had arrived safely at a north-east port and been greeted by the high commissioner. Gifts of money were pouring in from the Colony.

Will you please convey to the Southern Rhodesia Tobacco Industry my heartfelt gratitude for the contribution made towards the aircraft production of this country. Coming in a week when we have welcomed the second contingent of Rhodesian airmen to our shore, this most generous gift brings yet another striking proof of the single-minded determination of our Empire to see this struggle through to victory. (Lord Beaverbrook, Minister of Aircraft Production quoted in the Rhodesia Herald, 26th Aug. 1940)

RATG comes to Bulawayo

In Rhodesia another school, No 21 Service Flying Training School, at Kumalo on the old Bulawayo Municipal Airport, opened on 8th September. One of the many young men taking enthusiastically to the air was Peter Sutton who kept a vivid record of the training in his diary:

12th September. Nearly everything is easier on Harvards actually and they are grand kites. The only difficulty is the vast numbers of instruments and controls to worry about. At first, I could never find the right knob, lever or instrument when I wanted it in a hurry, and all the various cockpit checks were an awful trial. Now that everything is more nearly a matter of habit it makes flying a lot easier and far less harassing.
23rd September. Oh! Dear! I'm thinking it's high time I made my will! I was doing some low flying this morning––real low flying, not the official 100 feet up stunt. Approaching a rather large gum tree whilst turning, I decided to change the direction of the turn to fly round it. Unfortunately, I rather misjudged a few details, such as my speed and the momentum of the kite and didn't turn quickly enough. The tree seemed to rush at me at 170 mph and, although I made a last minute effort to lift one wing over it by applying bank, it was too late. There was a lovely 'crump' and the kite shuddered a bit and carried on. Dead silence for some moments. Then a gentle voice over the intercom. (I was flying dual) "Have you seen your wing tip?" It was quite an effort to bring my eyes round as far as that wing tip, and then I quickly averted them. I said, "Crumbs, I am sorry, sir!" We flew back and landed safely at Cranborne. Then we had a look at the damage. About two feet of the wing tip was hopelessly buckled and torn, with

jagged bits of metal here and there, and part of the leading edge of the main wing was dented too. Luckily, though, the fitters decided the wing could stay on, and after knocking out some of the dents, merely fitted a new wing tip. I hung round apologetically in the background and they roped me in to screw up some of the 64 bolts that hold the wing tip on. I am still flying the same plane and always have that shiny new wing tip, and the dents in the wing covered roughly with grey paint, to reproach me. Then there was the beastly written report to concoct––'Sir, I beg to report that …' It was a bit awkward to make up, especially as low flying should be done 100 feet above the tree tops. However, we managed something by saying that although I was at 100 feet, I lost height in an erratic turn and touched the top of a tall tree on rising ground. Not bad? I feel sorry for the instructor though as he was in charge of the kite, and only hope no one asks too many awkward questions. He has been really decent to me about it all and doesn't seem to bear me any ill-will at all. He says it was his fault as much as mine and just passes it off with a shrug and a 'such is life'. I really think it's awfully sporting of him. I only hope I manage to get Above Average in my assessment to repay him slightly.

2nd October. *I have a free morning. I have been up since 06h30 (it is now 09h00) in a large formation looking for a bloke who got lost on night flying the night before last. There were eleven of us in line abreast searching for him from Bromley north to Shamva and Mrewa and east as far as Mtoko and Headlands. The eleven kites (each about ten miles apart) covered the ground pretty thoroughly but there was no sign of the chap. I wonder what has happened to him. They had searching planes out all yesterday morning and afternoon, too, and I suppose they will continue all this morning and over the weekend until they find him. He's costing us quite a lot in petrol, and in instructors' and pupils' time wasted. Still I expect a pilot is worth it––provided they do eventually find him.*

7th November. *Since writing last, two things have made me devilishly keen to get cracking at the Hun. One is that I have done my first dive-bombing with practice bombs and fired a Browning in the air for the first time at Inkomo yesterday. I don't think my scores were particularly brilliant but I am not worrying unduly as I seem to have started slowly at everything I have learned in flying. Anyway, I had bags of fun and still have another 60 bombs and countless rounds of ammunition to use up in the near future. Soon we begin flying from Inkomo landing ground…*

16th November. I've come to the conclusion I'm a menace… I've just finished off my third wing tip, and incidentally an oleo-leg as well, in a glorious twizzle right in the middle of the 'drome. I was coming in nicely, determined to show the instructor, for whom I was safety pilot, that I could land well, when about ten feet up and just checking, the kite suddenly hit an air disturbance of some sort and dropped like a stone. It hit slightly sideways and went straight round in an unstoppable twizzle. The strain was too great on the undercarriage and one oleo-leg was bent, although luckily it didn't break off…

17th November. *A very sad thing has happened. JF—a bloke I knew well on our course—was killed on night flying last night. He was on cross-country to Gatooma and crashed into the deck quite heavily. There are various reports of the accident, ranging from engine failure to his having inadvertently fired his Very pistol inside the cockpit. Two pupils on the same cross-country noticed it…one heard a faint R/T message about someone going down and another saw an explosion on the ground near Beatrice, which must have been the crash. Whatever the cause, it is a darn shame––old Jack was one of the best and well liked by all of us. He was the last chap, I should say, to do anything stupid or to lose his head, so goodness knows what did happen. They aren't likely to find out either, I don't think, as the kite is a complete wreck…*

19th November. *I know it is awfully easy to get into all sorts of queer positions at night and not to know about it. Last night was pitch black––I did a cross-country myself––and there was not a sign of the horizon on which to keep straight, and owing to thick cloud you couldn't see any lights on the ground that might have given you a clue where you were, or whether you were the right way up.*

Perhaps J panicked and trusted his senses rather than the instruments until it was too late. Gosh, it's a poor show that we should lose two blokes on two successive flying nights. They say these things always go in threes—I wonder who's next? Yes, it's a bad business. It wouldn't be a bad thing at all to be in some nice safe job like the Paratroops! (Part of a diary kept by a Rhodesian pupil pilot Peter Sutton who subsequently served with No 237 Squadron and died in Italy.)

It was on 8th October that Lieutenant Colonel Lucas Guest welcomed the first RAF men to be stationed in Bulawayo. The same day came the first of many stories of courage and cooperation between trainee pilots and the local population. An aircraft crashed at Ruwa and burst into flames. The pilot of a second aircraft, which landed next to the crash, appealed for help to a number of Africans. Only one, Pasirayi was prepared to approach the burning machine. He helped drag the pilot clear. In July of the following year, the prime minister presented him with a bicycle in recognition of his courageous act.

On 2nd November the first pilots to be trained by the RATG passed out at Cranborne Station. Five of these men were Rhodesians and they were probably the first pilots to complete their training under the Empire Training Scheme.

Meanwhile yet another school was getting under way. On 9th November, Sergeant G.E. Tolmay, accompanied by Mr Campbell the superintendent of the Roads Department, arrived at the site of Heany Camp, and, after a search of the bundu found peg No 40 (later the site of the station headquarters flag staff). The campsite was surveyed and it was discovered that one borehole was operating. Four days later, the first 500 labourers arrived to prepare the ground for construction. A grass hut situated in the vicinity of what was to be the golf-club house accommodated the administration office, ration store and hospital. From that date workmen arrived at a rate of 300 a week until a peak of 4,000 was reached.

By December the housing scheme at Belvedere was complete, making life considerably more comfortable for the married members of the RAF and in the same month the first Rhodesian bomb was manufactured, not for use against the enemy but for training air crew.

Squadron badges
In the middle of December 1940, the Rhodesian public was asked to suggest suitable designs for squadron badges. There were some irreverent comments about some of the suggestions: The Zimbabwe soapstone bird is trying to fly. Rhodesians in all parts of the country are trying to have him incorporated into one or other of the designs for the Rhodesian squadrons of the RAF. Whether they succeed or not remains to be seen.

The Zimbabwe bird met with keen competition from sable, kudu, springbok, eagles, assegais, mine stamps and even the humble mosquito. Qualities were found for all of these to suit the spirit of a fighter or bomber squadron. One humorist at Shamva suggested the mosquito for the fighter squadron, the Zimbabwe bird for the bomber squadron and the locust for the army cooperation squadron. He added the following remarks: Mosquito—if the Pasteur Institute cannot supply a really vicious specimen there are innumerable specimens to be obtained at Shamva. Soapstone bird—I have always felt this broody-looking fowl was on the point of laying an egg. Locust—though not fast in flight, this farmer's friend can do a lot of damage in a very short time. For mottoes he suggested local language equivalents of My bite is death for the mosquito. We fling the thunderbolt for the soapstone bird and Where we have gathered they are destroyed for the locust. No 237 (Rhodesia) Squadron, then at battle station in the Sudan put through a request that no decision be made until the members had been given a chance to submit their own ideas.

During those final months of the year 1940, the thoughts of Rhodesians had been with family and friends in the United Kingdom. First there had been the Battle of Britain won at a terrible cost in aircrew. Then the threat of invasion, which had diminished as autumn drew on, followed by the winter of the bombs when night after night German bombers thundered overhead to drop their loads of death and destruction on London, Coventry, Southampton and many other cities. During the month of October, 6,334 civilians were killed and 8,695 injured in air raids but as far as breaking the spirit of the people was concerned, they were as ineffectual as raids on Germany were to be later in the war.

Budget report—4th May 1940

Southern Rhodesia war bill in 1940 – 41 is estimated to amount to £2,502.203 of which £1,422.203 will be defrayed from revenue funds and £1,080,000 from loan funds. Building for air training absorbed the bulk of the £1,080,000. £810,000 for air stations and bombing ranges and £250,000 for quarters. £1,060,000 in all. The estimate includes £5,000 for the acquisition of commercial aviation concerns and £15,000 for the buildings for military forces. Of the £1,422.203 of war expenses to be defrayed from revenue funds, £877,900 will be absorbed by air training. A sum of £25,000 is allotted as the cost of winding up the local training scheme and service squadron prior to absorption into the Empire Air Training scheme in the RAF. Barrack equipment £52,000 and contribution to the maintenance and operating costs of the training school, make up the £852,000 allotted to the air training scheme. The estimate of air force HQ costs £29,300 in pay and allowances. (*Rhodesia Herald*)

Report prepared for Inspector General—11th October 1942

Archives S 800

Rhodesia Air Training Group

Times taken for construction of stations.

School Station	Commenced	Opened
25 EFTS Belvedere	*4.3.40*	*24.5.40*
20 SFTS Cranborne	*4.3.40*	*19.7.40*
26 EFTS Guinea Fowl	*24.5.40*	*16.8.40*
21 SFTS Kumalo	*25.3.40*	*20.9.40*
27 EFTS Induna	*15.8.40*	*17.1.41*
22 SFTS Thornhill	*5.10.40*	*4.4.41*
24 CAOS Moffat	*14.12.40*	*7.41*
23 SFTS Heany	*1.12.40*	*1.6.41*
28 EFTS Mt Hampden	*16.11.40*	*4.4.41*

Lists of RATG Units for Southern Rhodesia

Disposal Depot, Bulawayo
Central Maintenance Unit, Bulawayo
No 31 Aircraft Repair Depot, Cranborne
No 32 Aircraft Repair Depot, Heany
Rhodesian Air Askari Corps, Belvedere
Communications Squadron (SRAF) Belvedere
No 20 Service Flying Training School, Cranborne
No 21 Service Flying Training School, Kumalo
No 22 Service Flying Training School, Thornhill
No 23 Service Flying Training School, Heany
No 24 Combined Air Observers School, Moffat (also includes Elementary Air Observers

School and Airgunners School)
No 25 Elementary Flying Training School, Belvedere
No 26 Elementary Flying Training School, Guinea Fowl
No 27 Elementary Flying Training School, Induna
No 28 Elementary Flying Training School, Mount Hampden
No 33 Rhodesian Central Flying School, Belvedere. In May, the name was changed to No 33
   Flying Instructors School. In November 1942, the school moved to its own home at Norton.
(See map showing location of units—if required S 800)

Organization of pupil flow
Pupils mainly from UK (small numbers from other places).
Local recruitment supplies about 15 in every six-week intake.
1) *Reception Depot at Hillside Camp. Initial Training Wing is at Hillside. Divided into Primary and
   Secondary courses. Each six weeks. On successful completion of the Initial Training Wing Course pupils
   pass to either Post Initial Training Wing Pool or direct to the Elementary Flying Training School.*
2) *Each EFTS intake 320 pupils. 50 from Post Initial Training Wing Pool and 270 direct from ITW course.
   Wastage at ITW average 6%. Approximately 35% of these are accepted for Airgunner Training and pass to
   No 24 CAOS. Balance given trade training and absorbed into Group or sent to Middle East or UK.*

RATG flying hours
Total flying hours per pupil per phase.

EFTS
Aim   Actual
80   81 half (average over three months
Grand total per pupil)

SIFTS
Aim   Actual
160   158 (average over three months
Grand total per pupil)

Total actual revenue expenditure incurred in the Colony of Southern Rhodesia
Year end.   31 March 1941   800,370
*   31 March 1942   2,230,000*
*   31 March 1943 Est. 4,025,000*

Salvage
*An aluminium reclamation plant has been set up in Bulawayo for the melting down of scrap aluminium
   and alloys and the production of these materials. Scrap obtained from Flying Schools and the Union
   and from Salvage Committees.*

Aircraft in use
Tiger Moth—at EFTS—Approx 295
Oxford and Harvard at SFTS—Oxford 217, Harvard 222
Oxford—33 Battle—19 Anson—19 at CAOS
Hornet, Leopard Moth, DH Rapide, Gauntlet—2 and 1 Hart
One Vega Gull—Communications Squadron.
(Cost of running this squadron including cost of spares borne by Southern Rhodesia government).

CHAPTER 8

The East African Campaign: June 1940–November 1941

A ceaseless struggle against both the terrain and the elements was as much a feature of the 17-month East African Campaign as the fighting. It was a conflict that demanded originality, improvisation and extraordinary endurance. The war zone covered a vast territory centring on Ethiopia, a mountain fastness and one of the most inaccessible areas on the African continent. To the north of Ethiopia lay the Italian colony of Eritrea—47,000 square miles of mountain and desert wasteland—while to the east and forming a wide coastal strip lay Somaliland, part British, part Italian and part French wholly undeveloped.

Theoretically, the territory should have favoured the defenders. In fact, the near impossibility of moving road transport, and the complete lack of modern communications, together with the vast distances involved imposed severe restrictions on both defender and invader.

Neither the Italians nor the British were ready for a war in this area but following their declaration of war, the Italians had attacked north-west across the border into the Sudan, capturing Kassala and Moyale before their advance became bogged down.

No 237 (Rhodesia) Squadron began the campaign by patrolling the border of northern Kenya and supporting ground forces engaged on the border with Italian Somaliland, but in September 1940, orders were received to move to the Sudan. The air parties with eleven aircraft arrived in Khartoum on 20th September. All squadron aircraft were now Hardys with K numbers, the last of the old Southern Rhodesia aircraft having been sent back home or dumped. Eric Smith recalls:

> The only incident was the running battle of wits, 'B' flight versus the rest of the squadron. 'B' flight had on return from detachment, boldly claimed nine months' rum ration and had been rewarded with 56 jars of lovely rum. They were quite determined to preserve this for themselves. The rest of the envious 200 Rhodesians had other ideas. That those 56 jars survived the journey was indeed a miracle and 'B' flight jubilantly claimed victory. When we arrived in Khartoum the war position was somewhat dicey but, fresh from the Highlands of Kenya, we were more concerned with temperatures of up to 127 degrees, than what the Ities (Italians) might do.

Less fortunate members of the squadron travelled by motor convoy to Juba and then by paddle steamer. A Rhodesian serving with No 237 wrote:

> The paddle steamer had a barge tied on each side and it pushed two barges lashed on in front. This conglomeration was controlled by the paddle steamer and a very difficult job the steering was! The Sudanese navigator was never relieved. He stayed at his post, squatting cross-legged on his charpoy, day and night. He dozed in the straight stretches of the river but automatically

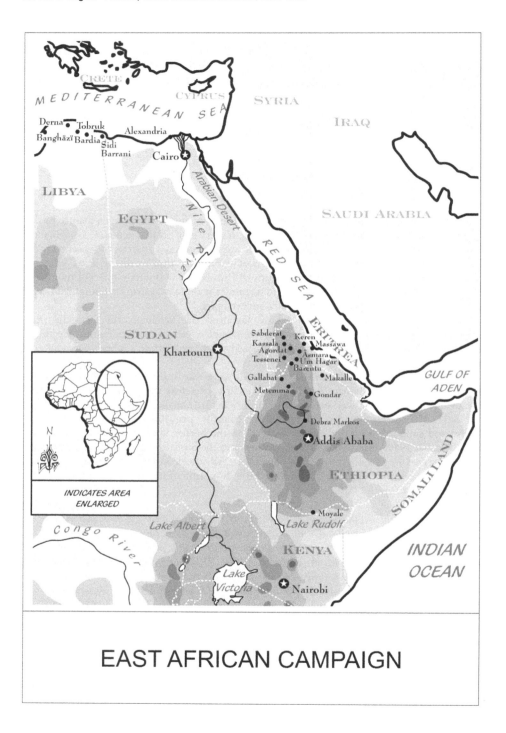

EAST AFRICAN CAMPAIGN

*woke again when the steamer came to a bend. He would go round sharp bends by bumping us
on to the riverbank at just the right spot.*

Obviously, the transfer of ground crew took time and it was 30th September 1940 before
the last members of the squadron left Nairobi.

*Gordon's Tree (near Khartoum) was the first camp at which the complete squadron was on its
own. The sleeping quarters were cool. These were mud-walled buildings, the walls being at least
18 inches thick, camel-dung plastered and whitewashed inside. The roofs were made of split-
palm tree trunks, covered with swamp grass matting, with a layer of mud on top of the matting.
The mess buildings and the canteen had corrugated iron roofs but the walls were just plaited grass
matting nailed on to a wooden framework. Unfortunately, stray goats used to eat up our mess
buildings and one had to be everlastingly chasing the animals away.*
(The War History of Southern Rhodesia)

One unhappy event that occurred about this time was the death, owing to blackwater fever,
of Corporal John Frederick Dreyer, cook and butcher. He was buried in the new Christian
Cemetery at Khartoum.

Life in the Sudan
Taking up the story of those first few weeks in the Sudan, Eric Smith records:

*No sooner did the ground convoy arrive than we were sent out on detachment to the front. 'B'
flight in the north, 'A' flight in the centre and 'C' in the south. The front was about 150 miles
[240km] long pivoted on Kassala, which the Italians had captured in their first push. This Italian
desert equivalent of 'The Rock' contained tanks and armoured cars and was backed by at least
6,000 troops with defended strong points to the north and south. It was rumoured that there were
at least 18,000 Italian troops in the line. Facing them, and only in the north, was Gazelle force,
commanded by Lieutenant Colonel Masservy (later general) with a total ration strength of just
under 1,000. This force was specifically charged with the task of bluffing the Italians that we had
defence in strength. Kassala was an easy two hours' drive across firm desert to Khartoum, posing
a deadly threat to our communications. Colonel Masservy tackled his task with great enthusiasm,
initiative and audacity achieving remarkable results. While 'A' and 'C' flights were fully occupied
doing reconnaissance and dive-bombing in the centre and south to keep up the illusion (of strength)
'B' flight in the north had been placed under the direct tactical command of this adventurous
colonel. They were immediately involved in a whirlwind of wild escapades from stampeding and
herding mule caravans into our lines, to the more serious low-level strafing and bombing of strong
points as a prelude to attack by Masservy's mobile force. Modern tacticians would raise eyebrows
at our techniques and it might be of interest to describe the pattern of these attacks. The mobile force
consisted of seven Rolls-Royce armoured cars (1914 – 1918 vintage), nine ordinary Dodge trucks
with wooden platforms on the back mounting a single Vickers water-cooled machine-gun. In
addition, there were five Howitzers also of 1914 – 18 vintage, always tagging a mile or so behind.
'B' flight mustered eight Hardys carrying 16 20-lb(9kg) anti-personnel bombs, one Vickers firing
through the propeller and one Lewis gun in the rear, fully guaranteed never to fire more than one
pan without a stoppage. Special equipment of the Hardys consisted of a fine pitch wooden airscrew,
which over-revved in a dive, set up a beautiful scream, flying wires deliberately set off true, making
more vibrations than any amplified modern pop band, and a sack of empty beer bottles for the
gunner to throw overboard when his Lewis gun finally and inevitably stopped. Seriously, these
had an effect. They whistled like bombs, made a satisfactory bang on hitting a desert rock and the*

glass splinters were equally as lethal as our 20-lb bombs, i.e. nil. The plan was that 'B' flight would attack first, dive-bombing and machine-gunning. To prolong the suspense some dummy attacks were thrown in for good measure. Under cover of this, Masservy would race his column in, in line astern and keep circling. The Howitzers, being more discreet, shelled from a distance but with remarkable accuracy—as well they had to, not to knock out the circling cars. From the air, this was not unlike the modern cowboy films with the Red Indians circling covered wagons. Meanwhile the flight would hop back a few miles where our three trucks were waiting at a convenient spot, to land, refuel, rearm and off immediately, back to the attack. Side bets were laid by both ground crews and pilots as to who could land nearest to the trucks. This led to heated arguments when the drivers took evasive action and moved. Pilots claimed that this was unnecessary, drivers being adamant that it was imperative. Under cover of our second attack, Masservy would break off at high speed, collecting the Howitzers and our trucks en route. This sort of escapade and other oddities from Masservy's fertile brain had a somewhat depressing effect on the Italian troops and soon we were warned by our Intelligence that the Duke of Aosta had issued an order of the day to his fighter pilots, 'Destroy the Hardys at all costs'. In passing, this charming and courteous gentleman confirmed this to me personally when I escorted him down to Nairobi and a POW camp much later. For 'B' flight life became somewhat tedious. Under considerable harassment, they moved to a new strip every three days. These strips were mere clear spots in the scrub—the smaller and more crooked the better— but they were confined to the vicinity of the Atbara River for water and this the Italians well knew. Sorties became a trifle dicey and often we had to scuttle home flying so low that dust trails became a menace. Fortunately, the Italian love for a 'Balbo' made them less effective. A few sections scattered around would have been deadly to us. All flights now began to suffer casualties and the war took a much more serious turn.
(Eric Smith, History of No 237)

In fact, one of the first losses after the move to Sudan occurred on 16th November when Pilot Officer Colin Thomas Campbell and Sergeant Alan Ponsonby Burl failed to return from a dusk bombing raid in the Metemma area. The following day a search was mounted but it was not until 18th November that Flying Officer Alec Hutchinson located the aircraft near the Atbara River. A ground party was immediately dispatched and rescued the crew the following day but were unable to reach the aircraft owing to the nature of the country. Campbell's face was slightly injured but Burl was unhurt. Apparently a bullet had pierced a water manifold causing a partial seizure of the engine, which compelled the pilot to force-land.

Also on 19th November, Eric Smith led 'B' flight of five Hardys on a mission from Khartoum to attack an Italian garrison at Gubba, a pass in western Abyssinia. Eric says of this operation:

I understand, though I'm not absolutely sure, that it was a diversion to assist Wingate to rescue Emperor Haile Selassie. My personal rating of this sortie is high because it was the first trial by fire of my flight after a year of training and I was proud of their performance. Also it was probably the longest raid ever carried out by the squadron. It involved seven and a half hours flying and two landings both ways to pick up fuel and about half an hour in the target area under constant fire. Finally, the AOC took the unprecedented step of sending for us and being embarrassingly complimentary. My personal recollection of the action was that in the pullout from my first dive, Flight Sergeant Jack Hall, my gunner, had his legs buckled under the pull of 'g'. He hit the floor of his cockpit with a frightening thud. I thought it was a direct hit by flak. One of his knees was dislocated and despite terrible pain, he continued to fire effectively while standing on one leg. Unfortunately (I believe) he was never operationally fit again. My aircraft was hit several times. One shell went through my auxiliary petrol tank without bursting and without setting fire to the tank. Another burst against my tailplane making the aircraft a little lazy in the pull-out. Luckily, that Rolls-Royce engine continued to run like a sewing machine because, had I been forced to break off, the flight would automatically have followed me and aborted the raid . (Eric Smith)

On 27th November the squadron experienced its first fatal battle casualty.

Hardy K3411 flown by Flying Officer Paul Alan Holdengarde with Sergeant Alan Ponsonby Burl as airgunner encountered a Caproni CR 42 east of Metemma.

During the ensuing attack, the aircraft was considerably damaged and Sergeant Burl was shot through the head and killed. The aircraft eventually force-landed in our territory at Guriangana. The pilot was uninjured. The aircraft was transported to Khartoum for repair. Sergeant Burl was buried at Gedaref the same day... (Operations Record No 237)

This aircraft was attacked by two Italian planes but despite losing his gunner and having his aircraft severely damaged, Pilot Officer Paul Holdengarde managed to fly the Hardy 18 miles (28.8km) to land safely in allied territory. It was a sad day for the squadron but spirits were raised a little by the arrival of five Mark II Lysanders from 102 Maintenance Unit.

According to the Official War History of Southern Rhodesia, these were the Westland Lysander Mark IIs, an army cooperation aircraft. An improvement on the Hardy, it had an accredited top speed of 220 mph (352 km/h) and a ceiling of 26,000 feet as against the Hardy's 21,000. The Lysander had a range of 600 miles (960km) and three guns. It was a particularly useful machine for message-dropping, dive-bombing and ground-strafing because it had excellent manœuvrability and a low landing speed.

Eric Smith comments: These speeds and ceiling are optimistic but the pattern of the rear gun was good. It was a Vickers air-cooled gas-operated gun and did not jam like the Lewis.

According to Rhodesia and the RAF:

The enemy flew Savoia (SM 79s) and Caproni bombers. The highly manœuvrable CR 42 fighter must have provided our pilots with some hair-raising incidents, but the squadron's spirit was good and they kept Rhodesia in mind by naming a new HQ site 'Umtali'.

A typical day's flying was noted in the Operations Record for 5th December 1940:

Flying Officer Robinson, Sergeant Stowe—0530 – 0820
  Landed at advanced landing ground Aroma. Recce over Wadi Khor-Girger. Machine gun emplacement dive-bombed and machine-gunned.
Flying Officer Spence, Sergeant Collins—1445 – 1600
  Jebel Dobabob—Sabderat—Jebel Kapon Sherifi. Two salvos of 4 x 20-lb high explosive released on Jebel Melassa and Jebel Kapon Sherifi.
Flight Lieutenant E.T. Smith, Sergeant Gray—1500 – 1725
  Aroma—Khor Girger—Tellai—Jebel Serobatib—Aroma. Bombs dropped at point 649—junction Khore Idris Dorit Sana and Wachai roads. Pamphlets dropped at Jebel Serobatib.
Flying Officer Holdengarde, Sergeant Maltas
Flying Officer Tyas, Sergeant J. Burl—0935 – 1205
  Tactical recce and photo recce. Gallabat—Metemma.

Early morning attack

November gave way to December, with the harassment of Italian gun positions and motor transport continuing unabated. Towards the middle of the month, the Italians took revenge.

On 11th December, a lone SM 79 was spotted at about 25,000 feet apparently taking photographs. No one paid this aircraft any attention. The following day, the reason for this flight became obvious.

Operations Record December 12th:

'B' flight 237 attacked. 'B' flight at Gez Regeb were attacked by one SM 79 and five CR 42s and CR 32s at 0610. The SM 79 dropped one stick of bombs across the camp and three CR 42s made a low-flying front-gun attack on the aircraft of the flight, all of which were set on fire and destroyed. They were Hardys K4053, K4308, K4307 and K4055. No casualties or other damage was sustained. One CR 42 was hit by ground defence guns of a landing-ground detachment of the Sudan defence force and force-landed east of Aroma. One of the accompanying CR 42s landed alongside and flew off with the pilot, after setting fire to the force-landed CR 42. The engine of the aircraft was subsequently salvaged by 'B' flight and sent to the RAF. It bore the date stamp of August 1940 as date of manufacture.

Eric Smith recalls:

*The men kept the guns wrapped up by their beds because of the dust. These were whipped out complete with wrapping and held to open fire on the attacking aircraft. The Italian shot down was the commander of the flight. The man who landed to pick him up was Mario Versintin** who had been credited with 14 kills by the British.*

Also on 12th December, Flying Officer John Walmisley and Leading Aircraftman Peter George Payne force-landed owing to lack of fuel. Unfortunately, the ground was soft causing the aircraft to flip but it was later salvaged and taken to Khartoum for repair. The motto of No 237 being as always—waste not want not. Incidentally, this seems to have been the only occasion during December on which the Lysander flew.

Christmas 1940 had arrived and it was celebrated with the drama of the bumph drop. Pamphlet-dropping was not popular with aircrews, who felt that while they were risking their necks, something more substantial might be handed out. For this reason there was always a backlog of bumph waiting to be unloaded. This was to result in some drama at Christmas time. The story, as recounted by Eric Smith:

It was during this period that the incident took place resulting in the now-recorded signal doggerel rhyme being sent to HQ by 'B' flight. What happened was that HQ fondly believed that propaganda pamphlets should be dropped on every target attacked. Life over these targets was far too hectic for us to have time to heave bumph around. We dutifully sent reports that the leaflets had been dropped rather than face the wrath of HQ but of course, the pamphlets accumulated. Masservy then informed us that he was definitely closing down the war over Christmas from 24th to 26th inclusive and we were free to amuse ourselves. I decided to have a grand bumph raid and to get rid of the offending pamphlets once and for all. 'Targets' were drawn for and a cheer went up when Sandy Mac (Flying Officer Sandy MacIntyre later killed in action) drew the 'hot spot' Kassala. Not only was the flak so thick that one could put wheels down and taxi on it but one could also clearly see the dust trails of Italian fighters taking off from Tesseni some ten miles [16km] away. Sandy Mac went in but despite the desperate heaving of his gunner, Oliver Collins (later killed in action with Flying Officer Billy Cooper over Amba Alagi), he faced the dismal prospect of having to make another run. Taking a wide circuit to

---

* Versintin was eventually shot down and killed during this campaign.

catch his breath, he suddenly saw bursts on our side of the line and wandered over to find five Capronis bombing. He attacked without hesitation believing he could get in before the escorting fighters could intercept. He pressed home the attack and broke away downwards fully expecting to be kept busy by the fighters. To his amazement, the fighters had disappeared. He turned back and went after the Capronis again but now there were only four; the damaged one was missing. He attacked again closing right in but on his second burst his solitary gun stopped firing. He continued to close and frantically signalled to Collins to take over with the Lewis gun from the rear. By now he was in close formation with the Capronis, a manœuvre that effectively shielded him from the fire of the 21 gunners in the other three Capronis. Collins concentrated on the port engine but so close were they that he was forced to fire between the Hardy's wings, shooting all the interplane struts away but bringing the Caproni down in flames. Immediately they were exposed to gunners from the other Capronis and Sandy Mac broke away in a hurry. Back at the flight, by unanimous vote it was decided that this was a worthy occasion to breach our much-treasured 56 jars of rum. One wireless operator and the Orderly Officer, Flying Officer Jack Taylor (later killed over Keren) remained on duty. After all Masservy had officially closed down the war. Belatedly I remembered that HQ should receive an operational report but by now ciphers were unmanageable and in plain language I sent the doggerel:

Happy Xmas unto thee,
We have downed a 133
If we only get our due
We will down a CR 42

Thus was born the tradition of sending 'special' messages in rhyme such as our welcome to 'A' flight when they were sent up to give us a hand and again when we eventually got our 42. At 4 am on Christmas Day, just when the rum party had developed into fire walking, a worried Flying Officer Jack Taylor brought in a signal ordering us to destroy the original Caproni attacked by Mac. It had been seen to force-land by our forward troops. I decided an immediate take-off was the only solution and was not in the least worried to see my gunner, Sergeant Green, being carried out, dumped paralytic in the gunner's cockpit. I merely ordered him to be roped down in case he woke up and fell out. Accompanied by Flying Officer Jack Taylor in another Hardy the mission was accomplished. (Eric Smith)

At this stage, the campaign in the desert was still a rather gentlemanly affair. For example the funeral of an Italian airman, Captain Stephano Castignoli, took place in Nairobi with full military honours, the pallbearers being Italian airmen from the prisoner of war camp, including three non-commissioned officers from Captain Castignoli's squadron. The firing party was supplied by the SAAF and members of No 237 (Rhodesia) Squadron were present. Captain Castignoli who was a flight commander, died from injuries he received when his aircraft was shot down over Garissa on 22nd November. 'A' flight relieving 'C' flight at Blackdown and 'C' flight returning to squadron headquarters at Gordon's Tree.

A minor tragedy has befallen the Rhodesian squadron, whose exploits in the Sudan are so often reported nowadays from Cairo. To brighten life in the desert sand, the squadron organized a homemade canteen with walls of dried grass. It had dartboards, table tennis and other games besides a restaurant stocking cigarettes, chocolate, sausages and the like... soon after midnight on Old Year's Night the place caught fire, probably a cigarette with a good desert wind to help the flames. The Rhodesian squadron canteen was gutted in five minutes. Everything was lost including all the stock and a wireless set presented by the State Lottery Trustees...I owe the

SUDAN AND ERITREA

news of this loss to a letter sent by the officer in charge of the canteen to Mr J.W. Keller, minister without portfolio. (Rhodesia Herald, 17th January)

Also lost in the fire, according to Eric Smith were unpaid accounts for Christmas cheer of more than £1,000. A levy of a penny on beer was decreed by the adjutant and very soon the shortfall was made up. The State Lotteries and the National War Funds also offered to help restock the bar but an announcement in the Cabbages and Kings column on 1st March reported that £100 was still needed. A week later the Rhodesian Squadron Canteen Fund was closed, £125-10s-2 having been raised.

Suddenly we were rolling rich. This was to stand us in good stead later in the desert. Every time we came back to the delta to re-equip, we were promptly issued with three truckloads of gas equipment and equally promptly we dumped it behind some sand dunes, loading the trucks so freed, with booze. We were forced to take continued evasive action to preserve our reserves from robbery by the RAF to assist newly formed squadrons. We argued loudly and clearly that our funds were a gift from the 'women and children' of Rhodesia and as such inviolate! However, to keep the funds reasonably static we hit upon a novel idea. When the opportunity arose, the whole squadron could drink on the house for 24 hours. All ranks were abolished from 0600 to 0599 the next day. I was no longer 'sir' but 'you b...y b...d Eric'. Let me record, however, that never once was there ever the slightest hint of any unpleasant incident, mainly, I think because the officers being more practised, could invariably outdrink the other ranks and carried their unquestioning respect! Let me also record that it enabled me to pick up many individual problems that would never have come to light because 'there is a war on'. It must also be remembered that very many of the officers and men were personal friends from civilian life but everybody accepted and respected the changed status because of the war. (Eric Smith, History of No 237)

On January 4th 1941, Flying Officer Ron Christie with Sergeant Ken Murrell as gunner, took off at 14h10 to dive-bomb the slopes of Jebel Miriam Waha. During this attack, the Hardy was hit by anti-aircraft fire. Sergeant Murrell was wounded in the knee but dug the shell splinters out with a screwdriver. He then discovered that the airscrew covers had been set alight, apparently by red-hot shrapnel, and had fallen on the floor of the rear cockpit. He threw three of the blazing pieces overboard. Then, finding that he could not operate the extinguisher, attacked the flames with his hands. The pilot signalled to him to abandon the machine by parachute but Sergeant Murrell refused. He continued to attack the blaze until Flying Officer Ron Christie succeeded in making a forced-landing. The fire was then extinguished with water and the aircraft flown safely back to base. Sergeant Ken Murrell was later awarded the DFM for courage and dedication to duty.

Eight days later came the first of what was to be known as late arrivals. Pilot Officer Peter Simmonds and Sergeant John Gray failed to return from a sortie. Their aircraft had been damaged by a CR 42 and forced to land a mile south of Tessenei. They made it back to Allied lines safely—on foot.

Meanwhile 'B' flight had been getting their own back on the Italians.

Flying Officer Eric Spence carried out a ground reconnaissance with Masservy, which took them some 50 miles [80km] on foot behind the lines and they had holed up for the day in the hills overlooking Agordat, a fighter base. He had meticulously observed the habits of the Italians and, in particular, noticed their officers' mess. When the surviving Hardy returned we promptly dispatched it with a full load of bombs for personal delivery to the mess. We later had the satisfaction of inspecting the accuracy and the Chianti stained walls. (Eric Smith)

The Battle of Keren

By the beginning of January 1941, preparations were complete for an operation, which would see the heaviest fighting yet in East Africa and some of the Italian's most resolute defence.

The major British offensive against the heavily fortified Italian position at Kassala was scheduled to begin on 19th January. Several days previous to this date Masservy called for an aerial reconnaissance. Thus alerted, the Italians, instead of coming out to the attack began to pull back.

> *Masservy with his Gazelle force pounced on them like a pack of bull terriers, calling on his personal 'air force' namely 'B' flight for support. 'B' had a hilarious time keeping up with him, breaking up rearguard actions, constantly harassing the fleeing Italians and feeding him with reconnaissance reports. Worthy of note was the performance of the three drivers of 'B' flight's Chevrolet trucks who under Corporal Cecil Messina drove round the clock for a week or more, sleeping and eating in their cabs, to bring up petrol, bombs and ammunition from Khartoum.*
> (Eric Smith)

The Allies swept 40 miles into Eritrean territory before they met any Italian defence. This was near the town of Keru, which was bypassed, leaving 900 Italian troops cut off. Only 'A' and 'B' flights were involved in this advance. 'C' flight was collecting five new Lysanders from Abu Seuir. The main aircraft in use was still the Hardy with very occasional flights by Lysanders. However, after the arrival of the new Lysanders on 21st January approximately half the sorties were flown by Lysanders.

On 24th January, 'B' flight moved from Sarum to Sabdurat. The Operations Record for that day records:

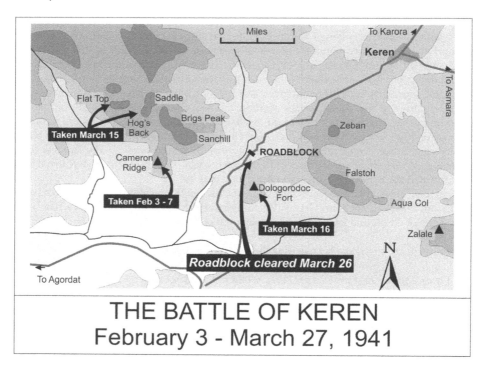

THE BATTLE OF KEREN
February 3 - March 27, 1941

'B' flight moved from Sarum to Sabdurat.
Four Hardys carried out tactical recce 15h00 – 16h45 Biscia.
Formation encountered three CR 42s over target area.
Three Lysanders—Dive-bombing 15h30 – 17h10 Umm Haggor.
Dive-bombing and ground-strafing of enemy troops and trenches. Grass surrounding trenches fired.
Lysander. Flying Officer Christie Sergeant Strickland 06h30 – 10h25.
Tactical recce. Tessenei-Eladel. Numerous tracks in vicinity.
Four Fiats observed—dropped to treetop height and returned Tessenei.
Visibility hazy.

'B' flight was heavily involved, scouting ahead of the advancing troops and dive-bombing enemy positions, harassing the retreating Italians all the way from Kassala to Agordat, which they reached on 28th January, nine days after the start of the advance. When the Italians, who had been resisting strongly at Barentu, heard that Agordat had fallen, they retreated towards Keren and orders came for the allied troops to pursue with all speed. Eric Smith, flight commander, was awarded a DFC for fine leadership during these operations.

On 28th January, the squadron headquarters moved to a landing-ground near Butana bridge on the Atbara River. The countryside was reminiscent of the Sabi Valley and so it was suggested that the new headquarters be named Sabi but it was eventually christened Umtali.

Some of the reconnaissance flights were now being escorted by Gladiators:

Operations Record January 30th:

Tactical recce ... escorted by two Glads. No movement seen Gardat/Barentu road. Intercepted by five 42s. Three attacked escort. Two attacked Hardy (flown by Eric Smith with Aircraftman Taylor). Evasive tactics successfully adopted.

On that same day, 30th January, Flying Officer Samuel Henry (Billy) Miller failed to return from a non-operational flight but was later reported, together with Aircraftman MacIntosh, as a prisoner of war. Their burnt-out Lysander was found later at Barentu.

On 2nd February, there occurred what the *Rhodesia Herald* described as One of the most amazing feats in the succession of battles over the Eritrean front...In less extravagant but more dramatic terms the Operations Report tells it this way:

In the course of a Tactical Reconnaissance patrol along the Scipitale/Tole road, Flying Officer M.A. Johnson, with Airgunner J.G.P. Burl, in a Lysander encountered three CA 133s. Failing to observe any escorting fighters, the pilot attacked the enemy formation forcing one to land and crash. The Lysander was then attacked by three CR 42s. The airgunner was injured in the right wrist but succeeded in firing off three pans of ammunition and damaging one fighter, which was seen to leave with smoke pouring from the engine. In the course of the attack the Lysander's flying controls were shot away, compelling the pilot to land and crash east-north-east of Tole. The airgunner succeeded in extricating the unconscious pilot while the CR 42s continued to machine-gun them. When the pilot recovered, the crew set off on foot in a northerly direction and were eventually met by natives who led them back on donkeys to our forward troops. (Operations Record No 237)

It so happened that a *Daily Express* correspondent was at the station when the two men staggered in. He reported that Burl, though in great pain and suffering from loss of blood, had carried the pilot a considerable distance on his shoulders. It had taken the men two days to reach British lines. Flying Officer M.A. Johnson received the DFC and Sergeant J.G.P. Burl the DFM for this exploit.

Masservy's rapid advance was abruptly halted a few miles before he reached Keren, where the mountains rose in a rugged sweep up from the desert floor to a height of 6,000 feet. The solitary road ran for two and a half miles along the bottom of a narrow gorge. The only route through the wall of mountains was dominated by eleven peaks, rising 2,000 feet above the level of the road. Seven of these peaks lay on the left of the road: Cameron Ridge, Sanchill, Brigs Peak, Hog's Back, Saddle, Flat Top and Samanna. The four on the right were Dologorodoc (with a fort), Falestoh, Zaban and Zalale. Between Falestoh and Zalale there was a rise towards a low ridge forming a gap, Aqua Col. This was obviously a point where a strong defensive position could be held and crack Italian troops were placed here.

Troops of the 4th Indian Division went into the attack, supported by No 237 Squadron and No 1 Squadron SAAF, flying Hurricanes, commanded by Colonel Laurie Wilmot. The first attempt to force a passage through the mountains began on 3rd February. The 4th Division stormed Sanchill, Brigs Peak and Cameron Ridge. They were driven off the first two but managed to hold Cameron Ridge despite murderous fire; at the same time, determined efforts were made to retake Brigs Peak and Sanchill.

The battle raged for four days. During this time, the Indians reached the top of all three peaks at least once only to be driven back by determined counter-attacks. No 237 Squadron was deeply involved. 'A' flight was employed mainly on artillery observation and spotting duties. 'B' and 'C' flights carried out dive-bombing and machine-gun attacks on enemy positions.

The Operations Record for 5th February is typical:

Flying Officer Storey, Aircraftman Quincey did four flights—
location of enemy forward positions.
Flight Lieutenant Smith, Sergeant Gray —11h50 – 13h10
bombed railway track ahead of stationary engine in Keren area and a convoy of enemy troop
lorries on Keren/Asmara road.
Flying Officer Flett and Sergeant Stowe
with Flying Officer Robinson and Sergeant Thomas—13h50 – 15h00
bombed railway bridge two and a half miles south-east Habi Mentel. Machine-gunned five
enemy motor transport vehicles on Keren/Habi Mentel road.

The following day, 5th February, was one of the busiest to that date with eight sorties flown while 'B' flight moved forward from Sabdurat to Agordat. So far the Rhodesian squadron had been remarkably fortunate but their luck was not to continue. On 7th February, Flying Officer Jack Taylor and Sergeant Garth C.D. Stowe in Hardy K4314 were intercepted and shot down in flames by a CR 42 while on an early morning tactical reconnaissance patrol over the Keren area. Both pilot and airgunner were killed. Their bodies were found later in the burnt-out remains of their aircraft by ground troops about 17 miles (27km) east of Agordat.

On 9th February, five CR 42s carried out a dawn attack on Agordat, during which two Hardys and two Lysanders were destroyed. Eric Smith recalls that pilots caught in the open dodged behind trees to escape the bullets, while one rear gunner firing a Lewis gun from the hip, brought down one of the raiders.

The fighting on the ground around Keren continued day after day with casualties mounting and no significant advance taking place. But while the war on the ground had bogged down, the Rhodesians maintained their dive-bomb and machine-gun attacks on the

Italian defenders. On 10th February, Alec Hutchinson had a lucky escape. He had been sent to collect a replacement Lysander for 'A' flight. Taking off from Umtali he flew to Tessenei, which had recently been captured from the Italians and then to Agordat. On take-off from Agordat on the return flight, the engine of his aircraft cut out and he crashed. He was extremely fortunate to escape serious injury but the aircraft was a write-off. For No 237 to admit that an aircraft was irreparable meant that it really was a complete wreck. In fact, it was incredible that Hutchinson got out of it alive.

The Gladiators arrive

At the beginning of March, 'B' flight was re-equipped with Gladiators that were no longer required by No 1 Squadron SAAF. The Rhodesians retained one flight of Hardys for bombing operations.

The Gloster Gladiator had been Britain's principal fighter at the time of the Munich crisis in 1938, but even when it was later replaced by the Hurricane and the Spitfire its career was not over. Gladiators served with the Allies in Norway, and for a time four Gladiators—three of which were known as Faith, Hope and Charity—were the only fighter defence of Malta against Mussolini's air force. Gladiators were flown by the Finnish air force and Swedish volunteers fighting the Russian air force in the winter war. For the RAF Gladiators, however, the final theatre was the Middle East. Last of the British biplane fighters, the Gladiator enjoyed the biplane's manœuvrability but in terms of speed and firepower, the Gladiator was no match for the monoplane fighter. Its maximum speed was 246 mph (394 km/h) and it carried four .303 Browning machine guns.

The first recorded No 237 (Rhodesia) Squadron operation with a Gladiator occurred on 10th March when Flight Lieutenant Eric Smith dive-bombed suspected anti-aircraft positions around Dolgorodoc and Falestoh. 'B' flight officially arrived back at Agordat on the next day and Flying Officer Sandy MacIntyre did a second sortie in a Gladiator, making a dive-bomb attack on a motor transport concentration four miles east of Keren. By 12th March, the Glads had taken their place beside the Lysanders and Hardys in the Battle of Keren.

The air commanding officer at this time was Air Commodore Bill Slatter. It seems that the Rhodesians were his blue-eyed boys and he came to know all the pilots individually, always addressing them by their nicknames. The members of 'B' flight were his favourites for the simple reason that they discovered his weakness for Plymouth Gin and no matter how dry they were, always managed to have a bottle for Bill on his frequent visits. However, a severe strain was put on the relationship by an incident that occurred over Keren. As Eric Smith later told the story:

In fairness to the flight, they were having a pretty frustrating time doing standing patrols over our bombers, coming in waves of three, at five-minute intervals. On this particular morning, the flight of five Gladiators had already mixed with 26 Fiats attacking two waves of bombers. The Fiats used their superior speed to avoid the Gladiators and to try to pick off the bombers. The Gladiators had discovered that the Italians were allergic to direct fire and had loaded their ammunition one tracer to three, instead of one to thirty. They then merely hosed a wall of tracers ahead of any attacking Fiat and this invariably made him change his mind. On our third patrol that morning, (we were doing up to eight sorties per day), we suddenly saw a low-wing monoplane some 5,000 feet below us. As it was not a Hurricane, it could only be a Macchi 202. Our intelligence had warned us to watch out for these new aircraft. We peeled off in line astern to attack. Imagine my horror when clearing fast from underneath I saw RAF roundels! All I could do was to roll off the top, straight into the path of the diving flight, forcing them to break up. We now recognized the Proctor, a two-seater communications aircraft with some rubber-necking fool driving it. We promptly dealt with him by barrel rolling round him and trying to roll him by flipping his wing. This aircraft had arrived ex the Middle East that morning and the AOC had promptly taken off in it to see how 'his boys' were doing over Keren, without a word to anybody. All this made not a whit of difference to the blast I got from Bill. Some say two baobab trees were uprooted behind me but I dared not turn to see. However, the lure of Plymouth Gin was too much and about nine that evening he wandered into the flight mess and we knew all was forgiven. (Eric Smith, History No 237)

The fight for Keren continues

The lull on the ground continued until 15th March, when both 4th and 5th Indian Divisions once more went into the attack. The plan was that the 5th Division should storm Dologorodoc on the right and then advance towards Falestoh and Zaban. The attack began with a heavy bombardment. In the Operations Record Eric Smith comments, attempted to range guns on target but unable to do so as too many batteries engaging same target. While Flying Officer Brian White remarks: Impossible to pinpoint shell burst owing to continuous air bombardment. Fort Dologorodoc and Sanchill dive-bombed and machine-gunned.

In all, the squadron flew some 21 sorties on 15th March, dive-bombing, artillery-spotting and tactical reconnaissance but despite a gallant effort that carried them to the top of the peaks, the Indians were once again thrown back by a counter-attack. Fighting continued all night. At first light Fort Dologorodoc was stormed, taken and held. All day the battle raged. There was no further advance but no ground was lost. This day, 16th March, was to be the day on which No 237 (Rhodesia) Squadron was to get its first CR 42. Eric Smith's log-book reads:

Glad 5820 Agordat—Keren—Agordat 45 minutes
Bombs on Sanchil—Wellesley down in flames—too far for us to help. Peter shot down a CR 42 and then force-landed.

Meanwhile the 9th Brigade of the 5th Indian Division was pinned down, exposed to well-directed fire from across the gorge. Major General (Piggy) Heath, commanding 5th Indian Division made an urgent request for 'B' flight to attempt to silence the machine guns and mortars that had his men pinned down. The men had been in this exposed position since the previous evening. They had no water or hand grenades and were desperately short of ammunition. The leading elements of this force, which were within 30 yards (33m) of the enemy positions, could not move back or forward and were suffering heavy casualties.

Eric Smith says:

I baulked at the order, claiming that under the intense light machine gun and flak we would encounter, I could not guarantee this sort of accuracy. Piggy overruled my objection and ordered us in. With its, by now, proverbial luck 'B' flight not only silenced the specific mortars and guns but proceeded to keep all the Italians heads down along the whole sector while the battalion very rapidly retired, bringing all their wounded and dead with them. The Gladiators did not escape unscathed and five out of the eight were unserviceable mainly from splinters from their own bombs, because while the orders were to bomb from 300 feet we went down to 100. Our men on the ground were told to flash metal to show us where they were. (Eric Smith)

The battle for Keren had now been raging for two weeks. The fighting had been fierce and the losses heavy. On 18th March, the Rhodesian squadron suffered another loss. Both Flight Lieutenant Tickey Tyas and Sergeant Rhodes William Horobin died when their aircraft was shot down by a CR 42.

The Operations Record for that day makes exciting reading:

Search made for enemy movement and motor transport. Own battery contacted and shoot carried out...called up battery—no movement seen—dive-bombed and machine-gunned suspected gun emplacement south east Falestoh...many fighter aircraft—CR 42 attempted to attack but broke off as Glad, flown by Eric Smith, turned to meet attack. Dive-bombing attack on east slope Sanchill. Dive-bombing attack Mt Zaban. Dive-bombing/machine-gun attacks on retreating enemy motor transport.

The heavy fighting continued up and down the mountainsides for another five days of attack and counter attack. There were severe losses on both sides and both General Platt and General Fresco, the opposing commanders, were beginning to wonder how much longer they could stand the casualty rate. By 20th March, the Italians were down to one third of their original strength. On 21st March, Flight Lieutenant Graham A. Smith was slightly wounded during a scuffle with a group of CR 42s, one of which was damaged by Smith's gunner, Sergeant Ken Murrell. Flying Officer Evert Kleynhans had an unhappy experience on 25th March. He was flying a Gladiator when he was attacked and badly damaged by a Hurricane. He tried several times to break off the engagement but the Hurricane pilot seemed to be determined to shoot him down. He was extremely lucky to survive the attack, which left him badly shaken.

The Italians' defence had been heroic but now they were beginning to waver and in spite of heavy fire, the Indian troops managed to clear a gap through a roadblock late on the afternoon of 26th March 1941. Early the following morning a squadron of tanks pierced the Italian defences. The Italians immediately pulled back and British tanks rolled triumphantly into Keren that same morning. The battle for Keren had lasted eight weeks. The British force had suffered 536 dead and 3,229 wounded while the Italians suffered more than 3,000 dead. But now the line was broken and once more the British advance was under way.

On the road to Asmara

The Rhodesians now turned to attacking roadblocks and keeping the Italians on the move. By 30th March, the attacking forces had reached Asmara, which fell without resistance on 1st April 1941. On the previous day, Pilot Officer Simmonds flying a Gladiator, had gone missing on a patrol over Ad Teclesan. Describing the event Peter Simmonds said later:

On March 31st, three of us were on a fighter patrol. (Flight Lieutenant Smith, Flying Officer Eric Spence and Pilot Officer Peter Simmonds). I had to break away before time was up as the engine started giving trouble. I realized I would not get home, so flew over a dry river bed roughly in the right direction but clear of the mountains. The trouble developed and I had to go down. I got things fixed up after a couple of hours and took off again. But by now I had got so far off my course, I was lost. All I could do now was fly on with my back to enemy territory and pray that I should pick up a landmark. I didn't and made a second landing with no petrol. I was now well and truly lost with no shadow of an idea where I was. I had to walk, so took the two tins of bully we carry and set off on a long and nearly fatal journey. I kept going with intermittent rest, until four o'clock next morning when I found the remains of a fire. I built it up and got warm and when it grew light a native appeared. I had a long, long drink of water and half a tin of bully, and then tried to get him to guide me back to Agordat. He wouldn't so I started the weary trudge once more. That Tuesday was sheer hell. The country was the wildest I have ever seen—strewn with sand and broken rocks. Under the scorching sun with no vestige of shade, no water and a desperate feeling of futility, I struggled on, towards the end by will power alone, for 26 solid hours. By now I was feeling weak and ill—nearly exhausted. Lack of water in that scorching heat had so swollen my tongue as to make it fill my mouth. When daylight came on Wednesday morning I had got to the stage where I would stumble over some silly little stone and take an age to get up again. Then at 7 am I found a waterhole. My God what a sight! Then and there, just as I stood, I flopped into it. I now decided to wait for some natives to turn up and ate the second half of the tin of bully. Soon a couple of natives came along. I managed to explain that I wanted them to guide me home to Agordat and that I must have a camel. This seemed all right and at about nine o'clock on Wednesday morning, I started off with them to get camels. I lasted only half an hour when everything went black and I flopped out. I knew nothing more for three whole hours. When I came to, I was lying under a tree, deliciously cool, soaking from head to foot. If this is paradise, thought I, at least it's comfortable. As I gathered my scattered wits, I realized an old native—he must have been about 60—was bathing me with gallons and gallons of cold water. What appears to have happened is that the two natives, when I fainted, decided I was dead, took the remaining tin of bully, the signal pistol and cartridges I had taken from the machine, what few odds and ends were in my pockets and beat it. The old man, passing that way, saw me lying there and proceeded to bring back my departing spirit. I lay there all day and the old fellow brought me gallons of goat's milk. That evening I felt better and trudged off to the old boy's hide-out. He had a little tent all alone where he lived with a few goats, some cattle and a couple of camels. He apparently migrated into Eritrea from the Sudan, many, many years ago and had lived there ever since. He did not know Agordat, so far from home had I got, but said he would take me to a British post. Early next morning we set off west on camels. From then until Sunday night April 6th we travelled, as I hope never to travel again. Resting only in the extreme heat of midday, riding by the moon as well, we came out at a small siding on the Sudan Eritrea border. From there I hopped a goods train up to Kassala and was able to get in touch with the squadron. (Peter Simmonds, The War History of Southern Rhodesia)

Story has it that when Peter Simmonds was reported missing, Cyril (Dopey) Sindall laid claim to Simmonds's most prized possession—a collapsible bath which was the envy of the flight. Despite being pleased to see Peter back—Sindall was not so happy about having to return the bath, feeling that he had more right to the bath than Peter did to be alive. The story according to Eric Smith was that the bath was never returned!

After the fall of Keren the squadron moved forward to Asmara. The journey was not without difficulty as one man who took part recalls:

6th April 1941. *Up at dawn and left Agordat at 06h30. First hitch about ten miles out—stuck in a drift and had to be helped out by 'B' flight who passed us. On to beautiful tar road and started the climb through pass into Keren, which Ities (Italians) had held so stubbornly; barren, rugged country, hillsides fairly blasted away by shellfire. Road had been blown up on steepest part but Royal Engineers had cleared the block. We stuck on a steep bit and had to be towed out. Made Keren about midday and stopped for some tea at NAAFI—pretty little village rather knocked about by our bombers. From there to Asmara, one long climb over superbly engineered tarmac road through rugged mountain scenery up on to a plateau seven to eight thousand feet above sea level. At Teclesan we had to negotiate some more road blocks—vertical cliff on one side, sheer precipice on the other and a narrow loose-surfaced track, bumpy as hell, to negotiate. Several trucks and gun-limbers had already failed to make the grade and had been pushed over the edge to keep the road clear! Low gear and prayers saw us safely through and we got to Asmara about 19h30. From Teclesan we had travelled with a convoy of guns, light and medium, on their way to batter Massawa and a friendly race to Asmara had developed between us and the gun convoy. Our stop to refuel gave them a lead but we caught them again on the outskirts of Asmara and passed them amid cheers and shouts of 'Will the circus be showing tonight?' Asmara by*

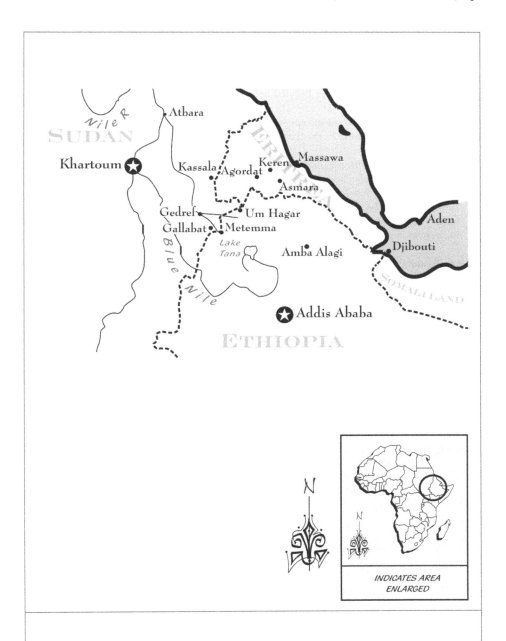

THE ADVANCE TO AMBA ALAGI

lamplight (electric) looked a lovely spot, with a decidedly bracing climate—especially after the heat at Agordat. (The War History of Southern Rhodesia)

With the advance came a happy release for some South African and Rhodesian prisoners of war. Among them Flying Officer Billy Miller and Aircraftman Alfred John MacIntosh who had been missing since 30th January when their aircraft had been shot down over Barentu. They had had a very unpleasant six-day journey from Barentu to Asmara because all the roads between the two towns were in the hands of the British:

The consequence was that our guards had to take us through the bush where there were no roads of any sort and we had to walk most of the 80 miles [128km] with a little assistance from some mules. Our own aircraft flew over us very low on many occasions and we were kept busy taking cover. We had to sleep out at nights and there was little food, while water was extraordinarily scarce. I had 24 hours in Asmara—half the time I was cast into goal; the other half I was being interrogated by the Italians. (Rhodesia Herald, 15th April 1941)

From Asmara the British forces swept on to the Red Sea port of Massawa, which Admiral Bonette refused at first to surrender. The town was attacked with close support from the air. On 8th April 1941, the Italian admiral changed his mind and handed the town over, complete with 9,600 men and 127 guns. This ended the Eritrean Campaign. The threat to East Africa and the Red Sea was over. No 237 (Rhodesia) Squadron had acquitted itself with honour winning two DFCs, two DFMs and five mentions!

The first weeks of May were passed mostly in mopping-up operations. Dive-bombing attacks were carried out against Toselli Fort and Amba Alagi where the squadron suffered the loss of William McGregor (Billy) Cooper and his gunner, John Oliver Collins.

At eight o'clock on the 15th (May) Bill set off to bomb the Duke's stronghold, which he did with great success. Just after he had dropped his last egg, the engine failed (cause unknown) and he commenced to make a forced-landing in a very difficult country—owing to this, he crashed. The aircraft was completely written off and Bill was rendered unconscious immediately, in which state he remained until three hours after when he died. He and Collins were picked up within five minutes of the crash by British troops and the doctor assured me that Bill never suffered, thank God. Collins died two days later. (Letter written by Pilot Officer Samuel Henry 'Billy' Miller who was himself to die in July 1942 as a result of an aircraft accident)

By the middle of May 1941, all fight had gone out of the Italians and on 19th May the Duke of Aosta and his 5,000 remaining troops laid down their arms. This surrender was watched by members of the Rhodesian squadron.

Eric Smith tells the story:

When the Duke of Aosta was standing on the tarmac at Khartoum ready to be flown to a POW camp in Kenya by a South African Air Force Ju 52, Air Commodore Slatter, in full ceremonial uniform came up and smartly saluted him. "Sir, would you mind if one of my Rhodesian pilots going on leave (me) travelled in your aircraft?" The Duke replied, "I will indeed be delighted." He gave me a message for the governor, Brooke-Popham, which I was unable to deliver. "Tell Popham that the map he gave me of Kenya and Uganda for my shooting safari was most useful (in the war)!"

Reporting on the campaign the *Rhodesia Herald* remarked:

In the type of machine used, the pilots' safety from hostile air attack rests largely with his airgunner and in their airgunners the pilots of the Rhodesia squadron have been well served. The aircrew have also been magnificently served by their Rhodesian ground staff. During the thick of the fighting, the whole ground staff went without meals and sleep to keep the squadron's machines in the air. The spirit, like the quality of their work, was first class. The squadron too, has been lucky in casualties. Regrettable though the loss of four pilots and five airgunners is, it is a low figure for 18 months of operations, particularly when it is remembered that the squadron's reconnaissance aircraft were often inferior to the fighters of the enemy and that they were constantly in action in some of the heaviest fighting of the East African Campaign.
(Rhodesia Herald, 31st Oct. 1941)

So the East African Campaign ended and a few days after the fall of Amba Alagi a convoy of No 237 (Rhodesia) Squadron vehicles left Asmara for Kassala to entrain for Wadi Halfa and the next adventure.

CHAPTER 9

The focus shifts

"Southern Rhodesia has 4,500 men and women on full-time military service today," declared Mr T.H.W. Beadle addressing a United Party meeting on 17th January 1941. He then gave facts and figures about the Colony's war effort. One thousand four hundred and sixteen men were serving in the air force within the Colony including 17 pilots working as instructors or with the Communications Squadron. Ninety-two pilots were serving outside the Colony and 259 men were in training. There were also 64 Rhodesians waiting to be absorbed into the Empire Air Training Scheme. The aim was to have about 400 pilots on active service. In the same proportion, that would be 400,000 pilots for the population of Great Britain. About 70% of the young Rhodesians joining the forces were choosing the RAF but the absorption rate was only about 10 to 15 a month. In a memo written after the war Colonel Meredith, commanding officer of the RATG, says:

> *The original programme of an initial training wing and six schools was increased, during 1941, to eight Flying Training Schools and in addition a bombing, navigation and gunnery school for the training of bomb-aimers, navigators and airgunners. To relieve congestion at the air stations, six relief landing grounds for landing and take-off instruction were established. Also set up, were two air firing and bombing ranges.* At a later stage, another air station was established for the training of flying instructors and this brought the total to ten air stations. Two aircraft and engine repair and overhaul depots were set up and also a Central Maintenance Unit to deal with bulk stores for a whole group. In addition to the three initial sections, works, finance and supplies, of RATG HQ, other sections were formed as development progressed. These included air staff, air training, signals, armament, administration, equipment, engineering, personnel, medical and legal, and were expanded as required until the total staff at peak was in the region of 400, of which 120 were commissioned officers. Stationed in Cape Town and Durban, there were two small units to deal with aircraft arriving by ship, and unpacking and assembling for flying to Rhodesia. Also in Cape Town was a movement control officer handling arrivals and departures of personnel. This involved, in the case of personnel arriving, the arranging of a number of special trains. At Port Elizabeth, there was a representative to deal with the incoming consignments of equipment. These units were under RATG HQ.* (Meredith memo)

As was mentioned earlier, accidents are bound to occur when such a vast programme of pilot training is undertaken and with the accidents came stories of outstanding bravery.

---

* The two bombing ranges near Bulawayo were named Mias and Myelbow. Strange names at first glance, but because the pilots and navigators had great difficulty in distinguishing between the two they coined the phrase: I didn't know Mias from Myelbow.

On 14th February, an aircraft crashed while night-flying and caught fire. Trapped in the burning wreckage were Flight Lieutenant Greenshields (RAF), the instructor and Sergeant Ian Jenkinson, the pupil pilot. Flying Officer Morris (RAF) was waiting to take off when the crash occurred and he taxied towards the scene, where he found the fire tender already in attendance, spraying the base of the fire in an effort to damp the flames sufficiently to allow rescuers to reach the trapped men.

Greenshields managed to free himself but Jenkinson was still caught in the burning aircraft when the supply of foam suddenly ceased. Despite the searing heat and the fact that the petrol tanks could explode at any moment, Morris with the help of Leading Aircraftman Goldsmith (RAF) lifted the aircraft, allowing Goldsmith to put his head and arms inside the burning cockpit and cut the harness straps, but the injured pilot still could not be released. By this time, the fire tender was in action again and Goldsmith directed the foam to dampen the heat. Once more, they tried to lift the fuselage and this time they succeeded, pulling the injured man to safety. Morris and Goldsmith worked with complete disregard for their own safety. Unfortunately, Sergeant Jenkinson's burns were too extensive and he died soon afterwards. In September 1941, King George VI awarded the George Medal for Conspicuous Gallantry to Flight Lieutenant Morris (RAF) and Leading Aircraftman J.L. Goldsmith (RAF).

In March 1941, work began on Myelbo Bombing Range, Crocodile Valley, White's Run and Imbezu. Just about everyone in Rhodesia was making some war effort—Rhodesia Railways even turned its hand to making practice bombs. These contained chemicals that produced a volume of dense smoke when they exploded, thus helping the bomb-aimer to judge his accuracy.

Estimated revenue in the 1941/42 Budget was £6,058,000 of which £2,282.958 was to be spent on the war effort. Of this £600,000 was to be spent on married quarters for RAF personnel. It is interesting to note that the Rhodesian government not only agreed to build special housing for the RAF men but also to furnish the accommodation. Speaking during the debate on the 1941/42 Budget, the prime minister said that the Colony's contribution to the war effort was a great deal more than the British government expected and that he believed that the very liberal and generous contribution was as much as the country could afford. The housing schemes were completed at Cranborne in June and Kumalo in July. Meanwhile Heany was getting under way.

News from the stations

March 25th saw the official opening of Thornhill, though the first two trainloads of young men had arrived the day before. However, it was to be almost a month, 19th April, before the RAF advance party, under the command of Flight Lieutenant Cox (RAF) arrived. The first station commander was Group Captain J.S. Chick (RAF).

Flying at Heany had already begun during the occupancy of the advance party, with No 2 Course taking to the air in mid-May. The urgent daily task of the advance party and first attachments was to unload the trains as they arrived at Heany siding and unpack the vast quantity of equipment. Much of the camp was still being erected and many of the billets were not yet habitable. On 7th July, the advance party of the RAF arrived and work began in earnest.

The life of a cadet at Heany provided him with little respite from the intensified schedule of lectures and flying. If a trainee's schedule could be arduous, so could the work of the men who kept his aircraft in the air. All labours had their compensation. Heany amenities for off-duty hours were far in advance of what might have been expected. What other RAF station could boast a change of cinema programme five nights a week or a hotdog stall for refreshment of

night-flyers or a tarmac ice-cream service during the hot summer months? In these happy days, too, before petrol rationing, the motorcar industry at Heany was remarkable. Heath Robinson-looking vehicles, capable of making the 16-mile [25-km] evening trip to town with a minimum of disintegration, would spring up almost overnight, and car parks would be replete with angular futuristic and variegated cars, uniform only in having four wheels and an engine.
(RAF Heany Archives)

Heany was also responsible for Rhodesia's first service newspaper. Born on board ship on the way from Europe its name, derived from the words RAF in Africa, was *AFRAF*. The newspaper was aimed at the whole command and not only the personnel of Heany itself. The first edition, price threepence, was dated 7th August 1941 and was on sale just one month after its parents arrived at Heany. The joint editors John K. Tither and Alan Brian Chalkley both had journalistic experience and their paper reached a peak circulation of 2,300 copies a week.

Moffat Air Station was now swinging into action. The advance party arrived on 2nd August with Group Captain J.K. Summers MC as their first commanding officer. Two weeks later, the first cadets arrived to train as navigators. The initial course consisted of 19 Rhodesians, ten men from the United Kingdom, one South African, three Australians and one lone Yank. The day after their arrival a game of soccer was organized. Over the following years, Moffat maintained its tradition for enthusiasm on the sporting field, with teams playing cricket, rugby, hockey, taking part in boxing matches, and swimming in the pool that was dug by the men themselves and named Moffat-by-the-Sea. The first course of gunners from Moffat passed out in September.

If Moffat was renowned for sport then Heany took the dramatic palm. The motivating force was Kenneth Keeling who had been a professional actor for ten years. The first show was staged during September 1941 and was followed by the announcement that regular fortnightly entertainment would follow. Early in November, the members produced their first show for the general public, Irksome Erks, which was staged in the Bulawayo City Hall.

However, the serious side of training was never neglected for the fun and games.

We have been discussing with the Air Ministry the air training scheme that the government of SR have established so successfully in the Colony and it is right that your ministers should be made aware of the fact that the Air Ministry have expressed their high appreciation of the speed and efficiency with which, despite the difficulties inseparable from war conditions, the scheme has been developed. (Message Sec of State to SR Govt)

Women's Auxiliary Air Service
On 1st August, 106 female recruits attested in to the Southern Rhodesia Women's Auxiliary Air Service.* Flying Officer Roxburgh-Smith was appointed commandant. The WAAS uniform consisted of a skirt and a belted tunic with long sleeves. It was worn with a field service cap, a black tie and black shoes. The girls were posted to the Communications Squadrons and to the Central Maintenance Unit in Bulawayo. They were trained in clerical duties, fabric working, parachute packing, elementary mechanics, and as equipment assistants and motor transport drivers.

Air Askari Corps
Also on 15th August, the Rhodesian Air Askari Corps under the command of Wing

---

* The formation of a Women's Auxiliary Services had been announced on 1st June 1941.

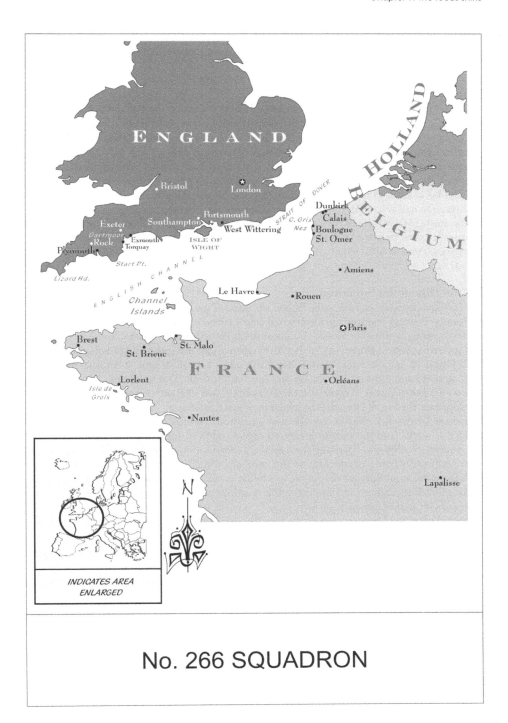

No. 266 SQUADRON

Commander T.E. Price, was formed to provide armed guards and non-armed labour for the airfields. Members of the corps were all volunteers and did valuable service guarding and protecting air stations.

Rhodesian aircrew in Britain

By September 1941, a steady stream of trained aircrew was leaving Rhodesia, but what was happening to them? At the outset of the war, Rhodesia had undertaken to supply the men to operate three squadrons, which would bear the name Rhodesia in their title. The first squadron to take the field, before the actual declaration of war, was No 237 (Rhodesia) Squadron whose exploits in the East African Campaign have already been detailed.

It had also been intended to form a fighter and a bomber squadron in Britain and as trainees became available, they were shipped to the United Kingdom with this in mind. The first recruits had arrived in the summer and autumn of 1940 for training with the RAF and by the spring of 1941, these men were completing their training. Rather than start a special squadron, it was decided to draft them into existing squadrons and gradually build up the Rhodesian content until eventually, it was hoped, the entire squadron personnel would be Rhodesian.

No 266 (Rhodesia) Squadron

No 266 Squadron was chosen as the fighter squadron. This squadron was originally formed in 1918 and was then a seaplane squadron based on the island of Lemnos. It was disbanded in 1919 after a campaign against the Russian communists at Petrovosk on the Black Sea. The squadron was revived at Sutton Bridge in October 1939 when under the command of Squadron Leader W.A. Hunnard, it took charge of 16 Fairey Battles. In a very short time, it became operational with Spitfires and went into action on 2nd June at Dunkirk. The squadron's record that day gave a foretaste of things to come, four Messerschmitt Me 109s and one Me 110 were probably destroyed for the loss of two pilots in battles fought at 22,000 feet.

Squadron Leader R.L. Wilkinson, the new squadron commander, took over on 29th June and a few weeks later the squadron entered one of the fiercest phases of its existence. From 8th August, No 266 was operating from forward aerodromes in the south of England, which were continually being attacked by enemy bombers. On 22nd August, the squadron moved back from the front line but the action was by no means over. During the heavy night raids on London, Birmingham and Coventry, the squadron provided night-fighters to combat the waves of German bombers.

According to the Squadron Diary, the first Rhodesian to join No 266 Squadron, which was at this time based at Wittering on the Sussex coast, was Pilot Officer E.O. (Colly) Collcutt. He joined the squadron as adjutant on 14th April 1941. Three days later he was joined by Sergeant Cyril J.L. Whiteford who arrived from 58 OTU and made his first operational flight on 5th May, taking off at 19h40 to orbit the base. Whiteford was to be killed in a flying accident on 13th October 1941, while he was serving with No 41 Squadron.

The commanding officer of the squadron was a New Zealander, Squadron Leader P.G. Jameson DFC, described as a dour fighter and great leader. He was one of the survivors of the aircraft carrier Glorious that had been sunk during the evacuation of Narvik, Norway.

During May, there was an influx of Rhodesians: Pilot Officer Allen J.F. Allen-White, Pilot Officer Hugh L. Parry (Northern Rhodesian), Sergeant Gordon William Lash Matthews, Pilot Officer George Andrew Forsyth (Zulu/Buck) Buchanan, Flying Officer Charles Green (later to command the squadron) and Sergeant Paul Devenish. Already the squadron was beginning to take on a Rhodesian personality and the young pilots were quickly involved in the day-to-day tasks of enemy intruder raid interception, dusk and dawn shipping patrols—

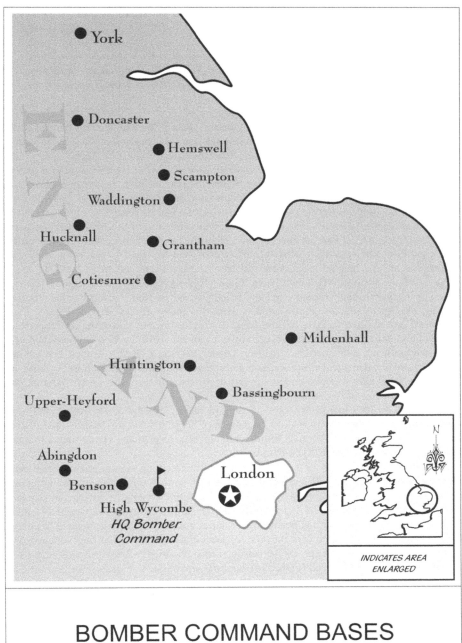

BOMBER COMMAND BASES

with the odd wing sweep across the channel for variety. Of course, in those early days, a great deal of time was spent in training for combat flying.

Non-operational flying consists of; camera gun, interception exercises, formation flying, night flying, practice formation and dog-fighting, practice fighting, climb, dusk landings, air fighting, cloud penetration, practice scramble, circuits, battle climb to 20,000 feet, weather tests, aerobatics and target-towing. (Operations Record)

Early in June 1941, Squadron Leader P.G. Jameson (RAF) who had been the commanding officer, was posted to Wittering as wing commander, and his place was taken by Squadron Leader T.B. de la Beresford (RAF) who had joined the squadron on 17th April.

First blooding for the Rhodesians came on a hot day in July when the squadron took part in a wing sweep over northern France. Taking off at 14h45 on 3rd July, the Spitfires of No 266 Squadron joined other aircraft from No 257 Squadron and No 401 Squadron. Leaving West Malling behind, they headed out over the Channel, crossing the French coast in the region of Boulogne and approached the Hazebrouch area, which is south of St Omer. Here the wing encountered something like 50 Me 109s and soon the air was full of whirling screaming dogfights. Pilot Officer Allen Allen-White's aircraft was damaged by a cannon shell, but making a tight turn, he got the enemy in his sights and saw his bullets strike the 109.

Pilot Officer Gordon Matthews Barraclough (RAF) saw Sergeant Matthews's aircraft struck by a cannon shell in the cockpit and subsequently the Rhodesian pilot was reported missing. However, Barraclough managed to shoot this enemy aircraft down. Sergeant Cyril Whiteford engaged two separate 109s probably destroying one and damaging the other. Pilot Officer Hugh Parry's aircraft was damaged by two cannon shells but he continued the fight, apparently with no great success. Squadron Leader Beresford (RAF) claimed one aircraft destroyed and one damaged, while Sergeant Thorburn (RAF) was reported missing, believed killed. The final tally was two enemy aircraft destroyed, one probably destroyed and four damaged for the loss of two squadron pilots.

The arrival on 19th July of Sergeants George Elcombe, Ian Mackenzie Munro and John Agorastos Plagis together with that on 1st August of Sergeants Alistair Spence-Ross, Victor Lawrence Carine, Wilfred Reginald Smithyman and Reginald Albert Hardy meant that the squadron was now just about 100% Rhodesian.

The days of early August 1941 passed mainly in intercepting enemy intruder raids and carrying out the occasional offensive strike across the Channel. Often this involved meeting up with returning bombers and escorting them home. On 19th August during a dusk patrol flight, Lieutenant McMullen (RAF) and Sergeant Ian Munro sighted and attacked a Heinkel He 111 flying at sea level. Both pilots made repeated attacks from different angles. The enemy aircraft dropped its nose and went into the sea leaving no survivors. On the following day, 20th August, almost in tribute, the squadron record shows the following announcement Squadron now entitled No 266 (Fighter) (Rhodesia) Squadron.

The problems of rendezvousing with returning bombers, sometimes in very adverse conditions was demonstrated just over a week later, when the squadron took part in a sweep 20 miles (32km) off the Dutch coast to cover the withdrawal of bombers returning from a raid on Rotterdam. The Rhodesian squadron took off from Coltishall in cloudy weather at 18h50 and was led to the correct position by a Blenheim. They patrolled the area at sea level but did not make contact with any of the bombers; neither did they sight any enemy aircraft or hostile shipping.

The month of August ended on a sombre note when Sergeant Victor Laurence Carine was killed while taking off on an interceptor operation. His port wing struck the maintenance hangar, and the aircraft caught fire. During the cool misty days of September, squadron activity increased with almost daily patrols from Docking across the Channel towards the Dutch coast. Enemy aircraft were frequently seen and Pilot Officer Hugh Parry claimed a probable on 21st September followed by another probable for Sergeant Eric Sydney Dicks-Sherwood three days later. In the latter half of the month, the patrols reverted to northern France with offensive sweeps in the Calais, Cap Gris-Nez and Dunkirk areas. During September, the squadron was re-equipped with Spitfire Mk IIBs that carried cannons, the first of these new aircraft having arrived on 3rd September. By 19th September, there were 12 of the new aircraft operational but then came the news that the squadron was to be equipped with Spitfire Mk VBs.

On 28th September 1941, 12 aircraft and 14 pilots together with a large number of ground personnel, left Wittering by road for Martlesham Heath to carry out manœuvres in cooperation with the army. This exercise was code named Bumper.

No 44 (Rhodesia) Squadron

The bomber squadron that had been chosen to bear the name Rhodesia was No 44 Squadron. This squadron had been formed at Hainault in Essex on 24th July 1917, and was then equipped with the famous Sopwith Camels. Its primary role was the defence of London against German air attack and even in those early days, the squadron made history. Its pilots were the first to fly single-seater fighters at night. The CO of No 44 Squadron who had Rhodesian connections was Bomber Harris, later to become commander in chief of Bomber Command. The squadron was resurrected as a bomber squadron on 8th March 1937 and equipped with Hinds but after only a few weeks, the Hinds were replaced with Blenheims, which remained the squadron aircraft until December 1939. In that month, No 44 Squadron was supplied with Hampdens. These were medium bombers with a top speed of 200 miles per hour (322 km/h), a ceiling of 18,000 feet, and a range of 1,700 miles (2,750km). The Hampden could carry a maximum load of two tons. Describing the activities of the squadron up to December 1941, the *Rhodesia Herald* reported:

> *Since the beginning of the war, the squadron has flown many thousands of miles over enemy territory, as far east as Danzig, and as far north as Norway. The squadron has also participated in many night attacks on enemy occupied ports in France, Belgium and Holland. It played a part in the big daylight attack on Brest in July. During the attack, the squadron alone shot down five Messerschmitts for the loss of only one of their own aircraft. Sixty-seven decorations have been won in this war.*

The daylight attack on Brest was an attempt to sink the German pocket battleship the Gniesenau which was then in Brest Harbour. Eighteen Hampdens of No 44 Squadron dive-bombed the battleship but they failed to sink her.

At the beginning of the war the squadron was stationed at Waddington, under the command of Wing Commander J.N. Boothman AFC (RAF), of Schneider Trophy fame, and was equipped with Hampdens. Waddington was commanded by Group Captain K.L.H. Cockey (RAF), who later became the senior air staff officer in the Rhodesian Air Training Group (RATG). For the first few months, the squadron was engaged in leaflet raids, security patrols and mine-laying over the enemy coasts and the North Sea. No 44 Squadron also played a part in the attempt to delay the Germans in their drive through France early in 1940. During the German air attacks in the autumn and winter of 40/41 the squadron was used to attack the incoming raiders and helped to disorganize raids on such towns as Birmingham and Bristol.

It was during July 1941, that Rhodesians began flying with the squadron and in fact one Rhodesian, Pilot Officer Kenneth Gordon Tew, actually took part in the attack on Brest. The Operations Record for that day reads:

> *24th July. Six Hampdens, piloted by Squadron Leader Collier, Squadron Leader Nettleton, Flight Lieutenant Ridpath, Flying Officer Clayton, Sergeant Gammon and Pilot Officer Tew, took off from Coningsby at 11h00 to form part of the strong force of 149 aircraft detailed for a daylight attack on the 'Gneisenau' and 'Prince Eugen' at Brest and the 'Scharnhorst' at La Pattice with Blenheims acting as a diversion. Five enemy claimed destroyed for the loss of one Hampden.*
>
> *1st August. A fatal flying accident occurred, which involved the loss of five personnel. At approximately 17h10 hours, Sergeant Le Blanc Smith while testing a Hampden aircraft crashed near South Park, Bracebridge Heath, Lincoln.*
>
> *Crew: Sergeant G.M. Le Blanc Smith (Rhodesian) pilot, Sergeant G.D. Dodds (Canadian), Sergeant A. Forsythe, AC 1 Jeffcote, AC 1 Clark Wireless Operator.*

This was the first Rhodesian fatality with No 44 Squadron.

On 6th August, the target was the docks and shipping at Calais and among the pilots was Sergeant Albert Denis Charles Dedman, flying his first operational duty with the squadron. Sergeant Dedman was later to take part in the historic Augsburg raid. On 11th August, five Hampdens went back to Calais, one of them piloted by Rhodesian, Sergeant Stafford Arthur Harvey, reported to be on his second operational trip. On 14th August, the target was Brunswick. The last day of the month saw ten Hampdens detailed to attack Cologne. Six of them reached their target.

> *Our aircraft met stiff opposition from enemy fighters. Flying Officer Sauvage was very badly shot up. It is not known if the aircraft piloted by Sergeant Stafford Arthur Harvey (Rhod) reached the target area, as at 03h30 hours a signal was received from the aircraft that he had lost height and was falling into the sea. The fix was given as 52° 06N 02° 11E. The aircraft flew for approximately 16 minutes; then there was complete silence. The assistance of Air Sea Rescue was immediately sought and, in addition, aircraft carried out continual searches throughout the day but the crew were not located.* (Operations Record)

That same night another Hampden collided with a Spitfire. Both aircraft crashed killing everyone on board.

During September 1941, the Hampdens were busy most nights attacking the Deutsche Works Shipyards at Kiel, bombing Kassel Railway Workshops, the Neptune Shipyards at Rostock or the docks at Le Havre. In the autumn and early winter months not all the problems stemmed from enemy action.

Operations Record 2nd September 1941:

> *Two objectives selected. First was to attack Berlin and the second Frankfurt. Nine Hampdens were detailed to attack Berlin with 128 aircraft from other Templehoff groups. Five reached the target. Pilot Officer Anekstein reported bombs dropped Templehoff area. Squadron Leader Nettleton in vicinity of railway station. Squadron Leader Burton Gyles and Pilot Officers Bell and Tew attacked the town. Sergeant Henry Dobbs (RAF) encountered Me 110 20 miles [32km] east of Norderney and his aircraft was badly shot up and Sergeant Shipton, Wireless Operator/Airgunner and Sergeant Durnan, Rear Gunner, were injured. Fire was exchanged between these aircraft and both Sergeant Shipton and Durnan reported Me 110 damaged.*

Widespread fog was experienced and the return journey was unpleasant, forcing many aircraft to land away from their home bases.

Numerous cuckoos nested at Waddington that night. One visiting aircraft wrote off 'Q' for Queenie, 44 Squadron's most operated aircraft, by undershooting and landing on top of this battle-scarred veteran, parked in the dispersal area at the edge of the airfield. After the airfield had been completely obliterated by fog and no further aircraft were being accepted, figures were looming out of the fog at the foot of the Watch Office and the station commander on the balcony anxiously called down, "Where are you from?" "Scampton" or "Luffenham" came the reply. "Where is your aircraft?" The figures would point vaguely behind them into the fog. Next morning, when a watery autumn sun had dispersed the fog, the scene was almost unbelievable. Aircraft were strewn all over the airfield, some in ditches, others poking their noses inquisitively over hedges; in fact, everywhere. Having landed and turned clear of the lighted flare path, the pilots were unable to see where they were taxiing; so they had switched off the engines when they estimated that they were not a danger to other aircraft, afraid to go further lest they strike an obstruction, even one as large as a hangar, which they could not see.
(The War History of Southern Rhodesia, confirmed by Venables)

On that same night, Rhodesian Sergeant Edward Killeen Eugene Knight had a narrow escape when his port engine was hit and cut out while he was over the target, Frankfurt. He brought the aircraft back on one engine but that cut out somewhere over Dorking and the Hampden had to be abandoned. All the crew baled out and landed safely with the exception of Sergeant Stevens (RAF) who was killed.

One of the squadron's main activities was mine-laying, otherwise known as gardening. A typical operation took place on 6th September when ten aircraft took off at 15h30 from Lossiemouth to lay mines in Oslo Fjord.

Duty gardening...Target One gardening onions. One assembly vegetables successfully planted in allotted position from 700 feet at 01h35 hours. (Operations Record)

The vegetables and sometimes flowers, were code names for mines dropped by parachute in the enemy shipping lanes. Losses were not always due to enemy action. Derek Venables who was then serving with ground crew attached to No 44 Squadron remembers:

The Hampdens had radial engines, which were inclined to cut out at certain temperatures. One night an aircraft loaded with mines, attempted to take-off and failed. The pilot made a second try and again failed to get off. He was warned not to try again but he made a third attempt, achieved some height but not enough and crashed back to earth. (Venables)

The aircraft was completely destroyed and her crew all killed when the petrol tanks and the mines she was carrying exploded. The pilot was Archibald Alan Watt of Bulawayo, who was buried at Waddington. One sad note was that Archie's fiancée arrived in England from Rhodesia the day after the accident. She later joined the WAAFS.

It was on 12th September that the squadron became officially known as No 44 (Rhodesia) Squadron and four days later came another historic day. The prototype Lancaster BT308 was demonstrated to the enthusiastic members of the squadron. By this time, 128 out of a total complement of 490 ground crew were Rhodesians. The squadron was under the command of Wing Commander R.A.B. Learoyd VC who was posted temporarily to Boscombe Down to familiarize himself with the new Lancaster.

In fact, some members of the aircrew had gone to Boscombe Down in July to get to know the new aircraft. Derek Venables was one of the ground crew who transferred temporarily to Boscombe Down in September. This was only the beginning of the slow process of changeover and the Hampdens continued in active service until the end of 1941.

Operations Record 20th September:

Ten Hampdens to attack Berlin. Take-off approximately 20h00 hours. Owing to weather conditions rapidly deteriorating recall signal sent. Four reached target. Bomb-bursts seen at west end of Unter den Linden and half a mile south of the Air Ministry. Fires started and seen for 30 miles [48km].

One of the pilots to reach Berlin that night was Squadron Leader John Nettleton (later to command No 44 Squadron). These raids were more in the nature of pinpricks than serious attacks but they did achieve a major morale boost for Britain at a time when it was desperately needed and also while the RAF proudly disproved Hitler's much repeated promise that Berlin would never be bombed. The German people were to learn his sad mistake the hard way from the hands of this squadron later in the war.

In October 1941, the targets were chiefly Hamburg, Bremen and the Ruhr cities and during this time, the Rhodesians serving with No 44 (Rhodesia) Squadron began to collect some gongs. The DFC was awarded to Flying Officer Kenneth Gordon Tew and the DFM to Sergeant Henry Dobbs.

In December, the squadron was called on to make another attack on the Gneisenau. Very much earlier in the year, on 22nd March, the German battleships Scharnhorst and Gneisenau had entered Brest Harbour. They had been in need of minor repairs but on 6th April in a suicide raid, RAF torpedo-bombers had attacked. The result was a six-month repair job on the Gneisenau and three months' work on the Scharnhorst. By July the Scharnhorst was able to leave Brest on trials and it was then that she was attacked at La Pallice. The Gneisenau was once again bombed at Brest, this time by the Hampdens of No 44 Squadron. Both ships needed yet more repairs. Meanwhile Hitler was having raging arguments with his High Command. He wanted those ships moved out of Brest away from the attentions of the RAF. His advisers told him it was impossible and so it was that the month of December came with the two battleships still in harbour at Brest. An attack was ordered for 13th December. Three Hampdens, from No 44 (Rhodesia) Squadron took part in this attack, one being piloted by Commanding Officer S.T. Misselbrook DSO, another by Sergeant Thomas Gerald (Tommy) Hackney, a Rhodesian from Gwelo and the third by Squadron Leader Peter Robert Burton Gyles.

Apparently, there was an argument about which aircraft should attack first and it was decided that a coin should be tossed. Hackney won but Misselbrook pulled rank, went in first and did not come back. The aircraft piloted by Burton Gyles* was so badly damaged that it was only by an incredible effort on the part of the crew that it got back. (Venables)

The Hampden was certainly not a luxurious aircraft and it could be almost unbearably cold in the cockpit. Derek Venables remembered that Therald Kaschula was flying on a raid one night and his window misted up. He opened it only to find a Jerry night fighter flying right alongside. He closed his window fast. Kaschula and his Rhodesian wireless operator/airgunner, Sergeant Kenneth Elser Hall, were killed on 17th December during yet another attack on Brest.

By the end of December 1941, the Japanese attack on Pearl Harbour had brought the

---

* Burton Gyles later received the DFC for this incident.

Americans into the war. Hitler's advance into Russia had bogged down but his troops had reached the outskirts of Moscow, were invading Leningrad and had captured Stalingrad. For some reason, the German leader became convinced that the Allies intended to invade Norway and so he issued orders that every available battleship be stationed along the Norwegian coastline. This entailed moving the Scharnorst, Gneisenau and the Prince Eugen, (which had joined them), out of Brest and through the English Channel. Every single one of Hitler's advisers warned that it would result in the destruction of the ships but Hitler would not listen. Just before Christmas, Naval Intelligence reported that activity in the port indicated that the German battleships were preparing to move. As a result, half the members of No 44 (Rhodesia) Squadron were placed on stand-by over Christmas. Lack of Christmas cheer was all in vain—it was February before the battleships made their dash, and to the lasting shame of the British navy, they negotiated the English Channel safely.

The best Christmas present the squadron could possibly have received arrived on Christmas Eve, Lancasters L7537, L7538 and L7541. Apart from odd diversions to the experimental establishment, the whole of AV Roe's Lancaster output was earmarked for No 44 Squadron to bring the aircraft strength up to 24.

On 26th December, Boxing Day, the order was received that no further operations were to be carried out in Hampdens and 22 of the old aircraft were handed over to No 420 (RCAF) Squadron! The last few days of 1941 were spent in training on the new aircraft. The gunners were familiarizing themselves with the turrets, while the armourers were experimenting with the various combinations of ammunition and bomb loads.

Derek Venables tells one amusing story about his first flight in a Lancaster, as ground crew. The pilot came out of the cockpit and asked if he would like to go up front and look around. He nearly fainted when he got there and found the cockpit empty. The plane was apparently flying itself! This was the first time he had come face to face with an automatic pilot!

Two days after Christmas, Colonel Lucas Guest, the Rhodesian Air Minister, and the newly promoted Air Vice-Marshal Meredith, who were in England for discussions on defence matters, visited the squadron. They took the opportunity of a flight in one of the newly acquired Lancasters and presented the squadron with its new squadron badge, which had been approved by King George VI. The bomber squadron badge had an elephant in the centre with the motto Fulmina Regis Justa, loosely translated as The King's thunderbolts are righteous and not as some wit suggested: Elephants never forget!

Autumn 1941 with No 266

To return to autumn, No 266 (Rhodesia) Squadron had been involved in shipping patrols, a monotonous task, which was interrupted on 13th October when the squadron joined a wing sweep from West Malling to cover the withdrawal of Allied forces after a seaborne attack on Boulogne. About 40 Me 109s were seen and various combats ensued. Flight Lieutenant McMullen destroyed one enemy aircraft and damaged another while Flight Lieutenant Charles Green also claimed to have done some damage to an Me 109. All the allied aircraft returned safely. After this excitement, it was back to dusk and dawn patrols enlivened occasionally by strikes on the Dutch coast.

On 18th October 1941, Flight Lieutenant Charles Green received his promotion to squadron leader. His first success as squadron leader came nine days later, while he was flying convoy patrol with another Rhodesian pilot, Sergeant Eric Sydney Dicks-Sherwood. Green spotted a German y Dornier 17 bomber, about 1,000 yards (900 m) ahead and only about 500 feet above sea level. Green attacked and his first burst caused an explosion in the enemy's starboard engine. The German dived to escape but Squadron Leader Green fired a second burst, setting fire to the fuselage. The bomber then cartwheeled into the water. No survivors were seen and the aircraft was claimed as destroyed.

With success came the inevitable losses; one of these was Sergeant Robert Gordon Goodenough Gain who had been with the squadron since August. He was killed when he crashed in a snowstorm near Grantham on 29th October.

On 3rd December, No 266 (Rhodesia) Squadron was awarded its badge by Mr O'Keeffe, the High Commissioner. This was a bateleur eagle (volant) with crossed assegais and the motto was the siNdebele word Hlabezulu meaning Stabber of the Skies. The *Rhodesia Herald* was claiming that all the ground personnel were Rhodesian but this was not entirely correct. By the end of 1941, 15 of the 34 pilots were Rhodesian and out of the other ranks, 128 out of 490 were Rhodesian.

CHAPTER 10

The desert war

While No 237 (Rhodesia) Squadron was helping win the war in East Africa, the fighting elsewhere was not going well. Initially General Sir Archibald Wavell had won lightning victories in the Western Desert, cutting off Marshal Graziani's army at Sidi Barrani in December 1940 and capturing 20,000 Italian soldiers. Successes continued through January 1941 with the capture of Bardia and Tobruk and a further 25,000 prisoners. But then on 12th February, General Erwin Rommel arrived in Tripoli, followed by units of the German army and air force.

This was to signal the end of easy conquests in North Africa. The Germans also came to Italy's aid in the Balkans—invading Greece and Yugoslavia on 6th April. Two days later Rommel recaptured Bardia and began advancing on Tobruk. By the end of April, as the campaign in East Africa was approaching its end, the Greek army had surrendered, Belgrade was in German hands and Rommel had captured Halfaya Pass and encircled Tobruk. Obviously, this was going to be no short and easy war. Then towards the end of May, the German attack on Crete began.

In the summer of 1941 the North African air front was, at best, of secondary importance, Allied air forces in the area were stretched to the limit. No 237 (Rhodesia) Squadron was still flying the obsolete Gladiator whilst ranged against them were the German bombers, the Junkers Ju 88, the Heinkel He 111 and the Junkers Ju 87. As far as fighter aircraft were concerned, the Germans were using Messerschmitt Me 110s and Me 109s while the Italians mainly employed the Savoia SM 79 bombers and the Fiat CR 42 fighters.

However, the Allies had one major advantage. Royal Air Force personnel had more experience in the maintaining of aircraft in desert conditions than their German counterparts, in adjusting engines to tropical conditions and keeping them free from sand particles. The air bases in North Africa were vast stretches of dust and stones in summer and cheerless boggy marshes in winter. Desert airfield amenities were primitive compared with the well-equipped sites in Britain. Living quarters were usually small shanties knocked together from empty petrol cans and packing cases and graced with bits of tent-cloth to act as sunshades. Beer was warm and rare. The nights could be bitterly cold while the day's sun burnt the skin black. When the rain fell, it came down in torrents leaving personnel struggling to release aircraft from the heavy mud.

The men of the desert air force lived in combat conditions of real hardship. Water was short and often severely rationed and the corned beef was fly-infested. The extremes of temperature, the lack of a varied diet and the prevalence of amoebic dysentery all told on the health of both air and ground crews. Under these conditions it was a miracle, owing entirely to the skill and determination of the ground crews, that operational flying could be sustained.

Late in May 1941 the Rhodesian squadron moved to Wadi Halfa, where the tents were

WESTERN DESERT

pitched at Khor Musa on the west bank of the Nile, six miles south of the Wadi. One Rhodesian wrote:

> *The sand temperature goes up to 140 degrees F and the shade temperature is often 116 degrees F as it was at midday today. The pullovers, balaclava helmets and scarves that have been coming in the comfort parcels are not a lot of use here. This afternoon I watched a sergeant unravel a complete pullover; he wanted some wool for darning his socks!*

During June, the squadron provided defensive patrolling of the Kufra area that lies 600 miles (960km) to the west of the Nile. The flights undertook this duty in turn, finding it a pleasant change. The journey by motor transport was long and tiring, taking about ten days but, apart from this disadvantage, Kufra was like heaven after the dismal stretches of barren wilderness.

It seems that because of these pressures, the feeling between Squadron Leader Maxwell and some of the squadron personnel came to a head. The problem was resolved when Maxwell was promoted and posted. He was succeeded by Squadron Leader Graham Smith. Graham held the command for about a month, before he was boarded back to Rhodesia, owing to a knee injury sustained during a rugby match. His place was taken by Eric Smith who had returned to the squadron in October following a posting to the RATG.

No 237 receive their Hurricanes

Meanwhile, No 237 Squadron had been relieved at Khor Musa by a RAF squadron and on 21st August 1941, the main party embarked on a river steamer. Their route took them from Wadi Halfa to El Shellal by Nile steamer and then from El Shellal by rail to Kassfareit where they arrived on 24th August. The rear parties took about another ten days to complete the journey, arriving on 3rd September. On 17th September, an advance party was dispatched to 'Y' landing ground near Abu Sueir, which had been selected as the squadron's next home. It was here, on 26th September, that the squadron received its new aircraft, six Hurricane Mark Is and the next few weeks were spent on intensive training. As the airgunners were no longer needed, they returned to Rhodesia to undergo training as pilots.

Eric Smith rejoined the squadron as commanding officer on 10th October and on 24th October Alec Hutchinson returned after his bad accident in East Africa. By the last days of October, the squadron had completed its training on the new aircraft and was ready to move back into battle, just in time for the excitement of a big campaign.

The squadron helps lift the Siege of Tobruk

The Allied garrison at Tobruk had been holding out against the Germans for five months. Now an all-out attempt was to be made to break through the German lines and lift the siege. Code-named Operation Crusader, the attack was planned for the middle of November 1941. 'A' flight was stationed at landing ground 122, 40 miles (64km) south of Sidi Barrani and close to the wire, which marked the outer perimeter of the British-held area. At 06h00 hours on 18th November, 450 tanks of the 7th Armoured Division with support groups from the 8th Army, moved out to Gabr Saleh; by midday they had reached their first objective, 30 miles (48km) west of Sidi Omar. By the following day, the 7th Armoured Brigade was only ten miles (16km) from besieged Tobruk. Hardly any Axis aircraft had been sighted during the first two days of the offensive because heavy rains over the coastal area had flooded the aerodromes. The Stukas and Messerschmitts were all bogged down.

On the afternoon of the second day, the 4th Armoured Brigade on the left flank came under heavy air and ground attack. Sixty-six tanks were put out of action and the brigade was

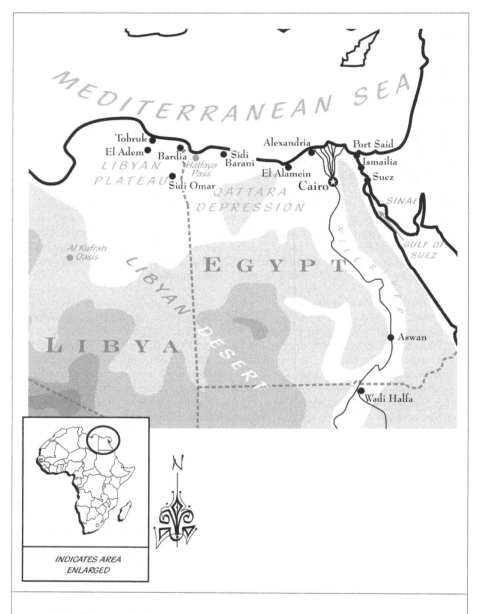

THE GERMAN COUNTER-ATTACK
23 November 1941

forced to withdraw. From this point the battle became confused. For two days, the fighting raged round Gabr Saleh and Sidi Azeiz and the British advance slowed to a halt.

Meanwhile, the Rhodesian squadron was heavily involved carrying out reconnaissance sorties. Hostile aircraft were constantly spotted and losses occurred. Eric Smith says:

> *On the whole, pilots preferred to try to bring the aircraft back rather than bale out. Partly because they didn't really trust parachutes and partly because in the desert you stood more chance if you stayed with the plane.*

Paul Sindall was one of the lucky ones. He was reported missing but arrived back at base the following day. On 22nd November 'B' flight was detached to No 451 Squadron Australian Air Force at Air Field 132. While flying a recce from this airfield, the Rhodesians were attacked by seven Macchis and Fiats. Alec Hutchinson's aircraft was hit and caught fire; there was nothing to do but bale out. It was about 09h00 and Hutchinson came sailing down alongside some ambulances. Not knowing whether he was friend or foe, the ambulance men tumbled out, guns at the ready. Hutchinson called out, You'd better pull that bit of four by two out of the muzzle or you'll split the barrel!

The ambulances were on their way to join the New Zealanders so Hutch hitched a ride and a tot of medicinal brandy from the doctor. Lunch was provided by the New Zealanders who arranged a lift back by truck. Even the ride back had its excitement because they were caught up in an Indian attack on Sidi Omar. As Alec Hutchinson tells it, the story had a happy ending, I got back in time to stop my water ration from being scoffed. And as soon as he reached base he went into the parachute packers, waving a pound note in their startled faces and saying, Here, take it! It opened!

The Germans counter-attack

By 23rd November 1941, although the situation was still confused, the balance appeared to be shifting in favour of the Germans and the air force was called in to attempt to deal with 40 German tanks that were doing damage to allied forces.

> *Rommel's tanks were waiting to attack Tobruk. 237 were sent to look for them. Rommel in his sweep round through the desert had collected the supply trucks of a South African Division and was making use of them, so when we found the column there were South African trucks all mixed up with the tanks. German light flak was very accurate and it was difficult to identify which vehicles were which. We had to come in very low and hold our fire until we got close.*
> (Eric Smith)

The Germans now made a rapid advance, so rapid in fact that Eric Spence found he was under fire from a convoy where no enemy convoy should be. Forced to land, he rushed into an Indian casualty clearing station nearby and gave warning but there was no time to move the wounded. Eric Spence was accosted by the driver of an armoured car: For you the war is finished! Taken prisoner, Spence was later transported across the Mediterranean to Italy aboard a submarine. By this time, the Germans had swept south and reached the wire. One Rhodesian anti-tank gunner says: We had assumed that the Germans had got behind us and would be holding the gaps in the wire but everything was normal at Maddalena so we went there and found 237 Squadron. We had a great welcome and copious amounts of tea to drink. This was at squadron headquarters at Landing Ground 128. Life at 'A' flight Landing Ground 122 was not nearly as peaceful. The Germans had reached the wire a few miles south of Sidi Omar at 17h00 on 24th November. Confusion was rife!

The Allied army was in retreat but we had been given no orders to pull back. German tanks were spotted only six miles [9km] from our landing ground. However, we knew they didn't like moving at night. A group captain flew up in a Gladiator and ordered us to move back to El Adem, but this would have meant a night landing. I asked if there were lights. He said he would organize it and disappeared. I decided not to take the squadron off. We sat in our cockpits all night, while various members of the ground crew organized what defence they could, mainly in the shape of Molotov Cocktails. During the night, a British tank arrived. It had been disabled but the crew had got it going again. We stopped it and got it to hole down for the night between the Germans and us. Four Bofors guns also arrived later. Next morning we took off in convoy with the tank and the guns bringing up the rear. (Eric Smith)

After his early successes, Rommel in his turn began to slow down. He reached Halfaya Pass on 25th November and Bardia on 26th November but then he was thrown back and by 27th November the Germans had abandoned their Siege of Tobruk and were retreating west. Soon the German army was in full flight. This retreat was to take them right back to the Libyan border. The problem with the war in the desert was that neither army could hold a line where the southern end could not be protected. Tanks moving across the sand could always sweep round, threatening to encircle any defenders. However, for the moment, the danger for the Allies was over and there was a breathing space.

By the end of November, 'A' and 'B' flights were back at headquarters at Landing Ground 128. During a recce on 1st December, Hutchinson spotted the wreckage of Flight Lieutenant Eric Spence's aircraft and it was assumed, correctly, that Spence must be a prisoner of war. On the 2nd, Flying Officer Cyril Sindall went missing only to reappear safely on the following day. The next casualty was Flight Lieutenant D.A. MacIntyre who was hit by ack-ack fire

INDICATES AREA
ENLARGED

THE GERMAN RETREAT
27 November 1941

and forced down but he was seen to land safely and join Allied troops. Three days later, he returned to the squadron reporting that his aircraft had not been too badly damaged.

On 7th December while on a recce, Flying Officer Brian White was shot down in flames over Sidi Omar and killed. On the same day, a new draft of 30 Rhodesians joined the squadron. They received a special and not very friendly welcome the day after.

Squadron landing ground was bombed and machine-gunned at 13h00 by six Me 109s and six Me 110s. Bombs were dropped on and around the aerodrome. During this attack, one bomber dropped two bombs on HQ flight cookhouse, killing three airmen and injuring eleven others. In the evening, the three airmen were buried one mile west of the camp. (Ops Record 8th Dec 1941)

Otto Gericke who was serving with the ground crew remembers:

We were having a meal, lunch, when the Jerries came over and strafed. Ralph Parry had a tin mug over his head. Later he said, 'Hey, there's a bullet hole in my mug!'

R.M. Thomson who was a medical orderly with the squadron says:

Leading Aircraftman Andrew Gordon Ednie and Aircraftman Heyworth (RAF) were dead when I arrived on the scene and Leading Aircraftman Andrew Ralph Meldrum died ten minutes later. A splinter caught him in the throat. Seven lads were taken to hospital—Corporal Smith, who died at 21h00, Sandy Marshall, Lilford Frederick Houlton, Ernest Gerart Lenthall, who died three days later, Timber Wood, Rogers and James. Laurence Brook Morton, Gert Oliver Smit, Maude (RAF) and Chelwynd Piggott were slightly wounded and were attended to by the medical officer of a nearby squadron, the 237 Squadron MO having been posted, despite the CO's strenuous complaints.

Eric Smith comments on this incident:

At our landing ground there was an MO with the Australian No 3 Squadron. He was there in a matter of about 15 minutes and worked at incredible speed.

On 10th December, 'B' flight left Landing Ground 128 for Sidi-bu-Amud where they were joined by HQ flight on 13th December. HQ flight then continued to Gambut leaving 'B' flight at Sidi-bu-Amud. During the move the convoy was bombed by enemy aircraft but no casualties were sustained. It was an unlucky day, however, for Flying Officer Miles Johnson who was shot down over Tmimi while on a tactical recce. He became a prisoner of war but was released when Allied troops captured the town.

On 12th December 1941, headquarters and 'B' flights left for Tmimi where they received a visit from Miles Johnson who was proceeding to Base Hospital having just been released by the Allied advance.

On Christmas day came notice of yet another move—to the Benghazi area.

Operations Record 27th December:

Squadron HQ and 'B' flight packing up for move. Main party convoy leaving on 28th. Bypass around Derna very wet and muddy through the hills. Both convoys (fast and slow) camped for night at El Faidia. Weather very wet, roads terribly muddy. The aircraft of the whole squadron left during the day as instructed by CO and arrived safely at new aerodrome.

To add to the problems of rain and mud, the slow convoy was also attacked by enemy aircraft and the orderly room trailer was damaged although fortunately there were no casualties.

> *I spent Christmas on the road to Berta, then on to Benina near Benghazi, but settled in before the New Year. On 27th December, we had a little bit of beer, some liqueurs and Chianti from the Italians. Then the Indian engineers got a brewery going and everyone got so drunk we stood and watched an air raid. There had been so much rain that the landing grounds were quagmires and the Hurricanes sank up to their axles; so, looking for some amusement, we went into Benghazi and found a post office that had been wrecked. There were stamps all over the place. I collected a few and borrowed some brown paper from the Fascist HQ to wrap them up. I dumped them into a parachute bag and the liaison officer kindly provided transport to Cairo. I flogged them later to a stamp dealer for a handsome profit!* (Hutchinson)

Speaking about this period, a report in the *Rhodesia Herald* read:

> *The Rhodesian air squadron, engaged in army cooperation work, is doing what an army intelligence officer described as a 'pretty useful job'. With the exception of three pilots, one Scot and two South Africans, all the personnel of this squadron are Rhodesians. Many are from Salisbury and they fly Hurricanes on vitally important missions working in pairs. These fighter pilots are the eyes of the army. They are especially trained to recognize troop movements, to identify our own and enemy columns and to notice features of the surrounding country. Unlike ordinary fighters on patrol, these specialists are doing something more than look for trouble and it is often more important to bring back information than to engage in combat.*

The Rhodesian Service Club
Incidentally, earlier in December 1941 it had been announced in the *Rhodesia Herald* that steps were being taken to establish a Rhodesian Service Club in Cairo. In fact there already was a Rhodesian Club in Cairo—unofficial but effective. It was the cocktail bar of the Hotel Ex Morandi and at this bar, imperial army rigidity about officers and men never drinking together was forgotten. Not only did the assembled exiles drink together, they exchanged Christian names as they had before the war. The Ex Morandi was a good hotel patronized by many besides the Rhodesians but the cocktail bar was almost entirely a Rhodesian preserve. It was the one place in Cairo apart from the office of Colonel J.B. Brady, the liaison officer, where Rhodesians could be sure of meeting one another. The Rhodesians coming together after months apart in various Imperial regiments, often under extremely uncongenial conditions, were quick to let their hair down and the occasional British officers who dropped in found themselves obliged either to leave or drop their narrow rules of etiquette and join in.

Attack and counter-attack
In January, airfields and landing grounds near the coast had been transformed into seas of slithering mud and so, on 3rd January, came orders to move back from Benghazi to El Adem. The advance party and one lorry of 'A' flight left the following day with the rest of the squadron leaving on 5th January. According to the Operations Record, the Crossley lorries gave trouble on the road and the slow convoy was attacked by enemy aircraft while climbing over Tocra Pass but with no losses. While they were still on the road, fresh orders came for the squadron to return to Tmimi instead of El Adem.

The Rhodesian squadron was still on its way back when the slow convoy was again attacked by enemy aircraft on 6th January but suffered no damage or casualties and arrived safely at Tmimi on 7th January. During the next two weeks there was very little operational flying owing to the constant moves, but Hutchinson did manage to locate the grave of Flying Officer White. His aircraft, which had been badly damaged, exploded on landing. The burial service had been conducted by Father Costello of the 2nd South African Division.

Meanwhile the German retreat continued until 6th January 1942, by which time Rommel's forces had been pushed back to the Gulf of Sirte. It seemed that the battle for Libya had been won by the Allies. But then, at 08h30 on 21st January, the Germans launched a surprise attack. The 8th Army was sent reeling. By 22nd January the Germans had reached Agedabia; by 19th January Benghazi had fallen. Marawa was taken on 1st February and by 6th February, the German army had reached Tmimi only about 50 miles (80km) from Tobruk. Here Rommel paused to regroup.

Rommel was preparing for another attack, which would take him skimming back across the desert, across the Egyptian frontier and to the gates of Alexandria, but the Rhodesian squadron was not to be involved in this campaign. On 19th January the squadron moved to El Firdar in the Canal Zone, a distance of 800 miles from the battlefront. Here Pilot Officer Wilfred Walsh was killed on 2nd February when his Hurricane crashed in a severe sandstorm.

On 6th February came orders for a move to Ismalia Air Station, where all ranks enjoyed a little local leave before being warned to prepare for yet another journey, this time to Iraq. Indeed the men of No 237 (Rhodesia) Squadron must have wondered when, if ever, they were to settle in one place for more than a few weeks.

CHAPTER 11
New aircraft

The year 1941 had ended on a black note for the Allies, the only good news having come from North Africa where the Germans were in retreat. Germany had invaded Russia in June 1941 winning lightning victories, which took her army to the outskirts of Moscow. Russian casualties were given as 350,000 dead, 378,000 missing and 1,020,000 wounded. By the end of November, the German Panzers were only 19 miles (30km) from the centre of Moscow but then came the winter and the German offensive froze. On 7th December, the Japanese attacked the American naval base at Pearl Harbour. This was followed by the American declaration of war on Germany and Italy as well as Japan. By mid-December the Japanese were advancing down Malaya and on Christmas Day Hong Kong fell.

Operational training in Britain
In Europe, the RAF continued to attack German cities with whatever aircraft were available and a steady stream of trained air and ground crew was arriving in Britain from RATG. On 9th January, an article in the *Rhodesia Herald* carried a report about life for the Rhodesian trainees once they reached the United Kingdom.

> *After passing through various training schools in Rhodesia, the flyer emerges as a fully-fledged pilot, observer or wireless-operator/gunner and with a group of other lads in air force blue he embarks for England. But although he has been through the full course in Rhodesia and wears his crested wings, flying O or AG badge, as the case may be, he is not ready to go into action immediately upon arrival in Britain. There is still more training awaiting him at an operational training unit ... to the pilot trained in Rhodesia finding his home aerodrome is no problem...in England he has to learn to look for camouflaged aerodromes and to make landings in the blackout.*

Then there was the climate! Learning to cope with the European weather was not easy for the Rhodesians, and there was the chance that a trainee pilot might unexpectedly find himself in combat. The newcomer from Rhodesia is destined for one of the four main RAF commands—Bomber, Fighter, Coastal Command or Army Cooperation and each of these has its operational training units, (OTUs) as they are called. As a RAF station commander defined it to me, 'The function of the OTU is to turn a qualified pilot into an operational pilot under the very nose of the enemy'. A young pilot might run into the enemy at any moment—so trainees are allowed to fly only within a certain radius from the aerodrome. (*Rhodesia Herald*)

The Lancaster arrives
One of the squadrons to which Rhodesian aircrew were being posted was No 44 (Rhodesia) Squadron. The group commander, Air Vice-Marshal, Sir J.C. Slessor CB DSO MC visited

the squadron on 7th January 1942 and took a flip in one of the new Lancasters (L7536). He found the Rhodesians very pleased with their acquisition. However, with new aircraft and bad weather conditions, accidents were inevitable and it was Squadron Leader Nettleton who had the first mishap. The cold weather had brought snow and ice. These conditions had severely curtailed flying, but sweeping the runway clear of snow allowed limited training. On 6th February, Nettleton had a tail wheel break after hitting a mound of swept snow that had frozen hard.

On the following day, Sergeant Dennis Franckling Nicholson suffered a more serious mishap when he crashed while landing at Skellingthorpe. According to the Operational Record, the pilot misread the wind indicator and landed downwind. His aircraft struck a pile of concrete posts and swung round. The undercarriage collapsed and the aircraft slid backwards into the mud. This necessitated major repair work but, fortunately, no one was injured.

So far the Lancasters had not been in action, although they had been placed on stand-by on 25th January for an attack on the German battleship *Tirpitz* at Trondheim. However, this operation had been cancelled owing to bad weather.

On 3rd February, the squadron was again warned for stand-by. Loaded with mines that were to be laid at the mouth of a Norwegian Fjord at Trondheim, they waited all day, only to be stood down once again because of bad weather. This experience was repeated on 24th and 25th February. It was 3rd March 1942, before the Lancasters actually set off on their first mission, and Air Vice-Marshal Slessor, knowing that it was definitely on this time, visited the squadron. He watched Nettleton take off in L7546 at 18h15 followed by L7547, L7568 and L7549 at three-minute intervals. Their gardening activities, code-named Yams and Rosemary, were carried out in the Heligoland Bight and very little opposition from flak was encountered, according to the Ops Record.

So No 44 (Rhodesia) Squadron had achieved the honour of being the first squadron to go operational with the Lancaster.

In rather the same way that pilots new to operations were given 'freshman' operations—local runs to say, Paris, to drop leaflets—so squadrons' introduction to operations in new types normally consisted of initial mining runs but this, of course, like leave, was subject to the exigencies of the service. An exigency came up on March 8th—the 'Tirpitz' again. After two days of standing by, eight Lancasters were ordered to Lossiemouth. This first gaggle of Lancasters—they did not aspire to a formation at this early stage—did not have a very friendly reception. An Allied convoy escort dotted the sky around them with ominous puffs of smoke. There was a view held by the RAF crews—entirely without foundations of course—that to the navy if an aircraft had a single tail fin it was a Heinkel or Junkers and you fired; if it had twin tail fins, then it was a Dornier and you fired—and if it had three or more fins it was an unidentified enemy aircraft and you fired. However, the RAF could not afford to be smug about this, for a Spitfire that very day had fired at one of the Lancasters, fortunately without causing serious damage. (Lancaster Ops Record)

Derek Venables talking about this trip to Lossiemouth says that the local engineering officer did not understand the undercarriage of the Lancaster and put all the aircraft unserviceable because their wheels leaned on the uneven ground. On a lighter note he adds: For some of us who went up there, this was our first taste of the best fish and chips when we were off duty and went into Lossiemouth for a break.

With eight aircraft away at Lossiemouth, the balance of the squadron at Waddington was asked to join in a raid on Essen on 10th March. This explains why only two Lancasters participated in this raid that marked the first bombing operation by Lancasters. The Operations Record reads:

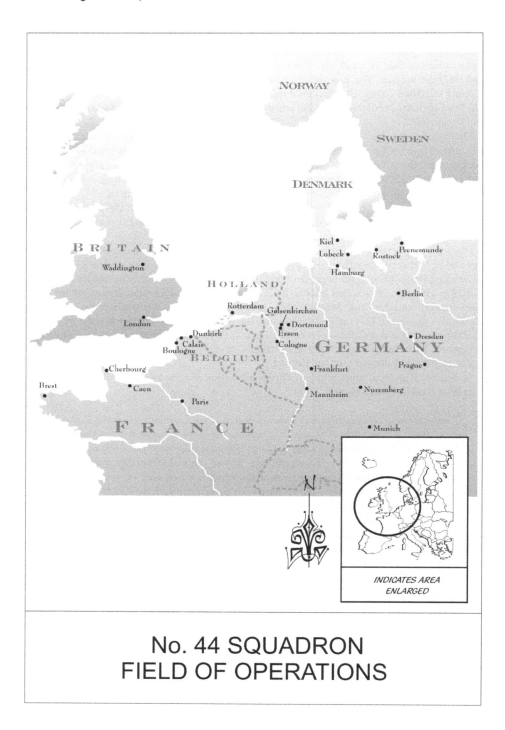

No. 44 SQUADRON
FIELD OF OPERATIONS

L7526 Flying Officer Bell and L7566 Flying Officer Wilkins were detached to carry out bombing operations over Essen, with 52 other aircraft. Lancaster aircraft loaded with a maximum load of incendiaries. 44 Squadron carried 14 small bomb containers, each container holding 90 x 4 lb (1.8kg) incendiaries. Total 1,260 = 5,040 lb [2,288kg].

The order of attack was for the incendiary-carrying-aircraft to form the first wave, starting fires that could be used as aiming points for the bombers that followed. Both the Rhodesian squadron aircraft reached the target area and dropped their incendiaries. The weather was unfavourable, cloud 8/10—10/10 which made absolute identification of the target difficult. A number of small fires and several large ones were observed. Both the squadron's aircraft returned safely but L7536 was hit by shrapnel when flying at 18,000 feet—the first Lancaster to be blooded.

Air attacks carried out during the first years of the war had been somewhat hit or miss. The organization of these raids was now becoming more scientific. Two days before the Essen Raid the Gee Campaign had begun. Gee, a radar aid, was carried by aircraft flying ahead of the main bombing force; they were known as pathfinders. These bombers dropped flares that marked the target area for the first wave of attack aircraft carrying the incendiaries The main force then bombed the area set alight by the incendiaries.

The second Lancaster bombing operation took place on 13th March 1942, when a single aircraft joined 61 Wellingtons, 13 Hampdens, ten Stirlings, ten Manchesters and nine Halifaxes in a raid on Cologne. This lone Lancaster was L7548 flown by Sergeant Rhodes (RAF—later shot down on the Augsburg Raid). Sergeant Rhodes suffered a mishap on return. He signalled for the runway lights to be switched on and when there was no response, he landed without lights overshooting the runway and causing slight damage to his aircraft.

So far, the squadron had been fortunate but casualties had to come.

Operations Record 24th March 1942:

Two Lancasters detailed for mine-laying operations near Lorient (with 23 Hampdens). The Lancasters carried six mines each and took off at approximately 19h50. Prior to departure, they were warned that on the return journey they would be diverted to St Eval. Warrant Officer Osborn, (R5484K) carried out the task successfully. Flight Sergeant Warren-Smith (R5493N) failed to return. A No 420 (RCAF) Squadron pilot reported that he had seen a four-engined bomber heavily engaged with anti-aircraft fire over Lorient and the Royal Observer Corps reported flares out to sea. A search was made without result and Flight Sergeant Warren-Smith (first pilot), Sergeant Richard Alfred Marston (second pilot) (Rhodesian), Sergeant Clive Edward Wigram Clifford (first navigator), Sergeant Alastair Fraser Murdoch (second navigator) (Rhodesian), Sergeant Edward Burgess Cluff (first wireless operator), Sergeant John Boyd (second wireless operator), Sergeant William Harold Flower (mid upper gunner) and Flight Sergeant John McNally Davidson (rear airgunner) were reported missing.

The crew composition of first and second pilots reflects the fact that crews were still training on Lancasters but a first and second pilot was normal at this time. However in the spring of 1942, the second pilot was considered superfluous but a new and important crewmember was introduced: the flight engineer. Both the first and second pilots on that unlucky aircraft were Rhodesians, as was the second navigator.

Only one day previously, a story had been printed in the *Rhodesia Herald* telling of Dick Marston's exploits.

Dick came back from an op one night and was lucky…his kite started a spin from 16,500 feet and pulled out at 5,000 feet right over the target area. The kite was declared a complete write-off the next day—old Dick just laughed. The next night he was over Cologne giving them a few thousand pounds of high explosive. (Rhodesia Herald)

Two days later, all the Lancasters were grounded because of a crash near Boston in Lincolnshire. Examination of the upper wing surfaces showed buckling and forcing of the flush rivets, resulting in a modification being carried out immediately on the wing tips. King George VI and Queen Elizabeth visited the works of A.V. Roe where the Lancasters were manufactured and the king named Lancaster R5489 George; this aircraft was later flown by No 44 (Rhodesia) Squadron.

It is to be expected that with the advent of new aircraft there will be teething troubles and towards the end of March all leave was cancelled for ground crews while 54 engines, which had been diagnosed as having supercharger problems, were replaced.

During this month, March, a new pilot was posted to the squadron. His name was H.H. (Happy) Taylor. He had attested in November 1940 and trained at Belvedere and Guinea Fowl where he completed his training in April 1941. His first posting was to Upper Heyford in Oxfordshire where he flew Hampdens. Happy says that there were more crashes during the training with Hampdens than there were in combat. The aircraft had some vicious faults including a stable yaw that was not easy to rectify. In fact, Happy's first task at Upper Heyford was to act as pallbearer to a pilot on the previous course. Taylor completed his training in September 1941 and joined No 144 Squadron at North Luffenham where he flew ten operations. He was posted to the Rhodesian squadron in March and took part in a few coastal sorties before his first big raid, which was on Cologne on 30th May 1942.

March closed with an attack on Lubeck. The squadron seemed to be swinging into a routine, but what the men of the squadron did not know was that one of the most famous operations of the war was about to come their way; one of those do or die attacks that make history.

Meanwhile the daily training and familiarization flights continued and on 12th April, a pamphlet raid over Paris was detailed. This was carried out by Pilot Officer Gerald MacLagan in aircraft R5510* and it is interesting to note that his crew was entirely Rhodesian. As this was the first and only all-Rhodesian crew to fly an operation, their names and crew positions are listed as follows:

Hubert John Sant Sturgess	Flt Eng 2nd Pilot
William Frederick Belton	Nav
William McDonald Crane	Obs bomb-aimer
Robert Duncan Olver	WOP AG
Bertram Llewellyn Nesbitt	WOP AG
Gilbert Walter Hough	Mid upper gunner
Thomas Douglas Moore	Rear gunner (the only survivor, was taken POW, is still alive and living in Harare).

The Augsburg Raid

The day before the Paris flight, 11th April, No 44 Squadron began, without knowing the reason, to prepare for an epic raid. They were ordered to make long-distance flights in formation in order to obtain endurance data on the Lancasters. Two days later ground crew were instructed to prepare eight machines to move to an advance base. Similar instructions

---

* Less than a month later, this aircraft went down in a low-level attack on the Heinkel Aircraft Factory at Warnemunde.

were given to No 97 Squadron. On 15th April, the Lancasters, flying in groups of three in Vee formation at extremely low level made their way south to Selsey Bill. There they turned and headed north to Lanark, across country to Falkirk and on to a point just outside the town of Inverness where they feigned an attack. They then returned to base following the route they had taken on the way north. A spate of complaints from all over the country was received by the Air Ministry castigating the pilots for the dangerous prank of flying large four-engined aircraft at treetop height over the countryside. A tactful letter was sent to all police stations but the aircrews of both squadrons already realized that they were in training for a special operation and bets were placed on the possible target.

It is doubtful if any of the squadrons' members guessed correctly. The target was in fact Augsburg in southern Germany, the other side of the Danube, involving a flight of some 1,500 miles (2,400km) over enemy occupied territory. The specific factory to be destroyed was the Maschinenfabrik Augsburg Nürnberg AG, where diesel engines for submarines were being manufactured. These submarines were threatening Britain's lifeline across the Atlantic. Somehow, the war at sea had to be won. It was felt that if the diesel engine works could be destroyed, it was worth the losses that would be involved.

On the morning of 17th April, operation orders were circulated. Briefing of No 44 (Rhodesia) Squadron was at 11h00 and the crews attending were instructed to take their tin hats, more correctly known as steel helmets, with them on the raid. Meanwhile the armourers received their instructions to load each aircraft with four 1,000-lb (450kg) general-purpose bombs, fused to give an eleven-second delay. Ground crews were ordered to top up the tanks to a maximum—2,154 gallons (9,693 l). These figures were to be quoted significantly by crews for the next three years—I hear they're filling up 2,154 portended a long run. For take-off the duty aerodrome control pilot, Sergeant Knight, had to be aware of the timing of the raid and in the cookhouse for Duty Ration Detail, Aircraftman Shaw, preparing sandwiches and flasks, had to know how many crew would be involved and roughly how long the operation would last. It would be dark when the crews returned and so the officer in charge of night-flying, the duty flare path assistants and floodlight operator, together with the duty electrician, Aircraftman Saunders, had to be aware of possible timings and numbers of aircraft involved in case of snags. An operation of this importance involved the whole squadron.

The plan was for six aircraft from each of the two squadrons, Nos 44 and 97, in formations of three to cover the distance at low level. In this way it was hoped to escape the German radar and reach the target safely. As the Lancasters prepared for take-off just before 15h00 on 17th August, 30 Bostons were carrying out diversionary raids on French targets while hundreds of Allied fighters swept the Pas de Calais, Cherbourg and Rouen areas. The plan was to involve the German aircraft in prolonged combat so that the passage of the Lancasters would coincide with the time at which the German aircraft would be refuelling and rearming. Unfortunately, all this activity also had the effect of putting the Luftwaffe on the alert.

Eight Lancasters from each squadron warmed up and as all the aircraft were serviceable, the crews detailed as second reserve cut their engines and watched the others take off. Over Selsey Bill, the first reserves noting that all was well, swung round and returned, leaving 12 Lancasters flying away low over the water.

Squadron Leader John Nettleton took his leading formation down to 50 feet (15m) over the waves as the French coast came into view, but this ruse failed because just after crossing the coast, No 44 Squadron's Lancasters were heavily engaged by fighters.

The Lancasters tightened formation, flying wingtip to wingtip in an effort to provide added protection. They skimmed low over villages, rising and falling to the contours of the countryside. So the Messerschmitts were forced to attack from above, their cannon shells exploding on the ground and causing consternation among the French villagers. Despite the Lancasters' efforts at evasion, the German attack took effect. L7536, flown by Sergeant Rhodes was first to go. Hit at that roof top height and travelling at 200 mph (322 km/h), there was no possible chance of baling out. Now the first formation was reduced to Nettleton's aircraft and one other.

One by one the Messerschmitts took out the second formation; R506, L7548 and L7565 flown by Flight Lieutenant R.R. Sandford, Warrant Officer H.V. Crum DFM and Warrant Officer J.F. Beckett DFM. All crashed and burst into flames.

John Nettleton and Flying Officer A.J. Garwell DFM carried on. With four aircraft down before they had even skirted Paris, there appeared to be little hope of reaching their objective but the German fighter controller was now perplexed. The bombers were getting beyond the range of the coastal fighters and there was no indication of where the Lancasters were going to strike. Would it be the Ruhr or would they switch to northern Italy? There was no radar cover over central France. Nettleton led the way across the French countryside; hedge-hopping all the way, skirted the Swiss border and flew low in the afternoon sunshine across southern Germany until he sighted the River Lech, which he followed to his target.

The warning sirens were now sounding in this remote corner of Germany and the Augsburg factory had been alerted. Coming over the brow of a hill onto the target, the two Lancasters were met with heavy opposition from the quick-firing guns. The bomb-aimers could not miss. At chimney height, with a target that covered an area of more than one square mile (over two square kilometres) Garwell went in and blasted the target but his aircraft was hit and set on fire. He landed in a field two miles west of the town, coming down so hard that the fuselage of R5510 broke at the mid-turret.

The six aircraft from No 97 Squadron had taken a slightly different route and had managed to avoid the fighters over France. A hail of fire greeted them as they appeared in view two miles (3km) from the factory. They swept in just as Nettleton had finished his bombing run. In good visibility they attacked from 400 feet (120m) through heavy opposition. Two aircraft were hit over the target.

As the survivors turned westward, the light began to fade and over France they had the cover of darkness. Four aircraft returned from No 97 Squadron's six Lancasters but of No 44 (Rhodesia) Squadron's group, only Squadron Leader Nettleton in R5508 came back. He had taken off at 15h00 on 17th August. He landed back at Squire's Gate on 18th August just before 01h00, ten hours later.

The British Prime Minister, Winston Churchill, sent a message to the commander in chief of Bomber Command:

We must plainly regard the attack of the Lancasters on the U-boat engine factory at Augsburg as an outstanding achievement of the Royal Air Force. Undeterred by heavy losses at the outset, the bombers pierced in broad daylight into the heart of Germany and struck a vital point with deadly precision. Pray convey the thanks of His Majesty's government to the officers and men who accomplished this memorable feat of arms in which no life was lost in vain.

After this operation, Squadron Leader John Nettleton was awarded the Victoria Cross. The Rhodesians decorated were Pilot Officer Patrick Arthur Dorehill—DFC. Sergeant Laurence Laver Dando, who flew in Flight Lieutenant Sandford's aircraft and was captured by the Germans when the plane was forced down two miles (3km) from the target, was awarded the DFM as was Sergeant Donald Norman Huntley.

The Rhodesians killed in this operation were: Pilot Officer Haworth Anthony Peall;* Sergeant Pilot Brian Douglas Moss and Sergeant Wireless Operator/Airgunner Peter Johannes Venter. Sergeant Pilot Albert Denis Charles Dedman was reported missing at the time but was in fact taken prisoner. Losses were exceptionally high and in Purnell's History of World War Two the comment is made:

> *Daylight precision raid on MAN Diesel engine factory—of 12 Lancasters involved seven destroyed and five damaged. Main assembly shop and other buildings damaged but production hardly affected. Raid showed that it was impractical for heavy bombers to make precision attacks in daylight and reinforced RAF faith in night offensive.*

The British public now heard about the Lancaster for the first time and the Germans, examining the smouldering remains of seven aircraft, knew that the British had a new four-engine bomber in service. Much more was to be heard about the Lancaster.

While No 44 (Rhodesia) Squadron was making news with the Lancasters, No 266 (Rhodesia) Squadron was also breaking in a new aircraft: the Hawker Typhoon.

Teething problems with the Typhoon

In its teething stages the Typhoon was to cause many more headaches than the Lancaster. The first Typhoons had been delivered to No 56 and No 601 Squadrons at Duxford. The engines were initially cleared for only 25 hours flying time between major overhauls but few reached that total. Intake fires on the ground were frequent and so were engine failures in the climb. Of the initial 142 Typhoons delivered to the RAF, 135 suffered serious accidents.

The Rhodesian squadron received its first Typhoons on 6th January. John Deall, later to command No 266 Squadron, who flew the new aircraft in February said:

> *At first, it was a most unreliable aircraft. The average life of an engine was eight hours, so most pilots suffered a forced landing at some time. It was not really a suitable fighter. It was too heavy but it was 50 miles an hour (80 km/h) faster than the Spitfire Mk V. The Typhoon also had the edge on the Focke-Wulf 190 at lower altitudes but not high up.*

David Garrick who was serving with the squadron wrote:

> *Johnny Deall was a great lad. I can confirm his remarks about the Typhoon teething troubles at Duxford. The Napier Sabre Engine was a terrific job but caused many headaches...even the civilian engineers attached to Napiers had their headaches too.*

While the Typhoon was being broken in, sorties were still being carried out in the Spitfires and on 11th January came the first loss of the new year.

Operations Record 11th January:

> *Three aircraft on convoy patrol took off from Docking having heard that enemy aircraft might be expected. When near convoy's position, told of enemy aircraft approaching—then saw a Ju 88 and chased it in line. Closing to 200 yards (180m) Pilot Officer Small opened fire as enemy aircraft crossed 100 yards (90m) in front of him and continued firing following enemy aircraft into cloud. On emerging from cloud, Pilot Officer John Small and Sergeant Norham Lucas rejoined and tried to call Flight Lieutenant Allen Allen-White on R/T but without success. Flight Lieutenant Allen-White is missing. Three aircraft searched for two hours, refuelled and searched for another one and a half hours and air/sea rescue has also been informed and has searched.*

By the end of January the squadron had received seven Typhoons. Towards the middle of February came an event that has already been mentioned in connection with No 44

(Rhodesia) Squadron. The Scharnhorst, Gneisenau and Prince Eugen, after ten months skulking in Brest, made their famous dash through the English Channel. The weather was extremely foggy and their escape was not noticed for several hours. Immediately all available aircraft were mustered.

No 266 Operations Record 12th February 1942:

Ten Spitfires (still being used) flew to Coltishall again. Nine taking part in operation connected with attack on Scharnhorst and Gneisenau. Covering withdrawal of our bombers 40 miles [64km] from Dutch coast. Saw the bombers but no enemy aircraft.

All in all the episode was something of a fiasco for the British. The following day, 13th February, six aircraft searched the North Sea for survivors of the previous day's battle. None were seen. According to John Deall the weather was very bad, and continued without letup into the following month. As a result, only four flights took place during the whole of March. Two Rhodesian pilots were lost in February and March. Pilot Officer Maurice Victor Denver Derwent Devereux was killed on 19th February and Pilot Officer Charles Ernest Lees died in an accident while on a training flight in a Typhoon on 8th March.

On the plus side, the squadron was notching up some successes. A Rhodesian, Flight Lieutenant Ronald H.L. (Rolo) Dawson, beat off four Dorniers, which were about to attack a convoy off the east coast. He picked out the nearest of the bombers but before he could get a shot in, the Dornier jettisoned its bomb load and made off, skimming low over the waves. Flight Lieutenant Dawson gave chase and opened fire. According to Dawson's account, In no time the Hun was thoroughly on fire all over the fuselage. Then he heeled over and dived into the sea leaving a great patch of burning wreckage and oil. Meanwhile the other three bombers had left the scene and the convoy was able to continue undamaged.

By March 1942, Typhoon MK 1Bs had been in action against Focke-Wulf FW 190s. At low level, below 10,000 feet, there was scarcely an aircraft to match their speed, while at treetop height, they proved the scourge of the tip-and-run Focke Wulfs but at 20,000 feet the Typhoon was easy prey to the German fighters. The lesson was obvious. The Typhoon had failed as an interceptor, the fault lying as much in accelerated engine development as in abbreviated aerodynamic development. However, it was the very weaknesses in the Typhoon's interceptor qualities that brought success when its operational role was changed to that of ground attack. The thick wing and high wing loading that placed the aircraft at a disadvantage at altitude, bestowed upon it the very qualities it required to survive tremendous punishment from light flak, and to provide a steady aiming platform under turbulent conditions. So it was that the Typhoon came to be armed with rocket projectiles.

The British three-inch (7,62cm) rocket projectiles, called initially UPs (unrotated projectiles) were simplicity itself. A length of three-inch (7,62cm) mild steel pipe containing the propellant charge, a 60-lb (27kg) high explosive warhead screwed in front and cruciform rectangular fins at the rear. It required long practice to hit a moving target with them. Theoretically a vertical dive was the best expedient—but the problem came when pulling out of the dive! During the next three years the pilots of No 266 (Rhodesia) Squadron were to become masters at rocket attack and also at handling the temperamental but brilliant Typhoon.

The last letter

This letter was written by 21-year old H.A.P. (Buster) Peall to his mother the day before he set out on the Augsburg Raid. The letter was only to be posted in the event of his death. It was never completed.

Officers' Mess
Royal Air Force
Waddington,
Lincolnshire.
Tel. Waddington 464

Tuesday, April 15th 1942

My darling mother,

I knew from the start that this was bound to happen in the end, and I have always thought that my only regret would be not saying thank you and good bye. It seems strange writing so but I feel. I must.

I will not begin to thank you for everything because words cannot express it, and anyway tt would take far too long.

Like Dad I am not afraid to die but just don't want to. But 'God's will be done' so instead of coming home to you I go and meet Dad. I have heard how brave you were when Dad left us so I have no fear now. It is rather strange I should mention those words about God's will as I remember so well when I last said them. I was just before I past out when in the sea that time.

I should have loved to see you all once again Tricia, Guy and little Anthony, but that's how it must be, I suppose. You are a wonderful 4 and I hope you stick together and see Hitler beaten. But for you people there would be nothing in life to live for. Dear, 'Fatty' I wonder if he really

Remembers me or if he has just heard you talk of me so often. Actually I think he does remember me—perhaps in the swimming bath. God, what a home-life I have had. Everything a man could wish for and I don't think I appreciated to the full.

You remember, Mum how I used to say, 'When I find a woman like you I would marry her to-morrow'. I now realize that if I had kept to that and if I had lived, I should never have been married ...

CHAPTER 12

Bomber's moon

Spring of the year 1942 came to Europe. News on all fronts was grim. The German battleships had escaped from Brest. The Japanese had achieved lightning successes in the Far East. Having taken the Philippines in March, they landed in New Guinea in April and captured Bataan on 9th April. In Russia, the campaign had been halted by the winter with the German army besieging Leningrad, standing at the gates of Moscow and in possession of Stalingrad. Even in the forgotten war in the Middle East, Rommel had launched a counter attack, which was to take him skimming across the desert and into Egypt.

Only in the air could the Allies retaliate in any way and with the limited numbers of aircraft available, they began mounting heavier and heavier attacks on the Germans in Europe. Often these attacks were suicidal and seemed to achieve little or nothing, but it is important to remember that at this stage in the war, morale among the Allies counted for more than sheer weight of bombs dropped.

Attack on the *Tirpitz*

One of the seemingly forgotten raids of the war, possibly because it was on such a small scale and was unsuccessful, was the first Lancaster attack on the *Tirpitz*. This German capital ship, together with two cruisers, was at Trondheim, because of Hitler's fallacious intuition that the British intended to invade Norway. The move suited British strategy very well, but the presence of German naval units in Norway was an acute embarrassment to the convoys making their perilous way to Russia with vital supplies. Lancasters from Nos 44 and 97 Squadrons were detailed to attack the assembled ships. On 21st April, a special train steamed north towards Scotland carrying ground crews, stores and spares. Two days later the Lancasters flew up to Lossiemouth, which was to be their springboard for the operation, to be mounted on the evening of 27th April 1942. The Operations Record gives a vivid picture of the briefing.

> *Crews were briefed for an attack to be made on the German battleship 'Tirpitz'. Briefing was as follows: The target is the German battleship 'Tirpitz', which is lying at Aavinkannet in the Foetten Fjord, the most southerly inlet of the Aasen Fjord (Norway) approximately 18 miles [30km] east-north-east of Trondheim. The alternative target, if the 'Tirpitz' has moved or cannot be located, is the German ships 'Admiral von Scheer' and 'Prinz Eugen' in Lo Fjord. At the same place there is believed to be a cruiser of the Hipper class. The 'Tirpitz' is a vessel of over 40,000 tons, very heavily armoured and of the most modern design with armament of eight 15-inch guns, 12 5.9-inch guns, 16 4.1-inch AA guns, plus heavy calibre machine guns. Four aircraft are carried. The battleship lies in a narrow part of the Fjord close against the land on the northern bank. She would be difficult to find except in good visibility in moonlight.*

She is protected by a double boom spaced by floats parallel to and 55 yards (50m) from the southern side. Another boom protects the stern. The other enemy warships, 'Von Scheer' and 'Prinz Eugen' lie in the Lo Fjord and crews are warned that they may open fire. The route to be followed is Base—Herma Ness – 63,25N 06,00E—thence to target. Return to Base via Outskerries. The attack is planned in two phases plus a diversionary effort by Beaufighter aircraft to deal with enemy aircraft. The first phase of the attack is for 12 Lancaster aircraft (six from each of squadron Nos 44 (Rhodesia) and 97, plus 12 Halifax of No 76 Squadron to attack with special 4,000-lb (1,800-kg) bombs. The 4,000-lb bomb attack is considered an essential feature of the operation and the necessity of accurate bombing is stressed. The Lancaster and Halifax aircraft are instructed to enter the main Trondheim Fjord at 6,000 feet and to proceed straight to the Aasen Fjord and if necessary to identify the target by flares. As soon as the target is located, it is to be marked by a red flare. Bombing is to be carried out with precision from 6,000 feet from east to west or west to east at the captain's discretion but as many aircraft as possible should be concentrated during the early part of the stipulated period. Having dropped their 4,000-lb bombs, aircraft are then to attack, with their 500-lb (225-kg) bombs, any active flak or searchlights in the vicinity to neutralize anti-aircraft fire. The second phase of the attack is to be made by Nos 10 and 35 Squadrons. They will drop special mines from a height of only 150 to 200 feet which, if dropped close to the stern and between the ship and the shore, should sink the ship. Twenty Halifax aircraft will carry out the mining attack.

Air Vice-Marshal Carr spoke to the crews and stressed the major importance of this operation, which if successful would release British naval units then patrolling the northern Atlantic. Unfortunately, although many explosions were seen close to the ships, not a single direct hit was achieved and subsequent photographic reconnaissance revealed little damage. The attack was repeated on 28th April when one hit was reported. A few days later, the Lancasters dispersed to their bases.

Early problems with the Lancaster

Meanwhile No 44 Squadron ground crews were experiencing teething troubles with the Lancaster. Not as severe as those encountered with the Typhoon but still there were problems. The Lancaster had been brought from prototype into service in less time than any other bomber, and in the early stages servicing manuals were simply not available. The centre section of the wing leading edge was hinged at the top of the front spar. This allowed easy access for inspection and maintenance of the cabin heater and other equipment. When the maintenance handbook eventually became available, it pointed out in bold letters that failure to screw this component down before the engines were run, would result in serious damage to the aircraft. There is a story behind this warning.

The incident happened when Squadron Leader T.H. Boylan was air-testing L7531 at Coningsby on 23rd April. This machine, formerly of No 44 Squadron, was being used for conversion flights by No 97 Squadron. It behaved normally until it gathered speed and then the leading edge suddenly flew off. The machine crashed just beyond the bomb dump. An investigation was held and the rigger was placed under close arrest. Later he faced a court martial and the flight sergeant and another rigger were also charged. Within a month, a similar accident happened to L7581 belonging to No 44 squadron. The leading edge flew back on its hinges just as the aircraft was about to become airborne, careering out of control and crashing into two Hampdens belonging to No 420 Squadron. Hence the addition of the dire warning in the handbooks.

While part of No 44 Squadron was operating from Lossiemouth, the remainder was visiting Rostock. On four consecutive nights from 23rd April, the target that was attacked was the Heinkel works just outside the town. Only a few aircraft operated the first night, but on the second occasion 60 bombers attacked with 4,000-lb bombs. After the final attack, photo-reconnaissance revealed considerable damage to the factory. Among the Rhodesians who took part in these raids were Pilot Officer Grimwood Cooke, Pilot Officer William Picken, Flying Officer Norman Goldsmith, Squadron Leader Francis Robertson and Flight Lieutenant William Whamond.

Loss over Warnemünde

On 28th April, the target changed to Kiel and then to the Gnôme-Rhône Works at Gennevilliers. Nineteen Lancasters, the largest number to operate as a group so far, went gardening on 2nd May, followed by three successive nights (4th – 6th May) when Stuttgart was the target. The greatest force of Lancasters to operate so far over German territory set out on the evening of 8th May. Their destination was Warnemünde and it was to be a particularly sad night for the squadron and for Rhodesia.

Of the 14 Lancasters taking part in the raid, one carried an all-Rhodesian crew. It was the first and only bomber to be manned by an entirely Rhodesian crew and it failed to return from the raid. All but one of the crew was killed, the survivor being Sergeant Thomas Douglas Moore, the rear gunner who was taken prisoner of war.

The other seven members of the crew were buried in the New Cemetery at Rostock. They were Flying Officer Gerald MacLagan of Marandellas (pilot), Flight Engineer Hubert Sturgess of Salisbury (second pilot), Pilot Officer Frederick Belton of Ruzawi (navigator), Sergeant Bertram Nesbitt of Bulawayo (mid upper gunner/bomb-aimer), Sergeant Robert Duncan Olver of Bulawayo (wireless operator/airgunner), Sergeant Gilbert W. Hough of Bulawayo (wireless operator/airgunner) and Sergeant William McDonald Crane of Shabani (air observer).

Missing from the same raid were Flight Lieutenant Charles Surtis Cranmer McClure (who had won the DFC for the Augsburg Raid three weeks earlier), Sergeant Leonard Raymond Webster and Donald George Mackay. In all, ten Rhodesians died in this raid. As far as the squadron was concerned, it lost its commanding officer, Wing Commander P.W. Lynch-Blosse DFC who had arrived only 24 hours earlier to assume command.

The Operations Record states bluntly:

> It is difficult to record the squadron's activity in this operation as four of our aircraft failed to return to base. The loss of a further four very experienced crews severely handicaps the squadron's operational capacity, until such time as fresh crews can be trained. The present crew position is three fully experienced crews plus two 'freshman' crews plus five under training with the conversion flight. It means, therefore, that if the squadron is called upon to continue with normal operations, the same experienced crews will fly on each occasion. For this reason it was suggested that the squadron should be 'stood down' for one month and carry out intensive training by day and night and so bring the crew strength to normal again.

The first thousand-bomber raid

Nevertheless, by May 30th the squadron was ready to take part in the first thousand-bomber raid. One eye witness to this historic attack was Pilot Officer Arthur Friend of Salisbury, a cheerful giant of a man, over six foot (2m) tall:

> We could see clearly the dykes, towns and sometimes even the farmhouses of Holland as we flew towards Cologne, soon after midnight on Sunday morning. The moon was to our starboard, and straight ahead there was a rose-coloured glow in the sky. We thought it must be something to do

with the searchlight belt, which runs for about 200 miles [320km] along the Dutch/German frontier. As we went through this belt, we saw by the light of blue searchlights, some friendly aircraft going the same way as ourselves and a few coming back, but the glow was still ahead. It crossed my mind that it might be Cologne but we decided between us that it was too bright a light to be so far away. The navigator checked his course—it could only be Cologne. It looked as though we would be on target in a minute or two; we opened our bomb-doors. We flew on—the glow was as far as ever. We closed our bomb-doors. The glare was still there like a huge cigarette-end in the German blackout. Then we flew into smoke—through it the Rhine appeared, a dim silver ribbon below us. The smoke was drifting in the wind. We came in over the fires. Down in my bomb aimer's hatch I looked at the burning town below me. I remembered what had been said at the briefing. "Don't drop your bombs on buildings that are burning best—go in and find another target for yourself." Well, at last I found one right in the most industrial part of the town. I let my bombs go. We had a heavy load—hundreds of incendiaries and big high explosives. The incendiaries going off were like sudden platinum-coloured flashes, which slowly turned to red. We saw many flashes going from white to red and then our great bomb burst in the centre of them. As we crossed the town, there were burning blocks to the right of us and to the left. The fires were immense. They were really continuous. The flames were higher than I had ever seen before. The buildings were skeletons in the middle of the fires. Sometimes you could see what appeared to be the frameworks of white-hot joists. The blast of the bombs was hurling the walls themselves across the flames. As we came away, we saw more and more of our aircraft below us silhouetted against the flames. I identified Wellingtons, Halifaxes, Manchesters and other Lancasters. Above us there were still more bombers lit by the light of the moon. They were doing exactly as we did—going in according to plan and making their way home.

This was Happy Taylor's first big raid: The only Rhodesian in my crew was Les Edwards, the navigator. He had a camera. We flew around, quite illegally and took pictures but they didn't come out.

Other Rhodesians from No 44 Squadron who took part in the thousand-bomber raid on Cologne, were: Squadron Leader Francis Harold Robertson, Flight Lieutenant William Whamond, Pilot Officer William Picken and Pilot Officer Grimwood Cooke DFM.

What seems to have impressed the Rhodesians most about this raid was the fact that so many British aircraft were in the sky about them, before, during and after the operation. Until this time, the diametrically opposite fact had always been a feature of their trips over Germany. They had always seemed to be flying alone after take-off. Darkness was partly responsible for this impression but it was also true that where smaller raiding flights were concerned, the aircraft could become dispersed in what appeared to be a limitless sky. However, on this night, an impressively brilliant moon illuminated the aerial armada so clearly, as it winged its way to and from Cologne, that the various types of bombers were easily identifiable. One pilot remarked: It was the first time in a raid that I could see any of the others.

Apart from the sheer numbers of aircraft involved, a new tactic was first tried on this raid. This was that the attacking force was streamed. All the aircraft took the same route and the period of attack was cut from seven hours to two and a half with an average of seven aircraft bombing each minute.

The Cologne Raid on 30th May was a first-time major air attack on Germany. One thousand and forty-six aircraft took part in the raid. Forty aircraft were lost and 116 damaged. Nearly half the city of Cologne was devastated: 474 people were killed and over 40,000 made homeless. This was the start of the bomber offensive and it compelled the Luftwaffe to redeploy their aircraft from the Russian and other fronts to protect German cities and industry.

One very personal view of the raid came from Sergeant Donald Norman (Buzzer) Huntley, whose cousin had received a DFM for the Augsburg Raid.

Now I can tell you why I, and the rest, were confined to camp. We were standing by for over a week, expecting to go each night, to Cologne or Essen, being disappointed and hopes raised again, as we got out of bed saying, "Yes—today is the day." As it does not get dark until nearly 11 o'clock, the take-off was not until 10.30. I had my own crew and one of the staff pilots, a chap by the name of Pilot Officer Sleight. He is a fine lad and the ground staff got busy with our kite, 'G' for George. On his side they had painted a 'Wimpy'* with bomb under one arm and he was kicking another, with the words 'A Sleight bit of trouble'. On my side they had 'Reserved for Huntley and Palmers—but they're not dropping ruddy biscuits'. In front was Greta Garbo. Well, 10.30 approached and having got our sweets, coffee and other rations stored in the aircraft, we started up and taxied to take off. It was a grand sight to see all the machines one behind the other. Soon we were crossing the English coast and were above the clouds. We got a good pinpoint, which enabled us to find a good wind and began heading straight for no-man's land. We spied the Dutch coast some time afterwards and very soon the ack-ack and searchlights began playing all round us. As we got on, it was really magnificent. We saw the different colours of the tracer bullets, sometimes almost within reach of us—the bursts of shells, and on the ground, fires of all descriptions. Some of the fires were genuine, where the fighter boys had been blasting the defending aerodromes, but many were faked to try to trick us. Finally we located the target and as we were to go in 15 minutes after the first machines, it was already blazing away. We got right in the thick of it then, and the bomb-aimer singled out a large building that looked like a factory, just past the big bridge that spans the Rhine. We dropped our load and skittled for home. It was then we saw two night-fighters, but good evasive action on our captain's part shook them off and we came back safe and sound. I did not have much time to think, but once or twice I had a feeling that I was somewhere where I should not be. Then I also had a feeling that I was right on top of Hitler's head with a wooden mallet tapping his head to pieces with slow even strokes. It was rather weird but I soon got over that, as I proved on the next night over Essen. And believe me if ever you see it on the screen, or in the paper, don't think that they have overdeveloped the film. It was the most devastating piece of work ever done in any air raid known.
(Rhodesia Herald, 28th July 1942)

Sergeant Gunner Alan Smith whose first two operations were Cologne and Essen remarked: It's a wonder the planes did not bomb one another for there were so many bombing at the same time and from different heights. I like these raids; you are always sure of bacon and eggs when you get home!

Incidentally, Sergeant Smith, who was to celebrate his 20th birthday the following month, had had an amusing adventure during his training. He had force-landed in Scotland, miles from anywhere in most beautiful scenery. He and his fellow airmen tramped for miles until they reached the country town of Forfar. By this time they were in a pretty bedraggled and very thirsty state, so they dropped into a local pub to refresh themselves with a beer. Mine Host, not realizing that his customers were airmen, discoursed at length about flyers, Wonderful chaps, those airmen, but they're all half daft, he commented. Oh, said Smith, but we are airmen. Rather taken aback, the innkeeper covered his embarrassment with the offer of a free beer. Mind you, he added, I still say you're all half daft!

No 44 (Rhodesia) Squadron supplied 12 aircraft for the second thousand-bomber raid,

---

* Wimpy was the universal nickname for the Wellington, named after the cartoon character J. Wellington Wimpy.

which took place on 1st June when the target was Essen. Flight Lieutenant William Nelson (Bill) Whamond was involved in this attack:

> *Once returning from Essen where we had evaded searchlights and done our bit successfully, we got caught at 10,000 feet in a cone of searchlights. For 43 minutes they held us, passing us from group to group while we turned, dived and twisted, keeping a general homeward course. We came so low, that we could see gun flashes horizontally in front of us, and shells passed between the main and tail planes. Then we passed over a town where the lights and shells could not follow us so we escaped. It was the longest 43 minutes ever. I felt all the time like a bird with its wings held.*

Six Lancasters with their crews and 70 airmen from the Rhodesian squadron were lent to Coastal Command on 11th June 1942 for long-range anti-U-boat escort, and commenced operations next day. They were attached to No 15 Group of the command at Nutts Corner in Northern Ireland until 6th July.

During that month, in which 61 hours were flown, two attacks were made on U-boats, both on 15th June, when an unidentified U-boat was attacked without result and in another attack the U 442 was claimed. The day before Lancaster R5858 had ditched in the Atlantic when an engine caught fire. An outward-bound convoy picked up the crew, who were later reported safe—in Africa! Incidentally, the German navy seem to have been as hazy on aircraft recognition as the British, because at least one Lancaster was contacted by a U-boat, whose commander evidently mistook it for a friendly Focke-Wulf FW 200.

For the stay-at-home section of the squadron, Emden was the target on 19th, 20th and 23rd June while on 25th June it was the Focke-Wulf works at Bremen. This was a particularly successful raid, in which a 4,000-lb bomb from one of the Lancasters hit the machine shop, and other buildings were gutted by fire. Warrant Officer Stott claimed three enemy aircraft shot down on this raid. This was the third of the mass attacks and the last in which Manchesters operated. The fact that 83 Lancasters were among the 1,006 aircraft dispatched, demonstrated the speed of build-up of Lancasters within No 5 Group. Bremen was the target again on 27th and 29th June.

In mounting these thousand-bomber raids, Bomber Command gave the appearance of being more powerful than it actually was. The front-line strength of the Command was actually less than that of the previous year by nearly 25%. The precise figures were 878 for July 1941; 670 for July 1942. The thousand-bomber raids were achieved only by bringing in the operational training and conversion units. The depletion in numbers was due to aircraft being diverted to Coastal Command, the failure of the Manchester as a bomber and the introduction of the Lancaster, inevitably slowed output during changeover periods on the production lines.

By mid-July the Lancasters of No 44 Squadron had returned from Coastal Command and were ready to take part in main force raids on Duisburg on 21st and 23rd July. Then Hamburg, followed by Flensburg where the target was the submarine works where a large workshop was demolished.

However, it was the final night in July that was to prove the most exciting of the month. For the first time more than 100 Lancasters, 104 to be exact, took to the air on one raid. Their target was Düsseldorf and they represented 25 percent of the total force on that clear moonlit night. Considerable damage was done to the Schiess A.G. Works, the largest machine tool production plant in Germany. Two Lancasters failed to return. Squadron Leader Nettleton VC, who had recently returned to duty after his honeymoon, did not participate in the Düsseldorf Raid, but among the Rhodesians who flew over Düsseldorf that night was Pilot

Officer Patrick Dorehill DFC who at the age of 20 was a veteran of 17 operational flights. Missing as a result of this raid were Sergeant Peter Rix, Flight Sergeant Norman Tetley, Sergeant Charles Norman Gardner and Sergeant John MacIntyre MacMahon. Norman Tetley's wife had recently arrived in England to join her husband. She was lost at sea returning to Rhodesia.

August started with a bang. There were raids on three consecutive days, 4th, 5th, 6th August, the first two on the Ruhr and the third on Duisburg. A day or two later, Happy Taylor brought a Lancaster back with a full bomb load, including a 4,000-pounder.

Talking about the incident later, Happy said, When I told the CO that I had brought them back, he nearly had a fit. A signal went out that no 4,000-lb bombs should be brought back. They must be dropped into the sea. Taylor added, You had to drop them from a height above 4,000 feet to be safe from the fragments and you had to turn well out of the bomber stream to avoid damaging other aircraft. Two days later Happy crash-landed the same plane after dropping his bombs!

Towards the middle of the month came a break in the main force bombing raids, while the Rhodesian squadron carried out a gardening operation. Mines were laid in the Baltic to prevent the battleship Prinz Eugen breaking out into the Atlantic.

August 20th 1942 was the date of the last raid of the first tour of duty for Happy Taylor. It was an attack on a submarine supply tanker off the Spanish coast. This was one of the only two daylight raids in which Taylor was involved. The other was a hit-and-run raid on Terschelling to bomb radar and flak installations. Using low-level cloud the plan was to belt in, drop the bombs and clear out. Remarking on the operational organization, Happy Taylor says:

A tour averaged 30 trips. My first tour was split between Hampdens and Lancasters. Altogether I did 58 trips on two tours and took part in two abortive raids; one owing to engine trouble, the other to bad weather. In summer we would average three raids a week, fewer in winter owing to bad weather. Hampdens did more operations on moonlight nights. With the Lancs it didn't matter, though with raids like the Stettin one, where we were flying long distances over enemy territory, the moonlight helped because we could hedge-hop all the way to avoid German radar. When we went to Stettin we hedge-hopped all the way and climbed over the Baltic. During summer, when the nights were short, most raids were made on the Ruhr, which was close. This area was protected by a 25-mile [40km] broad band of searchlights and ack-ack, which had to be flown through. As well as bombs, we carried fake ration cards and leaflets, which had to be dropped. In the very short mid-summer nights, even a short distance raid meant leaving in daylight. I think the Ruhr must have been the most heavily defended target in the world. We called these raids the 'milk-run'.

Squadron pilots had one week off in six and two stand-down periods of two days each with no operational flying. Taylor says that to start with he spent his leave in London but later made friends in Scotland. Talking of the luck of coming through two tours, Taylor says:

If you got through the first six raids successfully, there was a reasonable chance. You can't buy experience. You've got to know. For instance if a main searchlight is seeking you out, you must swing into it not away. If you are caught in a flak box, a small area where concentrated ack-ack is coming up, you have to work quickly, dive or climb out of the way. We didn't work in formation at night. Each pilot made his own way to the target and flew his own course over the target. Many a time a chap would take avoiding action and zoom past inches away from another aircraft. However, the losses from collisions were comparatively light compared with the protection given by large numbers of aircraft converging on the target at the same time. Someone dropped a bomb on my turret once and creased it. As far as height was concerned: Lancasters went in high about 17,000 to 20,000 feet over heavily defended targets such as the Ruhr. It was pushing the aircraft a bit to take it above 20,000 with a full bombload and you might find you hadn't enough fuel for the return flight if the trip was a long one. The Halifaxes came in slightly lower and the Stirlings had bottom position.

The latter part of 1942 failed to fulfil the promise of the raids on Cologne and Essen. The effectiveness of Gee, the new navigational aid based on a grid of radio signals, was reduced in the course of the summer. The Germans had discovered the frequency on which the system operated and jammed it. German night-fighter strength more than doubled, becoming the major threat to the RAF bombers. German flak units, too, seemed to multiply like virulent bacteria. German fighters and flak claimed 1,404 bombers during 1942. Fortunately, British factories managed to keep slightly ahead of losses.

So, if it was proving impossible to increase bomber numbers, could bombing accuracy be improved? The main problem was finding and identifying the target. This problem was addressed in August 1942, with the formation of the pathfinder force under Air Commodore Donald C.T. Bennett. Initially this force consisted of crews from five of the squadrons, which had been most successful in finding targets. Their task was to precede the main force, and flying at low level, mark the target area with flares and the aiming point with incendiaries.

At first, there were problems with the pathfinder force. The fires they started often spread, masking the target area. Sometimes the Germans themselves lit decoy fires to lead the raiders astray. However, as the autumn passed, the pathfinders' techniques improved. Special target indicator flares were developed that burst with unmistakable coloured patterns.

No 266 claims its first 'kill' in a Typhoon

It is now necessary to turn the clock back to the summer months. No 266 (Rhodesia) Squadron had been mainly engaged in intruder patrols over the occupied territory of France and anti-intruder activity over the English coast. Re-equipping and training with Typhoons had proceeded apace. It was during a training operation on 13th June that Sergeant Edward Hugh Welby crashed and was killed.

A week later, the squadron flew its first operation using the new aircraft. Taking off from Duxford they flew over the Calais and Boulogne areas before returning to base. The object of this exercise was to provide support for returning Spitfires but the rendezvous did not take place. All the aircraft returned to base without incident. The same result was obtained from a wing operation over the French coast three days later, and equally unsatisfying was a scramble on the following day to investigate an 'intruder' that turned out to be a lone Wellington!

By the month of July, No 266 (Rhodesia) Squadron was under the command of a Rhodesian, Squadron Leader Charles Green. Two flight commanders, Flight Lieutenants, Anthony Collyer Johnston and R.H. (Rolo) Dawson were also Rhodesians. It is interesting to note that Spitfires were still the main operations aircraft at this time. Hours flown in July—according to N.J. Lucas's log-book was Typhoon: 99.10; Spitfire: 158.45.

From time to time, welcome breaks occurred, such as the visit, on 10th July, to Napiers Works at Acton to see production of Sabre engines. This was followed by A rendezvous at the Final where tanks were refilled frequently and then pilots went on sorties in loose formation, some weaving more than others. All our pilots got back to their respective bases safely although somewhat after ETA!

August was to prove an exciting month for the squadron; on 9th August, Norham John Lucas and Ian Munro shared the distinction of making the first kill in a Typhoon. According to the Operational Record:

It was a day of 4/10 cloud with rain showers and bright intervals. Two operations were carried out. One raid and one sea patrol. In the latter (19h25 – 20h45) Pilot Officer I.M. Munro and Pilot Officer Norham John Lucas, patrolling north and south about 50 miles seaward of Cromer, saw a Ju 88 at zero feet pass almost under them. They turned and chased it, overtaking it very easily and firing more or less both at once, gave very short bursts at 600 and 400 yards (550 and 360m) and then a longer burst at 200 yards (180m), Pilot Officer Munro from dead astern and Pilot Officer Lucas from port quarters. The Ju 88 caught fire and went into the sea. This is the first victory for any Typhoon aircraft. Good show!

Their action was rewarded with a bottle of champagne from Group Captain Grady and drinks in the mess from Hawkers Ltd, the manufacturers of the aircraft. Four days later came a second success, this time on the part of Flight Lieutenant Johnston.

On a day of heavy cloud, the squadron carried out a dawn and dusk sea patrol. During the dusk flight, a Ju 88 flying at zero feet was spotted about 30 miles (50km) east of Lowestoft.

Flight Lieutenant A.C. Johnston flying in line abreast saw it first, so turned quickest and got in front of the other three aircraft. The Ju 88* started firing at 1,200 yards (1,100m) but kept flying straight and level making for a rain cloud. Flight Lieutenant Johnston gave it some short bursts at 1,000 yards (900m) and 600 yards (550m). He saw strikes on the water and got a strike on the starboard engine at 400 yards (370m) and then closing from 200 to 20 yards, set it properly on fire and had to break away violently to prevent ramming its tail. Sergeant Gerald Glasson Osborne and Pilot Officer W.J.A. (Susie) Wilson flying astern of Flight Lieutenant Johnston had pulled up and out of the way but the enemy aircraft was already well on fire. Enemy aircraft crashed into the sea, one man baled out but was apparently not found. One Ju 88 to Flight Lieutenant A.C. Johnston!

The Dieppe Raid

The first large-scale action in which the Rhodesian squadron was involved was the landing at Dieppe. The date was 19th August 1942. The object was to destroy enemy defences and aerodrome installations, radar stations, power stations, dock and rail facilities, also to capture secret documents and prisoners. It was not to be the start of an invasion but it was to be a landing in sufficient strength to test the German defences and to determine the feasibility of capturing a heavily defended port in the event of a full-scale invasion. The troops used were mainly Canadians, who were eager to see some action.

The day of the landing was fine and hot with good visibility. In the Operational Record the story continues:

In the night and very early morning, the combined operational landing at Dieppe took place and the land fighting continued there most of the day. This squadron went on three wing sweeps with Nos 609 and 56 Squadrons. The first in the morning was a diversionary attack. Our wing was to protect nine Defiants that were arranged to look like a large bomber force attacking east of Calais. No enemy aircraft were seen and the sweep was quite uneventful except that everybody was short of petrol and had to land at West Malling. The second sweep was from West Malling down to the battle area near Dieppe. Flight Lieutenant Dawson, Pilot Officer Smithyman and Flying Officer Munro saw and attacked three Do 217s and it is believed that Flight Lieutenant Dawson destroyed one. Also Pilot Officer Munro claims one probably destroyed. There were

---

* This Ju 88 was in fact an Me 210, the first to be shot down. Information came from a survivor. (Operations Record) *some FW 190s in the vicinity and Pilot Officer Munro saw tracer going past his wing at the end of the combat. Pilot Officer Smithyman is missing. From R/T interception several pilots understood that Flight Lieutenant Dawson destroyed one. Flight Lieutenant Johnston dived after ten FW 190s and probably destroyed one in a dive from 1,500 feet to near the deck at 480 mph (770 km/h). Pilot Officer Munro and Flight Lieutenant Dawson returned home at zero feet when, half way over the Channel, suddenly met a squadron of Spitfires all of which looked as if they were attacking. One fired at Flight Lieutenant Dawson whose aircraft went straight into the sea. Squadron Leader Green with three others came out from the French coast at 14,000 feet and they also complained that four Spitfires flew at them in a very menacing manner but fortunately did not open fire. Results of the day: One Dornier 217 destroyed by Flight Lieutenant Dawson. One Dornier 217 probably destroyed by Pilot Officer Munro. One FW 190 probably destroyed by Flight Lieutenant Johnston. Our losses: Pilot Officer Smithyman missing and Flight Lieutenant Dawson missing believed killed by a Spit. Poor Rolo (Dawson). He was a topping lad.*

The Dieppe exercise proved beyond doubt the difficulty if not the impossibility of mounting an attack on a heavily defended port. More than 9,000 casualties resulted, which in the case of the Canadian force was 68% of the men involved. But the lessons learned at Dieppe were well applied when it came to planning the D-Day landings. Field Marshal Mountbatten has said that for every soldier who died at Dieppe, ten were saved on D-Day.

The Rhodesian airmen who took part in the first thousand-bomber raid were:[*]

Squadron Leader F. Robertson
Flight Lieutenant W. Whamond
Flying Officer N. Goldsmith
Flying Officer D. Taylor
Pilot Officer R. Alan
Pilot Officer W. Cook
Pilot Officer G. Cooke
Pilot Officer T. Hackney
Pilot Officer C. Holland
Pilot Officer W. Picken
Pilot Officer W. Rail
Pilot Officer S. Young
Flight Sergeant J. Parry
Sergeant A. Coley
Sergeant L. Edwards
Sergeant R.I. Gruber
Sergeant E. Lincott
Sergeant W. Rickards
Sergeant P. Rix
Sergeant W. Rose
Sergeant N. Shattock

---

[*] Of these 21 men 12 were to die in air operations.

CHAPTER 13

The forgotten squadron

On 6th February 1942, No 237 (Rhodesia) Squadron moved to Ismalia, in the Canal Zone and two weeks later they continued on their way through the Sinai, Judea, Turba, Habbaniya, and up the Tigris Valley to Mosul in Iraq, where a new headquarters was established on 3rd March. In the overall strategy of the war, this area was of immense importance. Hitler needed oil in order to keep the wheels of industry and transport turning and the vast oilfields of the Middle East might lure him into attacking Iran and Iraq from southern Russia.

Incident at Mosul
Eric Smith tells an amusing story of the squadron's arrival at Mosul:

> *I contacted the colonel of an Iraqi Cavalry Regiment. They had magnificent Arab horses and I thought a bit of riding would amuse the chaps. He agreed and we arranged for eight horses the following Sunday. We arrived in casual khaki shirts and shorts to find the colonel and his officers in full dress. I immediately sensed that this was no casual outing and Rhodesia's honour and prestige were at stake. How lucky it was that I had picked six pilots. 'Pop' Bryson, our veteran adjutant, the six pilots and I were ushered into the mess with the courtesy normally accorded VIPs. We were then ceremonially served numerous small cups of weak black tea for what seemed ages and ages. Suddenly there was a tremendous commotion outside, punctuated with what sounded like violent Iraqi oaths. There were eight most magnificent white Arab stallions harnessed with martingales. Two grooms, at each head, were desperately trying, but not succeeding in keeping at least one hoof on the ground.*

From here 'Pop' takes up the story:

> *The CO and the pilots turned a slight tinge of green but the CO quickly gave us our 'operational briefing'.*
> *Chaps, this is serious so listen carefully!*
> a) *Go through your preflight drill meticulously. In particular check and recheck your safety harness and flying controls—you are going to need both.*
> b) *Signal when you are ready but do not wave your chocks (grooms) until I signal to you.*
> c) *When I signal slam, and I mean slam your throttles through the gate.*
> d) *Maintain your station in close formation; I want no straggling.*
> e) *If you force-land you will be on your own. I will not stop to give you air cover, but I expect you to salvage your aircraft.*
> f) *Good luck! And remember 'Rhodesia expects…'*
> *In two jumps the Arab stallions were in full stride and the CO was yelling for us to close up and*

maintain stations! Later, we were to learn that these stallions were never ridden by the cavalry officers. They were too spirited. The colonel had personally selected them for us! Who was it who said that Iraqis had no sense of humour! ('Pop' Bryson as retold by Eric Smith)

Unfortunately, the squadron had only been at Mosul just over two weeks when the first fatality occurred. Pilot Officer Gerald Edward Robert Lock was killed on 20th March, when his Hurricane crashed on returning from a training sortie with the army. He was buried the following day in Mosul Cemetery. It was at Mosul on 30th March that the squadron received their official crest from Air Marshal Sir A.W. Tedder KCB.

'The Bullytin'
The squadron had moved to this remote area in order to foil any possible German move through the back door into the oil rich areas of Persia and Iraq. However, this Axis attack never materialized and for the next few months, the squadron was almost forgotten. The Rhodesians grew more and more frustrated as the days passed with no sign of action. One escape valve for their 'browned off' feelings was *The Bullytin* a squadron newspaper.

An example from this newspaper dated 13th March 1942 reads:

Food for thought—promotions.
The topic of the week has certainly been 'promotions' and we feel that congratulations are due to those who have been fortunate in obtaining credit for efforts made. At times like these there are always regrets and sympathies galore and one kind of feels that it is high time that the authorities introduced a system whereby everybody at the Bottom moved up automatically whilst those at the Top moved down. This would ensure that people with the brains eventually got their chance of messing things up like their predecessors. It would also give those at the Bottom an opportunity for Home Leave, and other set-backs (!), which those at the Top have to face from day-to-day. We fully appreciate how difficult it is to please everybody in these matters, but it must be a weight off some Erks' minds to know that, where formerly they had to buy three stripes* to get into the cabarets in Palestine, they get them for nothing now, and can walk in upright.
(Extract from The Bullytin, 13th March 1942)

The main work carried out by the Rhodesian squadron was cooperation training with the recently formed 10th Army and on 14th April Peter Hugh Swaine Simmonds was killed in a Gladiator crash while on manoeuvers with the army. As far as aircraft were concerned, the squadron was still awaiting the arrival of additional Hurricanes from the Western Desert. On 8th May, the squadron provided an escort of six Hurricanes for the Duke of Gloucester who was visiting the area. This was not purely ceremonial as German aircraft were well within striking distance.

When we got to Teheran the air attaché asked us to show the flag. He suggested formation flying, aerobatics and a beat-up of the town. The last suggestion frankly terrified me. I knew the mood of my pilots. I asked for written orders and locked them in the safe of the Shell Company representative for safekeeping. We circled the town a few times in very tight formation to draw attention. Then broke into two flights of three to do formation aerobatics. We broke again for each individual to display his own skill. On my order to beat up the town all hell broke loose. I think it's true to say nobody moved except perhaps to dash for safe cover. (Eric Smith)

---

* Some places of entertainment were only open to certain ranks. So it was necessary to 'buy' the stripes to wear for a night out.

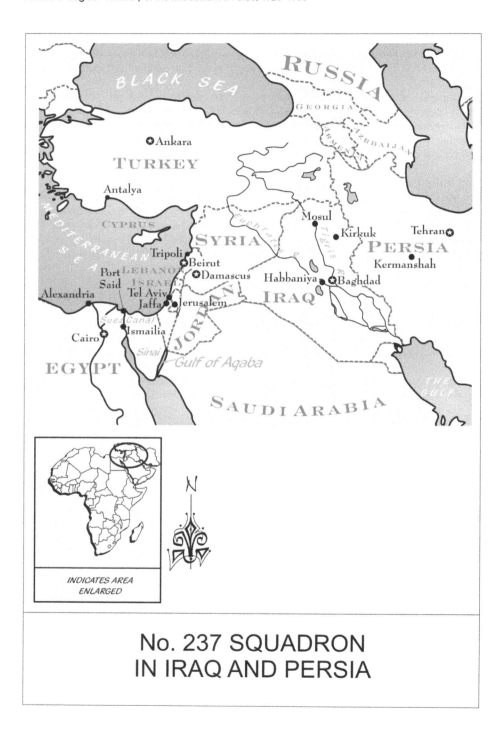

No. 237 SQUADRON IN IRAQ AND PERSIA

The Rhodesians found that this part of the world could be exceptionally hot, and during June, temperatures of 115° Fahrenheit (46° Celsius) in the shade were frequently registered at Mosul. Welcome relief was offered at a holiday rest camp high up in the mountains on the Turkish border. Clear ice-cold water from melting snow ran through the camp. The Rhodesians built a swimming pool by the simple expedient of placing two 500-lb bombs (225kg) in a cave and blasting a cliff down to block the stream. Members of the squadron on leave travelled up to the rest camp and back with the weekly mule-train delivering supplies. For two weeks the heat of the plain was forgotten as the men lazed, swam, climbed, shot grouse and became proficient trout fishermen.

One of the features of squadron life at this time was the variety of fauna, which they accumulated. Some were destined for the pot, others enjoyed a more permanent position with the squadron. As one pilot recounted:

We have a tame magpie named Joe Stalin. He delights in alighting on one's helmet when one isn't expecting him to do so. He is a great believer in camouflage and detests anything that shines. One has to be careful not to leave coins or nail scissors lying around. He will pick up these objects, fly away with them and bury them. He also delights in upsetting boxes of matches. He knows how to open the flaps of one's pockets and he fishes round inside for something to play with. He goes to the aerodrome every morning on one of the lorries but doesn't like to leave till someone has given him a drink of tea. Often he will fly over the top of the lorry keeping pace with it.

Joe Stalin obviously enjoyed a long and happy existence. Other members of the squadron were more temporary.

Our camp is like a farmyard these days. Some of our lads have bought geese to fatten up, others have invested in turkeys and there are always a lot of chickens about. On Sunday mornings we usually sleep an hour or so later, but this morning I was awake early; it was impossible to sleep because of geese screeching, turkeys gobbling and cocks crowing.

The Rhodesia Club

For those Rhodesians who could wangle a visit to Cairo, facilities had been greatly improved by the opening of their own club. Colonel J.B. Brady carried out an unofficial ceremony on 22nd May; the official opening was in July. This home from home was overseen by Mrs Kiley, the housekeeper, who was regarded with great affection by the Rhodesians. She devoted herself to their care and comfort, even sewing the coverlets and curtains herself, to save funds. There were 12 rooms, with sleeping accommodation for 25, dining facilities for 40 and a large roof garden. It proved an oasis for every Rhodesian in the Middle East by providing—during the first month of operation—959 dinners, 741 teas, 508 lunches, 419 breakfasts and 434 beds!

According to a report in the *Rhodesia Herald*, the club had one of the finest views in Cairo, occupying two luxury flats on the 15th and 16th floors of the tallest building in the city. The roof garden offered clean clear air while in the bathrooms there was always abundant hot and cold water, a boon to men who had gone unwashed for days or even weeks. The charge for a bath, bed and morning tea was two shillings a night, the all-in rate being nine shillings, with free laundry. There was a completely informal atmosphere, with only one unwritten rule: no officers allowed in the bar. There was no fixed time for breakfast, allowing men back from the desert, with a backlog of sleep to catch up on, to have breakfast in bed and go back to sleep. If a man wished to remain in bed for 24 hours, he could.

In July, No 237 (Rhodesia) Squadron was posted to Quiara, where the advanced party arrived on 7th July. On the following day, Captain E.C. Rowlette ceased to be attached to the squadron as medical officer. During August, Warrant Officer Charles (Darkie) Horton received his promotion but remained with the squadron as an engineering officer. Warrant Officer Horton had been one of the original ground crew seconded from the RAF to help in the training of Rhodesian airmen, before the outbreak of war. Prior to this he had refused numerous offers of promotion so that he could remain with the squadron.

Towards the end of August came yet another move, this time to Kermanshah, in Persia (Iran) where squadron duties included guarding against raids by local tribesmen. The main ground party arrived in Kermanshah on 13th September where the squadron headquarters was to remain until the end of November. At this stage the flight commanders were: 'A' flight—Flight Lieutenant Alexander James McBarnet; 'B' flight—Flight Lieutenant A.O.G. (Archie) Wilson; 'C' flight—Flying Officer Panico Hercules Christopher Theodosiou. The squadron was still fully engaged on ground/air cooperation training with the army and during November, a total of 409 hours and 50 minutes was flown. On 29th November came the move to Kirkuk, in Iraq and it was here that Ian Douglas Smith, later to become prime minister of Rhodesia, joined No 237 (Rhodesia) Squadron.

The squadron celebrates its third year 'in the field'

Towards the end of 1942, the squadron staged a magnificent celebration in honour of the third anniversary of leaving home. The squadron had actually left home in August 1939 but the heat in Iraq at that time of year was too overwhelming for outdoor sporting events. So the celebrations were held several months after the correct date. The events began in the evening with a Loony Park carnival, all the sideshows being homemade. Pay had just been received, so the money flowed. The following day featured a sports meeting in the morning, donkey races in the afternoon followed by a braaivleis and concert, ending with a campfire singsong. Everybody took part in the sporting events that ranged from flat races, to obstacle and three-legged events.

About 60 donkeys had been begged, borrowed or stolen for the donkey races and there were almost as many riders as spectators with the result that at the start of each race the competitors were strung out across a course that was a hundred yards wide. This meant that the outside riders had the handicap of riding on the edge of the runway. Artificial aids to motion, mechanical or vegetable, were strictly forbidden. Only impassioned shouts could be used to urge on the slow ambling of the stolidly philosophic beasts. The main event of the afternoon was the Derby in which little Tich Edwards, dressed for the part, ran away from the field on Honey Bee. As he had started odds-on favourite the bookies did not do too well on that race. Five races were run, if the sedate pace of the donkeys could be called running.

Towards the end of the meeting, the proceedings were enlivened by the sudden appearance of a grey mountain bear, which had apparently been chased down from the mountain by wolves. With about 300 men after it, the bear just did not have a chance and brother bear came riding back to camp on a lorry, held by the scruff of the neck in the powerful grip of Bob Hulme who had hopes of taming it as a squadron mascot. The bear was placed, for the night, in a stout crate but during the hours of darkness, it managed to break out.*

During their stay in Kirkuk, the Rhodesians managed to play a good deal of sport, beating all-comers at rugby, with the exception of the London and Scottish. Having been unable to teach them anything on the rugby field, the squadron gave their pipers a new tune: 'Sarie

---

* Eric Smith later admitted that the bear was released on his orders, for the good of both the bear and the squadron.

Marais', which apparently was a tremendous hit with the Scots.

So the year 1942 drew to a close and 1943 commenced following the same pattern—army cooperation exercises, tactical reconnaissance and photographic surveys. The only excitement came on 11th January when three aircraft from No 237 Squadron joined aircraft from No 52 Squadron to search for Flight Lieutenant Panico Theodosiou who was found unhurt at Khanaquin having force-landed there.

The squadron had now spent almost a year in Iraq and Iran and the men were itching to get back to active duty, so it was with great enthusiasm that they received the 'A' and 'B' flight aircraft left for Habbaniya, while the commanding officer, Eric Smith, made the trip by car. The main convoy set out on 20th January arriving in Baghdad on 25th January and Habbaniya the following day. Their route then took them through the Transjordan and Palestine to Shandour where they arrived on 6th February 1943.

One sad piece of news that reached the squadron reported the death of Dr C.W. Robertson in No 29 British General Hospital. Dr Charles Wilson Robertson, well known throughout Rhodesia, was a rather silent man who did not make friends very easily but when he did, his friendships were lasting and sincere. He was born in Sinoia on 14th December 1901, educated at Prince Edward School and studied medicine in Edinburgh. He had assisted as medical officer with the SRAF when it left for Kenya in August 1939 but after serving for several months, he returned to Rhodesia to continue his radiological work. However, in November 1942, he had five months' leave due, and as No 237 Squadron was without a medical officer, he volunteered to rejoin them. It was during this attachment that he contracted the illness that ended in his death from pneumonia.

News from 'home'

Meanwhile, back in Rhodesia things were settling into a steady pattern. The Budget for 1942/43 set aside over £4,000,000 for war expenses out of a total expenditure of £9,736.269. As far as the Women's Auxiliary Air Force was concerned, after the initial intake, recruiting proved disappointing. The average monthly intake from 1st September 1941 to August 1942 was only 32. The strength of the unit at the end of September 1942 was 505 women including seven officers.

The inspector general, Air Marshal Sir Edgar Ludlow Hewitt KCB CMG DSO MC, arrived in Rhodesia on Saturday October 10th 1942 to inspect the training schools. A report had been compiled for him, which makes interesting reading and covers all aspects of the RATG up to this date. (See end of chapter)

Incidentally, one rather amusing point was that, shortly after this visit, the name for the Combined Air Observers' School at Moffat was changed. The commanding officer felt that the initials CAOS were a rather unfortunate combination. The official title was changed to Royal Air Force Station, Moffat, with three resident units:

No 24 Bombing, Gunnery and Navigation School
No 29 Elementary Navigation School
Aircrew Pool

Another interesting point is that Moffat became the main centre for training Greek aircrew—men who had escaped from Greece. They had their own interpreters who remained at the station for a considerable time. A small number of trainees also came from Yugoslavia, some having fled from Belgrade and Zagreb across the Mediterranean to Cairo, after escaping from 'slave' factories. They understood the philosophy of Nazism and did not care for it.

Report on RATG, October 1942. Prepared for the Inspector General

Pupils come mainly from the United Kingdom, with small numbers from other places. Local recruitment supplies about 15 in every six-weekly intake. Reception Depot is at Hillside Camp. Initial Training Wing is at Hillside, where the pupils are divided into primary and secondary courses. Each six weeks, on successful completion of the initial training wing course, pupils pass to either post initial training wing pool or direct to the elementary flying training scheme. Each EFTS intake is 320 pupils: 50 from post initial training wing pool and 270 direct from ITW Course. Wastage at ITW averages 6%. Approximately 35% of these are accepted for airgunner training and pass to No 24 CAOS (Moffat). The balance are given trade training and absorbed into Group or sent to Middle East and UK. EFTS intake is 80 pupils (at each school) every six weeks (though it was lower at the start). The wastage is 10.25%, half of which is accepted for air observer training and 1.475% for airgunner training at No 24 CAOS (Moffat). Pupils failing EFTS ground examination are posted to initial training wing for coaching and re-examination. On qualifying, they are posted to SFTS (percentage of failures is low). SFTS—normal intake at present 64 every six weeks (at each school); wastage 2.94% pupils of which a third are accepted for air observer training and a sixth for airgunner training at No 24 CAOS (Moffat). Pupils failing are held back or sent forward with special coaching depending on the discretion of the CO. CAOS (Moffat) intake 35 every six weeks. 5% pupil wastage. 40% trained as airgunners. Pupils principally from pupil pilot wastage; also from other commands and local recruits. Airgunners intake was 37 every six weeks. Wastage 2% pupils. Intake is now 50 per course, 5% being provided by pilot wastage. The balance from other commands, locally serving airmen and recruits.

Instructors

Twenty-two instructors including the group link trainer officer have been posted from UK since May 1940 to the beginning of 1941. Air Ministry could not supply more until 1942. Group authorized by Air Ministry to train instructors. Fifty instructors now trained and present strength 68 (including two Greeks additional to establishment). (Instructors have been obtained from Rhodesian civilians and RAF ground personnel who have the necessary flying experience and from aircrew training and medical wastage).

Flying instructors' school

Twenty-four pupil instructors given six weeks course, which includes instrumentation and elementary and one service type. Hours flown 80. Twenty hours ground lectures given by staff flying instructors.

Rhodesian Air Askari Corps

On the inception of the air training scheme, it was decided to set up a native labour organization and enlist such natives as would be required in the various establishments. In consequence, The Rhodesian Native Labour Corps was formed. Later when the Rhodesian African Rifles was raised under the Defence Department, it was hoped to use men from this source for guard duty. This scheme did not materialize and the formation of the Rhodesian Air Askari Corps was authorized.

a)   Military Section (Askari)

b)   Labour Section

RAAC provides Askari for military duties, guards etc. and natives for general labour. Establishment of two Askari Rifle Companies at each SFTS and one at EFTS. Also Pioneer Section doing minor building works. Total establishment provides for 64 European officers, 178 European other ranks, 2,331 Askari and 2,205 labourers.

Buildings

What began as an expedient for providing temporary shelters for native construction gangs, has developed into a system of construction for accommodating European personnel also, and

this latest station to be built at Norton is approximately 50% 'Hessian Construction'. This consists of outer walls and partition, framed up on gum poles and lined on both sides with hessian, treated with lime wash or cement wash to weatherproof this material. The roofing is generally of thatch but where grass is not available, hessian is also used for roofing, with a layer of Malthoid stretched on wire netting below it to ensure protection against rain. This is an inexpensive though purely temporary type of construction, the cost being about half that of brick or wood and iron, and construction being much speedier. Early stations soon showed wear and wind erosion and tailskid wear made surfaces uneven and dangerous. By November 1941, Cranborne, Kumalo and Heany had taxi-ing tracks and runways in tar macadam. Stocks of bitumen began to run out and a search was made for a better method; molasses was not a success. Cranborne tried American soil cement stabilization. This proved successful, producing a hard, dust-free surface. This was not, however, considered suitable for EFTS on account of wear to tail skids. Mt Hampden officers carried out tar-emulsion tests.
Aeroplane shelters
These were used instead of hangars to protect the engines—leaving wings and tails exposed. The cost was £160 against £7,000 for a Bellman Hangar.

As a result of his visit, Air Marshal Sir Edgar Ludlow Hewitt submitted the following report:

I believe the Rhodesian Training Group is recognized as being the most satisfactory and trouble-free of all the Empire training formations. My visit to these schools confirmed these impressions and there is little to be said in criticism of this admirable training organization. Much of the credit for this very admirable state of affairs belongs to the Rhodesian people themselves and to their government. The contribution that this relatively small community of people, some 60,000 in all, has made to the war effort is truly remarkable. The government of Rhodesia is responsible for the whole of the capital expenditure for all the works required and for the design, construction, provision, maintenance, equipping and furnishing of the accommodation for all the air stations. In addition, they pay a substantial contribution towards running expenses including the complete cost of the Group headquarters. Estimated expenditure for 1942 is over £4,000,000. Sir James Ross, in a note to me states: 'This means that virtually the whole of the local expenditure is being met by Southern Rhodesia'. The estimated expenditure for the current year is over £4,000,000 and I was informed by one of the ministers that the entire revenue of the country before the war was only £2,500,000. In 1939 – 40 the total revenue was just over £4,000,000. This, therefore, is an exceptionally fine performance for so small a colony.

The report concludes:

The visit to these Rhodesian schools was a pleasant experience. The accommodation* is good and at almost every station beautifully kept. There are fewer complaints by airmen at these schools than at any other station I have visited abroad.

E.R. Ludlow Hewitt, Inspector General
Richmond, Surrey
16th November 1942

---

* The Inspector General was particularly impressed with the use of electricity for cooking and water heating. British stations still used coal.

CHAPTER 14

Punishment for the enemy

On 13th August 1942, when General Montgomery took command of the 8th Army in the Middle East, the German army, commanded by Irwin Rommel was threatening Alexandria. Although it did not seem like it at the time, this was to be the turning point in the Desert War, and in fact on all fronts. The German army was stretched to its greatest limits in Russia, having reached the outskirts of Moscow and Leningrad, and having captured Stalingrad. There were to be no further advances. In the Middle East, Rommel was to be held and repulsed at El Alamein.

No 44 Squadron take the fight to the enemy
In Europe, the summer of 1942 had seen the disaster of the raid on Dieppe, which seemed to prove the invincibility of the German Atlantic defences. However, in the air the Germans were not so invincible. Night after night, the heavy bombers of No 44 (Rhodesia) Squadron roared into the attack and stories of their exploits appeared in the *Rhodesia Herald*:

> *Pilot Officer Grimwood Cooke DFC DFM, one of the best-known Rhodesian bomber pilots, told guests at Rhodesia House in London, the other day, that he had never regretted choosing bomber-flying, if only because of the comradeship among the crews. His navigator is a New Zealander, his wireless operator a Scot and his gunner a Canadian. "A bomber gives a wonderful panoramic view of interesting country," he said, "and an opportunity to study and see the whole drama of the operations. Take that attack on the Renault works in Paris. To time the attack correctly, we toured Paris for half an hour. There was a bright moon and the whole city was lit up with flares from the earlier arrivals. Flak and searchlights were almost negligible." "While watching the earlier squadrons do their stuff I saw the Arc de Triomphe, the Eiffel Tower and the famous boulevards. When our turn came, we easily found the target, but the air was so full of our own machines we had to keep careful watch to avoid collision. After dropping medium bombs, we circled for some time to watch the heavy bombs dropped by the later arrivals. As we left the scene my wireless operator said 'Gosh! What a lovely sight!' so we turned for another look. Finally, setting a course home, he started singing 'The Last Time I saw Paris'. We all joined in." "My worst experience was on my fourth raid over Kiel. It was a stormy night with some mist and no horizon. I came down to 11,000 feet but as I still could not see much I went to 9,000 and then saw another aircraft caught in the searchlights. We went in but half the searchlights turned on us and we flew blind throwing the aircraft about to avoid the flak. My instruments toppled and I asked the navigator, 'Are we upside down?' He replied, 'By gosh we are! The stars are below us!' I dived to 1,500 feet, righting the machine and climbed up again to 8,000 feet but again the searchlights got us. Fortunately, there was cloud just near the target area. We circled it and then made our own attack, dropped our bombs, climbed above the clouds and made for home."* (Rhodesia Herald, 11th Sept. 1942)

Of course there were casualties. On the night of 13th/14th September, a Lancaster went down over the Zuider Zee, taking with it: Flying Officer Christopher (Chips) Thomas Holland; Sergeant Wireless Operator Donald Norman Huntley DFM; and Flight Sergeant Robert Ernest Williams (all Rhodesians). Other members of the crew were Pilot Officer Lovegrove, Sergeant Murphy and Sergeant Fidler. The bodies were later washed up on the Dutch coast. Sergeant Alec Goodyear, a Rhodesian, was the only crewmember to survive. He managed to swim to the coast and was taken prisoner of war.

Operation Robinson

To put every operational Lancaster into a single attack in daylight, seemed questionable to say the least but this is what was planned for the middle of October 1942. At this stage No 5 Group was the only bomber group operating Lancasters, apart from those allocated to the pathfinders, that could put nine Lancaster squadrons into the air. On 1st October, the four-engine bombers flew in magnificent procession across the English countryside, while fighters made mock attacks and wallowed in the slipstream. The Lancasters fanned out over the Wash and reconverged to drop their bombs on Wainfleet bombing range. This was the trial run. The real thing was planned for two weeks later. It was to be a daylight attack on the extensive Schneider Armament Works, the French equivalent of Krupps, located at Le Creusot near the Swiss frontier.

Secrecy was vital and the code name given to this operation, Robinson, was perhaps too allusive. The flight was planned to proceed at zero height, in order to evade German radar, and to arrive at the target area as the sun was setting. This would enable bombing to take place as dusk was falling and allow the aircraft the cover of darkness for the return journey. A total of 94 Lancasters, including nine from No 44 Squadron, took part in this raid.

The weather report on the morning of 17th October was good and Operation Robinson received the go-ahead. Security being of top priority, crews were only informed of the target minutes before take-off, while visitors to No 5 Group stations were only allowed to leave after the bombers were airborne. Once in the air, the Lancasters, coming from many different airfields made rendezvous over Upper Heyford. Meanwhile, Whitleys from Coastal Command, were sweeping the Channel to spot any E-boats that might radio a warning and to ensure that any prowling U-boats kept their noses down.

No 49 Squadron, under the command of Wing Commander L.C. Slee, led the bombers over Land's End, and, skimming the waves, headed south-west across the Bay of Biscay, to turn in over the French coast. It was exhilarating for the gunners as the scene below flashed past: chickens scattered and took to the air as the slipstream hit them; a team of oxen stampeded with the result that a neat pattern of furrows ended abruptly in a wild zigzag; some French civilians waved, but most were apprehensive.

The only opposition came from a covey of partridges, and resulted in slight damage to two aircraft. It was a tiring flight at this low level. The pilots had to maintain vigilant watch for any obstructions, while the navigators checked locations and times and the gunners assisted as additional lookouts to warn of higher ground or large buildings.

Forty-four miles (70km) from their objective the aircraft fanned out, and, precisely to the minute [planned], 18h09, the first Lancaster dropped its bomb load. Seven minutes later, the last bomb hit the ground and the Lancasters turned for home. A further group of bombers hit the Henri Paul transformer and switching station at Monchanin.

As darkness fell, 93 Lancasters raced back towards England and safety. At Command and Group headquarters and at the home bases their return was awaited with apprehension. When the scheduled time of return came and went, 23 aircraft were overdue. Inevitably, some would have strayed off course, or had engine trouble. The minutes ticked by and one by one the overdue aircraft checked in, until, after a further 15 minutes only 12 Lancasters were still unaccounted for. Gradually news was heard from these. Finally, only one aircraft, W4774 flown by Squadron Leader W.D. Carr, which had been seen to crash near Monchanin, had not returned. Apart from the members of that crew, one flight engineer had been killed by the only German opposition in the air, three Arado Seaplanes, which the Lancaster met as they crossed the coast near Brest. The navigator of this bomber, Flight Sergeant William James Rose of Melsetter, was later awarded the DFM. His aircraft was flying just four feet above the sea when it was attacked. In the resulting action, two enemy aircraft were shot down and a third driven off. According to the citation, it was due to Rose's assistance and subsequent navigation that the damaged aircraft was brought safely to a British aerodrome. This raid certainly resulted in light losses but the damage that had been done to the target was vastly overestimated, and later it was shown that in fact the factory was hardly harmed at all.

First flights over the Alps

Later in the same month, on 22nd October 1942, came the first over the Alps flight. A strong force of aircraft from Bomber Command attacked the port and naval base at Genoa, in Italy. The weather over the target was good and in the bright moonlight, many large fires were seen. Two days later the target was Milan. Flight Lieutenant Bill Whamond gave a first hand account of the raid:

Milan was my only daylight raid. At first the Lancs and fighters flew so low we had to swing round a convoy in the Channel. There was cloud over the French coast so we went high up and when the cloud broke, found the Lancs still there in formation. Then down we went to treetop level across France, where for a long time I flew alone. The people did not seem to be aware of us till we had passed. I saw a farmer ploughing straight furrows but the horses got scared and the furrows zigzagged. I saw crowded railway platforms and the open mouth of an amazed Gendarme. Children playing in school grounds ran to shelter but some grown-ups waved to us. There were no enemy fighters. After keeping close to the ground for as long as possible we climbed the French Alps, seeing Lake Geneva and Mont Blanc. As we descended on the other side flak was already bursting above the clouds as the first Lancs were attacking. It was an amazing picture for me who had never before seen a target clearly laid out in daylight. The flak was very wild. I located my target, dropped my bombs, and then circled for 15 minutes. The homeward journey was uneventful except for flak over the French coast. Most of the aircrew, in fact, seemed more impressed with the grandeur of the Alps than the raid.

Pilot Officer Thomas (Tommy) Gerald Hackney, who was awarded a DFC for his part in raids on Italian targets, died on the night of 6th/7th November over Genoa. No 44 Squadron carried out one further attack on Turin and then it was back to German targets again.

Raids during November alternated between German and Italian targets. On the 6th Osnabrück was bombed in daylight, and the following night, as troops formed up for the North African landings, Lancasters attacked Rommel's main supply base at Genoa. This was followed by a particularly heavy attack on Turin on 21st November.

On 6th December 1942, Grimwood Cooke celebrated his 21st birthday. Two days later, he and Bill Picken attended their investiture at Buckingham Palace where Grimwood was invested with the DFC and DFM and Bill with the DFC. On 11th December, Grimwood rejoined his old squadron, No 106, for his second tour. The crew bombed Duisberg on 20th/21st December, but failed to return from a raid on Munich on the 21st/22nd. His twin brother, Sergeant Airgunner Harold Cooke, had died six months earlier on the third thousand-bomber raid on Bremen on 25th/26th June.

INDICATES AREA
ENLARGED

No. 44 SQUADRON
GOES OVER THE ALPS

Details of Flight Lieutenant Cooke's death were later given to the Red Cross by a prisoner of war, Pilot Officer Philip Moore, who had been the navigator on Cooke's aircraft and was the only survivor. Pilot Officer Moore said that the Lancaster was so seriously damaged by enemy action that it turned over and plunged vertically, breaking up as it dived. Owing to the condition of the aircraft and the speed at which the disaster occurred, it was impossible for any of the crew to bale out. Moore literally fell out through the broken fuselage. His parachute opened just as he came down in the branches of an oak tree. The aircraft crashed a few hundred yards away and no one else managed to escape. Flight Lieutenant Cooke and four members of his crew were buried in the municipal cemetery at Beaufort en Argonne, in northern France. The grave site of the seventh man is unknown but his name is listed at Runnymede. Closing the year, 1942, Air Chief Marshal, Sir Arthur Harris, paid tribute to the men under his command:

> There are no words with which I can do justice to the aircrew men who fought under my command. There is no parallel in wartime to such courage and determination in the face of danger over so prolonged a period.

By the end of the year, British bomber strength was only 78 medium and 261 heavy bombers but the pathfinders were proving their worth. On clear nights they were marking the targets with 75% accuracy. However, when clouds obscured the ground, it was still largely a matter of hit or miss. The men who manned the bombers during 1942 had a one-in-three chance of surviving a tour of 30 operational flights. On an average, four to six percent casualties could be expected on each raid. To bale out of a crippled fighter over the sea had its risks; but the chance of surviving was good. The imprisoned crew of a bomber, flaming crazily down towards a blazing city in the Ruhr had less hope.

The courage required by the bomber's crewmen can only be compared with an infantryman who month after month was launched into heavy attacks twice a week. Strangely, the greatest source of strain seems to have been the cancelled mission, and frequently in the Operations Log-book the words: 12 aircraft detailed but operation subsequently cancelled appeared.

Prisoners of war

What of the fate of the men who baled out, survived and became prisoners of war? Writing from Stalag VIII B, Sergeant Observer Basil Henry Glasse says:

> The Christmas decorations are occupying everyone's time at present, making all the barracks cheerful in aspect. It is amazing what can be done with cigarette packets, coloured paper off Red Cross boxes, silver paper and raffia straw. Most designs are air force in theme. Some have even built creditable model aircraft. One section in our old barrack even made a sort of coat-of-arms in red, white and blue. In the four quadrants are: an aircraft 'coned' in searchlights; a big liner; an airmail letter and a Red Cross parcel. Vertically up the middle is inscribed: 'A little piece of England in the heart of Germany'. Across the middle is 'Greetings 1943'. On a scroll is 'Salute those giving life for their country' (in Latin). Altogether a work of art!

In a January 1943 letter, he wrote:

> The snow has come to stay but we keep warm by chopping wood for our fires. It is still remarkably mild. Am playing in another bridge competition. My partner and I were knocked out in the quarterfinals of the last through going down 1,700 in a slam—a bit of bad management. We were able to visit other compounds in the camp over Christmas, quite a pleasant change! School

has started again and I am continuing with Spanish and economics. I gave a talk on Rhodesia the other day to a discussion group, here. They all seem interested and full of questions. Had a lively discussion on the native question with a philanthropic member. Alan Hurrell of Hunter's Road helped greatly with information, being a pioneer's son. I believe he has a great future. In parcels, don't bother to send anything but chocolate and perhaps a towel or a pair of socks. The former has more value than clothes. (Basil Glasse)

Fighters over France

While the Lancasters were thundering over Germany and Italy, the men of No 266 (Rhodesia) Squadron, flying Spitfires and Typhoons were engaged in fighter sweeps over occupied France and Belgium. One typical sweep took place on 15th September 1942 when the Operations Record reports:

Rain early. Rest of day fine. Ops. Flying 12 aircraft with Nos 609 and 56 Squadrons under Wing Commander W.E. Gillam took off from Exeter to cover withdrawal of bombers after bombing Cherbourg. Swept just off north coast of Cherbourg peninsular and saw Sergeant (John Llewellyn) Spence's aircraft smoking and heard him say he would bale out. He did so about 25 miles from Cherbourg and was seen sitting in a dinghy. Six aircraft orbited him for nearly 30 minutes and got fixes, had to leave then as aircraft out of petrol, Air-Sea Rescue tried to get him but no luck. Wind north-west 7. Sea roughish. Half squadron landed at Ibsley. Other half Warmwell. On taking off to fly back to Duxford, Sergeant Peter Blackwell's engine failed and he crash-landed. Aircraft smashed but pilot although trapped in the aircraft for 20 minutes was not hurt. On landing near dusk at Duxford, Pilot Officer Barney Wright's aircraft, the first to land, swung and the undercarriage broke. The other aircraft landed successfully. Sergeant Wally Mollett's aircraft was run into by a Spit at Warmwell early the next day and was smashed; the pilot was not in it.

16th September. Windy. Fine. Visibility good. Ops: No news of Sergeant Spence. Eight aircraft swept from Matlock out to within 20 miles of Dutch coast. Then patrolled along it up to De Koy and then back. Bombers should have bombed harbour but returned as weather u/s. Nothing of interest. Pilot Officer (George) Elcombe caught wheel in wire fence on landing at Matlock but although oleo support broke aircraft remained on wheels.

Life at Warmwell

On 19th September a terrific party was held in the evening, beginning in the mess and concluding at the Bull Hotel, to celebrate the squadron's move from Duxford to Warmwell.

21st September. Train Party, Flying Officer Pickard in charge, marched to station with band and was seen off by Station Adjutant. Various motor cars off. Aircraft held up by bad weather till 16h25. Then 13 aircraft off without mishap.

22nd September. Warmwell. Cold and rainy. Except for this disappointing change in temperature, all personnel pleased with new station. Officers' mess is fine and sleeping quarters attractively situated on a millstream. Bit overcrowded and as yet rather sparsely furnished.

23rd September. Warmer. Sunny. Operations: three patrols scrambled but all without incident. Dusk patrol by two aircraft without incident but landing procedure with new lights considered incorrect by our pilots. Party for CO's birthday.

October 1942 came and went with little activity but one morale raiser when Squadron Leader Charles Green and Flying Officer Monty Bell, on a weather recce were chased by three FW 190s. All aircraft were flying at zero feet and:

Owing to high closing speed, it was impossible to get sights on the enemy and they passed through our sector. The FWs turned and started to chase us but could not catch up and abandoned the chase after a minute. It is pleasant to know that we are faster than the FW 190 on the deck.
(Squadron Diary)

There was also one unfortunate, though luckily not fatal, incident soon after the squadron's arrival at Warmwell. Pilot Officer J. Dennis Miller, failing to see the direction of the Glim lamps ran crooked off the flare path and crashed into a quarry. The aircraft turned over on its back but owing to the strong construction of the Typhoon, the pilot was unhurt. Dennis Miller was a tall man but Charles Green managed to haul him from the tangled wreckage through an incredibly small hole. John Deall remarked: Looking at it later, no one could imagine how we'd managed it!

A typical story from around this time was told by an unnamed squadron pilot, who was escorting Flying Fortresses on a bombing raid over Belgium, when he was jumped by a number of Focke-Wulf 190s. There was a bang behind him and a burning sensation in his left arm:

"Without further hesitation I broke left in a steep turn and saw six streams of bullets go flashing by to starboard—not really very healthy." Two machine gun-bullets had come in through the door. One had hit the pilot's arm, the other had grazed his knee and ended up in the self-sealing petrol tank. The controls didn't feel too good in the steep turn so he decided to 'get out of the way and quick too'. Down he went in a vertical dive, starting at about 25,000 feet. "Owing to the controls being ropey, I think the aircraft assumed a past-the-vertical attitude and no amount of winding the tail-trim back or pulling on the stick would rectify it. This continued down to a height of about 5,000 feet with me battling the whole way to try to get the thing right way up and getting tossed about like a pea-in-a-pod." "Finally it became evident that something drastic was necessary if a smoking heap of debris somewhere in Belgium was to be prevented. I wound the elevator trim forward and pushed the stick in the same direction. We came out of the dive, inverted and doing about 500 mph (800 km/h). My feet left the rudder bars. I was lying against the hood so hard that I could hear the perspex or the glass in my goggles crackling despite the fact that I was strapped in tightly. The seat mountings on the wing roots creaked and groaned; the pressure of blood in my head caused some small blood vessels in my eyes to burst making the whites bloodshot but otherwise doing no harm." During all this activity, the cockpit window had become so blurred that the pilot could see nothing. Eventually it cleared enough for him to realize that he was now heading almost vertically upwards and upside down. With another effort he righted the plane and began to think about heading home. "I wiped some of the muck off the windscreen and saw Dunkirk ahead so shoved the nose down and flew low over the place and out to sea. The compass glass was cracked but fortunately the 'woiks' were ok for eventually I rolled up at Manston, where I landed. On the way across the sea I got rid of the hood, for I was feeling sick and thought that I might feel faint later and have to bale out. Owing to the fact that I wasn't feeling too hot and nearly collapsed after climbing out of the plane, I didn't make an examination to see how much damage was done, but I have since heard that there were chunks of the tail missing." (Rhodesia Herald, 7th Nov. 1942)

During November, the weather deteriorated and on one occasion after an operations scramble in 10/10 cloud, rockets had to be fired to guide the aircraft back to the airfield. Scrambles, after real or imagined enemy aircraft, were an almost daily occurrence, but it was following a recce over Cherbourg that Flight Lieutenant Tony Johnston experienced his most embarrassing moment. He spotted an aircraft that appeared to take evasive action by flying into a cloud, and as it emerged, Johnston gave it a short burst of fire from about 600 yards (550m). Fortunately, none of his bullets hit the mark because the aircraft turned out to be a Typhoon. To compound his embarrassment, on his return to base Johnston collided with a steamroller while taxiing in. According to the squadron log-book: …the driver of which baled out. The steamroller was not damaged. Two days later, on 20th November, the squadron log-book reported: Flight Lieutenant Johnston promoted to Squadron Leader of No 56 Squadron. Not as a result of his exploits two days ago!

A pilot who was not so lucky was Ossy Osborne. On 28th November, on a training exercise, the squadron flew into cloud. Ossy lost formation and hit the deck. During the same exercise, Flying Officer Monty Bell also ran into trouble in cloud and tried to bale out but when the door jettison lever failed to operate he was forced to fly on, and he came out of the cloud safely with the rest of the squadron.

At Warmwell the first officers' billets were in a water mill. According to squadron members it was a wizard spot with plenty of fish in the stream.

David Garrick who was with the squadron during that period revisited the area in 1974:

Just recently (1974) I went to Weymouth and on the return journey passed through Warmwell where we had a good billet for the squadron. The two main blister hangars and several of the huts are still in good condition after approximately 32 years. The squadron's sojourn at Warmwell and at Harrowbeer, were periods of good friendship and hard-working times for all personnel.

The last few days of the year, 1942, saw the squadron, over Bayeux in France, carrying out its first attacks on locomotives, a feat for which 266 pilots were to become famous. The squadron log-book reads:

> *Squadron Leader Charles Green made one attack on a loco and was met by concentrated fire from a Bofors gun but was not hit and saw strikes on a loco and a quantity of steam issue from it. Flying Officer Frederick Brian Biddulph could not make the attack because of oil on the windscreen.*

The year ended with the roof of the King's Arms at Warmwell lifting to the strains of Sarie Marais, while in the mess the Rhodesian officers and sergeants were soundly and ingloriously thrashed in a beer-drinking relay match by their comrades from another squadron.

CHAPTER 15

Limelight on 266

The year 1942 had ended with Hitler facing his first major defeats. Rommel had been thrown back at El Alamein and was in retreat. By 18th January 1943, Montgomery's 8th Army had entered Tripoli. Meanwhile, a wide offensive had been launched by the Russians, forcing the Germans to withdraw from the Caucasus. By mid-January the Siege of Leningrad had been raised and on 31st January General Paulus surrendered the frozen, starving, ammunitionless remnant of 21 German divisions in Stalingrad. In their encircling movement, the Russians took 90,000 German prisoners. During the previous November, American troops had landed in Algeria, a move that resulted in the Germans moving troops into previously unoccupied areas of southern France.

Despite these successes, British civilians were still being killed in German air raids, with a death toll of 743 for the last five months of 1942. The winter and early spring of 1943 saw No 266 (Rhodesia) Squadron heavily involved endeavouring to intercept the German raiders. In fact, 1943 began with orders for yet another move, this time to Exeter in Devon.

This was not welcome news to anybody. We have now got settled at Warmwell and like it. It takes us still further from enemy-occupied land. We are to leave our maintenance behind which has done us very good service and is partly Rhodesian. The idea of having the squadron split half at Exeter and half at Bolt Head does not sound convenient. (Squadron Record)

Orders are orders and so after a farewell binge at Warmwell, the move to Exeter was carried out. Remembering the time in Exeter, David Garrick said:

Damage by forced landings ran in cycles, I think, and replacements were not quick in arriving. Whilst at Exeter we had four planes awaiting replacements of engines. It was said that when the fitters got them they had to clear out birds' nests, which had been built in the frames, before they could start work. Several funny things happened at Exeter. On one occasion, one of the squadron armourers (Webster by name) overlooked unloading one cannon, pressed the gun button and sent cannon shells shooting all over the countryside. Luckily, a search revealed no damage to anyone. On another occasion, Flight Lieutenant Barney Wright's fitter, a Rhodesian, Bob Tink, was running up the Tiffy engines, and failed to notice a poor WAAF passing the back of the plane. The force spread-eagled the poor girl against the wall, and all the savings stamps etc. she was carrying to our office went miles away. The squadron was encouraged to buy savings stamps and on instructions from the adjutant, I sat near the pay table taking the money. We had a barometer in the building showing how much the boys were saving and this went up one wall and started across the ceiling. We did not, however, know just how many stamps were redeemed so that a good night out could be had in Exeter. (David Garrick)

No 266 makes its first 'kill' of the war

Early in the year the Germans began a series of tip-and-run raids, aimed at the south coast of Britain and it was during one such raid, on 10th January, that the squadron got its first kill of 1943. The story was carried in the *Rhodesia Herald*:

A 31-year-old Shamva pilot, Flying Officer John Small, former manager of a gold mine in Southern Rhodesia, this afternoon destroyed a Focke-Wulf 190 in full view of people on the front at a coastal resort (Torquay). Another Rhodesian pilot, aged 21, from Salisbury Flying Officer Peter Blackwell was in the same engagement. It was a bright day with good visibility when eight FW 190s made their raid, dropping their bombs not on Torquay as reported but on Teignmouth. Flying Officer Small and Pilot Officer Peter Blackwell gave chase and closed fast, firing finally at a distance of 100 yards, as the raiders were actually over the Torquay beachfront. As the raiders turned and streaked for home, Small fired another burst shooting the enemy aircraft down into the sea 500 yards from the coast. Johnny Small said later, "The last burst caused a big flash in the raider's fuselage and he crashed into the sea with a tremendous splash. I was following so closely that I flew straight through the fountain of water, which the Focke-Wulf threw up." The debris and waterspout caused slight damage to his radiator and cowling but he returned to base safely. Peter chased the other Focke-Wulf 20 miles out to sea and "Got close enough to see my fire striking the radiator and causing flashes, but could not claim a second victory, and was forced to return to base when my ammunition ran out. Still one FW destroyed and one damaged was 'a damn good start at Exeter'!"

The following day the squadron endured a loss which marred their high spirits.

11th January. Lost our 'B' flight commander today. Flight Lieutenant Tommy Thompson. Four aircraft took off at dawn. Went over France. Tommy, flying 'Q' developed engine trouble and landed OK in France. Last message on R/T 'Goodbye boys. Write to Ma'. Believed to have destroyed his aircraft and been taken prisoner. (Peter Penfold)

Four aircraft, Squadron Leader Charles Green, Flying Officer Deall, Flight Lieutenant James Clack (Tommy) Thompson and Flying Officer John Robert Dison (Bob) Menelaws took off at first light to do Rhubarb (railway attack) at St Brieuc. Just after crossing the French coast, Thompson said on R/T that he had had it and must force-land and his aircraft was seen emitting smoke and glycol. He slowed down and the other three aircraft drew ahead. They were just going to turn round to see how he had managed, when some ack-ack opened up on them, so Squadron Leader Charles Green ordered the task to be abandoned, and they headed east for the coast, getting quite a bit of AA, which may have come from the Le Lain, St Brieuc Aerodrome, but returned safely to base. (Operational Record)

Later comment states:

Tommy Thompson now a POW. Very browned off.

The squadron carried out patrols several times a day whatever the weather. On 26th January their persistence was rewarded, despite an unfortunate mix-up earlier in the operation.

Fine and warm. Ops: Squadron Leader Green and three others went on shipping recce. One section to Cape Brehat, thence to Sept Isle. The other from Sept Isle to Isle de Batz. No shipping or enemy aircraft seen. On returning to base, heard another section being scrambled, so these four aircraft joined in the hunt but saw nothing. Flight Lieutenant Barney Wright on a scramble was vectored over Torquay and all AA opened up on him. His R/T procedure for the next few minutes was highly incorrect and it became obvious that he was being vectored after himself. The camp also at this time had some excitement as while 12 Venturas were taking off for an offensive sortie, the camp siren blew and then machine-gun fire was heard (let off accidentally). When the Venturas and the Spitfire escort were returning, Flying Officer Monty Bell and Sergeant Noel Vincent Borland were scrambled to intercept six FW 190s, which had crossed the coast near Torquay. After passing the Spitfires, Flying Officer Bell saw one FW 190 going south from Dartmouth. He chased it at zero feet, overtaking it easily and shot it down with three bursts. It plunged smoking into the sea about 12 miles south-south-east of Start Point. One FW 190 destroyed by Flying Officer Bell. Sergeant Borland had had trouble in starting but arrived just in time to see the smoke from the downed enemy aircraft and a Spitfire pilot came and took a ciné film of the wreckage. While Monty Bell 'bagged' a 190, Flying Officer Susie Wilson only collected a car with his propeller while taxiing. Peter Penfold remarked, "It didn't do either the plane or the car much good." (Operations Record)

February 1943 was a bad month for the Rhodesian squadron. On 2nd February Flight Sergeant Edgar Vincent Horne died when his Typhoon crashed into a hill at Brampton while on a non-operational flight. On the following day, Flying Officer (Dinger) Bell died during the fourth of five anti-raider patrols. His aircraft engine failed at 500 feet while he was ten miles (16km) out to sea over Torbay. He jettisoned the hood and doors and ditched his Typhoon, apparently successfully but did not get out in time, although the aircraft floated for five seconds. He may have been knocked unconscious. The aircraft sank, leaving nothing but a patch of oil on the surface.

Bell's No 2, Sergeant George Eastwood, orbited the position until he was relieved by Yellow Section. Later a Walrus and a Defiant joined the search and finally a motor launch was sent out from Torquay but nothing was found and Flying Officer Bell was presumed drowned. According to Peter Penfold, Dinger had a premonition that this would happen and he often pulled the emergency door release to test it. He'd damaged several doors this way as they hit the concrete when the aircraft was parked. (Peter Penfold)

This inability to land the Typhoon safely on water was a serious drawback. The Typhoon had been designed with a large scoop-like radiator. When the aircraft was ditched, this took in water causing the aircraft to dive straight to the bottom.

Four days later, Squadron Leader Green had engine failure over the sea. He reported that he would try to reach the coast in a glide, but would bale out if his aircraft dropped below 4,000 feet before reaching land. Fortunately, his engine continued to tick over and he reached Bolt Head Aerodrome where he made a wheels-up landing. Even this was a considerable feat, because the large propeller tended to bite into the ground, causing the aircraft to roll.

Sergeant Eastwood, the No 2 on this occasion, on his second flight with the squadron, seems to have been a bit of an albatross, because his first flight was in company with Dinger Bell.

Another prang, on 13th February, involved Pilot Officer J.D. Tusky Haworth. Following an operation to provide high rear cover for aircraft returning from a bombing attack on St Malo, Tusky's throttle control broke and he was forced to land on the football pitch next to the cookhouse. Somehow he managed to bring the Typhoon in under the high-tension wires but hit a tree with his starboard wing. The pilot was unhurt but the aircraft was almost a write-off.

The first successful 'ditching'

It seemed that all news was bad until an event occurred that lifted squadron morale considerably. The whole story was detailed jubilantly in the Operations Record:

20th February. Fine warm. Ops. Four anti-raider operations. On one of which the section saw an aircraft going fast at zero feet out to sea. Flying Officer John Small was sure it was a Hun by the way it was behaving and 'Tally-hoe'd' but when near saw it was a Liberator. They had been going fast and Flying Officer Mike Furber's engine suddenly cut. He said he was baling out and undid his straps but had insufficient height and had to ditch with his straps undone. Somehow or other he got away with it and got out of the sinking aircraft and into his dinghy. Flying Officer John Small did not hear him baling out and was on his way back to base. Then both he and Yellow Section went back and found Furber in his dinghy and eventually got a trawler-mine sweeper from a nearby convoy to pick him up. Lucky man!

This event proved to the men of No 266 (Rhodesia) Squadron that a ditching at sea could be accomplished. More good news was reported in the *Rhodesia Herald* on 6th March but referred to an event which took place on 26th February as told by Squadron Leader Green:

"We were flying off the coast, when we were told that FWs had just dropped bombs. We hared off in the direction given and suddenly saw pinpoints on the horizon. We guessed they were the Huns beating it for home so we set off in pursuit." "We went flat out at sea level for ten minutes gradually drawing up. There were eight FWs in line abreast, so I stalked up to within 150 yards of the one on the left and gave him a burst of cannon fire. His wheels dropped, his hood flew off and there was a big flash from the engine." Squadron Leader Green then saw a stream of something white, probably petrol, pouring from the aircraft, so he transferred his attack to another FW. "Once again my first burst brought the same result. His wheels dropped and pieces flew off but he was not done, so I closed to about 50 yards and sent him crashing into the water." Squadron Leader Green then turned to see what had happened to the first FW and found his No 2 just about to finish it off. I yelled on the radio 'Close well up to him!' No 2 took me at my word and blew the Hun into the water in pieces. For a moment I thought he would be brought down himself by the showers of debris and water through which he had to fly, but he came out all right and we flew home with our tails up." In fact, in this engagement Sergeant (Bundu) Thompson who was flying as No 2 had his aircraft damaged by pieces, which flew off the 190. (Rhodesia Herald, 6th March 1943)

The following day, 27th February, Sergeant Charles Baillie force-landed in a field six miles (10km) from the aerodrome with a broken throttle. This was the third such accident in a month and resulted in the squadron being grounded on 1st March, pending the fitting of a strengthened unit. This order was, however, rescinded on 2nd March owing to the need to continue with the anti-intruder patrols. Meanwhile serviceability was terribly low so no ops flying. On one patrol, a seagull put Flight Lieutenant Ian Munro's aircraft unserviceable and Sergeant George Eastwood's unserviceable from the same cause the day before. Even the birds conspire against us! (Operations Record)

As far as catching the enemy raiders was concerned, it was largely a matter of luck. John Deall says:

The 190s flew in low to avoid the radar, popped in over the coast, dropped their bombs and headed back. With this kind of hit-and-run raid, there was little hope of catching the enemy unless you were in the air at the time. My first taste of action occurred when Scottie-Eadie and I were patrolling on 13th March and saw the Germans bombing a village near Dartmouth. We actually saw the smoke from the bombs. We went in to the attack, destroying two and damaging one. Scottie was known as the 'Old Boy' because he was 27 years old. There were twins on the squadron too. Name of Borland. Came from Northern Rhodesia, like Scottie.

During March 1943, Sergeant Peters cheated fate when his engine cut at 50 feet as he was coming in to land. He was not so lucky in April when he crashed into the sea about four miles (6km) off Prawle Point. Flight Lieutenant Ian Munro witnessed the crash and later spotted an open parachute and a body floating on the water. An Air Sea Rescue launch was called and Peters's body was recovered. He made no R/T transmission so the cause of the crash could not be determined but he was flying at zero feet at the time and it is probable that he misjudged his height and flew into the sea accidentally.

A busy day

Two days later, Flight Sergeant George Eastwood had an experience, which could have proved more serious than it did. The incident occurred just after dawn on 17th April, when Flight Sergeant Eastwood encountered five Spitfires escorting a motor torpedo boat. One of the Spitfires broke away and flew into attack Flight Sergeant Eastwood's Typhoon. Squadron Operations Record remarks tersely:

> *Why on earth the Spitfire should break away from its formation and carry out a long drawn out attack on a Typhoon at short range is difficult to understand. Flight Sergeant Eastwood managed to fly his aircraft over land and baled out successfully. He would have crashed if he had tried to force-land as his aileron had been shot away.*

Commenting on the event, Peter Penfold said He was brought back on a farm cart giggling his head off. No doubt from shock. In the evening of the same day, Squadron Leader Charles Green and Flying Officer John Deall scrambled after two enemy aircraft attacking Plymouth.

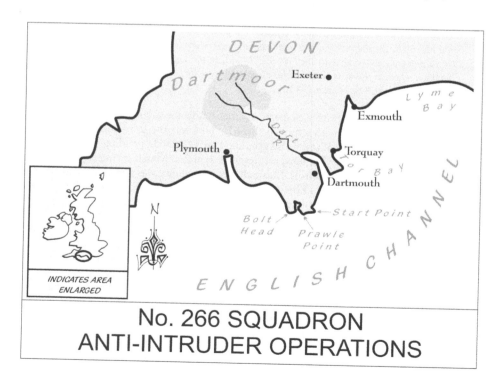

INDICATES AREA ENLARGED

No. 266 SQUADRON
ANTI-INTRUDER OPERATIONS

The enemy aircraft were chased back over the English Channel. About 40 miles (64km) from the French coast a dogfight occurred. As the Operations Record relates:

The Jerry pilots showed themselves to be experienced and a very hectic five minutes was spent by our pilots, who were severely handicapped as only one cannon on Flying Officer Deall's aircraft was firing. Each pilot claimed one FW 190 damaged.

And the day was not over yet as the log-book reported:

At 23h00 that night, a Whitley bomber crashed within a few yards of the servicing flight billets. It was a near miss for about 50 men who were in their beds at the time. Two crewmen in the bomber were killed in the fire and resulting explosion.

The end of April and beginning of May saw two further accidents. On 30th April, Sergeant Henderson had engine failure on take-off, tried to force-land, hit a tree, cartwheeled and was severely injured. Three days later, Flight Lieutenant Ian Munro was test-flying an aircraft when, during a dive, his wing appeared to break off, followed by the tail. After this, the aircraft spiralled into the ground. He had no chance to bale out.

Flying during May 1943 was curtailed owing to aircraft modifications but the time was spent profitably practising dinghy drill, using new sails. Squadron members also visited West Lulworth to view new types of tanks and take a ride in a Churchill Tank. The bumpy trip, over rather rough ground, was followed by a slap-up party in Weymouth. Another first-class binge was held in May to celebrate the double weddings of Squadron Leader Charles Green and Flying Officer John Small. The month ended on an exciting note of a different kind:

On 30th May there was a big panic 'scramble'; all the squadrons went up, when 24 FW 190s bombed Torquay. No 193 Squadron knocked down six. Our squadron was just too late to engage. Pilot Officer Wally Mollett ran into the tail of a High Altitude Spitfire of 124 Squadron. We had several wheel changes to do on the squadron's return. (Peter Penfold)

During the scramble, John Deall was fired at by a Spitfire. It seems that Spitfire pilots have a grudge against Typhoons. (Operations Record)

Bombphoons

In June 1943, the squadron moved back to Harrowber, in South Devon. From this airfield fighter sweeps over the Channel and into northern France were conducted flying Typhoons, which had been modified to carry bombs, and renamed Bombphoons.

On 17th June, it was Flying Officer Haig Allenby Cooper's turn for a lucky escape. Following a scramble after a possible enemy aircraft, his No 1, Flight Lieutenant Barney Wright, was 26 miles (42km) south of Bolt Head, flying at zero feet when Cooper called on the R/T to report engine failure, and to say he was going to bale out.

However, on trying to escape from the aircraft, Cooper became entangled in the wireless aerial and was only able to free himself at about 500 feet. By the time his parachute opened, he was only about 300 feet above the sea. On hitting the water, he became badly snarled in the shroud lines of his parachute and it was several minutes before he could free himself. During this process, he was forced to undo the dog lead which secured his dinghy and it floated out of reach.

Flight Lieutenant Barney Wright orbiting to get a fix, spotted the problem and cut his own dinghy clear of his parachute with the intention of dropping it to Flying Officer Cooper.

Unfortunately, the partly opened dinghy fouled Wright's tail plane making his aircraft difficult to control but despite this Wright continued to orbit the area until he was relieved by other aircraft. About 50 minutes later a Walrus arrived on the scene and landed to pick Cooper up but then was unable to take off again and was forced to taxi until an Air Sea Rescue launch arrived. Whereupon Cooper was transferred and the Walrus was able to get back into the air. The operational account ends with the laconic comment: He is ok.

Two further engine failures, resulting in successful bale-outs occurred on 19th and 20th June. The first involved Pilot Officer Bundu Thompson and the second, Pilot Officer Noel Borland. Comment in the Ops Log-book sums up the squadron feeling, A very successful bale-out but two bale-outs and one forced landing all caused by engine failure in five days are most discouraging. These engine failure problems resulted in the Rhodesian squadron having to enlist the support of No 183 Squadron in mounting its anti-intruder patrols.

Charles Green leaves the squadron

The following day, 22nd June, Squadron Leader Charles Green travelled up to London to collect his DFC. The citation stated that he had an impressive record of operational flights, had displayed outstanding leadership together with an intense desire to engage the enemy. By his example and keenness, he had raised the effectiveness of his squadron to a very high standard. But even Squadron Leader Green could not improve the serviceability record of the Typhoons, which had been pushed into combat before sufficient development had been done on the newly designed engines.

Following the award of his DFC, Charles Green was promoted to wing commander and was posted as chief flying instructor to an operational training unit in the north of England. Charles Green had joined No 266 (Rhodesia) Squadron as a flying officer in May 1941, becoming a flight commander in the following month. Five months later he became the squadron's first Rhodesian commanding officer. Wing Commander Green was succeeded as commanding officer by another Salisbury pilot, 24-year-old Squadron Leader A.S. (Sandy) MacIntyre. Sandy initially trained with the air unit, but completed his training in England, before going to East Africa to serve with No 237 (Rhodesia) Squadron where he took part in the Abyssinian Campaign, and in the 1941 advance on Benghazi. At the time, No 266 Squadron flight commanders were Flight Lieutenant John Deall from Umtali and Flight Lieutenant Barney Wright of Salisbury.

An all out bombing campaign

In January 1943, Casablanca was chosen for a top-level meeting between the British Prime Minister, Winston Churchill and the President of the United States, Franklin D. Roosevelt. The discussions that took place over ten days involved British and American heads of staff. These talks resulted in two major decisions, the first being that the defeat of Germany was to be the first priority; the second was that a strategic bombing campaign must be supported by a land offensive. By this stage in the war, it had become obvious that a bombing offensive alone would not achieve victory. The primary objectives of a bomber offensive were stated as:

The progressive destruction and dislocation of the German military, industrial, and economic system, and the undermining of the morale of the German people to a point where their capacity for armed resistance is fatally weakened.

No 44 (Rhodesia) Squadron was a vital part of this plan and on the 16th and 17th January their target was the German capital, Berlin. An eyewitness account from Sergeant Airgunner Maxwell Garnet (Maxie) Hall was carried in the *Rhodesia Herald* on 2nd February 1943:

There was cloud cover, but over the target the sky was clear. The moonlight reflected by the snow on the ground pushed the town and the street into our faces like a map. It was like daylight so the flares and incendiaries dropped by the pathfinders ahead, were hardly necessary. The bombers easily located the targets and dropped 4,000-pounders (1,800kg) with precision. Our bombs caused a terrific explosion. Flak and night fighters were suprisingly sparse on the Saturday but more formidable on Sunday, especially the fighters. There was also some cloud, but this attack was also successfully pressed home. (Rhodesia Herald, 2nd Feb. 1943)

The raid on 16th January was an all Lancaster affair but the aircraft were dispersed owing to snow and haze and only scattered damage was caused but losses were light, only one aircraft failing to return. The following night, Sunday, night defences were alert and fighter activity was heavy, resulting in the loss of 22 aircraft and damage to another 30. In fact, on that Sunday, Sergeant Hall's aircraft was hit at least twice, which perhaps was the reason he was so enthusiastic about the strength of the Lancaster: It is extraordinarily strong and can stand terrific strain and punishment. The pilots, evading flak, throw them about like fighters. Hall also mentions the teamwork of the crew with the pilot relying on his crew to keep him posted on the position of fighters, flak and searchlights, while in turn the crew have to trust their pilot implicitly. The crews of No 44 Squadron were a mixed bunch. One aircraft had a Canadian pilot, an Indian navigator, a New Zealander as a wireless operator while the rest of the crew came from the United Kingdom. Hall's pilot was a Canadian, the wireless operator, Ignatius Terblanche (Bob) Rademeyer, a Rhodesian.

H2S and IFF

On 30th January a new radar device, code named H2S, was used for the first time. H2S distinguished darkened or cloud-hidden cities from open countryside. Since H2S sets were mounted inside the bombers themselves, the system did not have the range limitations of ground-based radar and any number of bombers could use the sets simultaneously. However, H2S was to prove of limited value as a bombing aid.

As the months of the war passed, the electronic equipment carried by the heavy bombers became increasingly complex and each new aid, while helping accuracy, created its own problems. One vital item carried by the bombers was the IFF, Identification Friend or Foe. This device emitted signals that the Allied defences could receive and identify. IFF necessitated an aerial, one of eight aerial systems carried by a Lancaster, slung from the tip of the fins to the IFF instrument near the mid-turret. Damage to this piece of equipment or to the aerial system often resulted in the Lancaster being given an unpleasant reception when it returned to Britain. Obviously, the IFF system was highly secret and to prevent it falling into enemy hands the pilot, navigators or wireless operators could activate buttons, which would fire detonators destroying the equipment. In the event of a crash, the detonators blew automatically but to safeguard the crew in the event of a forced landing in friendly territory, there was a cut-out switch.

February 1943 brought raids in several different directions: Hamburg on 3rd February and Turin, with a total complement of 198 aircraft, on 4th February. Among three attacks on Wilhelmshaven, a raid was carried out on Lorient, and then on 14th February an all-Lancaster force returned to Milan; two of the 142 aircraft involved failed to return. Discussing the Lorient Raid, which was his first, Sergeant Air Observer Douglas Lindsay Thomson says:

There was a bit of flak and light cloud as we crossed the French coast but coming out we could see the objective, which was already lit up by the flares and incendiaries of the pathfinders. It was perfectly clear over our objective and it was obvious the first wave had rattled the defences for the flak and searchlights were very inaccurate. My moment came when, giving instruction to the pilot during our comparatively easy run-up, I dropped my 4,000-lb (1,800kg) cookie and watched it falling dead for our particular target. We circled about a bit to make observations and for about 25 minutes on the return journey we were unmolested by fighters and could see the fires burning.

Five days later, on 18th February, Thomson had a tougher trip when his bomber was attacked on four occasions by fighters while it was returning from Wilhelmshaven.

One Ju 88 couldn't be shaken off. We exchanged fire and the next thing I knew we were doing a breath-taking dive at 400 mph (640 km/h) and the enemy plane made off. Our crew is English except for one Irishman and me. All have got to know their jobs and trust one another so well that the team needs only the minimum of talking when at business.
(Rhodesia Herald, 12th March 1943)

Such constant activity was bound to incur casualties and during the months of January and February, the squadron lost eight aircraft,, while hardly a single raid was carried out without several Lancasters being damaged. The weather was bitter; at 18,000 feet the temperatures were frequently well below zero. In Squadron Operations Record there are references to severe icing conditions causing bombers to return to base without accomplishing their mission. In these conditions, a trifling mishap could have dire results:

19th February. *Bird hit turret of one machine and caused intense cold and frostbite for the crew during the whole of the trip.* (Operations Record)

On 1st March it was back to Berlin. Sergeant Thomson says:

Except for a slight ground haze, the weather perfect on the continent when on the night of March 1st we raided Berlin. The journey out was entirely uneventful owing to the skill of the navigator and pilot. Our Lancaster was in the first wave and arrived ahead of our zero hour, so in the capacity of reconnaissance aircraft, we circled the city for observation before making our run-up. I saw the first batch of incendiaries going down and three strong fires start up in the city. By the flames and the gun flashes the river was clearly outlined. Then from another quarter, we took our position for the run-up. By that time the flak and searchlights were well under way. There were some fighters up but they seemed to be chasing their own tails. Perhaps they were confused by the magnitude of the attack. At first it was difficult to pick out our particular target owing to much smoke, but I soon located my landmarks, made calculations and gave the necessary directions. The pilot made a normal run-up and I released my 'cookie' which, with our load of incendiaries, I watched falling outlined against the fires. I am pretty certain we 'pranged' the target. We continued our run on over the target and as we made our run out we were able to observe a lot of very widespread fires. On looking back, when once clear of the city, I could see masses of flames and the quarter of the city we had bombed canopied by a pall of black smoke. Observations made at intervals on the way home showed that the fires were visible up to about 200 miles away [320km]. The return trip was uneventful, again owing to the skill of the pilot and navigator faithfully adhering to the route given when briefed. (Rhodesia Herald)

Other Rhodesians who took part in this particular raid on Berlin were Pilot Officer Bernard le Sueur, Sergeant Pilot George William Oldham and Flight Lieutenant William James (Bill) Picken DFC, who was killed over Essen four days later.

The Battle of the Ruhr

The so-called Battle of the Ruhr began on 5th March 1943 with a 412 strong raid on Essen. This force included 140 Lancasters and was the first large-scale attack in which Oboe was employed. Oboe made use of two radar stations on the ground to guide a bomber to its target. Despite its uncanny accuracy, Oboe's range was only 300 miles (480km) and a pair of radar stations could direct only one aircraft at a time. So the system was used mainly to guide a pathfinder force and enabled them to mark the target blind. Depending on the weather conditions, the target was marked either with ground flares or sky flares. The following main force then bombed on the target indicators.

From the beginning of March, the main aim of Bomber Command was to eliminate the huge German industrial complex in the Ruhr or Happy Valley as it became known to bomber crews. If this vital area could be devastated, it would cripple the German war effort. In return, German tactics centred on the effort to inflict so many casualties that the raids would become impracticable. Hitherto, Germany had relied mainly on anti-aircraft fire, but late in 1942, the Lichtenstein apparatus was introduced. This was an airborne radar system carried by German night-fighters and was comparable to the radar used so effectively by British fighters in May 1941. This system, by which a main German radar station directed fighters into the bombers' path, until the fighters' own radar systems took over, caused a mounting casualty toll among Allied bombers. Another problem was the weather. Icing conditions on the wings affected lift and control, while ice forming on the windscreens and windows affected visibility. To ensure that the pilots' windscreens and the bomb-aimer's panel could be kept ice-free, glycol sprays were fitted. The nozzles for the main windscreens could be seen sticking up from the nose like antennae.

Bombing-up

Bombing-up was a technique in itself. Depending on the target and the role a particular unit was to play, the load could vary from 14 x 250- or 500-lb (112 or 225kg) to a single 8,000-lb (3,600kg) bomb. In general, all Lancasters built from early 1943 could accommodate the 8,000-pounder. Lancasters carrying the later 12,000-lb (5,400kg) and 22,000-lb (10,000kg) giants were classified as Specials.

The Lancaster was the most effective heavy bomber employed by the Royal Air Force. It was tough and dependable. It carried a heavier load and could fly further than most other aircraft. The only serious drawback was that it was considerably out-gunned by German fighters and carried little armament on its underside.

> *Coming back at night was when the fighters normally attacked, when the crews were tired and relaxed as they crossed the coast. At one time Flying Fortresses flew with the Lancs. They carried no bombs, but were extra heavily armed and acted as decoys for the fighters, showing lights and flying on the outside.* (John Deall)

This technique did not last long. Most of the time, the bombers relied on surprise and vast numbers to swamp the German defences.

April 1943 began with attacks on Essen and Kiel. Then, following a few days of cloud, came a raid on Duisburg. As technical aids increased, so also the attacks were becoming more scientific as the Operations Record shows:

> *8th April. Twelve aircraft detailed for a bombing raid on Duisburg. Squadron Leader Ingha, Flying Officer Pilgrim, Flying Officer William Douglas Rail (Rhodesian), Flying Officer Arthur T. Moodie (Rhodesian), Pilot Officer Taylor, Pilot Officer Raymond, Sergeant*

Drysdale, Sergeant Harding, Sergeant Haines, Sergeant Smith, Sergeant Pennington and Sergeant Ellis. Sergeant Haines's aircraft failed to return from this operation and no messages or signals were received. Sergeant Ellis did not attack any target owing to severe icing. Bombs jettisoned and aircraft returned to base. The remaining ten aircraft reached and bombed the estimated position of the target. Actual identification of the target was impossible owing to existing cloud formation and in many cases, crews were unable to observe pathfinder flares. Gee fixes were obtained and bombs released on DR and ETA. Flak was intense and accurate but otherwise there was little indication that the operation would prove successful. Flying Officer Pilgrim states that before their run-up to bomb, a blinding flash was seen and his aircraft was blown on its back. Control was regained at 6,500 feet when bombs were released. He observed incendiary fires whilst at this height. Flying Officer Rail reports seeing a big red flash followed by a red glow that could be seen for ten minutes. The failure of the operation was considered to be due to the very unsatisfactory weather conditions. (Operations Record No 44 Squadron)*

The following night the target was Duisburg again, this time with more success. Then came a strong attack on Frankfurt with no squadron losses, followed by a raid on Spezia, where ships and harbour installations were left burning. The following night it was back to Stuttgart, and the night after, Pilsen received a visit, which according to Happy Taylor was a flop.

The first raid on the Skoda Works at Pilsen on 16th April was a failure. The pathfinders were off target and most of the force dropped their bombs on a small village. My navigator decided that the markers were off target so we unloaded our bombs on a marshalling yard. It was later discovered that a small Czech village had been completely flattened and we had to go back to Pilsen during the following month. (Happy Taylor)

Collision over the target

A more successful attack was carried out two days later on Spezia, where visibility was good. On 20th April, Happy Taylor lost one of his nine lives over Stettin.

I was trying to get out of the slipstream of a Halifax, when a Stirling appeared in front of me. It all happened so suddenly that there was nothing I could do about it. We bashed a fin of the Stirling and knocked a 6 foot (2m) hole in our fuselage between the front turret and the bomb bay. It shook us quite a bit, but the only member of the crew who was injured was the bomb-aimer, one of whose eyes was scratched by a bit of metal. The Stirling appeared to be as right as rain, going on as if nothing had happened. Certainly my Lancaster stood the test. We carried on, bombed the target and returned without further incident. The only problem was the cold air, coming in through the hole. We stuffed our Mae Wests into the breach. The Stirling, however, began flying in circles. The engineer had to go back and cut the rudder wires, so the only control the pilot had for turning was by using the engines. The pilot of the Stirling, a sergeant was awarded the DFM for getting his damaged aircraft back. Later we chanced to meet at Mildenhall and chatted over the occurrence, which had been due to congestion over the target. Average time over the target on big raids was about 15 minutes. You had to bomb during that time so that the defences would be overwhelmed; stragglers would be picked on by fighters. The only real protection the bombers had was the solid mass of aircraft. Bombers were supposed to avoid dogfights but if a fighter attacked a bomber, then every aircraft in range would open up. The Germans soon learnt to leave the bomber streams alone. Apart from the collision, the thing I remember most about the Stettin Raid, is flying in half moonlight, at treetop height over Holland and seeing the farmhouses flicking the 'V' for Victory sign. (Happy Taylor)

On 28th April, during an operation to the Baltic, Happy Taylor had an extra passenger, a naval officer.

The navy thought the RAF was haphazard with its mine-laying, so this chap was detailed to go with me and see how efficient our mine-laying was. The technique varied, but on this operation we fired Very lights to pick up a landmark. Then flew a set course, at a set height and speed for a set time. At the exact time, we dropped our six acoustic mines. The officer was most impressed. He offered to take me on a submarine to watch a mine-laying exercise. "Wouldn't you like to come?" "No. Thank you!" I said. He was most hurt. "I came with you," he said. Another time I took an American observer to see how the squadron operated. He learned one thing, that it was best to stay away from the navy because we were shot at by a destroyer. (Happy Taylor)

The month of April 1943 closed with a further attack on Essen, which cost the squadron one aircraft. May began with cloudy weather and the repeated Operations Reports that read: Aircraft detailed for operations but op subsequently cancelled. Weather cloudy. Fog during night. But, on 12th May, the squadron returned to Duisburg and on the following night it was back to the Skoda works at Pilsen with Wing Commander Nettleton leading the squadron:

A considerable amount of black smoke, but if the Target Indicators were in the right place, then it was an excellent show. (Operations Record)

Sadly, two aircraft failed to return, the pilot of one was Flying Officer William Douglas Rail of Umtali. Apparently, he had a West Indian gunner named Gus, who came from Jamaica and was as black as the ace of spades. Rail claimed, He's going to put the Germans off. All they'll see are two white eyes!

Eight days of training in fighter affiliation and practice bombing were followed by an attack on Dortmund and then one on Düsseldorf, where, according to Flying Officer Pilgrim, The pathfinders put up a disgusting show. On the way to the target, two reds were seen to go down at least 30 miles (48km) apart. Sortie unsuccessful though scattered fires observed.

Essen was attacked on 27th May and Wupertal on 29th May. According to the Operations Record: Crews very enthusiastic about prospects of success but on the second raid two aircraft failed to return. One of these was piloted by a Rhodesian, Pilot Officer David William Erickson.

On the final day of May 1943, aircrews and ground crews moved from Waddington to Dunholme Lodge. This change of location was followed by ten days of typically English summer weather when operations were cancelled on every occasion, owing to cloud, and so it was 11th June before the squadron took to the air again. This time to visit Düsseldorf where, Several crews praised the technique of the pathfinder force and reported the raid a success. The following night the target was Bochum and two days later it was Oberhausen where, The night-fighter activity was heavy round the target and two aircraft, flown by Squadron Leader Haywood and Sergeant Shearman failed to return.

The shuttle services

A new phase in the bomber offensive began in June 1943. This was the 'shuttle-service' raid carried out first by Lancaster squadrons. Advances in North Africa had brought airfields, where refuelling could be carried out, within range of aircraft based in Britain, allowing more distant targets to be attacked. The Zeppelin factory at Friedrichsafen, on the shores of Lake Constance, was the first target chosen. Zeppelin production had long since ceased but the factory was an important centre for the manufacture of radar equipment. The operation order, detailing new techniques of attack, was received on 16th June only four days before the planned date of the attack. This allowed very little time for training in the technique which was to be used for the first time on this raid, that of receiving instruction by radio-telephone over the target from a master bomber. This method had been used with great success by Wing Commander Guy Gibson during the raid on the Mohne and Eder Dams and was to become a standard part of large-scale raids from this time on.

Five aircraft took off from Dunholme Lodge, carried out the raid and flew on to North Africa where they landed. They again took off on 23rd June carried out an attack on Spezia and returned to base on 24th June. (Operations Record)

Altogether 60 Lancasters took part in this operation, and although defences were light because the Germans did not expect a long distance raid on such a short June night, the attack was a limited success.

Not more than six crews scoring direct hits in the target area, but these did considerable damage. Six aircraft were damaged but not one was lost. (Operations Record)

While five crews were flying to North Africa and back, the rest of the squadron visited Krefeld, Mulheim and Wuppertal again. The following night over Gelsenkirchen there seems to have been some confusion. Flight Lieutenant Bailey arrived at position 'x' punctually and shortly afterwards the rear gunner reported red flares going down behind the aircraft. The pilot assuming he was on the wrong course made a correction and then saw green flares going down to the north of the reds, instead of to the south. He realized that something was radically wrong and just dropped his load on a concentration of fires.

The final raid in the month of June was on Cologne, from which Sergeant Hulbert failed to return. There was a large amount of flak round the target and for some reason the marker flares were 14 minutes late, which caused a hold up in the bombing. So the first six months of 1943 ended with bombing having become more precise and concentrated though mistakes were often made resulting in needless losses.

RAF Fairey IIIDs of Pulford's flight. Airfield not known.

The citizens of Bulawayo drove, rode or walked to meet the *Silver Queen*, the first aeroplane to land in Rhodesia. March 1920. Van Ryneveld and Brand had completed most of their journey from Brooklands to Cape Town.

"... it is difficult to realize that the pitiful wreck is the remains of that thing of wondrous beauty that shot out of the northern sky on Friday and cicled down to earth before the enraptured gaze of thousands." *Bulawayo Chronicle*

Units of the 1st Battalion the Rhodesia Regiment preparing to emplane in the RAF Vickers Victorias/Valentias at Salisbury on an exercise that was to take them to Rusape. 27 March 1934.

ACM Sir Arthur (Bomber) Harris, Commander-in-Chief Bomber Command spent his formative working years on a farm outside Salisbury. He wished to return to live in Rhodesia.

Major Dirk Cloete MC, AFC.

Mr D.S. (Pat) Judson, son of a Rhodesian pioneer and Mashonaland Rebellion hero, photographed while on a flight to Porto Amelia in Mozambique, 1930.

Aeroplanes were a fascination to the general public in the early years. The Vickers Victorias/Valentias lacked many aerodynamic design considerations and the pilots were subjected to the discomforts of an open cockpit.

Left: Lawrence John Walter (Jack) Keller MP (Labour) for Raylton, who was a thorn in the side of many parliamentarians.

Left: RAF Fairey IIID biplanes at Salisbury on a *Showing the Flag* exercise in the early '30s.

Left: Members of the 1st Battalion Rhodesia Regiment board the Vickers Valentia at Salisbury to fly to Rusape on a combined RAF exercise in 1931.

Below left: The second DH Moth of the Rhodesian Aviation Syndicate. December 1927.

Below right: Wing Cdr C.W.H. Pulford OBE, AFC. *Bulawayo Chronicle,* 4th May 1926

RAF Fairey Gordons accompanied by a Victoria/Valentia on one of the many RAF pioneering flights to southern Africa.

RANA's de Havilland Leopard Moth VP-YAZ outbound from Salisbury heading east.

Above left: An even-tempered and cheerful bunch of de Havilland technicians. (From left): Nevin Strickland, Doug Simpson, Theo Posselt, Davies, Chummy Page, Steve Prentiss, Hugh Gundry. John Scott-Robertson, the flying instructor, is seated in the rear cockpit of the Tiger Moth.

Above right: Jimmy Powell in pith helmet inspects Hawker Hart SR 1 being assembled in the hangar at Cranborne. 1938

Left: The hangars at Cranborne with five Hawker Harts on the apron. 1938.

The first Rhodesian air apprentices learning the ropes. Ralph Parry and Mick Gibbon are on the left. The others are Otto Gericke, Ron Boswell, Ron Cashel and Stan Young (not in order).

Maxi and Jimmy were the first flying instructors in the air unit. Flight Lieutenants V.E. Maxwell (RAF) and J.A. Powell (RAF) stand beside their beautiful, polished aluminium Hawker Hart SR 1. 1938.

Three of the six Hawker Harts of the air unit waiting to fly at Cranborne. 1938.

This delightful SRAF 1950s picture of a Tiger Moth shows the path that every pilot and pupil must take to mount this exceptional trainer.

The men of the first pilots' course of the Southern Rhodesia Air Unit with their Tiger Moth. 1937. From left, standing: Lt Graham Smith, D. de Waal (instructor), Lt Ron Marshall,

The first technicians to arrive in Southern Rhodesia, mid-1937: Sgt C.P. Horton who was to serve on No 237 Squadron, F/S A. Greenwood, Cpl A.P.B. Simpson and Sgt V.J. Royce.

No 1 Course after the First Wings Presentation. From left: Capt C.S. Style DFC, Lts John Holderness, A.B.T. Cazalet, Ron Marshall, Graham Smith, Eric Smith, Sgt M.C.H. Barber.

Five Hawker Harts in formation in typical Rhodesian summer flying conditions.

Maxi was a past master at picking up messages. Here he demonstrates the technique to members of the territorial force on exercise.

In a banked turn over the Rhodesian bush, SR 5 displays its lines.

Above: The radial-engined Gloster Gauntlet.

Right: The first de Havilland Rapide was purchased for the use of the governor of Southern Rhodesia. It was flown out from the UK by Dirk Cloete with Martin Madders and A. Higham as technicians. Initially registered as VP-YBU, it became SR 8, and was subsequently numbered 300 in the SRAS. It was returned to the air unit after the war and was re-numbered SR 23.

The pilots of the first and second courses of the Southern Rhodesia Air Unit, 1938. Back row, from left: Flt Sgt A. Greenwood, Sgt C.P. Horton, A/C K.L. Wilson, Cpl A.B.P. Simpson, Cpl A. Higham, LAC M. Madders, A/C R.C. Palgrave, Sgt V.J. Royce, A/C R.H. Krahner. Middle row: Lt J.B. Holderness, 2Lt H.C. Peyton, 2Lt E.W.S. Jacklin, 2Lt R.J.D. Christie, 2Lt A.T.R. Hutchinson, 2Lt E.E. Spence, Lt E.T. Smith, 2Lt N.S.F. Tyas. Seated: Lt M.C.H. Barber, Capt C.W. Robertson, Flt Lt. V.E. Maxwell, Maj D. Cloete MC, AFC, Sqn Ldr J.A. Powell, Capt C.S. Style DFC, Lt G.A. Smith.

F/O A.M. Bentley and P/O G.O. Ross, Bulawayo men who joined the RAF and who visited Southern Rhodesia again as pilots of a Vickers Wellesley bomber.

All that was needed for the Travelling Flying School training was a car, a tent, an aeroplane and an airfield (Gatooma). The PK (picannin kia/ little house/outside toilet) behind the tent, was an added luxury.

Hardy in flight over northern Kenya.

The officers' mess at Cranborne was constructed from the packing cases that the Harts arrived in from the UK. There was a lounge and, of course, a bar.

Personnel of the second air section of the SRAU. 1938. Standing: 2Lt R.J.D. Christie, Instr J.F.F. Finnis, 2Lt. H.C. Peyton, 2Lt E.E. Spence. Front: 2Lt E.W.S. Jacklin, 2Lt N.S.F. Tyas, 2Lt A.W.R. Hutchinson.

You fly 'em, so you fill 'em and fix 'em. Ted Jacklin and Eric Spence attend to their Audax SR 13 at Kisumu on the delivery flight in 1939.

Butt-firing was the method used to harmonize and synchronize the guns of the Hawker Harts. Note the ring and bead sight on the front cowling.

Wing Cdr Jimmy Powell DSO, OBE, after the presentation of the OBE by HRH King George VI.

Two Hawker Harts, and an Audax with its distinctive exhaust about to leave for Kenya.

Audaxes/Hardys at Kisumu. Note the slipper tanks.

On the second Audax ferry, two Hawker Audax aircraft arrive in formation with the government Rapide. These three aircraft had flown down from Cairo. This is a lovely picture of the Rapide SR8.

Hawker Audax No K 7534 of No 1 Squadron SRAF at Garissa in late 1939.

No 1 Squadron 'B' flight officers' mess at Garissa in late 1939.

Above left: Part of 'B' flight's camp at Garissa in late 1939. "Lo kia ka lo Boss!" ("The Boss's house!")

Above right: Mbeya, a halting place on the north road, well known to Rhodesians who passed that way either by air or by road.

Left: "B' flight's tented and grass hute camp at Garissa.

Far left: 'B' flight's duty pilot and lookout at Garissa, late 1939.

Left: Eric Smith, Alec Hutchinson and Eric Spence standing outside the officers' mess at garissa.

This was not a private hunting safari, but part of No 1 Squadron's detachment at Isiolo. The sand desert beginds quite close to Isiolo. The technician standing on the port main wheel is about to start the Hawker Hart.

The signboard at Namanga River Camp on the Great North Road near Kilimanjaro. Distances of interest in kilometres: Vic Falls 1908; Cape Town 3398; Cairo 3507; London 7638. The placard below states New York 10638.

Staff and pupils of Southern Rhodesia Air Force in the Cranborne hangar. 1939. Jimmy Powell is seated at centre; Charles Prince is ninth from the left; Keith Hensman is sixth from the right.

'B' Flight of No 1 Squadron SRAF at Nairobi under the command of Eric Smith. From left: Hutchinson, B. White, Hales, Christie, Kleynhans, Ted Jacklin, Eric Smith (Flight Commander), unknown , unknown, Sandy McIntyre, Eric Spence.

No 1 Squadron journeys north.

It was a pilot's dream come true to fly a Hawker Hart. Today it is just a pilot's dream.

The hangar at Cranborne under construction. Industry was well advanced in remote Rhodesia in 1939.

A face full of character if ever there was one—F/O Greenslade.

No 3 Wartime Course in perfect formation with Tiger Moth in line astern. From left, standing: G.E. Bedford, R.D. Cairns, N. Bowker, G. Cumming, J.S.S. Bazeley, N.F. Booth, J.M.G. Hooper, S.A. Wells, R.R. Webley, J.T. Berridge, G.F. Talent. Seated: S.J. Barbour, T.H. Scorror, P.O. Bates, P. Brunton, S.M. Moore, G.O. Reynish, J.P. Elsworth, J. Still, Sheppard, D. Milne, C.D. Ripsher, P. Donaldson, J.C.R. Hooper. (The two Hooper brothers were both awarded the DFC and George Reynish the DFM).

Above left: Mt Kenya from Isiolo with a Hawker Hardy taking off. Note the underwing slipper tanks.

Above right: A water point on the Isiolo road that led to the forward areas of the Kenyan front.

Left: A view of the immaculate, whitewashed Wajir Fort.

The Corps of Signals Band marches past the PWD Headquarters, Jameson Avenue, Salisbury. This building was the HQ of RATG in WWII and still stands today.

Far left: Lieutenant Hugh Peyton, No 237 Rhodesia Squadron's first casualty, He and his gunner, Corporal Freddy Kimpton, were killed in action.

Left: The badge of the Rhodesian Air Training Group (RATG). The literal Shona translation means *We will be strengthened in hundreds.*

Air Vice-Marshal C.W. Meredith was, amongst many other things, instrumental in setting up the Rhodesian Air Training group in Rhodesia. The apparently quiet and unassuming Lieutenant Colonel Ernest Lucas Guest was in fact an incredibly forceful character and was later to become Minister of Defence.

1st 'B' Flight, No 1 Squadron SRAF at Garissa under the command of Capt Marshall. The Hardy's long exhaust pipes are particularly prominent.

The badge of the RATG, with the eagle surmounted by the lion and tusk may be seen today above the doorway on one of the buildings of the RATG complex, facing 4th Street.

Above right: Bok-bok—a traditional game that is usually played after the consumption of alcohol, and the cause of many an injury. A contingent of Rhodesian pilots en route to the UK aboard the T. SS Diomed. These included John Deall, Grimwood Cooke, Bull Friend, Happy Taylor and Bill Picken.

Left: A Harvard IA with the fabric-covered fuselage is guided out of the apron at Cranborne. The duty pilot is in attendance in the tower on the hangar roof.

The first draft of Rhodesian aircrew on board ship, bound for the UK and an uncertain future.

Left: The Mount Hampden 1942 Rugger XV was captained by the CFI, Wg Cdr Bill Sykes. Seated on the right is Roy Simmonds who was to rise to the rank of wing commander in the technical branch of the Rhodesian Air Force.

Below: Almost identical in design to Thornhill was Heany Air Station, about 20 miles out of Bulawayo off the Salisbury road. It is better known today as Llewellin Barracks.

Insert below: Three Harvards from Heany in Vic formation over the familiar wide streets of Bulawayo.

Above: *Rumbavu* and *Inez* were presented to the SRAF by Mr John McAlister Smith on 28th March 1940 and 10th June respectively. They cost £1,250 each.

Thornhill Air Station was situated on the north side of the Gwelo–Umvuma road/railway. The married quarters section is yet to be built on the south side.

Rhodesian aircrew leaving Cape Town on the T. SS *Diomed*.

The pitiful remains of a Harvard after it crashed near Cranborne in 1942.

Above left: RATG Harvard IAs at Thornhill about to taxi out for a bumpy midday sortie.

Left: DH 82 Tiger Moth *Rumbavu* at Belvedere, Salisbury.

Kumalo Air Station was just a few miles out of Bulawayo on the Salisbury road. The main complex and the two runways can be seen clearly. It was renamed Brady Barracks.

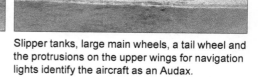

The Oxford, with the sun glinting off its wings, watches over the fledgling Harvards at Cranborne in the early days. 1940/41.

Slipper tanks, large main wheels, a tail wheel and the protrusions on the upper wings for navigation lights identify the aircraft as an Audax.

A ferry on the Nile River approaches Khartoum, carrying the technical backup for the 237 Squadron aircraft.

Khartoum. A dust storm would preclude any form of flying.

A-16

Staff officers and instructors of the SRAU at Cranborne. From left, standing; Lt John Holderness (No 1 Course), Lt Peter Fletcher (to become air chief marshal RAF), Lt Maurice Barber (No 1 Course), Lt Neville (Tickey) Tyas (KIA), Lt Keith Hensman (instr), Dr Ross (MO). Seated: Capt Charles Prince (instr), Capt Jack Finnis (instr), F/L Ron Marshal (No 1 Course), Capt. unknown (admin), Major Jimmy Powell (commanding officer, a squadron leader seconded from the RAF), unknown Fynn (radio and electrical), Capt Saunders (armament), Fg. Off. unknown (RAF), Humphrey-Davey (admin).

This is how we spent Boxing Day, Gederef, December 1940. From left: Paul Holdengarde, Tickey Tyas, Jim Storey and Ted Jacklin.

A horse designed by a committee . . . What the Lysander lacked aesthetically, it made up for in operational effectiveness.

A study of the redoubtable Hardy shows its larger wheels, and the extended exhaust, which made night flying easier.

The burnt-out wreckage of a Hardy in northern Kenya. 1940.

A group of Rhodesian pilots from No 1 Squadron SRAF relaxing on the banks of the Nile River. They were soon to tackle the Italians in the early part of the East Africa campaign.
From left: Ted Jacklin, Sandy McIntyre, A.T.R. Hutchinson, Cyril Sindall, E. Kleynhans, Eric Smith and Brian White. Top: Stan Flett. Bottom: Graham Smith.

Below: 237 Squadron's Early Warning System—a fully rotating stereophonic receiver with interlinked immediate voice response.

Asmara aerodrome after our bombers had finished with it.

The type of road the KAR and RWAFF had to contend with in central Abyssinia.

Behind the crest of Dologorodoc, Brigadier Messervy poses with Colonel Denys Reid and an Indian jemadar during a brief lull in the incessant bombardment.

Men of the West Yorkshire Regiment who dramatically stormed Fort Dologorodoc, the key to the battle, face up to another counter-attack.

The unchanging skyline of the Sebakwe hills will be remembered by all pilots who did weapons training at Kutanga Range. Two Harvard Mk IIs overfly the range.

Left: The Duke of Aosta, a skilled and honourable general, was accorded full honours when he surrendered.

Right: A Harvard Mk II at Heany on an open day.

Right below: Carriers of the King's Royal Rifle Corps. November 1941.

The War Cemetery at Sidi Rezegh with hundreds of graves.

The gun panels of the 266 Squadron Spitfire are off and three armourers are hard at work. What the other five men are doing is open to question.

Douglas Leggo sitting in his *Eva*. The squadron code letters UO were for the 266 (Rhodesia) Squadron Spitfires. This was changed to ZH with the acquisition of the Typhoons in January 1942. Doug Leggo was later to lose his life over Malta.

Pilots of 266 Squadron on stand-by.

Members of 266 Squadron. Standing: Johnny Small, Tusky Haworth, Tommy Thompson, Bob Menelaws. Sitting: George Elcombe, Susie Wilson, Ossie Osborne and Dennis Miller.

The armourers of 266 Squadron.

Three 44 Squadron Hampdens flown by Rhodesians, before the squadron was equipped with Lancasters.

Pilots of 'B' Flight 266 Squadron (all seated). From left: Ian Munro, Les Barlow, John Whiteford, P/O Penny, F/L Roach, P/O Johnston, Tommy Thompson, Bill Hagger, George Elcombe.

Above: A Handley Page Hampden, prior to bombing up.

Right: Speed 190 mph. Sgt Taylor flying the Hampden on 16 OTU.

The cockpit of the Hampden was only three feet wide. Before one could get into the cockpit, the seat back had to be lowered.

Fins and delay fuses are fitted by the armourers before loading up a Hampden. In a few hours, the bombs will become scrap metal.

A Hampden of 16 OTU on which many pilots of 44 Squadron were trained.

Wing Cmdr John Plagis DSO and Bar, Netherlands Flying Cross. John joined 266 (Rhodesia) Squadron in July 1941 and served as a sergeant pilot until he was posted in early 1942 to Malta. He was one of the pilots who flew the Spitfires off an aircraft carrier to Malta to serve with 249 Squadron. Whilst serving on the island, he gained credit for shooting down enemy aircraft, four of which fell to his guns in one sortie. John Plagis also served on 64, 65 and 185 Squadrons, and commanded 126 Squadron from June to Dec 1944, and 266 (Rhodesia) Squadron from Sept 1946 to Dec 1947. He was Rhodesia's leading Fighter Ace, and was credited with 16 victories.

A mass of Harvards (nearly 50) at Thornhill 1942-43. The prevailing wind is from 130°, the direction in which the RAF Lockheed Lodestar is facing. It is curious that the aircraft on the hardstand are facing downwind. The building amongst the aircraft is the control tower.

Above: No 266 Squadron, Kingscliffe. Mr S.M. Lanigan O'Keeffe CMG, High Commissioner for Southern Rhodesia, presents the squadron badge to Squadron Leader C.L. Green.

Left: No 237 Squadron camp at Wadi Halfa in the desert heat.

Hurricanes of 237 Squadron taking off to go on patrol.

Regular servicing of aircraft was essential in the desert. Technicians of 237 Squadron service a Hurricane.

No 237 Squadron's orderly room with the officer commanding, E.T. Smith, in attendance. The unofficial Southern Rhodesia Air Force badge with the lion and tusk is embroidered on the banner.

A montage of the Hurricanes, Lysanders and Tiger Moths provides a nostalgic, if not entirely accurate, representation of 237 Squadron against a desert sunset.

A garden of explosives enhances the 237 Squadron accommodation in the Western Desert.

A German 88mm is destroyed by the bombardment of the Rhodesian anti-tank battery at Thompson's Post.

Alec Hutchinson and two other 237 Squadron pilots are briefed for a recce flight by the army. The fleece-lined flying kit seems incongruous but it could get cold . . .

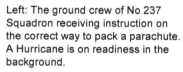

Above: The view from the Rhodesian Services Club showing the Blue Mosque and Moqattam Hills in the distance.

Left: The ground crew of No 237 Squadron receiving instruction on the correct way to pack a parachute. A Hurricane is on readiness in the background.

Hawker Typhoon ZH-B. Peter Blackwell's aeroplane—so he claimed ...

... but he didn't want to claim this one!

A parade of flying kit. Pilots of 237 Squadron pose in front of their steed, a Hurricane.

Far left: P/O H.H. 'Happy' Taylor DFM.

Left: Sqn Ldr Nettleton's Lancaster km-B of No 44 Squadron over the English countryside practising for the Augsburg raid.

Below left: The main wheel and undercarriage of the Lancaster—a formidable piece of engineering.

German High Command were most interested in the wreckage of a Lancaster shot down over Berlin. What technical secrets would they find?

Standing under the huge intake of the 266 Squadron Typhoon are John Deall and Charles Green. The Borland twins are on the right along with Peter Blackwell and 'Tusky' Haworth (pointing).

Four pilots of No 44 Squadron admire their badge. The motto means *The king's thunderbolts are righteous*, and the elephant symbolizes the squadron's heavy attacks. Happy Taylor is second from the right.

Group Capt Chris Dams and the Reverend Norman Wood attend the Nettleton School annual memorial service. The headmaster addresses the school.

Above: A dramatic night photograph portrays the menacing character of the Lancaster. This scarred veteran of No 44 (Rhodesia) Squadron has flown on 71 operations.

The 'Lanc'.

An artist's impression of the Augsburg raid of the No 44 Squadron Lancasters, bombing the German MANN diesel factory in daylight. Squadron Leader Nettleton who led the raid was awarded the Victoria Cross for this daring operation.

An unusual photograph of Lancasters queuing up to take their turn for take off, to go on a thousand-bomber raid. They left at one-minute intervals.

Not all the aircraft returned, but some of the crews that nursed their stricken aircraft home ended in an inferno. Many heroic deeds were performed away from the targets.

'S' Sugar celebrates its 21st raid. The technicians record the event on the fuselage of *Good Health Then*.

Members of No 266 Squadron, 1942. Back row: Dennis Miller, Stan Howard (KIA), Johnny MacNamara, Susie Wilson, Ted Welby (KOAS), Wilf Smithyman(KIA), Arthur Chaplin (KIA), Don McGibbon, Norham Lucas (KOAS). Middle row: Monty Bell, Johnny Small (KIA–– baled out and gunned down in parachute), Bob Menelaws, Neil Allen (KOAS), Barny Wright (POW), Bill Hagger (KIA), Colly Collcutt, Doctor Cook (MO), Tidders Tidmarsh (IO). Front row: Pick Pickard (Eng off), Dicky Sherwood, Jimmy Thompson (POW), Tony Johnson (POW), Charles Green (CO), Rolo Dawson (KIA), Paul Devenish, Les Barlow (KIA), Ian Munro (KOAS), George Elcombe, John Deall. (Note: KOAS—killed on active service. KIA—killed in action. POW—prisoner of war. MO—medical officer. IO—intelligence officer.)

The Duke of Gloucester visits 237 Squadron in Persia, 8th May 1942.

No 237 Squadron celebrates an anniversary in Iraq.

Far left: No 237 Squadron passes through Baghdad on their way from Iraq to Egypt.

Left: Transport of 237 Squadron halted on a road beside the Suez Canal.

Above left: A member of the Women's Auxiliary Air Service packing a parachute.

Above right: Personnel of the Rhodesian Air Askari Corps.

Left: A Harvard finds temporary abode in Queensdale either before landing at, or after take off from, Cranborne.

This RATG Harvard was found in a remote area of north-eastern Rhodesia in March 1975. After much investigation, it was established that the pilot had survived. The damage to the airframe was caused by the local population.

The control tower on top of the hangar keeps a watchful eye on 20 Harvards at Cranborne.

Above: The RATG barracks at Cranborne in 1944 appear simple yet comfortable.

Left: F/O Bill Picken and F/O Grimwood Cooke after their investiture by King George VI at Buckingham Palace on 8th March 1942. Bill Picken was invested with the DFC and Grimwood Cooke the DFC and the DFM. Both were members of 106 Squadron. Cooke turned 21 on 6th December, was invested on 8th December and was killed in action on 22nd December 1942. Picken was killed on 5th May 1943 over Essen.

No 266 Squadron Typhoons at RAF Exeter.

The aircraft overturned on coming in to land after a sweep over Cherbourg. (Blackwell)

Flt Lt Sandy McIntyre. Promoted to Sqn Ldr, he took over command of 266 Squadron on 28th May 1943, and was killed in action on 15th August 1943. He also served on 237 Squadron.

A Typhoon being refuelled.

A bit of cheesecake. Mess art from Peter Blackwell's album.

Shown to good effect here is the Napier Sabre engine that brought Peter Blackwell to this point.

Peter Blackwell enters his Typhoon. Perhaps the designer of the aircraft used to work for Ford.

Flt Lt E.O. Collcutt, Adjutant of No 266 (Rhodesia) Squadron.

The squadron pilots of No 266. John Deall and Charles Green are prominent figures in the group.

Charles and Betty Green at their wedding reception. The officer in the background is Barney Wright.

Members of No 266 relaxing at the skeet range, Exeter. Charles Baillie and one of the Borland twins are on the right.

To be attacked on the ground by this beast of an aircraft must have been very daunting. No wonder the Germans hated them.

During a lull in operations, 266 Squadron puts up 12 Typhoons for a formation flypast.

CHAPTER 16

The return of 237

For a very long 12 months, from February 1942 until February 1943, No 237 (Rhodesia) Squadron had been kicking its heels out of sight and largely out of mind in the faraway deserts of Iraq and the mountains of Persia. Now the squadron was returning to what was hoped would be a more active role.

On 6th February, the main convoy rolled into Shandour and 12 pilots proceeded to Kilo 61 to collect the new Hurricane Mk IIC, which had been fitted with long-range tanks. Training and familiarization began immediately. Just one week later, Flying Officer Henry Boyer* crashed and was killed while carrying out stern and quarter attacks.

It appeared that the long-range tanks and heavy guns that the Hurricane now carried, made the aircraft difficult to manœuvre in tight turns. Wing Commander Aitken from headquarters Middle East arrived to test the squadron's aircraft and, according to Eric Smith, the wing commander also had difficulty in the tight turns and very nearly wrote himself off when the aircraft he was flying stalled.

On 23rd February, 30 ground crew who were Tour Expired left the squadron prior to posting back to Rhodesia, while the advance ground party moved to Landing Ground 106 in the Western Desert. This was to be the squadron's home for the next three months. At the beginning of March, the squadron once more resumed operational duties, which consisted of shipping patrols, and scrambles after enemy aircraft. The record shows a rather disheartening repetition of the phrase One scramble—no contact.

A visit from the prime minister

A welcome break in routine came on 15th March when according to the *Rhodesia Herald*:

> *A Rhodesian Fighter Squadron (No 237) sent out an escort of four Hurricanes to welcome Sir Godfrey Huggins when he flew across the desert to visit them. The escort flew in astern when the distinguished visitor was some distance from the base and closed in to a tight formation on his plane. The planes included 'Bulala' with its painted emblem of a native shield and crossed assegais and 'Bonnie Scotland'. The four machines were piloted by men thoroughly representative of their country for their homes are in Bulawayo, Flight Lieutenant Archie Wilson; Que Que, Flying Officer Lynn Hurst; Salisbury, Flying Officer Ralph Ashby and Selukwe, Pilot Officer Ian Smith. Over the aerodrome, the escort peeled off while the transport plane slid down to a perfect landing and stopped near the canvas.*
> (Rhodesia Herald, 16th March 1943)

---

* Henry Boyer was born in Bulawayo, trained in Rhodesia and proceeded to the Middle East in February 1942.

During his visit, the prime minister received a thoroughly sustaining meal. The board groaning under a variety of curried dishes with unlimited rice and bully beef, garnished with tomato; cake and coffee in earthenware cups.

Squadron Leader John Walmisley takes command

Towards the end of March, Wing Commander Eric Smith, the squadron's commanding officer, underwent a spell in hospital and during his absence, Squadron Leader John Walmisley assumed command. It was during his command that the squadron received a visit from the Colony's military observer in the Middle East who reported:

> It was nearly dusk by the time we had found the desert track that would lead us to our destination. Battered tins and bits of wreckage pointed the way through an area where enemy mines still await the unwary. Against the murky skyline reared the crumpled, burnt-out skeleton of an Axis bomber; a mangled truck lay across the sand-bagged breastwork of a gun-emplacement on a sand dune; and nearby, a tank was visible with gaping wounds in its sides, its turret awry, the gun abjectly pointing at the sand as if in surrender. It is not long since General Montgomery strode triumphantly through these parts towards the west. A dust storm synchronized with our arrival and as we stood in the mess tent partaking of hospitality at the hands of Squadron Leader John Walmisley, who is in charge, in the temporary absence of Wing Commander Eric Smith, and Flight Lieutenant G. (Pop) Bryson, the adjutant. The faces and hair of the inmates began to take on that pale yellow frowziness that comes from the powdering of the fine dust. There were little trailings of dust at the bottom of our glasses and one could hear it grating between the spoon and the bottom of one's soup plate. By evening, rain was hitting the canvas in fitful squalls and though it laid the dust, it brought the cold. I was awakened before first light by the stuttering roar of engines, steadily mounting to a reverberating crescendo as a section of fighters scudded across the landing-ground into the dust that was again in evidence, and circled up into the low-lying murk. The day's work had begun. Only recently has the squadron changed from army cooperation to fighter operations. (Officially, the unit designation was changed to Fighter/ Reconnaissance on 21st March 1943). The changeover was achieved after two weeks' conversion training, which says a lot for both pilots and ground staff. Their main job at the moment is to provide protection for shipping on a particular sector of the Mediterranean. On the day on which they became operational as a fighter unit, their pilots were over a convoy giving high and low cover for a total of 67 hours. Combined with shipping patrols is the continuance of training as a fighter squadron. These occupations entail a considerable amount of flying. On a visit to one of the flights, I met Corporals John Frederick Wiid, Leslie Frederick Copland Alexander and Bennie Israel whose exacting duties still give them time to be salvage conscious. They showed me the dump from which they regularly dispatch loads to centres where the various articles are made good use of. A number of the chaps in their leisure time help in this salvage work and the efforts of Stanley Bates Jones (Que Que) and Corporal Eric Edward Glasby (Bulawayo) led to a surprising spectacle late one evening during my visit. Amid cheers from the onlookers there appeared on the perimeter of the landing ground, moving at a smart pace, a Nazi reconnaissance tank, its guns swinging about as if seeking a target! It had been found a few miles away with petrol still in its tank, having been abandoned by the enemy probably because of clutch trouble. It is to be taken under its own power, as a Rhodesian contribution, to a tank salvage centre.
> (Rhodesia Herald, 7th May 1943)

Wing Commander Eric Smith, who had been in command of the squadron for 18 months, was posted back to the Rhodesia Air Training Group for instructional duties and Squadron Leader John Walmisley took his place as squadron commander on 23rd April 1943.

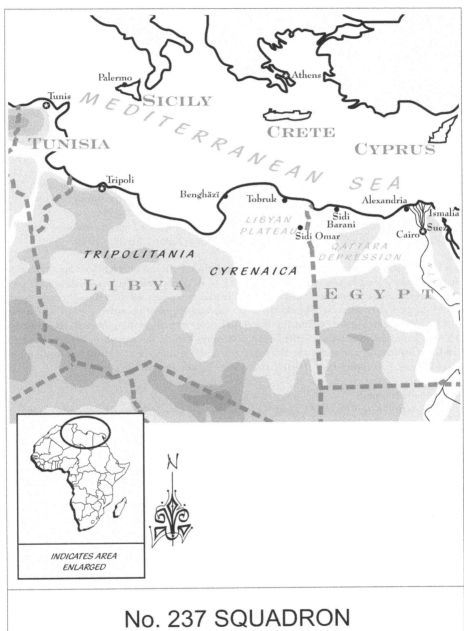

INDICATES AREA
ENLARGED

No. 237 SQUADRON
OPERATIONS IN THE MEDITERRANEAN

The most common entry in the log-book during May reads: Two scrambles—no contact. These scrambles after elusive high-flying German aircraft were interspersed with sorties, convoy escort duties and fighter sweeps with little or no real action. Although, on 26th May, Flying Officer John Michael Crook probably found he had more than enough excitement when he was forced to bale out of his Hurricane owing to a burst coolant pipe. HMS *Easton* picked him up and deposited him ashore at Alexandria.

Despite these occasional spurts of activity, this was proving to be a rather dull time for the men of the Rhodesia squadron and as a result, some members requested postings. Among these was Ralph Parry who was posted to the European theatre where he arrived in time to take part in the D-Day landings. As is always the case when there isn't enough excitement, odd mutters began to be heard. Middle East Liaison Officer reported:

> *Attention is again drawn to the fact that there are so few Rhodesians in No 237 Squadron. At the present rate, it will lose its identity as a Rhodesian unit. The men naturally are very displeased at the present trend. I am told by RAF Middle East that they have asked for SR personnel from time to time from RATG. I press this matter because I have the assurance that RAF Middle East will cooperate.* (M/E Liaison Officer report, 4th May 1943)

A further grumble was that members of the squadron believed they had lost opportunities for promotion owing to transferring from SRAF to RAF and felt that less-qualified officers were being promoted over their heads. Another matter that occupied their thoughts was: what would happen after the war? Would there be any employment opportunities in a postwar SRAF? Then suddenly the excitement of action thrust every other thought from their minds. On 10th June, the invasion of Sicily began. Two days earlier, the squadron said goodbye to Landing Ground 106 and moved to Bersis, where on 15th June, the squadron was on all night stand-by owing to rumours of Italian paratroopers in the close vicinity.

Operations Record:

June 16th. *Flying Officer I.D. (Ian) Smith force-landed (wheels down) six miles north-east of base owing to glycol leak. Three sorties failed to contact convoy at dawn partly owing to cloud. Convoy of 21 ships escorted from noon to dusk with a last light sweep. One successful interception exercise carried out. Flight Lieutenant Panico Theodosiou and Flying Officer John Michael (Boy) Crook scrambled after a Ju 88.* Crook returned from 22,000 feet owing to lack of oxygen. Flight Lieutenant Panico Theodosiou 'tally-hoed' and closed in to 1,000 yards [900m] and then lost consciousness and spun from 30,000 feet to 20,000 feet owing to lack of oxygen.*

Long distance raid on Crete

On 23rd June, No 237 (Rhodesia) Squadron took part in a long distance raid on Crete. Bruce Anderson covered the operation for the SABC:

> *At their briefing the night before the Crete 'party', the Rhodesians found that they were to be part of a force that included RAF, SAAF and Greek squadrons. It was unusual, I think, for land fighter aircraft to fly so far across water to strike at a target far from Africa. To Crete and back must, in this case, have been about 500 miles [800km]. Long-range petrol tanks were fitted beneath the wings of the fighters to enable them to achieve the distance. The planes took off in the night with a waning moon as illumination, and in perfect formation flew out to the three-pronged attack. The Rhodesians were led by the squadron's commanding officer, Squadron*

---

* The Ju 88 was pressurized and could fly at far greater altitudes than the Hurricane.

Leader John Walmisley. The pilots accompanying him were Flight Lieutenants Archie Wilson and Panico Theodosiou and Flying Officers Lynn Hurst, Basil Deall, Arthur Davies, John Crook and Arthur Coulson. The formation of which the Rhodesian squadron was part, headed for the western tip of the island, and just after dawn broke, saw its towering mountain standing out like a vast, sheer rock in the ocean. They came in from the northern side, the planes just skimming the water. It became necessary to jettison the reserve petrol tanks to enable a rapid climb to the top of the 5,000 feet mountain on top of which were the targets. They split up according to instruction to seek individual targets. Cretans welcomed the attackers and stood on the roofs of their houses waving to them as they roared low overhead to swoop with blazing guns on Axis concentrations in buildings, tents and gun emplacements. From all accounts, the enemy endured considerable losses and damage to installations of all descriptions. Flight Lieutenant Theodosiou is credited with having knocked out a wireless station and Flight Lieutenant Wilson with having put out an anti-aircraft position. The Rhodesians did their stuff with the best, and though they encountered heavy flak, got away without loss. Flying Officer Davies' plane was badly holed and he himself received a few slight shrapnel wounds but he flew his craft safely home. And now the Rhodesians are hoping for another show like the last to relieve them of the monotony of convoy patrols. The so-called monotony, however, was broken for Flying Officer Crook the other day (26th May) when he had to bale out owing to engine trouble when he was 30 miles [48km] out at sea. Soon after his parachute had deposited him in the sea, he was picked up by one of the convoy's escorts and got a taste of real navy hospitality. For he had no sooner set foot on the deck than he was conducted to a bathroom, where a hot bath, heated towels, a drink and a freshly opened tin of cigarettes awaited his attention. And while he was dealing with these, his clothes were being dried and pressed. In due course, he was landed at a North African port (Alexandria). (Rhodesia Herald, 28th Aug. 1943)

Commenting on the mass fighter attack on Crete, Ralph Parry says that it was in retaliation for the murder of commandos that they took part in a raid on the island.

August saw the squadron back on convoy protection duties and no-contact scrambles. The squadron lost one pilot on 5th August, when Flying Officer George Reid's Hurricane spun in and caught fire. He was buried the following day in the military cemetery at Barche.

Members of the ground crew go 'home'

It was in August 1943 that a large detachment of 65 ground staff arrived back in Rhodesia having served with No 237 (Rhodesia) Squadron since the outbreak of war. They travelled by sea to Durban and then by train to Bulawayo where they arrived on Saturday morning 14th August. In this contingent were men who had left the Colony in August 1939. They received a large and enthusiastic welcome. And by a happy coincidence that same day, the Women's Auxiliary Air Service held its first public parade to mark the second anniversary of its inception. This parade drew the population of Bulawayo not only out of doors but also onto rooftops and window ledges that commanded a view of Main Street. The Heany Air Station Military Band led the WAAS parade comprising five flights representing all stations and units. The Minister of Air, Colonel E. Lucas Guest, took the salute.

The men from No 237 Squadron returned to a country where higher income tax and more expensive beer and cigarettes were the order of the day. The extra taxation was necessary in order to finance an interest-free loan of £3,000,000, which had been offered by Britain. The loan was to be used in the Colony on RATG and internment camps. In fact, Rhodesia's Budget for 1943/44 allowed for an expenditure of £14,948,000. At the end of July 1943, there were 248 officers and 3,256 other ranks serving in the Colony, while a further 722 officers and 1,752 other ranks were serving overseas.

CHAPTER 17

A war of attrition

From March to July 1943, Bomber Command had endeavoured to make Happy Valley (The Ruhr) a hell for those below. Most raids were mounted by between 300 and 700 aircraft. But however much the Germans had endured during these five months, nothing had happened to force Hitler's advisers to consider an end to the war. No German city had been so shattered that it could not recover. During the same period, Bomber Command was also suffering losses. Between March and July 18,406 sorties were flown; 872 aircraft failed to return; a further 2,136 were damaged. Eight hundred and seventy-two aircraft missing translates as 6,000 men killed, wounded or taken prisoner. For the aircraft damaged but brought home by disciplined and courageous men, read a similar total in crews broken up. The Official History remarks: These were grave losses and the margin left to Bomber Command with which to preserve the future fighting efficiency of the force was narrow indeed.

The bomber offensive continues

On 3rd July 1943, 15 Lancasters from No 44 (Rhodesia) Squadron attacked Cologne. Five days later, the squadron returned to Cologne. This time 17 aircraft took part in the raid. The fact that no aircraft was lost on either occasion was sheer luck, because several aircraft were hit by flak and attacked by fighters. Sergeant Campbell's cockpit shield was damaged by flak and his bomb-aimer's perspex panel was shattered. The port outer engine of Squadron Leader Robert Grant Watson's aircraft was hit by heavy flak and the starboard outer engine caught fire, causing both turrets to become unserviceable. This aircraft flew back on two inboard engines crossing the French coast at a height of about 7,000 feet. The gunner of Flying Officer Pilgrim's aircraft was commended for promptness and efficiency in attacking a Ju 88. Sergeant Moffat returned with a hole four inches (10 cm) in diameter in the back of the port bomb door. Often it was only the amazing strength of the Lancaster that brought the aircraft and their crews back safely.

Gelsenkirchen was the target on 9th July. Happy Taylor says: It was my last operation and I was determined to stay out of trouble. I had a good aircraft and I climbed to 22,000 feet and bombed from 27,000. Pilot Officer Aldridge was forced to jettison his bombs but brought his aircraft back with the starboard outer and port inner engines, port generator, intercom and mid-upper turret unserviceable. There were holes in three engines, the wing, fuselage and bomb bay. There was one flak hole in the port wing of Pilot Officer Harding's aircraft but miraculously no casualties and according to the Operations Report: This route was reckoned to be quiet!

The Germans take the upper hand

It was the turn of Turin on 12th July, with Wing Commander John Nettleton leading the squadron. He failed to return from this raid. Happy Taylor says, Nettleton took a number of senior men on this trip: senior navigation officer, senior bomb-aimer etc. It was chaos when he didn't come back. One fortunate man was Des Taylor DFC who should have been a member of Nettleton's crew. It would have been his last trip but Nettleton called him in and said, We'll let you off the last trip. This was probably because Flight Lieutenant Taylor's wife was visiting. As soon as Nettleton's loss was reported, Squadron Leader R.G. Watson took over, and remained acting commander for three days, until Wing Commander E.W. Williamson arrived from No 106 Squadron to assume command.

On that same day, 16th July, three aircraft were detached to RAF Scampton for a raid on Leghorn in Italy scheduled for 24th /25th July.

The loss of Wing Commander Nettleton, highlighted for No 44 Squadron a fact of which Bomber Command had become increasingly aware during the first half of 1943: that the Germans were winning the war of attrition in the air. By July, German defences were shooting down 5% of the Allied bombers attacking their homeland and the rate was rising steadily. Three quarters of these losses could be attributed to German fighter aircraft; the rest to flak and accidents.

The Germans had in fact perfected a defence system. From a series of radar stations strung out across northern Europe, at 20-mile (32km) intervals, a long range, early warning system, Freya, could pick up approaching bombers. Another system would fix onto the German night fighters orbiting the station. The fighters would then be guided towards the bombers until the fighters' own Lichtenstein radar system had made contact with the quarry.

The British had developed a counter-measure, but until the middle of July, it had not been used. The authorities were afraid that once it became known, the Germans would use it against British radar. However, bomber losses were so high that some retaliatory measures had to be taken. On 15th July, at a meeting of the War Cabinet presided over by Winston Churchill, permission was finally given for the new method to be employed.

A top secret anti-radar 'weapon'

At 00h25 on the morning of 25th July 1943, as the leading bombers in the stream passed the island fortress of Heligoland on their way to Hamburg, the first window bundles were dropped. German radar screens were suddenly covered with snow. Window was the magic counter device; simply clouds of aluminium foil strips.

When the first wave of bombers, 110 Lancasters from No 1 and No 5 Groups, arrived over Hamburg at 01h03, their crews were struck by an air of unreality. Instead of the precise control, which had been a case over the past few months, the searchlights now seemed to be groping blindly in the dark. Where beams did cross, others would quickly join them, and as many as 30 or 40 beams would build up to form a cone—focusing on nothing. What had happened was that the aluminium foil had confused the radar operators and made precise measurement impossible. This affected the radar sets that controlled the searchlights making them useless, as were those that controlled the guns. So the gunners were forced to abandon predicted fire and take 'pot-shots'. On this, the first raid on which window was used, only 12 aircraft failed to return. Had the Allies lost their normal 6%, 50 bombers would have gone down, so 38 bombers together with their crews were saved by the dropping of 40 tons— 92,000,000 strips of aluminium foil.

The same technique was used with equal success on the following night during a raid on Essen, and against Hamburg on 27th July. Two days later the target was again Hamburg.

Flying Officer Parsons stated that the whole city appeared to be burning. Fires from previous raids could be seen 60 miles [96km] away. There was a pall of smoke up to 15,000 feet. Window used effectively against searchlights. Searchlight defence operating in conjunction with night fighters was greatly increased. Many searchlights went out when the window was dropped. Whole operation appeared to be a success. (Operations Record)

Aircrews had not been told the exact reason for dropping the aluminium foil, so that if they were taken prisoner they would have less to tell German interrogators. In fact, most of them presumed that Window put searchlights out. From the start of the Window Campaign, not a single aircraft from No 44 Squadron had gone missing. On 30th July, the scheduled target was Rhemscheid. Wing Commander Williamson chose to take his place for the first time as leader of the squadron on an operation. He failed to return and once again Squadron Leader R.G. Watson assumed command.

August 1943 proved a wet and cloudy month and many operations had to be cancelled, but on 2nd August, despite severe electrical storms and very bad weather, 14 aircraft took off for Hamburg. Many cookies were jettisoned in the sea. Sergeant Moffat and his crew were lost on this raid. (Operations Record) On the following day Wing Commander R.L. Bowes,* who had been an instructor with the RATG, took over command of the squadron.

Master of ceremonies
Following a break owing to bad weather the squadron attacked Mannheim on 9th August and Nürnberg on 10th August, without loss. Two days later came an all-Lancaster attack on Milan, where No 44 Squadron had their first taste of a Master of Ceremonies Raid. This was a technique that had been used successfully on the Dambuster Raid. The idea was that a master bomber, usually in a Mosquito, circled above the target for the duration of the raid. His job was to control the bombing and direct the aircraft precisely onto their target. According to the Operations Record: The pilots state that it is a helpful technique though there are complaints that his instructions were unsuccessful owing to jamming. This method of controlling the bombing was to be used increasingly for the rest of the war.

No 44 attack on Peenemünde
August 15th 1943 saw the Rhodesian squadron again over Milan, and then came a top-secret target—Peenemünde. Hitler had already hinted that Germany was preparing new and devastating weapons. Allied intelligence had pinpointed Peenemünde as the experimental establishment and factory, where a rocket weighing 80 tons, carrying a warhead containing 10 tons of explosives was being developed. The destruction of Peenemünde became a top priority and under the code name, Operation Hydra, the attacks began on 17th August. Five hundred and ninety-seven aircraft were detailed for this first raid. Group Captain John H. Serby, commanding No 83 Squadron in his Lancaster high above the target, was director of operations. Searby reported that the markers had been accurately placed and that the attackers were to bomb directly on the flares. During the final stages of the attack, German fighters began to concentrate on the area and caused heavy losses. Forty aircraft, including three from the Rhodesian squadron failed to return. Derek Venables says:

Tickey Baggot, from Rhodesia House, was at Dunholme Lodge on a visit during the raid. Aircraft 'J' Johnny, with Pilot Derek Aldridge, Mid-upper Gunner Derek Welensky and Rear Gunner Derrick Palmer, was late back. Sergeant Bryant, who was ground staff in charge of the plane, kept watching the sky. At length he gave a shout "'J' Johnny is coming!" Ambulances stood by as she touched down and veered to one side. The aircraft was riddled with bullet holes. There was a gaping hole in one side and one engine was gone.

---

* Wing Commander Bowes was awarded the DFC while in command of 44 squadron.

The Lancasters had paid a heavy price but the raid was vital. Five days later No 44 Squadron joined in attacks on a chemical works at Leverkusen but the pilots reported that the raid was disappointing owing to the bombing being scattered. On 23rd August, it was back to Berlin where visibility was good with a bright moon. 1,700 tons of bombs were dropped in 50 minutes. German night-fighters were busy, with 31 combats reported during the raid but the Rhodesians had no losses. Once again Lancasters proved their worth with losses of 5.4 percent against 8.8 percent for Halifaxes and 12.9 percent for Stirlings where gun positions had been sacrificed.

There followed two raids, one on Nürnberg and one on München-Gladbach and then on the last day of the month it was back to Berlin with nine aircraft. Pilot Officer Stephenson failed to return. Flying Officer Parsons's* Lancaster was attacked by enemy aircraft and his rear gunner, Flying Officer Pascoe, was wounded in the foot but elected to stay in his turret although his intercom had been severed and he had to take his lead from the actions of the mid-upper gunner. Later, the mid-upper gunner was wounded in the eye and his place was taken by the bombaimer, who manned the guns and kept excellent watch, despite the failure of the guns. As a result of this action, the mid-upper gunner lost an eye and Flying Officer Pascoe lost a foot. The pilot and the rear gunner both received immediate awards of the DFC.

The BBC makes a historic recording of a raid in progress
The first raid in September 1943, on the 3rd was an all-Lancaster attack on Berlin carried out in good weather from 21,000 feet, during the final hour of the day. The BBC commentator, Richard Dimbleby, actually made a recording that was broadcast later, aboard a Lancaster over Berlin. This was quite a feat in the days before magnetic tape, when making a recording involved cutting a vinyl disc! Unfortunately, 22 aircraft were lost on this raid, including two from the Rhodesian squadron. One of these aircraft was piloted by Flying Officer Rundle, the other by Squadron Leader Robert Grant Watson, who had been educated at Plumtree School and had entered RAF College, Cranwell in 1931.

On the following day, three aircraft went out to look for dinghies in the North Sea but five hours' searching brought no success, though Flying Officer Burr did spot a black object about the size of a mine. He did an orbit but failed to see it again. The next night, 5th September, it was the turn of Mannheim which cost No 44 Squadron one aircraft. Large numbers of hostile fighters were reported.

For two weeks during September 1943, the weather closed in with intermittent rain and low cloud, which caused the cancellation of many operations, though training exercises went ahead, including, practice bombing, fighter affiliation, air/sea firing and cross country. Then on 22nd September came the most concentrated attack so far on Hanover, in which 12 aircraft from the Rhodesian squadron took part.

All aircraft reached target. Weather clear. No moon or cloud. Visibility good. Fires numerous. Fires visible from Dutch coast 250 miles [400km] away. Deep orange colour with lots of smoke. Pilot Officer Snell observed nine columns of thick black smoke. A 4-lb (1,8kg) bomb dropped from above, made a hole in the tailplane of Squadron Leader Lynch's aircraft. Port outer engine of Flight Sergeant Barton's aircraft caught fire while crossing Dutch coast on the return journey. Did not affect mission. Spoof attack on Oldenburg was going well. Fires still burning at 22h30. Attack successful. (Operations Record No 44 Squadron, 22 Sept.1943)

★ Flying Officer Parsons's crew were: Sergeant Lewis, Warrant Officer Smythe, Pilot Officer Marshall, Sergeant Mann, Flying Officer Hartung and Flying Officer Pascoe.

The 'spoof' attack

The technique of mounting spoof attacks now began. The idea was that a diversionary raid would be made on a secondary target in order to confuse the enemy. Sometimes the spoof worked, and other times it did not.

On 23rd September, nine aircraft attacked Mannheim; on 27th September the target was Hanover again. Two days later the squadron paid a visit to Bochum. During this raid, Flight Sergeant Derek Welensky from Salisbury was mid-upper gunner in a Lancaster that was attacked by two enemy aircraft. Derek and the rear gunner together succeeded in destroying both enemy planes. Both gunners were awarded the DFM.* All aircraft returned safely but Pilot Officer West pranged aircraft rather badly on landing back at base—bad bounce—worse recovery! (Operations Record No 44 Squadron)

Reconnaissance flights and bomber escort

While the giant bombers were roaring further and further afield the Typhoons of No 266 (Rhodesia) Squadron were making their presence felt closer to home, as they carried out reconnaissance flights across the Channel and attacked shipping with bombs and cannons. Another of their tasks was to provide escort for returning bombers, sometimes extending their protection to the Flying Fortresses of the United States Air Force returning to their British airfields after attacks on Brest, Lorient or La Pallice. The Fortresses would come, some struggling back, one or more propellers feathered, with control lines shot away and tail assemblies torn to ribbons by the 20mm cannon shells of the German fighters. Then a flight of the RAF boys came out to meet us. Brother, they looked mighty good!

One entry in the Squadron Operations Record says:

Twenty miles [32km] south of Torquay found a Fortress with two engines u/s. Escorted it to Exeter. Crew very grateful.

During these rendezvous and escort operations, any target that presented itself was attacked. On 9th July, it was a small convoy off the French coast near St Brieuc Bay. The six aircraft of the squadron turned south, and increasing speed, attacked. Each of the aircraft selected one of the five ships, which turned out to be armed minesweepers. Bombs were seen to burst close but were all probably near misses and not very damaging.

Flak was moderate but Mike Furber's aircraft was evidently hit in the engine and he had to ditch. He made a good job of it, landing about 200 yards from the rocky shore but his aircraft turned over and he was not actually seen to escape. Pilot Officer Norham Lucas thought he saw something that might have been Furber come to the surface. He had got away with it in just the same circumstances in his last ditching on February 20th so there is quite a good chance.

In fact, 20-year-old Frederick Michael Furber of Plumtree who had attested in February 1941 and trained in Rhodesia was later reported a prisoner of war in Stalag Luft III in Germany. The crash occurred two weeks before his 21st birthday.

Increasingly during June and July, the war was carried into France with the Typhoons attacking French coastal aerodromes in an attempt to prevent German hit-and-run raids on England. On occasions, these sorties were carried out solely by aircraft from the Rhodesian squadron; sometimes No 266 Squadron aircraft joined in a Circus with other squadrons.

---

* The squadron's record since September 1939 stood at one VC, three DSOs, and 84 DFCs and DFMs.

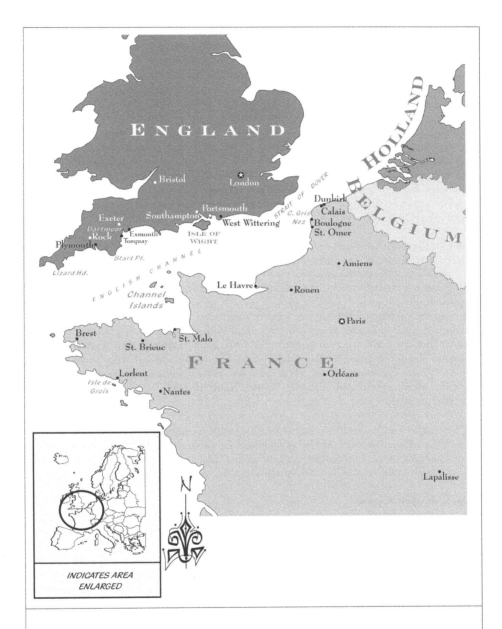

No. 266 SQUADRON CARRIES OUT RECONNAISSANCE & BOMBER ESCORT

Operations Record:

30th July. Fine and hot. Operations: 12 aircraft taking off from Portreath took part in a Circus. On this occasion, No 266 was joined by aircraft from Nos 183 and 193 Squadrons. The plan was that No 266 aircraft were to arrive over the target, Guipavas aerodrome, four minutes ahead of the Bombphoons of 183 Squadron. 266 was on time but did not bomb owing to the fact that there was 10/10 cloud at 8,000 feet. We saw a fair amount of flak. Flying Officer (Bob) Menelaws spun when the squadron flew into cloud and on recovering at 2,000 feet flew straight home alone. When he came out over the French coast, Flying Officer Haig Cooper's engine cut completely. He jettisoned his hood and doors and was just going to bale out when the engine picked up again. The squadron climbed and escorted him home. He looked very naked sitting in his open cockpit. On making a normal approach to land, he nearly spun in, owing to having no hood and doors, apparently. So he made a faster approach downwind on the longest runway, which was under repair and broke his port wing when he ground-looped on overshooting. Pilot not hurt. (Operations Record)

John Deall recalled that during July and August 1943, the squadron was frequently detailed for specific operations that required moving to Northolt (near London) or to the east coast for a day. It was also in July that the squadron received its first two Typhoons fitted with connections for long-range jettisonable fuel tanks, an improvement, which was to give the machines vastly increased range.

During the evening of 3rd August, while flying escort to returning bombers of No 263 Squadron, Squadron Leader Sandy MacIntyre and Pilot Officer Bundu Thompson became involved in a dog-fight with six or eight FW 190s. Sandy's aircraft was hit twice causing damage to the ailerons and fuselage and Bundu Thompson was last seen spinning down from 4,000 feet. The commanding officer, who was uninjured, landed at Portreath while the rest of the squadron returned to Exeter. Richard Keith 'Bundu' Thompson* was never seen or heard from again.

Shortly after this (incident of 3rd August) the squadron was warned about a move to Gravesend, in Essex. There was much packing of equipment for the move—but instead of Gravesend several aircraft went to Predannack in Cornwall and did an op. from there. In fact the move to Gravesend was cancelled. No 193 Squadron went instead. Such is war. (Peter Penfold)

A black day for No 266

August 15th was described as a black day by Peter Penfold. It was to be one of the worst days of the war for the Rhodesian squadron. All began well. A fine sunny summer day, with a Circus planned, during which the Whirlwinds of No 283 Squadron with an assorted escort were to carry out a bombing raid on Guipavas Aerodrome while aircraft of Nos 266 and 193 Squadrons, flying as one squadron, were to freelance. However, the bombers and their escorts were recalled before bombing the target owing to heavy cloud cover. For some reason Nos 266 and 293 Squadrons were not informed of this decision and continued with their operation.

About seven enemy aircraft were sighted near the target and six of the Rhodesian squadron aircraft turned to engage them, presuming that No 193 aircraft were close and would give

---

* Richard Thompson, born in Yorkshire had been farming in the Marandellas area before he joined up in February 1941. While training with RATG, Richard was lost in the bush after making a forced landing. He managed to survive by eating roots, fruit and insects. It was 12 days before he met a tribesman who guided him back to 'civilization'. His aircraft, a Tiger Moth, was never found. This incident gave rise to his nickname 'Bundu'.

them back-up. However, the No 193 Squadron pilots had not seen the German aircraft and were well on their way home. The whole engagement was a disaster.

Squadron Leader Sandy MacIntyre was shot down early in the encounter by an FW 190, which closed to about 50 yards. This aircraft was engaged by Sandy's No 2, Flight Sergeant Charles Erasmus who shot it down in flames. Flying Officer John Small's aircraft was evidently also hit because he was seen to bale out. Charles Erasmus continued his attacks on the enemy aircraft and claimed a further FW 190 damaged.

Finally, the remaining four Rhodesian aircraft turned for home. As they flew low over the French coast, they spotted two aircraft approaching. Uncertain whether or not these were hostile, the Rhodesians turned hard to intercept. In making this manœuvre, Flying Lieutenant Frederick Brian Biddulph's aircraft stalled and spun into the sea. Meanwhile Barney Wright and Tusky Haworth had become involved in individual dogfights with the enemy aircraft during which they were separated. Eventually Barney, after inflicting damage on one of the enemy, found himself alone in the sky with no aircraft in sight. Tusky, whose starboard cannons had jammed, was repeatedly attacked by the two Germans and was hit in the tail plane by a high explosive cannon shell. Eventually, after some difficulty, he found an opportunity to break off the combat and streaked for home. The Operations Record ends:

We are claiming one enemy aircraft destroyed and one damaged by Flight Sergeant Erasmus and two damaged by Flight Lieutenant Wright, but this is a poor set off against losing the CO Squadron Leader MacIntyre, Flying Officer Small and Flying Officer Biddulph.[*]

David Garrick, talking about the events of 15th August:

I must add that we lost four pilots that day. To the three listed must be added John Dennis Miller[†] *(of Bulawayo) who also went down in flames. My wife was staying in Exeter for a few days and on this Sunday the Adjutant, Flight Lieutenant Collcutt had given me the day off but sad to relate I had to help him sort out the four pilots' belongings and see to the necessary details for the Air Ministry. After Flight Lieutenant Collcutt was transferred to No 44 Squadron he wrote to me several times. He said that on 266 we were upset about losing one pilot but on 44 he sometimes had to see to the effects of 20 or more aircrew lost in one raid on Germany.*

Also telling of the events of 15th August, John Deall says,

The squadron moved to Bannock in the south-west tip of England and from there took part in a combined operation with several other squadrons. The Typhoons were to fly escort for twin-engined bombers carrying out a strike on the continent. In order to escape radar detection, the aircraft flew at wave-top height across the Channel. Halfway across, the bombers had to start their climb in order to pass over the cliffs. As they collected and began to climb, orders came through that the weather was unsuitable and the operation was called off. The enemy was by

---

[*] Frederick Biddulph was born in Johannesburg, educated at Prince Edward School in Salisbury and trained in Rhodesia before proceeding overseas in August 1941. John Small was born in Scotland, worked on a mine in Rhodesia before attesting in November 1940. Trained in Rhodesia before proceeding overseas in August 1941. Charles Derek Erasmus was born in Salisbury, attested June 1941 and trained in Rhodesia before proceeding overseas in May 1942. He later became CO of No 193 Squadron but was attached to No 266 Squadron when he was killed during air operations near Raathe, in Holland on 9th March 1945.

[†] John Dennis Miller, born in Johannesburg, employed by the Rhodesia Railways in Bulawayo before attesting in March 1940 and proceeding overseas for training in July 1940.

now alerted to the attack. Owing to some oversight, No 266 were not recalled and ran straight into the full enemy defences.

Following the loss of Squadron Leader Sandy MacIntyre, command went to Squadron Leader Peter Lefevre. During August the people at home learnt a little more about the activities of the squadron through an article in the *Rhodesia Herald*:

The squadron now specializes in attacking enemy ships especially small warships of the E-Boat type, enemy aerodromes and similar targets and also escorting Bombphoons (bomb-carrying Typhoons) on a variety of sorties. Up to the middle of July this year the squadron's total bag was 41 enemy aircraft destroyed, 21 probably destroyed and 30 damaged. Eight locomotives destroyed and scores of attacks on enemy shipping and other targets. The squadron now has Rhodesian flying personnel throughout. As well as protecting the shores of Britain, the men of No 266 found time to throw a party for 'blitzed' children in Exeter.
(Rhodesia Herald, 3rd Sept. 1943)

Early in September 1943, orders came for the long-awaited move to Gravesend.

This is terrific news especially after the disappointing cancellation of last month.
7th September. *Fine 6/10. Ops nil. 17 Typhoons took off from Exeter and flew to Gravesend. Sergeant (Chimbo) Hulley had to force-land, wheels up, in a field near Haslemere. His aircraft category 'B' - Sergeant Hulley slightly hurt. Officers billeted in the huge Cogham Hall, which* **is a most interesting mansion.**
8th September. *Fair—no flying. In the evening the pilots were briefed for tomorrow's job; a large convoy of invasion craft will be leaving Dungenees and heading for a point nine miles [14km] off Boulogne. Eight aircraft of No 266 with eight of No 193 and eight of No 257 squadrons will patrol the convoy. This is only a 'feint' landing, the object being to make the Hun attack in force and fight him on level terms over the Channel. All aircraft taking part in this operation have their wings painted in black and white stripes.* All went to bed early.*
9th September. *Fine. Ground mist. Ops. Because of the weather at base, ops postponed and finally cancelled. Patrolled Boulogne and saw convoy and masses of friendly aircraft. No enemy aircraft.*

And with that—it was back to Exeter the following day.

Norham Lucas qualifies for the Caterpillar Club and the Goldfish Club. On 21st September 1943, the squadron moved to Harrowbeer in South Devon, on the edge of Dartmoor. Two days later, nine aircraft were detached to Predannack in the early morning for a sweep. Flying Officer Norham Lucas was hit by an FW 190 on returning and had to bale out over the sea. Everything worked perfectly for him. He judged his height from the water while descending by dropping a book! His diary says: Baled out 33 miles south of the Lizard. Picked up by Walrus.

Flying Officer Norham John Lucas was trained at Guinea Fowl Air Station in 1941, where he flew solo after only five hours 50 minutes, which was a record. He flew Harvards at Cranborne and proceeded overseas in June 1941. In England he joined No 19 Squadron, which had been Douglas Bader's squadron but unfortunately Bader was then a POW so they never met. On 15th November 1941, his 21st birthday, he joined No 266 Squadron. He

---

* Obviously it was decided that the practice of identifying Allied aircraft by painting them with black and white stripes worked because it was later used on D-Day.

remained on the squadron until he took an instructors' course in 1944. He was subsequently posted back to Cranborne, where he instructed on Harvards until his death in a flying accident on 5th April 1945. While with No 266 Squadron he had four and a half confirmed victories. His worst ordeal was baling out over the sea, in bad, or duff to use RAF slang, weather. He was forced to remain in his dinghy for a considerable time before he was picked up. This experience qualified him to become a member of the Goldfish Club, open to any one who escaped death by using his emergency dinghy. Norham also qualified for membership of the Caterpillar Club having made use of his parachute to save his life.

Towards the end of September, 'A' flight received a new version of the Typhoon, which was a few miles an hour faster. However, the squadron pilots did not get a chance to try the machines out at Predannack because the weather turned bad with heavy mist and rain. There was, therefore, very little flying as the month of September 1943 drew to a close.

CHAPTER 18

Winter 1943

The Italian people had never been enthusiastic about World War II. The Italian army had been defeated in North Africa and on the island of Sicily where the city of Palermo fell to the Allies on 22nd July 1943. By 17th August, the island was in British and American hands with a loss to the Italians of 160,000 men killed or captured. Italy was in a bad position. She had lost 200,000 soldiers killed or captured in North Africa. A quarter of a million Italians were engaged in the Russian Campaign and another half a million were fighting against partisans in the Balkans.

Mussolini was summoned to attend a meeting of the Fascist Grand Council. This council, which was supposed to be the supreme policy-making body of Italy, had not met since the beginning of the war. Mussolini alone had made all the decisions. Suddenly the council found the strength to depose him as commander in chief of the Italian armed forces. Mussolini was replaced by King Victor Emmanuel, who immediately ordered the arrest and detention of El Duce. Negotiations with the Allies began and on 3rd September, a fateful date for Europe, Italy signed a secret act of surrender. On that same day, the Allies crossed the Straits of Messina and landed on the Italian mainland in Calabria.

News of the Italian surrender was released on 8th September 1943. At dawn on the following day, British troops made a landing half way up the leg of Italy, close to Rome. Two days later, 11th September, No 237 (Rhodesia) Squadron began a move to Idku, in Egypt. The move had been completed by 15th September and it was back to convoy escort duties. According to one pilot serving with the squadron:

> *The things I remember best about this period are not operations at all, but the more ordinary things of everyday life: the heat and the red dust of the desert, which got into everything, including food; parties at the Alexandria Sporting Club, when the beer flowed freely; moonlight nights over the Mediterranean as you flew to pick up your convoy; the picturesque scenery and the good wine of Cyprus; the endless living in tents and the sand and waiting for the Spitfires, which we had been promised and which never seemed to arrive.* (Official History)

One break in monotony came when the Rhodesian squadron was asked to provide an escort for units of the Italian fleet, which wished to surrender. A less fortunate episode occurred on 4th October at Idku, when Flying Officer Ian Douglas Smith's aircraft scraped the top of the sandbag wall shielding the parked aircraft. He was seriously injured in this accident and it was to be four months and much plastic surgery before he was back in the air again. Day after day during the month of October the squadron log-book reads:

> *Five convoys protected. One escorted*
> *Three convoys protected and escorted*
> *One convoy protected. Three convoys escorted.*

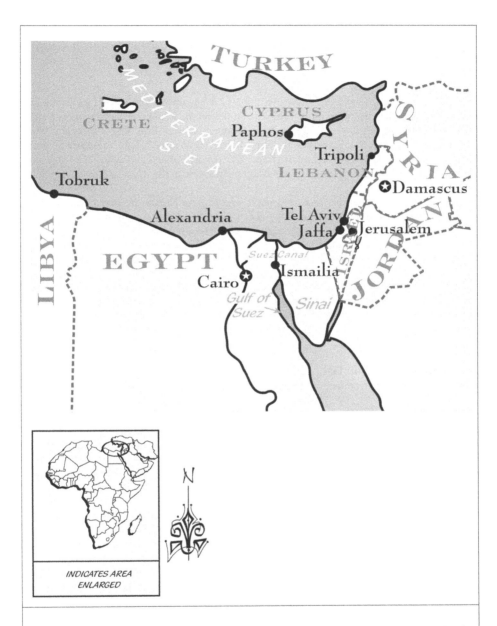

No. 237 SQUADRON - SHIPPING PATROLS AND CONVOY ESCORTS

Sometimes the code names of these convoys seemed to have been chosen by someone with a strange sense of humour: Convoys Nursemaid, Nostril and Paper escorted. Convoys Raven, Announcer and Nigeria protected.

No 237 move to Cyprus

On 30th October came welcome news: At 20h30 the squadron was ordered to proceed to Paphos, Cyprus, next morning on detachment. At 08h30 the following day Squadron Leader John Walmisley, Flying Officers Robert John Moubray, Harley Ernest Lew Petersen, Cyril George Lannin Hurst, Roy Francis Gray, John Michael (Boy) Crook, L.G. Paine and Sergeant McDermott proceeded with eight Hurricane IIC (Long Range) to Paphos. Ground staff followed later in the day travelling in two Dakotas. An article in the *Rhodesia Herald* reported:

> *Rhodesian fighter pilots have been operating in sweeps in the Aegean Sea recently but have found time too for sport and celebration on the ground. The island (Cyprus) on which their squadron is based was the scene on the night of 11th November of a braaivleis to celebrate the anniversary of their first action in Africa, four years ago. Sheep were slaughtered and spitted to supply the meal.* (Rhodesia Herald, 22nd Sept. 1943)

The article goes on to comment that the Rhodesians had been doing well at soccer and rugby—but they had one big grumble—the severe shortage of cigarettes on the island. News got back to base hospital. The men in the ward had a whip round amongst themselves and got together a large parcel, which they sent to the Rhodesian liaison officer for onward transport to Cyprus.

The Spitfires arrive—at last

Towards the end of November, the squadron returned to the African mainland.

> *The Rhodesia fighter squadron in the Middle East had had its prayers answered by the announcement that it is to be re-equipped with Spitfires. I (Rhodesia's Military Observer) was on a visit together with Lieutenant Colonel Thompson, Rhodesian Liaison Officer to the squadrons stationed on the North African coast when that historic signal was received, so I know it is absolutely 'gen'. On that day, too, the squadron's two flights, which had been on an island somewhere in the Mediterranean engaged for several weeks on fighter sweeps, were ordered to return to Africa. In the early afternoon, we stood on the edge of the runway with the station commander, a youthful New Zealander, and watched the flights come over in massed formation. "Every plane was in the air at a few hours' notice," said an officer of the ground staff, as he counted them off. The aircraft had no sooner landed than the first pilot I spoke to, said, "The squadron has got the finest ground staff in the Middle East. The ground personnel with us on the island kept our machines in tiptop order and we took off this morning en masse at very short notice. When one has nothing but the blue Med beneath one and a single engine pulling one's kite along, then it is a reassuring thing to know the quality of one's ground staff. They are a grand lot of chaps." Those members of the ground staff who had been sent to the island for maintenance work returned in transport planes next day.*
> (Military observer, Rhodesia Herald, 10th Dec. 1943)

On 1st December the squadron received an early, much appreciated Christmas present— the Spitfires that had been so long in arriving! Hastily all personnel received familiarization on the new aircraft and nine days later the squadron was on the move again—this time the destination was Savoia, in Libya, where once more convoy escort became the order of the day.

Savoia, Libya

The Christmas Eve service was held in a tent lit by hurricane lamps, the candle on the little altar relieving the partial gloom. An air force padre, wearing pilot's wings conducted the service and among the guests were Colonel Lucas Guest, Rhodesian Minister of Air, Air Vice-Marshal Charles Meredith, Lieutenant Colonel Thompson, Lieutenant Don Elliot and the military observer from Cairo. On Christmas Day, the ground staff Christmas dinner with the officers as waiters was held in a little village on the Barbary coast. The menu was: cream of tomato soup; roast pork and apple sauce; roast turkey and stuffing; potatoes, cauliflower and green peas; Christmas pudding and brandy sauce; mince pies and Christmas cake; oranges and beer. How the men managed to play a football match after that, heaven only knows.

On Boxing Day, Flying Officer William Basil Deall and Flight Sergeant J.H. McDermott scrambled. The bogey was a Ju 88, which No 33 Squadron tally-hoed but was unable to intercept. In the evening, it was the officers' turn for Christmas dinner, which was attended by Air Vice-Marshal Meredith and party. The year ended quietly for the squadron with the now only too familiar pattern of convoy escort and scrambles.

While No 237 (Rhodesia) Squadron was keeping a watch on the Mediterranean, the other Rhodesian fighter squadron, No 266 was busy patrolling the Channel.

Channel patrol with No 266

On 9th October Flight Lieutenant Barney Wright, Pilot Officer George Eastwood and Flying Officer Norham Lucas had an unpleasant experience when they found themselves in thick cloud with little or no petrol left, after an operational sweep into France. Coming through a hole in the cloud, they discovered that they were directly above St Merryn Aerodrome. They came in to land immediately, despite the fact that the runway was under repair and partially obstructed. Fortunately, they managed to bring the aircraft to a halt without hitting anything, but in their words it was A very shaky do!

Six days later a new arrival on the squadron, Sergeant Dougal Drummond, from Salisbury, had his first taste of action. It was 15th October—a beautiful day—when Flying Officer Norham Lucas and Sergeant Drummond were scrambled from stand-by to intercept two FW 190s that had been spotted crossing the coast in the Brixham area of Tor Bay.

The pilots were vectored south of Bolt Head and at a height of 8,000 feet spotted the two enemy aircraft, which promptly dived to 1,000 feet and headed south. Lucas and Drummond went after them and overtook them easily. Lucas selected one enemy and Had a bit of a turning match with it, but then it very obligingly straightened out and Lucas was able to get in several good bursts from dead astern. The enemy aircraft's starboard undercart dropped and after another burst the pilot baled out. His parachute was seen to open.

Meanwhile Sergeant Drummond had taken on the other FW which, after weaving a bit, straightened out allowing Drummond to fire a number of long bursts at it. He saw strikes and smoke. The enemy started weaving again and after several more bursts Drummond ran out of ammunition. He called Norham Lucas up on the R/T (radio transmission by voice) and told him what had happened and Lucas took over the pursuit getting in one short burst. The FW exploded and crashed into the sea. Norham did not know it but that final burst was the last of his ammunition as well. He circled the area and spotted floating wreckage from the two German aircraft less than a mile apart. He climbed and reported back saying that one German pilot was in the sea and gave the operations centre a fix.

Four No 266 Squadron aircraft with Squadron Leader Lefevre leading were detailed to patrol the area where the German aircraft had gone down. Unfortunately, two of these aircraft had to return to base almost immediately when one of them developed engine trouble. The

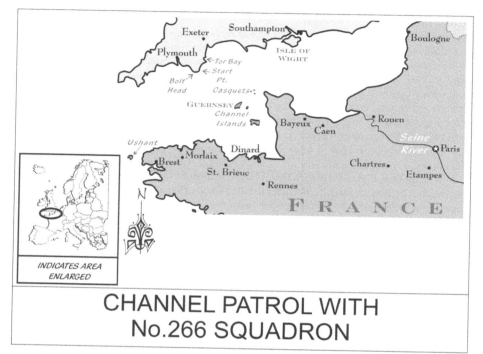

INDICATES AREA
ENLARGED

CHANNEL PATROL WITH
No.266 SQUADRON

two remaining pilots, Squadron Leader Lefevre and Flight Sergeant Ivan Olliver (Chimbo) Hulley, approaching the area at zero feet, spotted six enemy aircraft approaching. The enemy pilots spotting the Typhoons turned and made off towards the Channel Islands. The two Rhodesian squadron pilots gave chase, despite the fact that they were closer to France than to England. Squadron Leader Lefevre was slowly overtaking the fleeing enemy when he spotted the second enemy aircraft coming in to attack him. Lefevre broke off his attack on the first aircraft but managed to get a very short burst at the second, with no visible result. Meanwhile Hulley had closed on the commanding officer's original quarry, unmolested. He fired several bursts, starting from long range and closing to 200 yards (180m). He saw a strike but had to break off the combat as he very rightly considered that he must rejoin his No 1.

The enemy aircraft continued to belt for home, the island of Guernsey, but by then they were only a few miles ahead. As far as No 266 was concerned, it was a missed opportunity because had the other two Typhoons been with them they might have secured a good bag. According to the Operations Log-book: It is said that today's victories are the first by any aircraft taking off from Harrowbeer.

Long-range fuel tanks for the Typhoons
Later in this same month, the long-range fuel tanks were employed for the first time on an operational flight. These tanks gave the Typhoons an extended range, but in the event of a contact, they could be jettisoned to allow greater manoeuvrability. On this occasion, they were not jettisoned as no contacts were made with the enemy.

An attack on shipping in the St Malo Estuary was followed by a riotous party in the mess. It gravitated to Rock Hotel and back to the mess and ended in an attack on the moustaches of a number of the squadron members. Flying Officer John Dennis (Dusty) Miller's being a complete write off, the others—repairable! Peter Penfold remembered: The CO ran into 'S' whilst taxiing 'Q'. But to make up for it—plenty of drinking took place at the Leg of Mutton, Yelverton, on the edge of the airfield. Incidentally the pub is still there but is now called The Hunter.

By November 1943, the long-range tanks were being used on most operations and the early problems that had been encountered over jettisoning them seem to have been ironed out. Occasionally it was not only the tanks that were jettisoned.

> **11th November**—*fair. Operations: Four aircraft led by Flight Lieutenant J.D. Wright went on Rhubarb to railway east of Granville. Beat up two locos and freight train and continued eastwards but as cloud was down to the deck, turned about and attacked the same target a second time. Flying Officer Norham Lucas was hit in his port long-range tank, which was knocked off. As he was running on this tank, his engine immediately cut. Not knowing the cause, he jettisoned his hood and doors to bale out, but just before doing so, he tried switching over to the main tanks. The engine picked up and all was well. Claiming two locos damaged, one German A/A gunner killed and one light A/A post damaged.*

On this day, the Rhodesians of No 266 Squadron lost a good friend. Flight Lieutenant Colly Collcutt, who had been one of the first Rhodesians to join the squadron and who had served as station adjutant since March 1941, was posted to No 44 Squadron.

In November 1943, the squadron Typhoons started carrying bombs. These were usually 2 x 1,000-lb (450kg) or several of lesser weight. The task of shipping strikes with bombs was added to escort and reconnaissance work. The very first bombing operation, which took place on 16th November, was rather disappointing as, weather over target u/s so bombs jettisoned and operation abandoned. The target was to have been Poulmic, in France. The following day, on a shipping 'recce', the squadron had more luck. Saw and attacked a small armed trawler, seeing many strikes. This attack took place in the Lezardrieux Estuary. The month ended with a couple of shipping patrols and an escort for 18 returning Boston Bombers. Flying Officer Lucas once again, Lost his door! And there was a visit from the Rhodesian squadron's old commanding officer, Charles Green. He'd come from Alnwick in Northumberland in two hours, Penfold remarks. We thought that was fast, in those days.

'Roadstead' operation near Isle de Groix

December 1943 began with a bang. On the first day of the month, eight No 266 Squadron aircraft took off from Predennack and joined up with four aircraft from No 193 Squadron and one Mosquito. The weather was fair and the pilots were detailed for a Roadstead. This was a code name for an operation against shipping in a partly sheltered anchorage. Their specific target was a motor vessel of 4,000 tons near Isle de Groix in the vicinity of Lorient. Flying at zero feet, they located a large merchant ship, as well as several armed trawlers and minesweepers. No 193 Squadron planes attacked the ships. The flak was heavy and the Mosquito dropped its bombs a bit short, was hit and dived into the sea.

Meanwhile Red Section, led by Squadron Leader Lefevre, with Flight Sergeant Chimbo Hulley, Pilot Officer Wally Mollett and Flying Officer Peter (Blackie) Blackwell, had spotted a Ju 52 fitted with a mine-detecting ring approaching at about 300 feet. Hulley and Mollett attacked and the Ju 52 was seen to hit the sea.

Red Section continued flying round the island, attracting a great deal of flak from the ships and the island. Blue Section, meanwhile, which had passed to the south of the island and attacked the two minesweepers, was heading for home and was some distance ahead of Red Section.

As Blue Section approached Cape de la Chevre (near Brest) in company with two aircraft of No 193 Squadron, two Ju 88s were sighted. One disappeared into cloud but Pilot Officer Pressland of No 193 Squadron attacked the other, setting its starboard engine on fire. Flight Lieutenant John Deall and Flying Officer Dusty Miller then followed up this attack and each got a burst off at short range. The Ju 88 plunged into the sea.

As this combat was taking place, Red Section flying near Gleman Island saw yet another Ju 88. Peter Blackwell went into the attack firing from long to very short range. The other pilots of the section saw strikes on the enemy aircraft. Then they saw Blackwell break away. He was not seen again and it was presumed that his aircraft had been hit by the enemy's rear gunner. Squadron Leader Lefevre, Mollett and Hulley continued their attack until their ammunition ran out. Following Mollett's final burst the enemy aircraft crashed into the sea. During the combat, Pilot Officer Scott-Eadie heard someone say, I'm getting out and this could have been a message from Peter Blackwell.

Peter's story

A search was carried out, on the next day, of the area in which Peter went missing but nothing was seen. As always on these occasions there was a hope that the pilot had baled out successfully and this was the case with Flying Officer Samuel John Peter Blackwell. The men of his squadron had no means of knowing what had happened but after spending five hours in his dinghy, Blackie was picked up by a German flying-boat and taken to base for questioning.

I was in a room with my bodyguard and he switched on the wireless to a German station. While his back was turned I tuned to the BBC for the commentary at the end of the 6 o'clock news. This caused a great stir, and the guard rushed over to switch it off, saying, "It is forbidden for us Germans to listen to English programmes. The English propaganda is better than the German." Then I was marched off and given some food—what food! Macaroni boiled in water, black bread, heavy as a brick, which broke with a click, and some marge. I felt very depressed and hated even the voices of the Germans. They never smile. They are all so serious. I slept in a hospital ward (empty) and around the walls hung pictures of Hitler, Himmler, Goering and other Nazi bosses. I felt like turning them all back to front but thought they would not appreciate the joke.

The following morning Peter was dispatched in the direction of Germany, with an officer and a soldier as escort. For the long journey he was given half a loaf of bread, some margarine and a red sausage, but he couldn't complain because his escort received the same rations.

They were pleased at the privilege, as it meant a chance of going to Germany, but I don't think they got their leave. I expect they are now on the Russian front.

Because that night Peter jumped from the train.

It took a lot of organization, but it was not so difficult. My escorts were not very bright. I was on the go all that night and all the next day. I was very tired and my uniform was torn from crawling through hedges. I wished I could have brought the sausage and bread with me. Eventually I met some French people who looked after me. What I hated most about those two long months were the days of hiding when I could not go out of my room except for meals. I travelled quite a lot and how nervous I was on my first train journey, but I got a thrill from walking past German soldiers in the streets and watching them march through the town. One day the Germans visited a house in the country where I was staying and I had to leave in a great hurry, as they decided it would make a very nice officers' mess. I hid when I heard their car outside and they even went into my room and failed to notice an English book I was reading. When I could, I went for walks in the fields and one Sunday afternoon three of us were rolling logs, which the Germans had cut, down a hillside when six Germans on horseback came round the corner. They left the path and came straight towards us. I thought they were going to speak and stepped behind my two friends, but apparently they were only learning to ride and were taking the horses over the logs for practice. (Peter Blackwell)

By 30th January Peter was back with No 266 Squadron, none the worse for his escapade.

The war of attrition

While the fighter squadrons were busy on their anti-intruder patrols and attacking shipping, No 44 (Rhodesia) Squadron was still engaged in the war of attrition. Every night, weather permitting, the bombers thundered off from their bases in Britain to attack the industrial heart of Germany and every night the Luftwaffe, backed by ground defences, endeavoured to shoot some of the aircraft down. Often the missing rate was over 6 %. As the targets became more distant, so the likelihood of being shot down increased, but also the German fighter pilots were being stretched to breaking point. Clear heads in command on both sides realized that this battle would be won by technology not by brawn—it was up to the scientists.

Meanwhile day after day the men of No 44 Squadron were taking to the air. Early in October, the targets were Hagen and Munich. The second attack was not a success owing to inaccurate marking, and one aircraft piloted by Sergeant Smith failed to return. The rear gunner on this aircraft was a Rhodesian, Sergeant Kenneth Roy Watt.* Raids followed on Kassel, from which Pilot Officer Norton did not get back; then Frankfurt and Stuttgart. On the Stuttgart Raid, Flight Sergeant Lyford had problems. He was forced to jettison his bombs at 23h10, Owing to the rear turret becoming u/s and a glycol leak in port-inner, port-outer and starboard engines. This pilot also encountered flak over the London area and was coned by searchlights. He immediately fired recognition flares but it was a very unpleasant few minutes for the pilot and his crew. The next night, Sergeant Evans was forced to return from Hanover on three engines when one engine caught fire.

After this, there were nine days of no operations, owing mainly to cloudy, wet and foggy conditions. On 18th October, the squadron lost one aircraft over Hanover and two days later came a maximum range attack on Leipzig. Seventeen Lancasters did not return. No 44 Squadron lost one aircraft.

A Lancaster ditches

Flight Sergeant Watts, having attacked the target successfully, began the return journey. Shortly after the flight engineer had switched over to the centre fuel tanks, after the main tanks had been drained to about 80 gallons each, the engines began to splutter. The balance cock was opened allowing the engines to run on the port-centre, port-inner and starboard-inner tanks, in turn, until each was dry. It then became necessary to take fuel from the starboard centre tank which, it was suspected, had a damaged pipeline because of flak.

Almost immediately the two port engines cut and could not be restarted, but the port-outer engine was windmilled at intervals to enable the navigator to obtain Gee fixes—the

---

* Kenneth Roy Watt was born in Norfolk and educated at St George's College and Bulawayo Technical School before attesting in October 1942. Trained in Rhodesia and proceeded overseas in February 1943.

port-outer engine carried the alternator, which ran the navigational radar (Gee). The aircraft had been flying at 16,000 feet but now height was rapidly lost and the captain warned the crew that he might have to ditch.

The navigator continued to obtain Gee fixes and the wireless operator transmitted the aircraft's position to Heston control. When the aircraft was at a height of 2,000 feet, the engineer assisted the captain to remove his parachute harness and strapped him in to a partially inflated Mae West. The front hatch was jettisoned and the remainder of the crew took up ditching positions. About two minutes later, the pilot ditched the aircraft approximately into the wind, which was south/west.

The aircraft broke its back near the mid-upper turret and the rear half sank immediately. The dinghy inflated automatically and the crew boarded it, with the exception of the captain, Flight Sergeant Watts, who failed to get out of the aircraft, and the navigator who fell off the leading edge of the wing. They paddled the dinghy round to the front to look for the navigator and blew their whistles but in the dark and with a heavy sea running, he drifted away and was lost. The aircraft sank in about 15 minutes.

The sea was rough, the crew were violently seasick but they knew that the coast was not far away so it was decided to put out a sea-anchor and wait for dawn. Some lights could be seen so the Very pistol was removed from the emergency pack and fired, without result. During the night, a large merchant ship passed within 100 yards (90m) without spotting the dinghy. It was a heartbreaking moment but then the airmen caught sight of another ship. This was HMS *Lock Moidart,* a minesweeper, which carried a searchlight, and was actually looking for the dinghy.

This ship picked up the airmen three hours and ten minutes after they had ditched. They were landed at Grimsby early in the morning and taken to the naval hospital but were found to have no injuries beyond shock.

The Operational Record ends:
Raid appears MOST unsuccessful effort. Static/electrical storms encountered, icing heavy. Bombing widely scattered—Wanganui flares as much as 70 miles apart. General opinion— wasted effort!

Wanganui was a variation on Oboe in which the main force approached the target in the same direction as the Oboe run-in and bombed blind using the sky markers flying at 165 mph (265 km/h) with zero wind velocity on bombsight.

On 3rd November, 15 aircraft went to Düsseldorf on a raid, which was difficult to assess, but the pilots appeared fairly content. For the next six days the weather closed in and constantly the phrase, Operation cancelled appears in the Operational Record. The weather lifted on 10th November allowing 14 aircraft to attack Modane, but the following six days were again cloudy with rain.

During this lull, news was received that Flying Officer Happy Taylor had been awarded the DFC to add to his DFM.

The Battle of Berlin
In the middle of November 1943, what was known as the Battle of Berlin, began. This was a series of 16 large-scale operations against Germany's capital city, air raids in which Lancasters played a major part. No 44 (Rhodesia) Squadron launched its first attack in this battle on 18th November when 18 aircraft took off, among a total of 444. Nine aircraft failed to return, but none of the missing came from the Rhodesian squadron. Some 1,500 tons of bombs had been dropped. The extent of the damage could not be immediately assessed but was believed to be

considerable. However, the Berlin raids were less effective and more costly than the attacks on Hamburg and the Ruhr, owing mainly to the increased distance and the strength of the defences.

After three nights' break, it was Berlin again on 22nd November with 16 aircraft from the Rhodesian squadron taking part with no losses. On 23rd November, it was back to Berlin with 16 aircraft but three failed to return. The pilots were Flight Lieutenant Hill, Pilot Officer Buckel and Pilot Officer Hanscombe. Three nights later, the squadron was again over Berlin with 14 aircraft. This was to be the final operation in this month as fog and low cloud closed in, but Berlin was again attacked in great strength on December 2nd, when two aircraft from No 44 Squadron failed to return. William Paul Johnson (Rhodesian), the rear gunner in one of these aircraft, did not return.

Defences had been strengthened and extended but the raid was reckoned to be a success. On the following night Leipzig was the target and the attack time was 04h00 with the result that the Lancasters were landing back at their bases well after dawn. On 16th December, there was an all-Lancaster attack on Berlin in very bad weather, so bad in fact, that 12 Lancasters were wrecked trying to find their way home. Once again, the Rhodesian squadron was lucky.

It has now been further disclosed that out of four enemy fighters destroyed by British-based bombers in the last attack on Berlin on the night of December 16th, three were shot down by the aircraft of the Rhodesian Lancaster bomber squadron, two of them by the same aircraft. Since June, this squadron has shot down 13 night-fighters and damaged many more, a considerable number of which were unlikely to have reached their bases. Bombers attacking Germany by night, evade fighters whenever they can, their object being to reach the target, not to fight it out with the German air force, so the figure of 13 fighters actually destroyed by this one squadron since the end of June, is a measure of the enemy's desperate resistance, and of the great number of fighters the Germans have put up to meet this attack. (Rhodesia Herald, 23rd Dec.1943)

The Lancaster, which shot down two night-fighters on 16th December, was 'Z' for Zebra, flown by Pilot Officer Oakley. The first fighter was sighted just after the bomber had crossed the enemy coast and was shot down before it could fire a single shot. The second fighter, a Ju 88 was spotted 15 minutes later and dispatched with equal speed. Sadly, this successful trip was marred by the fact that Pilot Officer Rollin failed to return. The rear gunner in this crew was Flying Officer Arthur T. Moodie from Bulawayo. He had trained in Rhodesia and had been posted overseas in October 1942.

On 20th December, the target was Frankfurt and again the Rhodesian squadron lost one aircraft, flown by Pilot Officer Evans. Three days later, it was Berlin again for the loss of two aircraft. Christmas brought bad weather and there was to be only one more operation in 1943. That was an attack on Berlin on 29th December:

Clear starlight. Visibility good. Sky markers and route markers well placed and concentrated. No enemy fighters and flak slight over target, though heavy round Leipzig.
(Operations Record)

CHAPTER 19

The buildup

January 1944—the year may have changed but the role played by No 44 (Rhodesia) Squadron remained unchanged—almost nightly attacks on Berlin, Hanover, Hamburg or some other German city. Whatever the target, the routine was much the same. Wing Commander Bowes, commanding officer of the squadron explained:

As CO, I am told what the target is to be and the strength of the raid. I inform my Group of the number of aircraft that I can supply for the operation; fix details of aircraft to be used and quantities of petrol to be carried, which may be as much as 2,000 gallons (9,090 litres) or more, to each aircraft, according to the route they will take. Aircrews are selected for the night's work. The armoury staff is preparing the bombs and ammunition to be loaded up later. The ground staff are re-examining and testing the planes that are going to be used. The aircrews take the aircraft up for a final flying test. In the mess kitchen, sandwiches are cut and coffee made. Emergency dinghies are checked and the hundred and one other pieces of equipment packed carefully into their special stowage places aboard the aircraft. By midday or soon after, if all goes smoothly, everything will be practically finished and ready for the night's operation. The ground crews are as keen as the aircrews that nothing should prevent an aircraft taking off at the appointed time. I have been discussing the routes to the target and the general plan of attack with the station commander, and the met. officer, who tells us all that can be predicted about the weather. We may start with as many as three alternative routes, the final route to be selected nearer the time of take-off. The longer the route to be followed, the more petrol will be needed and the smaller the bomb-load can be carried. Every aircraft's part in the attack, exact time of take-off and required arrival over the target. Finally, at what is known as the Flight Planning Conference, details of the group plan of attack are settled by telephone among all the squadrons taking part. By lunchtime, all that remains to be done is the briefing of the aircrews. This is a very intricate affair particularly for the navigators, who are responsible for bringing the aircraft to a point perhaps 600 miles [960km] over Germany within one and a half minutes either way of a given time. Any straggler may find himself in Queer Street, as he will at once be made the individual target for the defence organization, so accurate navigation is all-important. The bomb-aimer gets a ground plan of the target and information regarding pathfinder technique for the attack. Then, the main briefing, which follows, makes the opportunity for all crews to get together and pool their individual information. Every man knows exactly what he has to do and when he has to do it. As dusk fall, the whole sky seems to vibrate with the roar of the bomber force as it climbs to gain altitude before setting out. The ground crews will be waiting again to take over in the icy winter night when our planes return in eight hours time.
(The War History of Southern Rhodesia)

So much for the men who watched the take-off. What was it like to fly on one of these large-scale raids?

The mid-upper turret is just about the best place in a bomber to see everything that is going on. My first trip to Berlin was on a cold night with big patches of cloud. About five minutes after take-off, I saw ice was forming on the guns. As we left the cloud the ice disappeared, but I had to keep a watch-out for it the rest of the trip. As we reached the French coast, flak opened up and a stray piece hit the exhaust on the starboard inner engine, which burst into flames. From the mid-upper turret, I could see the flames shooting out for nearly two feet and lighting up the clouds around us. I reported to the skipper, who could also see the damage from his cabin. The great danger was that the flame might reach the petrol tanks, but as it was not blowing that way and the engine was still working, we decided to carry on, the flight engineer keeping a careful watch on the temperature of the engine. No one made any suggestion of turning back. We went on and made our bombing run. Cloud was thicker over the city, but this was to our advantage, because their searchlights couldn't get through to us. Flames were still streaming from the exhaust, lighting up the clouds around us, and my turret in particular, I felt conspicuous but luckily, cloud kept the fighters down. We didn't see one—only a couple of fighter flares on the way back. By the time we got to base, the exhaust was burning merrily, but we landed safely and were pretty glad to see the ground again. But taking it all round, it was one of the quietest trips I ever made. (The War History of Southern Rhodesia)

On 1st and 2nd January 1944, the target was Berlin with a loss of just one aircraft. 5th January the squadron went to Stettin and then the weather took a hand. Ten days of no operations owing to fog, cloud and rain. However, the squadron did enjoy the officers' mess dance, which apparently was a great success.

The weather lifted briefly in mid-January, allowing eleven aircraft to take part in a raid on Brunswick, from which one failed to return; then clamped in again until 20th January, when Berlin received its heaviest pounding to that date. Twelve aircraft from No 44 Squadron took part and all but one reached the target. A spoof attack on Kiel was well timed.

The following night, when Magdeburg was hit, there were heavy losses of both Lancasters and Halifaxes. The Rhodesia squadron sent in nine aircraft. Seven attacked Magdeburg and two went to Berlin. Flight Lieutenant Ruddick was reported missing, while Flight Lieutenant Patrick Dorehill's aircraft was damaged by fighters. He brought the plane back with a large hole in the starboard wing, damage to the hydraulic system, and the rear part of the fuselage. Dorehill was forced to make a crash-landing at the base. Flight Lieutenant Wiggin, after making the bombing run, was attacked by two Me 109s. Three of his rear turret guns failed to fire and the fourth was a runaway. The result was that his aircraft sustained hits and considerable damage and had to make an emergency landing on three engines. It was partly because of this operation that Patrick Arthur Dorehill was awarded a bar to his DFC.

The month of January ended with three visits to Berlin. One of the Rhodesians who took part in the Berlin Raid on 28th January was Flying Officer Terence Hugh Fynn of Gatooma. It was his eleventh operational flight and his seventh visit to Berlin.

I thought it was a very good attack. When we arrived, many fires were burning. The whole attack seemed well concentrated. I saw two explosions, the second just when we were about to come away from the city. In each case, the cloud was lit up for miles around. The ground defences fell off as the attack developed and at one stage they seemed to be overwhelmed.
(Rhodesia Herald, 1st Feb. 1944)

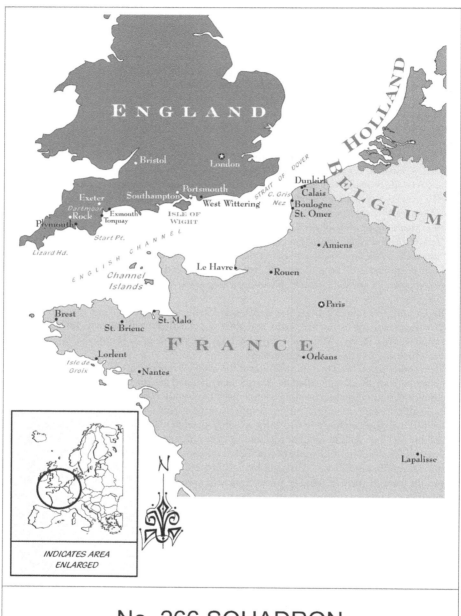

No. 266 SQUADRON
SWEEPS OVER FRANCE

The Operations Record for 30th January stated:

Pilot officer Lyford and Pilot Officer Johnston failed to return. Pathfinder flares excellent. Target identification by Gee and route markers. Wanganui flares red with green stars and red and green target indicators on ETA. Pilot Officer Bradburn had three combats and claims Me 210 destroyed. His bomb doors damaged by cookie owing to violent corkscrewing over target, while being pursued by a fighter. Attack concentrated. Cloud cover thick. Fires could be seen 100 miles [160km] away. Route from Danish coast to target, very busy all the time with heavy flak and fighter flares. Pathfinder flares on route and Wanganui very good.

H2S was used to good effect on this raid, proving the operational value of this tool and resulting in the speed-up of production and installation.

February began quietly with a fortnight of No Ops. Training was carried out when the weather, which was mostly cloudy with drizzle, fog and snow, permitted. On the third of the month, Wing Commander Bowes was posted from the unit to No 52 Base. His place was taken by Wing Commander Frederick William Thompson, a Rhodesian from Gwelo. The weather cleared briefly on 15th February allowing a raid on Berlin, followed by three days of cloudy drizzle.

On 19th February 1944, 18 aircraft attacked Leipzig flying through thick cloud and encountering severe cold. The next night the target was Stuttgart, which according to the Operations Record, was one of the best attacks seen. Pathfinder flares concentrated. As we turned for home, fires were developing into something big.

Three nights of No Ops and then 17 aircraft carried out a raid on Schweinfurt from which one Lancaster failed to return. Of course, the loss of an aircraft did not necessarily mean there was no hope for the crew. Frequently news was received of Rhodesians who were alive in prisoner of war camps in Germany; for example, during January, word came from Flight Lieutenant E.E. Spence, Pilot Officer Richard Galway (Dickey) Bennett, Flying Officer David Oucherlong Cowland-Cooper and Flying Officer Grenfell Godden, (later to be killed in a flying accident on 23rd November 1945). The target was Augsburg on 15th February for the loss of one aircraft, piloted by Flying Officer Bartlett.

Wing Commander Thompson becomes the commanding officer

March 1944 began with a 14-aircraft attack on Stuttgart, the first raid to be led by the new commanding officer, Wing Commander Thompson.

There were many big fires on the ground. We could see the glow very clearly through the thick cloud. Very few enemy fighters seemed to be up—the weather must have grounded many of them. Searchlights were blocked by cloud and flak was never very strong. Halfway on the return journey one of the engines failed but we came back all right on the remaining three.
(Rhodesia Herald, 3rd March 1944)

Another Rhodesian pilot on this raid was Pilot Officer Frank Levy whose Lancaster was attacked by a fighter.

My rear gunner opened fire at long range. Then, he was followed by the mid-upper gunner. They saw tracer bullets hit the fighter, which replied to our fire. But we were not hit. The fighter broke off the engagement and was last seen going down in a deep dive. We all think it must have been badly damaged. (Rhodesia Herald)

Flight Lieutenant Terrence Hugh Fynn of Gatooma described two large explosions:

We had just finished our bombing run, when we saw the first of them. It was in the target area right underneath us and at first I thought it was our own 4,000-pounder (1,800kg) going off, but it was too big for that. It lit up the whole sky above Stuttgart and something very big must have gone up to show through the clouds in that way. The second explosion was five minutes later and again there was a great red flash. We also saw fires glowing through the clouds. Fires were joining up quickly while we were there. (Rhodesia Herald)

Wing Commander F.W. Thompson, the new commanding officer of the Rhodesia squadron, had taught Science at Chaplin School before joining the SRAF in 1939 as a sergeant. He was commissioned in December 1940 and awarded the DFC in April 1942, the AFC in 1944 and the DSO in September 1944. His citation reads:

Wing Commander Thompson has completed numerous sorties against a variety of targets. On one occasion, en route to Stuttgart, his aircraft was hit by anti-aircraft fire, disabling one engine, which caught fire. The fire was eventually extinguished although not before considerable height had been lost. Nevertheless displaying the determination and efficiency that has characterized his operational career, he continued his mission and completed a successful attack. On the return journey, a second engine gave trouble necessitating a landing in adverse weather shortly after crossing the English coast. By his personal courage and enthusiasm, this officer raised the efficiency and morale of his squadron to a very high level.

Incidentally, Pilot Officer Oakley's aircraft was shot down by a night-fighter over Stuttgart, but Pilot Officer Oakley and his crew, with the exception of the engineer, Sergeant Jock Campbell who was killed when his parachute failed to open, all landed up in Stalag Luft III.

After this Stuttgart attack, the weather clamped in again and it was not until 10th March, that the squadron took part in another operation, an attack on Essen. Once again, the technique of a master controller was used and from reports, this seems to have been clear and helpful.

The next raid was also on Stuttgart on 15th March, when 3,000 tons of bombs were dropped in an hour. Flight Lieutenant Terrence Hugh Fynn failed to return. Pilot Officer Smith remarked that the concentration of aircraft over the target was tight and he spent all his time avoiding other aircraft. There were in fact 1,000 bombers in the air during the short bombing period. Two days later the target was Frankfurt. Once again the squadron lost an aircraft, that piloted by Flight Lieutenant Phillips. Flight Lieutenant Wiggin says: "800 aircraft in 15 minutes is too tight to be comfortable, particularly since the pathfinder flares were very late at Position E and aircraft were flying across each other's tracks at right angles."

Four days later, the squadron went back to Frankfurt. Sixteen aircraft from the Rhodesia squadron took part and two failed to return. After one day's break, the squadron was off again to attack Berlin. Yet again, two aircraft were lost. Only two more raids were carried out in March, on the 26th March to Essen and on 30th March to Nürnberg, from which Pilot Officer Charlesworth and Pilot Officer Frost did not come back.

A bit sticky over the Ruhr…a lot of night-fighters…many of our aircraft had combats with Ju 88s. Pilot Officer Bradburn claims one enemy aircraft as damaged. (Operations Record)

In all, March had not been a good month for Bomber Command. Seventy-three aircraft missing from the raid on Berlin on 24th March and 96 bombers lost in the Nürnberg attack on

30th March. The Rhodesian squadron alone had lost nine aircraft in eight raids. Contributory causes for these heavy losses were: often the Germans correctly guessed the target; vapour trails led fighters to the incoming bombers and severe icing conditions caused several crashes. But now spring was on the way and with the improved weather came a change in tactics aimed at preparing the way for the great offensive, The Invasion of Europe, which everyone realized must come this year.

The flying bomb—V-1

While No 44 (Rhodesia) Squadron was hitting German cities night after night, No 266 Squadron was waging a different type of warfare. From the squadron base at Harrowbeer in South Devon, aircraft were speeding on fighter sweeps over the Channel and northern France, taking cover in the low cloud and swooping to attack enemy airfields, rail or road traffic. Long-range tanks, holding 45 gallons (200 litres) of fuel, had been fitted to most of the squadron's aircraft giving them a much greater range. These tanks could be jettisoned if extra speed or manoeuvrability was required.

At the beginning of the year, the fighter squadron was heavily involved attacking the V-1 launching sites. These 19-foot long (6m) stub-winged flying bombs needed a launching ramp. Dozens of these ramps had been photographed in France pointing directly at London. New ramps were constantly being exposed by reconnaissance photographs, and these came under attack. It was not possible to destroy all the sites because they were often hidden deep in well-wooded areas and to put these ramps out of action required pinpoint bombing. But the attacks carried out by the Rhodesian squadron undoubtedly saved London and the southern counties from more serious flying-bomb attacks later in the year. These raids were code named No Ball.

> **4th January**. Four aircraft took off with four of No 193 Squadron to bomb No ball target. Found target area covered with 7/10 cloud. Our aircraft think they located the village of Flottemenville, 500 yards (450m) south of target so bombed just north of it. No results seen. Not very satisfactory. Moderate flak. (Operations Record No 266 Squadron)

Wing Commander Baker DFC and Bar arrived to take command of the wing on the same day. In addition to the No Ball raids, the squadron was involved in wide sweeps over France seeking any target, which might offer. These sweeps were known by the code name Rodeo. The squadron was also required to stand by to take on any enemy aircraft, which might try a daylight intruder raid on southern England. Often the squadron was scrambled, only to find that it was a friendly aircraft or even that there was nothing at all.

> **5th January**. Nine aircraft with No 193 Squadron swept at 8,000 feet from Treguter to St Brieuc, Gael, Rennes, Dinard. There were no aircraft seen on any of these airfields. Between Gael and Rennes, four of our aircraft detached to ground level but did not find a target, so returned independently. One scramble. (Operations Record No 266 Squadron)

Often, at this time of year, the weather caused problems and occasionally the attack would shift from flying-bomb sites to railway yards, railway lines and rolling stock, known by the code name Ramrod.

> **16th January**. Four aircraft led by Wing Commander Baker took off on a small Ramrod operation. The target was a store, being four large sheds beside a railway at St Theggonneg four miles [6km] east of Landivisiau. The attack was low-level, using eleven-second delay bombs, and was highly successful. At least four bursts seen slap on the target, shattering parts of the

buildings and one burst right on two trains standing in the siding. Bombing height 150 feet. Rest of trip at zero level. No flak.
20th January. *Fine day! One scramble just as sections were changing over stand-by. Sirens went but enemy aircraft were miles away. Four aircraft on shipping recce. Swept Isles—Batz and round to the west of Ushant to Cap Chevre and back to base. No shipping seen and no excitement. Recce carried out at zero feet.* (Operations Record No 266 Squadron)

A typical sweep on 21st January brought the squadron's first real success of the New Year:

Flew past Gael then turned north. When approaching Lannion, saw two Me 109s commencing to land, one with its undercart down. Squadron Leader Lefevre detailed 193 Squadron to attack one and he attacked the wheels down one. He fired just 20 rounds per cannon, from 200 yards (180m) closing to 100 yards (90m), saw a lot of strikes, and the enemy aircraft flew on quite straight at an angle of 25 degrees to the horizontal, as though it were going to land, but continued, and hit the perimeter track and exploded. Nice shooting! Flying Officer Douglas Charles Borland, his No 2, with his finger hovering over his firing button, saw the enemy aircraft explode and realized that his services were not required and got 'quite a dose of flak' as he flew at zero feet over the airfield. Meanwhile Flying Officer John (Gedunks) Meyer flying with No 193 was overtaking the other enemy aircraft too fast, 'had a squirt' but saw no results. He says he could have slowed up and had another squirt but thinking that No 266 Squadron pilots were following him, he broke away and Flight Lieutenant Cassey and Flying Officer Inglis of 193 between them came in attacking and the enemy aircraft exploded in the air and crashed in flames. The formation formed a defensive circle very smartly and returned to base. The same day there were two scrambles but in neither case could the enemy aircraft be reached in time. (Operations Record No 266 Squadron)

23rd January 1944 during a sweep:

All six pilots had squirted at the enemy aircraft, which kept turning into our attacks. From the camera-gun films it has been decided to share this among Lefevre, John Deall, Vernon Sanders and George Eastwood. Three enemy aircraft destroyed by this station in three days! Very lucky encounters!* (Operations Record No 266 Squadron)*
24th January. *Pouring with rain all day. Visibility less than one mile [1.6km]. No flying. Barney Wright 'A' flight commander is due to leave and become a test pilot. He joined the squadron in August 1941 at Collyweston and has been on every operational flight that he could wangle himself onto. He has bags of guts and most charming personality. The squadron will miss him. News had been received that Johnny Small, identified by the number on his aircraft, shot down nearby, has been buried at Le St Goet near LesNeven. Barney Wright said at the time that he saw Small bale out and his parachute open.† He also said that enemy aircraft flew round the parachute. We all thought that Johnny Small had got away with it. Several pilots attended a party at the WAAF officers' mess and it was a very hectic party.* (Operations Record No 266 Squadron)

Bad weather continued to 28th January when a sweep was carried out, without much luck.

★ Flight Lieutenant George Merriel Rubidge Eastwood of Mrewa was later awarded the DFC partly as a result of this operation.

† The inference of the remark about Johnny Small seems to be that he was shot by a German airman while coming down on his parachute.

29th January. Visibility good. Eleven aircraft led by Wing Commander Baker to Beaulieu at first light with 193 Squadron. Flight Lieutenant Deall crash-landed near Hurn; petrol block; pilot unhurt. Aircraft badly damaged. Nine aircraft took off from Beaulieu with one of 193, led by Squadron Leader Lefevre because the wing commander had a tyre burst. Flew zero feet climbing to 1,500 feet. Made landfall north-east Bayeux. Saw Caen Air Field clearly. No aircraft on it. As weather clear to the south climbed to 4,000 feet to near Chartres; turned soon after, and returned, leaving coast near point of entry. Slight flak at coast. No enemy aircraft seen. Pilots returned from Beaulieu to Exeter where they spent the night and 20 ground crew went in the evening from Harrowbeer by road to Exeter, taking long-range tanks to service the aircraft the next morning. The following day, ten aircraft with the wing commander leading, took off from Beaulieu to sweep the Paris area but on reaching the Needles they were recalled as 50 enemy aircraft were reported operating and our formation was considered too small. A telephone call to the officers' mess in the evening announced that it was Peter Blackwell speaking from London. He had just arrived back in England after being shot down south of Brest on 1st December. This is a terrific show! Nothing much was said at the time about the ways in which airmen managed to return to England from occupied France so as not to compromise the lives of the French Underground workers who made these escapes possible. (Operations Record)

February continued with Rodeo and Ramrod attacks when the weather permitted. By now, the squadron was only using Typhoons on operational flying, although Spitfires were still being used for training exercises.

6th February. Weather cleared. Wing commander and aircraft of 266 went on a weather recce. Then eight aircraft with 250-lb (113kg) bombs followed eight from 193 Squadron in an attack on an H class minesweeper at Aber-Wrach Estuary. 193 plastered the boat with cannon fire. Then 266 bombed it and it is thought that one direct hit was obtained and two very near misses. The boat was left covered in smoke. During the attack, considerable light flak came from an H-boat nearby. Squadron Leader Lefevre said he was hit and was seen to bale out about three miles [4.5km] out to sea. He had insufficient height and his chute did not fully open. He was seen motionless in the water. We are afraid that there is not very much hope that he can have got away with it. He has been a damn good CO to this squadron, keen as mustard and a really experienced leader in the air. His incredible slang expressions have come into general use by the squadron as can be seen from this book. He flew on practically every offensive operation in which the squadron was engaged from the day he arrived. Four aircraft went out and searched but saw nothing. They did see the Minesweeper lower in the water and down by the stern surrounded by oil.

9th February. A fine day. Three aircraft took-off from Beaulieu with three of No 193 Squadron followed five minutes later by six of No 486 Squadron. Wing Commander Baker had to return at once so Flight Lieutenant Cassey led; climbed rapidly to 8,000 feet to cross the French coast near Isign; then dived to zero feet for the rest of the sweep. When five miles [8km] from Chartres an enemy aircraft was seen approaching at 5,000 feet. Pilot Officer Charles Derek Erasmus attacked and shot the enemy aircraft down in flames. Enemy aircraft was a Me 109 type not known. Formation rejoined and got back onto course. When passing west of Dreux Pilot Officer Lucas saw and attacked a Dornier Do 24 flying at 200 feet, setting its pontoons on fire and his No 2, Flying Officer Dusty Miller, then attacked, setting fuselage on fire and saw it crash. Formation rejoined; flew north-west, climbed to 7,000 feet to cross out north of Caen.
(Operations Record No 266 Squadron)

Describing the surprise meeting with the Dornier, Norham Lucas said:

The pilot seemed to see us as soon as we saw him, and came in as if he wanted to play and we got him almost on the deck. I went in first and gave him a quick burst and watched his engines and pontoons burst into flames! Then Flying Officer Miller let him have a burst. The back half of the fuselage exploded and the rest of the aircraft floated down to crash blazing in a wood a quarter of a mile away. (Rhodesia Herald, 11th Feb. 1944)

Next, it was Norham Lucas's turn. The Wing was doing a sweep south of Chartres.

Straight ahead was a target really worth our attention—an aerodrome (Etamps-Mondesir) with many twin-engined aircraft dispersed on it. We dived in and I attacked a Ju 88 and set it on fire. Looking back I saw a heart-warming sight—four aircraft were burning and others smoking. Getting near Paris, I attacked a Ju 88 and it went down in flames. Then we saw three German planes landing, when a Rhodesian, Don McGibbon, weaved into them like a maniac, shooting the three down in almost the same number of seconds. (Lucas's log-book)

Flying Officer Haworth, who was one of the group, damaged another aircraft as it was landing. The section then reformed and proceeded north-west where they ran into bad weather with low rainstorms, so they climbed to 8,000 feet and crossed the French coast at Cap D'Antier landing at Tangmere.

Meanwhile Wing Commander Baker and his No 2 had lost John Deall at Bretigny Air Field, when they ran into a violent snowstorm. On breaking the cloud all alone, Wing Commander Baker saw a Do 217 flying east and shot it down in flames. Some time later having negotiated another snowstorm, he saw an FW 190 and destroyed that too. He finally landed safely at New Church. As Lucas says in his log-book, Good day for 266!

The following day was spent in aerobatics and dummy attacks on a Sunderland. Obviously preparing for the next Dornier they might meet. A sweep on 12th February brought no result with the weather being unserviceable.

14th February. Rain. No flying. Party in the officers' mess to celebrate the victory over Paris and to say farewell to No 193 Squadron.
15th February. Cloud low. A rush to briefing for an operation to intercept some Ju 88s, which had attacked a Sunderland in the Bay and which we hoped would be landing back at Kertin Bastard or Poulinio Air Fields. Nine aircraft were to go but the wing commander could not get his engine started and took off four minutes after the others and could not catch up owing to poor visibility. Flying Officer Lucas led. Flew at zero feet; climbing to 400 feet to cross cliffs at Tregastle; continuing at fewer than 200 feet aircraft suddenly flew over Morlaix Air Field in hazy conditions. Immediately light, medium and heavy flak of moderate intensity, but very quick and accurate, opened up on the formation. Flying Officer Lucas had a large hole blown in his rudder. Flying Officer Miller's aircraft was seen to be on fire and crashed in flames just off the south side of the airfield. Flight Sergeant Dougal Drummond's* aircraft was seen on fire and crashed in flames also south of the airfield. Flying Officer Wally Mollett was seen lagging behind and then was heard on the R/T to say that his aircraft had been hit but that he had sufficient height to bale out or force-land. Pilot Officer Scott-Eadie and Pilot Officer Ken Rogers took avoiding action flying so near the deck that they both hit some treetops but sustained no real damage. Formation flew at zero feet to cross the coast west of Kertin Bastard when they turned east passing within two or three miles to the north of the airfield and so back to base at zero feet. (Operations Record No 266 Squadron)

---

* Flight Sergeant Dougal Drummond was killed.

February 16th brought nothing but a false alarm when the squadron scrambled only to find that the bandit was a Defiant towing a drogue over a convoy for ack-ack practice and the note that:

Flying Officer Norham Lucas has been posted to 59 OTU for a rest. Norham has been with us since Kingscliffe days and is a quiet efficient pilot who always manages to bring his aircraft home despite having it badly shot up on several occasions. A most popular member of the squadron and one who has very steadily done his job and done it very well indeed.*

The weather now turned very cold and with No 193 Squadron having left, the Rhodesia squadron was on stand-by all day, every day, until No 263 Squadron arrived on 22nd February.

22nd February. No 263 arrived, were briefed and took off from here on a sweep. It was abandoned early and on the way home, near Guernsey, Squadron Leader Barns DSO DFC ditched and his No 2 seeing him in difficulties in the water baled out to help him. This is surely the most amazing effort. Six aircraft searched the area between Guernsey and Casquits for Squadron Leader Barns and his No 2 and another pilot of No 263 who was also reported in the drink. Saw nothing. (Operations Record)

The month closed, bringing very cold weather and a welcome surprise:

28th February. In the evening, we were amazed to hear Mollett's voice on the telephone. He's back in England. Thirteen days after being shot down near Marlaix. What a show! (Operations Record)

The speed of his safe return says a great deal for the courageous help and efficient organization of the French Underground movement.

2nd March. It was intended to fly only four aircraft but at the very last moment we were told to take five. Formation, led by Flight Lieutenant Healy, climbed to cross French coast at Cabourg, then dived and flew the rest of the way at zero feet and this was really low! At Ramouillet Flying Officer Derek Erasmus, in avoiding another aircraft of the section struck a tree and severely damaged his wing and radiator cowling. His temperature rose and so the formation about-turned for base and, because of Erasmus's damage, could only fly at 230 miles per hour [370 km/h]. Before crossing the coast, the formation attempted to climb to the clouds, but Erasmus was unable to do this, so the formation went down to zero feet again. And then about 25 miles [40km] inland, on the French coast, Flight Lieutenant Healy said that he had also hit a tree and doubted if he would be able to get back. Formation flew towards Cabourg and then broke. Chimbo Hulley and Charles Baillie going to the left, Vernon Sanders, Derek Erasmus and Healy going to the right and so they crossed the coast separately. Almost immediately Flight Lieutenant Healy said that he must "Get out. Get a good fix and send out the Air Sea Rescue boys." Flight Lieutenant Sanders at once orbited and transferred a fix but could see no sign of Healy. This was four or five miles [6-8km] west of Le Havre. Erasmus still with high engine temperature made straight for home. Sanders orbited for eight minutes then set course for home and about six minutes later heard 'Maydays given in a sing-song voice'. This was also heard

---

★ Norham John Lucas attested in November 1940, trained in Rhodesia and was posted overseas in June 1941. He returned to Rhodesia in November 1944 to take up Flying Instructors' duties. He was killed in a flying accident on 5th April 1945.

by Chimbo Hulley and Baillie. If it was Healy, then he evidently kept flying quite long after his original message. Air Sea Rescue was laid on but nothing was seen. Flight Lieutenant Erasmus managed to get back to Frinton and brought off a successful landing. Sanders landed at Tangmere. Flight Lieutenant Healy was reported missing. (Operations Record)

Snow and scrambles followed, mostly without incident, and Flying Officers Doug Borland, James (Jimmy) Haworth and Don McGibbon were transferred to OTU which left the squadron short of pilots. Then came a detachment to Bolt Head. Eight aircraft moving at first light on 7th March, followed by seven more as they became serviceable. There was one scramble on arrival, which proved to be a flock of gulls on the water, picked up by radar and mistaken for a rowing boat! The air section was followed by a land party of 55. The weather was good but very cold. The exercise, which took place on Slapton Sands, was a Combined Operations landing rehearsal, in preparation for the invasion of Europe which, everyone knew, must come with the summer. The Rhodesian squadron was present in a defensive role, to keep all enemy aircraft well away from the scene. In fact, there was little for the squadron to do during the five days of the exercise.

One scramble to lead home a Dakota, one scramble on which there were Huns but they were below cloud and we were above, so we did not see them, and two convoy patrols without incident. This brings our stay at Bolt Head to an end. As regards Huns, it has been disappointing but everyone has enjoyed themselves. (Operations Record No 266 Squadron)

Early in March, news was received that Peter Blackwell had been awarded the DFC for his escape from the enemy and that John Deall, 'A' flight commander was to leave the squadron.

Flight Lieutenant Deall has been with the squadron since Colley Weston days and he has a score of kills and is one of the old guard. A hell of a nice bloke. He deserves the rest but we all hope that he will be back again in the squadron at some future date.
(Operations Record No 266 Squadron)

John Deall did in fact return to the squadron on 6th October 1944.

12th March. Fine. One morning patrol. Whole squadron back to Harrowbeer in the afternoon to hear that we are to go up to Acklington for a gunnery course for about ten days and shall then move to Thorney Island to an airfield in 20 Wing. Flight Lieutenant Deall and Flying Officer Lucas have been awarded DFCs. They both thoroughly deserve it having been on a great number of ops and this will sweeten the pill of their leaving the squadron for a rest.
(Operations Record 266)

Actually the squadron's departure for Acklington was delayed until 15th March owing to bad weather. The next few days were spent training at Acklington with gunnery and bombing practice and 'Cab Rank' exercise in the evening. On 22nd March, the squadron left Acklington in two flights, each of nine aircraft, led by Flight Lieutenant Sanders. The new squadron commanding officer, a non-Rhodesian, Squadron Leader Holmes having left the day before, bound for the Palace to receive the DFC. The squadron flew direct to Tangmere through some extremely bad weather, arriving 90 minutes late. This move brought No 266 (Rhodesia) Squadron into 20 Wing, Tactical Air Force.

No one was quite sure when it would be, but everyone knew that the new grouping was in preparation for the great adventure—the invasion of Europe.

CHAPTER 20

The great invasion

By the spring of 1944, the German armies were retreating on all fronts. A strong Russian advance had recaptured Odessa on 10th April and the Red army was well inside the borders of Rumania. The British and Americans were advancing slowly up the leg of Italy, and in the United Kingdom, a build-up of men and material heralded the Great Invasion. So, as the days grew longer and warmer, attacks by No 44 (Rhodesia) Squadron shifted from German cities to tactical raids on rail communication centres and strategic sites in the occupied territories.

No 266 prepares for the great day

The Rhodesian fighter squadron, No 266, was now part of the Tactical Air Force Fighter Group in the Allied Expeditionary Force; when the invasion began they would be in the spearhead. Already the squadron was carrying out fighter sweeps into northern France and so contributing to the intensive air campaign, which was being conducted against the enemy. The Rhodesians were also gaining valuable experience for the day when the Allied Expeditionary Air Force would be asked to give close support to the invading Allied armies. However, during April, No 266 had variable luck. On 6th April, Flying Officer George Eastwood aided by Flight Sergeant Chimbo Hulley accounted for a Ju 88, but his comment was:

> *A month ago, potential Hun victims were not hard to find in northern France. At the moment our luck is out. It is like looking for a needle in a very large haystack. The Ju 88 that Flight Sergeant Hulley and I got, was the only enemy aircraft that any of us saw in a sweep of two airfields. In that sort of party about a month ago the enemy were as thick as flies and the chaps swatted them down at the rate of one a minute for ten minutes.*
> (Rhodesia Herald, 15th April 1944)

The Rhodesian squadron had already moved under canvas at Needs Ore Point. We look forward to our next move—France! Meanwhile the emphasis was on training with an occasional day off:

> *16th April. Everyone went to Lymington to have a bath and a beer. No bathing facilities and no beer here! Poor show indeed! BO prevalent!*
> *18th April. Flight Lieutenant Vernon Sanders and Flight Sergeant Donovan Hedley Dodd detailed for exercise Smash could not locate their target and returned to base. During this time, several aircraft were vectored on to a Hun in the vicinity. Flight Lieutenant Sanders and Flight Sergeant Dodd on entering the circuit at base and not knowing an enemy aircraft had been reported in the vicinity, saw flak concentrating at a particular spot. Proceeding to investigate, they found a Ju 88 stooging around at 2,000 feet. Sanders and Dodd attacked despite the enemy*

aircraft firing two reds. The Ju 88 soon crashed in flames about three miles [4km] from base. On investigating the crash, it was found the aircraft carried a crew of seven and must have lost its way in bad weather. Flight Lieutenant Sanders and Flight Sergeant Dodd thus destroyed the first Hun on English soil, for 266, since the Battle of Britain. Time 07h45. One Hun before breakfast—great show! (Operations Record)

On 21st April, the squadron visited Thorney Island where the pilots met Dwight D. Eisenhower, Allied Commander in Chief. Spring was now well established with one fine day following another; perfect weather, in fact, for the job at hand—attacking bridges, marshalling yards and railway workshops. April 27th brought a move, not to France but to Snaith in Yorkshire to brush up on smoke laying. The CO, who came from the district, was able to lay on some wonderful 'sorties' after the day's work. The Black Swan at Holsmanton was the favourite.

The days were filled with intensive training, high dive-bombing, strafing, smoke-screening with the army and evasion tactics. As far as the pilots were concerned, Snaith had one major advantage over Needs Ore Point: for seven days they lived like civilized people—sleeping in beds, tin roofs over their heads and a bath every day. One day they even received a visit from two old friends, Johnny Deall and Doug Borland who were persuaded, quite easily, to stay the night, the early part of which was spent at the Black Swan and later at the commanding officer's home.

On 6th May, the squadron bade farewell to Snaith, with regret, and returned to Needs Ore Point, where they were joined by Flight Lieutenant Robert (Paddy) Nesbitt, ex No 237 Squadron. Operational flights began again on 7th May with an attack in cooperation with Nos 197, 257 and 193 Squadrons on Arras. Earlier in the day, bad weather had caused the operation to be aborted but later the sky cleared.

9th May. Fine day. Eight aircraft in the morning bombed what was supposed to have been an ammunition dump. The bombing was excellent but unfortunately, the dump wasn't there! Flying Officer Charles Baillie had engine trouble over the target area and was last seen heading inland having called up to say he was going to bale out. He has an excellent chance of being safe.

Early in the evening of the same day, eight aircraft attacked the marshalling yards at Rouen.

Results excellent. Sergeant Ogilvy McMurdon was possibly hit by light flak and headed south at 6,000 feet with glycol streaming from his engine. Two in a day is a bit much!* (Operations Record No 266 Squadron)

The following day two sorties were carried out, the first against flying-bomb sites and at teatime, against bridges and canal barges at Rouen. On the same day the squadron welcomed another ex 237 Squadron member, Flying Officer Edward (Ted) Cunnison who had had a very hectic time in the Middle East. Shot down three times. Walked back to his unit once, returned by camel and once by Air Sea Rescue.

A visit from the prime minister

On 11th May, the targets were trains and marshalling yards in the morning and a radar station at Le Touquet in the afternoon. As the invasion date approached, radar stations became a major target. It was now less than a month to D-Day and it was imperative that the German

---

* Both Baillie and McMurdon were taken POW.

radar system should be rendered inoperative or at least unreliable. Unfortunately, towards the middle of the month, there came a period of duff weather when no operations were possible. It was during this break that Sir Godfrey Huggins visited No 266 and presented them with a new aircraft bought with funds collected by the Ndebele people. While he was with the squadron, the prime minister listened to the odd grouse and watched a formation flypast.

> **May 19th**. *The target was flying-bomb sites. The target was hard to locate owing to excellent camouflage; flak heavy and accurate; bombing poor. Flight Sergeant Holland was seen to lag on the way back and when about 40 miles [64km] out apparently tried to ditch but dropped a wing at 50 feet crashing into the sea and on fire. He was obviously hit by flak as were three other aircraft. Position orbited but nothing seen.* (Operations Record No 266 Squadron)

The weather continued good and most days two operations were mounted. It was during this week that news drifted through that 47 air force officers had been shot by the Germans at Stalag Luft III. The story was that the Germans had executed the men because of escape attempts. The feeling was that it was too incredible to be true. Swedish Red Cross officials were requested to investigate and of course the rumour proved to be correct.

The date for D-Day had been set for early June but it was a closely guarded secret. The weather was perfect through May but as the month drew to a close, conditions deteriorated. The Operations Record for 30th and 31st May and June 1st reads: Clamp in am. No ops. No activity on account of bad weather. Would the weather change in time? It was imperative that a period of at least a week of clear, fine weather should follow the invasion to give the Allied forces time to build up on the continent. What with the news from Germany and the drizzle outside, May did not end on a happy note.

No 44 take part in tactical attacks

No 44 (Rhodesia) Squadron had also been involved in the tactical attacks leading up to the invasion. The squadron was still stationed at Dunholme Lodge. April 1944 had started slowly with training exercises, a raid on Toulouse on 5th April, and then three days non-operational flying, during which the news came that Ignatius (Bob) Rademeyer had been awarded the DFC.

Vegetables were successfully planted off Hel Point on 9th April, followed by raids on Tours and Aachen. After a spell of bad weather, 13 aircraft went to Juvisy and Paris on 18th April.

On 20th April:

> *It was Paris again, this time La Chapelle. It was a good attack; smoke to 2,000 feet; glow seen over French coast; marking of target accurate; definitely a good prang.** (Operations Record)

The aircraft piloted by Pilot Officer Skinner was posted missing. Two days later the target was Brunswick and two days after that Munich, when Flying Officer Smith had the unpleasant experience of being caught in a searchlight cone for 15 minutes and had his aircraft damaged by flak. On 26th April, 16 aircraft went to Schweinfurt and on 28th April, for the first time the Rhodesian bomber squadron was called on to attack Norway; the target was Oslo.

During the Merry Month of May, the attack power of the Lancaster was largely switched from German targets to French. Toulouse Powder Factory was hit on 1st May and Mailly-Le Camp on 3rd May, from which raid Warrant Officer Nolan failed to return. A regular pattern

---

* Prang was used at this stage for an attack as well as an accident.

now was to have the raid controlled by a master bomber, but for some reason this failed at Mailly-Le Camp.

> *Marking fair and control though late was effective. No results seen by pilots but if markers were correctly placed then it should have been successful. Most crews did not receive any instruction on either W/T or R/T* and bombed merely because they saw other aircraft bombing the target.*
> (Operations Record No 44 Squadron)

Of the 362 Lancasters dispatched on this raid, 42 failed to return. To add to the confusion, the operating wavelength clashed with a civilian broadcasting station and one crew reported that they operated to the strains of Deep in the Heart of Texas. However, electronic counter-measures prevented crippling losses and roving Mosquito intruders did much to help. One new headache for Bomber Command was that German night fighters now had Naxos, a radar device that enabled them to home in on the H2S transmissions at a distance of 32 miles (51km).

Three days of training were succeeded by a highly successful attack on Salbris, a town in France about 40 miles (64km) south of Orleans. This was a night raid on an ammunition dump. The bombers went in at low level and hit the target so squarely that the glow of the explosions flooded the sky with such light that the reflection in his aircraft even at 10,000 feet made one pilot think his plane was on fire. During this attack, Pilot Officer Lloyd the mid-upper gunner in Flying Officer Bradburn's crew was wounded in the right leg by flak but continued to work the turret. Squadron Leader Colin Harvard Hunter failed to return.

Two days later, it was back to Paris for a successful attack on Gennevilliers from which Flying Officer Bradburn was reported missing. Bourg-Leopold on 11th May was largely abortive owing to bad radio transmission control and a faulty meteorological report. Only seven aircraft out of 16 dispatched reached the target and these were told not to bomb. This was to become increasingly common because the bombers were working over occupied territory not over Germany itself and every possible effort was made to limit civilian casualties. If the controller had any reason to believe that the markers were off target or if he could not identify the target with complete certainty, the raid was called off. Often this meant jettisoning the bombs over the sea or attacking an alternative target.

Rademeyer, who flew with Squadron Leader Cockbain on this abortive attack on Bourg-Leopold says:

> *Target identified by yellow flares over target and one red spot fire at 00h10. H2S confirmed target not marked correctly as red spot fires were in a field surrounded by woods. No yellow proximity marker. No green spot on other target. 1 x 4,000-lb high explosive jettisoned at 51 58N 00 53E from 14,500 feet. 16 x 500-lb general purpose bombs brought back. Cookie jettisoned to reduce weight on landing. Pilots' remarks: route good; met. inaccurate; cloud over target and wind 90 degrees out. Controller ordered to stop bombing twice on W/T and then ordered aircraft back to base at 00h34. Bombs continued to fall regardless of requests to stop.*
> (Operations Record No 44 Squadron)

Some of the later aircraft seeing nothing happening at Bourg altered course and joined in the attack on the alternative target of Hasselt. This fiasco was followed by a week of no operations, when the weather was cloudy and heavy rain fell. This time was spent in training.

---

* W/T—HF radio message in Morse Code
  R/T—radio message by voice

On 19th May, 16 aircraft were detailed to attack Amiens. Eleven of these aircraft did not bomb as orders were received to return to base. Pilot Officer Vivian Frances Hobbs's aircraft collided with another over the target. The crew, which included Stuart Biddulph Ingram, the Rhodesian rear gunner, were given orders to bale out, which they did successfully. Unfortunately, some of the crew landed in marshy ground. Stuart was heard to call repeatedly but was never found. The survivors were later reported prisoners of war.

On the last day of May, the target was Maisy, and the attack was led by Wing Commander Thompson (Rhodesian). Again, none of the aircraft bombed the target as orders were received to return to base. The weather was very bad with the Lancasters battling home through electrical storms. Lancaster ME794, piloted by Flight Sergeant Oswald, did not make his home base and was forced to land at Westcott. Coming in at 130 miles per hour (210 km/h) with a 13,000-lb (5,900kg) bomb load, the aircraft rumbled across the road, jumped a ditch and landed heavily, causing the undercarriage to collapse. It then slithered to a stop, burst into flames and exploded taking with it a Wellington, belonging to No 11 OTU. Because of this accident, the airfield at Westcott was closed and Flight Sergeant Canty was ordered to land at the satellite airfield, Oakley. Unfortunately, he too overran the short runway owing to the weight of his bomb load. The port wheel went into a ditch. The aircraft caught fire and was wrecked.

All in all, it was a most unfortunate night. Some of the aircraft were actually over the target when they received orders to return; others were crossing the French coast or at various points over the Channel. Some Lancasters were fortunate and managed to land at Dunholme Lodge before the weather clamped in. Flight Sergeant Canty was only about 100 miles (160km) from base when he received his orders to divert to Westcott.

> **2nd June**. *Fifteen aircraft detailed for Wimereux; three attacked the target. All other aircraft reached the target but did not bomb as the controller ordered them to return to base. Weather very bad. Most crews jettisoned their bombs.* (Operations Record)

This is hardly surprising when one considers the hazards of landing a fully laden aircraft in bad weather.

The prime minister welcomed by No 44

On 2nd June, Sir Godfrey Huggins, in Britain for a Dominion Prime Ministers' conference, paid a brief visit to the squadron. He was only able to stay for 17 minutes, which was rather a disappointment for squadron members who had been looking forward for weeks to the occasion. There were many matters of vital interest that they wished to discuss such as repatriation, allowances, decorations and the possibility of immigration to Rhodesia after the war.

However, any regrets felt at the short visit were soon forgotten in the excitement of the great event that was now only days away. Everybody knew that an attack on Hitler's Europe must come this year but only a few people knew exactly when. In fact, the Allied commanders had very little leeway about the date. They knew that a sea-borne attack on the strong German defences would be a hazardous operation. Apart from the assault itself, there was the sea-crossing, nearly 100 miles (160km) of treacherous water. If the troops were to seize the well-defended French beaches, they would need every piece of equipment that could be made available.

This equipment included amphibious tanks, which had to come ashore on a tide that reached its halfway mark 40 minutes after first light giving the warships and aircraft a vital period of daylight to blast the defences. It was also necessary that the night should be moonlit,

"D-Day"

so that airborne troops could identify their targets. These necessary conditions existed for only three days each lunar month. In 1944, June 5th, 6th and 7th were those particular days. If the invasion could not be mounted in June, it might be too late to exploit the landings before winter made the Channel dangerously stormy.

Operation Overlord—D-Day

So Operation Overlord—the invasion of Europe—was set for June, and 5th, 6th or 7th was given as D-Day. Every part of the plan worked back from that date to permit all the preliminaries, which included assembling the men and their equipment in the coastal areas and the massive embarkation operation.

D-Day was provisionally set for 5th June. But the fine weather of May became dull and rainy with the possibility of high winds and low cloud. Some of the troops had already embarked when orders came for a postponement. Eisenhower, the supreme commander knew he could only delay for a day. Meteorologists predicted a brief improvement in the weather for 6th June. Eisenhower gave the order: 6th June with the attack time set at 03h59. The aircraft were scheduled to land back at base at 06h00, just as the first assault boats were due to put ashore.

Meanwhile No 266 (Rhodesia) Squadron also received the long-awaited news.

> *5th June. A day full of operational sorties and surprises for the boys. Briefed for the big event we have all been waiting for. Morning attacks on radar…evening attacks on German HQ Chateau at Hareville. This mission was abortive owing to bad weather.*
>
> *6th June. D-Day. Everybody tense—boys over the beaches when first landings were made. A wonderful sight! Sergeant Percival Keith Mitchell crash-landed on the beachhead. 07h10 – 08h30 Rocketed gun post near Bayeaux—invasion beachhead. 18h00 – 19h25 Armed recce near Caen. Armoured cars were then attacked and two damaged. The road was cratered by bombs. Sergeant Donne baled out successfully five miles [8km] north-west Caen. 21h10 – 22h25 Armed recce Caen. The squadron split into two sections. One section attacked two M/T, and destroyed four M/T that were parked. Stationary armoured cars were strafed and bombed. Three parked together were observed to smoke. 150 mm gun attack and many strikes observed. Other half squadron destroyed two full open troop carriers and one empty one. Troops were de-busing at the time.* (Operations Record No 266 Squadron)

Approximately four hours later, 16 aircraft of No 44 Squadron were over the same target, Caen, where harassed Allied parachute battalions were hanging on to a slender bridgehead. The Lancasters went in to the attack at 02h44; their targets were bridges, which had to be demolished to prevent German reinforcements from reaching the front line.

> *Too much smoke to observe results on bridges—a few fires but not thought to have damaged town very much. If markers were correctly placed, bridges should be demolished.*
> (Operations Record No 44 Squadron)

D-Day plus one: the Rhodesian fighter squadron was in the thick of the fighting.

> *7th June. Fine day. Our aircraft on ops all day. Starting at 07h00 in the morning with an armed recce near Lisieux. One section of four aircraft saw nothing. The other section attacked a light armoured car and six-wheeler on the Mount-Vimont Road. There was a near miss on the M/T and many strikes on the armoured car. When returning to base, Sergeant Mitchell crash landed near St Aubin as his petrol tanks were punctured.*

Lunchtime brought an armed reconnaissance near Bayeux.

The section was diverted by the control ship, to attack tanks south-west of Bayeux. One left in flames near Ballenvy. Three more were bombed and seen to burst into flames, which rose to a hundred feet. They were claimed as destroyed. Teatime and another armed recce to Lisieux where a road and rail junction was bombed. (Operations Record)

The 7th June was a quiet day for the bomber squadron. They were detailed for a raid that was cancelled.

D-Day plus two: No 266 Squadron was sent out to dive bomb and block main roads round Caen. Squadron aircraft attacked motor transport south of Caen with cannon and claimed two flamers. There was intense light flak, and Flying Officer Hugh Chicheley Balance was forced to bale out 40 miles (64km) north of Caen over the sea but was seen to climb into his dinghy and was picked up by a boat about 40 minutes later. That night, 8th June, No 44 Squadron joined the fight, attacking bridges at Pontaubault. Three direct hits were claimed.

June 9th dawned grey and drizzling, Rhodesian bomber squadron pilots were forced to fret the day away on the ground but by the evening aircraft were able to take off, carrying out a raid on Etampes. Pilot Officer Thomas Bryan Richards claimed one Me 109 destroyed. Flying Officer Desmond Ernest Balsdon was shot down over France and Pilot Officer Dewhurst Graaff lost control of his plane over the Thames estuary and ordered his crew to bale out. The two gunners, wireless-operator and navigator jumped but then Graaff managed to bring the aircraft under control and back to base safely. All four crewmembers were drowned. One of the gunners was a Rhodesian, Sergeant Clive Hore.[*]

Most of the Lancaster operations during the next few weeks were aimed at preventing German reinforcements from reaching the battle area. It was during this period that Tallboy first came into use. This was a 12,000-lb (5,400-kg) penetration bomb and was a smaller version of the Grand Slam that had been planned but not, as yet manufactured. Bombs of this type had been used earlier in the war but the later versions had been redesigned to penetrate railway tunnels and bridges.

The weather had not improved and No 44 Squadron was unable to take any part in the fight during the days of June 10th and 11th.

The fighter squadron received good news in the morning and got back into the fight at lunchtime.

10th June. Weather clear. Edward Henry (Ted) Donne arrived back from France intact with a German rifle and helmet. Lunchtime activity took the shape of an armed recce south of Caen when the squadron 'bagged' one M/T. Two petrol bowsers, a staff car and an armoured car were damaged. Late in the evening, another armed recce was made towards Falaise when three flamers and two damaged M/T were claimed as well as direct hits on guns and a tank. (Operations Record No 266 Squadron)

Both squadrons were grounded on 11th June, but by early morning on 12th June the weather had cleared again and an armed recce was made by No 266 Squadron in the direction of Caen where strikes were carried out on motor transport. Flight Lieutenant Robert William

---

[*] Clive Hore, born in Bulawayo, attested in August 1942, trained in Rhodesia and proceeded overseas in July 1943. His brother Eric Vivian Hore had been reported missing believed killed as a result of air operations over Hamburg on January 14th/15th 1942.

(Paddy) Nesbitt* was seen to crash in flames during this operation.

Early in the evening, another recce was made towards Caen with excellent results and that night No 44 Squadron were also able to operate in the area of Caen. Conditions over the target were such that it was difficult to assess results and five of the 15 aircraft returned without bombing. Squadron Leader Cockbain's report gives some idea of conditions over the target.

Aircraft on fire as a result of flak. H2S u/s. Damaged by flak. Port-inner engine caught fire— other damaged. Very little icing; marking was not good. Target indicator was only visible when almost over it. Carried out three dummy runs. No avail. On reaching target indicator on third run up, we were hit by flak. Fumes filled the aircraft and the port-inner caught fire. We turned out and jettisoned. Disappointing trip.

The Allied beachheads join in

By 12th June, the Allied forces had fought their way clear of the beaches and linked up, resulting in an unbroken front of about 50 miles (80km).

June 13th was again a no-flying day for the bomber squadron. No 266, however, was engaged in close support action round the Tilly/Au Seul area. Sergeant Percival Keith Mitchell landed on a forward strip, as he was short of fuel. Later the same evening Ted Cunnison was also forced down. "Boys making good use of strips in France!" said the Operations Record.

The following day saw both squadrons taking part in the fight. The fighter squadron carried out close support at Couerville while the bombers were attacking Aunay. Next day was a day of rest and the squadron received the sad news that Wing Commander Baker had been lost in France. Meanwhile No 266 Squadron was maintaining its dive-bombing and cannon attacks on bridges, roads and canals near Caen.

On the ground, Montgomery's men were engaged in a desperate struggle to hold the bridgeheads they had established. It was vital that before the autumn weather set in, the Allies should be in control of a major port.

Jimmy Powell brings a Liberator home

While the two Rhodesian squadrons were fighting in France, news was received of one of the men who had helped to establish the SRAF, Jimmy Powell. Group Captain Powell was attached to the United States Air Force in the Mediterranean and had gone aboard the Liberator as an observer. The target was bombed successfully but on the way back to base the aircraft was attacked by fighters and flak. The bomb-aimer was killed, the pilot's leg was almost shot off, the navigator was seriously wounded and the co-pilot was injured in the foot. Despite his wounds the co-pilot managed to hold the aircraft steady while Powell slipped into the pilot's seat.

They asked if he'd flown a Liberator before. He said, "Yes" although he hadn't. No one guessed because he was so calm. The starboard engine was out of action. There was petrol leaking, as was the hydraulic fluid from the brakes. The instrument panel and the throttles had been shot away. As they spotted the North African coast, the last engine failed. However, the unwounded men in the crew refused to bale out and leave the injured. They lifted them and held them in their arms to save them from the shock of the crash. By some miracle, the battered plane came in to a level space among some orange trees and rolled safely to rest. Powell remarked that it was the roughest trip he'd had in 17 years of flying. (Rhodesia Herald, 17th June 1944)

★ Paddy Nesbitt was born in Ireland but attested and trained in Rhodesia before proceeding overseas in December 1941.

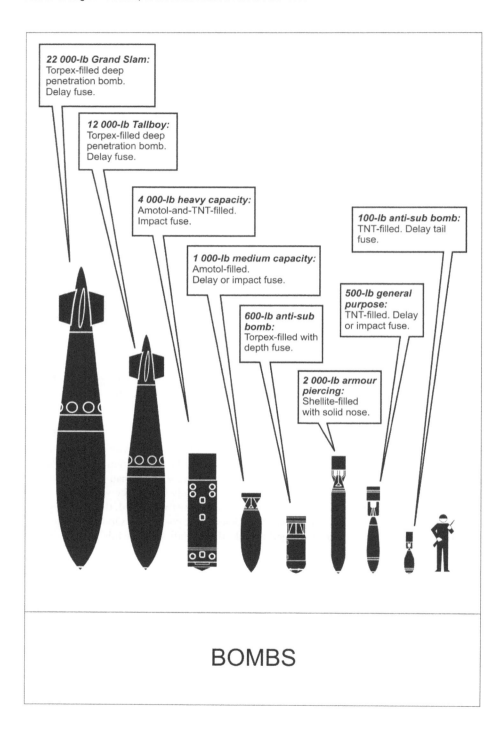

22 000-lb Grand Slam: Torpex-filled deep penetration bomb. Delay fuse.

12 000-lb Tallboy: Torpex-filled deep penetration bomb. Delay fuse.

4 000-lb heavy capacity: Amotol-and-TNT-filled. Impact fuse.

100-lb anti-sub bomb: TNT-filled. Delay tail fuse.

1 000-lb medium capacity: Amotol-filled. Delay or impact fuse.

500-lb general purpose: TNT-filled. Delay or impact fuse.

600-lb anti-sub bomb: Torpex-filled with depth fuse.

2 000-lb armour piercing: Shellite-filled with solid nose.

BOMBS

The battle for Caen

The days passed and still the battle for Caen was being fought with the utmost ferocity. On 17th June, No 266 Squadron was at its usual task of armed recce south of Caen but the following day, by way of change, was spent dive-bombing bridges at Harcourt. Then once more the weather clamped in so the boys took the opportunity of a trip to Christchurch in the evening.

On 20th June, it was the flying-bomb sites that received attention while later in the day the squadron carried out a dive-bombing attack on a railway embankment and were rewarded with two direct hits.

After this, there was a day of rest for No 266 Squadron but it was to be the worst day in the history of No 44 (Rhodesia) Squadron.

June 21st/22nd 16 aircraft were detailed for an attack on Wesseling. Six of these aircraft failed to return and Pilot Officer Mitchell was unable to bomb the target because his aircraft was damaged by flak. Two of the six lost aircraft were captained by Rhodesians, Pilot Officer Thomas Bryan Richards and Pilot Officer Neville John Wingrove Scholtz with mid-upper gunner, Sergeant Harry Moxon Greenfield and gunner, Pilot Officer William Donald Barnett respectively. Thus three Rhodesians died, and Barnett became a prisoner of war.

Squadron Leader Cockbain reported:

> *Route out good. On approaching the target, we were attacked by enemy aircraft. The control column jammed in a forward position and we started to dive. I warned the crew to put on parachutes. No sooner had I said this than the aircraft dived vertically. I ordered the crew to jump. Whilst waiting, I trimmed right back and with my feet on the instrument panel hauled on the stick, which gradually started to move back. I then told all those who had not baled out to stand by. We then jettisoned the load and the aircraft became controllable at about 8,000 feet. Three members of the crew remained. All parachutes were seen to open. I then asked my bomb-aimer to come back and navigate, which he did most successfully. The remaining members of my crew behaved admirably and they contributed largely to our safe return.*

(Operations Record No 44 Squadron)

One of those who jumped was Flight Lieutenant Bob Rademeyer DFC:

> *"I think I must have caught the tail of the plane with my leg, jumping. I lost consciousness and regained it just before reaching the ground. It was some time before I had medical attention and by then it was too late to save the leg. I was sent to a hospital run by British staff where it was amputated."* From there he went to a rehabilitation centre and after that to a camp which was an improvement on the ordinary POW camp because it was only for men intended for repatriation. Situated between Berlin and Leipzig, it gave a grandstand view of the Allied air raids. (Rhodesia Herald, 7th Feb 1945)

Among those who died that night were the Rhodesians: Pilot Officer Neville John Wingrove Scholtz, Pilot Officer Thomas Bryan Richards and his mid-upper gunner, Sergeant Harry Moxon Greenfield from Que Que.* The Rhodesian fighter squadrons were

---

* Neville Scholtze was educated at St George's College and Umtali Boys' High School. Thomas Richards was born in Kent but educated at Plumtree School and Prince Edward. He attested in April 1942 and, after training in Rhodesia, proceeded overseas in April 1943. Harry Greenfield was born in Que Que, attested in June 1942 and trained in Rhodesia before proceeding overseas in July 1943.

more fortunate—their armed recces of 22nd, 23rd, and 24th bagged two staff cars, one large motor transport, a supply dump, a railway tunnel and four tanks without loss.

No 44 Squadron in close cooperation with the army

Despite the losses, the fight went on and the bomber squadron attacked Pommerval on June 24th for the loss of another two aircraft, those piloted by Flight Sergeant Oswald and Pilot Officer Aiken. Losses were heavy because the Germans were bitterly contesting every inch of territory. Added to the strength of the defence, there was the fact the bombing had to be carried out with pinpoint accuracy to avoid hitting friendly civilians and Allied troops. Attacks were made from the lowest possible levels. The military situation also demanded that the Lancasters work in close cooperation with the army. This placed an added strain on crews who would often be briefed and then left to await a final decision. The weather at the target might be unsuitable or the military situation might have changed owing to an advance or a counter-attack. It was often a matter of—wait and see—or in military terms—hurry up and wait. Such a day was 25th June. Twelve aircraft were detailed and then at the last minute the operation was cancelled.

No 266 Squadron personnel were, in many ways, better off. They were being kept so busy that they did not have any time to sit around and think. In fact, a day off came seldom and was a welcome relief. June 26th reported, "No activity. Boys getting in a few sleeping hours!"

One of the pastimes, which had become a speciality with the Rhodesian fighter squadron, was attacking enemy headquarters and during the next few months this type of operation was to bring them renown. June 27th reported, "Half main building destroyed and all outbuildings razed of army HQ."

On the same day, the bomber squadron had another loss: the aircraft piloted by Flight Lieutenant Merrick failed to return from an attack on Marquise. There followed three days of cancelled operations.

Cherbourg falls to the Allies

On June 29th, Cherbourg fell to the Allied forces. Although the Germans had carried out a thorough demolition before they surrendered, the Allies now had a major port and 3, 000 German troops were in the bag. Meanwhile the fighter squadron was packing for a move to Eastchurch and a conversion to rocket-firing Typhoons.

> **30th June**. *Weather clamp. Boys have squadron party in village. Everybody nicely thank you.*
> (Operations Record)

And so No 266 (Rhodesia) Squadron said, "Goodbye to Needs Ore Point and after two weeks of intensive training—on 17th July—Moves to FRANCE—great day for all!"

No 266 somewhere in France

On their second operation as a Rocket Typhoon squadron, the Rhodesian airmen were attacked by 25 Me 109s. As result of this action, the squadron claimed one enemy aircraft destroyed and one damaged while No 266 had three losses: Flying Officer Gedunks Meyer, Flight Sergeant Harrold and Flight Sergeant McElroy. Both Flight Sergeant Ronald McElroy and Flight Sergeant John Cheshire Harrold* were later confirmed killed in action. However,

---

* John Harrold born in Umtali, attested October 1941, trained in Rhodesia and proceeded overseas in April 1943. Ronald McElroy, born in London educated in Rhodesia. Attested November 1940, trained in Rhodesia, proceeded overseas in October 1942.

the squadron was proving the value of its new equipment, doing vast damage to troop transports and barges crossing the River Orne, as well as providing support for the army by attacking mortar emplacements, troop concentrations and observer posts.

It was 25th July before the Rhodesians were in action again, this time in an army support capacity near the River Orne. There was one operation in the early morning and another later in the day, when the pilots carried out rocket attacks on a convoy of lorries four miles (6km) west of Thury Harcourt. During this attack, Flight Lieutenant Allen's aircraft was seen to dive straight into the ground.

Motor transport and railway trucks were the target again on the following day and the day after that it was a concentration of tanks in a wood near Roquancourt.

> *28th July. Ken Rogers back. Peter takes 'B' flight. Don McGibbon takes 'A' flight. Army recce Vire-Domfront and Alencon. Abortive owing to weather. Lost Pilot Officer Ian Hugh Forrester;* engine failure, crashed into building.*

The next day, the weather was bad and there was no operational flying. However, the month of July closed with two days of intense activity as the Rhodesian fighter squadron gave the Allied armies close support, making rocket attacks on tanks, motor transport and railway trucks.

August 4th brought a welcome break when Wing Commander Green visited the squadron and a big swing was held. According to the squadron diary: incapable all round!

Wing Commander Green joined the RAF shortly before the outbreak of war and was posted to No 266 Squadron in May 1941. He was given command of a flight in the following month and five months after that command of the squadron. He was awarded the DFC in January 1943 and the DSO on July 31st 1944. During the pre-invasion blitz, Wing Commander Green attacked German transport across France, scoring one particularly valuable victory near Le Mans in May when he wrecked oil and supply trains jammed in a siding. He was among the first pilots to go to Normandy and became known as the baker's boy when having visited England for repairs to his Typhoon he returned with a load of fresh bread. One of the greatest luxuries for troops in the field.

Wing Commander Green's father, Flying Officer Luke Green who was serving at Belvedere Air Station won the DSO during the First World War. He commanded a battalion of a Rifle Brigade in 1914 and took part in an expedition to Russia. He fought in the Anglo-Boer War and took part in the Siege of Mafeking when he was 16 years old. In 1939, he dyed the gray out of his hair, went to enlist and was accepted as an airgunner, until someone recognized him!

The Falaise pocket

General Montgomery's plan was to keep the Germans heavily involved at Caen drawing enemy reinforcements to the area and so allow the Americans to carry out an encircling movement. Despite pressure from his superiors, Montgomery held to his aims and the Germans fell into line. The day before the American general, Collins, began his successful breakthrough in the west, seven German Panzer divisions and four heavy tank battalions were facing the British armies at Caen. Only two Panzer divisions faced the Americans. Collins began his attack on July 26th driving south to Le Mans and then east. The chances of encircling a large number of German troops at Falaise were good. Hitler helped the plan by ordering a German counter-attack, which not only failed forlornly, but also ensured that

---

* Ian Hugh Forrester was born in South Africa and worked for the Standard Bank in Bulawayo before attesting in February 1941. He trained in Rhodesia and proceeded overseas in October 1941.

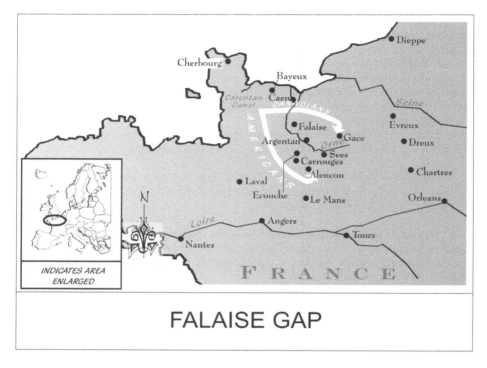

FALAISE GAP

more German troops would be caught in the trap. By 16th August, the Canadians in the north and the Americans in the south were only 15 miles (24km) apart. The gap closed on 20th August leaving 50,000 German soldiers caught in the Falaise pocket.

No 266 Squadron played a leading part in the attacks in the Falaise area, harrying the German forces as they vainly tried to pull back through the rapidly tightening pincer formation of the Allied advance. Although there were few enemy aircraft in the air, flak was always intense resulting in losses for the squadron. The first casualty in August occurred on the 7th , which was a very busy day. Flight Sergeant Harry Hiltan Wheeler was badly shot up by flak during an attack on motor transport but managed to force-land on the Allied side of the front line. Later in the same day, two attacks were launched on tanks concentrated east of Vire.

The following day the target was tanks again: 20 of them parked in an orchard at Fontaine Le Pin. On 9th August, tanks were the target once more with some motor transport hits and two horse-drawn guns damaged. During this attack, which was carried out just after lunch, Flight Sergeant Peter Charles Nightingale Green force-landed 10 miles (16km) north-east of Falaise, behind enemy lines and Squadron Leader Wright crash-landed at base; both owing to flak.

No 266 gains a reputation for pinpoint attacks

The target, in a joint attack with No 263 Squadron, on 10th August, was a German headquarters near Montpoint when pilots saw numerous strikes hit the main building. Later in the day, there was an attack on gun positions. The squadron had another busy day on 11th August with four operations on assorted targets such as motor transport, gun positions, radar stations, tanks and infantry.

12th August. *Another fine sunny day. Very successful attack on Jerry HQ at Epanay. A little hazardous owing to concentrated flak. As well as the attack on the Chateau, the Typhoons had a go at troop concentrations and parked vehicles in the area.*

13th August. *Boys very busy again. Successful attack on Chateau south-west of Lounguy, which was reported to be a Jerry HQ. Complimented by the army on the success of blowing up of observation tower that was causing them trouble. A few of the boys damaged by flak.*

14th August. *More success for the squadron. Complete destruction of gun sight, two tanks and four heavy guns at St Pierre. Few of our aircraft hit by flak. Released in afternoon, giving the lads an enjoyable afternoon on beach.*

15th August. *Bad luck hits again. Flight Sergeant Wheeler* believed killed by direct hit (flak) during an armed recce in Falaise-Argentan area. Destroyed four tanks, five M/T and a staff car. Flak very heavy.*

16th August. *Armed recce. Fifteen tanks attacked—four flamers. One large gun seen moving south.*

17 August. *14h30 – 15h20. Attack on barges on River Seine. Four barges attacked. One destroyed, three damaged. Ten barges south side and six north all strafed. One barge destroyed. 18h35 – 19h30. Armed recce of Vinoutiers gap area. A very successful wing op. Led by Group Captain Gillham flying with No 193. Other squadrons involved were Nos 263, 266 and 197. A skirmish took place with 15 Fw 190s. Resulted in two being damaged by Flight Lieutenant Don McGibbon and Flight Sergeant Ellis Palte. Flight Sergeant Wilfred Royce Love† was not seen again after this dogfight. Flight Sergeant J.L. Luhnenschloss (Rhodesian) badly shot up by Jerry. 20h55 – 21h40. Armed recce. One tank flamer. One M/T damaged.*

18th August. *Another field day for the squadron. Jerry on the run. Attack on 1,000 M/T, tanks, staff cars. Many M/T destroyed. Flight Lieutenant Peter Blackwell on rest. Flight Lieutenant Derek Erasmus has taken his place.*

19th and 20th August were again busy days harassing the German attempts at retreat.

Two Rhodesian Typhoon pilots left Normandy very reluctantly this weekend for 48 hours' leave. (This was Saturday 19th August.) Pilot Officer David Hughes and Flight Sergeant Archibald Paisley Knoesen of Bulawayo took their turn and in doing so missed something of 'the most marvellous prang we've ever had'. They came straight from the terrific attacks against the encircled Germans, an attack in which the Rhodesian squadron flying rocket-firing Typhoons has taken a large share. For the Typhoons, which specialized in attacking enemy transport, it was a 'piece of cake'. Vehicles of every sort, lorries, tanks, staff cars, horse-drawn carts, jam the roads, sometimes bumper to bumper and when the Typhoons, Thunderbolts and Spitfires sweep down on them, "the fires we raise look as though the road was strung all along with street lamps," Pilot Officer Hughes told me. He added, "Flamers, smokers, vehicles overturned into ditches and twisted bits of cars are what we leave behind. It's a wonderful show." From dawn to dusk, the Typhoons have been at the Germans struggling to get away and on every sortie rivalry is keen among the pilots to go out. Pilot Hughes said, "Our ground crews are wonderful. Though most of the pilots of our squadron are Rhodesian, our ground staff are English. I've two Englishmen in my crew and I couldn't want two better fellows." Team spirit and perfect training are the keynotes of the squadron's success, which recently gave them the highest score of transports

---

* Flight Sergeant Wheeler survived, evaded capture, and returned to his squadron on 30th August.

† Sergeant Pilot Wilfred Royce Love was killed on Air Operations over St Marguerite Des Loges, France. 17th August 1944. He was born in Bulawayo, attested in September 1940, served in the meteorological section until April 1942; then trained as a pilot and proceeded overseas in May 1943.

destroyed by their Wing and the recent battle raised their scores tremendously. The attack on the fleeing enemy was the culmination of the work they've done in France ever since D-Day, hunting down enemy transport wherever it was found. Often, also, they are sent out to deal with a strong point or fire-concentration holding up the army. They've had many messages from the army thanking them for their help. Pilot Officer Hughes said, "We are awfully pleased when we hear from the army that the target we went after has been completely destroyed. When a battle is as fluid as this, it is a tricky business sometimes when the target is near your own troops, and with the plan of battle altering quickly, we have to be very careful about identifying the transport. From the air, we get a much better idea of the battle than the men on the ground and it makes it much more interesting and exciting. But this terrific attack going on against the Germans is the most amazing sight I've ever seen. The air is humming with our own aircraft and the roads and fields below are strewn with wrecked, burning vehicles of all sorts."
(Rhodesia Herald, 22nd August 1944)

With regard to constantly changing battle lines, there is a note in the Operations Record for 20th August, recounting an episode in which American tanks could have been the target.

Briefed to attack infantry and tanks. No Red Smoke. No attack. Six Sherman tanks with white stars and cerise stripes seen going east.

On that same weekend, 19th/20th August, the public relations officer from Rhodesia House paid the squadron a visit and wrote an account that was published later in *The Herald*.

I spent last weekend with the Rhodesian Typhoon squadron in France. There is only one non-Rhodesian pilot. He is an American officer, Captain Norman Crabtree. If the trees over their tents had been laden with Mahobohobo, instead of cider apples, the scene would have been indistinguishable from a holiday camp off some dusty road in the Hartley or Gwelo districts, except that the Huns had left skillfully built dug-outs, in various stages of completion, made by Russian prisoners. I shared breakfast, lunch and afternoon tea and dinner with them at tables in a big marquee serving as mess for the Wing. It is a strange life our men are leading—ease and comfort, sunbathing, reading, letter-writing and leisurely personal chores, interspersed with short periods of intense energy. The London morning papers are received the same afternoon and home mails are coming forward satisfactorily. Sometimes on off-days, visits are paid to French towns and villages and a supply of French wines brought back to the squadron. As their turn comes round there are 48-hour passes with air transport to and from England. At first, when the front was nearer, it was possible for an aircraftman to light a cigarette after seeing his machine off to battle and have it still alight when the pilot returned. Even during my visit when the front was much further away, the tremendous speed of these aircraft made the interval seem very short, as I watched our men take off and waited for their return from action. The squadron may do four operations a day, or two for each flight. A pilot's total spell on duty pounding hell out of the bewildered Hun may be two or three hours a day, but each hour contains sufficient adventures for a lifetime. (Rhodesia Herald, 25th Aug. 1944)

The Canadians and the Americans closed the gap at Falaise on 20th August. The Germans who had managed to escape, mainly the remnants of the 5th and 7th Panzer Armies, made their way north-east towards the Seine, hoping to hold a line there. However, General Patton in a lightning move reached the river before them. Those Germans who managed to cross, were forced to leave most of their equipment behind. After a few days' rest the Rhodesian fighter squadron was once more in the thick of battle.

The race to the Seine

25th August. 07h55 – 09h05 Attack on Seine traffic and approaches. One barge attacked. No results observed. One tank flamer. Two M/T flamers. One M/T flamer. Stores park seen on south bank of Seine…tent seen in clearing surrounded by numbers of light guns. 12h25 – 13h40. Armed recce of Seine crossings. 16 rocket projectiles fired at staff car going east; destroyed and several occupants hit. Two direct hits on three barges. One ship beached. One ship with three barges adjacent—seen but not attacked. Moderate light and heavy flak from area. 15h50 – 17h00. Seine patrol with two aircraft of No 197 Squadron using cannon. One barge sunk; corpses in water. Moderate heavy flak from Duclair. 16h20 – 17h20. With aircraft from No 197 Squadron. One barge-ferry midstream hit and exploded. Other salvo hit jetty causing explosion. One tank damaged. 17h45 – 18h50.One barge. No claims. One barge damaged. Three barges, two steamers. One steamer damaged. Two barges stationary—near misses. 18h15 – 19h10. Rocket projectile attack on cable ferry barge moving north. Hit on stern claimed probable. Light flak. 19h45 – 20h40. Transport. One M/T bearing white stripes attacked. Rocket projectiles. No result observed. 20h10 – 21h15. Transport. No claims 20-30 M/T moving north. 8-10 moving on to ferry. Attacked. Seven rocket projectiles fired on S. Rouen as ordered. (Operations Record No 266 Squadron)

Following that day of feverish activity came a lull. Targets grew seemingly scarce. Only occasional scattered motor transport was spotted on 26th August. So a change of target was ordered, with disastrous results.

27th August. The squadron had a very successful shipping strike. Destroyed two destroyers and one minesweeper, damaging one other. Unfortunately, Royal Navy shipping ordered by the mistake of the Admiralty to be attacked and destroyed. Admiralty took full responsibility. Owing to doubt as to identity, controller was asked four times whether to attack and told that ships fired colours. Controller said that no friendly ships in area and ordered attack. No 263 Squadron claim rocket projectile salvos on two ships. No 266 on three ships. Also strafed. Ships were our own. Later in the day on a happier operation. One ferry was destroyed and a barge damaged. (Operations Record No 266)

August ended with heavy rain. Pilots took the chance to visit the forward area by jeep.

News from the bombers

Not only had the Germans been putting up a fierce rearguard action on the ground, they had also mounted savage attacks in the air, using the V-1 known as the flying bomb. Hitler pinned a final forlorn hope on this terror weapon. On 6th July, Winston Churchill announced that so far 2,754 flying bombs had caused 2,752 casualties in England. On the following day, 7th July, No 44 Squadron was given the chance to retaliate.

Eighteen aircraft flew to St Leu D'Esserant to attack a flying-bomb base. The bombing was highly concentrated and there were several combats with German fighters. No claims were made but Flight Lieutenant Carnegie, Pilot Officer Gowing and Pilot Officer Graaff* all failed to return. This costly operation was succeeded by four days of inactivity. Then on 12th July, 15 aircraft were sent to Chalindrey; again there was a loss: Flying Officer Arnold's aircraft was reported missing.

On 15th July, the squadron again lost an aircraft, this time as a result of a gardening

---

★ Dewhurst Graaff was born in Bulawayo, attested in February 1942 and trained in Rhodesia before proceeding overseas in April 1943.

operation. A heavy attack was carried out on Caen on 18th July, preceding the ground assault. Fourteen aircraft from the Rhodesian bomber squadron took part in this raid, which was successful from a tactical point of view, but again there was a loss.

The following night, 19th July, the target was Thiverney, which was Flight Sergeant Reginald Watson Heath's first operation with the squadron. As Heath joined, so Wing Commander F.W. Thompson left. He had flown unscathed since joining the squadron in January 1944. His final operation was an attack on the marshalling yards at Courtrai on 20th July. Night-fighters came after the Lancasters and half the credit for bringing down a FW 190 went to a Rhodesian mid-upper gunner, Flight Sergeant Derrick John Norman Palmer. This was Palmer's second tour and he had been credited with one kill during his first tour. A correspondent from the *Rhodesia Herald* was there to witness the take-off.

> *Before take-off I watched the careful preparation of the aircraft by the ground crews, many of them Rhodesian. Sergeant Andrew Newby Wawn of Salisbury, is in charge of the good running of 'Z' Zebra and Sergeant Alan Rubenstein of Bulawayo, a fitter has taken care of 'Y' York ever since she came to the squadron. Sergeant Lumsden (Rhodesian) of Bulawayo heads the ground crew of 'S' for Sugar and Sergeant Alan Baldwin Le Blanc Smith of Salisbury that of 'V' for Victory. After the take-off, we went back to the mess to wait for their return. It seemed a very short time before we braved the cold wind again and saw the planes sweep down from the sky. Then the crew came streaming into the interrogation room, carrying large mugs of coffee. "A very good prang," when the last plane returned the Group Captain said quietly, relieved, "They're all back."* (Rhodesia Herald, 26th July 1944)

After three days' rest it was back to Germany again with two raids on Stuttgart. Flying Officer Ibbotson failed to return from the second raid, while Flight Lieutenant Belasco did not attack because his aircraft was damaged by fighters. Belasco said in his report:

> *At a position 53 degrees east of Paris, the mid-upper gunner gave me a warning of a fighter coming in on the starboard but before I could take any action, another aircraft opened fire on us in a diving attack from above. Both turrets were rendered u/s but we luckily lost the enemy aircraft. We decided to return to base taking advantage of some low medium cloud on the way. In spite of this, we were pursued by at least three enemy aircraft by the time we were 40 miles [64km] south-east of the bridgehead at Caen—so we jettisoned load.* (Operations Record No 44 Squadron)

On the following night, 26th July, the target was Givors with 17 aircraft. Flying Officer Donald Neil McKechnie,* a Rhodesian, was reported missing. He had only been posted to the squadron on 22nd July and he died on his first mission. Flight Sergeant Reginal Watson Merrick Heath says the weather was very bad with thunderstorms and heavy rain.

After one day's break it was back to Stuttgart for the loss of two aircraft. July 30th brought an unusual daylight raid with 12 aircraft going to Cahagnes but none attacking as they received Marmalade, the call sign for abort, just before they reached the target. The month of July closed with a night raid on Joigny Laroche. Belasco says:

> *The gaggle on the way to the target from position E was beautifully concentrated. One stick fell across village north of canal; otherwise well on target, which could be identified visually.* (Operations Record No 44 Squadron)

---

* Donald Neil McKechnie born in South Africa attended Chaplin School in Gwelo and worked on a mine before enlisting in April 1942. He trained in Rhodesia, proceeding overseas in July 1943.

August commenced with a daylight raid on Stracourt and Le Breteque, which was pretty depressing because none of the aircraft attacked the target and either jettisoned bombs or brought them back. On the following two days, the target was Trossy, where on the second occasion the aircraft were so tightly massed over the target that accurate bombing was impossible and it was positively dangerous. Flying Officer Freestone's aircraft was actually hit by a bomb from another plane. During the following three days, the Lancasters were involved in daylight raids on Leu D'Esserant, Bois De Casson and Secqueville. Of this last occasion, Flight Lieutenant Ralph Albert Newmarch reported:

We were ordered to abandon the mission over the target by the controller, so we returned to base. Other crews continued to bomb in spite of repeated orders to stop.
(Operations Record 9th August)

The Rhodesian bomber squadrons were now being given a variety of targets. On 14th August, battleships and tankers in Brest harbour; on 15th August Deelen Air Field; on 16th August six aircraft went mine-laying and eight went to Stettin, followed on the next day by a daylight attack on Foret de Lisle and then the weather clamped in. Day after day comes the report, so many aircraft detailed, subsequently cancelled. Finally, there was a fine night and 18 aircraft were assigned to attack Darmstadt:

Flying Officer Freestone did not attack target owing to petrol leak. Flying Officer Lewis attacked Russelsheim and Squadron Leader Millington attacked a built-up area between Mannheim and Mainz. Operation appears to have been a complete failure owing to bad marking and lack of control. Flying Officer Anning in his report says, 'A masterpiece of organized chaos'.
(Operations Record)

Apparently, 190 Lancasters had a rather aimless flight over Darmstadt as a result of the master bomber's aircraft having an electrical failure and his two deputies being shot down. Squadron Leader Millington had this to say:

Controller failed to contact the force. Deputy was late. Markers failed to find target. Flare force ran out of flares, so on deputy controller's instructions we bombed what appeared to be a built-up area in the neighbourhood of the target after making four orbits.

Newmarch says that he heard pathfinders asking for controller and markers. Heard discussion on doubts about target. Our H2S took us well east of the fires and flares.

Next came two night attacks on Königsberg and a mine-laying operation as a result of which Squadron Leader White was reported missing. The final day of August saw the squadron making a daylight attack on Auchy les Hesdin.

During the month of August, Rhodesian airmen had received the sad news that their one-time teacher and friend, Jimmy Powell, had been reported missing presumed killed in air operations over Italy. He had been seconded for duty to the Southern Rhodesia Air Section before the war and had received the OBE and the DSO for a raid on Venice and Padua in 1941 when he had machine-gunned Padua Aerodrome from a height of 20 feet. On the lighter side, he had taken the part of a wing commander in the film, Target for Tonight.

CHAPTER 21

The Italian Campaign

Turning back the clock to January 1944 and changing the location to the Mediterranean, we see that the British and American armies had become bogged down in the rain and cold of the Italian winter. In the narrow mountainous area of central Italy, the Allied advance slowed from a bloody crawl to a full stop at Monte Cassino. This small town that lies on the main road between Naples and Rome, is dominated by a Benedictine monastery. Standing on a promontory above the junction of two rivers, it commands the surrounding countryside. Monte Cassino served as the pivot of the German Gustave Line and as long as the Germans held it, the Allied advance could not continue. One obvious way to break the stalemate was to launch an out-flanking, seaborne invasion north of the Gustave Line.

This landing took place on 22nd January when 50,000 British and American troops stormed the beaches at Anzio. However, instead of pushing inland and cutting the German supply lines the commander, Major General Lucas, dug in and remained on the beachhead. And so, once again it was stalemate. However, the Anzio landing did divert German forces away from western Europe where plans were already afoot for an invasion in May or June.

Back in the Western Desert
Meanwhile No 237 (Rhodesia) Squadron was still based at Savoia in Libya under their commanding officer John Walmisley, engaged on the somewhat monotonous tasks of convoy escort and patrol work. The weather during the first weeks of the New Year 1944 was against much flying of any kind and certainly delayed the squadron's training programme. On 8th January, for example, Flight Lieutenant John Haarhoff and Flying Officer Derek Guy Hallas scrambled after a low-flying bogey but made no contact and returned to base. That was the end of flying for the day. A hailstorm hit the aerodrome, followed by rain and low cloud, while on 17th January there was even a fall of snow that rendered the runway unserviceable for several days. In all, the squadron more than welcomed the news of a move...perhaps to better weather! The new base was Sidi Barrani, where the main party arrived on 2nd February. Once again, the squadron settled down to the routine of convoy escort, spiced occasionally with an exercise in cooperation with No 15 Squadron SAAF. On February 7th night flying practice began on Spitfires but then after the snow and hail came a dust storm that lasted all day. The weather certainly was not being kind to the Rhodesia squadron!

Towards the end of February, the squadron was divided into two sections, ready for yet another move. The main party proceeded to Aboukir, while the squadron's aircraft went back to Idku, where they were held in shipping readiness for the first week of March. Action began again on March 7th when a search was made for a missing Beaufighter of No 46 Squadron, with no luck. On 11th March, the squadron had its first loss for some time when Flying

Officer Eric Geoffrey Rapkin was lost at sea during a training exercise involving air-to-air practice interception.On 14th March the squadron was re-equipped with 16 Spitfire Mk IXs.

One pleasant diversion in March, on 17th, was the wedding of Squadron Leader John Walmisley and Rosemary Duke, a member of the Wrens at the Church of All Saints, Ramleh, in Alexandria. The following day, Flight Lieutenant John Haarhoff and Flight Lieutenant Duncan (Dinks) Moubray were posted to RATG, while Flight Lieutenant Basil Deall* assumed command of 'A' flight.

No 237 arrive in Corsica

At last, the months of dull patrolling and intensive training were over. On 20th March squadron personnel proceeded from Aboukir by train to Port Said where they embarked on HMT Circassia for transport to Ajaccio in Corsica arriving on 30th March. The squadron aircraft remained at Idku for a further two weeks while they were air-tested and fitted with long-range tanks. There was a series of tyre-bursts on take-off, probably because the aircraft had been standing for a while. In any events all tyres were changed and on 17th April, the squadron left in two sections for Corsica via El Adem and Tunis.

All 16 aircraft arrived at Poretta Air Field without incident on 19th April. The Spitfires were in fact due for their 40-hour inspection and it is saying a great deal for the aircraft and the ground crew that all 16 aircraft were serviceable by 24th April, the day on which the squadron was scheduled to make its first sortie. The commanding officer comments: "This was due to fine work by the ground crews."

The Rhodesian squadron was now part of the Tactical Air Force operating under the Mediterranean Air Command of Air Chief Marshal, Sir Arthur Tedder. The squadron's new home was at Poretta Aerodrome near Serragia on the eastern side of the island of Corsica. Here, based within 70 miles (112km) of the coast of Tuscany, the Rhodesian Spitfires began their active participation in the Italian Campaign. Their first operation, on 24th April 1944, began at 11h00 and was a sweep by 12 aircraft over occupied Italy, penetrating 50 miles (80km) inland. There was no incident but at least the squadron could feel it was back in the war.

The following day brought greater excitement, with 12 aircraft escorting 24 Martin B-26 Marauders with eight aircraft of No 451 Squadron on a bombing sortie, their target being an aqueduct. The raid was comparatively uneventful but the Allied planes encountered heavy and accurate flak on their return over the area south of Leghorn. Later in the day, 12 aircraft led by the commanding officer went on an armed recce of the Piombina road. Flight Lieutenant Panico Theodosiou claimed a three-ton truck as a flamer, while strikes were also observed on railway flat trucks and a signal box.

Two days of low cloud kept the squadron grounded and then on 28th April came the busiest day yet. It began at 08h00 with a fighter sweep during which attacks were made on Empoli station by Flight Lieutenant Basil Deall, Flying Officer Easton, Flying Officer Harley Petersen and Flying Officer Tore Rickland. A large gush of steam enveloped one railway engine when it was hit in the boiler. Two hours later squadron aircraft took off on a bomber escort and then at 18h25, came a second fighter sweep led by Flight Lieutenant Panico Theodosiou.

On the way out Flight Lieutenant Theodosiou said on the R/T that his cockpit was filling with glycol fumes. He baled out over the sea, by inverting his aircraft, three miles [5km] east of the island of Gorgonia (enemy-held). Pilot Officer McDermott and Flying Officer Derek

---

* Basil Deall's brother, John, was serving in Europe with No 266 Squadron.

No. 237 SQUADRON IN CORSICA

Hallas saw the parachute open. Pilot Officer McDermott signalled 'Mayday' on channel D, over the spot, enabling a fix to be taken, and then descended to 1,000 feet. He saw the canopy in the water but could see no dinghy. Flying Officer Hallas also had engine (boost) trouble, but returned safely. The Air Sea Rescue Service dispatched a Walrus and an Air Sea Rescue launch immediately; also Beaufighter, but could find nothing. During this sortie, while flying top cover, a section of four aircraft led by Flight Lieutenant Ipsen, experienced heavy, accurate and intense flak, east of Leghorn. Flying Officer Burne's aircraft was holed at the rear of the fuselage damaging only the skin. (Operations Record No 237 Squadron)

On the credit side, the pilots claimed one truck, a flamer, four trucks damaged as well as three railway coaches and two engines hit. On the following day, search was carried out for Flight Lieutenant Theodosiou* but with no joy.

On 17th April, two aircraft flew escort to 24 North American B-25 Mitchells on a bombing mission north of Lake Bolsena and in the evening, Basil Deall led an armed recce during which the aircraft strafed a German troopcarrier, lorries, a Bren gun carrier and several railway trucks. The final sortie of the month, on 30th April, was led by the commanding officer and was a fighter sweep to Lake Bolsena and Florence.

The squadron's main task was to attack road and rail communications from Pisa through Leghorn and so keep supplies from reaching the German divisions holding the mountains around Cassino. Further east, squadron pilots were also hitting the vital line of transport from the Alpine passes through Bologna and Florence to Rome. German fighter defence was almost non-existent but ack-ack fire was often heavy and extremely accurate.

During the first month of operations, new tactics were being constantly devised.

At the beginning, squadron take-offs required some organizing. It was finally decided to line the aircraft up along the edge of the runway, switch off and then start up ten minutes before the time of rendezvous in the case of bombers, or of departure from base in the case of fighter sweeps. It was then found simplest and most efficient to form into sections of four in line astern, until the whole squadron was in position, when, in the first case, each section would come in on the right of the No 1 and into battle formation. In this way, it was never necessary to make more than one circuit of the airfield. Aircraft have always taken off in pairs on this airfield, thus halving the nuisance created by dust on the runway. (Operations Record No 237 Squadron)

The first four days of May passed in what had now become routine missions—bomber escort and tactical reconnaissance but on 5th May, the squadron had its first brush with an enemy aircraft since coming to Corsica.

18h30 – 20h15. *10 aircraft led by Wing Commander Morris (Yellow section) went on a fighting sweep of the Civitavecchia—Orvieto-Piombino area. The CO was leading Red Section and Flight Lieutenant Ipsen, Green Section. While at 12,000 feet Pilot Officer Francis Girvan Barbour reported two unidentified aircraft three miles [5km] off at 12,000 feet. Wing Commander Morris ordered Green 1 and 2 (Flight Lieutenant Ipsen and Flying Officer Burne) to jettison tanks and investigate. The two aircraft then turned and were identified as FW 190s (long-nosed). The enemy aircraft turned east and after 20 minutes when Flying Officer*

---

* His dinghy was found open and floating, but Flight Lieutenant Panico Hercules Christopher Theodosiou was later presumed dead. Born in Cyprus, Panico attested into the Military force in November 1939 and transferred to the SRAF in February 1940. After serving in East Africa he returned to Rhodesia for pilot training and went back to the Middle East in October 1941.

Burne was within 700 yards (640m) of one, it disappeared into cloud and he was forced to turn into the other FW 190 that attacked him. Flight Lieutenant Ipsen was about to open fire on the latter aircraft when it too went into cloud. They were not seen again and the engagement was broken off at 2,000 feet. Flying Officer Burne landed at base with only five gallons (22 litres) of fuel. (Operations Record No 237 Squadron)

Problems with baling out

Four days later, on 9th May, the squadron had its second loss since coming to Corsica. The commanding officer led a fighter sweep over the Siena area, the return flight taking the Spitfires over Elba. The commanding officer, Squadron Leader Walmisley and his No 2, Flying Officer Tore Rickland, dived to recce the harbour and as they pulled clear, Rickland was heard to say that he was having trouble. Flight Lieutenant Deall saw white smoke pouring from Rickland's aircraft. Tore was then heard to say, Baling out. His aircraft turned on its back and then righted itself and Rickland was seen to bale out while the aircraft was in a steep dive before it hit the water. The commanding officer circled at 9,000 feet while the Germans were plastering the sky round his aircraft with very accurate flak. Then he detailed Flight Lieutenant Cyril Hurst as his No 2 to take over and the latter circled at 7,000 feet while Squadron Leader Walmisley went down to investigate. He reported seeing something yellow in the middle of an oil patch. Later in the morning, two aircraft searched for an hour and were joined by an Air Sea Rescue Walrus and a launch but nothing further was seen of Rickland,* who was later presumed dead.

This was apparently the second pilot to have been lost while baling out and John Walmisley, in a meeting with his pilots stressed the routine for baling out safely.

1. The first thing to do is jettison the hood by pulling forward on the black ball, and then exerting pressure with the elbows.
2. Open the side door.
3. If intending to invert the aircraft, trim right forward.
4. Pull out the pin from the safety harness before inverting the aircraft.

He was not in favour of inverting the aircraft, preferring to put the flaps down and climb over the side with the aircraft in a glide, or doing a stall turn and falling out at the top through the side door. He also suggested that goggles and oxygen mask should be used until the last moment to protect the pilot from the glycol fumes.

The No 237 Squadron log-book for 10th May 1944 carries an interesting note:

Flying Officer Ian Douglas Smith arrived on posting ex Middle East, 30th April 1944, having been non-effective for six months owing to a crash while night flying in a Hurricane IIC at Idku, Egypt.

Part of the day was spent at a nearby river practising dinghy drills, probably as a result of the recent losses. On the following day, several other pilots joined the squadron from RAF Middle East. One of these new arrivals was a young man who trained in Rhodesia and was later to die flying with the squadron, Peter Sutton. His diary gives a vivid description of life on the squadron. The entry dated 14th May 1944 reads:

---

* Tore Rickland was born in Natal and educated at Plumtree School. He attested in October 1941 and trained in Rhodesia before proceeding to the Middle East in 1942.

Well, here I am on the squadron at last. We flew over from Algiers in a Dakota, stopping at two places in Sardinia and flying round the coastline of Corsica, so we saw quite a lot of our surroundings. Corsica looked lovely from the air with its green grass and trees, and all the hills. When we landed, we found it as good as and better than it looked ... The first day passed uneventfully, filling in arrival forms, seeing the CO etc., but that night things began in earnest. I think Jerry must have heard we had arrived, for he sent a large number of Ju 88s over and laid hell out of us. It began with someone hearing the beat of an aircraft's engine out to sea at about 11 pm. He said, "I bet that's Jerry" and sure enough the ack-ack began to open up on the coast. We watched the gun flashes with great interest and saw the shells bursting nearer and nearer to us as a Ju approached. Soon, he was overhead and we could hear him quite plainly. We jumped a bit when the Bofors gun beside us went off, but we weren't a bit frightened—not yet! Soon more Jerries were overhead and the whole sky was filled with tracer and bursting ack-ack shells. Then the kites began dropping lots of parachute flares, which lit up the whole scene marvellously. We were still standing round in the open enjoying the show. At this stage, the first bomb fell with a whistle exactly like the sound in films and we fell down flat until it burst some way off. Then we heard odd bits of shrapnel from the ack-ack falling to earth, so we went into the tent to try to find our tin hats. We could only find mine, so 'J' just said, "Maleesh" and went without, though we decided that it would be wise to find a slit trench somewhere. We couldn't find any empty trenches, so we went and sat under the water-bowser, which we thought would keep us safe from falling shrapnel at least, though it was no protection from the bombs that were falling in sticks here and there. By now the parachute flares had floated down quite low and Jerry began to do his stuff. Down came the Jus dive-bombing our aircraft dispersed on the 'drome. We could see them coming screaming down in twos and threes, lit up by their own flares. They were dropping clusters of very small shrapnel bombs, though we didn't know it then. They went off with a succession of sharp pops, like a heavy machine gun. Shortly afterwards the flares burnt out and Jerry cleared off—the whole raid only lasting 20 minutes or thereabouts.* It was only when we'd picked ourselves up and walked round the aircraft that we realized what a lot of damage had been done in that short time. Not one aircraft had escaped entirely, and some were sorry wrecks filled with shrapnel holes and leaking petrol, oil and glycol. Yes, Jerry did a thorough job and we weren't the only ones to suffer. He got about six flamers (amongst the other squadrons) including a Liberator that happened to be on the 'drome. The ammo from the burning kites went on popping off long after he'd gone. If I'd known he'd dropped such a lot of bombs I wouldn't have been sitting so happily under the bowser. At about 12.30, we went to bed feeling a little bit weak at the knees and soon dropped off to sleep. But no, at 3 am back came Jerry again and we all hopped out of bed like scared rabbits. This time I knew what to expect and was really frightened and trembling like a ruddy leaf with cold and fear! But our panic was unfounded, and Jerry went right over us and dropped his load on the next 'drome down the island. I, for one, was more relieved than words can say, and we went back to bed feeling weaker at the knees than ever. I awoke at dawn next morning with a start and seeing the light outside called out, "Look out, boys, he's dropping more flares." Thank heavens no one was awake to hear me—I'd never have lived it down. At breakfast, we all discussed the raid and I was glad to hear everyone was as frightened as I was, and that most of them had been in slit trenches. After breakfast, you should have seen us getting down to digging one for ourselves. When we'd dug ourselves to a standstill, we wearily helped the others picking up shrapnel from the runways to prevent burst tyres. There was an amazing amount of it everywhere and a lot of unexploded bombs too. With so many of our kites out of action our spirits were very low that day, but we heard later that a squadron of Lightnings had found the base of the Ju 88s and had strafed them thoroughly, getting 14 flamers.

---

* Ops Record reports that of 17 aircraft all but one was holed in this raid.

This cheered us up a lot, and now that most of our kites are repaired again and we can give them tit-for-tat ourselves, we feel better than ever. I think Corsica must be rather a thorn in the flesh for Jerry. (Peter Sutton)

Particular mention is made in the Operations Record of Aircraftman Alfred Wheeler who stayed at his post throughout the raid and continued to operate the telephone exchange. Corporal Dixon stood by to take over in case Wheeler was wounded but although the tent in which they were working was hit, neither of the men was injured.

On 14th May Peter Sutton had his first flip in a Spitfire IX:

Which I enjoyed. The power of these Merlin engines is amazing and I frequently had the feeling that the kite was flying itself and didn't care a hell what I wanted to do. I did some general flying and then went to have a look at the snow on a nearby mountain. It was great fun flying through the passes with the snowy peaks on either side. I came in to land rather too fast and also like a clot, forgot to lower the flaps and I went streaking right across the 'drome bouncing like hell and wondering when the kite was going to slow down a bit. In the end, I went careering off the end of the runway and into the bundu with brakes full on before I could stop. By God what a mad landing it was. Unfortunately, the flight commander saw it. He was very nice about it, but he thinks me one hell of a useless pilot. What a pity to start off so badly. (Peter Sutton)

The first 'kill' in Corsica

May 15th turned out to be the best day for the squadron since arriving in Corsica. Twelve aircraft, led by Squadron Leader Walmisley, were detailed to escort 12 B-26s on a bombing attack on Voltri harbour. On the run-in to the target, Flying Officer Brian Wilson reported an aircraft at the same height, 12,000 feet, flying towards the formation. Four pilots were requested to investigate and they reported that it was a Dornier Do 217. All four pilots fired, hitting the German aircraft, which dived and took evasive action. The pilots attacked again, and Flight Lieutenant Ipsen's last burst was rewarded with a sheet of flame from the starboard engine. The Dornier went into a dive and hit the ground. The squadron was awarded three-quarters of the credit for destroying the enemy aircraft, so were able to chalk up the first kill in Corsica.

It seemed the Rhodesian squadron was on a winning streak. On the following day, 26th May, during a fighter sweep in the Piombino-Orvieto area Flying Officer Dinks Moubray, spotted a camouflaged landing strip with four dummy aircraft on it. Moubray and Sergeant Paul Pearson dived to strafe. Moubray put a cannon shell through the wing of an Me 109 hidden in the trees, while Sergeant Pearson strafed a camouflaged tent from which a number of enemy airmen were seen to leave in a hurry.

There were three further sorties that day, one armed recce and two escort operations, on the second of which the four aircraft were led by Flying Officer Ian Douglas Smith, flying his first mission since rejoining the squadron. The task was to escort 24 B-26s to attack a target at Pontedera. During the next few days, the squadron was kept busy flying fighter sweeps and escorting heavy and light bombers.

The Germans retreat to Rome

Since January 1944, the Allied advance north had been stalled at Monte Cassino. The monastery was completely destroyed by bombing but the German troops continued to hold out in underground passages and cellars. They withstood attacks by British, Canadian, Indian, New Zealand and US troops, until a fourth offensive led to its capture by the Poles and the British on 18th May. Some of the most bitter fighting of the war raged round Monte Cassino, but once it fell the route was open to Rome. Five days later, an offensive from the bridgehead at Anzio linked up with the 5th Army advancing north along the main road from Monte Cassino. The Germans now began a full-scale retreat and No 237 Squadron was called upon to harry the armoured columns as they pulled back.

The squadron Operations Record for 20th May 1944 tells a typical story:

08h25 – 10h05. Eight aircraft led by Flight Lieutenant Cyril Hurst on strafing mission. One section—Flying Officer Arthur Canisius Coulson and Pilot Officer Miller attacked a ten-ton lorry and trailer stationary in a valley. It was left smoking. Several trucks seen travelling towards Pisa. Trucks north-east of the town were strafed. They immediately came to a standstill and attacks on them were made by each pilot. Flying Officers Coulson and Miller each got a flamer. Three-tonner, fully loaded with sacks and two more badly damaged; also a small staff car. Flight Lieutenant Ipsen and Pilot Officer John (Jack) McVicar Malloch strafed a five-tonner and trailer carrying oil drums near Pisa. Flight Lieutenant Ipsen left the trailer blazing and damaged the truck. Pilot Officer Malloch made a flamer of a five-ton truck and damaged three more three-tonners and two 15-hundredweight trucks with cannon and machine guns. Flying Officer I.D. Smith and Pilot Officer Allan John Douglas strafed motor transport on roads north of Lucca. Flying Officer Smith strafed electric-powered train with six coaches that were moving out of a station. His first burst caused the engine to blow up. Both pilots then strafed three of the coaches that were full of passengers. Flying Officer Allan Douglas then damaged two three-ton trucks and Flying Officer Smith strafed a five-ton truck, which went into a ditch and caught fire. He also obtained hits on a red three-ton bowser, which poured liquid but did not ignite. A staff car containing four army types, was also badly damaged. Flying Officer Coulson's aircraft was hit by a bullet, which damaged the oxygen pipe and bounced off the armour plate of the seat before going out through the side of the cockpit. This was probably collected near Pisa where he experienced some scant but accurate light ack-ack.

12h15. Eight aircraft led by the CO were airborne on a fighter sweep of the same area, a few miles north of Pisa. Flying Officer Boy Crook and Pilot Officer Byron Peter Rainsford damaged two of what appeared to be nine railway bowsers. Two three-tonners were damaged, one leaving the road and landing in a ditch. Flying Officer Alan Edward Smith damaged six of 14 railway trucks. Thirty-plus motor transport were observed near the outskirts of a town. One three-tonner loaded with wood and a small staff car were damaged. He also saw a radar station and fired, observing hits on one square building. Flying Officer Dinks Moubray again strafed the ten-ton vehicle and trailer that had been damaged in the morning. A wheel was blown off into the road. The CO damaged three 15-hundredweight trucks. Flight Lieutenant Basil Deall* 'B' flight commander got separated from his No 2 and was heard to call over the R/T "I have been hit. Am force-landing." His position was then ten miles [16km] north of Leghorn. A search was made to locate his aircraft.

On 21st and 22nd May the pressure was intense with several sorties being flown each day. Then on 23rd May, the whole squadron moved from Poretta to Serragia. On the following day, it was business as usual:

24th May 10h30 – 12h15. Ten of our aircraft led by Wing Commander Morris in his own aircraft escorted 24 B-25s to bomb road and railway bridges north of Arezzo. 14h50 – 16h25. Eight aircraft led by the CO did a fighter sweep of the Pisa-Florence-Viterbo area. Much damage done to M/T. 18h40 – 20h10. Nine aircraft and Wing Commander Morris were airborne on a fighter sweep of the Piombino area. Again, havoc was caused among the retreating German transport. (Operations Record No 237 Squadron)

---

* William Basil Deall was later reported a POW.

On 26th May, there was another squadron loss:

> *Eight aircraft led by CO were escorting 24 B-25s attacking bridges at Incisa. A great deal of accurate flak was encountered near the target and an unidentified aircraft was spotted in the distance. Flying Officer Ian Smith and his No 2, Pilot Officer Jacobus Ignatius de Wet, were dispatched to investigate. They could not find the aircraft but spotted two five-ton trucks, which they strafed and damaged. As Pilot Officer de Wet* turned in for a second run, he was hit by flak and called up to say he was making a forced-landing.*
> (Operations Record No 237 Squadron)

The last few days of the month were spent on escort duty, with one unpleasant incident when Flying Officers Burne and Eaton were attacked by four Mustangs near Rome. They managed to evade the three determined attacks made upon them but such mistakes did not always end so happily. Operational flying now occupied all available time, 713 operational hours being logged during May. As a result the Keep Fit regime had fallen by the wayside although the men still found time to swim. Two rugby fixtures had to be cancelled during May owing to operational commitments. The Rhodesian squadron could not complain any more about being under-utilized.

The first days of June brought the usual pattern of two or three operations a day, mainly bomber escort. By now the front was in a mobile state with the Allied forces making a rapid advance towards Rome, which was taken by the 5th Army on 4th June 1944. Field Marshal Kesselring, the German commander, was now pulling back as fast as he could. The highways leading north towards Viterbo and along the Tyrrhenian coast, were clogged with German transport, presenting easy targets for American Mitchell and Marauder bombers. Peter Sutton, in his diary gives his comments on flying escort for these bombers:

> *5th June 1944. For the past week we have had 90-gallon [409-litre] tanks on and have been doing some tiresome bomber escort. It's not much fun lugging all that extra petrol about on such a small aircraft—the poor old Spit skids all over the sky to show her disgust. Today though, the 90-gallon tanks came off, and the squadron has been out all day on strafing sorties, as Jerry is pulling out of Rome. We have had very good hunting, getting 20 flamers and 30 M/T damaged during today, not to mention a train damaged. I myself flew two sorties, having 'bags of joy'! On the first trip, I fired at an ambulance in error and then had several goes at a convoy of 25 large army trucks. I hit two of them and they both burst into flames at once. When we left that convoy, seven trucks were burning merrily.* (Peter Sutton)

Meanwhile the fame of No 237 Squadron had spread, even rating an article in *Stars and Stripes* the American forces newspaper: "If this Rhodesian Spitfire squadron isn't the most travelled and experienced fighter outfit in the world, it will do until something better comes along."

Sergeant Pearson's story

Although the Luftwaffe was conspicuously absent from the Italian skies, German ground defences were formidable, as several of the Rhodesian squadron pilots were to discover:

> *5th June 16h00 – 17h45. Twelve aircraft (Wing Commander Morris) on fighter sweep in Viterbo area. Seven vehicles were destroyed and eight damaged. Sergeant Pearson's aircraft was hit by flak and he was wounded in his thigh. He force-landed 20 miles [32km] north of the line*

---

* Jacobus Ignatius de Wet was later reported a POW.

and Flying Officer Brian Carson Moubray Wilson, his No 1, saw him run for the woods. He strafed Sergeant Pearson's aircraft and set it on fire. (Operations Record)

Sergeant Pearson's story continues. The wound in his thigh was not serious but the damage to his aircraft caused the engine to overheat and he had to make a quick landing. The machine was actually on fire when he got it onto the ground. As he landed, he knocked his head on the reflector sight and was so dazed by the blow that he did not remember getting out of the aircraft. The next thing he does remember is seeing about 30 German soldiers running towards him, shouting. He raised his hands but they opened fire so he changed his mind about surrendering, and making a quick dive behind the burning aircraft, took off into the nearby woods. A bullet hit him in the thigh and he fell but regained his feet and managed to find shelter among the trees.

He kept running for a while, with Germans close on his heels but then, just as he reached thicker undergrowth and what could be greater safety he spotted another group of Germans approaching from the opposite direction. He dived for the nearest cover, a tree with foliage reaching to the ground and stood against the trunk pulling the small branches around him. His pursuers sprayed the bushes with their machine guns and came within yards of his hiding place. Then the party grew tired of the hunt and returned to the crashed aircraft, leaving only one man to guard the spot where they had last seen Pearson. From his hiding place, Pearson could see the Germans clambering over his aircraft. Then Flying Officer Brian Wilson, who had been his No 1 returned and, screaming down in a dive, strafed the stranded plane and the Germans who were clustering round it. There was a scramble for cover, made even more desperate as a second Spitfire appeared and began to shoot up the truck in which the soldiers had arrived.

In the meantime, the sentry who had been left to guard Pearson, came and sat in the shade on the opposite side of the tree, which Pearson was using as a hiding place. The soldier leaned his rifle against the tree relaxing after the heat of the chase. In fact, he was half dozing, when Pearson crept round the tree, a stone in his hand, and hit the German on the head. Then he set off as fast as he could down the road south, heading for the Allied lines.

Catching sight of some Italians working in a field he attempted to hide, but one of them spotted him and they all came to have a look. Finding that he was hurt, they carried him to a nearby house and bandaged his injuries, using German field dressings, which they had obtained somehow. He was given milk to drink and as soon as it was dark, they improvised a litter and carried him to a hiding place in thick scrub, only about 200 yards from a German heavy artillery post. Pearson could see the soldiers walking about in the gun pit and hear them talking. He remained in this hiding place for five days, during one of which he was delirious. Each night the Italians brought food and water for him. Each day the shelling grew heavier and on the fifth day, the German position was overrun by the advancing Allies. Pearson by now was too stiff to move, and the Italians arranged for a Partisan group to bring an ambulance for him.

Now it seemed that his problems were over, but on the way to a field hospital, the ambulance was attacked by Italian Fascists who shot it up and then threw a grenade into it. The force of the explosion literally blew Pearson out through the open door, but except for a thorough shaking, he did not receive further injuries. He crept into a ditch and hid there while the fighting moved away. Not long after, a jeep came along, carrying four American soldiers who had been celebrating the capture of a nearby town. They were a bit dubious at first, when this dirty, ragged, bloodstained man told them he was a Royal Air Force pilot. Finally, they took him aboard and drove him with maximum speed towards medical help. In this case their speed saved them because they detonated a mine but did not suffer the full force of the explosion, merely experiencing the sensation of travelling through the air and landing upside down in the ditch. Once again, Pearson escaped injury. The four Americans put the jeep back on the road and this time managed to deliver their wounded comrade to a medical officer who dispatched him to hospital where he stayed one day before taking French-leave and hitch-hiking to Rome. Here he was once again sent to hospital, and once again, he deserted his bed and found an aerodrome from which he hitched a lift back to his squadron.

Paul Pearson was also missing from a sortie on 24th March 1945, but he made good his escape. For his actions on this and subsequent days, and for his escapade detailed above he was awarded the Military Medal—the only Rhodesian airman to be so honoured.

On the same day, 5th June, that Pearson crash-landed, Flying Officer Arthur Coulson was also hit by flak near Lake Bolsena. He reported that he intended to make a forced-landing but his No 2 lost sight of him while taking evasive action and nothing further was heard of Coulson* for a while.

More lucky landings
Four days later it was the turn of Flying Officer John Michael (Boy) Crook.

> **9th June 19h00–20h50.** *Eight aircraft (CO) did a fighter sweep. One armoured car and eight large lorries were destroyed. Flying Officer Crook's aircraft hit a lorry he was strafing and he said he would have to force-land. He did so. He was seen to land in a field, but not seen to leave the aircraft.* (Operations Record No 237 Squadron)

In fact, he did land safely and walked south-east until he reached the village of Rocca-Tideright. There he joined up with Italian partisans and stayed with them until the Americans arrived. He was then able to make his way back to the squadron. Two days later Flying Officer Byron Rainsford also had a lucky break. During an armed recce, he was hit by light flak but managed to reach friendly territory before he was forced to land. On 14th June, it was Peter Sutton who ran into trouble:

> *Littorio Air Field, Rome. 15th June 1944*
> *Up to yesterday I regarded this war as a little show designed for my amusement, but now my ideas have been shaken up a bit. I was out for my usual strafing and had already got three flamers when our section suddenly got mixed up with a hell of a lot of Jerry light flak. I dodged bullets for a couple of minutes, using every trick I knew and they weren't able to hit me, though Ian Smith and his No 2 were both hit. The flak petered out, and I relaxed and prepared to go on with the job. Just at that moment, I saw red tracer streaking past the cockpit and there was an almighty bang right underneath me—evidently hit by a 22mm shell. I pushed the throttle wide open and made off like a mad thing, twisting and turning and climbing and was surprised to see that all was well in that department. I thought I had better climb up while I still had an engine, so up I went, calling up on the radio "Blackball green 2 hit by flak. I am heading south." It was only then that I realized that all this evasive action had caused me to lose my bearings entirely. I sought inspiration from the compass but that too had suffered from my violent manœuvres and was idly spinning round and round. So I just went on climbing, feeling decidedly unhappy. At a few thousand feet, I could make out a stretch of water that I thought might be Lake Bolsena. Anyway, I made for this as it seemed to be roughly south-west of me, as far as I could tell from the sun. I got up to 9,000 feet and began to take stock of things. The engine was still OK and I began to feel I had made a bit of a fool of myself. After a short debate with myself, I decided it*

---

* Arthur Canisius Coulson was later reported a POW.

would be best to keep on south and get over friendly territory even if I did get laughed at. Shortly afterwards, my glycol temperature started rising so it's just as well. I found that by throttling back a bit I could make that temperature drop down to a reasonable figure, so I kept straight on. Soon the temperature went up again and I throttled back some more and then still more. At minus 4 boost I at last managed to persuade the temperature to stay put…relief! On we went, losing height very slowly, but still getting nearer to our own troops. At length I could see a welcome sight: shells bursting on the ground, and I knew that the precious line was not far away. Still we limped on and I blessed that engine quietly turning over with a fraction of its maximum power but nevertheless keeping me in the air. The line came nearer and nearer and at long last I was over it and I began to breathe again. The gallant engine was still ticking over peacefully, and I began to have hopes of reaching Rome or some other aerodrome. But the engine evidently thought it had done enough and the little temperature needle went sailing round the dial, so I switched off to prevent the glycol catching fire and glided down towards a large field with a road nearby that I could see. I was at 4,000 feet so I had plenty of time to think, and was able to radio my position and intentions, jettison the long-range tank, tighten my straps, lock the hood open (it wouldn't jettison) and generally get ready. I decided to leave the wheels up. When I was right down low, I could see the field wasn't as flat as it had looked and I was just able to hop over a small hillock and dodge some telegraph poles. I held off OK and managed to get the speed down to about 70 mph (115 km/h) before we hit with a wallop. The air was filled with dust and small stones. I was thrown forward on my straps, then jammed against the side and lastly forced back hard in my seat again. I afterwards saw that this queer feeling was because the kite skidded round and stopped facing the way it had come from, stopping in a space of 15 yards or fewer. I was out of the cockpit in a flash, dragging my parachute behind me. The plane did not burn, however, so I mopped my brow and waited for an Italian farmer who came running up. After some unsuccessful attempts at explaining I wanted to see British or American soldiers, some Yanks came along, followed by some French officers, more Yanks in a jeep and finally a British officer. What a crowd there was round that kite, all asking questions and jabbering together. The British officer asked me if I would like a drink, which turned out to be neat whisky. I nearly burnt my throat out swallowing it, but it made me feel good. After a bit more jabbering, we got a Yank to guard the plane and I drove off with the Americans. They treated me very well and an officer named Robinson (a lootenant) was especially decent. He drove me round the countryside in a jeep until we found a French Piper Cub Unit that offered to fly me to Rome the next morning. Robbie fixed me up with a much-needed wash, some supper and a mattress and blankets. These Yanks were an advanced ack-ack post, incidentally, and next morning they showed me all over their 90mm guns and the range predictors. (Peter Sutton)

Peter Sutton's story has a strange ending. When he boarded the aircraft in Rome that was to take him back to his squadron, he was greeted by Sergeant Pearson, who had been shot down ten days earlier.

Ian Smith lands behind the lines

After a brief period spent in shipping patrols, it was back to the old routine, bomber escort, fighter sweeps and low level recces. Then came 22nd June:

16h30–18h30. Twelve aircraft (CO) on armed recce in the Alessandria area…electric train and two vehicles were destroyed and four electric trains; three railway trucks and seven vehicles were damaged. Flying Officer I.D. Smith said that his aircraft had been hit by flak. His aircraft was seen to turn on its back and burst into flames. Pilot was seen to bale out and land safely in the mountains north of Spezia. (Operations Record No 237 Squadron)

Speaking of the incident, Ian Smith said:

We were strafing trains. Blowing up trains in the Po Valley and this was our job. It was not very flamboyant—the attraction was always for the chap who managed to shoot down another aeroplane but that seemed comparatively safe to the people who used to have to do the strafing because you were right down near the flak on the ground. Most of our work was train-busting and convoy-busting and that sort of thing. So we were strafing trains and I collected flak, a shell from an ack-ack gun very near the ground. Well, you see, you were comparatively safe if you were up on top, so I had to bale out. It hit my oil sump and my oil went, and I could see my temperature coming up. And the chap who was flying as my No 2 (Alex Douglas) eventually said to me: "Your plane's on fire." So there was only one thing I could do. I stepped out of the thing and landed in the mountains.

Ian Smith hid his parachute, wings and badges in some bushes and later met up with a group of Partisans who were operating from a nearby village. He spent five months with this group, helping plan hit-and-run strikes, sabotage etc. During that period, he learned a little Italian and decided to trek north over the Alps to join the American army, which had landed in the south of France. It was a rough journey in sub-zero temperatures but Ian Smith and his three companions all survived and 23 days later stumbled down the last slope to the American lines. So, although the Rhodesian squadron had been unlucky enough to lose six aircraft during the month of June, no pilots had been killed and only one, Arthur Coulson, had been taken prisoner.

July saw the continuation of the now familiar pattern, escort for bombers and fighter sweeps but, on 3rd July the squadron got a little of its own back and won a DFC.

3rd July 1944. Twelve aircraft (Flight Lieutenant Cyril Hurst) on area cover for 18 B-25s attacking targets in the Po Valley. One aircraft returned with engine trouble escorted by another. Twenty Me 109s were sighted behind and 5,000 feet above. Flying Officer Dinks Moubray shot one down. The pilot was seen to bale out, after it had been chased down to 1,000 feet. (Operations Record)

No 237 move to Calvi
On 9th July, the squadron said goodbye to Serragia and 22 aircraft took off for their new airfield, St Catherine's at Calvi. Calvi lies on the north-western side of Corsica, a distance across the sea, of 120 miles (200km) from the French Riviera.

10th July 1944. Once again the squadron have moved. We have crossed the island and are now near Calvi. We have a lovely spot for our tent, on a ridge overlooking the sea, which is about a mile [1.6km] away. The 'drome itself seems pretty good, though it is surrounded by mountains on three sides, and it is very tricky dodging all the peaks while coming in to land. We were all packed up and ready to leave our last 'drome at Serragia two days before we actually did go; so for two days we lived homeless as the tents had gone on ahead. The first of these days was very hot but, luckily, we were free to go off and swim in the sea all afternoon, and were quite happy. That evening we raided all the farms in the vicinity and came back laden with fruit, and best of all, some mealies, which we cooked over a campfire. We slept under the stars that night and loved it. But it rained on and off all the next day. All our kit, and incidentally ourselves, got soaked and we felt pretty wretched. At long last, we got the order we'd been waiting for and were able to get cracking. We piled in the truck and got down to the 'drome, into our kites and off in record time. But our troubles weren't over, for the weather on the other side at Calvi was vile. The 'drome was surrounded by low clouds, it was pelting with rain, and visibility was practically nil. We made a very perilous circuit, narrowly avoiding mountain tops in the rain and cloud, but we all got down safely though some of us made shocking landings. We got out of our kites and became wetter than ever, and covered with mud into the bargain. How thankful we were to find that the advanced party had put up the mess tent and had tea waiting for us. (Peter Sutton)

The squadron's main task at Calvi was bomber escort, though the weather had turned unreliable and, on occasion, the fighters were unable to make contact with the bombers they were detailed to escort. Added to the problem of the weather, July was to close with two most unfortunate mishaps.

25th July. Nil ops. Ciné-gun and air-to-air firing. Flying Officer Brian Wilson and Pilot Officer Francis Barbour missing from one of these trips. Flying Officer Wilson was picked up by Air Sea Rescue launch very slightly injured. (Operations Record)

It is not clear exactly what happened but it appears that during a practice dogfight, Barbour's aircraft had a head-on collision with Wilson's plane. Wilson said that he baled out at 400 feet. Francis Barbour's* body was found floating near some wreckage.

On the next day came another loss.

26th July 05h50 – 12h05. Twelve aircraft on standing patrol. Sergeant Malcolm McKenzie on his first operation and flying No 2 to Flying Officer Roy Francis Gray reported that he was having trouble and said he was below second blower height. Nothing more was heard of him. A French Merchant ship reported seeing an aircraft explode in the air fairly high up in approximately the same position but there is no reliable evidence as to what exactly took place. Sergeant McKenzie[†] had reported his engine trouble to Flying Officer Gray when he was some distance behind, so that Flying Officer Gray lost sight of him when he turned back to try to make base.

In all a sad month with two pilots killed and not by enemy action.

On 31st July, Peter Sutton and Sergeant Pearson took some leave and revisited Italy in an effort to contact the Partisans who had helped them the previous month. Now that it was firmly in Allied hands, many Rhodesians took advantage of their arrival in Italy to spend time in Rome. A Southern Rhodesia Liaison Office had been established in the city and accommodation was available at the Minerva Hotel or the Springbok Club. The former was a seedy hostelry in the Piazza Minerva, a dismal square notable only for a small ornamental elephant on a pedestal supporting an obelisk, which, as a pagan symbol, Holy Church had suitably sanctified by superimposing a metal cross.

At the beginning of August, Southern Rhodesia's Minister of Defence, Captain F.E. Harris DSO, paid a visit to the forward areas and met many Rhodesian servicemen, among them the men of No 237 (Rhodesia) Squadron, which was now commanded by Squadron Leader Ian Hardy Robertson Shand DFC. Ian Shand joined the squadron on 7th August and assumed command on 12th August, replacing Squadron Leader John Walmisley[‡] who had completed his second tour of operations.

---

* Francis Girvan Barbour born in Salisbury attested in February 1943 and proceeded to the Middle East in December the same year. He was buried in the Military Cemetery at Bastia in Corsica.

† Sergeant Pilot Malcolm McKenzie was later presumed dead.

‡ John Walmisley who assumed command of the squadron in April 1943, had been on active service since November 1939 and had twice been mentioned in dispatches.

Allied landings in the south of France

It was becoming obvious that something big was in the air but no one knew exactly what, until the evening of 14th August, when Ian Shand addressed all personnel on the future commitments of the unit. There was to be a second invasion, an Allied landing in the south of France. It was to begin the following day, 15th August.

> *15th August. Twelve aircraft led by Flight Lieutenant Ipsen gave area cover to 396 C-47s (Dakotas) en route for south of France. Throughout the day, standing patrols were maintained over the beachhead in southern France from St Maxime to Cap Benat. No enemy air opposition was encountered.* (Operations Record No 237 Squadron)

> *Our own part in the invasion seems very small and insignificant—just maintaining a constant air cover over the beaches. I wouldn't mind betting that Jerry doesn't send anything up, anyway. Once again we are reminded what a wizard job we pilots have compared with that of the PBI (Poor Bloody Infantry). Last night while they were all packed into troop ships like sardines, cramped, as hot as hell no doubt and feeling pretty queer inside, not knowing whether they would be killed as they waded ashore next morning, or not. While they were like that, where were we? Why, sound asleep in comfortable beds with not a care in the world. And at zero hour, 08h00 this morning (15th August), when the troops were battling their way onto the beaches through minefields, gunfire and the rest, where were we? Still asleep in bed!* (Peter Sutton)

However, during the next five days, the squadron was fully occupied flying beachhead patrols and then it was back to bomber escort while preparations went ahead for another move.

> *25th August. Twelve aircraft led by CO escorted 18 B-26s attacking a railroad bridge south of Bologna. A second formation of eight aircraft again led by CO Ian Shand provided cover for 18 B-26s bombing La Rateneau Island. On the return journey, the CO's aircraft began to cut, and he was forced to bale out at sea, 40 miles [64km] from base. He was eventually picked up by an Air Sea Rescue launch after abortive attempts by a Walrus and a Catalina, the crews of which were picked up by the launch.* (Operations Record No 237 Squadron)

Ian Shand recalled the incident with great clarity:

> *When baling out, you always tried to turn the aircraft into a climb so that it would not fall on top of you. As I jumped, I must have hit the tail of my own aircraft because when I got into the water I found that my head was bleeding—not badly but enough to be a nuisance so I bandaged it. The Walrus came on the scene and circled low. The water was very rough—too rough for easy landing. However, the crew of the Walrus seeing my bandaged head thought it was a matter of life and death and put down, only to find that they couldn't take off again. Next on the scene was the Cat, which did likewise...put down and couldn't get off because of the bad weather. So we all had to wait for the Air Sea Rescue launch. And the aircraft had to be towed into harbour when the weather calmed down. I can tell you I wasn't very popular!*

No 237 move to Cuers

On the same day, 25th August, 'A' flight ground crew disembarked in the south of France, having left Calvi on 22nd August. All the aircraft flew across to Cuers in southern France. 'B' flight ground crew arrived on 31st August. The pilots went to work at once maintaining standing patrols between Marseilles and the Gulf of Fos.

The invasion of southern France had proved relatively easy and there was little excitement

ALLIED LANDINGS
IN THE SOUTH OF FRANCE

for the squadron pilots, except when they flew over the border into northern Italy. In fact, during the early part of September the main talking point was a gale that swept the camp area causing havoc among the tents and wrecking the operations room. Welcome visitors were four American Lightnings, which were forced into the airfield by bad weather while on their way from the United Kingdom to Foggia in southern Italy. And an even more enthusiastic welcome was given to a three-ton truck, which returned from a foraging mission in Marseilles with 2,000 bottles of beer. The weather continued bad and the squadron pilots took the opportunity of one day's stand down to take a look at Marseilles. By 9th September, the weather had cleared sufficiently for recces to be flown across the Franco-Italian border into the area north of Cuneo where road and rail transport was strafed with good results.

> *21st September 1944. Eight aircraft led by CO strafed M/T etc. on roads in the Franco-Italian border area, getting six M/T with about one damaged; also about half a dozen horse-drawn vehicles were destroyed. Flight Sergeant Hackett's aircraft was hit by flak and he had to bale out, which he did successfully and was seen to get out of his chute harness and run away. Flying Officer Miller's aircraft got a 40mm shell burst under the fuselage. A lot of Hun bodies were claimed.* (Operations Record No 237 Squadron)

By the end of the month, the French episode was drawing near to its close but it had been a break that everyone had enjoyed.

> *On arrival in southern France, the adjutant, Flight Lieutenant David Prentice Howat, spoke to the squadron about fostering good relations with the French people, stressing our responsibility in this connection, for two main reasons:*
> 1. *that the RAF are held in very high esteem by the locals and that we have a great reputation to uphold and—*
> 2. *that the few RAF units in this show are the only British forces that these people have encountered or will encounter and that consequently the impression they gain of us will 'go' for all Britishers.*
> *It can now be put on record that everyone took the tip, as evidenced by the tidiness, smartness and correct manners of the men and the extremely friendly and cordial relations existing wherever we have gone. Informal dances were held almost nightly at both Pierrefeu and Cuers and attended by numerous 'Jeune Filles' and their chaperones from the district. The squadron's orchestra consisted of Leading Aircraftman Lark on our £15 piano and Sergeant England, violin, Leading Aircraftmen Coppin, banjo, and Ford on his drums. The adjutant's contributions on the pipes were, if nothing else, a novelty in these parts.* (Operations Record No 237 Squadron)

Reluctantly, therefore, the ground crew packed up on 29th September and moved to a staging camp near Marseilles for four days, where a good time was had by all, and on 2nd October they embarked on LST (Landing Ship Tank). The air party left for Italy on the following day and ran into trouble. The aircraft were to land at Cecina but the aerodrome there was unserviceable so they landed at Grosetto, where they were serviced by the Americans. From there, all except four aircraft took off, and landed again at Jesi for the night. The following day, they flew on to their new base at Falconara and later in the day the ground crew sailed from Marseilles in their landing ship tank.

From the very beginning, the weather at Falconara was bad. Finding hard ground on which to place the aircraft proved a problem because the whole airfield was covered with soft mud and the rain continued to fall. In fact, squadron activities were severely curtailed during the first half of October but it was to be only a brief lull before the final storm.

CHAPTER 22

The beginning of the end—autumn '44

On 20th August 1944, the Canadians and Americans had closed the Falaise-Argentan pocket. Caught in the bag were 50,000 German prisoners and 10,000 dead. The German Fifth Panzer and Seventh armies had been destroyed. Meanwhile on 19th August, the citizens of Paris rose in revolt and the German garrison in the city surrendered on 25th August. The following day, General Charles de Gaulle, leader of the Free French forces, walked in triumph down the Champs Élysées. The battles of Normandy and central France had cost the Germans half a million casualties and everywhere the Allies were surging forward. Patton was racing through Lorraine while Montgomery was speeding north-west towards Brussels and Antwerp.

During the first days of September 1944, Europe basked in a glorious Indian summer. But the fact that the enemy had retreated so suddenly left No 266 (Rhodesia) Squadron temporarily out of a job, doing little or no operational flying. By 3rd September the battlefront was totally out of range so the pilots took the opportunity to visit Rouen and the next two days saw them making a recce of the Deauville are …by jeep! On 6th September, the squadron broke camp and moved to airfield B 23. The weather had broken as well and the rain came down continuously forcing the pilots to find shelter in sheds and barns until the delayed ground crew arrived. Incidentally, despite the weather conditions the squadron managed a flypast with 20 aircraft at B 23.

Next day the rain continued to fall from a leaden sky. The runway resembled a bog so squadron personnel visited the sites of the previous months: bombing operations, self-propelled guns (SP) and a tunnel at St Andne. After which they were entertained at a chateau by a French family. It was indeed a good life—but it was not to continue. On 8th September, the Rhodesian squadron prepared for a move to Abbeville but found the strip unserviceable so the aircraft landed at Manston in England and there was no further activity that day.

The next day the assignment was a shipping strike towards the Channel Islands but no enemy shipping was sighted and the pilots landed back in England, at Tangmere, where they spent the night. Although there had been no operational activity there was something to celebrate that night, the award of the DSO to Acting Wing Commander Charles Llewellyn Green and DFCs to Flying Officers Hugh Balance and Charles Derek Erasmus.

No 266 Squadron at Lille

Operating from Manston on the following day, the squadron attacked shipping round the Dutch coast, scoring direct hits on large and medium barges. Then it was back to France on 11th September where the squadron was based temporarily at Lille Aerodrome, undertaking strikes on military targets of all kinds, trucks, guns, marshalling yards, water transport and motor transport.

The weather during the rest of September proved unpredictable and on 15th September,

No. 266 SQUADRON
OPERATIONS FROM LILLE

a ground recce of the local countryside was carried out, searching for eggs and other fresh produce for the mess. Members of the squadron also took advantage of the non-flying time to throw a party. Use was also made of an old rifle range and a rugby ball to break the boredom.

On 22nd September two sorties were carried out. The first against Dunkirk and, later in the day a gun emplacement north of Antwerp where the attack was not put in because of bad weather. The bad weather continued for the next two days allowing squadron members to make a trip by jeep to Reims where they procured some champagne. A party followed!

Not much happened then until 26th September when the weather cleared and the squadron carried out three operations against guns north-east of Antwerp and in the Calais area. The following day the weather was still good and four tasks were carried out in support of the army. Attacks were again made in the Antwerp and Calais areas.

The next day, 28th September, the squadron attacked and destroyed a blockhouse at Cap Gris Nez and guns at Mexplas.

> *Lads very flak happy. Attacked church, being used as an observation post, near Calais and destroyed same. Congrats from army!* (Operations Record)

The final day of the month saw a spectacular attack led by the wing commander on a suspected German headquarters. During the attack, direct hits demolished most of the building. Earlier in the day, there was a narrow escape when one aircraft landed wheels up but the pilot was not hurt.

It was quite common at B 51 (Lille) to have Spitfires taking off on one runway and Typhoons on another. Very interesting to onlookers. An added complication was that Bowser Liberators began operating from the aerodrome in their hundreds. They could only be controlled from the ground by the use of Very pistols, which meant that occasionally we were entertained to wizard fireworks displays.

On 2nd October, following an attack on radar installations at Berkenbosch, the squadron moved to Antwerp, which had been liberated by the British Second Army on 4th September. 'A' flight flew direct, but 'B' flight carried out a shipping strike on the way, during which Squadron Leader Wright led the attack on a medium-sized ship near Maas/Uis in the islands off the Dutch coast. Barney Wright was the only one to fire his rockets, because the vessel suddenly became airborne in front of him and, flying through the debris he sustained a hole in his radiator. Barney flew north leaving a white trail behind him and later force-landed north-west of Rotterdam. Reginald Culverwell (Skid) McAdam, the commanding officer's No 2 returned to base with 18 holes and several dents in the fuselage. Doug Borland managed to get a magnificent ciné film of the entire short sharp engagement. Squadron Leader Barney Wright was later reported a prisoner of war.

Barney Wright's story

Barney Wright told the whole story later in a letter home.

> *October 1st 1944. The Wing was on the move again. I went along to intelligence to find out orders for the following day. I charged in out of the deluge and asked, "Any big stuff we can go and prang? Something nice and juicy?"*
> *"No, nothing as yet Barney—a few ships about though."*
> *"Good, we are first off tomorrow."*
> *October 2nd 1944. I was awoken by my batman at 06h30, and with his help, soon had my tent down and my things packed in the jeep. I reached intelligence to find that we were to attack two ships, the very thing I had been longing to do once again. But then things started to go*

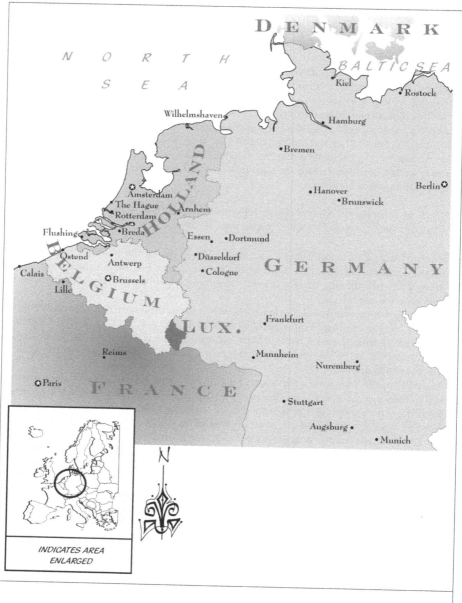

AUTUMN 1944
WITH Nos. 266 AND 44 SQUADRONS

wrong. For the first time the lads let me down! One of my flight commanders thought that as we were moving, it was not necessary to do an operation, for which he was thoroughly rapped over the knuckles. Consequently, I repeated our plan for the operation seven times owing to odd pilots turning up every five minutes. By then, I was really angry and let them all know it. We ran over to our parked aircraft only to find the engines stone cold. We had a devil of a time starting them—how I cursed my engineering officer. We taxied out and somehow or other managed to get airborne amongst the other four squadrons who had decided to move to the new airfield at the same time as we were trying to do an operation! I think I cursed everyone for the first three hours of that morning and I sincerely hoped it would never happen again. Not that it will, now that I am in Stalag III. I had set course and climbed to 7,000 feet towards Antwerp, with the rest of the squadron flying in perfect battle formation around me. We cut our way through the cumulus cloud but on reaching our target south of Rotterdam, there was no sign of movement. Blue One then reported two large trawlers on the river near a small village. As I turned to attack, I spotted something better—a large ship steaming up the river towards Rotterdam. It was about five miles from the Hook of Holland, a heavily-defended area. We came in out of the sun, all eight of us. I passed through 3,000 feet doing about 460 miles per hour, the ship increasing in size by the second. Holding it until the funnel filled my sights, I pressed the firing button and away went eight rockets. I pulled out of the dive, blacking out, when all of a sudden there was a terrific bang and a ripping of metal. The aircraft lurched and I hit my head on the hood. I then found myself on my back heading straight for the earth. I managed to right the aircraft and hold it in a flying attitude. I had time to look back and see the ship exploding. This is what had damaged my aircraft. I then looked at my aircraft in horror to see petrol pouring out of a huge hole in the wing, and my engine belching white smoke. The port aileron was gone and there were large tears in the elevator. I tried to bale out but it was too late. My life flashed before me as I went under some telephone wires, past a few houses—crash and then silence. (Barney Wright)

John Deall takes command

On 2nd October in the afternoon, 'A' flight carried out an armed recce in the same area and claimed a number of barges destroyed or damaged. John Deall took over command of the squadron after Barney Wright's forced landing. No 266 (Rhodesia) Squadron was now operating as a ground attack squadron in support of the army. Its main weapon was the rocket and its targets were bridges, enemy headquarters, railway bridges, tanks, gun positions, radar stations, trains and motor transport as well as shipping on the canal networks and on the River Rhine. Sometimes the target was a German observation post, which was usually located in a church spire, this being the best vantage point in the flat countryside of Holland and Belgium.

No 266 at Antwerp

Although we moved into static quarters at B 70 (Antwerp) we had been getting rather well organized at Lille what with electric light, beds, mattresses, tables, armchairs, mirrors and what have you. For most of these amenities we had the Boche to thank! Some members were too particular to dine at the mess, preferring their own eggs, chips and tomatoes, varied occasionally by the inclusion of partridges on the menu. Grapes, apples, pears etc. were not plentiful but could be obtained. A wireless-building craze seized the squadron, led by Geof Henderson, but at B 70 (Antwerp) the 'building' changed to 'buying'. (Operations Record No 266 Squadron)

3rd October brought bad weather, allowing the squadron time to settle in at their new base.

Everybody out scrounging stoves and light-fittings for their houses, and making themselves comfortable. Squadron allotted two adjoining houses for aircrew billets, and the orderly room is

situated in one of the ground floors. Occasional shells whistle eerily over head.
(Operations Record No 266 Squadron)

Late in the evening of 8th October, 'B' flight took off in appalling weather to disorganize a counter-attack by German infantry and tanks south of Bergen. The aircraft flying in extremely adverse conditions, went in at low altitude and riddled the target area with rockets and cannon fire despite intense anti-aircraft fire. Congratulations and heartfelt thanks were later received from the Canadian troops who managed to repel the enemy counter-attack. Flying Officer Doug Borland burst a tyre on take-off and was a bit shaken; otherwise the operation went off without trouble.

Back to Barney

Meanwhile Barney Wright was on his way to a stalag:

Then came the sound of rifle fire. I started to run for some trees and with the ricocheting of bullets around my feet I decided to hurl myself into a canal. Up to my neck in green slime and the blackest of mud, I found myself looking down the barrel of a sub-machine gun. My cigarettes were taken and distributed amongst the villagers and the Huns then led me off. I was allowed to wash from a barrel, and then dried out under the midday sun. I was taken to the local ack-ack HQ where the officers gave me bread, butter, jam and coffee, followed by wines and spirits! The general and his staff were very friendly and congratulated me on my fine shooting and the sinking of one of their ships. Apparently they had watched the whole show. They questioned me on the war and hoped it would be over soon. They thought it would be a good idea if the British joined forces with them and fought the Russians—their one great fear. Expecting a comfortable bed, I was shown a straw mattress with one blanket. The next day I was marched to a sedan car and was driven through the night to a village near Hengals where I was searched again and relieved of my watch—another debt to collect. I was taken to a large barn surrounded by barbed wire, with guns pointing inwards, in which there were about 200 airborne troops. I was greeted by the only officers there, British and American who told me what a hell of a time they had had, poor devils. We were all driven across the border in buses and then packed like sardines into a train, which took us on a never-to-be-forgotten journey. We saw the devastation that bomber command had wrought as we passed through the country on our way to Frankfurt—bomb craters everywhere, railway lines twisted grotesquely and vehicles unrecognizable. Frankfurt itself was in ruins, a dead city. Eventually we reached Oberhersal where we were stripped, searched and interrogated, and then locked in a small cell. What misery. Interrogations started with a vengeance and I was often threatened with torture by the Gestapo and goodness knows what else if I didn't answer all the questions. To hell with them was all that was in my mind. "I am only allowed to give you my name, rank and number." Nine days later I was marched off to a barrack where I met about 100 US and RAF flying people who had had the same treatment. Next day, 15th October, I left the 'Cages of Starvation' for the final disposal centre where we were to be sorted out into nationalities and forces, before going to our permanent camps. We arrived, disembarked and were treated to our first real meal in 13 days. Boy! How we ate. I was allotted a very spacious room with bed, mattress, sheets, three blankets, two chairs, a washstand and a fireplace. Heaven. What now? First the brutal treatment with threats of starvation and then absolute kindness with every comfort. "Would you like a hot shower?" I jumped at the opportunity and off I went with soap and towel to have a shower that lasted an hour. And on the way back I chose a book to occupy my mind. After further interrogation, I was given some clothes and was then marched through the barbed wire gates into the main camp. I thought of that poster of the prisoner leaning against the wire and the poor men who had been behind it for years. I was now determined to escape. (Barney Wright)

A visit from King George and Field Marshal Montgomery

Meanwhile Barney's squadron were spending their time, weather permitting, attacking shipping in the Flushing area. Then came the most memorable day of the month, possibly of the squadron's history.

October 13th 1944. A big day—Wing visited by HM King George and Field Marshal Montgomery. His Majesty spoke to Squadron Leader Deall, and Monty remarked upon Flying Officer Edward Terrence Cathcart (Ted) Cunnison's Africa Star and Rhodesian Wings. The king was present at the briefing of the day, which was for an attack on a German HQ south of Breda. (Operations Record)

Royalty or no royalty the war had to be fought.

'Rockphoons of the Tactical Air Force (TAF) led by Squadron Leader John Deall of Chicongas Farm, Umtali, kept a date today with a German General and razed his meeting place', says Reuter's special correspondent with the TAF. *'Information reached the TAF that the corps commander with the German forces defending the Breda zone had been holding conferences with senior staff officers in a house in the village of Ginneken near Breda. Today during a conference two Typhoon squadrons, one with rockets and the other with 500-lb (220kg) bombs roared over houses in the village at rooftop level and left them almost completely wrecked. After the first attack, the Typhoons turned and raked the wreckage with rocket fire to kill off survivors. Squadron Leader Deall said, "My squadron was second to go in. By then, although the air was full of dust and debris, I could see the middle of one house blown out."*
(Rhodesia Herald 14th October 1944)

The Rhodesians serving with the squadron at this time were:

Squadron Leader John Deall
Flight Lieutenant Peter Blackwell
Flight Lieutenant Don McGibbon
Flying Officer Hugh Balance
Flying Officer Doug Borland
Flying Officer Ted Cunnison
Flying Officer Jimmy Haworth
Flying Officer Ken Rogers
Pilot Officer L.D. Hughes
Pilot Officer Chimbo Hulley
Flight Sergeant Donovan Dodd
Flight Sergeant A.C. Henderson
Flight Sergeant Archie Knoesen
Flight Sergeant J. Luhnenschloss
Flight Sergeant Ellis Palte
Flight Sergeant Douglas Shepherd
Warrant Officer A.W. Paul
Sergeant Paddy Culligan
Sergeant Pilot Ted Donne
Sergeant Fred Day
LAC James Laing
AC George Cowan
AC C.G. Whittall

The battle of hedgerows and haystacks

And then, of all things, haystacks began to be targeted! It had been discovered that the Germans were making a habit of setting up pillboxes and camouflaging them with hay and so the order went out—hit the haystacks!

> **14th October.** *'B' operated twice. Both ops. Army support attacks on haystacks off which bullets were observed to bounce! This phenomenon was mentioned in the papers.*
> (Operations Record)

The report in the *Rhodesia Herald* was headlined: 'Rhodesian Typhoons Make Hay'.

> *The Rhodesian Typhoon pilots who attacked a group of 'haystacks' on the western front, after discovering that they were German pillboxes, were led by Squadron Leader J.H. Deall, says a message from Rhodesia House. After obliterating a gun emplacement south-east of Terneuzen with rockets, they had turned again to strafe the area with cannon fire, when German soldiers scurried out of a 'haystack'. The squadron immediately made for base to refuel and rearm with rockets. With a minimum of delay a second attack was made. "At least 24 rockets hit the three haystacks," said Flying Officer Reg McAdam of Salisbury, who was on both missions. "We released our rockets from 200 or 250 feet and lots of concrete debris flew in every direction as the haystacks crumpled up. They were completely flattened. It was a strongly fortified gun position with a network of slit trenches and foxholes. We didn't sight any huns on the second trip but to make sure, we strafed the hedges and trenches where they had hidden."* (Rhodesia Herald)

During the second half of October, the squadron lost two aircraft. Flight Lieutenant Don McGibbon was hit by flak and forced to bale out but landed safely. Flight Sergeant Cambrook was not so lucky. He was killed when he attempted to force-land after being hit by flak. Also during the second part of the month the squadron received two more distinguished visitors: Air Chief Marshal Leigh Mallory, who said he was on his way east and hoped to see the squadron there. And Lord Trenchard who autographed the flag and spoke mostly about the state of Belgium and France in the winter under war conditions.

> **24th October.** *Quite an impressive day in the Wing's history, owing to the outstanding attack on the German 15th Army HQ at Dordrecht. No 266 was the first squadron in. According to information received through underground channels, the HQ and staff were virtually wiped out and the resulting funeral was the biggest ever seen in Dordrecht. Two generals, 167 senior officers, 50 officers and 200 other ranks were said to have been killed. Bombs that went astray, also did useful damage in a motor transport yard. The attack had noticeable effects on the fighting qualities of the 15th Army.* (Operations Record)

V-2 rockets

From their airfield in Antwerp, the men of the Rhodesian squadron could see the smoke-trails of the V-2 rockets as they streaked up from their launching pads to the north-east. The rockets were sent off in pairs and it took just three and a half minutes for them to reach Antwerp. Pilots would see the smoke, and most of the time, could reach the shelters before the rocket hit but during one spell of bad weather towards the end of October a V-2 landed on the billets killing five men and injuring Corporal H.P. Offley-Share and Leading Aircraftman Gold from No 266 Squadron. The reason why Antwerp received so much attention from the Germans was that the port facilities were vital for the transport of supplies for the Allies' final push into Germany.

During November, Europe suffers notoriously bad weather and 10/10ths cloud over the target made life difficult for the squadron pilots at the beginning of the month, but when they could, they hit gun positions and observation posts. On 4th November, the squadron paid a visit to Gestapo headquarters in Rotterdam. Two days later, Flight Sergeant Land was hit by debris or flak but force-landed safely in friendly territory. He was soon back with the squadron.

November 7th. Flight Lieutenants Colly Collcutt, Tickey Bagott and Squadron Leader Joe Holmes arrived from England to pay a social visit. What a shout went up when it was discovered that they hadn't brought across any beer. Nevertheless, the party was a huge success. (Operations Record)

John Deall gave the visitors a briefing:

We are very busy just now. We have been gradually winkling out the enemy, who are established on the Scheldt Islands. By winkling we mean that lines of smoke are drawn with smoke shells between the enemy and our forward troops. Then our aircraft strafe and bomb everything immediately on the enemy side of the smoke. Then before the enemy have time to recover, our troops advance. We also do a certain amount of anti-shipping work on barges attempting to sneak out carrying men and materials. We often have to make these attacks at a very low level.

Flight Sergeant James Laing showed the visitors a trophy he had brought back from an operation. It was a piece of the railway bridge he had attacked.

I noticed an unusually shaped triangular hole in my plane and found it had been made by a jagged six-inch (15 cm) steel bolt complete with washer, of the sort used for fixing railway lines to sleepers. It must have flown up as a rocket struck the bridge and carved its way right through the gun panels of my mainplane.

On 10th November 1944, the British Prime Minister, Winston Churchill, made the first statement about the V-2s in the House of Commons. Both the V-1 and the V-2 had been developed at Peenemünde, where the first tests of the V-1, a small pilotless aircraft, took place as early as 1941. The V-1 was cheap and quicker to manufacture but the V-2 was a supersonic rocket and although it carried the same payload, the damage inflicted was greater because of the high-pressure shock wave produced by its speed of landing—roughly Mach 4, or four times the speed of sound. The V-1 was slow-moving and could be shot down or even tipped into the Channel by the wing of a fighter aircraft, and it ran on cheap low-grade petrol. The V-2 required alcohol and liquid oxygen but it was a world first, a highly sophisticated rocket projectile, an unprecedented weapon of war.

After much consideration, the Germans decided to go ahead with both projects and when the installations at Peenemünde were damaged in air raids the facility was moved to the Hartz mountains where subterranean workshops were established which proved to be undetectable. Of the 5,000 V-1s fired at Antwerp only 211 detonated on target and only one fifth of the weapons fired at England reached the target area owing mainly to the unreliable guidance system.

The V-2 offensive began on 6th September 1944 when two rockets were fired at Paris. Both failed in flight. Two days later the assault against England began but insufficient time had been spent in development and many of the rockets failed, some of them even detonating on the launch pad. Roughly 4,000 V-2 rockets were fired against England but fewer than 1,500 reached British shores. Even so, they caused considerable damage and claimed 2,500 lives.

In November 1944, priority was given to search-and destroy missions against the V-2s and their sites. On 11th November, No 266 Squadron went in search of rolling stock carrying V-2 rockets in the Utrecht area but finding none, attacked a rail-road bridge.

> *12th, 13th, 14th, 15th, 16th November. A very bad spell of weather; considerable amount of rain which played havoc with the aerodrome surface and made it necessary to move some dispersals. Model plane building became a popular pastime during the poor weather. Numerous wireless sets bought in Antwerp, very necessary with long winter nights approaching. Very sorry to lose Derek Erasmus to 193 Squadron as their CO. Doug Borland now commands 'B' flight.*
> (Operations Record No 266 Squadron)

On November 17th, 'B' flight managed to sneak in a raid before the weather closed in.

> *Army support by attacking observation post in church steeple. Village 3 miles [5km] east of Groesbeck just this side of German border. Church received direct hits but steeple still stood. Attacked a second time with cannon, in line. Heard the bell ringing, so low did we fly. (Operations Record)*
> *19th November. A train was caught east of Gouda by 'B' flight and well pranged. Flak effectively silenced by cannon fire. Flight Sergeant James Nelson Laing had to force-land behind enemy lines, unfortunately, with engine failure, thought to have been brought about by debris from attack. He called up on R/T to say that he had landed safely. Figures seen running towards him turned out to be members of the Resistance Movement who organized his safe return. Returned to us 14th December. Nice work 'Zombie'.*
> (Operations Record No 266 Squadron)

The rain came down again during the next few days and so the squadron members took the opportunity to visit Brussels where they were presented with a Citroen saloon salvaged from the Falaise Gap. They also managed to find a playing field and organized a game of rugby.

> *Pilots versus ground staff and some of the latter had to be briefed on how to play the game. Nevertheless, the score: three-all was very fair. Afterwards to swimming baths. Before retiring we had a beer on Flying Officer Ted Cunnison who had been grounded pending posting home!*
> (Operations Record)

Gestapo headquarters hit by No 266

On 26th November, the first operation for the day was on Kronenburg north of Leichswold where the target was successfully hit with cannon and rocket projectiles.

> *The next show, mostly 'B' flight was a very big Wing Operation. The Gestapo HQ and mess south of Amsterdam. It was scheduled to take place at about midday to catch the staff at lunch. As there were schools in the neighbourhood, this would also have been the best time had it been a weekday. After the group captain marked the target with phosphorous rockets 266 with the wing commander leading were first to attack the furthest building i.e. the mess the port side of which was left on fire. During this time, No 2 Squadron was dive-bombing flak positions to the west and flak ships in the harbour. We saw not a single burst of flak. Unfortunately, documents which it had been hoped were kept in the HQ were elsewhere, but an eye was being kept on their movements. In the evening 'A' flight made a successful attack on the Marshalling Yards at Gouda. (Operations Record)*

Following two days of bad weather the Wing again attacked a Gestapo headquarters, this time at Rotterdam. Intelligence had been received that important documents were being stored there and that prisoners with valuable information were being interrogated under torture.

> **29th November.** *A wing attack of Gestapo headquarters in Rotterdam. 266 played the role of anti-flak diversion during an attack on marshalling yards to the north-east of the city. Flying Officer Donovan Dodd flew No 2 the wing commander, marking HQ with phosphorous rockets. No 193 Squadron, low-level attacked the building with 1,000-lb (453kg)] delay bombs, few of which exploded. Another squadron did anti-flak diversions on the west side of the city. The operation was a success in that it enabled eleven prisoners to escape who would otherwise have been forced to divulge valuable information. Under German methods it is not an insult to say that almost anyone would eventually talk. Eight aircraft from each flight attacked, with success, an observation post in a church at Kronenburg. While this operation was in progress another panic army support target came through, and four aircraft, two from each flight, took off with four bombers as top cover during an attack and vice versa. (The Typhoons acted as top cover for the bombers).* (Operations Record No 266 Squadron)

The last operation of the month was carried out against marshalling yards at Bussum.

December opened with a return of the bad weather and there was no operational flying until 5th December when the squadron had one busy day and then there was a weather clamp-in which lasted for most of the month. The tedium was broken by the odd armed recce or army-support strike, by mess parties and by the welcome news that Flight Lieutenant Donald McGibbon had been awarded the DFC and that Bob Allen was safe although a prisoner of war.

Autumn and winter with No 44 Squadron

The weather, which had been so variable during the European autumn, had also inhibited the operations of No 44 Squadron. On the first day of September, 16 aircraft had successfully attacked Brest and 17 went to Deelen on 3rd September but on the second occasion the bad weather made it difficult to assess results.

There were no operations for the next five days and then came a dawn attack on München-Gladbach. The following day the target was Le Havre, also in daylight. The next night 240 Lancasters went to Darmstadt. In all, 12 aircraft, including two from the Rhodesian squadron failed to return. From the Stuttgart Raid, which took place the following night, one of the squadron's aircraft went missing. Four days of no operations. Then came a daylight raid on Boulogne. Twenty aircraft were detailed for this operation but eight of them did not attack the target as they received orders to cease bombing and return to base. At this stage in the war, precision bombing was vital because at times bombing attacks were being made only 200 yards from Allied lines. To ensure accuracy the master bomber would sometimes descend from the customary height to 3,000 feet at which range, the flak was often intense and accurate.

General Eisenhower, Commander in Chief of the Allied forces in Europe, wanted a swift closure to the European Campaign. To this end, Operation Market Garden was planned. Three airborne divisions were to be dropped into Holland to capture key bridges and open up the way for the British Second Army to outflank the Siegfried Line.

The American landings on 17th September at Eindhoven and Nijmegen were completely successful allowing the Allies passage over the Maas and the Waal Rivers. It was only at Arnhem that this ambitious plan failed—largely because the 9th SS Panzer were resting in the area and could react swiftly. The Guards Armoured Division fought with outstanding bravery to break through to the beleaguered airborne men but it was impossible and on the night of 25th/26th September orders were given for the position to be abandoned. Just over 2,000 survivors managed to escape through the German lines. Of the nearly 10,000 who had landed, 1,130 had been killed and 6,450 captured.

The Rhodesian bomber squadron took no part in the Arnhem landings. The target on 18th September was Bremerhaven and on the following night, it was back to München-Gladbach. Five Lancasters were lost on this raid but none from No 44 Squadron. However, there was a sad loss for the RAF. One of the missing aircraft was the Mosquito flown by Guy Gibson who was acting as master bomber for the attack. Bad weather again curtailed activities towards the end of September. On 30th September, the squadron moved from Dunholme Lodge to RAF Station Spilsby, near Skegness, where their first operation, on 4th October was mine-laying. Pilot Officer Evans failed to return.

During October, the squadron was out day and night

5th October:	daylight attack on Wilhelmshaven
6th October:	night attack on Bremen
7th October:	daylight attack on Walcheren
11th October:	daylight attack on Veere Flushing
14th October:	night attack Brunswick
17th October:	daylight attack Westkapelle Dyke
19th October:	night attack Nürnberg
23rd October:	day attack—gun positions Flushing. Flying Officer Henry Russell* missing
24th October:	mine-laying operation
28th October:	attack on Bergen. All aircraft reached target but did not attack as, owing to bad weather conditions, it was not possible to identify the target
30th October:	attack on Westkapellen Air Field.

Those days on which there were no operations were more often than not bad weather days when aircraft were detailed and stood by only to have the attack called off at the last moment.

Conspicuous gallantry

On the first day of November 1944, there occurred an event that demonstrated the courage and comradeship of the men who flew the bombers. Flying Officer John Haworth was bringing his Lancaster in on its bombing run, at about 17,000 feet, over the city of Hamburg when the aircraft gave a sudden lurch. A stray anti-aircraft shell, fired blind through the cloud layer, had hit the plane. John Haworth was mortally wounded and died within five minutes. The flight engineer had also been hit, but said nothing to the rest of the crew. Three of the four engines were unserviceable but the Lancaster was a tough machine and kept on flying until the bomb-aimer could take control. With the help of the rest of the crew he nursed the aircraft back on one engine until the British coast was in sight.

The damage was too bad for a landing to be considered; the crew would have to bale out. Hoping that the pilot might still be alive, they gave him a shot of morphine and arranged his parachute so that it would open, and pushed him out. Then one by one the crew jumped. The flight engineer, who had said nothing about his wound, hauled himself from the plane

---

* Henry Alfred Scott Russell born Berkshire, England attested December 1941, trained in Rhodesia before proceeding overseas in April 1943.

and pulled the ripcord but his parachute failed to open. It had almost certainly been damaged by the shell fragments, which had caused his wounds. Now only the bomb-aimer was left aboard the desperately crippled aircraft. He put the Lancaster on a heading out to sea so that it would crash in the water and jumped himself. Thanks to his courage and the self-sacrifice of the flight engineer, everyone landed safely except for the flight engineer and the pilot, John Haworth.* The bomb-aimer, Flight Sergeant S.W. Walters was awarded the Conspicuous Gallantry Medal on December 3rd. He was killed during a raid over Heilbronn on the following day, 4th December 1944.

On 2nd November the target was Düsseldorf and on the 4th November the Dortmund Ems Canal, in daylight, from which raid, Flying Officer Allwood failed to return. His crew included the Rhodesian airgunner, Maurice George Beckley.†

Wing Commander F.W. Thompson left the squadron on 9th November and the command was taken by Wing Commander Ralph A. Newmarch, who came from Salisbury and attested in 1940. On 11th November, there was an unfortunate accident when Flying Officer Caryer's aircraft, returning from a raid on Hamburg, collided with an aircraft from No 207 Squadron, while on his landing circuit. All crewmembers were killed.

During the next two weeks the weather began to deteriorate, although attacks were made in daylight on Düren and Gravenhorst and by night on Trondheim. Early on the morning of 26th November the target was Munich. Flying Officer Robert Kidson Hart, from Livingstone, who at that stage had flown 28 missions said:

I think my most successful raid was one on Munich. The defences absolutely packed up when the big bombs started to drop. But the weather on the way to the target was the worst the command has ever flown through. All the way across France, there was a belt of solid icing cloud from 2,000 – 20,000 feet and we had to stay on the deck below it until we reached clear skies beyond. We got more excitement that flight from the weather than the attack itself.
(Rhodesia Herald, 26th Jan. 1945)

One further comment from Flying Officer Hart was that he was a bit taken aback when he arrived on the squadron to find that two of his old school prefects were working as ground crew. Flying Officer William Keith Dives made a similar comment, "A lot of us were either at school together or trained together at home in Rhodesia. It's certainly great to work and play with old friends."

Occasionally news filtered through about the doings of men who had served earlier with Rhodesian squadrons: Three Rhodesian airmen from Salisbury were celebrating the 'gonging' of one of them that week in London (27th November): Squadron Leader Maurice Barber‡ DFC who won a decoration in the Middle East in 1942 and came to England early in 1944; Squadron Leader John Holderness (ex No 237 Squadron) who accompanied him to Buckingham Palace; with the third man being Flight Lieutenant Walter Kay, pioneer of Rhodesian and Nyasaland Airways, who piloted the first airmail from Croydon to Cape Town. Kay, who claimed to be the oldest pilot on active service, celebrated his 40th birthday recently.

---

* John Herewood Titley Haworth was born in England and educated at Prince Edward School. He attested in August 1942 and trained in Rhodesia before proceeding overseas in July 1943.

† Maurice George Beckley was born in London and educated at Umtali High School. He attested in May 1942 and trained in Rhodesia before proceeding overseas in January 1944.

‡ the three Barber brothers, Maurice, Roger (Jock) and Geoffrey all won DFCs. Geoffrey served with the SAAF.

The last days of November and the first few in December were spent in enforced inaction while the cloud lay low and the rain fell in a typically depressing British drizzle. In fact, a big dam raid had been scheduled for 2nd December with No 5 Group squadrons dropping tallboys. This operation was to have been made in support of American troops on high ground by flooding out the German positions. It had to be cancelled owing to heavy rain and it was 4th December before No 44 Squadron took to the air to attack Heilbronn. Nineteen aircraft took part and two failed to return. The pilots were Captain G.W. Hirschfield (SAAF)* and Flying Officer Dann. Apparently the damage was done by German night fighters.

On December 6th, 18 aircraft went to Geissen. One of the pilots who took part in the raid was Flying Officer Walter Dudley Barlow, who had worked in a bank before joining the RAF and was at the age of 20, a veteran of 23 operations.

There were a lot of fighters up when we attacked Giessen, and as we were making our bombing run-up my rear gunner reported an Me 410 coming in from the port quarter. I took evasive action as the fighter and my gunner simultaneously opened fire. The Me shot away to starboard without damaging us but my gunner thought he had scored a hit. However, the fighter appeared again, this time from starboard. This time my gunner got his burst in first and the Jerry went spinning down in a cloud with his port engine on fire. As we didn't see him hit the ground we only claimed him as damaged. All this took several minutes and after it was over we turned and made our bombing run. (Rhodesia Herald)

On 8th December came the delayed dam raid, and an attack on Heinbach Dam on the Urft River. It was fairly successful, but the bombers had to go back three days later and it was not so successful the second time. Of the 15 aircraft, five did not attack for one reason or another.

Crews were able to identify ground detail around the target and some could see the dam although this was obscured by smoke at times. Bombs appeared to circle the target at up to 500 yards radius although there were a few loose sticks that were wider. It was fairly well concentrated and it is believed that the target was hit repeatedly. The force leader went down to 3,000 feet to investigate the cloud en route and could not find any breaks at 5,000 feet. He therefore gave the order to the force to abandon the mission, and those aircraft that received the instruction, did not bomb. The leader, however, found the gap in the cloud on arrival at the target and bombed through it. Defence negligible. Three guns. No fighters. One aircraft seen to explode over target. (Operations Record No 44 Squadron)

Five days of cancelled operations were followed by another visit to Munich and a raid on the seaport Gdynia in the Gulf of Danzig (18th December 1944). This raid involved the Lancasters in a 2,000 mile (3,200km) round trip, which meant taking off from their base at Spilsby between four and five o'clock in the afternoon and arriving home at about three the next morning. December 21st saw eleven aircraft attacking Politz, in bright moonlight but then fog kept the bombers grounded up to and including Christmas Day. On Boxing Day, the target was St Vith. Flying Officer Terance Spencer reported:

Gee was u/s. Came in low over the sea. Climbed to cross the coast at 1,000 feet. Hoped to go between Ostend and Dunkirk. Got too near Dunkirk and was hit by flak and machine

---

* The navigator in Hirschfield's aircraft was Flying Officer Peter York who was educated at Prince Edward School and attested in August 1942. He received his preliminary flying training in Rhodesia before proceeding overseas in May 1943.

guns. Port outer engine feathered u/s. Large flak hole in port wing. Trimmers all shot away. (Operations Record)

Flying Officer Freeland reported seeing one Lancaster hit by flak and go down in the target area but parachutes opened. The last few days of the year passed with shipping attacks, mine-laying and a somewhat unsuccessful raid on Houffalize.

Autumn with No 237

To change the scene from northern Europe to Italy, in October 1944, No 237 (Rhodesia) Squadron found itself with its main base at Falconara in northern Italy and a detachment at Pisa. The weather was foul. The airfields were, for the most part, deep in thick sticky mud. In fact, it was not until 20th October that a run-in was constructed at Falconara. Up to that time, aircraft had to be parked with their tail wheels on the edge of the runway to stop them sinking belly deep in the mire. The squadron's main task was coastal reconnaissance, attacking any target that presented itself. The main enemy was the weather.

The Pisa detachment was billeted on the aerodrome, about 400 yards from the runway and in constant fear of American Beaufighters, which persisted in swinging off the runway and penetrating amazing distances into the rough. Pisa Air Field, like that at Falconara, was a sea of mud. However, there was room to park the aircraft on a taxi-way just off the end of the runway and the men made themselves reasonably comfortable with home-made stoves in their tents and duck-boards to keep some of the mud out.

November began with various scrambles but no contacts. There was one search by Flying Officer Peter Sutton and his No 2 for a Liberator crew whose aircraft had been seen to crash. It was later confirmed that all the crew had baled out much earlier. It was in fact George the automatic pilot that had been in control when the plane crashed.

On 2nd November there was a slight panic when news arrived that the River Arno was likely to burst its banks, in which case Pisa Air Field would find itself under water. All aircraft of the detachment were scrambled and flown to Florence. Falconara Aerodrome was also rendered completely unusable by the heavy rain. By 4th November, however, the squadron was flying again and despite continual rain managed to enjoy a party in the airmen's mess to celebrate the squadron's fifth anniversary on 6th November. With the threat of flooding having passed, the Pisa detachment returned from Florence and took up duties which were mainly coastal reconnaissance and Air Sea Rescue patrols, with the odd unsuccessful chase after a bogey, thrown in for good measure.

> **13th November.** *Pisa detachment moved to Rosignano Air Field where future ops will be carried out. Four Spitfires and the Hurricane flown down. Two Spits left behind (u/s) with two airmen. The squadron personnel are living in billets down at Cecina-Marina—right on the beach.* (Squadron Record No 237)

The squadron members found that the airfield was certainly no improvement on the one they had left. The following day it was reported that the runway was unserviceable owing to the rain and it was quite evident that it would be unserviceable whenever there was any rain. When the weather allowed the same pattern continued, with Air Sea Rescue and search operations, reconnaissance of shipping, strafing of enemy vessels and scrambles after bogeys, most of whom turned out to be friendly.

Peter Sutton suffered from the muddy condition of the runway at Falconara on 2nd November, when his aircraft turned over on landing. The aircraft was a write-off but Sutton escaped unhurt. This was to be a continuing hazard for the next few months with two further casualties owing to mud at Rosignano later in the month. Flying Officer Ewart John Seagrief flew straight into a lorry that was parked on the side of the runway. He was taken to hospital but had only a cut on the head. Then Flight Sergeant Hummer hit a patch of mud and turned the aircraft over, breaking his arm in the process. It seemed as though the mud was going to be more of a problem than the Germans. Not only did the weather curtail military operations, but it also placed severe restrictions on the squadron's sporting activities. In fact it was a disappointing month all round.

December saw the main base on readiness day after day but with little actual activity, while the detachment at Pisa flew escort to Beaufighters attacking the lake areas north of Venice. Then once again the rain moved in rendering the runway at Rosignano unserviceable for days at a time.

From Falconara, attacks were carried out on barges in the Grado and Trieste areas, as well as the, by now commonplace, Air Sea Rescue operations.

> **9th December.** *Aircraft led by CO, escorted six Beaufighters to the Grado area. One Beaufighter crashed in flames and another had to return on one engine. A Liberator ditched near the area. The CO covered it and sent out a Mayday. Only two survivors were seen to take to a dinghy. Both were later picked up by a Catalina. Flying Officer Peter Warren Sutton and Flight Sergeant Beville Charles Mundy were scrambled ASR.* (Operations Record)
>
> **13th December.** *(Falconara) Pilot Officer Allan Douglas and Sergeant Richard Mervyn Lushington Morant scrambled after a bogey. A visual obtained after about 20 minutes but it immediately disappeared into cloud. The chase continued for about 30 minutes but the hostile stuck to the layer of cloud and the plot faded. It was thought to be a Ju 88. They landed at Rimini owing to shortage of fuel. Pilot Officer Douglas damaged a flap on landing owing to mud. Put up for the night by No 45 Squadron.* (Operations Record)

Still the repetitive reports came from Rosignano—runway unserviceable. On 17th December, the commanding officer, Ian Shand had a near call. He was flying a shipping recce over the northern Adriatic when his engine cut. He pulled the aircraft into a climb with the idea of baling out but then decided against it. As he was gliding down, his engine picked up and he was able to make a safe landing. Meanwhile, something obviously had to be done to improve the runway at Rosignano. It was suggested that perforated steel planking could be laid and American engineers commenced work. It was hoped that the work would be completed in about four weeks, providing an all-weather runway. However, rain, mist and a cloud base of 500 feet made flying tricky and chasing enemy aircraft a waste of time. In fact, it may have been bad visibility, which caused the loss of Flying Officer Little who disappeared into some cloud on 19th December and was never seen again.

Despite the unhelpful weather conditions, some flying was carried out almost every day from Falconara although landing still presented problems and yet another aircraft was written off on 22nd December, through sliding on the mud.

So Christmas 1944 arrived and even on Christmas Day there was no let-up. A first light recce was carried out with a low-level attack on a railway engine, and later the squadron took part in a search for a Mustang pilot but with no sighting. In the evening, the senior officers served dinner in the airmen's mess and a welcome visitor to the festivities was Wing Commander William Francis Bryanton, who had been adjutant to No 237 Squadron during the early part of the war.

Boxing Day brought an armed recce, scrambles after bogeys, and an escort for Beaufighters on a low-level shipping recce. A Fortress in difficulties was reported and two pilots were detailed to guide the aircraft in to Falconara Air Field. The bomber reached the aerodrome

No. 237 SQUADRON OPERATING IN ITALY

safely but instead of landing, it turned out to sea and was unable to make land again. It ditched off the coast but all the crew, except the first pilot who had been killed by flak, escaped unhurt. A further search was mounted for a Liberator crew who had disappeared on Christmas Day but with no result.

On the last days of the Old Year, squadron pilots turned their attention to barges in the Corzone Canal as well as armed recces of the Padua area. All in all, it had been a reasonably good month for the main base and work was going ahead to render Rosignano more weatherproof.

News from 'home'

Meanwhile, back in Rhodesia in August 1944, the first Spitfire had been put on show.

The Spitfire will fly over Salisbury on Monday morning at 11 o'clock. It will be preceded by seven Harvards flying in formation. The Spitfire will then do aerobatics over the racecourse area and should be easily visible from the city. (Rhodesia Herald, 25th Aug. 1944)

Another exciting occasion came on 21st October when His Excellency the Governor presented the SRAF with a gold cup bearing the inscription: To the Southern Rhodesia Air Force from the RAF as a token of comradeship and esteem. To celebrate the occasion there was a flypast at Moffat Aerodrome. An interesting sidelight was a report from the Balkans Campaign, which claimed that 90% of the Greek airmen taking part in the liberation of their homeland had been trained or re-trained in Rhodesia.

By the end of the year, the pace of training was slowing down. A large reserve of trained aircrew had been built up and, obviously, the war in Europe would soon be coming to a close. Increasingly, in Group Routine Orders there appears the following remarks: is transferred to the SRAF Reserve of Officers.

On 14th November1944, came orders for the closing of 25 EFTS, Belvedere:

No 25 EFTS Belvedere will cease to exist as an independent unit after 20.11.44.

And on 14th December 1944, in a letter from the office of the minister of Air to the AOC air force headquarters came orders for closing down stations.

Cranborne to be retained as EFTS. ITW move from Bulawayo and the Central Flying School from Norton to Cranborne. Thornhill is to be retained as a Service Flying School. BOAC to continue to use Thornhill. Heany Central Repair Depot, Central Maintenance Unit to be at Bulawayo. All other stations to be closed.

In fact, the whole training scheme was being gradually brought to a halt. The secretary of Air had stated, however, that the training scheme in Southern Rhodesia had been the most efficient and successful of any, and hoped that some measure of air training might be retained in the Colony after the war.

CHAPTER 23

The final months

During the winter of 1944/45, No 266 (Rhodesia) Squadron was billeted near Antwerp and they experienced heavy German V-1 bombardment. The commonest operational task was interdiction, that is cutting railway lines and blocking communications, especially those leading to the V-2 sites. The Rhodesians regarded themselves as experts at the destruction of road and railway bridges but they were equally ready to have a go at chateaux or villas housing German headquarters.

Blind bombing using airborne radar had been used on a limited basis since September 1943, the main objection to the technique being that in German-occupied territory, considerable damage could be caused to civilian areas if the target was not correctly identified. However, as the occupied countries were liberated and the attacks centred more and more on Germany itself this objection did not carry so much weight. By the winter of 1944/45, blind bombing became the rule in bad weather.

December 1994—a German attack through the Ardennes

Everyone believed, in December 1944, that the war in Europe was almost over. Germany had been beaten and it was only a matter of time before the Allied armies entered Berlin. Hitler did not see it this way. He had built up a small reserve—250,000 men. Under cover of the bad winter weather that kept observation aircraft on the ground, the German military commander, Field Marshal Gerd von Rundstedt, massed all the available armour and aircraft in the Ardennes. On 16th December, he struck in a vain effort to swing the war in Germany's favour. The thunder of 1,000 heavy guns shattered the air. A German armoured column broke through the Allied lines and sped towards the strategically vital port, Antwerp, narrowly missing the main Allied fuel dump on the way. One hundred and fifty German soldiers dressed in American army uniforms caused confusion behind the Allied lines. So began the Battle of the Bulge.

Grounded by bad weather, the Rhodesian squadron was unable to participate in this battle until 23rd December when they had some joy with rail-traffic round Dortmund. But the German advance had been halted and an Allied counter-attack was under way.

On Christmas Eve, the commanding officer had a mishap while 'A' flight was attacking trains near Dulmen. He was struck by flak and forced to land, fortunately behind Allied lines. His No 2, Flight Sergeant Howell, also landed away from base because he ran out of fuel.

Christmas Day, 1944, proved to be a sad occasion. 'B' flight took off to attack trains in the Dortmund area and itself came under fire from 150-plus Me 109s and FW 190s. Pilot Officer Scott-Eadie and Flight Sergeant Green failed to return. Scott-Eadie was later reported a

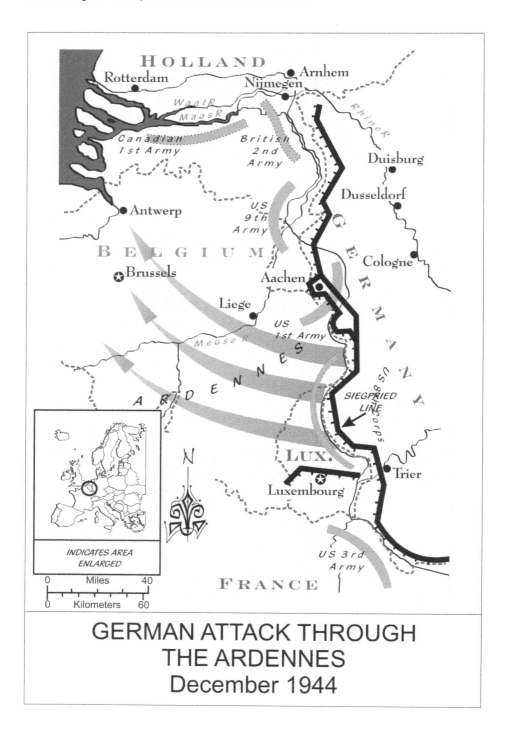

GERMAN ATTACK THROUGH
THE ARDENNES
December 1944

prisoner of war but Flight Sergeant Peter Charles Nightingale Green* was later presumed dead. No 193 Squadron, which was operating in the vicinity, attacked the attackers and claimed one enemy aircraft destroyed and another damaged.

That afternoon, after they had served the Erks their Christmas dinner, 'A' flight made an unsatisfactory attack on a V-2 site. The officers and sergeants had their Christmas dinner in the evening followed by a session in the bar. On Boxing Day the squadron again attacked V-2 sites at Steenwijk and news came that Wing Commander Charles Green was missing. Later the story was told that, spotting some tanks in deep snow in the Ardennes, he had gone down to attempt to identify them and had been hit by flak. He baled out and hid in a tree but the Germans cut the tree down to get him. Charles Green had been commanding officer of No 266 (Rhodesia) Squadron and had been awarded the DSO for leading an attack on German tanks attempting to flee through the Falaise Gap. He later received a bar to the DSO for exceptional leadership, skill and bravery of the highest order.

On 29th December, the Rhodesian squadron took part in a Wing Show, attacking a German headquarters in Biltoven, east of Utrecht and the following day it was a shipping sweep during which five or six barges were pranged. The year ended with a flurry of activity, with attacks on shipping and rolling stock.

A New Year shock

So the year 1944 ended with heavy fighting still taking place in the Battle of the Bulge. The new year began with a rude shock.

> *New Year's Day (1945) starts by 50-odd Jerry 109s and 190s strafing the 'drome. This resulted in our losing one aircraft in our squadron (fortunately the most clapped-out one). 'A' flight 'pranged' barges with rocket projectiles and cannon at Heidrecht. 'B' flight then demolished a German barracks and a factory at Kiezersveen with rocket projectiles and cannon. 'A' flight took off after 'B' flight and again gave the barges at Stiedrecht bags of punishment with rocket projectiles and cannon.* (Squadron Report No 266 Squadron)

Speaking of the New Year's Day attack by the Germans, John Deall says:

> *The Luftwaffe attacked with everything that could fly. Thirty 109s attacked 266 Squadron but did little damage. The runway should have been salted the night before but being New Year's Eve this hadn't happened, so the squadron was waiting for the ice to melt before taking off. The planes were just littered around on the edge of the runway not in position for take-off. If they had been caught in the process of taking off, a number of pilots might have been killed; as it was there was no loss of life and little damage.*

Early January was spent mainly in armed recces. The squadron was then converted back to bombers and given work cutting railway lines and demolishing embankments with 1,000-lb (450kg) bombs. On 6th January, the squadron was rewarded with one of the most unsuccessful sorties of its career.

> *Armed recce. Escorted by four 'Spits' of No 145 Wing. Operation abandoned through bad weather and intercom unsatisfactory owing to language difference. Polish versus Rhodesian! (The pilots of the Spitfires were all Polish.)* (Operational Record No 266 Squadron)

★ Peter Charles Nightingale Green, born in the Transvaal, educated at Plumtree School, attested in March 1942 and received his preliminary training in Rhodesia. He proceeded overseas in May 1943.

The biggest complaint during January was lack of activity owing to poor weather conditions.

Mud, ice, snow and aircraft muffled in warm jackets, marked the airfield where 266 Squadron is stationed. The damage done by the RAF when the Germans were there and by the Germans when they abandoned it, made it more desolate still, but the Rhodesians are fit and cheerful. Squadron Leader Deall of Odzi who commands the squadron had gone off for a hot bath at a neighbouring town. Deall had force-landed recently, luckily inside our lines, though he came down on the only cleared strip—in a minefield. Some pilots collected round a heater in the office, where a large poster hangs as a souvenir of their last party, to talk to me: Flight Lieutenant Hugh Balance DFC (Bulawayo) one of the flight commanders; Flying Officer George Eastwood, who married an English girl last December; Sergeant Robert Albert Clack; Flight Sergeant George William Godley; Flying Officer David Hughes, Flight Sergeant Ian Ernest Thompson Anton and Flight Sergeant J. Luhenschloss, all of Salisbury; Pilot Officer Ted Donne of Umtali and Flight Sergeant James Nelson Laing of Bulawayo. One of the biggest operations the squadron carried out in the last few weeks was close support of the landing on Walcheren, otherwise the targets are generally all forms of German transport and HQs. (Rhodesia Herald, 26th Jan. 1945)

Most of the rest of January and the first days of February were spent waiting for the weather to clear.

Everyone brassed off with the consistent bad weather. No flying.
1st February. *No comment—forgotten day.*
2nd February. *The squadron started the day by sending a pair of machines on a weather recce. The weather was pretty duff—but later on 'B' flight set off to bomb the line north-east of Appledoorn. No direct hits were claimed but on the way back, they saw some motor transport. They attacked and claimed one staff car destroyed and one truck—another damaged.* (Operations Record No 266 Squadron)

No 44 Squadron—and the new year
As far as No 44 Squadron was concerned, the new year had brought plenty of activity. On the first day of 1945, it was considered that the time was right to carry out another attack on the Dortmund-Ems Canal, a major German waterway. Because of its vital importance to the German war effort, barges loaded with ballast were strategically stationed so that any breach in the canal could be repaired almost immediately. Therefore, once the water had drained from one section, there was little point in bombing again until the banks had been repaired and the water had risen to its normal level, so that any breaches in the bank would be widened by the outward flow.

Nine No 5 Group squadrons, including ten aircraft from the Rhodesian squadron, were dispatched in daylight to breach the canal at Ladbergen, a section that contained a number of aqueducts and was therefore highly vulnerable. It was also heavily defended. The attack was so successful that the original course of the canal was difficult to trace from photographs taken later.

January brought its usual ration of bad weather and there was no flying until 5th January, when the squadron took part in a night attack on Royaan. This was followed by a visit to Houffalize and a gardening operation on 6th January, with a return visit to Munich the next night. Wing Commander Ralph Albert Newmarch, who led the 17 aircraft from No 44 Squadron said that the main danger on the Munich Raid was from aircraft cutting across the main track over the target. Another problem was that target-marking was late owing to the meteorological report being inaccurate and several aircraft having to wait over the target.

The second week of January brought snow and drizzle and five days of enforced idleness. Then came a long journey to Politz on 13th January. Seventeen aircraft took part in what was a highly successful attack. According to the Operational Record, marking and controlling were efficient. Only two more raids, one on Meesburg and one on Brux were possible in January owing to inclement weather, which included rain, gales, snow, frost and fog.

On 1st February 19 aircraft went to Siegen:

*The weather over the target was 10/10ths st. cu. Tops 4 – 6,000 feet. Aircraft arrived on time. One green Target Indicator seen a considerable distance from illuminating flares. H-hour put back by two minutes. Then four minutes. Aircraft orbited. Controller ordered, "Bomb red glow direct." Then assessed Reds as south of target and ordered five secs overshoot. Results difficult to assess but appeared scattered. High-bursting Target Indicator's marking would have been preferable and if ordered half an hour later target would have been clear. Defence negligible. Some fighter flares seen, and one Ju 88 seen in target area. Flight Lieutenant Gallivan complained about a 'close cookie!"** (Operations Record No 44 Squadron)

The following night, 2nd February, 16 aircraft raided Karlsruhe and two of them failed to return, one piloted by Flying Officer Gallivan. A Rhodesian, Sergeant Albert Balloch,[†] was flying as the flight engineer in his crew. The pilot of the second aircraft was Flying Officer Charles Worrall,[‡] a Rhodesian, who was on his 22nd operational flight.

The Red army had begun its final offensive on 12th January and achieved a swift break-through. By 17th January, the Russians had captured Warsaw and on 3rd February they reached the Oder River, only 36 miles (57km) from Berlin. Meanwhile in the west, the Allies had concluded the Battle of the Ardennes on 28th January, leaving the Germans facing seven great armies. The end was now inevitable; it was only a matter of time, but the armies in the west still faced the challenge of crossing the Rhine.

Meanwhile during February, No 44 Squadron continued with its attacks on the canal at Ladbergen and raids on Politz (where one aircraft was lost), Dresden, Rostz, Bohlen and Gravenhorst, interposed between periods of bad weather typical of Europe in February.

News from the POWS

During the final months of the war, 674 prisoners were repatriated under a scheme arranged by Count Bernadotte. Among these men was Flight Lieutenant Bob Rademeyer DFC who had lost a leg after baling out of a Lancaster while serving with No 44 (Rhodesia) Squadron.

For the other prisoners of war information that filtered through was exciting:

On 3rd January 1945 came the news we had been waiting for—the Russians had begun their offensive. On 18th January, the road alongside Sagan became very active—refugees from all walks of life, all fleeing west. The traffic never stopped right up until it was time for us to leave. We prepared for the march out of the camp by making packs for carrying food, and collected clothing and blankets for the trip. Then a very noticeable feature—aircraft of every description

---

* *cookie* was the nickname for a 4,000-lb bomb.

† Albert Balloch was born in Salisbury, attested in July 1943 and trained in Rhodesia before proceeding overseas in December 1943.

‡ Charles Worrall was born in Durban and educated in Rhodesia. He attested in June 1942 and trained in Rhodesia before proceeding overseas in July 1943. He was buried in the British Cemetery Durnbach, Bad Colz in Germany.

filled the skies: Stukas, Ju 88s, He IIIs, 109 Fs and Es in their scores, 190s and even the old Ju 52s. These all flew over the camp going east. Then they would come back, land at the airfield not far from us and take off with their loads, all day and all night, every day and night, a continuous roar of engines. (Barney Wright letter home)

The Germans mount last-ditch air attacks

Although the power of the Luftwaffe was waning, there were three occasions in these last months when a concentration of German aircraft took the Allies by surprise. The first had been on New Year's Day, during the Battle of the Bulge when a mass ground-strafing attack by some 800 German aircraft was carried out. This affected No 266 Squadron but not No 44 Squadron whose aircraft were safely tucked away in Britain.

The second surprise came at the end of February. A number of No 6 Group's Lancasters and Halifaxes were approaching Hanover when they were attacked at about 18,000 feet by 30 to 40 Messerschmitt Me 262s. For the first time in many cases, flight engineers took over the front gun turrets. Several crews claimed Me 262s shot down but eight bombers were lost. Once again, the Rhodesian bomber squadron was not involved.

They were, however, caught in the middle of the third surprise attack—a large-scale German intruder raid carried out during the early hours of 4th March 1945. The pilots of 13 aircraft from the Rhodesian squadron, returning from a raid on Ladbergen and mine-laying operations, found to their consternation that owing to the intruders, landing had been suspended at airfields in East Anglia, Lincolnshire and Yorkshire. Runway lights had been extinguished and aircraft waiting to land orbited in the darkness.

Obviously, plans had been formulated for just such a contingency but there was a delay in transmitting the code word scram, which would have effected the dispersal of the circling aircraft. For 30 minutes the heavy bombers were subjected, not only to the hazard of collision but also to fire from home defences, which were trigger happy that night, not to mention the possibility of attack from one of the enemy intruders. When scram was finally broadcast, crews were directed to airfields in the Midlands, chiefly Bitteswell, where, incidentally, part of Armstrong Whitworth's Lancaster output was tested, but also to Husbands Bosworth. One No 44 Squadron aircraft was shot down by an intruder over Brocklesby Park in Lincolnshire and all the crew were killed. Commenting on this operation, Flight Lieutenant Michael L.W. Wood said:

> *'Scram' procedure appeared to be thoroughly disorganized and this is especially criticized in view of the frequent warnings and instructions to crews at briefing and the apparent pre-knowledge that intruders were likely to operate.* (No 44 Squadron Operations Record)

Yet another crew had a serious problem, which was not connected with the enemy attack. A mine that had failed to release over the sea, dropped into the bomb bay just as the aircraft was orbiting base. The crew was forced to go back out over the sea, open the bomb doors and deposit their deadly load, unprimed, into the dark waters.

No 266 during the final months

Meanwhile No 266 Squadron continued with its campaign of attacking German supply lines.

> ***3rd February.*** *Was a busy day with three sorties on bridges, railway lines and goods yards; then no flying until 6th February when the squadron again attacked bridges, this time east of Gouda. Flight Sergeant John Oliver Pascoe made a good job of landing his aircraft on one wheel!*
> ***7th February.*** *Flying Officer Noel V. Borland and Warrant Officer Noel (Noompie) Phillips*

set out in the evening for the new strip B 89, which was at Mill. Billets were nissen huts and were quite comfy. Taxiing of aircraft was made difficult by the fine dust on the 'drome (Operations Record No 266 Squadron)

Actually, the airfield was surfaced with pressed steel plating which had been laid to make a suitable landing area as quickly as possible. On 8th February, the rest of the squadron moved to the new base and 'B' flight started operations from B 89. At Mill, a new technique was tried. Flying a set height and speed the aircraft were steered to the target by radar and told when to drop their bombs. It was hoped that this method would prove useful during days of heavy cloud but it did not prove to be all that successful. It was a busy time for the squadron with the two flights taking part in four or five sorties a day. The main task was to soften up the enemy ahead of the Allied advance.

Life in the POW camps
As the Allies moved closer, the spirits of the prisoners of war rose—Barney Wright described the feelings of the prisoners.

The Russians reached the Oder. If they could only surround our camp. German troops, tanks and armoured vehicles were all going in one direction—to the Front to stop the Russian onslaught. (28th Jan. 1945). We were given the order to move out within half an hour. There was panic. The goons told us to get out. Then we waited at the main gate for an hour before being told to get back inside again—we were to move out at one in the morning. During this six-hour delay, we decided to make sledges; so we ripped down the bookshelves, bust up the tables, beds and cupboards and made sledges of every conceivable size and shape. My feelings on getting outside were twofold: Free! But where on earth were we going? We got to North Camp but it was deserted and we watched the Germans looting the Red Cross parcels. The commandant helped himself to four Red Cross boxes, each containing 20 parcels and placed them in his car. Eating our food—how we hated his very existence. It started to snow and even with three pairs of socks, two shirts, three vests, and a lumber jacket over my battle dress and greatcoat, I was still frozen. The column moved forward—one long line of men all with packs on their backs and pulling sledges. There were 1,400 RAF and American officers stretching some three miles along the road and this is how we marched. The road was cluttered with refugees and vehicles (mostly Panzers) passing in either direction. What bedlam! The wind was bitterly cold. God it was miserable—I felt like screaming. The goons made us line up in front of a barn to count us. We stood for an hour in the snow and the rain and were soaked through, boots and all. Then there was a mad scramble—I found a pigsty which I filled with hay, had something to eat and went, or rather tried, to sleep. It was a long and bitter night and one that I will never forget. I really thought the end was coming if this continued. The next day, 29th January, we were on the road by eight. It was still dark and miserable and we took turns pulling the sledge, caring little about our fate. Just after 12, a blizzard started to blow but we continued until 3:30 when we came to a village called Gross Selter, 17km from our last halting place. Again, we had to find shelter in the pigsties and hencoops. Every day I thought "God, how much longer?" and prayed that the Russians would overtake us. How I thanked the Red Cross for the food in our parcels. They saved our lives!
Thursday 1st February*. That evening it began to thaw. We had one thought in mind—would we be able to pull our sledges? It soon became obvious that we could not, as the roads were streams of water and mud. That meant another 12 pounds to carry on our shoulders.*
There were a lot of us who wanted to escape but there was a certain crowd of useless individuals who had the maps and compasses and who would neither part with them nor share them. It was infuriating. The organization on our side, against the goons, was shocking—instead of delaying

and making a nuisance of ourselves, and disorganizing as much as possible the retreat, hoping the Russians would catch up, we were treating the Germans as our protectors. Conditions could not have been any worse no matter how much we antagonized them.

Friday 2nd February. The Americans, 800 strong, were marched off to where, we did not know. We set course too, marching through the green fields. It was a perfect spring day. However, we learnt that we had 25km to do, then another seven the following day, then onto a train to our final destination. That day was our worst—25km was a long way to walk especially having lived on scant rations for the past four months. We were not fit men. We were paraded through the main street of a small town called Mauskau to raise the morale of the local populace, but just before this, we passed the Yanks going in the opposite direction, with bags of cheering, and whistling Tipperary. We were the happy ones, not the long-faced townsfolk. The last 17km was heartbreaking—we thought the journey would never end. Most were limping and those who fell out had to be picked up by the Doc and his horse-drawn cart. My feet were badly blistered and had lost all feeling, so I wrapped them in plasters and in agony put my boots back on. Eventually we came to a small farmyard where we were given food and hot water for a brew. With only 100 of us to share the accommodation, we settled down for the night and were soon asleep.

Saturday 3rd February. We were woken at 7:30, having been told 12, but at the point of a gun you don't argue. After marching seven kilometres we found ourselves in Spremberg. We learnt that this was where we would embark on a train for Luckenwalde, 50km to the south of Berlin. We were given Red Cross parcels, and then whom should I meet up with but Tommy Thompson who used to be on the squadron, one of the original members—he had been shot down two years ago. We had a long chat and were very excited about seeing each other. Conversation was strained as we did not know where to begin, and during our meeting, another member of the squadron turned up—Tony Johnston, and of course the same took place. He was shot down at the same time as Tommy but was leading No 56 at the time. That afternoon the goons marched us the four kilometres through town and loaded us onto cattle trucks, where we scrambled for corners and the best seats. Cramp soon set in and we spent most of the time standing. The engine was connected and we spent an agonizing night. At midday we were allowed an hour's exercise and I went to the engine and swapped some cigarettes for hot water and made a wizard brew. A few stops later and we were at Luckenwalde where we were marched in the dark to a concentration camp. We stood in the rain for an hour while they searched us and all our belongings, and at about 1 am arrived at a barrack where I made one dive for this pit and have been in it now for a fortnight. The conditions are appalling and cannot be described—in this block are 216 men, where we wash, eat and sleep! We are terribly hungry and getting weaker and weaker. Most of the days are spent in our pits as it is too cold outside and we are too weak to do any exercise, except going out on appel to be counted twice a day. Things are grim. The Red Cross representative has been, so it shouldn't be long now. Coal has been cut again so the fires don't go on for as long. It's horribly cold again with snow on the ground. The Norwegians gave our Offlag a gift of 170 parcels, which worked out at one-seventh per man and we soon went to town on the contents. That evening I had a cold shower and my frame looked like a skeleton that had swallowed a watermelon. I think I must weigh about ten stone. Heartening news that 157 parcels have arrived in Luckenwalde to be shared among 40,000 men. They were an absolute godsend. I shall never forget the day. The parcels will last another three weeks, so our only hope is that the relieving armies will be here soon. News has been received that they are across the Rhine and sweeping north. Let's pray it won't be long. I'll give it a month. So, on the first of May, I hope to be home with all this behind me. I shall return home, treating this period as though I had died, and start a new life, appreciating all things good. (Barney Wright)

INDICATES AREA
ENLARGED

THE ADVANCE TO THE RHINE

John Deall, who had replaced Barney as commanding officer of No 266 Squadron had received his promotion and been posted off the squadron and there was conjecture as to who would be the new commanding officer.

> **7th March**. *No flying. Weather duff all day. Wing Commander Davidson, Air Liaison Officer, paid us a visit after seeing the AOC who discussed with him our future CO. We consider the squadron very fortunate in having Squadron Leader Sheward as our CO. Squadron Leader Sheward hails from the Argentine and is well known to No 266. Wing Commander Davidson was taken into Germany sight seeing, visiting Aspersen and Goch. Squadron Leader Sheward was initiated in the evening.*
>
> **9th March**. *Eleven aircraft 'A' flight on Interdiction. Followed by eight aircraft 'B' flight also Interdiction. Both were successful and cut lines in northern Holland. Derek Erasmus* CO of No 193 Squadron was carrying out a low-level bombing attack on a railway line in northern Holland when he was seen to crash and the aircraft exploded soon after. The causes are yet unknown. It was a sudden end to a most promising career. His gay and cheerful nature and ready answer to the call of duty will long be an inspiring memory to all who knew him. He was 22.*

On 12th March 1945, there was a brief break from the war when the squadron carried out some simulated attacks for a film that was being made for the RAF. Then it was back to the fight again. The good news was that the weather was improving: "This is the first day of the year that the sun has shone all day and had any bite in it. Things are quiet. Limited flying obviously working up for something really big ... once and for all we hope."

But it was March and the good weather did not last so the squadron had to wait impatiently for the Big Do. (T 1 T).

> **17th March**. *No ops. Weather unsuitable. Stood by for a T 1 T show. A few air tests carried out. Flying Officer Desmond Quick of Bulawayo joined the squadron.*
>
> **18th March**. *The long-awaited T 1 T show came off at 3.30 pm. The weather eventually clearing. Nine aircraft 'A' flight together with Nos 193, 197 and 263 Squadrons, took off. Wing Commander Deall led the show. Group Captain Wells flew as Master of Ceremonies. The target was a HQ south of Deventer, said to house three generals and staff. All the buildings were dealt with in the thorough No 146 (Wing) manner. Photographs taken afterwards proved bombing more successful than thought at first.*
>
> **19th March**. *A very successful day's operations. 'B' flight represented No 266 on another T 1 T show. The Wing led by Wing Commander Deall clobbered a big motor transport repair works at Doetinchen, 3,000 feet. The flak was plentiful but was avoided. 'A' flight sent off four sections of two aircraft at 15-minute intervals on armed recce up to northern Holland—resulting in five vehicles destroyed and five damaged. 30-plus troops attacked while marching down a road. Many casualties observed. Pilot Officer Ted Donne who carried out this attack reported that aerobatics such as theirs are seldom seen.*
>
> **20th March**. *Nothing doing—real summer day—but strong crosswind rendered runway u/s. Quite a good session in the officers' mess. The Royal Games, including bok-bok† were played. No casualties.*

---

* Charles Derek Erasmus DFC was born in Salisbury, attested in June 1941 and trained in Rhodesia before proceeding overseas in May 1942.

† *bok-bok* is a game in which members of one team leap-frog onto the backs of the other team, which is arranged in a long line. Has been known to cause quite severe back injuries when the supporting team collapses under the combined weight of the other team members.

21st March. Eight aircraft of 'B' flight together with the rest of the Wing pranged the HQ of the General and his staff who dealt with the withdrawal of troops and equipment from Holland. The show went off at first light, and it was considered that the big hotel on the outskirts of Bossum in which the HQ were situated was completely wiped out. A hell of a lot of flak came up from Hilversum. It was intense but inaccurate. Four aircraft of 'A' flight led by Flight Lieutenant 'Killer' Miller (Aussie) did Interdiction on a bridge north-east of Zwolle. Near misses were scored. A composite of eight aircraft 'A' and 'B' flights went after a fuel dump in some woods south-east of Deventer. All bombs into the target area, but no fires observed. This was a Wing show. This is the first day of spring and the day itself couldn't have been lovelier. Flying Officer Noel Borland pranged his much-troublesome 'H' for Hardluck on landing in a 20 mph (32 km/h) crosswind. Pilot unshaken and unhurt.

22nd March. Interdiction was the order of the day. Weather perfect. 'A' flight was sent to cut the line from Amersfoot to Buarnvelt. The bombing wasn't up to the usual standard and no cuts were claimed. 'B' flight later got two cuts on a line north-east of Deventer. They went after a bridge but cut the line either side of the bridge. One motor transport was pranged through fear. Flight Lieutenant Doug Borland went down after it, but before he could open fire, the vehicle broke hard to starboard, pranging itself amongst trees lining the road. A really beautiful cloudless day. We are still on limited ops. Waiting for the last big bust—we hope. (Operations Record)

The Italian Campaign

While the Typhoons of No 266 Squadron were harassing the retreating Germans in Holland, Spitfires of No 237 Squadron were engaged in the same activity in Italy. For attacks on bridges, ammunition dumps, factories and warehouses, the Spitfires carried a bomb-load of 1,000 pounds (450kg); for strafing transport or troops concentrations they relied on their 20mm cannon and heavy machine guns.

Some days, as many as ten sorties were flown on a variety of operations including bomber escort and Air Sea Rescue. By the end of February, the whole squadron was back together again at Falconara where they were to remain for the rest of the war. Sadly, the last few weeks of the conflict were to cost the squadron dearly.

The first loss of the new year

22nd February. Scrambled. Bombed HQ and radar station south-west of Parma. Bombing improving. Recce in the afternoon. Genoa and Parma. One M/T destroyed for the loss of one aircraft. Flying Officer Jack Malloch was hit and baled out. Believed to be safe. (Operations Record)

John Crook wrote about this incident later:

Although the engine kept going, it was only a matter of time before the engine seized up. However, he climbed away heading south-west towards our lines about 200 miles away. The terrain over which he had to fly is very rugged with mountain peaks up to 9,000 feet and dropping steeply into the sea in the form of cliffs and no beaches. After 15 or 20 minutes, he had coaxed the aircraft up to about 12,000 feet when the engine seized so suddenly that it twisted its mounts and Jack had no option but to bale out. He landed badly and broke his leg. I am not sure of this but I think I remember his telling me that he had landed in a cemetery on a hillside and it was one of those ornate Italian tombstones that did the damage. The Italians in the area were sympathetic towards us and hated the Germans, so they got a doctor to set the leg in plaster, then put Jack on a mule and sent him deeper into the mountains where the Partisans had their hideouts. (John Crook)

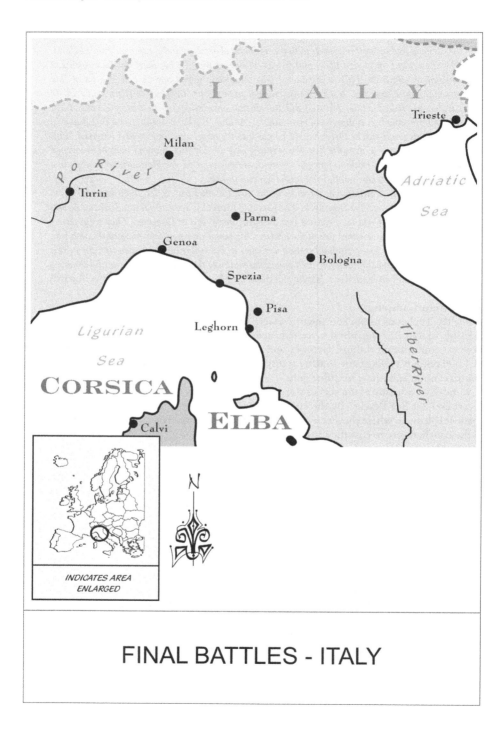

FINAL BATTLES - ITALY

Three days later Peter Sutton, whose diary has so often been quoted, was the unlucky one.

25th February. Sutton and Cornish on patrol. 16h20 – 17h50. Two aircraft on armed recce Spezia. Light, scant and accurate flak experienced. Flying Officer Sutton* pulled up to 8,000 feet and turned out over the sea; white smoke began to pour from his aircraft and he began to lose height. At 17h10 he baled out. His position was fixed by his No 2 who did not see a chute open at first but saw the plane and another object hit the water. Afterwards something white was seen in the water. The pilot was later picked up by a Walrus, dead. (Operations Record No 237 Squadron)

Back to the bombers

The Rhodesian bomber squadron was being kept as busy as the two fighter squadrons. March 5th saw 17 aircraft detailed for an attack on Bohlen and on this occasion six of the Lancasters were piloted by Rhodesians. They were Flying Officers Hennessy, Bill Dives, Dudley Barlow, Michael Wood, Lester Hayler and P.W.B. Morgans. Two aircraft did not attack because of the difficulty in identifying the target. One aircraft failed to return.

On the following night came an abortive raid on Sassnitz when a gap in the clouds closed three or four minutes after the raid began, causing the controller to halt the bombing. The next night it was the turn of Hamburg where the weather was clear with just a slight haze. Marking was undertaken in good time and the flak was only moderate, obviously inhibited by the presence of German night-fighters, which were plentiful.

Searchlights illuminated the bombers, which were then attacked by groups of seven to ten fighters at a time. Several aircraft were shot down over the target. Among those reported missing were Flying Officer Jetson and Flying Officer Morgans, a Rhodesian who had two fellow Rhodesians, Warrant Officer Charles Henry Dayton and Flying Officer Noel David Nicolle, in his crew. Later Flying Officer P.W.B. Morgans and his crew were reported safe:

'We were shot up by two German fighters just after we'd dropped our bomb load and lost both port engines. We decided to try to get back to England or France on the remaining engines, but after three-quarters of an hour we were down to 1,000 feet and over the sea, and the pilot found he couldn't fly the aircraft straight and level and decided to ditch. We came down on the sea and found we were on either some rocks or a sandbank. This was very lucky for us, because the dinghy hadn't come out as it should have done and we had to hack it out of the aircraft'. In fact they had come down in the North Sea about 15 miles [24km] from Brenenshaven. For eleven hours they tossed about in their rubber dinghy with icy seas soaking them, until they were rescued by a German Red Cross boat. After internment at Frankfurt, they were taken to Dulag Luft Wetzlar most of the way on foot, carrying heavy German officer's kit with very little food to eat. Dayton who was ill with 'flu fortunately got a lift on a petrol truck. The end of the adventure came, when they were liberated by the Americans. *'We knew that the Allies were coming. The artillery bombardment started and became more or less constant. Then, two weeks after we had arrived in Frankfurt, two American soldiers strolled up to the camp and we knew our worries were over'.* (Rhodesia Herald, 7th April 1945)

'Y' Yoke celebrates its 100th operation

On 10th March 1945, the squadron held a full-scale celebration. 'Y' Yoke Lancaster Mk III ND578 had completed its 100th operation. It was the first aircraft serving with No 44 Squadron to achieve its centenary. Air and ground crews held a party in her honour at the

---

* Peter Warren Sutton was born in Umtali. Attested in January 1943 before proceeding to the Middle East in December 1943. He was buried in the British Cemetery at Florence.

local and the landlady made a 100-candle cake. The cake was cut by Flight Lieutenant Lester Hayler who had captained the grand lady on 30 of her missions, and was in command for her 100th mission. Hayler was born and educated in Bulawayo and completed his flying training in Rhodesia before going to Britain to join No 44 Squadron in August 1943. His wife was serving with the WAAMS. Speaking about the aircraft Flight Lieutenant Hayler said:

> '*Y*' *Yoke is as good as any aircraft they make today. She has never given me any trouble at all. Once during a daylight attack on Düren (16th November 1944) a heavy ack-ack shell went clean through the port-outer engine and exploded above the aircraft but she came home with no trouble at all on three engines. Sergeant Alan Rubinstein, an old friend of mine in Rhodesia, is in charge of the ground crew. '*Y*' *Yoke has had the same ground crew all the time and they have done a fine job of work. Between us, we do all we can for this fine aircraft with 17 daylight attacks to her credit. She has been through the bombing offensive before and after D-Day. Her first trip was to Berlin. Wing Commander F.W. Thompson who won his DSO and DFC in her, was the captain when the gunners shot down a fighter on '*Y*' *Yoke's 21st trip. I reckon she must have carried at least 500 tons to Germany. Her two longest trips were to Königsberg and she was airborne for over eleven hours on one of them.* (Flight Lieutenant Hayler)

The final months

The final few weeks of the war took a sad toll on the Rhodesian squadrons. The target for 11th, 12th and 13th of March was Essen, Dortmund and Lutzkendorf. Then on 16th March, the squadron went to Würzburg when Flight Lieutenant Shephard's aircraft crashed shortly after take-off killing everyone on board. Bomber Command was hitting the Germans hard but, at the same time, the Luftwaffe were hitting back with everything they had and 24 aircraft were lost on this raid. March 20th and 22nd the Rhodesian bomber squadron visited Bohlen and Hamburg for the loss of one aircraft.

No 237 (Rhodesia) Squadron also suffered as the Germans put up a desperate defence around the town of Pisa. On 24th March, Paul Pearson was the leader of a section that took off at first light. The main purpose of the sortie was to check on weather conditions in the Po Valley. This proved to be less than good with almost unbroken low cloud. However, as the aircraft turned for home, Paul spotted a small hole in the cloud cover:

> *We spiralled down through it, over a town called Piacenza. There was a rail and road bridge across the river at this point that had been repaired and a supply train was just about to cross it. We attacked with our cannons and machine guns, getting some very satisfactory explosions and fires from the ammunition and fuel wagons. We took turns to beat up the train until our ammunition was exhausted and then headed south for home and breakfast. I knew that my aircraft had taken several hits from the small-arms fire put up by the troops who had jumped from the train and were in the ditches on either side of the line; but as they were all in the wing and tail I was not particularly concerned, and my No 2 said he had not been hit at all. However, ten minutes later just as we were climbing up over the mountains on the south side of the Po Valley, my engine, without any warning signs, quit dead. There was no hope of baling out as we were too low among the mountain tops. I managed as much by good luck as good management to make a belly-landing in a very small clearing in a pine forest on the side of the mountain. My aircraft was undamaged except for a broken propeller and dented wing, bending edges from hitting the tops of pine trees as I glided in over the clearing. My No 2 was circling above in a bit of a tizzy, and screeching over the radio about what the hell was I playing at, and that he thought we were going home for breakfast. I was able to tell him that I was unhurt and he would have to find his own way home, as I would not be having any breakfast. Then it was a matter of*

taking off up the mountainside to put as much distance between the aircraft and myself before the inevitable arrival of German soldiers. I found friendly Italians before the Germans found me, and they put me on the pillion of a stolen German army BMW motorcycle which was driven by a suicidal Italian at great speed over the most hairy mountain paths. It really was the most terrifying ride I have ever had and I was very relieved when we stopped in a little village and I was told I would have to walk the rest of the way. After two days walking and climbing, I was taken to a farmhouse in a tiny village high in the mountains where my rescuers said there was another English pilot living. I knew it was Jack from their description of him, where he had come down and that he had parachuted from a Spitfire. (Paul Pearson)

On 29th March during an attack on storage facilities at Pizzighettone, Flying Officer Sam Aylward's* aircraft blew up when the bomb he was carrying was hit by flak while he was diving on the target. This really was a one in a million tragic occurrence.

On 6th April, Sergeant William Alexander Maxwell's† engine cut out on take-off, his aircraft spun out of control and he was killed. A week later during an attack on a tank formation, Sergeant James Hogg Bennie called up saying that his engine had cut and he was jettisoning his long-range tank and bombs. He was last seen gliding down towards the ground near Lodi. Sergeant Pilot James Bennie‡ was later presumed dead.

Two days later while bombing a factory, Sergeant Patrick Adsero's aircraft was hit on the starboard side of the cockpit. The pilot was badly injured in both arms but despite considerable pain and loss of blood, he managed to bring his aircraft back safely. Two days after this remarkable effort, four aircraft led by the commanding officer were strafing motor transport when Flying Officer Michael Cuthbert Ward called up on the R/T *They've got me.* Flying Officer Keith James Burrow searched the area but could find no trace of the aircraft or the pilot. Flying Officer Michael Ward§ was later presumed dead.

Next day Flight Lieutenant Carlyle returning from a strike on some marshalling yards, dived through cloud and hit a mountain north-east of Pisa. And exactly one week later, four aircraft were on a shipping recce bombing and strafing, when Sergeant Bell noticed that his No 2 Sergeant James Keir Allan was no longer behind him. He called up on R/T but got no response. The area was searched with no result. Sergeant James Allan¶ was later presumed dead.

Finally, on 25th April, during attacks on a rail bridge, Flying Officer Neville Brighton Mansell was seen to hit the roof of a house and somersault into the back garden. Nothing further was seen owing to the dust but Flying Officer Neville Mansell** was later reported

---

* Harold Edgar Cecil (Sam) Aylward was educated at Plumtree School. He attested in January 1943 and trained in Rhodesia before proceeding to the Middle East in November 1943.

† William Alexander Maxwell was born in Salisbury and educated at Chaplin School. He attested in May 1943 and trained in Rhodesia before proceeding to the Middle East in September 1943. He was buried in Florence.

‡ James Hogg Bennie was born in Finland and educated at Prince Edward School. He attested in April 1943 and trained in Rhodesia before proceeding to the Middle East in 1944.

§ Michael Cuthbert Ward was born in London and educated at St George's College. He attested in June 1942 and trained in Rhodesia before proceeding to the Middle East in November 1944.

¶ James Keir Allan was born in Blantyre educated at Prince Edward School attested in July 1943 and trained in Rhodesia before proceeding to the Middle East in September 1944.

** Neville Brighton Mansell was born in East London, South Africa and educated at Umtali High School. He attested in November 1939 as ground crew and went with the first contingent to Nairobi. He returned to Rhodesia in March 1943 to train as a pilot and returned to the Middle East in December 1944.

missing presumed dead. Incidentally, Squadron Leader Ian Shand who was the commanding officer, remarked that it was only too easy to hit some object on the ground while dive-bombing. The pilot had to put the plane into a steep dive in order 'to sight' the target, release the bomb and then pull out. Often his eyes would be so fixed on the target that he would fail to see other objects in his line of flight. Ian Shand himself had many brushes with treetops. (See photographs)

So it was that between 25th February and 25th April 1945—exactly two months—No 237 Squadron lost seven pilots, killed. However, during that period they had carried out unrelenting attacks on enemy transport, marshalling yards, ammunition dumps, bridges, barracks and factories.

Crossing the Rhine

Now the build-up was in progress for the final great offensive, the crossing of the River Rhine. The Allied commanders were apprehensive, expecting the Germans to put up a desperate resistance in defence of their homeland. However at one vital point, the German guard on the eastern bank was less than vigilant, and on 7th March 1945, an American sergeant, finding the Ludendorff Bridge at Remagen intact and unguarded, led his platoon across and established a bridgehead on the eastern bank. The Germans fought back with everything they had but the bridgehead held long enough for the Americans to push several divisions across the river.

Meanwhile General Patton's forces had been clearing the western bank of the Rhine and by 22nd March, he was ready to make the crossing. During the hours of darkness his forces swept across the river losing only 28 casualties. Further north, General Montgomery encountered greater problems. Here the river was between 400 and 500 metres wide increasing to 1,000 metres at high water with a current running at three and half knots. On the same afternoon, the 22nd March, Montgomery ordered a massive bombardment on the town of Wesel, which was his first objective.

Seventeen Lancasters, from No 44 Squadron attacked the town at 15h30 and again at 22h30 just as the 1st Commando Brigade followed by the 51st Highland Division closed in on Wesel. The town was finally taken with only 36 Allied casualties. Field Marshal Montgomery said: The bombing of Wesel last night was a masterpiece and a decisive factor in making possible our entry into that town before midnight. This foothold was reinforced with airborne landings involving thousands of aircraft and gliders. Once across the Rhine, the Allies could strike into the industrial heart of Germany.

No 266 Squadron was also on the offensive. The squadron pilots spent 23rd March attacking an ammunition factory and dropping anti-personnel bombs on aerodromes at Enschelde and Steelewigh. The last operation of the day was an attack on Heldern, three miles (5km) east of the Rhine.

> ***24th March.*** *D-Day for the crossing of the Rhine today. 'A' flight was rudely awakened at 04h30 and proceeded with eight aircraft to attack the village of Kudenburg East of Wesel. The attack, made with eight aircraft of No 193 Squadron was successful and the target was left in flames. Our next detail was an anti-flak patrol to cover the airborne landings. Eight aircraft of 'B' flight and four aircraft of 'A' flight forming 'Pink', 'Grey' and 'Blue' sections, got some transports and the section of 'A' flight, a large flak position, which was attacked three times and left with a decided twitch. The next detail eight aircraft of 'A' flight and four aircraft of 'B' flight held plenty of excitement for 'Dusty' and 'Killer' Miller. Dusty's engine packed up on the way out and he force-landed east of Goccg [sic]. Killer was hit by flak in the port aileron, which jammed. He had sufficient control to make a right-hand circuit and pulled off a good landing. Several flak positions were attacked and hits with bombs and cannon seen. Killer finished off a*

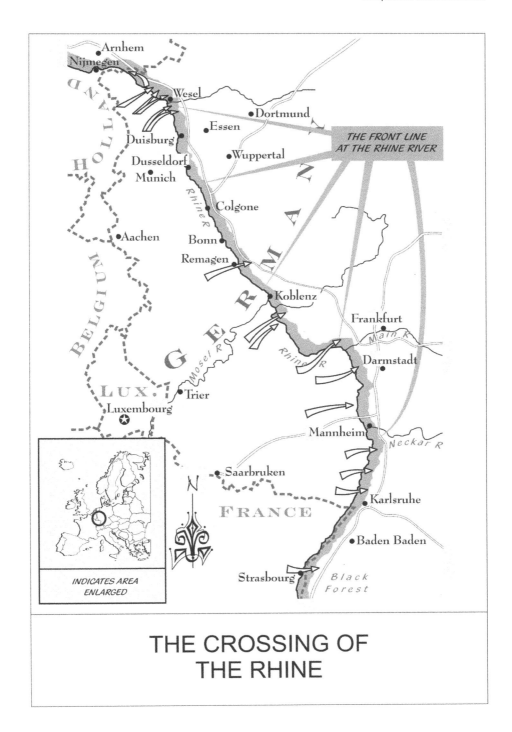

THE FRONT LINE
AT THE RHINE RIVER

INDICATES AREA
ENLARGED

THE CROSSING OF
THE RHINE

dispatch rider before he was hit. Blind bombing was laid on for the next show to be done by 'B' flight but the weather was too bad and they did not take off. A good day's work.

March 25th. *Eight aircraft from 'B' flight led by CO attacked HQ at Auholt very successfully. Three direct hits were scored. The building was adorned with a large Red Cross and protected by batteries of light ack-ack. The Hun up to his tricks again. Bad weather prevented further sorties over the battlefront but Dave Hughes, Killer Miller and Ted Donne wrecked their constitutions by doing a tail-chase and some fancy formation flying.*

March 26th. *In the middle of a great offensive, we are released for the day to do a practice bombing. A truly amazing war! In the morning, four sorties were flown by 'A' flight, 'B' flight taking over in the afternoon. After lunch, four aircraft of 'A' flight and four of No 193 Squadron made a very successful attack on some SS HQ south-east of Rhenen. The four buildings containing the headquarters were flattened. Pilot Officer Paddy Culligan* met with a fatal accident. Burst a tyre on take-off and cartwheeled. Paddy was most popular on the Wing and his death is a sad blow to all who knew him.* (Operations Record)

The last few days of March were passed flying armed recces and hoping for better weather. The weather had also affected the work of No 44 Squadron and following the brilliant raid on Wesel, the day before the Rhine crossings, the squadron was grounded for the rest of the month. Meanwhile to counteract the problem of bad visibility, No 266 Squadron were flying low-level reconnaissance.

1st April. *Though the cloud base was only 1,000 feet, we were sent off in pairs on armed recces. The first pair turned back early owing to engine trouble. Our second pair, Pilot Officer Ted Donne and Warrant Officer 'Noompie' Phillips, set off for some motor transport which they beat up, in the process of which Ted Donne[†] was hit by flak and seen to gain height and then stall and spin in. Something was seen to leave the aircraft before it spun. It is considered that Ted has a chance. Only time will tell. Ted Donne was a 'hell of a good bloke'. It's a pity there aren't more like him. This suicide low recce was stopped at midday, after the Wing had lost two pilots and the group, 19 pilots all told.* (Operations Record No 266 Squadron)

On 2nd April, 'B' flight carried out a dive-bomb attack on the village of Hussen; then once again the weather turned against the Allies and no operations could be carried out until 7th April, when it was back to hitting the railways in Holland, and strafing ground transport.

9th April. *In the early evening, a section of 'A' flight led by Pilot Officer Luhnenschloss proceeded to an area north-west of Oldenburg. Very early, a staff car was spotted. The driver spotting the aircraft, took cover in a front garden. However, the car's days were numbered, the pilot satisfied that it was finished after seeing a large tree fall on it. Later four trucks were breached on a crossroad. Three damaged claimed also north of Oldenburg. Some trucks were spotted and this was reported. No 197 Squadron attacked these. At 13h35 the CO and a section set out for an area west of Emden. This was very successful for they scored five flamers, four smokers and an unknown quantity damaged. The effect was dampened considerably by the*

---

* Patrick Joseph Padraig Culligan was born in Calcutta and educated at St George's College in Salisbury. He attested in March 1942 and trained in Rhodesia before proceeding overseas in March 1943.

† Edward Henry Donne was later presumed dead. He was born in England and educated at Prince Edward School. He attested in January 1942 and trained in Rhodesia before proceeding overseas in March 1943.

loss of 'Noompie' Phillips whose engine packed up and he had to force-land in the Leewaden area. After his plane had come to a stop, he was seen to leap out and run for it. The aircraft then proceeded to burn furiously.*

The other section was not very successful but scored on horse-drawn transports. 'B' flight then went out, one section led by George Eastwood proceeded to search for suitable targets between Emden and Bremen. Their effort was rewarded by belting one flamer and two smokers. These were motor transport; also horse-drawn. Then Flight Lieutenant Borland's section went from their airfield towards Groningen for the gain of one large motor transport that was destroyed.

News from Barney

As No 266 Squadron zoomed around in the spring skies above Germany, its old commanding officer, Barney Wright, languished below:

> *It is now 10th April, the weather has improved and we are sunbathing. The news we have received is excellent—spirits and morale are high. The Allies should be here within 14 days. On 14th April, we moved down to Luckenwalde to board a train—cattle trucks as before—but only 40 instead of 50 to a truck this time. They couldn't rake up an engine, so after a most enjoyable 48 hours on a railway station, we were marched back to camp where we managed to trade 60 cigarettes for a loaf of bread! Rumours are that the Americans are only ten miles from us—great excitement. But this was not to be. Bombing all around us and we see our planes in their hundreds all day long. I cannot believe that in about a week we will be free men again and on our way home. Please hurry up. It can be quite agonizing at times. The Russians have eventually liberated us, but nothing has turned up to take us home. Food is short, Red Cross parcels have run out and my patience is at an end. On 30th April, Bob and I set off towards Jutterborg, following the railway line and not daring to look back. That night we found a farmhouse where we were given a good meal. We slept well.† (Diary ends)*

266 in Germany

Meanwhile on 16th April 1945, No 266 Squadron moved to Dorp in Germany. Here the tactics were changed slightly, with aircraft going out in pairs in search of any target which presented itself, mainly motor and horse-drawn transport and barges at Wilhelmshaven.

> ***20th April***. *Shipping recces were the order of the day. Flying Officer George Eastwood and Flight Lieutenant Dusty Miller did the first one round Emden/Wilhelmshaven area. They saw no shipping but did one motor transport. Flight Sergeant Harry Wheeler and Flight Sergeant Percy Mitchell set out but saw nothing. No further flying was carried out until 23rd April. Pilots carrying out ground recces obtained several radios at Delmenhorst.*
> ***23rd April***. *Flight Lieutenant Hughes led a section and took off for the south-east of Stade to attack a train; cannon strikes were seen on the train and on nearby barracks. Later Flying Officer Noel Borland and Killer Miller carried out a shipping recce. On the way back some motor transport were seen and attacked. Flying Officer Borland‡ was hit and went straight in. He did not call up. His loss was a blow for he was very popular. Sympathies were extended to*

---

* Phillips was later reported safe.

† Squadron Leader J.D. (Barney) Wright hitchhiked his way back to England from Germany. It took him nearly three months.

‡ Noel Vincent Borland was born at Nylstroom in South Africa and employed on Nkana Mine before attesting in May 1941. He was trained in Rhodesia before proceeding overseas in April 1942.

*his brother Doug. It was later found that he had been buried near the crash and later his body
was removed to a nearby village cemetery near Leer.* (Operations Record)

The final operation of the war, for No 266 (Rhodesia) Squadron, was a Wing show. Twelve
squadron aircraft attacked a barracks north of Bremen. Later Flight Lieutenant Roy Gray and
Flight Sergeant Johan Heinrich Moll did a shipping recce while Pilot Officer Henderson and
Dusty Miller took off to photograph the results of the morning's activity.

This, although they did not know it at the time, was to be the end of the war for No. 266
(Rhodesia) Squadron. On 27th April, the squadron personnel packed up for the return to
England. The commanding officer led two sections of 'A' flight; the rest of the squadron
was led by Doug Borland and Dave Hughes. The weather was not good, the ceiling being
about 150 feet. Doug and Dave turned back but the commanding officer and two sections
continued, landing at Courtrai. The weather was so bad over the Channel, that the pilots
were forced to remain at Courtrai overnight, taking off the following morning and reaching
Manston in time for lunch. After lunch, they set course for Fairwood Common where the
rest of the squadron joined them on the following day. The boys immediately began to
indulge in good British beer with real enthusiasm. The rest of April and May was spent in
training and the squadron was disbanded early in August 1945.

No 237 Squadron's final operation was on 25th April because of strong crosswinds, which
rendered the airfield unserviceable for the final days of the war. On 30th April, Squadron
Leader Devenish took over from Ian Shand as commanding officer and so was in command
when the war in Europe came to an end on 8th May 1945.

April 1945 with No 44 Squadron
On 1st April, Wing Commander Stan Flett assumed command and on that day, 20 aircraft
took off to attack the barracks at Nordhausen. 'Y' Yoke had a lucky escape during this
operation. Flight Lieutenant Allan managed to bring her back on two engines. Flying Officer
Terance Spencer (a Rhodesian) reported: "Bombed western side of town. Unable to attack
planned target owing to evading bombs from other aircraft."

An abortive raid on Molbis on 7th April was followed by a more successful attack on
Lutzkendorf on 8th April. Two days later, the squadron visited Leipzig with eleven aircraft
from which raid Flying Officer Kennedy (with Flying Officer Woodhouse[*] in his crew)
failed to return and was later presumed dead.

Mine-laying on 13th April was followed by a dawn raid on Pilsen on 16th April and on
the next day 'Y' Yoke took part in its final operation—a dawn raid on Cham with Flying
Officer Parkin as pilot. Eight No 44 Squadron Lancasters were piloted by Rhodesians: Wing
Commander Flett, Flight Lieutenants Alastair Mackay, Tom Victor Webster, John Alfred
Konschel and Alan White, Flying Officers Robert Chelwynd Piggott, Terance Spencer and
Noel Plint.

On 23rd April, during an evening raid on Flensburg, eight of the 12 Lancasters involved
were piloted by Rhodesians. Unfortunately, the mission was abandoned by the controller
owing to heavy cloud over the target. Pilots: Flight Lieutenants Webster and Mackay, Flying
Officers Coom, Graham, Rodger, and Parry, Flight Sergeants Gerrard Graham and William
Hall.

---

[*] Geoffrey Clayton Rance Woodhouse was born in Surrey. He was farming in Rhodesia when he
attested in August 1942 and he trained in Rhodesia before proceeding overseas in December 1943.

No 44 Squadron's final wartime mission

The squadron's final wartime mission took place on 25th April 1945. This was an attack in daylight on SS Barracks at Berchtesgaden. Eight aircraft from the squadron took part and all but one carried a Rhodesian pilot.

The Rhodesians on this final raid were:

Wing Commander Stan Flett
Flight Lieutenant Leslie Edwards
Flight Lieutenant T.D. Kelley
Flight Lieutenant Alastair Mackay
Flight Lieutenant Tom Webster
Flying Officer Geoff Cranswick
Flying Officer H.L. (Mollie) Maltas
Flying Officer Robert Piggott
Pilot Officer Stewart Henry
Warrant Officer Keith Peters
Flight Sergeant S.T. MacLarty
Flight Sergeant A.P. Owens
Flight Sergeant George Bredencamp
Sergeant Dudley Hendry

For once, the BBC was permitted to report on the raid while it was in progress:

It was just before dawn when the great bombers took to the air, on operations, for the last time. Flight Lieutenant Edwards, flying with Wing Commander Flett remembers, "Our last operation in Europe was the famous Berchtesgaden Raid on 25th April. It had always been my special ambition to have a crack at Hitler's hideout. We were briefed soon after midnight and took off at a quarter-past four, while it was still dark. In the first light, we formed up over France near the Pas De Calais. It was a perfect day and not a cloud in the sky, and navigation was fairly simple, just a question of following the leading formation. We flew over France and crossed the Rhine just south of Strasbourg. All the way we could see slit trenches, bomb craters and ruined towns and villages, and near Ulm clouds of smoke and burning villages showed where the French army was in action. We could even see tank tracks through the fields, the dark brown lines converging at the gates and then spreading out again into the next field." "Passing the northern tip of Lake Constance, we came at last to the Alps. The mountains were covered in snow right up from the valley bottoms and patches of fog were lying in the fields. We made a right-angle turn to port and so came to the target. Berchtesgaden lies in a valley with mountains on three sides rather like a horseshoe. At the far end of the valley lay the village, with a little stream running down to Hitler's chalet at the near end and just where we crossed the mountain ring. To the right of the chalet were the SS Barracks, with a Czech workers' camp near by, and a dark patch on the mountains about six miles [10km] away marked the site of the chalet. Our leading formation was detailed to attack the Eagle's Nest, the second lot the chalet, and our own target was the SS Barracks. Everything was covered in snow and all we could see was the parade square end of the building." "As we got up to the target we saw vapour trails left by our American fighter escort above us, and for one horrible moment we thought they were enemy jet-aircraft. But the only opposition was one six-gun battery, which fired off salvoes at intervals. No one was hit as far as I could see. We dropped our bombs and turned sharply, to see a cloud of black smoke right over the barracks, so we assumed our aim had been correct. We didn't know then it was the last operation the squadron would do in Europe, but it certainly was an excellent climax to our five years of bombing." (BBC)

However, for some of the aircrews this raid came as an anti-climax. Maltas reported:

Abortive sortie. All bombs brought back. Weather good. Ground mist up valleys. Did not identify target. No Markers. Controller said, "You can't see target. It's behind the hills." Difficulty in pinpointing. Shambles. Aircraft going in from all directions. Controller confusing with chatter about orbiting.

Wing Commander Flett also remarked about the difficulty of identifying the target and added, "Gaggle not good. Particularly return home." In fact, only 53 bombers attacked the primary target that was, however, left in ruins. On 2nd May, Berlin fell to the Russians and four days later the Act of Unconditional Surrender was signed. The war in Europe was over. Then, for the Rhodesian bomber squadron came a new and satisfying experience: the evacuation of Allied prisoners of war, under the code name Operation Exodus.

We have changed from a destructive force to a passenger-carrying service. The Rhodesian squadron has brought back nearly 3,000 liberated prisoners of war from France and Belgium. Many of the chaps have said that it's the most pleasant job they've ever had to do. The prisoners wait in queues on the airfields, many of them wearing the queerest assortment of clothes—trilby hats, leather jackets, Russian bearskin coats and anything else they can lay their hands on. Some of them have been away for as much as five years and many have never seen a four-engined bomber before. As the plane approaches the English coast, the excitement grows and the navigator passes back messages…"Ten minutes, five minutes, three minutes, one minute to go," and finally, "We're back in England!" (Operations Record No 44 Squadron)

Westcott was the main reception base and there were many touching scenes as soldiers, sailors and airmen jumped out of the Lancasters onto British soil for the first time in several years for some cases. Every effort was made to provide a welcome and military bands played the Lancasters in. At one reception station, the response was measured in the rate of rations consumed in one day: 1,000 cups of tea and half a ton of cakes.

Operation Exodus continued through the VE Day celebrations on 8th May.

8th May 1945. Hostilities with Germany ceased at 00h01 today. VE Day was declared to be 8th May 1945, squadron personnel remained on duty as usual until 15h00 hours when a full station parade was ordered. A VE Day speech by the Right Honourable Winston Spencer Churchill was relayed through the Tannoy system and was followed by an address by Group Captain S.H.V. Harris, station commander who also read over a message of congratulations to all ranks from the air officer commanding in chief HQ No 5 Group. This was followed by a thanksgiving service led by the vicar of Great Steeping assisted by the station padre. The rest of the day was declared a holiday, which as far as the station activities were concerned was spent quietly and almost normally. A welcome note was struck when it was stated that a 48-hour pass, termed VE 48, was to be granted to all ranks on condition that it was taken within two months of VE Day. (Operations Record No 44 Squadron)

Operation Exodus and training continued for the rest of the month of May. Meanwhile in London, the population went on a mad spree of celebration. On VE Day the Lord Mayor of London attended a reception at Rhodesia House while on the floor above, a less decorous party was held, where Rhodesian service men on leave in London took it in turns to throw sweets and monkey nuts at the excited crowd below. Some of the guests were utterly bewildered by the sudden change from prison camp to celebrating mob. Flight Lieutenant Ray Hill who had arrived in England only the day before from Stalag Luft III in Silesia said: "This is like pandemonium let loose. I'm still dazed from being bottled up in camp with not even a walk for a change, except marches from camp to camp. It seems I have been jostled about in madly excited crowds ever since the Scots Guards released us."

Life on the ground

For some prisoners of war the return was almost too sudden; for others it was painfully slow. Squadron Leader Tony Johnston DFC, Flight Lieutenant David Cowland-Cooper, Flight Lieutenant Bert Bryson, Flight Lieutenant James Thompson and Flying Officer Dennis Booth who had all been imprisoned at Lukenwalde had this story to tell:

> *We were about 35 miles [56km] from Berlin and the final battle raged round us for two weeks. Then early one morning a small car arrived driven by a Russian major. In great excitement, he told us that the Germans had gone and after embracing anyone in sight, he asked the man at the gate to sign a chit to say he was the first in the camp. I believe they got some sort of special reward for being first in. Shortly after, a spearhead of enormous Russian tanks came roaring through the camp knocking down the wire and the barricades and everything that came in their way. On the leading tank rode a Russian girl armed with a tommy gun and two terrified German prisoners were clinging behind. There was more rejoicing and waving of Red flags. We threw cigarettes to the Russians and they rolled on. We were told to stay in the camp for the time being but the Russians supplied us with everything we asked for. VE Day was dangerous as well as exciting. The Russians fired off everything they had: rifles, pistols, sten guns—even mortars, and you wondered where the shells might come down. The Russians were very quick on the draw, and if we looked like breaking regulations, they fired over our heads just to let us know where we must stop. We were very fed up one day when American trucks arrived and we were not allowed to go with them. The Russians were very keen on making a show and I fancy they wanted to make a big gesture by sending us off themselves. In the end, they provided transport and we were seen off with presents of cigars and lots of flag waving. They took us as far as the Elbe, where we crossed the pontoon bridge on foot and were taken by the Americans the rest of the way.*

(Rhodesia Herald, 6th June 1945)

And so after so many years and so much adventure the Rhodesians came home.

> *Sixty-three Rhodesian ex POWs were given a great welcome when they returned to the Colony yesterday (6th August 1945). A crowd of 3,000 packed Bulawayo station to greet them when their train arrived yesterday afternoon (nearly seven hours late owing to an engine breakdown between Marula and Sandown). Heany Band played. Group Captain Charles Green in answering the mayor's address of welcome said, "One just doesn't know what to say and what to think. It has been a long cry from home and all this welcome takes one's breath away and leaves a lump in the throat."* (Rhodesia Herald)

Just one week later, the Japanese surrendered unconditionally following the dropping by the Allies of two atomic bombs, one on Hiroshima and the other on Nagasaki. The Second World War had finally come to an end.

The wind-down of RATG

In fact from late 1944, the war effort in Rhodesia had started to wind down. The training camps had begun to close and the activities of the Rhodesian Air Training Group were gradually curtailed. Air Vice-Marshal Meredith, his staff and the whole Colony could look back with pride at what had been, undoubtedly, Rhodesia's greatest single contribution to the Allied victory, the training carried out under the Empire Training Scheme, of tens of thousands of aircrew members. Looking back on the achievements of the RATG, Meredith wrote:

> *A total of 16 units was formed. At peak when all units were operating fully, there were about 12,000 adult male white personnel and about 5,000 adult male Africans employed. There were also about 200 white women in the Women's Auxiliary Air Service who were employed in post office and on clerical duties at various stations.* The white male personnel figure includes pupils under training. These came from Britain principally but also from Australia and South Africa in addition to the Rhodesian intake. There were also pupils from the Royal Hellenic Air Force. The African figure includes about 2,000 armed Askari for guard duties and about 3,000 for general duties ranging from work in the hangars and workshops to cooks, waiters, messengers, grounds men and cleaners. Incidentally, at one stage, during the building of the Air Stations, the African labour force was very much greater. These hands were employed on a civilian basis, but had to be housed and fed and to get the numbers required, special recruiting visits to various chiefs were paid by Wing Commander Thomas Edward Price.*

Finances

The final financial responsibilities accepted by the Southern Rhodesia government were for:

1. the capital expenditure on land and buildings and ancillary works for the whole of the Air Training Scheme including quarters and housing.
2. the cost of all barracks, equipment at air stations.
3. the cost of RATG HQ.
4. all pay and allowances for Rhodesian personnel serving in Rhodesia.
5. make-up pay and family allowances for Rhodesians serving abroad.
6. a cash contribution of £800,000 per annum towards operating costs of the Air Training Scheme.

All other costs, including the provision of aircraft, equipment, petrol, oil, transport and the pay and allowances of RAF personnel, other than those employed at RATG headquarters, were met by the Air Ministry, except in so far as they were abated by the Southern Rhodesia government's contribution of £800,000 per annum. The pay and the allowances of pupils from Australia, South Africa and Greece and other expenses were recovered from either the government concerned or the Air Ministry.

In addition to the buildings required for the air stations and ancillary units, a number of dwelling houses—possibly in the region of 160 and at least one block of flats—were built at Southern Rhodesia government expense to house the RAF married personnel. In effect, this was a contribution to the evacuation of women and children from Britain.

An expense incurred by the Department of Defence and therefore met by the Southern Rhodesia government was that of the SR Supply Corps. This unit organized bulk supplies of foodstuffs available at Salisbury, Bulawayo and Gwelo from which air stations drew their requirements and were debited accordingly.

> *It is very likely that the SR Supply Corps would not have come into existence at any rate on the scale it did, but for the Air Training Scheme and the large quantities of foodstuff required. The cost of this army unit largely serving only the air stations was borne by the Department of*

---

* They also undertook many other duties.

Defence and in effect, was a further contribution by SR government to air training. The total SR government war expenditure related to air was £11,215.220. (Meredith)

Of course, the trade was two-way as Sir Godfrey Huggins was to remark:

The Air Training Scheme in fact formed SR's greatest individual contribution to the war and in an unexpected way also proved a major economic boon. Farmers and industrial firms suddenly found an almost insatiable market and Guest [Sir Ernest Guest] calculated that Imperial's expenditure on the scheme alone almost equalled the indirect benefit that the country derived from its entire gold mining industry.

In 1970, Lord Malvern (previously Sir Godfrey Huggins) was making notes on Notable Events in the History of Rhodesia. This was not to be a book, but only memories of the main events that had occurred during his long career. He asked Sir Charles Meredith to write a memorandum on the Rhodesia Air Training Group and it is from this memorandum that most of the previous comments have come. Having completed the memorandum, Meredith then added some extra points:

The RATG that started with nothing—no staff—no organization as a base on which to build—was unusual, even unique. It combined in one command not only Air Stations for flying and aircrew training, but also aircraft and engine overhaul and repair facilities, controlled its own works and buildings and supply section and its own finance, both local and Air Ministry funds. An aspect of which I suggest sight should not be lost is that the whole effort originated in Rhodesia. It was Rhodesia that put forward the idea. True, Air Ministry quickly saw the possibilities, but even Air Ministry, with all its resources, could have achieved little without Rhodesian cooperation. In short, it was Rhodesia that made the whole affair possible. (Meredith)

One branch of wartime flying in Rhodesia that has received little publicity was the SR Air Service, whose aircraft were flying 100,000 miles (160,000km) a month by early 1945. From 1940 they covered seven territories from South Africa in the south to Kenya in the north and they maintained a remarkable record under difficult conditions. Flying for nearly five years in aircraft that were due for replacement in 1939, improvising spare parts and equipment, the SRAS made a name for Rhodesia with its enterprise and reliability. SRAS aircraft carried, without loss of life or serious accident, 33,000 passengers during the five and a half years of war and covered 6,600,000 air miles, a record as magnificent as that of their more dashing brothers who flew in Europe, the Middle and Far East.

CHAPTER 24

A phoenix rises

The excitement was over. The Rhodesians who had served with so much credit in the ranks of the Royal Air Force were returning home, where, for the most part, they were transferred to the Southern Rhodesia Air Force Reserve and settled back into civilian life with little difficulty. It had been agreed that former members of the forces were to be paid in rank until they obtained employment, up to a limit of three months. Sir Godfrey Huggins, then Prime Minister of Southern Rhodesia, had made it absolutely clear all along that he would do his utmost to prevent a repetition of the sad state that had occurred in 1918 when returning servicemen found themselves unemployed. In fact, the organization seems to have proceeded smoothly with most men making a reasonably easy transfer from the world of combat to that of civilian pursuits.

Men wanting to serve in a new air force

So much for the men who wished to leave the armed forces. What about those who wanted to remain in the services? These men, as far as the air force was concerned, fell into three categories. Firstly, there were the men who had signed on before the war. The six apprentices who had gone to Halton in 1936 were typical. They had originally signed long-term contracts with the Southern Rhodesia Air Force and they had never transferred to the RAF. Secondly, there were men such as Archie Wilson and Ted Cunnison who had attested in the newly designated SRAF at the outbreak of war completing their training to Wings on Nos 1 and 2 Courses of the SRAF. These men had been absorbed into the RAFVR in May and June 1940, an arrangement that had been agreed between Sir Godfrey Huggins and the British government to ease administrative problems. Thirdly, there were men like John Deall who had attested into RAF, trained with the RATG in Rhodesia and served with the RAF throughout the war but who now wished to join an air force in Southern Rhodesia. In 1945 there was nothing on offer for these men and many of them gave up their ideas of military flying and took employment on the ground in the civvy field. Some of them were to return to the SRAF later when the force began to expand. Others remained with the RAF for a while and then joined the Southern Rhodesia Staff Corps, often at a vastly reduced rank.

Aircraft for a new air force

A record compiled in January 1946 gave the strength of the SRAF still awaiting demobilization as 69 officers and 50 men, some of whom wanted to continue flying, but what about aircraft? In 1939, the SRAF had owned, among other assorted aircraft, six Hawker Harts that had been purchased from the RAF. Amazingly, one of these aircraft was still operational at the end of the war. There were also the aircraft that had flown with the Southern Rhodesia Air Services during the war, as well as a large number of RAF Tiger Moths lying around. The Southern

Rhodesia government was interested in using these machines but there were problems.

18th May 1945
From: HQ RATG
To: Wing Commander J. Davison
SR Liaison Officer
London

Will you look up the Air Ministry signal OX 2865 of 15/5/45 about the disposal of surplus Moths? There are still many departments of the Air Ministry, who do not understand that Rhodesia is not part of South Africa and that the Mission have no interest in us except financially. MAP (Ministry of Aircraft Production) seems to have no clue at all. There are over 130 Moths here in various stages of condition. There are many people who would jump at them at a reasonable price i.e. £100 – 200. They are not worth more and if local people could offer a price that MAP authorizes us to accept or otherwise, they might get something out of them, but that is probably too practicable a suggestion to consider.

A reply came eleven days later.

29 May 1945
From: SR Air Liaison Officer
To: Air Commodore L.H. Cockey CBE HQ RATG, Salisbury

I have your (letter) of May 18th asking me to try to race forward the question of disposal of Tiger Moths. I know there is a very annoying delay over this, but I assure you that the general question is under very active discussion by MAP. They are up against all sorts of snags in regard to negotiations with manufacturers and the Munitions Assignment Board. I will, however, keep close check on it for you.

In fact, two years later 181 Cornells, which had been standing on a two-acre (0,8 hectare) stretch of land on the eastern boundary of Kumalo Aerodrome in Bulawayo, were destroyed. They had been sent from America under the Lease-Lend agreement and many of them had never flown in Rhodesia because they were not suited to the altitude. All these machines were hammered, slashed and battered so that neither the aircraft nor any of their components could be used. It had been part of an agreement, made at the time of supply that the aircraft would be broken up when the RAF had no further use for them.

Cranborne 1945

According to Ralph Parry, the men at Cranborne (formerly SRAF Station, Hillside) in 1945, were Keith Taute, a pilot, Ted Jacklin, later to become the first CO of the new Rhodesian air force, Gordon Norris, an ex RAF man who was in charge of equipment, Otto Gericke, and Mick Gibbons who had been among the original six Halton apprentices, as had Ralph Parry. These men came under the command of the Southern Rhodesia Staff Corps.

At Cranborne, they found a building, which they appropriated. Their first aeroplanes were the government Leopard Moth SR 22 and the Rapide, which had been part of the Communications Squadron. Using their own tools and whatever else they could beg, borrow or steal, they set to work. They found that the RAF who had left in a hurry had abandoned a great deal of valuable equipment; for example, in one of the hangars they discovered a petrol bowser, which they used for many years to refuel aircraft.

The RAF also left behind a large stock of aircraft spares, quantities of which had been sold to scrap-metal dealers. Enterprising members of the air force toured the scrap merchants buying back the often-unopened boxes of precious aircraft parts.

By the end of 1945, although there had been some suggestions that RAF training should continue in Rhodesia, most of the RATG stations had closed down. Cranborne was the only station still employed in flying training, on a reduced commitment, and this station was due to close its doors on 5th April 1946. Thornhill had been closed, except for care and maintenance. Heany had also been closed, while Kumalo (Bulawayo) was operating as a staging post for civilian aircraft landing in the Bulawayo area. Before the war, this had been the Bulawayo Civil Airport.

Ralph Parry toured the stations and selected six Tiger Moths that were in the best condition. These were to be replacements for the aircraft Rhodesia had made available to the RAF in 1939, that is, the aircraft that went to Nairobi with No 1 Squadron SRAF. Parry organized the dismantling of these machines, which were then loaded onto rail trucks for the journey to Cranborne. These six Moths, together with a war surplus Anson presented by the RAF, formed the backbone of the first postwar air unit.

Writing many years later, Air Vice-Marshal Raf Bentley who was, in 1945, RAF liaison officer in Rhodesia said, "Everything had to be done from scratch and the air force's future rested heavily on the persistence and ingenuity of the men." This ingenuity took many forms and soon all air force personnel came to be regarded with some suspicion by those who had any material or equipment that could be of use in rebuilding activities. Tools, raw materials, all manner of odds and ends, even trained staff, filtered through to the air force headquarters at Cranborne. "No one asked where things came from in those days," Bentley remembered. The men went on forays to the old RAF maintenance depot at Bulawayo and to the former RAF scrap dump off the Salisbury Road, just outside town. They came back with, among other items, the salvaged wrecks of Tiger Moths, which were then reconstructed and pressed into service for recruit pilot training.

Eventually, using scratch tools and equipment, the air force ground staff rebuilt the two crashed Tiger Moths. The result of all this hard work was that, in the first years after the war, the air force's actual assets far outweighed its book value, which was zero. Within the oil-stained, petrol-soaked bowser shed at Cranborne Air Field, the small group of trailblazers set about planning a viable programme for a new air force. "We asked ourselves," said Bentley, "How does one build an air force? We pondered on this for a while and then went into action. As it turned out, we did just about everything at once. We had a budget of £10,000 but even this was controlled by army headquarters; we could not purchase a thing without army permission. This was difficult for us because the army could not always understand our plans for forming the new air force."

Even the original air force buildings at Cranborne had been cordoned off behind barbed wire for use as accommodation for immigrants and as a workshop for the CMED (Central Mechanical Equipment Department), the Irrigation Department and the Public Works Department. Speaking of this period, Bentley continued:

I must add that I am intensely proud to have belonged to the Rhodesian air force, for it contains the finest body of officers and men it has ever been my privilege to work with. While I held the position of chief of air staff, the only problem I had on the discipline side was to stop my men from working too hard. The ground staff regarded any assignment as a challenge; they never failed. In fact, they always did better than one dared hope. The whole outfit was intensely resourceful; everyone was full of invention and innovation. Most of the officers who joined the air unit after the war took a tremendous drop in rank, some from wing commander to sergeant [John Deall]

and this was indicative of the type of chaps we had in the air force in those early days.
(Rhodesia Herald interview, 25th May 1971)

The staff strength was around a dozen officers and men, led by Ted Jacklin, a South African-born veteran, who had joined the Southern Rhodesia Territorial Air Unit with the second intake of pilots in 1937. On 31st March 1946, he relinquished his commission with the RAF and joined the Southern Rhodesia Staff Corps. However, in November of that year, he was seconded back to the RAF and granted a temporary commission in the rank of wing commander to be held concurrently with his staff corps commission. This action was taken because in December 1946, he was appointed RAF liaison officer at Defence headquarters in Salisbury and, in April 1947, he was posted to the Air Ministry in London. He returned to Rhodesia in September 1947 to join the headquarters staff at RATG Kumalo.

Postwar air-training scheme

Meanwhile, discussions were still going on between the Southern Rhodesia government and the United Kingdom government on a future air-training scheme, which was to be Rhodesia's contribution to Empire defence. It was suggested in a memorandum drafted by Sir Ernest Lucas Guest early in 1946, that the scheme should begin in January 1947 and that the Southern Rhodesia government would make an initial contribution of £25,000. The RAF was to have the use of Heany and Thornhill, while accommodation was to be provided at Kumalo for a Wing headquarters. Fixed assets were to remain the property of the Southern Rhodesia government.

On 29th January 1946, the Group Routine Orders of the old RATG ceased, and were only replaced after almost a year's break, on 10th December 1946 by Wing Routine Orders: Air Training Wing, Southern Rhodesia. By the end of March 1946, all Southern Rhodesia personnel had terminated their service with the RAF. Those wishing to stay on, had joined either the RAF, with RAF conditions of service, or the Southern Rhodesia Forces. As from 1st April 1946, in the absence of any definite policy pronouncement, all RAF stations were placed on a care and maintenance basis and from the same date, a nucleus headquarters covering Air requirements was merged with Defence headquarters. (Loose Minute signed Wing Commander Mason, 12th Feb. 1946 Archives S798)

Six days earlier, a letter of complaint had appeared in the *Rhodesia Herald* about the noise caused by flying training at Cranborne. In reply, J.H. Ralston, the Minister of Air and Defence said: "The continued use of this station as a training centre or not, will be considered by the Cabinet when the whole question of postwar training is decided." In other words, no firm decision of any kind had been made. However, it was felt privately that if the RAF training programme was to be re-introduced it would not be economical to maintain a purely SRAF training organization. (Archives S 798 Memo on Postwar Defence Scheme)

On 5th April 1946, the Colony went to the polls for the first time since the outbreak of the Second World War. The result gave no clear majority to either side, the United Party taking 13 seats, the Liberal Party 12, the Labour Party 3 and the SR Labour Party 2. Sir Godfrey Huggins as leader of the party with the largest number of seats, remained in office as prime minister.

Early in May 1946, a large contingent of ex RAF and SRAF men went south to take part in the Rand Victory Parade on 6th May, and two days later an Air Ministry mission arrived in Salisbury to discuss the proposed flying training scheme. It was during the Budget debate at the end of May, that the first definite statement was made about Rhodesia's defence commitments and future plans for the air force.

The Colony is under a definite and specific obligation to provide a force adequate to cope with local disturbances and incidents, which may occur on our borders however remote they may appear to be. In addition, there is a moral obligation, which the Colony would wish to discharge as fully and effectually as possible to make a contribution towards the defence of the Empire. Negotiations have taken place during recent weeks for the establishment of a modified form of the Empire Air Training Scheme. (Rhodesia Herald, 31st May 1946)

A block vote of £400,000 to include the cost of a Permanent Staff Corps, Territorial and Cadet Training, Civil Aviation, Meteorological Services and SR Supply Corps, was arranged.

First postwar air search

The first call on the services of the men at Cranborne came in the middle of June 1946 when a Harvard disappeared while on a flight from Salisbury to Fort Jameson. The aircraft had taken off from Cranborne at 09h30 on Friday 14th June with Flight Lieutenant L.J. Murphy and Flying Officer B. Boswell DFM on board. Nine aircraft took part in the search, which was organized from bases at Fort Jameson, Lilongwe and Salisbury. The airmen were found on Tuesday 18th June, in a desolate part of the Luangwa Valley, roughly 83 miles (133km) north-west of Fort Jameson. The country was too rough and wooded for an air rescue but ground parties were guided to the spot by aircraft.

With the closing down of RATG, Air headquarters moved out of the buildings on Jameson Avenue, which it had occupied since 1940, and joined Defence headquarters. This was to be regretted because during the preceding six years, RATG and the Public Works Department, between them, had turned what was an official slummery into a neat and pleasant group of buildings. The ancient offices, which had long been overdue for demolition, some having been erected in pioneer days, were kept going from year to year pending the development of the government's plans for the area. The first part of these plans had been the erection of Vincent and Milton Buildings around the site where Cecil Rhodes's statue then stood.

A further part of the winding-down process occurred in August 1946 when the Air Liaison Office at Rhodesia House, in London was closed, and Wing Commander Maurice Barber DFC returned to Southern Rhodesia. The final and perhaps the largest job undertaken by the Air Liaison Office had been demobbing Rhodesians serving with the three British Services and repatriating them, along with their wives and children.

Agreement on RAF training in Rhodesia

The agreement on peacetime RAF training in Rhodesia was signed on Thursday 12th September, 1946 in the Air Council Chamber at the Air Ministry, London. Signatories were the Under Secretary for Air, Mr de Freitas on behalf of the Air Ministry and the Southern Rhodesia Minister of Air, Colonel Sir Ernest Lucas Guest on behalf of the Southern Rhodesia government. The scheme was intended to provide 350 trained pilots and navigators every year. On his return to Southern Rhodesia, Sir Ernest gave a brief outline of the Colony's local defence plans and projected contributions to Empire defence. He said that agreement had been reached with the British authorities regarding the Colony's contributions to Empire defence and that a training wing of the RAF would be established in the Colony. Training would begin in the new year, 1947. Rhodesia would provide airfields, buildings and a cash contribution, as well as essential services. Provision would be made within the scheme for the training of Rhodesian airmen. Meanwhile, Rhodesia had become, as far as air matters were concerned, an independent command of its own as it had been before the war. (*Rhodesia Herald*, 5th Oct. 1946)

Once the final decision had been made, things moved fast and the first 20 officers and men to take part in the new Empire Air Training Scheme, arrived in Salisbury by air on 9th October and left that same day for Bulawayo.

In November 1946, Air Commodore G.G. Banting, the new chief of the Empire Air Training Scheme, arrived to assess the situation and just after Christmas, the first RAF draft of 73 young men, 64 of whom were to train as pilots and navigators, arrived in Bulawayo. Meanwhile the man who had done most to make the running of the wartime RATG the success it was, Air Commodore Sir Charles Meredith, left military flying to become Chairman of Central African Airways.

In some ways the advent of the training scheme was to Southern Rhodesia's advantage, but it also posed problems—not the least of which was, that the hard-working men at Cranborne did not want to see the aircraft which they had built with such loving care, grabbed and sent to Bulawayo for the RAF. A way round this problem was suggested by Maurice Barber, in a memo to the secretary of the Department of Defence and Air.

30th October 1946

Aircraft for Southern Rhodesia Government Communications Work
With the move of aircraft and personnel from Cranborne to the RAF Wing at Bulawayo, there is an urgent requirement for aircraft for government communications work (aircraft cannot be supplied by RAF Wing or CAA, too expensive to hire). The only solution appears to be the formation of a small communications flight, organized preferably within the SRAF. An estimated establishment on the basis of six aircraft is:
Air communications requirements
VIP visits, movement of Defence Staff Officers, liaison visits to RAF, liaison visits to South Africa, Northern Rhodesia and Nyasaland, search and rescue, meteorological work, photography and survey, police and medical work.
Aircraft
Anson Mk I
Harvard Mk IIA
Cornell
Tiger Moth
208 flying hours per month
Two officers, staff pilots
Fourteen ground crew
Radio operator (possibly NCO)
Equipment and stores
The Air Ministry would probably accede to a request for the aircraft named, and a certain amount of equipment, to be handed over as a free gift or, for a nominal sum, as a replacement for the eleven aircraft (Harts, Audax and Gauntlets) purchased by SR government, and used by 237 Squadron in the early days of the war. The flight to be located at Cranborne.

Signed M.C.H. Barber (Wing Commander)

This plan was accepted. Later the six Tiger Moths, obtained from the RAF, with two rebuilt Tiger Moths, were joined by two Harvard Trainers bought from the RAF Training Group. It is interesting to note that the first aircraft given a postwar number was a Communications Squadron Leopard Moth. The number SR 22 was issued on 6th November 1946.

Conspicuous Gallantry Medal for John Casson

There was a sad reminder of the cost of war on 22nd November 1946 when Mr Harry Casson of Inyanga received the Conspicuous Gallantry Medal (Flying)* that had been awarded posthumously to his son John.

During the battle for Rome, Flight Sergeant John Casson led a Kittyhawk bomber squadron in an attack on a German transport column. There was heavy anti-aircraft fire. On his first run-in, he was fatally wounded. For 15 minutes, he flew over the enemy lines and across the mountains, losing blood rapidly from the wound in his leg. When he reached his airfield, aircraft were lined up on the runway to take off. John Casson did not ask for an emergency landing. He circled the field three times and then came in to land. As the aircraft touched down it slewed violently across the runway and ground crews ran to see what was wrong. They lifted John unconscious from the cockpit. His leg was amputated but he died a few hours later. His brother, William Harry Casson, was an airgunner with No 102 Squadron and was killed in December 1942.

The Communications Squadron personnel

It was 1947. The idea of creating a Communications Squadron had been accepted and officially there was one aircraft available. What about pilots? Two men were immediately available— Keith Taute and Doug Whyte.

Keith Taute had joined the RAF in 1938 on a Short Service Commission and on his demobilization in September 1946, he joined the Department of Civil Aviation. By March 1947, he held the rank of captain. Doug Whyte joined the RAF in January 1941 and after serving overseas, he returned to Rhodesia as a flying instructor with RATG. He was demobilized on 14th January 1946 and later attested into the Staff Corps ending up as a sergeant in the Ordnance Depot, with Sergeant Chisnall, issuing uniforms. In addition, there was also WO II Harold Hawkins (ex RAAF) who was an air traffic controller at the civilian airport at Belvedere.

On 22nd March 1947 operating out of Belvedere, Sergeant Doug Whyte converted to Leopard Moth SR 22 and WO II Harold Hawkins went solo. Some time later, he was transferred to the Communications Squadron and in June he was promoted to lieutenant. As for the ground crew, there was Ralph Parry, Mick Gibbons and Otto Gerricke. On 19th April, another aircraft joined the fleet, an Avro Anson numbered SR 21. The squadron was based at Cranborne using the airfield, a hangar, the control tower and an office block.

A Royal visit

On 7th April 1947, the British Royal Family arrived by air at Belvedere Airport. During this visit, King George VI opened parliament and held an investiture at Government House. Air Vice-Marshal Sir Charles Meredith received the KBE. Mr Erasmus, the father of Flying Officer Charles Derek Erasmus, was presented with his son's posthumous DFC, Mr Oldham was given the DFC that had been won by his son Gordon, and Mrs Albertson, the widow of Flight Lieutenant Arthur Ian Albertson, received her husband's AFC. Wing Commander John Deall, Wing Commander H.H.C. Holderness, Squadron Leader Ian Shand, Flight Lieutenant Geoff Cranswick, Flight Lieutenant George Elcombe and Flight Lieutenant Don McGibbon were also at the Investiture although their decorations did not arrive in time for

---

* the Conspicuous Gallantry Medal (Flying) may be considered a rare award, only 109 medals being awarded during the Second World War. All, with the exception of two, were awarded to members of Bomber Command. The two exceptions, strangely enough, went to fighter pilots on No 250 (Sudan) Squadron, one of whom was John Casson.

the presentation. The Royal Family left by train on 16th April 1947.

During the Budget, which was presented on 29th April, provision was made for a contribution of £240,000 towards the cost of the RAF Training Scheme. Provision was also made in the Defence Vote for the establishment of a Communications Squadron at a cost of £44,000. The Government Gazette dated 20th June 1947 contained a notice requiring men to register for peacetime training.

The prime minister flies to South Africa

On 21st July 1947, Prime Minister Sir Godfrey Huggins flew to Pretoria for a meeting with South African Prime Minister General Smuts, travelling in the Anson SR 21 flown by Sergeant Doug Whyte. The story goes that General Smuts wanted to know why the Rhodesian prime minister was flying in such an old aircraft. The reply was, It is the only plane we have. To which General Smuts remarked: We will have to do something about that! Not only did he arrange for a Dakota to be sold to the Southern Rhodesia government at a ridiculously low price but also for the supply of 12 Harvard Mark IIBs at a nominal price of £500 each.

With effect from 15th September 1947, the Communications Squadron, Cranborne, became known as the Southern Rhodesia Staff Corps, Communications Squadron with Captain Keith Taute as unofficial officer commanding and Sergeant Otto Gericke in charge of maintenance. As far as aircraft were concerned, the squadron had in addition to the Leopard Moth and the Avro Ansons, a Rapide SR 24, acquired from RANA and the Dakota SR 25, purchased from the South African government.

Archie Wilson, later to become commander of the air force says:

> *At this juncture, the establishment of pilots was four and the strength three, namely Warrant Officer II Harold Hawkins (ex Squadron Leader RAAF), Sergeant Doug W. Whyte (ex Flight Lieutenant RAVR) and Sergeant A.F. Chisnall (ex Warrant Officer RAFVR). Whyte and Chisnall had, since the end of hostilities, been members of the Army Staff Corps at the Ordnance and Supply Depot. Harold Hawkins was also on the army strength. At the time of transfer, he was serving as an air traffic controller at Belvedere Airport. To bring the establishment up to current strength the vacancy was advertised in the national press and I was the successful applicant, so I became the first 'demobbed' pilot to re-enter the new air force, re-attesting as a sergeant, having reached the rank of squadron leader with the RAF. I began flying in November 1947. Incidentally, all four of us had seen operational service and Hawkins, Whyte and I were qualified flying instructors.*

Archie continues: "My log-book confirms my first flight was one of familiarization on 22nd November 1947, with Harold Hawkins as my conversion tutor in Dakota SR 25. My next entry reveals that on 24th November, I flew a refresher sortie with C/Sergeant Doug Whyte in Tiger Moth SR 26. In fact, two Tiger Moths SR 26 and SR 27 were flown that day from RAF Heany to Cranborne to join the squadron. The other pilot was Doug Whyte."

The air unit is officially established

The Government Gazette dated 28th November 1947 carried the following notice:

Department of Defence
The following Government Notice is published for general information.
S. Garlake, Colonel
Acting Secretary Department of Defence and Air.

No 945

It is hereby notified that His Excellency the Governor has been pleased, in terms of section 97 of the Defence Act (Chapter 111) as amended, to make the following regulations relating to members of the SR Air Force:

1. *An Air Unit of the Permanent Force is hereby established which shall be styled the Southern Rhodesia Air Force.*

2. *The SRAF shall consist of those persons who were attested in the Permanent Staff Corps (Air Section) as provided in Government Notice 527 of 1936 as amended and such persons as may be attested in the Force on or after 27th June 1947.*

3. *The principal regulations known as 'The SR Staff Corps regs. 1947' shall apply to all members of the SRAF.*

4. *The Regulations published in Government Notices Nos 527 of 1936, 602 of 1936 and 515 of 1938 are hereby repealed.*

This momentous event, the re-establishment of Southern Rhodesia's own air force, passed unnoticed by the *Rhodesia Herald* but was reflected in a speech made by Sir Godfrey Huggins, in which he stressed the need for Southern Rhodesia to be independent in matters of defence.

CHAPTER 25

The SRAF tries out its wings

In the first instance, credit for the creation and initial expansion of the postwar Southern Rhodesia Air Force must go to Sir Ernest Lucas Guest, the Minister for Defence, together with Colonel (later Major General) Storr Garlake CBE, who was Commander Military Forces, Southern Rhodesia.

Colonel Garlake, General Officer Commanding Central Africa Command, was responsible for the air force until 1956, when it became autonomous, by which time the air force was operating Vampires and had acquired the title Royal Rhodesian Air Force. The first commander of the air unit was Captain Keith Taute, who was succeeded by Lieutenant Colonel E.W.S. Jacklin (later Air Vice-Marshal)—a dynamic leader and the driving force behind the tremendous task of rebuilding the force. On his retirement, he was paid the compliment, never before accorded to a Commonwealth airman, of being invited to inspect the Royal Air Force. During 1961, he visited and inspected every Home Command of that force, as well as the RAF stations in Germany. A trophy was presented to the officers' mess at New Sarum to honour this occasion.

Two other men played outstanding parts in the spectacular growth of the immediate postwar period. One was Doug Whyte (one of the first pilots to serve with the resuscitated air unit) and the other was Harold Hawkins who afterwards became Air Vice-Marshal, chief of Air Staff and subsequently Rhodesia's accredited diplomatic representative in South Africa.

The new air unit carried out its first casualty evacuation (casevac) just before Christmas 1947, when Police Trooper Bruwer, taken seriously ill at Gokwe, was transported to Gatooma aboard an aircraft of the Communications Squadron.

During his speech from the throne at the opening of parliament in May 1948, the governor, Major General Sir John Kennedy foreshadowed increases in the Colony's permanent force. He reported that discussions in this regard had been held with the chief of the Imperial General Staff, Field Marshal Viscount Montgomery, who had recently visited the country.

In June, the Colony welcomed the visit of six Lancaster aircraft /Lincoln bombers of No 44 (Rhodesia) Squadron. Only one Rhodesian crewman, an airgunner, was flying with the squadron then, but many of the other men had relatives in Southern Rhodesia.

During the Defence and Air Vote hearing-in committee in June, Mr G. Hackwill (United Party member for Lomagundi) asked whether an auxiliary air squadron was to be formed for the men who had recently left the air force but wished to continue flying. The prime minister replied that it was hoped that such a squadron would be inaugurated during the following year, 1949. It had apparently been intended to make a start earlier but the proposal had been axed in an economy drive. One of the problems related to the economic situation was that of a petrol shortage. This was due, not so much to a lack of petrol itself, as to a severe shortage of railway tank cars. In fact, from 12th to 23rd August, sales of petrol were limited to a maximum of one gallon per customer. This problem was to continue until 1950.

The Anson ferry

The British government had agreed to provide compensation for the Rhodesian aircraft and equipment that the Southern Rhodesian government had made available to the RAF at the beginning of World War II. This compensation took the shape of three Avro Ansons and it was decided that these aircraft should be flown out from Britain by Rhodesian pilots. These ferry flights were to become commonplace during the next 15 years. The Anson flight was under the command of Captain Keith Taute, who was accompanied by Brigadier S. Garlake. The other pilots were Doug Whyte, Harold Hawkins, Archie Wilson and Tony Chisnall, who had transferred from the Ordnance Depot to the Communications Squadron in December 1947. The men left Salisbury aboard Dakota SR 25 with Archie at the controls and Harold Hawkins as second pilot. While they were in the United Kingdom three of the airmen attended the RAF Central Flying School at Hullavington to upgrade their flying instructor categories.

On the return flight, the three Ansons were to be piloted by Tony Chisnall, Archie Wilson and Keith Taute with Brigadier Garlake and Otto Gericke as passengers. Doug Whyte returned to Rhodesia as second pilot to Harold Hawkins in SR 25.

By 8th June, the three Ansons were in position at Manston but their departure was delayed when it was announced that the flight could not proceed unless each aircraft carried a qualified navigator! When it was pointed out that the air unit establishment did not have navigators as such, the RAF agreed to release three recently qualified RCAF navigators to accompany the ferry team as far as Egypt.

On the day of departure, 12th June, fog was thick over Manston and the Channel, with low cloud extending across central France. As the weather reports showed no promise of an early improvement, the pilots decided to take off and fly independently via Calais, their designated checkpoint for entering French airspace, to Bordeaux. As they approached Calais, Archie asked his navigator for a course to steer. Archie remembers: "The course given appeared to be grossly inaccurate and so I decided to fly by my own reckoning. The cloud cleared as the flight was approaching Bordeaux and the three aircraft landed within a few minutes of one another."

While the aircraft were on the ground the weather deteriorated to such an extent that the pilots decided to remain overnight and make an early departure next morning. Came the dawn and the navigators had not returned from their night out on the town. The weather was still bad with heavy cloud and rain between Bordeaux and Istres (Marseilles), their next destination, and airfield control made it clear that should the flight proceed it would be at their own risk. The pilots decided to take off and follow their own course to Istres.

At 07h00 as the crews were boarding the aircraft the three navigators arrived, looking rather the worse for wear. It was agreed that they would continue as passengers to Egypt. The Ansons took off with Keith Taute and Tony Chisnall opting to fly below the cloud, and heading north of the direct route. Archie Wilson chose to fly through the cloud following the shorter path. About 15 miles out of Istres, the cloud broke up and Archie let down well ahead of the other two aircraft.

After refuelling and flight clearance, the aircraft took off from Istres and were able to fly in a loose Vic formation in relatively clear weather to El Aouina, in Tunisia. A short break to take on fuel and it was off again to Castel Benito (Tripoli) where there was a night stop.

On 14th June, the first leg took the flight from Castel Benito to El Adem in Libya and the second leg on to Fayid in Egypt. Here the three navigators were thanked for their part in the exercise and given a farewell. June 15th was a non-flying day spent carrying out maintenance and planning the run down Africa.

During the day of 16th June, flying over the desert, the aircrews could see the relics of the battles that had raged backwards and forwards over the sand during World War II. In some

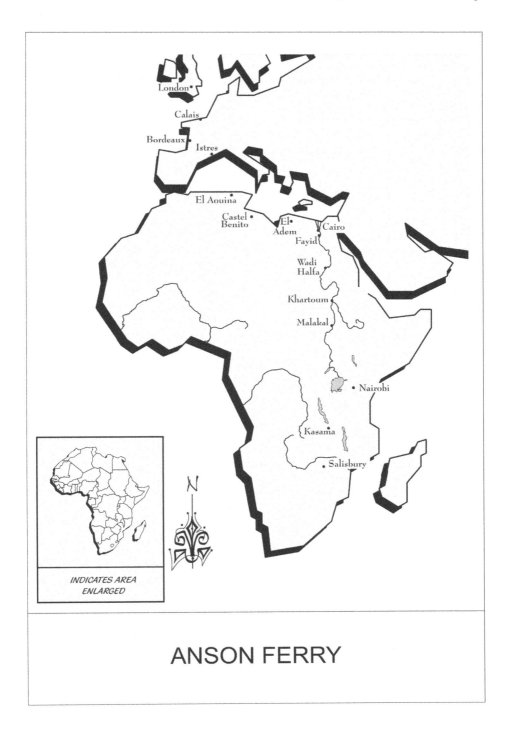

London•
Calais
Bordeaux•
Istres
El Aouina•
Castel • El• Cairo
Benito Adem
Fayid
Wadi Halfa
Khartoum
Malakal
• Nairobi
Kasama
• Salisbury

INDICATES AREA
ENLARGED

N

ANSON FERRY

areas the burnt-out shells of tanks, armoured vehicles and trucks littered the ground, a mute reminder of the waste of war. From Wadi Halfa, the flight continued to Khartoum and a welcome night stop before take-off on 17th June for Malakal in the Sudan.

It was at Malakal that the gremlins again intervened. Ready for departure, they sought the usual clearance, but the airfield controller refused to give it. He regretted that as the aircrews were without a qualified navigator he could not allow the ferry to proceed. This unexpected turn of events left the team speechless. Archie decided that the only course was to brazen it out. Confronting the chief controller, he asked indignantly what the problem was. He was the fully qualified navigator appointed to the ferry team, and there had been absolutely no problems this far on the flight so why this ridiculous hold up. The airfield controller apologized and the team prepared for take-off.

At Malakal the tarmac runway lies in wet marshland. Led by Keith Taute the three Ansons taxied out line astern. On reaching the end of the runway, the lead aircraft turned and took off. Archie had proceeded no further than a few metres along the fringe of the runway when the left wing dropped with a lurch and the nose slewed 30 degrees to port.

On inspection, it was found that a section of the runway had collapsed and the left wheel had slid into the hole. Although the aircraft had been moving fairly slowly, the sudden jerk had caused the oleo leg to twist. No spares were available either aboard the Ansons or at Malakal so Keith Taute decided that VM337 would have to remain where it was until spares could be flown in, but aware that the prescribed navigator would be staying on the ground, decided that he and Chisnall should leave at once. Subsequent examination showed that water erosion had undermined the runway, causing the crust to give way under the weight of the aircraft.

It was a dreary wait of ten days before Dakota SR 25 flown by Lieutenant Harry Hawkins arrived with the necessary spares and a relief crew for the Anson. But then the gremlins stepped in again. The Dakota developed a problem and so it was another six days before Archie and Otto Gericke were able to depart en route for Nairobi, Kasama and home. The first Ansons landed at Cranborne on 19th June while the third, reached base on 4th July. These aircraft were given the numbers SR 29, 30 and 31. (Information from Archie Wilson)

Later in the month of June 1948, the government, which had been in a weak position, not having a clear majority, was defeated on a confidence motion, and resigned. General Election polling day was set for 15th September and it was hoped that the country would give a clear mandate to either the Liberal Party or the United Party. The winner was the United Party with a landslide victory.

As well as being polling day, 15th September was Battle of Britain Day and at the Royal Air Force Association dinner held in Salisbury, Sir Ernest Guest announced that arrangements had been completed for the establishment of an auxiliary air force. "We have the aircraft, our establishment of personnel is rapidly filling up. They are being trained and the government that was elected today should have no difficulty in putting into effect the scheme that has been planned," he said. Sir Ernest continued that when the unit was functioning, it should be possible to re-establish the air cadets and so encourage the young and stimulate their interest in the air. He described the Royal Air Force Training Group as permanent and the base for a larger local air unit should it be necessary. He went on to say: "We have no territorial ambitions, nor do we wish to impose our ideology on the world, but if our honour is at stake or our security threatened, there can be no doubt whatever that we must accept the challenge, whatever the consequences may be." (*Rhodesia Herald*, 16th Sept. 1948)

Once again, the world situation was such that at any moment some incident might light the fuse of a World War III. In Europe, Russia had instituted the Berlin blockade, hoping to force the West into backing down and handing the city over to them. However, the Americans, showing more determination than they were to evince later, mounted a huge airlift of supplies into the beleaguered city. Russian pilots, flying wingtip to wingtip with the Allied planes, continually harassed the supply aircraft, but the airlift was maintained until eventually the Russians eased the situation.

In October 1948, Sir Godfrey Huggins attended the Commonwealth Prime Ministers' Conference in London. In view of the serious world situation, the decision was taken to strengthen the armed forces of the Empire and lengthen the term of compulsory military service in the United Kingdom. While the world was busy preparing for a new conflict, thought was being given to those who had died in the recent war. On Sunday 26th December, the Dean of Westminster, Dr A.C. Don, dedicated a frontal cloth on the new altar of the Holy Cross in Westminster Abbey to the memory of Rhodesian pilots of the RAFVR killed during the war.

As the New Year 1949 began, not only were Rhodesian men being called back to service but the recruiting of women was under way, although the campaign did not get off to an auspicious start. Rhodesian girls seem frightened of the services was the reported comment of Miss P. Wibberly, commandant of the SR Women's Military and Air Service.

Again, owing to world conditions, the Defence Estimates were increased in the 1949 Budget and it was announced that the Territorial Force Air Section was to begin training in July. In fact, the vote for Defence was for £857,684, an increase of £178,584 over the previous year's allocation, and included £350,575 for the RAF training scheme. Mr R.A. Ballantyne (United Party) said that the vote was already large and wondered if it would be necessary to increase it further in the future. The prime minister replied that like other parts of the Commonwealth, Southern Rhodesia was preparing for any emergency that might arise. Everybody hoped there would not be a war but this was an expense and an insurance, which the country had to face in common with the rest of the Empire.

Mr Wise (Liberal Party, Hartley) thought the vote was too small, and added that it seemed as if the Colony was not paying its full share in defence matters, only a miserable £4,000 having been voted for the SRAF. Mr G.H. Hackwill (United Party, Lomagundi) asked if the Harvards bought from the SAAF at £500 each for territorial purposes, were airworthy; to which the prime minister replied that he doubted if the South African government would sell planes to Southern Rhodesia that were not airworthy.

The Harvards arrive

The first two Harvards were collected from the SAAF towards the end of May 1949.

SR Staff Corps Air Unit
Cranborne Air Station
Salisbury
Dakota SR 25 will be required to transport an SR Staff Corps Selection Board to Durban and Johannesburg. Take off Cranborne at 0800 hours Sunday 29/5/49. Ferry crew to collect two Harvard aircraft from Zwartkops Air Station. (Return date for Dakota 5/6/49).

Dakota Crew	**Harvard Crew**
Lieutenant Colonel Jacklin	*Major Taute*
Captain Hawkins	*Lieutenant Whyte*
Colour Sergeant Wheaton	*Captain Webster*
Sergeant Ballinger	

Signed E.W.S. Jacklin Lieutenant Colonel (SR Staff Corps, Air Unit)

On 13th February 1949, Ted Jacklin's secondment to the RAF was terminated and he relinquished his RAF commission. On 1st March, he was appointed commanding officer of the Southern Rhodesia Staff Corps Air Unit with the rank of lieutenant colonel.

Until this time, civil aviation had been using Belvedere Airport but the city of Salisbury was growing and as the height of the buildings and the size of passenger aircraft increased, it became obvious that a new site had to be found for a civilian aerodrome. It therefore came as no surprise when, on 18th June 1949, the government announced that the construction of a new national airport was being planned. The cost would be in the region of £2,000,000 and the site chosen was south of the city beyond the suburb of Hatfield. This site was to become not only the home for Salisbury Airport but also the main base for the air force under the title of New Sarum.

No 1 Course SRAAF

During July 1949, flying training of territorial volunteers began and No 1 Squadron, Southern Rhodesia Auxiliary Air Force was formed. This squadron was to be manned by ex-combat pilots resident in Salisbury who volunteered to carry out flying training before work in the morning and after work in the evening. Despite the difficulties of fitting the training in with a day's work, the air force managed to retain its training maxim: Quality before quantity with only the best men available being selected. (Bentley)

The pilots of No 1 Course were: Owen M. Love; Dennis A. Bagnall; I.J.S. (John) Bridger; W.H. (Bill) Smith; Colin D. Graves; Peter E. Potter; Gordon J. Merrington (SR Artillery); J.B. (Bruce) Mackenzie and Gordon R. Rowley.

Training camp at Sinoia

On 20th August 1949, the following report appeared in the *Rhodesia Herald*:

> *Troops moved to the attack under a smoke screen while aircraft engines roared, and machine-guns rattled grimly. A demonstration of air and ground cooperation was watched this morning by the 800 cadets of the 3rd and 4th Battalion Royal Rhodesia Regiment, now in camp at Ikwani [Sinoia].*

The demonstration was a realistic and dramatic affair. Four Harvards, led by Major Keith Taute, representing rocket-firing Typhoons, swept down on the enemy strongpoint—a mud hut. As they did so charges were detonated, giving out clouds of smoke, under cover of which men of the Rhodesian African Rifles, led by Lieutenant R. Griffiths pushed home the infantry attack. A running commentary was supplied by Major Raf Bentley and Captain R.J. (Sam) Putterill. On Monday, 21st August, the prime minister paid a visit to the camp, arriving at Sinoia Aerodrome in a Rapide.

The training exercise was carried out in cooperation with the East African Command, and Lieutenant General Sir Arthur Dowler, General Officer Commanding East African Command. Brigadier Hirsch, military adviser to the British High Command, also attended the manœuvres. During this camp, the SRAF took part in one unscheduled exercise when it was called upon to assist in the evacuation of a patient with a suspected fracture. As *The Herald* commented: "The first stretcher case was evacuated by air this morning, a Rapide being used, and although this was not a serious case, it gave valuable experience in evacuating this type of patient." (*Rhodesia Herald*, 14th Sept. 1949)

Overall, the Southern Rhodesia Staff Corps Air Unit figured largely at this camp.

> *There is a daily service from Salisbury and more often if required, for officials' and troops' mail, while the Rapides are also used for personnel whom it may be necessary to send into town and for evacuation of hospital cases. Small Auster aircraft are also flitting about carrying out*

reconnaissance work in connection with the various schemes and next week's big exercise. The Banshee wail of the siren at the airstrip sounding ten minutes before the aircraft is due to land is, therefore, heard with some frequency. The duty pilot's control car is in touch by wireless with Cranborne and with machines in the air. While this work in connection with Ikwani is going on, the air unit is running its own full-time fortnight of training for the volunteer pilots of the Auxiliary Air Force at Cranborne. (Rhodesia Herald, 15th Sept. 1949)

Battle of Britain commemoration

The anniversary of the Battle of Britain fell during this period and the RAF joined the Southern Rhodesia Staff Corps Air Unit in a display to mark the occasion.

First to arrive soon after 10.30 am were three Southern Rhodesia Ansons* which, swooping down on the brigade parade ground and true to their mission as supply-droppers, proceeded to drop a few light expendable stores as souvenirs of their visit. Aircrews appeared to be using the regimental sergeant major of the Staff Corps, who happened to be in the centre of the parade ground at the time, as an aiming mark, though the items dropped were too light to do any damage. The RSM palpably shocked at such unorthodox goings-on, rallied to the emergency and was heard even above the roar of the engines giving vigorous orders to have the debris cleared immediately. Then the rest of the SR aircraft— Harvards—appeared, and after, in turn, swooping down on the parade ground, the pilots proceeded to give an impressive display of flying round the camp, giving a general impression that Brigade HQ was being attacked by a swarm of giant wasps. In the midst of the excitement, the RAF arrived in double-engined Ansons flying in precise order of four successive flights and in the stateliest fashion over the training area. The whole demonstration was over in 15 minutes after which the aircraft flew off towards Salisbury. (Rhodesia Herald, 16th Sept. 1949)

The entire exercise ended with Operation Lion Cub. This consisted of military manœuvres and a battle in which the air unit took part, acting as spotters and air observers. It was probably the air activity during the training session at Sinoia that prompted the *Rhodesia Herald* to do a follow-up report on the pilot training that was taking place.

A working day, which begins at 5.30 am and a wealth of flying experience is the lot of eleven young pupils who are undergoing training with the SR Air Unit at Cranborne. These young men have been chosen from territorial troops and will have to put in 300 hours or more of flying, as well as many long hours of theoretical instruction before they gain their Wings. They are out at present in full-time training along with the other territorials. Under the command of Lieutenant Colonel E.W.S. Jacklin AFC, the pupil pilots are put through a course of instruction, which will make them the equals of any air force pilots in the world. The air correspondent of the 'Rhodesia Herald' who visited Cranborne, saw pupils receiving instruction on Tiger Moth aircraft while others were at a lecture on engine maintenance and instruments. Throughout the school, there was an atmosphere of eagerness and willingness to learn. One thing, however struck the correspondent forcibly and that was the lack of facilities normally provided for a school of this kind. The air force has 28 aircraft to maintain and this task necessitates over-time work for the majority of the personnel. The instruction too, demands the sacrifice of many hours on the part of instructors and other senior staff members who on an average work a 60-hour week. The men themselves, however, appeared to have no complaints and their main object was the turning out of good pilots with the minimum of wastage of man-hours. In addition to the training section, the SR Air Unit

---

★ One of these Ansons had been a gift to the prime minister from the British government.

at Cranborne is responsible for transport. The training section is under the command of Major K. Taute AFC. The unit at Cranborne is still in need of ground staff and it is hoped that when these vacancies have been filled, the capacity of the school will be so enlarged as to be able to cope with a greater number of pupils next year. (Rhodesia Herald, 21st Sept. 1949)

Meanwhile the Communications Squadron was carrying out its tasks with it usual efficiency. In October, these included a trip outside the Colony to Lourenço Marques (Maputo) carrying the minister on an official visit.

In November, the Southern Rhodesia Auxiliary Air Force staged its first official display at Zomba Air Field in Nyasaland (Malawi). Four Harvards piloted by auxiliary pilots left Salisbury on Saturday morning, 5th November and gave a demonstration in support of a meeting organized by the Nyasaland Branch of the British Empire Service League, to raise funds for Poppy Day. Three of the Harvards, led by Sergeant John Deall, demonstrated various types of formation flying and Major H. Holderness performed aerobatics.

In December 1949, the petrol ration was cut again owing to a deteriorating supply situation, while on the political scene, Sir Godfrey Huggins was working hard to bring about his great dream—federation between the two Rhodesias and Nyasaland. However, the Labour Party was in power in the United Kingdom and its members were strongly opposed to the idea even though the three territories already maintained close links. These included joint participation in Central African Airways and the Hydro-Electric Power Commission as well as common defence arrangements.

As the year 1949 drew to a close, reports were appearing in local newspapers of terrorist incidents in Malaya, including the death by burning of a policeman. These events seemed far removed then, but they were to have a profound effect on Rhodesia's future.

Early in 1950, the air unit received a new recruit, Corporal (later to become Air Commodore) James Pringle ex-RAF and a past member of the RATG. In fact, it was while serving with the RATG that he married an Umtali girl, which accounted for his urgent wish to become a member of the air unit, even at a considerably reduced rank. Remembering his arrival at Cranborne in January 1950, he lists the aircraft as:*

Nine Tiger Moths SR 26, 27, 32, 34, 35, 38, 39, 40, 41 and one Leopard Moth SR 22.
One non-operational Anson Mk I—a wooden job that was so distorted it never flew.
Four operational Ansons SR 21, 29, 30 and 31.
One Harvard Mk IIA SR 42.
Two Dragon Rapide Transports (one ex RANA) SR 23, 24.
One Dakota that had been purchased from South Africa SR 25
and the first of our Air Observation Post aircraft, an Auster J1 that was terribly under-powered.

Subsequently a considerable amount of horse-trading went on with the RAF, to bring about a standardization so that the Rhodesian aircraft would all be Mk IIBs while the RAF had Mk IIAs. During the month of February 1950, the British electorate went to the polls, returning the Labour Party with a very small majority, so small indeed that by the end of March it was down to three, a situation that obviously could not continue for long. However, by bringing halt, maimed and virtually dead members to the house to vote, the Labour government managed to stave off defeat until the latter part of 1951, when a general election held in October returned the Conservatives with a small majority.

Meanwhile in May 1950, during the Rhodesian Budget debate, the Defence Vote was

---

* Also 12 Harvards ex-SAAF bought during 1949.

increased to £925,558. During the debate Mr Stockil said: "No doubt we will have to increase our Defence Vote, but I feel also that Southern Rhodesia can be proud of the active service of her men in the past, which has set an example to the rest of the dominions. One of the main advantages of being a member of the Commonwealth lies in defence. It is inconceivable that if any member of the Commonwealth became involved in any conflict, Southern Rhodesia or any other member of the Commonwealth would not go to her aid. I doubt whether there is any Dominion including Britain herself capable of defending herself alone."

Mr J.W. Keller rose during the debate to complain that the Defence Vote had been increased at the expense of Social Services. The prime minister replied that that was not true, and even if it were, it would not matter. It was a starving of the Defence Vote in the old country that had largely led to the last war. Until the world was more stable, it was necessary to spend money on defence. In fact, he said, it might be necessary to increase the Defence Vote even further. He pointed out that in the Air Wing much improvisation was necessary because of lack of equipment. The country was lucky to have such energetic people. He concluded: "So I hope the Honourable Member for Raylton will allow us to have this modicum of defence here." (*Rhodesia Herald*, 5th May 1950)

The energies of the members of the air unit were made visible early in June when, during King George VI's birthday celebrations, No 1 Squadron SR Auxiliary Air Force was able to put seven Harvards into the air for a flypast.

In June, it was reported that the Australian government was sending a transport squadron to help Britain in her campaign in Malaya. Then abruptly, in the last week of the month, attention shifted dramatically to Korea, where friction between Russian-dominated North Korea and American-sponsored South Korea broke into open warfare on 26th June 1950. The North Koreans launched a dawn attack and by the following day, North Korean troops were entering the South Korean capital, Seoul. The United Nations called for an instant cease-fire and when this call was ignored, a United Nations force was dispatched to aid South Korea. A possible war in the Far East had become a fact.

On the home front, one new member of parliament who had a particular interest in air matters was Mr Ian Douglas Smith (Liberal Party MP, Selukwe), who had been a member of No 237 (Rhodesia) Squadron. Taking part in a debate on subsidies to private flying clubs, Mr Smith said that he could not support the amendment entirely because it might have a detrimental effect on the permanent Air staff. He pointed out that the permanent force was not up to strength, especially as far as numbers of aircraft was concerned, owing to a lack of money. It seemed wrong to ask the government to support what could only be described as a sport, when members of the Auxiliary Air Force needed new aircraft. Any money available should be spent on obtaining Spitfires.

The first nine men to train with the Auxiliary Air Force had completed their training on Tiger Moths and on 29th July, they carried out a cross-country flight from Cranborne to Gatooma. The purpose of the flight was to test their ability to fly an unfamiliar route and carry out a landing at an airfield away from base. All the pilots who trained in their spare time had completed 80 flying hours, which included 40 hours solo, in a little over a year. The cross-country was uneventful, but a large crowd at Gatooma witnessed some rather bouncy landings owing to gusty winds. Later in the day, Sergeant Major Charles Paxton gave an aerobatic display, looping, rolling and executing low-level passes.

No 2 Course SRAAF

The second intake in the Auxiliary Squadron had now begun training. They were D.O. (Des) Anderson, K.A.S. (Ken) Edwards, D.B. (Don) Macaskill, M.J. (Mick) McLaren, W.H. (Billy) Duncan, D.A. (Doug) Bailey, L.A. (Les) Deall, M. (Marshall) Robinson, D. (Des) Peckover and R. (Ray) Fisher. What was only training in Rhodesia had become the real thing in Korea, and despite the fact that 28 countries, including South Africa, had offered aid to the United Nations, the communist north was making rapid gains.

The annual camp at Inkomo

Against this background of mounting world tension, Southern Rhodesia's military forces assembled at Inkomo north of Salisbury, in August for their annual training, and on this occasion the SRAF, which now had 38 serviceable aircraft on its books, played a major part.

> *After the weapon firing display, five Harvard aircraft from Cranborne carried out a low-level bombing attack on armoured cars which, for the purposes of the demonstration, were supposed to be moving towards Inkomo Siding. Flying low, behind the cover of trees, the aircraft attacked the armoured cars. Owing to the nearness of the cadets, live bombs could not be used, but the impression of reality was increased by explosions on the ground around the cars. Smoke poured from the tail of one of the aircraft which, cadets were told over the loudspeaker, had failed to take an elementary precaution. The aircraft plunged towards the earth below the level of the trees. After repeated bombing attacks and the loud explosion of a direct hit, flames and smoke belched from the turrets of two armoured cars. Their mission accomplished, the aircraft left the area.*
> (Rhodesia Herald, Aug. 1950)

This, the biggest peacetime exercise held in Rhodesia to this date, culminated in a five-day battle in which Rhodesian and East African units took part. During this battle, 300 infantrymen attacked a hillside under cover of heavy artillery fire, with air support provided by the Harvards of No 1 Squadron SRAF. Spectators included Major General Sir Arthur Dowler, General Officer Commanding East Africa, Sir John Kennedy and Sir Godfrey Huggins who had flown from Bulawayo to the camp airstrip in an SRAF Anson. At the end of the exercise, a ceremonial parade was held at Inkomo during which six Harvards flew low over the saluting base.

By the end of September, the tide had turned in Korea and the United Nations troops were advancing on Seoul, which was recaptured after bitter street fighting on 26th September. Optimists were reporting that the Korean War was all over bar the shouting as the United Nations forces approached the 38th Parallel, the border between North and South Korea. The question was, would the United Nations force stop at the border, or would it continue north into North Korea. China issued a warning, that she would consider any attack on North Korea as wanton aggression. The South Koreans disregarded this warning, and, crossing the border, seized a town 30 miles (48km) north of the 38th Parallel, while the American General MacArthur demanded the surrender of North Korea.

By the middle of October, the North Koreans were battling to hold their capital city, while a United Nations paratroop force of over 4,000 men had been dropped to trap fleeing North Koreans. The United Nations forces reached the Manchurian border on 27th October, and then the Chinese army joined the battle. The United Nations force found itself facing 60,000 Chinese soldiers. Within days, the pattern reversed and the United Nations army was in full retreat, with the eastern flank having been turned, bringing the Chinese and North Koreans into a position where they could encircle the United Nations force. By 6th December, the trap was closing on 20,000 United Nations troops.

In Southern Rhodesia, Sir Godfrey Huggins announced that a military force was to be raised for service in the Far East: "We have offered the UK a token force for the Far East and this has been accepted. The men were to be volunteers and unmarried and they were to serve with the Special Air Service not in Korea but in Malaya where the fight against the guerrillas continued unabated."

The photographic unit

It was during this year, 1950, that an important and largely unnoticed new section of the air force came into being. This was the photographic unit, which was established at Cranborne and housed in a single large room next to the aircrew living quarters. Conditions were primitive to say the least. The nearest running water was an outside tap some 30 metres away, from which water was collected in buckets. The whole section was converted into a darkroom by the simple action of switching off the light. However, according to one early photographer:

> *There were so many cracks in the ceiling and window frames that it was never really black— ideally suited to photographers who were afraid of the dark! In spite of the problems, many square miles of photographic cover were flown and supplied to various government departments using the Harvard and Rapide aircraft.*

Processing the film, which was 165 feet in length and nine and a half inches wide, was quite an adventure:

> *After posting a large 'Keep Out' sign on the door, the photographers hurried the film through the developing process before it became affected by the extraneous lighting. Final film washing was carried out under the hydrant behind the Fire Section before the film was placed on the huge darkroom drying drum, five feet (1,5m) in diameter and eight feet (2,4m) long, which occupied a large percentage of the floor space.*

Other activities carried out by the photographic section included the production of ciné-gun training films, defect report photography, photographs for boards of inquiry, and pictures for service history and publicity displays.

The Southern Rhodesia Air Force

The photographic unit was just one part of the growing activities of the young air force and just before Christmas 1950 came recognition of the force's increasing importance when it was announced that the title Southern Rhodesia Air Force would be used in future for the regular military air service. This was to supersede the title Southern Rhodesia Staff Corps, Air Unit, which had been used until that time.

CHAPTER 26

The halcyon days

It was the year 1951. On the world front, news from Korea continued grim, with the United Nations forces falling back to a point south of Seoul and the Chinese advance continuing at an ever-increasing pace. In Southern Rhodesia, all men between the ages of 19 and 39 were required to register for service. Despite all her efforts, the country was not in a position, early in 1951, to provide an air force squadron but she could make ground forces available and on 12th March, a contingent of 100 young volunteers left for the Far East to serve in Malaya.

Late in 1950, an Air Agreement was concluded between the United Kingdom and Southern Rhodesia, under which Britain contracted to sell 22 Spitfires to the SRAF at a cost of £12,000 for the aircraft and £8,000 for spare parts. The aircraft were to be ready for collection in February 1951. Announcing news of this agreement, the prime minister said that he was confident that within two years Rhodesia would have sufficient trained pilots to make a useful contribution to Commonwealth defence.

Plans were also afoot to change the Auxiliary Flying Training Scheme into a Short Service full-time course. It was suggested that the Auxiliary scheme should continue, until the pilots then under training were fully qualified, at which time the Auxiliary scheme would cease. Meanwhile a full-time training scheme would be started for men in the age group 17 – 20, with pupils reaching operational standard in two years. The first course, with 15 cadets, was scheduled to begin in September 1951.

It soon became obvious that there was not going to be a place in the Southern Rhodesia Air Force Short Service scheme for all the young men who wished to fly. A further agreement was, therefore, drawn up between the Southern Rhodesian government and the Air Ministry in London under which suitable young Rhodesians between the ages of 17 and 26 could train as aircrew with the RAF, thus continuing the close association that had been established during World War II.

With the increase in flying training, more ground personnel were also needed and the government set about actively encouraging members of the Coloured community to enlist. Archie Wilson remarks that only one application was received, as far as he could recall. The mess that was built at New Sarum and earmarked for the Coloured intake, became a mess for corporals and airmen. It seemed that the Coloured community was suspicious of government's intentions. As Archie adds, Sad but there you are!

The area around the military airfield at Cranborne was becoming more built-up making it increasingly unsuitable for flying training. Obviously another site had to be found for a military aerodrome. The government had been negotiating the purchase of a farm named Woodvale near Bulawayo with the aim of constructing a civil aerodrome on the site. It was now decided to utilize this site as a military station for training the two-year air force men.

First Spitfire ferry

In February 1951, a party of 15 airmen and eight ground crew travelled to England to collect the first eleven Spitfires. The total number of regular pilots serving with the SRAF was fewer than 20 so some members of the Southern Rhodesia Auxiliary Air Force were needed to join the ferry team so that a nucleus of staff could be left behind to carry on with pilot training and transport flying.

The composition of the ferry team was:

Dakota crew

Captain	*Harold Hawkins*
Co-Pilot	*John Moss*
Flight Engineer	*Newland-Nell*
Navigator	*Alan Atherton*
Radio Operator	*W.J. Jenkins (on loan from the army)*

Technical team

Captain	*Mick Gibbons*
Warrant Officers	*Titch Nesbitt*
	Pat Patrick
	Cyril Jones
	Frank Burton
	Charlie Goodwin

Spitfire pilots

Regular
Ted Jacklin
Jock Barber
Bobby Blair
John Deall
John Hough
Charles Paxton
Mike Schumann

Auxiliary
Dave Barbour
Ben Bellingan
Dicky Bradshaw
Jack Malloch
Ossie Penton
Basil Hone

Lieutenant Colonel E.W.S. Jacklin was in command of the flight, which was expected to take about a fortnight, though there were sceptics in the RAF who considered that the SRAF pilots would be lucky to get six out of the eleven machines safely back to Rhodesia.

Captain M.H. Gibbons was in command of the ground staff servicing the Spitfires during their long flight. These nine men, without whose hard work and dedication the flight would not have been possible, were given a maintenance course while they were in the United Kingdom. The pilots, some of whom had flown Spitfires operationally during the Second World War, completed a minimum of six hours flying in the Spitfires. Incidentally, while the pilots were in the United Kingdom, they were also given the opportunity to try their hand at flying the new Meteor jet fighter.

One of the pilots on this ferry was Sergeant John Deall DSO, DFC who had commanded

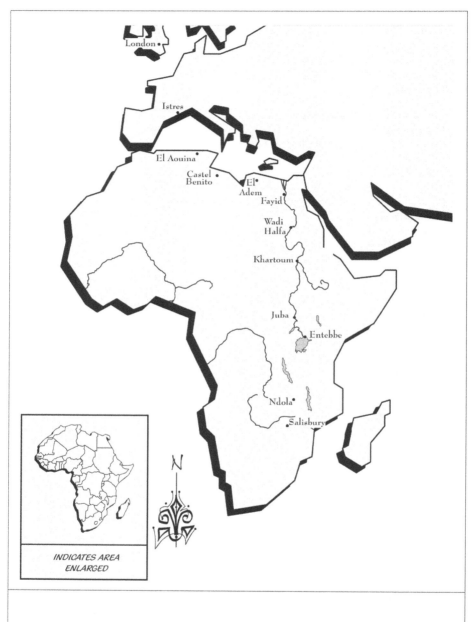

London

Istres

El Aouina

Castel
Benito

El
Adem

Fayid

Wadi
Halfa

Khartoum

Juba

Entebbe

Ndola

Salisbury

N

INDICATES AREA
ENLARGED

FIRST SPITFIRE FERRY

No 266 (Rhodesia) Squadron and had risen to the rank of wing commander before being demobbed. When he enlisted in the SRAF, it was as a sergeant, although he was given the rank of acting warrant officer for the flight to the United Kingdom. Deall tells the story that one day he was having a drink in a London pub, when he noticed a man looking curiously at his medal ribbons and badges of rank. Eventually, the man approached Sergeant Deall, obviously unable to contain his curiosity any longer: "I say old boy, you must have made a black!" Towards the middle of March the *Rhodesia Herald* reported on the new aircraft:

In the Spitfire Mk 22, Southern Rhodesia will have a machine that, though out-dated by the latest jet aircraft, is capable of more than 400 mph (640 km/h), and is ideally adapted to its role of ground attack. The Spitfires flying to Southern Rhodesia are powered by Rolls-Royce Griffon engines and equipped with 4 x 20mm Hispano guns. Rocket-firing equipment will be added in Rhodesia. The planes fitted with supplementary petrol tanks to extend their limited cruising range will fly to Rhodesia via France, Tunis, Egypt, the Sudan and East Africa. (Rhodesia Herald)

It was Wednesday 14th March, when the Spitfires took off from the RAF base at Chivenor in Devon on the first leg of the 6,500-mile (10,450-km) delivery flight. Their route was to take them via Istres, in the south of France, El Alouina, Castel Benito, El Adem, Fayid (in the Canal Zone), Wadi Halfa, Khartoum, Juba, Entebbe and Ndola. It was probably the most ambitious flight schedule ever laid down for and adhered to by a squadron of Spitfires. The longest hop of the journey was the 645 nautical miles (1,196km) from Khartoum to Juba. Two night landings were made, one at Castel Benito and the other in the Canal Zone in Egypt.

Ten of the eleven Spitfires reached Salisbury without mishap, landing on 22nd March, just nine days after leaving Devon. One aircraft had technical problems. The pilot, Ossie Penton, left Juba with the formation but soon after take-off, the aircraft developed a leak in one of its glycol glands, which then burst. Loss of this cooling agent could have caused the engine to seize. An SRAF officer remarked: "Lieutenant Penton did a fine job getting the Spit down without mishap. John Deall together with technicians and spare parts were flown to Juba in an SRAF Dakota piloted by Archie Wilson. They put the Spit in order and John Deall flew it back to Salisbury, with the Dakota in attendance, landing safely on 7th April."

The arrival of the main force of Spitfires caused a great deal of excitement in Salisbury.

Hundreds of people gathered at Cranborne Aerodrome yesterday morning to watch Southern Rhodesia's first Spitfire squadron land after its flight from England. Wives, parents and friends of the pilots and technical staff stood and sat in little groups round the tarmac, listening to the Spitfires' wireless messages which were relayed by loud speaker from the aerodrome tower. As the time of arrival neared, the waiting crowd heard the voice of the wireless operator calling: "Cranborne tower to Red Leader, what is your approximate position and ETA?" After a crackle, a clear voice from the Spitfires replied: "We are over the Umvukwes Range of mountains. Our ETA is 9.55." An expectant murmur ran through the crowd as further messages showed the progress of the Spits. The voice from the squadron said: "We are over Inkomo" and a few minutes later: "Crossing Mount Hampden now." Soon after that message, the drone of the aircraft turned all heads upwards towards the grey, cloudy sky. The Spits had arrived. In close formation, the ten aircraft roared over the aerodrome at 300 miles per hour (480 km/h). Four Spits in the lead were followed by two flights of three. They split up after they had crossed the aerodrome and circled out of view before landing. First to touch down was the Spitfire flown by the commanding officer of the SRAF, Lieutenant Colonel E.W.S. Jacklin. He taxied his aircraft across the tarmac to the spot where Sir Godfrey Huggins and Brigadier S. Garlake were waiting to receive the pilots. The other aircraft touched down at short intervals afterwards and lined up with the leading Spitfire on the tarmac as relatives and friends moved forward to greet the pilots. (Rhodesia Herald, 23rd March 1951)

Speaking to a reporter from the *Rhodesia Herald* Ted Jacklin said: We had a good trip but it was very tiring. Still, we have done it in nine days including two non-flying days. And we arrived with more than 90% of the squadron. He paid tribute to the technical and ground staff who accompanied the Spitfires in a Dakota. The Dakota was always there when we wanted it. There was a lot of maintenance work to do and the engineers did a really first-class job. It is difficult to work out our average flying speed for the whole flight but it would be somewhere in the region of 200 mph (320 km/h). We have flown all the machines at more than 400 mph (640 km/h) but on this trip we had to fly as economically as possible. Jacklin said that all the pilots had flown jet fighters while they were in England and had found them easy—easier than the Spits in fact.

After greeting the pilots, the prime minister congratulated them: I must thank you for putting up such a fine show. The RAF said you would be lucky if you managed to bring six Spits to Salisbury and that if you brought eight here it would be a miracle. You have brought ten, which indicates what a very high standard you have achieved. This result has been due to the skill of both pilots and engineering staff. He remarked that the auxiliary pilots were particularly deserving. (Photo *Rhodesia Herald*, 23rd March 1951) When the eleventh Spitfire arrived safely on 7th April, it made the ferry 100% successful and Ted Jacklin received a cable from the Rolls-Royce Company: "Heartiest congratulations on a magnificent flight!"

Provision made for two SRAF squadrons to be created

The new session of parliament opened on 10th April 1951 and one of the first pieces of business to be dealt with, was the second reading of the Defence Amendment Bill. Part one embodied legislation, which had been on the statute books since June 28th 1940 and covered the relationship of Southern Rhodesian forces with visiting military and air force personnel. The second part of the bill allowed for a programme of military training, the expansion of the territorial forces and the extension of training for territorials to rural areas for the first time. Previously only men between the ages of 18 and 22, living in the towns had been liable for this training. The bill also provided for call-up of men between the ages of 41 and 60 in times of emergency. Clause 18 covered the establishment of the new air force, and regulations for the control of the new force were gazetted on Friday 20th April 1951. It was proposed that Southern Rhodesia would have two fully operational squadrons within two years.

During the committee stage of the Defence Act came the first recorded suggestion that helicopters should be acquired for use in Southern Rhodesia. The suggestion came from the prime minister in reply to a question from Mr P.A. Wise (Liberal member for Hartley) about the establishment of a Yeomanry. The prime minister said he favoured helicopters for internal defence but that at this stage costs and numbers had not been considered—It was merely a suggestion.

The Budget brought no shocks. The Defence Vote was up to £744,936 of which the largest single item was the addition of £303,000 for the SRAF to enable two fighter squadrons to be formed and maintained.It had been decided to proceed with the construction of a national airport at Kentucky, a farm south of Salisbury, where it was hoped to accommodate the two Spitfire squadrons early in 1952. A sum of £350,000 was provided on revenue votes for the construction of military buildings at Kentucky, while a further £77,000 was made available to the Public Works Department for military buildings elsewhere in the Colony.

When the House considered the Defence Vote of £1,697.494, Mr Dendy Young, referring to the £45,100 for the SRAF said he understood that the United Kingdom was converting its fighter command to jet aircraft. In view of this situation, he wanted to know whether the Spitfires the government had purchased had been acquired at a reasonable price. Mr Hackwill said the officer commanding, and the pilots who brought the Spitfires from England should be congratulated on the short time they had taken and the fact that the planes had been delivered safely. He went on to say that he had been told that a committee was going into the question of air force salaries. He wanted to know whether the committee had completed its work and if so, what the committee's recommendation was.

Donald MacIntyre said he was concerned about the enormous increase in the Defence Vote and queried its justification. The Prime Minister, in his reply, said that the reason for the added expense was that this department also met civil requirements: "A certain amount of stockpiling is going on. The question of whether a reasonable price has been paid for the Spitfires the country has acquired, was a matter of individual opinion. I told the house at the last session, that we are getting these Spitfires at a reasonable price. I am not at liberty to say the price, as there are other people in the world interested in getting them." He went on to point out that conversion from Spitfires to jet fighters was a relatively simple matter compared with conversion from a Harvard where a lengthy training period was required. Finally, he stated that the committee examining air force salaries was still busy and its recommendations were not yet to hand.

On the wider scene, a conference had been held in London in March, to consider closer ties among the three central African territories of Northern and Southern Rhodesia and Nyasaland. This conference had recommended federation. Meanwhile, Southern Rhodesia was involved in the East African Defence system and the Minister for Mines and Transport, Mr G.A. Davenport, representing Southern Rhodesia at a meeting held in Nairobi in August, promised speedy and efficient transport of military forces and material should the need arise.

News from the Korean War improved a little as the year progressed. Having been nearly driven from the southern-most beaches by the Chinese, the United Nations forces fought back and by 29th March 1951, United Nations troops had retaken Seoul and were clearing the road north, in their advance towards the 38th Parallel. That line was crossed on 4th April, a victory that was succeeded by the shattering news that General McArthur had been relieved of his command. A new communist offensive followed during which, despite a gallant stand by 29th Brigade, the United Nations forces were thrown back across the 38th Parallel. Once again, towards the end of May, the tide turned, and the United Nations forces began advancing on all fronts. At the United Nations, Soviet delegates proposed a cease-fire and talks about ending the Korean War had begun towards the end of July 1951.

Meanwhile at the end of May,* a Government Notice was published giving details of the Short Service Unit: "The unit will be known as the Southern Rhodesia Air Force (Short Service Unit). Men wishing to take service in this unit must be between the ages of 17 and 21, unmarried, British subjects, and must serve eight years with the SRAF Reserve."

SRAF and SRAAF air display

On 7th June, the SRAF and the SR Auxiliary Squadron staged their first air display at Cranborne Air Station before a crowd of more than 20,000 excited spectators.

For more than two hours, streams of cars converged on Cranborne and by 3.45 pm when the flying events were scheduled to begin, the four car parks were packed to capacity, and the 900 yard (823m) tarmac frontage was thronged with spectators. The aim of the display was to demonstrate the flying ability of the air force and to show off the different types of aircraft. During the afternoon,

---

★ One Tiger Moth SR 39 piloted by Doug Bailey was written off on 3rd May 1951 but the pilot survived.

the crowd watched enthralled as the pilots performed aerobatics, formation flying, flew Spitfires in mock attack on a ground target, and carried out an air race. Static displays had also been set up in two hangars. Two stripped-down engines lay on their specially constructed 'test-beds' revealing to the layman a bewildering array of pistons, crankshafts, carburettors, cogs and valves. In the other hangar, items on show included instruments, a parachute, stripped-down airframes, a miniature wind tunnel and general 'flying paraphernalia'. While outside, lined up on the tarmac stood examples of the different types of aircraft then in use by the air force. Pride of place had been given to one of the newly arrived Spitfires, which was surrounded by hordes of small boys who examined every rivet with consummate interest. The air display proper began with a flypast of four Tiger Moths, three Austers, two Ansons, a Rapide, three Harvards, a Dakota and three Spitfires. This was followed by a 'slow' flying race between three Austers, to illustrate how slowly it was possible to fly this type of aircraft that was used extensively for air observation work. The Austers, in fact, made their way across the airfield at the sedate pace of about 20 mph (32 km/h) ground speed. Four Tiger Moths then gave a display of aerobatics and formation flying. As they landed, three Spitfires (piloted by regular air force men) and three Harvards (piloted by Auxiliary Squadron pupils) took off and demonstrated standard formation drill. An exhibition of formation and solo aerobatics was given by the Harvards and two Spitfires and then came the highlight of the afternoon: a demonstration ground-attack by six Spitfires on a dummy tank. A lone Harvard flew in to attack the Spitfires, a dogfight ensued and the Harvard was 'shot down' most realistically. The grand finale was an air race between an Auster, a Rapide, an Anson, a Harvard, a Dakota and a Spitfire. Although heavily handicapped, the Spitfire reached the finishing post well ahead of the others. No doubt the excitement of this afternoon filled many small boys' heads with dreams of being a pilot. (Rhodesia Herald, 8th June 1951)

Following their success in Salisbury, SRAF pilots gave a display at the Karoi Flying Club on 11th August, it unfortunately drew only 250 spectators, probably owing to the petrol shortage.

Perhaps the most spectacular part of the show was the formation loops by three Harvards. These aircraft kept perfect alignment throughout two consecutive loops. Then there was a 'dead-stick' landing by a Tiger Moth. From 1,000 feet its pilot-instructor brought the Moth down into a perfect landing, which brought further murmurs of admiration from veteran pilots on the airstrip. A Dakota feathered one engine and was demonstrating to spectators the art of flying on only one motor when there came an unintentional hitch: the pilot was not able to unfeather the propeller. It made no difference, however, for as the announcer, Captain H. Hawkins stated: "You will now see how easy it is to land on one engine." One Spitfire had engine trouble but the other delighted spectators with its speed-runs across the airfield.
(Rhodesia Herald, 13th Aug. 1951)

The following weekend it was the turn of Gatooma, where 2,000 people attended the Saturday afternoon display. This occasion marked the end of a year's training for the pupil pilots of the second Auxiliary intake who flew their first cross-country from Salisbury to Gatooma in ten Tiger Moths. A newsletter had been started with the aim of keeping the Rhodesians serving in Malaya in touch with home. Occasionally these letters shed light on the off-duty activities of the airmen. For example in the newsletter dated 28th August 1951:

The SRAF have decided to run their own baseball team. A tender has been put out for a ton of chewing gum. The name of the team has not yet been decided but I've heard the words 'Makabusi Braves' mentioned.

The later career of this team seems obscure.

First Short Service Course

The end of the first year's flying for the second intake of Auxiliary pilots marked the beginning of the first Short Service Course, on Saturday 1st September 1951. Fifteen young men reported at King George V1 Barracks in Salisbury for training. Their names were:

Keith Kemsley	Basil Myburgh	Arthur Hodgson
John Mussell	John Rogers	Brian Horney
Bob d'Hotman	Clive Wilcox	John Cameron
Dave Harvey	Nigel Bridges	Ray Reed
Peter Piggott	Alan Murray Hudson	Ralph Weeks

The course, which is the first of its kind in Central Africa, will last two years and at the end of that time successful trainees will be qualified pilots. t present, they will be accommodated at King George V1 Barracks until the SRAF moves to Kentucky early next year. Their ground training and flying, however, will be done at Cranborne. Training starts on Monday 3rd September 1951. (Rhodesia Herald, 1st Sept. 1951)

Once again annual training time had come round and Lieutenant General Sir Arthur Dowler, General Officer Commanding East Africa was a guest. "I hope very much that we shall have some Rhodesian representatives in our brigade training in East Africa in February and March next year and I know if it takes the form of an SRAF Squadron it will be very much liked!" he said in his address.

Meanwhile delegates had gathered at Victoria Falls for yet another conference on federation. The meeting opened on 18th September and lasted for three days and then adjourned until the following year. It appeared that while most of the white delegates were in favour, the black representatives were mostly against the idea.

No 1 Course SRAAF are awarded their Wings

27th September 1951 was a memorable day for the SRAF. For the first time since the end of the war, men trained by the SRAF were awarded their Wings. The ceremony took place at Cranborne Aerodrome. These were the men of No 1 Course of the SR Auxiliary Air Force:

Owen Love	Dennis Bagnall	John Bridger
Bill Smith	Colin Graves	Peter Potter
Gordon Merrington	Bruce Mackenzie	Gordon Rowley

When the prime minister, who was accompanied by Lady Huggins, arrived at the aerodrome, the pilots were in the air. They flew past in eight Harvards followed by a single Auster in which Cadet Merrington had trained as an air observer pilot for the Southern Rhodesia Artillery. He was the first air observer pilot to be trained and awarded his Wings with the SRAF. After the flypast, the Harvards split into two flights and crossed the aerodrome in line astern. They then went into shallow dives and performed a Chandelle; a manœuvre in which each aircraft in turn peels off and pulls up vertically.

Veteran SRAF and SRAAF pilots who had come to watch the ceremony were surprised at the high standard of aircraft handling shown by these cadets who had only two years part-time flying experience. The Harvards and the Auster landed, forming the third side of an open square of aircraft with Tiger Moths and Spitfires flanking the cadets' planes. Each of the cadets, who were wearing white flying overalls, stood in front of his aircraft and then marched to the centre of the tarmac. Behind them were men of the SRAAF No 2 Course and the No 1 Short Service Course. (Rhodesia Herald, 28th Sept 1951)

The pilots were inspected by Sir Godfrey Huggins, accompanied by Brigadier S. Garlake.

SSU pilots go solo

With full-time training now in operation, it wasn't long before the first pilot of the Short Service Course went solo. An event reported in the *Rhodesia Herald* on 30th October 1951: "He is Officer Cadet Keith Kemsley, who yesterday earned the distinction and a ducking, by being the first cadet of the SRAF Short Service Commission Course to fly solo. He soloed in the morning and swam in the afternoon. These men started their training nearly two months ago and began flying training three weeks ago. Cadet Kemsley soloed after eight hours, 55 minutes' flying." (*Rhodesia Herald*, 30th Oct. 1951)

Commenting on the young pilots, Chief Flying Instructor, Archie Wilson, said: "They are all progressing quite well and are good material." The training programme started with a month's general service training—and lectures in elementary aerodynamics in preparation for flying. Then the cadets began their flying training on Tiger Moths, converting to Harvards for more advanced training after the first six months. On completion of 120 hours flying time in Harvards, they would qualify for their Wings. Although Keith Kemsley had been the first to fly solo, it was Officer Cadet John Mussell who flew solo with the least number of flying hours to his credit. When he first took an aircraft up alone, he had completed only seven and a half hours flying time. During the second year of service, it was planned to post the pilots to other squadrons and allow them to convert to Spitfires. These men were to form the nucleus of the first ground attack squadron of the SRAF.

Later in the month, the SRAF lost an aircraft. It happened on 21st November when an Auster SR 55 piloted by Lieutenant W.J. (Budge) Henson crashed in thick bush near St Mary's Mission in the Prince Edward Dam area, now known as Seke, south of Salisbury. Lieutenant Henson, shaken but unhurt, walked four miles (6km) to the mission for help. The aircraft was badly damaged, part of the undercarriage being ripped off in the landing and both wings smashed. An eyewitness said that the plane circled the area so low that it brushed the top of a tall tree and then disappeared. A few seconds later she heard a crash and saw dust rising. When she arrived at the scene the pilot had climbed out of the wrecked aircraft, and she showed him the way to the mission.

December's News Letter to the Rhodesians in Malaya reported that all the short-service cadets except two had now gone solo. The first and last pilots to solo, had been thrown into Salisbury swimming bath in all their clothes: "This is evidently a very necessary propitiation to the gods of aviators." It contained the news that Kentucky had received some Harvards and Spits for housing and had also got its first batch of living-in personnel safely housed in one of the completed billet blocks.

Also that, "A great deal of interest and some yearning was aroused in the hearts of our flying staff when four Vampires and a Mosquito landed in Salisbury recently. They unfortunately also took off again leaving us with slight feelings of contempt for our feeble piston-driven ships." (Newsletter to Malaya S 815) In fact, the SRAF had been using Kentucky since mid-October because, although the facilities were not yet complete, there was more space and less likelihood of taking the top off a tall building.

Second Spitfire ferry

Eleven Spitfires had been ferried to Southern Rhodesia earlier in the year; now a further eleven were ready for collection. The ferry pilots were:

Regular Pilots

Lieutenants	Bobby Blair
	Ted Cunnison
	Bill Smith
Sergeant	Ossie Penton

Auxiliary Pilots

Lieutenants	John Campbell
	Alan O'Hara
	Peter Pascoe
	Dave Richards
	Ray Wood
Sergeant*	Owen Love

They left Cranborne on 9th November 1951 in a Dakota piloted once more by Captain Harold Hawkins. While they were in the United Kingdom, they attended a RAF Central Fighter Establishment and were given the chance to fly Meteor jet fighters. The technical personnel took brief engine magneto and propeller courses, while the pilots went to Abingdon where they each completed six hours' flying time in Spitfires.

The Spitfires, accompanied by the Dakota carrying spares and technicians, had been due to leave on 6th December but did not get away until the following day owing to winter weather over western Europe. In fact, the weather was not good for most of the trip. Fifteen miles (24km) from Beauvais, the Spitfires flew into cloud and Owen Love encountered difficulties. Few pilots on the ferry were current on instrument flying or night flying. Love apparently lost contact with the formation and had to convert onto instruments, an extremely difficult operation when disoriented. His aircraft crashed in a field and he was killed. He was buried with military honours in the village of St Marguerite des Logos in the Calvados district of France on Friday 14th December 1951. His grave lies next to that of his brother, Flight Sergeant Wilfred Royce Love, who was killed in France during the Second World War while serving with No 266 (Rhodesia) Squadron. A padre from the British Embassy in Paris took the service and there was a firing party from the French air force.

This, the first fatal accident since the war, delayed the rest of the flight and they only reached El Aouina on Sunday 9th December and Fayid on 10th December. More trouble occurred on 16th December when another of the Spitfires flown by Dave Richards crashed on landing at Entebbe in Uganda and was fairly extensively damaged. The pilot, however, was unhurt. The remaining Spitfires and the accompanying Dakota proceeded on their way bringing the pilot of the crashed machine. At Tabora, in Tanganyika, which they reached on 17th December, they were once more delayed—this time by a waterlogged airfield.

Between Tabora and Kasama, the Spitfires provided an impromptu fighter escort for a CAA Viking on a flight from Nairobi to Salisbury. No doubt the Viking pilot, Captain P.B.G. Davies DFC, got a special thrill because he had flown Spitfires during the Battle of Britain.

The bad luck, which had dogged this flight, continued to the bitter end. The Spitfires were unable to land at Ndola, on the night of 18th December, because the runway was waterlogged and so they continued to Lusaka. On the final landing in Salisbury next day, There was one

---

* Change in rank was due to the fact that he had left the SRAAF and joined the regular force.

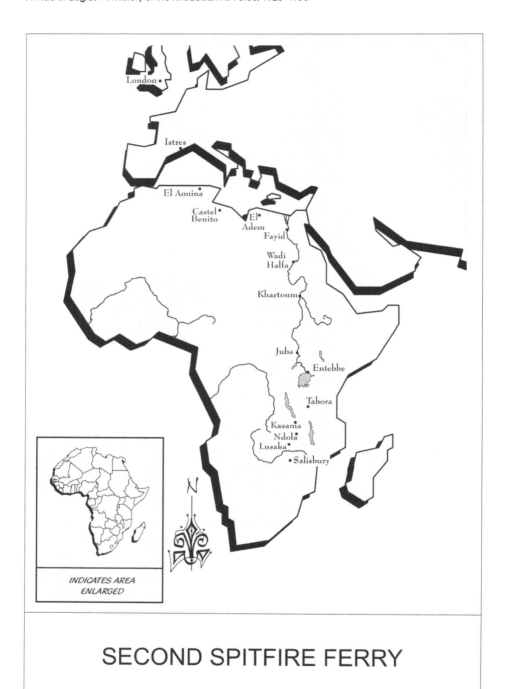

London

Istres

El Aouina

Castel Benito

El Adem

Fayid

Wadi Halfa

Khartoum

Juba

Entebbe

Tabora

Kasama

Ndola

Lusaka

Salisbury

INDICATES AREA ENLARGED

SECOND SPITFIRE FERRY

mishap. The tail wheel of one Spitfire failed to lower into position. But despite the fact that the machine had come in to land at about 100 mph (160 km/h), the pilot kept it under control and stopped the machine before any serious damage was caused.

James Pringle, the engineering officer accompanying the ferries in the Dakota remembers:

It was a splendid job. We were flying to the limit; if anything went wrong, faulty navigation, diversion, bad weather, we had no reserve. There was precious little fuel left on each leg. And you have no idea what those cockpits were like, because we had to carry our Mae Wests, shooting irons, and the whole of our survival paraphernalia as well as our flying helmets. It was bloody uncomfortable. On the second ferry, it was a no-go on the first attempt to get across the Channel. The weather was very much against us. We ran into icy conditions with the escorting Dakota and we had problems starting the aircraft in Istres in southern France. Landing at Tunis, we had a most expensive night stop in what had been Field Marshall Rommel's headquarters, now a very attractive hotel. These Spitfires had not had their first major service. The cycle, if I remember correctly, was in the order of 800 hours between services and not one of these aircraft had more than 50 or 60 flying hours. They had been in hangars because the RAF had switched to jets.

Speaking about the trip, Harold Hawkins said: The RAF were first rate. They gave us excellent service including meals, accommodation and flying rations. At Tunis, Marseilles and Dijon there were RAF liaison officers who gave us assistance in conjunction with the French air force who were also very helpful. He paid tribute to the SRAF ground crew who on two occasions worked right through the night to make certain the Spitfires would be ready to fly the following day. His final word of praise was for the Dakota. We did not even touch it with a screwdriver. Just filled it up with petrol and it went.

Meanwhile in the same month, December 1951, the first postwar course left to attend the RAF School of Technical Training at Halton. This course started in January 1952. The apprenticeship was three years. The apprentices were: F.J. (Johnny) Gent who attended the Radio School at Locking, Geoff P. Proudfoot, eventually to become a squadron leader, Rob Schley also retired as a squadron leader, J.G. (Chinky) Stewart, Danny van der Merwe and B. Wallace who did not complete the course.

Report of the commander military forces for the year ended 31st December 1951*

    Technical Wing

(i)   *Technical Headquarters*
        Technical Records
        Technical Training Staff
        Airframe Repair Section
        Stressed Skin Section
        Carpenters' Shop
        Engine Repair Section
        Spitfire Squadron
        Electrical Section
        Instrument Section
    Radio Section
    Fire Section
    Machine Shops

---

* It is of interest to note the increase in the size of the technical wing, which was necessitated by the arrival of extra aircraft and the training of the short service men.

Metal and Welding Shop.

(ii) In order to maintain the increase in aircraft, Technical manpower was increased during 1951 by 23 tradesmen and as a long-term policy, recruits were attested and seconded for three years to the Royal Air Force in the United Kingdom for training as technicians.

(iii) Maximum technical effort has been curtailed to a certain extent by technical staff having to undertake various extraneous duties. An example of this was the necessity of six tradesmen having to accompany each of the two Spitfire ferries, which resulted in six men being non-effective for a period of approximately four and a half months. The transportation of equipment to the New Salisbury Airport and the carrying out of five road convoy trips under conditions of self help, in order to uplift stores from Royal Air Force sources in the Colony, are further examples of tasks that this section had to carry out.

Schedule of aircraft fleet state during the year 1951

Type of Aircraft	Strength on 1st January 1951	Acquired	Struck off	Strength on 31st December 1951
Anson 12 VIP	1			1
Anson 19	3			3
Auster J1 and J5	5		1	4
Dakota DC-3	1			1
Harvard, Mk II and IIA	11	4(IIB)		15
Leopard Moth	1			1
Rapide DH89A	3			3
Spitfire, Mk 22		20		20
Tiger Moth DH82A	11		2	9
Total	**36**	**24**	**3**	**57**

No 1 Course Southern Rhodesia Auxiliary Air Force

No 1 Squadron SRAAF formed July 1949
Commenced Training: July 1949
Wings: 27th September 1951

Dennis A. Bagnall	Continued in his civil employment.
I.J.S. Bridger	Unknown
Colin D. Graves	Later joined the regular force. Killed in a Vampire flying accident.
Owen M. Love	Killed on the second Spitfire ferry. Buried in France.
J.B. (Bruce) Mackenzie	Served in the Royal Navy, then the Southern Rhodesia Staff Corps before joining the air force. Continued in civil employment.
Gordon J. Merrington	Southern Rhodesia Artillery Territorial Force Air Observation pilot. Continued in his civil employment.
Peter E. Potter	Continued in his civil employment.
Gordon E. Rowley	Continued in his civil employment.
W.H. (Bill) Smith	Later joined the regular force. Retired as wing commander.

Wg Cdr Eric Smith DFC (commanding officer).

P/O Peter Pistorius

F/O Jack Harrison (equipment officer).

P/O Joe Brander (cypher officer).

P/O Doug Coulson.

Flt Lt Sandy McIntyre.

P/O Ian Smith, later to become Southern Rhodesian Prime Minister.

F/O Brian White. Many young men gave their lives in WWII.

Brian White's simple desert grave.

The stark remains of F/O Brian White's Hurricane after he had been shot down in flames.

The funeral of P/O Boyer at the British cemetery at Geneifa in February 1943.

The firing party at Boyer's funeral.

German aircrew relax in the sun by their Bf110. Desert air warfare held little romance—both men and machines faced grim and wearying conditions.

No 237 Squadron at Idku, Egypt, 1943. From left, standing: F/O Polly Payne, Flt Lt D.P. Howat (Adj), Flt Lt P.H.C. Theodosiou, Flt Lt Basil Deall, P/O Roy Gray, Flt Lt Lynn Hurst, Sqn Ldr John Walmisley (CO), Lt Col J. de L. Thompson, F/O Paul Fick, Sgt J.H. McDermott, P/O George Millar, F/O Ipsen, F/O Bob Moubray, P/O Dinks Moubray, P/O A. Coulson. Front row: P/O Geoff Rapkin (KOAS), Flt Lt J.E.S. Harrison, Flt Lt Taffy Williams, F/O Boy Crook, P/O Tore Rickland (KIA), F/O Ronnie Napier, P/O Derek Hallas, P/O Allan Smith.

When they briefed us that we were going do a 'sweep', I didn't really think they meant it ... A Borland twin enjoying a mundane activity.

Below: KM-J arrives back with fewer aircraft before take-off. The Lancaster could survive a fair amount of flak.

Briefed to *go right in* when pursuing an enemy aircraft, 22-year-old Rhodesian Flight Sergeant Derek Erasmus shoots down an FW 190 over Brest, recorded by his ciné-camera-gun. *Four of them dived on us. We turned into them and a general dogfight ensued. I had him nicely in my sights and I went right in pressing the button all the way. He blew up just in front of my nose.*

Left: 'Q' Queenie is caught in the lens of a professional.

After I had been pulled out of the 'drink' and flown to the 'drome, is the scribble on the back of the photograph. Norham Lucas was picked up by a Walrus, 33 miles south of the Lizard. German cyphers would have had a time decoding that one.

Winter in Harrowbeer. John Deall is under the map.

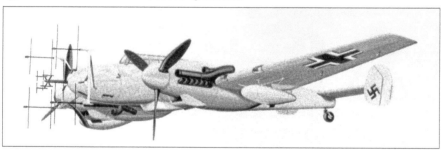

The Messerschmitt Bf-110G, although unsuccessful as a long-range fighter and fighter-bomber, was used successfully as a night-fighter. It carried two 30mm and two 20mm cannons and two machine guns.

The Junkers Ju 88G6 was a variant of the famous medium bomber. As a night-fighter, it carried an upward-firing cannon mounted in the fuselage. It had five 20mm cannons and three machine guns.

The Dornier Do-217J was developed as a night-fighter and was armed with four 20mm cannons and six machine guns.

The Heinkel He-219A first flew in 1942 but never achieved widespread operation. It had a formidable armament of four 30mm and two 20mm cannons.

German captivity map.

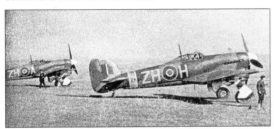

Two No 266 Squadron Typhoons prepare to go on an anti-rhubarb patrol from Warmwell.

Sandy McIntyre recounts his recent anti-'rhubarb' patrol to a spellbound audience at Warmwell. The door and canopy combination of the Typhoon cockpit is interesting.

The complete crew of seven of a Lancaster of 44 Squadron are briefed on their next operation.

Not much to salvage when a Typhoon crashes.

Left: A most unusual view of a Lancaster with the crew assembled about the rear turret. The sheer enormity of this famous Merlin powered four-engine bomber is testament to the skills of the designers and manufacturers. Although it could certainly do with a good wash and have the props 'dressed' correctly!

There is many a story hidden in this jovial 266 crowd at Bolt Head. Sitting on the fuel bowser is one with his head swathed in bandages and another with a shotgun. The tall one at the rear is presumably a ground crew member who has had his fuel truck commandeered by the air crew.

Bolt Head, March 1944. The 266 Squadron ground crew prior to the D-Day invasion.

"You don't know what's coming to you FRITZ!" is the simple yet heartfelt message on the 266 Squadron Typhoon's 500-pounder that will soon end its existence in Germany.

Sir Godfrey Huggins, Prime Minister of Southern Rhodesia, is watched by the aircrew as he walks across to inspect a Typhoon of No 266 Squadron in May 1944, prior to D-Day.

Typhoon Mk IB of 266 Squadron with unusual black and white stripes on the undercarriage fairing. Once the gear has been retracted, these markings will blend into the well known D-Day stripes that were painted on the aircraft for easy recognition. The idea of the stripes was not new—it was borrowed because of its effectiveness.

Sir Godfrey Huggins and two officers of the Royal Air Force are dwarfed by the Typhoon. The Matabele shield with the inscription *Hlabazulu* can be seen between the 20mm cannons.

A German photograph of the substantial Atlantic wall built to prevent an invasion from across the English Channel.

An RAF ground crew prepares to load the bomb bay of a Lancaster with 1,000 pounders. Famed by its adaptability, the Lancaster was eventually modified to carry the *tallboy* and the *grand slam* bombs.

This wartime publicity photograph displays the RAF's awesome arsenal. Of note are the 40-lb GP (top centre), the 8,000–lb cookie, the 12,000-lb tallboy and the 22,000-lb grand slam. The offset fins of the grand slam spun the projectile to stabilize it in its supersonic flight.

American troops drive the last of the enemy from St Lô after which the way was clear for Patton's advance.

The Germans cannot escape the holocaust erupting around them in the Falaise pocket. They were surrounded by the British, Canadians, Poles, Americans and Free French.

The convenient size of the V-1 meant it could be transported to the launching ramp easily.

Not so for the far bigger V-2, which had to have a specially designed vehicle to take it to the launch site.

The special V-2 trolley was used to lift the rocket to the vertical position for launch.

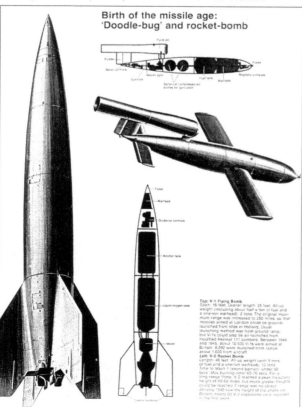

Birth of the missile age: 'Doodle-bug' and rocket-bomb

The V-1 flying bomb or *doodle-bug* had a one-ton warhead, carried half a ton of fuel and was powered by the simple Pulse Jet engine which gave it its distinctive noise. It had a range of 250 miles, which enabled it to be launched from Holland to hit London. It was normally launched from a ground ramp but was also air launched from modified He 111s.

About 10,500 V-1s were aimed at Britain, 1,600 of which were dropped from aircraft.

The V-2 Rocket Bomb also had a one-ton warhead but it required nine tons of fuel. It took 30 seconds to reach the speed of sound and had a burn time of only 70 seconds. Its peak trajectory was 50-60 miles. In the first week of the attack on Britain, 60 V-2s were reported.

Fighting the flying bomb menace. Flying straight and level, the V-1 crossed the Channel at speed, a fast moving target for either the AA guns or the fighters. Once contact was made, there were two choices— either tip it over or blow it up with gunfire. Both were effective but when the deadly rocket was tipped, it was still armed and going to cause destruction.

The V-1 is sighted ...

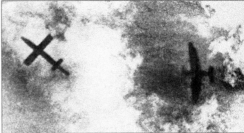

A Spitfire closes in ...

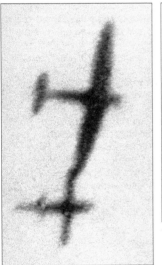

The Spitfire unbalances the
V-1 with its wing tip.

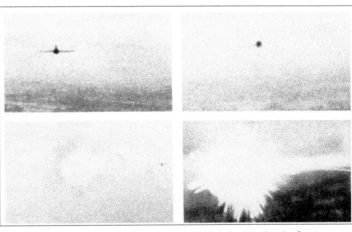

The orthodox way—a camera-gun records the destruction by front gun.

But many got through ...

No 266 Squadron out in full force in France. There are more than 30 aircraft on the airfield.

The tented camp at Needs Ore Point did not please the crews. They complained bitterly.

Left: The obliteration of the town of Cassino by massive aerial bombardment was the curtain-raiser to synchronized attacks at Anzio and on the main Italian front.

Below: 237 Squadron at Calvi, north-west Corsica, August 1944. Back row: Allan Douglas, Brian Wilson, Roy Gray, Dinks Moubray, Polly Payne, Red McDermott, Adrian Burne, Harry Murdoch-Eaton, H.E.L. Peterson, Jack Malloch, Keith Burrow. Middle row: Spy Hughes, Boy Crook, Dave Howat (Adj), Lynn Hurst (CO 'A' Flight), John Walmisley (CO), Ippie Ipsen (CO 'B' Flight—Danish), Doc McCaw, Don Currie, Taffy Williams, Peter Rainsford. Front row: Bill Musgrave, Will Ford, Jack Hackett (Aussie), Bevil Mundy, Paul (Junior) Pearson, Peter Sutton, Derek Hallas. Not in photo: Sam Aylward, Arthur Taylor.

Spitfire Mk IX of 237 Squadron armed with two 250-lb bombs underwing and one 500-pounder under the fuselage. Italy 1944.

HM King George VI pays a visit to No 266 Squadron, 13th October 1944.

Appearing on the BBC were two Bulawayo boys—Flt Lt D.R. Taylor DFC and F/O H.H. Taylor DFM. The young lady is Driver Dorothea Fazakerley (MTC) who was Miss Dorothea Rodwell, the daughter of Sir Cecil and Lady Rodwell.

No 266 Squadron in the Ardennes, in a very cold Europe after D-Day.

Gp Capt Charles Green introduces a group of Rhodesia airmen to HM Queen Elizabeth at a garden party at Buckingham Palace. Princess Margaret is in attendance. The man on crutches is Bob Rademeyer who had returned from being a POW. When he baled out of a Lancaster, his leg struck the tailplane and was so badly damaged it had to be amputated.

The seven members of a Lancaster aircrew at Spilsby in May 1944. The second pilots were dispensed with and replaced with flight engineers.

Huggins, in the dinghy, has a bit of fun with the members of No 266 (Rhodesia) Squadron on his visit in May 1944.

Above: Gp Capt Doug Whyte OBE. Doug served with No 237 (Rhodesia) Squadron during the World War 11 and was the first NCO pilot in the postwar era. He was also the first OC of No 4 Squadron RRAF formed in January 1956. He was awarded the OBE in June 1962, and retired from the force in June 1966.

1st left: The first aeroplane of the postwar air force photographed at Belvedere. SR 22, a Leopard Moth registered as VP-YAT, was taken on charge in March 1947.

2nd left: The first de Havilland Rapide, SR 23 had a checkered history. It was ferried out from the UK in 1938 by Dirk Cloete for use by the governor of Southern Rhodesia. It was registered as VP-YBU. It then became SR 8, and was transferred to military service with the SRAU/Air Service (SRAS) and was renumbered 300. After the war, it reverted to VP-YBU and was fittingly returned to the postwar air force in 1947 as SR 23.

Below: The Royal Air Force visits Southern Rhodesia in a wartime-camouflaged Dakota in late 1944.

The first three Ansons, numbered SR 29, SR 30 and SR 31 respectively, arrive at Salisbury in 1948. The story of the ferry, written by one of the pilots, is to be found in the text.

Many of those who had only heard about the famous Lancaster bomber had a chance to see one for the first time. The 44 (Rhodesia) Squadron aircraft KM-M flew out from the UK to do a survey of the Zambezi Valley in preparation for the massive Kariba Dam project. Here it is at Heany, 1947.

A Dakota, Rapide and Tiger Moth make the perfect backdrop for an inspection of the SR Staff Corps Air Unit by Colonel R.E.B. Long OBE in January 1947. From left: Lt H. Hawkins, Capt K.D. Taute DFC, Col R.E.B. Long OBE, WO II A.F. Chisnall, Sgt N.V. Phillips, WO II G.H. Norris, Sgt Frobisher, Sgt C.J. Cubitt, Sgt C.H. Paxton.

SR 25, the Dakota that was presented to the air force by Field Marshal Jan Smuts in late 1947. It served the air force faithfully for 30 years before being destroyed by an RPG-7 rocket at Mapai airfield in Mozambique in May 1977.

SRAF crews with their Harvards in an army cooperation exercise held at Gwebi. From left, standing: John Moss, John Campbell, unknown , Dicky Bradshaw, unknown, Jack Malloch, Ossie Penton, unknown. Front: Roger Brackley, unknown, Neville Brooks, John Deall.

A striking shot of a Harvard formation over typical Rhodesian terrain on a clear day.

The First TF Course of Pilots trained postwar. August 1949 - September 1951. Back row, from left: Graves, Henson, Rowley, Fitzgerald, Love, Smith, McKenzie. Seated: Paxton, Phillips, Hawkins, Jacklin, Wilson, Moss. Front: Fleming, Bagnall, Potter, Bridger.

The Southern Rhodesian Air Force, 1st April 1950. Even this large group is overshadowed by the Dakota. Back row: Rompani, Borlase, Chambers, Budd, Forsgate, Taylor-Memory, Smith, Butterworth, Dawson, Ford, Cuttler, Pringle, Skinner, Atherton, Wood, Rumbelow, Kavanagh, Nimmo, Vine, Stockwell. Second row: Goodwin, Horrex, Powell, Weston, Minks, Ballinger, Simpson, Cubitt, Burton, Hamilton, Fowler, Rowe, Patterson, Doig, Simmons, Webster, Watson, Hope, Morgan, Nicholson. Third row, seated: Coffin, Parry, Campbell, Gerricke, Moss, Wilson, Taute, Jacklin, Hawkins, Gibbons, Erwee, Norris, Weisner, Gundry, Chisnall. Front row: Pattrick, Cunnison, Phillips, Bennett, Forshaw, Nesbitt, Jones, Paxton, Mateer.

The officers of the SRAF on the occasion of the visit by His Excellency the Governor, Major General Sir John Kennedy and Lady Kennedy to Cranborne, May 1951. From left, standing: Capt F.H. Taylor MBE, Capt B.H. Gibbons, Maj A.M. Bentley OBE, AFC, Brig S. Garlake CBE (Commander Military Forces), His Excellency, Lady Kennedy, Lt Col E.W.S. Jacklin AFC, Maj K.D. Taute DFC and Bar, Capt C.W. Hyslop MBE, Lt D.M. Whyte. Front: Lt L.T.P. Coleman, Lt A.O.G. Wilson DFC (American), Lt J.H. Deall, DSO DFC NFC, Lt J.P. Moss, Lt C.H. Paxton, Lt M. Schumann, Lt G.N. Dawson, Capt H. Hawkins, Capt R.H. Barber DFC, Capt M. Wheaton (ADC).

Line-up of Spitfire F 22s on the hardstand outside New Sarum Headquarters. They were soon to become obsolete with the dawning of the jet age.

Left: Capt Johnny Deall DSO, DFC, NFC, Deputy Squadron Commander No 1 Squadron Southern Rhodesia Auxiliary Air Force. A true officer and a gentleman who was admired and respected by all.

Below: Twelve SRAF Tiger Moths in perfect symmetry at Cranborne in the early '50s, ready for the day's flying.

Formation break by four Harvards of the SRAF. The upper surfaces of the mainplanes were painted dark green while the remainder was silver.

Johnny Deall flies SR 69 over Seke. Note the green and gold flashes of the Southern Rhodesia Air Force on either side of the roundel.

An incredible escape for both pilots whose Harvard put a wing in while low flying and cartwheeled wingtip to nose, leaving the engine behind, and depositing the wing in one of the few trees left in the Seke Reserve. Peter Potter had concussion while Basil Hone, the instructor, was only recognized an hour after his surgeon and friend, Jos Nangle, had put 140 stitches in his head. There was a misunderstanding as to who had control at the time of the accident.

Members of the first postwar Halton Course who attested on 30th November 1951. From left: K.B. (Keith) Preedy, D.J.C. van der Merwe, G.P. (Geoffrey/ Goofy) Proudfoot, B Wallace, J.G.(Chinky) Stewart, F.J.(Johnny) Gent, R.E.(Rob) Schley,

The Spitfire always looked beautiful, especially from this unusual angle. The polished aluminium finish on the Spitfires was a welcome change from their wartime colour schemes. The bulges on the wings are to house the 20mm cannons.

SR 41 and SR 45 in a small contretemps—Doug Whyte had just come in to land in the paddock reserved for the Tiger Moths at Cranborne. Dicky Bradshaw was doing an instrument take off when the student swung off the runway. Dicky corrected the swing but hit the Tiger Moth. There were no casualties. Doug said that this was his only flying incident in 43 years, and even then, he was not to blame.

The 2,000 horsepower of the Spitfire F 22's Griffon engine had its own distinctive sound, though pundits will argue that the noise of a Merlin engine could never be surpassed for sheer ecstasy. An Anson can be seen in the background on the hardstand at New Sarum. The Salisbury control tower is yet to be built to the left of the frame.

CHAPTER 27

Southern Rhodesia joins the jet age

News of the progress of Salisbury's new airport was given in February 1952 by the then Director of Civil Aviation, Lieutenant Colonel M.C.H. Barber. He reported that the secondary runway was already in use by the SRAF which had a large proportion of its aircraft based at Kentucky. The sixth hangar was in the process of being erected. Some of these hangars had been brought from Cranborne. "As more hangars and equipment are removed from Cranborne and taken to the airport, the SRAF will gradually transfer more of its staff and operations there. The Resident Engineer, Mr A.H. Ashworth reported that the rapid progress was being maintained and about 90% of the basic work, involving the movement of 800,000 tons of soil, had been completed. No cement was to be used in the construction of the runway, which was to be composed of layers of compacted earth and gravel. The main runway was to be 2,800 yards (2,560m) in length but provision had been made to extend the length to 5,000 yards (4,570m)."

Short Service Courses

The second batch of Short Service trainees began their two-year course on 1st March 1952, These men were:

Frank Mussell	Roy Morris	L.A.S. 'Rex' Taylor
Barry Stephens	Vince King	Vic Watt
Bernard du Plessis	Charlie Jamieson	Ray Maritz
Vic Paxton	John Essex-Clark	Wally Hinrichs

Two days later, the first Short Service Course cadets completed six months' training and became eligible for promotion to the rank of second lieutenant. By this stage in their training, each man had completed 80 hours in the air and 485 hours on the ground at lectures and drill.

In April, a second party of five apprentices left for training with the RAF at Halton and a further very welcome piece of news was that Southern Rhodesia had finally sorted out the transport and storage problems, and petrol rationing would be lifted on 25th April 1952.

Early in the year, Sir Godfrey Huggins, had paid a visit to the Victoria Falls, flying to the venue in the SRAF Dakota, for yet more talks about a possible federation. This time the talks were being held with a conservative government, following a general election on 25th October 1951, when the Tory party was returned with an overall majority of 17 seats. The Conservatives were more inclined to favour the idea. Therefore it came as no surprise when at the opening of the new session of parliament in March, the governor referred to a possible referendum on federation. Further talks were held in London in April, and Sir Godfrey Huggins flew the first stage, to Livingstone, in an SRAF aircraft. The white paper on the proposed Federation of Rhodesia and Nyasaland was tabled in the Legislative Assembly on 18th June.

SRAF move to Kentucky—the New Salisbury Airport

Officially, the move to Kentucky had been made on 1st April 1952.

> **10th April.** *SRAF set the fashion when, at the beginning of this month, they struck camp at Cranborne and removed themselves bag and baggage to Kentucky. (Now called New Salisbury Airport). The reason for the change in name, we imagine, is to prevent bewildered pilots touching down in the Deep South of the USA.* (S 815)

By the middle of June, the SRAF had been ensconced at New Salisbury Airport for over two months but facilities were still somewhat Heath Robinson-ish as the June newsletter makes plain:

> *The runways are not completed but it is necessary on occasion to fly aircraft in and out. This can be both interesting and hair-raising as there is usually the odd grading machine or bulldozer to avoid.*

But if the runways were not all that could be desired, there was apparently nothing wrong with the most important parts of the new complex.

> *Those of you who remember the little mess at Cranborne must visit the mess at the New Salisbury Airport on your return. A member of the Rhodesia Railways who visited it, was so impressed that he has recommended to the Railways Authorities that the 'shack' known as the Victoria Falls Hotel should be replaced with a new building modelled on the warrant officers' and non-commissioned officers' mess. Incidentally, all messes at the New Airport are of identical design.*

The June newsletter also sheds light on the activities of individual members of the air force.

> *The Second Short Service Commission Course is now well under way. Essex-Clark, latterly an instructor at the Salisbury Drill Hall is on the course and is throwing himself all over the sky in a Tiger Moth. He has flown solo and is endeavouring to emulate the antics of Keith Kemsley who is now a 'fundi' on the Harvard aircraft and should get his Wings in September. The Short Service Unit is able to field a useful friendly rugby side and two members—Jamieson (son of Fred Jamieson former president of the Mashonaland Rugby Board) and B. du Plessis of Bulawayo, were picked for the Mashonaland under-19 trials. Du Plessis has since been selected to play flyhalf for his side. Captain Archie Wilson, who was holding the SRAF flag in the forces' rugby team, was unfortunately injured in the first game.* (S 815)

One of the students of No 1 Course SRAAF, Colin Graves, came to ground rather unexpectedly at the beginning of July 1952, when the Tiger Moth he was piloting made an unscheduled landing in Rhodesville Avenue. Fortunately, neither he nor his instructor was hurt. The undamaged aircraft was flown out later in the day by Archie Wilson using the strip-road as a runway, while the BSAP kept the road clear of traffic.

Wings Parade for the first Short Service Course

Construction work on the main runway at New Salisbury Airport was nearing completion after 15 months' effort, and on 12th August 1952, G.A. Davenport, the Minister for Mines and Transport, visited the site to see the last of the pre-mix concrete carpet laid. Nine days later, on 21st August, the airport was the scene of a Wings Parade and the passing-out ceremony for the first Short Service Course.

The eleven graduates of the First Short Service Course who had completed one year of training were:

Second Lieutenants:

John D. Rogers	Basil Myburgh	John Mussell
Brian Horney	Arthur Hodgson	Dave Harvey
John Cameron	Robert d'Hotman	Nigel Bridges
Peter Piggott	Keith Kemsley	

The six graduates of No 2 Auxiliary Course who had completed two years of part-time training were:

Corporals:

Des Anderson	Ken Edwards
Mick McLaren	Don Macaskil

Cadets:

W.H. Billy Duncan	Doug Bailey

The parade commander was Captain A.O.G. Wilson and the parade adjutant, Lieutenant J.H. Deall. The four corporals had in fact become regular members of the Southern Rhodesia Staff Corps and it was planned that their promotion to sergeant would have been promulgated before the parade. However something went wrong and they were only promoted on the day after receiving their Wings.

The Governor, Major General Sir John Kennedy who presented the Wings, said:

> *I am glad to be here today because it gives me an opportunity to express my admiration for the way in which the SRAF is carrying on the glorious tradition that was established by Rhodesian airmen in the last war. The achievements of 237, 44 and 266 Squadrons, as well as of the Rhodesians who served in other squadrons of the RAF were outstanding and will never be forgotten. The Rhodesian airmen who fought the war provided a shining example, and that example is being followed, and worthily upheld today in our air force.*

(Rhodesia Herald, 22nd Aug. 1952)

Two overseas visitors who attended the Wings ceremony were Air Marshal Sir Francis Fogarty, recently appointed inspector general of the British Air Council and Air Chief Marshal, Sir Arthur Saunders, Commander in Chief Middle East.

On 1st September 1952 intake No 3 of the Short Service Unit began their training. These men were:

C.W. (Chris) Dams*	M.S. (Mike) Saunders	C.J. (Chris) Hudson
J.C. (John) Allen	Solly Ferreira	B.F. (Barry) Raffle
T.N. (Tommy) Robinson	D.E. (Dare) Broughton	R.J.W. (Dick) Purnell

---

* Later to become an Air Vice-Marshal.

| C.T. (Colin) Miller | R.H. (Ron) Westerman | W.J. Lowery |
| P.A. Huggett | B.J. (Bennie) Kerstein | N.F. Allen |

On the world scene, the news was not good. War still raged in Korea while in Egypt, army officers had seized power in a bloodless coup, which led to Colonel Nasser taking control in July. Mau Mau troubles broke out in Kenya in September while in October, British aviation was severely affected when a Comet crashed soon after taking off from Rome Airport. A happier event occurred on the local scene at the end of October when a de Havilland dual control jet trainer Vampire paid a visit to New Salisbury Airport while on a flight from South Africa. Nearly every member of the SRAF was there to see the aircraft land and in the afternoon, Lieutenant John Mussell was fortunate enough to have a chance to fly the Vampire.

New Sarum

During the month of October 1952, Southern Rhodesia Air Force headquarters moved out to New Sarum* as the military side of the New Salisbury Airport had been named. Archie Wilson says that this title was suggested by Keith Taute, Sarum being the old Roman name for Salisbury in Wiltshire England.

Air Vice-Marshal Raf Bentley remarked later, "This was our first permanent home and it was the first time we had the complete buildings, equipment and other facilities necessary to operate as a fighting air force." The transport squadron, which had been known as No 1 Squadron, and had been based at Cranborne, also moved out to New Sarum and was redesignated No 3 Transport Squadron. Belvedere Airport was still being used as the civilian aerodrome but whenever it proved unsuitable owing to weather conditions, aircraft were diverted to the new airport where passengers and freight were handled by No 3 Transport Squadron.

First postwar civil air display

Unfortunately, the new airport was not completed in time for the first Civil Air Display to be held since the end of World War II and so this event was staged at Cranborne on 1st December 1952. A crowd of 10,000 flocked to the aerodrome to watch the fun that began at 08h00. The event was organized by the Department of Civil Aviation with the help of various flying clubs, together with the SRAF and SRAAF. As far as the crowds were concerned, the outstanding events were the aerobatics and formation-flying of the SRAF Spitfires. Flying at high speeds, the aircraft wheeled, looped and roared low over the heads of the spectators. The Spitfires were led by Captain Charles Baillie SRAAF, acting officer commanding No 1 Squadron; the other pilots were Lieutenants Ben Bellingan, Jack Malloch and Ray Wood; individual aerobatics were performed by Captain John Deall. Members of the public were allowed to go into the control tower and request various aerobatic stunts. These requests were relayed to the pilot by Lieutenant Dicky Bradshaw.

Safety equipment section

On 24th November 1952, the *Rhodesia Herald* carried an article on the work of the Safety Equipment Section at New Sarum. This article described the special packs, which would now be fixed to the harnesses of the emergency parachutes carried by the flyers. In the past, these packs had been carried in the aircraft in a tin box and so were only of use if the aircraft

---

* Although the new military base had been given the name New Sarum, it was referred to as New Salisbury Airport right up to late 1956. Only then was the name New Sarum officially used.

made an emergency landing. The kits contained first aid equipment, a compass, water bottle, leather gloves, knife and small hone, matches, spare water bag and signal cartridges as well as a heliograph, fishing line and hooks, socks, burning lens, mosquito hat, signal strips and code instructions, razor blades and rabbit snares. The article commented that no one in the SRAF had ever had to use a parachute and ended with the words, There have been no flying fatalities in the SRAF within the Colony since its inception. (That is since the war). Sadly, this state of affairs was not to continue. Lieutenant Raymond Vivian Corruthers, artillery observer pilot, was killed instantly when his Auster hit high tension cables and crashed into the Hunyani River near Prince Edward Dam on 14th December.

The SRAF had a further mishap in February 1953 when Officer Cadet Bennie Kerstein dropped his Tiger Moth in the grounds of Bothashof School, Lytton, south of Salisbury. The aircraft rolled over and was badly damaged, finishing up back on its belly with its nose in a vegetable garden. The pilot was unconscious when help arrived but was pulled from the wreckage, which fortunately did not ignite even though petrol was dripping from the fuel tank.

Meanwhile, talks had commenced in London between the Southern Rhodesia Defence Department and the Air Ministry concerning a possible switch from Spitfires to Vampires. The feeling was that whether the federation came into being or not, Southern Rhodesia had to come into line with British Air Policy. The Korean War had emphasized the need for jet aircraft. If Southern Rhodesia was to play a part in any future war in the air side by side with the RAF and other Commonwealth territories, the SRAF must have up-to-date machines. So the military needs were clear but there were other factors. On the financial side, what might be too heavy a cost for Southern Rhodesia alone could be borne by a federation of the three central African states. Balanced against this, however, was the problem of maintaining the Spitfires, which would become increasingly difficult as the aircraft spares became harder to obtain.

Following the talks in London, it was announced that RAF air training in Southern Rhodesia was to cease. George Ward, Under Secretary for Air, said that after the RAF Training Schools in Southern Rhodesia were discontinued, on the expiration of the existing agreement in March 1954, the close partnership between the air forces of Britain and Southern Rhodesia would continue. "In part it is hoped that some of the Short Service SRAF officers who have learned to fly modern aircraft will afterwards join the RAF." Part of this close cooperation was displayed by the fact that small parties of apprentices regularly left Rhodesia to train with the RAF. The third party to leave in 12 months, departed in January 1953, seven of the cadets being destined for Halton and one for Cranwell.

Wings for the second Short Service Course

On the penultimate day of February 1953, the prime minister inspected the men of 'A' flight and presented them with their Wings; these were the cadets of the second Short Service Course. Sir Godfrey Huggins told these men that, a decision regarding future training would be taken by the Southern Rhodesia government in April, after the result of the referendum on federation was known.

> *I wish I could tell you something definite now but I cannot. The big question is how we are going to re-equip this station. All I can tell you is that we will know in April. Those of you who have just received your Wings must realize that this is only the first step in your careers. You have done so well so far I have not the slightest doubt that you will last the course. We in Southern Rhodesia have a commitment to fulfil and although the tax-payer may groan a little, it is our duty to fulfil that commitment.* (Rhodesia Herald)

Recalling this time, James Pringle said:

> *The Royal Air Force was progressively withdrawing during the course of '53, and opportunity was taken to do a bit of aircraft 'horse-trading'. We took over a number of their Harvards, on an exchange basis, in the interests of standardization. It worked quite well. We took over 14 I think. The reason for this was that one type had the American electrical installation and the other had British. We took over the American IIAs and gave them the IIBs. The RAF always wanted their pound of flesh but they always gave us the option to tender when they were getting rid of equipment. I recall one particular case, where we spent thousands of man-hours rebuilding Tiger Moth mainplanes, a very man- hour consuming task. The RAF put a large number of Tiger Moth mainplanes on the market. We knew the local scrap dealers would tender for them. I was sent to do an evaluation and I made a bid of ten shillings per mainplane, bearing in mind that there were four mainplanes or wings to each Tiger Moth, two top and two bottom, left and right. We collected sufficient unused Tiger Moth mainplanes to last us for the time we operated the aircraft.*

On 9th April 1953, the Colony voted in a referendum* on whether to join a federation with the two Northern Territories. Counting took some time and the new parliament opened on 14th April, while the issue of federation was still in doubt. The decision on whether to train SRAF squadrons on jet aircraft was therefore delayed, but Edgar Whitehead, in his Budget speech said that this decision had an important bearing on the Defence Vote.

> *The Colony undertook to provide two SRAF fighter squadrons as its contribution to imperial defence. Recently, discussions with the United Kingdom have made it evident that modern practice in training would render this force entirely useless for its purpose unless training on jet aircraft were undertaken. In fact we were advised that if the Colony were financially unable to undertake jet training it would be better to disband the SRAF entirely rather than to continue with obsolete machines. The government has now decided that as this is likely to be the only effective contribution to imperial defence that can be made by the Federated Territories in peacetime, the project should continue especially in view of the fine record established by the SRAF. Northern Rhodesia has been kept informed of the position and has volunteered £200,000 towards the cost in the current year before the Federal government is able to take over defence. The net effect of these transactions on the Defence Vote will be a gross increase of about £200,000, which will be brought back to almost exactly the actual expenditure for 1952–53 by the Northern Rhodesia credit in aid. The net amount provided is £1,740,166.*
> (Rhodesia Herald)

The Hunting Percival Provost and the Pembroke

While a final decision on jet fighters was hanging in the balance, Southern Rhodesia did commit itself to new basic training aircraft. These were the Hunting Percival Provost and the Pembroke, which was a general purpose twin-engined aircraft. The Provost was already in use with the RAF and Southern Rhodesia became the first Commonwealth air force to follow the RAF lead and adopt it as its basic trainer. Both the Provost and the Pembroke were fitted with Alvis Leonides series 12600 engines which developed 550 horsepower at sea-level. These engines were believed to be particularly suited to the high-altitude airfields and warm climate of Rhodesia. Although the first Pembroke had flown in November 1952, it was not shown to the public until the Farnborough Air Show in September 1953.

★ Result of referendum: majority of 10,832 in favour; 25,560 for, 14,728 against.

The Pembroke had a wingspan of 64 feet 6 inches (19.5m). The cabin accommodated eight passengers in rear-facing seats and the fittings allowed for quick conversion to freighting or casualty evacuation for six stretcher patients. Supply-dropping by parachute could be carried out through large removable cabin doors. Dual controls and amber screens could be fitted for instrument flying practice and a flying classroom version was available for training radio operators, navigators and bomb-aimers. The aircraft was also designed for photographic survey and reconnaissance for which the high wing layout was particularly suitable. It had a maximum speed of 220 miles per hour (354 km/h) and could remain airborne for seven hours. The Provost was the new standard basic trainer of the RAF, the prototype having made its first flight in 1950. It had a top speed of 200 miles per hour (320 km/h), could climb to 10,000 feet in seven minutes and had a service ceiling of 25,000 feet.

For the United Kingdom the most exciting event of the year was the coronation, on 2nd June of Queen Elizabeth II. King George VI had died at Sandringham on 6th February 1952 but the coronation of the new queen had been delayed by over a year. A flypast of six Spitfires, led by John Deall, celebrated the event in Salisbury.

First air rally at the new airport

Later that month on 13th and 14th June 1953, the first air rally was held at New Salisbury Airport. Military and civil aircraft converged on the airport but it was No 266 (Rhodesia) Squadron of the RAF flying Venom fighters that drew special interest.

The display, under the control of Archie Wilson, began with formation aerobatics performed by Tiger Moths flown by Doug Whyte, Colin Graves and Bill Smith of the SRAF. The team executed line-astern loops, aileron turns, barrel-rolls and other manœuvres with impeccable precision. This was followed by a display given by nine Harvards of the Royal Air Force Training Group. Later, John Deall piloting a Spitfire, demonstrated the art of rocket-firing before he was joined by another Spitfire, flown by Charles Paxton for a remarkable display of aerobatic flying that included hesitation rolls at a dangerously low altitude. Finally, the SRAF pilots gave an exhibition of pinpoint bombing, and staged a dogfight. Unfortunately, the weekend was marred by a tragic mid-air collision between two RAF Harvards, which resulted in the deaths of three RAF personnel.

A step forward in the intended conversion to jet aircraft took place in June, when a group of 12 technicians, led by their senior technical adviser, Major Mick Gibbons left for the United Kingdom to undertake a course of instruction at the Hatfield factory of de Havilland. Archie Wilson, Officer Commanding Flying, and Mike Schumann also left Rhodesia to attend a Vampire jet technical course at de Havilland, followed by a Vampire jet conversion course at RAF Merryfield near Taunton. They were joined later by Flying Instructors Dicky Bradshaw and Charles Paxton. These four pilots took acceptance of the first four Vampire FB 9s and ferried them to Rhodesia in December 1953.

Within Southern Rhodesia, the highlight of the year was the visit of Queen Elizabeth, the Queen Mother and Princess Margaret for the Rhodes Centenary Celebrations in July. They were flown around the territory in an SRAF Dakota that was piloted, on most occasions, by Doug Whyte.

Wings for the third Short Service Course

A story that had begun 13 years earlier, came to a close on 6th August 1953 when the RAF ensign was lowered for the last time at Thornhill, marking the final graduation parade for the Royal Air Force Training Group. But although RAF training in Southern Rhodesia had come to an end, the close association between the two countries continued. Military pilot training within Southern Rhodesia was now completely in the hands of the SRAF and this was demonstrated towards the end of August when a Wings Parade for the men of No 3 Course of the Short Service Unit took place at Salisbury Airport. In a speech of congratulation, Sir Godfrey Huggins said:

This ceremony marks the end of your first year and indicates that you have had a successful year. In your final year, you will convert to operational machines and learn how to use them as weapons of war. No doubt, you will be among the first young Rhodesians who will fly the Vampire jet fighters, which are to replace the Spitfires in the course of the next year.

To the men of No 1 Course, Sir Godfrey said:

You are just about to complete your short service term. You are the originals of this short service commission scheme. You have done extremely well and I am told that you are now fully trained squadron pilots with about 400 flying hours each. You have used Spitfires in the ground-attack role, achieving good results. I am confident that you will be a credit to Rhodesia wherever you may go. You will of course be posted to the reserve when you have completed your term this month. I hope and expect that while you are in the reserve, it will be found possible to convert to jets. (Rhodesia Herald)

Sir Godfrey said that the Auxiliary Squadron would now be disbanded. This was because the Short Service men were now being trained on a regular basis and would be able to perform the duties that the Auxiliary Squadron had been so ably performing up to this point.

He went on to say that it was a pity that the Auxiliary Squadron could not be maintained but this would mean additional ground staff. However, suitable officers would be posted to the Reserve. Sir Godfrey complimented the technical staff on parade saying that it was due to their efforts that the SRAF flying programme had been maintained. He also paid tribute to the RAR (Rhodesian African Rifles) attached to the SRAF, saying that they had made a valuable contribution to the smooth running of the service by providing men for security and other ground duties.

On 4th September 1953, Lord Llewellin, first governor-general of the Federation arrived in Salisbury, and four days later Mr Garfield Todd, as leader of the United Party, became prime minister of Southern Rhodesia, Sir Godfrey Huggins having relinquished his position as prime minister on 7th September. A general election was held for the first Federal Assembly with a majority of the seats going to the Federal Party under the leadership of Sir Godfrey Huggins and so he became the first prime minister of the Federation of Rhodesia and Nyasaland.

The RAF ensign had been lowered for the last time at Thornhill in August. Now it was the turn of Heany, near Bulawayo, where at the end of October the Royal Air Force Training Group officially closed and the last of the many young pilot officers were presented with their Wings by the Governor of Southern Rhodesia, Major General Sir John Kennedy. This was among the last of his official functions because towards the middle of November he and Lady Kennedy left for the United Kingdom. Sir Robert Tredgold became acting governor.

The Pembrokes and the Vampires arrive

Once again, the SRAF was gearing itself for the excitement of an aircraft ferry. On 12th September, Major Hawkins and Captain Cunnison had taken off in SR 25, one of the aircraft of No 3 Transport Squadron, to fly to England in preparation to escort the first Vampire jet fighters and the new Percival Pembroke aircraft back to Rhodesia. On 23rd November 1953, braving a steady downpour, a big crowd of SRAF personnel, wives and children, gathered on the tarmac of Salisbury Airport to witness the arrival of the first of four Percival Pembrokes.

THE FEDERATION OF
RHODESIA AND NYASALAND

The occasion was both an opportunity to see the new aircraft, a sleek twin-engined communications plane, and for a re-union. Six of the SRAF men aboard the Pembrokes were returning to Rhodesia after nearly six months' training in Britain. An excited murmur rippled through the crowd as the Pembroke made its first appearance through low, grey rain clouds and swept over the aerodrome. For most of the crowd, the new aircraft took second place after it had landed. First there were welcomes and exchanges of news. After a few minutes, however, the Pembroke came into its own as SRAF personnel inspected their new acquisition.
(Rhodesia Herald, 24th Nov. 1953)

This, the first of the four Pembrokes to arrive was flown from the United Kingdom by Captain Ted Cunnison. It was followed by the infinitely more exciting arrival of the Vampire FB 9s. These aircraft took off from a RAF base in the south of England on Friday, 4th December. The flight was under the overall command of Lieutenant Colonel Ted Jacklin, commanding officer of the SRAF. The flight of four Vampires was led by Major Archie Wilson, while the other three pilots were Lieutenants Dicky Bradshaw, Mike Schumann and Charles Paxton. The Vampires were supported by a Dakota of No 3 Squadron piloted, as usual, by Major Harold Hawkins. Flying virtually the same route as that pioneered by the Spitfires, the Vampires stopped in at Istres, Tunis, Tripoli, El Adem, Fayid, Wadi Halfa, Khartoum, Juba, Entebbe, Tabora and Ndola. One hour and 12 minutes after their take-off from Ndola on 12th December, the aircraft were landing at Salisbury. This time included circling Ndola twice after take-off, passing over Lusaka at 30,000 feet and circling Salisbury twice before landing. Remarking on the event the *Rhodesia Herald* said:

The high-pitched scream of jets has come to stay in Southern Rhodesia. Yesterday four Vampire ground-attack jet fighters circled over Salisbury twice before landing at New Salisbury Airport. Travelling at about 450 mph (724 km/h) the planes were transformed in a few seconds from dots on the horizon to screeching jets overhead. (Rhodesia Herald, 13th Dec. 1953)

The Vampire trainer first flew at the end of 1950. By 1953, it was in production for the RAF and the air forces of 12 other countries. Although the Vampire FB 9 had been outclassed by later jet aircraft and was no longer regarded as a frontline fighter, it was well suited to the role of ground attack. It was armed with 2 x 20-mm cannon and could carry both rocket projectiles and bombs. It had a maximum speed at sea level of 538 mph (866 km/h) and an operational ceiling of 40,000 feet.

An important benefit, which came with the re-equipping was a simplification of maintenance. Both the Vampire trainer and the Vampire fighter carried the same type of engine: the Goblin 3. Similarly, the Provost and the Pembroke were both powered by 550 horsepower Alvis Leonides piston engines. This was a nine-cylinder air-cooled radial engine. The twin-engined Pembrokes were intended to take the place of the Ansons and Rapides then being used for transport duties.

No 2 Course Southern Rhodesia Auxiliary Air Force
Commenced training July 1950
Wings: 21st August 1952

Des Anderson	After attending a flying instructors' course he left the force and returned to civilian life. Later joined DCA and became an air traffic controller.
Ken Edwards	Joined the regular force. Retired as group captain.
Don Macaskill	Joined the regular force.

Mick McLaren	Joined the regular force, retired as an air marshal having commanded the Rhodesian Air Force.
Les Deall	Attached from SR Artillery.
And Cadets:	
Billy Duncan	Continued in civil employment.
Doug Bailey	Continued in civil employment.

No 1 Short Service Unit Course

Commenced training 1st September 1951

Wings: 21st August 1952

Nigel Bridges	Joined CAA on completion of course.
John Cameron	Joined RAF on completion of course.
Bob d'Hotman	Flew commercially—later flew with RRAF and Rhodesian Air Force.
Dave Harvey	Joined CAA.
Arthur Hodgson	Killed in a civilian accident in 1955.
Brian Horney	Joined regular force.
Keith Kemsley	Joined regular force. Retired as air commodore.
Alan Murray Hudson	Did not complete the course.
John Mussell	Joined regular force. Retired as group captain.
Basil Myburgh	Joined regular force. Then resigned.
Peter Piggott	Did some commercial flying and rejoined RRAF in 1962.
Ralph Weeks	Did not complete the course and returned to civil employment.
John Rogers	Joined CAA and rejoined the RRAF in 1958. Retired as air commodore.
Ray Reed	Did not complete the course. Later killed in a flying accident.
Clive Wilcox	Did not complete the course and returned to civil employment.

No 2 Course Short Service Unit

Commenced training: 1st March 1952

Wings: 27th February 1953

Bernard du Plessis	Joined the RAF and flew with No 266 (Rhodesia) Squadron. Rejoined RRAF in 1960. Then went to Air Malawi and the Sultan of Oman's Air Force, then back to commercial flying.
John Essex-Clark	Did not complete the course. Continued serving with the army, then joined the Australian military forces, saw service in Vietnam and rose to rank of brigadier.
Wally Hinrichs	Joined RAF and served on No 266 (Rhodesia) Squadron. Rejoined RRAF in 1960. Retired as wing commander.
Charlie Jameson	Did not complete the course. Returned to civil employment.
Vince King	Completed course and later joined the regular army.
Ray Maritz	Killed in a Spitfire flying accident 1953.
Roy Morris	Joined RAF and served on No 266 (Rhodesia) Squadron. Rejoined RRAF in 1960. Retired as wing commander. Served in the Sultan of Oman's Air Force.
Frank Mussell	Retired as an air marshal having commanded the Rhodesian Air Force.

Vic Paxton	Joined the Kenya Police Air Wing—killed in an accident while on operations.
Barry Stephens	Joined the Kenya Police Air Wing—killed in an accident while on operations.
Rex Taylor	Joined Kenya Police Air Wing—rejoined RRAF in 1957. Retired as wing commander.
Vic Watt	Did not complete the course—later joined VR.

No 3 Course Short Service Unit

Commenced Training: July 1952
Wings: August 1953

Chris Dams	Later to become an air vice-marshal.
Mike S. Saunders	Left as squadron leader 1965. Went commercial flying.
Christopher Hudson	Left force after completing course. Rejoined 1/12/54. Left force again in 1963.
John Allen	Joined RAF No 266 (Rhodesia) Squadron.
Solly Ferreira	Joined RAF No 266 (Rhodesia) Squadron.
Barry Raffle	Joined RAF No 266(Rhodesia) Squadron.
Tommy Robinson	Returned to civilian employment—later joined VR.
Dare Broughton	Returned to civilian employment.
Dick Purnell	Returned to civilian employment.
Colin Miller	Went commercial flying.
Ron Westerman	Returned to civilian employment.

Ted Jacklin was to become the first Rhodesian Chief of Air Staff.

Raf Bentley in a relaxed mood

CHAPTER 28

The Royal Rhodesian Air Force

It was mid-December 1953 when the people of the Federation of Rhodesia and Nyasaland went to the polls to choose their first parliament. A heavy majority was scored by the Federal Party, and in fact, Dendy Young was the only Confederate returned to the Federal Assemby. Ian Smith, later to become prime minister of Southern Rhodesia, was elected as the Federal Party member for Midlands.

In January came the Southern Rhodesia elections and the United Rhodesia Party was returned with a big majority, 26 out of 30 seats, with Raymond Stockil leading an independent opposition.

Troubles there were soon to be for the Southern Rhodesia Prime Minister, Garfield Todd and his government. In February, a strike broke out at Wankie Colliery among the African mine workers. The territorials were called out and transport was provided by the SRAF. Todd's ultimatum was, return to work or be signed off. Nine hundred and twenty strikers went back to work.

In March, Admiral Sir Peveril William Powlett was appointed governor of Southern Rhodesia and in the same month defence became a Federal matter and, therefore, the SRAF came under Federal government control. It was in April that the Governor-General of the Federation, Lord Llewellin, made his first official trip outside the Federation when he visited Lourenço Marques (Maputo). His party travelled in an SRAF Dakota. Towards the end of the month, a contingent of 12 SRAF pilots and technicians left Salisbury for the United Kingdom to fetch the second group of Vampire fighters and another Percival Pembroke aircraft.

During the Southern Rhodesia debate on the Budget, the subject of internal security was raised, and it was pointed out that the air force could play a vital part in the maintenance of internal security as had been proved in Kenya, Malaya and Indo-China.

The Southern Rhodesia Minister of Defence, Mr G.A. Davenport, said that the Federal government was in fact dictating Air policy. H.D. Wightwick commented that if a major war took place, Southern Rhodesia might be faced with internal security problems and he wondered about the correctness of the present training and organization of the armed force. Indications were, he continued, that what was needed was a mobile force. Even though well trained along commando lines, no modern military man was really a soldier unless he could be dropped by parachute. On the question of the air force, Humphrey Wightwick said: "We have a ground attack squadron but a squadron, possibly manned by Territorial or Auxiliary Air Force personnel which could be used for transporting airborne troops would be useful." In reply, Mr Davenport said that Southern Rhodesia had certain obligations, one of them being to maintain the Rhodesian African Rifles (RAR) in a state of readiness to go anywhere, and the other being to maintain a certain number of air force squadrons.

Second Vampire ferry

It was 10th May 1954 when a further five Vampires, four FB 9s and RAF T 11 left the RAF station at Benson, near Oxford. They had an uneventful flight to Khartoum where it was found that minor faults had developed in the long-range fuel tanks and they were delayed for six days awaiting spares from the Middle East. The Vampires arrived in Salisbury on 20th May, shortly after 11h30. Major Raf Bentley of the SRAF commanded the flight and the other pilots were Captain Doug Whyte, Lieutenants Charles Paxton, Mike Schumann, Noompie Phillips. Flight Lieutenants J. Upton and E. Richards accompanied the flight in a RAF Vampire T 11. These two pilots had been seconded to the SRAF to help with the familiarization of the SRAF pilots.

Major Bentley said, on arrival, that the Vampires were absolutely marvellous. He paid special tribute to the untiring efforts of the ground crew, both in taking over the machines in Britain and on the flight out to Africa. He said: Nothing was too much trouble for them. Although they were fatigued and they often worked 15 hours a day, they never failed to diagnose faults. They just would not give up until the job was done . This delivery brought the number of Vampires to eight with an extra two-seater Vampire, on loan from the RAF.

June 1954 brought further industrial problems in Southern Rhodesia when railway workers came out on strike. A state of emergency was declared, and the striking firemen's leader, Mr Taylor, was jailed. The strike ended after five days and Taylor was deported.

The first Federal Budget was introduced by Donald MacIntyre, the Minister for Finance, at the end of June. In his speech he reported:

> The Federal government has assumed full responsibility for the defence in the north, towards the maintenance of which the liability of the Northern government (Northern Rhodesia) was previously limited to contributions to the War Office. Not only does the full cost of the establishment have to be met from the Federal purse, but also a considerable additional cost arises in setting up the command HQ that will take over military control of the forces of the Federation. One item alone, an installment of the purchase price of the jet aircraft with which the air force is being equipped accounts for £450,000 in the 1954 estimates. (Rhodesia Herald)

He went on to say that the air force was being reorganized on the basis of two fighter squadrons and one Communications Squadron. Initial provision had been included through the Defence Vote for a system of national service training. According to an article which appeared in *Flight* magazine:

> The first duty of the SRAF is to train and hold in readiness, two ground-attack squadrons. One of these is equipped with Vampire FB 9s and the second is working up on Vampire trainers. In an emergency, these squadrons would expect to operate with the RAF having been re-equipped with first-line fighter/bombers, probably Venoms. As a sideline, the SRAF trains AOP pilots for the army, using Austers. (Flight,2nd July 1954)

Update on the SRAF

By July 1954, the SRAF headquarters at New Sarum could boast a two-storey administration block, designed to take a further floor later, with a first-class road leading, most of the way, to the city, thanks to the visit of Queen Elizabeth the Queen Mother in 1953.

At this stage, the SRAF still came under the command of Army Defence headquarters and could be regarded as an air arm of a joint defence force. Chief of the General Staff was Major General S. Garlake CBE. Senior air commander at New Sarum was Colonel E.W.S. Jacklin. Lieutenant Colonel K.D. Taute had gone to Rhodesia House in London as air liaison officer, while the senior air force staff officer was Major Raf Bentley. In addition to the pilots being trained inside the country, 12 apprentices were being sent each year to the RAF stations at Halton, Cranwell and Locking. Nine members of the Women's Military and Air Service (Wams) were serving with the SRAF. By the middle of 1954 the SRAF's aircraft strength was:

Spitfire F 22	19
Harvard II	19
Tiger Moth	12
Anson	3
Rapide	3
Auster	3
Dakota	1
Pembroke	2
Vampire FB 9	8
Leopard Moth	1

Towards the end of July 1954, Sir Godfrey Huggins, gave a broad outline of the new Federal Defence plans. Regarding the air force, he said that the Federation's contribution towards imperial defence would be two fighter squadrons. If war broke out, they would be transferred to the RAF as the Federation would not be able to run its own air force in the event of war. Replying to a point raised about the sum of £470,000 on the estimates for the purchase of aircraft, he said that £20,000 was for a second Dakota. The remainder was part of the amount required for re-equipping the air force with 55 aircraft: Vampire trainers and fighters, Provost elementary trainers and Pembrokes. The Defence Vote of £2,982,465 was accepted.

Third Vampire ferry
On Wednesday, 4th August 1954, a further six de Havilland Vampires were ferried out by Captain John Deall, Lieutenants Dicky Bradshaw, Bobby Blair, Harry Coleman, Colin Graves and Mick McLaren. This was the third and largest formation of Vampires to make the ferry and the aircraft all landed safely at Salisbury Airport on 10th August 1954.

The use of the civil airport by military aircraft was in fact the subject of a question put in the Federal Parliament by Dendy Young (Confederate member for Sebakwe). The Minister for Transport and Commerce, Sir Roy Welensky, replied: I am quite satisfied, provided there is no elementary training taking place at the New Salisbury Airport, that there is no greater risk or danger to flying than there is under normal circumstances.

No 5 Course Short Service Unit pilots receive their Wings
Once again, on 20th August, it was time for the annual Wings ceremony. This was the fifth occasion on which Wings were presented to Short Service Course pilots. Sir Robert Tredgold, deputy to the governor-general, made the presentation and spoke of the high standard of the SRAF. "It is not enough nowadays," he said, "that we should have courage and dash in our airmen, but it must be coupled with a high standard of technical training." For the first time at a Wings ceremony the flypast included Vampire jets, which were led by D.A. Bradshaw.

A big attraction at the Salisbury Show, a few days later, was another flypast by six Vampires, once again led by Lieutenant Bradshaw, during which the aircraft buzzed the showground three times in different formations.

The large crowd at the show was able to hear the control officer speak to the Leader of the flight by wireless and Lieutenant Bradshaw replying and giving his position. The other pilots were

Lieutenants Harry Coleman, Bobby Blair, Colin Graves, Mick McLaren and Flying Officer Sandy Mutch. The commentator summed up in the words, 'The planes of today and the pilots of tomorrow'. (Rhodesia Herald, 27th Aug. 1954)

In September 1954, the SRAF was in the news again when its Anson took part in the search for a missing Piper Cub. A report was received at midnight on 18th September, stating that Charles Dunn was 30 hours overdue on his first solo cross-country from Mufulira to Luanshya. A search was conducted throughout the daylight hours of 19th September by aircraft of the Mufulira Flying Club. On 20th September, the SRAF Anson joined the search, while other SRAF aircraft stood by in case additional assistance was required. As it turned out, they were not needed as news came through the following day that the pilot was safe, having made a forced-landing in the Belgian Congo.

The annual training camp

September brought the annual combined territorial exercises, this year titled Catchem and Killem. The camp was staged in the Magondi district 40 miles (64km) from Sinoia. Describing the exercise in detail the *Rhodesia Herald* reported:

On Tuesday morning early, a group of bandits (played by a company of RAR) was spotted and an air strike was immediately called for from Salisbury. Harvard aircraft took part in the strike. The bandits were found and bombed with flour bags and the strike was considered a success. There were further air strikes later in the day and more flour bombs were employed with great accuracy. The directing staff agreed that the support of the SRAF had been magnificent and that air strikes would have caused many casualties. In fact, an important contribution towards the success of Exercise 'Catchem and Killem' was made by the SRAF under the command of Brigadier E.W.S. Jacklin. Pilots of the force put in more than 50 flying hours in ten aircraft, which flew a total of over 6,500 miles [10,500km] during the exercise. They played a vital part in finding the bandits and inflicting heavy casualties on them. With the first report of the bandits, a reconnaissance flight of three Harvards and two Austers at the forward airfield at Sinoia were called upon to assist the troops in locating the enemy. The rugged bush country of the reserve, 100 miles [160km] from Salisbury providing excellent cover, made this no easy task. At first, the spotting aircraft, under the command of Captain John Moss, were rewarded by only occasional glimpses of their quarry. However, as captured bandits acknowledged, they were seriously embarrassed by the aircraft, which made it difficult for them to break cover. On the final day of the exercise, the aircraft succeeded in keeping the bandit gangs under constant surveillance from dawn until the end, radioing back valuable information on which the army acted. Brigade HQ were also able to call upon 'strike action' by four Harvards standing by at the main base at Kentucky where Major A.O.G. Wilson was the senior air staff officer in charge. The aircraft immediately went into action carrying out two sorties in which they strafed the bandits with their .303 forward guns and dropped light anti-personnel bombs in the shape of flour bags, coming in as low as 30 – 40 feet over the bush. They would undoubtedly have inflicted heavy casualties. In one instance, so accurate was the bombing, that a bandit was hit by a flour bag, about 50 of which were dropped. Meanwhile, reports had been received that forward elements among the troops were not having it all their own way, being cut off from the main body and short of food and water. Again, the air force was called in. Lieutenant Charles Paxton taking off from Kentucky in a Pembroke, dropped supplies by parachute. Two loads of 150 pounds (68kg) of rations each, were dropped to the relief of the troops, about 80 men. Finally also playing its part was the ambulance Rapide, flown by Lieutenant A.F. Chisnall, which stood by throughout the 'ops' and flew back to Salisbury a test 'casualty' brought in to Sinoia by an Auster from the airstrip at Brigade HQ 40 miles [64km] away. (Rhodesia Herald, 25th Sept 1954)

Altogether about 30 pilots and ground crew took part in this exercise, gaining valuable experience, not only in carrying out reconnaissance and supply drops but also in providing essential communications between the airstrip at brigade headquarters, Sinoia and Salisbury. This was to be the last exercise in which the SRAF was to take part.

The Royal Rhodesian Air Force

Before the Federation came into being, it had been decided that the defence of the three territories should be controlled by the Federal government, which meant that the Southern Rhodesia Air Force would cease to be. This became official on 15th October 1954, when it was announced that the new title of the air force would be Royal Rhodesian Air Force (with the permission of Queen Elizabeth II). Simultaneously, the Southern Rhodesia Women's Military and Air Service became Rhodesia and Nyasaland Women's Military and Air Service. It was also announced that the Royal Rhodesian Air Force would adopt RAF ranks in place of the military ranks, which had been in use since the end of World War II.

The first Percival Provosts arrive

On October 26th 1954, four Percival Provost training aircraft piloted by officers of the Royal Rhodesian Air Force took off from RAF station Benson, in Oxfordshire on a delivery flight to Salisbury. They were the first Provosts to be collected by the RRAF under its re-equipment programme, 14 Vampires and two Percival Pembrokes having already been delivered.

The Percival Provost carried an instructor and pupil pilot side-by-side in an enclosed cockpit. It was powered by a 550-horsepower Alvis Leonides engine providing a cruising speed at sea level of 194 mph (312 km/h). The wingspan was 35 feet (10.55m) and the length was 29 feet (8.84m). A jet-propelled version of the Provost had recently been built and had flown for the first time earlier in the year at the Society of British Aircraft Constructors' Show at Farnborough, England.

On their ferry flight from Oxfordshire to Salisbury, the Provosts were under the command of Flight Lieutenant John Moss and as usual, the flight was accompanied by a Dakota, piloted on this occasion by Flight Lieutenant Peter Pascoe. The ferry pilots were Flight Lieutenants Tony Chisnall, Brian Horney, Chris Dams and Mike Saunders. The scheduled route was the old faithful, pioneered by the Spitfires. Leaving Benson on 25th October, the aircraft flew via Dijon, Cagliari, Tripoli, Benghazi, Tobruk, El Fayid, Wadi Halfa, Malakal, Entebbe and Kasama arriving in Salisbury exactly on schedule on 4th November.

The Dakota pioneers a West African route

Also in October 1954, the RRAF took delivery of a second Dakota, which was collected from Prestwick in Scotland by Squadron Leader Archie Wilson. This ferry turned out to be quite an adventure as Archie himself told the story. It seems that Air Commodore Jacklin was anxious to have an alternative, economical ferry route up his sleeve and so decided to utilize the Dakota delivery flight to help crystallize his thinking on the subject. It was decided that an exploratory route should be followed by the new Dakota flown by Archie and carrying Ted Jacklin as passenger, with Warrant Officer Max du Rand as wireless operator, Warrant Officer Titch Nesbitt as engineer and Sergeant James as French-speaking-interpreter. The aircraft was to fly through France, across the Sahara Desert, via West Africa and the Congo to Salisbury.

As the flight plan involved landings at remote airstrips in the Sahara Desert, Jacklin enlisted the support of an old friend, a general in the French air force. He obtained the willing agreement of the authorities who promised to provide all available assistance including the cooperation of elements of the Foreign Legion manning outposts along the proposed route.

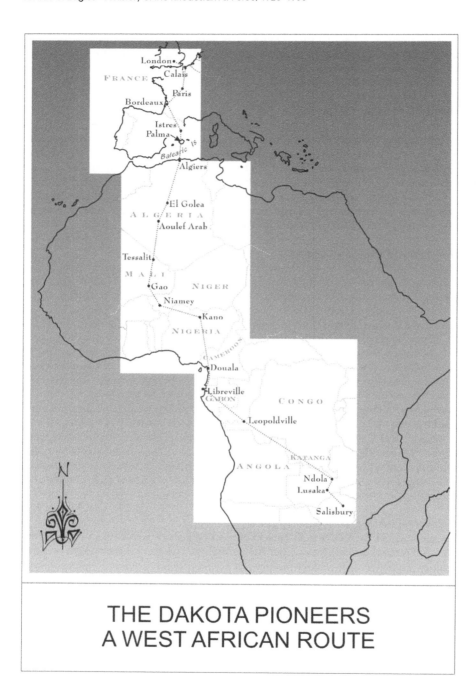

THE DAKOTA PIONEERS
A WEST AFRICAN ROUTE

A final itinerary was prepared and diplomatic clearance sought and given.

The aircraft was air-tested and accepted on 24th October 1954, and positioned at RAF Benson for departure. Leaving from Benson on 26th October, the scheduled flight was via Palma in the Balearic Islands, Algiers, El Golea, Aoulef el Arab (both in Algeria), Tessalit (in Mali), Gao (on the Niger River in Mali), Niamey (also on the Niger), Kano (in Nigeria), Doula (in Cameroun), Libreville (in Gabon), Ndola, Lusaka and so to Salisbury.

Apart from the failure of the automatic pilot over France, which necessitated flying the Dakota manually for the rest of the journey, the aircraft performed well. However, according to Archie Wilson, the trip had its interesting moments, such as having to land in a sandstorm at Aoulef el Arab, and touching down in a 40-knot cross wind at Niamey. The very short, rough and stony airstrip at Tessalit, in the southern Sahara was made all the more challenging when on their arrival, they found that the position of the landing T called for a downwind approach. No amount of coaxing by the French-speaking Sergeant James, could persuade the airstrip controller to divert from his ruling that the aircraft must land in the direction indicated by the T. The Dakota landed safely albeit making use of every last metre of the runway in the fresh, gusting tailwind. The difficulty of the landing was more than compensated for by the mortification of the controller when he realized his mistake—it seems that he had been firmly convinced that he had placed the T into the wind.

Ted Jacklin was deeply touched, when on alighting from the aircraft, he was met by the outpost commander, a corporal of the French Foreign Legion, who had drawn up his entire complement of six men as a Guard of Honour, which he invited Air Commodore Jacklin to inspect! But the pièce de résistance was to come. On arriving at the mess, the RRAF team were confronted by a three-course luncheon with hors-d'œvres, asparagus, cold roast chicken and pudding, supplemented by bottles of premier French Champagne. It was revealed that the French general, friend of the commanding officer, had had these rations especially flown in. To the Legionnaires it was a mirage come true and they enthusiastically turned the occasion into a gala event. After toasting Rhodesia and France in neat whisky, everyone wined and dined in style. It was a very happy crew that took off on the next leg of the journey.

The final appreciation of this alternative route was that with its spartan facilities and inherent hazards, it would only be feasible for use in an emergency. In fact, such an emergency was to occur quite soon.

According to a report in the Citizen, the Southern Rhodesia and Federal governments had spent more than £1,000,000 since 1948 on the purchase of new aircraft. However, for that very reasonable sum, they had maintained two squadrons of combat aircraft. It was intended that the Provost should replace the Tiger Moths and Harvards for training purposes. Cadet pilots would now start training on Provosts and convert to Vampires. Following the excitement of the arrival of the Provosts, the remainder of the year passed in routine fashion, only broken in November by a search for a missing aircraft.

The last Spitfire

With the arrival of the Provost and Vampire, the Spitfire seemed to be on its way to the scrap heap. It was a sad end for a well-loved machine but some of the aircraft did escape the final indignity of being melted down. For many years, a Spitfire graced the entrance to New Sarum Air Force Base. In the late 1970s this aircraft was taken down and after much tender loving care, was put back into flying condition and flown by Jack Malloch before enthusiastic crowds in 1980. Chris Dams, talking about this aircraft said:

I was the last (air force) pilot to fly the Spitfire that Jack Malloch refurbished. The Spitfires were used post-Wings for operational training, and No 3 SSU Course, which was my course, was the last to fly them. There were only a couple left serviceable and we used to air test them on Saturdays. The last flight by SR 64, which was Jack Malloch's aircraft, was on Saturday 18th December 1954. All the others were u/s. It was the propeller that caused them to be grounded. This was made of wood and its pitch-change mechanism was operated by a ring gear attached to each blade root so that they changed pitch in unison. When the wood shrank there was movement, which caused problems.

Sadly, SR 64 crashed after flying into a storm cloud on 26th March 1982, killing the pilot, Jack Malloch. Seven of the Mk 22 Spitfires were sold to the Syrian government for £200 each. Not wishing to take the chance that the SRAF took in ferrying them out, the Syrian government arranged for them to be crated in Salisbury and shipped via Beira in April 1955.

In January 1955, the Federal Prime Minister, Sir Godfrey Huggins, flew to Cape Town in an RRAF aircraft on his way to attend the Prime Ministers' Conference in London and during the same month, Wing Commander Keith Taute returned to Salisbury after his stint at Rhodesia House. His place as air attaché was taken by Wing Commander Harold Hawkins.

Vampire T 11

Flight Lieutenant Charles Paxton undertook his sixth ferry in March 1955, when he commanded the flight, from England, of the first five two-seater Vampire Jet T 11 training aircraft. The ferry pilots were Flight Lieutenant Ossie Penton, Flight Lieutenant Keith Kemsley, Flying Officer Frank Mussell and Flying Officer W.H. (Bill) Smith. The jets took off from Benson on Saturday, 5th March, and touched down at Salisbury Airport a little after 13h00 on 10th March, having been held up at Ndola by bad weather.

As all these new aircraft had been purchased, it was decided that the public should get a chance to see what their tax money had paid for and so began the first round—the Federation flag showing exercises.

> *Over 5,000 spectators watched an air display by RRAF Vampires at Chileka Airport yesterday afternoon. (3rd April). This was the first time jet aircraft had been seen in Nyasaland. The detachment was led by Flight Lieutenant J.H. Deall and the display was organized by the RAF Association on the occasion of its birthday.* (Rhodesia Herald, 4th April 1955)

A week later, it was the turn of Lusaka.

> *Four Vampire jet planes of the RRAF stole the show at the Lusaka Flying Club's rally here today with high-speed flying and aerobatics that thrilled the crowd.* (Sunday Mail, 10th April 1955)

Meanwhile, yet another flight of five Vampires was on its way from Britain. The aircraft had been due to arrive on 4th May but were delayed by bad weather over France. This consignment, which consisted of three T 11 two-seater Vampire Trainers and the two FB 9 single-seater Vampires, brought the total Vampire strength to 24. But while the aircraft arrived with the greatest of ease the spares came by a more laborious route, as a Port Elizabeth newspaper reported:

> *Two Rhodesian army NCOs will face a long and difficult test of driving skill when they leave Port Elizabeth on Friday. They have to drive a large trailer 66 feet (20m) in length, loaded with the crated wings of a jet fighter plane, all the way from Port Elizabeth to Salisbury, 1,500 miles [2,400km] by road. The wings will be used as spare parts for Vampire fighters of the RRAF.* (Rhodesia Herald)

A major effort was now being made to complete New Salisbury Airport and one of the greatest concentrations of heavy earth-moving machines ever to assemble in the Federation was working almost non-stop. Tenders had been received for the terminal building of which the lowest was £393,578. Of course, the air force had been using the airport since October 1953 but it was not yet ready to receive civil passenger transport, except in cases of emergency. Civilian aircraft had become larger and faster and it was necessary to strengthen the runway further. In order to carry out this work, the Vampire jet-training squadron had to move away from Salisbury and it was decided that the squadron should be posted to Livingstone Aerodrome on detachment from June until September 1955. The advent of the Vampires at Livingstone caused problems for the Livingstone Flying Club. There was no room for their three light aircraft in the hangars so they had to be moved to Victoria Falls Aerodrome where they were parked in the open, under some trees.

On 4th July, an article appeared in the *Rhodesia Herald*, written by W.E. Arnold, of the Federal Information Department. Giving a resumé of the state of the RRAF, he pointed out that the pilots being trained on the Provost would find conversion to Hunters and Canberras a relatively easy matter. While the accent was on jet aircraft, the transport work was also important. For a number of years the air force had relied on a single Dakota, presented to the prime minister of Southern Rhodesia by Field Marshal Smuts at the end of the Second World War. The Dakota fleet had now been expanded to three and it was planned to acquire another five. When the fleet was complete, it would consist of two Dakotas equipped for VIP transport and six freighter-troop carriers. The RRAF also had two Pembroke eight-seater aircraft and three Austers in service. The Rapides and Ansons were due to be disposed of. The two Harvards equipped for passenger carrying, were largely used for flying doctor service and had done valuable work for ten years. The rear cockpit of the Harvard was fitted with a comfortable plush seat for the doctor or passenger.

In 1955, the RRAF logged an average of 1,000 flying hours a week. There was a total of 31 staff pilots and 60 pupils. The RRAF also had 14 staff officers who had been trained as pilots and still flew five hours a month. Two thirds of the pilots had seen battle during the Second World War or in Korea and they held 15 decorations among them.

RRAF ground staff had the highest reputation. Their workshops could carry out any job on their aircraft from daily inspections to the overhaul of engine and airframe, except for a complete overhaul of the jet engines which, after 450 hours, had to be sent back to the factory. The average length of service of the ground crew was between 11 and 12 years. (*Rhodesia Herald*, 4th July 1955)

At a dinner in Ndola in October, Sir Roy Welensky, then acting prime minister, outlined the Federal Defence commitment.

> *The Federation's principal war commitment, he said, was its air force and its immediate contribution would be two day-fighter ground-attack squadrons, backed up by a transport squadron. These squadrons would be battle-trained and capable of immediate action. We have at home the obligation to maintain law and order and internal security. We have also the self-interest of defending our borders. The Middle East is likely to be a battle ground in any future war and such is the pace of development in the air that in a few years' time, aircraft based in the Middle East will be well within range of the Federation.* (Sunday Mail, 23rd Oct. 1955)

The last Vampire ferries

Meanwhile another ferry had been taking place. Once again, the Vampires were collected from Benson Air Field in Oxfordshire and made the first leg to Istres Air Field near Marseilles. Flying at 30,000 feet at an average speed of over 300 mph (480 km/h) their route took them to Tunis, on the North African coast, Khartoum and Juba in the Sudan, Entebbe on Lake Victoria and so through Northern Rhodesia to Salisbury. The Vampires landed at New Sarum on 1st November 1955.

The worst part of the journey was from Khartoum to Juba, 656 nautical miles [1,216km] with no alternative airfield in case of trouble," said Air Commodore Jacklin. On one occasion the flight ran into a heavy hail storm, receiving dents in their metal work but never a Vampire failed to complete the journey. (Rhodesia Herald)

Just over a month later, on 16th December after a three-day wait for the weather to clear, a ferry flight of eight Provosts accompanied by an RRAF Dakota left Benson. Even with special long-range tanks, the Provosts had to make frequent refuelling stops and only arrived in Salisbury on Christmas Day. This final ferry brought the total strength of new aircraft to: 16 Vampire FB 9s, 16 Vampire T 11s, 16 Provosts, seven Dakotas and two Pembroke light transports.

The whole operation of bringing the Vampires, Provosts and Pembrokes to Africa had been completed without a single serious mishap.

In April 1956, a silver model of a Vampire fighter was presented to the RAF Ferry Wing of Benson Air Station by Sir Gilbert Rennie, High Commissioner for the Federation of Rhodesia and Nyasaland as a token of appreciation from the Air Officer Commanding, E.W.S. Jacklin, and all ranks of the RRAF. On the plinth below the aircraft are the badges of the RRAF and RAF station Benson and the words: "In appreciation of the valuable assistance given during the re-equipping of the RRAF."

The RRAF is re-formed into four squadrons

January 1956 saw the re-formation of the RRAF into four squadrons in place of the existing three. The formation of No 1 Squadron took place at New Sarum. This squadron was equipped with Vampire T 11s and Vampire FB 9s and its major tasks were to train pilots as PAIs (pilot attack instructors) and to meet the RRAF Middle East commitment to Commonwealth Defence. The first officer commanding of the newly-formed squadron was Squadron Leader D.A. (Dicky) Bradshaw with Flight Lieutenant A.W. (Sandy) Mutch as flight commander while the PAIs were Flying Officer Frank W. Mussell and Pilot Officer E.J. (Ted) Brent.

No 2 Squadron, also formed at New Sarum was under the command of Squadron Leader Charles H. Paxton. Its prime role was that of instruction and it was responsible for the Advanced Flying Training of Short Service Unit pupil pilots. This squadron was also equipped with Vampire T 11 and FB 9 aircraft.

No 3 Squadron, the old transport squadron, had been the first squadron formed after the war. Its commander was Squadron Leader E.T.C. (Ted) Cunnison and apart from transport duties, it had the task of carrying out reconnaissance and photographic work. In this capacity, the pilots of the squadron worked in close cooperation with the photographic section, which had been transferred from its primitive quarters at Cranborne to New Sarum in 1952. During 1955, the section had moved into its permanent home at New Sarum and the photo-recce Rapide was replaced with a newly converted Dakota. Consequently, the photographic staff had been increased to cope with the steadily increasing workload. This included photographing the upper reaches of the Zambezi during flooding, to record high-water levels; a route survey of the new road to Kariba and a low-level survey of Salisbury city for a new large-scale ordnance map. The photographic section was producing 25,000 contact prints and enlargements each year.

No 4 Squadron, which came into being on January 3rd 1956, was also initially based at New Sarum. Its role was both internal security and pupil pilot training. The squadron was equipped with Provost aircraft. These were originally designed as trainers but those belonging to the RRAF had been modified to carry armament in the form of .303 Browning machine guns, rocket projectiles, bombs and anti-riot tear-smoke grenades. Supply canisters could also be fitted for dropping medical supplies and rations. Squadron Leader Doug Whyte commanded the squadron. The flight commander was Flight Lieutenant Ken Edwards. Squadron Log-book for January 3rd reported:

> *Today was the first day of the new system. In the morning, the squadron commander called a meeting of all squadron staff pilots. At the meeting, he explained at some length the requirements for the squadron for the future and gave some intimation of a projected move for the squadron as a whole to station 'X'.*

Thornhill—Gwelo

The mysterious station 'X' was soon revealed as Thornhill, Gwelo.

> *The Federal government decision announced yesterday to move the RRAF Training Unit from the New Salisbury Airport to Thornhill, Gwelo was criticized by Northern Rhodesian members of the Federal Parliament, who felt the training unit should be moved to Livingstone, reports SAPA's parliamentary service. Lord Malvern (Sir Godfrey Huggins) said that an important reason why Gwelo was chosen instead of Livingstone was that the move to Gwelo would cost £398,000 against a cost of £1,124,000 for a move to Livingstone.*
> (Rhodesia Herald, 23rd Feb.1956)

News of the move to Gwelo was received with joy by the squadron concerned.

> *27th February. Nothing much has occurred out of the ordinary since the last entry. Squadron training has been progressing according to plan with the accent on instrument flying, instrument approaches and letdowns. AFTS (Advanced Flying Training School) chaps are just about finished now and fly their tests at the end of this week. The squadron has been participating in parade rehearsals for the Wings Parade that was held on Saturday last. Went off very well indeed. There were numerous 'congrats' (many of them from the top army brass!) and generally everyone enjoyed themselves. A very enjoyable Wings Dance was held in the officers' mess on Saturday night—much drunken revelry. Great News—station 'X' has officially been proclaimed as Thornhill, Gwelo. Things are moving now and a great deal of work is envisaged preparatory to the actual move. 4 squadron will be the first to go, followed at a later date by the rest of the RRAF—should be good fun indeed.*
> *5th March. The advanced party for Gwelo will be moving down in the first week of April, to be followed by the rest of No 4 Squadron towards the end of April. Some consternation has been caused amongst the married men by the announcement that married accommodation will not be available for about three months. Squadron starts armoured training this week. Next week we move to Inkomo to operate from there. (No 4 Squadron Diary)*

However, in Africa even the best-laid plans gang aft agley.

> *14th March. On Monday, we flew four aircraft out to Inkomo to start our range programme. Two aircraft ended up in holes (undamaged) made by white ants and the programme was cancelled until the Roads Department could service the airfield and fill up the holes. Yesterday*

we started in earnest. Scores were reasonable to begin with. Then the Event. Chris Hudson was just about to turn on for an attack when his engine chopped. He turned back and tried to make the airfield but didn't have the height. He put down in a field but ended up on his back because of the extremely soggy nature of the ground. He was rescued unhurt by the rest of the squadron chaps who in their efforts to get there fast were in a far worse physical condition at the end of the day than Chris Hudson himself—especially the bumph-jugglers!

27th March. *Quite a bit of excitement since the last entry. Bombing programme finished with fairly reasonable averages and the squadron started ABC TS Training (Airborne Carrier Tear Smoke). This consists of dropping hand grenades from low level. Yesterday while loading up, a grenade dropped out. Flight Sergeant Jock Howie took off like a startled hare only to find that the pin was still in. For the rest of the day, he shame-facedly bore the brunt of the squadron's 'chaffing'. Today as Mick McLaren and Ken Edwards started their take-off run on a sortie, four grenades dropped out of the canister. All of them went off and ironically only Jock Howie was injured, receiving a minor flesh wound. Alan Bradnick's aircraft was peppered by shrapnel but Alan himself was unhurt. The dates for the move to Gwelo have finally been fixed. The Adjutant, Flying Officer Basil Myburgh goes down on 7th April with one fireman to take over fire and crash rescue services from DCA (Department Civil Aviation). He will be succeeded on 23rd April by the advance party and the station starts operating on 14th May. The accommodation situation is still a little unhappy but appears to be improving (as various people vacate houses).*

Most of the buildings at Thornhill were in use by various government departments. When the Royal Air Force Training Group closed down, everything movable was sold and the buildings were divided among the Ministries of Agriculture, Education, the Public Works Department and the Gwelo Municipality. The officers' mess had been taken over by Glengarry School for mentally-handicapped children. Thornhill High School had been established in the domestic area while many other buildings had been used for the bulk storage of maize. The runway was still in use, as the Central African Airways Beaver flights touched down there each week and so the fire-fighting equipment operated by the Department of Civil Aviation was still functional. However, there was no air traffic control in operation.

26th April 1956. *A full month since the last entry and a lot has happened. On 7th of this month, Flying Officer Basil Myburgh proceeded to Thornhill with Sergeant Tom Crow and two native drivers by road. On Monday 9th April, he took over all fire-fighting equipment held at Thornhill by DCA and from that date continued to provide fire services for the CAA Beaver aircraft landing there. (Tomorrow DCA takes back their equipment to open a landing strip at Kariba). Apart from this function, Flying Officer Myburgh and Sergeant Crow had one or two other small jobs to do, such as: making messing contacts—taking over buildings and married quarters—using the 18 other fire-crew boys who were flown in on 9th April to clear up round the various buildings. They lived at the Midlands Hotel. Flying Officer Myburgh's wife arrived at Thornhill on 14th April and they took over and moved into house No 40. Sergeant Crow continued at the Midlands until 19th. On that date, the mess caterer Flight Sergeant Noland moved down and he and Sergeant Crow moved into House No 9 using House No 11 as the mess. On 23rd April, when the advance party (per schedule) arrived, the mess was in full operation and able to supply everything from hot meals to cold beer. On that date also the OC brought down the first Provost No 148. On 26th April, four more Provosts were flown in by Ken Edwards, Mick McLaren, Mike Saunders and Alan Bradnick. Thirty minutes after they had arrived, the Dakota carrying the governor-general touched down. This is the first official visit to the airfield. The OC took him around and showed him the RRAF section and then handed him over to Mr Todd, headmaster of Thornhill School. Equipment has gradually been* *coming down in odd loads on the 15-tonner and three-ton lorries. On Sunday (or Monday) another 15-tonner and still another are expected today. We are still, however, short of many things both for the airfield working side and for the messes (e.g. curtains that won't be here for another six weeks or so). There have been many harsh words spoken between the OC and Air HQ over the question of equipping Thornhill and Air HQ have made a few concessions. (Though not very many).* (No 4 Squadron Diary)

The idea was to carry out basic flying training on the new Provosts at Thornhill. Pupils would then return to Salisbury to complete their advanced flying training on Vampire jets. First to be trained under the new scheme were the cadets of No 9 Short Service Course, who were eventually to receive their Wings from Her Majesty Queen Elizabeth, the Queen Mother in 1957.

30th May 1956. Quite a lot has happened since the last entry. Generally everybody has arrived here at Thornhill and except in one or two cases all the married men have their wives and families with them, occupying air force houses in the Thornhill housing estate. The houses themselves are very attractive and clean. The messes of the officers, WOs and NCOs are functioning and already there have been one or two rather good parties. A very nice sundowner party was thrown by the town council of Gwelo to welcome the RRAF and it is hoped soon to be able to return the hospitality by way of a station dance. The members have organized themselves with the various sports clubs, including the golfers—and members of the RRAF have already been selected to play for the Gwelo side. Flying training with No 9 Course started on 11th May. So far nothing exciting has happened and all the pupils seem to be coping reasonably well. The station has settled down into its work pattern and things are going reasonably smoothly although we are still having a bit of hardship with regard to spares and equipment. Tomorrow—the Queen's Birthday Parade—14 cadets commanded by Flying Officer Myburgh will be participating on the ground and a flypast of five aircraft is being led by Flight Lieutenant Edwards.
31st May. Parade went well. One cadet fainted on parade but was forgiven, as he did so strictly at attention! (No 4 Squadron Diary)

Meanwhile No 1 Squadron was showing the flag at Lusaka where members took part in the Lusaka Flying Club's Air Rally on Whit Sunday. A Vampire staged a mock battle with two Tiger Moths and there was a demonstration of formation flying, the first to be given by the squadron. This was followed on May 31st, Queen Elizabeth II's official birthday by a military march past, a 21-gun salute and a flypast by No 1 Squadron Vampires. On the lighter side, a Rhodesian air speed record was set up early in June when two Vampires on a casual training flight from Bulawayo to Salisbury flew at an average speed of more than 480 mph (772 km/h) completing the journey of 194 nautical miles (359km) in 27 minutes.

Meanwhile in Gwelo all was progressing well.

6th June 1956. Sick quarters are by now well established under the new MO, Captain Jock Davidson. Happily, he has had little business as yet. Charlie Goodwin arrived today to take up his appointment as Station Technical Officer with us. Golf is taking hold. Sunday RRAF are playing in a competition match against Gwelo Golf Club.
11th June. RRAF lost four games to one. However, all the chaps say their golf is improving!
18th June. A six-inch naval shell was picked up on the Victoria Falls road last week and had been brought to us by the police for examination and possible disposal. (How that got there will forever remain a mystery.) We've received our first consignment of arms and ammunition (.303) and it is hoped to start a range programme fairly soon.

22nd June. There remain now only four out of 14 pupils to solo.

26th June. Only three pupils remain now—of these one has been suspended from further flying training—the other two are being persevered with. Saturday RRAF played Nomads Cricket Club—disaster—but enjoyable. All remaining pupils were got off solo. A most enjoyable solo party was given by them and the majority lived up to the tradition of the service i.e. of having to be put to bed. That was on the 29th (Friday). On Saturday morning pupils played staff at seven-a-side hockey and beat them 4–3.

Friday 6th July. We had our first fatality. Officer Cadet Richard J. Nahke was killed when on a solo detail. He crashed 10 miles [16km] west of Selukwe. The findings of the court of inquiry are not yet out but it is generally supposed that he was low flying. Four of our T 52 aircraft (armed version) have been withdrawn and replaced with T 1s. A not very popular move.

16th July. Flying programme a little behind schedule owing to bad weather.

24th July. Sunday we had our first visit from the GOC. He was accompanied by the AOC and was shown round the station by the OC. 'Reasonably impressed'. The swimming pool is progressing and it is expected that we will be able to use it by the end of August. A start has been made on the golf course. (No 4 Squadron Diary)

Not all the training was being done in the air.

30th July. On Saturday night or rather Sunday morning, the students took part in an exercise with the territorials at Ngamo Dam. The idea was that the 'enemy' were holding a line of approx. 400 yards (366m) and the students presumed shot down in enemy territory were to infiltrate the line in an attempt to reach safety. Having four hours in which to cover some 200 yards (183m), they took their time and were reasonably good in their efforts at concealment. However, the line was so heavily defended that it was literally impossible for anyone to get through. They were all caught but, nevertheless, seemed to have enjoyed themselves. All officers on the station now occupy officers' quarters, although two of them still require renovation.

During the next years, a regular stream of VIPs from overseas was to visit the various RRAF stations. In August 1956, accompanied by a small army of plainclothes policemen, the president of Portugal, General Francisco Higino Craveiro Lopes, himself a qualified pilot, toured RRAF station New Sarum and fired some rounds from the guns of a vampire jet trainer in the butts.

At Thornhill, a second station parade was held on the morning of 18th August.

The delay being caused by the non-arrival of 'blues' for most personnel. At the last moment, the tailors let us down again and a motley of uniforms was worn. Drill is still not a strong point. As the doctor said to the officers afterwards, "You certainly can't drill, so your flying must be terrific." (No 4 Squadron Diary)

Next day came some compensation.

A Thornhill Cricket XI took on the Gwelo odds and sods headed by the local butcher, Mr Butt, and won a hilarious game. Proceedings were considerably enlivened by the bowlers having to sink a pint every time they took a wicket and the batsmen having to do the same every 10 runs scored. Officer Cadet Malcolm Bolton who scored 54 eventually had to be helped off the field 'retired drunk'. A Thornhill VI competed in the BSAP reserve weapons meeting at the local range. Considering the handicap of lack of practice, and using drill purpose rifles, the team put up a good show ending up 6th out of eight teams competing. (No 4 Squadron Diary)

No 2 Squadron had its first fatal accident on 21st August, when a Vampire FB 9 crashed on a training flight in the Seke Reserve about 40 miles (64km) from Salisbury. The pilot, Officer Cadet David Paul Garrett, had been due to receive his Wings in three weeks. The aircraft RRAF 110, which was one of a formation of four, left a trail of wreckage for more than half a mile (0.8km). Officer Cadet Garrett was buried with full military honours on 23rd August.

During the same month, August 1956, two Provost aircraft from No 4 Squadron had a lucky escape when they ran into a freak storm. Damage to one of the aircraft was extensive.

And we are led to believe they (the hailstones) were about the size of Mount Everest. However, both pilots got home safely—the main thing in such events. (No 4 squadron Diary)

Now, at last, just over ten years after the end of World War II, the air force was about to come of age and be allowed to run free of the apron strings of the army. This was the effect of the Defence Amendment Bill put before parliament in August. Major General S. Garlake, who had been commander of both forces, would in future be general officer commanding the army, while Air Commodore E.W.S. Jacklin would assume command of the RRAF as air officer commanding and chief of Air Staff. Moving the amendment, the Federal Prime Minister, Lord Malvern said: It was also clear that the air force now that it was fully re-equipped had reached the stage where it ought logically to manage its own affairs. And the air force, must have added about time! for benign as army control may have been, there must often have been a conflict of interest and aims.

No 4 Course Short Service Unit
Wings: 12th February 1954

Buster Webb	Joined the RAF No 266 (Rhodesia) Squadron.
Cyril White	Joined the RAF No 266 (Rhodesia) Squadron—rejoined RRAF in 1961.
Doug Bebington	Joined RAF and rejoined RRAF in 1962. Later left to join Qantas.
Gary Falk	Returned to civil employment.
Ted Brent	Continued serving. Retired as squadron leader.
Cliff J. Cary	Returned to civilian life.
Robin Hood	Joined CAA.
E.T.L. Jones	Returned to civil employment.
Arthur Spann	Unknown
Lindsay Kipps	Joined RCAF, then went commercial flying.
Brian Ault	Returned to civil employment. Later joined Rhodesian broadcasting.

No 5 Course Short Service Unit
Wings: 20th August 1954

Nick Bey	Returned to civil employment.
Alan Bradnick	Continued serving. Retired as flight lieutenant and served as a reserve pilot. Later joined an insurance company.
John Cragg	Joined Department of Civil Aviation.
Bruce Gledhill	Returned to civil employment. Served in VR.
Mark Smithdorf	Continued serving. Retired to farm and mine. Joined VR.
John Stern	Joined Department of Civil Aviation.

Digby Sinclair	Returned to civil employment—rejoined March 1963—then resigned to go commercial flying.
Tony Aldridge	Joined RAF and served with 111 Squadron. Was a member of the Black Arrows Aerobatic Team.
Norman Walsh	Temporarily returned to civil employment before rejoining in June 1956. Retired as air marshal, having commanded the air force from 1981 to 1983.
Paul Hodgson	Returned to civil employment.

No 6 Course Short Service Unit
Wings: 26th February 1955

Cliff Booth	Returned to civil employment.
Mike Bracken	Returned to civil employment, then went commercial flying.
Peter Cooke	Continued serving. Retired 1976 as wing commander. Rejoined and finally retired in 1983.
Arthur Downes	Returned to civil employment.Then went commercial flying.
Jerry Dunn	Continued serving—left as squadron leader to go commercial flying.
Bill Jelley	Continued serving. Retired as wing commander to go commercial flying.
Jock McKenna	Joined RAF.
Dave McLaren	Joined the army.
Nils Prince	Joined the Civil Service. Later served in VR.
Mike Reynolds	Returned to civil employment—rejoined 1957—retired 1967 to join SAA.
Peter Ross	Joined RAF.
Stan Schur	Attended Gwebi Agricultural College and became a successful cattle rancher.

No 7 Course Short Service Unit
Wings: 25th February 1956

Eric Ehrlinger	Joined civil aviation.
Mick Grier	Continued serving. Retired as group captain.
Alan Ruile	Returned to civil employment.
Chris Spalding	Joined CAA.
Pat Meddows-Taylor	Continued serving—retired in 1967 to go commercial flying.
Ted Stephenson	Continued serving—retired as wing commander.
John Evelyn	Joined CAA. Served in VR.
Roger Brackley	Continued serving—joined RAF in 1961—rejoined RRAF September 1966. Then resigned to go commercial flying.
Graham Lindsay	Returned to civil employment.

No 8 Course Short Service Unit
Wings: 24th September 1956*

Eric Atkinson	Joined CAE.

---

* This course did not have a Wings Parade. It was cancelled as a mark of respect to Pilot Officer W.D.P. Garrett who was killed in a flying accident late in August. The Wings were presented by Colonel A.M. Bentley in his office.

Pete McLurg	Continued serving—retired as wing commander.
Walter Garrett	Killed in a Vampire flying accident.
Eddy Wilkinson	Continued serving—retired as wing commander—went to Oman and flew for the Red Cross in Mozambique.
Justin Varkevisser	Continued serving—retired as flight lieutenant to go farming. Served in VR.
Basil Green	Continued serving—flew as VR and commercial pilot.
Randy du Rand	Continued serving—left to join SAAF—rejoined RRAF and retired as wing commander.
Mike Rigby	Returned to civil employment.

The FB 9 and T 11 in battle dress—not as attractive as the high-speed silver livery though.

CHAPTER 29

The Old Lion's sharpest claw

During the year 1956, the four squadrons of the Royal Rhodesian Air Force had been reorganizing and building up to strength. Between January 1956 and June 1957, pupil pilots of No 8 and No 9 Short Service Units (SSU) were trained to Wings standard, while Nos 1 and 2 Squadrons grew in strength through the posting in of pilots who had completed the Operational Conversion Unit (OCU).

Two important events occurred towards the middle of 1956. On 30th June, the New Salisbury Airport was officially opened to civilian traffic which meant that the RRAF would be sharing the airfield, and in August the RRAF became autonomous, free at last from the control of the army.

During the second part of the year, Northern Rhodesia had some industrial unrest, with strikes and riots, followed by a declaration of a state of emergency in the Western Province. In September the RRAF were requested to help the Northern Rhodesia government by transporting two companies of the Second (Nyasaland) Battalion of the Kings African Rifles, to restore order. Seven Dakotas were utilized in this operation and later 55 European members of the BSAP were flown to the Copperbelt where they stood by in case of need.

Thornhill

At Thornhill Aerodrome, where No 4 Squadron had now settled in, a new runway was in the process of being built. This had become a number one priority because the old one was rapidly falling to pieces.

> *Visible evidence of activity on the new runway is the roar of heavy earth-moving equipment and the large clouds of dust on the far side of the aerodrome. Flying activities are now restricted to a triangle between the old runway and the tower.* (No 4 Squadron Diary, 17th Oct. 1956)

Towards the end of October the officers' mess held its first large-scale entertainment, a dinner/dance. Despite inadequate facilities, a thunderstorm and a power cut, was a great success!

The month ended in panic when all Provosts were grounded until their rudder bar pivot spindles had been examined in Salisbury for suspected fractures. A cross-country to Fort Victoria had been planned for the first weekend in November and now there were grave doubts as to whether it could be flown. Hastily, all the Provosts were stripped and Flying Officer Chris Dams flew the spindles to New Sarum for inspection. This was on 31st October. By late in the evening of 1st November, all the spindles had been checked, and at the crack of dawn on 2nd November, Chris flew them back to Thornhill, where work began fitting the spindles back into the aircraft. At 16h00 that day, a No 3 Squadron Dakota arrived to transport the spares, staff and supporting personnel to Fort Victoria for the cross-country. The Provosts were ready! A combination of organization and sheer hard work had won through. The only worry now was the weather.

On 4th November, despite a menacing thunderstorm near the aerodrome and intermittent light rain, the five Provosts piloted by students on No 9 Short Service Course, returned on time from Fort Victoria. Next came the Dakota carrying the other six pilots and staff. Despite the weather, the exercise had been both successful and enjoyable.

A 'bundu' survival course

Towards the middle of November 1956, the officer cadets from No 4 Squadron were subjected to a three-day bundu (bush) survival exercise. The plan was that two groups should be dropped by road transport at Ngamo Dam, and at a point west of Gwelo and should find their way home using only a walkie-talkie set for communication with the Provost aircraft, which was to observe their progress from the air. Although one party did get itself a little lost, excellent time was made in covering the 40 miles (64km) back to base.

On the afternoon of the penultimate day of the exercise, 14th November, while returning from a reconnaissance of the bundu bashers, Squadron Leader Doug Whyte ran into extremely widespread bad weather. With visibility restricted to a few yards by heavy rain, Doug landed safely on the main Bulawayo/Gwelo road. The aircraft was picketed at the roadside and remained there, under guard for the night. Early on the morning of 15th November at 06h30 to be exact, he returned to the scene, took off from the road and flew the aircraft back to Thornhill. The survival exercise ended successfully at noon on 25th November.

After 23 years' service as prime minister, first of Southern Rhodesia and then of the Federation, Lord Malvern (Sir Godfrey Huggins) retired at the end of October 1956 and Sir Roy Welensky became the new Federal prime minister. One of his first acts was to engage in defence talks with Sir Robert Armitage, the Governor of Nyasaland and Sir Arthur Benson, the Governor of Northern Rhodesia, flying to these meetings in an RRAF transport aircraft.

News from Thornhill

Entries in the Thornhill Squadron Diary for December make continual mention of heavy rain. The downpours had reduced the aerodrome to a sorry state and made it vital that something be done to provide hardstandings for the aircraft. This work was started on 3rd January.

Machines are working hard on the runway and at last, things are taking shape. Gravel for the hardstandings is being off-loaded by the truck-full and it is hoped that it won't be long ere work commences on these standings. (No 4 Squadron Diary)

On 5th January 1957, the main party of No 10 Short Service Course arrived by Dakota and two days later, started their training. After a quiet break, the station resumed full activity, though there was still time to enjoy the swimming pool that had now been refurbished.

As staunch supporters of the Provost, No 4 Squadron had some derisive words to say about the Pembroke when it arrived on a visit to Thornhill in February.

Who said Pigs can't fly! Thornhill was visited today by the Pneumatic Pig (alias the Pembroke) bearing a party of staff officers from New Sarum. When time came for take-off after lunch 'the elastic appeared to have broken'. The necessary mending was done to the accompaniment of much 'kindly' advice from the members of No 4 Squadron. (No 4 Squadron Diary)

When the Vampires first arrived in the country, it had been reported in the *Rhodesia Herald* that all the aircraft were equipped with Martin Baker ejector seats. On 8th January, two of these seats were used successfully, for the first time in the Federation, by an instructor and a pupil pilot of No 2 Squadron when their Vampire jet trainer crashed near Marandellas. The instructor was Flying Officer Brian Horney, and the pupil was Officer Cadet Rob Gaunt, son of John Gaunt, member of the Northern Rhodesia Legislative Council and territorial leader of the Dominion Party.

On 24th January 1957, the first Governor-General of the Federation, Lord Llewellin died, and it was an RRAF Dakota that flew from Salisbury to Bulawayo, to bring Sir Robert Tredgold to the Federal capital, where he was sworn in as acting governor-general. The Dakota landed at the New Salisbury Airport which, since its official opening in the previous July, had become one of the busiest airports in Africa south of the equator. It was estimated that an aircraft was landing or taking-off every six minutes and that the newly opened terminal building was handling 20,000 passengers a month. This was 5,000 fewer than at Jan Smuts, Johannesburg, but for various technical reasons the Salisbury Airport passengers were carried in a far greater number of aircraft. In addition, the RRAF were making increasing use of the runways.

VIPs were flitting in and out of, and around about the Federation, usually making use of the VIP Dakotas of No 3 Transport Squadron. First to arrive in January 1957, had been Air Commodore E.M. Donaldson, who brought with him an RAF team to discuss Commonwealth defence. He was tight-lipped about the talks but said he had formed the highest impression of the RRAF. A more popular visitor was Sir Jack Hobbs, the famous England opening batsman, who was treated to a bird's-eye-view of Salisbury from an RRAF Pembroke. He was followed by the United States air attaché, who was stopping over between Pretoria and the Congo, by way of Salisbury and Kariba.

Meanwhile Gwelo was still enduring an over-abundance of rain.

8th March. Flying Officer Mick McLaren flew down to Kumalo today to tie up the details of the Internal Security exercise scheduled to take place at Plumtree next weekend. Shortly after he returned, the heavens opened and the deluge soon made the aerodrome look more like a flying-boat base. A Dakota of No 3 Squadron was unable to take off owing to the state of the grass runways, so the occupants spent the night at Thornhill being lodged in the camp hospital owing to a shortage of mess accommodation.

9th March. Today 2,84 inches (72mm) of rain were recorded on the aerodrome. The Gwelo River rose above the bridge on the road to town and its valley looks like a lake.

11th March. It has rained continuously during the weekend. Flying has been cancelled because of the waterlogged state of the airfield.

12th March. The aerodrome is still u/s because of the rain! Which shows no sign of diminishing. Several days of dry weather will be needed before the ground dries sufficiently to enable flying to start again.

At last some sunshine! Flying training was resumed today.

On the following day a road convoy consisting of staff corps vehicles, the new fire tender, a Land Rover and a flying control van from New Sarum left for Plumtree to take part in the internal security exercise 'Red Coat'. The exercise lasted until 17th March, when the Provosts returned at 11h30 and the road convoy trailed back at 19h00. The exercise has provided useful experience of internal security operations. One of the lessons learnt was the difficulty in detecting well-camouflaged personnel and vehicles from the air. In fact, it was proved that one could walk through an area without being aware of tents, vehicles or troops. (No 4 Squadron Diary)

This was a lesson, which was to become painfully obvious in later years.

Just after the middle of March, work finally began on the much-needed hardstandings for the aircraft and on the new runway, which would not be completed until the end of October. No 10 Short Service Course began flying training in May and by 22nd May the first member of the course had gone solo. First off was Officer Cadet John Barnes, closely followed by Peter Petter-Bowyer and Eric Cary.

In June to facilitate projected re-equipment and reorganization plans No 2 Squadron was temporarily disbanded and the staff pilots were posted to No 1 Squadron. Advanced flying training was undertaken by 'A' flight of that squadron.

The time had now arrived for the transformation of Thornhill into a fully-fledged air force station. This necessitated providing the administration necessary to operate both training and operational squadrons up to medium bomber standards as well as providing sophisticated facilities such as a photographic section, which could make available ciné gun training and assessment. Additional officers were posted to Gwelo at the beginning of June. On 8th June, the squadron said goodbye to Squadron Leader Doug Whyte, who had been officer commanding since the formation of the squadron. His place was taken by Wing Commander Archie Wilson, with Squadron Leader Jock Barber arriving later to take up the duties of station administrative officer. Archie Wilson initially filled the dual roles of officer commanding flying and officer commanding No 4 Squadron which latter duty was delegated, for all practical purposes to Flight Lieutenant Ken Edwards, the flight commander.

The high point of 1957 occurred in July when Queen Elizabeth, the Queen Mother, visited the Federation. During her visit, No 4 Squadron was on stand-by to cover the movements of Her Majesty. Pilots and ground staff were in readiness for take-off on search and rescue duties throughout the periods that the Queen Mother was in the air. No 3 Squadron was given the task of flying the members of the local and overseas Press contingent, the entourage and the baggage. They did not, however, carry the royal family as Queen Elizabeth flew in a Viscount. On 16th July, the Queen Mother presented seven officer cadets of No 9 SSU Course with their Wings. This was the first Short Service Course to be trained at Thornhill.

The RRAF had now taken over most of the station at Thornhill, although Glengarry School continued to occupy the old officers' mess. It was decided that something special should be done for the Gwelo Show in August. So between 06h30 and 09h30 one quiet Sunday morning, a Provost aircraft was walked into Gwelo along the main road. Operation Show Plane involved a good deal of manœuvering particularly in the first lap from the hangar to the air station gate and for most of the distance the Provost actually proceeded backwards. However, the effort was worth it, because the aircraft proved to be the main attraction at Gwelo's three-day show.

The contractors were hard at work on the new runway at Thornhill and this contributed to a serious fire, which broke out just after midnight on 19th September 1957, when the bitumen pre-mix plant ignited, fatally injuring an African employee. The fire crew was quickly on the scene and soon extinguished the blaze. Later in the day another fire started in the south-east hangar, which was still being used by the Grain Marketing Board. Once again prompt action was taken by the fire section, which prevented any heavy loss of the stored maize. By then the new runway had been laid up to base level and 80% of the work had been completed in the apron area. The Public Works Department then turned its attention to the second phase of building rehabilitation renovations to the Safety Equipment Section. These were completed by September, when work began on the battery charging room.

With the advent of the rains, Gwelo's seasonal thunderstorms once again began interfering with training. However, by the end of October 1957, the new runway was almost complete, requiring only its final carpet. The surface of the eastern taxi-track was finished and all the cables for the runway and taxi-track lighting had been laid. In fact, the new runway was used for the first time on 1st November, when a Dakota piloted by Squadron Leader Ted

Cunnison landed and took off again. Meanwhile, the Cinderella squadron, No 3, had been quietly going about its work, to-ing and fro-ing, carrying everything from VIPs, through medical cases to supplies. As an example of the quantity of work carried out by this squadron, during October 1957, 75 sorties totalling 173 hours were flown and 140 passengers carried.

Canberra jet bombers
However, the really big news, at the end of the year, concerned No 1 Squadron. This was, that in January, the squadron would fly to Aden to take part in operational training with the RAF. Following this announcement, Sir Roy Welensky, the Federal Prime Minister and Minister for Defence, announced during the Budget debate that they hoped to acquire two squadrons of Canberra jet bombers. There was immediate criticism from Mr John Graylin who said he felt the money, £1,000,000, would be better spent on internal security. Sir Roy replied: "We have decided that providing two squadrons of Canberras stationed here in support of the Baghdad Pact signatories is the best part we can play in Commonwealth defence." And after further objections, he remarked, "I am not prepared to change my mind on this. I consider it is our bounden duty to make a contribution to Commonwealth defence." (*Rhodesia Herald*, Oct. 1957)

The 18 English Electric Canberra bombers purchased from the British government were to become the basis for a new squadron, No 5. The Canberra B2 currently held several world records. The aircraft was powered by Rolls-Royce Avon 1 engines, which gave a static thrust of 5,500 pounds (2,500kg). Its normal cruising height was between 45,000 and 50,000 feet and its range was in the region of 2,000 miles (3,200km). Remarking on this fact alone, Sir Roy commented: "The Canberra with its range and speed, is the answer to what has been called the 'air barrier' which has existed since the Suez crisis across the north end of Africa."

All the aircraft, three of which were T4 trainers and the remainder B2 bombers, had spent several years in service with the RAF but before delivery they were completely refurbished by English Electric Ltd and were virtually in new condition. All the aircraft were to be supplied complete with ground handling equipment, spares and tools. Following the announcement about the purchase of the Canberra, 16 RRAF pilots were nominated for Canberra conversion training at Bassingbourne RAF Station. These pilots were selected from the senior ranks of the other squadrons, a decision that was to have a profound effect on the whole air force in the years that followed. There was, at that point, only one Canberra-trained navigator serving with the RRAF, Flying Officer Pat Addison. The other 15 navigators to complete the Canberra crews were recruited primarily from the RAF, while a few came from the SAAF. All crews attended No 231 OCTU at Bassingbourne. The first course began on 23rd October 1958.

As the year 1957 drew to its end, the RRAF gave a weapons demonstration at Inkomo. Among the spectators were Lord Dalhousie, Governor-General of the Federation and the Federal Prime Minister, Sir Roy Welensky. "On the eve of their jaunt to Aden, the members of No 1 Squadron were in frisky mood. The atmosphere was enlivened by the scream of two Vampires, which made several low passes over the aerodrome this morning (28th November). The leading culprit was Group Captain Bentley." (No 4 Squadron Diary)

The first Vampire lands at Thornhill
At Thornhill, the final surface of the airfield was complete except for 500 feet (150m) at the west end of the runway, the western taxi-track and a small part of the western end of the apron. About 50% of the verges had been planted with grass but lack of rain had disrupted the planting schedule.

At 11h00 on 11th December 1957, the first RRAF Vampire landed at Thornhill. The pilot was Raf Bentley and the passenger, a very important person indeed, was Dr Vincent Grainger, consulting engineer to the government on airfield construction. The purpose of his visit was to test the newly completed runway.

Before departing for Salisbury, Group Captain Bentley did a most lively beat up of the aerodrome causing the crowd of spectators to duck. (No 4 Squadron Diary)

Towards the end of 1957, the political scene in Southern Rhodesia claimed attention. At the beginning, Garfield Todd had seemed a reasonable choice for prime minister, dealing strongly with the problems that cropped up. However, as time passed he showed himself to be headstrong and dictatorial, making decisions with little or no consultation with his cabinet. Rumours began to circulate that he was having talks with African nationalist leaders without the approval of his colleagues. He began to lose support and his followers voted against him during several crucial debates. Matters came to a head late in 1957, when most of his ministers resigned. Garfield Todd did not step down as prime minister, but decided to go it alone and appointed a new cabinet from among the members of parliament still loyal to him. A party congress was called, and Garfield Todd was deposed as leader of the party.

There was some difficulty in finding a successor but eventually the position of party leader and therefore prime minister was offered to Edgar Whitehead, the Federal representative in Washington. He accepted and arrived in the Federation to find himself a prime minister without a seat in parliament. It was decided that he should stand for the safe seat of Hillside, Bulawayo. To the consternation of the party, Whitehead lost the seat to his Dominion Party opponent. There had to be a general election, which resulted in the United Federal Party, led by Edgar Whitehead, winning 17 seats, the Dominion Party under the leadership of Winston Field gaining 13, while Garfield Todd failed to win a single seat, even losing on his home ground of Shabani.

First trip to Aden
This was all in the future. New Year 1958 for the RRAF meant all the excitement of the trip to Aden.

At dawn yesterday (4th January) five RRAF Dakota aircraft of No 3 Squadron, took off from New Sarum Airfield, Salisbury, loaded to the safety limit with all the hundreds of bits and pieces of spares, provisions and accoutrement necessary to maintain an up-to-date jet fighter bomber squadron in the air. Squadron Leader Charles Paxton said, "Every rocket, every cannon shell we fire will be paid for by our own country and we are self-contained in every way, taking all our own spares, provisions and such-like. What we cannot take with us, we will buy from the RAF." (Sunday Mail, 5th Jan. 1958)

No 3 Squadron was used to place spares along the route and to ferry servicing teams. Chileka, Dar es Salaam and Mogadishu were used as staging posts and during the whole time that the Vampires were operating in Aden there was a regular shuttle service. In fact, some members of the RAF were ferried from Aden to Rhodesia for leave. While they were in Aden, the Dakotas were attached to No 84 (Transport) Squadron RAF and during this period, they often had to fly over extremely rugged country to reach forward airfields. On one of these sorties, Flight Lieutenant Bill Smith lost one engine and had to fly for over an hour on the remaining engine to reach base.

As the transport squadron was somewhat stretched during the Aden exercise, local flights were restricted to the carrying of VIPs, but even so during the month of January, with the

Aden ferry in progress, the squadron logged 397 hours, 309 passengers and 169,650 pounds (77,000kg) of freight.

Although the RRAF's main duty in Aden was training, the squadron could be called on for operational work at any time. The Rhodesian force of 16 Vampire jet fighters, under the command of Squadron Leader Charles Paxton, was staffed by 22 officers and 72 other ranks and came under the overall control of the air officer commanding British Forces Arabian Peninsula. This was a new land/air defence responsibility stretching from Kuwait and Bahrain to Somaliland. The operational training undertaken by the RRAF consisted of ground-attack work with rockets. It was the first occasion on which the RRAF operated outside the Federation and it provided invaluable training.

On the eve of its departure, 9th January, No 1 Squadron was inspected by Lord Dalhousie, who said: "I give you my best wishes, for your forthcoming detachment to Aden. I am sure that you will maintain the fine record that you have achieved in the past and prove to be one of the Old Lion's sharpest claws." At the same time, a message was received from the air officer commanding Middle East. "We are all very proud in the knowledge that the RRAF will soon be operating side by side with the RAF in the Middle East and I am confident that this is only the renewal of a long and happy relationship."

The first flight of Vampires arrived in Aden on 15th January, while the second flight left Salisbury on that same day, spending the night of 15th January at Dar es Salaam, before proceeding to Aden where they arrived on 16th January 1958.

During their spell in Aden, the RRAF men were not only taking part in a training exercise, but they were also a squadron standing by to reinforce that particular area under the Commonwealth Air Defence Scheme and so it came as no surprise to hear that they had been in action against marauding tribesmen. There were no casualties but on one occasion Flying Officer John Mussell, who was working as squadron liaison officer with the British army formation combing the mountains for bandits, came under fire from Arab snipers for several hours. Chris Dams said:

When we went to Aden on that first detachment we had to be shown round, to become familiar with the countryside. The first sortie I did, on Monday 20th January, was with Charles Paxton and John Mussell. We were following an RAF Venom to a place called Dalla. It was a cloudy day, heavily overcast. In the vicinity of Dalla, there was a hole in the cloud. The Venom went down through the hole and we followed. The pilot was briefing us about the airfield, the army camp and the hospital at Dalla. Our duties were in support of the British army, so obviously we had to know where things were located. Anyway, we came down low over the town because of the cloud. Then the Venom pilot said, "Pull up!" And we pulled up and went right into the cloud. Now as soon as you pull up your speed is going to drop very swiftly. Next thing, I heard Charles Paxton, who was ahead of me say, "Break!" So we hauled into a turn and during the course of the turn I came out of the top of the cloud, and there, right in front of us, was this huge great mountain. The Venom had been able to climb faster and had cleared the cliff but with our slower rate of climb, we were going directly into it. Fortunately, Charles climbed out of the cloud in time to warn John and me. It would have been a very inauspicious start to write off three Vampires on a familiarization trip. (Chris Dams interview)

Charles Paxton commented later: "The serviceability record of the squadron always surprised the RAF. They just couldn't understand how we could keep our aircraft, in a state of 100% serviceability all the time." Jock Watson who served in Aden with the ground crew and later became a group captain and chief technical officer with the Rhodesian Air Force had the answer: "We achieved 100% serviceability by working till all aircraft were serviceable.

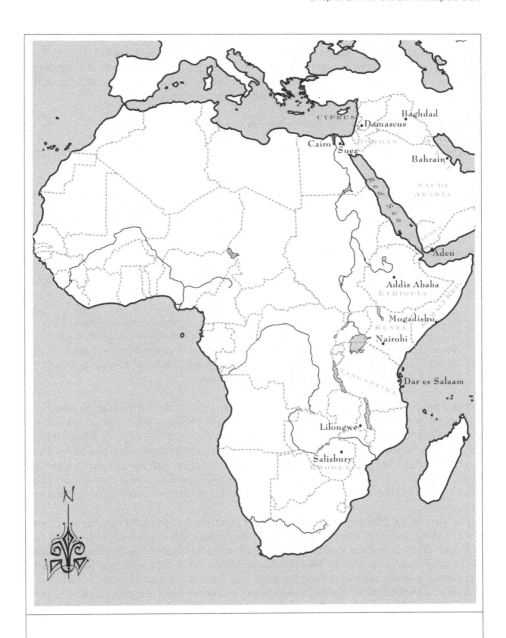

FIRST FLIGHT TO ADEN

You didn't work so many hours a day—you worked to achieve a state of readiness—all day and all night if necessary—and we obtained an efficiency level without equal."

During the first detachment, Charles Paxton shared an office with the squadron commander of the local RAF squadron, Squadron Leader George Eliot. One evening in the mess the subject of serviceability came up and George Eliot made a boast.

George: I bet that I can get as many aeroplanes into the air as you can.
Charles: When?
George: First thing tomorrow morning!

Next morning at seven o'clock Paxton had every Vampire in the air. Eliot admitted defeat but the officer commanding flying was not impressed because Paxton and his squadron had taken off without any kind of authorization.

When the time came for the squadron to return to the Federation, it was decided the men should throw a party for everyone in Aden who had been so friendly and helpful. It was arranged that No 3 Squadron would fly out the beer, (provided by the breweries) and also meat for a real Rhodesian braai on the beach. As there was no wood in Aden No 3 Squadron was also deputed to fetch some of that. However, something went wrong with the arrangements.

We invited everyone who'd shown us hospitality and that was virtually the whole of Aden. The beer arrived, the meat arrived but unfortunately the wood didn't. And there's no wood in Aden. We couldn't let it fall through so we hired the services of a local charcoal-griller-type chap at so-much a head. He did a fantastic job of feeding about 500 people. There was plenty of meat and he cooked it all in an incredibly short space of time. (Paxton)

While No 1 Squadron was settling down in Aden, the men of the RAR under the command of Major Peter Walls were returning from Malaya. In February 1958, the general officer commanding the Federal army, General Garlake, was flown to Beira by No 3 Squadron to welcome the men home from Malaya. Also in February, the Federation's Chief of Air Staff, Air Commodore Ted Jacklin made a trip to Cyprus for talks with Air Marshal Sir Hubert Patch, Commander in Chief Middle East. Although no one was saying very much, it was believed that the talks covered the use of Rhodesian bombers for the defence of the Baghdad Pact countries.

The first of the Vampires arrived back from Aden on 5th March 1958, having proved that Rhodesia could get air-reinforcements to the Arabian Peninsula within one and a half days and that a squadron could be maintained from Salisbury. Ted Jacklin, welcoming the squadron back, remarked: "We now know that we can keep a squadron supplied with everything it needs without having to strain our line of communications." During this operation, a weekly Dakota flight operated from Salisbury to Aden carrying a total of 350,000 pounds (158,800kg) of freight. Some people within the Federation still grumbled about the cost of maintaining a modern air force, even one as small as the RRAF. The *Rhodesia Herald* air correspondent put another point of view.

It is a financial impossibility for any country other than Russia and possibly America to have a balanced air force, but by regarding the Commonwealth as a single entity, Rhodesia is helping to provide a defence force with aggressive as well as deterrent capabilities—a force second to none.

The correspondent continued:

Admittedly, ground forces are cheaper but, an air force gives economy of manpower, hitting potential, state of readiness, mobility and flexibility. To put these points into practical terms look at No 1 Squadron. This consists of 16 Vampires, capable of flying 100 miles [160km] in 20 minutes and then delivering salvos of rocket projectiles, each salvo the equivalent of a broadside from the turret of a heavy cruiser. Each Vampire carries 8 x 60-lb (27kg) rockets and 4 x 20mm-cannon, capable of firing 650 rounds a minute. As an alternative, the fighter can be armed with 2 x 1, 000-lb (454kg) bombs to be dropped either from low level or in a high-dive attack. And all this strike power is provided with 100 men.

The air correspondent concluded:

A promise of help from Rhodesia in the time of one, two or three weeks, would be pleasant but useless. Vampires can be sent within a day and a half—Canberras less.
(Rhodesia Herald, 15th Feb. 1958)

For No 3 Squadron, the return of the Vampires meant the beginning of a tidying-up operation as the remnants of spares and supplies were collected from the various staging posts along the route. Personnel and ground crew had to be flown back to the Federation.

Another step towards improving Commonwealth cooperation was achieved during February when new radio equipment was installed in Salisbury enabling the RRAF to enter the Commonwealth Air Force communications network for the first time.

No 1 Squadron moves to Thornhill

The recently returned No 1 Squadron soon found that its sojourn in Salisbury was to be brief. On 21st March 1958, 15 Vampires took off and flew over Salisbury in formation en route to Thornhill, where the new Pyrene Mark 6T airfield crash and fire tender, an impressive six-wheeled fire-fighting appliance glittering with chromium, glass and brilliant scarlet paint, was on show to greet them. More that 70 ground staff and 22 officers were involved in this move, which brought No 1 Squadron to its new permanent home at Thornhill.

Towards the end of April, just 16 months after the air force became an autonomous unit, and As a result of the growth of the RRAF and its contribution to Commonwealth defence, Air Commodore E.W.S. Jacklin was promoted to the rank of Air Vice-Marshal, an equivalent rank to that of Major General S. Garlake, Chief of General Staff.

Mrs Jeannie Boggie of Gwelo, who will be remembered for her protests about aircraft noise during the Second World War, had been quiet until the arrival of the Vampires. But now she complained long and loud that her cows did not at all like the sound made by the jets screaming overhead. She received some unsympathetic comments from Cliff Allen, re the letters section of the *Bulawayo Chronicle* who said that his uncle's cows, near York, gave 10 percent more milk because of the noise of jet aircraft. Other suggestions included placing cotton wool in the cows' ears. Jeannie's cows received a respite towards the middle of May when some of the Vampires went north to Ndola in order to give a demonstration of air weapons at a site seven miles (11km) from the town.

Nos 1 and 4 Squadrons of the RRAF will attack old armoured fighting vehicles with cannon, rockets and machine-guns. A mock railway station will be attacked with fragmentation bombs, tear smoke and machine-guns, and a mock radar station will be attacked by high-diving Vampires using 250-lb bombs with instantaneous and delayed action fuses. In conjunction with troops from 1st Battalion, the Northern Rhodesian Rifles, Dakota aircraft of No 3 Transport Squadron will take part in a supply drop. (Northern News, 12th May 1958)

The display was so realistic that rocket fragments injured two spectators and narrowly missed others. One 12-year-old girl was injured in the leg and a man was struck on the temple. During the following month, Rhodesians had their first chance to take a look at Britain's Vulcan bomber, when it arrived, bringing Air Chief Marshal Sir Harry Broadhurst, Air Officer Commander in Chief, RAF Bomber Command, for discussions on air defence.

Crisis in the Middle East

When No 1 Squadron left Aden, its members eagerly looked forward to the next time presuming that it would be the following year—1959. This was not to be the case; the call was to come considerably sooner. First news of a crisis came on 15th July 1958. Iraq Army Stages Coup was the banner headline in the *Rhodesia Herald*.

> *Baghdad radio claimed today that army officers had overthrown the pro-Western Iraq monarchy and had arrested King Faisal. The radio claimed that Crown Prince Abdul Illah, King Faisal's uncle and General Nuri Es Said, 70-year-old 'strong man', prime minister of the Jordan-Iraq union, had been killed.* (Rhodesia Herald, 15th July 1958)

Meanwhile it was reported from London that the British Embassy in Baghdad had been ransacked and set on fire. Next came word that the Americans had landed marines at Beirut and the Russians had warned of a possible world war. Sir Roy Welensky, the Federal Prime Minister, made a statement in parliament as the tension heightened. "The Federal government welcomes the American action in the Middle East and will back the United Kingdom in any line, which it takes. We have not been called upon to provide any armed forces yet, but the UK government can be assured that our forces are available."

The RRAF, of course, had only short-range ground-attack Vampires capable of going immediately to the scene, but the fact of the Iraqi revolution brought about an instant accentuation of the Federal role in the front line of Middle East defence. It was obvious that the British-manned air bases at Habbaniya and the Iraq air force's Vampires, Venoms and Hunters would no longer be available for the defence of the other Baghdad Pact countries. Following the war in the Canal Zone, the United Arab Republic had erected an air barrier across North Africa. Now this Yashmak curtain as it had been called, had been extended across the Middle East as far as the frontiers of Iran.

As a precautionary measure, No 1 Squadron was brought to a state of readiness. On 18th July 1958 came the news that 2,000 British paratroopers had moved into Jordan, that Iraq, not surprisingly, had quit the Baghdad Pact and that warning noises were coming from Red China. The United Nations Security Council went into emergency session but rejected a Soviet resolution demanding the withdrawal of British troops from Jordan and United States forces from Lebanon.

In Salisbury there was talk of possible mobilization. In Moscow Krushchev said, referring to the Middle East situation, "It is the most serious moment in the world's history." Then came the news that King Faisal was dead. Together with other members of his family, he had been wiped out in a tommy-gun burst fired by a rebel army captain. The officer commanding of No 1 Squadron, Charles Paxton, received secret orders. "We were ordered to move to Aden. The whole thing was so shrouded in secrecy, I think no one knew. One hand didn't know what the other was doing."

On his arrival in Nairobi, Paxton reported to the RAF liaison officer, a group captain. His remark was, "What are you doing in Nairobi?" When Paxton said that they were on their way to Aden, the group captain replied: "Are you? Nobody told me. Well, if you've got orders to go to Aden, I suppose you'd better go but you'll have to organize your own move. We're far too busy!" So Charles Paxton and the others set about organizing their own move from Nairobi to Aden. One of the main problems was obtaining fuel. The squadron had to find a refuelling stage somewhere between Nairobi and Aden. The navy finally came to our rescue and positioned fuel at Mogadishu for us, so we managed after three or fours days to reach Aden. (Paxton)

No official statement had been made about the move and the Federal capital buzzed with rumours. Gwelo, the hometown of the jets was goggle-eyed. The *Rhodesia Herald* reported:

> *Secrecy surrounds the reason for the appearance in Kenya of a group of Rhodesian airmen who arrived at RAF Eastleigh in a Dakota aircraft. Air force and army spokesmen have been unable to disclose the reason behind the manœuvre or the strength of the party. All they say is that the airmen are 'just passing through'.* (Rhodesia Herald, 10th July 1958)

Obviously some official statement had to be made and it came on 4th August 1958, when Sir Roy Welensky disclosed that No 1 Squadron was operating in Aden, together with several Dakotas from No 3 Squadron. In fact, by this time, 150 Rhodesians were based in Aden.

Aden and the Arabian Peninsula had been a centre of unrest for some time. Apart from chronic troubles with communist-armed Yemeni tribesmen on the frontier, discontent was also being stirred by the exiled Mohammed El Jiffri, president of the Southern Arabia League, who alleged British aggression in the Peninsula. Then there was the problem of the Sultanate of Muscat and Oman, where Omani nationalists continued to defy the Sultan and his British-officered troops. As soon as No 1 Squadron arrived in Aden they started work.

> *We relieved the local RAF squadron, which had moved out—so we were the only fighter squadron on the base. It was fairly routine really. We were more ground-attack than day-fighter, working in conjunction with the army. When suitable targets cropped up we were briefed and off we went.* (Paxton)

As in all war situations, unpleasant jobs had to be carried out. On one occasion, orders came through to attack a camel train moving north near Daula. The squadron was commanded to knock the train out with rockets.

> *It was messy and most unpleasant, a bit of a nasty thing to do, but we had positive instructions to go and hit this thing. Then having written this camel train off, when we came back there seemed to be conflicting orders and we shouldn't have done it. However, it was discovered a couple of weeks later that we had in fact put paid to a possible up-rising, as the camels were running arms and ammunition through. They are very brave people the Arabs up there. There's no doubt about it.* (Paxton)

Jock Watson, later to be promoted to group captain and senior technical officer was in charge of the ground crew. He remembered:

> *Arming and turning the aircraft round became the job of everyone, irrespective of their trade, and we all became first-class at rearming. The speed at which we could get an aircraft turned round and prepared for the next mission was something quite unheard of.* (Jock Watson)

The main problems on this detachment were heat and corrosion. Aden stands on rocky soil containing gypsum, or calcium sulphate, which forms a dust.

We had to keep our aeroplanes serviceable. They were the only ones we had. The RAF Venoms flew 800 hours and then the engines were thrown away. Well, to keep ours serviceable meant washing down regularly and keeping everything well- lubricated. (Paxton)
I think we set a bit of a precedent. We washed our aircraft down with cloths and buckets of water. All ranks would be there to help out. (Watson)

Of course, this would not have been possible had the squadron been stationed in Aden for a year or more. The Rhodesians knew that they would only be in Aden for two or three months and that the aircraft were needed back at home when the detachment was completed, so they took meticulous care of the Vampires. "And it paid off. We're still flying those aircraft today," a remark made by Group Captain Watson in 1972 but it was to be equally true in 1980.

Apart from the gypsum dust there was the intense heat, which often rose to 120° Fahrenheit (49° C) in the shade. The men suffered from heat fatigue even when no heavy work was being done. Once they were airborne, the Vampire had a very efficient cooling system but this could not be used on the ground.

My chaps in the ground crew suffered all the time. I mean we didn't complain. We knew that the chaps in the air had to be efficient, had to keep cool, but our offices and workshops, in those concrete buildings, were like ovens. I remember the STSO Jimmy Pringle, was in his office one day, a concrete cell really, and I walked in and there he was throwing buckets of water over the walls. "It's as good a way of air-conditioning as any, Jock," he said. And certainly it did drop the temperature a few degrees—for a while. (Watson)

Jock Watson remembered a barracuda cooked whole in the sergeants' mess, trips to the duty-free port of Aden for cameras and binoculars, a dose of Aden tummy but mainly work, work, work and more work. But it was a challenge. Charles Paxton remembered one incident concerning the Ethiopian Emperor, Haile Selassie.

The RAF hierarchy were trying to make pals with him. They wanted to route aircraft through Ethiopia and in fact we did use one of the Ethiopian air force bases on one of our trips. It was about 30 miles [48km] from Addis Ababa. Anyway, the Emperor wanted to see a demonstration of firepower for some unknown reason and so two of us, John Mussell and I went through, taking a Dakota and some rockets and 20mm ammunition. The Swedish air force was, at that time organizing the Ethiopian air force and we cooperated with them in this weapons demonstration. Whether they were trying to pull a fast one on us, I don't know, but they wanted us to attack an Ethiopian village, which of course I refused to do. They said they would evacuate the village. We could use it as a target. I said no. Finally it was agreed that they would erect some targets for us, which we demolished on our first attack—all of them. The hierarchy of Ethiopia was suitably impressed. (Paxton)

Back in Aden, in September, came a typical operation. Two forts standing on a ridge, close to the Yemeni border near the town of Am Sauma, had been firing at passing convoys using heavy machine guns.

Well, the forts in that part of world were not particularly well-built, just large stones piled one on top of the other, but they were pretty effective against small-arms fire. The first time we attacked one of these forts, our rockets went clean through the wall and out the other side, just knocking a couple of stones out. Then, after a while we got the trick. We discovered that by firing rockets into the base of the fort, we could make the whole thing collapse quite easily. (Paxton)

One final comment on the second Aden detachment came from Mr R.A. Butler, British Home Secretary. Addressing a lunch hour meeting of the Rhodesian National Affairs Association in Salisbury on 18th September 1958, he said: "I want to thank you for sending your squadron to Aden. It has been of the utmost help and has shown a feeling of solidarity. You have, in fact, been one of our most loyal friends."

No 9 Course Short Service Unit

Wings: 16th July 1957
These officer cadets had the privilege of having their Wings presented to them by Her Majesty the Queen Mother.

Tusky Britchford	Joined East Africa Airways.
Mike Murray	Returned to civil employment.
Mike Pollard	Returned to civil employment.
Ian Hutchinson	Killed while crop-spraying in UK.
Frank Gait-Smith	Continued serving—left to join Qantas.
Bob Spandow	Went commercial flying in East Africa—joined Aer Lingus.
Rob Gaunt	Continued serving. Retired as a wing commander. Then entered politics.
Gerry Craxford	Continued serving. Then resigned to go commercial flying.

No 10 Course Short Service Unit

Wings: 19th August 1958

Ian Ferguson	Went farming.
Murray Hofmeyr	Continued serving—retired as wing commander.
Peter Petter-Bowyer	Continued serving—retired as group captain.
Ian Law	Continued serving—left in Jan. 1965 to join CAA. Served in VR.
Dave Thorne	Continued serving—left January 1965 to join Qantas—rejoined later and retired as Air Vice-Marshal.
John Barnes	Continued serving—retired as air commodore.
Eric Cary	Continued serving. Killed in a flying accident 9/2/1961.
Gordon Wright	Continued serving—retired as group captain.
Keith Corrans	Continued serving—retired as group captain. Went to commercial aviation and then joined RAF.
Bill 'Wally' Galloway	Continued serving—retired as flight lieutenant and then went commercial flying.

CHAPTER 30

Emergency in Nyasaland

On 25th September 1958, No 2 Squadron was re-formed at Thornhill Station, Gwelo, from 'A' flight of No 1 Squadron and placed under the command of Flight Lieutenant Ossie Penton. The squadron was initially equipped with Vampire T 11 trainers and was responsible for the advanced flying instruction of No 11 Short Service Unit. Meanwhile 16 senior RRAF pilots, mainly from No 1 Squadron, had proceeded to the United Kingdom to undertake a conversion course to Canberra bombers. The course began on 23rd October at 231 Operational Conversion Training Unit, Bassingbourne.

No 3 Squadron was still quietly and efficiently going about its job of ferrying VIPs around, both inside and outside the Federation. In fact, during 1958, the squadron's flying hours approached 3,000 and though the number of passengers carried was down, the freight load was up to 836,000 pounds (380,000kg). It was during November that the squadron answered an emergency call to fly an iron lung from Gwelo Isolation Hospital to Fort Victoria where a case of paralytic poliomyelitis had been diagnosed.

Ground Control Approach Radar for Thornhill

By the end of 1958, the installation of Thornhill's new Ground Controlled Approach Radar System (GCA) was complete. This system was designed to assist pilots on their approach and landing at the airfield and enabled aircraft to make a landing irrespective of the weather conditions prevailing by day or night. The full GCA equipment consisted of two complete and independent radar systems: the area surveillance or search radar (ASR) and the precision approach radar (PAR), both systems being situated on the airfield. The ASR system operated on the ten-centimetre band and scanned through 360° in azimuth. This enabled the ground controller to see fighter aircraft within a radius of 50 nautical miles (93km) and larger transport aircraft up to 100 nautical miles (186km) away, and in elevation from ground level up to 40,000 feet. He could also see all high ground and hazardous obstructions within this area. The PAR system operated in the three-centimetre band, scanning in azimuth 10° either side of the centre line of a selected runway and 7° in elevation, to a range of 15 miles (24km) from the touchdown point on the runway. This gave the ground controller a three-dimensional picture, which enabled him to talk down an approaching aircraft accurately in azimuth and elevation from 15 miles (24km) away on the final approach, to touchdown. Many aircraft and perhaps lives were saved by this equipment.

Added to the latest radar facilities, Thornhill now possessed a theatre and in January 1959, members of the drama group staged their first production: Rose and Crown by J.B. Priestley.

Thornhill also had many first class sportsmen. This led to the development of excellent sporting facilities and to the participation of station teams in Midlands sporting events. As well as demonstrating their superiority over the army in rugby and cricket, Thornhill's 1st

XV proved to be one of the premier sides in the national first league. Unless Thornhill was engaged in inter-service fixtures, the Club was home to a few stalwarts from the army's Central African Command Training School, which was not able to raise its own rugby team. It was this sort of inter-service cooperation that strengthened service ties and provided the incentive for the founding of the Combined Services Sports Control Board, which arranged for coordinated sport at international level.

A temporary halt to flying training

Members of No 11 Short Service Unit received their Wings on 19th December 1958, following an intensive training period. From this date, No 2 Squadron once again became ineffective, as the staff pilots were posted to the United Kingdom to attend Canberra Conversion Courses, before the formation of Nos 5 and 6 Squadrons. This, in fact, was to be the end of flying training by the RRAF until November 1960.

Boxing Day 1958 brought an event that could have been the most appalling tragedy but was alleviated by the prompt action of men on the spot. A UAT airliner with 63 passengers and a crew of seven was taking off from Salisbury Airport when it ran into a storm-front just as it was leaving the ground. The aircraft dropped back onto the tarmac, crashed and burst into flames. Heavy rain blocked sight of the crash from the control tower but the alarm was given by a security guard at the end of the runway, and RRAF fire tenders rushed to the spot. Three people died in the crash and many were injured. The victims were taken first to the RRAF hospital at New Sarum where more than 50 received treatment. Those seriously hurt were then rushed to the general hospital in Salisbury.

Early in 1959, No 4 Squadron moved back to New Sarum and assumed a new role, that of Light Ground-Attack and Reconnaissance. No sooner had squadron members settled in, than they were dispatched to inspect all the airfields in the Federation—a task that provided aircrews with valuable first-hand knowledge of the facilities available.

Nyasaland emergency

Despite its many advantages, Federation was bitterly opposed by African leaders in Northern Rhodesia and Nyasaland. One of these was Dr Hastings Banda (later the first prime minister and then president of Nyasaland) who had returned to Nyasaland in 1958 after an absence of 40 years, and had assumed leadership of the African National Congress Party (Nyasaland). At the beginning of 1959 the storm broke. The African National Congress parties in each of the component territories began a deliberate campaign of riots and intimidation. In Nyasaland, the position was particularly serious and in February, a plot to murder Sir Robert Armitage and other top officials, was revealed. Sir Robert requested help from the Federal authorities. A state of emergency was declared and RRAF squadrons were placed on stand-by.

A composite Tactical Air headquarters under the command of Wing Commander Archie Wilson was established at police headquarters in Zomba and a base airfield was set up at Chileka under the command of Wing Commander Doug Whyte. No 4 Squadron was positioned at this base together with elements of No 3 Squadron. The TAC HQ commander and his staff, which included Wing Commander John Deall and Officer Cadet Vic Wightman with Flying Officer Peter Cooke as the detachment adjutant and air traffic controller, were responsible for all air support in Nyasaland. Brigadier R.E.B. Long was commander of the Federal army deployed in the territory and both he and the air force commander served on the Security Council chaired by Sir Robert Armitage, Governor of Nyasaland.

On 20th February, No 3 Squadron was called upon to uplift 129 members of the security forces to Blantyre. This request came at a difficult time because two Dakotas were at Africair on major overhauls. Luckily, Africair was able to lend the squadron a replacement, but it was in poor condition and was nicknamed The Flying Drip Tray. Further troops were flown to Blantyre on 21st February and four Provosts were moved north to Chileka while Vampire jets took part in show-the-flag flights over Nyasaland on 22nd February.

Sunday saw bloody riots in Blantyre where 60 people were injured. Troops and aircraft assisted the police but the disturbances severed all communications between Blantyre and Limbe for three hours. After a morning meeting called by the African National Congress, the crowd moved to the clock tower square in Blantyre. A Provost spotter aircraft circled overhead and the crowd, which at that stage was in a fairly good humour, broke off shouting Congress slogans to give the aircraft a cheer. However, when officials of Congress arrived and addressed the gathering, the mood changed and stoning followed.

On February 24th 1959, the territorial force was called up and more troops had to be flown from Heany to Lilongwe as trouble spread. Rumbles of discontent were felt the following day at Kariba, where a strike began, mainly among workers from Nyasaland. As a result, No 3 Squadron was called upon to airlift 100 troops to Kariba. The squadron was being really extended.

On that same day, 24th February, the RRAF went into action in Nyasaland for the first time, when a Provost was called in to drop teargas canisters on rioting crowds at Lilongwe, after troops of the King's African Rifles opened fire. By the following day, Nyasaland's main road link with East Africa was in the hands of rioters. African mobs had taken over the custom's post at Fort Hill (now Chitipa) on the road to Mbeya and Dar es Salaam. The airfield at Fort Hill, the only field in the Northern Province capable of taking troop-carrying Dakotas, had been blocked with barrels and tree trunks. The Federal government was, therefore, unable to fly in reinforcements.

The government of Tanganyika, which was a United Nations Trust Territory, moved troops up to the border but found the road blocked. On 26th February, a state of emergency was proclaimed in Southern Rhodesia, the African National Congress was banned and its leaders flown by No 3 Squadron to Khami Prison, in Bulawayo. Meanwhile Fort Hill was still in the hands of African rioters and the road north continued closed. A group of former military parachutists offered their services to the Federal government. Gerald Gordon, a committee member of the newly formed Central African Parachuting Association suggested that, given the use of two RRAF Dakotas, parachutes and arms, they would recapture the airfield with minimum casualties.

In Southern Rhodesia, the first day of the state of emergency passed quietly, but in Nyasaland one rioter was shot dead and four were injured at Chigaru 20 miles (32km) from Blantyre when the KAR opened fire on a mob advancing with iron bars and sticks.

On February 28th news reached Salisbury that a police force from Tanganyika had crossed the border and cleared the Fort Hill runway of obstructions. Members of the force were now waiting for the RRAF to make a test landing. A check was carried out from the air and the runway declared safe for troop-carrying Dakotas. It was only then that the story of what had happened on February 20th became known. That morning, a Dakota with security force personnel on board had taken off from Chileka Airport on a flight to Fort Hill. As the aircraft was nearing its destination, a message was received from Mrs Connie James that Africans were attacking the Fort Hill radio room. Suddenly the signals ceased. The aircraft circled the airfield three times and finally landed. The runway was clear but there was a crowd in and around the nearby store.

Shell Company and Witwatersrand Native Labour Association (WNLA) employees met the aircraft and told the commander of the security forces that the mob had damaged the signals office, petrol stores and pumps. A patrol from the aircraft started towards the WNLA agent's house, which was nearby. On the way, it encountered two crowds of Africans, one of

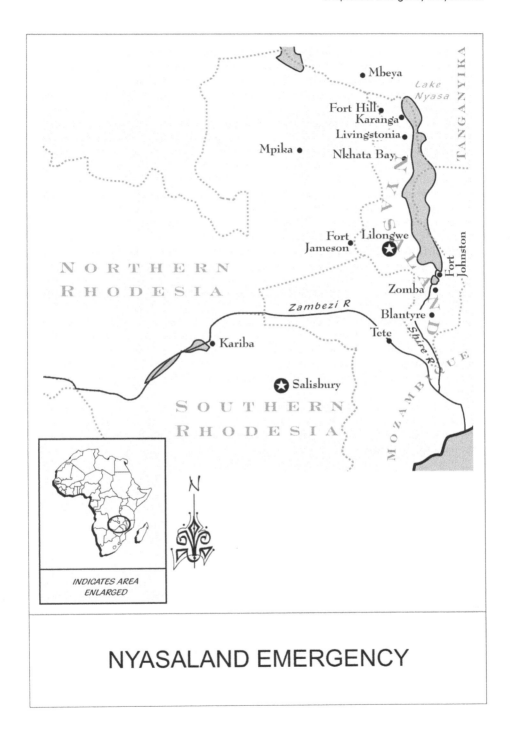

NYASALAND EMERGENCY

which showed signs of agitation. Many of the men were carrying axes and pangas. When the patrol reached the house, it found that Mr and Mrs James, and Mr Douglas, Mr McIntosh and Mr Basil Pettifer were there. They told the members of the patrol that a crowd had arrived at the airfield signals office, threatened Connie James with weapons and damaged the equipment. Mr James and the other two men had also been threatened and told to leave the house.

One armed guard was left behind, while the group from the house, together with the rest of the security force, set out in three trucks to carry out a reconnaissance of the area. They soon came upon a roadblock that had been erected by an unruly mob. The riot act was read and the patrol then opened fire with tear gas canisters. The crowd drew back and members of the patrol began removing the drums that were blocking the road. But, as the security personnel were engaged in this activity, the crowd began throwing stones. Both Mr and Mrs James were injured. The patrol opened fire. After only eleven rounds, the mob dispersed. They then decided to return to the airfield, but on the return trip, the patrol was subjected to more stoning, and further road blocks had to be removed.

At the airfield, Connie James climbed aboard the Dakota, which took off. Messrs James, Douglas and McIntosh left by truck for Makonde in Northern Rhodesia. The security force patrol remained at the airfield until 02h20 and then, after collecting the guard at the house, drove to Karonga. Following the withdrawal of the security forces, the rioters blocked the runway, using barrels and trees.

On 2nd March 1959, No 3 Squadron flew Dr Hastings Banda and Henry Chipemberi to Gwelo for restriction after the banning of the African National Congress in Nyasaland. Further riots followed. Twenty-six rioters were shot dead and many African National Congress leaders were arrested. In a number of incidents on 5th March, mobs fired on security forces. Fire was returned and five rioters were killed, bringing the death toll to that date to 35.

An RRAF Provost dropped teargas on an unruly crowd and later in the day, a leaflet drop was carried out in the Central Province. Thirty thousand leaflets were released, warning the rioters that they would have to pay for any damage caused to roads, bridges, buildings and other installations. The message read:

'Take heed. Police and troops are being used because you are breaking the law. You will pay for this. A fine will be levied on the people of all areas where the police and troops are being used to keep you in order.' 'The money to pay for these fines will be deducted from the prices for your tobacco and groundnuts. If you do not stop these disturbances and damage now, the tobacco market in your area will not be opened and you will not be able to sell your tobacco'.
(Rhodesia Herald, 6th March 1959)

Three days later, while armoured cars and Bren-guns guarded the approach roads. The Governor of Nyasaland, Sir Robert Armitage, Sir Roy Welensky, the Federal Prime Minister, and the Prime Minister of Southern Rhodesia, Sir Edgar Whitehead, discussed the fate of Nyasaland at a secret meeting held at Chileka Airport. Sir Robert flew the 40 miles (64km) from Zomba to Chileka rather than risk driving the route in his easily recognizable car.

While further reports of arson were coming in from the Northern Province, the RRAF dropped 300,000 leaflets throughout the Southern Province telling the people they had nothing to fear from the security forces.

By Monday 9th March, the worst seemed to be over. Reports were coming in of local people removing the roadblocks, following extensive patrols by armoured cars, jet aircraft, troops and special police in the Southern Province.

On Tuesday 10th, the RRAF were called in to help with a supply drop along the shores of Lake Nyasa. It was the first operation of its kind carried out by the air force but despite difficult weather, it went according to plan.

The aircraft left Salisbury at 07h00 and dropped supplies at Karonga and Fort Hill. On the return journey, it released packages of mosquito nets at Nkata Bay and Salima. The supplies included one day's ration of fresh meat, potatoes, vegetables and nine days' supply of tinned rations, as well as medical stocks of camoquin and mosquito repellent. Motor transport stores of fan belts, truck parts and other items were also delivered, some by parachute, others by free-fall, depending on the stores. (No 3 Squadron Diary)

Trouble flared again in Nyasaland during the middle of March 1959, on the northern extension of the railway line and on the road to the Lower Shire Valley. On this occasion, the Nyasaland Flying Club helped with security operations. Members, who had built their own airfield at Luchenza, were enrolled as special constables and flew their small biplanes under the command of the RRAF.

During this emergency, No 3 Squadron had been at the very centre of operations. From the time when the first airlift began, on 20th February, until 4th March when all forces had been withdrawn, the squadron flew a total of 2,094 passengers and 153,650 pounds (69,650kg) of freight in a total of 479 hours—nearly 37 flying hours each day. No 4 Squadron had also been put to the test. Detachments visited Chileka, Mzuza, Lilongwe and Fort Hill, where they rendered invaluable support to the army and the police. It was this emergency, which saw the birth of the close cooperation between air and ground forces that was going to prove so important in the future.

It was the extensive experience gained in this operation that led to the introduction of the Joint Operations Centres (JOCs). This was a highly mobile and efficient self-contained command and control system, which was to prove one of the best methods conceived for the joint command and control of forces in a counter-insurgency (COIN) environment.

With the return of peace came the pullout. One thousand and seventeen troops were moved from Nyasaland to Southern Rhodesia in three days and by 26th March, the RRAF had completed the airlift. Important lessons had been learned during the emergency about the process of loading and the amount that a Dakota could carry. This was after some pilots had taken off with excessively heavy loads, accordng to the No 3 Squadron Diary.

The Canberras arrive

Almost forgotten in all the excitement was the fact that new aircraft were on their way from the United Kingdom. Four Canberras had taken off on 10th March 1959. They were flown by RRAF crews who had been attending conversion courses in Britain. They flew via Idris, Kano and Luanda where they landed with dangerously low fuel supplies.

The arrival of the Canberras meant that the Federation had superior bomber power to any country in Africa south of the equator. It is interesting to note that not even the Union of South Africa had jet bombers. With a Canberra squadron available, the Federation was very much better equipped to play a strong role in Commonwealth defence. Following the arrival of the Canberras, the RRAF put on a special jet show to demonstrate the latest additions to its force, and to display the jet fighters that had returned from service in Nyasaland.

What about helicopters?

One point which the emergency in Nyasaland did raise, was: Why no helicopters? Early in April 1959 came the news that a British company had applied to the Air Authority in Salisbury for permission to operate four helicopters, including one jet version. An application was also received from a company operating in Northern Rhodesia to increase its force from two to five.

The subject of helicopters was raised in the Federal parliament, and the Minister of Defence, Sir Roy Welensky, replied that he considered troop-carrying aircraft better value. However, on the quiet, the defence department was watching with interest the performance of the commercially operated helicopters and probably had in mind the fact that these aircraft could be chartered in time of need.

The new company wishing to introduce helicopters was Helicopter Services, Rhodesia. It planned to import one Bell 47G, one Bell Jet Ranger, one Hiller 12E and one jet-engined French-built Alouette. A constant criticism of the helicopter as a security force vehicle was its short range and small load-carrying capability. It was pointed out that the Alouette, the largest of the machines to be imported, had a range of only 375 miles (600km) and a carrying capacity of four passengers. The military mind, tending to think in terms of large-scale engagements, was against the idea of putting down a handful of troops in a trouble spot, with no ground transportation. Squadron Leader Dowling, an Air Ministry official and pioneer of the anti-terrorist helicopter squadrons in Malaya, disagreed.

> *Things have reached a stage where you just cannot get the same results without helicopters, in these internal security operations. There are several machines suitable to conditions in the Federation, where small helicopters are needed. Where you have sporadic outbursts of violence in different parts of the country, and when people need to be evacuated in a hurry, it is much better to have small machines that can deploy small groups of troops to different areas. In fact, it really increases the effectiveness of your forces in the field. They can drop troops into small landing zones in the bush or down rope ladders with little or no warning, whereas ground troops give insurgents hours to disappear.* (Dowling)

On the same day that the air correspondent of the *Rhodesia Herald* was considering the merits of helicopters, 3rd April 1959, the Right Honourable G.R. Ward, British Secretary of State for Air, arrived in Salisbury on board a Comet of RAF Transport Command. One of his first public pronouncements was to defend the Canberra B2 bomber. He denied that it was obsolescent and said he was glad that the RRAF had become a force with some teeth in it.

From March, Canberras arrived at the rate of four per month. With the appearance of the bombers, came the official formation of No 5 Squadron, on Monday 13th April 1959. It comprised eight crews under the command of Squadron Leader Charles Paxton, who held this position until September 1960. Meanwhile Mrs Boggie, the terror of the RRAF station at Thornhill, announced that her cows liked the Canberras: They didn't hear a thing!

The aerobatics team

The decision had been made to train a formation aerobatics team using the Vampire FB 9s of No 2 Squadron. This was partly to improve flying skills but also to be a national showpiece for the air force. The first public display was to be at an air show in Elisabethville (Congo) to which the Royal Rhodesian Air Force had been invited. The pilots selected for the team that was led by Colin Graves, were Peter McLurg as No 2, Mike Reynolds No 3 and Randy du Rand No 4. There had been weeks of hard work and on 6th May, a few days before the team was due to leave for Elisabethville, a final rehearsal was held at Thornhill Air Station. Talking about this rehearsal, the team members said:

> *For some unknown reason Colin was in a great hurry before getting airborne. He wrote the names and the numbers in the authorization book and I was given number 103. This was*

Colin's aircraft as it was underpowered compared with the others. (The leader normally takes the least powerful machine, which makes it easier for those formatting). Colin took 108. I had no time to wind my altimeter back up to 4700 feet—Colin had been using it on QFE (reading zero on the ground). From my position as number four, behind the leader, the display was poor. I had great difficulty holding this position in many of the manoeuvres because of the lack of power. I consequently found myself having to fly further forward than normal in order not to be left behind. After the final loop, which was to be performed over the runway, we were to turn out left, break and land.
(Du Rand)

The formation team carried out its sequence of loops and barrel rolls, but on exiting our final loop of the show, I saw out of the corner of my eye the nose of Randy's aircraft move under Colin's tailplane. Colin's aircraft suddenly pitched down and went straight into the ground. The formation broke up immediately, the three remaining aircraft becoming individuals. Looking around after regaining level flight, I was relieved to see that the other two aircraft were all right.
(McLurg)

A low-pressure area could have been set up between Colin's tailplane and my canopy. This would have sucked the two aircraft together and regardless of my pushing forward and applying negative 'G' the two aircraft collided. My canopy and windscreen were damaged and I could not see out. I pulled the stick back carefully to complete the loop, hoping my wings were level. They were. I had no idea of speed, only the deafening outside noise.
(Du Rand)

At this point, there was a barely discernible voice coming over the radio against a very noisy background. It was Randy saying that he could not see, and that he was proceeding to the large vacant farmland between Thornhill and Selukwe where he intended to bale out. I happened to be flying close to Randy so I formatted on him and observed that his front windscreen had been flattened and the nose of his aircraft crumpled. His visor was missing from his helmet, his face covered in blood, and his head bobbing about in the slipstream that was now blowing directly onto him.
(McLurg)

I was pretty shaken up, and not being able to see clearly or hear the radio above the noise, added to my bewilderment. After some time I could make out the artificial horizon and airspeed indicator (ASI). I confused the altimeter reading, and remembered too late that I hadn't changed it to the correct setting before take-off. So I nearly flew into the ground twice. At this stage, I thought it best to bale out.
(Du Rand)

We all knew that the statistics showed few, if any, successful bale-outs from the Vampire FB 9, which did not have an ejector seat. I suggested to Randy that this wasn't really an option for him and that I would talk him down to land on the grass runway.
(McLurg)

Mac was of tremendous help and it was also reassuring to be able to speak to someone. Without his advice I would have gone for the bale-out.
(Du Rand)

Randy formatted on me and we proceeded to reduce speed and position ourselves for a long shallow approach. Our undercarriages were lowered, but on Randy's aircraft only the main wheels came down. (McLurg)

Having put the wheels down unsuccessfully, I pulled them up and left them up. At this stage, I had had enough, and my main aim was not to save the aircraft but just to get safely back on the ground. (Du Rand)

The approach went very smoothly and was a credit to Randy's formation flying ability, as his vision was considerably impaired. As we got to the round-out, I overshot and Randy carried out a super landing, coming to a stop in a very short distance. (McLurg)

Randy was rushed to the station hospital where the medics painstakingly removed glass and perspex from his face. It was a miracle that his eyes were not damaged. It wasn't long before he was back in the air as well as in the formation aerobatic team. The Elisabethville display that subsequently took place was the first in which the Canberras took part.

It was apparent that the pilots were still not completely familiar with the Canberra and at least one aircraft was badly over-stressed during the display: 200 rivets 'popped' on the mainplane, and another burnt its brakes out on landing. (No 5 Squadron Diary)

A further four Canberras arrived early in June, bringing the total to 15. One crew: pilot, Flight Lieutenant Frank Mussell and navigator, Flying Officer Don Brenchley, had every reason to be proud. They had carried off one of the most coveted awards in RAF Bomber Command, the Rapier Prize for outstanding results on a bombing course. It was the first time that the prize had been awarded to a Commonwealth aircrew.

Now that the crews had returned from their conversion courses, another Canberra squadron could be formed. This was No 6 Squadron, which came into being at Thornhill in June 1959. First officer commanding was Squadron Leader Dicky Bradshaw, who had led the most recent ferry. 'A' flight commander was Flight Lieutenant Ossie Penton and 'B' flight commander was Flight Lieutenant Frank Mussell.

No 11 Course Short Service Unit*
Wings: 19th December 1958

Alan Waterson	Joined RAF.
Vic Wightman	Continued serving—joined RAF in January 1961. Later rejoined RRAF and retired as squadron leader.
Ian Harvey	Continued serving—took a short break—rejoined. Became AVM and chief of the AFZ
Fred Roberts	Continued serving—retired as group captain.
Tol Janeke	Continued serving—retired as group captain.
Meis Nederlof	Continued serving—resigned to join Qantas.
Oliver Sutton	Joined Fleet Air Arm.
Geoff Kruger	Continued serving. Joined the SAAF in 1969.
Rich Brand	Continued serving—retired as squadron leader.

---

* No 11 SSU Course was the last one; after this they became Pilot Training Courses. There were 22 PTC courses between 1958 and 1980.

CHAPTER 31

Chaos, misery and death in the Congo

By the middle of the year 1959, the solid progress of building activities at Kariba seemed to coincide with Salisbury's recovery from the slump. Commercial broadcasting had come to stay but on the health scene, the country was suffering from the horrors of poliomyelitis outbreaks. Since 1957, the numbers of sufferers had been increasing and vaccine had been flown from Britain to help combat the plague. During the months of high summer, the swimming pools were closed to try to help stem the wave of sickness and death.

On 7th July 1959, No 6 squadron, now stationed at Thornhill, Gwelo, moved into its own building. Before this date, the offices and crew room had been shared with No 5 Squadron, because a visiting RAF squadron, No 208, had been using the quarters originally allocated to No 6 Squadron. Having a place of their own gave a boost to the morale of squadron members and it was not long before a crew room, offices and even a coffee bar had been organized. Flying training commenced during the month with crews engaged mainly on navigational exercises, night-flying and familiarization flights.

Flight Lieutenant Keith Kemsley and Flying Officer Fred Roberts, while flying a general handling operation on Wednesday 23rd July, had an alarming experience, which was never satisfactorily explained. They were returning to base, flying at a height of 10,000 feet when there was a loud report accompanied by violent oscillations lasting several seconds. Their first impression was that they had hit another aircraft. A Vampire flying in the area was called in to inspect their machine but the Vampire pilot could not spot any external damage. The subsequent circuit and landing were uneventful and the aircraft handled normally apart from a feeling of roughness. The aircraft was grounded for investigation but nothing out of the ordinary was ever found.

A life or death flight

On 23rd August 1959, No 5 Squadron took part in a life and death drama. In Gatooma, Mrs Rix, her three sons and their cook had been struck down by a sudden and mysterious illness that was diagnosed as botulin poisoning. This is a rare but exceedingly dangerous form of food poisoning caused by a toxin produced by the bacterium Clostridium botulinum. It is a common microbe, which may contaminate incorrectly preserved food. It multiplies only in the complete absence of air as, for example, in a closed tin or preserving jar. A very small dose of the toxin paralyses the nervous system and is commonly fatal. There were no supplies of the anti-toxin in the Federation, the nearest available source being Johannesburg. RRAF Headquarters Salisbury was approached for help. The message was relayed to Thornhill where it was received just after 23h00 on Sunday 23rd August. By midnight, a Canberra was ready for take-off. The pilot, Squadron Leader Charles Paxton, made the trip to Johannesburg and back with the entire stock of anti-botulin serum available in South Africa, within three hours.

Further supplies were flown from Europe on a civilian flight. The happy sequel to the story was that Mrs Rix, her sons and the cook all made complete recoveries.

First 'Rover' flights

Exchanges had taken place in July 1959 between the Rhodesian Canberra squadron and a RAF Canberra squadron, the purpose being to train RRAF pilots with the Middle East Air Force in Cyprus and to allow RAF pilots based in the Middle East to visit the Federation. During their stay in Cyprus, the RRAF officers took part in discussions aimed at increasing the close liaison between the RAF, Middle East and the RRAF. These flights to Cyprus were known as Rhodesian Rover flights. In August, the flight was piloted by Flight Lieutenant Frank Mussell, with Flying Officer Don Brenchley as navigator. They ran into bad weather after leaving Brazzaville and had to divert to Kano, where they found that the wood-fabric leading edge of the fin had been damaged by hail. A temporary repair was carried out by a Nigerian airways engineering officer and the flight continued to Cyprus. The return flight was uneventful and the aircraft landed back at Thornhill on 25th August.

These single aircraft jaunts to Cyprus were in preparation for a squadron visit, which took place in September 1959. The first Cyprus detachment consisting of six aircraft from No 5 Squadron left on 9th September and returned on 24th October. No 6 Squadron was called on to supply reserve crews. These were Flight Lieutenant Keith Kemsley, Flying Officer Fred Roberts, Flying Officer 'Porky' MacLaughlin and Flying Officer Pete Oosthuizen; these two crews were consequently combat rated before the official departure of No 5 Squadron on 9th September. In fact, one member of the No 5 Squadron crew went sick on the eve of departure and so Flight Lieutenant Kemsley and Flying Officer Roberts left with No 5 Squadron.

The following day, 10th September, Porky MacLaughlin and Pete Oosthuizen were detailed to take a reserve aircraft to Brazzaville for No 5 Squadron. The unserviceable aircraft was left at Brazzaville while the squadron continued its flight to Cyprus with the replacement aircraft. MacLaughlin, Oosthuizen and Corporal Dave Panton who had travelled up in the reserve aircraft, replaced a faulty fuel tank pump and brought the aircraft back to Thornhill next day.

During their third tour of duty, which lasted six weeks, the RRAF pilots flew alongside Canberra bombers of the Middle East Air Force and took part in extensive bomber and fighter exercises, both by day and night, often at high altitudes. This operational training carried them as far as the borders of the Union of Soviet Socialist Republics with Charles Paxton, officer commanding No 5 Squadron, carrying out a Lone Ranger trip to Teheran, Iran.

On 17th September, while No 5 Squadron was in Cyprus, all the Canberras in Rhodesia were grounded for undercarriage checks. They were not put back into service again until 7th October. This delayed training programmes and resulted in a shortage of combat crews. Flight Lieutenant Ossie Penton and Flight Lieutenant Brian Horney and their crews were given priority as far as flying training was concerned and were combat rated by October 22nd. On 26th October, they departed for Cyprus to join the RAF for an exercise in Pakistan.

In Cyprus, Penton and Horney were attached to a RAF squadron selected for air operations in connection with the Central Treaty Organization (Cento), which had as its members Turkey, Iran, Pakistan and Britain. The two RRAF machines left Cyprus, overflew Turkey and night-stopped in Teheran before flying on to refuel at Karachi. Penton said later, "We flew on to Peshawar, a Pakistani air force station near the frontier, arriving there on 2nd November. Before the exercise began, we attended a briefing and got to know what the exercise was about. In fact, we had no time to get into town. For the next few days we did fairly intensive flying. The weather was pretty grim with storms and rain. We were all

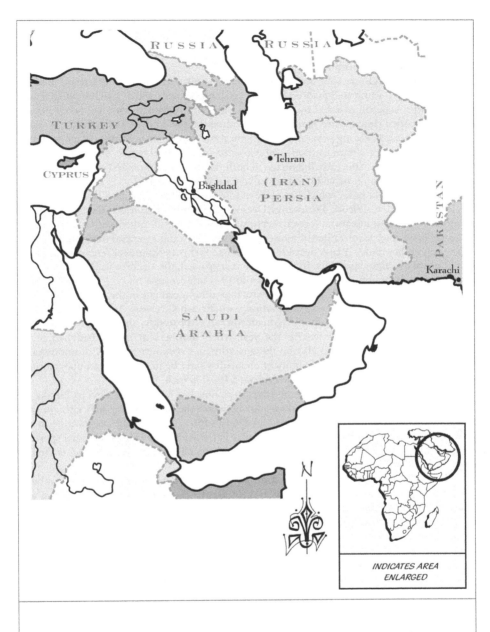

INDICATES AREA
ENLARGED

RHODESIAN ROVER FLIGHTS

particularly impressed with the efficiency of the Pakistani air force." The two aircraft with their crews and technicians were back in the Federation by 20th November.

The third Aden detachment

The Canberra squadrons were not alone in their involvement in overseas visits. During November, No 1 Vampire Squadron left the Federation for its third detachment to Aden. The squadron was commanded by Squadron Leader Sandy Mutch who had taken part in the previous Aden flight. Once again, No 3 Squadron did the donkey-work of placing spares and ground crews at staging posts along the flight route. Unfortunately, this detachment had one accident, when a 20mm cannon shell exploded in the barrel, while the aircraft was on an operational sortie. This caused damage to both the 20mm cannon and to the nose of the aircraft. The squadron returned to Thornhill on 3rd December 1959.

November brought news, which was to be of interest to former members of the SRAF and the RAF. Mr J.M. Caldicott, Minister of Defence, announced that it was the government's intention to set up a territorial force to serve with the RRAF. In other words, there was to be an air force reserve, or rather two reserves, an auxiliary and a general division including officers and other ranks. A later decision was made to form one volunteer reserve. This force was to prove its value repeatedly. In fact, as the years passed, the air force in Rhodesia was to rely increasingly heavily on the men of the air force volunteer reserve.

Several days later, John Caldicott made a further announcement in the Federal Assembly that the Federal government was negotiating with British Overseas Airways Corporation (BOAC) for the purchase of four Argonaut aircraft. Apparently, this decision had been influenced by experiences earlier in the year when numbers of troops had had to be transported to Nyasaland, and also by the government's commitment to Commonwealth defence, where the speed and flexibility of an airlift would be of the utmost importance. It was stated that the cost of the aircraft was about £400,000 each.

Although the future of the Federation was in doubt, No 5 Squadron flew to Lusaka on 21st November for an affiliation ceremony during which the squadron was officially adopted by the city. Formation flying and individual displays formed part of the programme in the air while on the ground there was a dinner/dance at the Ridgeway Hotel and social sporting competitions. The weekend was thoroughly enjoyed by all and was perhaps one of the last completely relaxed periods in an increasingly difficult time.

Added to their training and defence commitment, the RRAF were always ready to lend a hand at any task that needed doing. Photographing the country for accurate mapping was one such chore. Another, in December 1959, was to provide a Provost and crew to take part in rain-making experiments using Australian apparatus. Admittedly in Rhodesia, this had been carried out on the ground for hundreds of years but now a more scientific approach was to be tried. Rockets were fired at suitable cloud formations in the hope that rain might be encouraged to fall in drought-stricken areas.

On 11th December, Porky MacLaughlin and Pete Oosthuizen of No 6 Squadron left on a Rhodesian Rover flight, the seventh, to Cyprus via Nairobi, Khartoum and El Adem. After take-off from Khartoum, on their way north, a large bird struck the leading edge of the starboard wing, making a slight dent and causing a few rivets to pop. This was repaired while the crew was in Cyprus.

The Canadair DC-4M-2 (Argonaut)

The year (1959) ended with the arrival of new aircraft for No 3 Transport Squadron. These were the Canadair DC-4M-2 Argonauts. The first aircraft G-ALHW was handed over at a ceremony held at London Airport on Monday 14th December, when Air Vice-Marshal

E.W.S. Jacklin, Chief of Air Staff RRAF officially took delivery. This aircraft had been used for Royal Flights and was to be employed as a VIP machine. Following the hand-over, the aircraft was flown to Nairobi where four pilots and members of the ground crew had been taking a conversion course with East African Airways. The first Argonaut was flown into Salisbury on 31st December by Squadron Leader Harry Coleman. It was in this aircraft that Princess Elizabeth (Later Queen Elizabeth II) had flown from Entebbe to London after hearing of the death of her father, King George VI, while she was touring East Africa in February 1952.

This Argonaut was used by British Prime Minister Harold MacMillan when he visited the Federation in January 1960, making his historic 'Winds of Change' speech in Parliament in Cape Town. MacMillan remained in the Federation for a week and was flown from Salisbury to Lusaka, the Copperbelt, Blantyre, Livingstone and of course Kariba by members of No 3 Squadron, before leaving for the United Kingdom from Jan Smuts Airport on 25th January.

On 20th January 1960, Flight Lieutenant Chris Dams and Flying Officer J.M. van den Burgh, from No 6 Squadron departed on the monthly Rhodesian Rover exercise to Akrotiri Air Field (near Limassol) in Cyprus. They flew via Nairobi, Khartoum and El Adem, returning along the same route and landing back at Thornhill on 27th January without incident. They were accompanied by an aircraft from No 5 Squadron.

Parachute training

For the time being, the subject of the purchase of helicopters for the air force seemed to have been shelved. However, the training of a parachute force was still very much on the cards. It was obvious that, had trained personnel been available, they could have been used when Fort Hill Air Field was seized by rioters. As it was, the airfield in the remote Northern Province of Nyasaland was in the hands of the rioters for almost two weeks.

The RAF had been approached for help and in January, Squadron Leader E. Minter, an RAF officer experienced in parachute training, arrived in Salisbury to advise the government. The squadron leader, who had been born in Bulawayo but had left the country 12 years before, had 364 parachute drops to his credit. His first task was to reconnoitre possible dropping zones. He was assisted by No 3 Squadron making use of a Pembroke captained by Flying Officer George Alexander.

This initial reconnaissance was followed on 11th February 1960 by an experimental drop from a Dakota at New Sarum in which a dummy was used. It had previously been believed that parachute jumps at these altitudes using standard parachutes were risky because the air was too thin. Squadron Leader Minter was obviously happy with his tests and the first live drop was carried out on 3rd March 1960. Exercise Evaluation then swung into action, with 20 volunteers from the Federal army and air force, half of them black, taking part. This scheme was designed to discover the advantages and disadvantages of setting up a defence force parachute unit.

Remarking on the exercise, Group Captain Raf Bentley, Deputy Chief of Air Staff, said, "We want to discover the not-so-obvious. Not only the military aspects but also the matter of air–ground rescue operations in such emergencies as plane crashes or serious accidents in the bush. We are getting down to the bones of the case in a completely practical way. It is the only way to do it."

At New Sarum, a hangar was converted into a parachute-packing department, and a team of packers was trained. The training of the volunteers began and on 11th March, the first jumps were carried out from RRAF No 3 Squadron Dakotas by nine African Askaris and four Europeans. Commanding Officer No 1 Group RRAF, Group Captain Harold Hawkins was among the observers. The leading man out was Sergeant Manikayi, who therefore became the first black man to make a parachute descent in the Federation. These trainees went on to carry out jumps in various centres throughout the Federation and they qualified for their Parachute Wings in June and July 1960. This was the initial phase of the RRAF's Parachute Training Wing, which was to be formed in 1961.

In April 1960, an air supply platoon was formed. Again, the need for a unit of this kind had been made obvious during the Nyasaland riots. The task of the unit was to provide an emergency supply of equipment such as food, ammunition, blankets and medicines from the air.

Also, during April, the most widespread exercise ever carried out by the combined Federal defence forces took place. Code named Treble Chance the exercise involved 800 men of the territorial force, together with members of the Parachute Evaluation Detachment. They were flown to areas in Northern Rhodesia and Nyasaland by No 3 Squadron in Canadair Argonauts that were being used as troop carriers for the first time in the Federation. These aircraft were, according to the troopies, much more comfortable than the Dakotas. Treble Chance gave the Joint Staff of the Federal army and air force an opportunity to assess the potential of parachute troops as part of the overall defence strategy. Army spokesmen were as usual tight-lipped but the RRAF reported: "Undoubtedly the experiment has been a success. Many valuable lessons have been learned."

While all was progressing satisfactorily in the air, life on the ground was not so happy. In February 1960 the Monckton Commission, headed by Viscount Monckton of Brenchley, and including representatives from the United Kingdom, Australia, Canada and the three Federal territories began its work. This Royal Commission had been set up to investigate the Federation and to suggest alternatives, which might make it more acceptable to African leaders in Northern Rhodesia and Nyasaland. The commission members flown by No 3 Squadron, visited every part of the Federation and heard evidence from every interested group with the exception of the extreme African nationalists who refused to cooperate. Commission members were impressed by the obvious economic benefits to all three territories and made some reasonable recommendations. However, stepping outside the terms of reference they then recommended that, in view of the obvious African hostility, a territory should unilaterally be able to secede. The African nationalists were delighted. This obviously meant that sooner or later the Federation would come to an end.

No 6 Squadron disbanded

During March 1960, No 6 Squadron was disbanded and its members amalgamated with No 5 Squadron. No 6 Squadron was not to be resuscitated until 1st June 1962. This disbandment meant that several crews were available and No 5 Squadron strength increased to eleven crews.

It was also decided to re-form No 2 Squadron as a training squadron, to pave the way for the reintroduction of flying training. The squadron was re-formed at Thornhill under the command of Flight Lieutenant Bob Woodward, with Flight Lieutenant Chris Dams as flight commander. The squadron role was to train flying instructors on both Percival Provost T 1 and Vampire T 11 aircraft, before commencing the basic and advanced flying training of pupil pilots under the new Pilot Training Scheme. The squadron's other roles were internal security using Provosts, and defence and ground-attack using Vampires.

The official opening of Kariba Dam

The official opening of Kariba Dam had been scheduled for 17th May and it was estimated that 700 VIPs from all parts of the Federation and beyond would have to be transported to the dam site. In preparation for this exercise, No 3 Squadron began carrying out trial runs early in May, using the Canadair Argonauts.

The most important visitor was of course Queen Elizabeth, the Queen Mother, who was piloted by Squadron Leader Harry Coleman of No 3 Squadron during her five days in the Federation. On 16th May, Her Majesty visited Thornhill where she inspected the Guard of Honour and witnessed a flypast of six Canberras of No 5 Squadron and nine Vampires from No 1 Squadron. On 17th May, she was flown to Kariba and was able to enjoy a superb view of the dam when the Argonaut flew low over the dam wall. Incidentally, the road from the airfield to town was specially tarred for the visit and so Kariba was left with a permanent reminder of the royal advent.

During the Royal Tour, No 3 Squadron flew 190 sorties, carrying 2,533 passengers and 22,700 pounds (10,300kg) freight. The high point of the five days, as far as work was concerned, was 17th May when the squadron carried out 53 flights, carrying 700 passengers in and out of Kariba. Peter Knobel's aircraft had a fire in one engine while taking off and had to return to Salisbury. As his passengers were members of the Press, the episode received wide coverage.

Flying Officer Peter Knobel of the RRAF, was the pilot of a Dakota carrying 25 pressmen to Kariba yesterday. The plane was barely airborne when flames were seen to leap from the port engine. F.O. Knobel immediately feathered the engine and brought the plane safely into an emergency landing at Salisbury Civil Airport. Fewer than ten minutes later, the Press party was once more on its way to Kariba in a reserve plane. (Rhodesia Herald, 18th May 1960)

A further description of the giant airlift read:

Just before 7 o'clock last night a Canadair aircraft landed at New Sarum with the last of nearly 700 guests flown to Kariba and back to see the Queen Mother open the hydro-electric scheme. It was the end of the greatest airlift ever carried out in the Federation. The RRAF used five Dakotas, four Canadairs and one Pembroke to fly 101 movements between Salisbury and Kariba. The first aircraft left for Kariba at 5 am. The last of the guests reached Kariba shortly before the Queen Mother arrived. (Rhodesia Herald)

At the end of the Queen Mother's tour, on 29th May, members of No 3 Squadron were presented to Her Majesty at Government House during a cocktail party. The cost of the airlift was estimated to be £1,732 but on the credit side, it resulted in much favourable publicity.

In June, the municipality of Blantyre/Limbe adopted No 3 Squadron as part of a scheme launched the previous year to promote friendship, good feeling and understanding between municipalities and squadrons. And, during the same month, it was announced that No 3 Squadron had been presented with the initial award of the Jacklin Trophy for the most efficient squadron of the year. Specific mention was made of its efforts during the Queen Mother's visit.

1960 saw a substantial increase in the vote from revenue funds for the defence forces. Total Defence Votes were up by nearly £900,000. The bulk of this sum £650,000 went to the RRAF bringing its total vote up to £2,400,000 compared with £1,700,000 in 1959/60. The increase was largely required for the installment due on the Canberras. The Federal Minister of Defence, Mr J.M. Caldicott also announced the purchase of additional equipment such as wireless sets and ammunition.

Trouble in the Congo

Independence was due in the Belgian Congo and in anticipation of problems in that country, a large-scale exercise was mounted towards the end of June at Kawambwa in the Luapula province of Northern Rhodesia (Zambia) close to the Congo border. Air support included a supply-drop by Dakotas, the laying of a tear-gas smoke screen by Provosts and formation pattern-bombing by Canberras. There were also dive-bomb attacks by Provosts and Vampires.

In fact, the blow-up in the Congo came during the Rhodes and Founders holiday weekend in mid July, 1960. An army revolt broke out in what was then the province of Katanga; four Europeans were killed and hundreds of others panicked and fled into Northern Rhodesia. By Sunday 10th July, Kitwe had become a huge refugee camp. Leave for all RRAF personnel was cancelled and the stations were brought up to full operational strength.

As the fleeing Belgians poured south, No 3 Squadron flew night and day sorties carrying the men, women and children from Ndola to Salisbury. Return aircraft were loaded with blankets, bedding and rations for those camping at Fort Rosebery, Solwesi and Mwinilunga.

At Fort Rosebery where there was no radio communication or other night-flying aids, the RRAF borrowed 15 gooseneck flares from Ndola and laid an emergency flarepath so that a Dakota laden with blankets supplied by the army, could land and take off again.

Help was requested at Mwinilunga, a tiny airstrip about 100 miles (160km) west of Solwesi, where two wounded refugees were sheltering. A Dakota took off from Salisbury at 02h30 but had difficulty finding the airstrip that was ringed with bush fires. The strip was finally located and the Dakota landed at first light unloading supplies of blankets and food and uplifting the two casualties, together with six other refugees who were transported to Ndola.

It was estimated that by Sunday 10th July, there were about 600 European refugees. By 11th July, the stream of refugees had become a flood. All available RRAF transport aircraft were put into the air to carry the evacuees from the Copperbelt to Salisbury.

The first of the air fleet to arrive in Salisbury today, an Argonaut with 61 on board, took off again half an hour later to return to Ndola for another batch of refugees. This procedure is being followed by all aircraft throughout the day. Air Vice-Marshal E. Jacklin, Air Officer Commanding, and Chief of the RRAF and Group Captain H. Hawkins who is in charge of the operation watched the aircraft come in. Each aircraft, as it returns to Ndola is carrying supplies for the Federal troops standing by, in or near the Copperbelt.
(Evening Standard, 12th July 1960)

Peter Plain writing in the *Evening Standard* gave this description of the scene at New Sarum.

RRAF corporals' mess was the clearing centre for the biggest emergency operation in Southern Rhodesia so far. They started to come in yesterday afternoon, in RRAF planes from Ndola. However, it was not until late last night that the trickle grew to a flood as plane after plane landed at New Sarum. From lumbering Dakotas to the bulking majesty of the US Air Force Globemaster, they landed and all were dealt with by ground crews and staff who had not even been asked to volunteer. "They just turned up," said Group Captain Harry Hawkins, who was there with AOC in Chief, Air Vice-Marshal Jacklin, to see that the operation went smoothly. "Our chaps are a good lot. They don't have to be ordered around," said the Air Vice-Marshal. It was after 2 am this morning when I left the corporals' mess and there was still one plane to come in with 30 more on board. (Evening Standard, 12th July 1960)

The RRAF could only wait at the border. They could not send aircraft across to help the desperate mobs in Elisabethville because under international law, military aircraft were not allowed to cross the frontier without governmental permission. The refugees were transported to the border by Sabena and Central African Airways aircraft chartered by the mining company Union Minière. By 14th July, more than 1,500 evacuees were safely in

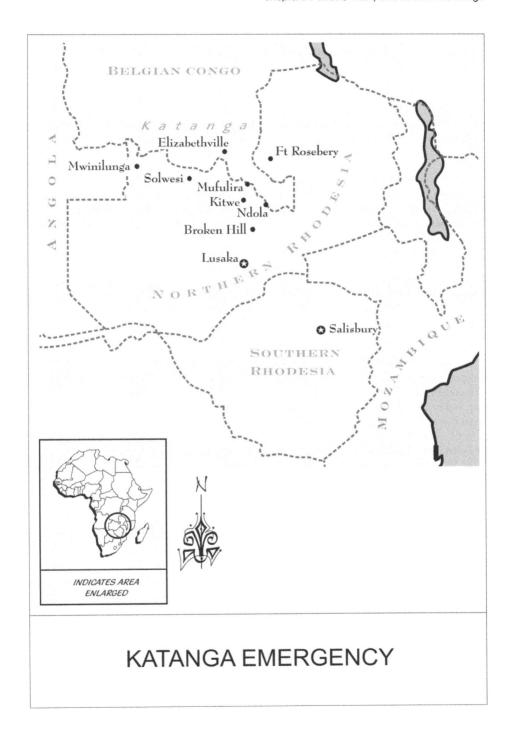

INDICATES AREA
ENLARGED

KATANGA EMERGENCY

Salisbury and some had been moved on to Bulawayo. Temporary camps were set up in the showgrounds where the bewildered human beings could be welcomed and given assistance.

By 15th July, the worst was over.

> *For the first time last night since the holiday weekend there has been a temporary halt to the number of refugees arriving in Salisbury by air. Three flights arrived yesterday bringing in a total of 110 men, women and children. RRAF HQ stated that a total of seven flights, carrying 332 refugees had arrived at Bulawayo. At Gwelo, three planes landed with a total of 105 refugees.* (Rhodesia Herald, 16th July 1960)

A sequel to the story occurred in December when the Belgian Consul General to the Federation, Mr J. Houard, presented eleven medals and 500 flower bulbs as a mark of gratitude from the Belgian government to the Rhodesians who helped the refugee operation. Mr Houard said that in thanking the Federal Prime Minister, Sir Roy Welensky, his government decided on something special—a gift of the bulbs from Belgium for the official residence. Ted Jacklin, who had by that time retired, drove up from Johannesburg for the occasion.

In July 1960, No 5 Squadron left Thornhill on its annual detachment to Cyprus. The squadron, under the command of Charles Paxton was destined, once more, for Akrotiri, where it would undertake training with the Middle East Air Force. The first four Canberras left Nairobi on 22nd July and arrived in Cyprus the same night. A second flight of four machines left RRAF Thornhill on the same day but night-stopping in Nairobi and reaching Cyprus the following day. The ground crew followed in a Canadair Argonaut flown by No 3 Transport Squadron.

The polio epidemic was still in full force and in September, a combined RAF and RRAF mercy flight team rushed a new type of portable breathing apparatus from Sweden to Salisbury. The patient was 21-year-old Philip Handford. An RAF Canberra carried the equipment from England to Nairobi and an RRAF Lone Ranger Canberra from No 5 Squadron brought the apparatus to Salisbury landing just after 05h30 on 7th September.

In October, No 1 Vampire Squadron left Thornhill Air Station for its annual attachment to Aden. On this occasion, the RRAF detachment was under the overall command of Wing Commander Archie Wilson who was attached to the staff of Air Marshal Sir Charles Elworthy at RAF Tarshine.

It appears that the air marshal was impressed by the squadron's operational preparedness and all-round professional approach both to air and ground matters. As usual, the move was supported by No 3 Squadron using Canadair Argonauts and Dakotas.

Technical and pilot training

Early in the new year 1961, eleven young men went to Britain to begin a three-year training course at RAF establishments. An indication of the high standards set by these apprentices is that in December 1961, a Rhodesian was one of the 150 young men and women to be presented with Gold Standard awards by the Duke of Edinburgh. He was Leading Aircraft Apprentice Douglas Charles Payne, then at Radio School in Locking, Somerset. Within the Federation, more youngsters were undergoing technical training with the RRAF. Added to this, flying training that had been in abeyance for about two years, was re-started with ten young men beginning an 18-month course at Thornhill. The training, both basic and advanced, was the responsibility of No 2 Squadron and during 1961, Nos 14 and 15 Pilot Training Courses were taken to Wings standard.

1961 started on a less happy note for Central African Airways when its four Vickers Viscounts were grounded. The decision was taken on 8th January after a metallurgical expert, especially flown from the United Kingdom, discovered minute cracks in the wings of one Viscount. The RRAF came to the rescue, not only lending four No 3 Squadron Canadair Argonauts to CAA but also supplying the pilots. One current joke going the rounds was Join the RRAF and fly CAA. Nineteen scheduled runs were carried out between 18th January and 24th March. In appreciation for this assistance, CAA presented No 3 Squadron with a silver rose bowl.

RRAF Volunteer Reserve established

The news passed almost unnoticed at the time, but a vital decision had been reached during 1960. A decision that was to have ever-increasing importance during the next 20 years. On 14th January 1961, the RRAF Volunteer Reserve was officially established. The formation of this unit had been authorized during 1960 in an amendment to the Defence Act. On 13th January, regulations allowing recruiting to begin and setting out conditions of service were published in a Federal government notice. The commanding officer of the reserve was to be Group Captain Charles Green who was then farming in the Beatrice area. Charles Green had joined the RAF just before the Second World War and had been the first Rhodesian to command No 266 (Rhodesia) Squadron.

The RRAF Volunteer Reserve headquarters was established in Dolphin House, Salisbury and recruiting was initiated, covering both Northern and Southern Rhodesia. Two regular officers, Wing Commander Dicky Bradshaw and Flight Lieutenant Don Holliday flew to Lusaka to open an operational centre for the use and training of VR members in Northern Rhodesia.

There was a magnificent response to the announcement, even though it was stated that reservists would not be given flying duties as: Pilots cannot be kept in training by weekend flying. In an emergency, the reservists will take over such duties as operational rooms, signals and other control work to release men for flying duties. Possible exceptions to this non-flying decision were commercial pilots who could take over, without training, such duties as transport flying.

During 1961, No 3 Squadron was doing its usual sterling work ferrying VIPs round the Federation, among them the chief of the United Kingdom Defence Staff, Earl Mountbatten of Burma, who paid a flying visit in October. No 5 Squadron had flipped off to Bahrain and Aden, where it took part in Operation Sea Sheik in cooperation with No 8 Squadron RAF. This exercise began in February and continued into March. Also in March, No 5 Squadron carried out an interception exercise in conjunction with the Royal Navy. The target was HMS *Victorious*, then positioned in the Mozambique Channel. No 5 Squadron operated from Thornhill and Invato in Madagascar.

Good and bad news about the Canberras

This same month saw the long-awaited arrival of the Canberra T4 trainers, which had been delayed so that the Mk 3 CT ejector seats could be fitted. No 5 Squadron's role had now changed from that of high-level, to medium and low-level attack and in January it was suggested that rocket projectiles be fitted to the Canberras. The plan was to fit four rocket rails under the nose of the aircraft, utilizing the outboard rocket rails from the Provosts. Despite gloomy predictions from the manufacturers, English Electric, the modifications were carried out. The first aircraft fitted with the projectiles flew on 6th April 1961, and successfully completed trials at Kutanga Range.

During the early part of the year, No 5 Squadron Canberras experienced five wheels-up landings, three of which were found to be due to a failure of the sequence valve in the hydraulic system, which raised and lowered the undercarriage. The sequence valve was triggered by the leg so that the final movement of the leg operated the valve, which re-routed hydraulic pressure to the undercarriage doors. Sometimes, in flight, the leg could droop releasing the sequence valve, so that when the pilot tried to put the undercarriage down nothing would happen. When this occurred, the only course open was to belly-land, which only caused damage to the bomb-bay doors but was annoying. RRAF technicians finally came up with a solution that was later incorporated by the RAF and the Royal New Zealand Air Force, both of which had encountered a similar problem.

First experiments in 'rainmaking'

Meanwhile, as a change from training pupil pilots, the men of Thornhill had begun trying their hand at rainmaking and in March 1961, they carried out the first experiments in the Gwelo area. The man in charge of the team was Harvey Quail, officer in charge of the Meteorological Department at Thornhill. Using Provost aircraft, the rainmakers carried out cloud-seeding activities. According to a report in the Gwelo Times:

> Small cartons, just like ice-cream cartons, will be fitted to the aircraft bomb racks and, at the right moment, these will be released to shower a mixture of salt and sand onto the cloud.

The team also intended to use a silver iodine burner. There is no report on the success or otherwise of these experiments.

The RRAF gets its own General Service Unit

In April 1961, the air force celebrated 25 years of flying. It was in 1936 that six young volunteers from the Southern Rhodesia territorial force took their first flying lessons at Belvedere Air Field. By 1961, the air force strength was in the region of 1,000 personnel and 70 aircraft, including jet bombers and fighters. A further step towards total independence was taken on 14th April, when a General Service Unit was gazetted. This meant that the RRAF now had its own GSU like the RAF regiment.

About 150 men, formerly Askaris seconded for special duties at New Sarum, were transferred from the army to the air force. Some of them had served the air force as guards and drivers for almost eight years. Flying Officer Basil C. Lederboer, an ex-heavyweight boxer, was placed in charge of the new unit.

Also in this month, the RRAF placed two of its aircraft on show at the Federal Manufacturers Fair at the Drill Hall in Salisbury. On the Monday following the show, came the problem of taking the aircraft home.

> The aircraft, a Provost trainer and a Vampire jet fighter have been on show. Now they have to be towed at walking pace 10 miles [16km] along the main roads during Monday morning rush hour. "We have to get these aircraft back to the airport on Monday—to do this we are appealing to the motoring public to cooperate and avoid using the Hatfield road in particular on the way to work," the police appealed. (Rhodesia Herald, 29th April 1961)

Cooperation with the SAAF

Since its inception, the air force in Rhodesia had worked in close cooperation not only with the RAF but also with the South African Air Force, and in June 1961, it was announced that the RRAF and SAAF were to carry out joint training exercises. Sabres of the SAAF would intercept RRAF Canberra bombers during long-range navigational flights. A statement issued on 25th June, said:

> Long-range navigational training exercises form an important part of the routine training of the RRAF Canberra bomber force, and, in order to achieve as much variety as possible in these

exercises, an approach was made recently to the South African government for permission to carry out training flights over South Africa. Both the RRAF and the SAAF welcome the opportunity to carry out training interceptions that this scheme offers. (Rhodesia Herald, 26th June 1961)

It was also during 1961 that the first trials were undertaken using the Canberra for high altitude aerial survey and photographic reconnaissance.

In June, the members of the RRAF bade a sad farewell to the founder and creator of the postwar air force, Air Vice-Marshal E.W.S. Jacklin. On 30th June, a flypast of 44 aircraft was staged at Thornhill in his honour. In an interview Ted Jacklin said: "The day we changed from our army uniforms to the air force blue, which we now wear, was a token of the acceptance of our air force as a competent striking power."

Politically a great deal of activity had been taking place against a background of growing unrest. In February 1961, a new constitution had been negotiated between the Southern Rhodesia government and Britain. This constitution widened the franchise bringing African voters onto a 'B' roll, which would elect 15 members to the Territorial Parliament. So, for the first time in Southern Rhodesia's history, Africans would sit in parliament and have a say in the day-to-day running of the country. At first, the African nationalists approved the proposals, but later, following an overseas visit, their leader Joshua Nkomo, changed his mind. Edgar Whitehead, Prime Minister of Southern Rhodesia, went ahead with the plan despite this setback and a referendum was held on the proposals. Troops were dispersed throughout Southern Rhodesia to deal with any possible outbreaks of violence on polling day, 26th July 1961. The electorate approved the new constitution by 41,940 votes to 21,826 votes.

At the same time, widespread disorder broke out in Northern Rhodesia and Nyasaland. Civil servants were attacked, schools and government buildings destroyed. Defiance of authority and intimidation was rife. Federal troops and the RRAF were called in to help control the civil disobedience and long hours were spent in the air by No 4 Squadron crews. Often the squadron's Provosts were the only means of reaching outlying districts cut off by damage to bridges, the obstruction of roads and the destruction of telephone lines. By 20th August, the death toll stood at 16. No sooner had the disturbances subsided inside the Federation, than the trouble that had been simmering for a year, erupted again in the Katanga Province of the Congo. Katanga, under the leadership of Moise Tshombe seceded. In September, a United Nations force seized power in Elisabethville and President Tshombe fled. A Battle of Britain Week flypast, which was to have been held on the weekend of 9th September, was cancelled because of the crisis and Vampires and Canberras were dispatched to Northern Rhodesia. Troops of the Rhodesian Light Infantry were moved from Salisbury to Ndola aboard No 3 Squadron aircraft. Nos 1 and 5 Squadron aircraft were also involved carrying out daily reconnaissance flights along Northern Rhodesia's border with the Congo. On 13th September, the Federal Prime Minister, Sir Roy Welensky, announced the troop movements in parliament. Speaking on the Katanga situation he said, "We have no alternative but to prepare for the worst."

The first aircraft to arrive in Ndola were three Provosts with guns and tear gas bombs slung under their wings. As dusk fell, four rocket-carrying Vampire jets screamed over the airport before taxiing into the rapidly filling parking areas. Finally, in the darkness, six Canberra bombers touched down to round off what had been the busiest day since the previous year's evacuation from Katanga.

Dag Hammarskjöld's plane goes missing

On 18th September, the RRAF was called upon to search for a missing aircraft. It had been carrying the Secretary General of the United Nations, Dag Hammarskjöld. That day the *Evening Standard* carried the following report:

Hammarskjoeld's plane missing. RRAF search. Northern Rhodesian planes of the RRAF are searching for Mr Dag Hammarskjoeld's DC-4 aircraft, which is missing on a flight between Leopoldville and Ndola. The RRAF is investigating a report that the wreckage of a plane has been sighted about ten miles [16km] south of Mufulira on the Copperbelt. A search party has also set out overland to the scene of the reported wreck.

Next day the *Rhodesia Herald* carried confirmation of the tragedy:

The Secretary General of the United Nations, Mr Dag Hammarskjoeld, died in an aircraft crash today just north of Ndola. He was on his way to have peace talks with President Tshombe of the Katanga. The lone survivor of the crash, Sergeant Harold Julian, an American member of the UN Security Force, said that when the aircraft flew over Ndola, Mr Hammarskjoeld changed his mind about landing and told the pilot to alter course for another destination.

Mr Hammarskjöld's body together with those of the other 16 victims was flown to Salisbury on 26th September aboard a No 3 Squadron aircraft. Commenting on this crash Archie Wilson writes:

The authenticity of the statement attributed to Sergeant Julian who was barely alive when found and who soon died of his extensive injuries is clearly suspect as was later revealed. Evidence at the site of the crash and that produced during the Board of Inquiry established that the aircraft with lights off was on a final approach to the main Ndola runway with undercarriage and flaps down when it descended into trees with tragic results. Certainly all at Ndola Air Field that fateful night assumed from the pilot's behaviour that Hammarskjoeld had at the last moment changed his mind and instructed the captain of the aircraft to divert; this assumption arose out of the fact that the aircraft was seen to fly at altitude over the airfield with its navigation lights on, only to switch these off and discontinue radio contact when directly overhead and then to alter course towards Katanga. There was nothing at that juncture to suggest that the pilot was about to attempt an unorthodox letdown. Despite repeated attempts, the airfield controller was unable to get a response from the aircraft and at no time during those early stages was there anything to indicate a mishap. It was expected that the pilot would eventually report his whereabouts and give the reasons for his extraordinary procedure. However, overdue procedures were instituted in due course in accordance with international practice, followed by the Department of Civil Aviation activating their Search and Rescue organization. Meanwhile the air force on its own initiative had, in conjunction with its patrol-duties along the Congo border, carried out extensive searches and in the event did find the wreckage where least expected—relatively close to the airfield on upward-sloping ground out of sight of the airport control tower. From the subsequent Inquiry, it was established that the aircraft had in all probability entered the standard Letdown Pattern for Ndola in an attempt to avail its passengers of maximum security at a time when they were most vulnerable to attack i.e. whilst on the approach to land. Whatever the cause of the pilot's behaviour there was absolutely no doubt that the aircraft had descended into trees miles short of the main Ndola runway in what appeared to be a standard final approach with power on but lights off. A very significant piece of evidence was that the pilot's facilities chart was clipped open at a page marked NDOLO (as opposed to NDOLA). Ndolo, the Leopoldville [Kinshasa] airfield, has the same Letdown Pattern as that laid down for Ndola, the vital difference being that Ndolo is about 3,000 feet lower in altitude than Ndola. One can draw one's own conclusions from this revealing piece of evidence but it does give one the impression that the pilot had selected the wrong airport information and that on his final approach thought he still had 3,000 feet in hand. It was known that Hammarskjoeld's crew were unduly worried about possible attacks from Congolese rebel aircraft and this was borne out to some extent in that the aircraft was not flown direct to Ndola but chose to enter Northern Rhodesia by the shortest route and fly all the way down to Ndola inside the borders of that territory. Hence the situation where the aircraft arrived over Ndola well past its ETA and had never given position reports until almost overhead. The fact that the Swedish government took such pains to dispute the Board's findings was presumably because of their reluctance to accept that a Swedish National was indirectly responsible for the death of a national hero of the calibre and status of Dag Hammarskjoeld. The allegation that the RRAF could have done more to search on the night in question is nullified by two facts. Firstly, the Civil Aviation authorities were and are responsible for initiating and directing Search and Rescue operations within the area under their jurisdiction. In defence of the civil authorities, it should be recalled that there was nothing in the early stages to suggest that the aircraft had crashed or was indeed missing. Secondly, the RRAF Detachment at Ndola under the command of Squadron Leader John Mussell did respond immediately, when the report was received that something was amiss. A most unfortunate aspect of the saga is that the actual crash was witnessed by an old African who, in his naïveté and confusion, did not report the matter to the authorities, but waited for his employer to return from Ndola in the morning to announce the tragedy.

A court of inquiry, costing the Federal government £8,000 was set up in February 1962. Members of the court were flown to Ndola in a Canadair of No 3 Squadron piloted by Flight Lieutenant George Alexander. Using this aircraft, George Alexander performed letdowns in which he simulated the descent of the United Nations aircraft. During this operation, the flight path of the Canadair was photographed by a Dakota of the same squadron.

At the end of the month, Sweden told the United Nations inquiry that on the evidence available it was not possible to establish with any degree of certainty the cause of the crash. Also a memorandum submitted by the Swedish government stated that it was not possible to establish with any certainty that pilot error was responsible. The Swedish government also criticized the RRAF for not doing more to speed up the search for the plane after it had been reported missing. However, despite the accusations, the RRAF were requested to provide a fighter escort for a United Nations aircraft flying high-ranking United Nations officials from Leopoldville to Ndola on 19th September.

Alouette III helicopters

During the last week of September 1961, Air Vice-Marshal Raf Bentley, the Federal Chief of Air Staff, who was attending the annual conference of Commonwealth Service Chiefs in London, announced that the Federal government had signed a contract for the purchase of five Alouette III helicopters. Two were to be delivered in February 1962 and the others in October. The total cost of these machines was given as £300,000, the price of each helicopter being £50,000 with a further £50,000 allocated for spares. The Alouettes were capable of being armed with machine guns, cannon, with the option of rockets and air-to-air missiles. Manufactured by Sud Aviation of France, the Alouette III would normally carry a pilot and six passengers but over short distances, eight passengers could be transported. The range was about 300 miles (480km) with a maximum all-up weight of 4,600 pounds (2,087kg). The normal cruising speed was given as 120 miles per hour (193 km/h) with a service ceiling of 15,000 feet. The SAAF already had seven Alouette IIIs. It is interesting to compare these figures with the actual operational capability of the Alouette III. It could carry five troops and a technician, without a side-mounted weapon. Later, when the machine gun was fitted and the troops were fully kitted out, the maximum load was four troopies and in some circumstances, if the men were carrying heavy equipment, only three.

Parachute Training School established

Meanwhile, the RRAF plans for parachute training were going ahead. On 5th October 1961, five members of the force returned after completing a four-month training course for instructors at the RAF Parachute School in Abingdon, Berkshire. It was intended to use these men to instruct the Federation's new crack unit of airborne commandos, the Special Air Services. Although the SAS was to be an army unit, the RRAF had the responsibility of training the men in the use of parachutes at the new Parachute Training School, which had been established at RRAF station, New Sarum, under the command of Flight Lieutenant Ron Smith AFM on secondment from the RAF.

On 1st November 1961, seven of these instructors gave a display of jumping techniques in front of 20 SAS recruits, when they leaped from a Dakota flying 1,000 feet above New Sarum Air Field. Eight days later, on 9th November, the first 16 members of the SAS No 1 Parachute Course performed their first jump. Jumping with them was station commander, Group Captain Archie Wilson who wanted to familiarize himself with the techniques. After a further eight days they had completed the course and been awarded their Parachute Wings.

Describing the event, the *Bulawayo Chronicle* reported:

> The only casualty at New Sarum Air Station at Salisbury yesterday, when 16 men of the SAS completed their final parachute jumps before qualifying as parachutists was the course mascot 'Fred'. When Fred, a large uniformed teddy bear was thrown from the RRAF Dakota to test wind drift, his parachute failed to open and he plunged into the ground losing his head as he hit. The 16 recruits will be presented with their Parachute Wings by Sir Malcolm Barrow, Federal Deputy Prime Minister, at a passing out parade today.

The RRAF brings aid to Kenya and Somalia

All round, November 1961 proved to be a busy month. Vampire pilots of Nos 1 and 2 Squadrons were detached to Ndola to patrol the border with Katanga Province where unrest continued. Then from 16th November to 16th December, came the detachment to Aden. No 1 Squadron flew via East Africa to the RAF station at Khormaksar where they undertook operational training and familiarized themselves with some of the forward areas in the Aden Protectorate. There were disastrous floods in Kenya at the time and No 3 Squadron was detached to Embakasi to drop food supplies and other aid to thousands of marooned villagers. Partly as a result of this flooding, famine hit parts of Kenya and Somalia, and the RRAF Dakotas transported 213 tons of food, using the free-drop technique in hilly, inaccessible country, mostly during poor weather conditions.

Acting Prime Minister, Sir Malcolm Barrow, commented, "This move is simply part of our positive policy of providing assistance whenever possible when asked to do so by the British authorities." On one occasion, the Chief of Air Staff, Air Vice-Marshal Raf Bentley, who was on his way to Aden, was an interested observer when the aircraft in which he was travelling made an air drop of 6,000 pounds (2,720kg) of maize meal at Kibisi Hill in the Sultan Hamid area.

The three RRAF Dakotas were described by the AOC Nairobi as, "A most welcome reinforcement in a serious situation". On 29th November, the *Evening Standard* carried a report on the RRAF activities:

> Three RRAF Dakota aircraft operating in Kenya's food-lift, dropped more than 66,000 pounds (29,920kg) of supplies to stricken tribesmen during the weekend. Round the clock work by the 17 RRAF ground crew based in Nairobi enabled the aircraft to fly a total of 23 hours and 50 minutes on Saturday and Sunday to bring urgent famine relief to the Loitokitok, Lake Natron and Selongai areas near the Tanganyika border. In difficult flying conditions, pilots

swooped their aircraft low over isolated villages to drop food from 200 feet. The RRAF aircraft also carried 30 passengers on their mercy flights. Most of the passengers were service personnel responsible for the distribution of supplies. (Evening Standard)

A further Dakota was dispatched with medical supplies to the Luapula Leprosy Colony in the Kawambwa area. By 5th December, when two of the Dakotas returned to Salisbury, 73 sorties had been flown with a flying time of 1,455 hours. Aid continued to be given until the end of January 1962.

No 3 Squadron must have thought that they had flown just about every kind of freight possible, what with maize meal to starving villagers, meat for a braai in Aden, motor parts to the army in Nyasaland and breathing apparatus for a polio case in Fort Victoria—but there is always something new—and in February 1962, it was ostriches.

A new role came to the squadron this month when 12 ostriches were flown from Wankie National Park to Salisbury, where they were transported by road to Lake McIlwaine National Park. The journey was successful and they all thrived in their new abode.
(No 3 Squadron Diary)

An airman wins the British Empire Medal for Gallantry

A member of the RRAF was involved in a rather different kind of rescue operation towards the end of November 1961. This time the incident took place within the borders of the Federation. On Wednesday 22nd November, a Rhodesian Air Services DC-3 (Dakota) took off from Salisbury Airport at 11h00, had a port engine failure and crashed into the New Sarum bomb dump killing both pilots: Captain Larry Owen and First Officer Noel Stewart. Aircraftman Kawilila of the General Service Unit was working in his maize patch when the crash occurred. He scaled a high fence and ran to the rescue. Miss Crosby, the air hostess, was lying among the wreckage. She was pinned face to the ground, still strapped into her seat. Kawilila loosened the safety belt and carried her more than 40 yards (37m) to safety. She survived with minor burns and lacerations. Kawilila was then joined by Sergeant Bishop of the Rhodesia and Nyasaland Medical Corps. Together they removed the body of one of the pilots and carried it away from the crash, having checked that the other pilot was also dead.

In June the following year, Aircraftman Kawilila was awarded the British Empire Medal for Gallantry for his action in twice entering the plane despite the risk of fire and explosion. Aircraftman Kawilila, who was born in Angola, had served with the RRAF since April 1961, when the General Service Unit was formed. Before that date, he had served with the army in Rhodesia for more than seven years.

Later a story grew up that ghosts could be seen at the New Sarum bomb dump. One security guard on night duty even reported seeing two pilots in uniform sitting on the branch of a tree doing cockpit drills. He apparently was able to recite what the pilots had said even though he had never been in the cockpit of a Dakota.

It was now over a year since the inception of the volunteer reserve and although initially it had been decided that the reserve should not supply pilots, it was later agreed that a small number of current pilots with service Wings, should be attached to No 3 Transport Squadron. The first pair to express an interest in flying were Flying Officers Archie Knoesen and Jerry Lynch. The former was shown a computer and decided not to continue; the latter who had joined the VR Squadron in January 1961, was still eager. However up to the end of 1961, he was still employed as an ops assistant on the ground and no final directive had come through about his future role.

The Rolls-Royce Trophy

Appreciation of the RRAF's technical excellence came in January 1962 from Rolls-Royce Ltd. The trophy, which was to be awarded each year to the best technical apprentice, was a replica of the famous Spirit of Ecstasy more commonly known as the Flying Lady that decorates the radiators of all Rolls-Royce cars. It was handed to the High Commissioner, Mr A.E.P. Robinson by Air Marshal Sir Colin Weeden, a senior representative of Rolls-Royce Engines in London, at a ceremony in Rhodesia House. Sir Colin said that it was only the third occasion on which a trophy had been awarded in the last ten years. "We like to set a rather high standard and it comes with our respect and admiration for the qualities of the RRAF. Everybody knows the part played by the squadron in the last war and the help given in the recent build-up in Kuwait."

CHAPTER 32

The birth of No 7 Helicopter Squadron

No 7 Helicopter Squadron came into being officially on 28th February 1962 with the promulgation of RRAF orders, issue No 3 of that date. Squadron strength was just two pilots: Squadron Leader Bill Dowden DFC, officer commanding, and Flight Lieutenant Rex Earp-Jones, who had recently completed a helicopter conversion course in France. The squadron technical officer was Flying Officer Wilf Wood, who had four technicians serving under him; Senior Technician Jim (Boggy) Marsh and Corporal Technicians Tony Atwell, Ned Kelly and Jim Brown. Aircraft strength was nil because none of the Alouettes on order had yet arrived.

Five more pilots, Flight Lieutenants Rex Taylor, Gordon Nettleton and Peter Cooke, and Flying Officers John Barnes and Peter Piggott were undergoing a conversion course with the SAAF and were due to join the squadron towards the end of May. A further three technicians: Chief Technician Jim Harries, and Corporal Technicians Sandy Steele and Peter Haddon were under training with Sud Aviation in France and were due back at the end of March. The helicopters were expected to arrive at about that time.

In fact, the first Alouette III arrived in Salisbury on 27th March 1962. The partly dismantled machine was freighted from the factory directly to New Sarum in a specially converted UAT DC-6. The aircraft touched down at 13h15 and left again at midnight, carrying eight RRAF technicians who were on their way to Britain for a maintenance and repair course on the Hunter jet fighter, it having been announced that the Federation was to acquire Hunters. Work on the assembly of the first Alouette began the following day, 28th March and by 16h00 it was ready to fly. At approximately 16h30 Bill Dowden and Rex Earp-Jones lifted 501 off from the apron—No 7 Squadron was airborne.

One of the first people to have a close-up view of the new Alouette was the Governor-General of the Federation, Lord Dalhousie, when one of the aircraft paid a flying visit to Government House on 30th March. It seems that the visit to Government House caused some pandemonium. The downwash of the rotors looked as though it was going to obliterate the rose blooms completely, so Bill Dowden took his chopper across the lawn. On the way, his hovering machine passed over the fishpond whereupon the goldfish started leaping from the pool onto the grass. Government House staff came rushing out to retrieve the shell-shocked fish that were flapping around in the grass and in the flowerbeds. Apparently, the noise and increase in pressure on the water had caused panic among the fish.

The second RRAF Alouette to fly was test-flown on 4th April. Two days later Peter Piggott, who had been on a conversion course with the SAAF, reported for duty and the third RRAF helicopter took to the air.

Most of the early flying took the form of demonstrations for police and army, together with flights for VIPs of whom the governor-general was one. Large numbers of RRAF personnel were also carried during routine training and by the end of the first month, 307 passengers had been transported and a total of 69 hours logged by the three helicopters. At this stage, the only operational equipment possessed by the squadron was the cargo sling and associated equipment. On 12th April, one of the machines travelled as far as Thornhill but none had yet ventured outside the borders of Southern Rhodesia.

First pilots of the ten-year Medium Service Commission

For the major part of 1962, No 1 Squadron remained at Thornhill on routine training, with only such extra activities as flypasts for Queen Elizabeth's birthday and Wings Parades to break the routine. In March, seven pilots of No 14 Pilot Training Course received their Wings from Air Vice-Marshal A.M. Bentley. They were: Terry Ryan, Brian Strickland, Keith Clarke, Tony Smit, Mike Hill, Alec Roughead and George Wrigley. These were the first pilots fully trained to Wings standard by No 2 Squadron and it was at this ceremony that the custom of awarding a Sword of Honour to the top student was inaugurated. These were also the first pilots to qualify under the new RRAF, ten-year Medium Service Commission. As these men went on to OCU, 12 new pilots began their training at Thornhill. At the end of the month an affiliation ceremony, with march-past and flypast, was held to "Give formal expression to the close and cordial relationship and mutual interest that has existed between the town [Gwelo] and the air station [Thornhill] for so long". (*Gwelo Times*, 30th March 1962)

In March, Flight Lieutenant George Alexander of No 3 Squadron was involved in an interesting experience. While flying five visiting Portuguese officers round the Federation, he was forced to land his Dakota at Sanyati following an engine failure. According to the Squadron History, "There was no damage to crew, passengers or aircraft. The five passengers were taken by vehicle to Sinoia, where they were uplifted the next day to Bulawayo and on to Thornhill. George and his crew remained with the aircraft and a supply-drop was carried out. The crew stayed at Sanyati until a new engine had been fitted and then flew the aircraft back to Salisbury."

Once again, in April, No 3 Squadron was called upon to drop food. On this occasion it was to the villagers of Kashiba, in Northern Rhodesia who had been cut off by the flooded Luapula River. Another request came from Impresit, the Italian Company, which was building Kariba Dam, to help in the search for three of its employees who were missing on the lake. A Dakota located a boat but was unable to confirm that it contained the missing men. An Autair helicopter was guided to the scene and hovered low over the waters of the lake while a check was carried out. In fact, all was well, and the boat carrying the men was able to make its way to harbour under its own steam.

No 7 Squadron assists police patrols during unrest in Salisbury

Helicopters, on this occasion those from No 7 Squadron, were again in the news when they gave a demonstration of their practical uses at the School of Infantry in May 1962. An interested spectator on this occasion was the Chief of the Imperial General Staff, Sir Richard Hull who was on a goodwill visit to the Federation.

It was only a few days later, that the helicopters gave conclusive evidence of their abilities when politically-inspired unrest broke out in the African townships of Highfield, Harare and Mufakose, near Salisbury. At first light on 14th May, two aircraft of No 7 Squadron were called out to assist police patrols. One of the pilots was attached to the central police operations room, while the other two carried out reconnaissance patrols with police observers, circling the townships to pinpoint trouble spots. Tear-gas was fired at strikers. The police were full of praise for the help they received from the choppers. One story, confirmed by the police, told of a factory official who telephoned the police to report a case of intimidation, while in mid-sentence he broke off, "Never mind—a police truck is just arriving." It had been guided to the scene by one of the helicopters whose crew had spotted the intimidators and radioed the information back to the police vehicle.

The riots, during which one black man was killed and four were injured, flared as a result of a 20-hour strike called by the Southern Rhodesia African Trades Union Congress. Many Blacks who defied the strike call were beaten up by intimidators. The police reservists at the scene were particularly impressed with one attribute of the helicopters—having thrown their stones and half bricks, the trouble-makers leapt into the cover of the long grass to hide. However, as the helicopter descended, its downdraft flattened the grass, and the rioters, stones in hand, were left in full view and much discomfited.

By 16th May, the trouble had subsided and army and police reserve units were stood down. That morning, a lone helicopter did an early morning patrol over the townships but finding everything peaceful returned to base. No 7 Squadron's first operational task had been completed satisfactorily.

Four more pilots joined the squadron in May 1962, while Rex Taylor left to complete an instructor's course with the SAAF. On completion of the course, he was appointed the 'A' flight commander and the squadron QHI (Qualified Helicopter Instructor). Flight Lieutenant Peter Cooke was appointed 'B' flight commander. Work now commenced in earnest to increase the flexibility of the squadron and discussions took place with the BSAP regarding the setting up of landing zones (LZs) at all police stations. Other subjects considered were the carriage of police tracker dogs, the fitting of police radios, and the possibility of dropping tear smoke from helicopters. The BSAP seemed to be taking a far greater interest in the capabilities of helicopters than the army.

Meanwhile, night-flying trials were being carried out to determine the most satisfactory flare layout and numerous systems were tried, until the standard 'T' of torches or flares, five paces apart was agreed upon. These findings were passed on to the police and the army and from then on the squadron was able to operate anywhere at night with the knowledge that the ground party would know how to lay down an acceptable landing 'T'.

Repair and maintenance
It had been arranged that No 5 Squadron should stage a flypast at Ndola on 2nd June, for the birthday of Queen Elizabeth II. Unfortunately, the formation flew into a flock of birds, probably hawks, which resulted in suspected damage to three of the four aircraft. The Canberras were forced to land at Lusaka Airport and an RRAF Dakota of No 3 Squadron carrying a technical crew flew from Salisbury to effect repairs. At first it was feared that the damage was extensive, because as an air force spokesman said: Even small birds—and these were large ones—are capable of tearing large holes in an aircraft. It's as if the birds were fired from a giant catapult. When they hit, the velocity is the same as that of the aircraft. An investigation on one aircraft found that it had sustained damage to the leading edge of a wing and to its tail plane.

It was vital that the Canberras be placed in first-class condition as quickly as possible because their annual detachment to Cyprus was due to take place later in the month. The squadron, under the command of Squadron Leader Frank Mussell, left on 15th June. During their stay in Cyprus, the squadron took part in bomber and fighter exercises with the RAF. As usual, No 3 Squadron supplied backup for the Canberras, ferrying technicians and spares and anything else that was required.

On the subject of repair and maintenance, the RRAF had switched its contracts from overseas to local companies. Transactions worth thousands of pounds were involved; the immediate effects were a golden harvest for companies in Southern Rhodesia and greatly increased mobility and self-reliance for the air force. Four major companies benefited from the new scheme. They were Rhodesia United Air Carriers (RUAC), Field Aircraft Services, Central African Airways (CAA) and Africair.

It was agreed that RUAC should undertake the major overhauls to aircraft such as the Vampires and Canberras, and the Hunters when they arrived. To deal with this extra work, RUAC imported 30 specialists and technicians. Field Aircraft Services, which had in the past carried out a certain amount of air force work, was to get a larger share of the piston engine overhauls, together with the maintenance of ancillary equipment. CAA was to service radio gear, propellers and associated equipment, while Africair, a firm based in Bulawayo, was to handle major overhauls on transport aircraft frames i.e. Dakotas and Canadairs.

News from No 7 Squadron

June 13th 1962 saw No 7 Squadron's first deployment outside the borders of Southern Rhodesia when an Alouette flew to Lusaka and Ndola to take part in emplaning and deplaning drills. The helicopter then proceeded to Mkushi, where it was joined by a second aircraft for the squadron's first participation in an army cooperation exercise. Five days later, a helicopter went to Nyasaland to participate in training with the King's African Rifles (KAR).

Meanwhile, in the Mashonaland area, No 7 Squadron Alouettes were visiting police stations to photograph the newly constructed landing zones, completing index cards, noting details such as fuel stocks, accommodation and medical facilities. This practice continued until the squadron had a complete record of every official landing zone. Additional areas were cleared on farms and at country clubs that could be used as police reserve bases.

Now that the squadron had an instructor, continuation training and standardization flights were carried out and for this purpose, two training squares were marked out with whitewash in Seke Reserve. During June, police radios were fitted to all Alouettes and trials were carried out. At first, only one person in the aircraft could use the police radio, which was independent of the normal radio and had only one lead. Modifications were carried out later so that the police radios fed into the normal intercom system and pilots could listen to both sets concurrently, although transmission still had to be separately selected.

By July 1962, No 7 Squadron was independent of SAAF training and it was decided to explore the feasibility of instrument flying. After some experimentation, a canvas screen was fitted so that it obscured the vision of the pilot in the right hand seat, without hampering that of the safety pilot in the centre seat. This method proved successful and became standard practice, so that pilots could be instrument rated on helicopters, although actual instrument flying was not permitted, as the Alouette was not fitted with a stand-by instrument system. The main purpose of carrying out instrument flying was to ensure that pilots were familiar with flying the aircraft on instruments, in the event of finding themselves in cloud or in conditions of very thick haze with no visible horizon.

The remaining two Alouette helicopters arrived on 6th July aboard a UAT French Airlines DC-6 and were soon assembled, bringing the squadron up to its establishment of five machines. Low-level oblique photo reconnaissance was added to the squadron's roles with the mounting of an F 24 electrically operated camera in the rear doorway. This proved quite successful but was never used to any large extent. (No 7 Squadron Diary, July 1962)

First No 7 Squadron casevac

One important helicopter capability that still had to be tested was casualty evacuation. An opportunity arose on 3rd August. An item in the *Rhodesia Herald* began the dramatic story:

An RRAF helicopter was due to leave Salisbury early this morning to rescue a 26-year-old

Rhodesian Railways engine driver lying stranded with a broken leg in a remote area of the Chimanimani Mountains. The man, Mr B. Garde, was one of a party of climbers who set out to scale some of the Chimanimani peaks. He is stranded where he fell and a spokesman for the Chimanimani Hotel said it would take at least four days to rescue him if he had to be carried out manually. The spokesman said that a medical officer would be on board the helicopter. It was hoped that Mr Garde would be rescued by 7 am. He was as well as could be expected.
(Rhodesia Herald, 3rd Aug. 1962)

The tale was, later in the day, taken up by the *Evening Standard*:

An RRAF Alouette helicopter touched down in a disused football field outside Salisbury Hospital today and so ended a dramatic mountain rescue early this morning. The accident happened at 5 am on 2nd August, when Mr Garde's leg was apparently broken by falling rock. He was made as comfortable as possible under shelter and Ron Searle went for help. It was 16 hours before he managed to contact the police who got in touch with the RRAF. Meanwhile a patrol had been dispatched to render first aid. It was late in the afternoon before the RRAF were told of the accident. With night approaching, it was too late to risk the hazardous mountain rescue by helicopter. Finally, at first light today, Squadron Leader W.A. Dowden put his helicopter down on a narrow, jutting outcrop of rock on the mountainside. Below the outcrop was a sheer drop into a gorge. The RRAF senior medical officer, Major D. MacIntyre, congratulated the climbers on their first aid work and gave Mr Garde a sedative. The helicopter refuelled at Melsetter and flew to Salisbury. (Evening Standard, 3rd Aug. 1962)

This was the first of many hundreds of casualty evacuations carried out by No 7 Squadron. The cases ranged from serious illness or accident in remote areas, to battle casualties inflicted during counter-insurgency operations. Casualty evacuation is one of the primary roles of any helicopter squadron and it proved an inestimable morale-booster for troops engaged in active service. Helicopters were later to land in frontline areas while fighting was still in progress to uplift dead and wounded, carrying them back to casualty clearing posts within minutes of their being hit.

From July until September 1962, No 7 Squadron was hard at work flying cooperation sorties with police and army units, practising trooping drills and also training police dogs with their handlers in the art of emplaning and deplaning. At the same time, as part of a public relations exercise, the helicopters staged displays at agricultural shows throughout the country.

In September 1962, No 1 Vampire Squadron took part in a flypast in honour of Battle of Britain Week. No 2 Squadron commenced basic flying training with No 16 Pilot Training Course. No 3 Squadron was engaged in paratroop training. No 4 Squadron was affiliated to the city of Umtali, in a very impressive ceremony that cemented a blossoming friendship between the town and the squadron, and No 5 Squadron was taking part in training exercises in South Africa.

No 6 Squadron, which had been resuscitated on 1st June 1962 under the command of Squadron Leader Chris Dams, had at first been unable to do any flying as it possessed no aircraft, pilots or ground crew. This strange state of affairs was partially remedied on 14th June with the arrival of ground crew, and on 20th June, four pilots and one navigator began an OCU, which they completed on 14th September. So it was that No 6 Squadron only became operational on this date.

Earlier in 1962, new constitutions had been granted to Northern Rhodesia and Nyasaland, which ensured the return of African nationalist governments. On 26th March, the British government created a new office of Central African Affairs headed by Mr R.A. Butler, Home Secretary, to oversee the Federation, and general elections to obtain a new mandate on the future of the Federation. The official opposition, the Rhodesian Front (formerly the Dominion Party) did not contest the election, which was held on 17th April. The result was that the UFP won 54 out of the 59 seats in the Federal Assembly. In May, Mr Butler visited the Federation and indicated that Nyasaland would be allowed to secede and a team of advisers appointed to investigate the consequences of the impending Federal breakup arrived in June 1962.

Unrest in the Chipinga and Melsetter areas

Meanwhile, there had been a sharp increase in political intimidation, violence and acts of sabotage in Southern Rhodesia. On 19th September, RRAF squadrons were placed on alert and volunteer reserve pilots were called up. The following day, the Prime Minister of Southern Rhodesia, Sir Edgar Whitehead announced the banning of the Zimbabwe African People's Union (ZAPU). Nos 4, 5, 6 and 7 Squadrons took part in leaflet drops and flag-waving flights over remote areas. *The Chronicle* in Bulawayo printed a news item on September 21st, which stated:

> *About 750,000 leaflets in English, Shona and Sindebele were dropped in various parts of Southern Rhodesia by the RRAF: 'ZAPU is dead. You have cried to the government for a long time that something be done to bring back happiness and a peaceful life. Government forces—the police, the army and the air force—are in your district to help you. They are your friends. You have nothing to fear from them. They are here to remove the bad people who have intimidated you and damaged some of your homes and schools. When part of the pumpkin is bad, the bad part is cut out and thrown away by the farmer who reaps it. ZAPU has been cut out by government law. We throw it away. ZAPU is dead and finished. It is now against the law to be a member. The terror they fashioned on lies is over'.*

Another leaflet told the people they could arrest anyone committing a crime or starting a fight. The Chipinga/Melsetter area was proving to be particularly troublesome with a great deal of general disorder taking place and numerous reports of arson. It was decided that tough measures were needed, and on 20th/21st September members of the Special Air Services, making their first operational parachute drop, jumped into the area from a No 3 Squadron Dakota. The following day, they were uplifted and dropped again at Kutama Mission, followed by another uplift and drop at Inyanga on 26th September. Reporting on the situation in the issue of 24th September, the *Rhodesia Herald* had this to say:

> *Armed troops of the SAS and special police, also armed, set up roadblocks ringing the Melsetter area today, (23rd). The search for fire-raisers intensified after more than 120 acres (48,6 hectares) on the BSA Company's Thornton Forest Estates were destroyed early this morning by three fires started deliberately just off the Melsetter/Chipinga road. This time the arsonists were nearly caught. RRAF men in a helicopter on early morning patrol saw an African lighting one of the fires. On the ground, a police reservist was bringing his rifle into line when the man dived into the undergrowth. The helicopter could not continue the search because it was running short of fuel and the man escaped. The police theory is that the fire-raisers are being brought in by car from the maze of valleys near the Portuguese [Mozambique] border. A patrolling aircraft spotted two cars speeding away along dirt roads shortly after the fires were started. Police reservists were sent after them but it is understood that the search was unsuccessful. During this season, the forests are tinder-dry and fire-raisers have an easy task.* (Rhodesia Herald, 24th Sept. 1962)

Further leaflets were dropped and on 3rd October, thirty paratroopers of the SAS jumped from a Dakota of No 3 Squadron into Chinamora Reserve, just north of Salisbury, to assist security forces in a search of the area and to set up a cordon. A police spokesman said that the combined police and military operation was to follow up cases of arson that had been reported from the reserve.

Wings for No 15 Pilot Training Course

Meanwhile, a further nine fully trained pilots, members of No 15 Pilot Training Course had received their Wings from the Federal Minister of Defence, the Honourable Sir Malcolm Barrow, at a ceremony on September 29th 1962. These men were Dave Becks, Dave Currie, Henry Elliot, Dave Hume, Brian Jolley, Bruce Smith, Harold Griffiths and Tony Gassner. In his speech at the ceremony, Sir Malcolm said that the importance of the armed forces, especially the RRAF, could not be over-emphasized.

We have both an internal and an external commitment to meet with our air arm and we have our part to play in the overall pattern of Commonwealth and Western defence. Should the need arise, the country also has to be able to meet any threat that might eventuate on the African continent and, finally, other forces engaged in dealing with attempts at insurrection within our midst have to be assisted. We must be ready to counter the lawlessness, unrest and instability that totalitarian and quasi-military organizations such as the late and unlamented ZAPU endeavour to foment. We must be able to render immediate and effective aid to the civil authorities of any territory whenever and wherever they may require it.

He congratulated the RRAF, the RRAFVR and the territorial force on the invaluable role they had played during the ten days preceding.

Following this Wings ceremony, No 2 Squadron was able to expand into a further, third flight, which was formed in October, and to carry out operational conversions on the Vampire with pilots selected from the previous training course.

Photographic reconnaissance

During 1961, the first trials had been undertaken, using No 6 Squadron Canberras for high altitude aerial survey and photographic reconnaissance. The project manager at Thornhill was Don Brenchley. The only camera available was an Mk I Williamson 6-inch survey camera that had been used in a No 3 Squadron Dakota to produce 1:25 000 scale mapping negatives for the Survey Department. It had to be manually operated and worked well enough in a Dakota flying at 12,500 feet.

The first trials using a Canberra crewed by Chris Dams and Don Brenchley were flown in October 1962. Some were successful and others were not and Don came to the conclusion that the photo survey could be accomplished if the Canberra was modified but that the camera was unreliable. The main problem was that the area where the camera would be housed was not pressurized or heated. The camera would only operate efficiently between temperatures of zero and 15°. Trials were moved to New Sarum and the decision was taken to buy a Wild RC-8, a Swiss-made camera that was perfect for the job. However there was one difficulty. It would cost £6,000. Where was the money to come from? Obviously all the security forces would benefit from having accurate maps—so the army and the police as well as the air force contributed equally—£2,000 each and the camera arrived. To date, it had only been employed in civil aircraft, in pressurized cabins with an operator hovering close at hand to operate the controls. The air force were going to place the camera 40 feet back in the fuselage, remotely controlled and subject to temperature variations of 80°.

Warrant Office John Cubitt, in the drawing office was roped in. He designed a support frame but when the contraption was put in place, it wouldn't fit. The only solution was to allow the lens to protrude into the slipstream. But what about the film, which had to be kept at a steady temperature of between 0° and 15°. Don devised a glass panel in a frame that was attached to the fuselage to protect the camera.

The next problem was weight. Having a heavy camera in the tail would unbalance the aircraft. The simple answer—add weight to the nose. Now Don was ready to fly a test, despite the dire prophecies that the lens would crack under the extreme temperatures. A test flight was authorized and history was made—a world first. Wild sent the air force a congratulatory telegram and a silver pen. No one had lifted a Wild RC-8 to such altitudes, subjected it to such temperatures and obtained such good survey negatives at 1:80 000 scale. Eventually three Canberras were modified to take the camera. Much later, F52 36-inch focal length recce cameras were fitted and finally the F96 36-inch and 48-inch cameras became available.

So No 6 Squadron was able to begin its task. A large proportion of the hours flown in December was spent in bringing crews to a fully operational standard and in preparing them for their new role. A visit was paid to the Federal Survey Department in November 1962 as part of this training. Towards the end of the year, Squadron Leader Chris Dams flew extensive photo reconnaissance over Angola, Mozambique and Nyasaland.

Interest focused on the Safety Equipment Section of the RRAF in November when a report in the *Rhodesia Herald* told how the parachute packers at New Sarum had proved their confidence in their own handiwork by making parachute descents. This was the first opportunity that the backroom boys had of testing their own parachutes in a live jump. Those same packers were put to a further test on 27th November when the SAS carried out their first night-drop at Ndola. Transport was provided, as usual by No 3 Squadron.

News from the VR

The month of December 1962 passed quietly with very little flying, except the routine VIP trips and training. However, there was interesting news on the VR front. Group Captain Charles Green had retired. He was succeeded by Group Captain Graham Smith who had commanded No 237 Squadron briefly and was a founder member of the VR. It had become obvious that if the scope and responsibilities of the VR were to be increased, the squadron must recruit young flyers as well as veterans. It was also necessary to place the training on a professional basis. The appropriate directive had been issued to the new commander and the VR rapidly became indispensable to the regular force in almost all facets of operational deployment, enjoying the high esteem of the armed services and being accepted rank for rank by all concerned.

> *The volunteer reserve pilots were by this time being allowed to do more than 'just raise the wheels' so there was a lot of circuit work being done, followed by instrument flying from the right-hand seat. The VR were then converted to left-hand seat flying, which made instrument flying easier. The way was now open for VR pilots to become fully-qualified second pilots. One new regular pilot arrived at Christmas time to join the squadron. He was Flying Officer Jim S.G. Weir from Britain, who had originally trained in this country, at Heany, after the Second World War.* (No 3 Squadron History)

The 5th January 1963 was a big day for the VRs because that was the date on which they commenced routine flying as second pilots. The first three men to qualify were Flying Officers Jerry Lynch, John Matthews and Roy Cooper.

The Hunters arrive

No 1 Squadron had been eagerly awaiting the arrival of their new aircraft, the Hawker Hunter FGA 9. At last, on 20th December 1962, the day came. The aircraft were flown from the United Kingdom by Flight Lieutenant Saunders and Flying Officer Gait-Smith. Other squadron pilots were either in the United Kingdom doing three-week conversion courses or preparing to go to the United Kingdom.

The Hunter, a front-line fighter and ground-attack aircraft with supersonic capability, could carry bombs weighing from 25 lbs to 1,000 lbs (11–444kg) plus various types of rockets employing different warheads. The Hunter could also fire air-to-air or air-to-ground missiles. Its cruising speed was given as 470 mph (750 km/h).

The *Rhodesia Herald* announced the arrival of the Hunters on its front page:

> *The latest addition to the RRAF arrived in Salisbury yesterday with the biggest bang ever heard over the city and brought a stream of protests from people in the Salisbury area. The air force's two new Hawker Hunter jet fighters screamed about 1,000 feet (sic) over the city at an officially estimated 400 mph (640 km/h). Then the trouble started. City buildings reverberated with the deafening noise of their engines. In a medical surgery, a crowd of children were so frightened that they burst out crying. City dwellers called the 'Rhodesia Herald' to complain. In the Salisbury Magistrates Court, proceedings came to a halt as the jets screamed overhead and people in the court ducked their heads in alarm. They sat bolt upright in the Salisbury City Council meeting, reported the municipal correspondent. But it was learned that the noise made by the aircraft when they first flew over the city on arrival from Nairobi was unavoidable because of the low cloud ceiling, which was down to 500 feet. Unofficial reaction seems to be that the public will have to get used to the noise of the aircraft. Ten more are due here early next year. Leading Federal government officials headed by the Federal Prime Minister, Sir Roy Welensky, were at New Sarum to greet the pilots of the new green and grey aircraft.* (Rhodesia Herald, 21st Dec. 1962)

Obviously the Hunters were well below 1,000 feet if they were below a 500-foot cloud level. Bill Sykes remembers: "I was on the fifth floor of a building in town on that day and I reckon it was 100 feet at 550 mph! It made me join the air force."

One unfortunate casualty of the Hunter beat-up of the city was a budgerigar that seems to have died of fright. He belonged to 88-year-old Mrs Beatrice Postlethwaite, who lived at Fairways old people's home. She had owned Diddums for eight years until the fateful day when the Hunters flew over the city. As the aircraft screamed overhead, Diddums fell off his perch and stood speechless, with feathers fluffed out. A few days later he died. This story eventually reached the ears of members of the RRAF, who individually and collectively felt responsible. Air Vice-Marshal Raf Bentley contacted the secretary of Fairways and arrangements were made. A day or two later, Raf Bentley appeared at the home with a perky, upstanding young budgie, whose feathers were a brilliant shade of air force blue. The bird was named Blue Peter, partly after his colour and partly after the flag. It was hoped that Mrs Postlethwaite would have many happy hours teaching him to speak.

Yet more trouble in the Congo

Towards the end of December 1962, trouble flared again in the Congo province of Katanga, when United Nations forces tried to oust the President, Moise Tshombe. As a result, Nos 1 and 2 Squadrons were detached to fly border patrols. No 6 Squadron was also on detachment in Ndola for Congo border patrol in support of the army. No 4 Squadron carried out reconnaissance operations from its base in Ndola and No 7 Squadron also assisted in border control activities.

When Flight Lieutenant Peter Cooke and Senior Technician Jim (Boggy) Marsh flew to Ndola on 29th December, and then to Chingola on 1st January with Squadron Leader Chris Dams as the Forward Air Support Operations Centre (FASOC) commander. Peter Cooke handed over to Rex Earp-Jones on 11th January having flown some ten hours in support of the army. The versatility of the helicopter was amply proved to the army. It was in the middle of the rainy season and most road communications were in atrocious conditions. Peter Cooke remembers:

I flew over miles and miles of waterlogged country. I had to land at Mokambo village, on the border—the 'browns' in their wisdom decided to mark the LZ with sheets of corrugated iron laid out to form the letter H. The marking was perfectly correct but the use of corrugated iron was potentially very dangerous, not only to people on the ground but also in the helicopter. I tried to indicate that they must remove the sheets but they did not see my frantic signals. So I decided to show them what would happen and descended a bit—whereupon the corrugated iron started to get airborne. I climbed away. They had finally got the message.

No 3 Squadron flew President Tshombe to Salisbury for talks. By the end of January 1963, all was quiet again.

On the technical side, the year ended well with an RRAF aircraft apprentice passing out top of his three-year course at an RAF training establishment and winning three awards. He was Sergeant Aircraft Apprentice Erroll V. Bennett, whose father Warrant Officer Derek Bennett and his brother Terence Bennett were also serving with the RRAF. RRAF technicians were now also being trained in the Federation at No 1 Ground Training School, New Sarum and they were proving to be comparable to if not better than those trained overseas. The local Technical Training Courses were termed LAR Courses (Local Airmen Recruit).

In December 1962, it was officially announced that Nyasaland would be allowed to secede. The British decision was bitterly attacked by the Federal Prime Minister, Sir Roy Welensky, who charged Britain with bad faith. The adoption of the new constitution had not helped the Southern Rhodesia government. Pressure continued from all sides and no credit was given for the immense advances achieved in the realms of health, education, social services and the standard of living. The demand for one-man-one-vote grew louder. White Rhodesians, who felt that they had gained nothing in return for the concessions they had made, went to the polls in a territorial election on 16th December 1962. The result was a Rhodesian Front victory with 35 seats to the 29 won by the UFP. All the RF seats were 'A' roll (White) Constituency seats while the UFP seats were divided between the 'A' and the 'B' (Black) rolls.

The new prime minister, Mr Winston Field, faced a difficult task. During the previous 18 months, there had been an almost complete break down of law and order with racial unrest and lawlessness rife throughout the country. The African nationalists represented by the Zimbabwe African People's Union (ZAPU) led by Joshua Nkomo and the Zimbabwe African National Union (ZANU) led by the Reverend Ndabaningi Sithole had created a reign of terror in the townships as each sought to increase its hold over the black population. From the beginning of 1962 until February 1963, there had been 73 incidents in which petrol bombs had been used.

Welcome news for No 7 Squadron, on 17th January, was that three more Sud Aviation Alouette [Mark] III helicopters had been ordered. These helicopters arrived in the Federation on 6th August 1963 and incorporated slightly improved modifications. The main difference was all-transparent front cabin doors and a larger transparent centre panel at the pilot's feet, allowing improved visibility. With the new aircraft came three sets of hoisting equipment. This added immensely to the squadron's capability in the field of search and rescue because all the Alouettes were wired to take the hoist, which could be fitted in about ten to 15 minutes.

At the end of February 1963, the Vampires joined the helicopters in Northern Rhodesia (Zambia) to take part in the last major Federal army exercise, Brown Water. By this time, most members of the Rhodesian Light Infantry had been combat-trained on helicopters, but in March, the RLI received first hand experience of the helicopters' mercy role when a seriously injured troopie was flown from Kariba to Salisbury for treatment.

The same month, March, saw the first major accident involving a RRAF helicopter when scores of frightened children at Macheke School scattered to safety as the aircraft, apparently entering a vortex ring state, landed extremely heavily, breaking the tail boom. Fortunately, no one was hurt. Eyewitnesses reported that the aircraft, which had just taken off from the playing field, climbed to a height of 100 feet before plunging back onto the ground damaging the tail rotor and undercarriage.

No 2 Squadron was, meanwhile, continuing its instructional role. No 4 FIS commenced in March and No 16 Pilot Training Course OCU in July. Earlier in the year, the serious business of training had been interrupted when a flying display was staged in Lusaka and a civic ceremony was held in Livingstone to mark the affiliation of the squadron to that town. Chris Dams said he hoped cooperation between Northern and Southern Rhodesia would continue. Sadly, this was not to be the case. In the same month, March, No 6 Squadron was affiliated to the town of Ndola and two more Hunter jet fighters arrived from Britain bringing the Hunter strength to six with six more on order. During the following month, April, No 6 Squadron aircraft flew to Cyprus on a Rover Operation.

The end of the Federation

Events were now moving fast towards the demise of the Federation. In March 1963, representatives of the Federal government and the governments of Northern and Southern Rhodesia were invited to London to prepare an agenda for a conference on the future of the Federation. Kenneth Kaunda demanded that Northern Rhodesia should be given the right to secede and this was officially granted on 29th March.

Through the months of April and May, No 3 Squadron flew the governor-general and his wife, Lord and Lady Dalhousie, on a series of whistle stop trips to say goodbye to the people of the three territories. The final farewell was reported in the *Rhodesia Herald* on 7th May 1963:

As the aircraft, an RRAF Canadair (No 3 Squadron) began moving along the tarmac, the crowd waved enthusiastically. Lord and Lady Dalhousie waved back through the windows of the aircraft. A few minutes later, the aircraft circled the airport and flanked by an escort of six RRAF Vampire jets, flew over the airport building at about 500 feet before heading for Nairobi.
(Rhodesia Herald, 7th May 1963)

Following the departure of Lord Dalhousie and his family to Nairobi en route for Scotland, Sir Humphrey Gibbs was made acting governor-general until the end of the year.

As might have been expected, arguments had already begun about the future role of the Federation's air force. On 6th May, speaking on television, Sir Roy Welensky, the Federal Prime Minister stated that it was beyond argument that the RRAF must go back to Southern Rhodesia on the breakup. However, a speedy reply came from Kenneth Kaunda in Lusaka, who said that it must be realized that the Federal army and air force had been built mainly on Northern Rhodesia money. Kaunda as head of Northern Rhodesia's leading political party, UNIP, declined to say what action Northern Rhodesia would take if Southern Rhodesia tried to take over the whole air force. He also refused to say whether he would request Britain to intervene.

Two days later, Mr Winston Field, whose Rhodesia Front party had won the Southern

Rhodesia territorial elections in December the previous year, made a broadcast. Referring to suggestions that the Federation's armed forces should be placed under the control of a commission consisting of the British government together with the governments of Northern and Southern Rhodesia, he said: "This we reject. The forces must remain under the Federal government to whom they now owe allegiance, until such time as our defence, which was our own function prior to Federation, is returned to us." Replying to timorous critics who said Southern Rhodesia could not afford a worthwhile defence force, Mr Field said, "In this day and age in Africa we have got to."

The conference, convened to preside over the breakup of the Federation, opened at the Victoria Falls in June. At the beginning of July, discussions began on one of the thorniest problems on the agenda—defence. The *Rhodesia Herald* announced the outcome of these discussions on 4th July 1963:

> *When the Federal government ceases to be responsible for defence, the operational control of the defence forces will revert to the pre-Federation position. Agreement on this at the Victoria Falls conferences was announced last night by Sir Roy Welensky in a radio broadcast. "Perhaps the most important agreement reached was that there would be no attempt to split the physical assets of the forces, and that these will in general remain with their present units," Sir Roy said. "There will thus be no partition of the RRAF," he said, "Naturally there will have to be subsequent financial settlement that will be dealt with in the context of the general arrangement of the apportionment of Federal assets and liabilities." It was also agreed that arrangements would have to be made to permit all members of the forces to declare in which territory they would in the future wish to serve.* (Rhodesia Herald, 4th July 1963)

It would seem that this had settled the matter but it was only the beginning of a bitter wrangle. At the beginning of September, a demand that Great Britain should take over the Southern Rhodesian army and the RRAF was put forward by 32 African member states then represented in the United Nations. This was followed by an accusation from Ghana that Portugal, South Africa and Southern Rhodesia had agreed to maintain a powerful Southern Rhodesia air force that could be used against other African countries. The outcome of this criticism was discussed in the *Rhodesia Herald* on 12th September 1963:

> *Ghana is criticized by two British newspapers today for seeking to use the UN Security Council to hold up the transfer of Federal armed forces to Southern Rhodesia. The 'Daily Telegraph' said: 'This is the second time that President Nkrumah has sought to intervene in the dissolution of the Central African Federation'. "Britain's delegate to the United Nations, Sir Patrick Dean, has made a forceful speech completely demolishing the Ghanaian case on the danger of a transfer of armed forces to Southern Rhodesia," the Prime Minister of Southern Rhodesia, Mr Winston Field, told the House.*

Still the argument continued. Alex Quaison-Sackey of Ghana speaking in the United Nations Security Council remarked that: "The Rhodesian Air Force is more powerful than even that of South Africa. It is stronger than the combined metropolitan and colonial air force of Portugal." He went on to say that the proposed transfer of the armed forces to a white-dominated government in Salisbury would result in conflicts on the African continent.

These remarks were contested in the *Sunday Mail* of 22nd September 1963:

> *The RRAF is a 'near-perfect pocket air force' but it is not the most powerful in Africa. Egypt, with Russian MiG fighters and the latest bombers and transport planes is very much larger, and*

both Abyssinia and Algeria have air forces comparable with Southern Rhodesia's. The South African air force is also larger, but has less firepower.

The actual strength of the RRAF at this date was given as 91 aircraft none of which have nuclear capabilities. The total of 91 was made up as follows:

No 1 Squadron	Twelve Hunters F(GA) 9s. Fighter/ground attack.
No 2 Squadron	Twelve Vampire T 11s and FB 9s. Fighter bombers. Together with 14 Vampires of both types in storage owing to No 1 Squadron being re-equipped with the Hunter.
No 3 Squadron	Four Canadair C4s. Eight Dakotas. Two Pembrokes.
No 4 Squadron	Thirteen Provost T 52s. Light ground attack.
Nos 5 & 6 Squadrons	Eighteen Canberra B2s. Medium bomber and photo reconnaissance.
No 7 Squadron	Eight Alouette III helicopters. Light transport and ground assault.

The *Sunday Mail* article continued:

With the exception of the Hunters, all these aircraft are second generation (3 – 5 years out of date). Compared with the NATO powers, the RRAF is a tiny and largely obsolescent force. But by African standards it still represents a 'capable and very effective defensive air force'. The RRAF has 207 officers and 951 other ranks, including a substantial number of Africans. It can also call on a small volunteer reserve, including a handful of pilots, most of whom have had previous service experience. (Sunday Mail, 22nd Sep.1963)

On 11th October 1963, any speculation came to an end when the Federal Ministry of Defence made an official announcement. This stated that Southern Rhodesia was to retain the RRAF although slightly reduced in strength, and just over half of the Federal army. The SAS paratroops were to be stationed in Southern Rhodesia and the Selous Scouts (armoured cars—not to be confused with the later force) were to be disbanded.

This decision had been made with the agreements of the governments of Britain, Northern and Southern Rhodesia and Nyasaland, despite the protests made by the representatives of the Afro-Asian block at the United Nations. As far as the aircraft were concerned, Northern Rhodesia was to receive four Dakotas and two Pembrokes, while the RRAF, which was to revert to Southern Rhodesia would consist of 75 aircraft, including the Hunters, Canberras, Vampires, Dakotas, Canadairs, Provosts and Alouette helicopters. Kenneth Kaunda promptly called an emergency UNIP caucus on the unfair allocation of aircraft.

Chief of Air Staff, Air Vice-Marshal Bentley remarked that it was sad but inevitable that the affiliation between squadrons of the RRAF and municipalities in Northern Rhodesia and Nyasaland would be brought to a close. In some hearts, the feelings of regret may have been tinged with relief, because back in May during an air rally and army parade, Flight Lieutenant Norman Walsh of No 1 Squadron had dropped a real boom. The crowd thought it was great but certain householders and businessmen in Lusaka did not. In one case, damage of more than £100 was done to plate glass.

RRAF cooperation and assistance to the British government
Carrying out trials on a different kind of boom in May 1963, No 5 Squadron had developed

a bomb box that enabled the Canberra to carry 96 fragmentation bombs in one aircraft. This apparatus was no doubt given further tests in June when the squadron left for a month's training with the RAF in Cyprus. The squadron, commanded by Squadron Leader Keith Kemsley took part in bomber and fighter exercises and managed to carry off the first prize in the Near East Air Force Medium Level Bombing Competition. No 5 Squadron were still in Cyprus when the Victoria Falls Conference opened and some hasty plans were drawn up to bring the squadron back to base. However, these proved unnecessary.

Further assistance was rendered to the British government in June when United Kingdom troops were flown from Kenya to Salisbury on their way to strife-torn Swaziland. RRAF Dakotas and Canadair C4 aircraft of No 3 Squadron helped to move the troops who night-stopped in Salisbury before being ferried on to the British Protectorate. Federal military authorities and RRAF officials refused to comment, saying, "This is purely a British operation." Security at Salisbury Airport was tightened even further when President Tshombe of Katanga passed through on 14th June on his way to Paris.

On 27th September 1963, an Order in Council signed by Queen Elizabeth II detailed the functions to be handed back to the territorial governments.

Even though the northern territories were beginning to go their own way, No 3 Squadron did take part in a flying display and parachute drop for the SAS at Ndola in October while No 6 Squadron visited the town for an Armistice Day Parade in November. However, as the inevitable breakup approached, Southern Rhodesia sought greater cooperation with South Africa and in October, clearance was granted for Rover flights to major airfields in South Africa. SAAF bombing ranges at Roodewal, De Wet and Hopefields were offered for training purposes.

As far as the Southern Rhodesia Air Force was concerned, details were released on 14th November 1963. Air force headquarters was to remain in Salisbury, with air stations at New Sarum in Salisbury and Thornhill in Gwelo. The force would consist of six squadrons, a transport squadron and squadrons of Hunters and Vampire fighters, Canberra bombers, Provosts and Alouette helicopters. The strength of the force was to be slightly more than 900 officers and other ranks. The air force territorial force and the volunteer reserve would be maintained.

There was some speculation as to whether Southern Rhodesia would have the men to maintain the operational effectiveness of the aircraft and also whether the force would be able to sustain its role in Britain's Middle and Near East Defence strategy. It was pointed out that the Hunters, Canberras and Vampires had been sold to the Federal government on easy terms and that this form of hire purchase included an agreement by which the aircraft were detached for short periods of duty with the RAF in the Middle East. In fact, from 1958 onwards, the RRAF had not only taken part in every major training exercise, it had also maintained a state of readiness and taken part in actual operations resulting from various Middle Eastern crises. The question was, could this cooperation be continued?

It was sad for everyone who had believed in the Federation. As 1963 drew to its close, there came the inevitable round of farewells. On 3rd December, the air force held a parade for the Federal Prime Minister, Sir Roy Welensky. For this event, No 3 Squadron, flying in miserable weather, ferried 213 personnel from Thornhill to Salisbury and back. Five days later, the army staged their parade for Sir Roy, during which No 3 Squadron carried out a flypast using one Canadair and five Dakotas. It was also the task of No 3 Squadron to fly the Federal Chief of General Staff, Major General J. Anderson, Mrs Anderson and the Parliamentary Secretary to the Minister of Defence, Mr Sydney Sawyer to Ndola, Lusaka, Bulawayo and Thornhill to make their farewells to all military units.

For reasons of economy, it was decided that No 6 Squadron should be disbanded and the personnel combined with No 5 Squadron. Chris Dams who had been No 6 Squadron officer commanding since June 1962, became officer commanding of No 2 Squadron. No 6 Squadron was to be re-formed on 1st August 1967.

All members of the RRAF were given the choice to stay or to leave the force at the end of 1963. The options were: to leave the force with a commuted pension; to join the new Northern Rhodesia Air Wing; to apply to the RAF or to remain with the RRAF. The situation varied from squadron to squadron. For example, No 5 Squadron strength was considerably reduced, and several technical personnel from No 7 Squadron took advantage of the opportunity to exploit their helicopter experience in the more lucrative civilian field. But No 7 Squadron History remarks: No aircrew showed any inclination to change their lot, which speaks well for the morale of a busy squadron during an uncertain period. Owing to a surplus of aircrew over establishment, No 3 Squadron did lose flying personnel. Squadron Leader Ted Cunnison took over command of the new Northern Rhodesia Air Wing and three of the squadron pilots joined him.

On 30th December, two Pembrokes and one Dakota were ferried to Livingstone. The following day, three more Dakotas were flown to Livingstone but had to wait ten minutes before they could land. The delay was caused by Flying Officer Czaja (ex RRAF) who had trouble getting one of his engines started on a Pembroke after an asymmetric landing practice. He kept going round in little circles completely blocking the runway so that no one could land. (No 3 Squadron History) The VRs acted as co-pilots on this operation. No 3 Squadron was now reduced to an aircraft strength of four Canadairs and four Dakotas.

On the final day of 1963, the Federal Minister of Defence, Sir Malcolm Barrow sent a farewell message to all ranks of the RRAF through the Chief of Air Staff, Air Vice-Marshal A.M. Bentley. He said: "I am proud to have been associated with you in the past and I am confident that the benefit of the fine spirit and morale built up in the RRAF will carry on with you in the future."

Sydney Sawyer also sent a message: "As Parliamentary Secretary for Defence over the past 18 months and having had the privilege of meeting so many of you, it is with great personal regret that I now say farewell. A great force has been built up and I know that the qualities and traditions that have been established will not die with the Federation. Sad as 31st December will be, we should now look to the future and the beginning of a new era."

CHAPTER 33

The Rhodesian Air Force goes it alone

The great experiment of Federation had ended and as the year 1964 began, Southern Rhodesia was once more on its own. This applied also to the air force in Southern Rhodesia. During the ten years of the Federation the air force had grown strong and more self reliant—now at the end of that period the force had reverted almost completely intact to Southern Rhodesia.

It was announced during January, that references to the Southern Rhodesia Air Force were incorrect. The name remained the RRAF. This decision had been made in the well-founded belief that Northern Rhodesia would soon change its name and that Southern Rhodesia would then be able to call itself Rhodesia.

The air force in Southern Rhodesia

The year 1964 was an exciting one for the men of the air force in Southern Rhodesia. No 1 Squadron, based at New Sarum, in Salisbury continued with its Hunter training on weapons, navigation and formation flying.

No 2 Squadron commanded by Squadron Leader Chris Dams had the roles of advanced flying and operational conversion, plus defence and ground attack on the Vampire T 11 and FB 9.

No 3 Squadron did little routine flying during January though three new pilots were trained. The four Dakotas that remained were augmented, towards the end of the month by two ex SAAF machines and a further two from the same source were taken on strength during February, making eight in all—Nos 702, 703, 704, 705, 706, 707, 708, 709.

The basic training role reverted to No 4 Squadron, commanded by Squadron Leader John Mussell (until October 1964). This squadron combined its pupil-training activities with internal security and reconnaissance. The squadron had been based in Salisbury but now that it had resumed pupil pilot training, the authorities did not want the pupil pilots using the same runway as civilian airliners. So No 4 Squadron was moved to Thornhill—which meant that a Thornhill squadron would have to move to Salisbury. It could not be No 1, the Hunter squadron. No 2 Squadron was also involved in pilot training, and so the displaced squadron had to be No 5, the Canberra squadron.

No 4 Squadron, having no furniture or telephones, appropriated those left behind by No 5 Squadron when it moved back to New Sarum. Even so, it was a week before the squadron personnel settled in and two weeks before the telephones were working. The squadron had a strength of 12 pilots (on paper), 15 ground crew and 13 Provost aircraft. It was a somewhat trying period with pilots familiarizing themselves with new ground crew, preparing wall charts, scrounging furniture including a coffee bar, and generally clearing up. Flying only began on 21st January and there was still a shambles at the end of January. Only 100 hours flown for the month.

No 5 Canberra Squadron, commanded by Squadron Leader Dermott Wilmot (Porky)

MacLaughlin, who had taken over from Squadron Leader Keith Kemsley, had a strength of ten pilots; Flight Lieutenant Ian Donaldson 'A' flight commander, Bill Jelley 'B' flight commander, Wally Hinrichs, Brian Jolley, Justin Varkevisser, and Pete Nicholls, Flying Officer Brian Strickland and Pilot Officer Keith Clarke.

The navigators were Squadron Leader Len Pink, Flight Lieutenants Alan Cockle and Roy Wellington, Flying Officers Archie Conlin, Jim Hunter, Doug Pasea and Phil Schooling, Pilot Officers David (Polly) Postance, Bernie Vaughan, Terry Bennett and Roger Blowers. Once the squadron had settled down at New Sarum and the new crews had been established, training continued as normal.

The commitment to Commonwealth defence continued although exercises to the Middle East were a thing of the past; on the other hand, cooperation with the SAAF became stronger. During the year, the silver paint of the Canberras was replaced with camouflage on the upper side and the light blue of the underside was replaced with dark brown.

On 1st January 1964, Squadron Leader Ossie Penton was appointed to succeed Squadron Leader Bill Dowden as officer commanding No 7 Squadron. And at 00h01 that day, during a magnificent New Year's Eve Ball, it was announced that Squadron Leader Penton had been awarded the AFC. A great day for the squadron! Penton left shortly afterwards to take a helicopter conversion course with the SAAF. Later conversions were to be carried out by No 7 Squadron.

Meanwhile life was returning to normal after the unsettling events of 1963.

8th February. Party in the 'Grog Spot' most enjoyable. Followed by a cricket match on Sunday. Invited team versus 4 Squadron. We lost. Our first stand-by at Thornhill 28th February. Nine aircraft on the line fully-loaded with tear smoke on the Friday—but situation calmed down. February was very much the same as January—shambolic. Things were not really as bad as they appeared, however, and we did nearly twice as much flying in February as we did in January. (No 4 Squadron History)

On 21st February, No 7 Squadron was called in to assist the police in a hunt for two Africans who had assaulted a 26-year-old mother of five at her home. After the attack, the men ran off in the direction of the Henry Chapman Golf Course. The police request for assistance was answered by the arrival of a helicopter and lunch-hour traffic was held up for several minutes while the machine landed on the Umtali Road. To the excitement of the watching public, three policemen, including a detective accompanied by a black Alsation police dog, scrambled in through the door, and within seconds the helicopter was making a low-level search of the surrounding grassland.

On the subject of No 7 Squadron, four VR officers, Derek Purnell, Brian Patten, Derek Whellaman and Trevor Ruile, were posted to the squadron as observers, forward area helicopter controllers and administrators. However, they were not fully exploited and by 1967 their services had been withdrawn. It was probably more a lack of continuity than a lack of enthusiasm that caused the problems.

In March 1964 during a mine-workers strike at Wankie Colliery, Dakotas from No 3 Squadron were used to carry members of the BSAP to Wankie and also to transport European miners from Fort Victoria, Gwelo, Salisbury and Mangula to keep the mine operational while the black workers were on strike. The strike was over by 10th March. During the same month, a weekly shuttle service from New Sarum to Thornhill and Bulawayo was inaugurated by No 3 Squadron. This proved so successful that two weeks later, a three-weekly shuttle to Grand Reef and Thornhill was added and it was hoped to include visits to Fort Victoria later.

News from No 4 Squadron

The big event of April 1964 was the RRAF Tactical and Air Weapons Demonstration for which preparation had begun early in March.

No 4 Squadron Diary—March/April

Warning of a big weapons drill due to take place at Kutanga Range in April. This means a lot of armament practice—especially the ex 2 Squadron chaps who have never done any weapons work in Provosts.

3rd March. Start bombing practice—scores, in the main, not bad.

6th March. Panic stations again. The stand-by* was called on Friday evening but there had been a stand-down at the station. Therefore, most of the single chaps were away for the long weekend. Chris Dixon was reached in Salisbury for the stand-by. Oh boy was he charmed! On Sunday, we were taken off stand-by without any aircraft getting airborne. Chris? He was even more charmed.

9th March. As is normal for this time of year at Gwelo, in came the guti. The flying programme goes for a ball of chalk, but it is good instrument flying weather ... so off we go.

10th/11th March. Weather as above but the instrument flying (IF) hours are piling up; so is the work! We have just been given a project to do and this is to be presented to the whole of the flying wing in three weeks' time. The project? How to attack Southern Rhodesia!

21st March. We presented our project to Flying Wing and it seemed to go reasonably well but it's hard to say. In two weeks No 2 Squadron have their project to put over—How to stop this attack on SR. This will give us some idea of how good or bad our plan was.

April. 'The Weapons Demo'—this is all that can be heard round the station at present. The Weapons Demo is being blamed for everything! Jobs outstanding? Oh, it's because of the Weapons Demo!

April 12th. The big day had arrived. The Weapons Demo! No 4 Squadron contribution was as follows: four aircraft tear smoke. Their job was to lay a thick screen. Each aircraft dropping 80 grenades on the first and only run. Two aircraft front gun—Squadron Leader John Mussell and Prop Geldenhuys. They were joined by Mike Saunders and Spaz [David] Currie on completion of the tear smoke. The front gun aircraft demonstrated the 'air pin' technique. As they cleared the target, the bombers arrived to do two attacks each. Four bombs were dropped by each aircraft on both attacks. Bombs were 20-lb (9kg) fragmentation.

No 1 Squadron also took part in this demonstration as did No 2 Squadron, while No 3 ferried personnel from the various centres and performed a supply drop.

Owing to servicing problems with the computer units of the Canberra T3 bombsights, all bombing, from the middle of 1963, had been carried out using the fixed head sight. Not associated with this problem but still on the weapons theme, No 5 Squadron recorded mixed scores at the demonstration. The rocket projectile and low-level bombing operations were very successful but the 1,000-lb (454kg) and the fragmentation bomb box attacks were both well off target.

Giving a less technical assessment of the demonstration the *Rhodesia Herald* reported that:

Provost, Vampire, Hunter and Canberra aircraft demonstrated their versatility in a number of limited war situations. The important functions of helicopter and supply aircraft were also seen to advantage. The aircraft used machine-gun and cannon fire, rockets and bombs with

---

* This would have been for the strike at Wankie.

devastating effect against a variety of targets, including concrete forts, dummy oil installations and a convoy of vehicles composed of wrecked cars and trucks. The use of 'live' weapons added spectacle and tested stocks. (Rhodesia Herald, 13th April 1964)

A blue Monday for No 4

The continuing saga of No 4 Squadron as recorded in the Squadron Diary makes amusing reading for the rest of April and early May.

13th April. Some chaps have all the luck! Four aircraft and five drivers with five ground staff left for Kariba today on a ten-day detachment. The army is having an exercise in the area south-east of Kariba and our chaps are flying the usual recce sorties out of Kariba.
On 22nd the detachment got back from Kariba—the only complaint—not enough of the right sort of flying.
Monday 27th April. Blue Monday. OC flying goes hairless. To start off with, the nose wheel of a T 11 of No 2 Squadron collapses while being towed out of the hangar. The 'D' doors bent horrifyingly. A Hunter abandons take-off when No 2 of the second section calls to say the leader is streaming brake fluid. He abandoned take-off and found himself without brakes and stopped well into the overshoot—just missing five or six obstructions but no damage to aircraft. A call is then received from Peter Petter-Bowyer who is in the flying area taking Chris Dixon on a standardization check, saying he is force-landing—engine cut! When coming in on finals for the forced-landing the engine restarts so he heads for home. It was found that a ball valve in the collector tank was unseated so that when the aircraft was inverted, which it was just before cut, all the fuel 'vents', and cut-out occurs. It takes quite a time for the tank to refill and that is why the engine only restarted on the final approach.
Thursday 30th April. Between Monday and Thursday, all has been well. But Thursday—to start with, the guti rolled in so all flying was delayed. Eventually at 10h30 we got airborne—all of us (except the boss who is on a day's leave). We had planned a nine aircraft formation with one extra aircraft to take photos. We formed up in various formations including flying a figure four. Petter-Bowyer who was flying the photo aircraft was naturally using high power settings to get himself into the right position, but also using up fuel at a terrific rate. Towards the end of the detail we got a range check from GCA (Ground Control Approach) 40 NM (Nautical Miles) [74km] from base! And Peter was down to 75 pounds (34kg) of fuel!* Panic stations in the control tower resulted but Peter got home OK with his very sick passenger. It appears that this passenger had been sick for most of the detail and this was why the photography had taken so long. The rest of the formation had no problems. Four aircraft did night cross-country to Fort Victoria.
Thursday 14th May. Peter Petter-Bowyer in 312 lands on the main road at Shangani. Oil pressure began to drop very low and the oil temperature was going up—all attempts to keep it down and the pressure up, failed—so down on the road he went.
Friday 15th May. Peter back to collect 312. The techs drained the oil etc. and said they could find nothing wrong. Peter flew it home and it seemed OK. (No 4 Squadron Diary)

On 22nd May light aircraft from all over the country headed for Fort Victoria for the annual Police Reserve Air Wing Exercise.

At 8 am an RRAF Provost from Gwelo touched down to be followed at five-minute intervals by 24 light aircraft of varying makes. Planes were clocked in as their wheels touched the ground in front of the control tower, specially erected for the exercises. The mayor announced that the town

---

* This would have been fewer than 10 gallons (45 litres).

would be adopting No 7 Squadron, RRAF, in two weeks.
(Rhodesia Herald, 22nd May 1964)

In April 1964, Winston Field resigned as prime minister of Southern Rhodesia and his place was taken by Ian Smith, the first prime minister to have been born in the country. On 14th May, Ian Smith toured the RRAF base at New Sarum, being shown radio and radar equipment in operation, guard dogs in training, and the cadet training school. Four weeks later Mr Smith paid his first official visit to Thornhill, Gwelo. "I don't think we quite convinced him we were the best squadron in the RRAF." (No 4 Squadron Diary)

On the previous day, six Provosts had left to fly via Salisbury to Umtali, where, together with aircraft from No 3 Squadron they took part in a display to celebrate the town's Diamond Jubilee, on June 11th and 12th. On 17th June, No 2 Squadron took part in a flypast to celebrate Queen Elizabeth II's official birthday and No 17 Pilot Training Course flew its final navigation exercise to Waterkloof, arriving in snow and ice. These pilots received their Wings at a presentation on 27th June. In June 1964, Chris Dams left No 2 Squadron to take up the position of director of Air Plans and Intelligence at air force headquarters in Dolphin House. Talking about his posting, Chris Dams said:

> *Director of Air Plans and Intelligence meant that I worked for the chief of Air Staff, as his long-range planner. I had connections with the Joint Planning Staff and I was responsible for planning secret operations. I held the position for about 18 months.*

Cooperation between the RRAF and the RAF was still strong and between the months of June and September, RAF Bomber Command Valiants of No 543 Squadron carried out an aerial photographic survey of Southern Rhodesia, Northern Rhodesia and Bechuanaland. The Valiants that were based at New Sarum, photographed some 400,000 square miles (1,000,000 sq km) of territory from 33,000 feet.

Meanwhile No 1 Squadron gave Bulawayo citizens a thrill when they flew a diamond nine formation over the city following a letter to the newspaper from a local inhabitant, saying that Bulawayo never saw the Hunters. There was also a short detachment by squadron pilots to Aden where they flew standardization sorties in RAF Hunter T 7 aircraft.

The Oberholzer murder
Terrorism and anti-terrorist operations first became part of No 7 Squadron's way of life with the murder of Mr Petrus Johannes Andries Oberholzer on the night of 4th July 1964. The story was told by Mrs Oberholzer:

> *In the afternoon of Sunday 4th July 1964, we were returning from Umtali to our home at Silverstreams Wattle Factory. My husband was driving, and our four-year-old daughter, Elizabeth, was standing on the front seat between us. It was about six pm, as we climbed the hill towards Skyline Junction, but, although it was getting dark, we did not have our lights on as we saw the road block—big stones. We could not cross over it, and they were right across the road; so my husband stopped to take the stones away. He got out and they threw stones at him. I can remember seeing four Africans around the car. They came up to him and I saw one raise a knife above his head and stab downwards at my husband. It was so quick and all in such a rush that I did not see how many times he stabbed. It was quite a long knife. Stones were coming from all round. I could not see very well. They broke the windscreen with stones. I got a stone on my jaw. They threw petrol over my husband and in my eyes. After a while, I said, "Let's go or they will pour petrol over us." He said, "I can't. They have stabbed me in the chest." I said, "Please*

try" and so he did. He closed the door, started the car and drove over the stones. He drove until the car turned over in the ditch onto its side. They ran up to the car and tried to put fire to the car. They threw matches on and in the car. Too bloody inside I think for the matches to ignite... too much blood inside. He sat on my lap when we fell over.

I said, "Please, you are too heavy. I can't get out."

He said, "Can't you open the door?"

I said, "The car is on its side."

He got up, flung the door open. He stood up until he could no longer stand. As they tried to put fire to the car, it caught alight on the roof. I rubbed it with my hand to put it out. I first thought I'd put the little girl out. Then I thought it would be dangerous, so we sat down. My husband then sat down as he could stand no longer. I saw the lights of another car coming. I stood up slowly and so stopped it and asked for help. I put the girl out and the man asked me to get out. I spoke to my husband, taking his arm; but he did not answer me. So I got out and I said, "What shall I do about my husband?" He said that there was nothing that could be done, but that we should phone the police.

Initially one helicopter was called out to assist the BSAP investigations and was based at Nyanyadzi. Two days later a further three aircraft were dispatched, supported by a Forward Air Support Operations Centre (Fasoc). Although on this operation the helicopters had no success in helping to catch the culprits, the aircraft proved extremely useful, bringing in large numbers of suspects and relatives of the wanted men for interrogation, as well as transporting teams of detectives to kraals in remote areas. In this way, a wealth of vital information could be gathered with speed. The helicopters were withdrawn on 13th July 1964.[*]

The Parachute Training School

At the time of the break-up of the Federation, only 20 or so members of 'C' Squadron SAS elected to remain in the Rhodesian army. The squadron was re-formed to comprise five troops and a headquarters staff—120 men in all. The staff of the Parachute Training School was reduced to a total of six. The school had been going through a rather quiet period and use was made of the spare time to carry out evaluation tests on a Caribou aircraft and also to conduct trials, during June, July and August, using the 32 PX parachute. It was decided that this parachute had little to offer in comparison with the 'X'-type in current use. However, a number of 'X'-type parachutes were modified into double blank gore parachutes and in November 1964 the first successful live jumps were carried out. These parachutes proved most successful and were used by Parachute Training School staff for demonstrations.

An unsuccessful attempt to hover over water at night

In August 1964, No 7 Squadron personnel were instructed to carry out an evaluation on the feasibility of hovering over water at night, using both natural and artificial visual references. The idea was that either a rope or a hoist could then be used for a descent from the hovering aircraft to a fixed point—presumably a boat. This request led to a somewhat unfortunate incident, which was reported in the *Rhodesia Herald* on 25th August.

A 17-year-old Umvukwes youth, Bryan Martin, dashed by speedboat across Lake MacIlwaine last night to rescue three airmen from an RRAF helicopter that crashed into the lake shortly after seven o'clock. The Alouette helicopter landed in shallow water near Dassie Island, half a mile (800m) north of the Ancient Mariner boat jetty. The crew climbed out before it sank and swam

---

[*] No 1 Squadron was also involved.

about 50 yards (46m) to the rocky island. They were rescued unhurt by Bryan in his boat. "I was lucky to reach them so quickly," said Bryan, "But I was guided to the spot by a searchlight from the second helicopter. The rest was easy." He said he had found the men cold and shivering on the shores of the island. One of them had to be helped into the boat. Bryan's father said he was proud of his son. (Rhodesia Herald, 25th August 1964)

Peter Cooke who was a member of the crew on the ill-fated flight recalls how cold he was. "It is not recommended that you go night swimming in August!" He also recalls that in the salvage operation the helicopter having been partially floated in an upside-down position suffered even greater damage than it received in the initial accident when it was towed, by accident, into a submerged obstruction. It was three days before the helicopter could be rescued from its resting place on the muddy bottom of the lake. It was necessary to strip the machine down completely and rebuild it. The operation was complicated by the need to obtain spare parts from France and it was 1st March 1965 before this helicopter was once again airworthy. Flying Officer Dave Becks, who with Warrant Officer Taff Powell had been aboard when the machine ditched, carried out the test flight and reported the helicopter "as good as new".

PCC and ZANU banned

By the end of August 1964, intimidation and political violence in the townships had risen to unacceptable levels. The Minister of Law and Order announced the banning of the *Daily News* and two African Nationalist parties: the People's Caretaker Council (PCC) and the Zimbabwe African National Union (ZANU). Security officers swooped on the Enkeldoorn home of Mr Zimbewe, chairman of the local branch of the PCC. He was driven to Gwelo and then placed aboard a Dakota for the journey to a restricted area. Mr Joshua Nkomo had been detained in April 1964. Highfield African Township, near Salisbury, was declared an emergency area and extra troops were brought to Salisbury by No 3 Squadron. These men were used to seal off the township early on the morning of 26th August, in order to round up intimidators and thugs. No 7 Squadron was called in to provide support for the ground forces and to prevent any incidents. No 4 Squadron stood by with tear smoke. In fact, the flying involved was purely reconnaissance and the mop-up was carried out with no major problems. As far as No 3 Squadron was concerned, the remainder of August and the first half of September was occupied in transporting restrictees to Wha-Wha, a prison near Gwelo.

The indaba of chiefs and headmen at Dombashawa

In September, Ian Smith went to London for talks with the British (Conservative) Prime Minister, Sir Alec Douglas-Home. The Rhodesian prime minister was told that if he wanted independence under the 1961 constitution he must show that this constitution was acceptable to the people as a whole. Shortly after this, however, a general election in Britain brought the Labour Party to power with a new prime minister, Harold Wilson. Despite these changes, Ian Smith went ahead with his plans to consult the people of Rhodesia. An indaba of chiefs and headmen was held at Dombashawa Training College, near Salisbury, and a referendum was carried out on 5th November 1966, to test the electorate. The exercise to transport the chiefs and to protect their families was designated Operation Phoenix. Most of the RRAF squadrons were involved in this operation.

16th October. All systems go. Operations on exercise 'Phoenix' probably the largest passive exercise yet, involved continual recces of all African tribal areas. This was to provide close support for the army that had small sections in every chief and headman's village throughout the country to prevent arson, intimidation etc. from the 'thug' element, while the chiefs were congregated at Dombashawa discussing the independence referendum. This exercise involved a good deal of flying and a good deal of new experience. At Thornhill, the instructors helped out by flying afternoon recces. (No 4 Squadron Diary)

No 3 Squadron ferried the chiefs from Fort Victoria, Wankie and Binga and took them home again after they had given a unanimous Yes to independence under the 1961 constitution. No 5 Squadron Canberras were also heavily involved policing outlying areas. To conserve fuel and give greater endurance and range at low level, most of their flying was done asymmetric (i.e. with one engine shut down). One crew had a flame-out on its live engine but managed to re-light. In all, the squadron flew over 400 hours during October, an all-time record. Most crews logged over 80 hours during the last two weeks of October.

No 2 Squadron continued reconnaissance and flag-waving patrols over tribal areas through November and December 1964. The year was marred by a fatal accident when Flying Officer Henry Elliott flying a Vampire FB 9 crashed about 15 miles (24km) west of Thornhill, while on a night instrument recovery. Operation Phoenix ended officially at the beginning of November. Although, both the chief's indaba and the referendum gave a clear vote in favour of independence, Harold Wilson refused to accept the indaba as a valid indication of African opinion.

1964 was to have ended with a final cross-country for the student pilots of No 4 Squadron, but this was cancelled at the last moment.

HQ not happy to have the cadets flying solo around Umtali with the weather hazard and not happy to have them fly dual either. This being the second time we've cancelled all Umtali's plans at a moment's notice, we're all of the opinion that our popularity is probably on the wane with that fair city. (No 4 Squadron Diary)

New Year 1965 got off to an exciting start when, on 7th January, RRAF spotter aircraft were called in to help the police in a country-wide manhunt for African prisoners who had escaped from jail in Bulawayo. The men were said to be dangerous and a £250 reward was offered for information leading to their capture. The RRAF airlifted police officers who could identify the missing men, to strategic border posts and the operation ended with the recapture of three of the men at 08h20 on Friday 8th January, a few miles from the Bechuanaland (Botswana) border. In February, following a final flight by Squadron Leader Keith Kemsley, Officer Commanding No 2 Squadron, the Vampire FB 9 aircraft were phased out of service.

During 1965, No 5 Squadron abandoned shallow dive-bombing in favour of low-level techniques for which a special bombsight was developed by the squadron technicians. The biggest problem with low-level bombing proved to be flying at the correct height and methods for achieving this were researched.

On 23rd February, No 2 Squadron lost a second Vampire (a T 11) during an uncontrollable spin, but both pilots, Flying Officer Tol Janeke and his pupil, Officer Cadet Bill Buckle, ejected safely to qualify as members of the world famous Caterpillar Club.

The Secretary for Commonwealth Relations, Mr Arthur Bottomley and the Lord Chancellor, Lord Gerald Gardiner, arrived in Salisbury on 21st February, to sound out public feeling regarding independence. No 3 Squadron uplifted chiefs from all parts of the country and brought them to Salisbury to listen to Mr Bottomley's spoutings. Three days later, the chiefs were returned to their homes. The Commonwealth secretary was then taken on a visit to the Lowveld where he met various nationalist detainees and on to Bulawayo for a dinner party with the Governor, Sir Humphrey Gibbs, all by kind courtesy of No 3 Squadron.

Coppers on the ground, choppers in the sky

An example of police/air force cooperation, or 'Coppers on the ground, choppers in the sky', occurred in March, when a RRAF helicopter on night operations over and around Salisbury Airport, spotted a car parked in the bushes. The pilot decided there could be a murky reason so he radioed the control room at New Sarum. The message was relayed to the police. "Within seconds, police patrol cars were racing to the spot. By the time they reached the area, the buzzed vehicle was on the move towards the city. However, the whirly bird had it in sight and its every twist and turn was reported from aloft, which was promptly reported to the prowling police cars. Finally, the vehicle was neatly intercepted in the Rhodesville area. Probably only a young couple—but it demonstrates the cooperation possible." (*Rhodesia Herald*, 18th March 1965)

The army exercise Broken Arrow that took place during the same month was a further example of inter-service cooperation. No 3 Squadron arranged a large supply-drop in the Tjolotjo area and No 4 Squadron sent two Provosts on detachment. It was to prove an unfortunate detail as Pilot Officer Barry Matthews and Chief Technician Sandy Trenoweth were killed when Provost 306 crashed while doing a low-level beat up of the airfield. "They did a barrel roll and couldn't pull out in time—striking the ground very near a large crowd." (No 4 Squadron Diary, March 1965) Peter Cooke remarks: "Matthews was No 4 in line astern, a very difficult formation position to hold in a tail chase."

Exercise Panther

In July, the RRAF held its own two-day training weekend, Exercise Panther. This was the first full-scale operation for the force's volunteer reserve following reorganization after the breakup of the Federation. About 200 VRs and some territorial force men took part, with aircraft and self-contained road convoys deployed to six advanced and main bases throughout the country. The task was to occupy the fields, establish and man communications, distribute fuel and equipment, and generally make the bases operational. Hawker Hunters, Canberra bombers, Provosts, Dakotas and helicopters took part in the exercise.

Wing Commander Dicky Bradshaw, who commanded the exercise, said: Within the space of six or seven hours, we were able to activate and deploy 16 field force units throughout the country. Six widely separated civilian airstrips were turned into advanced air bases by units consisting of 12 to 18 reservists. Arriving at its allocated airstrip on Saturday, each unit set up an operations tent bristling with maps, codes, logistic tables and a large generator-powered radio. Armed guards patrolled the camp area. Equipped with everything from fire extinguishers to floodlights and medical supplies to camp chairs, the men were set to stay in the field indefinitely, if necessary.

In cases of real emergency, the VRs will man certain airstrips chosen by the air force from which support and reconnaissance aircraft can operate. This exercise is giving the VRs an opportunity to put into practice what they are learning in training, said Group Captain Graham Smith, officer commanding (VR).

At set times during the exercise, the VRs opened envelopes that contained papers presenting them with various administrative problems ranging from pay requests to plane crashes. "Valuable flexibility would be hard to achieve without the VRs," was Graham Smith's final comment on the exercise.

Meanwhile in May, Rhodesia had gone to the polls in the country's first general election since the break-up of the Federation. The result was no surprise. The Rhodesian Front (RF) secured all 50 'A' roll seats while for the first time in the territory's history a black man, Mr Josiah Gondo, became leader of the opposition.

In July, Mr G.L. Guy, curator of Queen Victoria Museum in Salisbury was able to keep a long-standing promise to present a bateleur eagle to the RRAF. The bird, a seven-year-old male, had been shot while raiding a chicken run. It had been presented to the Museum, where it was preserved and mounted, before being housed in a place of honour at RRAF headquarters.

Civilian casevacs

During 1965, No 7 Squadron demonstrated its capabilities in the field of rescue and mercy flights. On 26th April, Mrs Catherine Boshoff, wife of the field officer in the Tsetse Fly Control branch of the Ministry of Agriculture was taken seriously ill at remote Kariangwe Camp, near Binga. A helicopter piloted by Flying Officer Murray (Hoffy) Hofmeyr, landed at Salisbury Central Hospital, collected a doctor and nurse, and flew to the camp. Mrs Boshoff was taken on board and transported to Wankie Hospital where she was given an emergency blood transfusion. Five days later she was released, but relapsed and was subsequently flown to Salisbury. During May, a Chaplin School pupil, Ronald Allen fell from a wire slide at his home in Gwelo and was brought by helicopter, flown by Peter Cooke, from Gwelo to Salisbury for treatment for injuries to his back.

A further drama was reported by the *Rhodesia Herald* in July; this time the starring role was taken by No 3 Squadron.

> *9 pm Monday (12th) night. Mrs Moebius falls ill aboard a launch, anchored in Binga Harbour. Mr Moebius races on foot two miles [3km] over the hills to the local District Commissioner's house. An orderly from Binga Hospital, which has no doctor, is taken to the launch. Word is sent back for medical advice.*
>
> *2 am yesterday (13th). Police make an SOS appeal to Bulawayo General Hospital. A European doctor gives radio instructions. The messages are written down and taken one by one to the African orderly who stands by Mrs Moebius. 5.45 am. Mrs Moebius, only partially conscious is gently carried to an RRAF Dakota on the grass airstrip. A midwife watches anxiously on the flight to Salisbury, while Mr Moebius snatches two hours sleep on a camp bed in the aircraft.*
>
> *7.30 am. Dakota is met at Salisbury by an ambulance with police car escort. Mrs Moebius is still semi-conscious. 2.50 pm. Daughter is born! Weight 6 pounds 6 ounces (2.8kg). Mother and child doing well. Mr and Mrs Moebius were apparently enjoying a lake holiday when the trouble began.* (Rhodesia Herald, 14th July 1965)

The following month it was once again the turn of No 7 Squadron. Game Warden Rupert Forthergill was involved in an operation on the shores of Lake Kariba to shoot rhinoceros with drugged darts and relocate them to Wankie Game Reserve.

The game ranger was out with three African game scouts when he spotted two rhino. As he shot at one animal with his compressed-air gun, a third rhino charged him from behind, injuring him quite severely. He managed to crawl to a nearby tree and with the help of the scouts, walked back to his truck, which was parked about a mile away (1.6km). One of the scouts drove him back to camp on the Sengwa River. The National Parks and Wild Life Management radio network sent out a call for help. The message was passed from Wankie headquarters to Bulawayo and from there to the RRAF base at New Sarum. A Provost dropped supplies of morphine at Sengwa; meanwhile a helicopter flown by Flight Lieutenant Peter Cooke picked up Dr Laidlaw from Salisbury General Hospital and flew him to Sengwa where Rupert Forthergill was taken onboard and flown to Salisbury. Thanks to the prompt help he received, Rupert survived his injuries, which included stomach wounds and a fractured right arm.

The helicopters had proved themselves invaluable in the casevac role; now it was decided to give them a sting as well, for the purpose of defence and, if necessary also attack. FN 7.62 MAGs were fitted to the port running board, adjacent to the rear door. A reflector sight was fitted to the gun and squadron technicians were trained to operate the gun. Those qualifying were issued with an Air Gunner Badge, and an additional allowance.

The Unilateral Declaration of Independence

On the constitutional issue, nothing much had happened since March 1965 and on 3rd October, the Southern Rhodesia Prime Minister, Ian Smith, accompanied by the Minister of Justice, Desmond Lardner-Burke, flew to London for discussions with Harold Wilson, the British Prime Minister. Ian Smith pointed out that the constitutional uncertainty was harming his country's economy and that Rhodesia had made considerable concessions, including the formation of a senate in which chiefs had a voice, and what amounted to universal adult suffrage on the 'B' role. The British government countered with its own plan for Rhodesia. On 9th October came the announcement that talks had broken down. Ian Smith returned to Rhodesia and was given an unofficial flypast by five Canberras, which resulted in the squadron commander, Squadron Leader Porky MacLaughlin being carpeted by the chief of Air Staff!

The Rhodesian government came forward with further proposals on 20th October. These included a treaty to guarantee African rights. The British prime minister agreed that this offer could provide a fresh basis for negotiations and on 25th October, Harold Wilson arrived in Salisbury for more talks. He also met the African nationalist leaders Joshua Nkomo and the Reverend Ndabaningi Sithole. He reported that he found them unwilling to accept any grant of independence that was not preceded by majority rule. During this visit, the British prime minister and his party were carried by helicopters of No 7 Squadron.

On 5th November 1965, the Minister of Law and Order, Desmond Lardner-Burke announced that a State of Emergency had been declared for a period of three months because the security of the country was threatened, stating, "This is not a prelude to UDI,"—a blatant lie. On 9th November 1965, aircraft of No 7 Squadron were detached to Gwelo, Kariba and Wankie. It was obvious at this stage that relations between Rhodesia and Britain were extremely strained and this move was to forestall any possible outbreak of violence by extremists.

No 4 Squadron Provosts were deployed to Wankie and Kariba to assist the army in guarding installations. Added to this, all squadrons were placed on stand-by. Aircraft were in position when the prime minister, Mr Ian Smith, announced the assumption of Rhodesian independence on 11th November 1965, but despite the outcry overseas, there were no local incidents.

CHAPTER 34

Rhodesia goes it alone

On 11th November 1965, Prime Minister, Ian Douglas Smith, announced that Rhodesia had, unilaterally, assumed sovereign independence. Perhaps, to the surprise of Britain and other overseas countries, there were no outbreaks of violence within the country and no signs of panic. For the air force, as for the whole country, this was to be the end of one era and the beginning of another.

Two days earlier, on 9th November all the RRAF squadrons had been placed on stand-by. The aircraft of No 7 Squadron had been detached to Gwelo, Kariba and Wankie while No 4 Squadron Provosts were deployed to Wankie and Kariba to assist the army in guarding installations. Following the Declaration of Independence, No 5 Squadron undertook low-level reconnaissance patrols along the country's northern border. These flights were carried out below 200 knots (370 km/h) and on one engine to conserve fuel.

Southern Rhodesia's African nationalist leaders believed that the United Kingdom government would intervene militarily. They had no understanding of how unpopular this would have been with many people in Britain. Conversely, an attack on Southern Rhodesia by British forces would have placed members of the Rhodesian army and air force in an invidious position because, as members of the Federal armed services, they had sworn loyalty to the Queen. As it was, this did not happen. Harold Wilson's government preferred to rely on sanctions. Rhodesia's assets in London were frozen with immediate effect and she was expelled from the Sterling Area. Economic sanctions were also applied banning the import of Rhodesian tobacco and sugar.

One interesting story concerning the Declaration of Independence involved Wing Commander Tony Chisnall, the RRAF's air liaison officer at Rhodesia House in London, and Group Captain Archie Wilson, who was attending the Imperial Defence College. Both men were approached by the British but they refused to desert Rhodesia and they, together with their families, were expelled from the United Kingdom in December 1965. On his return, Archie Wilson was appointed DCAS with the rank of air commodore, while Chisnall was posted to air headquarters. Eight members of the RRAF who were training with the RAF actually ended their course on 17th November and returned to Rhodesia on 18th November. André du Toit had taken all the top prizes at the end of his course at the RAF Air Navigation School. Not only was he deported, after refusing offers of a commission in the RAF, but also his prizes were taken away from him!

Another member of the RRAF whose plans had to be changed at short notice was Chris Dams, Director of Air Plans and Intelligence at air force headquarters. He had been scheduled to attend Staff College in the United Kingdom during 1966. Obviously, this was no longer possible. Instead, he was transferred to Thornhill as officer commanding Admin Wing (OCAW) and in April 1966 was appointed to command No 1 (Hunter) Squadron.

In Britain, there was no suggestion that the RAF's No 44 (Rhodesia) Squadron should change its name or drop its badge—an African elephant. In fact, the officer commanding of the squadron flatly refused to change anything and the squadron still proudly carries the full motto and emblem. There were then no Rhodesians on the squadron, Flight Lieutenant J. Robertson of Bulawayo, serving with the RAF, having been posted to another unit during the previous month.

As far as the RRAF was concerned, it was encouraging that only one officer, a former RAF navigator who was on leave in England at the time of UDI, broke his oath of allegiance and joined the RAF. So it was that the RRAF's effectiveness and order of battle remained intact and ready to meet any challenge the future might bring.

On 6th December 1965, sanctions were extended to cover 95 percent of Rhodesia's exports, and the Commonwealth Trading Preference was withdrawn. Eleven days later, the British government announced an embargo on oil supplies to Rhodesia, and a tanker actually en route to Beira was diverted. As a result, petrol rationing was introduced on 28th December. The initial ration was three – five units (13,64–22,73 litres) a week for most private vehicles. At this stage, a unit was worth one gallon (4,54 litres) but on 25th January the value of a unit was cut to six pints (3,4 litres) an effective reduction of 25%. However, as the supply position improved, restrictions were relaxed and finally rationing became a formality as petrol flowed into the country through South Africa and Mozambique. The immediate effect of the fuel embargo on the air force was to reduce flying hours during the early part of 1966, though normal training was continued. No 5 Squadron flew sorties to South Africa and Mozambique in addition to its low-level patrols along the Zambian border, an activity that led to accusations of incursions. The RAF based a Javelin squadron at Lusaka but this did not affect the reconnaissance flights. In fact, *Flight* magazine, in an article on the RRAF termed the number of hours flown as surprising. An RAF liaison officer, Wing Commander Evans, who returned to the United Kingdom after UDI wrote a report concluding that, "The RRAF won't last as an operational force once the United Kingdom replacements and spares cease under sanctions." He had obviously not reckoned on the Rhodesian flare for ingenuity.

Canberra starter cartridge

For the RRAF, as for the rest of Rhodesia, sanctions encouraged innovative thinking. For instance, No 5 Squadron technicians found that starter cartridges were at a premium. The cartridge produced gases which turned a small turbine in the starter motor. This drove the shaft of the starter motor, which in turn engaged the shaft of the aircraft's engine through a bendix-type arrangement. When the aircraft's engine was rotating fast enough, it would draw in air from the front, through the compressors, and into the combustion chamber, where fuel (and a spark) was introduced when the engine reached a particular rotation speed. These British-made cartridges cost £7 each, when they were available, and had the disadvantage of fouling the engine with cordite and sometimes even exploding, causing considerable damage. When this occurred, the starter units had to be sent back to the United Kingdom to be cleaned and repaired at incredible expense. Added to which, it was necessary to have stand-by units to replace any that had become damaged. In January 1966, the squadron began employing a new technique, developed by squadron technicians. This was to use a high capacity industrial cylinder (oxygen/acetylene type) filled with pure, clean, Rhodesian high pressure, industrial, compressed air. Several other Canberra operators had tried unsuccessfully to use air starts but this was the first workable system to be developed. The new system reduced the cost to about five shillings to start both engines and did away with the wear and tear. In fact, unusually heavy rains caused more problems than the sanctions at the beginning of 1966 and No 3 Squadron endured the indignity of having Dakota 707 bogged down for a week at Sinoia.

February proved an interesting month for No 4 Squadron. On 8th and 9th February, Flight Lieutenant Pat Meddows-Taylor and Flight Lieutenant Justin Varkevisser organized a squadron low-level exercise based on past experience with the Police Air Wing. The exercise proved hard going, especially as cloud level was very low during the two days, but those who took part agreed that it was well worthwhile. Points were awarded on merit, 105 being the maximum. The winner was Flying Officer Harold Griffiths with 83 points.

On 13th February 1966, came the Challenge Boat Race held on the flooded Gwelo River, organized and sponsored by No 2 Squadron. Teams from RRAF Thornhill competed, together with members of the public in ships of various designs some of which showed a good deal of ingenuity. In fact, 17 assorted craft took to the water in a mass start from below the bridge on the Umvuma Road, east of town. The finishing line was the Salisbury Road Bridge. The event, which was won by No 4 Squadron's Pilot Officer Mark McLean in Rat Fink, was held to celebrate the flowing of the Gwelo River after many years of drought. It was hoped that the race would become an annual event.

Water was also in the news as far as No 3 Squadron was concerned when, in conjunction with the Parachute Training School, the first descents were made into the drink. Fifteen aircrew from New Sarum spearheaded by the station commander, Group Captain Charles Paxton and Wing Commander Ossie Penton, Officer Commanding Flying Wing, dropped into Lake McIlwaine, near Salisbury, on 22nd March. This experience was enjoyed by all participants and all elected to try it again—but this unfortunately was not permitted. According to the Squadron Diary, "All survived." This was a one-off exercise. The reason for doing the drop into water was to reduce the possibility of injury on landing. There were in fact few volunteers who were prepared to jump out of a perfectly serviceable aircraft.

The volunteer reserve increases its numbers

In addition, during March 1966, the RRAF Volunteer Reserve numbers increased considerably when No 105 Squadron was formed in the Lomagundi area. Talking about this squadron Peter Cooke says:

> No 105 Squadron had its headquarters at Preston Farm in the Banket area. The farm had strong connections with the air force. Michael Ward who owned the farm before and during World War II served on No 237 (Rhodesia) Squadron and was killed in action in Italy in April 1945. During the post war years, the farm was owned and run by John Haarhoff who also served on No 237 Squadron. John's sister, Dorothy was the wife of Ted Jacklin.

Although the VR was a non-flying unit, more and more of its members were to be called upon to undertake flying duties as the years went by. In fact, the first man to qualify as a VR captain of an aircraft was George Walker-Smith. George explained later how he became involved with the VR.

> I was walking down First Street in Salisbury when I met a colleague with whom I'd flown during World War II. He said, "Why aren't you in the VR?"
> And I said, "Why the hell should I be?"
> So he said, "There's going to be a war and we are going to be in trouble and we need people like you." Well, that made me feel good. Then he went on, "You don't want to be in the police or some low stuff like that. Be with the elite, be in the air force." So I said, "All right! What do I do?" He said, "I'll fix it!"
> Well, I didn't hear anything. Six weeks went by and I bumped into my friend again. I was a bit fed up, "What's happened about your miraculous bloody air force!" Two days later, I got a

call to present myself at an office in Salisbury. The chap said, "I believe you want to join the VR. What were you in the last war ?" And I told him. Then he said, "Well, let me tell you here and now, joining the VRs you will not fly. We are ground operations only." I said, "OK" and I applied to go into the Operational Branch, which I thought would be the most interesting thing to do. Then I met another friend, who was a VR pilot, and he said, "What are you doing messing about on the ground? Why don't you come and fly?" So I went to the group captain and I said, "I want to fly." And he said, "Push off." Well, the next thing was, I ended up at a party with the officer commanding No 3 Squadron. He said, "I believe you have the qualifications to join our squadron as a pilot." I told him what had happened. He said, "I'll fix it. Just write a letter requesting transfer to the VR Pilots Pool." After a couple of days I got a call, "Your first day's training will be on Thursday." So after a break of 20 years I was back in the air again, which was quite interesting. But flying's like riding a bicycle. You get back into it and after a while, there is no problem. During World War II I'd flown fighters, never anything as big or heavy as a Dakota so that took a little getting used to but if you like flying and you know that you are doing something worthwhile it's fine. (George Walker-Smith)

The Battle of Sinoia

No 4 Squadron was caught napping in the early hours of 13th April 1966, when there was a practice station alert. For a few hours chaos reigned. The faults in the call-out system were only too apparent and there was a long debrief afterwards.

The need for this kind of exercise became evident towards the end of April when the lull came to an abrupt end and insurgency activities took a new and ugly turn. Earlier in the year, 47 heavily armed members of the Zimbabwe African National Liberation army (ZANLA), the military wing of ZANU, had crossed from Zambia. North-west of Sinoia they split into two groups. One of these groups, code named Armageddon and comprising seven men, had attempted to blow up a number of pylons about seven miles south-west of Sinoia.

No 7 Squadron was called in and helicopter pilot Peter Petter-Bowyer with Ewart Sorrell as his technician flew to Sinoia to be briefed by the police superintendent.

During the first afternoon, I found that, for all my training, I had not been properly prepared for operations. To fit a helicopter into an opening among trees with no more than six inches to spare all round was fine in training; yet here I nearly fell out of the sky as I had a full load of police reservists and their operational equipment on board. Many of my training flights had been fully laden flights but obviously these were insufficient. Right there and then, I made my mind up that when I started instructing, my students would do most of their training at maximum all-up weight. Where there's a will there's a way, however, and I was soon flying with proficiency having developed a safer technique when entering into tight landing zones. (Petter-Bowyer)

Information had been received from a police source that the Armageddon group had made camp close to Sinoia between the old strip road and the new main road. The police contact was due to arrive from Salisbury by car. It was arranged with Air headquarters that a helicopter, piloted by Murray Hofmeyr, should keep watch on the car, flying high so as not to alarm the insurgents, while three more helicopters stood by at Banket, 12 miles away. At this stage, the authorities considered that it was a civil matter and that the police should handle the situation.

The commissioner of police, Mr [Frank] Barfoot, was adamant that the police could handle the situation. He regarded it as no more than a criminal case necessitating armed action to kill or apprehend law-breakers, notwithstanding the fact these men had automatic rifles and grenades; to call in the army would suggest a state of war existed. The morning of 28th April dawned like

most Rhodesian dawns, cool, bright and clear. Soon a stream of private vehicles started arriving at the Police Sports Club with all occupants in civilian clothing. Here they changed into their police reserve uniforms. These two-piece dark blue denim outfits were intended for riot control situations in which clear identification was necessary but were not suitable for armed action in the bush as the wearer was transformed into an easy target for any marksman.
(Petter-Bowyer)

The plan was that the reservists, together with a sprinkling of regulars would be divided into three groups. A northern stop-line would be set up along the main road. The southern group would be placed on a line from the strip road to the main road and would sweep towards the west. The third group would act as stops along the river. The insurgent group would be caught neatly in the middle. The weapons issued were 7.62 mm SLR assault rifles for the regulars, and self-loading shotguns, Sten guns and the odd .303-inch Enfield for the reservists. Peter Petter-Bowyer was listening out on the radio in his helicopter for news from the aircraft trailing the contact's vehicle.

At about 10h45 Hoffy Hofmeyr called to the three other aircraft that the 'contact' had passed Banket. Gordon Nettleton, my flight commander, acknowledged and said he would be landing in three minutes. I told Hoffy that ground forces were all set to move. Hoffy's next call which seemed to take an age, but probably no more than ten minutes, came through saying, "The 'contact' vehicle has stopped at the road junction; stand by." He then called to say that a man had climbed into the car that was now moving slowly down the strip road. He had just completed this transmission when he came back on the air, "The vehicle has stopped and the occupants have gone into the bush on the south side, repeat south side of the road, not north into the expected area." This really put the cat amongst the pigeons and my immediate reaction was to thank the Lord I had asked for the extra helicopters. I acknowledged Hoffy's transmission and told him we were standing by for confirmation that the 'contact' vehicle had left the area before we moved. At this stage, Hoffy was holding his height at 6,000 feet above ground and flying very slowly but continuing his heading westwards. (Petter-Bowyer)

Now the original plan had to be reversed, but the sweep was still to be westward. In this changed situation John Cannon, the police superintendent realized he would have to rely on Petter-Bowyer to control the operation from the air.

The stop-groups and sweep-lines were not quite ready when Hoffy called, "The 'contact' vehicle has turned and is leaving the area in the direction of Salisbury." Right away, the three helicopters at Banket were called forward to start an immediate lift of police reserve 'sticks'. A stick was the name given to one helicopter load of six men. (Petter-Bowyer)

Quickly the reservists were helicoptered to their new positions and the choppers returned to the soccer field where fuel had been positioned the previous evening.

When Hoffy landed I found his aircraft was fitted with a side-firing 7.62 mm MAG machine-gun. This was a very crudely mounted affair with no sighting system suited to air gunnery. His technician, Sergeant George Carmichael, had, however, fired this gun in its embryonic airmount form and had a reasonable clue on 'laid-off' aiming in flight.

Following deployment of the reservists, Petter-Bowyer flew a recce over the sweep area. To his horror, he found that the group of men who had been dropped at the power line was sweeping north. This meant that the reservists in the stop-line would be immediately in front of the sweep line.

What made this situation especially dangerous was the fact the terrorists were expected to be in black. Police reserve dark blue uniforms, particularly in shadow, looked very much like black. Also, in this, our first operational experience in combat against terrorists, a major difficulty was the lack of radios on the ground. The sweep commander was in the centre of the line with his extremities over 200 yards to left and right. Although he learned of the danger, there was no quick and accurate way of getting the message to his right flank. So, Dave Becks landed his helicopter, and his technician ran to tell the men to watch his helicopter, which would hover over any policeman directly ahead. In these circumstances, they should not shoot but move up and absorb the stops into their line. With difficulty I managed to halt the stop-line by moving down along it, often hovering, to hand-signal the men to hold their positions. It was an awful mess that tied Dave Becks up for almost an hour before the danger had passed. Without his assistance, I am certain police reservists would have suffered casualties from this fiasco.

Once the danger was over, Petter-Bowyer commenced a general reconnaissance of the area.

I was orbiting a small outcrop of trees when suddenly a black man in a white shirt and black slacks appeared with a weapon pointed at the aircraft. Sunlight vaguely reflected faint puffs of smoke from his weapon before it dawned on me that this was one of the terrorists firing at me. Had he remained crouching in the long grass in the vlei, I doubt I would have seen him. The terrorist squatted a couple of times to recharge his SKS magazine, then rose again to fire as I continued to fly around him. This happened at least four times when suddenly the man started to run like the devil towards the south-west. Only when he was at the edge of the vlei did I realize he was under fire from Hoffy who had arrived unnoticed above me. In the grass, the helicopter's machine-gun strikes had not shown up. As the bare ground was reached, the terrorist disappeared in the dust raised by an angry swarm of bullet strikes that raked from his rear to his front. I was shattered to see the man emerge going even faster than before. Again, a burst engulfed him but he came out running still faster. At a speed that must surely have exceeded any Olympic record, the terrorist again disappeared in another dust cloud, but, when he emerged, his weapon was no longer in his hand. Yet another burst and the man was down. The air force had made its first kill; it was also the first by Rhodesia's security forces. Being in the air made it all seem unreal. The horror of it all was lost by detachment from the gory spectacle of this unfortunate man's corpse. It was more a case of one down and six to go. (Petter-Bowyer)

The police sweep line moved forward and two insurgents rose from cover and were killed before they could get off a shot. As the reservists swarmed towards the dead men, another two armed men began firing from behind an anthill. One raised his arm to throw a grenade and a shot took him in the chest. The grenade fell back to the ground killing the other man. The seventh ZANU man fell shortly afterwards.

Peter Petter-Bowyer wrote a full report on the operation as he had witnessed it. He was critical of the police's reluctance to make use of professional soldiers, the lack of radios and the dark blue uniforms.

The police were not at all pleased by my report. The army was delighted. The air force acknowledged it but severely criticized the excessive amount of ammunition used to kill one man. 'The use of 176 rounds to neutralize one terrorist is excessive. Such expenditure of precious ammunition is clearly unacceptable and too expensive'. This was a laugh coming from senior officers who had no concept of the difficulties involved in using open sights on a wobbling mounting within the confines of a helicopter cabin. At least the report accepted the need to sort out a decent side-mounted gun arrangement, which I got cracking on immediately the approval came through. (Petter-Bowyer)

The Battle of Sinoia, (Chinhoyi) as this operation was named by the Zimbabwe nationalists is now commemorated as the opening shot in the War of Independence, the Second *Chimurenga* (the First *Chimurenga* having taken place in 1896). Flight Lieutenant Peter Petter-Bowyer was awarded the Military Forces Commendation (Operational) for his part in this incident.

The Viljoen murders
The second ZANLA group, armed with PPSH sub-machine guns, a Sten gun, a Schmeisser and Tokarev pistols, and led by a man named Gumbashuma, made its way to the Hartley district. The insurgents spent some time in the compound at Nevada Farm, where they were fed by farm employees. At 01h00 on 17th May, they knocked on the homestead door. Johannes Viljoen went to investigate. The gang members opened fire, killing the farmer and his wife. The seven ZANLA members then retreated into the nearby Zowa Tribal Purchase area. At 05h00, the Viljoen's gardener's attention was attracted by the crying of the Viljoen children, nine-month-old Yolande and three-and-a-half year old Tommy. Police units discovered ZANU pamphlets at the scene, calling on Africans to use violence against Europeans.

While the Nevada Farm incident was still being pursued, two more groups of infiltrators crossed the Zambezi. However, they became lost, and ventured into Mozambique, where they were picked up by local people who handed them over to the authorities. During this period, No 7 Squadron operated freely across the Mozambique border carrying Rhodesian army personnel and police, as well as members of the Portuguese army who were assisting in rounding up the remaining insurgents.

To return to the ZANLA members led by Gumbashuma, one of them was a local, and information from his father led to watch being kept on a kraal in the Hartley area, where later the youth was ambushed and wounded. Information from this youngster led to the discovery of the ZANLA main base on the Umfuli River. Two members of the gang were killed when the base was attacked and Gumbashuma who was wounded, returned to Zambia. The rest of the gang made their way to Salisbury where they were eventually arrested.

This operation was complicated by the deployment of forces to the Karoi area where three Europeans had been found murdered on their farm. It was at first believed that this was also a terrorist attack but it proved to be a domestic incident and the African servant was arrested.

Incident on the Zambezi
As a result of these incursions, pilots of the Canberras flying border patrols became particularly sensitive to activity on the banks of the Zambezi River and this nearly led to an unfortunate incident in July 1966. A pilot on a regular patrol spotted two men paddling across the river in an army assault craft. Flying lower, he saw armed men in strange uniforms on the riverbank. The pilot did not know it, but the men were extras in a documentary about Rhodesian army counter-insurgency operations being filmed by the Ministry of Information.

Frantically, an army lieutenant tried to radio the aircraft not to attack, but the Canberra flew low over the river in two more passes before the radio message got through. Feeling very naked and defenceless in the rubber assault craft, were the film's director Steve Knight and producer Peter Armstrong. They had just finished a sequence in which infiltrators crossing the Zambezi were supposed to have been ambushed by an army unit.

During September, the infiltrations continued with small groups of up to 12 men crossing

Zambia's border with Rhodesia at points from Wankie north to Kanyemba. In most of these cases, the helicopters of No 7 Squadron were used in conjunction with ground forces to capture the gangs and recover arms and ammunition.

The Tiger talks

On 1st December 1966, Rhodesians were startled to learn that at 05h30 that morning, Prime Minister Ian Smith, J.H. (Jack) Howman (Minister of Information), Sir Humphrey Gibbs and the Chief Justice Sir Hugh Beadle had boarded an RAF Britannia to fly to the Mediterranean in order to meet British Prime Minister, Harold Wilson aboard HMS *Tiger*. Once again, negotiations broke down when Harold Wilson insisted that the British proposals be accepted or rejected as a whole. The British government then withdrew all offers, stating that, "In future no grant of Independence will be contemplated unless African majority rule is already an accomplished fact." It was to be nearly two years before the two prime ministers were to meet again aboard another ship of the Royal Navy, *Fearless*.

By the end of 1966, insurgency activity appeared to have ceased and No 7 Squadron was able to concentrate on routine training and projects designed to increase flexibility. All technicians received training on the MAG side-mounted machine gun and were designated airgunners, some very good scores being achieved on the range. They were allowed to wear a very distinctive RRAF-designed Winged Bullet on the left arm. This was modelled on a pre-1939 RAF aircrew badge.

A self-contained pressure refuelling system

A significant development in the operation of No 7 Squadron was the fitting of a self-contained pressure refuelling system devised by Flight Lieutenant Petter-Bowyer.

We used to have to refuel with a hand pump in those days, and frankly, I found I was pooped especially when we were on the go with trooping. Half the time I didn't have a technician because we were carrying six troops. It was no joke having to roll drums, lift the damn things and pump. I thought, why not make the aeroplane fill itself? I got into trouble with some senior technical officers who said that when they were in the desert they'd refuelled by hand, and, what was wrong with it? I believed if we could refuel faster, we could ferry more troops and improve our efficiency. I took a pressured air tapping off the engine, and it worked like a charm, pressurizing the fuel drum and forcing the fuel in. But the authorities refused to accept it, initially, because there was a ruling that you do not refuel with the engine running. This ignored the fact that the helicopters used paraffin as opposed to highly inflammable aviation fuel. Anyway, with the connivance of a master technician, Frank Oliver, we designed and made a superb little unit, which you removed from the aircraft, stuck the suction pipe in the fuel drum, the delivery pipe in the fuel tank, turned a handle, pressed a button and she refuelled herself. With the hand-pump, it took 15 minutes of sweat and blood to refuel one drum. But we could refuel this way in three and a half minutes. Then I arranged a demonstration to prove the idea would work. My squadron commander, Norman Walsh, called senior members of the technical staff to No 7 Squadron on the pretext of some urgent problem. Two helicopters landed next to the fuel drums. One refuelled the old way, and one the new way. The helicopter that refuelled the new way was airborne before the other crew had even started to pump. Obviously, I personally couldn't gain anything financially from the idea but I did hope they would patent it and use any patent money to help Rhodesian Security Force personnel. Actually, it seems we gave the full rights to the French, no doubt for something we needed in return. Later we heard that the French sold the patent to the Americans who used the idea in Vietnam. (Petter-Bowyer)

The Beech Baron

During the years of UDI, Rhodesia was to find that she had many good friends in different parts of the world but the closest links were with Mozambique (until 1974) and South Africa. During November 1966, No 3 Squadron strength was increased by the arrival of a much-appreciated Beech Baron Model B 55, presented by a South African organization.

The Beech Baron, R 7310, was used by Prime Minister Ian Smith to fly into small bush airstrips. It was gloss white, with air force markings and a thin blue cheat-line along the fuselage. The Baron—damaged when the undercarriage was inadvertently retracted after landing—was sold after the Britten-Norman Islanders were acquired in 1974. From then on, the prime minister made use of the Britten-Norman Islanders, and although this aircraft was slower than the Baron it was better suited to small airstrips and could carry more passengers and luggage. The Baron, now registered as VP-WHF, was sold to a member of the VR, Robin Fennell, who had a coffee farm in Chipinga.

On the subject of aircraft serviceability, the annual report issued by the chief of Air Staff, Air Vice-Marshal Harold Hawkins for the year 1966 made comforting reading. He stated that there had been no unserviceability of RRAF aircraft, as a result of shortages of spare parts, during the year.

> *Though the application of sanctions affected some of our normal sources of supply, the equipment staff displayed considerable ingenuity and resourcefulness in the maintaining of a satisfactory flow of items to the air and technical branches. The potential of Rhodesian industry was explored diligently during the year and a firm policy is to be adopted of purchasing wherever possible locally-manufactured articles in preference to imported ones.* (Rhodesia Herald, 20th July 1967)

In fact, this policy proved its worth during the following years, and air force technicians working with local industry proved that the country could make or make-do with almost anything that was needed. If a particular item was no longer available, a substitute could usually be found and in some cases the substitute proved better and was certainly cheaper than the original.

Sanctions were now in full force and the *Sunday Mail* reported in April 1967 that the French government had banned the export of snowploughs and dirigibles to Rhodesia. Hawkins kept a stiff upper lip. "It's some time since the RRAF used air ships—in fact, I can't remember our ever having used them and we haven't got any on order at present. As far as we are concerned it all sounds like a lot of hot air. The subject of helicopters was not mentioned!"

Static line descents and free fall

The Parachute Training School continued to render invaluable service largely owing to the work of one man, Squadron Leader M.J. (Boet) Swart, who had transferred from the Rhodesian army on 15th January 1963. He qualified as a parachute jumping instructor in June of that year and was promoted to acting squadron leader in January 1964 when he became commander of the school. In September 1966, he was also appointed survival training officer.

The first static line descents using RLI members had been made on 12th June, 1966 at the Delport's farm a few miles to the east of New Sarum. By the beginning of 1967, the school was working with the new TAP 665 French parachute that had been received in November 1966. This was of a revolutionary design and proved to be superior to the 'X'-type. Trials were held carrying equipment in various types of containers and with different attachments.

On 31st March 1967, Flight Sergeant Frank Hales carried out the first free-fall parachute descent at the school, jumping from a Dakota flying at 15,000 feet. This was the start of trials conducted by the army into free-fall parachuting. The training and dispatching was carried out by staff at the school with Hales as the instructor and with descents being made from between 9,000 to 15,000 feet. In addition to this free-fall training, two basic courses took place during the year to bring the Special Air Services up to full strength. Later in 1967, a number of American T 10 parachutes were obtained for evaluation and as the trials proved successful, it was decided to re-equip with the American parachute.

There was some excitement for No 4 Squadron in April when, during a weapons demonstration held for the Police Reserve Air Wing, live fragmentation bombs were incorrectly attached, with the result that once they were released they remained hanging from the aircraft by the fusing wire. One bomb was accidentally dropped on a farm and three others became detached as the aircraft was landing. Fortunately, no damage was caused to the aircraft or the runway. Later in the same month, a more successful demonstration was held for Portuguese visitors, followed by a first class party.

For the RRAF station at Thornhill, the end of an era came on Sunday 23rd April, when Mrs Jeannie Boggie died in Gwelo Hospital at the age of 91. For so many years, Mrs Boggie had been part of Thornhill life. The battle began during World War II and continued into the 1950s with her threatening to shoot down any aircraft that flew too low over her farm. Now at last the love-hate relationship had ended.

Counter-insurgency operations commenced again in June 1967 when Nos 7 and 4 Squadrons were called out on detachment to the Kariba area to search for infiltrators. No 4 Squadron Diary notes:

> This detachment marked a change in HQ policy towards the use of air weapons. This was the first time permission was given to use weapons if needed. Unfortunately, the detachment proved to be a rather quiet one, the basic job being continuous air patrols over the Makuti area. No weapons used.

At a passing-out parade held for eight officer cadets at Thornhill towards the end of June, the first chief of Air Staff, Air Vice-Marshal Ted Jacklin, paid tribute to the ability of the air force. He said that it was making an outstanding contribution to the security, peace and stability of the country. It was also announced that a new volunteer reserve squadron was to be formed in the Lowveld. It was to be designated No 107 (Lowveld) Squadron RRAF VR.

The Cockle-Shell

It was during 1967 that news was released of the invention of the RRAF Mark I Concrete Bomb or Cockle-Shell named after its inventor, Flight Lieutenant Alan Cockle, a Canberra navigator. This was a 130-lb (59kg) practice bomb that was cheap and could be made locally. The cost was about £6 compared with £100 for the British-made equivalent. The Cockle-Shell was just one of the many innovative ideas that came from members of the air force during the following 13 years. As Peter Petter-Bowyer remarked later:

> The range of our activities was from the very sophisticated electronic end of the scale to the very simple backyard type of solution, which in the right circumstances was just as effective—like Alan Cockle's bomb. Bombing practice was originally done with 'smoke and flash' bombs that were the same size as the 20-lb fragmentation bombs. They were carried in the bomb bay in a series of racks, which each carried five bombs. When doing level bombing, there are many factors that govern the trajectory of the bomb. Your true height above ground, and your track and groundspeed are critical. Also, there must be no sideways velocity at the moment of release. The small 20-lb bomb was extremely susceptible to all these conditions. Inside the bomb bay, there is a considerable amount of turbulence owing to the 300 knot airstream when the bomb doors

are opened. The 20-lb bombs were not only jostled about in the bomb bay, but were thrown 'all over the place' on leaving the aircraft, and the results were not a true reflection of the skill of the crew. The 130-lb concrete bomb was much less susceptible to turbulence in the bay and was far more stable when leaving the aircraft. It was thus more representative of the flight of the 1,000-pounder that the practice bombs were designed to imitate. Consequently, it gave a much clearer picture of the actual results. (Petter-Bowyer)

Trials with the new toy began in July 1967. At first the tails were found to be too weak but after some additional strengthening, it was agreed that the Cockle-Shell was a great improvement on the bombs then in use. It was even suggested that it might be used against thin-skinned targets such as road convoys, having the advantage that aircraft making low-level attacks would not experience any upward blast—as they would from high-explosive bombs.

The photo-interpretation section
A full-scale photo-interpretation section had been formed as part of the photographic section at New Sarum and the production of aerial photographs had been increased. By the end of 1967, about 130,000 square miles (200,000 sq km) of the country had been surveyed for the Surveyor General's Department, plus a considerable amount more for air force training.

The survey cameras being used had interchangeable lenses. These varied from a six-inch (15cm) wide angle lens and an 80mm RC 10 wide-angle lens, to a 36-inch (91cm) telephoto lens used on an F 52/F 96 recce camera. The six-inch lens was capable of taking a photograph at 50,000 feet showing 152 square miles (235 sq km) of territory on a single negative, while the 36-inch lens was used to obtain detailed reconnaissance information. In addition to the fixed camera installations, hand-held cameras were used in the Provosts and Alouettes to record oblique target photographs and carry out low-level reconnaissance.

The technique employed to obtain aerial photographs for map-making was precise. The Government Survey Department would designate the area to be surveyed and RRAF headquarters would detail No 5 Squadron. The survey would be flown using a Canberra equipped with a fixed vertical survey camera, which was remotely controlled from the bomb-aimer's position. The camera was electrically driven and triggered at regular time intervals determined by an interval meter under the control of the photo-navigator.

The area to be photographed would be divided into flight lines along which the aircraft tracked. The time interval of the shots was calculated so that the area of ground covered by each photograph overlapped the previous by 60%. In the same way, the strips of photographs overlapped by 30%. This over-lapping system was designed to ensure that all ground detail was covered by at least two photographs. This provided stereoscopic cover, which is the basis for any accurate map-making. It also ensured that minor navigational errors did not result in gaps.

The film was then brought back to New Sarum and processed, checked for defects and analysed for accuracy and overall cover. A cover trace was then produced from an existing map of the area, showing the actual track of the aircraft with the appropriate negative numbers and all the details of the flight crew, height, scale, camera operation and so on. The film was then dispatched to Government Survey for the production of maps.

Remarking on the aerial photographic work carried out by No 5 Squadron, Flight Lieutenant Peter Knobel, in the air force magazine *Ndege* (June 1967) concludes:

It is not generally appreciated what an extremely high standard of flying accuracy is required for aerial photography. Deviations in height, speed, aircraft attitude and navigational errors can all render the resulting film unusable. For example, a 1° heading error will result in photographic cover gaps on a long flight line. The camera never lies and all such flying errors are faithfully recorded on the film. Similarly, correct and precise flying is also recorded. (Ndege, June 1967)

The photographic section was also called upon to undertake an infinite variety of jobs from document and identity shots to recording hairline fractures of pipes located in inaccessible parts of aircraft. The men of the section had to have a wide-ranging knowledge of photographic theory, embracing both optics and chemistry as well as a thorough understanding of at least half a dozen camera types.

The Trojan ('Trog')

It was also during 1967, that the first Aermacchi Lockheed AL-60C aircraft began to arrive in the country. Known locally as the Trojan ('Trog'), the aircraft arrived in specially constructed crates. The fuselage was securely fixed to the floor of the crate and the main-planes were attached to the side walls with the tail plane fixed to the end walls. The undercarriage had been removed from the aircraft and fixed to the floor. The crates must have cost almost as much as the aircraft! The whole thing was like a meccano kit.

Ten of these aircraft had been ordered. They were capable of carrying six people or up to 1,000 pounds (454kg) of cargo or they could be converted to make an ambulance capable of carrying two stretcher cases and one medical attendant or a sitting casualty. The Trojan could also be used for paratroop drops. The aircraft was particularly valuable for reconnaissance, close support and security operations. The maximum speed was 125 miles per hour (200 km/h) with a range of 600 nautical miles (965km). The Trojan could be armed with rockets and in fact, the aircraft would be festooned with all manner of armament during the next few years.

Strict security precautions were in force when the Trojans arrived at New Sarum. Assembly began on 1st August 1967 and the ninth aircraft was completed by 24th August. There was some delay with the tenth machine, which was only completed on September 6th. An eleventh machine was supplied in 1973 from South Africa.

Petter-Bowyer tells an interesting story of how the Trojan got its name. Some time after UDI, the Rhodesian government had purchased 18 American T 28 Trojans.

> *These were massive beasts, used in the States as a training aircraft. We purchased them through the French and they were on the high seas when someone in Salisbury talked too loudly and they were turned around and sent all the way back to France. Later, when we got these little puddle jumpers they simply acquired the name Trojan—totally wrong. But the little low-powered Trojans scared the pants off me many times.* (Petter-Bowyer)

Of course, another reason for the name could have been that these vitally needed aircraft arrived concealed in wooden crates—rather like the attacking soldiers entering Troy in the wooden horse.

During 1967, Nos 1 and 5 Squadrons carried out long-range navigational exercises to bases in Mozambique and South Africa. In July, a Canberra returning from Durban with an unserviceable No 3 tank fuel pump, ran into severe icing problems over the Drakensberg. This resulted in a double flame-out (both engines out). The squadron commander, Ian Donaldson and his navigator, Alan Cockle were about to eject when a re-light was achieved and the aircraft returned safely to Salisbury.

1967 saw a considerable amount of reorganization taking place. No 6 Squadron was resurrected and took on the task of instruction. This left No 4 Squadron free to continue its conversion to the Trojan aircraft, a task that was completed by the end of September. However, for a short while, No 4 Squadron continued to operate a number of Provosts on loan from No 6 Squadron. No 6 Squadron, re-formed on August 1st and being purely involved in training, was allocated seven Provost T 52 aircraft.

Operation Nickel

In July 1967, a large force of 94 insurgents crossed the Zambezi River using rubber boats, and made their way into the sparsely populated area between the Victoria Falls and Kazungula at the point where the Zambezi and Chobe Rivers meet. This group was composed of members of the South African African National Congress (SAANC) and the Zimbabwe African People's Union (ZAPU), supporters of Joshua Nkomo. The operation was under the control of John Dube (ZAPU) and George Driver, a South African Coloured (SAANC). Chief of Staff was Leonard Mandla Nkosi who had spent a year in Moscow at a military academy. The aim of the SAANC members was to penetrate through Rhodesia and Botswana and infiltrate the Republic of South Africa.

Having crossed the river successfully with their supplies, the men made their way to the Wankie/Dett area, where several camps were constructed containing dugouts, weapons pits and observation posts. The first contact between this group and the security forces came on 1st August 1967 when one member of the group was captured in the Wankie National Park near Shapi Pans. This set in motion a full-scale anti-terrorist operation, code named Nickel in which the air force was heavily involved. Chris Dams, officer commanding No 1 (Hunter) Squadron was air force representative and W.A. (Bill) Godwin was brigade commander at the JOC (Joint Operations Centre).

Flying Officer Prop Geldenhuys was called out to set up a FAF (forward air field) at Kariba. He was replaced there by Pilot Officer Tudor Thomas on 9th August. This operation initially consisted of leaflet dropping and recces. (No 4 Squadron Diary, 5th August)

A contact had in fact been made on 1st August and initially the air force involvement consisted of leaflet drops and reconnaissance flights in the Makuti/Chirundu area. The leaflets called on the men to give themselves up and printed on the back of the leaflets, which were in English and chiShona, were photographs of two terrorists who had recently surrendered.

Meanwhile the infiltrators had moved towards the Bulawayo/Victoria Falls road where their tracks were discovered by game scouts searching for poachers. First Battalion Rhodesian African Rifles and members of the BSAP were deployed. Forward Air Field 1 (FAF 1) was established at Wankie on 12th August with two Provosts from No 4 Squadron piloted by Prop Geldenhuys and Chris Weinmann and one Alouette from No 7 Squadron piloted by Mick Grier. On the same day, No 4 Squadron aircraft were involved in a skirmish with the infiltrators resulting in one capture.

Soon after daylight on 13th August near Inyantue Siding, Section Officer Barry James Tiffin (BSAP) was leading a patrol through dense bush, with Prop flying top-cover, when contact was made with the group. The men were in a strong defensive position about 30 metres from the patrol. Tiffin and his men were pinned down. Fire was exchanged and reinforcements called in. Prop recalls:

We were itching to contribute with our 2 x .303 front guns, but the safety distance was not sufficient. In those days, a safety distance of between 100 to 300 yards was needed in order to discharge air to ground weapons from attacking aircraft. A helicopter crewed by Mick Grier and

Bob Whyte came to the assistance of the ground forces. Under heavy fire, Bob attacked the terrorist position. Despite continual fire from the helicopter, the insurgents kept up the attack. During our two-hour and 40-minute top-cover sortie, three terrorists were killed. Chris Weinmann, flying the second Provost, relieved me when I had to return to FAF 1 to refuel. Most of the time we flew at 1,000 feet in order to attack at an optimum 20° dive angle. Because of the high engine settings, the Provost endurance was significantly reduced. (Prop Geldenhuys)

Taking advantage of the distraction provided by the air attack, the ground party pulled back to a safer position. It was during this manoeuvre that casualties were sustained by the security forces. Section Officer Tiffin crawled forward to assist the re-enforcement group and was seriously wounded in the thigh. Private Simon Chikafu of the RAR emptied his 20-round magazine into the enemy position and then crawled forward to the wounded policeman, dragged him to cover and then carried him to the waiting helicopter.

During this engagement, five ZIPRA infiltrators were shot dead and two were captured. Two members of the RAR, Acting Corporal Davison and Private Karoni were killed in the initial encounter and three European and one African security force personnel were wounded.

On 18th August, contact was again established with the gang in the Angwa Vlei and there was an action in which three of the enemy were killed and five more were burned to death when there was an explosion in their hide. Six more members of this group were captured. One man managed to escape, only to be killed on the following day. The Forward Air Field was then moved from Wankie FAF 1 to Wankie Main Camp to be closer to the scene of operations.

Two days later, another man was captured and on 22nd August 1966, part of this original group was encountered in the Nata River area, at the extreme south-western point of the Wankie National Park. Prop Geldenhuys again takes up the story:

What a day the 22nd was. Rich Beaver and I got airborne early and proceeded with our armed recce in support of the RAR. By now, Lt Ken Pierson had deployed stop groups along the Nata River. Our airborne presence meant that the gooks could not cover a lot of ground. On each occasion that we came close, they had to go to ground and that allowed the army call signs to catch up. Whilst we were circling Lt Nic Smith's call sign, all hell broke out. Every time we flew over, we were subjected to a hail of lead. WO2 Timitiya came on the radio to say that the lieutenant had been hit. Then all contact was lost. It was then that an AK-47 slug hit my Provost. I was circling when my port wing 'opened up' right before my eyes. The bullet then struck my side of the canopy, just behind my head and rattled itself to death inside the cockpit—fortunately without striking Beaver or me. I banked sharply to starboard. Beaver thought I'd been shot and was trying to control the violent air manoeuvre. I thought he had been hit.

It was with considerable relief that both men realized that a miracle had occurred and they were uninjured. Prop called up Chris Weinmann to relieve him and made his way back to base where the techs confirmed that no vital organs (on the aircraft) had been damaged, applied several strips of masking tape to the bullet holes and refuelled. The Provost was soon back over the contact area. The two security force members mentioned in Geldenhuys's account, Lieutenant Nic Smith and Warrant Officer Timitiya, were killed. Five insurgents died in the contact and at least two more were wounded, their bodies being found the next day.

As the operational area had now moved south it was necessary to shift the Forward Air Field once more to bring the helicopters closer to the action. This time the site chosen was Tjolotjo, a village in Matabeleland South, about 100 kilometres north of Plumtree.

On 23rd August, a base camp suitable for 50 men was discovered on the Tegwani River. It

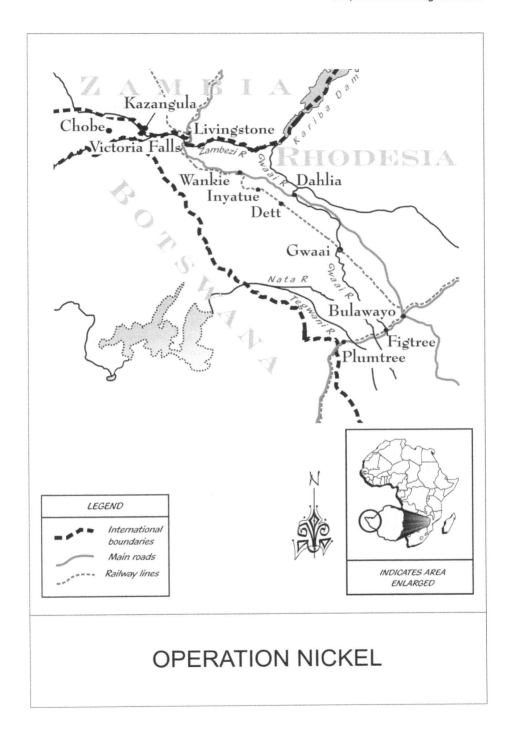

OPERATION NICKEL

was well-camouflaged and fortified. During follow-up operations, a group was sighted from the air and an air strike was called in. This was carried out by Hunters and Canberras.

Each Canberra dropped 96 fragmentation bombs. However, the insurgents had moved more slowly than had been expected and so the strike was not as successful as had been hoped and the terrorists were waiting in ambush as the security forces approached. At 17h15 the enemy attacked, pinning the security forces down. The fight that developed was carried out at extremely close quarters, and lasted more than an hour before the enemy pulled back. During this contact, movement of ground forces in the area was directed by a helicopter of No 7 Squadron, piloted by Mick Grier. Fire was directed on to the insurgents, who were in a strong defensive position only about 30 metres away. Mick's aircraft came under determined fire from the ground.

During the battle, communications were lost between the patrol and Joint Operations Centre (JOC) and it was only at 01h30 the following morning, 24th August, that the JOC received a radio message asking for immediate evacuation of a battle casualty. Flight Lieutenant Chris Dixon was detailed with this duty, which entailed making a night flight of about 40 miles (64km) over inhospitable country. There were the additional hazards of landing and taking off in a small badly lit landing zone. Despite all the difficulties, Dixon carried out the evacuation successfully and delivered the two casualties to hospital. Squadron Leader M.R. Grier and Sergeant R.C. Whyte were later awarded the Military Forces Commendation (Operational).

Meanwhile, on 14th August George Driver, the leader of the ANC group, had stolen a car in Dett, wounding an African security guard, and driven towards Bulawayo, evading several roadblocks on the way. His aim obviously was to make his way through Bulawayo to the South African border. By Friday, 18th August, Driver had reached Figtree, south of Bulawayo, where he took a farmer's wife and her six-year-old son hostage but the woman and child managed to escape with the help of their gardener. Security forces were called in, the house was surrounded and Driver was killed.

By early September, 30 insurgents had been killed and 47 captured in Rhodesia and Botswana. Only one member of the original group managed to reach South Africa, and he was caught later. Those taken prisoner were in bad shape. The official report said: "The incessant harrying by the security forces had forced them to abandon some of their equipment. They had been suffering from lack of food and water. They were completely disillusioned about the situation in Rhodesia, having been led to believe that they would not meet with strong opposition." Another surprise for them was the fact that local tribesmen refused to help them.

The final casualty figure for the security forces was seven dead and 12 wounded. As a result of these deaths, the captured men were tried for murder and for carrying arms of war, which under the Law and Order (Maintenance) Act carried the death penalty. Seven of the men were convicted on both counts and sentenced to be hanged.

As a result of patrols flown during Operation Nickel, the Zambian government accused the RRAF of violating her air space. Kenneth Kaunda, the Zambian President, warned that, "Zambia will take active measures with friends to defend her territory." In Salisbury, the Rhodesian Minister of Defence, Lord Graham, denied that there had been any infiltration into Zambia by Rhodesian forces, either by land or air. This denial was amplified in early October when the Chief of Air Staff, Air Vice-Marshal Harold Hawkins released the following statement:

The north-west border of Rhodesia for the most part runs approximately along the middle of the Zambezi River. My staff is well aware of the actual position of the boundary line as set in an order-in-council in 1953. It is across this boundary that many luckless terrorists have infiltrated in recent months. We are entitled to patrol our air space as and when we wish. I categorically deny, however, that any of our aircraft have breached Zambian air space, and I am sure that

anyone who knows the reputation of my force will accept this statement. It is possible that from the 'worms-eye' view right in the Zambezi valley, aircraft might sometimes appear to be on or over the border. This is an effect which height can give. Again some observers might not be aware of the location of the border but we are in no doubt of this.
(Rhodesia Herald, 10th Oct. 1967)

One major result of this joint ZAPU/ANC operation was that South African Police units were sent to operate in Rhodesia. During the next 13 years, South African involvement grew and eventually included army and air force personnel and equipment.

New Sarum Air Show
On a lighter note, an air show was held at New Sarum at the beginning of September 1967.

The thousands who reached the show saw four Hawker Hunter jet fighters, four Canberra jet bombers and a Vampire make a series of low runs across the air base. The Hunters made a series of low-level rocket strafing runs and then hurtled off over the heads of the crowd in a mock dogfight with the bombers. A demonstration of anti-terrorist warfare began with a mass parachute drop of more than 20 Special Air Service men. The men were dropped on the nearest 'strategic point' to their target—three houses near the central arena—then ferried by three Alouette helicopters into the arena. (Rhodesia Herald, 3rd Sept. 1967)

Three Provosts from No 6 Squadron also took part in the display. With everyone back at Thornhill, No 4 Squadron continued training with the new Trojans and made various modifications. A few live and dummy ammunition trials were carried out in conjunction with the RAR in order to develop suitable ground-attack patterns for use during counter-insurgency operations. In fact, the Trojan was proving its usefulness as a light transport and communication aircraft, as well as a valuable casualty evacuation machine.

At the end of the month, on a long cross-country, Pilot Officer Beaver [Trevor] Baynham distinguished himself by getting lost 'somewhere near Sanyati' and is to be awarded the Bamboo Shield. (No 4 Squadron Diary)

The hazards of operating from the bush
By the time 1967 came to an end, No 7 Squadron was committed to maintaining helicopters on a semi-permanent basis at forward air fields at FAF 1 Wankie and FAF 2 Kariba in order to provide quick reaction to any infiltration. Operating in the Rhodesian bush presented the helicopters with hazards quite apart from the man-made variety. A report in the air force magazine *Ndege* published in May 1968, tells of one such incident. The Alouette was landing in a bush clearing which was about 20 yards by 40. Ground contact had been made, but before the landing had been fully completed, the pilot noticed two adult and one young rhino entering the clearing. It seemed the animals were prepared to dispute possession of the clearing. The pilot decided that immediate lift-off was necessary and in the process, the main rotors struck a tree. The helicopter was landed about half a mile (1km) away and an inspection was carried out. Damage had occurred to the main rotor tips but after a hover check, the pilot flew the aircraft back to base at reduced air speed. Comment from *Ndege*:

To leap up into a tree would seem a natural reaction in these circumstances, although this procedure is not recommended for choppers! The mind boggles at the possible damage had the animals actually made contact with the aircraft and the pilot obviously worked fairly quickly at the transition from landing to lift-off. His subsequent actions were absolutely correct and the aircraft returned to base without further mishap. This accident is classified as Normal Operational Hazard—although this sort of normality we can do without. (Ndege)

During the first ten days of January 1968, a further two groups of infiltrators were mopped up, one near Kamativi, 60 kilometres east of Wankie, and the other near Makuti, 50 kilometres east of Kariba. The pre-positioning of the helicopters in the forward areas probably contributed to the speedy conclusion of these operations. No 4 Squadron was also involved in this contact and this was the first time that Trojans were employed on an operation. Following this call-out, the aircraft returned to Thornhill where message-drop trials were carried out and it was found that good accuracy was fairly easy.

Long-range tanks for the Canberras

Long-range tanks had been fitted in the bomb bays of the Canberras. These carried 2,000 pounds (907kg) of fuel each and were found to increase the bomber's range to 2,500 nautical miles (4,600km) and the endurance to five and a half hours. No 5 Canberra Squadron's roles were modified during the year to reduce fatigue and increase the life of the components. The use of rockets was discontinued and efforts were made to conduct most flying during the cooler hours of the day, whenever possible. Nose cones began bursting at high altitudes and this caused concern as the spare parts position was not easy.

The arrester barrier at Thornhill was initially used in February 1968 when a Hunter of No 1 Squadron overran the runway. Fortunately only superficial damage occurred.

Meanwhile No 3 Transport Squadron was carrying out trials involving sky-shouting apparatus. Two large loudspeakers were fitted in the rear doorway of a Dakota and beamed down to the ground. The aircraft was flown for endurance and in gentle turns to port at about 1,500 to 2,000 feet above the ground, while various tapes were played.

The strength of the squadron was increased by the acquisition of a Trojan for light transport work, and so now stood at eight Dakotas, one Beech Baron and one Trojan.

A detachment to Wankie by No 4 Squadron in February 1968 was used to evaluate the Trojans in the reconnaissance role and to train both pilots and flight engineers in the finer points of observation. Training on the ground by rangers from the Department of Parks and Wild Life was followed by reconnaissance flights to determine the difference between human and animal tracks and paths. "All the squadron gained first-hand experience with animals in the natural state and got some good photos!"

The month of March 1968 began with Exercise Spiderweb, designed to test the capabilities of the Trojan; however, training suddenly developed into the real thing when Operation Cauldron broke.

'I'd rather be flying' could well have been the sentiment of the duty pilot who had to do his stint in the control tower at Cranborne.

An RAF Canberra at New Sarum on the occasion of the Rhodes Centenary Air Display, 1953.

To the same air display came diverse aircraft such as Lancaster PF 4410 from the RAF.

The stub-nosed FB 9 was painted with the red flash, a purely air force design. The open hatch is the access panel to the 20mm cannon ammunition bay.

A huge RAF Hastings overshadows the tiny FB 9, though the crowds were probably more interested in the little'un.

Above: A sound that the residents of Hatfield were to become accustomed to was the scream of the Goblin engines. Two FB 9s in a formation take off with the New Sarum control tower behind.

Left: Seven Spitfires over New Sarum. The Spitfires flew in many ceremonial flypasts.

Lt Tommy Robinson appears to have little to do in the New Sarum tower. Controlling of air traffic for Salisbury was transferred to the civilian authority when the airport terminal opened. The new Salisbury tower had an air force ATC liaison officer (Peter Cooke was the first) to assist with military traffic.

The five-bladed propeller was needed to absorb the immense power put out by the 12-cylinder Griffon engine. The props were made of wood and one of the reasons for grounding the Spitfires was the shrinking of the blade roots owing to the harsh African climate. Taff Evans is one of the technicians.

Dave Harvey reflects the sentiments of all pilots who have had the opportunity to take control of a masterpiece of engineering. The Spitfire must have been the forerunner of the expression *Silly grin aeroplane*. (The expression is used to describe the look on the face of a pilot who has just completed his first solo in an awesome machine).

A Spit starts up to go on a weapons sortie carrying four 3-inch rockets with the practice 60-lb concrete heads. These inexpensive rocket heads were used well into the '70s by the Vampires.

Left and right: Ossie Penton and Mike Bracken came in a touch too low in a Tiger Moth on their approach to Cranborne. They got their wheels caught in the long grass, with the inevitable outcome. Righting the aircraft simply needed manpower. The only damage was to the fin and the propeller.

A photographic study of the silver FB 9 in its high-speed-silver finish. The white plastic strip over the nose was to allow the radio compass to function properly, although these were never fitted to the FB 9s.

Hunting Percival Pembroke SR 133 taking off from New Sarum. This aircraft accompanied the first Vampire ferry arriving November 1953. The lack of security fencing or revetments is very apparent when compared with photos taken in the '70s. The residents of Hatfield, especially the young boys, were able to stroll across the runway to look at the aeroplanes.

A wheels-up landing executed to perfection by John Mussell on runway 32 at New Sarum. The propeller is the first casualty as the individual blades fly off in all directions.

Same problem, same place, same result. This time it was Brian Horney.

John Mussell, apparently unperturbed by his recent incident ,poses with one of the blades that went AWOL during his shortest ever landing in a Spitfire.

Put your wheels into the soft sand and the tiny elevator has little chance of keeping you stable . . .

Governor-General of the Federation, Lord Llewellin, in full regalia, welcomes the Portuguese governor from Mozambique at New Sarum in 1953. SR 25 is the Dakota that Jan Smuts presented to the air force

Far left: Spike Owens (or 'Wobotoc'—Warrant Officer Bill Owens, Thieving Old C**t) was one of the more colourful characters in the force. His initial posting to Spitfires in the '50s lit the flame in him that restored the Spitfire Gate Guardian at New Sarum to flying condition. Here he inspects a Vampire T 11.

Left: Lt Bobby Blair retrieves his kit from the ammo bay of his FB 9 after the ferry from the UK in August 1954.

Seven silver Vampires grace the hardstand at Sarum. Some of them would still be flying operationally 25 years later.

The pilots of the third Vampire ferry. From left: Capt John Deall, Lieutenants Dicky Bradshaw, Colin Graves, Bobby Blair, Harry Coleman and Mick McLaren, all in SRAF uniform of khaki battledress.

The pilots of the first Provost ferry. From left: Lieutenants Brian Horney and Tony Chisnall, Capt John Moss, Lieutenants Chris Dams and Mike Saunders. 1954.

From under the wing of the Canadair C4 the photographer composes a worthy aviation picture featuring an RRAF Dakota at New Sarum.

Crowds gather to see the new acquisitions--Hunting Percival Provosts arrive from the UK, 5th November 1954.

A sorry sight for today's rebuild enthusiasts--Spitfire F 22s ignominiously sold as scrap. Seven Spitfires were sold to Syria, two were lost on the second ferry (Owen Love was killed in France and Dave Richards crashed at Entebbe), two were kept as Gate Guardians and the remainder went to the big aviation knackers' yard in the sky (Kopje Post Office area, Salisbury).

A fine photograph of a silver Provost showing the rocket rails and the post-Federal numbering 304. In the late '70s, many years after the Provs had been withdrawn from service, one was restored to flying condition and named the *Silver Provost*. The aircraft was still flying in 2000, piloted by AVM Ian Harvey.

These flying badges were introduced when the prefix 'Royal' was bestowed upon the Southern Rhodesia Air Force. They have the Queen's crown.

Six Dakotas were ferried from the UK in 1955, all having been prepared by Scottish Aviation at Prestwick. At the breakup of the Federation, four Dakotas were transferred to the Northern Rhodesia Air Wing. To make up the losses, four more were purchased from the SAAF in 1964, returning 3 Squadron to its original strength of eight Dakotas.

The main entrance of the new Salisbury Airport building from the car park, the cars being a dead giveaway for the era. The clock no longer works.

At 2, 800 yards, the 06-24 runway at Salisbury was then one of the longest in Africa. The new airport building can be seen on the upper side of the runway intersection with New Sarum on the lower. Runway 14-32 was only partially tarred, the rest being grass.

Above: Queen Elizabeth, the Queen Mother, is introduced to Wing Commander Mick Gibbons, RRAF Chief Technical Officer, by Air Commodore Ted Jacklin. 1957.

Left: Rugged terrain acts as a backdrop for a Vampire T 11 being pre-flighted by the ground technicians of No 1 Squadron RRAF in Aden.

Flying Officers Peter Cooke and Johnny Johnson welcome in the jet age to Thornhill. In 1961, Peter Cooke was the most qualified air traffic controller in the country.

Nine Vamps in three 'Vics' fly over a parade.

Six Vampires of No1 Squadron view the world from a different perspective as they relax the pressure over the top of a loop. Formation aerobatics was new to most of the air force pilots and manoeuvres were only done in the looping plane. They might have progressed to the rolling plane had there not been a fatal accident during one of the practices. Formation aerobatics was discontinued soon afterwards much to the chagrin of the pilots.

During the Nyasaland emergency in March 1959, the aircraft were stationed at Fort Hill in the north of Nyasaland. It was here that the Nyasaland disturbances first began when rioters roughly handled the woman radio operator. Three Provosts and a Dakota are on stand-by. There appears to be no shortage of fuel.

A Pembroke and three Provosts await orders at Fort Hill during the Nyasaland emergency.

Engine failure after take off was the cause of this accident at Fort Hill on 12th July 1959. The Dakota was dismantled by the technicians and transported by road back to New Sarum. The fuselage just managed to squeeze between the girders of the bridge over the Kafue River north of Chirundu.

Canberra number RRAF 165 shows its immense wing area as it arrives overhead New Sarum on completion of the ferry flight from the UK. The large wing (thus low wing loading) made it almost impervious to interception at high altitude, but extremely uncomfortable in the bumps at low level. The Canberras were to prove invaluable in both the operational and the photo recce/mapping roles.

The first Canberra lands at New Sarum on 12th March 1959 and disgorges all the crew's baggage.

Top right and above: AVM Ted Jacklin explains the cockpit to Sir Roy Welensky while Lord Dalhousie and Gp Capt Harold Hawkins show an interest in the power plant. The Federal roundel with the three assegais is prominent on the fuselage.

Lord Dalhousie chats informally with the pilot, Jerry Dunn, and navigator, Roy Wellington, as Harold Hawkins and Sir Roy Welensky approach.

The largest aircraft operated by the air force was the Canadair DC-4 M purchased from BOAC. Two of them stand at New Sarum with the fleet of Dakotas lined up near the main runway.

The installation of the Precision Approach Radar (PAR) at Thornhill was a blessing to the pilots as they could now fly when the *guti* (local mist) rolled in. Many an aircraft and possibly a few lives were saved as a result of this innovation. The checkered pattern on the shack was a warning to aircraft (a large obstruction) and to personnel (danger from micro-waves).

One of the Rhodesian Canberras taxies out at Akrotiri, Cyprus, throwing up clouds of dust with the jet blast from its Avon engines ...

The 'engine room' on the Canadair sported four Rolls-Royce Merlins.

... and gets airborne.

The RAF Air Vice-Marshal greets Charlie Paxton on arrival in Cyprus in 1959.

Three RRAF Vampire FB 9s at Aden in the presence of two RAF Meteors and an RAF Valetta, having its engines seen to.

Three Canadairs DC-4 Ms in formation. All four of the Canadairs were put up for sale in 1964 and were purchased by Air Links, UK.

Six Canberras fly over Glamis Stadium, timed perfectly with the 21-gun salute, on the occasion of the Queen's Birthday in 1960.

Katangese refugees glad to be in a safe haven after having been flown out of the Congo in an RRAF Dakota in 1960.

Katangese refugees leave the Dakota and walk past a Canadair about to take off for Northern Rhodesia.

A thirsty Canberra is refuelled by two bowsers at Aktotiri, Cyprus.

AVM Ted Jacklin followed by Gp Capt Harold Hawkins and their wives arrive at Thornhill for his farewell parade, June 1961. The two other officers are Flt Lt Bill Smith, ADC to the chief of staff, and Wg Cdr John Moss.

The Air Congo Dakota was hijacked by members of No 6 Commando and flown out of the Congo to Rhodesia. The aircraft landed at Kariba en route to Salisbury.

... have their cargo slinging capability tested by lifting a Mini Moke ...

The first eight Alouette IIIs arrive from France in a UAT DC 6 in 1962 ...

... are assembled in the No 7 Squadron hangar ...

... given full air tests ...

... and are finally lined up on parade with their crews, in front of No 7 Squadron for inspection. The squadron was operational by the end of 1962.

One of the first requirements was trooping drills; there were six soldiers per helicopter initially, but this changed to five, and then four when the men were fully armed and machine guns were installed in the helicopter.

Left: A PR exercise: the RLI deploys with Alouette III G-Cars.

Below left: A dog and his handler are dropped to look for tracks (a much later photo as the Alouette has anti-Strela shrouds fitted).

Bottom left: The first of two Hawker Hunter FGA 9s to land in Rhodesia taxies into dispersal at New Sarum, 20th December 1962 and (bottom right) is welcomed by Sir Roy Welensky, and OC Flying, Wing Commander Dicky Bradshaw. They were flown by Flight Lieutenants Frank Gait-Smith (above) and Mike Saunders. Their arrival over Salisbury at low level and high speed was "memorable".

Two Vampire FB 9s taxi out at Thornhill on a training flight, June 1961.

Above right: Four Hawker Hunters of No 8 Squadron RAF on a visit to Rhodesia, fly over Salisbury in July 1960. The photograph was taken from an RRAF Vampire T 11.

Left: A team that was to last right through to 1980—Canberra, Hunters and Vampire T 11 over Kyle Dam.

Below right: The Eastern Bombing Quadrant Tower at Kutanga Range near Que Que was the ideal vantage point from which to view weapons demonstrations. A Dakota of No 3 Squadron carries out a supply drop for the benefit of senior army and police spectators.

The Canadair carrying Lord Dalhousie is escorted out of the Federation by two Vampire T 11s and four FB 9s of No 2 Squadron.

A close-up view of the Cross formation that flew over the Anglican Cathedral in Salisbury on Battle of Britain Sunday, 15th September 1963.

An RAF Vickers Valiant in Salisbury, mapping the colony in 1964 when relations between Britain and Rhodesia were still good. There were serious considerations of building a base for the V-Bomber force between Bromley and Marandellas.

No 7 Squadron arrive at Fort Victoria on 6th June 1964 to take part in celebrations to mark their affiliation to that famous town. Eight Alouettes were met by the Mayor, Councillor O.C. George. Air Cdre Hawkins and Gp Capt Wilson took the opportunity to accompany the squadron.

The townsfolk of the beautiful Eastern Highlands city of Umtali honour the 4th Battalion Royal Rhodesia Regiment with the Freedom of the City. A Trojan of No 4 Squadron leads the aerial parade with four Provosts on its wings. No 4 Squadron was of course affiliated to Umtali.

The Oberholzer murders on 6th July 1964 affected the whole population and over 100 police and soldiers were called out on an extensive manhunt for the killers. The No 7 Squadron helicopter re-supplied the units in the field and uplifted SB officers to numerous kraals in the Melsetter and Nyanyadzi areas.

Alouette number 501 (5701) is salvaged from Lake MacIlwaine after an incident in which the crew inadvertently landed in the lake during an approach to Dassie island. The purpose of the exercise was to determine the feasibility of hovering over water at night! This same helicopter was also involved in an accident at Macheke School when the pilot encountered vortex ring conditions and crashed on the sports field. It was rebuilt after both accidents and was finally written off in a mid-air collision with another Alouette on fireforce operations.

Flt Lt Bill (Wally) Galloway shows a student the intricacies of the cockpit of a No 2 Squadron Vampire T 11. 1965.

"Clear to hoist," indicates the technician after he has been deposited on rock by an Alouette III during a training sortie. The pilot will return to uplift him.

In preparation for possible counter-insurgency, a Forward Air Support Operations Centre (FASOC) is set up to train members of the VR.

The dark clouds were perhaps a portent of things to come.

The Canberra tailplane area is much the same as that of a Hunter mainplane. The huge rudder surface is required to counteract the asymmetric effect of flying on one engine, either intentionally or in the case of an engine failure.

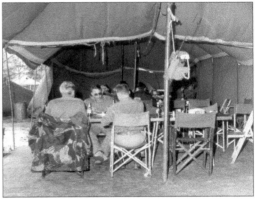

Tented accommodation was adequate although the metal canvas chairs tended to be more functional than comfortable. One could never get one's legs under them.

Absolute tranquility—seven Canberras in echelon flying above the clouds on a lazy afternoon. Not so for the pilots, however, who will be shedding gallons of sweat to maintain their station.

Wankie National Park—Main Camp airfield. On their final Alouette III conversion cross-country, Sqn. Ldr Norman Walsh and Flt Lt Petter-Bowyer happened upon a friendly lion cub belonging to a game ranger.

With thunderheads billowing beneath and surrounded by lines of cumulonimbus, the formation of Canberras, in this immaculate photograph, would do well to stay in clear air on a potentially stormy summer afternoon high above Rhodesia.

The Beechcraft Baron served the air force well. It was considered to be the prime minister's personal aircraft, but Ian Smith's wishes to visit the forward areas was to be served better by the Islander which could land at more rugged airfields.

Purchased under conditions of severe sanctions, the Trojans were the most maligned aircraft in the history of the force. They not only bore their burdens with stoic calm, but also proved to be workhorses of immeasurable value. They flew more than 35,000 hours. This Trojan displays its white 'T' painted on the upper surface, which indicated the direction of the target to the strike aircraft. It was easily visible from the higher-flying jets. The Provost looks on.

The Trojans were expertly packed in crates that made assembly ridiculously easy. Hardly had the crates touched the hangar floor when the aircraft were flying.

Police Reserve members on exercise watch an Alouette III get airborne in the Mazoe area. 1969.

An SAP Cessna 185 numbered 104, code-named Kiewiet, stands alone at the old Mtoko airfield. These aircraft were later, sensibly, painted in camouflage. 1967. They were used mainly for courier duties in the early years of the Bush War.

CHAPTER 35

Operation Cauldron

The most northerly point of Rhodesia is that area where the Chewore River joins the Zambezi. To the north, on the far side of a wide stretch of sandbanks and grey water, lies Zambia, while to the east, roughly 35 kilometres away, is the border of Mozambique. This wild desolate region, a place of dense thorn bush, was largely uninhabited by humans but heavily populated by wild animals, particularly elephant, rhinoceros and buffalo. In the area between the Chewore and the confluence of the Luangwa and the Zambezi, the animals reigned supreme, within the protection of the Chewore Game Reserve.

Down in the valley, the temperature is high all the year round and the thorn bush, though thick, gives the impression most of the year of being dry and lifeless, presenting a haze of grey branches. Underfoot, the ground is arid and bare with little grass. During the heat of the day the bush is silent, only awakening as the white-hot sun drops to the horizon. At night, there is a cacophony of grunts, roars, squeals and squeaks. Here there is no twilight. The sun sinks so rapidly that sunset to dark is a matter of minutes. But the nights are a glorious black velvet, lit by a myriad of bright stars or the great silver disc of the moon.

It was here in this desolate but strangely beautiful land, north of the rich farming areas of Sipolilo and Centenary that the RRAF fought an engagement in which Flight Lieutenant Mark McLean won the first Bronze Cross awarded to an airman.

The operation, code-named Cauldron took place in March 1968 but to set the story it is necessary to go back to 1967. During August of that year, Operation Nickel was mounted when a large group of the banned ZAPU party, together with members of the South African ANC had attempted to infiltrate Rhodesia. Their plan was to enter through the Wankie Game Reserve, to pass through Botswana and continue into South Africa. This large-scale incursion failed utterly so the African nationalist leaders decided to make another attempt, this time further east, through the Chewore area.

Six months were spent in detailed planning and a large number of men, many of whom had been trained in Cuba, Algeria or Russia, were selected from bases in Tanzania and moved into Zambia, where two camps were established. One was at a disused mine some distance from the Zambezi, the other only six kilometres from the confluence of the Zambezi and the Chewore. The plan was to cross the Zambezi River in the Chewore area, move down the valley and cross the escarpment into the farming areas of Sipolilo, Centenary and Mount Darwin, setting up bases and building alliances among the local people. Success here would give the insurgents strong backing for a swift move south towards the capital city, Salisbury.

In December 1967, a reconnaissance party crossed the river and infiltrated about nine kilometres where they found a suitable site for a base camp. By the middle of December, the combatants were moving across the river in considerable numbers but heavy seasonal rain brought the river down in flood and the men experienced some difficulty in bringing up supplies.

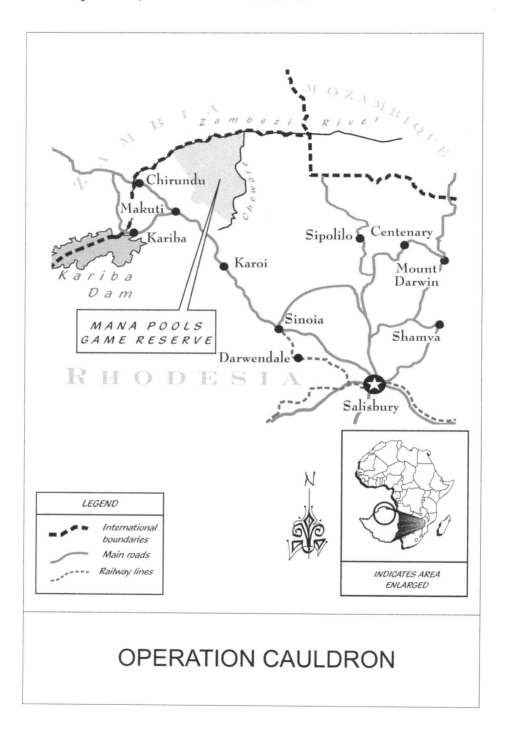

OPERATION CAULDRON

Having established Camp 1, which was to be the initial receiving station, the ZAPU cadre moved further south and set up a more permanent base, Camp 2. This covered a largish area and was fully fortified with a network of trenches and strong points. It was capable of housing over 100 men. During the next three months, the ZAPU forces consolidated their position, moving deeper and deeper into Rhodesia and establishing Camps 3, 4 and 5. Camp 4 was sited in a strategic position on the summit of a flat-topped mountain, which gave excellent all-round visibility. During this period, their movements had gone unnoticed. They had been extremely careful not to give themselves away to any European who might be in the area, nor had they made any effort to contact the local black villagers. They did, however, make one basic error. Because of supply problems, they often ran short of meat and so they got into the habit of shooting game for the pot. It was later estimated that between 21st January and 12th March they killed 105 animals, including elephant, rhino and buffalo. This, in a game reserve where shooting was normally only carried out by the National Parks staff, had a marked effect on game distribution and was noticed by the game warden when he carried out his regular patrols. It puzzled him. Then he came across unusual footprints, which he and his African game guards tracked for six hours. Increasingly there were signs of human traffic and it was estimated that at least 40 men had passed through the area during the previous few days. The game warden radioed the information back to base and within 24 hours, police and army patrols were on the scene. Obviously a serious situation had developed, with a strong, heavily armed, well-trained group somewhere in the area. The security forces swung into action. On March 15th 1968, the RRAF was placed on stand-by.

16th March. Cyril White and Brian Penton flew a tracking team of SAS to Karoi and later in the day set up a FAF (forward airfield) at Karoi. By 18h30, Chris Weinmann and Tony Smit were also at Karoi with two armed Provosts.
17th March. Recces carried out. (No 4 Squadron Diary)

It was on the morning of the following day, 18th March, that the first contact was made with the enemy. This occurred in the Mana Pools area. A small patrol of 13 troopers of 1st Battalion, Rhodesian Light Infantry (RLI) and members of 1st the Battalion Rhodesian African Rifles (RAR) were following tracks when they ran into a group of 14 ZAPU soldiers. An engagement ensued.

18th March. Provost was called in to a contact of eleven CTs (communist terrorists) and carried out a strike. Total killed during the engagement was eleven and one security force. During the afternoon, another contact was made and Provost, Vampire and Canberras were called in to strike at an estimated 100 CTs.

During a follow-up, members of the RLI and RAR came under fire, at close range, from a well-armed group of over 60 men. The security forces had stumbled on Camp 5. The small army unit was pinned down in open ground by concentrated fire from rifles and machine-guns. At the beginning of this contact, the only air support available was an unarmed Trojan, carrying out reconnaissance. Second Lieutenant Pearce, the commander of the army unit, called this aircraft up and requested air support, so that he could pull his men back.

Mark McLean, piloting a helicopter, answered the Trojan's call. Despite the fact that the two forces were uncomfortably close to each other, Mark mounted several attacks on the enemy position. Each attack was met by heavy automatic fire. These strafing runs enabled Second Lieutenant Chris (Dumpy) Pearce to pull his men back to safer positions.

Following this initial contact, Mark remained in the area flying low over the enemy position to mark it with smoke grenades, drawing heavy ground fire onto his aircraft. He stayed in orbit to direct air strikes, which were carried out by No 2 Squadron Vampires flown by Squadron Leader Bill Jelley and Flying Officer Prop Geldenhuys using squash head rocket projectiles and 20mm cannon. This was the first occasion that No 2 Squadron had fired a shot in anger and after years of training and innumerable stand-bys, the squadron was glad to have been blooded.

A Canberra from No 5 Squadron, piloted by John Rogers, also took part in the strike, using fragmentation bombs. This had a less happy conclusion because, owing to a misunderstanding, some bombs were dropped on security force positions, causing injury to two soldiers. As a result of this, the squadron's technique for fragmentation bombing attacks was changed from medium to low level.

While the battle was still in progress, Mark McLean and his technician, Sergeant Richard (Butch) Graydon, were called upon to evacuate five badly wounded men. The landing zone was close to the enemy position, which meant that considerable skill and courage were needed on the part of the helicopter crew. Having completed the evacuation, McLean returned to the contact area and gave valuable assistance to the ground forces, acting as their eye in the sky until darkness fell. For this operation, Flight Lieutenant McLean was awarded the Bronze Cross of Rhodesia.

When the ground forces were finally able to move into the enemy camp, no bodies were found, although the area had been torn by bombs, and the trees were stained with blood. The dead and wounded had obviously been removed. After this attack the insurgents broke up into smaller groups, some making their way back along the line of bases towards the Zambezi, others continuing south into the Sipolilo area. Among the second group was the operation commander Hadebe, an Ndebele who was later captured in Mozambique.

The air force squadrons stood by for another two weeks but were not called upon to take any further action. However, towards the end of the month, No 3 Squadron did make leaflet drops into the operational area calling on the remaining ZAPU members to give themselves up or die. The four-page leaflet was in English and Shona and carried the photographs of two men, one dead because he resisted, and the other alive because he surrendered. Of the 58 combatants killed in the various actions, which were part of Operation Cauldron, 43 were members of ZAPU and 15 belonged to the SAANC (South African African National Congress).

The operation was terminated towards the end of May 1968 and the helicopters of No 7 Squadron and the Trojans of No 4 Squadron reverted to border patrol duties. There was one stand-by at the end of May when a group consisting of members of the SAPAC (South African Pan African Congress) and a Mozambique nationalist organization skirted the eastern border, but did not enter Rhodesian territory. Four of these men were killed and ten captured, for the loss of three Portuguese soldiers, near Vila Pery in the Chimoio Province of Mozambique.

A memory of the early days of flying in Central Africa was revived in March, when representatives of the South African government and the SAAF attended the funeral, in Umtali, of Sir Quintin Brand, the pioneer airman. It had been 48 years earlier, in March 1920, that Christopher Quintin Brand and Pierre van Ryneveld landed their aircraft, the *Silver Queen* on the Bulawayo racecourse and so became the first airmen to visit Rhodesia. Sir Quintin Brand died at his home, Quo Vadis, and was buried in Umtali. The funeral was attended by his nephew, Flight Lieutenant Rich Brand, a member of No 1 Squadron RRAF, and also by members of No 104 (Umtali) Squadron of the volunteer reserve.

No 7 Squadron wins the Jacklin Trophy

With an average of one casualty evacuation a week, the crews of No 7 Squadron, which had recently won the coveted Jacklin Trophy for the second time, were getting plenty of experience in carrying out mercy operations. In every case, speed of reaction was vital and crews could be airborne within 30 minutes of an alert, complete with stretchers, blood plasma and medical kit.

In April, the squadron was called out to a mountain rescue when a Marandellas High School teacher, Anthony Stone, fell 100 feet (30m) while climbing in the Chimanimani Mountains. He was one of a party carrying out a week's exploration from a base at the Outward Bound Mountain School. He was taking photographs near Martin's Falls when the accident occurred. A physical training mistress, Glenda Flanagan, a pupil, Susan Lane and four school boys stayed on the mountain above the injured man, while two boys from the party walked 18 miles (28km) through very rough country to fetch help from the Outward Bound Mountain School. It was 16h30 on Sunday when the two boys, John Hansen and Peter Roberts, reached the school. Bill Bailey (ex-LRDG and PATU founder), the warden, organized a rescue team, composed of a police patrol officer and a local farmer, Sidney Gregory, and they left for the scene of the accident taking mountain rescue gear.

At the same time, a call was made to air force headquarters and a helicopter was dispatched from New Sarum. Thick mist kept the machine grounded in the Chimanimani area until late the following morning, 21st April. When the Alouette eventually reached the Martin's Falls area, the teacher was found lying dead on a ledge of the rock face.

No 3 Squadron comes of age

In May 1968, No 3 Transport Squadron came of age. During its 21 years of service, it had carried 1,000,000 pounds (453,600kg) of freight and several thousand passengers. "Not one passenger has been 'damaged in transit' despite often by no means ideal conditions." (No 3 Squadron History)

The squadron, at this date, operated eight Dakotas, one Beech Baron and one Trojan. These aircraft were flown by 12 regular pilots and six volunteer reserve co-pilots, under the command of Squadron Leader Peter Barnett. The squadron's role had grown, adding Paratroop Operations, Tactical Air Support, Casualty Evacuation, Air Search and Rescue, and Sky Shouting to the original roles of transport and carriage of VIPs.

No 3 Squadron was not alone in adapting to new roles in changing circumstances. Towards the middle of the year, the Rhodesian Breweries added canned water to their list of products. The water, contained in normal 12-ounce (340g) beer cans was intended for the use of troops in the Zambezi Valley. Commenting on the report, the CO 1RLI, Colonel Reg Edwards, said: "Water containers dropped by air, burst open and attempts to drop blocks of ice have also been unsuccessful. We feel the cans may be the answer. We will be carrying out various types of drops to see how they stand up. No doubt the troopies would rather have had the real thing! (Some troopies were known to swap these cans for cold ones at unsuspecting hotels or bars!)"

It was during Operation Cauldron that trials had been carried out on ice drops. Providing the ice was securely wrapped in sacking, there was not a problem. The troopies on the ground received chipped ice that they could put in their water bottles. The biggest problem was having the ice available and packed at the forward airfields.

Operations Griffin, Mansion, Excess and Gravel

During July 1968, to coincide with President Kaunda's visit to Britain and his request for missiles to defend Zambian air space, a concerted effort was made to infiltrate Rhodesia. The code-names given to these incidents were Operation Griffin, Operation Mansion, Operation Excess and Operation Gravel.

Three groups of ZAPU followers and one of ZANU crossed the Zambezi at different points. The ZANU party, numbering 16, crossed the river just above the point where it enters Lake Kariba. Two Batonka fishermen living on the Zambian side of the river were pressed into service as guides and porters. One of the Batonka was captured by the security forces and revealed useful information. Within 48 hours of their crossing the river, four members of the group were killed and the remainder captured.

The ZAPU contingent was a much larger force. It consisted of 91 men divided into three parties. One crossed at the point where the Gwaai River enters the Zambezi in Matabeleland, the second crossed the Zambezi in the Chirundu area and the third in the region of the Chewore junction.

The first group was dealt with by the South African Police, and all but one was killed or captured. The second group was stopped close to the Zambezi and all but one accounted for. The third, numbering about 30 men, was heading for Mount Darwin when the security forces made contact on 18th July 1968.

Operation Griffin
The ZAPU cadre had established itself in a deep gorge and engaged the security forces at close range with heavy fire from rifles, machine-guns and bazookas. Twelve Troop 1st Battalion RLI, commanded by Second Lieutenant Jeremy Strong, approaching along a gully, was pinned down by the weight of fire.

The air force was called in to support the ground forces and Squadron Leader Norman Walsh, flying an Alouette was given the task of deploying troops in the surrounding mountainous country. Having accomplished this, despite the difficult terrain and heavy fire, he then succeeded in manœuvring his helicopter into a position from which he could engage the enemy. His gunner, Sergeant Kevin (Tinker) Smithdorf, directed fire onto the enemy position even though heavy automatic fire was coming from close range on the ground. This action enabled the troops on the ground to withdraw to a better position. By then, a second helicopter, piloted by Flight Lieutenant Pete Nicholls with Sergeant T.J. van den Berg, had arrived on the scene. Flying low over the enemy position, Sergeant van den Berg directed accurate fire onto the ZAPU positions. Both helicopters were hit by enemy ground fire and Pete Nicholls was forced to return to base.

Meanwhile there were casualties among the RLI troops and Walsh was requested to evacuate a wounded troopie from the contact area. This proved an extremely hazardous operation as fighting was still in progress. The only possible landing zone was close to the enemy position and his helicopter was hit by ground fire as he was carrying out the casevac. Having completed the evacuation, Norman Walsh returned to the contact area and directed further air strikes, which were carried out by two Provosts, flown by Air Lieutenant Ken Law and Flight Lieutenant Tony van Rooyen-Smit. The nature of the terrain imposed severe restrictions on the Provost attack pattern, while the proximity of the enemy forced the pilots to release their weapons over the heads of the security force personnel. Norman Walsh, with Lieutenant Colonel Robert William Southey aboard, succeeded in pin-pointing the enemy position with such accuracy that the Provosts were able to carry out a successful strike inflicting many casualties.

That night, at about 22h00, two helicopters flown by Squadron Leader Mick Grier and Flight Lieutenant Pete Nicholls, were tasked to carry out a casualty evacuation. It was a difficult operation because the serious condition of the wounded meant that Mick's Alouette had to be flown into a narrow ravine, to land in a small LZ on a steep slope in the dark. Added to this, it was possible that the enemy would commence firing during the evacuation. In the event, the operation was carried out without loss.

No 2 Squadron was scrambled for an air strike on that same day, 18th July, but owing to fading light and the proximity of the security forces to the enemy positions no weapons were fired. However, on 20th July, the squadron had more success when squash head rocket projectiles and 20mm cannons were used at the junction of Zambezi and the Gwaai Rivers. The Hunters also took part in this operation.

The Trojans of No 4 Squadron had by now been converted into combat aircraft by the fitment of Matra rocket pods. This armament was initially used during Operation Gravel, by Pilot Officer Brian Phillips and resulted in two enemy dead and 13 wounded. The Trojan was hit five times by ground fire. Morale, which at this stage was badly lacking, especially amongst the junior pilots, went rocketing upwards. (No 4 Squadron Diary)

Operation Mansion
Despite the rude remarks, the Trojan was now given yet another role, that of airborne Forward Aircraft Control (FAC), an Eye in the Sky technique for spotting and directing the fire for faster aircraft. This proved highly successful during Operation Mansion, when a Trojan directed the Hunters and the Vampires on to a target on the south bank of the Zambezi.

This operation began when tracks were found on the north bank of the Gwaai River. Just before the Gwaai joins the Zambezi in Devil's Gorge, it flows parallel to the Zambezi for a few kilometres forming a peninsular of high ground with a flat top. Troops started tracking the spoor. Peter Cooke taking up the story says:

I was airborne on a recce and telstar (radio relay), and arrived over the area to find that our troops had followed the tracks up the southern side of the peninsular and across the top. As they started down the northern side, they came under fire. The sides were steep, sloping down towards the Zambezi and the area was strewn with large boulders that offered good cover. It became clear that the situation was a stalemate. I had no weapons but continued to orbit and called up Don Brenchley who was commanding the FASOC and suggested he request Thornhill for a heavy strike. In no time Vampires, Hunters and a Canberra were on the scene. An Alouette piloted by Mark McLean also arrived. I talked the strike aircraft onto the target giving them a full description of what they would see as they ran in for their attack. Mark was able to point out the position of the enemy by firing his MAG into the river close to their hiding places. After the pair of Vampires had exhausted their ammo, the Hunters went in, then the Canberra, which dropped a full bomb load. Our troops then moved down into the terrorists' positions and found that most of them had made good their escape. The large boulders had given them protection from the bombs. The stragglers were soon rounded up.

No 4 Squadron was triumphant.

The Trojan is coming into a field of its own. Its potential is beginning to be realized by all. However, it is still the butt of many jokes in the bar, i.e. 'If the Trojan flies past the drive-in cinema at normal cruising speed the pilot can watch the shorts; if it flies past just off stalling, the whole feature can be seen'. 'The birds are complaining of Trojan strikes'. These jokes, however, are no longer heavy with sarcasm and one can detect just a twinge of envy in the voices of the steely-eyed killers! (i.e. the Hunter and Vampire pilots) (No 4 Squadron Diary)

Other comments about the Trog that had been heard before Operation Mansion were: "The Trojans only get airborne because of the curvature of the earth", "They convert Avgas to noise", "The engines have one piston working and the other five clapping".

Incidentally, a point that was demonstrated yet again during Operation Mansion, was that men on the ground can survive heavy bombing if they have suitable cover, such as rocky outcrops, the ruins of buildings or dugouts. In this case, after the strike, when the area was cleared by police with dogs, some of the insurgents were found still alive, albeit rather shaken. During the following years, this was to be proved over and over again.

By the end of August 1968, 38 insurgents had been killed or captured. In fact, of the whole party of 91, only eleven survived and they presumably made their way back to Zambia. Morale among ZANU and ZAPU reached a low ebb and no further incursions were made for nearly 18 months.

As far as the air force was concerned, several awards were presented for its part in Operation Griffin*. Squadron Leader Norman Walsh received the Bronze Cross of Rhodesia, Squadron Leader Mick Grier, Flight Lieutenants Pete Nicholls and Tony van Rooyen-Smit, Air Lieutenant Ken Law, Sergeants T.J. van den Berg, Tinker Smithdorf and Butch Graydon were all awarded the Military Forces Commendation (Operational). This action probably resulted in more decorations for the air force than any other operation. These were among the first Rhodesian decorations, distinct from the Federal Awards and were made in October 1970. Incidentally, the gorge in which the action took place became known as Griffin's Gorge. Security force casualties were a South African policeman, Constable du Toit, killed and three South Africans and two Rhodesians wounded.

Commenting on these operations Mr James Spink, Commissioner of Police, said that a close bond had been created between the BSAP, the Rhodesian army and the RRAF. "At all levels the comradeship and cooperation among members of the three services is excellent." This view was reiterated by Air Vice-Marshal Bentley at the passing out parade of No 21 Pilot Training Course at Thornhill on 1st August 1968. On the whole, this cooperation was to continue throughout the period of the Bush War despite inter-service rivalry and some lack of coordination among units later in the campaign. The unwritten definition of a JOC (Joint Operations Centre) was Reasonable men acting in reasonable cooperation with one another.

In August 1968, school cadet organizations were disbanded. The Ministry of Defence had decided that all available personnel and funds should be channelled into more important military priorities. Included in this disbandment were the Air and Sea Cadets that had been operating on a trial basis since March 1965 at two Salisbury schools, Churchill and Prince Edward. However, as one branch of the service was closing down, another was expanding. In August, two new VRs joined No 3 Squadron. One was David Barbour who had been a member of No 1 Squadron Southern Rhodesia Auxiliary Air Force, and who had taken part in the Spitfire Ferry in 1952. The other was John Akester, who was RAF-trained and worked in Salisbury as a commercial photographer.

Vital help from South Africa

Cooperation between Rhodesia and South Africa was growing stronger. In October 1968, Air Vice-Marshal Harold Hawkins officially received, on behalf of the RRAF, a hydraulic self-loading truck, seven high-powered radio transmitters and three gas refrigerators from branches of the Friends of Rhodesia Association in Johannesburg, East London and Richmond in Natal. Harold Hawkins, thanking the donors, said that the loader would fill a gap in the RRAF's armoury and the transmitters had a vital role to play in modern warfare. These gifts were only the start of a regular flow of such presents from the generous people of South Africa.

HMS *Fearless* and the air force radio section

While it appeared to the man in the street that the break between Britain and Rhodesia was

---

* No awards were made for Operation Mansion.

complete, negotiations were continuing in secret. On 9th October 1968, came the surprise announcement that the Rhodesian prime minister and his team had departed, the previous evening, aboard an RAF Britannia aircraft to meet the British Prime Minister, Harold Wilson, on board HMS *Fearless* off Gibraltar. Both sides were anxious to reach a settlement but still the differences were too great and negotiations failed.

One interesting fact about the talks held on HMS *Fearless* and the earlier negotiations aboard HMS *Tiger* was that the Rhodesian Air Force Radio Section in cooperation with the Royal Navy provided the highly efficient radio link between Salisbury and the ships in the Mediterranean area. So efficient was the service that it took the British experts by surprise and it is on record that a senior Royal Navy officer used the system to send a message to his relatives in Salisbury and received a reply within an hour. The first radio tradesmen had been recruited into the air force in 1948 and their duties consisted of maintaining and operating air traffic control radio. By 1952, the complement was four wireless mechanics and one signaller/air traffic controller. The radio system was still very local. Soon afterwards came the move from Cranborne to New Sarum and an expansion into the field of ground-to-ground communications and the beginnings of air or ground radio specialization. In 1959, there was a further expansion with the need for radio-equipped general security vehicles.

From then on the demands placed on the radio tradesmen and the widening scope of their activities resulted in a steady increase in complement and a crystallization into definite air and ground divisions. By 1968, Ground Radio Equipment provided worldwide communication but was usually confined to the local sphere and consisted of maintaining and operating voice, CW and radio teleprinter contact with units round the country.

Vampire crash

In November 1968, No 6 Squadron lost its first aircraft, when Flight Lieutenant John Barnes and Flying Officer Guy Munton-Jackson ejected from a Vampire, following a fire warning. The aircraft crashed close to the Gwelo/Selukwe road. Squadron Leader Peter Cooke who was on a routine training sortie flew to the scene. Having confirmed that both men had ejected safely, he guided the Crash Rescue vehicles to the area.

No 3 Squadron begins 'rain making'

With the start of the rainy season, No 3 Squadron began rain-making trials. The background to these activities, which were to last four years, was related by Squadron Leader Len Pink:

> *A benefactor actually donated a substantial amount of money to the university to investigate the feasibility of cloud-seeding. No 3 Squadron carried out the trials in conjunction with the university, the Met department and the Central Statistical Department, so the results were verifiable from a statistical point of view. The man who was running it from the Met Department visited Australia because they were quite 'heavily' into the cloud-seeding scene and he wanted to see how they were handling the project.* (Pink)

The chief of Air Staff in consultation with the Ministry of Defence agreed to make an aircraft available for the project and government funds were allocated. A committee to coordinate the Cloud-seeding Experiments (CoCCSE) was set up to control the project, which was code-named Operation Tarpaulin.

> *There are a couple of ways in which you can do cloud-seeding. You can use dry ice, which the Russians and the Indians have used or you could do it the way we did it—burning silver iodide.* (Pink)

The technical problems were considerable. They involved manufacturing measuring instruments from scratch as well as carrying out major modifications to the aircraft. The extent of the task meant that the equipment would have to be fitted semi-permanently, and so a Dakota, 7307, christened Chaminuka, was chosen for the job and handed over for modification. Chaminuka was a Shona spirit medium who was reputed to have been a highly successful rainmaker.

The burner system consisted of two streamlined pods, into which the silver iodide/acetone mixture was pumped, atomized and mixed with air before being ignited. The pods were mounted on pylons, which were fitted on each side of the rear fuselage. The resulting smoke consisted of numerous tiny particles with a shape similar to snow flakes. These formed the freezing nuclei. The burners were fed from a 14-gallon (63.5-litre) reservoir tank inside the aircraft.

So what you actually do is create additional nuclei in the cloud, which is the way a cloud builds up. The water droplets coalesce into big drops. This starts the chain going and the drops increase until the cloud can't hold them and it rains. There were quite a few parameters: the cloud had to be formed before you did it; the temperature had to be minus 11° centigrade and the cloud top had to be above 10,000 feet. (Pink)

In order to obtain reliable statistics about the results of cloud-seeding, the statisticians had worked out a system to randomize the seeding operation. Once the pilot had picked a suitable cloud, he opened a sealed envelope, which contained the instruction to seed or not to seed. Finally the seeding was only done in areas where a wide network of rain gauges had been set up in conjunction with the Ministry of Agriculture, so that an accurate measurement could be obtained of how much rain actually fell to the ground.

Then we also designed two things in the aeroplane. We used an old camera with a serrated drum that revolved. We passed tinfoil over this drum. When we opened the aperture, the rain impacted on it. The statisticians could work out the size of the droplets because they made an indentation. They could count the number and the size of the water droplets and from this they could estimate how much it was raining. We also set up a gadget that caught the rain through a funnel arrangement on top of the Dakota. So, with the three ways of measuring, one on the ground and two in the air, they were able to determine whether there had been any significant increase. Over all, the results were very satisfactory. Subsequently, cloud-seeding was taken over as a commercial project. (Pink 67/68 Ndege)

Remarking on cloud-seeding activities, No 3 Squadron VR pilot George Walker-Smith stated:

We did three years of it. I did dozens of flights. We used to measure the height of the cumulus cloud and fly in one third of the way up above the base, fly through the cloud, open burners and come out the other side. Then close burners. One day, during a very dry season, we flew down this line of cumulus and when we got to the end, another line had built up about 10 – 20 miles (16 – 32km) away. And so we decided we would come back that way. As we came out of these clouds, we could see where we had flown originally. The first cloud was raining heavily. The next one slightly, the third one was just starting to rain. By the time we had finished, the whole lot were raining. That gave us a kick. It was one of the few times I was quite certain we were responsible. But I must say we were glad when they said we would not be doing cloud-seeding any more. It was a most unpleasant job because the turbulence was enormous. It could break off a wing and mess up the engine. Also you could get instant icing. Then the whole aircraft was suddenly a mass of ice. That happened to one Dakota. The only thing then is to get down to a lower, warmer altitude and melt it off. (George Walker-Smith)

New flag and roundel

On Monday 11th November 1968, Rhodesia's new flag was raised for the first time. However, it was announced in the *Rhodesia Herald* that:

> *The red, white and blue Royal Air Force roundel with a single silver and gold assegai, is to remain the official marking of the RRAF despite the change of national colours to green and white. The RRAF sky blue ensign with a quartering of the Union Jack on which the old Rhodesian flag was modelled, will continue to fly at RRAF headquarters, Milton Buildings in Salisbury.* (Rhodesia Herald, 11th Nov. 1968)

The article went on to give the history of the RRAF roundel, which had originated from the RAF roundel adopted by the Royal Flying Corps early in World War I. It had been discovered that the Union Jack painted on RFC aircraft wings looked too similar to the German black crosses in combat. French aircraft also adopted the blue, white and red roundel, making all allied aircraft easily identifiable. In later years, Commonwealth air forces varied the roundel by changing the centre spot to a red maple leaf, kangaroo or springbok. In Federal days, RRAF aircraft bore three assegais over the basic RAF roundel. In 1964, this was changed to the single upright assegai through the centre of the roundel.

Mozambique 1969

In March 1968, Frelimo (Front for the Liberation of Mozambique) had opened up operations in Tete. The Mozambique government requested help to police this vast area that lies between the borders of Zambia, Malawi and Rhodesia. Early in 1969, SAS teams began to operate in Mozambique but their presence was top secret. Commenting on the problems of working in this inhospitable region, Ken Flower in his book, *Serving Secretly*, says:

> *I recalled how, in January 1969, he (Kaulza de Arriaga, commander in chief in Mozambique) had seen for himself how our soldiers lived rough and tough in the worst of the Zambezi Valley for weeks on end, in contrast to the metropolitan Portuguese soldiers in Mozambique who rarely moved from their base or transport and remained dependent on supplies of bread and wine. I had heard Costa Gomes say to his military attaché: "But do the Rhodesians really expect us to follow their example, living like animals in the African bush merely to confront guerrillas?" The attaché replied: "No, senhor. It is the example that is quite magnificent, and it suits the Rhodesians who are Anglo-Saxons, but they don't really expect that sort of behaviour from us Latins!"*

Commenting on the same subject Peter Briscoe says:

> *The Portuguese army was an army of conscripts who had been hauled out of their native land to spend two years fighting an enemy they did not know, in a country they did not care about. They were poorly trained, poorly equipped and had abysmal leadership. The rank structure was based purely on class—the rich were the officers, the poor were the troops. They all spent their two years trying to survive—in order to return to metropolitan Portugal. Early in 1969 four helicopters from No 7 Squadron together with a command element consisting of Wing Commander Ken Edwards and Flight Lieutenant Nobby [Derek] Nightingale, a few subalterns and a dozen or so SAS, left Salisbury and headed for the town of Furancungo 'to*

make ze operation'. Living conditions were appalling. The food was instant dysentery and the mosquitoes could carry away the rats. The only favourable thing was that we were allowed to drink as much as we wished in the well-equipped canteens that stocked every conceivable liquor. One day, Portuguese Intelligence indicated a group of some 400 Freds (Frelimo) based in a massif 25 kilometres to the north. The plan was that our Hunters and Canberras would conduct a preemptive strike and then we would follow up by dropping Portuguese troops and our own SAS to do a sweep. A dozen soldiers, using felt-tip pens made copies for us of the master map in the Ops room. Our planned dawn strike took place well after sun-up and on the way to the target, we flew through heavy rain, which seeped into the cabin and smudged our maps, making them unusable. Fortunately, we managed to find our way and identify our landing zones. The jets, however, never located the target and returned to base with full bomb loads. As anticipated the 'operation' was a huge 'lemon', as they were to become known. It was during this sweep that our men realized that the Portuguese principles of war differed somewhat from ours—their troops wore bright blue scarves and as they advanced through the bush, they tapped the butts of their G-3 rifles, making a noise like marbles in a tin can. When we questioned the Portuguese major, his answer was simple—the scarves showed the enemy that they were up against a 'crack' commando unit and that on seeing the bright scarves at a great distance—they would tremble with fear and run away. The latter of course was true—it achieved the objective, but it became glaringly apparent that it was not going to achieve ours. (Peter Briscoe)

Frantan

During 1969, the air force carried out trials with its own version of a napalm bomb. The problem with the bomb, which was being used by other air forces, was that it consisted of a cigar-shaped tank fitted with detonators that exploded on impact. Because of its shape, the bomb could behave in an erratic fashion. The frantan bomb, short for frangible tank, devised by the director of Plans, was a plastic container strong enough to carry 50 gallons of napalm yet brittle enough to shatter on impact. The tank was fitted with four fins and streamlined so that it could be aimed accurately and when it hit the ground, the flaming napalm pitched forward. This was introduced towards the end of the year, as a standard weapon for use by the Vampires.

No 1 Squadron continued to experiment with No 4 Squadron on the airborne Forward Air Control (FAC), which had first been used during 1968. Time was spent at the beginning of the year on trials with the 18-lb (8kg) rocket projectile and it was adopted as No 1 Squadron's standard internal security operations weapon. Trials were also carried out on a towed target banner, which led to a suitable target being developed.

Throughout 1969, No 2 Squadron carried out border reconnaissance flights over the western, northern and eastern borders, using Provosts and Vampires, which they shared with No 6 Squadron. No 2 Squadron also took over the COIN (counter-Insurgency) commitment and the defence and ground-attack role from No 4 Squadron.

Cessna crash

An unfortunate start was made to 1969. A South African Police pilot, Lieutenant Johann van Heerden and an RRAF technical officer, Flight Lieutenant Don Annandale, were involved in a Cessna crash at the RRAF airfield at Kutanga Range, about 20 miles (32km) north of Gwelo, on 7th January. Johann attempted to do a low-level barrel roll (an illegal manœuvre in a C 185) and struck the ground. He was killed and Don Annandale suffered extensive burns. The aircraft was completely destroyed. A further accident occurred when the vehicle being used to take Don to hospital skidded into a ditch and overturned. A passing motorist took Don Annandale to hospital in Que Que and a specialist was flown in from Salisbury. Don died on 9th January in Que Que Hospital and was buried in Salisbury. The body of Johann van Heerden was flown back to South Africa. During the month of February, No 4 Squadron undertook a detachment to Wankie and Kariba where a new system of reconnaissance was brought into operation, each pilot being allocated his own area. Night reconnaissance flights from Kariba were begun towards the end of February.

Tony Smit's help in finding a lost patrol at night was greatly appreciated by No 1 Commando RLI (Rhodesian Light Infantry). Brian Meikle flew a heart attack victim from Bulawayo. The victim preferred to sit in the front seat and carried out a 'hearty' conversation for the duration of the trip. Several other casevacs were carried out throughout the month. Army cooperation exercises were carried out with the army, involving various methods of marking and target indication. One aircraft pilot and tech flew in support of our friends to the east doing Operation 'Success'. No 1 Squadron was bombed with 28 rolls of toilet paper on the 10th.
(No 4 Squadron Diary)

A heavy rainy season 1968/69

The rainy season 1968/69 was a good or bad one depending on which way you looked at it. No 3 Squadron spent much of its time resupplying troops whose transport had become bogged down. Many of the airfields became unserviceable owing to the heavy rains and at one stage two aircraft were stuck in the mud at the same airfield when a Dakota went to the aid of the Beech Baron that had starter trouble.

No 7 Helicopter Squadron was called out to rescue 12 villagers marooned on two islands in the flooded Lundi River near Triangle on 22nd March 1969. The helicopter, piloted by Flight Lieutenant Peter Briscoe, landed at Triangle and picked up Section Officer Phillip Graham who guided the pilot to the islands. First to be rescued were two men and two boys who were set safely on the banks before the helicopter flew off to collect eight men from another small island. The excessive rain hampered counter-insurgency operations being undertaken by the army. The continual soaking rain made the few roads in the border areas impassable.

If an area was inaccessible by road, there remained only two ways to move; on foot, which would have slowed down progress considerably, or by air. The RRAF helicopter clattered into our base early in the morning. By lunchtime about 30 men had been taken to the starting points of their patrols. The importance of air support had already been shown during the first phase of the operation when bad weather and difficult terrain had made communications by radio difficult. An RRAF plane had had to be called up to make contact with one platoon that had been out for five days and could not be reached by road. This vital lesson had been learnt by security forces early in anti-terrorist operations. In our case, air supply support enabled 'A' Company, Depot RRR (Royal Rhodesian Regiment)—the 100th intake's official title—to complete its task.
(Rhodesia Herald, 27th March 1969)

As far as No 4 Squadron was concerned, March 1969 was a quiet month with the detachment at Kariba and Wankie continuing and a further detachment to Salisbury taking place. Trouble was expected on 15th March, Freedom Day in Zambia, but the day passed quietly. However, there was an alert at the end of the month when a vehicle was shot up on a bridge in the Mtoko area and tracks were located nearby. The No 4 Squadron Trojan at New Sarum was placed on stand-by but nothing further was heard.

In April 1969, the air force was called to help when there was a serious outbreak of Rift Valley Fever. The prime minister, Ian Smith, authorized the RRAF to fetch urgently needed supplies of vaccine from the Onderstepoort laboratories near Pretoria. The first consignment of 100,000 doses arrived on 29th April and was available at 07h00 on 30th April from Salisbury Veterinary Research Laboratories.

May was another quiet month. No 4 Squadron's detachment at New Sarum came to an end, which was hard luck on all the Salisbury birds, according to the Squadron Diary. A malaria case was uplifted from Kanyemba and practice landings and take-offs were carried out at night using the headlights of two Land Rovers to light the threshold of the runway.

Rich Beaver from No 2 Squadron managed to damage a Provost when it flew into high-tension cables. He was court-martialled and Bill Sykes received a severe reprimand for low flying! No 3 Squadron was as usual busy transporting everything to everywhere and the squadron was so short of crews that VRs were used right throughout the month.

In June 1969, No 4 Squadron won the Jacklin Trophy for the year 1968, which was presented on the 27th by Air Vice-Marshal A.M. Bentley.

Otherwise, it was a quiet month. Two casevacs on 10th June from Kariba. On both trips there was a nurse on board. Brian Phillips is very proud of this fact. Airfield evaluation in Wankie. Meikle carried out a 'Jacko Jeep Crash' exercise, directing a vehicle by radio from the air to the scene of an accident. Low-level navigational exercise was organized, finding several pinpoints of interest and making notes of what was observed in a single low-level pass.
(No 4 Squadron Diary)

An otherwise quiet month was enlivened for No 3 Squadron when the wheel of a Dakota caught fire after landing at Chirundu while carrying some army VIPs. The ensuing grass fire was speedily controlled by the crew. The army were very impressed by the swift action.

Weapons exercises were held at Bumi Range early in July with Canberras, Hunters, Vampires and Provosts all taking part, the strikes being directed by Trojans doing airborne FAC. On the last day of the exercise, Brian Penton had a lucky escape when he went off the end of a narrow 700-yard (550m) strip south of Bumi Hills.

Frantan accident

Another less fortunate accident occurred on 23rd July, when Cyril White and Prop Geldenhuys on the final trip of a Special Weapons Course brought back a hang-up frantan. Bob Breakwell and three other technicians were busy taking the tank off, while the aircraft was still being run down. The frantan was dropped and went off. Bob Breakwell's body was engulfed in flames. Master Sergeant C.J. McIntyre, one of the technicians went to Bob's aid, dousing the flames by lying across his body. Both technicians sustained serious burns. The injured men were flown to Salisbury in two helicopters from No 7 Squadron. Master Sergeant C.J. McIntyre was awarded the Military Forces Commendation (Non-operational). Chief Technician Peter Poole also received a commendation for his action in combating the fire.

No 7 Squadron helicopters were again called in when a routine army patrol found a four-year-old African boy with a broken leg in a remote village in the Zambezi Valley. He had been lying in agony for three days before he was discovered by the patrol. Doctors said that if he had been left without medical attention much longer he would certainly have been permanently disabled and might even have died. As it was, within hours of being located, he was neatly tucked up in bed at Kariba District Hospital.

During the latter part of 1969, No 1 Squadron began a series of long-range cross-country exercises terminating at Cape Town. Landing-away flights to Mozambique and South Africa provided the pilots with useful experience in navigation over unfamiliar country and weapons proficiency was improved by practice on different ranges. Normal training and various security force exercises were also carried out.

No 5 Squadron puts the country 'on the map'

Security problems had highlighted the need for the efficient surveying and mapping of the entire country and No 5 Squadron was heavily involved taking the photographs for these maps. The Wild RC 8 camera was used extensively during the winter months on mapping activities, which led to overall improvement of the 1:250 000 and 1:50 000 coverage of the country.

A typical example of the value of the work done involved Lake Kariba. Over the years since the dam had been built, reports came in that Kariba weed (*Salvinia auriculata*) was forming on the lake. It was feared that if this growth continued, the weed would soon block the intakes to the turbines at the power station. A professor from the University of Rhodesia and Nyasaland was consulted and he requested an aerial survey of the lake. Private pilots were unable to help significantly and so the air force was called in. The application for the survey was made on a Thursday, it was authorized for Friday morning and the photographic prints were on the professor's desk the following Monday. The whole of Lake Kariba had been photographed at 1:80,000 scale. The exercise was repeated a few weeks later and comparison made. These photographs showed that the weed growth had stabilized but patches were drifting from one area to another.

Eventually the whole of Rhodesia and the surrounding territories had been photographed. Flight Lieutenant Bernie Vaughan, one of the No 5 Squadron navigators, spent a small fortune on a Hewlett Packard calculator into which he programmed reconnaissance/survey formulae that could do all the calculations in the air, at great speed and with outstanding accuracy.

Training, training and more training

Food seemed to be uppermost on the mind of Combined Operations in the latter part of the year when Exercises Pea Soup (August) and Irish Stew (October) were held. During Pea Soup, two Canberras of No 5 Squadron were deployed to Bulawayo and Thornhill respectively. The squadron did well, gaining top points. However, two occurrences marred the record. One aircraft was struck by shrapnel while delivering 250-lb (113,6kg) bombs, and another burnt out its brakes at Bulawayo while attempting a downwind landing. No 4 Squadron was also heavily involved during these exercises, so that at any one time only two or three pilots were available at Thornhill. However, the squadron still managed to maintain its role of casualty evacuation:

> One snakebite victim from Forward Air Field to Bulawayo. One army chap shot off toe —from Kariba to Salisbury. One army chap—severe head injuries—from Bulawayo to Sarum. Heart stopped on final approach but the medic managed through cardiac massage to start it again.
> (No 4 Squadron Diary)

During Operation Irish Stew, in October, Air Lieutenant Jim Stagman (pilot) and Flight Lieutenant Dave Postance (navigator) ejected from their Canberra over Wankie National Park. The trouble began just about dusk when they entered a line of storm clouds, unusual during that season. They experienced repeated flame-outs and re-lights each of which meant taking the aircraft to lower altitudes and then climbing again. During these emergencies, they made several changes in course, so that eventually they were unsure of their position and ran out of fuel. A Dakota from No 3 Squadron and aircraft from Nos 2 and 4 Squadrons were involved in the search and rescue and the crew were picked up early the following morning south of Victoria Falls, having spent a very uncomfortable night amongst the only too audible wildlife of the park.

The pilots of No 4 Squadron were continuing with night trials on runway lighting. In place of the old gooseneck flares, they experimented with discs faced with Scotchlite reflective tape that were illuminated by the aircraft's landing lights. This proved successful. They also practised water and message drops during the Irish Stew exercise.

December brought the regular Christmas goody flight to the troops in the forward areas, carried out by No 3 Squadron. One crew got more than they bargained for when a tyre burst on landing at a remote airfield in the Mtoko area and they were stranded for the night. Chief Mukota heard of their plight and sent an escort to bring the members of the crew to his kraal where they were given VIP treatment while a special guard was placed on their aircraft. The RRAF returned the compliment on 11th December 1969, when Chief Mukota and a group of 60 headmen and villagers were welcomed at New Sarum. The chief was presented with a plaque and a letter of thanks from the chief of Air Staff, Air Vice-Marshal Archie Wilson. He said in the letter: "It is this mutual assistance and cooperation which, blended together, means success prosperity and happiness for us all."

Operations Birch and Teak

Following a lapse of well over a year, a large-scale incursion took place in January 1970 resulting in Operation Birch in the north of the country and Operation Teak in the Victoria Falls area.

> *Operation Birch. A group of 22 crossed on 8th January west of Chewore mouth. First tracks found on escarpment west of Hunyani River. 16th January—first contact. 18th January— group divided into four groups. Choppers were of great value in moving troops into area and positioning stop lines in the very rough terrain. On one occasion, Cronners (Flight Lieutenant Graham Cronshaw) put Matra into suspected ambush site to speed up tracking. Chopper fired MAG both contacts. Cronners and Wenters (Air Lieutenant Chris Wentworth) providing top cover and telstar. Results: seven terrs killed (one in 'funny land'—Mozambique) six weeks later. Fourteen captured. One RLI killed in first contact. Two RLI wounded. One police dog shot. One terr outstanding.* (No 4 Squadron Diary)

Operation Teak was heralded by an attack on Victoria Falls Airport and the South African Police Camp at Sprayview.

> *Tracks found near Gwaai River mouth and police patrol boat was fired on from the Zambian side of the Zambezi. Tracks lost Kamativi area on the night 16th January. SAP camp at Chisuma attacked and shots were fired at Victoria Falls Airport building. Three pilots provided cover and carried out recces. One strike in a suspected area but with no results. Two terrs spotted in a village. Troops too slow getting there. Results five terrs killed, six captured out of a group of 20. Some got through to Botswana. One RAR troopie killed. Four SAP wounded. Railway line south of Falls Airport blown up.* (No 4 Squadron Diary)

Both these ZANLA operations were better organized than previous incursions. The soldiers had been well trained in anti-tracking measures and were working in smaller groups of four or five, attacking various points at the same time, thus spreading the security force strength.

During these operations No 3 Squadron Dakotas took part in a sky shout which seems to have been successful as some of the terrorists who were captured said that they were glad to know of surrender procedures because they had become disenchanted about being hounded round the country.

Operation Birch ended in the middle of February 1970, only to be followed on 20th February by Operation Chestnut, when a ZIPRA guerrilla was captured at Dett Siding in the

Wankie area. It appeared that he was one of a group of seven; patrols were carried out in the area to the south-west of Dahlia to find the others. No 4 Squadron set up a forward airfield (FAF) at Dahlia from which armed reconnaissance flights and leaflet drops were carried out.

No 2 Squadron had been concentrating mainly on operating Vampires, only four pilots remaining current on Provosts. In February 1970, after the squadron had experienced some difficulties in aircraft recovering from spinning, fuel flow checks were carried out on the Vampires for asymmetry, and large discrepancies were found between the two wings on some aircraft. This resulted in new pre-spinning requirements, that is not to spin with more than 800 pounds (363kg) of fuel in total.

In contrast to the previous season, 1969/70 proved to be very dry and No 3 Squadron's efforts to promote rain seemed to have had little effect.

March 1970 saw the 50th anniversary of the first flight by an aircraft in Rhodesia, which marked the end of another era—that of the Royal Rhodesian Air Force.

CHAPTER 36

A break with royalty

On 20th June 1969, the Rhodesian electorate had gone to the polls in yet another referendum. Two issues were involved:

1. the adoption or rejection of a new constitution
2. whether Rhodesia should become a republic

The new constitution was favoured by 72,5% of the voters and the republic received a Yes vote from 81%. At midnight, therefore, on 2nd March 1970, the new constitution came into force and Rhodesia became a republic with Mr Clifford Dupont, formerly officer administering the government, assuming the role of acting president. Rhodesia's 80-year-old link with the British crown had been severed.

The announcement of new rank structures and badges for the air force had been announced in the Government Gazette of 1st March 1970. The two junior officer ranks of pilot officer and flying officer were renamed air sub-lieutenant and air lieutenant respectively, while the rank structure for airmen was streamlined. The new badges carried a redesigned bateleur eagle and the lion and tusk that had been used in military insignia since the pioneer days. The roundel was also changed. It had a white centre on which was superimposed a gold lion and tusk, outlined in black with a dark green outer circle.

The new insignia, which had been designed by Warrant Officer Cedric Herbert, was unveiled on 5th March by Mr Howman, Minister of Defence, at New Sarum. RRAF aircraft would carry the green, white and gold roundel and a green tail flash with a narrow white stripe running down the middle. There was also to be a new ensign, which would carry a blue background, as in the old flag, with the Rhodesian national flag in the top left-hand corner and the new roundel in the centre.

Operation Pluto

During this period No 4 Squadron personnel were heavily involved in the latest counter-insurgency operation code named Pluto.

The operation began on 5th March, after a group of terrs attacked the Kariba Airport transmitter site on the night of 4th March. (Rockets were fired into the roof of the building). Wenters and Dick (Air Lieutenant Chris Wentworth and Air Sub-Lieutenant Dick Paxton) happened to be doing their tour at the FAF 2 and so became involved in the op. A Trog (Trojan) provided top cover, recce and telstar throughout Operation 'Pluto'. Two Provosts helped out with recce and dropped flares in the gorge at night. Wenters chased a Zambian Beaver up and down the gorge demonstrating the superior performances of the Beaver. This operation packed up on 13th March. Terr tracks were lost on the third day and in spite of patrols combing the escarpment no further signs were found. This group appeared to be badly trained in weaponry as very little damage was done to the transmitter site—the bazookas fired were not fused. Casevacs. On 15th March flew 19-year-old car crash victim from Que Que to Salisbury and a food poisoning case from Gokwe to Salisbury. On 26th March Cronners (Flight Lieutenant Cronshaw) located a lost patrol—brown jobs lost again! Night flying: nine cadets taken up to be frightened in Trog single line flare landings on 24th March. Enough night-flying by everyone to remain current and keep the adrenaline level steady. 27th March. Water drop to 24 Pilot Training Course on survival march Sabi-Lundi junction area. One Trog position at Silobela on 15th March in a Vampire timing exercise. Message bag and water drops practised by new pilots. (No 4 Squadron Diary)

Royal links suspended

The news came in the middle of March 1970 that the Royal family's links with the Rhodesian services had been suspended. The notice that appeared in the *London Gazette* on 13th March, said that use of the prefix Royal for the Royal Rhodesia Regiment and the Royal Rhodesian Air Force should be dropped. This order had been approved by Queen Elizabeth. According to officials in London, the links were only suspended and not severed, so that ties could be restored if the services at any time resumed allegiance to the Crown. On 8th April 1970, therefore, the air force once more officially changed its name and became the Rhodesian Air Force. This title was not to be shortened to RAF because that would cause confusion with the British RAF. However, it could be written as RhAF and was referred to as RHODAF in signals or verbally. The title CAS was superseded by that of Commander of the Air Force, in confirmation with the new rank structure. The ranks of the commanders of the army and air force were elevated to lieutenant general and air marshal. This facilitated the closer liaison between the commanders and their counterparts in the armed forces of nations sympathetic to Rhodesia's cause. A link with the past was broken at the end of March 1970, when Air Commodore John Deall, Deputy Chief of Air Staff retired from the force. Group Captain Mick McLaren was promoted to air commodore and appointed Air Officer Administration.

Operation Granite

The title of the air force may have changed but the tasks remained the same. April 1970 was a typical month for No 4 Squadron, as described in the Squadron Diary:

Operation Granite. The fifth operation this year got underway on 10th April resulting from two terrs being picked up at a store in the Matopos area. These two were originally from a group of seven. Arms and ammunition were found in a cave in the Matopos and tracks were followed south. One terr was captured by locals but escaped before security forces arrived on the scene. Tracks were lost and later Botswana Police reported having caught two. 'Cronners' provided telstar, recce and airborne stopline during this operation. Once again, terrs proved that their anti- tracking training has improved and managed to elude security forces. Four members were treated to a mortar firing demonstration by the RLI north-east of Shamva before doing airborne control. This was of great value as it gave pilots an insight into the problems facing the mortar crew while being controlled from the air. A GAC/FAC demonstration for the South African Police was laid on at Wankie. Done by 'Wenters', and involved one pair of Vampires and five Hunters. The 'slopies'* were very impressed. Casevacs: from Sprayview to FAF 1 on 4th April, a slopie who had shot himself through the groin, and slopies with food poisoning on 27th April. Roger [Watt] on the night of 30th April, flew from Kanyemba to Salisbury taking an

---

* Slopie/s—service slang for SAP.

African child with severe burns; the child died en route. FAF to Salisbury, on the night 8th May appendicitis patient and Chipinda Pools to Thornhill on 1st May, with a cadet from 24 Pilot Training Course who developed ankle trouble on survival march. Other: on 8th May Giles Porter dropped a pair of boots for one individual slopie on patrol who had his old ones pinched by a hyena. Night navigation by Roger and Dick Paxton on 7th May, and Roger and Ed Potterton on 14th May. Further rocket-training —formation flying. 11th May Tony Oakley journeyed up to Salisbury to lecture to brown jobs on Trog. The second Vasco da Gama: Cyril White and Boss Norman Walsh undertook a daring canoe trip from Beira to Vilanculos setting out on 12th May. No 5 Squadron dropped a newspaper to them. No 1 Squadron failed to find the two Robinson Crusoes. For the full story ask Vasco himself. Social life—rock bottom for months— hit a new high this month. (No 4 Squadron Diary)

Continuing with the diary, the month of May found No 4 Squadron involved in such varied activities as: dropping rations and water to a lost territorial force patrol near Pandamatenga; casevacing a troopie who had been stomped by an elephant; and transporting a doctor and two medics to deal with a typhoid outbreak at Kutanga. On the negative side:

Eight members practised mass bag and water dropping on a competitive basis here. Half the parachutes tore loose and with those that stayed intact, the water cans broke open on hitting the ground. As a result of this marvellous display, the cans are now being fitted with metal cables to ensure that they strike the ground squarely. No 1 Squadron took part in dropping toilet rolls—250-yard (230m) overshoot. Very Pistol Trials: following Dick Paxton's achievements, burning out 1,200 acres (500 hectares) of Meikles Ranch, Ed Potterton carried out trials with Very Pistol to see what height to fire them from so that they burnt out before they reached the ground. Verys continue to burn for approximately 500 feet when fired vertically with the aircraft in level flight. (Now you know Dick!) (No 4 Squadron)

The diary also notes that "It is disheartening to see that very little is being done about the defence of the forward airfields after what we have seen and learnt during this year."

Air Force Security Branch

In fact, the security situation was under review. Since its formation, the RRAF police had followed the pattern of the RAF police. The major difference was that all members were now provosts, which was a higher rank than that of a station policeman. The highest standards were set and this led to the creation of a small, highly efficient force with every RRAF policeman being capable of running a guard room as well as carrying out investigations. With UDI, the role of the air force police changed. The routine work of discipline, investigation and VIP escort was still necessary but the protection of airfields assumed primary importance. It was obvious that the army was not in a position to provide adequate airfield protection. The provost marshal at the time of UDI, Flight Lieutenant Don Graham, commenced a campaign aimed at the formation of an air force regiment modelled on the RAF Regiment. This unit would have the immense task of protecting not only the main bases at Thornhill and New Sarum but also the forward airfields.

In 1970, the title of the air force police was changed to the Security Branch and members became known as security/provosts. Initial training was carried out at No 1 Ground Training School, New Sarum.

The drill and weapons instructors were Flight Sergeant Ken Jackman and Corporal Don Junner. Instruction in all other aspects of the air force was carried out by regular members of the security branch, one of the foremost being Ken Salter. He was a man with terrific charisma. All who knew him came to respect him. They did not necessarily like him, but they respected him. As a lecturer he had no equal. (Paul Hill)

At the main stations of New Sarum and Thornhill, the role of the Security Branch continued more or less unchanged. It included the manning of the guard room, regulation of visitors and vehicles and the issuing of passes and permits, plus all the day-to-day duties of controlling parking and sorting out the problems of lost IDs, escorting VIPs and investigating petty theft. The titles of the incumbents changed occasionally but generally their duties were as follows: the station security officer (S Sec O) was in overall charge of station security; under him was an officer in charge of the General Service Unit, (this later became a regimental post) and the warrant officers in charge of the guard room and the dog section.

The defence plan at New Sarum was laid out as follows. In the centre was the security area, which contained the hangars, workshops, stores, photographic and motor transport sections, the fuel dump, armoury, fire section, communication centre, operations room and station headquarters. The security area was virtually closed off, access being through the two taxi gates for the passage of aircraft, and the vehicle gate from the domestic area. This gate was guarded by security personnel during normal working hours, and out of hours by pickets. The whole area was patrolled at night and at weekends by dogs and their handlers. The domestic area, which was outside the central security area, contained the training schools, parade ground, messes, single and married quarters, canteen, sports club, playing fields, car parks, general service unit living quarters and station sick quarters. This area was covered by irregular foot or vehicle patrols.

The Parachute School logs its 10,000th jump
On May 6th 1970, the Parachute School logged its 10,000th jump, performed by Flight Sergeant Tony Hughes from a Dakota flying at 1,000 feet above New Sarum, bringing Hughes's personal total to 155. He was, at the age of 26, the youngest staff instructor at the Parachute School. He had joined the air force in 1961 as a radio operator and transferred to the Parachute School in 1967. Dispatcher for the historic jump was Warrant Officer Bill Maitland, who had been with the school since its inception in November 1961, while the pilot for the flight was Flight Lieutenant George Alexander, who had been the first pilot to drop a paratrooper over Rhodesia. He had also been responsible for training other pilots in para-dropping techniques. George Walker-Smith, in the co-pilot's seat represented the VR. Of the 10,000 jumps on record, only eight men had failed the course and only one had refused to jump. During this whole period, there had been no casualties or permanent injuries. The accident occurrence rate stood at 1.39% and this included everything from a cut finger to a broken leg. The Parachute School was staffed by six qualified instructors and two trainee instructors.

No 5 Squadron demonstrates the 'bomb box'
During Operation Cauldron in 1968, there had been an unfortunate incident when an RLI trooper had been injured in a bombing attack by the Canberras of No 5 Squadron. As a result, a certain prejudice had been noticed amongst army personnel, particularly junior members, against using the Canberra bomb box. It was, therefore, decided to carry out a display using live bombs to demonstrate No 5 Squadron accuracy. The occasion was fully described in the army magazine *Assegai*.

It is a well-known fact, that one of the few things guaranteed to strike terror into the heart of RLI troopies is the sound of a Canberra opening its bomb doors. And even the blood of such stout hearts as that of 'killer Cronkie', whose exploits range from poaching on the front porches of the New Jerusalem to free fall minus parachute from a chopper, runs cold at the sound. Thus it was with great trepidation that support group greeted the news that their OC intended to rid them of the craven fear by planting them on a hillock and have a Canberra bomb a gully directly in front of them. Prayers of utter purity rose rapidly in volume, voltage and intensity as the sound of the Canberra grew nearer. It was obvious that 5 Squadron had put in 'maningi' homework and we are happy to report the troopies are all in one piece and extremely impressed with the result. Full credit must go to the 'blues' who positioned themselves well in front (presumably to encourage the 'browns'). No 4 Squadron provided some immaculate shooting and Ian Harvey gave a lively display in which he nearly shot himself down. His swift IA (Immediate Action) drills, which consisted of a rapid rewinding of elastic bands plus deft application of glue, saved the day and the 'troggie' fluttered out of trouble to the vast disappointment of the troopies.

One of the consequences of the sanctions imposed following UDI was that it became increasingly difficult to replace cracked nose cones on the No 5 Squadron Canberras. In order to decrease wear and tear, a restriction was placed on the maximum height, lowering it from 50,000 feet to 35,000 feet until a solution could be found. Air force technicians had been busy working on the problem and a new nose cone was designed and fitted; successful trials were carried out in the middle of 1970. The new nose cone consisted of three clear vision windows fitted to a modified fibre-glass nose section giving it a Dimple (Haig) appearance.

Helicopter crash at New Sarum

On 1st July 1970, No 7 Squadron suffered its first fatality when a helicopter crashed outside the main gate to New Sarum shortly before midday, killing pilots Squadron Leader Gordon Nettleton and Flight Lieutenant Michael Richard Hill. No real explanation was found for this crash. The theory was that the pilot was affected by what is known as flicker vertigo. He had been instrument flying, which meant that he was enclosed in a hood allowing no outside visibility. When he released the hood, the bright sunlight being interrupted by the rotating blades of the helicopter could possibly have had a stroboscopic effect causing him to have a type of epileptic fit. According to eyewitnesses, as the helicopter made its approach, it actually rolled onto its back and crashed immediately. Attempts by investigators from the French company that manufactured the Alouette to simulate the movement of the helicopter before its crash, failed.

During August, No 3 Squadron was involved in a sky shout, which took them north of Mueda in northern Mozambique for eight days. This was part of Operation Big Push that was in fact small by Rhodesian standards. Crew members stated that the food was of the usual unimpressive standard. However, they survived, but in September when another sky shout was carried out to the north, the Dakota crew suffered badly from the effects of the food and had to organize a rota system for the little room at the back of the Dakota. Cholera jabs were ordered for all members of the squadron, including the VRs, who had a double dose.

The Trojan bird strike

September also proved a busy month for No 4 Squadron:

September 1970 will not go down as having been the most quiet of months what with Beav Baynham's hairy forced-landing at night and at least two engines becoming weaker than usual at interesting stages of take-off. There have been times when we have had only one aircraft flying with the distinct possibility of getting our Tiger Moth airborne. Not to forget to mention Ian Harvey's almost amazing and unheard of bird (owl) strike from the front. (No 4 Squadron Diary)

It seems that this unusual occurrence took place while the Trojan was doing some night-landing practice using single-line flares. The notable point here is that it was always believed that the Trog flew so slowly that it only received bird strikes when some poor unsuspecting bird actually flew into the back of the aircraft.

He maintains that nothing was felt, so perhaps the contact took place during a rough landing. On the other hand though, No 1 Squadron maintain that the owl was probably about to roost on the strut and bungled its final approach. Judging by the surprised look on the owl's face, we suggest that this might have happened. Casevacs: 8th September. Dick Paxton at FAF 2 uplifted two casevacs from Angwa Bridge Air Field to New Sarum (troopie with eye injury). Nothing daunted, returned to FAF 2 and told to proceed immediately to Kanyemba for another 2 INDEP stretcher case. Did a hairy take-off in the dark for New Sarum. 13th September. Beav at FAF 2 Troopie to FRSB from FAF 2—back injury. It seemed that 4 Squadron 'Flying Doctor Service' could not fail but subsequent events were to show that it doesn't pay to count your 'hoekoos' before they hatch. (No 4 Squadron Diary)

Beav Baynham's 'hairy' casevacs

To appreciate Beav Baynham's most spectacular casevac it is necessary to sketch in a little background. In 1970, the government mounted a campaign to capture black rhinoceros in the remote areas south of Kariba Dam, where the animals were being threatened by poachers, and relocate them in the vast Gonarezhou Game Reserve in south-eastern Rhodesia. During Operation Rhino, 43 animals were darted and captured. Of these, 41 were successfully moved to their new home, a living memorial to the courage of the men involved.

The incident in question took place in the Tendi Springs area 50 miles (80km) south of Lake Kariba and about 200 miles (320km) north of Bulawayo in very difficult country. Not only are there steep ravines and rocky hills but also the low-lying country is covered by a dense tangle of jesse bush through which the only paths are tunnels made by the animals themselves. Visibility in such conditions is often limited to a few yards. It is dangerous country in which to track a rhino for the kill—suicidal if you wish to catch one alive.

Paul Coetsee, the game warden in charge of Operation Rhino in that area, had set up camp on the Nyandora River. On Monday 14th September, Coetsee, ranger David Scammell, and tracker Kapesa left camp to follow up a large bull rhinoceros. They were able to take the Land Rover about 12 miles; after that they were on foot.

It was 13h00 on the second day, Tuesday 15th September. They had been tracking the rhinoceros for five hours through waterless country. The bush was thick and Paul Coetsee could not see more than a metre or so ahead. They had spotted the animal they were tracking earlier as he broke cover and crashed through the bush but now they had lost him again. Then suddenly the rhino was there just three yards away and as Coetsee saw him the rhino charged. The beast hit the warden at full tilt, caught him in the thigh and flung him cartwheeling up. As the man's body came crashing down, the rhino slashed again catching him once more in the thigh and tossing him over his head again, so that he fell on the rhino's back. Bewildered, the animal retreated and then as Coetsee's body slipped to the ground, the rhino made off through the undergrowth.

The rhino had left gaping wounds in the warden's upper leg. Ranger Scammell managed to stop the bleeding and administered morphine. Then he tried to call base camp for help but could not establish contact. So, leaving Kapesa with the injured warden, Scammell walked back to [the point where they had left] the Land Rover, and then drove back to base camp where he radioed the Wild Life Department's Sinoia office. Having reported to base, he collected a group of labourers and a stretcher and drove the Land Rover as close as he could to the injured warden. From that point, David and the African labourers began to hack a road through the bush so that they could get the Land Rover to Coetsee.

Just after 16h00, Beav Baynham landed his Trojan at the Forward Air Field at Kariba (FAF 2). On a two-week detachment, he had just flown a routine flight from Kanyemba. He was immediately placed on stand-by for the casevac and five minutes later word came through that the Ministry of Defence had cleared the flight.

Because Coetsee's injuries were so severe, it was suggested that Baynham should take a nurse instead of a technician with him. The problem was time—if take-off were to be delayed, it would be dark before Beav could reach the landing strip. A nurse was available at Kariba hospital but it would take time for her to reach the airfield. It was decided that Baynham should take an army medic who was immediately available.

We got a medical orderly from the Rhodesia Regiment, a Corporal Boyens, who had never flown before. We got airborne from Kariba at about 16h30 and I plotted a course to Tchoda, the other side of the Sanyati Gorge. At about 17h30 I found the airstrip, just an ordinary bush strip. I had a bit of difficulty finding it because the sun was going down and there was a lot of haze. I flew over the airstrip, did an inspection run to make sure that it was clear of holes and warthogs and other 'skelms' that like to hang around there. Then I landed. (Beav Baynham)

Meanwhile, David Scammell taking the Land Rover along the track cut by his gang, reached the injured man just after 17h00 and drove him about 10 miles (16km) through the bush to the airstrip, where he found Baynham waiting.

We transferred the injured man to the aircraft, behind the two front seats. The medic sat next to me where he could turn round and attend to Coetsee if necessary. As we got airborne, it was 18h15 and getting dark. In fact, I did a semi-instrument take-off on a compass heading. The worst problem was the haze layer, which gave a false horizon. I went up to 6,000 feet. I wanted to contact the Kariba tower. I said when I left that I would give them information to pass on to Salisbury so that they could have a doctor standing by for us. I couldn't get a reply from Kariba so I tried Salisbury tower without any luck, so I decided to take the Trog up higher, hoping I could make contact. We had been in the air for about 15 or 20 minutes and I was trying to creep up in a cruise-type climb to about 7,000 feet, just to try to get radio range, when I heard a change in tone. You are very conscious of engine tone, particularly if you fly single-engine aircraft and I heard this change of tone, which was accompanied by a drop in boost pressure and I realized that something fairly severe was wrong. Then the vibration started. At first I thought I had a propeller coming off. I checked. Magnetos were OK. Pressure OK. Temperature OK. I hoped that it was just a bad fuel feed. I tried changing fuel tanks. It didn't help. In fact, things were about as bad as they could be. The vibration was getting worse. I couldn't raise anyone, not even with a PAN call, which means that there is imminent danger. I was flying in an easterly direction so I didn't even have the last light of the setting sun to help me. I couldn't turn back. True the landing ground was only about 20 minutes behind me but there would be no one there now and landing there in the dark would be impossible. There really wasn't anything to do but push on and pray. I couldn't see the ground below but I knew I was over very rugged hilly country where any kind of landing would be fatal.

Meanwhile in Salisbury, Flight Information Centre was waiting for news. Suddenly, breaking through the static they heard Baynham's Mayday call. He reported partial engine failure, said that he was unable to maintain height, and might have to make an emergency landing, that he could see nothing of the country below but knew that he was over the

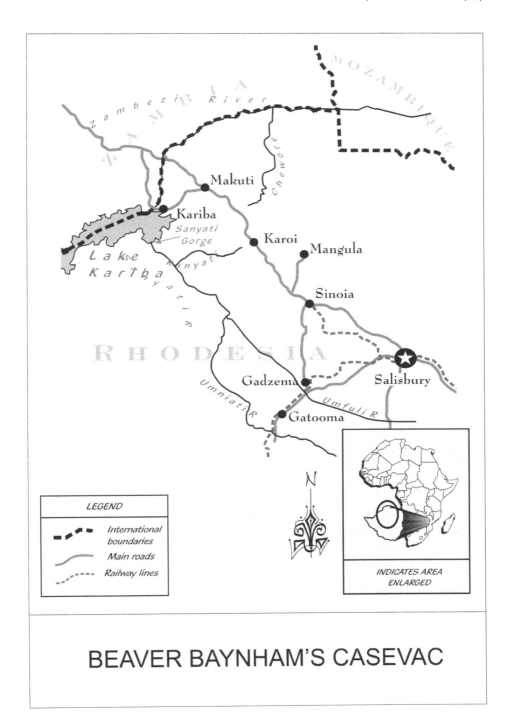

BEAVER BAYNHAM'S CASEVAC

escarpment in mountainous, broken country. Flight Control picked the Trojan up on radar. Three night-flying helicopters, and a Dakota en route from Kariba to Salisbury were alerted and Crash Rescue was placed on stand-by. During their conversation with Beaver, the men at Flight Control were startled to hear explosions coming from the engine of the stricken aircraft. There seemed to be no hope. And then the moon came up:

The moon made all the difference. It showed me a faint strip of dirt road. I informed Salisbury that I was going down and they pinpointed my position on radar. I asked the corporal to make sure the game ranger's stretcher was secure. I tried to do a positioning turn over the stretch of road I'd seen. I wanted to make an engine-assisted landing but by now the engine was so intermittent that I didn't dare trust it; if it cut as I was coming in I'd drop like a stone. So at about 800 feet I decided I'd better chop everything. I switched off all the lighting in the cockpit so that I had a better chance of seeing things outside. I was going to put this thing down by feel. I went through all the emergency procedures, fuel off, magnetos off. The only things I left on were the landing lights. As I got down towards the road, I saw some shapes on the right hand side. I thought, "The Kariba power lines cross here somewhere." To the left of the road was what seemed to be a vlei—it was a lighter patch of land. I wasn't absolutely blind now the moon was up but I couldn't see to any great extent. I could see that there weren't any trees to the left, so I made the approach having turned in fairly steeply. I started to dive the aircraft to get a bit of extra speed so that as I got closer to the ground I would be able to see things moving and have sufficient speed to take evasive action. As I got closer, I found I was going a bit too fast. I saw a tree in front of me and I managed to pull up over the top of it. I was still going fast and I lifted flap to stall the aircraft. I pulled the stick back and went in. It was quite funny—everything happened in slow motion. We hit. Bounced on a contour ridge and the aircraft went in nose first. The nose wheel came off. We slid along with the left wing on the ground. I thought we were going to cartwheel but we slewed round and she fell back on her undercarriage. I stopped in about 400 feet, I think. Unfortunately, the corporal had not secured his seat correctly and when we tipped forward, he slid down into the instrument panel like someone going down a ski run. We had to get our casualty clear fast because there was petrol everywhere. We stumbled through the bush with the stretcher until I reckoned we were far enough. Then we put him down. The aircraft didn't catch fire so I went back and switched everything off. Then I collected the medical kit, a blanket and the Very pistol. We'd landed in a semi-ploughed land. There were huts nearby and I found an African who told me that there was a Roads Department camp about a mile down the road. From this camp, I contacted Salisbury Control Room and reported that I'd landed alongside the Sinoia/Gadzema road. They dispatched a No 7 Squadron chopper, which I guided in with the Very pistol. It landed right beside my aircraft. We got Coetsee on board and on his way. Meanwhile a second chopper went to collect a police detail to guard my aircraft. It dropped them and took us out—about 21h00. (Beav Baynham)

No 4 Squadron Diary's version of the story goes:

Beav only got as far as the Sinoia/Gadzema road and had to force-land in a field after his engine gave up the ghost. No 5 pot blew off and the other 5 stopped clapping. Beav sounded a bit breathless (was that it) over the R/T. He has a tape-recording of the complete spiel. It must sound like sweet music, judging by the number of times he plays it. The Alouette from No 7 Squadron completed the task and got the injured warden to Salisbury safely. We believe too, that he is well on the way to recovery. So, by the way is Beav. He seems a bit chatty these days! The funny thing was that Beav had just taken out some fairly hefty life and death insurance and according to him this rather bothered him as someone else was going to get all that lovely money

so soon. The aircraft was only Category 3 damaged and is now venturing into the skies again.
(No 4 Squadron Diary)

Any remarks about Baynham's flying abilities were abruptly halted on 14th October when Gordon Wright had a similar engine failure.

Gordon Wright, doing his first bush tour at FAF 2 with Graham Cronshaw as 'fundi-passer on-er', attempted to uplift a troopie ill with sleeping sickness to Salisbury, but alas, as with Beav Baynham, he was fated not to get all the way there—by air anyway. Gordon had only been airborne for about 30 minutes when his engine developed similar symptoms to Beav's prior to failing: running rough, boost falling off and clattering badly. Fortunately the trouble developed while flying at 2,000 feet since at the time the country below was only full of big hills and Gordon was able to turn back to a farming area and select a suitable field. At this stage, the aircraft was descending at 300 feet per minute with full power set. A successful forced-landing with power was carried out, the nose-wheel only collapsing at the end. Ironically, the troopie being casevaced was the only one injured. He wasn't tied onto the stretcher and cut his head on the seat despite the fact that Mike Parker (the tech) was trying to hang onto him. No 7 Squadron, again, completed the journey for us. As a result of this second engine failure, all the Trojans were called to New Sarum for engine inspection. It is interesting to note that when questioned afterwards the troopie said that he thought the engine sounded like a machine gun. *
(No 4 Squadron Diary)

Throughout all this excitement, the squadron was carrying out cross-country flights to Victoria Falls and Umtali, bush tours to FAF 1 and 2 and practising formation-flying for the Independence Day flypast on 11th November 1970. According to No 4 Squadron Diary:

HQ want us to put up nine aircraft—laughing or is it crying. On the subject of formation, a Hunter and a Trojan managed to accomplish this at Victoria Falls. Speed 140 knots.

No 3 Squadron, while preparing for the Independence Day Parade, was also involved in airfield evaluation prior to the onset of the rainy season. Other activities included a casevac from the Mozambique port of Beira of a young Rhodesian girl who had been injured while swimming. She died of her injuries.

First Rhodesian honours
On 23rd October 1970, the first Rhodesian Honours were awarded. Before UDI, Rhodesians had been eligible for the full range of British Honours and Awards for Gallantry and Long Service. After UDI, these awards were no longer available. In 1969, under Rhodesian Government Notice No 893A, the award of the Rhodesian General Service Medal was announced with eligibility for the award dating back to April 1966.

The new system whilst not directly equivalent to the British system did have minor traditional similarities. For example, the ribbon for the Bronze Cross of Rhodesia for the air force was the same colours as the British Distinguished Flying Cross—violet and white. In the main, the ribbons took the force colours i.e. red for army and sky blue for air force and in

---

* During this period, HQ produced a directive concerning the inspection of engines for fractures of the cylinder heads. Beav and Roger were instructed to fly direct to Sarum along the main road—just in case. On calling Salisbury, they were instructed by the controller to turn right at the first set of robots and call the airfield in sight. Fortunately, though, Beav and Roger remembered that they had to turn left at these robots.

the case of the police the colours of the BSAP, blue and old gold, were added in the middle. The Military Forces Commendation was similar to the British Mentioned in Dispatches. In both cases an emblem—MID an oak leaf, and the MFC the pick taken from the shield of the Rhodesian Coat of Arms—was worn attached to the ribbon.

The criteria for an award were very stringent and in many cases, the award of a Military Forces Commendation was for bravery similar to that which would have merited a DFC in World War II. One major difference between the Rhodesian and British systems was that the Rhodesian system was across the board. There was no rank differential. The Bronze or Silver Cross could be awarded to both officers and non-commissioned officers. Among the first air force recipients were Tony Smit and Ken Law, who were awarded the Military Forces Commendation (Operational) for their part in Operation Griffin, on 18th July 1968.

Independence Day flypast—1970

Despite claims by the enemy to have shot down 33 Rhodesian aircraft, seven formations took part in the flypast on 11th November 1970. It was a credit to the ground crews that after five years of sanctions, No 5 Squadron could still put eight Canberras into the air. The well-known Carpenter's Column in the *Rhodesia Herald* offered a guide to the flypast:

As you will be craning your necks this morning to watch the air force flypast, here's a crash course on aircraft recognition and some interesting 'gen' on the planes involved. First come the helicopters. There will be a 'cross' formation of seven led by Squadron Leader M.J. 'Mick' Grier doing a steady 85 miles per hour (137 km/h) at 450 feet. These machines are jet-engined maids of all work and in their rescue role have saved 229 Rhodesian lives to date. Then come the Trojans, single-engined monoplanes used for communications and light transport support. Nine Trojans in three 'vics' of three in line astern, led by Squadron Leader Pete McLurg will sail past at 105 miles per hour (170 km/h) at 550 feet. The Provosts will follow. These aircraft are single-engined armed trainers, distinguishable from the Trojans by the set of their wings. Provosts are low-winged monoplanes; Trojans are high-winged monoplanes. Provosts are used as basic trainers and in close-support and ground-attack roles. The ten in the flypast will be in two 'vics' of five in line astern, led by Squadron Leader Eddie Wilkinson, doing about 140 miles per hour (225 km/h) at 650 feet. Then comes the original workhorse of the air, the Dakota, which has been around for so long I doubt if anyone will fail to recognize its profile with tapering wings and twin engines set fairly close to the fuselage. This is the air force's principal transport plane. Six in two 'vic' of three will be led by Squadron Leader Mike Gedye. They'll be chugging along at 155 miles per hour (250 km/h) at 750 feet. After them come the Canberras, easily recognized by their wing-tip fuel tanks and the breadth of wing inboard of the engine nacelles. These twin-jet medium bombers with the Hunters constitute the air force's return strike force. Seven led by Squadron Leader J.E. 'Ted' Stevenson will fly past in 'vic' and 'box' formation at 310 miles per hour (509 km/h) at 850 feet. The Vampires follow and these are unmistakable because of the twin-boom tail. These jet trainers are also used in an armed role in close-support or ground-attack. Twelve of them led by Squadron Leader F.J. 'Tol' Janeke will fly past in three 'boxes' of four in 'vic' formation at about 350 miles per hour (563 km/h) at 950 feet. Our fastest jet fighters, the Hunters, will bring up the rear. Nine of them led by Squadron Leader Roy Morris will be in a 'diamond' nine formation at 1,050 feet doing about 420 miles per hour (670 km/h). You can hardly mistake the Hunter because its single turbo-jet engine produces about 10,000 pounds (4,536kg) of thrust out of the rear end of the fuselage making it the fastest thing in the air hereabouts. It is in fact capable of supersonic speeds in a dive. All the aircraft will be approaching from the rough direction of Jameson Avenue East and perhaps you can guess at the careful timing required for the formations to arrive over the city centre at about

45 second intervals. Apart from this, each formation has a recovery procedure to follow soon after it passes Rhodes's Statue to prevent an unholy pile up somewhere above Glamis Stadium. (Rhodesia Herald, 11th Nov. 1970)

Indeed the timing had to be exact and it was. Low cloud looked like spoiling the effect but fortunately, it lifted at the psychological moment. Grudgingly No 3 Squadron Diary remarked: "The ground forces were also very impressive."

Operation Apollo

For some time, there had been little insurgency activity, so it was that when Operation Apollo began on 29th November 1970, it caught members of No 4 Squadron on the wrong foot. They were called at 06h30 following a "sterrek thrash" (big party) in the mess the night before. However, despite 'mag drops' way out of limits, they set off on a northerly heading to 'Funny Land far far away'. (No 4 Squadron Diary)

During 1970 with the help of Frelimo, ZANLA began establishing bases south of the Zambezi River in Tete Province. The African nationalist forces in Mozambique were for the most part faced by young conscripts shipped out from Portugal who had little enthusiasm for the fight. It was to help protect this soft north-eastern border area that the air force became more and more involved in operations in Mozambique or 'Funny Land' as it was called in the Squadron Diaries. Peter Briscoe of No 7 Squadron has vivid memories of this time.

We formed a detachment based at Chicoa on the south bank of the Zambezi just west of the Cabora Bassa Gorge. Chicoa was a hell-hole. We anticipated a lengthy stay and we had learnt to take our own field kitchen and cooks. It was the rainy season and the afternoons were punctuated with the usual thunderstorms. Cleanliness was a problem so we rigged up showers. These were serviced by a tank of water that was filled from the waters of the Zambezi. However, the water was chocolate brown and we ended up dirtier after the shower than before. So we found the answer— wait for a rainstorm, strip naked, bring out the soap and shampoo and use Mother Nature. Except for our feet and ankles, we were clean. The only person who enjoyed shower time more than we did, was the postmistress who watched from a distance. The thing we envied most about the Portuguese air force stationed at Chicoa was that their Alouette helicopter had a 20mm cannon. Compared with our 7.62 machine gun this was a real killing machine. It was patently apparent that they had little or no idea how to operate this weapon or even service it and this was graphically demonstrated one morning when the gunner's replacement arrived. The new incumbent had never seen a weapon like this before and he was given a quick tutorial. The tutor, demonstrating how to load the gun, pulled back the moving parts and released the breechblock. He had, however, forgotten to clear the weapon. It picked up a 20mm round that went off with a fearful bang, travelled across the open ground towards the Portuguese camp, entered a tent and hit the cook who was taking his post-breakfast siesta. It removed a large part of his skull and he was casevaced the 250km to Tete by chopper. That evening the commander came over to our camp to tell us that the cook was dead. Seeing the looks of dismay on our faces, he immediately qualified his remark by saying, "Oh, don't worry, he was a 'sheet' cook anyway!" We were stunned by this callous disregard for human life, but it was typical of the overall attitude. As there seemed to be little action at one stage, we threatened to pack up camp and return to Rhodesia, which was bad news for the Portuguese army colonel. We had just been to a scene where there had been a report of a Fred [Frelimo] camp but it was a 'lemon'. The Portuguese had to return by vehicle. No sooner had we landed back at Chicoa than the Portuguese army colonel came running across to our camp, in itself an unusual sight. Panting and puffing he approached Wing Commander Ossie Penton, and, scarcely able to contain himself, he blurted out what was to

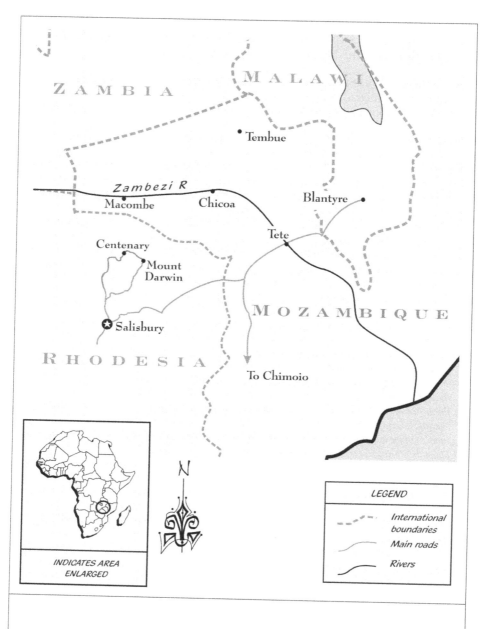

OPERATIONS INTO TETE PROVINCE

become the most famous words ever uttered at Chicoa. "Colonel Penton, good news, good news, we have just been ambushed!" Ossie's face was a picture. Recovering, he looked at the colonel and said, "Well Colonel, if that's the good news, what the hell is the bad news?" We deployed troops to the site but rain had washed the tracks away. One morning Captain Neves, their OC, gave the whole company a pep talk, telling them that convoys were going to be sent out on the three roads that led out of Chicoa to locate land-mines. This was a good plan—except for one small drawback—the intention was to discover the land-mines by hitting them. The plan also required volunteers to drive the vehicles. As these vehicles were not mine-protected, the volunteers were, in effect, going to their deaths. The troops got into a huddle and a group of volunteers stepped forward to loud applause from their comrades. They boarded the vehicles and drove off. Within the hour we were called on to pick up the casualties and drop trackers to search for spoor but even in the case of freshly laid mines, the rain soon washed any evidence away. The young people lost their lives needlessly but this did not seem to bother the officers. After a few days the exercise was called off—there were no more vehicles. There was one concession, however. The drivers of the Bedford trucks were allowed to remove the bonnets because if they hit a land-mine the bonnets would flip back and crush the driver! Then we were off again on our 'magical mystery tour', on this occasion to the picturesque resort of Tembué, an army camp encircled by a few mud huts. We were billeted in a corrugated iron shed, which had a hessian partition across the middle to separate the officers from the other ranks. A short walk found us at the officers' mess, next to which was an open air kitchen in which the chef was preparing our evening meal, surrounded by a host of flies. A severely malnourished cow that should have been put out of its misery months ago, was tethered nearby. On the second day, we returned to camp to find the cow missing. We decided not to risk it, so we dined on corned beef and 'dog' biscuits washed down with copious amounts of Cerveja (beer). The following morning the cow reappeared, so we needn't have worried, but the threat was ever-present that she would one day go missing for good. (Peter Briscoe, No 7 Squadron)

Operation Apollo took place south and south-west of the Cabora Bassa Gorge, inside Mozambique. No 3 Squadron was also heavily involved in this operation. At the beginning of the operation, VR pilots were used but authority for this was later withdrawn and only regular pilots flew. December 1970 saw No 4 Squadron "carrying out searches for brown jobs who fairly regularly seem to mislay themselves. (They don't make them as they used to!)"

Christmas Day, an aircraft of the Phyting Phourth (sic) was airborne to drop 'goodies' to the South African Police at Chirundu! Meanwhile at the front, Ed Potterton, Beav Baynham and Rog Watt flew armed top-cover for the troopies. Ed did courier and Beav casevaced, at night, an 'alien' troopie with a badly broken arm from 'Alpha' to 'Bravo'. The FAF folded on 15th December but was re-opened on 20th when Giles (Porter) casevaced a corpse from Binga to Bulawayo, a territorial who failed to answer a challenge. Dick Paxton casevaced a troopie who had shot himself. Beav casevaced a troopie with a broken arm from somewhere in 'funny land'. (No 4 Squadron Diary)

Along with their Christmas lunch, the security forces enjoyed wine donated by the commander in chief and all ranks of the Portuguese forces in Mozambique. Colonel J. Pavao Machado, the Portuguese Military Liaison Officer in Salisbury said, at the handing over ceremony, "This is a mark of esteem from my colleagues to their Rhodesian counterparts." In accepting the consignment, the officer commanding New Sarum, Group Captain Sandy Mutch said that the wine would be shared with the Rhodesian army personnel and would be enjoyed by all members of the security forces in the forward areas during the Christmas period.

CHAPTER 37

The calm before the storm

By the beginning of 1971, sanctions had been in force for five years and the Rhodesian Air Force was still flying high despite the dire predictions made in 1965. The men in the front line, when it came to keeping the air force in the air, were the technicians. It was their initiative and capability that was of ever-increasing importance, and a scheme was instituted by which monetary awards could be made to technicians for inventions. The awards were made in recognition of the airmen's ingenuity and skill in producing equipment that was either unobtainable or that would have involved the government in considerable expense.

On this same sanction-breaking subject, No 5 Squadron also achieved a breakthrough. Not only was an exceptional serviceability record achieved, resulting in a situation where the squadron had more aircraft available than aircrews, but also a Canberra was actually rebuilt during 1971 using parts from an aircraft that had been placed in storage as unserviceable. A further important innovation was the technique developed by Flight Lieutenant Rich Brand to harmonize the low-level bomb[ing] sight.

As well as local flying, No 1 Squadron carried out regular trips to South African and Mozambican bases and aircraft from other squadrons were operating across the Mozambique border on counter-insurgency operations.

As a security precaution, all roundels and serial numbers disappeared from the visible parts of Rhodesian Air Force machines during 1971. Serial numbers were still carried but greatly reduced in size and hidden away.

No 2 Squadron continued its dual role of operating both Vampires and Provosts and at the beginning of 1971, most flying time was spent carrying out conversions.

No 3 Squadron was involved with Operation Jacaranda, which had replaced Operation Apollo, while cloud-seeding Operation Tarpaulin, was still consuming a great deal of flying time. This was the third and final year of the cloud-seeding experiments, which had begun in 1968.

Among the casevacs carried out in the early months of the year were a ten-year-old African boy injured by a crocodile, an African constable run over by a train, an air force sergeant with an eye injury, and an RLI troopie.

In January 1971, during a weapons training exercise at Kutanga Range, the pilots of No 4 Squadron made an interesting discovery about the Trojan.

7th January. Converged on Kutanga. Dave Rowe and Ed Potterton were flying low-level, when Dave decided to run one fuel tank dry and then switch to the other. Indeed, when the engine spluttered, the fuel transfer cock was immediately switched over but the engine demonstrated a frightening reluctance to restart. While the ground rose up to smite these two intrepid aviators, Ed with sweating brow, frantically pumped mixture, throttle and other sundry controls. Then, just as all seemed lost, with the undercarriage tickling the grass, there was a round of applause from the engine and the Trog leapt away into the luft. Technical advice has since taught us that it is inadvisable (gross understatement) to run a tank dry unless there is sufficient height available to allow the motor to clear any possible airlocks in the fuel system as a result of completely draining a tank. (No 4 Squadron Diary)

There was a second exodus to Kutanga in February when an experiment was made using plastic fins on the rockets. It was a failure. The reason was that rockets that had already been fired heated the adjoining rocket tubes, melting the plastic fins. As a result, the rocket had no means of keeping straight. Some rockets, after having left the tube, arched back over the top of the aircraft never to be seen again.

During March 1971, No 1 Squadron members decided to keep fit by climbing mountains in the Chimanimani area and inter-squadron relationships were fostered when No 4 Squadron undertook a supply drop for them. It was also during March 1971 that No 4 Squadron took part in a Police Reserve Air Wing (PRAW) exercise in the Wankie area.

There was an unfortunate occurrence at New Sarum on 26th March when a fire broke out while practice bombs were being filled, resulting in injuries to five men, one of whom, Sergeant Harry Young, died later from his injuries. The following month there was another episode, which could also have had fatal results. This time the scene was Thornhill.

One fine dark evening during the course of night-flying circuits somewhere down-wind, something happened to Pete (Neddy) Nicholls's engine. Amid sparks, spewing oil, violent shuddering and dull explosions, Ned's falsetto voice announced over the R/T with an air of remarkable nonchalance, that he suspected a spot of engine trouble, and he would appreciate it very much if he could have immediate landing clearance as his machine refused to defy the laws of gravity and seemed intent on descending earthwards despite his efforts to the contrary. Calmly coaxing his stricken craft towards runway 13, the pilot skillfully alighted on the said runway and closed down. When the engine was examined, an unfamiliar bit of metal was observed projecting from the crankcase. A further detailed examination identified this 'bit of metal' as a conrod! (No 4 Squadron Diary)

During the month of April 1971, the air force was called in to locate a lost patrol in the Milibizi area, find a police patrol boat that had become mislaid in the Gache Gache area and also render assistance to some South African tourists. It seems that their boat became swamped while they were elephant-watching on Kariba. Two men were drowned but eight other people, a man, two women and five children were saved. The bodies of the two men were recovered after a ten-hour search by police and army personnel, and an air force helicopter.

Meanwhile No 2 Squadron had been carrying out take-off trials at Wankie National Park Air Field proving that it was suitable for limited Vampire operations.

May 14th was a great day for all Rhodesian motorists because it ended petrol rationing temporarily. Petrol had been fairly freely available for a while with extra coupons for sale at sixpence a unit for those who found the ration was insufficient.

The Rhodesia Air Force receives the Freedom of the City
Eleven days later on 25th May 1971, the Rhodesian Air Force enjoyed a very special day when they received the Freedom of the City of Salisbury from the mayor, Councillor T.E. Taylor. Commander of the air force, Air Marshal A.O.G. Wilson received the Deed to the City at the Town House at 15h00 and Salisbury city streets were closed to traffic while aircraft of

the air force carried out a flypast to coincide with the ceremony. Having been granted the Freedom of the City, the air force received the right to march through the city with bayonets fixed and colours flying. Three hundred men representing all units of the air force paraded with the BSAP Band. A civic cocktail party was held in the evening at Meikles Hotel. Archie Wilson took the opportunity to detail the roles of the air force. These were, he said, to defend Rhodesian airspace against hostile intruders, maintain a counter strike force, provide close support for the country's ground forces and to aid the civil power in the maintenance of law and order.

Meanwhile, No 4 Squadron had been bringing aid to the army. One had tried to ski down a hill with the result that he broke his arm, and another had been stabbed in the hand by a grunter while fishing and had suspected blood poisoning. A grunter is a small fish with toxic spines, found in the Zambezi.

During June 1971, the number of casevacs rose to three while the squadron also took part in low-level cross-country flights. Exercise Bird's Nest, an escape and evasion test was also staged in June. During this operation, Roger Watt and Dave Rowe had to make their way on foot from Chiredzi to Zaka using only their normal survival kit, and evade attempts to capture them. They were apprehended by two local African policemen but later escaped and managed to hijack a truck from an innocent African Internal Affairs driver, completing the exercise in style.

Operation Lobster

Following some months of calm, August 1971 saw a renewal of insurgent activity. On 3rd August, a train was derailed on the line near Victoria Falls, and ZAPU forces based in Lusaka claimed responsibility. A two-kilogram pack of Russian explosive was also discovered close to a culvert two kilometres from Victoria Falls but this had failed to detonate. Four days later, on 7th August, Radio Zambia stated that ZAPU had been responsible and that this incident was the beginning of a new offensive. At the end of the month, Mr Morris Element of Sinoia, driving his Citroën near Mana Pools detonated a land-mine. His wife and child were in the car but they escaped with minor injuries.

As a result of this activity, No 4 Squadron became involved in what was known as Operation Lobster:

> Action started at Rushinga and Dave Rowe made No 4 Squadron's presence known in the area mainly by dropping 48 supply boxes to starving brown jobs. Out of ten trips, nine were supply.

Operation Lobster continued into September and on 5th September, No 2 Squadron Provosts carried out two live strikes with .303s. On the second strike, both guns jammed after firing only 100 rounds. Operation Lobster came to a close at the end of September by which time 14 members of the armed band had been killed and the others had made their way back over the border to the north.

The Parachute Training School had maintained its busy schedule during 1971 and on 10th September, Sergeant Charles Buchan became a parachute-jumping instructor. Five days later, Dakota 7303 piloted by Flight Lieutenant Peter Bater, transported members of the SAS from New Sarum to Kariba for a descent into the lake, returning the following day. On that day, 16th September, the first free-fall drops were also made from a South African Cessna, piloted by Lieutenant van Rensburg flying at 5,000 feet.

During October and November 1971, intensive free-fall training was carried out at Cranborne using Dakota 7303 from No 3 Squadron, piloted on different occasions by Flight Lieutenants Peter Daykins, Mike Russell, George Alexander, Alan Bradnick, Peter Bater, Bill

Galloway and Bob d'Hotman and Squadron Leader Mike Gedye. Night descents were also carried out providing the Dakota pilots with a great deal of valuable training.

The Vampire T 11 was one of the few early jet aircraft that could get away with a belly landing. On 24th October 1971, the port undercarriage leg of Vampire R2424 refused to function. The pilot, Flight Lieutenant Chris Wentworth, contacted the tower and told the controllers that he would attempt a belly-landing. Fire and crash vehicles stood by as Chris burnt off as much fuel as possible and came in. The landing was an unqualified success. Damage to the aircraft was negligible and the pilot was unharmed. The air force technicians got the aircraft back on its undercarriage, towed it to a hangar and repaired it sufficiently to fly back to Thornhill. It was operational again some weeks later.

Following damage to two Vampires of No 2 Squadron during weapons training at Kutanga Range, it was decided that in future 20-pound (9kg) fragmentation bombs should not be dropped from Vampires.

Several casevacs were carried out by No 4 Squadron. One involved taking off before dawn with a Portuguese navigator who had been electrocuted and in another incident an aircraft landed at Chikwenya landing strip after dark with the aid of two Land Rover headlights, only to find that the stretcher case was able to walk to the aircraft.

At the beginning of November 1971, No 2 Squadron passed its Provosts on to the No 4 Squadron pilots who then took over the operational role. The changeover was noted in No 4 Squadron Diary.

> *The Provosts (all three of them)* arrived on the squadron this month (November) and conversion started immediately. The ground crews worked flat out all month to keep the three Provosts flying and something like 140 hours were flown in them.* (No 4 Squadron Diary)

As well as conversions, the squadron carried out three casualty evacuation flights, including a troopie who had injured his back falling from a helicopter, and a sick woman who was uplifted from Sengwa Gorge.

The rainy season 1970/71 had been intended as the final year for cloud-seeding trials, but a request came from the Meteorological Department for a bonus year, and despite pilot objections, No 3 Squadron once more found itself up among the clouds scattering crystals.

Frame 21 metal fatigue

On 16th November 1971, a No 5 Squadron Canberra crashed in heavy rain near Salisbury Airport. As the aircraft was carrying a full load of bombs that detonated on impact, wreckage was strewn over a wide area. A light aircraft and a helicopter had to be used to locate pieces of the bomber. Flight Lieutenant Alec Roughead and Air Lieutenant Guy Robertson died in the crash. There was a drop in squadron flying hours while the crash was being investigated. The result of the investigation was that the crash had been caused by metal fatigue in Frame 21.

Chris Dams who was station commander at New Sarum, said:

> *The fuselage of an aircraft is composed of a whole lot of frames that are joined together with stringers and then the whole thing is wrapped in a skin of aluminium. The frames give the aeroplane its shape and Frame 21 was particularly important because it was the frame to which the wings were attached. The frames are huge metal castings, very strong. On the Canberra they were constructed of a metal alloy, which was developed during the latter stages of World War II. At that juncture, the science of metallurgy and the knowledge of metal fatigue was in a very*

---

* During the year, ten Provosts arrived ex South Africa.

early stage. What happened over a period of time with this alloy was that a disassociation of the various elements of the alloy began to take place in an ageing process. This process was helped by the flexing of the whole structure and by changes of temperature and weathering and so on, as a result of which cracks began to develop in this frame. By the middle 1970s, we had a lot of trouble with this Frame 21 and it had to be inspected, by the end, almost on a daily basis. The inspection process was a very delicate and finely tuned scientific operation. We had to try to measure the extent to which the cracks had grown. We plotted the whole thing on graphs. The measurement process involved visual inspection, crack detection with a chemical that exposed the cracks, X-ray detection and electronic testing. If the structure became too weak, then it gave up the ghost and the wings or at least one of the wings came off—and that was it. The aircraft that crashed was undertaking a tight turn after take-off when the accident happened. The cracking problem had been known almost from the first day that we got the Canberras. The South African Canberras didn't suffer from the problem because they were built much later. Some Canberras even had the frame physically removed and a new frame put in but that has been beyond our capabilities—in fact, it would have been an uneconomic proposition. So we kept them on the go but carried out a close monitoring of what was happening. It meant that you could not fly the machine very fast at low levels, because that put extra stresses on the aeroplane. Nor could you fly it in bumpy conditions because again that put stresses on the aeroplane, so we limited operations to try to conserve the life that we had in the Canberras. (Chris Dams)

The accident had an adverse effect on squadron morale for a while. However, No 5 Squadron found itself so busy during 1972 that spirits soon lifted.

Parachute School

SAS tracker teams had been operating in Mozambique, at the request of the Portuguese, since 1969. By December 1971, No 3 Squadron, often using VRs as crew, was heavily involved in flying paratroops and resupply. For example, for the month of December 1971, the Parachute School log-book reads:

1	Dakota 7039	Flt Lt Jock McGregor	Demo
2	Dakota 3708	Flt Lt George Alexander	Seki pathfinder exercise
3	Dakota 7303	Flt Lt Peter Bater	Basic course air exercise
7	Dakota 3708	Air Lt Peter Woolcock	35 Basic 1st descent
8	Dakota 3708	Air Lt Peter Woolcock	35 Basic 2nd descent
9	Dakota 7303	Flt Lt Jock McGregor	35 Basic 3rd descent
9	Dakota 7303	Flt Lt Jock McGregor	35 Basic 4th descent. Cancelled—high wind.
10	Dakota 7039	Flt Lt Peter Bater	SAS Inkomo free fall
14	Dakota 7039	Flt Lt Nobby Nightingale	SAS Marlborough DZ
15	Dakota 3708	Flt Lt George Walker-Smith	35 Basic 7th descent
16	Dakota 3708	Flt Lt Mac Geeringh	35 Basic 8th descent
17	Dakota 3708	Flt Lt Alan Bradnick	SAS ex Condor
22	Dakota 3708	Flt Lt Peter Bater	Shuttle Thornhill
30	Dakota 3708	Flt Lt Alan Bradnick	SAS to Valley (a) Musengezi (36km inside Mozambique) (b) Sundi Gutsa
30	Dakota 3708	Air Lt Ed Potterton	Gutsa—New Sarum (heavy kit).

(Source: Charles Buchan, Parachute Training School)

Just before Christmas 1971, No 7 Squadron came to the aid of a truck driver, Cyrene Munengati, who, employed by a Salisbury-based transport firm, was on the road between Tete and Malawi when his vehicle detonated a land-mine. Mr Munengati was severely injured. He was taken by Portuguese army personnel to Nyamapanda by road but it was felt that the long journey back to Salisbury would be too much for the injured man. The local police called on the air force for help. A helicopter was brought in and Cyrene was whisked up and carried off to Harare Hospital where he made a complete recovery.

The Pearce Commission
The year 1971 had seen Rhodesia's economy booming with many sanctions-busting efforts succeeding but politically there had been a stalemate. Then towards the end of the year, Sir Alec Douglas Home, the British Foreign Secretary, visited Rhodesia. Following this visit, it was announced that agreement had been reached and that the proposals were to be submitted to the people as a whole. This testing of opinion was carried out early in the New Year 1972 when the Pearce Commission, under the leadership of Lord Pearce organized a test of acceptability. The commissioners were in Rhodesia for two months during which time they saw 6,130 Europeans and 114,600 Africans out of a total population of over 5,000,000. The Pearce commission completed its work in Rhodesia on 10th May 1972 and having examined, in London, the written evidence of Rhodesians living in Great Britain and in other parts of the world, it completed and published its report on 23rd May 1972. The commission came to the conclusion that the proposals were acceptable to the great majority of Europeans but that in its opinion the majority of Africans rejected the proposals as a basis for independence.

The arrival of the commission triggered riots in the black townships, particularly in Gwelo. No 4 Squadron was on stand-by for three days while on 17th January 1972, helicopters of No 7 Squadron were called out to help control the rioters. During this operation, one helicopter crashed killing Flight Lieutenant Guy Munton-Jackson and Flight Sergeant Peter Garden. Once again, there seems to have been no definite reason for this crash. However, a combination of bad weather and spatial disorientation were definitely contributory factors.

Apart from helping to control outbreaks of civil disobedience, the air force was not really involved in the work of the commission, although No 3 Squadron was called on to fly loads of pamphlets outlining the proposals to various outlying spots. In fact, No 3 Air Supply Platoon, which had been operating with No 3 Squadron perfecting supply-dropping techniques, was really put to the test. The squadron also carried out one sky shout over Gwelo after there had been arson and looting in the African township before the arrival of the commissioners.

The volunteer reserve
No 3 Squadron was also providing Dakotas for the Parachute School and the Special Air Services. During February, March, April and May 1972, 36 and 37 Basic Courses were completed including free-fall techniques. Added to this, an 'X' Parachute water jump into Lake MacIlwaine was carried out with aircrew members. The SAS also carried out a night drop at Makuti Air Field and training exercises with SAS pathfinders in Seki Reserve. With all this activity taking place, the squadron often found itself short of pilots and almost continuous use was made of the volunteer reserve pilots.

In March 1972, Group Captain Graham Smith, the second officer commanding of the reserve retired and was succeeded by Group Captain Ossie Penton. The *Rhodesia Herald* marked Graham's retirement by printing a long article detailing the work carried out by the VRs. There were eight VR squadrons and two flights, each of which was trained and equipped for specific tasks. The VRs helped to man tactical forward airfields, providing key personnel such as camp commandants, field security officers, intelligence and operations staff. Reservists also assisted with the movement of supplies and equipment, and provided essential support in many trade groups.

A man joined the VR for a minimum of three years, with the option of extending that period. Each recruit had to pass the normal air force medical test and a general service examination covering academic subjects. The recruit was then assessed on his results and channelled into one of a number of special training courses conducted by the individual VR squadrons. He then began training as an aircraftman, attending courses in both practical and theoretical subjects at elementary, intermediate and advanced levels.

Initially, reservists had been expected to spend eight hours a month on training, lectures and exercises but this length of time had proved inadequate and all the squadrons had increased this quota with regular fortnightly training evenings and occasional weekend field exercises. VRs came from all walks of life: lawyers, bank managers, businessmen, schoolteachers and so on. The VR squadrons were established throughout the country and were accommodated in existing military establishments where possible. (Reservists received no pay for the time and effort they spent in training but they were paid when they were called up for active service, which usually meant leaving home for up to three weeks at a time.)

101	(Bulawayo) Squadron	Brady Barracks
102	(Gwelo) Squadron	Thornhill Air Station
	Redcliff Flight	Under the command of 102 Squadron
103	(Salisbury) Squadron	VR Centre Cranborne Barracks (This included the VR pilots pool)
104	(Umtali) Squadron	Squadron HQ in centre of town
	'C' flight Chipinga	Under the command of 104 Squadron
105	(Lomagundi) Squadron	Preston Farm, Banket
106	(Air Movements) Squadron	VR Centre Cranborne Barracks
107	(Lowveld) Squadron	Buffalo Range Air Field
108	(Field) Squadron	VR Centre Cranborne Barracks

The squadrons were administered from the VR headquarters, which was part of air force headquarters. The VR headquarters staff consisted of, Group Captain Ossie Penton, Commanding Officer VR, and Staff Officer VR, Squadron Leader Peter Cooke who were regular officers, and a number of VR officers on full time call-up. In the mid-1970s, officer commanding VR took on the hat of staff officer VR, and staff officer VR took on the hat of Reserves 1. These two officers were responsible for the administration and control of the National Service Intakes, the Territorial Force A and B Reserves, and the Reserve Pilot Pool. They were assisted by a small staff of three regular NCOs supplemented by a couple of national servicemen and territorial force members on call-up. It is interesting to note that this small staff administered a force larger than the regular force. In late 1978, Ossie Penton retired and was succeeded by Staff Officer, Peter Cooke, whose post of SOVR and Reserves 1 was taken over by Squadron Leader Prop Geldenhuys.

One outstanding example of the hard work and enthusiasm of the VRs was the Training Centre for Nos 103, 106 and 108 Squadrons at Salisbury's Cranborne Barracks. The building had originally been the hospital and dental clinic for the RAF's RATG during World War II. It was in a very sorry state when the VRs took it over during 1971. There followed a great deal of spare-time work and a fair amount of scrounging, as well as a flood of contributions. The change was dramatic. By March 1972, each squadron had its own self-contained block with offices, lecture rooms and other facilities to cater for the individual squadron roles, as well as a comfortable recreation centre with that most important item—a bar.

During the early months of 1972, the usual casualty evacuations were carried out by Nos 4 and 7 Squadrons, sometimes with more than a few problems, as is shown here:

Sunday 28th May. *Mike (Plod) Litson carried out a night casevac from Binga to Wankie. He was having a few Chibulies (beers) in the Baobab when he was called out to uplift an unconscious brown job. He set course and landed up over Zambia. After much nervous tension he found Binga, uplifted the brown job and then on the way back ended up at Kamativi—that was his fourth mistake that month (which had included an unscheduled landing in Botswana on 5th May).* (No 4 Squadron Diary)

In May 1972, No 1 Squadron converted from the old 60-pound rocket projectiles to 68mm Matra rockets. They had the chance to put their new armament to the test in June during a force exercise code-named Blackjack. This was held on Lake Kariba with attacks taking place on a moving target on the waters of the lake. The Hunters and the Vampires had a unique experience in that there was no external reference for release height as was usual in ground attack. Consequently there were some alarming moments, one when Mark McLean went through his own spray on pull-out in his Hunter, and another when air headquarters personnel on the towing vessel kept shouting "STOP, STOP, STOP" because they thought the aircraft were targeting them. Some wag in the attacking aircraft asked, "Are you pulling the target or are you pushing it?" which caused great consternation aboard the vessel. There were others who joked about sinking the vessel on purpose so they could all go up a few ranks.

The Security Training Unit

Insurgent activity was increasing and with it the need for more security staff and larger training facilities. A Security Training Unit or STU was set up by Ken Salter in the old signals building at New Sarum. Training at the school could be roughly divided into the following categories: Police and Law, Field Craft, COIN (counter-insurgency), Weapon Training, First Aid, Physical Training, Armoured Fighting Vehicles and Air Field Defence. According to Paul Hill, second in command to Ken Salter:

Our weapon training was of a very high standard, particularly with the weapons peculiar to our work. While the MAG and rifle featured heavily, the sub machine gun and pistol were given greater emphasis than in the army for example. It is fair comment to say that in Rhodesia the air force was the leader in the training of pistol and SMG techniques. This may be gathered from the following examples, from amongst many. Ken Salter was teaching the two-handed 'weaver stance' with pistol in 1968, whereas the police only abandoned single-handed shooting in 1976. I was requested to instruct elements of the Selous Scouts in handgun techniques. There were several weapons peculiar to the air force, on which we had to train. One was the infamous 'Puza Monster', so named because it 'puzad' (ate up) .303 ammunition at an incredible rate, when it worked. It was two aircraft Browning machine guns fixed together, each firing at a rate of 1,200 rounds per minute. Probably the best slimming machine ever invented! The gunner held on to two handles like grim death and pressed his chest against a chest pad, besides trying to hit the target. His main preoccupation was to keep his feet on the ground! His number two meanwhile was rushing from side to side in a vain attempt to keep the thing fed! Usually the guns stopped solid with any one of a dozen types of stoppage before the number two collapsed from exhaustion or the gunner's fillings fell out of his teeth. Training was primarily for the defence of forward airfields, a boring, monotonous job. It was hard to maintain discipline because the guards became demotivated as uneventful month followed uneventful month. Only in the latter part of the war did things really hot up as far as the Security Branch was concerned. We did find, however, that with regular continuation training, we not only kept up the standard of our defences, but also were able to maintain, to some large degree, the keenness of the men. The great demotivating factor remained the fact that our men, no matter how well qualified, invariably found themselves under the command of men who knew little or nothing about security. We commenced training in earnest just in time to be given our eviction orders! The Signals Branch wanted the building back. So we got an office in a block beside the Parachute Training School, and directly opposite the office of the station signals officer, which was to have amusing consequences. (Paul Hill)

The saga of the armoured cars

To explain the background we have to go back about six months; it was then that Flight Lieutenant Jack Lewis-Walker (Boss Jack) had taken over as weapons instructor from Don Graham. Boss Jack along with Ken Salter sported an extravagant moustache and an unusual sense of humour. A South African liaison officer from the Southern Cross Fund had stopped by earlier in the year to ask for requests. The Security Branch had already received a lot of essential equipment donated by South Africa, in the way of radios and weapons.

This day the eminent gentleman stuck his head round the door and said, "I suppose more radios and machine guns?" Boss Jack replied dryly, "Of course and a dozen armoured cars, please." Six months later a dozen armoured cars arrived! Now we had a problem. What do you do with 12 armoured cars? The VRs were out for a takeover of these new toys. The Motor Transport Section grabbed all the back-up equipment, and the game was on! The Security Branch would never be the same again. We all trooped up to marvel at these wonders. 'Jack, the Tank', alias Squadron Leader Jack Walls VR said he would write an operation manual for them. He had served in Matildas during World War II. Air Lieutenant Alan Dewsbury, impetuous as ever, wanted to drive one immediately. Jack Lewis-Walker just wandered around the cars muttering to himself. Well, the problem was solved through the good offices of our friendly SA Liaison Officer. Arrangements were to be made to send us to Bloemfontein for training. When I was informed, by Boss Jack, that I had won 'first prize', 12 weeks in Bloemfontein, I immediately volunteered for the Russian Front. To which he replied, any more of that stuff and I would get second prize, i.e. 24 weeks in Bloemfontein. I could write a book on our exploits at Tempe, School of Armour. I think Lieutenant Kriek, our course instructor, later Commandant Kriek, was very relieved when we left. Another week of us and he would have had a nervous breakdown. On the course were Air Lieutenant Peter Cowan (later squadron leader), Air Lieutenant Alan Dewsbury, Sergeants Barry (Chimp) Webster and John Cox (later wing commander and one of the air force of Zimbabwe officers to suffer detention and torture), Charlie Bean, George Parson (later flight sergeant and the force driving instructor) Barry Taylor (later air lieutenant—also detained with John Cox) and me, Paul Hill (later master sergeant). (Paul Hill)

To return to the story of the STU (Security Training Unit) and its second home opposite the office of the station signals officer:

This gentleman (the station signals officer) did not like us. I don't think he liked anyone, not even himself. Amongst his endearing habits was complaining about everything we did, in particular about the noise our Eland armoured cars made. Well they did. Just as beauty is in the eye of the beholder, sweet sounds are in the ear of the listener! To confirmed 'armour nuts' like us, the sound of an air-cooled flat four warming up (a morning ritual) was the sweetest. Anyway, it made far less noise than a Dakota. One morning he had had enough, and shortly before Ken Salter and I arrived, he ordered our new, raw trainees to stop the racket and move the cars onto the road some distance away. I arrived first and blew a fuse. Ken Salter arrived shortly *afterwards and saw an opportunity for a little fun at our friend's expense! His conversation with the station signals officer went like this: "Well. I'm getting Paul to take the cars over to the Air Force Vehicle Section to see how much damage has been done to them. I'll let you know, sir, after I've reported to the CO and the Provost Marshal." Gasp. Pause. "What?" "Well," said Ken, "as you know, you do irreparable harm to an Eland by moving it on a cold engine." Pregnant pause. "And that is what you ordered the trainees to do." Gasp. "But…" said Ken, "they are expensive things. The engine alone costs $2,000. We should know by 12h00, sir." It was a very worried officer who waited for noon that day! Our new image did not go unnoticed by the remainder of the air force. Well, how can you not notice a noisy Eland rumbling around the place, upsetting the quiet routine of a well-ordered establishment, after all wasn't this the New Sarum Flying Club! MT Section didn't like us because we used all their premium petrol and more importantly I had run over their fire bucket. OC flying did not like us because we used his hardstandings as short cuts. We would damage them, he claimed as our cars were too heavy, a logic that eluded me. A 5.75-ton Eland will damage a hard-standing, a 15-ton aeroplane will not? Interesting! But most of all we were different! The sight of a goggled figure standing in the turret was too much for most airmen. The inevitable Sieg Heil salutes came almost as soon as the cars appeared. The parachute training instructors, always a high-spirited humorous lot, soon coined the title 'The Desert Rats'. One day they struck. Ken Salter and I were enjoying our lunch when I saw Ken stiffen and look out of the window. A furtive figure was moving between our parked Elands. We crept out and caught Flight Sergeant Tony Hughes spraying little black rats on the doors of the cars! He was sent on his way by a very (to all appearances) irate WO I Salter. A letter of protest was sent to the OCPTS saying that if a job is undertaken it should not be half done, and Flight Sergeant Hughes must spray rats on all 12 Elands! The parachute jump instructors went one better. Later that day a 'necktie party' arrived outside, and announced that as Tony Hughes had been caught (the only and most heinous offence in the airmen's book) he must suffer the ultimate penalty! They then proceeded with hanging the poor wretch from a gantry outside our office. As he was bound hand and foot, he really could not do much for himself except go funny colours. How far they would have gone I don't know; anyway Ken Salter then found himself pleading on behalf of Hughes! The Elands were decorated. We retaliated by kidnapping Fred, the parachute instructors' Teddy Bear, a hero of 113 fatal jumps (they never could get his chute right) and honour was restored. Later in the war, we adopted a motto to go with the 'rat' that had now become a 'mouse': 'Seek and Squeak', a parody of No 4 Squadron's motto 'Seek and Strike', much to their annoyance. It was then that we decided that there were three types of driver in the air force, driver armour, driver motor transport and driver airframe!* (Paul Hill)

Disaster at Wankie

The 6th June 1972 was a day that will forever be remembered at Wankie Colliery. A huge methane gas explosion tore through No 2 Shaft, trapping hundreds of miners below ground.

Under the headline Disaster at Wankie, the *Rhodesia Herald* told the story the next day:

A massive rescue operation was immediately started. Rescue teams from throughout Rhodesia converged on the scene and an elite 20-man Proto team from the South African Chamber of Mines, Johannesburg, is due to arrive at Wankie by charter plane at about 6.30 am. The Minister of Mines, Mr Ian Dillon left for Wankie after making a statement in the House of Assembly. Rhodesian Air Force aircraft and a number of other chartered planes flew in doctors, mining engineers and the BSA Police Support Unit.

Another headline read: 'Airlift of Oxygen':

Rhodesian Air Force planes, carried emergency supplies of oxygen and special rescue personnel to Wankie Colliery yesterday. As the underground ventilation system was damaged in the explosion, it was vital that liquid oxygen should reach the rescue workers as quickly as possible. "Some of the oxygen backpacks worn by the mine's rescue workers operate on liquid oxygen," said Mr Emil Vanderzypen, the manager (medical) of Rhodox. "The air force asked us if we could let them have containers of liquid oxygen to fly to Wankie," he said. "The only containers in the country suitable for transportation by aircraft are held by the Animal Breeders Co-op in Salisbury. They lent us six 25-litre containers, which we filled and sent to New Sarum Air Base." Mr Vanderzypen said Wankie Colliery had some containers, which were sent by road to Rhodox's Bulawayo branch for filling immediately after the explosion. "This rescue apparatus is brand-new and has only recently been issued to Wankie," he said. "We are also sending gas and apparatus designed for the relief of pain in rescue operations." On one of the air force planes was the chief government mining engineer, Mr Bernard Davey. (Rhodesia Herald)

The rescue teams were unable to reach the trapped men. Deadly methane gas and carbon monoxide seeped through the network of tunnels extending over seven kilometres below the surface. Only one man was brought up alive. Four hundred and sixty-five miners died and it was later decided that the risk in bringing the bodies out was too great. They were left where they had died, at the bottom of the Kamandama and Central Shafts, which were then sealed.

Cooperation with the SAAF
It was in 1972 that SAAF Canberras began operating together with Rhodesian Air Force planes from a Rhodesian base. No 12 Squadron SAAF detached two of its aircraft to New Sarum during July, August and September. In cooperation with Rhodesian Air Force Canberras, they undertook a survey task of enormous proportions. This happy combined operation was only the beginning of a long and beneficial liaison between the two forces.

The Hunters were also involved in detachment flights to Durban and Lourenço Marques. During a local flight to Bulawayo, Rickie Culpan lost his cockpit canopy. He was not impressed with open cockpit flying, as he was unhappy about falling out. (No 1 Squadron Diary)

The squadron also flew several sorties in support of the army during a training exercise, Countdown, with only limited success it seems:

The TF [territorial force] units filled the air with sarcastic remarks but fortunately for them we were not armed. From our side we did not know what the situation on the ground was, with regards to enemy and friendly forces … and the sorties did not seem to achieve much.
(No 1 Squadron Diary)

Vampire crash
On 4th August 1972, a Vampire T 11 crashed just off the Umvuma road, killing the pilot, Air Sub-Lieutenant David Brown. Writing later about this crash, Group Captain Bill Sykes says:

David Brown was my student on the OCU. He had recently returned from leave after gaining his Wings and had also been awarded the Sword of Honour. We had done two dual general sorties to familiarize him with the Vampire again and he was cleared to go solo. Aircraft were extremely valuable because they could not be replaced and to this end, pilots practised the manœuvre of making a 'horseshoe' after take-off. This was a simulated engine-failure, designed to train the pilot to land back on the runway, providing his airspeed was above 180 knots at the time of the failure. At any speed less than that, the pilot was briefed to land ahead, or eject. The Vampire ejection seat had minimum criteria of 200 feet above ground level and 120 knots. It was assumed that David Brown attempted the horseshoe at a speed below 180 knots and consequently was unable to complete the manœuvre satisfactorily. He managed to get the Vampire most of the way round the horseshoe turn but did not have enough speed to reach the runway. He did not eject and the aircraft crashed short of the threshold. Dave lost his life trying to save a valuable aircraft. (Bill Sykes)

Rescue at Mtarazi

The training sessions undertaken by No 7 Squadron were put to good use when, towards the end of August 1972, one of the squadron's helicopters was called upon to take part in a tricky rescue operation. The scene was the Mtarazi Falls, situated close to the scenic drive between Inyanga and Umtali. Rosalie Ashton and her husband were staying in a holiday cottage near the falls. At about 18h00 on Sunday evening, 20th August, Mrs Ashton went out for a walk and when she did not return her husband raised the alarm. Her father-in-law, Dr E.H. Ashton, her husband and the occupants of the neighboring cottages searched all night, without success. Next morning they were joined by members of the Umtali Dog Section (BSAP), local farmers and their employees. Two hundred workers from the Rhodesian Wattle Company were called in and members of the Police Reserve Air Wing helped in the search.

At about midday on Monday, rescuers spotted a small piece of cloth caught in a bush on the face of a cliff at Mtarazi Falls. This led rescuers to Rosalie, who had been seriously injured in a fall and had been lying in pain for more than 20 hours. That she was still alive was a miracle because she had plunged 30 metres down a cliff before her fall was broken by some bushes. She had then tumbled another 90 metres through undergrowth and small trees into a gully. In all she had fallen 125 metres. A mountain rescue team assembled in Salisbury, was flown to the area and they managed to reach Mrs Ashton but could not lift her out.

An air force helicopter, piloted by Flight Lieutenant John Annan, already in the area, was called in to help. The helicopter hovered 15 metres above the ledge, while a stretcher was lowered into a small clearing, which had been cut by the rescue team. Rosalie, gently strapped into the harness, was winched up to the hovering helicopter. During this operation, the rotor blades of the Alouette were whirring within three metres of the cliff face. The helicopter lifted the injured woman to the cliff top where a doctor administered emergency treatment and painkillers. Mrs Ashton was then flown to Umtali Hospital where she was found to be suffering from severe concussion as well as injuries to her right arm and left ankle.

Operation Sable

Operation Sable, which lasted through September and into October 1972, was largely conducted in what was known as funny land, in other words, Mozambique. Commenting in its usual lighthearted way, No 4 Squadron Diary remarks:

> *Tony Oakley was unanimously chosen, from a cast of hundreds, to take a liaison officer to Tete. He was eventually lashed down in the cockpit and launched into the wild blue yonder. One day, while at Tete, and with a few cervejas [Portuguese for beer] under the old belt, he was only just stopped from doing a low-level pass over the Frelimo HQ to drop a toilet roll. Provosts flew 30h10 on this op. Trogs trudged through 79h05. SAS clobbered a couple of terrorists and caused sufficient noise to disperse the rest.* (No 4 Squadron Diary)

On 13th October 1972, four aircraft were positioned at Nyamasoto to support the RLI (Rhodesian Light Infantry) and a further operation code-named Crater started on 30th

October, when two territorial force men were blown up by a mine in the Binga area. A few insurgents were captured and some arms discovered and the two operations were concluded by the middle of November.

Air force dog section
Towards the end of October 1972, a death was announced in the *Rhodesia Herald*. It was that of Chaka Zulu, better known as Chaka, the wonder dog, who had died at the age of eleven. Chaka's owner and trainer, Flight Sergeant Alec Mann, the Rhodesian Air Force Dogmaster at New Sarum was reported as saying, "I admit I cried after the vet put Chaka away. He was suffering from old age and had had a series of heart attacks. He had to go."

Chaka was born in Kariba and given to Alec Mann as a puppy by Mr George Davison. Chaka's excellent temperament and the patience of his trainer had enabled him to master some spectacular tricks, such as jumping through a flaming hoop, carrying a burning torch in his jaws and balancing while he walked along two parallel ropes.

It was probably because of the interest caused by Chaka's death that the *Rhodesia Herald* published an article on the Air Force Dog Training School. They interviewed Chaka's owner Alec Mann, who said, "We are at present about ten dogs below establishment and this is sufficient reason to recruit more. Especially when you consider that a good percentage of our trained guard dogs are reaching retirement age—that's about ten years old." He said that the air force was looking for male Alsatians aged between nine months and two years. Alsatians were preferred because they had the best natural qualities for training as guard dogs. Labradors were used as trackers.

The dogs were trained to work with a number of different handlers. But, as Alec Mann pointed out: "The dogs respond to secret commands so that any stranger who tries to order one of our multi-handler dogs around, is in for a big surprise. Training a guard or security dog to air force standards takes about three months, although a dog could be pushed to do guard work within six weeks. To us, they are weapons and we look after them just as a soldier looks after his rifle. Air force dogs are treated as part of the service establishment. They all have serial numbers and are posted just like service personnel."

The Air Force Dog Section at New Sarum, which was established in 1962, supplied trained dogs for guard and security work for all air force establishments. At this stage, the dog school relied on young dogs coming in from outside but later the school instituted its own breeding programme because it was unable to find sufficient canine recruits of the correct standard.

The air force celebrates its 25th anniversary
The air force staged its first major air show in five years, at home in Thornhill on 8th October 1972. Between 8,000 and 10,000 people attended the spectacular display, which included free-fall parachute drops from Dakota 3708 flown by Flight Lieutenant Ivan Holshausen; a tail chase sequence by four Provosts and an aerobatics display by a single Provost. This was followed by two formation displays, one by six Vampires and the other by four Hunters. There were also casevac demonstrations by an Alouette and supply drops from a Dakota.

This was a foretaste of what was to come on 28th November 1972, when the Rhodesian Air Force celebrated its 25th anniversary. This was 25 years from November 1947, which has been taken as the date of the reformation of the air force following World War II. In fact, No 1 Squadron could trace its history back much earlier. To mark this historic day, 300 air force men marched through the city of Salisbury with bayonets fixed and colours flying, a right they had received when they were granted the Freedom of the City in 1971. Nine Hunters took part in a low-level flypast overhead. Before the parade, the President, Mr Clifford Dupont, presented colours to the air force at Government House.

It is a tradition of the Royal Air Force that the Queen's/King's Colours, or in this case the President's Colours may only be awarded to a unit after it has been in existence for at least 25 years, and provided it is worthy and has earned the honour.

Summing up for the year 1972, in a report published mid-way through the following year, the Secretary of Defence, Mr J.A.G. Parker stated that nearly $24,000,000 (Rhodesian) had been spent on the defence of Rhodesia, and provision had been made for this sum to be raised to $28,000,000 but money used for defence should be considered well spent. Rhodesia was spending 2,1% of her gross national product on defence compared with 2,5% by South Africa, 7,9% by USA and 11% by USSR. In the light of these figures, there should be little cause for complaint. Mr Tony Parker continued:

Although one must respect the contention that Rhodesia is still a young developing nation, without the substantial industrial and technological backing of the older developed countries, and cannot therefore expect to bear lightly the burden of expenditure carried by such countries, there would appear to be scope for the payment of a higher premium in the interests of the assured security of this country. In terms of Africa today, the best deterrent to any would-be aggressor, most probably lies in the direction of a firm and conclusive indication that terrorism and subversion cannot succeed.

Shortage of finance and European manpower was, however, causing concern to the army and air force alike. The air force had lost many technicians in the senior grades to private companies. Men with these qualifications were constantly in demand in the civilian field, where they found little difficulty in obtaining better rates of pay and less onerous hours apart from less physical risk. The problem highlighted the need for a review of conditions of service, pay and pension schemes.

Air Marshal Archie Wilson also made the point that the air force was operating aircraft of increasing age and therefore it was necessary to increase technical vigilance, expertise and improvisation, as well as shortening maintenance cycles. "It is timely and appropriate to sound a note of warning that the upkeep of, and improvements to, the modern air force are expensive and we must be prepared for greater spending in this direction," he added.

As the number of flying hours increased, to nearly 20,000 during 1972, ever greater demands were placed on the members of the air force. The fact that there had been fewer accidents proportionately, reflected creditably on the aircrew and the technical branch whose ingenuity and effort had proved invaluable in the maintenance of standards and who were well supported by the equipment personnel.

It was reported on 16th December that national service was to be increased from six to 12 months starting on 1st January 1973. This was due to the establishment of nationalist bases in Botswana, increased infiltration by ZIPRA forces from Zambia and by ZANLA insurgents into Mozambique, events that were to be dramatically illustrated before the end of the year.

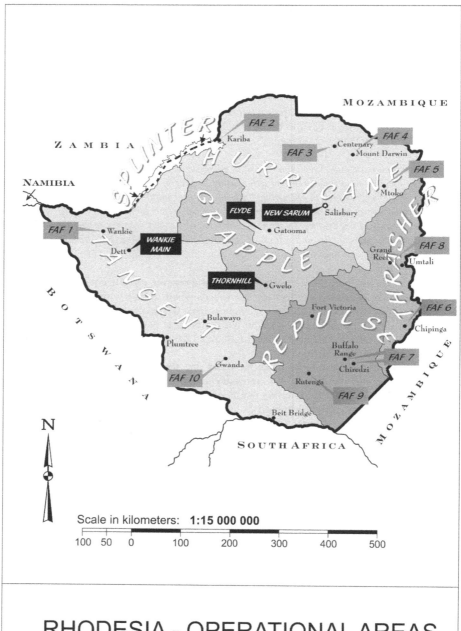

RHODESIA - OPERATIONAL AREAS

CHAPTER 38
Operation Hurricane

During the period 1970 to 1972 ZANLA cadres had infiltrated and cached armaments and stores in north-eastern Mashonaland. They had obtained by fair means and foul the help of local people. The words Chaminuka and Nehanda were appearing with increasing regularity in security reports. Chaminuka, a prophet and rainmaker, one of the most powerful spirits of the Shona people, inhabits a human male. Following the death of one Chaminuka, the spirit enters another body. Nehanda is traditionally another powerful spirit, which takes a female form, and is a medium and rainmaker. The Chaminuka and Nehanda who lived in the late 19th century were extremely influential leaders during the Mashona rebellion in the 1890s. They were executed by the authorities for their part in the rebellion.

ZANLA had stolen a march on the Rhodesian authorities by invoking Chaminuka in their anti-government campaign. They also abducted Mbuya Nehanda, the reincarnation of Nehanda. Some attempts were made to counter these moves by approaching local spirit mediums who were sympathetic to the legitimate government but these efforts were never pursued with any determination. So it was that slowly but surely ZANLA forces infiltrated the north-eastern areas. One large cache of arms was discovered near Mtoko late in 1972 following the arrest of three men but largely these covert activities went undetected.

Altena Farm attack

Early in December 1972, a ZANLA group, under the leadership of Solomon Mujuru (*nom de guerre* Rex Nhongo), crossed the border between Mukumbura and Musengezi. During the early hours on the morning of Thursday 22nd December, this group using RPG-7 rocket launchers and AK-47 automatic rifles attacked Altena Farm on the Zambezi escarpment near Centenary. This was the first occasion on which rocket launchers had been used within Rhodesia. The farm belonged to Marc de Borchgrave, but when the attack occurred, the farmhouse was occupied by Mr de Borchgrave's mother, Mrs Biddle (who was on holiday from England) and four children. The attack, which lasted only about 30 seconds, resulted in injury to eight-year-old Jane who was wounded in the foot.

Mrs Biddle smuggled the children out of the house and drove slowly away without using the vehicle headlights. She narrowly missed hitting a land-mine, which had been laid in the driveway and which detonated the following morning beneath an army vehicle injuring four RLI soldiers, one of whom, Corporal Norman Moore, died later. The injured child was taken to hospital while the other members of the family took shelter at the adjoining Whistlefield Farm, home of Archie Dalgleish. That night, 23rd December, this farm was attacked with rockets, hand grenades and rifles and once again land-mines were placed in the road. Mark de Borchgrave and his nine-year-old daughter Anne were injured in the attack.

After these attacks, a Joint Operations Centre (JOC) was set up at Centenary where air

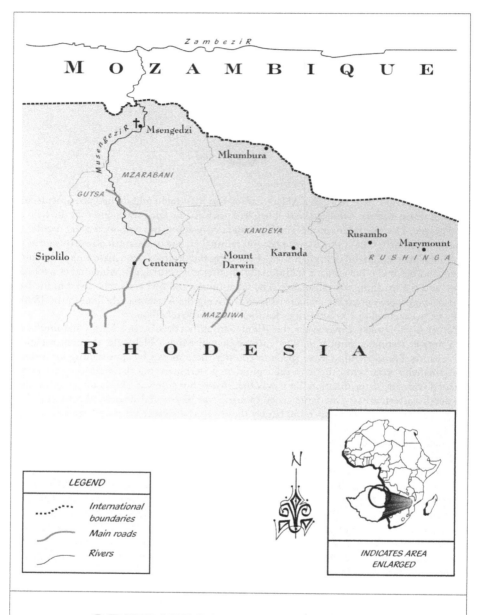

LEGEND

.... International boundaries
⌒ Main roads
⌒ Rivers

INDICATES AREA ENLARGED

OPERATION HURRICANE - THE START

force, police, army and Special Branch could pool their information, and Rhodesian Air Force squadrons were immediately placed on stand-by. This caused some disruption to the Christmas festivities, which were in full swing.

> *On 20th December all the guys had a bit of a thrash at the Sports Club over the lunch period, during which much drinking and eating of rolls, cheese and pickled onions took place with nearly all concerned getting R-soles by 3 o'clock. At this critical stage, there was a call-out. Alf Wilde and Peter (Simmo) Simmonds headed for the Burg [Salisbury] rather under the weather. This was the start of Operation Hurricane. Steve Kesby and Vic Culpan followed the next day in two Trogs [Trojans]. They all stayed at Centenary for Christmas and the New Year. Trojan flying consisted mainly of telstar, communications/courier flight, casevacs and the conversions for Greg Todd and Peter Simmonds. Provost flying consisted mainly of telstar, top cover and armed recce. Dave Rowe and Mike Litson went to FAF 2 (Kariba) and FAF 1 (Wankie) respectively, on 24th December for the normal FAF duties. Rob Tasker and John Blythe-Wood went to FAF 1 with the Provost to do stand-by.* (No 4 Squadron Diary, Dec. 1972)

No 1 Squadron was also placed on stand-by at 05h15 on 21st December. The squadron had to fly further recces over Christmas and New Year. During police, army and air force follow-up operations, three members of the ZANLA group were killed and three captured. One of those wounded in this engagement was picked up near Centenary on 27th December.

In February 1973, two men appeared in court for the attack on the Dalgleish farm. Security forces claimed to have killed or captured nearly all the members of this gang. In March, these two men received the death sentence for the attack and for the death of Corporal Moore.

Following the attack on Altena Farm and the intensification of the Bush War, the Vampire T 11 came into extensive use. Its top speed, considerably slower than that of the Hunter, was not a disadvantage because it could orbit closer to a target and get a better sighting. The Vampire T 11 two-seater was rock-steady and could deliver a formidable load of ordnance. Many Rhodesian pilots had not only trained on these aircraft but also had their first taste of combat in them during trips to Aden. To modern eyes the Vampire may look ungainly with its twin booms and fat fuselage but it was a sturdy aircraft and like all Rhodesian aeroplanes soldiered on long after its airframe was officially time-expired.

New Year 1973 began with something of a bang in the early hours of 8th January when the district commissioner's buildings in Mount Darwin were attacked. The offices were empty but in the Country Club nearby, a few late visitors were still celebrating. The ZIPRA attackers fired two rockets and sprayed the offices, the Country Club and the squash court with automatic rifle and machine gun fire. The result was two holes in the roof of the district commissioner's office, a few bullet holes in the Country Club and land-mine damage to a bridge on the road into Mount Darwin where a Bailey bridge had to be erected later.

On that same day, 8th January, a No 7 Squadron pilot, Flight Lieutenant Graham Cronshaw and Technician Sergeant Rob Blumeris were called out to Kazungula following a land-mine incident on the Kazungula/Victoria Falls road in which two South African policemen lost their lives. This aircraft and another piloted by Flight Lieutenant Ian Harvey eventually recovered to Victoria Falls when it was realized that the terrorists had crossed the border back into Zambia after laying the mine.

Rhodesia closes the border with Zambia
In the middle of the previous November, the Rhodesian government had warned Zambia about permitting insurgents to operate across the border and so, on 9th January at 22h00 Rhodesia closed the border posts at Victoria Falls, Kariba and Chirundu. All road and rail

traffic between the two countries came to a halt. Later, Rhodesia was to reopen her side of the border but the Zambian side remained closed, although freight trains carrying copper from the Congo were allowed through. The rolling stock was shunted to the centre of the bridge from where a Rhodesian locomotive was connected to move the goods through the country.

Operations into Mozambique

On 12th January 1973, Air Lieutenant Dick Paxton and Sergeant R. M. Cuttler, from No 7 Squadron were operating the Rushinga-based aircraft. During a routine patrol, they spotted an abandoned Land Rover, and landing their helicopter close by, discovered that the vehicle contained the bodies of Robert Edward Bland and Denis William Sanderson. These were two inspectors, employed by the Ministry of Lands, who had been reported missing earlier, and had been killed by members of a ZANLA cadre. Fortunately, the terrorists were no longer in the area, because the engine of the helicopter had been shut down after landing and it was an ideal position for an ambush. Had the ZANLA group still been close by they could easily have destroyed the aircraft. A third land inspector, Gerald Douglas Hawksworth, who was with Bland and Sanderson when they died, had been captured by the terrorist group, which appeared to be heading towards the Mozambique border.

Of the six No 7 Squadron helicopters initially sent to Centenary, two were deployed to the Gutsa area to operate with the RAR and two to Mount Darwin, following the deaths of Bland and Sanderson. The two Mount Darwin-based helicopters operating from Mukumbura were tasked to assist the RLI in its efforts to find Hawksworth.

The Centenary-based aircraft were available for allocation to any area as required. The Rushinga-based aircraft, while carrying out routine border control operations, was also available if required and was in fact used quite extensively in the initial efforts to prevent the departure of Hawksworth from Rhodesia. However, despite all the security force efforts, he was taken across the border into Mozambique, where he was held as a prisoner of war. He was released in December 1973.

The first airborne military operation outside Rhodesia

It was obvious now that ZANLA members were working in close cooperation with Frelimo, and so permission was obtained from the Portuguese authorities to mount an operation into Tete Province. Ostensibly, this operation was to intercept the group that had abducted Hawksworth, and obtain his release. Obviously, secrecy was of paramount importance, so it was decided to utilize paratroops employing both free fall and static line, and rehearsals were held at the Parachute Training School. By January 19th 1973, everything was ready for the first airborne military operation outside Rhodesia in the counter-insurgency campaign.

A No 3 Squadron Dakota 7303 piloted by Flight Lieutenant Ivan Holshausen with two pathfinder teams on board, took off from New Sarum at 17h30, the plan being to drop these men at last light. The two four-man teams were to free-fall into the area and select suitable dropping zones. They were to signal information back to the aircraft carrying out the main drop, about the direction of flight and give final dropping instructions. The leader of the first pathfinder group was Lieutenant Chris Schulenberg (Schulie) and he was to drop west of the Musengezi River 36 kilometres inside Mozambique. Captain Garth Barrett was in charge of the group dropping to the east.

Squadron Leader Derek de Kock of the Parachute Training School was in overall command of the drop. Ivan kept his Dakota above 11,000 feet to avoid detection from the ground and reached the dropping zone in perfect time—just after sunset. The first stick landed more or less where they had planned. Unfortunately, Frank Wilmot from the second stick was killed when his parachute failed to open. The surviving seven men had no time to grieve. They had to find suitable landing points for the main force of static line paratroops. As it turned out, in the time available only one dropping zone could be found, and that was uneven and littered with rocks and small trees, but it was midnight and the drone of the Dakota engines could be heard approaching.

Once more the pilot was Ivan Holshausen with 20 SAS on board. The pathfinder team directed the Dakota in and the drop was made, the only casualty being a trooper with a broken ankle. A helicopter crewed by Air Lieutenant John Smart and Flight Sergeant Steve Stead had been positioned at Musengedzi Mission specifically for casualty evacuation and this aircraft uplifted the trooper to Centenary. Meanwhile another No 7 Squadron helicopter was called in from FAF 3 (Centenary) to collect Frank Wilmot's body.

It was 04h00 when the Alouette, piloted by Flight Lieutenant Peter Woolcock reached the pickup point. As the pilot and his technician, Bob Mackie, flew along the Musengezi River, the moon disappeared into the clouds and when they reached the pick-up point it was completely dark. Would they be able to spot the pathfinder team?

Suddenly, Bob spotted a pinpoint of light flickering below. It was Schulenberg's torch flashing. Peter descended, cutting his way through a tree to land in the gully, the blast from the rotor blades sending the dust billowing. It was only in the final seconds before touch-down, that Peter switched on his landing light. As soon as he was safely on the ground, he cut his engine. It was a remarkable example of flying but something the army was to become accustomed to over the years.

Frank Wilmot's body was placed aboard the helicopter together with all the equipment he had been carrying, for the inquiry that would be held later.

The SAS remained in Tete for almost a month, causing consternation to their enemies who believed themselves to be in a safe area. No 3 Squadron carried out re-supplies, even dropping cameras to the SAS so that photographs could be taken of ZANLA soldiers to prove that anti-Rhodesian insurgents were in fact operating in Mozambique. A great deal of equipment was captured including the first RPG-7 rocket launcher. Enough solid proof was obtained of ZANLA operations to persuade the Portuguese authorities to allow Rhodesian security forces to remain in Mozambique.

Meanwhile, a number of incidents had been reported in the Kariba area. On Tuesday 16th January 1973, a Rhodesian security forces patrol had been fired on at a point near Nyamuomba Island between Kariba and Chirundu. The fire was not returned. On Thursday 18th January, at about 18h15, a Rhodesian police launch was hit by fire from the Zambian bank. On the following day a South African Police patrol boat was fired on while pulling out from moorings on the Rhodesian side of the river at Chirundu and during the same period a security force truck hit a land-mine near Mana Pools leaving two men slightly injured.

And then, on 24th January, came another farm attack in the Centenary area. A nine-man group of insurgents hit Ellan Vannin Farm using small arms and hand grenades. Mrs Ida Kleynhans was killed and her husband Chris was wounded. In the early hours of 25th January, Air Lieutenant Giles Porter and Sergeant Ted Holland, in a helicopter from No 7 Squadron, uplifted the injured Mr Kleynhans to hospital. Later a skirmish developed between this gang and the security forces.

The battle lasted for two hours and ended with the deaths of four members of the gang. Another man was wounded and died later in hospital. As a follow-up to this incident, a 16-year-old African appeared in court in September charged with the murder of Mrs Kleynhans. He gave evidence that an insurgent group had set up camp in Chiweshe Tribal Trust Land in December. Towards the end of January, there was a night attack on a South African Police post near the Zambezi.

Six policemen were wounded, none of them seriously.

No 1 Squadron Diary, January 1973:

The situation on our north-eastern border deteriorated during the month. There were three attacks on civilian homes resulting in the death of a farmer's wife and several people being wounded. Two land inspectors were also killed and one captured by terrorists. As a result of all these activities, the squadron was on stand-by with fully armed aircraft from dawn to dusk during most of the month. Several armed recces were carried out in the border areas. On three occasions, aircraft were on stand-by from Victoria Falls in case of any border violations.

No 7 Squadron Diary, January 1973:

Hours flown 1018h30 with 7,392 passengers carried during the month. This figure must be a record and could offer competition to quite a few airlines. Squadron serviceability 96%. Operation Hurricane continued throughout the month with 14 pilots participating at one time or another. Over and above the Operation Hurricane commitment routine, border patrols were carried out at Wankie, Binga and Kariba in addition to Rushinga. During the month, 631 hours were flown on Operation Hurricane, and of these Pete Woolcock flew over 110 hours; several other pilots got very close to this figure.

Casevac:

Following the overturning of an African bus near Rushinga on 23rd January, Air Lieutenant Dick Paxton uplifted eight of the injured to Karanda Mission Hospital. Apparently the driver of this particular vehicle had been drunk at the wheel and disappeared immediately after the accident.

Incidents:

Air Lieutenant Roger Watt struck what must have been a fairly large bird (feathered) while in flight at 400 feet. There was a loud bang followed by whistling sounds, so Roger says. Most probably it was a screech of rage at having its rear end shattered. Judging by the size of the dent in the tip, we assumed that the bird has definitely passed on to higher places. Following on from this bird-strike Roger again managed to feature. Coming into a landing zone, he managed to prove quite conclusively that helicopters do not cut trees down very effectively. The main rotors were damaged and had to be changed. (No 7 Squadron Diary)

No 4 Squadron Diary, January 1973:

Total flying hours for the Provost: 218; Trojan: 423hrs
The majority of the operational hours were still spent on Op Hurricane and the FAF commitment at the beginning of the month. The chaps at the FAFs were later released. We lost Dave Rowe and Steve Caldwell who have gone to the 'Egg Beaters' after giving their best on No 4 Squadron for two and a bit years. The new guys went to No 6 Squadron to do their Provost refamiliarization and then on to No 2 Squadron where Varkie Varkevisser and Des (sic) gave them a quick Provost OCU. Hope to get them back at the beginning of February. Alf Wilde, Tony Oakley and Planks Blythe-Wood spent the whole of the month at Centenary. Every now and then they saw a fourth and a fifth chap in the area. John Carhart, Planks and Vic Culpan spent a short peiod at FAF 1. Steve Stead did a bit of socializing at FAF 2 before going on to No 7 Squadron. We eventually got some new Sneb rockets for the Trogs and all the guys had a bash at firing them. The squadron average was about 17 yards.

As far as No 3 Squadron was concerned, its greatest contribution to Operation Hurricane was in the supply sphere. Often the terrain was mountainous or thickly wooded and the roads, when there were any, were impassable owing to heavy rain. Air transport was the only means of maintaining a constant flow of ammunition, fuel, food and medical equipment. This was clearly demonstrated at the outset of Operation Hurricane when excessively wet weather bogged down army vehicles with the result that movement of troops and equipment became well nigh impossible. No 3 Squadron played an indispensable role in this situation. In the absence of suitable landing strips, the Dakotas parachuted supplies in, or dropped them free fall if they were suitable for this method of supply.

On a lighter note, about a hundred people saw the air force take top honours when two members took first and second place in the six and a half kilometre inter-service swimming race held at Lake Kariba on 28th January. Kevin Sheehan enjoyed the prize of a cold beer, after swimming from Redcliff Island in two hours nine minutes and 12 seconds. Second was Danny Svoboda in a time of two hours 27 minutes and 20 seconds. Both of them said afterwards that they would not be entering again unless the prizes were substantially increased!

In February 1973, the Chiweshe Tribal Trust Land lying in the middle of the white farming areas of Centenary, Mount Darwin, Umvukwes and Bindura, was chosen as a testing ground for a new government policy. The entire population, about 50,000 people, was resettled in Protected Villages (PVs). While this system had worked well during insurgency problems in Malaya, it seemed in Rhodesia to be more a form of collective punishment than of protection and tended to alienate the local population.

Choana Farm, 15 kilometres south of Centenary Village was the target for an attack on Sunday 4th February. At about 21h30, Leslie Jellicoe, a 72-year-old visitor from the United Kingdom was watching television when the farm was attacked with hand grenades and rockets. Mr Jellicoe was killed. The attackers also assaulted the storekeeper and set fire to eight tractors and a motorcycle. In September 1973, Rivers Peter Chimumondo was sentenced to death for this attack and for placing a land-mine near a store in Kandeya Tribal Trust Land on 5th January.

It was given in evidence that Rivers Chimumondo had been handed over to the security forces by his father.

Sunday 25th February saw the first Hunter strike in Op Hurricane. Boss Gaunt and Ricky Culpan were called out to attack a terr base to the north-east of Centenary. The cloud base in the area was only 200 feet when the attack was carried out. The target was in a ravine, with the ground rising 100 to 150 feet at the far end, with the cloud base 100 feet above this. A number of attacks were carried out on target. Unfortunately, the terrorists had moved to a position 200 yards east of the target. (No 1 Squadron Diary, Feb. 1973)

No 4 Squadron Diary, February 1973:

Hours Provost: 349; Trojan: 341

Most of the flying this month was taken up by work at JOC Hurricane. The two Provosts were required at Kariba at the beginning of the month in order to try to intercept any Zambian aircraft violating our air space. The Boss and Planks had the pleasure of doing this. Unfortunately, nothing came of it and after three days they returned home. This month the squadron claimed two kills. Planks did an airstrike after sighting one terr and wounding him in the back and a few days later Greg Todd did an op with the SAS and wounded another terr. The only occurrence of the month was when Robbie Tasker noticed the oil pressure dropping on take-off, did a horseshoe, and on landing the engine seized up on him. All in all, a quiet month.

No 7 Squadron Diary, February 1973:

Total hours flown: 729

Operations:

Op Hurricane continued throughout the month with 16 pilots participating at one time or another. Six aircraft were deployed. Two are at Centenary, two at Sipolilo and two at Mount Darwin. The aircraft at Mount Darwin and Centenary have been sharing operations—based at Musengedzi Mission during the day and returning to their respective bases at night. Air Lieutenants Brian Phillips and Giles Porter were also called out for four days in order to help with the operation. Giving a total of eight aircraft on the operation at one time. The Rushinga-based aircraft carried out routine border patrols and helped out on Operation Hurricane on a couple of occasions. Aircraft were also based at FAF 1 (Wankie) and Binga while the SAP aircraft went for servicing. We now have an aircraft permanently at FAF 1. Casevacs this month were mainly concerned with troops on operations but Flight Lieutenant Graham Cronshaw went to Mount Hampden to uplift a land-mine victim to Salisbury General Hospital and Air Lieutenant Roger Watt uplifted an African female with a breached birth to Sipolilo.

No 7 Squadron suffered a loss on 21st February 1973, when Air Lieutenant John Smart and Sergeant Kevin (Tinker) Smithdorf were killed when their Alouette hit a tree during routine border control activities in the Rushinga area. These were the days before automatic crash beacons and it was only after five days of intensive searching that the helicopter was found in thick bush in the Ruya River area on the border with Mozambique, 150 kilometres north-east of Salisbury. Amongst many other aircraft, four aircraft from No 7 Squadron spent a total of 96h40 minutes on this search.

John Smart had trained with the Royal Air Force and joined the Rhodesian Air Force in 1972. Kevin Smithdorf had attested with the RRAF in 1964. He had received the Military Forces Commendation (Operational) in 1970.

Incident at Karoi

Richard Errol Robinson, Christopher Gumborinotaya and Amon Magiya Sibanda had been sent by ZAPU for training in the USSR where they had spent nine months. They entered Rhodesia early in 1973 and arrived in the Mukwichi Tribal Trust Land, just north of Karoi, at the end of February. There they had aroused the suspicion of two African district assistants who attempted to arrest them. The insurgents fired at the district assistants, wounding one in the arm.

The alarm was raised and a PATU (police anti-terrorist unit) stick was brought in. The insurgents were tracked to the Owl Mine where there was engagement on 9th March. A police reservist, David Michael Stacey, was wounded. On the evening of 10th March, Squadron Leader du Rand flew the injured man by helicopter from Karoi to Salisbury. Unfortunately, the man did not survive his wounds. During the afternoon of 10th March, members of the group held up a store owner, Judy Barker and her African assistant. They stole some food and other articles and abducted the African storekeeper. The security forces were soon on their trail and there was an engagement about a kilometre from the store during which one of the insurgents was killed.

No 7 Squadron Diary, March 1973:

Operation Hurricane continued with little respite for the squadron. The operation extended its area westward following incidents in the Karoi area with 12 pilots being involved during the month. However, the pressure was alleviated somewhat by the squadron commitment being reduced to one crew on one-hour readiness. The murder of a roads surveyor at Wedza resulted in one aircraft being detached for support but to date this operation has not been given a name. Deployments to FAF 1, Binga and Kanyemba for routine border control duties. This month once again the Rushinga-based aircraft assisted with support for Operation Hurricane for there is at present a lot of terrorist activity in the area. Graham Cronshaw carried out a night casevac at approximately midnight on 18th March. The casualty was Lieutenant Bob Warren-Codrington of the SAS who lost the fingers of his left hand in a parachuting accident. Bob is well known to the squadron and I am pleased to report that he is on the mend and that he will be returning to more intense soldiering in a few months. Bekker Homer trials and rope descents were carried out; also crash rescue beacons tested. The squadron received a new 'Bone Dome' for trial. It received a big 'yes'. Perhaps in the relatively near future we shall be equipped with a helmet that is specifically designed for use in a helicopter. HQ has also approved the use of Uzi sub-machine guns for those pilots who prefer it to the FN.

No 1 Squadron Diary, March 1973:

At the end of February, four aircraft from Thornhill were called to Salisbury for a strike. Five days later the Boss, Rob Gaunt, and Ricky Culpan attacked a 12.7mm post. Dag [D.A.G.] Jones and Baldy [Malcolm] Baldwin attacked a porters' camp. Unfortunately, it was found out later that both camps were deserted. After the strike, Dag and Baldy were required to photograph the areas.

Frolizi incident
No 4 Squadron Diary March 1973:

This month saw Frolizi, the Front for the Liberation of Zimbabwe, a quiet organization up until now, come to light with the first of their terror activities. The first incident was the holding up of a garage at Gatooma on 11th March. Then later on in the month they killed a farmer in the Wedza area. Bruce Collocott was positioned in Salisbury as a stand-by for the ensuing follow up. Operation Hurricane FAF 3 (Centenary). The Trogs were used mainly for courier trips, re-supply, telstar and recce tasks. The Trogs were also involved in ten casevacs during the month. The Provosts were used mainly for top-cover and telstar duties. On 16th March Alf Wilde and Greg Todd were used in a contact in the Mukumbura area both dropping their frantan.

The Frolizi incursion involved Thomas Harris Zerf and Cecil Paul Murtagh, two Coloured men who had crossed into Zambia where they had undergone military and political training. They crossed back into Rhodesia with six other men, on 17th February 1973. This group was armed with five AK-47 rifles, 2,400 rounds of 7.62 ammunition, six RDG hand grenades, anti-personnel mines, four pistols, maps and other ammunition. They made their way south stealing a car en route and raiding an empty farmhouse in the Mangula area for food and clothing.

They set up a camp in a rocky outcrop near Umvuma. From this base, on 11th March, they carried out an armed robbery at Car Mart Service Station in Gatooma threatening the petrol attendant with a pistol and robbing him of $218 (Rhodesian).

Four members of the gang went to Wedza where they established a camp at Laughing Waters Farm. Two members of this gang Hlidududzi Naison and Guvamayanga who was the commander of the group, were spotted by a herd boy employed by Mr Andries Hendrik Joubert. Joubert went to investigate, armed with a pistol and accompanied by two employees, one armed with a spear and the other carrying a heavy rifle. Guvamayanga shot Joubert through the head, killing him instantly. Later Guvamayanga was spotted on a bus travelling through Enkeldoorn. The bus was stopped at a roadblock and he took flight and ran across a vlei practically in the middle of Enkeldoorn. The police opened fire and he fell; as he did so a primed grenade fell from his pocket. He was badly wounded in the incident but recovered, was tried and sentenced to death.

No 4 Squadron Diary, April 1973:

Hours Provost: 171 Trojan: 274

Greg Todd spent a few days on stand-by for a follow-up going on in the Wedza area where some people had been killed by the Frolizi gang. Up at the sharp end we had Bruce Collocott, Plod [Mike] Litson, Pete Simmonds, Willie [Mark G.] Knight and Gaps [Kenneth] Newman doing their bit. Trojan flying was the normal courier, casevac and telstar sorties. No air strikes by the Trojans. Provost flying consisted of flights to and from the forward bases, a little telstar, top cover. No strikes, however, materialized. All in all a very normal month with very little action. The lull before the storm it would seem.

The air force took part in an incident in April, when two security force dog handlers tracking spoor on the Choana Estate in Centenary, saw a man running away. The alarm was sounded and when the man dived for cover, the security force patrol opened fire on what turned out to be a group of insurgents, who fired back. Air support was called in and the area ahead of the group was strafed. After this, contact was lost, but ballistic evidence recovered at the scene led to the conviction of three men captured later. They were Lovemore Dube apprehended in Chiweshe Reserve, Onias Garikayi captured in the Zambezi Valley and Mabonzo arrested while heading for the Midlands. Lovemore Dube received the death penalty; the other two were sentenced to 30 years.

Rover flights to South Africa

One of the advantages of serving with No 1 Squadron was the chance of a Rover flight to Durban or Cape Town and it is interesting to note how often a one-night stopover became two—for various reasons.

No 1 Squadron Diary, April 1973:

On 17th April Dag Jones and Steve Kesby night-stopped in Cape Town. The starter on one aircraft had seized before the start-back from Cape Town. This has happened on several occasions now! They returned with wine and crayfish. More serious business involved the squadron during Easter.

No 1 Squadron Diary, April 1973:

Over Easter, Friday 20th Gaunt, Culpan, Baldwin and Kesby were called to Salisbury for a briefing. Early Saturday morning they carried out a strike in the north-east. On the return trip, the Boss led the formation over Rushinga, Mount Darwin, Bindura and all suburbs in Salisbury at 500 feet and 400 knots in a very civilized manner. Ricky returned from the area after the others with news that the strike was good but, unfortunately, the camp was empty.

The air force had better luck on 29th April, when four Canberras and three Vampires attacked a Frelimo/ZANLA base in northern Mozambique. The RLI provided troops to man stop-groups to intercept insurgents leaving the area. The raid was highly successful.

Archie Wilson retires

Air Marshal Archie Wilson's retirement came into effect on 15th April 1973 ending an air force career spanning 32 years. He was the only serving member of the original Southern Rhodesia Air Force and his retirement marked the passing of an era. Making a speech on his retirement, he said: "Terrorism in Rhodesia will probably get worse before it gets better but the security forces will win. Terrorism cannot win. It cannot achieve its aim." The new head of the Rhodesian Air Force was South African-born Air Vice-Marshal Michael John (Mick)

McLaren who was to be known by the new title of Commander of the Air Force.

With the change to this title, came another change, and this was the uniform of air officers. In keeping with the army where officers of field rank wore red tabs on the lapels of their tunic, the air force now adopted a similar system. Tabs of air force blue/grey were added to the lapels of air officers. These were correctly called gorgets. Group captains wore plain gorgets on each lapel, air commodores had one bateleur eagle on each gorget, air vice-marshals had two eagles, and for an air marshal it was three eagles.

No 1 Squadron carried out numerous strikes during May—with mixed results.

On Wed. 2nd May, Rob Gaunt, Dag Jones, Chris Weinmann and Ricky Culpan were called out for a practice strike in the Gungwe area. A grid reference was given before take-off. On arrival, they marked out the target area and Captain Garth Barrett talked the Boss onto the target. This particular method worked very well. On Sat. 5th, Dag and Ricky were called out to a strike in the north-east. They were on target but after the strike the Provost doing FAC requested a strike north of their target, as the major part of the camp was in that area. However, the helicopters had moved into the area so a further strike was an impossibility. Once again, the camp had been deserted before the strike. On Sunday 13th, two pairs of Hunters flown by the Boss and Baldwin, Dag and Chris Weinmann were called out and required to carry out an airborne stand-by over Mount Darwin. The airborne stand-by continued through to last light. Unfortunately, a strike was not called for and the aircraft returned to Thornhill for debriefing. Chris and Baldy were called out to strike in the north-east on 15th May. A grid reference was given before take-off. The Hunters joined up with two Canberras who followed the Hunters in. Other than the grid reference the only identification was a smoke marker 800 yards from the target. Redirection was not given as the ground radios were u/s. Once again the camp was deserted. Twenty percent of the target was destroyed by the strike. Taking into account the accuracy of the maps, the plotting of the grid reference and the fact that the target marking was nil, this is considered to be a fair result. (No 1 Squadron Diary, May 1973)

Death at the Falls

The Rhodesian side of the border at the Victoria Falls was closed but tourists could still enjoy the spectacular view as the river tumbled into the gorge. Then on Tuesday 15th May 1973, there came a vicious attack. At about 14h00, a group of tourists, including two Canadian girls, Christine Louise Sinclair and Maria Drijber and two Americans, John Crother and his wife Carol, were admiring the view from the fourth gorge, when five Zambian soldiers on the far bank suddenly opened fire on them with automatic weapons. Christine Sinclair was killed almost immediately and John Crother was wounded. Maria Drijber fell or jumped into the water. From the cover of rocks and bushes, the five soldiers kept shooting at John Crother but he was reasonably well sheltered. Maria could be seen sitting on a half-submerged shelf of rock in the river, holding on with one of her arms to a higher rock with her head resting on her arm.

People on the Zambian bank could see her long blonde hair and they shouted to the Zambian soldiers that it was a woman. The soldiers said it made no difference. One spectator caught hold of one of the soldiers but was shaken off. The soldiers began shooting at Maria but finding that they were unable to hit her from the position they were in, moved up river and set up a machine gun. At this point, another Zambian soldier arrived and told them not to shoot because it was a woman. About ten minutes passed and then firing started again and at 15h45, Maria screamed and disappeared into the river. The soldiers continued to fire into the water after she had disappeared. As soon as the alarm was raised, the security forces proceeded to evacuate the wounded man and his wife. Throughout the rescue operation, Zambian troops kept their weapons trained on the Rhodesians.

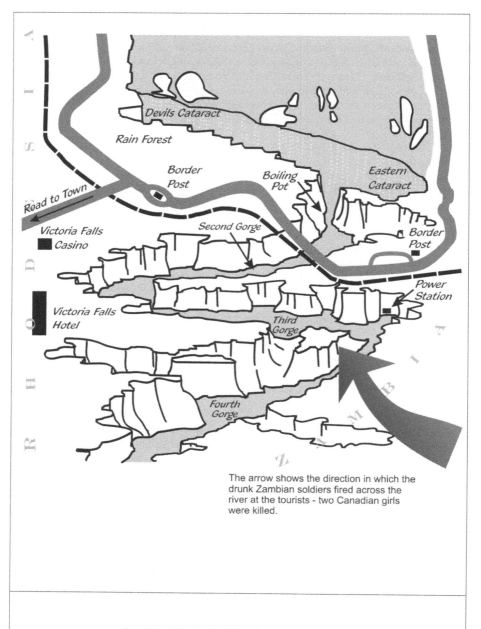

The arrow shows the direction in which the drunk Zambian soldiers fired across the river at the tourists - two Canadian girls were killed.

DEATH AT THE FALLS

No 1 Squadron Diary:

On the afternoon of 15th May, the Zambian army fired across the border at the Victoria Falls killing two Canadian girls and wounding an American man. The Boss and Dag (Jones) were called out on 16th May to provide top cover while rescue operations were in progress. If a shot was fired across the river during that period they were authorized to retaliate. They returned later in the morning with their armament intact. They were later accused by Zambia of violating Zambian air space.

The Hunters were an effective warning. Trigger-happy Zambian soldiers took a wary look at the jet fighters cruising overhead and held their fire. Armed cover was also provided by Alouettes of No 7 Squadron.

Operations to recover Miss Sinclair's body were delayed while the Rhodesian authorities waited for an assurance from Zambia that rescue teams would not be fired on. The attack had taken place on Tuesday 15th just after midday but it was only on Thursday 17th that Rhodesian security forces received the assurances they needed and were able to go ahead with operations to bring out the body and search for the missing girl. All this time Rhodesian Air Force aircraft were standing by to go ahead with the perilous task. During the operation, the six stretcher-bearers and accompanying armed security force members were exposed to the Zambian side for two and a half hours.

CID detectives with the rescue team recovered bullets for ballistic tests and made note of the many indentations in the rocks. Miss Sinclair's body was airlifted by a helicopter from an emergency landing zone halfway down the gorge and carried to Wankie Colliery Hospital for autopsy. Nineteen-year-old Maria Drijber's body was never found.

Navex to Luanda

During May 1973, No 1 Hunter Squadron carried out flights to Mozambique and Luanda.

The Boss and Baldy day-stopped LM on 14th May. They returned with 250 lbs of prawns and a few crayfish tails. On 23rd the Boss and Chris left on the first Navex (Navigation exercise) to Luanda. On the way up, Chris lost one radio and the Boss had recurring fuel transfer failure. At Luanda they enjoyed Portuguese beer and seafood. On the return, the aircraft would not start initially and when they did, the Boss had a generator light on. The Boss strapped in five times and Chris three. They departed Luanda 40 minutes late. The Boss lost a radio resulting in difficulties in communication with each other and with Luanda. After levelling off, the Boss experienced engine surge and decided to divert to Nova Lisboa. Communication with Salisbury proved difficult but eventually a Dakota arrived with a ground crew, and repairs were carried out. Gordon Watts then discovered metal in Chris's engine. Spares were flown in and an 'engine split' was carried out—the first occasion such an operation had been performed outside New Sarum. Clive Chard and Norman Ely from ERS and the squadron crew completed the job in two days, which was most commendable. The hospitality given to the crews by the Portuguese, in particular Col Cracae and Major Freitas, was quite outstanding. A tour round a pineapple wine factory was arranged for the Boss and Chris while Mr Ward proved to be a very generous host and a week later the crews returned. Subsequently two air tests were carried out on the Hunter. (No 1 Squadron Diary)

No 4 Squadron Diary, May 1973:

Hours Provost: 225; Trojan: 388
Accident 1 Trojan 3421
Welcome to the squadron, three new junior pilots, Clive Ward, Mark Aitchison and Kevin

(Cocky) Benecke who arrived on 20th May. Operation Hurricane Trojan flying consisted of limited recce, extensive courier and the usual casevac and re-supply flights. For the first time we used the Trojan for air strikes and FAC (Forward Air Control) for the Provosts. Plod Litson did a bit of recce in 'Funnies' (Mozambique) and located a few camps, which he reported to JOC. It was decided to zap the camps and he did FAC for two Provosts. Unfortunately, he did a few orbits in the air over the main camp before finding it and the terrs ran away before the strike went in. Alf Wilde and Plod did a few more strikes with Trogs and great fun was had by both. Provost flying was mostly top cover with a few air strikes and positioning at forward bases for daylight stand-by. The normal sort of stuff. While giving top cover to SAS who were surrounded, Greg Todd's Provost was hit through starboard seat and the starboard windscreen was smashed. A fairly close shave. Luckily there were no passengers. John Carhart had an unfortunate mishap and pranged 3421 our best Trojan at Sipolilo. Damage was assessed as Category 5 but apart from being a bit shaken up JC and Barry Badenhorst were unhurt.

Security Training Section

Back on the ground, the Air Force Security Training Section had once again been evicted and in June 1973, it took up residence in the old Registry at station headquarters, New Sarum.

Ken Salter reckoned that if it happened again he would either change his name to Moses or buy himself a caravan and call us 'Salter's Travelling Circus and Medicine Show'. I was inclined to agree. We had only been going one year and this was our third home. (Paul Hill)

And there was yet more to come:

We moved again! This time to the last resting place of Security Training Section as we were now. The building had been the recreation rooms for women members of the force, just after the war, then a Judo Dojo, then the canteen and finally the station library, prior to our moving in. This was quite fortuitous as a quantity of stationery and hard-to-obtain reference books fell off the truck in transit from our new building to their new location, the Security Training Section having generously offered to assist in the move! Training had been continuing despite our nomadic existence but now the school received an impetus and most importantly—finance. Two new classrooms, a cinema and a gunnery classroom were built. Our already large 'Terrorist Weapons Display' was expanded, as was our field-training section. We now undertook the training, not only of our own security personnel, but all air force recruits and national servicemen, in security matters. There had for a long time been good cooperation between the local BSAP member-in-charge and the air force police—this was passed on to the local police reserve and we had the pleasure of assisting in the training of these people. We always found them keen to learn anything we had to teach them. It was not always one-sided either. The guard force had been formed and along with the army and the police, we commenced training African guard force members. While their calibre might not have been quite as good as that of our own general service unit African servicemen, we did turn out a good product. We were fortunate in having remarkable internal affairs. They received all our basic training, plus lectures on specialized subjects from their own people. The training at Security Training Section was hard, much harder in fact for a national serviceman than he could expect with the army. We found this out in an unusual way. We planned our training programmes well over a year in advance, so we were surprised when we were informed at short notice that a territorial force intake would be arriving! Arrangements were made and we commenced training. A few weeks later the bombshell fell—they had been intended for the army! How do you tell an intake that you have been feeding on a diet of 'air force is best', that they must now go to the 'browns'! The officer commanding was a man of steel.

He volunteered! He gave the news to a shocked, and utterly dejected group of men. He broke it to them like a solicitor reading the last will and testament of a rich aunt who has just bequeathed you her 12 Pekinese and no maintenance! They took it well considering, and were marched off to hand in their kit, singing, 'I wish I was a blue job up in the sky!', a song that was popular then! Later I met some of them at the armoured car regiment. They thoroughly shocked me by telling me that they considered the air force training far better than that of the army, and that they found Llewellin Barracks to be soft by comparison. (Paul Hill)

The staff members at the Security Training Section were: Chimp Webster, Paul Hill, André van der Walt, Gordon Drake, Bob Jordaan, Ken Jackman, Don Junner and Ian (Stretch) Merrington.

No 1 Squadron Diary, June 1973:

An orange and grapefruit run (to the Lowveld) was carried out on 13th June and a prawn run to LM on 21st June. Rickie Culpan and Steve Kesby had difficulty in starting one Hunter resulting in a night-stop being forced upon them! The following morning the aircraft started after the first attempt. In the meantime, however, a Canberra had already left for LM. No 1 Squadron are still waiting for a letter of thanks for organizing the day-stop. Flight Lieutenant David Arthur (Ghuru) Jones became the first Rhodesian pilot to fly 1,000 hours on Hunters on 20th June 1973. For his efforts, devotion to duty and being so very brave, he was given a dunking in No 6 Squadron fishpond together with a glass of champagne, and was later presented with a memento of the occasion. On Sat 30th June, Dag, Chris Dixon and Steve carried out boom runs [supersonic flights] in the north-east, which was planned to coincide with the partial eclipse.

Towards the end of June 1973, there were several follow-ups going on in the Musengezi area that involved the SAS and the RAR. A contact took place on 22nd June with a group of ten terrorists. Air Lieutenant 'Beaver' Baynham and Sergeant Thomson flying a helicopter saw the group running away after an initial contact with ground forces. Thomson opened fire but, unfortunately, the gun jammed after about 50 rounds. However, the first helicopter had now been joined in orbit by a second flown by Flight Lieutenant Ian Harvey with Sergeant A.J. (Jim) Pawson, who also opened fire.

These two aircraft were joined by a Provost from No 4 Squadron flown by Alf Wilde who carried out a frantan attack. The helicopters broke off the engagement once the Provost had turned in to attack. One fran hung up and the other bounced over the insurgents' heads, exploding on the second impact and killing a man hiding in thick bush.

Twenty-six packs were recovered containing quite a haul of ammunition and explosives. The Provost was hit in the rudder by one bullet fired from the ground but the damage was not serious. Neither helicopter was hit. Air Lieutenant Baynham had a second contact a short while later with another group. Subsequently it was established that two terrorists had been killed and four wounded in the strike, most of them by frantan.

Airmen honoured

On 29th June, the Minister of Defence, Mr Jack Howman, presented the Defence Forces Medal for Meritorious Service to five men at New Sarum. They were Squadron Leader Peter Arthur Barnett, Squadron Leader James Cordiner Boyd, Squadron Leader Kenneth Mash Gipson, Master Technician William Gaitens and Warrant Officer William Henry Owens. According to their citations for the awards, Squadron Leader Barnett joined the Rhodesian Air Force in 1958 after previous service with the South African Air Force. In

1964, he took command of No 3 Transport Squadron. His flying skill and devotion to duty played a significant part in the then high standards and achievement enjoyed by his squadron. Squadron Leader Boyd, a staff signals officer, planned and directed the development of highly specialized and complex ground communications equipment and systems. Squadron Leader Gipson who was appointed staff armament officer in 1964 played a notable part in expanding the operational capability of the air force. As staff officer, he was concerned with the development of weapons and certain explosives and explosive stores. Master Technician Gaitens made an outstanding contribution to the specialized field of structural repairs to aircraft, and in the technical field. Warrant Officer Owens was responsible for aircraft maintenance, and maintaining the aircraft in a state of operational readiness.

First mass kidnapping

In July 1973, ZANLA changed its tactics. Seeking more recruits for training outside Rhodesia, its members undertook the first mass kidnappings of African school children. On the night of Thursday 5th July, a 17-man band armed with automatic weapons swooped on St Albert's, a lonely Jesuit Mission near Centenary. They looted a nearby store, cut the telephone wires to prevent an alarm being sent, and spent three hours at the Mission before moving out, taking 273 people, mostly children, with them. Father Clemence Freymer insisted on accompanying the group. He told the ZANLA men: "These are my people, I shall go with them." After the ZANLA members left, Father Rojek and a party from the Mission walked three kilometres to alert the security forces, which were soon on the scene. Father Rojek said: "We saw the flares drop. They were bright as daylight. Aeroplanes circled for one and a half hours and at 5.15 am the army arrived on foot. A few minutes later, they went into the valley in pursuit."

Meanwhile in the early hours of the morning, a search aircraft located the party and dropped four flares, three of which were exactly on target. The group scattered in confusion. The ZANLA men took cover under trees while the abductees made an attempt to escape, hiding behind trees and rocks. By the time the abductors regained control, one teacher and eleven children had got away, and were on their way home.

The remaining abductees were shepherded down into the Zambezi Valley where they split into two groups. Seven ZANLA members took the remaining children in one direction while ten other insurgents went another way with the adults. At dawn, the security forces caught up with the group containing the children. It was a difficult situation—if there was any exchange of fire, the children could be injured, but if the group was allowed to continue they would soon be across the border. The security forces moved in and there was a short gun battle. One of the seven abductors was wounded and the others fled, leaving the children unharmed.

By Sunday, a further 33 victims of the abduction, who had managed to escape, returned to the Mission. However, some primary school children and ten adults were still missing. On Monday this group, which was being constantly harried by the security forces, split up. Meanwhile one girl pupil had been killed by an accidental discharge from the gun of a member of the police unit. Two of the abductors had been killed, several others had been captured, and two members of the BSAP had been injured.

On 18th July, nearly two weeks after the abduction, another ten children and teachers were freed after a relentless chase over some of the roughest terrain in central Africa. Only one primary school boy and seven girls between 15 and 18 were still missing. This final group was apprehended in the border area, and despite the fact that the ZANLA members used the abductees as shields, one more terrorist was killed, and the children were rescued safely.

The abductions from St Albert's Mission marked a turning point in the insurgents' tactics. Increasingly they began to terrorize the local populations in order to command their respect, if not their loyalty. Among the many incidents, was one in which five ZANLA men went

MASS ABDUCTION FROM
ST ALBERT'S MISSION

to Mangare School in Kandeya Tribal Trust Land near Mount Darwin. They dragged the headmaster, Mr Chipara, from his home and took him to the school office where they forced him to hand over books and money. They then forced three African schoolteachers, one of whom was the headmaster's younger brother, to watch while the headmaster was beaten to death.

No 1 Squadron Diary, July 1973:

On 16th July the squadron started firing rocket projectiles again. The usual war stories were prevalent before the sorties, followed inevitably by the crestfallen looks of sheer disbelief after the sortie. On 19th July at about 11h00, the squadron was told to prepare for a Salisbury stand-by of approximately ten days. At 15h00 hours the Boss, Baldy and Steve left for Salisbury. The stand-by was to provide the SAS with airborne support if they required it. The SAS were operating in SHHH!—you know where. The stand-by was 'crew in readiness' from first light to 17h00 daily. On 20th July, a call-out was initiated at 16h30. Baldy prepared the maps while the Boss and Steve started the kites. What followed was perhaps one of the better comedies of recent years:

a)   The shackle was deciphered incorrectly. This was remedied after about five minutes.

b)   The Flot (Forward Line Own Troops) didn't tie in with the target. Once again an error in deciphering.

c)   Baldy ripped up two of the 1/50 000 series maps of the area and as we had only four sets of maps this proved to be the final straw. OC FW took a deep breath, then went white and nearly fainted. Squadron Leader du Rand nearly swallowed his briar pipe but, fortunately, he was absolutely speechless. Finally, the Boss and Steve got airborne. When they contacted FAF 3 they found it was a 'practice' call-out! This pleased the Boss no end. The Boss was then given various points to fly to, encoded in 'shackle'. As he had only a strip map to the op area the reader might well appreciate the Boss's feelings. At this stage the Boss, never at a loss for words made a statement that surprisingly never made sayings of the week. 'It is f...... obvious that no f..... knows how to operate a f...... Hunter in this f...... air force!'

On 28th July, a strike in the op area was carried out by the Boss, Steve and Baldy. After the initial strikes were said to have been 'on target'! the browns then stated that our strikes went 'over the top'. An interesting debrief is envisaged at the end of this exercise. Whilst in Salisbury a few parties were attended. Meanwhile back at Hooterville (Thornhill) Dag continued with a conversion of Don Northcroft, Danny Svoboda and Spook Geraty. Spook should be going solo early next month.

Air Rhodesia had acquired some new Boeing 720 jetliners and on 25th July a publicity flight was arranged over the country's main centres to give the Press an idea of the comfort and service that would be provided by the new aircraft. As the Boeing approached Gwelo it was joined suddenly by a No 1 Squadron Hawker Hunter from Thornhill. Flight Lieutenant Rick Culpan, the Hunter pilot, radioed to the Boeing skipper, Captain Gus Tattersall, "Welcome to our air space, Big Brother." Then he flew wing-tip to wing-tip alongside the Boeing and finally dropped the undercarriage, the standard interception signal. Finally, Culpan slipped from the Boeing's port to starboard wing, pushed forward the throttle and streaked off.

No 7 Squadron Diary, July 1973:

Total hours flown 593

2,725 passengers carried 95% serviceability

Two unfortunate incidents. Both resulting in nose wheel collapses occurred requiring very lengthy repair work on the aircraft involved. Sixteen pilots and 18 technicians were involved during the month and were all employed at some stage on either Operation Hurricane or Operation Dirk.

Naturally keeping the aircraft in the air for such long hours required an equally high servicing record. The average serviceability rate of 95 percent maintained by No 7 Squadron reflected great credit on the technicians who also flew as crewmen. The amount of work they carried out over and above routine turn-rounds is demonstrated by the fact that, during the month of July three engines, seven tail rotor heads, six tail rotor blades sets, three main blades, two clutches, one main rotor and one tail rotor gearbox, were changed. Two aircraft, damaged when their nose-wheels collapsed on landing, were recovered to Salisbury by road ultimately, one having to be cargo-slung out of the valley to the vehicle which was on the top of the escarpment.

Macombe—a forward base

For some time the SAS had been monitoring ZANLA and Frelimo movements south of the Zambezi River, and the air force had supplied backup on the Mozambique side of the border. There was a Forward Air Field at Centenary but now a tactical headquarters was established at Musengedzi, an old mission station on the Musengezi River north of Centenary. Helicopters and fixed-wing aircraft could be kept on stand-by at this airfield ready for cross-border air-strikes and casevacs, as well as being available to ferry troops and drop supplies.

The Musengezi Forward Air Field proved invaluable but the distance from the Zambian border where the ZANLA forces were crossing was still too great, so it was decided that a forward base should be set up inside Mozambique. The site chosen was Macombe, a protected village with an airstrip situated on the south bank of the Zambezi River. Aircraft remained on stand-by at Macombe during the hours of daylight and were pulled back to Musengezi at night, because they were too vulnerable to enemy attack during the hours of darkness on a dirt airstrip surrounded by thick bush.

From this strategic spot the SAS, together with detachments of the RAR could control the area south of the river and keep it clear of ZANLA forces. Then, moving north they could set up patrols to inhibit the entry points from Zambia. In a typical operation, air force Dakotas would ferry in a free-fall pathfinder group who would choose a single dropping zone for the main force. This group would split up into various patrols, which would then make observations, locate camps and carry out ambushes. The air force re-supplied the groups by parachute every 14 days, dropping food, batteries for radios, medical supplies and ammunition. At the end of their six weeks' stint the men would be pulled back to Macombe and airlifted out.

The tactic worked well and caught the enemy totally by surprise, but it was hard on the SAS soldiers, who were spending six weeks in the bush and ten days back home. The air force provided backup in the shape of helicopters for casevacs, Provosts for air strikes and Dakotas for parachute drops and resupply.

Jacklin Trophy

On 27th August 1973, Air Marshal M.J. McLaren, Commander of the RhAF, presented the Jacklin Trophy to No 5 Squadron. Speaking at the ceremony Air Marshal McLaren said:

> *For a year of outstanding achievement, and for its sound contribution to the balance of the force, and to the overall effectiveness of the security forces, No 5 Squadron has emerged clearly as the winner of the Jacklin Trophy. This is the third occasion the award has been presented to No 5 Squadron whose role includes high- and low-level bombing, photographic reconnaissance and survey, and courier and training activities.* *

---

* The squadron first won the trophy in 1965 and then again in 1966.

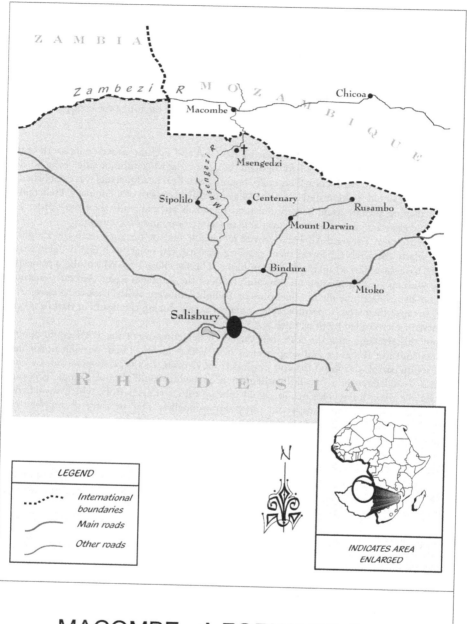

MACOMBE - A FORWARD BASE

No 7 Squadron Diary, August 1973:

Hours flown: 517h05; 2,855 passengers carried; 95% serviceability

Internal security. With SAP aircraft now manning FAF 3 and Rushinga, the squadron has two aircraft deployed at Musengezi and one each at Mount Darwin, Chiswiti and Sipolilo on operation Hurricane, plus one at FAF 1 (Wankie) throughout the month on Operation Dirk. It also became necessary to deploy a further aircraft at FAF 1 and one at Kanyemba during the servicing periods of the SAP aircraft. Two aircraft were hit by ground fire during operations, one of them having to force-land at a forward army base because of dropping oil pressure. However, no personnel were injured in either of these incidents. In another reported incident, two of our aircraft were fired on by terrorists when returning to Musengezi from Macombe Aldeamento. Troops lifted into the area located the firing positions and recovered items of terrorist equipment although nothing was seen of the terrorists themselves. Note: a mat designed to prevent loose items from blowing out of the cabin when flying without doors has been approved and is being manufactured for supply to each aircraft. Difficulties of opening the port baggage door have been experienced when the new ammunition boxes are fitted and this is to be modified on the squadron. Both baggage doors have also been fitted with special fasteners to prevent their being inadvertently opened in flight.

Ian Harvey clocks up 2,000 hours

Flight Lieutenant Ian Harvey became the first person to fly more that 2,000 hours in the Alouette in the Rhodesian Air Force. One thousand-hour badges went to Flight Lieutenants George Wrigley, Barry Roberts, Brian Phillips, John Annan and Brian Penton. These 'badges' were in fact tie clips and were given to the pilots by Sud Aviation, the manufacturers of the Alouette helicopters. The tie clips depicted the Sud Aviation logo, a silhouette of a helicopter contained in a shield the shape of the Alouette II and III tail rotor guard. One thousand hours was signified by one small diamond, 2,000 hours by two diamonds.

Air Vice-Marshal Ian Harvey had, by the year 2000, amassed over 9,000 hours on helicopters.

Month after month in the squadron diary the figure of 95% serviceability appears. In fact, the Rhodesian Air Force maintained the highest Alouette III utilization rate of any air force anywhere in the world. This was achieved by careful management of the aircraft so that major servicing such as an engine change was staggered. But the highest praise must go to the total loyalty, dedication and outstanding ability of the plumbers as they were sometimes called. They were neither clock-watchers, nor of trade union mentality.

CHAPTER 39

The fight for hearts and minds

The ZANLA insurgents entering the north-eastern areas of Rhodesia were using all manner of tactics to draw the local people into the fight on their side. They used indoctrination, abduction, political education, promises, force and local spiritual beliefs. They had invoked Chaminuka a revered spiritual leader and taken the spirit medium Nehanda into Mozambique. It was difficult for white administrators to work in this area of spiritual belief but some attempts were made to win local hearts and minds.

In September 1973, the air force put on a display to salute a young man, Joni Mtabeni, who had become the new chief of the Zhombe people. Paul Hill tells the story of when the air force security branch was requested to undertake the protection of a spirit medium, Mtota. A group of A and B Reservists was assembled and taken to the kraal. They carried out their duties impeccably and even though the river below the kraal was a known ZANLA infiltration route, they kept the old man safe until he died of natural causes 18 months later.

Once again, in the middle of September an attempt was made to abduct children, this time from Kuwondo School, about 30 kilometres east of St Albert's Mission. In four days of pursuit, security forces freed two thirds of the captives. In addition, in September, there were attacks on farms in the Mount Darwin area. Describing the attack on Kachitapa Farm, an eyewitness described the effect of having air support: "Every rock is a potential enemy and death lurks behind every bush. Someone cocks his head and I too, hear the faint drone of a far-off aircraft. Half a minute later, a light support aircraft is circling above and everyone's confidence returns now that the 'blue jobs' are spotting for us."

No 1 Squadron comes of age

On 21st September 1973, the air force was honoured when No 1 Squadron was presented with its Standard. Air Marshal A.O.G. Wilson made the presentation at Thornhill in a ceremony attended by senior officers of the army and police. Among the spectators were four Rhodesians who had been commanders of the squadron: G.A. Smith, John Walmisley, Eric Smith and Ian Shand. The occasion was celebrated with dinner in the mess when 120 baby soles and a large amount of liquor was consumed. These goodies had been brought back from Durban by a crew doing a night stop.

No 1 Squadron was by far the oldest unit in the air force having been formed in 1939 from members of the Southern Rhodesia Air Unit who were hurriedly dispatched to Kenya in August 1939, before the outbreak of World War II. It was on 19th September 1939 that the unit was officially designated as No 1 Squadron, the Southern Rhodesia Air Force. Seven months later, in April 1940, the squadron was re-numbered No 237 (Rhodesia) Squadron, RAF. It was not replaced by or absorbed by 237—it was renamed and therefore continued to exist as before under its new title. No 237 (Rhodesia) Squadron was disbanded in 1945. The air unit of the permanent force, the Southern Rhodesia Air Force, was officially established on 28th November 1947. In July 1949, No 1 Squadron Southern Rhodesia Auxiliary Air Force was formed. In January 1956, the force was reconstructed into four squadrons. They were No 1 Squadron (Training of Instructors and Commonwealth Defence); No 2 Squadron (Advanced Flying Training); No 3 Squadron (Transport); No 4 Squadron (Internal Security and Pupil Pilot Training). One interesting point is that the Transport Squadron, which became No 3 Squadron, had actually operated without a break from 1939.

No 4 Squadron Diary, September 1973:

Flying Hours: Provost: 174 Trojan: 315

Operation Hurricane continued into its tenth month at its usual intensity, all the junior pilots gaining 'Fighting Four' experience. Plod Litson while out in the bush had some excitement. He spotted five terrs and went in for the kill in typical Fighting Four manner. The terrs scattered and eager not to let them go he stalked them. Then, what HQ calls target affixation (sic) took control of Plod. We'd rather say he was bloody hungry. Eventually having added one more terr to his score and pulling out very low, he flew into a tree damaging the wing. Plod thought it was his last flight but he managed to keep control and landed safely. Guess who got the Booby shield this month? The other incident involved Al Bruce who on landing found the Trojan had no brakes, but in the normal fashion of a flying brick, it eventually came to a halt leaving a rather shaken pilot to recover from the ordeal. Eureka also had a fair share of excitement when a heavy storm hit Centenary. The storm settled the dust or rather washed it all away and just about took Eureka with it. Willie Knight was standing on a wet patch when lightning struck the area. It is said that sparks flew from his shoes in the immense static discharge. He also found a large bruise on his thigh where he had come to blows with a table.

Benji joins the air force at Centenary Air Field

With increased use, the condition of Centenary Forward Air Field was deteriorating and problems had been experienced during the rainy season 72/73. The strip was on heavy red soil and when it became wet was more than a little hazardous. As it was apparent that the air force stay at Centenary was going to be a long one, the decision was made to lay a tarmac strip. During this process, the FAF was moved to Eureka Farm, a few miles north-east of Centenary Airfield where there was a private airfield. The command element remained at Centenary. When the construction work was completed, the personnel and aircraft returned to Centenary from Eureka. One extra recruit was Benji, a scruffy mongrel of questionable parentage. During the FAF's stay at Eureka, Benji made friends with the security personnel and when they moved back to Centenary Benji followed. He was returned to his owners, Mr and Mrs Bez Bezuidenhout at Eureka Farm, many times but kept walking back to Centenary to be with his new-found friends. In the end, it was agreed that he could attest into the air force as a regular member. He enjoyed a long and chequered air force career.

Casualty evacuation and training

Apart from its involvement in the war, the air force was still involved in mercy flights for civilians. In October 1973, eight-year-old Norman Walter Fulton of Gwelo was injured when he was hit by a truck. He was carried by air force helicopter to Salisbury Central Hospital. A nursing sister from Gwelo hospital accompanied him and the helicopter landed at the newly completed pad at Andrew Fleming Hospital. The pictures of Norman on his stretcher, which were published in the *Rhodesia Herald*, struck such a chord of sympathy at air force headquarters, Milton Buildings that the staff adopted him. During his three-month stay in hospital, he had regular visits from air force personnel bearing sweets, toys and messages.

Other mercy flights in October involved Africans injured in a bus crash, a game ranger's wife who had birth complications in a remote game park, and African children kidnapped by insurgents. Some 500 mercy flights had been carried out during the previous ten years using both helicopter and fixed-wing aircraft. The air force was on 24-hour stand-by and provided a free service as long as it was a life or death situation and that the flight had been cleared with air force headquarters. The Alouettes could carry two stretcher cases or six seated patients. With the new landing zones at hospitals throughout the country, it was possible to transport seriously ill patients with the minimum handling and discomfort. Helicopters also played a major role in rescue work in difficult terrain. If there was insufficient room to land close to the patient, the helicopter could hover overhead, while a crewmember was lowered with a stretcher. Once the patient was safely strapped into the stretcher, it could be lifted back to the hovering aircraft.

Obviously, this kind of rescue required highly skilled flying by the pilot and No 7 Squadron prided itself on its flying abilities. To demonstrate the prowess of its pilots, the squadron staged a display for a *Rhodesia Herald* photographer at the famous balancing rocks near Epworth Mission south of Salisbury. Squadron Leader Eddie Wilkinson held the helicopter steady in the air above a 21-metre high rock while Herald reporter, Colin Blair, wearing a bright orange sling harness, was lowered at the end of a pencil-thin steel cable by the helicopter technician and winch operator, Sergeant Bernie Collocott.

Once Colin was safely on top of the balancing rock, Sergeant Jock Bain was lowered in the special canvas chair, which was used for a two-man lift. The two were hoisted into the helicopter together and then, with Bernie Collocott keeping a careful watch for obstructions, the Alouette came down to land in a nearby field. Commenting on the difficulties of manœuvring in a small space, Eddie Wilkinson said: "I have to watch this clearance question very closely. I have 36 feet of rotor blade above me and a 38-foot boom behind me to look after, so I need the technician as a second pair of eyes."

The fireforce concept begins to take shape

Until now, the helicopters of No 7 Squadron had been employed largely on an ad hoc basis, with one or two machines deployed to a base to fetch and carry as required. However, towards the end of 1973, with the increase in insurgency in the north-eastern areas the JOC, which had been established at Centenary (FAF 3), was upgraded with higher-ranking officers and moved to Bindura. The senior army representative was now a brigadier and the air force representative, a wing commander, later upgraded to group captain. Centenary (FAF 3) and Mount Darwin (FAF 4) became Sub JOCs with a lieutenant colonel and a squadron leader in command. The main JOC at Bindura was not a tactical base like the forward airfields and as such was not allocated an FAF number.

The Alouettes were grouped at Centenary and Mount Darwin with two regular battalions, 1 RAR and 1 RLI respectively, together with members of the BSAP. At first, helicopters ferried whatever troops were on hand but it soon became obvious that men and machines must be on stand-by to provide fast reaction when an incident or sighting was reported. These reaction groups later became known as fireforce and the aircraft that carried them went by the name of G-Cars.

Of the 50 or 60 men available at a JOC, a third would be on immediate stand-by, one third on 30 minutes call and the remainder available at longer notice. Each Alouette could carry a four-man stick so if three helicopters were available, 12 men could be dropped into a problem area within a few minutes. Up until now, the Alouettes had been used mainly as transport vehicles. The only armament they carried was one MAG or Browning .303 machine gun mounted on the port side of the aircraft. The fireforce concept with later adaptations proved a valuable tool in fighting the war.

No 1 Squadron Diary, October 1973:

On 2nd October, three aircraft shot up to Kariba to visit the Boss (Rob Gaunt), Jim Stagman and Bill Sykes who were taking part in the annual tiger fishing tournament. We dropped them a newspaper and took some pictures. Unfortunately, the film was of poor quality and didn't come out well. After 'bugging' the Boss, Dag Jones flew through the Sanyati Gorge, and from subsequent reports, the fishermen were 'impressed'.

Remarking on this incident later Bill Sykes remembers:

On the last day of the tournament, No 1 Squadron paid us a visit and did the most impressive low passes ever—the water on the lake rippled around us as it was disturbed by the Hunter's wake! No reports of low flying were received from either the Boss or the fishing fraternity.

No 2 Squadron Diary:

No 2 Squadron did the one-hour stand-by on the first weekend of the month, and this will now be a regular occurrence to give No 1 Squadron a bit of a breather. On 10th October, a dawn strike was carried out. Unfortunately, it was a bit of a shambles from the technical side so we did the same task the next day. On 12th October, Dag Jones and Baldy Baldwin put on a show for the installation of a chief at Mubayira [Mondoro]. Dag displayed; Baldy watched. Later in the morning came an air task for a strike in the operational area. No 1 Squadron had two targets: one Rudodo and Mapaiya. The Boss, Rob Gaunt, and Dag took Rudodo and Chris Dixon and Baldy Mapaiya. The strikes were successful Unfortunately, the hosts were out visiting.

No 4 Squadron Diary, October 1973:

Mark [Willie] Knight had an unfortunate accident on 25th October while carrying out a casevac at night. The particular airfield had no runway lights so two Land Rovers' headlights were used for the illumination of the runway. As Mark reached flying speed beyond the beams from the Land Rover, he struck three cows that had wandered onto the field. Damage incurred was to the prop, nose-wheel and tail plane. The prop was bent completely back into the cowling. The only army complaint was that no more cows had been slaughtered. Obviously, the carcasses didn't go to waste. Mark and his passengers got out unscathed.

In November, it was announced that defence costs were up by nearly $1,000,000 (Rhodesian). An increase in operational flying by the air force, because of armed incursions during 1973, was covered in a supplementary vote of $4,250,000 (Rhodesian).

No 4 Squadron Diary, November 1973:

The highlight of bush activities was the return to Centenary and everyone left Eureka with few regrets. The fixed accommodation, eating and toilet facilities being the most welcome change, not to mention a tar runway. The Boss was busy with recce training including the Lomagundi PRAW [Police Reserve Air Wing] flight. Several camps were found during the squadron training and two strikes resulted involving Nos 4, 5 and 1 Squadrons.

No 7 Squadron Diary, November 1973:

Squadron Leader Eddie Wilkinson crashed into telephone lines while returning to base after uplifting casevacs following a land-mining incident. Both Squadron Leader Wilkinson and Sergeant Duncan Woods received injuries in the accident. Squadron Leader Wilkinson was back at work after a few days but Sergeant Woods is off recovering from a variety of broken and cracked bones. The aircraft sustained Category 5 damage. Air Lieutenant Beav Baynham was involved in a fracas with terrorists and his aircraft was hit when he came under heavy ground fire after landing troops to investigate a suspected terrorist camp. Trials carried out on new FM radio sets. In addition, experiments with sky shouting from a helicopter were again tried.

Spotlight on No 3 Squadron

Since September, No 3 Squadron had been resupplying not only security forces within Rhodesia but also the SAS force stationed in the Macombe area of Mozambique. In December, it was decided to show the press something of what was going on in the Operation Hurricane area. A party of journalists was flown by Dakota to the north-eastern border area where a fence was being built from Kanyemba to Mukumbura. The reporters were also taken to see one of the new protected villages. Following this trip, Tom Ballantyne of *The Herald*, wrote a graphic description of the problems of resupply:

The aircraft lifted easily off the runway at the Rhodesian Air Force, New Sarum base. It tucked itself in between the low cloud ceiling, banked north and headed for the north-eastern border. The Rhodesian Air Force Dakota was carrying one and a half tonnes of supplies for the security forces. The men at the base, operating in bush country drenched with heavy rains, would be waiting for the supplies. The drop would provide them with food and other essentials needed to keep them going in the rugged bushveld country of the border area. On board the Dakota were two air force pilots and a team of four territorials who would literally push the stuff out of the plane over the target zone. All had been thoroughly trained in their job. Dropping supplies can be tricky on occasion. The plane settled down at about 1,000 feet above ground level just below the clouds. Ahead the weather looked murky. The aircraft closed in on the koppies of the escarpment and suddenly plunged into a blinding cloudbank. It was frightening for a while and the pilot flew by his instruments until we broke clear a few seconds later. The pilots fly by the seat of their pants, steering the plane visually through breaks in the weather. However, it was obvious they have done this often before. The tops of some of the koppies were actually above us as we wove our way through the weather, flying round the hills and heading steadily towards the edge of the escarpment. Periodically, you felt you could reach out and touch the trees but, in reality, the gap was a few hundred feet. Below us the bush was lush and green; the maize was looking tremendous. Suddenly the plane sneaked over the edge of the escarpment and the flat bush country spread away in front of us, where you could see it through the haze. Our target was about five minutes away and the dispatch team got ready for the drop. The Rhodesian Air Force makes these drops several times a week especially when roads are impassable. Sometimes the Dakotas land and off-load but more often than not, the drop has to be made by parachute. The supplies were in 14 separate crates or 'shooks' each with a parachute attached. They would be dropped from about 300 feet, and would take only seconds to hit the ground. Liquids can be dropped to the troops in specially-designed boxes and mealie meal can go out without a parachute. The air dispatch team stood by the open hatch as we closed in on the base camp. The crates were put on a conveyor of rollers, two at a time. As two men push the crates out, the others in the team haul the next crates to the conveyor for each drop. On this drop, all the crates were going out at the same base camp. With two shooks going out at a time, the Dakota would make seven circuits over the target, each taking about three minutes. The work is hard; each crate weighs about 140 kilograms and has to be man-handled on to the conveyor before being pushed out. Air speed at the moment of the drop is about 100 knots. Below us, troops stood around the camp watching the Dakota as it roared in low over the dropping zone. A red light came on and the sergeant major yelled, "Ready." Then the green one flashed, a buzzer sounded and it was go. Two shooks went lurching out into the air-stream, their 'chutes billowing open, and they hit the ground dead on target. The Dakota screamed as power was increased and it climbed and banked into a circuit bringing it back over the dropping zone again. And while the plane keeled steeply round, the dispatch crew was hauling another two crates into position for the next drop. It was a team effort and everything went smoothly. Finally, all the crates had fallen together near the base camp below to be picked up by army trucks. The Dakota pulled round again and came in low over the camp. We could see a couple of soldiers standing naked in makeshift showers. Another group waved their automatic rifles as our plane gained altitude and headed back towards the escarpment. The flight had given no trouble. Apart from dodging the weather and the koppies, it had been a fairly routine supply drop. The captain of the Dakota said, "The supplies have to get in. If the roads are bad, then the air force has to do it instead." He and the other Dakota pilots have been doing it regularly since the present outbreak of terrorism in December 1972. Keeping frontline troops constantly supplied is part of the war security forces are fighting. These planes continue to roar in over the terr-troubled north-eastern border despite weather. Our Dakota didn't have to screw its way round the hills on the way back. It flew high, and straight through the drizzle and blinding clouds back to New Sarum. Behind it was another successful and vital drop. (Rhodesia Herald, 28th Jan. 1974)

On 20th December 1973, Air Lieutenant Dave Rowe and Sergeant Carl de Beer were the crew of a helicopter engaged in a trooping sortie in the operational area. While approaching a landing zone, the Alouette came under heavy ground fire and Dave Rowe was seriously wounded in the right arm and right leg. Carl attempted to render first aid but it was obvious that Dave would not be able to fly the helicopter back to base. He briefed Carl on the use of the collective pitch lever, which he was now unable to operate himself, as he had to use his left hand for the cyclic. With both men operating the various controls, Carl using his right hand and Dave his left they managed to land safely, much to the relief of the troops who were being transported. The aircraft was slightly damaged, one round having gone through the cabin floor and the other hitting one of the rotor blades. It was flown back to New Sarum and was serviceable again the following day.

Both men were awarded the Military Forces Commendation (Operational). This incident drew attention to the fact that helicopter crews were extremely vulnerable to small-arms fire from the ground. Work was begun on improving the protection offered by the pilot's seat and evaluating suitable bullet-proof jackets to be worn by the crew.

As had become usual at Christmas time, Sally Donaldson, Sweetheart of the Forces, visited forward airfields to record troopies' messages. She was flown around by the air force, and included messages from air force personnel in her special Christmas radio programme.

1973 ended on a damp note with flooded rivers and disrupted road transport. In fact, during the Christmas period, Rhodesia recorded one of the wettest weeks in the history of the country. Once again, No 7 Squadron was called upon to provide help and support. In one case, seven Africans were marooned in the tops of trees in the middle of a swollen river. Unfortunately, one fell from the branches and was taken by a crocodile. The others were plucked to safety by a helicopter. In another incident, an 18-year-old herdsman stood for nearly 24 hours up to his waist in the Shangani River before being winched to safety.

During 1974, the Dakotas of No 3 Squadron continued to provide aircraft for the Parachute Training school, to ferry SAS personnel into action and to re-supply forward positions. One incident that is worthy of mention is that in January, a No 3 Squadron Dakota (R3708) collected a bullet hole somewhere in the north-east. This was the first No 3 Squadron aircraft to be hit by enemy fire.

No 1 Squadron goes night-flying in Salisbury

The beginning of the year saw the strength of No 1 Squadron increased by three. The Squadron Nominal Roll as at Jan 1st 1974 was Squadron Leader Rob Gaunt, Flight Lieutenants Chris Dixon, Chris Weinmann, Don Northcroft, Rickie Culpan, Air Lieutenants Vic

Wightman, Bill Sykes, Jim Stagman, Danny Svoboda, Malcolm (Ginger/Baldy) Baldwin and Air-Sub Lieutenant Paddy Bate. Squadron activities were curtailed by the bad weather. In fact, according to the Squadron Diary: "Overall, it was one of the quieter months that the squadron has had for a long time. But we did manage to put in 175 hours flying."

The squadron left Gwelo for a detachment to Salisbury on 28th January and on the morning of 12th February, nine Hunters and a Canberra got airborne from Salisbury runway. The Canberra's assignment was to photograph the Hunters in various formations culminating in a Diamond Nine flypast over Salisbury City. The pilots flying in the formation were Squadron Leader Rob Gaunt, Chris Dixon, Don Northcroft, Rickie Culpan, Vic Wightman, Bill Sykes, Jim Stagman, Danny Svoboda and Malcolm Baldwin. The next evening a night-flying programme was planned for four aircraft. According to the Squadron Diary:

> The evening ended with some close nervous-breakdowns in Salisbury tower. While flying was in progress, one transmission went over the air as follows 'This is a general broadcast to No 1 Squadron. Owing to the extremely poor conditions of navigation lights and poor visibility on the approach, the tower accepts no responsibility for separation of aircraft in the circuit'.

Bill Sykes, who was one of the pilots that night, says:

> The weather was very poor and worsening, with rain coming in from the south. We shouldn't really have got airborne, but we were all un-current on night-flying. The four of us completed a couple of circuits and landings but then, the tower became 'uncertain' of our positions in the circuit. This caused one Hunter to overshoot, causing excessive R/T chatter, which in turn forced another aircraft to fly an extended downwind leg. This in turn resulted in the aircraft behind him calling 'final' before the aircraft ahead of him. When the wrong aircraft called 'final', the whole thing fell apart. The controller could not really be blamed because he was endeavouring to maintain strict civilian separation of aircraft in the circuit. To be 'bounced' by four Hunters on a dark rainy night was a little unfair. As soon as the controller 'signed off', telling us to do our own thing, we decided to call it quits and land, which was just as well, as the storm broke as we were taxiing in.

No 1 Squadron Diary:

> The Boss (Rob Gaunt) had a rather unfortunate accident when landing at Thornhill in that he had to call for the barrier to stop his Hunter from ending up on the Umvuma Road. Six strikes went in during the month starting on 19th February. These were all concerned with Op Hurricane and the weapons used were the 30mm cannon and the 68mm Matra. Five of the strikes included Hunters and Canberras with a Vampire as the marker aircraft in one of them. The Canberras led on two occasions.* The sixth strike involved Hunters only but, unfortunately, it was aborted owing to weather. The squadron recorded its first kills since the camel train in Aden in the late 1950s. (No 1 Squadron Diary, Jan. 1974)

On February 1st 1974, fuel rationing was reintroduced largely as a result of a substantial rise in the price of crude oil, which meant that supplies were draining the reserves of foreign currency. Also in February, call-ups were increased and plans were announced for a massive increase in Rhodesian defence forces and a change in tactics from defence to attack. It was also announced that there would be a five-year grace period for new immigrants but that after this period, they would be liable to call-up on the same basis as the rest of the white population.

---

* The Hunters now had three-inch rocket rails fitted to them which enabled them to fire 18-pound rocket projectiles.

Selous Scouts—first operation

It had been long accepted that to be successful, the security forces needed reliable information. This meant infiltrating the enemy ranks, in other words posing as sympathizers or even pretending to be terrorists in order to gain this information. It was a tactic that had been used with success in Malaya and Kenya, and during the early days of the insurgency in Rhodesia, members of the Special Branch had tried the technique on a limited basis. Ron Reid-Daly had served in Malaya with General Walls, and towards the end of 1973, he was approaching retirement from the Rhodesian Light Infantry. General Walls invited Reid-Daly to set up and command a new regiment to be called the Selous Scouts. These men were to be tasked with the clandestine elimination of terrorism and terrorists both within and outside Rhodesia. In day-to-day matters, the new regiment would work closely with the director-general of the Central Intelligence Organization.

One of the first operations carried out by the Scouts was in Kandeya Tribal Trust Land, north of Mount Darwin. The local ZANLA contact man was persuaded that an incoming Selous Scouts team was in fact a group of insurgents. The team was directed to the local ZANLA camp, which contained about 12 armed men. The Selous Scouts team reached the vicinity of the camp during the night of 23rd/24th February. The Scouts commander on the ground talked the helicopter in and the troops landed on target. The battle was brief and ended with six ZANLA members dead and another badly wounded.

This fireforce incident is mentioned in Ron Reid-Daly's book as a hoax attack carried out by the Selous Scouts to establish the credentials of one of their members. The dead were apparently six African Scouts liberally doused in Blood Transfusion Centre blood. Reid-Daly comments:

> *Shortly afterwards six, air force helicopters came in, landed safely and disgorged their cargoes of fireforce troops, much to my heartfelt relief. There was a reasonable moon that night, but it is still not easy for a pilot to land a helicopter after dark particularly when, as it was there, the homestead was surrounded by bluegum trees of giant stature. It would have been a terrible cross for me to bear had one crashed, causing loss of life, for it was, after all, only a hoax call, even though a deadly serious one.*

The pseudo-terrorist concept did undoubtedly provide security forces with a great deal of valuable information but it also led to some bitterness among various arms of the security forces and confusion in the minds of Africans who supported the government.

The development of the K-Car

The fireforce concept with helicopter G-Cars transporting troops was now working well, but the fight on the ground was changing. The war was spreading and larger groups with more sophisticated weapons were infiltrating the country. To counter the danger of ground fire, the Alouettes were now carrying extra armour-plating and it was time for the next move—to use helicopters in an attack capacity.

No 7 Squadron Diary, February 1974:

> *A gunship with 20mm cannon fit, is awaiting the 'go ahead' from HQ before commencing trials. Trial exercises were carried out with Trojans to evaluate the possibility of concealing helicopter approach with the aid of fixed-wing aircraft.* These were generally successful. The flak jacket was reported on by members of the squadron and a recommendation to purchase the jacket was forwarded to HQ.*

★ The noise of the Trojan was used to drown out the sound of an approaching chopper.

Further trials with the 20mm cannon were carried out at Inkomo Range during March, and proved highly successful. As a result of the trials, minor modifications were carried out on the helicopters, leading to the development of the specialist K-Car. Initially the K-Car gunship was fitted with the 151/20mm cannon, and this served the squadron admirably for many years. A further development came about when four .303 machine guns were mounted together and operated hydraulically, the purpose being to saturate the target with lead. This ingenious design did, however, have its drawbacks and was never as popular or as effective as the morale-boosting (or morale-shattering) high explosive rounds of the 20mm cannon. All weapons were fired out of the port doorway, so the aircraft had to be flown in a left-hand orbit to bring the guns to bear. This meant that the pilot, in the right hand seat, had a limited but adequate view of the target. Later, these K-Cars carried an army commander aboard and so became an airborne tactical command post.

In March 1974, came the first free-fall training exercise carried out at night by the parachute jump instructors at New Sarum using a No 3 Squadron Dakota piloted by Flight Lieutenant Barry Roberts. The British SAS had carried out experiments on night-time free fall and they proved very helpful, (unofficially). The Parachute School now had a new mascot. The old one, Fred Bear, used as a wind and drift indicator, had bounced once too often. The replacement teddy bear was promptly christened Barbear, in honour of David Barbour, a volunteer reserve pilot.

Macombe airlift

Cabora Bassa, the new Portuguese hydroelectric dam upstream of Tete, was filling fast and places like Macombe, which the SAS had been using as a base, would soon be under water. The air force was approached for help in uplifting as many villagers as possible to the higher ground round the Musengezi River, just inside the Rhodesian border. Dave Thorne of No 3 Squadron was one of the pilots tasked with the airlift.

On 11th and 12th March 1974, Bob d'Hotman and I as co-pilot took Dakota 7053 into Macombe airstrip, which was just 800 metres long with barely-visible markers in the grass. Hundreds of villagers were assembled with as many of their worldly goods as they could carry. This included bicycles, blankets, boxes, baskets, boots and babies, not forgetting poultry in coops and goats on ropes. The villagers comprised all sorts from the very, very old to the very, very young. One elderly woman had a most unfortunate deformity—only half her face had a proper bone structure; the other half hung down making for a most grotesque appearance. Even more remarkable, she was obviously pregnant. Captain Rob Warraker was the SAS officer supervising the loading. This was the first time I had met him. His plan was to pile the worldly goods in a heap in the middle of the aircraft's cabin and then allow the owners of the goods to sit on and around them. As each flight was completed, we found it more and more difficult to clamber over everything and everyone to get up to the cockpit. However, all went well and the sorties progressed throughout the two days although, admittedly, we noticed that the aircraft felt heavier each time we took off. On the last sortie of 12th March, the same procedure was followed, except that Rob Warraker suggested that the pilots go 'up front' and let him finish off the loading. As it was getting late and time was of the essence with the fading light, we agreed. He eventually came under the cockpit window and shouted up to us that our engineer had managed to squeeze into the toilet and we were all set to go. Glancing back into the cabin, we saw only the usual mass of humanity and goods packed up to the ceiling. Sensible engineer, we thought. Bob wisely used a quarter of flap to help with the take-off and ran-up the engines to full power before releasing the brakes. Well, every metre of the 800 was used for that take-off. As we lumbered off into the air, Bob remarked that out of interest we must do a head-count when we landed at

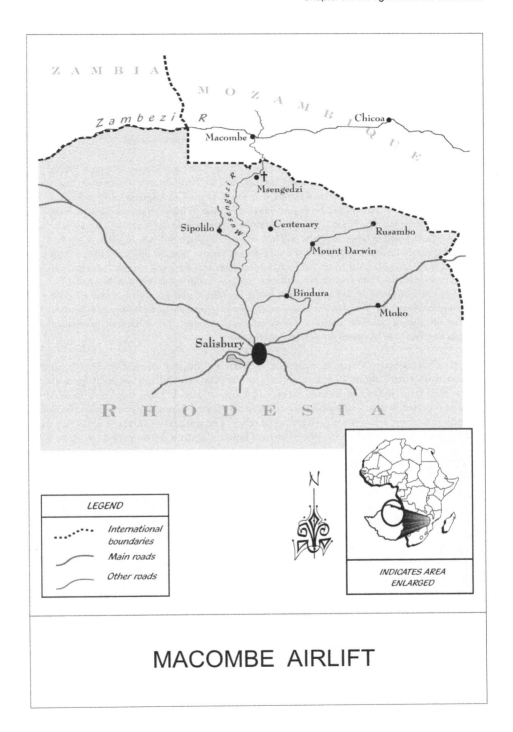

MACOMBE AIRLIFT

Musengedzi Mission. As I recall, 97 passengers were counted off at the Mission. The engineer was squeezed into the toilet because there was simply nowhere else for him to go. Although we suspected that Rob Warraker was stretching our good faith in him, he obviously had more faith in the Dakota than the rule books. The book 'The Dakota Story' has a record of 111 Pakistani passengers being carried on a Dakota but I think we came a good second, especially because of all the 'worldly goods'. (Dave Thorne)

Ian Harvey, a pilot with No 7 Squadron, was also involved in this airlift:

As the final day progressed, with time running out, I was able to pile more and more people into my Alouette III as the fuel burned off. My last load, with fuel down to 110 pounds, was a total of 29 passengers (surely a world record), with my tech Finn Cunningham sitting outside on the running board with his feet on the port wheel. This load included an old man with a crude type of skateboard. The RAR CSM approached me saying that the old man was a cripple who had trained a donkey called Reggie to pull him around the village and into the fields. It was his most treasured possession. In the fading light, I agreed to do one more lift. We set off with a cargo net and sure enough, there in the field standing all alone was Reggie, a riempie halter around his neck. We loaded him into the net without any fuss and with the donkey dangling under the chopper we delivered him to his owner who was beside himself with joy at having been reunited with his companion. The district commissioner, who was probably under orders, had specified that no livestock would be permitted. He summarily shot Reggie. The RAR were so incensed that they had to be restrained from evening up the score.

One of the most unfortunate episodes in March occurred when five South African policemen on patrol about 12 kilometres from Victoria Falls village, stopped for a swim, leaving their rifles in the camp's thatch-roofed picnic hut. Possibly they had been tracked by a group of insurgents who had crossed the river. In any event, the enemy came upon the South Africans as they were swimming, rifles out of reach. The policemen surrendered. They were then marched nearly a kilometre along the road before the insurgents opened fire. One SAP constable, Johan Kuhn, managed to escape the initial shooting. A No 7 Squadron helicopter was called out to search for him but he was never found.

No 1 Squadron detachment to Salisbury ended on 8th March and the men and machines returned to Gwelo. The squadron took part in three strikes during the month, one in conjunction with the Canberras, the other two carried out by the Hunters alone. The use of 18-lb (8,2kg) rocket projectiles began on the second strike, which occurred on 28th March. Some difficulty was experienced in harmonizing the sights for the 18-lb RPs but eventually a compromise was achieved.

Canberra crash
On April 4th 1974, Canberra 2155, on a low-level bombing attack north of the border in the Macombe area, crashed, killing the pilot Air Sub-Lieutenant Keith W. Goddard and navigator Air Sub-Lieutenant Richard Airey. The wreckage was ferried across the river by helicopter and then uplifted by No 3 Squadron aircraft and brought back to New Sarum for the Board of Inquiry. The crash was observed by pilots from No 1 Squadron involved in the same strike.

Remarking on this crash Chris Dams said:

The Canberra could carry 96 x 20-pound fragmentation bombs in a specially designed bomb box. These bombs were mostly tail fin and looked rather like large hand grenades. Because these bombs were so light, they tended to become wild in their flight when they were released from the bomb bay and hit the air stream. The priming device was a cap with vanes on it. Sometimes this cap would spin off in the airstream causing the bomb to become armed directly underneath the aircraft. With the bombs jostling and the caps flying off, there was obviously the chance that one bomb would touch another, and detonate, causing a chain reaction. Something of that kind must have happened to the Canberra we lost in April 1974. The Board of Inquiry didn't prove it but the aircraft was on a bombing run and there is a 99% probability that it was bombs detonating that caused the accident. (Chris Dams)

This possibility added to the Frame 21 metal fatigue problem resulted in the Canberra being rested for a while from its combat role. This proved to be a very significant part of air force history.

Towards the middle of April, intelligence was received that a group of about 50 ZANLA men had set up three bush camps in Chiweshe Tribal Trust Land. An attack upon these men was difficult to plan because the area in which they were operating was densely populated and the group moved continually among the three camps. An air force strike hit the first two camps at 11h30 on 13th April, but the ZANLA men were all at the third camp, and on hearing the noise melted away into the bush. During the night of 17th April, the Selous Scouts observer on the ground reported that about 40 ZANLA men were grouped in the Bobogarande area. A first light attack by the air force was requested but it was some time before a fireforce appeared. The fireforce commander was dropped by helicopter onto a rocky pinnacle but it soon became evident that he did not have a clear enough view of the area to control the action, so command was taken over by the Selous Scouts commander, Mick Hardy, and the senior helicopter pilot. A running battle commenced and by dark, eight ZANLA men had been killed and four captured. Two more bodies were found the next day.

The case of the missing Trog

On Sunday, 14th April 1974, a Trojan (3244) flown by Flight Lieutenant Chris Weinmann with technician, Senior Aircraftman Patrick Durrett was on a reconnaissance flight into Mozambique when it passed over a Frelimo camp. The aircraft was hit by fire from 14.5 and 12.7mm anti-aircraft guns and crashed. An air search was launched for the Trog during which two Hunters had a lucky escape. They were on a flight path using a rocky koppie as a turning point. As they reached the hill, one Hunter broke right and the other broke left. Between them, a dirty smudge appeared in the sky. They followed the trail of the smudge back to its source and plastered the hill with everything they had. It was pure luck that they were turning away from each other at the time, and the SAM-7 heat-seeking missile did not know which aircraft to follow! This was the first occasion that a strela missile is known to have been used against Rhodesian aircraft.

No 1 Squadron Diary recorded the incident—which comments:

The fighter recce course came to an abrupt halt when members of the squadron were deployed to Tete on 4th April. This is the first ever deployment out of the country for the Hunters. The flying in Mozambique consisted of several strikes and recce and top cover in the search for Chris Weinmann's aircraft. On the final of these recces, Vic Wightman and Rick Culpan were fired at by what is almost certain to have been a strela missile. Luckily, the missile did not achieve a lock-on and flew straight past them. Needless to say, both pilots had heart failure. One evening during the Tete deployment, the Portuguese decided to test their 40mm anti-aircraft guns. It was unfortunate that at the same time, Vic Wightman and Rick Culpan were in bed when the first shot was fired. Rick sat bolt upright in bed and blurted to Vic, "We're being attacked!"

(No 1 Squadron Diary, April)

The search for Chris Weinmann's aircraft continued and on 20th April a Provost and a Trojan (3427) flying in tandem were also the targets of a SAM-7. The Trojan was hit and went down. The Provost pilot marked the position of the crash and called in ground forces. The wreck of the second Trojan was quickly located, together with the bodies of the pilot, Air Sub-Lieutenant Robert John Wilson and his technician, Flight Sergeant Roger Stephen Andrews. Air force technicians, who had been escorted across the border by an army patrol, began collecting pieces of the wreckage, only to discover that they had two nose wheels—both apparently from a Trojan. They searched the bush a little further and came upon the Trojan that had crashed six days earlier. The two aircraft had come down some 400 metres from each other. The wreckage of the first Trojan had been tampered with and parts of the aircraft, equipment, and papers from the bodies of the pilot and technician had been removed.

That was when we started heat-shielding the helicopter engines. The Alouette exhaust normally came straight out leaving a large heat source. We made our jet-pipes turn upwards and blow the air into the rotor blades which dispersed the heat, and we put a simple aluminium shield round the engine so that it would not give off any infra-red reflection for a heat-seeking missile. The SAM-7 had a range of about five miles. It was a shoulder-borne weapon. Once a target was in sight the operator switched on the weapon aimed the missile at the target, waited for the lock-on signal, and fired. This took about seven seconds so a lot depended on the speed of the aircraft and the height. With a Viscount, there was time to lock on and fire—a Hunter skimming past at 420 knots was too fast. The Dakota was vulnerable, being slow, but flying at low altitude in and out of the hills, by the time it came into sight and the enemy tried to lock on, the aircraft was out of sight again.* (George Jansen)

As has been explained, the Selous Scouts made use of pseudo terrorists, men who could be smuggled into a suspected area and gain the confidence not only of the local people but also of any genuine insurgents who were moving through, or who had set up bases—in other words they were undercover agents. These men had to be introduced into an area without arousing suspicion and one way of achieving this was to ferry them into the general area by helicopter.

The helicopter pilots were all of an incredibly high standard and I cannot speak too highly of them. They never complained and were always willing to try anything if asked to, and they rarely asked why, either. Helicopters are particularly difficult aircraft to fly at night, for the pilot needs a horizon to work by, but the pilots, although they well knew that, also realized that the closer to night-time the pseudo groups were dropped off, the less chance there would be of a compromise. So, they invariably ignored their flying rulebook in the interests of the soldiers when going on an in-depth deployment, and it was common for them to have the problem of trying to beat the fading light on their way back to the safety of their base. Sometimes they took their helicopters into landing zones, which were so tight the rotor blades would tip the trees but they never demurred. They just went in like heroes to pick up the waiting call sign, or the prisoner, or the casualty, or whatever other funnies were waiting for them, and fly them back to wherever they needed to go. (Ron Reid-Daly, Selous Scouts: Top Secret War)

Early in May 1974, a ZANLA camp was located in the Madziwa Tribal Trust Land. The camp lay near a large village. The plan was that the air force should carry out a dawn strike on 7th May. Selous Scout leader, Dale Collett, was to lay out a fluorescent panel on the outskirts of the camp to act as a marker. It was a difficult operation because the camp was close to a

---

★ The Trojan exhaust was also shrouded to dissipate the heat source.

large village. Collett reported that the panel was in place. But at dawn the area was covered in thick mist. At 07h00 it lifted and the air force went in, but because the panel was too close to the target area, the strike aircraft overshot the camp. It turned and made another run—but the terrorists had been alerted. The ZANLA men had been lined up for a rollcall but they scattered before the RLI arrived. At the debrief, the air force requested that in future the marker panels should be laid out at least 800 metres from the target in order to give the pilot a chance to orientate himself.

One strike was carried out this month involving six Hunters, three Vampires, three Canberras and eleven choppers. The target was completely wiped out but, unfortunately, it was unoccupied. The estimated cost of the Hunter strike was about $30,000 Rhodesian.
(No 1 Squadron Diary, May)

Ten days later, the security forces received word that ZANLA leaders were holding a large meeting at Ruwani School in the Kandeya Tribal Trust Land, 35 kilometres north-west of Mount Darwin. A fireforce based at Centenary flew to Mount Darwin at first light on 16th May. The school was not marked on the map and so it was a matter of putting the troops down, as stop groups, close to the target grid reference and doing a sweep. The helicopters arrived overhead as the meeting was taking place and a running contact broke out over a large area resulting in the deaths of nine insurgents and the capture of seven. From information received, it appeared that 56 men had been attending the meeting when the fireforce arrived.

No 1 Squadron receives the Jacklin Trophy

The Jacklin trophy for 1974 was presented by Wickus de Kock, Deputy Minister in the Department of the Prime Minister, with special responsibilities in the security field. Speaking at Thornhill, on 17th May, he said, "Cohesion and cooperation among security forces are nowhere better demonstrated than here in Rhodesia. In the field of cooperation the air force has earned the reputation among the country's fighting men that is not only above average but I would go so far as to say, unique. In its own right too, as a deterrent to a would-be aggressor, the air force is a potent factor and in no small measure, the free skies of Rhodesia are mute testimony to its worth."

Squadron Leader Rob Gaunt, Officer Commanding No 1 Squadron, accepted the trophy. Later a celebratory party was held at Squadron Leader Gaunt's house.

Perhaps it was the news that the squadron had won the Jacklin Trophy that gave the impetus but during May, squadron members with Bill Sykes in control, redecorated the crew room. A partitioned seating area was designed, with a separate coffee counter and dartboard. A new carpet was obtained and when the work was completed, the squadron had a very attractive crew room, adorned with some very good photographs.

First VR captain

May proved to be a landmark month for No 3 Squadron VRs:

The last day of the month saw quite a milestone. Flight Lieutenant George Walker-Smith VR was appointed as captain. This is the first VR captain in the Rhodesian Air Force. We hope it's not the last! Congratulations George! (No 3 Squadron Diary, May 1974)

On 21st June, four helicopters and a Provost from FAF 4 (Mt Darwin) were tasked with deploying troops from No 1 Commando RLI. Flight Lieutenant Ray Houghton (SAAF) had dropped his stick on relatively open ground when his helicopter was hit by a RPG rocket fired from a small clump of trees about 35 metres away. The aircraft caught fire immediately. The crew abandoned the burning aircraft and took cover. The enemy came under fire from a K-Car piloted by Flight Lieutenant Dave Thorne who took command of the operation, while the crew of the downed helicopter was uplifted by Flight Lieutenant Erasmus (SAAF). A further three helicopters and one Provost from FAF 3 (Centenary) were called up to assist in the contact. All the weapons were recovered from the wreckage of the helicopter, which was unfortunately Category 5, having burned out completely.

Flight Lieutenant Houghton who had been wounded, was casevaced to Salisbury by a Trojan while the technician, Sergeant Ray Verniche, who escaped with minor cuts and bruises, was treated at the FAF. (SAAF pilots attached to 7 Squadron wore Rhodesian camouflage and badges of rank.) Deaths from this contact numbered fifteen. Three were armed terrorists. Eleven were recruits and one was a female who was feeding them when the attack occurred. In addition six recruits, most with slight injuries, were captured and casevaced to hospital.

No 1 Squadron Diary, June 1974:

Trials have been carried out on the new Global Navigation System GNS 200 [Omega] with the old Mark 1 eyeball as a stand-by. One airstrike was carried out by the squadron on 24th June. Nox Dixon was supposed to lead it but returned to the crew room because his aircraft went u/s. Rick Culpan finally led the strike with 68mm Matra and 30mm cannon. Two terrs were killed after being flushed out by the strike.

The GNS trials were carried out over a number of months, some successful, some not, but the limitations were found. One of the main problems was the shielding of the external aerial from the signal, in a tight turn at low level. The system then bombed and the pilot had to work like an octopus to get the thing programmed again. There is enough workload in a single-seater fighter for one man, without having to divert one's attention inside the cockpit to push buttons and flick switches with a gloved hand, at low level doing 420 knots—to get everything up and running again. (Bill Sykes)

'Flame-out' during a formation-flying practice

A Forces '74 Fête was scheduled to be held in Gwelo on 20th July at which four aircraft from No 1 Squadron were to perform formation flying. It was three days before the show while the squadron was carrying out formation-flying practice that Rickie Culpan received the shock of his life. Bill Sykes recounts what happened:

Soon after midday, the four of us got airborne for a practice formation. At the briefing, the Boss said that we would fly out past Somabula, find a straight section of the railway line, and use that as a reference to simulate the road past the Gwelo showgrounds. Purely by chance, the Boss spotted a straight bit of rail closer to Thornhill and changed his mind. We went through the various turns and formation changes as briefed, and then ran in for the 4g pull-up into the vertical bomb-burst. I was No 3 on the left of the formation and Rickie was in the No 4 position in line astern. As we got to the vertical, there was a high-pitched squeal over the radio from Rickie shouting, "I've had a flame-out!" Well, if things were to go wrong this could not have happened at a better moment. Rickie pulled over the top at 7,000 feet and rolled wings level. He was at 210 knots (gliding speed) and on the glidepath and also just about on the centre-line for Runway 31 at Thornhill. Perfect ... I just happened to be closest to him, put down two notches of flap, and came into a loose formation on his port side. The tower, meanwhile, was in a bit of a panic. The controller was inexperienced and on hearing the Mayday call from the Boss instructed all the aircraft in the flying area to return immediately and land. Wrong—should have told them to keep well away. Rickie, on his glidepath, was checking that he had carried out all his emergency procedures. One of these was to jettison the drop-tanks, so that the maximum gliding distance could be attained. Rick, conditioned as we all were to conserve equipment, refused to throw his 230 gallon tanks off, as there was only one set per aircraft. It took a lot of persuasion to get him to realize that if he kept his tanks on, he might not reach the airfield, and we would lose the aircraft as well. The tanks fell away and tumbled into an open field. Back at the airfield, things were hectic—the Vampires were landing and blocking the runway. One of the Vamps had already landed and turned off at the end of the runway, but there was another in the middle of its landing run and directly in the path of the oncoming Hunter. Rickie was getting a little agitated at this stage—"Get that b..... aircraft off the runway!" There was a pause of about five seconds while Approach, who were now on our frequency, relayed the information to the tower controller. The Vampire, still doing about 80 knots, thundered off onto the grass in a huge cloud of dust. Rickie then had the ideal set-up—lots of speed and an empty runway dead ahead. He dropped his undercarriage early to wash off the excess speed, crossed the threshold at around 170 knots, deployed his drogue 'chute before touchdown and then waited till the last moment to apply full brakes. It was a magnificent effort. The other three of us landed on Runway 13 and as we rounded out, we saw Rickie standing next to his lifeless aeroplane on the taxi track. The only 'downer' in this incident was that I, as the only witness, had to get airborne in a Provost to search for the drop tanks while Rickie was being fêted. By the time I got down to the mess, I was a good six beers behind. (Bill Sykes)

The flypast at the fête was flown by Boss Gaunt, Rickie Culpan, Danny Svoboda and Bill Sykes and consisted of the four aircraft in different formations culminating in a vertical bomb burst with the Boss and Rickie rolling out at the top and then pulling through for a 1,000 mph closing speed (1,600 km/h) cross at the bottom. Rickie didn't try any party tricks on this one. While the flypast was in progress, Don Northcroft and Jim Stagman were carrying out a photo task in 'Porco land' (Mozambique). The mission was a success, but Jim confessed that he didn't see much on the visual recce side. The next day, Nox Dixon and Jim Stagman escorted an incoming Dakota carrying the retiring minister of defence and soon after that they escorted an outgoing Viscount carrying the singers of the Forces '74 Show. Nox and Jim were dying to remove their masks so that the ladies in the Viscount could photograph them but alas, they were having too much trouble staying in formation to remove their hands from the controls. Vic Wightman spent most of the month at Mount Darwin. (No 1 Squadron Diary)

Incident in Madziwa

Earlier in the year, on 17th April 1974, a government animal health inspector, Hugh Gundry, was working in a village about eleven kilometres north-west of Rusambo Mission, near the Mozambique border, inoculating the villagers' dogs against rabies. A terrorist forced his way through the waiting crowd, shot the vet and disappeared into the bush. Soon afterwards, a land-mine exploded under an African bus injuring eleven people, six of them seriously. Follow-up operations were immediately launched but with no result until the middle of August, when information was received that infiltrators had been spotted in the Madziwa Tribal Trust Land. Early on Wednesday morning, 14th August, a report was made to the JOC. Within 20 minutes, the fireforce was on its way.

A flight lieutenant piloting one of the helicopters described how he circled over the area in which the terrs were sighted, but they had apparently gone to ground. "I decided then to drop the RLI chaps and as we came in, terrorists hidden in the surrounding rugged country opened up on us," the flight lieutenant said. "The way those RLI chaps took off after those terrs without worrying

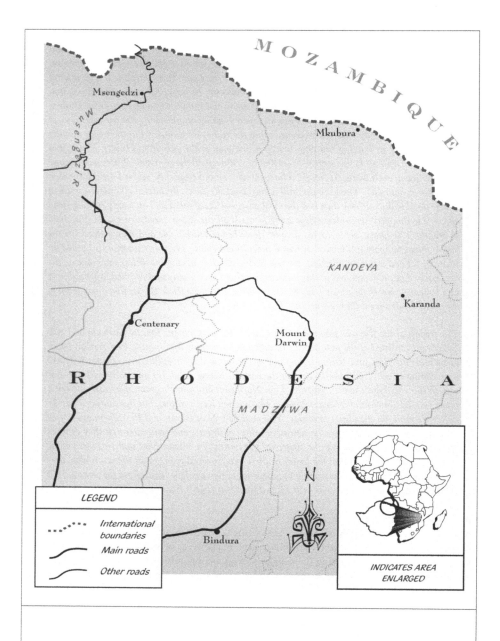

LEGEND

- ⋯⋯ International boundaries
- ⌒ Main roads
- ⌒ Other roads

INDICATES AREA ENLARGED

OPERATION IN MADZIWA TTL

about their own safety would do any army in the world proud," he said. With the troops in hot pursuit of the terrs who had scattered in the face of fierce retaliatory fire, the flight lieutenant and the pilots of the other helicopters turned to informing the troops where the pockets of the enemy were hidden. "A lot of the success must be due to the excellent cooperation between the pilots and the men on the ground," the flight lieutenant said. A lieutenant who was controlling the battle on the ground described how effectively the black and white troops worked together during the ensuing one and a half hours. "The action moved back and forward over the area of one kilometre square," the lieutenant said. "During this period the men were mingling together and helping support one another in every conceivable way. It was a classic example of cooperation between the fighting forces on the ground and those in the air." The battle continued to rage, with the terrs, after engaging in a stand-up fight at first, becoming intent on escape. The attempts of some were thwarted, however, with the arrival of fixed-wing aircraft called in to bomb and strafe the enemy positions. In the confusion of battle, it was impossible to gauge the success of the 'hit'. But when the dust had settled, eight terrs were dead. The one security force death was that of Major Ernest C. (Doomps) Addams who was hit by rifle fire. The terrorists were armed with RPG rocket launchers, RPD machine guns and AK-47 automatic rifles. (Rhodesia Herald, 16th Aug. 1974)

There were many factors that could influence the effectiveness of a fireforce operation. One major problem was the noise of the Alouette's jet engine, which in quiet bush surroundings, with the wind blowing in the right direction could be heard many kilometres away, allowing plenty of time for insurgents to melt into the bush. It was therefore vital, that the helicopters approached from down-wind and the ground forces had to take this fact into consideration when talking aircraft onto targets.

Centenary sunset
Peter McCabe, 16th August 1974:

The only down side to the Alouette III was the grease—the regular lubrication required by the rotor head was a pain. The grease that was pumped into the head immediately spread over the entire surface of the head and blades once they started to rotate and this film of grease picked up a layer of dust whenever the aircraft landed in the bush. One of the tech's jobs was to clean it, then pump in more grease thus starting the cycle all over again. In the early days at Centenary, immediately after the main airstrip had been tarred and the aircraft dispersal area was in the process of completion, the Alouettes were all parked alongside the main runway. On this particular bush trip, a Provost aircraft was in the area with an instructor and an up-and-coming 4 Squadron student pilot who was doing the operational side of his conversion. In the event of a call-out, the Provost would follow the fireforce aircraft into battle, remaining on the fringes of the action to gain experience. One evening just as the sun was setting, I was on top of my chopper, minding my own business and cleaning the head as usual. The Provost, with Flight Lieutenant Steve Baldwin and a student were on finals for the runway, landing from the golf course end. Unbeknown to the Provost crew, while they had been away during the day, a construction gang had dug a ditch across the threshold of the runway for a sewerage pipe. The student pilot, obviously wishing to impress his instructor, planned to put the aircraft down on the threshold. The aircraft was landing into the sun, and the ditch and spoil bank were not visible to either the instructor or student. The Provost touched down just on the spoil bank and both main wheels and undercarriage legs were immediately ripped off. The aircraft flopped onto its belly and ground its way down the runway directly towards my helicopter, which was positioned first in line—with me on top! The Provost finally came to a halt in a cloud of dust just two metres from the front of my helicopter. The hood was wound back and the two occupants climbed out and beat a hasty retreat. The Ford F-250 fire truck was right on the scene as the Provost slid to a stop. This was not by design but by good fortune—their swift reaction was due entirely to the fact that the fire crew were already on their way to light the flare path for some aircraft movement later that evening. The hasty exit of the Provost crew was followed very closely by me on my way to an immediate underpants change. (Peter McCabe)

Visits to Durban—successful and not so successful

Meanwhile the Rover trips to the coast were providing welcome relief:

No 1 Squadron Diary, August 1974:

Bill Sykes and Danny Svoboda left for Durban on 21st August. Much to Danny's disgust his aircraft would not start for his return trip the next day and he was forced to stay another two nights! As far as 3 Squadron was concerned—flying to Durban was just too easy!

No 3 Squadron Diary, Aug/Sept 1974:

August was hard work month with little social activity. Bob d'Hotman did three weeks at Bindura supporting JOC Hurricane in his own inimitable way. Dave Barbour set out to sail from Vilanculos to Durban with an untrained crew and without a chart, saying that he couldn't get a man from the squadron to crew for him!

The sequel to this report is as follows:

Four battered and bruised Rhodesian yachtsmen were stranded on a deserted Zululand beach for a day and a night after their 11.5-metre sloop capsized in high seas at the weekend.

The military coup in Portugal and its aftermath

Up to this point the situation in Rhodesia had been contained. The SAS personnel in Mozambique had succeeded in keeping the number of insurgents entering the country to a minimum and any who did make it through the cordon were soon picked up. But far away in Portugal events had occurred that were to change the whole war. The Portuguese people were tired of fighting wars in distant countries and on 25th April 1974, Dr Marcello Caetano's government was overthrown in a military coup. At first, it seemed that there would be no sudden hand-over in Mozambique or Angola but as the weeks passed the mood changed. There was talk of a transfer of power, but before anything could be organized, the Portuguese army collapsed leaving Frelimo in control of Mozambique. For Rhodesian security forces, this created a nightmare. Instead of a relatively small border area to patrol, there was now over a thousand kilometres of rugged terrain running right down the mountainous eastern border. Added to this, most of Rhodesia's imports and exports had been moving through the Mozambique ports of Beira and Lourenço Marques (Maputo).

Towards the end of August, there was a scramble by Whites to leave Mozambique because of the fear of a future black government, despite Frelimo's efforts to persuade the white community to stay. In the general confusion two hitch-hikers, Miss Forsyth and Mr Gunn were injured when the lorry in which they were travelling was blown up by a land-mine near the Nyamapanda border post. The Portuguese authorities transported them to the border where they were picked up by helicopter and taken to Karanda Mission Hospital. Michael Gunn's injuries were superficial but Hilary Forsyth died shortly after reaching the Mission.

By the beginning of September, the situation in Mozambique was deteriorating rapidly and Air Rhodesia was called to evacuate 56 Rhodesians and South Africans from Beira. On 11th September 1974, Frelimo troops marched into Lourenço Marques and assumed power.

One interesting sideline is that, as a result of the situation in Mozambique, Rhodesia acquired four Britten-Norman Islanders. These aircraft were flown across the border and hidden in a hangar at Mount Hampden airfield, until the legalities had been dealt with. After this, their bright markings were covered with camouflage and they were transferred to the Rhodesian Air Force. These aircraft were ideal for working out of bush strips and after their arrival, the Beech Baron was sold (it had been damaged in a landing accident). The top speed of the Britten-Norman Islander (120 knots) was less than that of the Baron's (180 knots) but they had a very good carrying capacity and proved to be of immense value to the security forces.

Helicopters to the rescue

While the war went on, No 7 Squadron still had its humanitarian role to fulfil. In the middle of September, an aircraft from the squadron was used to search for the body of a commercial pilot, David Charlton, who fell to his death while attempting to hang-glide from World's View in Inyanga. Rescuers could not reach the body and a helicopter had to be used to retrieve it from the mountainside.

On 21st September, helicopters were again called in for a rescue operation when a goods train careered head on into a stationary train at Trelawney Station at 09h00. Two No 7 Squadron helicopters airlifted firemen and equipment from Salisbury to the crash scene. There was the threat of an explosion because a fertilizer wagon had caught fire in the crash and the train was carrying fuel.

And some time before 07h00 on Monday 23rd September 1974, a crowded bus travelling along a dirt road detonated a land-mine near Combiro Protected Village in the Chiweshe Tribal Trust Land. An hour later, a medical orderly from Centenary arrived in a No 7 Squadron helicopter. He found two men dead and 29 people injured, including a child of two with a badly broken leg. The mother's leg had been amputated in the blast. Two other victims had lost limbs and one man had both his legs blown off. As soon as they received the report, security forces released more helicopters from operational duty and the injured were evacuated to Bindura Hospital. An air force helicopter was also used to ferry in extra supplies of blood during the afternoon. The sequel to this land-mine incident came on 2nd October just as the sun was setting.

> *The pilot [of a helicopter], an air lieutenant, who spoke to newsmen yesterday at the briefing said ground forces asked him to investigate two suspicious men who were apparently herding cattle. "We picked them up running across a ploughed field and as we got close to them they started firing at us with AKs." The gang commander Solomon Hokoko (25) was firing wildly into the air but the other man who has not yet been identified was calmer. The pilot said, "We dropped him in his tracks first and then got Solomon. We fired about 400 rounds." The attack was carried out in a difficult light because of the setting sun. The terrs fired first. The puffs of white smoke from their rifles identified them as terrorists. They failed to hit the aircraft with a single shot. Both men were badly wounded but alive when a helicopter landed to pick them up. They died later in Centenary Hospital. The pair were wearing civilian clothes recently stolen in a raid on a Glendale farm store. The pilot said it was unusual to catch terrs in the open. Another 300 metres and they could have reached thick cover.* (Rhodesia Herald, 4th Oct. 1974)

These two men were part of the eleven-man gang responsible for laying the land-mine that detonated under the bus on 23rd September, as well as several other incidents including one on 1st October during which a district assistant and a national serviceman were killed.

Kotwa capers

During October 1974, Nyamapanda came under a daily mortar barrage from inside Mozambique. To counter this threat, FAF 5 (Mtoko) was activated and No 7 Squadron aircraft also began operating from Kotwa (on the road north-east running from Mtoko to the border crossing at Nyamapanda). Two Alouettes, one G-Car and one K-Car, were detached from the fireforce at Mtoko and stationed at Kotwa, close enough to assist but not close enough to attract mortar fire. Graham Cronshaw and John Britten were in the K-Car, 'KC' Law and Pete McCabe were in the G-Car. The helicopters were based at the police station at Kotwa, which was very much a one man outfit. The pilots and techs slept under canvas and ate at the police station.

On the day in question, the K-Car was required at Mtoko and so Graham and JB flew off leaving the G-Car at Kotwa. Peter McCabe takes up the story:

> Soon after the K-Car had gone, an RAR call sign reported a contact not far away and we went galloping to their aid. A small group of terrs had opened fire on the patrol from a rocky koppie and had the RAR pinned down. When we arrived, the terrs, not unnaturally, started shooting at us. We returned fire with the MAG and soon sorted out the problem. We remained in orbit while the RAR swept the area and confirmed that the enemy had been eliminated. All without the use of the redoubtable gunship! When the K-Car arrived back from Mtoko, Graham and John were pretty upset that they had missed the action. Next, there was a callout to Mtoko. After the contact, Graham asked KC Law and me to take his K-Car back to Kotwa because he needed the G-Car to fly some VIPs round the area. On our way back to Kotwa, another RAR call sign radioed requesting a position check and telstar to their base. They had come across the very fresh tracks of 16 possible terrs. We over-flew them to identify their position and then orbited. As we climbed to get comms with base I saw the group of terrs lying in ambush along the edge of a maize field about 50 metres from the RAR stick. KC warned the stick to get into cover. And we called Mtoko for a fireforce. HQ requested we hold off until it arrived but seeing us orbiting, the terrs realized that they had been spotted and began to pull out. The RAR stick then opened fire on them—we joined the battle. We had accounted for most of the enemy before the fireforce, including a G-Car flown by one very browned-off Graham Cronshaw, arrived. Once again, he had missed the action! A couple of weeks later, a well-polished Bedford RL pulled up outside the squadron HQ at New Sarum. Out stepped an immaculately dressed sergeant major from the RAR. He requested the presence of KC Law and me and then very kindly presented us with a couple of crates of beer 'for looking after his lads'. Graham missed out on that, too! (Pete McCabe)

As the K-Car pilots and technicians gained experienced, so more modifications were suggested and put into practice. Changes were carried out on the commander's seat; the K-Cars were fitted with anti-strela shrouds and as they came in for servicing, they were given a matt paint finish to make them less visible to the heat-seeking missiles. Engine shrouds for the rest of the aircraft were fitted later. Templates were designed for an extension to the armour-plating on the pilot's seat to cover the pilot's head, back and sides, as well as an elliptical extension that provided protection for the pilot's left arm.

The Hunter squadron was also carrying out trials with new equipment. "Most of the flying time has been occupied by operational training and with trials on the Global Navigation System GNS 200, which have been fairly successful. One interesting point is the increasing reference to pilots joining the Rhodesian Air Force from countries such as Australia, America and the United Kingdom."

There was an echo from the past on October 16th, when the death was announced of Frank

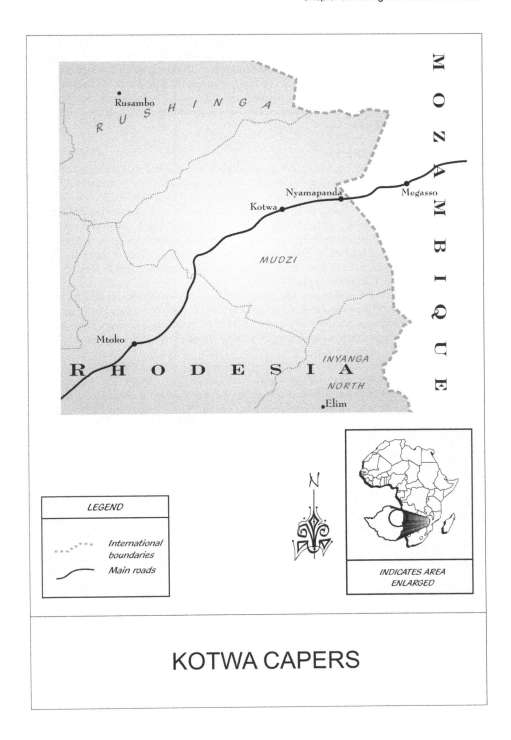

John Gericke. Born in Benoni in 1919, educated at Umtali Boys' High School, he was one of the six young Rhodesians chosen to attend the RAF Training Centre at Halton in 1936. After a three-year apprenticeship with the RAF, he returned to Rhodesia in 1939. Later he joined No 237 Squadron and remained with the squadron throughout World War II. Thereafter, he served in the postwar air force with distinction and ultimately commanded No 1 Ground Training School (Technical) at New Sarum. For his services to the force and the country, he was awarded the MBE.

Special Investigation Branch

During the year 1974, the Special Investigation Branch of the Air Force Security Unit was formed. The role of SIB was primarily the detection of crime or security offences within the air force. The founder members were Flight Lieutenant Jack Lewis-Walker, Steven Gale and Don Granger, the last two being ex-BSAP members. When they had completed their tour of duty, they were replaced by Bob Bishop and Paul Hill. Assistance was also provided by various VRs with specialist knowledge, such as lawyers, magistrates and even an ex-sheriff from Nevada County, Alex Konig. There were also two African members of the team. Whilst the investigators at station level were doing a good job, SIB could be called in if the case was considered serious or if it involved civilians.

Runways on forward airfields provided more than enough space for the smaller aircraft but the Dakotas could have problems and on Guy Fawkes day, Noel van Hoff ran out of brakes and then runway at Mount Darwin. His load of MP passengers emerged shocked but unharmed and perhaps a little more appreciative of the hazards of the north-east.

In the Independence Day honours list, George Walker-Smith received the much- merited Military Forces Commendation (Non-Operational) for his efforts in the VR, especially becoming the first VR captain. Well done George! Jerry Lynch becomes the second VR captain. The skies of Rhodesia are no longer safe! (No 3 Squadron Diary, November)

A far cry from the days when the volunteer reservists were told that they must not expect to be allowed to fly an aircraft.

CHAPTER 40

A sanctions-busting ferry

Events in Mozambique during 1974 had disastrous results for Rhodesia. It meant that the whole of Rhodesia's eastern border was now controlled by a regime that had close ties with ZANLA and was sympathetic towards its aims. The collapse of Portuguese rule in Mozambique also convinced the South African Prime Minister, B.J. Vorster, that black rule was inevitable in Rhodesia also, and that he must, therefore, loosen ties with White Rhodesia and seek a détente with Kenneth Kaunda in Zambia and Julius Nyerere in Tanzania. Vorster, therefore, set about forcing Ian Smith into declaring a ceasefire and agreeing to talks with the nationalists.

Leaders of Rhodesia's four nationalist organizations attended a meeting in Lusaka and signed a Unity Accord linking them under the banner of the ANC. These groups were ZANU, ZAPU, Frolizi (led by James Chikerema) and the ANC. The Prime Minister of Rhodesia, Ian Smith, made a broadcast on 11th December 1974, in which he stated that he had agreed to release detainees, that a constitutional conference was to take place, and that the terror war would cease. Talks and meetings were held in operational areas, and terrorist commanders said they would inform their followers about the agreement. Thousands of leaflets were dropped by the air force.

Meanwhile anti-terrorist activities continued, with the air force being called upon to cover an ever-widening area as incursions took place further to the south. No 7 Squadron helicopters were now operating regularly from Inyanga and Mudzi.

Casevac from Mashumbi Pools
Flying at night from airstrips in the bush could be hazardous. On the evening of 17th December 1974, a No 4 Squadron Trojan (4326), piloted by Air Lieutenant Brian Murdoch was tasked to uplift a casualty from a landing strip near Mashumbi Pools. The landing and take-off was carried out using a single-line flare path with mini flares. These had been developed for such emergencies and were one-litre tins filled with paraffin and fitted with [a] cotton waste and screw top. To lay the flare path, two flares were placed at the threshold of the runway i.e. one on each of the first runway markers and then one on each of the left-hand runway markers with two at the end. Unfortunately, the flare-laying party who were waiting to put out and collect the flares had parked their Land Rover in the overshoot on the line of the aircraft's take-off path. Shortly after becoming airborne, the Trog's undercarriage struck the top of the Land Rover. This must have distracted the pilot for the aircraft crashed a few moments later killing everyone on board: the casualties were Corporal John Mitchell Parker (8RR), Lance-Corporal Roger John Povey (2RR), the medic, and the pilot, Brian Murdoch.

Despite détente, acts of terrorism continued; just after Christmas 1974 came one of the worst incidents for some time. Five members of the South African Police travelling in a Land Rover near Victoria Falls were hailed by a group of insurgents. The South Africans stopped their vehicle and were taken prisoner. A member of the BSAP travelling with the SAP understood what was being said and shouted a warning that the terrorists were going to kill them. As they were crossing a high-level bridge the BSAP member and one member of the South African Police dived out of the vehicle and plunged into the river. Despite his wounds and being attacked by a leopard the SAP man survived. The BSAP man was never seen again. The remaining members of the SAP were paraded around the Tribal Trust Lands and then shot.

On 10th January 1975, it was announced that the release of detainees was to be halted because terrorist activities were continuing. The nationalists retaliated by saying that the terrorist war would not stop until all the detainees were released. In fact, an average of six incidents were being reported each day, including an attack on the Bulawayo/Victoria Falls railway line. The détente exercise had failed.

Apprenticeship scheme

Obviously first class technicians were required to keep the air force's ageing aircraft in the air and a new scheme was announced towards the end of 1974. All local airmen recruits who joined the air force after 1st January 1975 as trainees would be given the option of entering into a contract of apprenticeship, providing they agreed to serve a minimum of ten years. A trainee did not have to make the decision at the time of attestation; he could choose to spend one year in the force while he made up his mind. Anyone who did not wish to join the scheme could serve five years under a different training programme. In fact, 47 of the 59 recruits, inducted for training with No 34 Course, opted immediately for medium service engagement with the Indentured Apprenticeship Scheme. An agreement had also been reached with the Apprenticeship Authority that retrospective action could be carried out. This meant that qualified technicians could apply to the Authority for recognition of previous training and possible issue of indenture papers.

On 21st January, Air Lieutenant Mike Litson and Master Sergeant Geoff Dartnall were airborne in a No 7 Squadron helicopter when they heard a civilian aircraft transmit a Mayday call. Cessna 401 VP-WEC, with pilots Tony Birch (a DCA examiner) and Graham Keth, was on its way back to Charles Prince Airport when a fire broke out in the starboard engine. The Cessna crash-landed on the Warren Hills gliding strip. Litson landed his helicopter alongside the crash and casevaced the injured pilots to Salisbury Central Hospital.

Away flights and the consequences

No 1 Squadron Diary, January 1975:

In January, the squadron was put on 'one hour stand-by or less' on several occasions, but unfortunately never took to the air. Bill Sykes and Paddy Bate flew down to Durban on 15th January. To the disgust of both members, one of the aircraft would not start and an extra night was spent in Durban. The only swim of the trip was had on the hardstanding at Durban while changing batteries in the rain.

Extended night-stops were becoming a bit of a habit on the squadron and although most of them were genuine, there was the odd one here and there that put the Boss on his guard. We were briefed in no uncertain manner that a second night in Durban would not be tolerated. The Boss was not going to have the wool pulled over his eyes any more—he knew every trick in the book. Except one ... When we put the aircraft to bed, I, or one of the South African technicians, must have kicked the master switch to the On position. Needless to say the battery went flat. On start-up the next day—nothing. The solution—use ground power. Bingo! All the cockpit *lights came on, but still no start. A phone call to the squadron brought no immediate answer to the problem, so we decided to change batteries between aircraft. As a result, mine started but Paddy's didn't, even with ground power. We were stumped. It was now too late to get airborne so we were driven back to the hotel 'kicking and screaming', for another night on the town. As it turned out, we were NOT guilty. The problem, we discovered later, is that the ground power does not hold in the starter relay. There has to be a trickle of power from the battery to do that. We were reluctantly forgiven by the Boss, who now had what he thought was the complete list of loopholes for extended night-stops! Yes, and we did get thoroughly soaked, and we had to fly home in sodden flying suits. On the way out of Durban we broke a few rules by giving the tower and the helicopter squadron based there a beat-up that they would not forget for a while. We turned out to sea after take-off, and did a wide arc, coming in over the coastline between the sand dunes at 'nought' feet and doing well over 500 knots. We pulled up just above the fuel tanks and rolled away into the climb. The air traffic controller was elated. "The Mirages never do that," he said. "The pilots would be grounded immediately." It was only afterwards that we realized we had 196 bottles of wine in the 'loot' tanks.* All safe though.* (Bill Sykes)

No 1 Squadron Diary:

Another night stop took place on 22nd January. This time Vic Wightman and Pete Mason flew down to Cape Town and greatly enjoyed themselves. The members of No 1 Squadron from 1st January are as follows: Squadron Leader Rob Gaunt, Acting Squadron Leader Chris Dixon. Flight Lieutenants Don Northcroft, Bill Sykes, Vic Wightman and Ken Law. Air Sub-Lieutenants Paddy Bate, Pete Mason and Doug Reitz.

No 4 Squadron Diary, January 1975:

Provost flying hours: 163h50; Trojan: 159h25; Cessna: 14h40
Eleventh year of the squadron at Thornhill. Quite an action-packed month for aircrew. Willie Knight and Norman Maasdorp leapt to the border for two days. Dave Bourhill proved that the Provost doesn't fly on hot air alone, by making a successful precautionary landing on a road in the operational area. He has now registered his Provost with the AA (Automobile Association). Phil Haigh declared a new airfield at Chombira 'open' ahead of time by landing there on his way to FAF 3—just a courtesy call? The main event of February 1975, as far as No 3 Squadron was concerned, was an accident that occurred on 21st February, at the Rushinga Forward Air Field. Dakota 7307 (Chaminuka) ground-looped on the landing strip because of brake failure. Ed Potterton and Frank Wingrove VR, the pilots, escaped uninjured but the engineer John Mitchell received a gash on the head. The Dakota was badly damaged and it was not possible to carry out repairs. The aircraft had to be stripped and was taken to Salisbury on the Queen Mary, a large flatbed truck. After inspection at New Sarum, it was deemed to be a write-off.† One aspect that emerged from this accident was that the crews of No 3 Squadron would never again have to fly into dark, turbulent cumulonimbus clouds at 12,000 feet to seed clouds! On 25th February, Dave Barbour became the third VR member to be awarded his captaincy on the Dakota.

Air force reservists at FAF 5

Most of the forward airfields were organized and staffed by reservists. The story of one such air force reservist, Robin Fennell, was told in the *Rhodesia Herald* on 17th February 1975:

---

* In December the Hunters had started carrying out trials with 50-gallon frantan tanks—including one of Portuguese manufacture.

† *Chaminuka* lay alongside the Parachute Training Centre hangar for months after the accident.

When he is not doing reserve air force duty, Robin is taking care of his coffee crop in Chipinga. In February 1975 he was doing his call-up. "There aren't many problems on the estate during this season," said Robin, "although I have had a new tractor overturned and the staff are not keen on taking orders from my wife." As soon as his five or six week stint is over, he'll be back in Chipinga picking coffee until November. Robin is doing his service this time at Forward Air Field No 5, Mtoko, a cozy little canvas-and-caravan operation centre and airstrip. He helps to run the centre with six different means of communication. His fellow officers and men appear relaxed with their music, their games and grub. But the planes and helicopters that come and go, the weapons and paraphernalia of war are parked menacingly around and the sharp-eyed air force territorials doing guard duties dispel any thoughts of idleness. The camp is close to an area where there is still plenty of activity. Terrorists have been mining vehicles and ambushing others not very far away. The camp is run by Squadron Leader Preller Geldenhuys, South African-born, but Rhodesian by choice. His friends call him 'Prop' to go with propeller. In seconds, he can be in contact with the right people through air traffic control using three different radio systems, teleprinter, or telephone. He can have a plane or helicopter over the area within a few minutes. Prop's only other regular air force staff are the cook, the equipment NCO and telegraphist; the remainder are reservists from air force territorial force. The camp commandant is the marketing manager of the Rhodesian Wattle Company. There is another farmer in the operations room, by coincidence, also from Chipinga. Forward Air Field No 5 can be all packed up and spirited away somewhere else within 24 hours—lock, stock, barrel and everything else, except the shower, the only permanent structure in the place. This small forward airfield is as close as Rhodesian security forces can get to the Bedouin Arab tradition. It has not happened yet, but if military policy demands it, the first thing the locals will know is when they see a shower, an airstrip and some concrete slabs getting covered by blowing sand. Between one action and the next at present, there are new paperbacks to read—the air force buys them every month—and a tape recorder with new cassettes to use, but best of all perhaps comes the occasional bottle of wine. It all depends how the accounts are organized, for the air force mess is on a cash basis locally. Being away from the farm cannot be that bad, can it? (Rhodesia Herald, 17th Feb. 1975)

Bill Sykes comments:

The original FAF 5 learnt one lesson from Mount Darwin—the pub. It was a hole in the ground about three metres in diameter and one and a half metres deep. It was ten degrees cooler than the surface temperature and it served as a safe place during a mortar attack. Unless the mortar landed in the pit!

Talks with African nationalists were limping along, but on 19th March 1975 came the news that the chairman of ZANU, Herbert Chitepo and his bodyguard had been killed when his car was blown up by an explosive device outside his home in Lusaka. ANC President Bishop Abel Muzorewa and President Kaunda of Zambia visited the scene. Suspicions were voiced in Lusaka that dissidents inside ZANU were responsible; this led to the arrest on 27th March of the entire supreme council of ZANU with many of its military commanders, including Josiah Tongogara, commander in chief of the ZIPRA forces. He was held in a Lusaka prison for a year on suspicion of having planned the murder. Tongogara was later released and died under suspicious circumstance in Mozambique in December 1979, as a result of a car accident.

News from the squadrons
No 1 Squadron Diary, March 1975:
Four Canberras staggered into Thornhill on 6th March after being intercepted by five Hunters in a simulated dawn strike on the field. The squadron exercise involved a combined jet strike

on the range and later that day an 'intercept' in the north-east, and finished with a ten aircraft fly-past over Salisbury and a night-stop. On 26th Squadron Leader Dixon and Bill Sykes ventured down to Durban and as amazing as it may seem, they came back the next day. (Comment from Bill Sykes: "There were no more loopholes!")

Monthly Report No7 Squadron, March 1975

1215 passengers carried. A/c stationed at FAFs 1, 4, 5, Pfungwe, Mashumbi Pools, Makuti, Kariba, Umtali, Fort Victoria, Inyanga, Mudzi, Mount Darwin.

No 3 Squadron Diary, March 1975:

On the SAAF crew for Dakota 6878, André Steenkamp was replaced by Grant Rix but not before an incident that occurred at Chenje Air Field [Zambezi valley]. The aircraft got bogged down and while attempting to get it out under power, it nosed forward and the props hit the ground. The aircraft was there for a couple of days while repairs were carried out, including a prop change. A considerable period was spent this month rehearsing for the parade that is due to take place next month when 3 Squadron is to be presented with a Standard. A sky shout exercise was carried out in the Angwa River area. This was done by Noel van Hoff and Ian Rodwell. A posting list came out during the month and the effect of this on 3 Squadron will be as follows: Clive Ward from 4 Squadron, Peter Daykins from HQ, Ivan Holshausen from Ops, Thornhill. John Matthews has been awarded an 'A' Cat on Dakotas. Some members of the squadron, including VRs, bravely volunteered to carry out a static line paradrop into Lake McIlwaine on 12th March.

No 3 Squadron receives its Standard

No 3 (Transport) Squadron was the second squadron to receive its Standard, which was presented by AVM Frank Mussell on 7th April 1975. The squadron was formed in 1947, when it was known as the Communications Squadron Flight of the Air Wing of the Staff Corps. It was renamed No 3 Squadron in 1956. During the march-past, aircraft of No 1 Squadron, which had received its Standard in 1974, flew over the parade. The squadron once again lived up to its reputation when the nine Hunters passed overhead exactly on time and in perfect formation. The commander of the Rhodesian Air Force, Air Marshal Mick McLaren was present at the ceremony.

The parachute training school

Since the beginning of 1975, No 3 Squadron pilots had been involved in PTS and close cooperation with the SAS on dropping techniques and new parachute types. For example:

March 1975

11th	Dakota 3708	Flt Lt Barry Roberts	2,500 feet with Serviac Mk 2 (cumbersome)
12th	Dakota 7034	Flt Lt Barry Roberts	No 11 Basic free fall
12th	Dakota 7034	Flt Lt George Alexander	Aircrew water descent and booze.
18th	Dakota 7039	Flt Lt Barry Roberts	On end stick. Low cloud
19th	Dakota 7039	Flt Lt John Matthews	SAS Cont. Followed
20th	Dakota 7039	Flt Lt Mike Russell	Observer
20th	Dakota 7039	Flt Lt Mike Russell	Observer
21st	Dakota 7039	Flt Lt Vic Cook	No 11 Basic course
23rd	Dakota 7303	Flt Lt Dave Thorne	Op Hurricane. Uplift to Mount Darwin Drop OK. 1 x 5, 1 x 5, 1 x 10 Return

25th	Dakota 7303	Flt Lt Bob d'Hotman	Jump for fun!
25th	Dakota 7303	Flt Lt Bob d'Hotman	Followed
26th	Dakota 7039	Flt Lt John Matthews	No 11 Basic free fall. Pathfinder Ex Night Drop Inkomo
27th	Dakota 7303	Flt Lt John Matthews	No 11 Basic free fall Inkomo Box

Commenting on the use of boxes to drop supplies Charlie Buchan says:

By April 1975, we were experimenting with jumps from 12,500 feet and at that altitude we had to use oxygen. The parachute was supposed to open at 2,500 feet but sometimes it opened at 3,500. The men always followed the box down. In training, we put smoke bombs on the boxes so that we could find them. Gradually we got the hang of working with the boxes and we started working out systems for carrying large amounts of equipment down with us on long lines so that the equipment landed first. You had to be very careful not to get tangled up and hurt yourself. Speed-wise, it did not increase your speed but with all that equipment swinging underneath, you had to make sure that you didn't do a back somersault on landing.

Among the detainees released during the détente exercise were Robert Mugabe and Edgar Tekere. Robert Gabriel Mugabe was born in 1928 at Kutama Mission and brought up as a Roman Catholic. He qualified as a primary school teacher and won a scholarship to Fort Hare University in South Africa. After spending time in Northern Rhodesia and Ghana, where he married Sally, he returned to Rhodesia in 1960. When the government cracked down on ZAPU and ZANU in 1964, Mugabe was arrested and spent eleven years in detention. By 1975, he had become the secretary-general of ZANU while Edgar Tekere was secretary of the youth wing. Although they had been released from detention, neither man had any travel documents. They left Salisbury by car and crossed the eastern border into Mozambique and made their way to Dar es Salaam where they set about reconstructing ZANU.

Because of the efforts at détente, all external operations had been stopped and security forces had been ordered to take action only against insurgents heading into Rhodesia. However, it became increasingly obvious that there was no real ceasefire. In fact, the African nationalists were using the détente exercise to regroup, so word was passed that the SAS could move back into Tete province as long as they did it quietly and did not get involved with Frelimo.

The Jacklin Trophy is awarded to No 7 Squadron

In the monthly report for April 1975, it is recorded that No 7 Squadron carried 2,489 passengers in its helicopters. It operated from FAFs 1, 4, 5, Binga, Mashumbi Pools, Makuti, Inyanga and Bulawayo, but most important of all, for the third time in its history, it had been awarded the Jacklin Trophy. Previous awards were made in 1964 and 1968. The presentation was made by Mr E.A. Sutton-Pryce, Deputy Minister in the Department of the Prime Minister. The statistics given were that during 1974, squadron helicopters had flown 6,000 hours and carried 30,000 personnel. In the operational sector, the squadron had expertly fulfilled its main role of trooping and close support for the ground forces participating in the deaths of 130 armed insurgents and the capture of many more.

During the year, the squadron maintained a 24-hour stand-by for non-security force casualty evacuation. Its beneficiaries had included victims of land-mine incidents, brutal terrorist attacks, as well as road and rail casualties. Food and supplies had been dropped to needy villagers; hunters and mountaineers were rescued under difficult conditions and civilian plane-crash victims brought to safety. Describing the casevac procedure, Sutton-Pryce continued:

As soon as a call comes in over the radio in the operations room at a forward airfield, the 'scramble' hooter is pressed and pilots on stand-by drop their magazines, cards or volley ball to race to the helicopters. Meanwhile the operations room staff have worked out the grid reference of the site in question and as the choppers become airborne, this information, plus a heading and details of what they are likely to find, are radioed to them. From hooter shriek to take-off, the time lapse is rarely more than three minutes. Each helicopter can carry two stretcher cases. Sometimes, if the condition of patients to be uplifted is suspected to be critical, a doctor or medical orderly goes along in the chopper too.

An unusual rescue attempt on the lake

Soon after the award, No 7 Squadron played a role in an unusual rescue attempt. For a considerable period, a ZIPRA reconnaissance platoon had been based on the Zambian shores of Lake Kariba. Every now and then, they crossed into Rhodesia to gather information. The SAS planned a surprise attack on their camp, in order to take prisoners who could be interrogated. The plan misfired and the ZIPRA group resisted and then escaped, leaving one of their dead behind, and setting the house on fire. The SAS men grabbed all the documents they could find and made their way back to the boats. By now the house was blazing furiously and the stored land-mines, rockets and ammunition were exploding, added to which a violent storm had blown up on the lake. An urgent request for help went out and was answered by No 7 Squadron.

As dawn was breaking, the SAS men were still in Zambian waters. Fuel was lowered and the two smaller boats got going, but the engine of the largest boat refused to start. While the Alouette hovered, a line was passed down to the men in the boat. Then an attempt was made to tow the disabled boat back to the Rhodesian shore. But the waves were now higher than ever and as they crested, it seemed that the boat would smash into the bottom of the chopper. Then as the boat dived into a trough it threatened to drag the helicopter out of the sky. Reluctantly, the crew cut the rope. The men in the boat were once more on their own. The Alouette pilot circled, waved good luck and flew back to base leaving the men in the boat to struggle back on one engine. Fortunately, before too long, they cleared Zambian waters and spotted a friendly boat, which immediately came to their rescue and towed them to safety.

No 4 Squadron Diary, May 1975:

Provost: 111h45; Trojan: 289h50; Cessna: Nil

During the month, a Provost T 1 was literally flown to its limits by Ray Boulter. After finally landing in a disused mealie field and frightening the occupants of a kraal, it was agreed by all concerned that the endurance of a T 1 is fewer then three hours. Ray is now contemplating becoming a BP/Shell Rep.

No 3 Squadron Diary, May 1975:

On 31st May, a VR Pilot Navex (Navigation Exercise) was carried out in two aircraft, which included nearly all the VR members plus Peter Daykins. The two aircraft were captained by John Matthews and Bob d'Hotman. A night-stop was held at Chiredzi with the crews staying at the Planters' Inn. On the return journey, approximately four tons of grapefruit was uplifted for presentation to the forward areas. This trip was a memorable one for several reasons:

1. *The two aircraft completed 20 hours flying and carried out 96 landings.*
2. *The total age of one of the crews of six members came to over 300 years.*
3. *Richie Calder VR succumbed to air-sickness on the outward journey. He was de-planed at Rusape rather than fly one more minute. This trip was later to become known as the 'fruit fly-around'.*

Mauswa meeting

News was received early in June that a top-level ZANLA meeting was to take place between 16th and 23rd June in the general area of Mauswa Village, near Bindura. It was decided that a new tactic should be tried. The attack would be carried out at night using 40-pound (18kg) magnesium para-flares to light the contact area. Each flare would burn for four and a half minutes with the equivalent of 800,000 candle power. A Provost carrying six of these flares could provide illumination for 27 minutes. A relay of aircraft would remain overhead until the operation was complete. Troops would be dropped so that they could cordon off an area five kilometres by eight kilometres in the hopes of trapping the ZANLA leaders within this box.

Three fireforces were mobilized, one made up of a K-Car and five G-Cars, and the other two each consisting of one K-Car and four G-Cars, 16 helicopters in all. The air force also supplied three Provosts, seven Trojans and four Dakotas. Units of the RAR, RLI and the RR were involved in the fireforces and the cordon and sweep. It was to be an all-out effort.

At 10h00 on 24th June, large numbers of terrorists were spotted moving in the area but it was decided to wait, hoping to make an even bigger kill. All through the first day, the members of the fireforces did nothing but play cards alongside their helicopters. That night the strike came. The Provost circling overhead waited for instructions from his forward ground controller. The order came. The canister fell away. The parachute opened and the flare spluttered into life bathing the countryside below in brilliant light. The cordon started moving in and a contact developed.

In fact, the whole operation was disappointing. Only three contacts were made with six insurgents killed and one captured. Information received from the prisoner told of more than 30 ZANLA men who had been within the cordon but had managed to escape. This was one of the first occasions in which this 'box' technique was employed. Later it was modified to produce a triangle and the whole procedure could be carried out in virtual radio silence.

No 1 Squadron Diary, June 1975:

It has been a rather quiet month on the squadron with a large portion of the aircrew away. For the majority of the month the only pilots on the squadron have been Squadron Leader Chris Dixon, Vic Wightman, Doug Reitz and Pete Mason. Credit must once again go to the ground crew for maintaining aircraft serviceability at its record high level. Vic Wightman took Ken Law on a guided five-minute tour of the Cape Peninsula on 4th June and in the evening went to see some of his old friends on the docks. Later in the month, Squadron Leader Dixon and Pete Mason were intercepted by a SAAF Mirage F1 on the return route on the monthly liberty run to Durban.

No 4 Squadron suffered a tragedy on 19th June. Ray Boulter was killed when his aircraft crashed while he was performing a tail-chase in a Provost.

The BSAP comes to the rescue

On many occasions over the years, the BSAP had reason to be grateful to No 7 Squadron and in June 1975, members of the police force were able to make a small repayment. A helicopter was flying along the southern shore of Kariba when its engine malfunctioned. The pilot attempted to land on the shore but unfortunately set the aircraft down on a patch of Kariba weed and it sank in about 10 metres of water. The BSAP were called in to help. The force's sub-aqua section arrived on the scene, removed the rotor blades and attached empty drums to the body of the aircraft. The aircraft was then dragged some 350 metres through the water to a suitable position close to the lake shore where, with the aid of another helicopter and a caterpillar tractor, it was brought ashore. A rough roadway had been cut through the bush to enable suitable transport to reach the helicopter. Once the aircraft was safely on dry land everyone involved in the rescue operation believed that the battle had been won but as the fuselage of the helicopter was being driven away, the vehicle carrying it hit a land-mine. The chopper that had been rescued from the depths of Lake Kariba could not escape a second time.

Blue birds

The announcement that women were to be recruited into the army and air force came on 28th June 1975. The first training course for members of the newly formed Rhodesian Women's Service began in Salisbury on August 4th. Thirty women aged between 18 and 48 took part, six of whom were destined to join the air force at the end of the course. The first squad of airwomen passed out on 19th August. Initially it had been intended that their work would be limited to radio communications, air control and photography. However, as time passed the scope of their duties expanded, and the Blue birds, as they were known, became became part of all aspects of the force and were encouraged to take up a full-time career.

One of the first unofficial Blue birds was Nora Seear whose story was unique.

In 1975 before RWS was formed Carole, Marie Louise and I were recruited as civilians after answering an intriguingly vague advertisement. We had a day of aptitude tests and gruelling interviews but nobody actually said what the job was. We started out in Milton Buildings and moved later to a purpose-built unit at Sarum. We had 'security' and 'diligence' constantly hammered at us. The unit was always secured and nobody came there uninvited. And we were diligent—we even did our own cleaning and coffee-making; indeed we wondered if that was why we had been recruited. Weeks of training went by while we battled with the inmates of New Sarum, who had an inordinate interest in who or what we were. As civilians, we had problems with the Sarum drivers who refused at first to let us on to the bus. We were eventually allowed to eat the awful food in the officers' mess but were not allowed in the bar! As it was a Joint Service Unit, there was an establishment of three army and three air force posts. Bill Buckle, Jim Weir and Carole had the blue slots and John, Marie Louise and I had the brown. The army suddenly decided that a male army officer should take one of their civilian-held posts. John protested that nobody had time to train a new officer and they suggested sending me on a commissioning course. The first female course had been running for months and I was sent to KG VI for the last two days, before the passing-out parade. The eleven girls who had survived the course gave me a very frosty reception as a civilian. They were appalled at my presence on their course, and a deputation came to tell me that I wouldn't be marching on their final parade. I was very relieved as I don't know my left foot from my right. Convinced that I was going to lose my job to a male officer, I treated the whole thing as a joke. The colonel who interviewed me must have had a sense of humour—he said he was commissioning me, but only on condition that I personally broke the news to the other eleven girls. I don't think he fancied the task. I told the girls that the commission wasn't my idea and suggested they try to accept me as an 'expert' coming in, say, as a dentist or lawyer. They were still not impressed. Fortunately, New Sarum was a long way from KG VI and we seldom met. I was given a uniform and a number, and then I fled to Ken Salter's office and begged him to teach me some GD basics; surely there had never been a more ignorant officer and I had a very steep learning curve to climb. Sarum was not used to women in uniform, as there were not yet any air force RWS members. I took a lot of stick in such a blue stronghold, but strangely I found my credibility improved at briefing sessions, although the bus drivers still refused to let me on the air force bus. There was a dining-in night for Ian Douglas Smith at KG VI and I was given two days' notice to acquire a really ugly white, long dress, the first disastrous attempt at mess kit. As I was by far the oldest person present that evening,

I avoided the mad mess games but the inevitable pyramid of white dresses was formed while I wondered what we would collectively be charged with if a general's daughter fell off the top into the fireplace. Pressure at work increased daily, weekends vanished and stomach ulcers arrived. Long hours were the norm but we gained credibility and recognition as a unit, I doubt that I could have coped without husband Sid's constant support. In 1977 my award of the MFC (with army) came out of the blue—I knew nothing about it and thought it was intended for my son who had been doing some fancy flying. It was really an embarrassment as there was no civilian equivalent for Carole and Marie Louise who had worked just as hard as everybody else. Late in 1979, our unit was dissolved and we all went our own ways. An old army friend asked me to be his adjutant at Rhodesian Intelligence Corps in Cranborne. Then he moved on and I carried on with my own unit, which became ZINC. In 1980, I went to KG VI to resign, and on the way called in at Air HQ to say goodbye to all my blue friends. Boss Geoff Oborne offered me a job—so finally I got a blue uniform and another number and another learning curve.

Ambush

On 19th July 1975, two members of the RLI were making their way down a dry riverbed near Rushinga when a ZANLA group hiding in a small cave opened fire on them. From their position higher on the embankment, the other members of the patrol could not see where their comrades had fallen or whether they were still alive. A K-Car was called in, but the ZANLA position was too well hidden. In the silence, an RLI medic heard moans coming from the riverbed. He moved forward, was hit by terrorist fire, and fell. The RLI soldiers moved forward and one of them was shot dead, and two men, including the RLI officer, were wounded. They pulled back. No further attempts were made to reach the wounded men. Night fell bringing with it brilliant moonlight. Two Alouettes took off from Mount Darwin. As they began their approach to the river, the pilots switched off their navigation lights—now only a faint light came from their instrument panel. Outside the windows, the silver moon lit up the barren countryside. The two helicopters flew close to the riverbed and the pilots were given an update on the situation that had not changed for several hours. Hand grenades were thrown into the riverbed below the cave and rounds were fired at likely hiding places. Then three men went downstream and entered the riverbed. Cautiously, taking every opportunity for cover in the brilliant moonlight, they moved upstream. At one stage, thinking they had heard something, they opened fire but there was no reply. At last, they reached the place where the three men lay. They were all dead. Above them, they could see the cave hideout, which the ZANLA men had used. They lobbed a couple of grenades into the opening but with no result. The enemy had long since escaped. Killed in action were Corporals Jannie de Beer and John Coey, Rifleman Hennie Potgeiter (all RLI) and WO2 T.G. 'Taz' Bain (RR)

VIP Dakota

One Dakota, R7036, was fitted out as a VIP machine, and, among others, it carried the first President of Rhodesia, Clifford Dupont. With its white top and polished body, it was a credit to the force. Later, it donned camouflage like all the rest and it was this machine that was used by Peter Walls as commander of cross-border raids. It was festooned with aerials and equipped with high-power radios and a teleprinter, allowing the man in command of the operation to be in complete control of the action, so that any change of plan could be assessed and implemented immediately. It was this aircraft that carried the Rhodesian Prime Minister, Ian Douglas Smith, to the conference on the Victoria Falls Bridge in August 1975 for his meeting with the South African Prime Minister, John Vorster, and the President of Zambia, Kenneth Kaunda. Like all the other efforts at ending the war, this meeting that took place in a railway carriage in the middle of the bridge, failed to produce an agreement.

First bush trip for the new minister of defence

I had just completed a four-week trip on operations in Mount Darwin and was looking forward to 10 days' rest. So I wasn't pleased when Squadron Leader Eddie Wilkinson told me that he had an air task for me. There had been a recent cabinet reshuffle and P.K. van der Byl had become our new minister of defence. 'PK' had decided that the best way to get to know the military and to show how seriously he took his job was to tour the front line. My air task was to fly him around the north-east operational area, spending one night each in Mount Darwin, Marymount Mission and Pfungwe. I was then to drop him back at New Sarum where he would meet the commanding officer. On Tuesday 2nd September 1975, my tech Steve Stead and I prepared the Alouette II. We had a tiny bag each with clothes and toiletries for three nights and stretchers that we packed under the back seat. PK duly arrived wearing a full set of camouflage. His bed-roll was hauled out of the car boot and I wondered if we would ever get it in the Alouette. Then two large bags came out of the car—one obviously contained clothes—the other, much heavier, clinked suspiciously. Somehow we managed to squeeze everything into the cabin. PK was also carrying something that looked very much like an elephant gun. We took off. Before we had been in the air for ten minutes, he had informed me that when we came back we must drop him in the botanical gardens near his home. "It's all been arranged," he said when I tried to tell him that I had orders to take him back to New Sarum. As we approached Mount Darwin, I discovered that there was a contact going on and changed radio frequencies so that the minister could listen in. He became very excited and wanted to be put down in the area. There was no chance that I could do that but I did pass his request to 'The King' Colonel David Parker who was running operations at Mount Darwin. The colonel's reply was, "Get the minister to Mount Darwin, NOW, Simmo." After we landed, PK 'watched' the rest of the contact in the Ops room and spent the afternoon poring over maps, tactics, strategies and getting to know the men involved in the war. That evening he endeared himself to the officers in the mess with his quaint stories, along with three bottles from the clinking bag. The following day we set off for Marymount stopping in at Karanda Mission on the way. Recently, some seriously wounded soldiers had been taken to the mission where they were patched up by the American surgeon before being sent on to Salisbury General Hospital. PK wanted to thank him. We landed unannounced at the airfield where the Karanda Mission pilot was attending to his Cessna. I introduced PK and explained the reason for our visit. The pilot was impressed and insisted on calling PK 'Your highness' for the rest of the visit. We met the surgeon who was appropriately thanked and then we moved on in a cloud of dust to Marymount. Halfway there we flew over a group of African women carrying huge suitcases on their heads. PK immediately wanted to check them out, 'in case they were carrying weapons of war'. This was a minister like no other we had seen before. He was determined to be personally involved. So we landed and checked the suitcases. Having satisfied himself that all was well, PK climbed back on board. If Karanda was a mission prepared to help in an emergency, Marymount was a different kettle of fish. The missionaries were particularly 'anti'. Father Ignatius was well known for marching angrily about in his white socks and sandals, constantly complaining about the inconvenience of having military personnel around his mission. What was even worse for the troopies in this hot dry corner of Rhodesia, he absolutely forbade them to use the large swimming pool. Major Brian Robinson was in command of the SAS men based near the Mission, and they had lost a man in action the day before [Cpl Kelvin Storie (25), KIA on Luia River, Mozambique, 2nd September 1975]. So they were in no mood for exchanging niceties with new ministers. It crossed my mind that PK may not win over many hearts and minds on this day. I couldn't have been more wrong. PK knew about Storie's death, and he was determined to let these soldiers know he was on their side. He also mentioned to Brian that he was tired of his longs and would like some khaki shorts. The quartermaster was called and a few minutes later PK walked back into the room wearing a pair of very short shorts and sporting spindly white legs. Brian suggested that perhaps a larger size would be better. PK looked down and in front of the assembled men, announced, "You are quite right Brian, my cock sticks out of these." There was much discussion about tactics, strategies and troop movements, and then PK announced that he intended spending the night on ambush with a stick of RAR. It rained that night and I really hoped, while I was tucked up in my nice dry bed, that PK would get a chance to use his elephant gun. Of course it didn't happen and yet he was chirpy and unfazed by the wet uncomfortable night. Brian Robinson had somehow succeeded where other commanders had failed and grudgingly Father Ignatius had agreed that a few troops could use the pool for half an hour each evening. After a rest, PK asked some of the men if there was anything he might do for them back in Salisbury. Most of the soldiers were content to say no, but one of the troopies saw an opportunity and explained about the swimming pool. PK's reply was straightforward. "Corporal, go to Ignatius, give him my regards and explain to him that from now on my troops will have free access to the pool. He will be allowed to use it from 5 to 5.30 pm and if he doesn't like the new rules, I'll deport the fellow." We left Marymount a couple of hours later much to Father Ignatius' relief but with the complete support of every soldier within a hundred miles. Pfungwe was manned by an RLI commando, led by Major Bruce Snelgar, with two helicopters at his disposal. The camp was based on a low granite koppie at the western end of the Pfungwe Air Field. I had radioed ahead that I was bringing a VVIP and various members of the camp, thinking that I was bullshitting, lined up and gave me a bare bottoms-up salute as I landed. PK wanted to know if I always got that kind of welcome. The last of the clinking bottles was gratefully consumed that evening as the sun went down. The next day it was time to return home. As instructed by PK, I sent a message ahead saying I would be dropping PK at the botanical gardens—the reply was that he was to be taken to New Sarum. I wasn't going to argue—by now I was sure that as minister of defence his orders outranked everyone else's. We left Pfungwe at 4 pm and flew back over Avondale to PK's chosen LZ off Second Street extension. When we touched down all became clear. The adjacent four-lane-highway was packed solid with Friday going-home traffic. This came to a halt as our helicopter landed. Two servants dressed in freshly starched white uniforms stood to attention. One took the enormous bedroll. The other carried the bags, while PK resplendent in his new shorts, which carried the signs of days and nights in the bush, marched down the road with a demo (African axe), he had found in the bush, over his shoulder and carrying his elephant gun. The new minister of defence was seen to be doing his job. He must have won many votes that day. He certainly got mine though I was in the quagmire for not taking him to New Sarum! (Peter Simmonds)

Squadron update
No 1 Squadron Diary, September 1975:

September has been a heavy month for all squadron members in that flying hours this month have nearly doubled those of previous months. Practice in formation rocketing and bombing continued with very encouraging results. On a sad and sour note, one of our members, Sergeant Alex Bremner, was tragically killed in a motor accident on Friday 26th.

No 3 Squadron Diary, September 1975:

On 27th September, the squadron acquired a new aircraft, a Cessna 421A [7153]. Squadron Leader Alexander and John Matthews flew the aircraft to Rhodesia, after spending a few days in RSA being converted onto type by Tony Smit (ex No 3 Squadron, now with SAAF). The SAAF Dakota crew has now been withdrawn from Rhodesia. A new member joined the squadron—Stig Ohlsson attested with the rank of air lieutenant and is at present undergoing conversion onto the Dakota.

No 4 Squadron Diary, September 1975:

Provost: 142h35; Trojan: 233h50; Cessna: 85h00

A rather hectic month for the squadron with a number of conversion hours being put in at base, and a fair amount of flying being done in the bush. Ian Sheffield (ex-RAF) has eagerly continued his Provost conversion and should have it completed fairly soon. He informs us that he can now say he has flown the Provost, which he had previously only seen in an aircraft museum! New faces: Ed Potterton, Russell (Kiwi) Broadbent, Mick Delport (and technicians), Dave Crawford (another Irishman) and A.R.T. (Art) Smith. With these three new aircrew members, the squadron pilot situation has been alleviated and bush duties will become less frequent once all three become operational.

Monthly Report No 7 Squadron, September 1975

Hours: 584, 530 on ops; 1,541 passengers. A/c deployed to FAF 4, Marymount, Mutawatawa, Mudzi, Mukumbura, FAF 5 and Umtali. Flight Sergeant Finnbarr Cunningham, a helicopter technician, was injured when he came off his bike on the ring road at Salisbury Airport and died later. He had flown more than 1,500 hours in helicopters and won the Rolls-Royce Trophy as the best technical apprentice.

No 1 Squadron Diary, October 1975:

October has been a busy month for the whole squadron with flying hours at their highest since February 1974. The majority of hours were taken up by flag-waves—a combined squadrons exercise. Thirteen flag-waves were carried out this month, all successful from the air with very favourable comments from the ground. This was verified by Paddy Bate who was the squadron bushman for two weeks of the month as deputy ops commander at Mount Darwin. A small amount of squadron rivalry built up this month amongst the jet squadrons. Initially No 1 Squadron jebel cats were painted on the No 2 Squadron Vampires, which insisted on parking on our hardstandings. Their reply to this was the painting of a Vampire and a jebel cat linked together in a rather obscene position with the Vampire getting the better of things. Jebel cats were then painted on the Canberras while they were down here. No 5 Squadron reciprocated by painting an eagle's foot gripping an inverted jebel cat* in what appeared to be a very painful position.

No 1 Squadron Diary, December 1975:

In spite of all the normal end of year socializing, the squadron did manage to get down to some constructive work this month. The re-introduction of 30mm ammunition to the monthly weapons allocation enabled all pilots once again to get the feel of things and especially the smell of cordite. A special Christmas effort was made by the squadron who visited the north-east border area on the morning of 25th December.

Casevac

Early in December, the *Rhodesia Herald* carried the story of a typical casevac:

A Rhodesian patrol emerges from the bush and approaches a lonely kraal in the border war zone. The time is 9.05 am in the morning; the heat of sun mounting now as morning wears on and is broken by a few clouds. Though weary and dirty, after an all-night operation, the patrol is alert, weapons ready. Among the small cluster of huts, members of a terrorist group may be

---

* The jebel cat is a wild mountain cat found in and around Aden. It was rumoured to have been endowed with spectacular testicles. The cat was adopted as the No 1 Squadron icon.

resting or hiding. As the Rhodesians come closer, the terrorists may well be ready to spring an ambush. There is no ambush; instead the patrol find the villagers huddled round a bloody figure, sprawled in the dust outside one of the huts. Last night a group of terrorists entered the kraal and forced everyone out of their beds at the point of loaded Kalashnikov rifles and demanded to see the kraal head. After accusing him of helping the soldiers, and despite his denials, they beat him on the face with their rifle butts, stabbed him in the chest with bayonets and left him for dead, before walking away into the night. The Rhodesian patrol worked quickly. While a medic begins to treat the wounds, another trooper is already on the radio calling base. "We have a wounded man here. Head and chest injuries; tribesman beaten by terrs; need immediate casevac," he says, giving time and location. The Joint Operations Centre received the call in the operations room at 9.10 am. Four minutes later, helicopter pilot Kevin Peinke lifts his craft off the ground and heads north at top speed to the lonely kraal. "We can't afford to waste time. We do a fair number of casevacs and speed is essential," the young pilot comments. At the kraal, the wounded man is made comfortable on a blanket. The wounds are already cleaned and bandaged. Other members of the patrol question the small group of villagers about the night attack. When did they come? Did you recognize them? When did they leave? What direction did they take? The radio crackles again and information is passed quickly to base. The rebels may be spotted from the air or tracked down in follow-up operations. At 9.27 am, eleven minutes after leaving Mount Darwin, the helicopter lands in a field within metres of the kraal. Already, as the sound of the chopper is heard, the patrol on the ground has the casualty on the stretcher. They stand at the edge of the field and as the aircraft lands, they run forward crouched, to avoid the slashing blades, with the wounded man. Dust clouds the sky as the rotors slice through the air and the casualty is quickly placed in the helicopter behind the pilot, and the medic jumps in holding up the bottle which drips plasma into the victim's bloodstream. At 9.29 am the helicopter is in the air again and on its way back to Mount Darwin. The patrol, reorganizing, leaves the kraal and sets out into the bush on the trail of the rebel group. It could be a busy day. At Mount Darwin Major J. Ferguson, the doctor in charge of the base hospital, prepares to receive the wounded man. The small operating theatre is ready, and he already has a good idea of the injuries involved. "The casualties are not always brought here. If the wounds are very bad, we send them straight through to the hospital at Bindura or even Salisbury," he says. "But if the wounds do not appear too serious, then the base hospital can handle it. It's amazing how quickly we can get a casualty out, sometimes even in difficult conditions. I have done several night casevacs and they can be pretty hazardous." The last one Major Ferguson was on, at night, the helicopter chopped some branches from a tree as it landed. "But the pilots are magnificent. They will do everything they can if there is the slightest possibility of getting in, no matter what the conditions. They go out of their way to save a life even if it means risking their own," he comments. At 9.40 am the pilot lands on the small landing pad near the camp hospital. Two minutes later, only 37 minutes after being found by the security forces patrol, the wounded man is on the operating table being examined and prepared for treatment and somewhere in the bush north of here, Rhodesian troops are searching for the gang that attacked him. (Rhodesia Herald, 11th Dec. 1975)

There was a most unfortunate accident just before Christmas 1975, when a SAAF Alouette III piloted by Air Sub-Lieutenant Johannes van Rensburg hit a steel cable, which had been erected across a stream to carry goods from one side to the other. Major General John Ryan Shaw, Colonel David Gladwell Parker (commander RLI), Captain John Bourchier Lamb and Captain Ian Andrew Brampton Robinson were killed, while the pilot was seriously injured. The crash occurred about 10h00 on Shinda Orchards Farm about three kilometres from the Mozambique border between Umtali and Cashel, in very rugged country. Rescue workers had to ford a river to reach the crash site.

A thank-you from the police reserve

As has been remarked earlier, a spirit of close cooperation and camaraderie had grown up between the ground and air forces—this was particularly so with the police reserve and the air force. A typical story is told by Norman Maasdorp:

> On 30th January 1976, Mick Delport and I were based at Mount Darwin. I volunteered for that night's stand-by and around 21h00, a call came for assistance from some police reservists in the Rushinga area who were surrounded by the terrs and were being stomped. I got airborne in my Provost and through the sound of the engine and discreet use of the navigation and landing lights, the guys were able to guide me roughly overhead. We were armed with those big magnesium flares and I proceeded to drop these at intervals. While the flare was illuminating the ground the firing ceased, but as soon as the flare went out the barrage would open up again. Through judicious use of the flares, we kept the ground fire to a minimum. As the flares were running out, I called up Mount Darwin to scramble Mick who came and took over from me. I then returned to the field to re-arm. Mick and I kept the cab-rank system going until sunup, at which stage the terrs decided to leave. While the flares were descending, the relief for the chaps was obvious and it showed in the tone of the voices on the radio. They insisted that they would stop and buy us a drink at Mount Darwin on their way through. This I acknowledged with an "uhuh" and did not think about the remark again. About a week later after an all day assignment in the op area, I arrived back in Mount Darwin to receive a very warm reception from the police reserve guys that Mick and I had helped out that night. What was particularly warming was that the guys had just completed their six-week bush tour and were on their way home. They had purposely waited for nearly six hours just to see us and to say thanks, before continuing on to Salisbury. They very generously left us a crate of beers, which we shared with the techs who had armed the aircraft. The sacrifice of hours away from their families I thought was very gallant of them and it certainly renewed our faith in human nature and made us feel that the job we were doing was worthwhile. (Norman Maasdorp)

A sanctions-busting flight

The Rhodesian Air Force had achieved miracles with its ageing aircraft but it was becoming vital to acquire replacements. Peter Petter-Bowyer, who at this stage was primarily concerned with improving operational efficiency says:

> Military aircraft were virtually impossible to acquire. Those that were offered by the host of carpet-baggers, who regularly knocked on the door at our equipment branch, were highly suspect and their offers ridiculously expensive. It seemed our only safe bet was to identify a civilian aircraft type, which could be used operationally. One of these was the American-designed Cessna FTB 337 being built under licence in France. I flew the only one of its kind in Rhodesia and found the aircraft's handling and performance to be promising. (Peter Petter-Bowyer)

Because the Reims Cessna FTB 337 Milirole was designated a civil machine, sanctions could be circumvented. So the Air Force Equipment Branch set about negotiating a purchase deal direct from the aircraft manufacturer. Two contracts were signed in the middle of 1975, one for 12 aircraft and the other for six. All 18 aircraft were to be delivered in January and February 1976. The total value of the contract was $5,255,024 (US).

> It was my task to determine what equipment the aircraft should be fitted with. There was some resistance from one or two senior officers to what they considered to be unnecessary aids and comforts. This was because they had no experience of the difficulties and dangers that the pilots

of light, fixed-wing planes faced in the absence of good navigational and letdown aids, and with poor cockpit ventilation and heating. Fortunately, Air Marshal Mick McLaren, then an air force commander, ruled in my favour. (Petter-Bowyer)

Negotiating the purchase was one thing. Getting the aircraft safely into Rhodesia was another. No one wanted to take the risk of having this purchase turned round at sea, as had happened earlier with the T 28 Trojans. Eventually the decision was made. The aircraft would be flown out to Rhodesia from Reims, in France, where they were being manufactured.

To reduce the risks, considerable trouble was taken to disguise the ownership and destination of the aircraft. The Malagasy Republic was chosen as the ultimate destination for two separate flights; one down the western flank of Africa and the other down the eastern side. Of course the Malagasy government knew nothing of this plan. A fictitious company for fish surveillance was established and a very colourful company badge was designed and emblazoned on all the aircraft, which were to be painted in garish colours. The badge motto and all documentation were to be in French. French pilots would accompany the Rhodesian pilots to talk them through any awkward situations. Rhodesian pilots were to be passed off simply as civil pilots on hire and essential to transit southern Africa's stormy weather patterns, with which the French pilots were genuinely unfamiliar. (Petter-Bowyer)

The chosen pilots, all carrying British passports, made their way by different routes to Paris where Group Captain Alec Thomson was in charge. He briefed the men and then they all made their way to Reims. One of these pilots, Dave Thorne, tells his story:

It was stressed that we all must keep a very low profile. Our passports arrived from the CIO and it was interesting to see that I was born in Southend-on-Sea, England. My profession was commercial pilot. So off we went in separate groups to Paris. A cursory briefing from Alec the next day informed us that we were now required in Reims, as the aircraft were ready. We had never seen a Cessna 337G before and were pleasantly surprised: it has two engines in line, one in front and one behind, a real 'push-me-pull you' aeroplane. The propellers contra-rotate so there is no torque or yawing slip-stream effect. The Cessna 337G normally seats six, but immediately behind the pilots' seat was a huge 200 litre cylindrical fuel tank. It had no contents gauge, only a complicated system of pipes and pumps. We only just managed to fit an overnight bag between the tank and the back of the seat. Under the seat was a life vest and a small bottle for holding urine, for use on the nine-hour flight. To my knowledge, however, no one used the bottle—we preferred to forego morning tea or coffee. Besides, it is almost impossible to urinate from a seated position, in a cramped cockpit, even after loosening the seat belts. How one was supposed to fit a life-vest, let alone pull it out from under the seat, was beyond one's imagination. Our conversion consisted of an hour of circuits and bumps. A few days later, the leader of the French pilots called out five of our names and briefed us that the first five aircraft would depart very early on the morning of 15th January 1976. His briefing was sketchy, in broken English, but understandable enough for us to realize that we were actually on our way. (Dave Thorne)

It had originally been planned that Peter Petter-Bowyer would lead one of the formations but at the last moment this was cancelled owing to a commitment in South Africa. Peter was bitterly disappointed particularly as the South African plans were then postponed. He did, however, go with Wing Commander Len Pink and a small team to a base at Ruacana in South West Africa (now Namibia) to monitor the Cessna flight.

Describing the trip, Len Pink said:

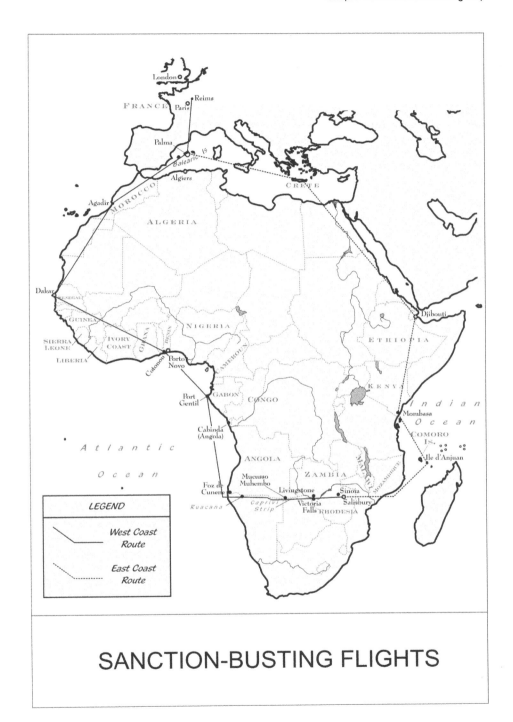

SANCTION-BUSTING FLIGHTS

We flew to Ruacana in an unmarked Dakota. We were all in civilian kit. I had a pair of ordinary shorts on, a t-shirt and slops. We arrived on the base and almost got arrested. The base commander was not available. I found the guy in charge and tried to explain to him—but he didn't seem to know too much, so I said, "Well, over the last few days have you received a fairly large supply of fuel?" And he said, "Yes." So I said, "That's why we are here!"

In fact refuelling during the ferry was a problem. From a security point of view the fewer the stops the better. In normal circumstances, this type of aircraft would have taken about 12 hops to complete the journey. It was planned for this first ferry to make only five stopovers for fuel and rest. This meant using the specially designed long-range fuel tanks, already mentioned. To accommodate these tanks, the rear seats were removed. One further problem was that these tanks were expensive. There were only sufficient funds for eight. This meant that only eight aircraft could be flown out at a time. The second flight would have to wait until these tanks could be air-freighted back to Reims. This increased the risk for the second flight immeasurably because there would be eight clearly identifiable aircraft in Salisbury before the second flight could take off. All the authorities could do was hope to keep them under wraps in the large hangar at New Sarum.

The first ferry left Reims at 23h00 on a clear night on 15th January, 1976. This first leg across Europe was flown at night in order to reduce the possibility of visual identification. Apart from this leg and the final hop into Rhodesia, all flights were made in daylight. My co-pilot was a young Frenchman named Jacques Bonte who was to turn 21 on 18th January. He flew the first leg—(thankfully, because the air traffic controllers used a lot of French that night)—from Reims to Palma on the Balearic Islands where we landed just before dawn. After a quick refuel, we flew over the Atlas Mountains in brilliant early morning sunshine and landed at Agadir in Morocco. The ten of us found our way to a hotel with several pools, scores of pillars and blue mosaic tiles everywhere. Some of us took the opportunity to study the rest of the route and found to our horror that several of the air routes that we were to navigate were closed, some for military reasons and some for no apparent reason at all. We asked the French leader about it, he said, "No problem. We get airborne—then tell air traffic they must direct us!" (Dave Thorne)

Meanwhile back at Ruacana Peter Petter-Bowyer and Len Pink were anxiously awaiting news of the flight.

We were depending heavily on Flight Lieutenant Chuck Dent and his specially designed radio aerial for two-way communications with the aircraft. Chuck was confident we would be able to hear and speak to the flight leader all the way from Reims as long as the aircraft were actually airborne. Having helped raise Chuck's rather simple-looking but very large aerial, Len Pink and I had unspoken doubts about Chuck's claims for its reception range. These doubts arose when we heard not a word for some four hours after the aircraft were airborne over France and Spain. It was a delight and relief when we first received a call from Squadron Leader Eddie Wilkinson who was heading the first formation of four aircraft. The other four, led by Wing Commander Rob Gaunt were only minutes behind him. Eddie reported he was landing at Malaga, in Spain, to refuel. (Petter-Bowyer)

Aboard the aircraft, things were proceeding relatively well.

On 16th January, our aircraft took off in a gaggle—we flew over the desert and down the coast, taking photographs of each other, to the most westerly point of Africa—Dakar in Senegal. This leg took seven and a half hours and was the first real test of our bladders. We found a hotel close to the beach and swam in a very cold Atlantic. Our next sector took us almost due east across Senegal, over Bamako in Mali, Ouagadougou in Burkina Faso, over the top of Ghana and Togo and then almost due south, down the length of Benin to its capital, Cotonou. I made the mistake of saying, "Nice place Dahomy." And the official replied, "We had a revolution. It is now called Benin!" We proceeded to Customs and Immigration where our passports were confiscated! We spent a miserable night at the hotel, imagining what a Benin jail would be like, especially after the revolution. Early the next morning, back at the airport, our French leader disappeared into the office of the immigration official. After a long and agonizing wait, he appeared with our passports, saying, "Let's get out of here!" Apparently there was nothing wrong with the passports, the official was just hoping to extract several thousand francs from us. (Dave Thorne)

Everything went exactly to plan until the aircraft were on their fourth leg and well past the mid-way point between Abidjan and Point Gentil.

The weather over the Bight of Benin was ominous and we flew below the massive cumulonimbus clouds, meeting heavy rain as we approached Port Gentil in Gabon. The sound of the rain on the windscreen was like continuous machine gun fire and the turbulence was considerable. About an hour after take-off, we had to start climbing into the cloud-cover to attain a safe altitude over the islands of São Tomé and Principe. Fortunately, the weather was easing slightly but the turbulence was unrelenting. Two hours after take-off, we were still in cloud and rain, when Jacques pointed to the rpm gauge for the rear engine. It was slowly dropping and did not respond at all to the rpm lever. Eventually it became obvious that nothing would revive it and I shut down that engine. The front engine was still purring along but it had to be pushed to the maximum to maintain height. We turned about 20° left, aiming for where I imagined Libreville to be. We radioed one of the other aircraft and told them we were heading for Libreville. The thunderstorms were causing the non-directional beacons to be unusable and VHF navigation instruments were out of range, so all we had was the good old compass. When we were quite sure by dead-reckoning that we had passed São Tomé and Principe, we descended to 1,000 feet and out of the cloud. About an hour after the engine failure, the VHF navigation instrument, the Omni-Range (VOR) started to pick up Libreville and, believe it or not, it was dead ahead. Another hour and we were overhead Libreville where we tried to re-start the rear engine, with no luck. The front engine was coping adequately and we had been able to throttle back a bit from maximum continuous power, so we decided to continue to Port Gentil, another 30 minutes down the coast. After a five hour thirty-five minute flight, four hours of which were in cloud and three and a half hours on one engine, we landed safely. Inspection of the rear engine showed that it had no oil in the sump. At first I was afraid that the engine had seized—but no—the propeller was easy to move. We filled the engine with oil—and it poured straight out—through the drain-cock! The drain-cock has a quick-release opening which comprises a round valve controlled by two feeble leaf springs. So we pulled the valve down, shut it, jammed a piece of twig into the gap and filled the sump with oil. We could only surmise that vibration and turbulence had caused the valve to move into the open position. The engine started immediately and all gauges showed 'green'. The engine had been saved by a very clever design feature, which takes oil to the propeller pitch control from a higher point in the sump than the take-off point for the engine lubrication. So, as the level of oil fell, the propeller pitch was the first to be affected by the lack of oil and gradually went into the fully-feathered position, causing the rpm to drop to zero with no damage to the engine. Jacques Bonte had a triple celebration that night! We had landed safely, and not in the sea! He had made his first crossing of the equator and it was his 21st birthday! (Dave Thorne)

One of the problems on the Port Gentil–Ruacana leg, flown on 19th January, was that the Russians were in Angola. They had fairly extensive radar coverage, which extended at least 80 miles (128km) out to sea so the plan was to fly 120 miles (192km) off the coast past Luanda and then cut back in across the north of South West Africa south of the Cunene River.

The next day we took off from Port Gentil in a loose formation, remained at low-level and headed out to sea in order to fly parallel to the coast, out of range of Angolan radar. Perhaps we were not as vigilant as we should have been—because suddenly we found ourselves flying over a low, flat tanker with smaller boats escorting her. Either they didn't see us or they were not concerned at the sight of five 'push-me-pull-you' planes dashing over the waves 100 nautical miles out to sea. At any rate no one came to intercept us. We remained more vigilant after that!
(Dave Thorne)

On the same subject, Peter Petter-Bowyer wrote later:

Bob d'Hotman was the skipper of the Dakota that had flown us to Ruacana. More out of curiosity than good reason we made a flight with Bob from Ruacana out westward to the South West African (Namibian) coast where the murky waters of the Cunene River, the boundary line with Angola, spills into the cold Atlantic Ocean. Our route took us over fascinating territory. Dry hostile bush country gave way to the strange Zebra Mountains. Then there were deep dry ravines and hostile open flats that changed, in a sharply-defined line, to pure desert whose shiny hot white sand dunes rippled steeply for a couple of miles before being cut off abruptly by the deep-blue, icy waters of the Atlantic. As if this was not sufficient to intrigue us, there ahead lay the most enormous Russian fishing fleet, spread over a large area just below the horizon and directly on the extended line of the international boundary between Angola and South West Africa (Namibia). Over 60 vessels appeared static with the so-called 'factory ships' prominent in the midst of this huge fleet monitoring South African and Angolan radio transmissions. Our excited reports back to the South Africans met with the polite reply, "Thanks buddy, but we know all about them. They have been there for over ten days now. For the moment their interests are more in the Angolan fighting than in us."

Much to the relief of everyone, the strange little aircraft eventually appeared in sight.

The arrival at Ruacana of the Cessnas left me with the lasting impression of how noisy and ugly they were. Both flights came in together in a gaggle, which streamed for a direct approach to land. Once on the ground, they looked somewhat better, all dressed up in bright colours. Nevertheless they certainly did not possess the grace or silence of a Lynx, whose name they had been given by the air force. (Petter-Bowyer)

The crews were delighted to be on 'safe' ground and celebrated with hot showers, a decent meal and French champagne that they had brought with them.

During the evening, we learnt that one Frenchman was required to return immediately to France. After much liaison with Air HQ, Bob d'Hotmann was tasked to fly him all the way to Pretoria by Dakota to catch his flight home. It just so happened that the man who left for Pretoria was the one and only French captain (all the others were co-pilots) who had been hired to make up the numbers. His departure at this late stage left us in a bit of a quandary. Whatever his reason for departure. Air HQ signalled, tasking me to fly in the French pilot's place. I sent a return signal reminding the Air Staff that I had not been instrument-rated for 18 months, I had not flown at night for about the same period, and I had received no training whatever on this aircraft type. The reply was that they were relying on my experience as well as the assistance I would receive from the Frenchman who was to be my co-pilot. I told Monsieur José (my co-pilot) of my position and asked if he wished to fly in the captain's seat, with me acting as his co-pilot. He immediately declined, pointing to the bad weather building up, saying I was the one who knew African thunderstorms. He preferred to operate the fuel transfer pumps and navigational equipment for me. I prepared to take-off number six in the line, having first been instructed by my assistant on how to start the engines. I found engine power checks much the same as a Cessna 185 and easier than a Trojan. Quickly enough I found my way round the controls and instruments, and opened both throttles wide. We had a long lumbering acceleration and eventually staggered into the air, because the aircraft was way over weight with the large long-range tank in the rear of the cabin. As the aircraft clawed for height, I found rudders and elevators easy and responsive, but the ailerons felt poor and awkward from a yoke so much narrower that I had known before. There was little opportunity to get used to the feel of the controls because we were ploughing head-on into the face of storm clouds only a matter of three miles out from the runway. When the cruise height of 11,500 feet was reached I levelled off and could not understand why the aircraft accelerated to a lower cruising speed than I had planned for. My co-pilot was of no help until I discovered that, in fighting the weather, I had failed to raise flaps in the climb. As soon as these were up, the aircraft settled into comfortable speedy flight. However, I had fallen back in line having been overtaken by the two aircraft that had taken off behind mine. (Petter-Bowyer)

The route taken was east along the Caprivi Strip clear of Angola, Botswana and Zambia. Most of the flight was carried out on dead-reckoning as NDBs (Non-Directional Radio Beacons) were few and far between. The weather cleared a little as the aircraft reached the end of the Caprivi Strip and Monsieur José got a good view of the Victoria Falls as the sun was setting. He was not so impressed with the visibly bad weather ahead.

The air traffic controller at Vic Falls Air Field confirmed storms along the entire route to Salisbury. I decided to head for Sinoia to stay north of the continuous line of flashing cumulonimbus clouds. Whilst Monsieur and I flew in calm starlight conditions, we could hear conversations among the crews who were ploughing through the very rough weather to our south. In the calm night, I flew mostly on instruments to get used to cockpit lighting and instrument layout in preparation for the final descent into Salisbury in bad weather. Up until this flight I had never flown an aircraft with any form of let-down aids, which provided glide-path and runway centre-line guidance. Having turned south for the final leg to Salisbury, Monsieur José set up the ILS-VOR and gave me a couple of pointers on how to interpret the needles. With such help, it was a piece of cake to handle my first-ever landing in a Lynx, at night and in stinking weather. (Petter-Bowyer)

As each aircraft landed it was whisked away into hiding. Petter-Bowyer's safe arrival meant eight Lynx's home and eight to go. There was one problem. According to Pink, there had been a possibility of using the same route for the second flight but he remarks that:

We blew the route on the first flight so we couldn't use it again. The authorities had caught on. Possibly it was the fact that although we had filed a flight plan to Windhoek, we never confirmed arrival there. So it was realized that something was wrong. (Pink)

It was then decided to fly the second ferry from Reims via Palma in the Balearic Islands to Crete and then by way of Djibouti and Mombasa to the Comoros Islands. From here the plan was to skip across northern Mozambique to Rhodesia. Wing Commander Keith Corrans led the second ferry. Again there were seven Rhodesian pilots and one new French skipper. All the co-pilots were Frenchmen who had been on the first ferry flight. The flight was scheduled to leave Reims on Wednesday 28th January 1976 and arrive in Salisbury on the 31st.

On this occasion, the flight was monitored from Salisbury by Chuck Dent. It was a longer flight with seven stopovers, the last refuelling and rest point being Ile d'Anjuan in the Comoros. The planned route was then to fly down the coast and come inland north of Quelimane. The aircraft would be flying low, and although Mozambique did have a couple of MiGs, they were in the south at Maputo. Seven of the aircraft touched down one day later than planned at 17h30 on 1st February.

The aircraft with the two Frenchmen, Ravello and Ferrand aboard, ran into trouble just before it was due to turn west across Mozambique. The rear engine caught fire forcing the pilot to close it down. The fire was extinguished but the pilot saw that a small airfield was marked on his map, near the coast at Mtwara, just inside Tanzania, and decided to land. He found the field but did not carry out an inspection run and so did not realize that the airstrip was unserviceable, until it was too late. A trench had been dug right across the runway, probably during the Portuguese/ Frelimo war.

The aircraft undercarriage hit the trench on its landing run and its nose crunched into the ground, collapsing the nose-wheel and damaging the front propeller, before it came to a halt in a cloud of dust. The Frenchmen were stranded but they were unhurt. As for the remaining aircraft, it was imperative to clear the area as soon as possible so, promising to send help, the other pilots headed for home.

The score was 15 Lynx home and one damaged machine sitting in, what was for Rhodesians, enemy territory. Fortunately, there was not a Rhodesian on this plane. Local African fishermen soon appeared on the scene and cared for the two Frenchmen until Frelimo officials arrived. The Frenchmen kept to their story of being en route to Madagascar and used language difficulties to maximum effect. Their story was confirmed by the senior French pilot on the ferry, who telephoned Maputo and requested Frelimo's permission to mount a recovery of the aircraft from Salisbury. He assured Frelimo that this was purely a civil aviation matter in which Rhodesian Civil Aviation authorities were assisting an entirely French commercial operation. Frelimo was new to government and took the Frenchman at his word. Amazingly, they made no attempt to contact the Malagasy government to confirm the story.

It was decided that Group Captain Paxton, who had taken early retirement from the air force and was working for a private civil aviation firm in Salisbury should be approached to deal with this unusual situation. Paxton, as well as the necessary spares, was flown in by helicopter.

Minimum repairs were carried out in order to get the aircraft out of enemy territory as soon as possible. The rear engine was replaced, the collapsed nose-wheel physically bolted to the airframe and a replacement front propeller was fitted. The aircraft passed ground power checks. A large box of goodies for Frelimo and the local people assured rapid repairs to the runway surface and the aircraft took off for Umtali with almost indecent haste.

The flight was a slow one because the landing gear was strapped down. All the same, the 16th Lynx arrived safely in Salisbury. With one aircraft to be repaired and three still awaiting camouflage paint, the air force defiantly rolled out 12 Lynx Reims Cessna FTB 337 Milirole aircraft and exposed them to public gaze. All that remained was to modify them for their armed role and this task had already been started. Within six weeks, all the aircraft were fitted with twin .303 Browning machine guns and underwing-pylons.

CHAPTER 41

The war moves south

The change of government in Mozambique caused considerable supply problems for Rhodesia. Now that access to ports in Mozambique was denied, the only road and rail links to the outside world were to the south through South Africa, and this in turn meant that the extreme south-eastern area where Mozambique, South Africa and Rhodesia joined had vital strategic importance. This situation brought about a shift in ZANLA tactics. Prior to 1976, cross-border infiltration had taken place mainly in the north-east. Now that there was a sympathetic regime in place, ZANLA forces could move easily and quickly down the eastern border and ZANLA commanders were quick to realize that to win the war they must cut the supply lines from South Africa. As a direct result of the increasing activity in the south-east, a new Joint Operations Centre (JOC) was established in January 1976 at Chiredzi in the lowveld with a forward airfield at Buffalo Range, known as FAF 7.

Operation small bang

In February 1976, information was received that ZANLA had set up a transit camp near the village of Pafuri. Reports also suggested that the camp could have been supplied with ZU23 triple mount anti-aircraft guns that fired 12.5mm shells, so it was decided that the attacking aircraft should be given the added protection of Hunters. In all, one K-Car and three G-Cars were allocated, to ferry a mortar detachment, an infantry company of the RAR, and a Selous Scouts reconnaissance team to the area, while two Hunters were detailed to strike as necessary.

The Scouts reconnaissance team crossed the border at dusk on 23rd February 1976. The RAR troops and helicopters were positioned on a bush airstrip at Mabalauta, about 35 minutes' flying time away. The Scouts located the ZANLA camp and placed their electronically detonated marker flares, but then, as they were pulling back, they were challenged by a ZANLA sentry. The Scouts opened fire and this alerted the men in the camp. An air strike was called in immediately, followed by the airborne assault. This was the first occasion on which the Hunters had been in action. However, the ZANLA men had heeded the warning given by the gunfire and only three bodies were found in the camp, although large quantities of arms, ammunitions and documents were recovered.

So, the pilots of No 1 Squadron had finally contributed to the war effort and were hopefully scanning the horizon for MiGs and the hills for tanks, after the newspapers had reported the arrival of both these armaments in Mozambique. The pilots of No 4 Squadron were taking advantage of any breaks in the weather to try out the new Lynx aircraft, which had now arrived on squadron. Despite the weather, they managed 50 hours flying time in the Lynx during the month. Meanwhile No 7 Squadron was being stretched to the limit operating from FAFs 1, 2, 3, 4, 5, 6, 7, Erin, Umtali, Melsetter and Mabalauta.

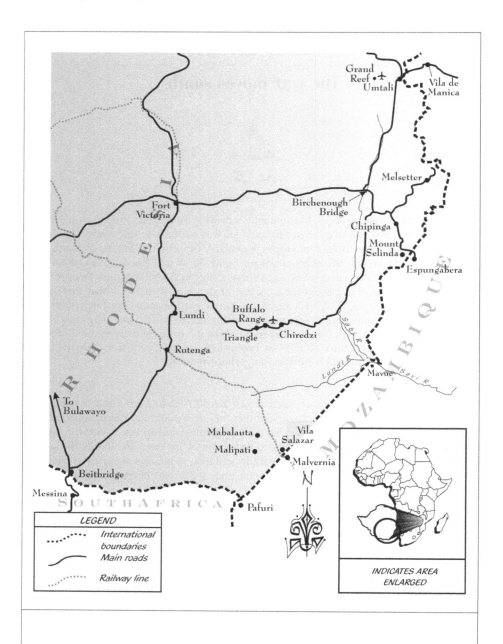

EASTERN BORDER AREA - RHODESIA

A fatal accident

On 16th February 1976, there was a flying accident at Umtali in which Squadron Leader G.A. (Rusty) Routledge was killed while flying as a passenger in a Cessna 185. Talking about this accident Peter Petter-Bowyer says:

> *Squadron Leader Rusty Routledge had no control over the flight leading to his sad death. He needed to visit Umtali on radio communications business and was flown to Perrems Air Field in a South African Air Force Cessna. The young pilot made a bad approach and at a late stage decided to overshoot for a second approach. The aircraft struggled to gain speed but could not achieve this, as the gentle rise of ground ahead proved to be too much. Control was lost as an attempt was made to turn left for lower ground. The port wing stalled and the Cessna rolled into the ground. Rusty did not survive an avoidable crash, which the Board of Inquiry found was caused by the aircraft being excessively overweight. This was the unfortunate and inexperienced pilot's responsibility.* (Petter-Bowyer)

Medical practitioners begin doing 'bush stints'

On 28th February 1976, in the north-eastern border area, a group of RLI soldiers was tracking a large number of terrorists when they came under fire. In the first contact, the tracker was killed and one officer and a corporal were seriously wounded. Soon after this, a sweep line made contact with a further group of insurgents in dense bush. Another member of the RLI was wounded. Flight Lieutenant Rob McGregor and Air Lieutenant Ginger Baldwin of No 7 Squadron were flying in support of the men on the ground. Rob supplied top cover while Ginger carried out the evacuation of the wounded men.

The landing zones were very small, and heavy enemy fire was directed at the helicopters. Trooper Kenneth Daly, the medical assistant helped with the evacuation, briefing the pilot on the nature of the wounds and the urgency of getting the casualties to hospital. Rob McGregor later returned to the contact area at night, under extremely difficult flying conditions, to re-supply the troops with ammunition. Both Flight Lieutenant Rob McGregor and Air Lieutenant Ginger Baldwin were awarded the Military Forces Commendation (Operational).

The increase in armed incursions resulted in enormous pressure being exerted on security force medical personnel. In order to alleviate the situation, civilian medical practitioners and specialists volunteered to do fortnightly stints in the operational areas. At the forward airfields, periods of sit around and wait were interspersed with intensive activity when there was a contact or a land-mine explosion. The doctors often travelled aboard the helicopters or fixed wing aircraft to the scene of a contact. They carried a medical kit that was fully equipped for minor surgery to be performed on the spot. They could set up drips in the field, remove foreign matter from a wound, dress it, administer morphine and antibiotics before the patient was flown to the nearest hospital. Patients with head or spinal injuries could be flown directly to the nearest city where a landing pad was available in the hospital grounds.

The dustbin saga

After reading an article in a South African magazine to the effect that Rhodesian Air Force pilots were so skilled that they could shoot up a dustbin in a jungle clearing, No 4 Squadron decided to have a joke at the expense of No 1 Squadron. A very ancient dustbin was acquired and presented to the Hunter squadron. Squadron Leader Rich Brand took up the gauntlet. The dustbin was placed in the middle of a clearing at Kutanga Range and Rich Brand, flying in at 480 knots from 2,000 feet, fired just one of the Hunter's 30mm cannons. One of the five rounds caught the dustbin amidships severely buckling the receptacle and leaving a gaping hole. The dustbin was later galvanized and given pride of place at air force headquarters in Salisbury.

The saga of the dustbin so impressed the Australia/Rhodesia Association that they commissioned a half-size replica which was sent to Ian Smith for presentation to the Rhodesian Air Force as a Marksman of the Year Trophy. Handing over the pewter model, on 18th May 1978, the Rhodesian prime minister recalled that many Australians (some 655) had received pilot training in Rhodesia with the RATG. The first recipient of the Dustbin Trophy was Flight Lieutenant Tony Oakley of No 1 Squadron.

No 1 Squadron Diary, March 1976:

This has been a fairly quiet month after the excitement of last month. 2 Squadron has thrown down the 'black glove of war' attacking 'innocent' formations, carrying out a 20-minute chase, and dive from 20,000 feet, and finally having the audacity to claim 'kills'! Needless to say, all pilots' 'lookout' is improving. The 'flag-wave' season is now in full swing. Already a few crowds have been thrilled, and gaze on in amazement and awe at those men in their flying machines. To date no 'midges' (MiGs) or tanks have shown themselves but we are always hopeful. Rumour has it that Kutanga Range has re-equipped with 3,000 dustbins to put in jungle clearings so that 1 Squadron can get 'to the point'. [To The Point was a South African news magazine.]

Operation Thrasher

The operational area Thrasher covering most of Rhodesia's eastern border area was opened in March 1976 because of increased ZANLA infiltration from southern Mozambique. And as the focus of the war switched to the south-east, so FAF 7, the airfield at Buffalo Range, in the lowveld became a major centre of activity.

FAF 7 Buffalo Range Daily Diary:

April 13th 1976. Fireforce was deployed to the Sabi-Lundi junction. Yellow section helicopters had an excellent contact of which ground fireforce claimed two and K-Car claimed two. Three others were arrested. Yellow section returned to FAF 7 at 14h30. Trog was used as telstar during this contact and Lynx as top cover. At 16h35, Yellow section and 2 RAR fireforce were called out to UM 502282 where terrs were sighted. Two terrs were shot dead and the K-Car once again came into its stride and claimed one fellow who decided to hide in a hut and was slotted. Lynx was flying top cover. Trog was requested to casevac a pregnant African woman.

From their bases south of the Sabi River, the insurgents could move with relative ease across the south-eastern part of Rhodesia and during the Easter weekend they set up an ambush on the main road south. The ambush happened at dusk on 18th April 1976, north of the Bubye River on the Fort Victoria/Beitbridge road. Four young people travelling on two motorcycles came across terrorists who were holding up three cars. The ZANLA group, numbering between 12 and 20, were armed with AK-47 rifles and they opened fire on the motorcyclists, killing the three men and severely wounding the girl. Douglas Plumsteed, on his way from Johannesburg, arrived on the scene and opened fire on the attackers who fled. Soon after this incident, a train on the nearby railway line detonated an explosive device, which caused some damage to the locomotive. A massive search including helicopters and fixed wing aircraft was mounted and on 23rd April, a group of insurgents was caught before they could cross back into Mozambique. One of the results of this attack was the institution of road convoys on the Beitbridge/Fort Victoria road. These convoys often had airborne cover.

In the same area, on 30th April, fireforce responded to a call that the army had made contact with a group of 30 insurgents, three of whom had already been killed. Corporal

Makuwa, 1st Battalion Rhodesian African Rifles, spotted 13 armed men attempting to escape from the contact area. He signalled the pilot of an aircraft and the gunner engaged the group. A fight developed, with the result that several terrorists were killed, wounded or captured.

The helicopter squadron was not the only one being stretched to breaking point. No 4 Squadron was also feeling the pressure. In April, the Provost clocked up 74 hours flying time, the Trojan 183 and the Lynx 453. Both aircrew and ground crew were creating records and the opening of FAF 8 at Grand Reef in Umtali stretched the deployment even further.

On 6th May there was a communications error that could have been fatal. A major trooping exercise was being carried out in the Sabi/Lundi junction area when Air Lieutenant Hilton (Slade) Healey (SAAF) was given in-flight instructions to proceed elsewhere. The exact message passed from FAF 7 was: "Healey to proceed to the Loc beginning with Mike Alpha Lima [Malapati] and to land there for further trooping instructions." Healey misunderstood these instructions and thought that the Mike Alpha Lima referred to Malvernia, in Mozambique. Fortunately for him he had called up the Lynx doing telstar to give him cover. According to FAF 7 Diary: "The pilot of this aircraft nearly had a heart attack when he saw they were orbiting Malvernia and he was able to convince Healey of the error. The two aircraft departed that loc. swiftly!" Small-arms fire was directed at them ineffectually.

FAF 7 Buffalo Range Daily Diary:

22nd May 1976. Flight Lieutenant George Sole uplifting casevac from mine incident in Boli area arrived back after dark in shocking weather conditions. Air Lieutenant Norman Maasdorp had to be diverted to Thornhill on his return from Inkomo because of weather. Trog positioned at Fort Victoria until further notice.
FAF 7 Daily Diary:
25th May. At 16h30, call sign 81 was ambushed while having tea. The fireforce was called from Rutenga and Flight Lieutenant Chris Wentworth was sent to the same area to casevac one security force wounded in the clash. No further details. Air Lieutenant Neil Liddell (SAAF) operating with the fireforce lost himself and landed out of fuel at the Triangle cricket field. Flight Lieutenant George Sole was sent out to ferry troops into the SE area. Not enough time was allowed for this exercise and he returned after dark with one casevac on board.

Contact

The FAF 7 Daily Diary in conjunction with a situation report for the same action gives a detailed picture of a typical contact. At approximately 14h30 on 27th May 1976, information was received at FAF 7 that security forces had boxed in about 13 ZANLA men. Air support was requested. Helicopters and Lynxes were dispatched. Unfortunately, the FAF 9 K-Car had a stoppage and assistance was requested from the FAF 7 Lynx and the FAF 6 K-Car. Another K-Car from Chipinga and the fireforce from Rutenga were also called in. Heavy and accurate ground fire was directed at all the aircraft with the result that a number of helicopters were hit, none of them seriously. The area surrounding the complex in which the contact took place was very open so the armed men were forced to remain within the buildings. Owing to the heavy resistance they were encountering, the ground forces requested a rocket attack on the target area and two Hunters were called in from Thornhill.

A description of the target was passed from the K-Car, via the Lynx to Red Section Hunters and it was good, despite a large amount of radio transmission chatter.

The Lynx was acting as Airborne FAC but it had already made use of its smoke markers and had only a 37mm HE rocket to mark the target. Unfortunately, this marker was not spotted by the Red Section Hunters. In the opinion of everyone concerned with this contact, the Hunters acquitted themselves exceptionally well and the strike was fully justified and resulted in five terrorists being killed and one wounded and captured. This was the first real success since the opening of Repulse. Another contact south of Mabalauta resulted in three enemy dead. This operation was essentially air force controlled and executed, with army follow-ups and sweeps.

Frantan was used but there was no evidence that it caused any injuries. Most of the wounds came from small arms and shrapnel, with the majority of deaths caused by air action.

During May another VR, Ian Rodwell obtained his Wings, Commission and Captaincy, reinforcing the fact that the air force volunteer reserve had come a long way since the early days when the volunteers were expected to perform only desk duties. No 7 Squadron carried over 2,000 passengers during May, not counting the four-footed variety used for tracking, but the pilots did have a slight problem with the army as it did not seem to realize that Alouettes needed fuel to fly: "FAF 7. May 31st Chopper ran out of fuel, landed in a cane field. Crusader not keeping us totally informed of distances."

No 4 Squadron Diary, May 1976:

Provost: 42 hours Trojan: 171 hours Lynx: 611 hours
The main point of interest in this month's flying was Ian Sheffield's forced-landing at night, in a Trojan! He experienced an engine fire and was very lucky to get away from the aircraft with no injuries, nothing except a few blisters from his long walk afterwards. Yet again quite a hectic month on the squadron with FAF 9 [Rutenga] being opened up halfway through the month. All chaps have been kept busy with Cocky Benecke doing recce training.

Casualty evacuation

The land-mine had become the terrorists' favourite weapon, particularly in the north-east operational area and victims became part of daily life in the field hospital at Mount Darwin. To the land-mine there is no friend or enemy—anyone travelling along the dirt roads and tracks could become a casualty.

A typical incident occurred late one afternoon when a fully laden bus was moving slowly along a dusty road 100 kilometres north of Mount Darwin. The vehicle had just crossed a bridge and started the upward climb to Rushinga when it detonated the land-mine. The air was filled with dust and debris and once the noise of the explosion died away, there was only a shocked silence.

The pilots of No 7 Squadron based at Mount Darwin were relaxing in the late afternoon sun, when word came through. The wail of the scramble hooter washed around the already running figures and was quickly obliterated by the whine of Alouette engines and the beat of rotors proceeding over the thick bush. As the helicopters climbed from the field, the base controller's voice called the magnetic heading, casualty figures and ground force movements.

Twenty minutes later, the helicopters arrived at the scene. One landed on the bridge behind the bus; another settled down in the bush alongside the wreckage. The pilots found an old man with a white beard sitting in the dust, both legs smashed. A woman's body lay at a grotesque angle while many others, including children, had been seriously injured. In all, 15 people needed medical attention. They were taken to nearby Karanda Mission Hospital and then on to Mount Darwin before completing the final leg of the trip to Salisbury, by air force Dakota.

But it did not require a heavy vehicle to set off a land-mine. Some were placed in such a way that the weight of a light cart or even a bicycle would detonate the explosive. On 11th June 1976, several children were riding on a Scotch cart, which was taking maize meal to a village north of Mount Darwin. The land-mine detonated blowing the cart 20 metres up the road. Three children died on the spot and one died later. The 15-year-old boy leading the animals and the animals themselves survived. Two helicopters were called in to evacuate three of the injured children to Karanda Hospital.

The aircraft based at Mount Darwin could be called in to provide assistance over an area of 16,000 square kilometres, supplying fire power for ground forces, lifting in fireforce troops and taking out casualties. If the need was urgent enough, a chopper could be flown in, whether it was a farmhouse under attack or a woman suffering a difficult labour. It was a tremendous morale booster for the security force members to know that if they were injured, they could be lifted out and receive medical help. One soldier wounded in a contact was flown to Bindura Hospital, operated upon and installed in bed, while his colleagues were still engaged in combat. The news of his successful operation was radioed back to the patrol in question.

Casualty evacuation work in these circumstances held as many risks for the helicopter crews as military operations. One of many such incidents occurred after a fireforce call out when, during the follow-up, a small stick of troops was ambushed by insurgents. One soldier was seriously wounded and required immediate evacuation. The helicopter arrived just as night was falling and it was about to touch down when terrorists, who had been in hiding, opened fire. It took four or five attempts before the aircraft was able to land safely. After finally routing the enemy by means of tracer and machine-gun fire, the injured man could be attended to on the spot by the doctor, and then flown to hospital.

Another perilous task was rescuing farmers and their families who had been wounded in terrorist attacks. Farmers in the operational area were encouraged to submit diagrams showing the position of a landing zone, which if they were wise, was constructed either within or close to the security fence. Obstructions such as farm buildings, trees, aerials, power lines and fences were marked on the map because the chances were that the helicopter would have to land at night, with the pilot flying by the seat of his pants.

In all probability, the pilot's only guide would be a flare sent up by the farmer—if that. The helicopter could be on the scene well ahead of any military backup and could come under fire from terrorists still in the area. Often during a farm attack, the surrounding roads would have been mined so troops would have to de-bus a few kilometres away and proceed with caution. Sometimes one or two sticks of troops could be choppered in so that if the insurgents were still close by and opened fire, they would get a sharp reply.

Buffalo Range
By June, Buffalo Range had become one of the 'hottest' spots in the country.

FAF 7 Buffalo Range, 1st June 1976:
Not enough accommodation for crews! Flight Lieutenant George Sole's aircraft unserviceable! Replacement engine flown in by Dak.

22nd June FAF 7:
This morning the weather was QBI (clampers) and halted the war for a while. However, at 09h30 the Dakota was able to get airborne to Boli for a resupply of the troops there. On the way back at low level, he was shot at and sustained one hit in the port wing. A Lynx en route from Fort Victoria was diverted and two others put into the air. The fireforce was also deployed from Rutenga but all to no avail.

23rd June FAF 7:
The Dakota was airborne at 06h15 for Boli. Then returned with one casevac (sick) and went to Thornhill for armaments. The Dakota went unserviceable on its last trip from Rutenga with

security force. This caused a trip up to Sarum for one Lynx (Norman Maasdorp) with the crew of the Dakota to collect a spare aircraft. They arrived at about 22h30. Whilst this was going on we were trying to raise Sarum ops on the SSB night frequency and the whole set-up in the ops caravan went unserviceable. One Vampire positioned here early in the morning with the other two arriving at 13h30. Pilots Roy Hulley and Brian Penton. (Daily Diary)

News from the squadrons
No 4 Squadron Diary, June 1976

Lynx: 760h25 Trojan: 89h55

No 4 Squadron had a very busy month: with the ever-increasing bush commitments, men and machines are fully-occupied. Thus Group Captain Charles Paxton (a reserve pilot on call-up) was a very welcome visitor and his help was greatly appreciated. Other welcome visitors were Armourer Sergeant D. Curwen and Engine Fitter Sergeant Brian McEnery, while joining us permanently we have Engine Fitter Sergeant Steve Mason and Armourers SAC Dennis Calvert and SAC Jurgen Schoeman. In the bush—air recce proved most successful.

No 1 Squadron Diary, June

This month has been a busy month in the operational field, though unfortunately the 'hurry up and waits' outnumbered the actual operations by up to 4 to 1. The big news was that Squadron Leader Rich Brand flew on his first strike at last, but we all know that this was only because Flight Lieutenant Tudor Thomas was not yet available for flying duties. Both Air Sub-Lieutenants Martin Lowrie and Mark Vernon had their first taste of operational flying this month. It appears from the amount of whistling heard in the air that No 2 Squadron are at last doing some work again. (The Vampire does have a whistling sound). We presume that the reason their latest bateleur contributions are so short is that they are trying to give the impression that they have been very busy. We hope for their sake that they won't try to steal any of the real jet squadron's range bookings in the coming months. Air Sub-Lieutenant Mark Vernon grabbed the headlines with 'Hunter does Victory Roll over City'. This incident has caused him to be the most popular air subbie on station. The squadron has received several letters of appreciation of the incident from a Salisbury school.

Attack on Mount Selinda and Zona Estate

Towards the middle of June, there was an unprovoked attack on the Zona Tea Estates. The estate, which runs parallel to the Mozambique border at Mount Selinda, came under a three-hour rocket and mortar bombardment. This was launched by Frelimo from the town of Espungabera, which overlooks the 300-hectare estate. The Mozambique army also hit the border post and a nearby farm with machine gun fire. Once again, the Hunters were called in. This time Tudor Thomas was flying in the op:

Thursday 10th June 1976 is a day that will live with me forever. I was 'A' flight commander on No 1 Squadron based at Thornhill and during the morning, I had flown an operation in support of the Selous Scouts. I was on stand-by for the rest of the day and around 15h00 I received a call from the duty officer for an air strike in the eastern side of the country. Air Lieutenant Martin Lowrie and I went up to the squadron where OC Flying Wing, Wing Commander Keith Corrans, briefed us. A platoon of brown jobs who had been patrolling the border near Espungabera had come under intensive fire from the Mozambique side of the border and were having a hard time trying to extract themselves. Some Eland 90s from Chipinga and the Lynx flown by Flight Lieutenant Russell Broadbent, a tame Kiwi, had done what they could in support but the fire continued unabated. Red Section, with me leading, armed with

68mm Matra rockets, and Martin with frantans, and both with full gun packs of 30mm, arrived overhead Chipinga at altitude. We were duly briefed by Squadron Leader Cyril White as to the latest developments and told to contact Russell in the Lynx who was in the strike area controlling the operation. On the edge of Espungabera was a tin hut that was thought to be a command post for the gooks so I was briefed to take it out with Matra. Russell would mark the target with a smoke rocket. We descended and split for the strike. The Hunter was a wonderful weapons platform and, having picked up the target from Russell's marker, I went in and fired eight rockets. I watched them heading for the tin hut and then started my pullout. And that's when things went awry! As I was pulling out, the hydraulic warning sounded and immediately the controls went into manual mode. I remember cancelling the warning, putting on full power and pulling out of the dive with both hands. There were some steep hills ahead and I wondered if I was going to make it over them. Having regained some semblance of control, I called Martin and told him I had lost my hydraulics and would be clearing the area. I continued towards Chipinga, assessing the situation. The aircraft was controllable and I had enough fuel on board to make it to Thornhill so I decided to return to base. During the long flight back, I observed that at normal throttle setting, my indicated air speed was about 40 knots less than it should have been. Then I noticed the 'dolls eye', which indicated that the air brake was extended. Without hydraulics, the air brake would have drooped, causing extra drag, and thus reducing the speed. Another problem I encountered en route was that I had to trim more and more left wing down. Checking the fuel indicators on the 230-gallon (1,045 l) drop tanks, I noticed that the starboard drop tank was not feeding. A quick calculation showed that I would still have enough fuel to make it back to base, even at the slower speed. The whole way back I tried to figure out what had caused all these problems. I made contact with John Digby who was on duty in the Thornhill tower and he informed me that they were already aware of the situation. It was starting to get dark as I descended, and about 20 miles [32km] out from Thornhill I decided to 'blow' the pods and drop tanks over a clear area, to give me better control for the landing. By this stage I had nearly full left aileron trim. I called the tower and told them what I was about to do. Aware that I would have to counter the roll to the left once the tanks had gone, I pushed the appropriate buttons on the instrument panel. The explosion of the two tanks and both pods being ejected simultaneously caught me completely by surprise and I found myself almost inverted as the left trim took effect. At that exact moment, John Digby called me for a check to determine my QDM. I missed the call as I was trying to recover from this totally unexpected unusual attitude, and it took another couple of calls from tower, each one becoming more and more frantic, before I had composed myself enough to reply. Having calmed down, my plan was to join direct right hand downwind for runway 13, blow the (landing) gear down with the pneumatics (the normal procedure when the hydraulics were lost) and land. I selected the gear down and pulled the pneumatic handle. Surprise! Surprise! Nose wheel green but both main gear lights bright red! I advised John and requested a low run past the tower for them to check my landing gear position visually. It was now fairly dark so a flare was fired as I flew past but they were unable to confirm things 100%. The nose wheel certainly looked down and maybe one of the main legs. What now? I decided to do a slow-speed handling check to determine the safe approach speed. And as the aircraft slowed to around 210 knots I found that I had to use full left aileron to keep the wings level. This meant adding ten to 15 knots to the airspeed to give some aileron control on finals. That was nearly 100 knots faster than a normal approach! And I had the undercarriage problem as well as a full gun pack of 540 30mm cannon shells right beneath my feet! Both low-level fuel lights had by now illuminated, which gave me little time to make a plan. A quick discussion with Wing Commander Keith Corrans, who had flown Hunters, confirmed that there was really only one course of action—a 'Martin Baker' letdown. Eject! I had had enough time on the flight home to ensure I was strapped in tightly, so I turned to the north of the airfield, shut the engine down, and pulled the ejection handle over my head. It seemed to take ages but finally the canopy blew off then the seat 'banged out'. My first sensation was the cold air hitting my face followed by a feeling of tumbling head over heels. The parachute deployed and I began my earthward descent. Looking down, I could see dark and light patches on the ground, which I decided must be trees and grass. I had recently done a parachute training course at New Sarum and remembered how to steer, which I did, towards the lighter patches. As it was quite dark now, it was extremely difficult to judge my height above the ground. I had remembered to release the survival pack underneath me but that did not seem to stabilize my swinging from side to side. Just as I was trying to work out whether to roll left or right on landing, I hit the ground. Having uttered a few appropriate words like 'gosh' and 'gee whiz', I checked to see if I was still in one piece and then thought about how I was going to get home. The aircraft had continued flying for about three or four kilometres when it struck the ground and was totally destroyed. Overhead I heard a Trojan that was obviously looking for me, so I took my RT60B (an emergency radio operating on 121.5 mHz) from my survival jacket, and tried to make comms with the aircraft. No luck! All I heard was the local radio station blasting through. Next plan. Ah yes! Flares! I took the 'pencil flare' gun out of my survival jacket, screwed in a flare, waited for the aircraft to circle back in my direction, pointed the device heavenward and fired. Nothing! So I changed the flare for another one. Same result—nothing! By this stage, Martin Lowrie was also in the circuit looking for me. He had continued with the strike and, once completed, had initially headed towards Bulawayo thinking that I might have diverted there. As I could not attract anyone either by radio or with flares, I decided to head towards a road where I could hear vehicle traffic in the distance. I spread my parachute out on the ground for future reference and headed off. Unknown to me, a nearby farmer had phoned the tower to ask if there was any parachute training being carried out as he had heard an aircraft go overhead and then seen a parachute descending. He was able to indicate the area to the fire jeep and ambulance. About 20 minutes later, I saw a red flashing light though the trees. It was the rescue team—the farmer had certainly got his directions right! Once they drew abeam, they did a left wheel and came thundering towards me, little knowing that between us was a large dry riverbed. I tried yelling at them but to no avail. It was only by running down into the riverbed and up the other side that I managed to stop the ambulance from plunging ten feet down the embankment. After a rather painfully bumpy ride through the bush, the ambulance dropped me at the station hospital for a checkup by the doctor, while the rest of the team continued searching for the wreckage. Squadron Leader 'Boots' Horsfall, the station doctor, did a thorough physical, pronounced me okay, and said I wasn't to have any alcohol for 24 hours and I must report to him next day! As I walked out of sick quarters, there was Chris Dixon waiting with an ice-cold beer, which I quaffed with great relish. He took me home where more beers were consumed and then said we were going across to the School of Infantry for a cheese and wine party with the army. On about my third glass of wine my hands started shaking uncontrollably. I had to put the glass down to prevent spraying everyone around me. This was the delayed shock setting in and was the end of my evening. I slept like a log that night. Once the wreckage had been found, it was ascertained that the aircraft had been hit in several places by ground fire. Rounds had gone through one of the main wheel wells and severed both the hydraulic and pneumatic pipes. The starboard drop tank had also been punctured by ground fire thus preventing the fuel feed. A very sad end for Hawker Hunter FGA 9 No 1280—such a beautiful aircraft. (Tudor Thomas)

Meanwhile, back on the border, Tudor Thomas's air attack had resulted in the deaths of eleven terrorists. One African employee of the Tea Estate said his people had been afraid of the rockets and did not know where to hide, but it was good to see the jets go in. Russell Broadbent later received the Militaty Forces Commendation for this incident.

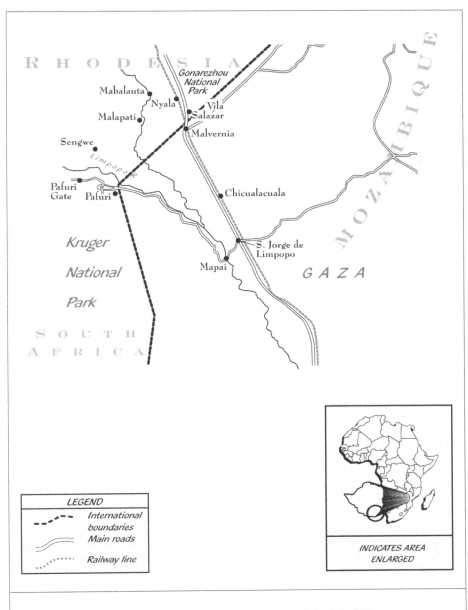

ATTACK ON MAPAI AND CHICUALACUALA

First motorized cross-border attacks

Until now, troops operating across Rhodesia's borders had either been airlifted or had gone in on foot—but the Rhodesian army had now acquired the Unimog, a vehicle similar to those in use by the Portuguese army. The idea was soon sown. Why not carry Rhodesian forces across the border in these vehicles, which were virtually indistinguishable from those inherited by Frelimo. The decision was taken to do a test run. Two ten-men teams using four vehicles were chosen to cross the border in the Chiredzi area and proceed 180 kilometres to the village of Chigamane.

The column left late in the afternoon of 13th May 1976. Its task was to lay mines, destroy stores or supplies and capture ZANLA or Frelimo soldiers for questioning. This limited operation was highly successful and led to the planning and carrying out of the major cross-border raids undertaken during the following three years.

Attack on Mapai and Chicualacuala

The next motorized attack was carried out on the transit camps at Mapai and Chicualacuala in June 1976. Again the starting point within Rhodesia was Chiredzi. The route was to be south-west along the border to the road and railway line at Malvernia, then south-east along the main road to Mapai. No one had any idea how this daring scheme would work out. Would the column walk straight into an ambush? Would Frelimo spot the hoax and call in the MiGs? It was a gamble. The date chosen for the attack was 26th June, a public holiday in Mozambique. During the night of 23rd June, a reconnaissance team made its way to the Malvernia area creating various diversions on the way.

On 25th June the Rhodesian road convoy crossed the border in four Unimogs with two Ferret scout cars. In the sky, high above the column was a Lynx from No 4 Squadron acting as telstar. Fingers were on triggers as the column turned onto the Maputo Road but the Unimogs caused no concern; a bored sentry at a railway siding watched the column pass. The vehicles refuelled at Jorge do Limpopo, which they had reached without incident, and pulled into Mapai at 06h00. Here the main point of interest was a building used to store arms and ammunition for ZANLA cadres. On the upper floor of this building, the Rhodesians met their first real opposition. One member of the Scouts was injured and WO2 J.A. (Jannie Nel) was killed in the ensuing exchange of fire. The Selous Scouts bombarded the upper floors with small-arms fire and RPG-7 rockets but the resistance was stubborn and another member of the Scouts was wounded. The officer in command, Major John 'Butch' Duncan, requested a casevac for his men. He liased with the pilot of the Lynx who called in Hunters to carry out a rocket strike on the building. A fierce fire engulfed the arms store and the enemy who had been resisting with such determination ceased firing.

Meanwhile a No 7 Squadron helicopter, which had been called in, landed to pick up the casualties and fly them out. Major Duncan re-formed the column and the ground forces withdrew, hitting the ZANLA staging post at Chicualacuala as they pulled back. Once again, the object had been achieved with complete surprise.

A technician dies in action
No 4 Squadron Diary, July 1976:

Trojan: 59h15 Lynx: 839h35

Yet again, a busy month for the squadron as indicated by the flying hours. The area of operations was also increased with the positioning of a Lynx at Wankie. The beginning of the month saw the arrival of Squadron Leader Mike Saunders (Reserve TF Pilot) and his stint at FAF 5 helped out tremendously. Also, back for another tour with the squadron is Flight Lieutenant Don Northcroft (reserve pilot) who is also at FAF 5. Congratulations to Norman Maasdorp awarded Military Forces Commendation (Operational). Well done Bam Bam (Maasdorp). John Bennie promoted to Squadron Leader. B.G. Graaff became 'A' flight commander. Ed Potterton 'B' flight commander. In the Bush: Phil Haigh and Mike Saunders had quite a busy time this month. On 9th July, both played a role in a contact in which five terrs and eight feeders were killed. On a not so happy note, during another contact on 18th July, in which Phil and Mike took part—three terrs and ten feeders were killed, a helicopter tech, Sergeant John Patrick (Pat) Graham, was killed and three troopers in the chopper were wounded. The chopper driver, Danny Svoboda, was lucky to be unharmed. One of our aircraft picked up a couple of hits in operational flying. Ed Potterton had the not so pleasant job of casevacing some hunters who had been in a land-mine incident. In the same blast, some Spanish tourists were injured and died before they could be casevaced to Salisbury.

The Hunter celebrates its 25th anniversary

On 19th July 1976, flights were made by No 1 Squadron Hawker Hunter jet aircraft over Rhodesia to commemorate the 25th anniversary of the first flight of a prototype of the Hunter at Boscombe Down Air Field in England by Nevil Duke.

The aircraft led by the officer commanding, Squadron Leader Richard Brand, left Thornhill Gwelo at 09h15 and flew in box formation at a height of 500 feet, passing over Bulawayo at 09h30 and West Nicholson at 09h45, Rutenga at 09h55, Chiredzi at 10h05, Shabani at 10h20 and back to Thornhill. The second flight flew from Thornhill to Fort Victoria where it arrived at 12h35, Chipinga at 12h45, Melsetter at 13h00, Umtali at 13h05 and Inyanga at 13h10, Rusape at 13h15 and Marandellas at 13h20. They refuelled at New Sarum at 13h30 and then proceeded to Mtoko where they arrived at 15h35, Mount Darwin at 15h50, Bindura at 15h55, Sinoia at 16h05, Hartley at 16h15, Gatooma at 16h20, Que Que at 16h25 and back to Thornhill by 16h30.

The Jacklin Trophy, 1976

In July, the commander of the air force, Air Marshal M.J. McLaren, presented the Jacklin Trophy to No 7 Helicopter Squadron. Addressing the 27 men and one woman of the squadron he said: "We have no quarrel with any of our neighbours. We ask only that they act in a responsible manner and within the accepted tenets of civilized states." McLaren went on to say that great sacrifices would continue to be asked of Rhodesians. "I cannot offer any consolation of a change in circumstances in the immediate future. It must be a total determination and dedication to rid this country of the terrorist menace in order to provide a stable base on which political endeavours to find a just and equitable solution for the peoples of Rhodesia can be found. Our duty is clear—to fight to preserve everything we stand for, and have built, in this great country. You will all have seen published very recently, the fact that the security force commanders have complete authority for the conduct of our campaign. I wish to assure you all, that my colleagues and I are conscious of this great responsibility and have every determination and intention to utilize all means at our disposal to achieve success. We will not, and in fact, do not, hesitate to carry out operations against our enemies, who hit and run and seek a safe haven in neighbouring territories, and those who harbour them."

The air force commander said the award of the Jacklin Trophy to No 7 Squadron would have the full support of army and police colleagues as well as many civilians, black and white, who had cause to be grateful for the squadron's evacuation and rescue services.

On 26th July, the *Rhodesia Herald* carried the story of one member of No 7 Squadron:

After more than five years in the air force, Air Lieutenant Mark Aitchison is well accustomed to terrorism and to the death and destruction it brings, but some of the scenes he was called to in the bush still sicken and horrify him. He was one of the first at the recent bloody scene at Mount Selinda, where two girls and their mother were killed by a land-mine and a third girl lost both legs. "That was an ugly scene—it made me extremely angry," said Air Lieutenant Aitchison. He was also a key figure in the Maranke Tribal Trust Land casevac operation when two African buses were blown up by a land-mine. "There was a lot of carnage with a lot of bodies lying around. Many people, including a woman and a little girl, had shattered limbs. It was all very gory." Air Lieutenant Aitchison who is back in Salisbury for a week's rest and recuperation (R & R) from No 7 Squadron after a month in the eastern districts, described the four hour long casevac exercise. "I was on stand-by when reports of two large explosions came in. Within minutes, a recce pilot, a fixed wing aircraft radioed the position of one of the land-mined buses in the Maranke Tribal Trust Land. With a medic on board, I landed my helicopter beside the wrecked bus and we found two people killed. When we got there it looked bad. There were lots of bodies all around and so I asked for another helicopter to bring a second medic. Apart from the two people killed, there were about 17 others lying about seriously injured." The wounded were ferried to hospital in Umtali in a series of flights. Air Lieutenant Aitchison said, "Most of the people in the bus were women and young girls but there were a few elderly men. Some of the women were wearing the white dresses of the Apostolic Sect. The most seriously injured victims were a woman with shattered legs and a little girl with shattered feet. It was a pretty lengthy casevac operation. We are accustomed to all this. We get hardened to death and tragedy very quickly." (Rhodesia Herald, 26th July 1976)

This was the kind of situation that few Rhodesian medical practitioners had been called on to face, and so at the end of July a demonstration was laid on for them. They were given lectures on the treatment of bullet wounds and shown the effects of land-mines and bomb blast on the human body. Flight Lieutenant Rob McGregor, showed how patients could be winched [hoisted] into a helicopter on slings and how they could be placed inside the aircraft using stretchers. The doctors were also given warnings about approaching the helicopter while the rotors were still turning. Approach should only be made from the front of the machine and only when the pilot had given a signal that it was safe. He showed, with the help of a tall doctor how it was possible for the rotor blades to dip and slice a man's head off.

Alpha—the bouncing bomb

At the beginning of 1976, Chris Dams had been posted back from South Africa to become director of operations at air force headquarters. One of the first tasks he was given was to get the Canberra back into operations. The Canberra had been virtually out of the war since November 1971. This was partly due to the Frame 21 metal fatigue problem but also because the 20-pound (9kg) fragmentation bombs that the bomber carried had not only proved to be largely ineffective but also dangerous to the aircraft carrying them. Group Captain Peter Petter-Bowyer, who was air force projects officer, and Denzil Cochran of Cochran and Sons Engineering Works in Salisbury, were consulted. First, they carried out tests to assess the effectiveness of the fragmentation bombs:

At Kutanga Range, we set up a hessian-enclosed area with figure targets and we organized a Canberra to drop 96 fragmentation bombs on this area. We did a careful examination of the result, checking the effectiveness of the bombs. We plotted the point of impact of all the bombs. We also took photographs from the ground, as well as filming the operation from inside the Canberra bomb bay, actually filming the bombs coming out—we could physically see what was happening—the way that the small bombs jostled around as the slipstream hit them. By the time the 96 bombs reached the ground, they were just a shower of metal falling out of the aeroplane. The bombs were going in all directions, and the more disturbed they were by the airflow, the further back they fell in the strike pattern. We decided that the most effective bomb we could devise would be one that detonated at about ceiling height giving an equal blast in all directions. So we decided that the bomb must be round, not pencil-shaped because a pencil shape is inclined to give blast in one particular plane. Then we said, "How do you get these bombs to detonate at ceiling height?" Obviously, the only way is to allow the bomb to hit the ground first and then bounce up. So, we came up with the concept of a sphere of metal, 155mm diameter, with another sphere, 120mm, inside. Between the two spheres we packed 240 super balls, each 15mm in diameter, made of rubber with high bouncing capabilities. As the bomb hit the ground, the outer case stopped, the inner case compressed the balls underneath, which then rebounded lifting the bomb back into the air again. As the bomb hit the ground, the fuse chain initiated and a quarter of a second later the bomb went off—by which time it was 12 to 15 feet in the air. The next question was: How does the aircraft carry these bombs? The old bomb box was no use. So we designed a cradle to hold 100 bombs. A Canberra bomb bay could carry three of these cradles, loaded. The one limitation was that you could only drop the bombs in batches of 50, not fewer. But when it came down to it, we never dropped anything less than a full load of 300. You could, if you wished, release the cradles a few seconds apart to increase the spread on the ground. Now we had a much more effective weapon. We tested the bombs at first by taking one or two of the earlier versions up and hurling them out of a helicopter, even, on one occasion I remember, down onto the grass runway at New Sarum. That way we could observe what happened when they hit the ground. We also used the bombing range at Inkomo Barracks. There was a lot of trial and error but we proved that it would work, so I went to see Mick McLaren, commander of the air force. I was then acting chief of staff as well as DG Ops, I explained to Mick what we had been doing and that this was a way to get the Canberra back in the war—but we needed money. He said I should go and see the secretary for defence—

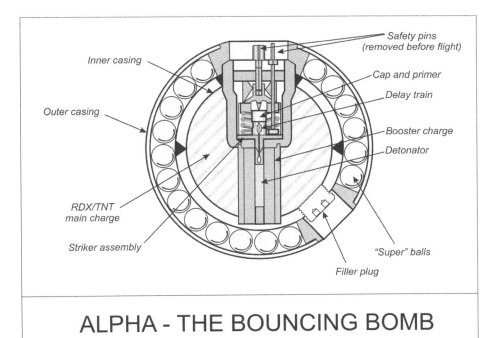

ALPHA - THE BOUNCING BOMB

which I did. We needed several tens of thousands of dollars. It was approved. Mick said he wanted the idea operational in six weeks—which, let's face facts, in terms of munitions development, was absolutely, totally impossible. I said we'd give it a go. We developed it from concept to fully operational in seven and a half weeks. (Petter-Bowyer)

Chris Dams recalled the day of the first large-scale demonstration:

We set up a test site at Kutanga Range complete with a few spectators, and the Canberra came in and dropped what looked like a shower of marbles. I tell you when those things started to go off it was like thunder, a roll of explosions that must have gone on for two or three seconds, a real growl of anger. Then we walked out to the test area, where we had dummies set up above ground, and in holes in the ground. The devastation, compared to the 28-pound (12.7kg) fragmentation bombs was unbelievable. There had been hot metal flying in all directions—if you had been anywhere in the target area you would have been very lucky not to have been hit—so it really was a truly devastating weapon.

The Canberra would soon be back in the war.

Hot extraction at Zamchiya

Early in August 1976, the Special Air Services undertook a reconnaissance patrol into south-eastern Mozambique to check information that a terrorist camp had been set up near Zamchiya town. A four-man team was choppered the 20 kilometres into Mozambique and put down some distance from the business centre, but they soon found that the area was densely populated. When dawn came, they managed to find a hiding place and that night continued to move towards the settlement. At dawn the next day, they were at the bottom of a small wooded hill. Whether they had been spotted the previous day or someone had come across their spoor will never be known, but with no warning, heavy firing suddenly broke out, aimed in the direction of the hill. The SAS men held their fire so as not to reveal their position. Meanwhile they called their base in Chipinga for a helicopter to lift them out—urgently.

Unfortunately, there had been a fireforce call-out and no choppers were available. By now the SAS position was rapidly being encircled by 100 heavily-armed men and the hill was coming under heavy attack from small-arms fire, RPGs and mortars. The team called again. Better news—no choppers but a Lynx was on its way. The approaching enemy were so close that the SAS men were forced to open fire. Now a running fight developed. The SAS group pulled back towards the border, with the ZANLA forces in pursuit. During a brief pause, the SAS called base again. On this occasion, the news was a little better. The Lynx would be there in an hour, the helicopters a bit later. But could they hold out that long? Somehow, they kept going until they found themselves in a wooded area close to a river. It was 14h50 and still about 20 minutes before they could expect any help. They were surrounded and vastly outnumbered.

The Lynx was still out of sight but approaching. The pilot requested an exact position. The men on the ground were not too sure, having entered the area at night but they managed to give a general direction and soon they spotted the Lynx way off to the north. As the Lynx came overhead, the ZANLA men began shooting at it with small arms and RPGs. The pilot circled fairly high but still in danger from a lucky hit. For what seemed an endless wait, the SAS men held their fire while the Lynx engaged the ZANLA forces below. Then at last came the wonderful sound, and soon after the sight of two choppers skimming low over the trees. The SAS men threw a couple of phosphorus grenades to keep their attackers busy while the choppers swooped and hovered. In no time, the men and their gear were aboard and the choppers turned for home.

This hot extraction was typical of the operations that No 7 Squadron crews would become increasingly accustomed to as hostilities increased.

Operation Eland—August 1976

In the early hours of Thursday 5th August 1976, an attack was launched by ZANLA forces on Ruda Base, on the Mozambique border, east of Inyanga. Between 60 and 70 attackers fired flares, heavy machine guns, RPDs, 82mm and 61mm mortars and 75mm recoilless rifles. Three mortar bombs fell within the police post. The attack lasted about 20 minutes and resulted in moderate damage but no casualties. The next day, while newspaper reporters were being shown round the camp, news came of a contact beyond a nearby koppie, and in the ensuing operation, four insurgents were killed. There was a further attack on Ruda Base on the following day and a mortar attack from across the border that killed four Rhodesian reservists. Three days later, there was a cross-border mortar attack in the Burma Valley during which four territorial soldiers were killed. Another territorial was killed during follow-up operations. As a result of these attacks, Prime Minister Ian Smith finally gave approval for the first major cross-border raid—Operation Eland.

Increasing mention was being made by captured terrorists of a large ZANLA base on the Pungwe River. It appeared that this was the point from which attacks into the Thrasher Operational area were being launched. The information was passed to the air force and they began flying intense photographic reconnaissance sorties over the area where the river bisected the main road from Chimoio to Tete.

For weeks nothing significant was spotted and then came the break. Wing Commander (Randy) du Rand, engaged in an unrelated photographic mission over Mozambique, was flying in the direction of the Pungwe River through heavy cloud, when a gap suddenly appeared, and there, below was a large complex. A Canberra was immediately dispatched to photograph the area in more detail, and actually flew over the camp while a muster parade was in progress. From the resulting photographs, it was obvious that nearly 2,000 men were based in the camp.

Careful photo reconnaissance revealed not only the exact location of the camp, 14 kilometres from the Pungwe River on the banks of a tributary, the Nyadzonya, but also a possible route by which the camp could be attacked. Aerial photographs revealed a meandering bush track winding through the mountainous border country, commencing at a farm in Penhalonga, just north of Umtali and progressing through hilly terrain until it linked up with the main Beira road at Villa de Manica. This was to be the route taken by the Selous Scouts.

Operation Eland was carried out by 72 Scouts, both black and white, divided into two strike forces, with helicopter gunships in support. Some of the men wore Frelimo uniforms and some of them spoke Portuguese. The raiders, Strike Force 1 and Strike Force 2, left Umtali at 04h00 on Sunday 8th August 1976. The motorized column included two Unimogs and one Berliet troop carrier, which had been captured on a previous raid. These vehicles had been fitted with 20mm Hispano cannons* from a grounded Vampire.

Strike Force 1 took the farm road and moved towards its target, a large ZANLA headquarters and base camp near the village of Andrada. Military Intelligence had established that the base was occupied by more than 250 trained ZANLA members, together with a smaller detachment of Frelimo troops, and according to a western diplomatic intelligence source, between 100 and 200 Tanzanian troops. Some civilian political personnel were also reported to be stationed at the base. Strike Force 2 skirted the Frelimo border post on the Umtali/

---

* These Hispano cannons were later mounted on a homemade armoured car, the Pig, and provided the heavy armament employed in Operation Mardon, in October/November 1976.

Beira road without raising the alarm, and driving along old farm tracks and across open veld, reached the main road and headed for Andrada. With light vehicles probing ahead, both strike forces reached the target without opposition. Before first light, the raiders were in position around the target—all was still quiet. Back in Umtali, two helicopter gunships and two casevac helicopters waited.

From their concealed positions, the raiders watched as the inmates of the camp went about their early morning activities. At 05h20, both strike forces moved in. They achieved complete surprise. The team swept through the base, gunning down sentries and blasting barrack buildings and huts. Supported by fire from the Hispano cannons and mortars, they brushed aside attempts at resistance. The base became a killing ground. The enemy who fled from the main thrust of the attack were caught by stop-line teams.

Within an hour, resistance was reduced to scattered pockets fighting back from the flimsy cover of buildings, and small groups trying to fight their way through to the safety of the bush. At 06h00, the helicopter K-Cars flew in to reinforce the raid but the ground attack had been so successful that their firepower was hardly used. The K-Cars circled the base eliminating survivors who were attempting to escape. Military Intelligence quickly collected all the documents and special weapons they could find, including a 12.7 Russian heavy machine gun. The casevac helicopters returned to base. They had not been needed on this occasion, any injuries sustained by the raiders being very slight. By 06h50, the operation was complete.

Leaving the camp, the strike force withdrew towards the main Tete road where they blew up the bridge across the Pungwe River to hold up any counter-attack. They then turned west and made their way back towards the border. Only six kilometres from the border, they passed through a village, which was guarded by Frelimo soldiers, who opened fire on them with mortars. Hunters were called in and strafed both the mortar positions and a 12.7mm anti-aircraft gun, which was firing from inside a roofless hut. There was a large explosion as the hut and a nearby ammunition store were hit.

Meanwhile, the security force column had become bogged down and were forced to make their own road back through the mountains. A helicopter brought in picks and shovels and flew out with a casualty, while a Lynx circled overhead giving the column instructions on the easiest way to proceed. It was now getting dark and the column were forced to spend the night and the following morning cutting, winching and digging their way towards the border, which they reached just after midday on Tuesday, 10th August.

Earlier that morning, a Canberra had been sent to make a reconnaissance run over the camp at Nyadzonya/Pungwe. The photographs showed hundreds of bodies in the devastated area.

On the security force side, two members of the column were reported missing. A Lynx carried out an air search of the last part of the evacuation route without success. It subsequently turned out that the two men, having been separated from the column at the camp had made their own way back by foot, crossing the border in the afternoon of Thursday 12th August, exhausted but unhurt.

As a result of this raid, Umtali came under rocket and mortar attack from Mozambique in the early hours of 11th August. The spasmodic fire lasted for about 30 minutes, bomb damage being inflicted on houses in Greenside and Darlington but there were no reported casualties. The inhabitants could see rocket and mortar fire interspersed with small arms and tracer bullets being exchanged across the border. Then just after 06h00, two Hunters swooped low over the city centre and patrolled up and down the border. The Cecil Hotel, in the centre of town, became a temporary evacuation centre for families from the affected areas. Border posts at Umtali and Vila Salazar were subjected to both rocket attack and small-arms fire and during the following week, two policemen were killed at the Nyamapanda border post.

Information had been received that ZANLA were making increasing use of the railway to move troops south into the Malvernia area. It was, therefore, decided that this line should be sabotaged and trains attacked. Small teams were dropped in by helicopter along the line of rail to place explosives that would derail trains. RPG-7s were also used to disable the locomotives.

Greater protection for airgunners

On 17th August 1976, Air Lieutenant Michael John Delport, was under operational instruction when his aircraft sustained considerable damage from ground fire during an attack on a terrorist target which resulted in the loss of roll control. The aircraft captain was injured during the attack and was forced to hand over control of the damaged aircraft to Air Lieutenant Delport during a critical stage of the attack. In spite of his limited experience on the aircraft type, he brought the crippled aircraft back to safe flight and nursed it back to base where he carried out a difficult landing. He was awarded Military Forces Commendation (Operational).

One of the crew members most at risk from small-arms ground fire was the air- gunner/technician on the helicopter. On 18th July 1976, Sergeant Pat Graham had been killed by fire from the ground. Another such incident occurred on 1st September when the FAF 7 fireforce was called out to the Matibi area after tracks of approximately 15 ZANLA members were picked up. At about 17h00 hours, the K-Car was running out of fuel when a contact took place. Unfortunately, Sergeant Herbert 'Beef' Belstead, a gunner in the K-Car, was hit in the contact. He was casevaced to Chiredzi Hospital but was dead on arrival. Peter Petter-Bowyer:

Airgunners were so difficult to protect without limiting their all important freedom of movement. I became involved in trying to solve this problem and succeeded to a large extent in my contacts with Robert Cleaves of Marina Del Rey, California. Robert acquired for me sample American SWAT vests suited to aircrew. Other items from the same source were Light Intensified Surveillance Viewers for night operations and Gyro-stabilized binoculars for air reconnaissance. The SWAT vests were a great improvement and actually saved a couple of gunners' lives. The trouble was that they were too expensive and slow in coming; which led to another project.

August 1976 saw several changes to No 3 Squadron. Pilots started Islander conversions and the first territorial pilots from Air Rhodesia and ATA (Air Trans-Africa) came across for refamiliarization on the Dakota.

There was an unfortunate occurrence on 23rd August when Alan Bradnick and Carlos da Silveira hit the power lines that cross the Sabi River north of Mutandahwe. They were lucky to be in a climbing attitude when it happened, otherwise it would have been a different story. The Dakota, although damaged, got back to Buffalo Range safely, even though it landed with one tyre punctured.

Frelimo becomes 'fair game'

At first, after Frelimo took over the government in Mozambique, efforts were made not to involve Frelimo forces in the war. However, it became increasingly obvious that Frelimo forces were actively supporting ZANLA and even engaging Rhodesian forces on their own account. One such occasion was the death, on 2nd September, of Flight Lieutenant Henry William 'Bill' Stevens flying Lynx 3414 in a hot-pursuit operation into Mozambique. A ZANLA group had infiltrated in the Inyanga North area where the mountain range dropped to flatter country drained by the Ruenya River. This group deliberately made its presence known and then withdrew, to draw Rhodesian forces across the border to a position where a large Frelimo force waited in ambush. Bill Stevens flew in to aid the ground forces that were in difficulties and was shot down by the Frelimo force. His aircraft crashed in flames along his attack line. His body was brought back by helicopter. During this incident, Detective Constable Aananude was wounded and Constable Nkube was killed.

FAF 7—hot weather

By this stage, at least one No 3 Squadron Dakota was stationed permanently at Buffalo Range for any duties that were needed. Often this aircraft flew long hours, for example on 4th September 1976: "Dakota Mike 3, Flight Lieutenant David Mallett as pilot, had a busy day starting at 06h40 with a fuel lift to Boli. Then to Devuli with five security force members and equipment uplifted from here. After lunch, the Dak went to Mutandahwe and Chisambanje to pick up trackers and dogs, then on to Malapati returning after sunset." This was a 12-hour day in somewhat uncomfortable flying conditions as FAF 7 Diary for 20th September points out, "Very hot weather 36/37°C on the ground. Darrel Squance confirmed a temp of 100 degrees F in the aircraft while flying."

And as the Diary goes on to confirm, the action could also be hot: "At 21h30 terrs opened rocket and small-arms fire on rancher Derek Henning at Ngwane Ranch, south-east of Lake MacDougal. The bedroom was extensively damaged. Henning was not in the room at the time and was unhurt. He returned the fire from a defensive position and kept the terrs at bay until a Lynx arrived and dropped illuminating flares."

The last week of the month proved very busy for the men at FAF 7. On 23rd September 1976 at about 12h30, a defence force vehicle hit a land-mine. Two G-Cars with trackers and one security force stick were sent to investigate. The helicopters were about one kilometre off line as they approached the scene. As they banked to go into the area, they were subjected to intense and accurate ground fire. A K-Car was deployed into the area immediately and engaged a group of about 15 insurgents. A lengthy contact ensued with follow-up troops being deployed by Dakota to Mutandahwe airstrip. Fuel and ammunition were also ferried in so that the helicopters could refuel and rearm at Mutandahwe. Despite this, one helicopter ran out of fuel in the contact area and another helicopter ferried fuel to him. The final count on this operation was seven killed and one captured.

Then a week later, at 10h15 on 30th September, FAF 7 was requested to get the fireforce airborne for a contact between a call sign and a group of about 20 terrorists. The fireforce was dispatched and the Dakota followed some ten minutes later when it returned from its re-supply task. The first contact with the insurgents occurred almost immediately. The G-Cars opened fire on a group of about ten men. The aircraft were subjected to extremely heavy ground-to-air fire. Leon du Plessis had a close shave when he was hit in the side and back by shrapnel. Cocky Benecke and Mick Delport were also involved. Benecke's Lynx was hit with five rounds, three in the starboard wing and two through tanks. One round hit the port boom and one went through the port wing entering the flap and exiting at the trailing edge of the main plane but the pilot managed to land the aircraft safely back at FAF 7.

The Rutenga fireforce officer commanding, and a Lynx from Chipinga were called in to help. They arrived at about 12h30. At 13h00, the SAS called for a paradrop and a Dakota carried out three static-line drops.

These men arrived at 15h30 and by 16h10, the SAS had been deployed as a stopline to prevent the ZANLA men exiting to Mozambique.

Next morning, there was a 05h30 take-off for all the aircraft except one K-Car and one G-Car. The troops were deployed into the area of the contact made the day before. One K-Car acted as top cover and the Lynx carried out reconnaissance. The Dakota left to take fuel to Chipinda Pools and lift a Selous Scout troop out. The G-Cars ferried troops into the area of 22

Delta for the Selous Scouts. The Dakota was in the middle of a trooping task for the police when the pilot was called back to ferry SAS members to Malapati for a very urgent task. Unfortunately after a long day's work by the pilots, the whole exercise was called off. The Dakota was back on ground at 19h30. Final tally for the two-day operation was 28 enemy confirmed dead.

The South African government withdraws its helicopters

During August, in an attempt to force the pace of détente with the black nationalist leaders, the South African government withdrew 26 of the 40 helicopters, which had been on loan to Rhodesia. Fifty pilots and technicians were also recalled. This placed an intolerable strain on Rhodesia's small group of helicopters and led to a greater use of Dakotas for transporting troops. Obviously, a Dakota could not land in the kind of areas that could be used by helicopters but they could drop greater numbers of parachute troops. One drawback to the normal paradrop was that the troops were vulnerable to fire from the ground as they drifted down and, depending on the wind conditions, they could find themselves widely dispersed. It was, therefore, decided to train RAR soldiers in the art of free fall. The first such jump occurred in September 1976.

Parachute Training School, September 1976

2	Dakota 7053	Flt Lt Smith	No 61 Basic. First jump
3	Dakota 7053	Flt Lt Bradnick	PJ1 Demo at Gatooma for No 3 Squadron
7	Dakota 7313	Flt Lt Ward	No 16 Basic. African free fall. First descent by Sergeant Chikonda
8	Dakota 7313	Flt Lt Russell	No 16 Basic free fall. Second descent
9	Dakota 7313	Flt Lt Culpan	No 61 Basic. A long way away
10	Dakota 7053	Flt Lt Lynch	No 61 Basic fall. Another long walk back
17	Dakota 7034	Flt Lt Russell	RSM turns slow and jerky
17	Dakota 7034	Flt Lt da Silveira	RSM again same trouble
23	Dakota 7313	Flt Lt Barbour	Follow Corp Stephen. Not too good
24	Dakota 7053	Flt Lt d'Hotman	No 16 Basic. At end
28	Dakota 7034	Flt Lt Mallett	After RSM. All over the place

The Parachute Training School was run and staffed by the Rhodesian Air Force, but the pupils were army personnel. There were nine instructors, and only 24 trainees were accepted at a time. The basic static line course took three weeks. The free-fall course lasted a month and enabled the parachutist to drop, in full combat kit, into the operational area from a far greater height—an obvious advantage in counter-insurgency work. In one trial, the officer commanding the Parachute Training School himself did a descent from 15,000 feet into a well-populated part of a reserve at 2 pm—and until the last few seconds before he landed, was not noticed by a single person. Another benefit of free falling was that the parachutist could control the direction of his drop. In its 15 years of existence, a total of 25,000 descents had been carried out, with one death and only a few minor injuries.

It was in this month, September, that Connie Cousins made her first official jump with the air force. She was a member of the Rhodesian Women's Service and worked in the Safety Equipment section as a parachute packer. Like any other parachute packer, she claimed and was given the right to jump. At this stage, about 40 women were serving with the air force. After training, they were employed on radio communications work, air control and as photographers processing air survey films, acting as ground photographers and specializing in industrial photography. They became known as the Blue birds and were able to make a full-time career in the force if they wished.

The technical wing

One of the most vital parts of any air force is the technical wing and this was particularly so with the Rhodesian Air Force, which by 1976 had to rely on the ingenuity of its own technical staff to make-do and mend the elderly aircraft it was flying. Technicians allotted to each of the seven squadrons dealt with the immediate requirements and problems of their units and attained a serviceability of over 90% in most squadrons. A Hunter, fresh in from the operational area could be serviced and re-armed in six minutes.

The technical wing, in addition to overseeing all work done on squadrons, included the Aircraft Servicing Squadron where complex servicing, renovation, rebuilding and modifications were carried out. Ninety-five percent of the all-important tools in the Engine Room Repair Section were designed locally and made in the machine shop at New Sarum. Apprentices attended No 1 Ground Training School (Technical) where they completed a five-week course in drill, weapon-training and air force history and administration. After this, each apprentice began his five-year tuition in his chosen trade: engines, airframes, electrics, instruments, radio or armaments. The pattern of training varied according to the trade.

Twenty-eight kills in the south-east

The month of September ended with a boost for air force morale. Until this date, the record kill had been 19 with one capture, in the Mount Darwin area. Intelligence had been received that a large group of insurgents would be crossing in the Gonarezhou area later in September. Efforts had been made to intercept this cadre but with no success. Major Nick Fawcett as OC RAR was the fireforce commander and his troops were based on the airfield at FAF 7. The SAS were deployed not far from Gonarezhou and were doing their own quiet thing there but were available should they be needed. The Grey's Scouts were also in the area, on the Mozambique border of Gonarezhou looking for tracks.

A wide swathe of countryside had been cleared all along the border and because the soil was sandy, it was impossible for a group of infiltrators to obliterate their footprints. Only wind or rain could do that. Consequently, when the Grey's Scouts came across the tracks of 100 men who had apparently crossed during the night, the alarm was raised. It was 30th September.

Pete Simmonds who was with No 7 Squadron at FAF 7 takes up the story:

> *We received a call saying that the Greys were close on the heels of the group, and that a sighting was imminent. We got airborne knowing that there wasn't much we could do against 100 terrs with only one fireforce. We requested the Rutenga choppers to join us as fast as they could but they were busy and took a while arriving. It took a while to get down to the Gonarezhou and the G-Cars had to refuel at the Browns' camp on the way. We flew direct in the K-Car as we had nearly two hours of fuel. We established radio contact with the Grey's Scouts only to find that they had come to a stop and were calmly watching the terr group.* (Pete Simmonds)

Pete McCabe also played a part in this operation—as the K-Car gunner.

> *The atmosphere in the K-Car was electric as we listened to the Grey's Scout whispering to us on the radio. Two of them were following the terrs on foot while the other 20 had stayed behind with the horses. The advance trackers were so close that they could read the slogan on the back of the last terr's t-shirt.* (Pete McCabe)

> *I remember being astonished that such a large group of enemy soldiers could be completely unaware that they were being watched from such a short distance. The terrain was flat and the Scouts had their horses to keep quiet. They had been following tracks since first light and their*

horses were very tired and thirsty. I couldn't believe our luck that they had found this huge group in an uninhabited piece of country where the bush wasn't too thick and there would be no need to worry about locals getting in the way. I was talked onto the target by a casual, relaxed Grey's Scout leader and immediately on arrival overhead, at about 1,000 feet, all 100 terrs opened up on us. The noise of gunfire was deafening and pretty scary. (Pete Simmonds)

When we finally burst onto the scene, it was like the start of the Comrades Marathon. Fortunately, in their initial reaction to shoot back, all the terrs stayed in bunches. This increased the ground fire but made our job easier. We had about 20 minutes to ourselves before any other aircraft showed up. (Pete McCabe)

The terrs then started to bombshell. Fortunately, I had an old stalwart, Pete McCabe, looking after the K-Car cannon. He made every one of the 20mm rounds count, while Nick Fawcett and I deployed our troops. The Grey's Scouts were to the west and therefore were able to act as a large stop group, but a bush fire, which was started by our K-Car ammo, and fanned by the prevailing wind, was travelling towards them. Ironically, it was this fire that prevented the terrs from escaping westward, but it also meant that the Greys were unable to join in the fight from that side when we sorely needed them. When the other G-Cars arrived, they positioned their troops to the north, east and south, and we arranged for fuel and ammo to be dropped nearby. Pockets of terrs were now spread everywhere and Pete Mac selected his targets. The return fire was heavy and even at 1,000 feet we picked up a few rounds through the fuselage and one through the blades. Once the initial commotion had subsided, we settled down to the task of eliminating the smaller groups that had gone to ground. I asked Cocky Benecke in the Lynx to have a go at a group of terrs. He had been flying around the outside of my orbit watching the punch-up develop. Anyone who ever operated with Cocky will know that he was never slow in coming forward in the most dangerous situations. He came in firing his rockets and guns. As he pulled out, his aircraft was badly shot up. He turned in again nonchalantly and promptly laid down another accurate burst with the rest of his ammo. Every aircraft was shot at that day. Cocky's Lynx was like a colander and he had a nasty fuel leak that forced him to return immediately to base. We refuelled and rearmed close to the scene. The pockets of resistance were now few and far between and the area around the contact was saturated with our troops. It was great to watch them chasing the enemy through the bush and around anthills. It was now 15h30, more that two hours after the initial contact, and so when Bill Sykes arrived on the scene, Simmo requested him to drop his troops about 12 miles ([9.2km] away to act as stop groups for any fleeing insurgents. To his surprise, Bill spotted a lone enemy soldier sheltering beneath a tree. His tech, Garry Whittal, opened fire. This lone terr turned out to be part of a group of ten who then went to ground by a large anthill. Our own troops were on the other side of this anthill only about seven metres away. This made it extremely difficult for us to open fire from the K-Car without hitting our own men. Grenades were being flung about by both sides and everyone seemed to be shooting but getting nowhere. The job was eventually completed by our guys on the ground in very dangerous circumstances. Before last light, SAS troops were dropped along the border to catch any of the enemy trying to cross back into Mozambique during the night. The following day, the contact area was swept. The score was about 28 with some captures. Major Grahame Wilson (SAS) was the army commander on the ground. He had been in charge of his own mission elsewhere when we called for help, and as was usual with him, he had to get involved himself rather than send his troops. He and his men opened fire a few times that day but he was magnanimous in saying that he had done little more than clear up after the blue jobs. In fact, none of it would have happened without a very professional Grey's Scout call sign who initiated the whole thing and did a fine job in tracking. (Pete Simmonds)

The picture of the lone terr is still vivid—a single tree, no other cover of any sort, with our terr trying to keep the tree between himself and the chopper. The scene was exactly like the cowboy movies, where the baddy in the saloon is made to dance to the tune of a six-gun. Gary kept firing but we kept getting stoppages. Every time our gun stopped, the terr would stand and fire back at us, which was very unnerving when you are at 30 feet and only 100 metres away. Our tracers had started a small fire at the base of the tree and this spread outwards encircling him. Simmo spotted the terr before I had finished taking him on. A few 20mm rounds and he was gone. We must have dangerously exceeded our red light fuel limit when we landed in the bush a few miles from the contact. And there we sat as a 'stop group' for a few hours with our twin .303s pointing into the tall grass for the rest of the afternoon until some kind pilot threw a drum of fuel at us, gave us the 'twos-up', covered us in dust and disappeared over the horizon. When we got back to Salisbury, they asked us how many we had killed. I choked on the word 'We'. 'They' got 28. (Bill Sykes)

A *clean* Trojan. No weapons hanging off it, no white 'T' on top. Things were about to change ...

Flying a Provost in and out of the clouds on a hazy afternoon was pure delight.

OC No 7 Squadron, Sqn Ldr Norman Walsh shows his pride and delight at winning the Jacklin Trophy. The squadron pilots and technicians are equally pleased. From left: Flt Lt Mick Grier ('A' Flight commander), Bernie Collocott, Cpl Tech Johnny Ness, Tinker Smithdorf, Sqn Ldr Norman Walsh, Johnny Norman, Flt Lt Ian Harvey, Flt Lt Peter Petter-Bowyer ('B' Flight commander). 1968.

Above left: Two RAR casualties are flown out from *Op Hurricane*, November 1974. The Alouette III has ample room for two lying and two sitting patients, with the attachment points for drips.

Below left: They said that even if we managed to get all 12 Hunters to Rhodesia we would never be able to get all 12 airborne at the same time! The air force managed to put up many Diamond Nines during the next 18 years, and in 1980, even after having lost three Hunters over the years, a Diamond Nine flew over the Opening of the Zimbabwe-Rhodesia Parliament.

Above right: *Our wings are as a fortress to our land.* The badge came about when the crown was replaced with the historical emblem of the lion and tusk.

Below right: Not much to commend it aesthetically on the ground, the T 11 certainly came into its own once airborne.

RRAF 7307, *Chaminuka* arrives home after yet another successful cloud-seeding sortie. The Silver Iodide dispensers can be clearly seen on the underside of the rear fuselage. The rugged Dak, an old faithful of so many countries over so many decades. The drone of the Pratt and Whitneys still has enthusiasts running outdoors to see history pass slowly by.

Named after the local rain god, Chaminuka the Rain Maker displays one of its Silver Iodide dispensers. Having to punch through turbulent thunderclouds to seed them, many pilots heaved a sigh of relief when Chaminuka crashed and was written off.

Prime Minister Ian Smith alights from the VIP Dakota and shakes hands with General John Hickman at one of the forward airfields. Assistant Commissioner Bill Buchanan was the senior police representative.

The Portuguese town of Chioco on the southern edge of the Ruia River. The Rhodesian Air Force helicopters operated from here in 1969/70.

Sqn Ldr Norman Walsh was the pilot of this Alouette III that hit a bird. It went through the left windscreen hitting the technician in the chest and knocking him out––the consequences would have been different had it entered the pilot's side.

The Minister of Defence Jack Howman studies the new Rhodesian Air Force roundel at the request of AVM Archie Wilson while WO Cedric Herbert, the artist, awaits his approval.

Air Lieutenants Chris Wentworth and Bill Sykes on the No 2 Squadron Detachment in Bulawayo. Two years later Chris was to do the perfect *wheels up* landing at Salisbury.

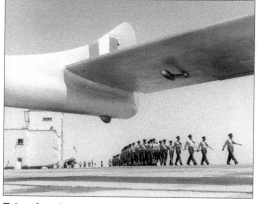

Taken from beneath the silver tail of a Vampire T 11, a parade of General Service Unit members swings round in front of New Sarum Headquarters. 1962

A beat-up by a Dakota is fun for those in the air, but is an awesome experience for those on the ground.

Eight Canberras of No 5 Squadron fly majestically down Jameson Avenue. All of the squadrons were within four seconds of their allotted time over Rhodes's statue.

The first Alouette III crash was a shock to the whole force in that two of its most professional men, Sqn Ldr Gordon Nettleton and Flt Lt Mike Hill, lost their lives. The crash occurred on the ring road to New Sarum close to the main gate. The cause of the accident was never formally established.

This study of the Dakota was the result of a Trade Test Board. The calibre of air force photographers was never in doubt.

Above: Members of 'C' Squadron Rhodesian SAS jump from three Dakotas of No 3 Squadron, September 1967.

Right: Formation aerobatics was banned soon after the fatal Colin Graves crash in 1960. 'Thornhill 72' was the closest the squadrons ever came to reviving the art. The six Vampires of No. 2 Squadron performed formation changes, steep wing-overs and high 'g' manoeuvres to the delight of the crowd and to the immense satisfaction of the pilots. But very hard work without power controls.

Nine Hunters climb to height out of Thornhill to position for a flypast over Salisbury.

The Portuguese Alouette IIIs operated in conjunction with the helicopters from No. 7 Squadron in Mozambique in the late '60s.

Twelve Vampires climb steadily out from Thornhill to position over Salisbury for the flypast. All the squadrons put up as many aircraft as possible.

'Tanks on - tanks off' - the technicians' nightmare. Easily transportable drop tanks await fitment at Thornhill.

A Vampire T 11 is towed off the main Salisbury runway into New Sarum after a wheels- up landing in October 1971. There was minimal damage, the gun doors were replaced and the aircraft was flying again a few days later. Flt Lt Chris Wentworth was the pilot.

Above right: The business end of the 68 millimetre Matra Rocket Pod fit on the Hunter FGA 9. The 18 rockets could be fired singly or in salvo. The weapon was used extensively throughout the bush war.

Right: 'Seek and Squeak' was a parody on the No. 4 Squadron motto 'Seek and Strike'.

Medic Air Lieutenant Mike Strauss receives from Mrs Walker, resuscitation equipment donated by the SA-Rhodesia Association who assisted greatly in the humanitarian side of the conflict.

A special stretcher (air mattress) that allowed an even distribution of weight for the patient along its length was donated by the Moths Committee for Hospitalised Troops to the RLI and the Air Force. Dr Cliff Webster (Major) of the RLI demonstrates the equipment.

Training on armoured cars took place in Bloemfontein in the Orange Free State. The Air Force were initially equipped with the Mark IVs which came up by train in 1972. These were replaced by the Mark Vs, but after Independence in 1980 were all returned to South Africa.

An armoured car with Sergeant Taylor and Air Lt Alan Dewsbury. Sergeant Paul Hill is driving.

One very useful accessory to the medical equipment was the mountain rescue stretcher, being admired here by the Donor, and Flt Lt Cocky Benecke and Squadron Leader Ed Potterton, OC 7 Squadron.

The armoured car with its low centre of gravity could negotiate most terrrain. Here the crews are on a training course at Inkomo Range.

The armoured cars were integral parts of the defence of the forward airfields.

Even on the ground the Hunter combines grace with aggression.

The assorted weaponry of the armoured fighting vehicle on display.

Air Lieutenant Ginger Baldwin taxies out of New Sarum, June 1972.

A Canberra flies past at Thornhill '72 with its wheels down.

Thornhill '72 was a most successful Open Day in which all the Air Force aircraft took part. The Canberra on static display has been fitted with the Rhodesian designed "Dimple" (Haig) nose cone.

No 1 Squadron Colours Parade, Thornhill. Air Vice-Marshal A.O.G. Wilson takes the salute. Steve Murray carries the colours.

The immaculate formation on parade in front of the Town House, Salisbury.

The Rhodesian Air Force parades its Colours through the streets of Salisbury on 28th November 1972.

An Alouette III about to get airborne at Centenary in 1972.

This aerial photograph of Centenary airfield shows just how few aircraft the Air Force put into the field in the early days of the war - two Provs, two Trojans for operations and a PRAW. And two armoured cars for airfield defence. The building was private hangar loaned to the Air Force. 1972.

Above: A Trojan flies off on a task while the other Trog, and two Provs armed with Frantans, remain on stand-by.

Above: The scene from the ground viewed through the hatch of one of the armoured cars.

Left: The Yellow Devil was the insignia for the Provosts. There was one painted on every tailplane.

And with sudden but not entirely unexpected 'crunch' (with apologies to Uncle Roger, *Flight* magazine.) The Aircraft Servicing Flight (ASF) recovery team salvage a South African Alouette III that hit a tree with its tail rotor in the bush near Wankie, 1973. Air Lt Terry Eaton with, amongst others: Craig Moore, Tony Cobbett, Geoff Cuttler, Errol Sheasby, Rob Sweeting, Nick Tselentis and Jerry Tasker.

The armoured car crews were always a cheery bunch. Centenary December 1972.

New Sarum has increased its security by erecting a fence between the main Salisbury runway and the Air Force base. 1973. Before the end of the war this will be increased to a high earth wall. On the 3 Squadron hardstand are a Canberra, two Hunters and a Vampire displaying their weapons capabilities for visiting army units. Among the six Dakotas are the Beech Baron and a Trojan.

An Alouette III picks up troops near the confluence of the Mazoe and Nyagui rivers, Shmava, north-east Rhodesia. 1973.

The technician/gunner leans out over his .303 in typical pose, warning the pilot of any obstacles that might damage the tail rotor on landing. Shamva area, May 1973.

Refuelling places were situated throughout the entire country. In the operational areas they were no more than 20 minutes' flying time apart.

The Devil finds work for idle hands - there was a lot of spare time in the bush ... The control tower at FAF 4.

The Hunter gunpack was designed to be replaced as a unit. The gunpacks were belted up with 540 rounds of 30 millimetre for the four Aden cannons, in the Station armoury before being taken to the squadron. To change the gunpack on a Hunter took less than five minutes.

An Alouette III with South African Police on board moves slowly along the Zambezi River gorge near Victoria Falls, looking for the bodies of the Canadian girls shot by Zambian soldiers from the opposite bank. 18th May 1973.

Major servicing of aircraft was a necessity. A Vampire T 11 is stripped down to bare essentials before being repaired, repainted and put back onto operations.

A Trojan at one of the Forward Air Fields. The exhaust shroud can just be made out above the nose wheel and the stain from the exhaust gas is clearly visible on the fuselage.

An Alouette III at one of the FAFs. Notice the security lights on the poles. These were to prevent the enemy from seeing into the camp, but to the more skeptical occupants it meant 'Here is where to put your mortars!'

The Provost was an ideal light strike/army coop aircraft. The pilot, with parachute, is about to fly off in support of ground troops, or to do top cover, recce or telstar. Its armament is 37mm rockets, Frantan and twin .303 front gun.

The view from the No 2 position in the formation off helicopters flying off to a 'scene' in the operational area.

An Alouette comes in to land at FAF 4, Mount Darwin. 1974. The chopper in the foreground shows its Bekker Homer aerials to good effect. The aerials were also a perfect place to keep the windscreen cleaning cloth.

Above: The Alouette sports its twin .303 Browning machine guns as it flies overhead.

Left: Free-fall training high over Rhodesia. Frank Hales uses a camera to record the performance of the paratroopers. The drawbacks were the strain on his neck when the 'chute opened, and that the 16mm film was only developed after the student had done further jumps.

The Leonides 550 hp nine cylinder Provost engine has its own distinctive roar as the pilot puts on full power and gets the tail up. The Provost, armed with rockets takes off from Centenary airfield. December 1972.

The Parachute School Instructors land safely at one of the many display jumps.

The Parachute Training School Instructors with (possibly) SAS on completion of their basic Para Course, 1972. Seated, from left - Charlie Buchan, Derek de Kock, Frank Hales, Ian Bowen. Front - 'Fred Bear' (the Drifter, with parachute). Fred, who had done too many fatal jumps was eventually replaced by 'Barbear', named after David Barbour, one of the VR pilots.

A more formal photograph of members of the Parachute Training School on the occasion of Kevin Milligan qualifying as a PJI, 19th September 1974. From left - Kevin Milligan, Ian Bowen, Squadron Leader Derek deKock, Mike Wiltshire, Ralph Moore, John Boynton, Dennis 'Charlie' Buchan, Frank Hales. Front - Sergeant Fred Bear in No 1 Dress with Wings.

The rugged, reliable Islander proved its worth. The short field performance in and out of bush strips doing courier, casevac or re-supply made it a useful adjunct the Force.

The original MAG machine gun with a rate of fire of only 650 rounds per minute soon became obsolete in the escalating bush war. It was replaced with the .303 Browning which had a rate of fire of 1,200 rounds per minute. Even when the twin Brownings were introduced it still remained largely a defensive weapon.

With the sun in their eyes on final approach to Centenary Air Field, neither instructor nor pupil noticed the recent earthworks at the threshold. The Provost's undercarriage legs were torn off and the aircraft skidded to a halt only feet from the parked helicopters.

Only accessible by helicopter, this pinnacle was an ideal place for a relay station or an OP. It is situated to the east of Marymount Mission in the north-east of Rhodesia. January 1975.

The .303 Browning machine guns mounted above the mainplane of the Lynx was yet another successful Rhodesian Air Force design and implementation.

The Internal Affairs keeps were a common sight for pilots flying around the north and north-eastern operational areas. They provided secure refuelling points for the helicopters.

The subsequent colours party went on into the wee hours.

For outstanding achievement—No3 Squadron are awarded their Colours at a ceremony at New Sarum on 8th April 1975. In the foreground is Squadron Leader George Alexander, Officer Commanding No 3 Squadron. No 1 Squadron did not have time to practise the difficult Figure 3 formation so it was decided to do a simple Roman III. Comment from one of the pilots: "Judging from the photograph we should have attempted the former!"

The Psyops war had its proponents and its detractors. The chiefs or the local population were gathered to listen to talks on the superiority of the Rhodesian forces. These exercises culminated in authorized low-level beat-ups by the Hunters, with few objections from the pilots. The Hunters were used on occasions to *plant* sonic booms on the crowds. 1976.

OC No 7 Squadron, Sqn Ldr Eddy Wilkinson is presented with the Jacklin Trophy by Deputy Minister of Defence, Mr Ted Sutton-Price, at New Sarum on 15th May 1975.

Above left: A/L Pete Simmonds takes Alan (Paddy) Gray, *The Herald* photographer, for a public relations photo-shoot in the Alouette II. The photo was taken by Paddy.

Left: Prime Minister Ian Smith is welcomed aboard the Rhodesian Air Force VIP Dakota at New Sarum, by the captain, Flight Lieutenant John Matthews.

A scene enacted countless times throughout the Bush War—choppers coming in to land in a Communal Land mealie field. Centenary North, 1975.

The Alouette IIs were loaned to No 7 Squadron by the SAAF for flying training, an agreement that alleviated the pressure on Alouette IIIs, allowing them to fight the Bush War.

Rolling take-offs made transition with a heavy load much easier although it was not recommended for rough, dirt airstrips as the nose oleos were not strengthened. This dramatic picture shows two Alouettes using this technique to get airborne with full troops on a narrow tar road in the bush. December 1975

Fitted with full anti-strela kit, Dakota 7307 *Chaminuka* displays its hot exhaust gas dispersal tubes below the wings, and the drab, low infra-red signature paint scheme.

A simple thing like brake failure has reduced this aircraft to scrap metal.

This Cessna 421 was purchased in 1975 to fulfil the light VIP role. Flown in by Sqn Ldr George Alexander and Flt Lt John Matthews, it suffered from continual unserviceabilities and had flown only 766 hours when it was sold in 1981.

The Provost stands proud, having done its duty in defence of its country for so many years. These aircraft were withdrawn from operational service after their airframe hours, which had been extended to the limit, eventually expired.

An interception exercise proved to the new pilots on No 1 Squadron, just how difficult it was to shoot down the massive Canberra at low level. Although the Hunters have the speed, the Canberras easily out-turn the fighters and watch derisively as they sail past without even getting a bead on the bombers. A photographer was standing by to catch the impromptu flypast on their return to New Sarum.

The night stops in Durban were always enjoyed by the pilots and were often extended to a second night due to a 'technical fault'.

The Cessna 185, on loan from the SAAF, in less visible plumage than the polished aluminium of before. One of the more notable pilots of this aircraft was Harry Morris who, from 1977 to 1979, accumulated over 500 hours flying as a volunteer with no military commitment. He was 54 when he was awarded the Commander's Commendation.

Left: Prime Minister Ian Smith presents the miniature dustbin trophy to Flt Lt Tony Oakley who obtained the best weapons results on No 1 Squadron. 17th May 1978. Flt Lt Vic Wightman, on the right, was to become the next No 1 Squadron commander.

Above left: Grant Domoney and Mickie Joss arm up the Lynx with 68 millimetre rockets, which packed a much greater punch than the 37 millimetre rockets on the inboard pylon.

Above right: No 4 Squadron invades the hardstand at New Sarum with Lynxes, in preparation for an external operation.

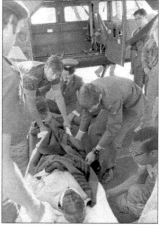

Wing Cdr Wally Hinrichs and Air Cdre Chris Dams study the damage to *That Jungle Dustbin,* which was placed at Kutanga Range and fired at by Sqn Ldr Rich Brand from a Hunter.

Army and air force medics make Mr James Mukwisiri from Mt Selinda comfortable before flying him to Salisbury in a Trojan, June 1976.

No 7 Squadron flies in cross formation down Jameson Avenue.

Sgt Hans Steyn, the technician, is well placed to attend to the needs of a stretcher case flown in from the operational area. Pete Simmonds looks on. The single MAG machine gun is shown to good effect.

At a refuelling point in the middle of nowhere—a K-Car and three G-Cars on stand-by.

Flt Lt E.O. 'Ted' Lunt and 'Beef' Belstead return from an operation in the K-Car. Note the technician's goggles on his flying helmet and his ammo pouch and water bottle.

A technician inspects the weapons pods under the port wing of a Lynx on readiness at a forward airfield. The fuel pump in the foreground was electrically driven and was a useful accessory for refuelling the fixed wing aircraft, especially the Dakotas.

CHAPTER 42

Attack on Madulo Pan

The South African government's hopes for a détente with Black Africa had come to nothing and early in 1976, the South African prime minister approached America for help in normalizing the situation. Henry Kissinger, then United States Secretary of State, began a spell of his famous shuttle diplomacy. He visited President Nyerere in Dar es Salaam and President Kaunda in Lusaka. And he met President Vorster twice, once in June 1976 and again in September. These talks resulted in a master plan for peace in southern Africa but no details were given.

On 14th September 1976, Ian Smith went to Pretoria for a meeting with Kissinger and Vorster. Following this meeting, it was announced that majority rule would come about in two years and that an interim government would be established to work out a new constitution. Meanwhile Robert Mugabe, in Lusaka, said that ZANU and ZAPU were working towards establishing a united military front. The news of the Kissinger proposals and their acceptance caused a certain amount of alarm and despondency in certain quarters in Rhodesia and Air Marshal McLaren felt it necessary to brief his senior officers.

The briefing was held at New Sarum and was attended by all senior officers of both main stations, Air HQ Staff and all operational commanders from the air detachment and forward airfields. The details of the proposals and the gist of the commander's remarks were then made available in further briefings at unit level so that all officers, NCOs airmen, reservists and RWS members were aware of the situation before the prime minister made the proposals public in radio and television broadcasts. The commander emphasized that the air force was not in any way being asked to accept or reject the proposals. "You are all aware that we have no political function whatsoever," he said. "The prime minister has accepted on our behalf, a package deal, which he believes can provide for a just and peaceful settlement. Our role is to combine with the police and the army in maintaining law and order and stability within Rhodesia, whilst the politicians sort things out. It has been made clear to all parties," said the commander, "that the prime minister's acceptance of the proposed package is conditional on the cessation of terrorist activity. If all those involved in the negotiations leading up to the Pretoria meetings keep their word, then we should expect an end to large-scale incursions from neighbouring countries. However, past experience has shown that we would be very wise not to assume any reduction in terrorist activity for the time being." (Bateleur, November issue 1976)

Dealing with the question of change to the structure or conditions of service of the defence force, the commander emphasized that no changes were envisaged for the immediate future. "We will go on as at present," he said. "We have a duty to Rhodesia, which will not change in the interim period of constitutional negotiations. All present conditions of service and engagements will remain in effect unless the Council of State introduces some constitutional amendment."

Far from decreasing, the terrorist war stepped up, and by early spring incidents became an almost daily event, with gangs rocketing farms, Europeans and Africans being ambushed and killed, attacks made on black policemen, and mines being laid.

Help from the skies came in many forms and was warmly appreciated by the recipients!

No 4 Squadron Diary, October 1976:

Ed Potterton dropped flares over a farm that terrs were attacking, forcing them to break off the attack. The grateful farmer and his wife presented him with a bottle of black and white, which must have put paid to the rest of his stand-by.

No 3 Squadron Diary for September and October saw continued operational effort. Pilots were few and far between in Salisbury. On 7th October, a Dakota was hit while dropping paratroops but only a battery was damaged. Also in October, helicopters were carrying more four-footed friends, this time sharp-nosed fox terriers, animals that the dog section was experimenting with for follow-up operations.

Contact at FAF 1

As the war moved south, so the north-eastern border area saw less action. By October 1976, one of the perks of serving with No 7 Squadron was to get a rest and recuperation trip for two weeks to FAF 1 (Wankie). This assignment meant a chance to do normal bush flying without the stress of fireforce call-outs. Squadron Leader Gordon Wright was the FAF commander and the only trips the pilots had to do were the odd trooping tasks for 1 Independent company who were busy training the territorials.

So it was that Chris Dickinson arrived at Wankie on Friday 1st October looking forward to a restful two weeks:

My tech, Mike Rochat, checked out the resident G-Car and put our flying kit ready for take-off on Monday. On Saturday, Mike and I had permission from Gordon Wright to go to the Wankie Show. "But you had better take a radio just in case we need you," Gordon had added. We laughed. At about 16h00 we got a call to return to FAF 1. Apparently, a call sign had come across suspicious tracks and felt that they needed support. Remember that this was FAF 1 where there were supposedly no gooks. The call sign, needless to say, was in a truck, not on foot. Gordon decided to fly there in his Cessna 185 and instructed Mike and me to follow in the G-Car. There was an experienced Scout tracker team in training at 1 Indep so we decided to take them along just in case. Gordon meanwhile was overhead the call sign, which was midway between Kamativi Mine and Wankie National Airport. We bundled along in our G-Car and eventually got to the area. After some animated R/T chatter with the TF call sign I dropped our Scout trackers. They reported that it looked like terrs. I then uplifted them to search for a likely line of flight. There was a deserted school some three kilometres ahead and I told the tracker team I would drop them there so that they could do a 360. The landing at the school was uneventful but as I lifted off, I heard the shout, "Contact, contact!" The terrs had been hiding in one of the classrooms. Pandemonium—Gordon Wright was trying to get a word in, the TF call signs wanted to know what was happening and Mike was saying that he had the terrs visual running down a path. We pulled up into orbit and I told Mike to open fire. And that's when it all became terribly amusing—Mike had consumed a couple of beers at the show and consequently his aim was not all that great. In addition, I don't think the gun sight on the MAG had been zeroed for some time and the rounds were going everywhere except near the terrs. Added to which, these weren't the type of gooks we had been used to—these guys were

ZIPRA trained in conventional warfare. As we fired at them, two of them would run, while the other two would take aim and direct some fairly useful ground fire at the G-Car. This made Mike all the more determined to try to hit them but to no avail. This cat and mouse game went on for quite a while with stray rounds flying all over the place and with the tracker team now in full pursuit. Then the telltale red light on the fuel gauge started to flicker. The nearest place was Wankie National and we had to leave the scene. After refuelling, it was too dark to continue, so we flew the 45-minute night trip back to FAF 1. The trackers remained in the area but the terrs had crossed the main Kamativi tar road and so tracks were lost. It was later discovered that the ZIPRA group had been on a recce in the area looking for support from the locals. When Mike got back to the squadron, the other techs gave him a really hard time for not even hitting one gook with 800 rounds. Although we were not particularly successful in our efforts to reduce the number of insurgents, we were very proud that the air strike report that went to Air HQ from FAF 1 was 'Air Strike Report Number One'. (Chris Dickinson)

The Genets arrive

In October 1976, 17 SIAI-Marchetti SF 260 C aircraft arrived in the country and a short while later a further consignment was received of SF 260 Ws. These machines were given the name Genet and were purchased to replace the Provost aircraft for basic training. The latter, the military version, were named Warrior and could carry armaments. These aircraft were ideal for providing top cover for the road convoys running between Fort Victoria and Beitbridge.

Whether it was complete but disassembled aircraft, spares or ammunition, all equipment now had to come in through South Africa. Sometimes the trucks would drive from Rhodesia to Durban and collect the material, in which case they would all be painted with a bogus South African company logo and address. They also carried two number plates so that a switch could be made at the border. The Genets were transported by rail from Durban to Pietersburg and collected from Pietersburg by the Rhodesian Air Force.

Meanwhile the air force had purchased an old tobacco barn at an auction and erected it at New Sarum, as far away from prying eyes as was possible. The mysterious crates were brought in under cover of darkness. The Genets were assembled under the strictest security, even to the extent that flight-testing was carried out late at night or very early in the morning. So, when these new aircraft suddenly appeared in the skies it was a complete surprise.

Fatal accident at Kutanga Range

On 21st October 1976, Flight Lieutenant Roy Hulley, of No 1 Squadron took part in weapons training at Kutanga Range. No one can be sure of exactly what happened on that day. Hulley turned his Vampire in for the attack, went down in a dive and delivered his weapon all in the normal way. He pulled out and turned downwind to position himself for the next attack. On downwind he rolled wings level. Then, for some unknown reason he commenced a shallow descent, suddenly banked right and crashed into the trees (narrowly missing an army training team camped in the bush).

The weapons selector switches are in an awkward position in the FB 9, and it was assumed that he was concentrating on selecting the correct switches for the next attack and as a result failed to notice the impending situation. The Vampire FB 9 aircraft is very sensitive on the controls and he could easily have made an input on the control column while his eyes were 'inside the cockpit'. (Peter Petter-Bowyer and Bill Sykes)

Operation Mardon, October/November 1976

There were two main targets for this operation. One was Jorge do Limpopo on the railway line from Maputo to Vila Salazar; the other was Massangena where the road from Mapai crossed the Sabi River on the way to Malvernia. The distance between the two was 250 kilometres. Two reconnaissance teams were dropped in by free fall to mark the southern target area. The first team was to position itself south of Jorge do Limpopo, 100 kilometres from the border, and the second team to the north of the town. As soon as the road convoy crossed the border, these two teams were to set up an ambush on the road and cut the telephone lines. After attacking their target, the main column were to pick up the two teams and bring them back to Rhodesia. The weather was bad and the countryside very flat with few visible landmarks. As a result, the second team was dropped about seven kilometres from the intended landing zone.

On Saturday night 30th October, engineers cut the border fence, cleared the land-mines, and more than 80 vehicles, together with horses from the Grey's Scouts advanced in a pincer movement—one arm aimed into the Tete area and the other into Gaza Province. As the columns passed through the countryside, camps were attacked, numbers of enemy soldiers killed and large quantities of arms and ammunition captured or destroyed.

However, the southbound column was delayed by ambushes along the road and did not arrive in the Jorge do Limpopo area until late on 31st October. There they surprised a troop train, blew up the vital water reservoir and, picked up the second recce team.

Meanwhile the first reconnaissance team, positioned in the area south of Jorge do Limpopo, was unaware that the column had been delayed and began creating diversions too soon. By late afternoon on 31st October, this three-man group found themselves in the middle of angry retaliation by Frelimo. During the running fight that ensued, one of the Rhodesians became separated from the other two. The road column had at last arrived in the area but was unable to find the recce team, which in fact had landed further south than was thought. A Canberra was, therefore, sent in to circle the area at 30,000 feet. Despite very weak radio batteries, the recce team managed to contact the pilot and give him their exact location. A helicopter was tasked to uplift the team at first light. At dawn, a helicopter escorted by a Lynx, flew in and picked up two members of the missing team. As the Alouette climbed, it came under heavy fire from Frelimo. The sun was rising as they turned for home, flying along the railway line. Just a few minutes later, the pilot spotted a man on the ground waving something white. Incredibly, it was the missing member of the recce team, leaping up and down to attract attention. Meanwhile the road column had successfully fought its way through a Frelimo ambush and returned to Rhodesia. Once again, but not quite so easily, the objects of the operation had been achieved.

One interesting point is that Air Lieutenant Benecke, one of the pilots of FAF 7 which had a great deal to do with this operation, was given a forced rest period after he had flown 22½ hours during a 36-hour period. The FAF 7 Diary for 30th October 1976 reads:

A hot chaotic day, with not a minute's peace from the early hours of the morning to dark. Flight Lieutenant Alf Wilde had to be casevaced to Bulawayo. Flight Lieutenants Bob d'Hotman and Bill Fergus [TF ex ATA] spent the day trooping and re-supplying around the countryside. Flight Lieutenant Ken Law on his way to the farm attack at Masapa's Ranch had a gearbox failure just north of Mkwasine and had to land asap. Flight Lieutenants Bruce Collocott and Bruce Smith flew down with spares from Salisbury. The Selous Scouts gave us grief today flying bodies around from A to B—insisting it had to be done immediately, if not sooner. Flight Lieutenant Ron Bull (VR) and his fireforce returned from Ruti in the Gutu district after a H/D (high density) operation. They finished up with a kill of nine out of ten. K-Car was Air Lieutenant Mark Aitchison. Kevin Peinke and Dick Paxton were the heroes of the day.

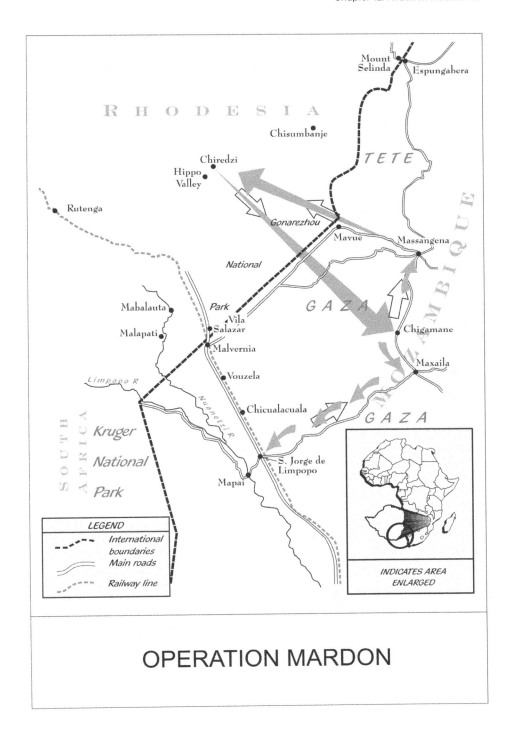

OPERATION MARDON

FAF 7, 31st October 1976 (Sunday)

An early call for the hot pursuit operations on the S/E border. Flight Lieutenant John Blythe-Wood was heard to say ecstatically (over the radio) as a shell hit a target in Malvernia, "Oh, most pleasant, most pleasant!" Flight Lieutenant Ken Law was unable to take part in the proceedings as he had lost all his gearbox oil at Mkwasine the previous day. Most of the pilots flew mammoth hours during the day. Flight Lieutenant John Blythe-Wood, eight and a half hours, Flight Lieutenant Dick Paxton, ten and a half hours. A couple of drinks and they were all in bed. However not all managed a reasonable night. The ops staff continued planning for Monday's flying and it turned out to be an all-night watch for Air Lieutenant Ian Stein, (the VR ops officer) and Flight Sergeant Cox, the No 4 Squadron armourer. We had a visit at 1 am from Squadron Leader Randy du Rand in a Canberra and after a debrief and cup of coffee, he flew back to Salisbury. Bob d'Hotman and Bill Fergus, the Gooney drivers (Dakota) had a long day with casevac roles. Fortunately, none of the casevacs were fatal. They arrived back from the last trip just in time for the coffee.

FAF 7, 3rd November 1976

35 hours flown by the two Lynx and fireforce. Air Lieutenant Cocky Benecke and Air Lieutenant Clive Ward together with No 1 Squadron providing top cover while Scouts moved back from their hot pursuit operations.

Casevac at Birchenough Bridge

As well as providing support for cross-border raids, No 7 Squadron was on constant stand-by for casevac within Rhodesia and sometimes the line between completing the evacuation safely or not—was hair-thin. Early in November, Chris Dickinson was stationed at Hot Springs, in the Sabi Valley. His technician was D.J. 'Wally' Wallace. The incident occurred on 7th November. They had carried out a few trips during the morning and were relaxing when there was a fireforce call-out. A sighting had been made near Birchenough Bridge.

A successful contact was made and the insurgents pulled back towards the river where they took up a strong defensive position. By now the G-Cars needed to refuel so they returned to Birchenough Bridge while the RLI sticks began to flush out the enemy. Then a report came through from an observation post that one of the sticks [seemed to] needed a casevac. However the radio was malfunctioning and while the transmit button worked the members of the stick could not transmit speech. Using a code of one click for yes and two for no the OP established that the stick leader had been shot through the ribs and was losing a lot of blood. The sticks were new in the field and this was one of their first contacts. It further appeared that they were close to the river line with the gooks nearby. It was decided that a casevac in daylight would be too dangerous for both the call sign and the chopper.

Chris Dickinson agreed to go in at last light. He continues the story:

I requested the OP to ask the call sign to fire a pencil flare on my run in to indicate their position. The OP told me that there was an LZ we could use just south of the river line. I plotted the LZ on my map and decided on an approach for the night landing. As we came in, the call sign fired the flare and we landed without mishap. Other groups nearby provided covering fire to keep the gooks' heads down but it was pretty nerve-wracking having all that tracer flying around while we were coming in. The members of the stick carried their leader on his poncho and placed him in the back of the chopper. They all wanted to climb in too. But Wally had to point out that we couldn't take them all and after a few tense moments, they moved away and we got airborne—without lights—and headed for Chipinga. The mountains in the area are thousands of feet higher than Birchenough Bridge and in order to reach a safe height we had to do a spiral climb to well over 9,000 feet before setting course for Chipinga Hospital. The journey took us the best part of an hour. As soon as we landed, the stick leader was whisked inside the hospital and we shut down. As I got out of the chopper, I saw Wally staring in horror. Wrapped around the starboard wheel was the poncho that had been used to carry the stick leader. Obviously, it had been thrown over him as we took off and during the flight it had blown out and wrapped around the wheel. We shuddered to think of the consequences if the poncho had fouled the tail rotor blades and caused a rotor failure. Needless to say, we consumed quite a few drinks that night at the hotel. Unfortunately, the stick leader died shortly after arrival. (Chris Dickinson) Air Lieutenant Chris Dickinson later received a MFC (Operational).

Attack on Mavue
Within days of the end of Operation Mardon, the SAS and RLI were back inside Mozambique attacking a ZANLA base at Mavue on the junction of the Sabi and Lundi Rivers. Once again, FAF 7 was involved.

FAF 7, 10th November 1976
A lot of to-ing and fro-ing today in preparation for the external operation tomorrow. Squadron Leader Graham Cronshaw carried out most of it.

FAF 7, 11th November 1976
What a day! Fortunately, it was cool because towards the end of the day everyone had nerves on edge. We mounted an external operation against Mavue and keeping the lot re-supplied during the course of the day and half the night proved no mean task.

Among the pilots included in this attack were Air Lieutenant Clive Ward, (who destroyed two heavy machine gun posts despite heavy fire from the ground), and Air Lieutenant Mick Delport, both of whom received awards for this action.

FAF 7, 12th November 1976
We finished with 84 hours flying in a day.

And the heat was not only coming from the combat. In this operational area, the temperatures during mid-November were 42°C, 24th November being the hottest on record with temperatures of 43° – 44°C.

The Battle of the Honde Valley
The first signs of an enemy build-up came early on the morning of 15th November 1976, when ground forces reported unusual activity in the valley. Flight Lieutenant Tudor Thomas, the senior pilot at Ruda, the police base in the Honde Valley about 55 kilometres north of Umtali was called on for support. The four helicopters were crewed by Flight Lieutenant Chris Wentworth and Sergeant A.M. (Tony) Merber; Flight Lieutenant Tudor Thomas and Sergeant Brian Warren; Flight Lieutenant Trevor Baynham and Flight Sergeant Ted Holland; and Air Sub-Lieutenant Nick Meikle and Sergeant J.J.B. (Hans) Steyn.

The helicopters with RLI, RR and RAR sticks were quickly deployed and the first contact came about 06h45 on the western face of a koppie. The crews came under fire as soon as they flew into the contact area and were under sporadic fire throughout most of the day. Despite the difficult and dangerous flying conditions with early morning cloud, they worked steadily, trooping men and re-supplying ammunition. During the day, vital supplies of ammunition and fuel also had to be ferried in to Ruda.

During the 12-hour battle, the four helicopters spent a total of 24 hours in the air. "It was good to be in on it," said Flight Lieutenant Tudor Thomas. A fixed-wing aircraft, piloted by Squadron Leader Dag Jones, also took part in the fight and put in several effective strikes on the enemy. "Afterwards, when we found out that the total killed was 31, the morale of the pilots and technicians was high. I had underestimated the number of terrorists and when we found out how many we had killed, it was fantastic," said Dag.

The size of the gangs crossing the border was now very much larger and in the middle of November, a group of about 100 crossed from Mozambique. On Wednesday 24th November at 11h00, a contact occurred with security forces. Acting on information from a call sign, a stick of four soldiers entered the area under cover of darkness. They were moving into position in thick bush when they heard movement. It was a group of 60 ZANLA men. The patrol went to ground and there was a similar reaction from the terrorists. The security patrol knowing they were in a curfew area, opened fire first. The group returned fire and beat a retreat dropping their equipment as they ran. The patrol gave chase.

Tudor Thomas who was once again at the scene said, "We picked them up quite easily and dropped troops into the area." He also reported that captured equipment had included anti-aircraft guns. "We haven't lost any planes," he said. "They don't seem to be very effective at using their guns." This fight, which included the army, the air force and elements of the police force continued for a week, taking place in rugged hilly country about 20 kilometres from the border in the Inyanga North area close to Avila Mission.

No 4 Squadron Diary, November 1976:

Yet again a busy month with operational flying quite heavy. Group Captain John Mussell joined us this month and was deployed to the bush only to be abruptly re-deployed to Salisbury Hospital with a bullet in the foot. This was a memento from a contact and we hope the recovery will be a swift one. Welcome to Air Sub-Lieutenants Rob Griffiths, Martin Hatfield, Mike Huson, John Kidson and Chris Tucker; also Air Lieutenant Roger Bowers from the USA. Clive Ward from 3 Squadron had his aircraft hit by a 12.7. This caused a hole in one of the tail booms and an even bigger hole in his seat (not caused by the terrs!!) He is now no doubt glad to be returning to the 'armchair' squadron—No 3—having been loaned to 4 Squadron temporarily to fly the Lynx.

Bateleur

It was in the month of November 1976, that the air force magazine *Bateleur* saw the light of day. Published by Air headquarters, it was the first journal produced by the air force since the cessation of *Ndege* early in 1969. (*Ndege*—Kiswahili for big bird). *Ndege* had been a glossy full-colour magazine, which essentially dealt with flight safety. Alan Cockle had been responsible for the last four issues but then in 1969, the Ministry of Finance changed its accounting system. Prior to this, the Government Printer had been doing the job at virtually no charge but from 1969 it was required to bill the air force a considerable amount for the work. Rather than reduce the quality, *Ndege* was suspended. The *Bateleur*, produced much more cheaply in newspaper format was edited by Squadron Leader A.J. Cockle.

The name *Bateleur* was chosen because the bateleur eagle was the adopted symbol of the Rhodesian Air Force and formed the main feature of the original RRAF badge approved by Queen Elizabeth II. It is doubtful that this particular bird would have been selected had a little more research been done. The dictionary defines bateleur as a mountebank, charlatan or swindler, a cheat or imposter—obviously not truly representative of the general character of the air force. The eagle is said to have been given the name bateleur because of its habit of somersaulting, slow rolling and performing other antics in the air.

Roberts Birds of South Africa, however, does produce some lighter insights into some of the traits that could perhaps be attributed to the force: "Solitary or somewhat gregarious, in flocks of up to 40 ... Spends much of its day in direct or circling flight, seldom flapping. Its striking appearance and colouring at once attract attention as it flies overhead, usually travelling fast across country. Seldom flies in wet weather. Hunts live prey by stooping in flight or parachuting gently. Robs larger (birds) of food; also scavenges, especially in immature stages. By day may sunbathe with wings spread. Voice: A variety of sharp barking calls."

In the first edition of *Bateleur*, it was announced that a new air base was to be built. This was the airfield later to be known as Fylde, situated approximately 30 kilometres west of Hartley off the Chakari road. Many people knew about it but it was never discussed openly until after the end of the Bush War. It was used as a training base from 1977.

During the latter part of 1976, in a new Anglo-American effort, Dr Kissinger visited South Africa. He offered Rhodesia a package deal. In return for majority rule in two years, there was to be an end to the terror war and a lifting of sanctions. A conference was scheduled for Geneva, during December 1976, but once again negotiations collapsed.

On 3rd December 1976, it was announced that Intake 146, which had been due for release on that day, would serve another three months. This unlucky intake had already had its call-up time extended. There were a lot of very unhappy people.

A happier event occurred early in December with the official opening of the new officers' mess at Thornhill. Squadron Leader John Digby, President of the Mess Committee, paid tribute to the Department of Works. "We had some very willing help from them on furniture too and the mess funds contributed over $5,000 [Rhodesian] to the alterations." The building was originally erected by the Royal Air Force at Thornhill as the officers' mess in the early 1950s and was taken over by the Glengarry School who occupied it until 1975. The officers, in the meantime, had been using the official sergeants' mess and they in turn had been using the airmen's mess. In 1975, all the messes had been returned to their rightful owners.

And still the war continued.

FAF 7, 2nd December 1976

A No 5 Squadron Canberra arrived at 05h10. Crew: Squadron Leader Randy du Rand and Air Lieutenant S.P. (Paddy) Morgan. At 10h15, they were called for by the Scouts at Vila Salazar who were under intense mortar, artillery and small-arms fire. The Canberra neutralized the fire very quickly, sustaining one bullet hole in the process. Another Canberra was sent down from Salisbury and ours went back for inspection. The Dakota was hurriedly sent up to Fort Victoria at lunchtime to go and get more shells for the gun battery down at Nyala siding as the battery was completely out of ammo after the morning's scene.

FAF 7, 9th December

One helicopter and the Lynx went off to do a Psyac demo in the Nyajena area. On the way back the helicopter, piloted by Mark Dawson, was diverted to a casevac near Renco Mine. Unfortunately, he developed a main gearbox oil leak and had to put his helicopter down in the middle of the Nyajena TTL. When he was about two hours overdue, we sent a Lynx out to search for him. He was found very quickly and a helicopter was dispatched with gearbox oil and a new oil seal. He eventually got home at about 17h00.

Operation Tangent

Towards the middle of December, it was announced that a new operational area had been opened. Named Tangent, it covered the whole of Matabeleland from Kazungula in the north to Beitbridge in the south.

The Fighting Cook

The story of the Fighting Cook received considerable coverage towards the end of December. On 20th December, an army patrol called for the casualty evacuation of a group of black civilians who had been injured. The task was assigned to Flight Lieutenant Vic Cook who set off on this errand of mercy, accompanied by his technician, Corporal Finch Bellringer, and an army medical orderly. However, as the No 7 Squadron Alouette approached the pick-up point, it came under heavy ground fire. Bellringer was hit in his flak vest by one bullet and another got through below the jacket and penetrated his back injuring him slightly. Vic said later, "I felt the controls going. There was vibration and I realized I had to force-land." The tail rotor drive shaft had snapped. Fighting to control the damaged machine as it came in, Vic saw a group of five armed men ahead of him. They were pointing their guns in his direction and firing. "I aimed the aircraft at them deliberately. We thumped down nose first and I lost sight of them." As the helicopter landed, a piece of the control column snapped off in the pilot's hand and his foot was badly gashed. After this, Cook is a little vague about events. He knew that the enemy were still around. His Uzi was unserviceable having taken a round in the base. "I knew they were coming back. I needed a weapon. Then I saw this terr lying beyond the chopper. He had probably been hit by the rotor when we came down, I don't know, but he had an AK and all I knew was that he was between me and the weapon. I grabbed his AK and shot him with it." Cook then shouted for his technician and the medic to run for it but the wounded technician could not move. Together, Cook and the medic dragged the injured man to higher ground. Meanwhile the insurgents were closing in. Cook took a position between them and his wounded technician who was being cared for by the medic. He remembers being angry at having been shot down and wanting to chase his attackers, but he kept tripping over. It was only then that he saw the deep gash in his foot.

A K-Car and three G-Cars soon arrived from FAF 7, followed shortly by a Dakota, which dropped an SAS stick in the area. Cook said later that the army patrol that arrived after about 45 minutes was a beautiful sight. Corporal Bellringer was casevaced to Chiredzi Hospital and Cook was flown to Sarum by Wing Commander Tol Janeke for some rest and recuperation (R&R). Subsequently the technician made a complete recovery and Vic Cook was awarded the Silver Cross of Rhodesia.

Christmas 1976

So the season of peace and goodwill arrived again. No 1 Squadron was busy with air tasks and readiness in fact from 24th to 27th December and again on 1st and 2nd January the pilots were on half-hour stand-by. The Hunters did a flag wave over the Beitbridge road convoy on Christmas Eve and on Christmas Day Reindeer Section visited as many FAFs as possible while the weather held. The squadron managed one Republic Rover, the first for some considerable time! Two shuttle aircraft from No 3 Squadron flew out of Salisbury carrying 3,000 kilograms of food and drink for the hundreds of airmen stationed at the forward airfields and on detachment throughout the operational areas.

No 4 Squadron Diary, December 1976:

The last month of 1976 was relatively quiet. Squadron Leader Prop Geldenhuys was deployed on the completion of his Lynx conversion. Squadron Leader Mike Saunders joined us again. Prop Geldenhuys had his aircraft hit by small-arms fire but made it back safely. Cocky Benecke had an engine failure but this was due to a fuel calibration problem. We had an incident with Ian Sheffield and his rabid pets from FAF 8. He is now on an anti-rabies course and naturally he is temporarily released from any bush deployments. Leon du Plessis got the monthly 'Boo Boo' shield for a small incident with a smoke grenade at Rutenga.

Apparently, the smoke grenade had, clearly printed on the canister, WP SMOKE, so Leon thought that it was a harmless white smoke grenade. Actually, the letters WP stood for white phosphorus. Had he known this, he would not have been so casual about chucking it into the room where the PRAW pilot was sleeping on the top of the bed, wearing just his underpants. Fortunately, the grenade went off close to the edge of the bed so the spray of phosphorus went up past him, hitting the wall and showering gently down on him. He was taken immediately to the army medic's tent, where the medic showed little interest.

What's the problem? asked the medic. Turn the lights out and you will see, said Leon. The medic, confronted with a half-naked figure, was a little suspicious, but he complied with the request. All was revealed. There standing in front of him, was a glowing pilot.

Cocky Benecke of No 4 Squadron received a welcome Christmas present when the Terrorist Victim's Relief Fund paid for him and his family to spend a holiday in Durban. Apparently, the requirement for the award was a) to have spent 229 days per annum in the bush or b) to have been wounded.

Cockleshell heroes

Cabora Bassa, lying on the lower Zambezi River is one of the largest man-made lakes in the world. The waters of the lake back up to the Rhodesian border, while the dam wall lies nearly 300 kilometres away down stream. Early in 1977, the SAS using canoes, spent six weeks on the lake attacking Frelimo bases and harbours, carrying out ambushes and laying land-mines.

During these six weeks, everything the SAS men needed in the way of food, ammunition, boat spares and equipment was dropped to them by No 3 Squadron Dakotas. The lake lies entirely in Mozambique so there was always the chance that the aircraft would be spotted despite all the diversionary tactics carried out by the pilots. There was also the problem of locating the tiny canoes in that vast area of water.

The SAS men maintained daily contact with headquarters but their messages had to be limited and in code. Ten minutes before the pilot's ETA overhead, the men on the ground would contact the pilot and again five minutes later. To hide their approach the Dakotas were flown with their navigation lights off and so the men waiting in their canoes or on an island nearby, would have to talk the pilot in using the sound of his engines. The only clue that the Dakota pilot had as to the whereabouts of the canoeists would be the flash of the strobe light below in the darkness. To the men in their tiny canoes, the black outline against the stars was their survival line. As the green light flashed in the back of the Dakota, the boxes of supplies would be heaved from the plane falling 800 feet to land often within metres of the waiting men. Then with a dip of its wings, the Dakota turned for home and the men on the water were left alone in the silence. At the end of the operation, the SAS men cleared a landing zone and left the lake in style aboard five Alouettes of No 7 Squadron. Bill Sykes remembers:

> *I was one of the chopper pilots who picked them up at the end of the six weeks and I was shocked by their state—on the way in, the SAS had been smartly dressed and clean-shaven. On the pick-up, no one would have recognized them. Their hair was long, some were sporting beards and their clothing was literally in tatters. But they were all sun-bronzed, healthy, smiling and very glad to be going home!*

Rams and alpha

On the technical side, work was constantly going ahead to improve Rhodesia's attack capability. By January 1977, the alpha bouncing bomb had been tested and enough bombs had been manufactured to allow six Canberra loads to be immediately available.

Work had also been going ahead on methods of signalling from the ground to aircraft overhead. One of these was Rams, a Radio Activated Marker System, which had been developed by the air force radio section at New Sarum. This ground receiver could be carried by special forces operating in enemy territory and set up in advance close to the intended target. A signal from a Canberra bomber triggered the device, which ignited one or two flares on the ground at the ideal moment during the final run up on the bombing run. Since Rams and the flares could not be set up in the middle of a large terrorist camp, the air force devised a system known as offset bombing.

Offset bombing was achieved by altering the angle of the bombsight to allow for the distance on the ground between the Rams and the target. The Rams was normally placed on the line of attack on the run-up to the target, for greater accuracy, but it was just as easy to adjust the bomb sight for a Rams laid beyond the target.

Operation Manyatela: the attack on Madulo Pan—January 1977

An ideal chance to test both the alpha bomb and Rams presented itself in January 1977. Intelligence reports had come in indicating a large transit camp some 80 kilometres west of the Maputo/Malvernia railway line in the vicinity of Madulo Pan. A photographic reconnaissance was carried out by a Canberra, and the existence of the camp was confirmed. From further information received, it appeared that a large number of men would be at the camp between 10th and 12th January. The siting of the camp made a successful ground assault difficult. A pattern of paths leading through the surrounding thick bush would enable the enemy to escape once an attack had been launched. It was, therefore, decided that the camp should be attacked from the air only.

Late in 1976, officer commanding 5 Squadron, Squadron Leader Randy du Rand and Peter Petter-Bowyer had a meeting with Captain Rob Warracker and Chris Schulenberg of the Selous Scouts to discuss the matter of launching an attack on Madulo Pan. The plan was to attack with Canberras, going in at night at about 300 feet above ground. The flat terrain of the region would make this a relatively safe operation, which was not the case further north where the countryside was more mountainous.

The long wait for Madulo Pans to become a worthwhile target ended when SB reported that they had a radio intercept, which indicated that Madulo Pan Camp would be occupied by 150 ZANLA comrades destined for Zimbabwe from 10th–13th January. This message arrived on 3rd January, which allowed time for a trial run. Hurriedly, Captain Rob Warracker set up an exercise with Schulenberg to test the Rams and the Canberras. The area chosen for the rehearsal was Gonarezhou National Park because it was the closest approximation inside Rhodesia to the real target area 90 kilometres away.

On the night of 6th January, Schulenberg made a free-fall descent into the game reserve and set up the Rams on a target area that related in distance and direction to the Madulo Pan Camp. Randy du Rand, flying the Canberra, struck the target with practice bombs precisely. The only hitch was a late response in the ignition of the flares.

The next morning, Peter Petter-Bowyer with Rob Warracker aboard, landed his Cessna 185 at an airstrip called Chikombedzi. They were lifted by helicopter to the strike area to assess the results. The strike was on target and the alpha bombs had bounced satisfactorily.

Meanwhile, at about 14h30, a Dakota (7304) with Flight Lieutenant Mallet and Squadron Leader Peter Barnett (reserve pilot) had taken off from Buffalo Range on a resupply paradrop.

Talking later, Peter Petter-Bowyer said:

Having finished our business on the ground in the growing heat of the day, we returned to Chikombedzi by helicopter. Here Schulie and Rob, both big men, plus a pile of parachutes and other equipment, squeezed into my little aircraft. The Cessna struggled into the air and I had a

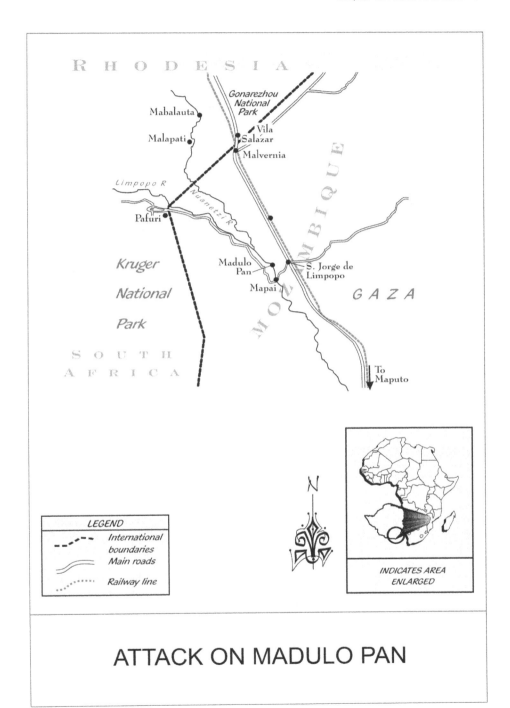

ATTACK ON MADULO PAN

bad moment when it refused to accelerate above the trees. We were on limits in hot conditions, which required some nifty handling before the Cessna slipped over the drag step and lifted her tail into comfortable flight. We were intending to fly straight back to Salisbury but when we checked in with Buffalo Range Air Field we were requested to divert to search for the Dakota 7304 that was overdue. It was thought at first that the Dakota may have proceeded direct to Devuli but when we checked with the choppers that were returning from Devuli, it became apparent that this was not the case. I dropped Schulie and Rob at Chiredzi Air Field.

At approximately 17h30, the army phoned through to say that the high tension wires across the Lundi were down and a G-Car was immediately sent to the approximate location. Petter-Bowyer then took off and flew back south to the Lundi, where he found the crumpled wreckage of 7304 amongst trees on the south bank of the river. The power cables crossed from bank to bank, but the pylons were hidden by surrounding river-line bush. One of the cables had sliced into the cabin killing both pilots outright. The flight engineer, who had been standing behind the pilot's seats, was saved by the bulkhead, which severed the cable before it reached him. He struggled to pull the aircraft out of its left-hand roll. The cables that were holding the plane broke but it was too late to avoid impact with the ground and the Dakota shed its wing as it slithered to an untidy dusty halt.

Fortunately, the cables had decelerated the aircraft almost to stalling speed before its impact with the ground and that probably saved the lives of the engineer and the four dispatchers. The other dispatcher, Corporal Bradley, was injured in the crash and died later.[*]

Peter Petter-Bowyer returned to Salisbury with Rob and Shulenberg to meet with Norman Walsh, Randy du Rand and Ron Reid-Daly who were awaiting at New Sarum. They were briefed by Flight Lieutenant Bill Buckle using the latest large-scale grid photographs of Madulo Pans. Recent radio intercepts confirmed that the ZANLA men would be at this camp during the period 10th–13th January.

The air attack was to be carried out by three Canberras carrying 900 alpha bombs and was timed for 04h00 on the morning of 12th January 1977 to allow for any Frelimo transport deficiencies. As a result of the trial run, Randy requested that two flares be used and that while three aircraft made the attack, a fourth Canberra should be overhead at height to activate the Rams. This would ensure the instantaneous ignition of the flares. He also requested that the two Rams units should be placed two kilometres apart to give an accurate final line-up to the target.

There was definite concern about the time factor. The attack had to be before 04h00 when ZANLA usually awoke and dispersed. The difficulty was that first light would not come until 05h15, which meant an hour and 15 minutes between air strike and helicopter force arrival. To cover the possibility of Frelimo's intervention during this period, it was agreed the fourth Canberra would carry a load of 300 alpha bombs and that a pair of Hunters would be on station over the target with back-up Hunters on immediate stand-by at Thornhill. Wing Commander Tol Janeke was positioned at FAF 7, Buffalo Range to direct operations. All normal operations were cancelled, and a Dakota was sent to Thornhill to uplift four 20mm cannons and extra ammunition.

Captain Schulenberg and Sergeant Mpoto were dropped by No 3 Squadron on Monday afternoon 10th January with their supply boxes and landed in a shallow escarpment some ten kilometres west of the camp. From here, they made their way cautiously towards the outskirts

---

[*] It was not until 4th February 1977, that a G-Car with a recovery crew visited this crash site to find out whether there was anything recoverable. On 26th February a G-Car ferried salvaged parts of the Dakota from the south to the north bank from where the pieces were recovered to base by road.

of the camp, which they reached on the evening of 11th January.

The Canberras were already loaded and at 03h10, they taxied out onto the runway at New Sarum. For the purposes of security, radio transmissions between the aircraft and the control tower suggested a routine training sortie. Squadron Leader John Digby was sitting beside the civilian controller. He would often be present for air force strikes. Having gained clearance from the Salisbury air traffic controller, the Canberras lifted off. Flight Lieutenant Ian Donaldson climbed to 40,000 feet from Buffalo Range while the strike formation levelled out 20,000 feet below him. On board Ian's aircraft was Air Sub-Lieutenant Dave Hawkes, the navigator and Selous Scouts Captain Rob Warracker.

The strike formation passed over Buffalo Range and headed towards Malvernia. The formation then commenced a slow letdown to the initial run-in height, having obtained the QFE (altimeter setting) from a call sign in the area.

Schulenberg had positioned the inner marker at the base of a big tree 400 metres from the camp, and had eventually managed to identify the clump of trees for the outer marker. He had been close to calling off the strike as he had experienced difficulty in finding the clump of trees but fortunately, all was well and both markers were set.

Randy brought his formation around and commenced the run-in to the target. The stepped-up formation crossed the border into Mozambique. Tensions were running high, as they always did just before a strike.

> *"Running in live," Randy called to Ian.*
> *"Stand by for ignition," Ian called to Schulie.*
> *"Send it," Schulie replied.*

Randy called his formation to accelerate to 330 knots. There was little change in sound as the aircraft picked up speed towards the target. In the utter darkness below nothing was visible.

> *"Bravo 5 this is Alpha 5, stand by Rams."*
> *"Standing by."*
> *"Rams go!"*
> *"Rams gone. Stand-by ignition."*
> *"Roger we have one burning."*
> *"Re-transmitting. Stand by!"*
> *"Roger you're Go on two."*

In that sea of blackness, a glow appeared slightly to starboard of track.

> *"Go ten right," Randy called to his formation. They had anticipated this having a better view of the flares from their slightly higher positions.*
> *"Stand by, left. Ten left. Go!"*
> *"Rolling out, check 172°, bomb doors Go!"*

As the bomb doors opened, the smoothness of flight was broken by a slight shaking of the airframes; throttles went forward to compensate for the drag caused by the open doors of the bomb bays. On the ground, Schulenberg heard the silence of the night change to a dull roar. The rumbling of Canberra bomb bay doors told him the bombers would be flashing overhead in just a moment.

The outer marker glow changed to direct light and the navigators strained their eyes to pick up the all-important inner marker. When it became visible, they knew the line up was perfect. The aircraft were now visible in the light of the flares and the spacing looked good.

The navigators called to their pilots, Bombs gone, bombs falling. The time was 04h00.

For a first attempt at very low-level bombing in difficult country, Randy's formation of three Canberras did a magnificent job and placed 900 bombs over the whole of the target area from an attack height of around 300 feet at 330 knots.

When the Alouettes arrived at first light they were met by determined fire from the ground. The anti-aircraft fire directed at the helicopters was so intense that the G-Cars were forced to back off. Everyone was astonished. The Canberras were supposed to have cleared the way for the safe arrival of the helicopters. Flight Lieutenant Mike Borlace, known for his daring, moved his K-Car in close. Although he came under heavy fire, his gunner took out a particularly menacing nest of 12.7mm guns before retreating with small-arms fire following them all the way as they climbed to a safer height. Further K-Car and Lynx attacks took place before troops could be placed around the target.

Once on the ground, the troops immediately found the reason for the Canberras' failure to neutralize the target. Almost all of the bomblets had penetrated the thin layer of sand in the ZANLA camp area and had buried themselves in gooey black clay before bursting harmlessly below the surface. Hundreds of black craters all over the area were evidence of a dismal strike failure. Only two of the bomblets had activated on impact, one against a tree and the other when it struck firmer ground. These two burst in the air and accounted for some ZANLA deaths.

The two Hunters were called in and delivered a rocket and cannon attack. Still the anti-aircraft fire continued. Unknown to the Scouts, a heavy Frelimo column had arrived to support the ZANLA men. The remaining Canberra was requested to bomb the Frelimo force. The weather was cloudy and the pilot, Flight Lieutenant Ian Donaldson made a slow turn, losing altitude as he did so, and came out of the cloud directly over Malvernia. Frelimo forces alerted by the attack on Madulo Pan opened fire with everything they had. The Canberra flew through a hail of fire. It rolled over and dived into the ground.

The pilot, the navigator Air Sub-Lieutenant David Hawkes and Captain Rob Warracker of the Selous Scouts were killed instantly.

On the following day, 12th January, a search and rescue operation was mounted from Buffalo Range. Intensive fire was experienced from across the border at Malvernia but the rescue and recovery operations continued all day with the pilots flying under extremely hazardous conditions. A ground recovery attempt initiated by the Selous Scouts and the army, came to nothing for the same reasons. For the security forces, it was a very sad and frustrating day. However, despite the loss of the Canberra, this operation proved beyond doubt the value of the bouncing bombs and as a result, the Canberra was back in the war.

Of course, the Canberra had never been completely out of service but had been used mainly for photo-reconnaissance. And it was during one of these sorties on 13th January 1977 that pilot Ed Potterton was faced with a dilemma:

Flight Lieutenant Terry Bennett and I were tasked with a photo-recce in the Malvernia area. Following a normal take-off, we settled into a long climb to our cruising altitude. Terry had crawled forward into the nose to sort out his maps and I was enjoying the flight—but then I looked down and saw that the starboard engine fire warning had illuminated. I told Terry and he replied "Bullshit." But just in case there was a grain of truth in my remark, he started reversing out of the bomb-aimer's position. As he did so, the warning light was shining just a few inches from his nose. Suddenly he became highly motivated and with the agility of an athlete half his age, he strapped himself into his ejection seat. I went through the drill of shutting down the engine. Then I pressed the fire extinguisher button. The fire warning light remained on. By now, I had turned back towards the airfield. It was a beautiful day and the airfield was clearly visible. It seemed ridiculous to abandon a valuable aircraft when we were so close to home. I called Salisbury and told them we had a fire and requested a straight in approach to runway 06. Once again, I ran through the checklist to ensure that I had done everything. The checklist stated quite clearly that if the warning light did not extinguish then the crew must eject. But for many years, the attitude among aircrews had been to save the aircraft at all costs. I asked Terry to look through his periscope and see if there was any evidence of fire. He couldn't see anything. A Vampire from No 6 Squadron was departing and the officer cadet kindly offered to see if he could spot a fire. I accepted his offer but I was maintaining maximum speed on my one engine. I wanted to get down on the ground fast—so our closing speed was nearly 700 knots. I don't think he was able to see much as we flashed past. I told Terry that I intended to try a landing—but that if there was any problem he must eject. After landing, we turned off onto the taxiway followed closely by a fleet of fire tenders. I shut down and we evacuated the aircraft. The investigation found that one of the flame detector switches in the starboard engine was shorting to earth causing the fire warning light to illuminate. There had been no fire. I was glad that I had decided not to follow the Emergency Checklist, ejected and lost a valuable aircraft. The event had in fact—fortunately—been a non-event. (Ed Potterton)

A priceless find
After all the talk of war and killing, a story told in the January 1977 Monthly Report of No 7 Squadron comes as a welcome respite:

The sharp eyes of a chopper crew saved a piece of Rhodesian history for posterity and gave the force a pat on the back. Flight Lieutenant Tudor Thomas and his tech Johnny Jacobs were recently briefed to drop some equipment on a hilltop in Inyanga. The only flat area in the vicinity was an obvious ruin site, in the middle of which a round object was partly visible. The object turned out to be a large earthenware pot, which the crew carefully retrieved and carried back to base at Grand Reef. Squadron Leader Cyril White arranged for the pot to be sent to the Umtali Museum. The staff burst into ecstasies. They dated the pot at around 1700 AD and pronounced it an important find. "It is very unusual to find such a large and ancient earthenware pot in such a perfect state," enthused Mr Cran Cook, the museum's Keeper of Antiquities. "Certainly this is the first time we have received an acquisition by helicopter and the first time a ruin has been reported from the air." In an area of frequent terrorist activity, a bit of 'pot hunting' makes a change from pot shots.

Rescue at the Bubye
During the summer of 1976/77, the rains fell and fell. In February 1977, 175mm of rain was recorded in the Rutenga area in three days. The Bubye River, normally a sandy bed with a trickle of water running beside the Lion and Elephant Motel on the road between Fort Victoria and the South African border, began to rise at an alarming rate.

The riverbed beside the motel was its usual sandy self on Sunday night, 6th February. Then the flood came down. A policeman who was on the spot said, "As I waited about 400 metres from the motel, I could literally see the water rising every minute. It went up 10cm in ten minutes and suddenly we realized we were in the midst of a flood. I radioed to base and the air force told me they were standing by, and shortly afterwards a spotter plane appeared, to assess the situation from the air. I was in radio contact with the pilot and he flew off, leaving me, Inspector Hennie Cilliers, and six security force men in our five-ton truck watching the water rising rapidly all round us."

Inside the motel the owners, Ray and Beth Torr, and their overnight guests had taken refuge in the bar—the highest point in the building. At first it was rather pleasant, according to one of the guests. "When the water reached waist level we all clambered on to the bar counter. The water still rose and the Torrs said we had better get on to the roof. So they all climbed out through the thatch."

Back at the air force base, Wing Commander Tol Janeke was in charge of the rescue operation. Three helicopters, crewed by Flight Lieutenant Dick Paxton with Corporal Ralph Harding, Flight Lieutenant Bill McQuade with Senior Aircraftman Rob Nelson and Air Lieutenant Chris Dickinson with Sergeant Alan Shields were dispatched to the Lion and Elephant to assist with the rescue.

By the time the helicopters arrived people at the motel had been on the roof for an hour, and the water was still rising. Then began the dramatic rescue operation as each Alouette in turn plucked people from the motel roof. The pilots manoeuvered their aircraft to the side of the thatched roof, wheels touching the water and as the helicopters hovered, 17 people were helped on board the choppers. It was a case of cool nerves and highly skilled flying by the pilots.

> We were at Chiredzi when we got the call. I was in a K-Car and we took the cannon out and went to Bubye. Tol Janeke was overhead in a Cessna 185 and he acted as telstar. There were a couple of G-Cars there already and they had uplifted people from the roof of the hotel by hovering next to the top of the roof. We had a rope, which we secured to the steps of the K-Car, and we uplifted a few guys who were caught in trees near the hotel. My technician also managed to rescue a sheep. In addition, we searched a few of the farmhouses upstream. The tech would jump out of the K-Car and wade to the house to check if anyone was inside and then wade back to the chopper. He would then grab onto the step of the K-Car and pull himself in. We didn't find anyone and the flooded river subsided very quickly so we went back to Chiredzi with our sheep. (Chris Dickinson)

Having carried the people from the motel to safety, the choppers returned to the area to direct rescue operations by local farmers using motorboats. Two security force men were picked up by boat from thorn trees where they had been clinging for nearly four hours. Other security force members were rescued by ropes trailed from the helicopters. At Nuanetsi, the district commissioner had been planning a massive civil defence rescue operation but the prompt action by the air force meant no other help was necessary. In all, more than 60 people were rescued by both the air force and the local farmers.

Meanwhile the war continued with larger groups of armed men moving closer to the city of Salisbury. A contact began at about 09h00 on Thursday 17th February 1977, when an observation post spotted a group of armed men in a rocky outcrop of a Tribal Trust Land in the Marandellas area about 80 kilometres from the city. The security force post opened fire and a helicopter was called in, together with a fixed-wing aircraft, which circled overhead. A second helicopter was soon on the scene and the bullets began to fly. About 90 minutes later, a Dakota roared in at low level, circled and dropped two sticks of paratroopers.

The contact ranged back and forth over an area of two square kilometres for just under two hours, until all the insurgents had fled, been killed or captured. By about 11h00 it was all over and only one fixed wing aircraft was left to keep a watching brief. In the mopping-up exercise, security forces picked up three battered AK rifles, an SKS as well as 10 stick grenades and ammunition.

Chioco garrison attack

Information had been received that ZANLA had established a major base near the town of Chioco in Tete province. The complex was well built with a protective network of trenches

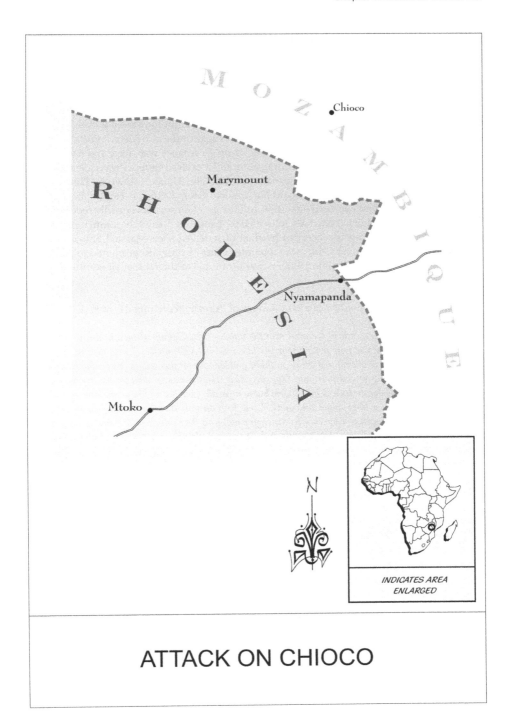

ATTACK ON CHIOCO

and bunkers. The attack was to be mounted from Mtoko Forward Air Field using the airstrip at Marymount Mission where the police had a base camp. It was set for first light on 24th March 1977.

Security force personnel were lifted in using three helicopters, which hugged the contours of the ground in order to remain out of sight until the very last moment. There was no suitable landing spot so the three machines hovered while the troops deplaned about 20 kilometres west of the town and then the choppers returned to Marymount for a second load. The plan worked well. The SAS men detonated their claymores against the two barrack walls while the rest of the attackers made their way through the camp. Resistance was fierce and Andy Chait was wounded. He was carried to the landing zone and a casevac chopper was called in, with the Hunters standing by in case there was any trouble. The Alouette flown by Dick Paxton touched down and Andy was placed aboard but, unfortunately, he died later. Despite this loss, it was a well-planned and executed operation and the garrison was never really reoccupied.

In April 1977, Air Marshal Michael John (Mick) McLaren retired as commander of the Rhodesian Air Force and was succeeded by chief of staff, Air Vice-Marshal Frank Mussell. Air Commodore Christopher Dams was appointed chief of staff and promoted to Air Vice-Marshal. Group Captain J.D. (John) Rogers was promoted to the rank of air commodore.

A scorching day at FAF 8
The April edition of the *Bateleur* carried the story of 'A really scorching day at FAF 8'.

> *Army vehicle becomes stuck in the mud near the railway line. Gallant airmen in the air force vehicle leap to the rescue only to sink four feet into mud holes themselves. Crew discard Rule Book and contrary to all training decide to think problem out for themselves. They dig out the vehicle of brown jobs who depart laughing, suggesting that the airmen wait for the dry season and then excavate own vehicle. Crew shovel but to no avail; crew hee and haw; air force vehicle sinks lower. Then a train comes into view. Crew leap on rails shouting, waving frantically; train stops; driver consults; crew connect the engine to the air force vehicle with a steel cable and retire to safety. Train driver opens throttle and air force vehicle pops out of the mud like a cork from a bottle; gallant airmen spend afternoon hosing out mud from vehicle; blessing railways and cursing brownies. 'Strue.* (Bateleur)

The April edition also carried news of a sporting highlight:

> *A team of reprobates from New Sarum furthered the holiday camp image of the air force by winning the Troutbeck Pentathlon during the weekend of 26th/27th February 1977. Competing against 23 other teams from all over the country, our heroes swept the board by winning the table tennis, squash, golf and tennis events, ceding victory only in bowls. The Sarum team comprised Flight Lieutenant Simon Maitland, Air Lieutenants W.M. 'Mo' Houston and Sammy Symes, WOs A. 'Barney' Barnes and R.W. (Ron) Williams, Sgts J.P. Corbett and Hedley Giles, and RWS member Joan Webster. It is not recorded where they came in the drinking competition but it is known that Ron Williams has since been driven to marriage by the stress of the weekend.*

DC-7C
No 3 Squadron obtained the use of a new type of aircraft—a DC-7C belonging to Jack Malloch. The terms of operation were never made public. From 6th April 1977, it was on more or less permanent loan and was used extensively for parachute drops of men and fuel, especially on trans-border operations. The DC-7C was flown by Squadron Commander George Alexander and was co-piloted by Flight Lieutenant John Matthews. Flight Lieutenant

Bob d'Hotman was supposed to come onto the pilot strength, but at this stage, he was so busy instructing that he did not manage to complete his conversion.

Before the DC-7 went into service with the air force, it had a medium green top and fin, with a metal-skin under-surface and a Gabonese registration. It was one of the aircraft that were used in sanctions-busting operations. It flew Rhodesian beef to Gabon and brought in items unobtainable in Rhodesia, both luxurious and mundane. Prior to its sanctions-breaking career, it was employed together with three or four other aircraft of the same type, and a Constellation, in flying food and weapons into Biafra. It sported midnight blue on its upper surfaces and fin, with a grey cheat-line. The registration letters were very small and always covered, when the aircraft was on the ground. Referring to the DC-7 Charlie Buchan says:

With the DC-3 we jumped using a cable, which ran along the roof, but with the DC-7 the parachutes flipped round the edge of the wing and caught the tail piece, so we moved the cable from the roof to the floor. This meant that the parachute came out underneath. The first time we used the floor cable we got the full blast of the engines up our arses as we came out. We then ran the cable down to the corner of the doorway with a longer static line so that the parachute opened well beneath the tail.

Operation from FAF 5

It began on the morning of 4th April 1977, when Flight Lieutenant Cocky Benecke spotted what looked like two terrorist camps in the bush. A fireforce was mobilized. Alouette Pilots Danny Svoboda and Vic Cook were already in their seats strapping on their blue flak vests. Technicians made last minute checks as the helicopter blades began to turn. On the runway, Flight Lieutenant Ed Potterton was warming up his Lynx. His job was to supply fire support for the troops, with rockets and bombs.

Flight Lieutenant Tom Tarr, a reserve pilot from Air Rhodesia, was starting up his Dakota as the parachute assault troops of the RLI filed aboard. Each man with his jump helmet, parachute, rifle and ammunition. It was the last day of this particular tour and this commando had notched up 67 kills. They were keen to make it 70. With a whine, the helicopters lifted off while the Lynx and Dakota roared down the runway. The assault force had synchronized their time of arrival so as to bring the total force to bear at the same moment. Twenty minutes after take-off the force was over the target. Circling high overhead was a Police Reserve Air Wing aircraft.

Below, the helicopters dipped in and out of the valleys. Higher, the camouflaged Lynx darted in ready for the fray, while in between lumbered the Dakota following its pre-arranged flight path, its belly full of paratroopers, awaiting the word to drop. First on the ground were the helicopter troops, only to be met with disappointment. It was certainly a ZANLA camp but three weeks old. The troops emplaned again and made for the second camp. On this occasion, there was a contact. The chopper-borne assault force went in, followed by the paratroops who were dropped into a maize field a few hundred metres from the action.

Meanwhile back at FAF 5, the FAF commander, Squadron Leader Kesby and the RLI commander Lieutenant Colonel Peter Rich were listening to the action:

One terrorist has already gone up the river, going west.
Where? Right. I've got him. What a pleasure.

Then came news that an RLI trooper had been shot and was being brought back by helicopter. The army doctor, a national serviceman, trundled up to the runway in his ambulance with medics ready to help. The injury apparently had occurred when one section of heli-borne assault troops encountered some women civilians. The stick leader called one of the women over and as he was speaking to her, a concealed terrorist opened fire with his automatic weapon. One round hit the trooper but he was only wounded in the shoulder and was sitting up in the helicopter smiling. The helicopter waited on the ground, with its engine running and the rotor blades flashing in the sunlight while the ground crew pumped fuel into the tanks and the pilot and his technician grabbed a cool drink. Then they were off again.

The next aircraft to refuel was the Lynx. Pilot Ed Potterton briefed the squadron leader and the colonel on the state of the action, while the technicians refuelled and rearmed his aircraft. By the end of the day, the terrorists who had escaped were far away. Trackers would be dropped later to follow their spoor. Four had been confirmed dead and others had been captured. The Dakota had taken off to collect the paratroops who had found their way to a convenient airstrip. It was quite dark before the last two helicopters come beating back, their red anti-collision lights flashing in the night sky. After debrief, it was time for a shower and then into The Chopper's Arms* for a well-deserved beer.

On the next day, No 7 Squadron helicopters went to the aid of a farmer near Odzi. The terrorists opened fire some way off at the side of the house. The farmer returned fire while his wife and young son manned the Agric Alert. The rockets and small-arms fire set part of the roof alight but two helicopters were soon on the scene and engaged the attackers who fled. About 20,000 kilograms of tobacco were burnt, two tractors damaged, and a store in the area burned and looted.

Spitfire SR 64

After 20 years of decorating the concrete plinth at the entrance to New Sarum, Spitfire SR 64 was removed so that is could be restored. The project team from No 6 Squadron, was led by Warrant Officer Spike Owens who had spent time during the early part of his 35-year service working on Spitfire Mk 22s. SR 64 was built in 1945 and given the number PK350 when it entered service with No 73 Squadron RAF. Acquired by the Southern Rhodesia Air Force, it was ferried out from the United Kingdom in February 1951 by Lieutenant Bradshaw and allocated the number SR 64.

After a short career in Rhodesian skies, the aircraft was retired on 18th December 1954. The pilot on this final flight was Chris Dams while the Form 700 was signed by Colour Sergeant Roy Simmonds. By the standards of 1976, SR 64 was still virtually brand new. Airframe hours totalled 462; the engine had another 150 hours before it needed an overhaul and the propeller had only operated for seven and a half hours. Added to this, the aircraft had been placed on its plinth complete with its engine and all its mechanisms. The enthusiasts at Thornhill were eager to see the aircraft flying again. However, the war took over and despite the enthusiasm, there never was sufficient time to work on the old aircraft and so it sat month after month in a hangar at Thornhill. Eventually Jack Malloch's company Affretair acquired SR 64, guaranteeing to restore it at the company's expense, but agreeing that the air force would still have control of the aircraft.

Restored to its former glory after 26 years, the aircraft took off once again on 29th March 1980 with Captain Jack Malloch at the controls. Two years later, on 26th March 1982, the aircraft was being filmed for a documentary. Returning to base it flew through an unexpectedly violent hailstorm. The aircraft crashed and Jack Malloch was killed.

---

* The Chopper's Arms got its name from an amalgamation of the nicknames for helicopters (choppers) and policemen (coppers), because the police at FAF 5 contributed one wing of the pub. The association was a happy one for many years.

SR 65, the engineless Spitfire, which had been adorning the gate at Thornhill Gwelo, was removed and taken to Salisbury to replace SR 64. After Spitfire SR 65 had been removed, a maze of supporting pipe framework was left decorating the plinth, one piece of which looked remarkably like the barrel of a cannon. Sure enough the Thornhill humorists set to work and one morning the station was greeted with the sight of a large white flag protruding from the 'muzzle', carrying the boldly stencilled inscription BANG. Eventually the empty plinth at Thornhill received a new decoration, a Provost, R 6300, painted in standard green and brown camouflage. (No 4 Squadron Diary)

CHAPTER 43
Fylde—the strategic airfield

By the beginning of 1977, the war was placing a heavy strain on Rhodesia's young white men and in April it was announced that, for the first time, men over 38 years of age must register for training and service. In fact, many men over that age had already volunteered and were serving in the police, army and air force volunteer reserve. Despite all the efforts at détente, the insurgents' campaign went on.

Meanwhile Ian Smith had gone ahead with legislation designed to do away with racial discrimination, and in March, eleven of his Rhodesian Front members of parliament rebelled over the Land Tenure Amendment Bill, which opened up European farm land to purchase by Africans.

Lynx crash—4th May 1977
Rob Griffiths had been posted to No 4 Squadron in November 1976. On his second bush tour, he was sent to Grand Reef (FAF 8). On 4th May 1977, he was tasked to carry out a GAC training sortie with a local army unit at Clydesdale Battle Camp. The Lynx was normally armed with one pod of 18 37mm Sneb rockets, two frantan bombs and twin .303 Browning machine guns. However, for GAC (Ground Air Control) tasks, the frantans were removed and two light series bomb carriers were fitted. Each of these held four small polystyrene cylinders filled with a white powder that exploded on impact. These carriers caused a lot of drag, which reduced the aircraft's performance. May 4th is a day Rob will remember all his life:

Lance Corporal Compton Brown was mad keen on flying and had been pestering me for a flip so, as this was not an operational flight, I agreed he could join me. I arrived over the target area at 14h30. After I had completed the exercise, the Browns asked me to give them a beat-up, which I did and then, remaining at low-level began the journey home. Low level in the operational area meant below 50 feet because above 50 and below 1,500 feet you were vulnerable to small-arms fire. As we approached the mountains near Grand Reef, I increased the engine power, aiming for the lowest point, which happened to be the end of a valley. Owing to my inexperience, I went up the centre of the valley instead of taking a route along the edge. About three quarters of the way up, I realized that the mountain was out-climbing me. I thought, "Not serious. I'll turn left—go down and try again. A bit embarrassing with Compton on board but still not serious." I started my turn but was forced to continue climbing to maintain my height above ground. I was concentrating on the ground, not on my instruments and didn't notice the speed falling. The wing dropped. I kicked rudder and hit the flaps. "Why are there no flaps?" The aircraft brushed through branches—a strange, unbelievably terrible sensation. I felt the Lynx jolt and shake. There was a solid buckling sound as we hit the trees. And a deafening scream. "No! God please—not now." I don't know who screamed. Thoughts of my family flashed through my mind—how will they take it? Flame leapt up from my left foot, over my left side and into my face. "I am being burned!" I lifted my arm to cover my face. I was flung forward. There was a bone-shattering jar as the harness halted my forward momentum. There were flames everywhere. "I must get out—quick!" But the catch on the harness wouldn't come undone! I felt the burning and pulled desperately. Now I was free but my left foot was caught. I kicked. Everything was exploding round me. There were flames everywhere—the .303 ammunition was going off—then the rockets. I was still burning. Smoke was coming from my left side. My whole body was unbelievably painful. I could hardly see. I tripped and stumbled as I pulled clear from the wreck. I ripped at my flak vest—and then struggled with my survival jerkin. I shouted for Compton but he didn't answer. My eyes had been fused shut by the flames—but fortunately a cut through my left eyelid meant I had some vision. I needed help. I tried to get the emergency radio out of my survival jacket but my hands wouldn't work. I realized then that my leather flying gloves had been charred stiff. I ripped them off with my teeth but I couldn't get the buttons of my jacket undone to reach the radio. I did manage to reach the day/ night flares and set one off. It looked pretty pitiful compared to the pyrotechnic display behind me. I hadn't had time to send out a Mayday call but I knew Grand Reef would soon be getting worried and search aircraft would be on their way. From my survival training I knew I should stay with the aircraft but inactivity made the pain unbearable—and if help didn't come soon we would both be dead. I could vaguely make out something white in the valley below, which looked like some sort of building. I called again to Compton—again there was no reply, so I started down the hillside. The descent was steep and strewn with boulders; not being able to see very well, I tripped and slid most of the way on my backside. As the sound of the exploding ammunition decreased, I became aware of voices. I called for help—but there was not even a lull in the conversation let alone a reply. I negotiated a barbed wire fence with difficulty and reached the building. Perhaps I would find a telephone! There was no answer to my knocking. I felt totally helpless. I was standing wondering what to do next when two young Africans appeared. They were wary and didn't come too close. They seemed afraid that they would be blamed for my condition. I asked them to go for help but they refused. While I was talking to them, a plane flew over. It was then that I found I couldn't lift my arms above my shoulders. The aeroplane disappeared from sight. An older man joined us. He offered to guide me to the nearest store. He was an absolute star. Apparently, he was a barman in Umtali and this was his house. He took my arm, and realizing that I was in intense pain did everything he could to distract me. Reaching a small stream, he suggested I lie down in it but it was very dirty. I did wade in and try to drink but I couldn't cup my hands, so he took water in his hands and gave it to me. The two young men who had accompanied us now agreed to go for help. At last, my guide and I reached the store. I asked for water but my friend insisted on a cola and held the bottle while I drank. When the storekeeper asked for payment, my guide told him to take a hike. It wasn't long before we heard the sound of a car engine and a vehicle screamed to a halt—the two young men jumped out. The driver was a Lands Inspector who lived in Umtali but had an office about a kilometre from the store. Normally he left the office in time to reach Umtali by half past four—but on this particular day he had forgotten his house keys and had to return for them. It was as he was leaving the office for the second time that the two men arrived with news of my crash. He told me that he had already alerted the authorities and would take me into Umtali. The drive into town seemed to take a lifetime. The pain was unbearable. My poor driver, the nurse at casualty and the doctor all got a fair list of expletives. I could not give Wing Commander Hugh Slatter, the officer commanding Thrasher, much help with the whereabouts of the wreck and they only found Compton about midnight. It was his death that was the most difficult thing to live with. A few days later I was transported to Andrew Fleming Hospital in Salisbury where I met two other people who were to have a profound influence on my recovery—Sister Midge Turnbull, sister in charge of the Burns Unit and Mr Bertwin Owen-Smith, my reconstructive surgeon. Apart from being brilliant at his job, the fact that made him special was that he had been badly burnt in a

World War II aircraft crash. His surgeon had been the famous Archibald McKindoe, the father of modern plastic surgery. Owen-Smith had no time for self-pity and always greeted me with a firm slap on some unbandaged part of me. I had burns over more than 65% of my body. The odds of my survival were reckoned to be about 50% but this didn't take into account the support I got from everyone and my own dogged stubbornness. The surgery began with my eyelids and worked slowly down taking over three months. The saline baths were the worst—excruciatingly painful. During those weeks, my spirits were raised by visits from among others, Richie Kaschula who had a bullet wound in his foot, Leon du Plessis, Mark Dawson and Darryl Squance. Air Marshal Frank Mussell visited me virtually every day. I was persuaded to work towards specific goals—the first was to be out of hospital for the 30 PTC Wings Ball and the second was to be back flying within a year of my crash. I made the deadline of the Wings Ball. I was back at work as No 4 Squadron adjutant by October 1977. The biggest hurdle was the scarring which affected my vision. But once again fortune was on my side and an eye specialist and golfing associate of my father's designed corrective lenses and I was cleared for normal flying. On 8th May 1978, I started flying again, and was cleared for day operations on the Trojan. I had missed my goal by just four days. On 24th November, I was cleared for operational flying in the Lynx. (Rob Griffiths)

Convoy ambush—Chipinga

On the morning of 12th May 1977, the Chipinga convoy was attacked by a group of insurgents and an army stick was deployed from Chipinga to do a follow-up. They tracked the terrorists and made contact with them on the north bank of the Bangwe River close to the Chipinga road. Martin Hatfield had been deployed from Grand Reef and was en route to provide top cover in a Lynx. The contact had occurred just before he arrived. After the attack, the insurgents moved east onto higher ground. Martin Hatfield continues the story:

I commenced circling, slowly moving eastwards when the call signal on the ground informed me that I was taking small-arms fire from the vicinity of Gondo hills. I picked up the terrs' movement and positioned for an air strike. By now there was a fair amount of popping around my aircraft and I can remember cursing the terrs on each attack. Every time I called "turning in live", I told the troops to keep their heads down, followed by "the f.....s are shooting at me." (I was informed after I landed that my choice of language was interesting!) The terrain was hilly with thick vegetation so I attacked the areas where I saw muzzle flashes. On my third or fourth run in, I took a hit through the cockpit. When I pulled out I could smell fuel, and I had no boost indication on the rear motor, so I shut it down and diverted to Chipinga Air Field about 10 minutes away. I had dropped two Frans, and fired 30 Sneb and about 200 rounds of .303. As I left the contact area, a G-Car from Grand Reef was already at the scene to assist. At Chipinga, I noticed the aircraft had been hit four times in the wings and fuselage. A tech was flown in to do a complete assessment of the damage and he did temporary repairs so that a ferry flight could be carried out. After being debriefed by the local army commander, we decided to night-stop. Chipinga was the most convenient place to effect repairs. The fact that I happened to be dating a nurse at Chipinga Hospital at the time was completely coincidental, although I have to admit that I would have used any excuse to divert and stay over. Of course I had my leg pulled by the squadron—that I would do anything—even get shot up—for a night-stop! That night-stop turned out to be quite pleasant! I flew to Thornhill the next morning with a hell of a hangover to carry out the aircraft change, and returned to Grand Reef the same day. (Martin Hatfield)

It was also a very busy day for the Dakota. As this aircraft was completing its final re-supply for the day, it was tasked on a casevac and eventually night-stopped in Salisbury because one of the two serious casualties was in a critical condition.

Casualty evacuations at night, using airstrips and FAFs with poor or non-existent lighting, were hazardous to say the least, one recurring problem being that ground forces often did not fully understand the correct way to lay out a landing area. During May, Chris Tucker a pilot with No 4 Squadron had a nasty incident at Pachanza when he found that the flare path had been incorrectly laid and he had to leave the runway damaging the aircraft. Luckily, he was not injured.

Certainly there was always a complete willingness by pilots to fly fixed wing or helicopters into difficult areas in order to bring wounded men out. This knowledge was a great morale booster to the men on the ground and the debt owed in lives was fully acknowledged.*

A Silver Cross action

The Silver Cross of Rhodesia had been awarded to Flight Lieutenant Watt for an action in which he was flying an Alouette with crewmember Sergeant Garry Whittal who was also awared the Silver Cross. Roger Watt tells what happened that day:

I was tasked to re-supply the radio relay station on top of a mountain in the area of Marymount Mission in the Mount Darwin area. My technician was Sergeant Garry Whittal. We delivered the goods to the relay and headed for home. Shortly after leaving the mountain top, we crossed a dry riverbed in which Gary and I, at the same moment, spotted about eight to ten armed men running. We both realized immediately that we had surprised a gang of terrorists, as they were sprinting to get to cover. I turned to bring the aircraft's machine gun to bear, and at that point, the terrs opened fire on us as they realized that they had been seen. Simultaneously the gang split into three groups and bomb-shelled, firing at us all the while. As soon as we got into the attack pattern, I ordered Gary to open fire. After only one shot, the MAG had a stoppage. Gary stripped the gun to see if he could get it working again but found that the only way to get it to fire was to re-cock after every shot. While all this was going on, I radioed FAF 5 at Mount Darwin and passed on the details. I knew that the fireforce were going to take about 20 minutes' flying time to get to us, plus five minutes to get airborne, so we were going to be on our own for at least 25 minutes. I increased my orbit to keep contact with, and try to contain, all three groups of terrs. I told Gary to forget about the MAG and use his FN rifle instead, by laying it on top of the MAG so as to make use of the offset gun sight. As a result, he was able to get in a few good shots and managed to place some rounds fairly close to the terrs, which had the desired effect of reducing the ground fire being directed at us. I was trying to keep track of where each group was running to, so that I could direct the fireforce onto them. The fireforce arrived led by Flight Lieutenant Trevor Baynham in the K-Car, and I briefed him as to what was happening on the ground. We were now in a position to turn the tables on the terrs. I indicated to Trevor where the three groups had gone to ground and shortly thereafter, he initiated a contact and deployed the troops to round up the terrs. In the meantime an RAR call sign about eight miles away made a gallant effort to reach the contact area, running all the way and arriving shortly after the fireforce. I was now low on fuel so I had to return to Mount Darwin. During the 25 minutes it took the fireforce to get to the scene, our aircraft was subjected to continual ground fire throughout our orbit, with limited means of returning the fire. Although the aircraft was never hit, there were a number of very loud cracks, which I was later informed were rounds passing close to us. Because of this action, nine terrs were either killed or captured, some of whom had been wounded. I was sure that I had

---

* From Op Hurricane—thanks to pilots, John Kidson and Chris Tucker, who were involved in last night's casevac from Mashumbi pools This JOC heartily endorses thanks for a difficult task carried out in the full tradition of the air force. [Comment from John Kidson: Nothing special—just in and out on a dark night.]

seen ten men initially, and I was vindicated when many months later a tenth man was found. He had been severely wounded but had managed to get to a nearby kraal, where the locals had given him refuge. (Roger Watt)

Alouette fire in Gokwe

Towards the middle of May 1977, a village in Gokwe was attacked by a gang of about 65 ZIPRA insurgents, and one African policeman was killed. The following day an Alouette III was flown from Thornhill, with Chris Dickinson as pilot and Rob Nelson as engineer/ gunner. Chris was doing his instructor's course on No 6 Squadron and as this was evidently going to be a protracted deployment, Roger Watt volunteered to take Chris's place so that he could return to his course.

On the evening of 17th May it was decided to base the follow-up operations at a National Parks Training Centre located north-west of Gokwe on the Sengwa River. The rest of the story is told by Roger Watt:

On the morning of 18th May, Rob and I loaded everything into the chopper and set off for our new base. About ten minutes out, we heard that an RAR follow-up group had contacted the terrs and was calling for more trackers, and a casevac for two slightly wounded men. I acknowledged the call—landed at base—refuelled, unloaded our personal gear and took off with four game rangers who were to be relief trackers. We arrived, dropped off two of the rangers, but the third told me he had spotted something in the bushes as we were coming in to land, so the four of us, two trackers, Rob and I went back to check. Suddenly, as we were climbing, the bush beneath us came alive—immediately the sky was filled with green tracers. I could feel the aircraft taking hit after hit as I desperately pulled power to get out of range, and at the same time tried to bring our twin Brownings to bear on the enemy. I remember seeing the altimeter at 1,200 feet— then suddenly the aircraft filled with white smoke—which turned black and was pierced with flame. I closed both fuel controls and started an autorotation. At this stage, everything seemed to slow down. It seemed I had all the time in the world to make decisions. Firstly, where to land? There were two obvious places, the dry riverbed or a ploughed field close to a deserted village. I chose the ploughed field. Secondly, I saw that the flames were being affected by the rotor wash and were passing through the interior of the aircraft in a clockwise direction. In operations we always flew with both rear doors and the front left door off, the pilot's door being the only one fitted. I decided to jettison this door to enable me to exit faster when we got down. As I reached for the lever, I saw that both trackers had climbed out to escape the flames and were standing on the step outside my door so I didn't jettison the door. I believe this decision actually saved our lives, as the flames were blocked by the door. I undid my seat belt. I could feel the back of my neck and my left arm being burnt and by unstrapping I could move forward away from the flames. Looking back I could see that the rear wall of the chopper had been burnt through and I knew that just behind that were the control rods to the main rotor. If the rods were burnt, then the controls would be useless and I would not be able to land the aircraft. I was either going to die on landing—or survive and be trapped in the burning wreckage. I remember my left arm burning but I knew that if I took it off the collective there would be no chance of putting it back into the flames in the final moments. As it turned out, I made a near-perfect forced-landing in the ploughed field, with just slight forward speed. The nose wheel dug in and the aircraft tilted forward about 40° and then settled back on all its wheels. The burning fuel then washed to the front of the cockpit and my hands, face and legs were burnt. As the aircraft nosed in, I was in a detached frame of mind. I heard someone screaming (which must have been me) and from then on I do not remember anything else until I was rolling on the ground outside the aircraft to put out the flames. I stood up. The two rangers had survived the landing. I moved towards the chopper to fetch Rob but one of the rangers said he had jumped from the aircraft while it was about 300 feet up. We stood a moment, pulling ourselves together and then realized that the ammunition was exploding so we moved away taking stock of the situation as we went. We had only one rifle and one full magazine among us and we knew that there was a fairly large group of terrs nearby. We decided to try to reach the village, which was on higher ground. We would have some shelter there if we needed it. At this stage, the shock began to wear off and the pain came in great waves. There was not much shade from the sun, or cover from the terrs. After about 15 minutes we saw, to our horror, that a group of men with black faces, was approaching the still-burning wreck. We prepared for trouble—but they were game rangers. They didn't have any morphine but they went and fetched water from the river for me and for one of the rangers whose arm was also burnt. I spent the rest of the time pouring water over our burns. Rob's body was found and brought back to the village. Forty-five minutes later, the two Hawker Hunters that had been scrambled from Thornhill arrived overhead. Using the RAR corporal's radio, I told Rob McGregor, who was leading the flight, what had happened. After a wait of about five hours, which seemed forever, a chopper arrived, having come all the way from Wankie. We were flown to an airfield nearby, where we were met by an Islander with a doctor on board and flown to Salisbury. I spent just over three weeks in hospital, where I was really well cared for. I declined a skin graft on my left arm deciding that I had had enough pain already and that I would rather live with the scar, which is now barely noticeable. The game ranger had a skin graft on his left arm. The three of us were very lucky. (Roger Watt)

Operation Aztec

Operation Aztec was staged at the end of May running into the month of June 1977 and was designed to restrict the movement of ZANLA forces into south-eastern Rhodesia. The plan was to mount a three-pronged attack. The 2nd Battalion, Rhodesia Regiment, was to penetrate ten kilometres across the border taking out any staging posts in the area. Concurrently, a group of RLI would be helicoptered into the ZANLA complex known as Rio, which was situated close to the Nuanetsi River. Another group would be parachuted into the ZANLA base area at Madulo Pan. Meanwhile, a Selous Scouts flying column would move along the line of rail taking out all ZANLA camps as far as Jorge do Limpopo.

The operation began at last light on 28th May 1977. The column crossed the border using a bush track. The going was difficult in the dark but soon after dawn, they reached the Malvernia/Maputo road. Once again, FAF 7 played a large role as the Daily Diary for Sunday 29th May shows:

Up before the lark at 04h00 to pass a weather check to pilots. Air Lieutenant Jan Mienie was airborne at 05h45 with our Jetset (Int Officer) Squadron Leader Steve Fenton-Wells and headed off into Mozambique territory to do telstar and top cover duties. The Canberras were over us at 05h50 and we eagerly awaited news of their efforts. Squadron Leader Cyril White took off from Malapati to act as telstar and passed on the welcome news that all strikes were on target. Several times during the day, the Hunters went in and there was a feeling of excitement as we listened in on the ops channel.

Following the air strikes on Madulo Pan, 40 commandos were paradropped into the area. Among other items discovered were a considerable number of skulls and human bones, presumably the result of the Canberra strikes on the camp the previous year. Leaving members of the RLI at Madulo Pan, the column continued to Jorge do Limpopo, where, on the outskirts of the town, it met with scattered resistance in the form of rocket and mortar fire.

Air support was requested and the Hunters of No 1 Squadron went in and dealt effectively with the enemy. Leaving members of the RLI to clear any pockets of resistance at Jorge do Limpopo and to hold this strategically important base against counter-attack, the column set out for Mapai. Only minor opposition was encountered until the column reached Mapai airstrip. Here a large Frelimo/ZANLA force armed with 14.5mm heavy machine guns was holding well-prepared defence positions. There was a short, sharp engagement during which the enemy forces withdrew and after a night's rest, the column moved on towards Mapai leaving a small force at the airfield.

It was now early morning on 31st May. At dawn, the Hunters carried out attacks on the Frelimo and ZANLA strong points around the town. Then the column moved in, coming under heavy but inaccurate mortar fire. The Hunters were called back but could not pinpoint the mortar positions. Large caches of arms, ammunition and equipment were discovered hidden around the village. The airfield at Mapai had not been damaged in the attack and so it was decided to send in a Dakota, carrying a team of mechanics who could repair captured ZANLA vehicles, which were then used to ferry valuable material back to Rhodesia. Jerry Lynch, Dakota pilot, picks up the story:

We were stationed at Buffalo Range (FAF 7) as part of the fireforce for that area. On the morning of 31st May, my crew and I (Flight Lieutenant Bruce Collocott and Flight Sergeant Russell Wantenaar) were briefed to take a team of mechanics and various supplies to the airfield at Mapai. We loaded the men and equipment and made the trip without incident. There was a lot of captured equipment at the airfield. We enjoyed tasting the Frelimo rations—not particularly satisfying but full of goodies by courtesy of various Scandinavian countries. We loaded all we could into the Dak and ferried it back to FAF 7 where we were ordered to return to Mapai with a team of demolition experts, under the command of Captain C.J.I. (Neil) Kriel of the Selous Scouts. Once again, the Dak was loaded to the gills with captured equipment. We arrived back at FAF 7 during the lunch hour—and had a bit of a problem finding men to unload and service the aircraft. The turn round which should have taken about half an hour— took two hours. In the meantime, we had been requested by Major John Murphy not only to load water, mortar bombs and ammunition for the defenders of the captured airfield but also to go to Malapati to collect various items and men. When we had eventually loaded at Malapati, it was getting close to last light, and it was dark before we were halfway to Mapai. We were flying at treetop height, standard anti-strela tactics, and were fortunately spotted by a high flying aircraft, which guided us onto the approach path to Mapai. The Scouts had arranged trucks with their lights shining on the threshold of the runway and they also had some Megablitz strobe light. The men at Mapai welcomed the supplies—particularly the water. The Dak was quickly unloaded and reloaded with equipment. Ammunition and brand new tyres were piled high in the front section and lashed down. The strobes were switched on and we commenced our take-off. The time was 20h00. The airstrip was narrow and very sandy but the bush had been cleared well back on either side. I had decided to do a short take-off, which entails applying full power at brake release, lifting off at 65 knots and then maintaining that speed until well above any obstacles. The Vmc of a Dak is 90 knots on one engine. We had just got airborne and were, fortunately, not more than ten feet off the ground, when there was the unmistakable 'tak-tak-tak' of bullets hitting the aircraft and the green flashes of tracer passing through the cockpit. There was a loud 'whoosh', most likely from an RPG-7 and we immediately lost the starboard engine. There was nothing I could do to correct the resulting yaw to starboard other than cut the power on the good engine and put the aircraft back on the ground. Fortunately, I was able to correct the violent swing with hard port braking. We came to a stop off the runway and short of the thick tree line on the verge. At this stage, the whole interior of the aircraft was in flames. It seemed that the hydraulic reservoir behind the co-pilot's head had been ruptured by gunfire and the resultant high-pressure spray of fluid had ignited. During the violent swing, Bruce had slumped from his seat and was lying across my lap. Everything had happened very quickly and it was only when I tried to lift Bruce out of his seat that I realized he was dead. There was regrettably nothing I could do and I had to leave him in the aircraft. I found my way out of the now fiercely burning cabin. It had taken a good three minutes to get into the cockpit clambering over the piles of cargo—I got out in three seconds. Russell Wantenaar and I ran into the bush on the left of the runway and took cover. We had no idea how many of the enemy there were or whether they were on our side of the runway. The only weapon we had was Russell's pistol—we hadn't paused to grab a rifle on our dash from the plane. We watched the aircraft burning. Russell, the ever-efficient engineer said, "Sir, you left the landing lights on." I said he was welcome to switch them off—and the Mags as well, if he liked. Just then the fuel tanks exploded and the fuselage dropped to the ground. Through the smoke and dust, we saw the approaching figure of a loan Selous Scout, firing his pistol into the trees and shouting obscenities. It was John Murphy, hotly pursued by two of the Scouts' vehicles. If we hadn't been delayed at FAF 7, we would have got in and out of Mapai in daylight. It was a very sad end to an otherwise successful day. The aircraft, Dakota 3702, which had been General Smuts's personal plane, was something the country could ill afford to lose. Bruce, with his ever-ready wit was a great loss to us all. His last words as we put on full power were, "One hour to beer time." (Jerry Lynch)

Next day at dawn, an air force salvage team flew in by helicopter, and recovered what they could from the burnt-out wreck. What could not be removed was blown up.

During the daylight hours of 1st June, the Selous Scouts column moved rapidly down the line of railway to Mabalane, some 200 kilometres south of Jorge do Limpopo and demolished a steam crane, ensuring that the railway line, which had been sabotaged, could not be cleared immediately.

For the six days that the Rhodesian forces were in Mozambique, the air force maintained daylight patrols with high-flying aircraft keeping a watchful eye on the countryside to monitor any enemy reinforcements being brought up from Barragem. These efforts were rewarded by the bonus of six Frelimo vehicles loaded with troops, which were destroyed in air strikes.

On 2nd June, the ground forces pulled back, having achieved the complete destruction of Mapai and Jorge do Limpopo, as well as a major disruption of the railway line. Final clear-up and regrouping took another couple of days.

FAF 7—Saturday 4th June 1977

The Mapai Operation was wrapped up today and all aircraft including the K-Car and G-Car based at Mabalauta returned to FAF 7. The Lynx were used as top cover for the withdrawal of the column (motorized) from Mozambique.

The Air Force Regiment

With increasing insurgent activity taking place over larger and larger areas of the country, airfield and airport security was assuming ever-greater importance. It had now become considerably more than a case of patrolling the immediate perimeter.

The air force had set up a security-training unit in the early 1970s and the establishment had rapidly increased in size. During 1977, it became responsible for training national servicemen, internal affairs and guard force as well as air force recruits. By the end of August 1977, about 200 internal affairs and 500 guard force personnel had passed through the school. The trainees were mainly used to guard forward airfields, but there were never enough men available and so the air force began to use members of the general service unit as guards.

Obviously, the training of these men had to be placed on a more professional footing and so it was decided to set up an Air Force Regiment. Formed along the lines of the Royal Air Force Regiment, this force would have the primary role of defending and securing all air force aircraft, installations, personnel and equipment against any form of intrusion or attack.

Squadron Leader Bruce Harrison, then personal staff officer to the commander of the air force, says:

> *Wing Commander Tol Janeke and I sat down in the officers' mess at New Sarum and worked out that we would need a bare minimum of $3,000,000 (Rhodesian) to start the whole thing off. There was no way we could do with less. We had discussions with Treasury on 24th June, just before the annual estimates of expenditure. They said, you can have one and a half. Tell us by five o'clock how you are going to spend it. By five o'clock that night, we had some kind of budget. It certainly was not enough but it was a start.* (Bruce Harrison)

The next important question was: Where should the training be carried out? What was needed was an airfield with a runway but not too much traffic. It was decided that the best location for the regiment would be Fylde, the new strategic airfield 40 kilometres north-west of Hartley. The runway had been completed but there was not much else there.

> *Fylde consisted of an airfield with very minimal facilities and a farmhouse with outbuildings, which had been the original Fylde farmhouse. I think the farm had been named after a place in East Anglia, in Britain. It was a large flat plain. So we had a typical airfield to practise on, with some farmland round it, well away from the bright lights. As we used to tell the recruits, "You can cry as much as you want. Your mothers are 90 kilometres away." I had a bit of a problem with Squadron Leader Derek de Kock, who was in charge of the works side. He was a great lad with explosives. He wanted to demolish all the old buildings and put up temporary accommodation. I said you won't demolish a single thing here unless I tell you to. Ultimately the garage became our armoury. The water tank became a superb Senior NCO's mess. The farm assistant's house that was roofless when we arrived became the instructors' single quarters and very comfortable they were. The pig pens were going to be the dog kennels but we didn't move the dog school down from New Sarum. John Cox who was then OC Depot wanted the dogs down, under his command, but we couldn't find the money. The farmhouse, a big spacious building, was the only one that the Public Works Department would accept as a government building. That became our command centre. In fact, the whole thing developed into the showpiece of the air force to the extent that visitors were regularly taken down and shown around to see the depot at work because it looked and felt like a military establishment—and ran like one. It was a training depot so we made it look like a training depot, with whitewashed stones and a parade square right in the middle. A lot of it was done on the scrounge. For instance, the parade square had been the tobacco seedbeds. The local Roads Department chap, who was building an access road, was persuaded, without the knowledge of his superiors, to use his equipment to grade and lay down decomposed granite to make a nice hard surface for the parade square. So we started off with no money, a physical place but no real development and a handful of instructors. Having the ear of the commander made a big difference and I must admit that we had Frank Mussel right behind us.* (Bruce Harrison)

The next thing to be decided was the training itself.

> *We didn't even have a syllabus. So we went to the RAR and they gave us the syllabus they had been using for many years to train our soldiers. Following this schedule they could convert the*

rawest civilian into a soldier in six months. Shock and horror from high up. You have to do it in six weeks, we were told. Fortunately one of the sensible things I did, was to stick to my guns. I insisted that if it took six months, that is what we had to have. (Bruce Harrison)

The first three courses went to Ground Training School at New Sarum. There they did general training and a basic physical fitness course. The rest of the six months was spent at the depot at Fylde doing infantry training plus practice with heavy weapons, 20mm cannon, Browning heavy machine guns and mortars. Following their six months, the men were deployed to forward airfields as well as to New Sarum and Thornhill. There were 100 men in the first intake and the intakes came in every six weeks from GTS. The first men passed out early in 1978 and began a tradition that was to continue until the end—of marching from Fylde to New Sarum carrying their equipment. The depot was actually responsible for the first formal drill and weapons courses since the closure of the School of Infantry. In 1978, the Security Training School at New Sarum ceased to exist as such with the formation of the Regimental Training Depot at Fylde.

Hunter flypast

The highlight of the opening of parliament on 21st June 1977 was a flypast by No 1 Squadron. The squadron made use of the opportunity to acquire some much-needed close-formation practice and to celebrate two notable events in the squadron's history. The occasion not only marked the 15th anniversary of the squadron's acquisition of Hunters but also the attainment of 1,000 Hunter flying hours by the squadron commander, Squadron Leader Richard Brand. The formation took off from Thornhill, overflew Bulawayo, their affiliated city, and then turned for a run over Salisbury for the presidential salute.

A tribute to a troopie

In July, Rex Taylor was on call-up with No 7 Squadron in the eastern districts.

The siren went and we attended the briefing. A bunch of terrs had been sighted. The sticks were already in the chopper when the stick leader and I arrived. Holding the pilot's door open was a fair-haired young man wearing a huge grin. "Your men are ready for inspection, sir!" he said. "All ready to go. If you have any problems just call me! We'll look after you!" He was always the same. His humour was infectious. I would return his salute with mock ceremony but my attempts at repartee were never up to his cheerful greeting that always relieved the tension of the moment. My tech, Adrian Rosenberg monitored the engine as it went through its starting cycle, and then made a circuit of the aircraft to check that all was OK before I engaged the rotors. While this was going on, the fair-haired troopie held my door open and pretended to scan the instruments, every now and again giving me a condescending nod of approval. As the rotors came up to speed, he closed my door and made some unheard comment that lip-read as, "Good show, sir. You're OK to go now!" Then he leapt into the vacant seat behind me and gave me the thumbs up sign. The smiles all round were reassuring. The gang we were about to engage had been active near Inyazura. They had evaded the security forces so far but now they were cornered on a huge granite outcrop, a geographic feature in the area. The initial assault took the gang by surprise, but a hard-core element was now holed up among the rocks of the koppie. The choppers having dropped the troops were no longer required, so we landed nearby and gathered round a VHF radio, listening intently. Shoulders drooped when we heard that the RLI Commando had taken a casualty. There was no call for medics and we knew instinctively that a troopie had been killed. Twenty minutes went by; the hard core had been winkled out and the troops were now sweeping the area for escapees. Overhead, the G-Car circled, controlling the sweep. The radio barked: 'Black Four, go to the lower slope and uplift a casualty'. That was me. Rosenberg and I started our chopper and landed near a small group of troopies standing round a silent bundle in a khaki sleeping bag. We were saddened, and cursed the senselessness of war. The soldiers lifted their lifeless comrade gently into the chopper. As they slid him in, the zipped-up sleeping bag opened to reveal the youthful face and rumpled fair hair of our happy cheerleader. My sorrow turned to tears. Head bowed, I avoided looking at Adrian as we flew our passenger home. Soon we were back in the contact area, taking over temporarily as airborne control while one of the other choppers went to refuel. We were in orbit with the army major on board when we got a call from one of the sticks: "Trooper Barclay has heard that his brother Dave has been hit. Can you tell us how he is?" I couldn't help feeling sorry for the major. There was a short pause, then the major's reply, clear and concise: "He's dead. I'm sorry." The simplicity of those words may be hard to understand, but together with the pause before he spoke—and the sombre tone of voice, those four words conveyed more sorrow, sympathy and consolation than any padre could have done. Young Dave Barclay died a week before his 21st birthday. I never knew his name until his tragic death—now I shall remember it always. (Rex Taylor)

The Blue birds
The first day of July 1977, was a significant date for the women of the Rhodesian Air Force. It was on that day that women members lost their temporary status within the Rhodesian Women's Service and became full regular airwomen. Perhaps the most obvious immediate change and possibly the most welcome was the appearance of badges of rank on women's uniforms. During the following years, women found their way into almost every type of job. They came to be respected and appreciated for the roles they undertook and rapidly became indispensable. One such was Corporal Arietta von Popering, who in July '77 was functioning as a general dog's body at No 7 Squadron. In practice, Arietta did most of the jobs of the squadron adjutant. Arietta claimed that it was the best job in the air force. "It's the immense variety," she said, "which attracts me. No two days are the same and there is always lots of work to keep me occupied, but I sometimes wonder whether the men will ever really get used to having me around and there is still quite often a distinct hush as I walk into a crew room." That hush was explained by one of the young squadron pilots: "The language around here," he said, "used to be a bit robust but since Arietta arrived we find ourselves toning it down. She is really terrific and we wouldn't know what to do without her." In the middle of August, a squad of air girls passed out after an intensive two-week training course at New Sarum. They were the first women recruits to have been trained entirely by the air force and their number included the first Asian woman to serve with the air force. She was Salisbury-born Miss Miriam Hassam who had started her career with the rank of sergeant because of her qualifications and secretarial experience, and was posted to the air force communications centre.

Air force dogs nab cons
It was in July that the air force dog section hit the headlines. While they were travelling to town, several members of the New Sarum Dog Training School staff learned by radio of the escape of two prisoners from Kentucky Prison. They immediately hurried to the scene. Warrant Officer Alec Mann and Flight Sergeant Terry Rubenstein carried out an assessment of the situation whilst SAC Le Grange went to New Sarum for appropriate canine assistance. Before long, one tracker dog and one attack dog had joined the chase. The spoor of bare-footed running men was found on a nearby dirt road and the party set off in pursuit. After one and a half miles of tracking, the escapees were overtaken and recaptured. After a delay of something less than an hour, the party was able to resume its journey to town. The *Bateleur* carried the story under the heading Dogs Nab Loose Cons.

Five-star hotels in the bush

Whilst not every inhabitant of the FAFs would agree with journalist Philippa Berlyn's description of them as 5-star hotels, it is still generally true that most of them were relatively comfortable places to live. For the most part, that comfort was due to the hard work and industry of the airmen who decided that since they had to exist in the bush, they might as well make the best of their surroundings. A great deal of the work at individual FAFs could be credited to the dedication of a few inspired individuals, at what might be termed grass roots level. Sergeant Gazimbi Tadious of the New Sarum Security Section was one of the pioneers of airfield construction. Sergeant Tadious was a well-known sight seated behind the wheel of a tractor or earthmover. He spent his time moving from FAF to FAF with the travelling circus building revetments and other protective earthworks around the perimeters. His dexterity with the tractor shovel resulted in a radical reduction of drum-filling time and much of the credit for the security of the FAFs must go to Sergeant Tadious and his colleagues who did such a vital job in the forward areas.

News from Cranborne

As far as the VR was concerned, their headquarters at Cranborne had been extended by the addition of a lecture hall, which was officially opened on 21st August by the commander, Air Marshal Frank Mussell. This building had been constructed in 1942 as a temporary hospital ward for RAF Cranborne with an intended life of five years. After a varied career, and having become a decrepit wreck, it was allocated to the VR, who spent a great deal of tender loving care on the old building. The new hall was named after the late Air Lieutenant Dan Murray, who had died in February 1975. Dan was a member of the RAF and had done part of his training at Cranborne during the RATG days. Following his demobilization in 1946, he purchased an aircraft in the United Kingdom and flew it out to Rhodesia where he took up a career as a farmer. He joined the VR in 1960. On the subject of Cranborne, Ian Dixon tells the following story:

106 VR (Air Movements) Squadron's headquarters was located in Cranborne. We had been allocated a building that had once been the Royal Air Force Camp Hospital, when Cranborne was an RAF training station during World War II. When 106 took tenure the building was in a shocking state of disrepair, and Air HQ told us categorically that there was no money to rehabilitate it. This gauntlet, thrown down to the squadron had an extraordinary result. Amongst our complement were some very competent tradesmen. The talentless like me could paint, wield demolition hammers, and hump furniture. In a very short time, by demolishing a wall here and constructing another there, painting everything in sight, begging, borrowing and stealing, we had transformed the building from an eyesore, to a classy suite of offices. 103 VR Squadron, our stable companion, famous as a refuge for the gentry, were not to be outdone by the ruffians of 106. But instead of dirtying their patrician hands, they employed artisans to reconstruct their offices. The end result was that both squadrons had HQs worthy of their endeavours and were not ashamed to invite visitors. The reaction of Air HQ was totally predictable. Firstly, they had proof that VRs lived in luxury, and secondly, the VR would not now need any cash to rehabilitate their accommodation. That's neither here nor there—what was relevant was that both the buildings were reputed to be haunted. I can personally testify that on two occasions while overnighting, I heard doors opening and closing, voices in the corridors, and even a telephone ringing! Some of my colleagues had similar experiences and would not stay in the building alone under any circumstances. As it had been the station hospital, there had obviously been a number of fatalities because of training accidents. Which takes me to the night of 30th March 1978—tasked with transporting stores to Rutenga by road, I camped in the

106 Squadron office. For security reasons our fully loaded truck was parked in the yard outside. At 23h00 following a few drinks in the SAS mess, I was snug in my sleeping bag. The quiet was disturbed by the sound of a key turning in a lock, a door opening, and the sound of heavy footsteps on a wooden floor. This was followed by another door opening, somebody flushing a toilet and then footsteps retreating. I was dumbstruck and my heart started beating like a drum. Considering my profound state of fear, I was very brave to get up and open the door to the corridor. All the lights were off except the parking lot lamp, which threw a dim glow down the corridor. Silhouetted against this glimmer was the outline of a man. Although the sound that came out was high and strangulated, I shouted "Halt!" The figure turned and came towards me. During World War II, RAF personnel in Rhodesia wore black shoes, khaki shirts and stockings, and either a peaked, or forage cap. There was sufficient light to see that my intruder was dressed like an old-time RAF man except for the headgear. My blood ran cold!
"Who are you?"
"Jock McGregor."
"Are you air force?"
"Yes."
'Where are you from?"
His Scots accent had prepared me for the reply.
"West Kilbride, Scotland."
I smelt a powerful waft of whisky and realized with alarm that he was moving closer.
My eyes, now more accustomed to the dim light, made out a very ordinary clean-shaven man shorter than I am. "Sorry to disturb you! I promised to fix Banjo's car, but I got waylaid." Banjo Brown, also a Scot and a dedicated drinker, was a member of 106. I had seen his battered old car parked in the yard when I checked into the building. After the fright that McGregor had given me, it was a relief to realize he was engaged on something so prosaic. I shrugged, Jock McGregor turned away and walked down the corridor. I went back to my sleeping bag. The following morning Banjo Brown was one of the security guards on our vehicle. When we stopped for lunch beside the road, I asked him why he hadn't told me that Jock McGregor was coming to sort out his car for him. He looked at me as though I was round the bend. "I don't know anybody called Jock McGregor!" (Ian Dixon)

Salisbury bombs

On 6th August 1977, Salisbury experienced its worst example of urban terrorism. A large bomb exploded in a crowded Woolworth's store at about 12h15 on Saturday morning. That particular branch catered mainly for black shoppers. Eleven people were killed and 76 injured. On the same morning, another bomb had been placed in the left luggage department at Salisbury railway station and a third in an underground parking area below Meikles Hotel. Both these bombs failed to go off and were later defused. The following Saturday, 13th August, another bomb exploded in the toilets at Chancellor House on Jameson Avenue. No one was injured in this blast but because of these explosions, tighter security was put in place in urban areas. Cordon and search operations, where a whole city block was cordoned off, and everyone in it subjected to a search, soon became common practice. The public were also asked to be on the lookout for any suspicious parcels. This resulted in frequent bomb scares and any unclaimed package was blown up. The operational area now covered the whole country and increasingly helicopters were coming under sustained and accurate ground fire.

FAF 7, 4th August 1977

The fireforce was called out to the south and a successful contact took place. Seven terrs were engaged, two killed initially and the K-Car killed another two during the ensuing engagement.

Pete le Roux was fired on and was lucky not to be hit as he was flying low. During the evening, the Islander arrived with the Combined Operations staff on board for another visit.

7th August

An Alouette III received ground fire in the Matibi No 2 TTL. The aircraft was badly hit but there were no casualties and the chopper returned to its base.

14th August

The first task of the day was only managed at 11h40 (owing to miserable weather) by Air Lieutenant Kevin Peinke who was tasked to go to Grootvlei to uplift a casevac from (VL 070485) to Grootvlei Air Field. This was followed by the Lynx to uplift the same casevac from Grootvlei to Buffalo Range. On return, Air Lieutenant Peinke was fired on by approximately 6 – 8 CTs. He ran out of ammunition and called the fireforce. He had to refuel at Chikombedzi with diesel while the fireforce continued with the search. The chopper flown by Air Lieutenant Peinke received one shot in the stabilizer. The Lynx carried out top cover for the contact. Trojan carried out a leaflet drop in the Matibi TTL.

Parachute training

The Rhodesian African Rifles had been undergoing parachute training for a year and two platoons had already been trained and were being used on operations. Squadron Leader Derek de Kock, Officer Commanding the Training School said he believed that every soldier should be a trained to use a parachute. "It makes a better soldier of that man even if he is never used in that role," he said. "It gives him esprit de corps. The best troops in the world are paratroopers with the result that the enemy, whenever he sees soldiers dropping realizes he is up against a crack force—so psychologically it is a good thing." But the psychological advantages apart, paratroopers offered a greater mobility to the army. Men could be put into a contact area quickly and be immediately available for combat. On average, a trooper could hit the ground, get out of his harness and be ready for action within 30 seconds, faster if the enemy were shooting at him. At the end of an operation he could be speedily lifted out and if necessary deployed elsewhere.

The training of African and European troops was identical. As Squadron Leader De Kock put it: "The parachute is no discriminator of colour or rank or creed. Some of the African soldiers come into the school straight from basic training and from the Tribal Trust Lands where mechanical things are not often seen. It is a giant leap forward for a soldier like this to take that long step from an aircraft, a machine he has probably only seen from a great distance. I think we have the best paratroopers in the world. We have more parachuting experience in the combat role than any other country. In the last eight years, the Parachute Training School has carried out 10,000 parachute descents. In the first seven months of this year, there have been 8,000 descents. It's a tremendous increase. And, in fact, during August, the school was training Nos 74 and 75 Basic."

The increase in parachute training meant an increase in the need to pack parachutes, which led to a shift system being worked so that the section could operate from 05h00 until 22h00. Master Technician John Wise reported that during the first seven months of 1977, the unit had packed 150% more parachutes than during the whole of 1976. During August the barrier of 2,000 parachutes a month was passed. More importantly, the massive increase had been achieved without impairing the unit's 100 percent safety record.

On 2nd September, Air Lieutenant Leon du Plessis and Sergeant John Stephen Underwood were killed when the Lynx (3042) in which they were flying crashed during a cross-border raid south of Umtali—a double loss for No 4 Squadron. Du Plessis had put in an attack on a group of insurgents and was attempting to pull out when the crash occurred.

Cross-border raids and the internal security situation were stretching all the squadrons to their limit. No 3 Squadron Diary for September reads: "Once again this month, pressure has been placed on the squadron. With the same number of flights being allocated to us, our techs have found it increasingly difficult to retain serviceability rates but fortunately they have managed to succeed. The arrival of reserve pilots has relieved a lot of pressure on the other aircrew."

October was again a busy month for the squadron, with more and more use being made of the Islander and the C 185. The FAF 5 (Mtoko) crew found themselves travelling all round the Hurricane area with the fireforce and were lucky enough to spend a night stop at the Cutty Sark Hotel in Kariba.

Radio dog trials

Long hours were also being flown by the helicopter pilots. On 9th September 1977, Flight Lieutenant Ian Harvey became the first Rhodesian Air Force pilot to notch up 3,000 flying hours in an Alouette. As well as their attack and casevac roles, the helicopters were also involved in radio dog trials, which started on 22nd September and continued into October at FAF 5 (Mtoko).

October 1977, FAF 5 Mtoko area

Radio control tracker dogs will be positioned at FAF 5 for operational duties. The dogs will be controlled through Wing Commander L.A.S. (Rex) Taylor and will only be utilized in the tracking role as laid down by Flight Sergeant Terry Rubenstein in liaison with the appropriate forces. They are not to be utilized for arms cache finding, cattle rustling, tracking or other duties but they may be used for conventional tracking and radio-control tracking. In this respect the advice of the dog handler is sacrosanct; otherwise valuable flying time will be wasted and lack of confidence in the dogs would result. Flight Sergeant Rubenstein and Wing Commander Taylor are requested to formulate operating procedure and ensure the education of personnel in the correct role of the dogs. This HQ should be notified as and when the dogs are used. The results obtained and other pertinent information will assist in assessing the value of the scheme and in the training of the other dogs.

Explaining the thinking behind this scheme Terry Rubenstein says:

Squadron Leader Petter-Bowyer and Warrant Officer Peter Allen of the Dog Section developed this concept before I joined the force. I just picked it up again. A dog, unhampered, can move at four times the speed of a man. For you to hang on and let him pull you through the bush slows him down. First we decided to try letting the dog run free and putting a homing device on him. That wasn't an operational success because it didn't give us an exact location, only a line, and if we circled in order to spot the dog we betrayed our presence. So then we tried attaching a microphone to the dog's collar and we trained him so that when he spotted someone hiding, he would sit down at a safe distance and bark. In the helicopter we could hear him bark. We also had a transmitter in the helicopter and the dog carried a speaker so that we could talk to him as well. At the beginning, we used one speaker but we found during training, that every time we gave the dog a command he veered off to the side on which he had the speaker. At first we could not understand why and then we realized that he was hearing the voice on one side of his head so he was naturally moving to that side. After that, we gave each dog two speakers, in stereo. It was a simple thing but it cost a lot of time to get it right. After that, we could use all the normal commands as though we were there with him. The main difficulty was the lack of immediate control. If you are there you can immediately discipline or reward. Dogs had to be trained to a very high standard before you could begin to retrain them on the radio control. The other difficulty was that you had to be able to see the dog all the time to give him commands. I became the Dog Master in 1977 and that interfered with this scheme. There was also a lack of time for training and the fact that helicopters were at a premium. (Terry Rubenstein)

However, trials were still being conducted in April 1978 as Peter Cooke reports:

In April 1978, I was asked to fill in as FAF commander at FAF 5. It was also decided to use me to carry out some operational trials with the radio-controlled tracker dogs. I reported to No 7 Squadron on 10th April, and was given a quick refamiliarization on the Alouette II. Over the next three days, in conjunction with Corporal R.M. Le Grange and Sergeant Chingodza, I carried out trials with the dogs and their handlers. I was then deployed to FAF 5 on 17th April. My brief was that should an opportunity arise, I should use the dogs operationally. After my take-over as FAF commander, I gave the dogs a quick practice in what was unfamiliar territory. As has been described, the dogs were fitted with a radio receiver and a transmitter, operating on different frequencies. The transmitter microphone was open at all times allowing us to hear the dog's movements—panting and barking and so on. The receiver was used by the handler to pass instructions to the dog. The dogs were also fitted with Dayglo orange jackets so that they were easily visible from the air. At a scene, the handler on the ground would do a 360° sweep—if the dog showed keenness to go he was released and the handler climbed back on the chopper. We would then follow the dog visually and hope to make contact with the men he was tracking. On 19th April, an opportunity arose. I deployed Corporal Le Grange and two Labradors, one white and one black. The dogs were soon on the scent and disappeared into the bush. We followed for about an hour and a half—at which stage the dogs lost the scent or got bored—because they discovered a water hole and decided to go for a swim instead—they were having high jinks when we arrived. The following day I deployed the dogs again but they did not pick up any tracks. On 23rd, I again deployed with Sergeant Chingodza—but this proved to be a repetition of the first occasion—the dogs found a water hole and play was more important than work! We returned to New Sarum after what I considered was a very interesting but unproductive exercise. My feelings were that Labradors were not suited to the task—being water-friendly and too playful. Fortunately, the radios were water-friendly too. (Peter Cooke)

Operations on the 'Russian' front

SAS operations had been working well in the Tete Province of Mozambique. With the land-mines, ambushes and attacks on ZANLA and Frelimo convoys, life had become difficult for anti-Rhodesian forces in the province. All in all, incursions into the north-eastern areas of Rhodesia had dropped to almost nothing. Now it was decided to withdraw the SAS from Tete and allow them to use the tactics that had proved so successful in the southern Gaza Province. The question was: how to get into the area without the enemy knowing.

Major Brian Robinson of the SAS put forward an ambitious scheme. His men would drop in from high altitude and the group would not be a small pathfinder team—it would be the biggest free fall operation carried out during the war: 24 men in one jump. They would go in at night taking enough equipment to carry out their first ambush. They would carry rifles, 60mm mortars and RPD machine guns, added to which each RPD gunner would take 500 rounds with him.

The men would land in a single dropping zone and regroup before first light. To do this they would have to exit the plane virtually touching each other and keep a tight formation in the air. The jump would be made from 12,000 feet, which was just on the oxygen level. In addition, they would take three boxes of extra kit to be used following the first ambush. The boxes with parachutes attached would be pushed out first and carry a flashing strobe light so that the free-fallers would know where they had landed. These parachutes would have automatic opening devices to release the parachute at a pre-determined height.

Each free-faller would wear a red or green light on his helmet. As the men jumped, they would turn left or right according to the colour. The drop was to be from the DC-7C piloted by Jack Malloch who would be required to find the LZ in enemy territory, at night, with no moon and without any special navigation aids.

At 03h00 on 11th October 1977, the aircraft's green light went on and the boxes went crashing out. One trooper who had collapsed owing to lack of oxygen did not make the jump. Of the 23 men who dropped that night, one paratrooper had a blackout on the way down and owed his life to the automatic opening device on his parachute, another broke his ankle, and two twisted their ankles on landing. They had all dropped on time and landed within five kilometres of the planned dropping zone—an incredible achievement on the part of the pilot. The injured men were left at the DZ while the others made their way to the ambush point on the road and railway line just south of Mapai.

The first convoy to come along the road consisted of three trucks. The leading truck, which was carrying weapons and ammunition, was destroyed. The other two trucks did an about turn but were destroyed by a Hunter strike. The casualties, including one seriously wounded member of the SAS were lifted out by No 7 Squadron, while a further 18 static line paratroopers were dropped to reinforce the free-fallers.

From then on until the final days of the war, the SAS operated in this area. Rhodesian forces found the going, in the southern province, much more difficult. The terrain was flat and sandy, water was in short supply and the local civilians were hostile. Added to this there was never enough heavy equipment to combat Frelimo forces with their tanks and armoured personnel carriers. A further difficulty was that bases for air support were a long way away. A helicopter flight from Mabalauta to the area of operations took about two hours. During the following two and a half years, Frelimo soldiers were stationed at all the sidings along the railway line. From these bases, they could carry out frequent patrols. Operations took the form of cat-and-mouse games between the SAS and Frelimo and their Russian and East German advisers, hence the SAS name for this area—the Russian Front.

Operation Melon—October/November 1977

As Rhodesian security forces radio communication was being monitored by the Russian fleet off the coast, so radio communications within Mozambique were monitored on a 24-hour basis by specialists in Salisbury. Towards the end of October 1977, information was received about a ZANLA convoy carrying top-ranking men and reinforcements, moving from Maputo by way of Mapai and then through to the Rhodesian border. Plans were made to intercept this convoy. Jerry Lynch takes up the story:

> We were stationed at Buffalo Range on fireforce duty when we were tasked, on 9th November, to fly SAS personnel into Mozambique at night. We were briefed by Captain Bob MacKenzie to proceed to a predetermined point and drop the team. There was no intelligence about enemy AA positions or troop movements. At the SAS briefing, we learned to our surprise that we were to carry alpha bombs as well as troopers. (This was apparently so that the enemy would be led to believe that the aircraft was on a bombing mission not dropping troops). My crew, Laurie Temple-Camp and Flight Sergeant Russell Wantenaar, planned our route to the target and loaded Dakota 3708. Once we were airborne, I asked the SAS officer, Percy Johnson, what he wanted to do with the alpha bombs. He said we would look for an interesting target on the way

home. We reached the area of the dropping zone and deposited the team, hopefully, where they wished to be and then sank down to 200 feet and started looking for a target to bomb. We had been following the line of rail northward but well to starboard. Bob and I spotted the light of a fire and decided to give it a dose of alphas. We told Percy that he should hurl his bombs out on the green light signal. As Percy dropped the bombs, I banked port to see what the results were. We had a rude awakening as the bombs bounced a lot higher than we expected and exploded with an almighty bang and frightening flash. Suddenly we were enveloped in an enormous fireworks display. Goodness knows how many weapons opened up on us—but we were surrounded by tracer of all colours and deafened by the noise of bullets hitting the aircraft. I dived to tree height and although the tracer followed us, we took no more hits. Shakily we assessed the damage. Unbelievably we had no casualties. It was a miracle because we found later that we had been hit 23 times! Bob was the only person to suffer any injury. He had been standing between the seats and a bullet or piece of shrapnel had grazed his cheek before continuing its flight to demolish the HF Radio behind Laurie's head. Everything in the aircraft seemed 'normalish' and we arrived back at Buffalo Range shaken and thirsty. Percy apparently decided that in future he'd leave flying to those who were crazy enough to enjoy it. On shutting down, we found that we couldn't stop the engines, because the control cables for the mixture had been severed by bullets. Before we swapped our Dak which now looked like a colander, for a new one, we inspected the damage. We were surprised at the size of some of the holes—up to 37mm in diameter. No weapon of that calibre had been reported to that date! On the following night, with a replacement aircraft, we went on another cross- border jaunt. This time Bob was well prepared, in his full American kit, Armalite, flak vest, GI helmet, water bottle etc. He said that the natives were distinctly unfriendly in these parts. Fortunately, nothing untoward happened on this sortie. We were subsequently told that we had overflown Mapai. I still dispute this as the rail line passes quite a few miles east and the fire we had a go at was on the line. I think it was a Frelimo mobile column, equipped with 12.7s, 23mm and 37mm, which we had not encountered before. Air HQ vehemently denied that Frelimo had any such weapons until the SAS captured one and donated a few rounds to No 3 Squadron. Bob d'Hotman gleefully sent them to HQ with a note: 'These are the things you say don't exist!' (Jerry Lynch)

Meanwhile the paratroopers were making their way 15 kilometres to the main Mapai/ Maputo road, which was once again the target for their ambush. About midmorning next day, the men were in the process of mining the road when they spotted three enemy soldiers moving down the road. The SAS opened fire, killing the men, but fearing that this gunfire might alert the enemy, they decided to move their ambush. While they were still in the process of finding another suitable site, they heard the convoy approaching, one day ahead of schedule. The ambush was not ready but at least the road was mined. A loud explosion, as the first vehicle hit a mine, was followed by an even louder detonation. The first vehicle had been a truck loaded with ammunition. This prevented any of the other vehicles getting past, and not wanting to turn back, the Frelimo and ZANLA commanders decided to make camp for the night.

It was now dark and the SAS commander decided that the opportunity was too good to miss. He reported the situation to the tactical headquarters at Mabalauta, in Gonarezhou National Park. The OK was given for No 1 Squadron to join the party. The SAS moved up so that they were in a good position to talk the aircraft onto the target and to ambush any vehicles that attempted to flee back down the road.

When dawn came the ammunition vehicle was still burning. The Frelimo and ZANLA commanders, realizing their danger, had prepared for an attack by moving the rest of the convoy into the cover of the surrounding bush. High overhead a Lynx came droning past.

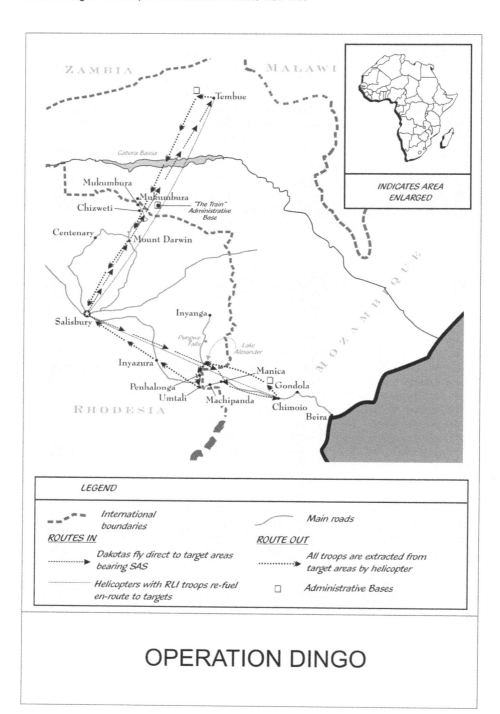

OPERATION DINGO

The SAS commander on the ground contacted 'A' Troop Commander Bob MacKenzie, who was on board the plane. Using the burning truck as a reference point, the ground commander passed information about the hiding places of the other vehicles.

From the air, Flight Lieutenant Giles Porter could not spot anything in the dense bush and he brought his aircraft down for a closer look. Despite warnings from the ground, Giles, flying at treetop height, passed directly over the heads of the SAS men and carried on down the road towards the blazing ammunition truck. At that moment, the early morning quiet was blasted by the sound of gunfire from hundreds of automatic rifles, several 23mm anti-aircraft guns, machine guns and various missiles, including at least one strela surface- to-air missile. The Lynx disappeared into a solid wall of fire. Once again, Bob MacKenzie thought his last hour had come. It was impossible to survive. But his guardian angel, or more probably the skill of the pilot, not to mention a small portion of incredible luck, meant that he lived to tell the tale. The Lynx pulled away from the killing zone with both passengers shaken but not stirred!

The heavily-armed men on the ground continued firing at the slow-moving Lynx and so revealed themselves to their enemy. Sighting on the pinpoints of light as the rising sun reflected from the windscreens of the partly concealed vehicles and on the muzzle flashes from the Frelimo and ZANLA guns, the Hunters turned in to the attack. Soon the bush was a scene of exploding ammunition, burning vehicles and wounded men. The smoke from the Hunters' 30 mm guns added to the spectacle. The whole attack lasted for five hours. The Hunters made strike after strike with one pair of aircraft replacing another as their ammunition was exhausted and they had to return to base to rearm and refuel. Meanwhile, the Frelimo and ZANLA forces kept up their heavy defensive fire.

This is just one example of the great bravery shown by many of the guerrillas. To stand up and fire your personal weapon or to maintain your station at an anti-aircraft gun while a Hunter is coming down in a dive at you, travelling at nearly 500 miles an hour with four cannons blazing, pumping out 30mm shells at the rate of 80 rounds a second, or firing a salvo of 68mm rockets, takes a very special kind of courage.

Quite early on, the SAS decided that the blues could be left to finish the job and discreetly withdrew from the area. However, when they reached the dropping zone they were requested to return to the site of the battle to give a report. It was a hazardous mission with the area full of enemy soldiers. Four SAS men volunteered do the recce.

What they found confirmed that their enemy had been the Frelimo Fourth Brigade HQ (Mobile), which had been moving up to Mapai to support ZANLA and set up a forward base. They found evidence that the convoy had been organized by Russian advisers. It was the first time that there was definite proof that the Russians were operating in Mapai.

The damage inflicted by the air strikes had been devastating with brand new Russian trucks, trailers, fuel and water bowsers, operations and command centres, support weapons and spares rendered useless before they had ever been used in action. The SAS men spotted a few vehicles, which might possibly be repairable, and the Hunters returned to the scene to render them useless. The four security force men withdrew to the dropping zone from which they were successfully uplifted by helicopter.

Field Marshal Lord Carver arrives

Against this background of escalating attacks and counter-attacks, a two-pronged attempt at peace-making was still going ahead. Within Rhodesia, attempts were being made by the more moderate African leaders to unite in order to solve Rhodesia's problems. This led to talks between the prime minister and these leaders who included Bishop Abel Muzorewa, Ndabaningi Sithole and Chief Jeremiah Chirau.

Meanwhile Britain and the United Nations were still intent on a détente with the leaders in exile. Field Marshal Lord Carver had been chosen as the prospective British resident commissioner. And, at the end of October, he flew to Dar es Salaam where he had talks with Nkomo and Mugabe. They said categorically that there would be no cease-fire unless their forces were placed in absolute control. Carver arrived in Salisbury on 2nd November 1977, wearing his field marshal's uniform, which outranked that of the Rhodesian commanders. Carver was accompanied by Lieutenant General Prem Chand who represented the United Nations. Neither of these eminent men could have found any fault with their reception.

> *It was a masterpiece of military precision. Hunter jets escorted his Hercules (Field Marshal, Lord Carver's) through Rhodesian airspace and smartly dipped their wings in salute as it touched down. Police and military guard snapped to attention as Carver stepped from the plane. A shining limousine swept onto the tarmac and drove the British appointed Commissioner for Rhodesia to the freshly dusted and polished British Residency in Salisbury, Marimba House.*
> (Rhodesia Herald, 3rd Nov. 1977)

Once again nothing came of the visit and before the end of the month, Ian Smith announced his intention of proceeding directly with talks between himself Muzorewa, Sithole and Chief Chirau—aimed at achieving an internal settlement.

Operation Dingo
The attacks on Chimoio and Tembué—November 1977
Some kind of internal settlement might be on the cards but the war continued with increasing ferocity. Aerial photographs supported by evidence from a captured ZANLA soldier who had been at the camp two weeks earlier, confirmed that Chimoio was the largest and most important base in Mozambique. Frelimo had allocated the entire Chimoio/Vanduzi/Pungwe area to ZANLA and since fleeing Rhodesia after the abortive détente exercise, Robert Mugabe had begun to reconstruct the war effort from Chimoio (formerly Vila Pery). The ZANLA leader and his two top commanders, Rex Nhongo and Josiah Tongogara, directed operations from their high command headquarters in an old farmhouse. It was believed that there could be as many as 9,000 men under training in this camp, supported by Frelimo-crewed Russian T 54 tanks and BTR 152 armoured personnel carriers. It was from Chimoio that the thousands of ZANLA members trained in Tanzania, China and Ethiopia deployed into Rhodesia. The camp covered five kilometres with many satellite bases fortified with, well-constructed trenches and bunkers. There were anti-aircraft weapons positioned in protective pits as well as lookout towers to give early warning of any attack. The camp was close to a large Frelimo base. The second area that came under scrutiny was Tembué, north-east of Cabora Bassa. Other camps had been hit by Rhodesian ground and air forces but because Chimoio was 90 kilometres inside Mozambique and Tembué 225 kilometres from the Rhodesian border, the ZANLA commanders believed they were safe.

The SAS commander, Brian Robinson and Group Captain Norman Walsh of the air force, believed that an airborne assault was feasible and eventually they persuaded a somewhat reluctant ComOps that the gamble was worthwhile. In fact, the plan was to be even more ambitious. There was to be a double attack, hitting both camps within days. The first target was to be Chimoio. The second, to be mounted as soon as possible after the first assault, was to be aimed at Tembué. The whole operation was code named Dingo with Chimoio as Zulu-1 and Tembué as Zulu-2. Obviously, for an operation of this size, the air force would have to commit the majority of its aircraft and should there be major losses it would be a disaster for the country. It was a dangerous gamble.

The Dakotas, carrying the paratroops, could reach both camps with no problem but the

Alouettes with their limited range, were another matter. They needed a point ten or 15 minutes' flying time from the target where they could refuel and rearm. This meant setting up temporary forward bases inside enemy territory. The administrative base for Zulu-1 was to be 80 kilometres inside Mozambique and only 10 kilometres from the target. The administrative base for Zulu-2 was to be 225 kilometres from the border and five minutes' flying time from Tembué. In addition, a transit refuelling area was also to be positioned on top of a flat-topped mountain, named The Train, just south of Cabora Bassa.

The raid was to be a joint SAS, RLI, air force operation and was to be controlled by Brian Robinson, commanding officer of the SAS. He would fly with air force officer Norman Walsh in an Alouette III above the battlefield. This helicopter would be in touch with Lieutenant General Peter Walls in the command Dakota, which would remain some distance to the north of the battle zone. Walls would be in direct contact with Prime Minister Ian Smith by teleprinter and would be able to take immediate top-line decisions should they be required.

The largest airborne force that could be put in to attack Chimoio was in the region of 200 men, so surprise was vital. The biggest problem facing the commanders was how to get the air armada into position around Chimoio without alerting the men inside the camp. The most obvious way was to disguise one noise with another even louder distraction. So it was decided to make use of Jack Malloch's DC-8. Timing would be critical. The plan was that the DC-8 would fly, as noisily as possible, over the camp, just as the ZANLA men were lining up for their morning parade. Fearing an air attack, they would dive for cover. Once the plane had passed harmlessly over the camp, the trainees would start emerging from their dugouts, thinking that the aircraft was only a civilian machine. At that point, the Rhodesian Hunters and Canberras would arrive.

Further, reports received after attacks like the one planned showed that during an assault, the enemy melted away into the bush and were able to regroup later with minimum casualties. To combat this problem, Brian Robinson and Flight Lieutenant Hales devised a technique, which was to box the area. This meant dropping troops either from Dakotas or from helicopters, on all four sides of the camp, effectively closing off all the escape routes.

Warrant Officer Geoff Dartnall, of No 7 Squadron was at New Sarum on 22nd November, the eve of the big raid.

Word had been out for a few days that a 'big one' was in the offing. Alouettes had been arriving from all over the country and were being prepared. The 'latrine rumour' (always infallible) was that we were going to have all our aircraft at New Sarum that night. Naturally, a party was organized—the war would probably last forever but we might never get everyone in the same bar at the same time again. The Corporals Club was requisitioned and declared 'all ranks'. Everyone was confined to camp 'for security reasons' but I think it was actually to ensure that they attended the party! But work had to be done first—we needed all 31 choppers serviceable and they would have to stay that way for up to a week! So all the aircraft were gone over with a fine toothcomb. Primary and primary star services that were due in the next ten flying hours were done. Components that were reaching the end of their life, were replaced. Refuelling pumps (putt-putts) were overhauled, and guns were cleaned and serviced. A general air of elation, anticipation and well-concealed fear, prevailed. A briefing had been held and everyone knew where we were going, whom we would be flying with and whether we were in a G-Car or a K-Car. And we had also seen the photographs of the 'refugee camp' with all the anti-aircraft weapons dotted around it. Finally, at about 18h00, the aircraft were as ready as they would ever be and were put to bed. The crews adjourned to the Corporals' Club and proceeded to drink it dry. Finally, at 22h30 it was my responsibility to shut the party down. We were due to be airborne at first light. (Geoff Dartnall)

Also taking part in the raid was Squadron Leader Steve Kesby (Vampire Squadron):

Our squadron was to fly two Vampire T 11s and four FB 9s. The briefing was held in the parachute hangar at New Sarum and was the largest and most comprehensive for any target to date. The enormity of the strike filled us with excitement and not a little apprehension. The FB 9s with no ejection seats were to be flown by Varkie, Ken Law, Phil Haigh and me.
The northern part of the Chimoio target comprising the training element was allocated to the Vamps—Varkie and I were to suppress flak by taking out anti-aircraft weapons while the others were to take out barrack blocks and other targets.

Came the dawn—23rd November 1977:

Ten K-Cars and 21 G-Cars began to wind up at about 05h00. There were a few sorry- looking individuals but most of them were handling their hangovers quite well. Anyway, there was a fair amount of adrenaline to compensate. I was in a K-Car with Vic Cook. (Geoff Dartnall)

The helicopters were to pick up 40 members of the RLI from Lake Alexander, a forward base just a few kilometres from the border. At Thornhill the eight Hunters with Squadron Leader Rich Brand leading, were awaiting their take-off time. The engines of six Dakotas roared into life and led by Flight Lieutenant Bob d'Hotman, taxied out onto the runway at New Sarum, carrying 97 SAS and 48 RLI paratroops who were to fly direct. The aircraft were overloaded and struggled into the air after a long take-off. The brief was to place three Dakota loads of troops on one side of the square and then turn 90° to drop the other three loads on the second side. The choppers were to seal off the third side.
The armada was on its way:

We flew high level from Thornhill to north Inyanga only to find extensive cloud cover over Mozambique right up to our eastern highlands. We decided to descend early to get beneath the cloud—easier said than done as the cloud base was very low. We threaded our way through the 'gomos' to find that the cloud base was higher on the other side but would still require us to enter the rocket profile at below normal height. (Steve Kesby)

The idea of using one noise to cover another worked perfectly. Having dived for cover as Jack Malloch's DC-8 passed noisily overhead, the ZANLA men were taking up their places on the parade ground once more as the Hunters dropped down from 20,000 feet to release their bombs and the Canberras came in fast and low with their alphas.

We left our IP on time and on pull-up I searched frantically for my target and experienced a huge feeling of relief at finding it exactly as in the photographs. On turning in to the attack, I saw vast numbers of 'swastikas' bombshelling in all directions. I called to my number two to concentrate on the parade square. We had been briefed to re-attack from different directions so as to confuse the gunners. As soon as I had loosed off my rockets and positioned for a re-attack with front gun, I heard Phil Haigh report that his aircraft had been hit. I formatted on him, climbing through the cloud. Phil said he had a very high jet pipe temperature. I did a close formation evaluation of his aircraft but couldn't see anything untoward, so we continued towards Salisbury keeping Marandellas in mind as a possible emergency runway. I crossed back into Rhodesia and changed frequency to Grand Reef to inform them that we were 'feet dry'. Phil did not check in. I descended to try to locate him while informing Grand Reef that there might be a possible bale- out or forced-landing and to send a chopper. There were two fields below suitable for a forced-

landing, and on turning towards the second field I saw a pall of smoke. Phil had conducted what appeared to be a perfect forced-landing but the aircraft had hit a ditch and burst into flames. Very sadly, I climbed away and made it back to Salisbury with minimum fuel. That day was certainly not over for us as we returned fully armed to Chimoio to provide top cover for the browns. There was a lot of activity over the target and this made for some very interesting flying. What with the haze, the cloud and the smoke, the individual targets were difficult to identify, but the briefings from the troops were good and the radios clear. It was amazing that we did not have any mid-air collisions. On one occasion when committed in the attack, a helicopter passed right though the centre of my gun sight. I called for him to 'break left' and then released my salvo of rockets. (Steve Kesby)

The helicopter gunships arrived on the scene just as this first wave of attack aircraft had gone through the target.

The flight to Chimoio was very quiet. As the target approached, we listened intently to reports from the fixed wing aircraft going in. Our only transmission was a query from Vic to a returning Vampire as to whether he had knocked out the 23mm that was guarding our specific target. His terse 'affirmative' was very reassuring. Over the target we were met by continuous ground fire from small arms. The tick-tick-tick of rounds going by could be heard for the entire seven hours. These were interspersed with, in our case, three loud bangs as rounds hit the aircraft. The camp had long thatched buildings that appeared to be deserted. The ground fire was coming from the surrounding bush that was extremely dense. Having planted a couple of rounds into each of the buildings to ensure that no one was at home, we commenced firing into the denser areas of bush. This was much more rewarding—several were being used as cover and a couple of 20mm rounds had the desired effect of driving survivors out into the open. (Geoff Dartnall)

The scene on the ground became chaotic, with desperately fleeing terrorists being gunned down, K-Cars continuing the attack on the main base, while enemy anti-aircraft fire split the air on every side. The Canberras and Hunters had returned to base to refuel and rearm, while the helicopters touched down within sound of the fighting.

After an hour of this, it was time to refuel and, more importantly, find out where the holes were. One was in a main blade and could be patched easily. Another was about two millimetres from the leading edge of a tail rotor blade. Had it cut the reinforcing strip on the leading edge, two thirds of the blade would have ripped off, which would have then torn out the tail rotor gearbox. The third strike was only found the next day in the self-sealing fuel tank. At the admin base, we had three injured helicopters. Mine needed new tail rotor blades, 7513 needed main rotor blades and 7506 had been hit in the engine. It had flown on without any problems, but refused to start. We cannibalized, to give us two serviceable aircraft out of three. We then had blades and a new engine flown in. One of the G-Cars went back to Grand Reef to collect the parts and anyone who was not required to fly helped change blades and the engine. Although the Alouette is designed so that repairs can be carried out in the bush, they have to be done with great accuracy. It was a very creditable achievement to put all three aircraft into the air and back over the target before the end of the day. Ground fire was still fairly continuous, but not so intense. Then we received a call from the ground "Cyclone 7—I don't know if you know it, but people are shooting at you." "Yes, we did know thank you!" One moment of stark terror was induced by a Vampire coming down in a dive at us obviously about to deliver his weapons. Another Vampire was not far behind. Then there was the most almighty bang. I thought the second Vamp had flown straight into us but in fact it turned out to be the explosions of the first Vamp's rockets hitting its target—a 23mm anti-aircraft gun, which was either shooting at him or us. We returned to the LZ after our last sortie, refuelled and set course for home. In the fading light, I thought of the beaches at Beira only an hour's flying away. The K-Cars were the first to arrive back at Grand Reef. The G-Cars still had to pick up troopies. This gave us the opportunity to watch all the other choppers come over the horizon with their beacons flashing. It looked like a mobile Christmas tree and is an abiding memory for anyone who saw it—real 'lump in the throat' stuff. Emotionally drained, I still had to change the starter/generator. At this point I began to sum up my condition: Here I was, 41 years old, a wife and four kids at home, filthy dirty, had fewer than three hours' sleep in the past 36, spent seven of the last 14 hours being shot at, had no idea where I was going to sleep tonight and now I have to work on a bloody aeroplane. It was probably the fastest starter/genny change that had ever been done on an Alouette! Even after the exhilaration and success of the first day, Grand Reef was not an anti-climax. Everyone will remember the dinner that John Creewel and his staff served up that night—a full three course meal with strawberries and cream. Amazing. The next few days were a blur—via Mount Darwin (FAF 4) to some godforsaken place called The Train; then across Cabora Bassa to a place called Tembué. I remember it was a successful operation too, but it was certainly an anticlimax after Chimoio. (Geoff Dartnall)

Next day while the bewildered and wounded guerrillas were making their way through the bush to safety, the big cleanup began. Everything in the camp was either destroyed or transported to the nearby refuelling base and then air-lifted via Lake Alexander to Grand Reef and then on to Umtali or Salisbury. Several 12.7mm guns were carried home and later allocated to airfield defence. Estimated enemy casualties were 1,200 dead for the loss of one Vampire and two security force personnel. But there was no suggestion of the security forces resting on their laurels.

Twenty-four hours after returning from the Chimoio Raid, the air force embarked on Zulu 2: the attack on the recruiting camp at Tembué north-east of Lake Cabora Bassa where it was believed there could be as many as 4,000 military trainees. Except for one helicopter and one Vampire the aircraft complement was the same as that which had attacked Chimoio. All the aircraft damaged on the first raid had been repaired and were ready to fly. The main fear was that the raid on Chimoio would warn the occupants of Tembué and the camp would be empty when the attackers arrived.

Zulu-2 was a far more complex operation than Zulu-1. Firstly, the distance was greater. Chimoio was only about 80 kilometres inside Mozambican territory. To reach Tembué the aircraft had to fly over 225 kilometres of enemy territory. Secondly, the target was not one camp but two, placed so close together that completing a box round each camp would be impossible. The distances involved meant setting up three refuelling and rearming bases north of Mount Darwin, two of which were inside Mozambican territory. One was situated between Cabora Bassa and the Rhodesian border; the second was west of Tembué Camp. Even so, the fuel situation was tight.

The paratroopers flew from New Sarum and established the best cordon they could before beginning their sweep towards the centre. Meanwhile the K-Cars began their strike on the unguarded side of the box. The death toll was estimated at 800.

During the afternoon, a report came in that there was another camp approximately 30 kilometres away where 500 men were under training. At 17h00 hours, the Canberras made a run over the camp dropping their devastating load of alpha bombs.

The helicopters withdrew from Tembué in the late afternoon and positioned back at Chiswiti, just inside Rhodesia. As there were no messing or sleeping facilities at this remote airfield, it was decided to return to Mount Darwin for the night, a short 40 minutes by chopper. However, on reaching the top of the Mavuradhona Mountains north of Mount Darwin, a thunderstorm was encountered and many of the helicopters could not make it through. They landed at any convenient place they could find before they ran out of fuel. Some landed on farmers' tennis courts while others managed to navigate to the haven of the Centenary Club. Club members said later that when they saw the navigation lights approaching from Mozambique, they believed they were being attacked. One pilot who ran short of fuel crossing the vast expanses of the lake, landed on an island and had to have fuel dropped in to him by the DC-7.

Most of the SAS men had to wait for morning before they could be uplifted by the helicopters and flown home.

All in all Zulu-1 and Zulu-2 had been a complete success. Rhodesia had lost one airman and one soldier was killed and eight men wounded. The enemy dead were reckoned to be over 2,000 plus several thousand wounded and vast quantities of equipment captured.

No 3 Squadron Diary, November 1977:

The most memorable activities of this month are undoubtedly the raids on Chimoio and Tembué. The writer is sure that he speaks for everyone concerned in that the operations were carried out with pride and professionalism, although we might admit being a little dubious at times about our survival. It appears that those who took part are pleased to have done so. Grateful thanks to the members of Nos 1 and 2 Squadrons for keeping the anti-aircraft guns away from us. Not one Dakota received a hit. The celebrations after the operations were unparalled!

The success of these raids convinced the security force commanders of the value of airborne control and this method was developed and improved. The only objection the commanders had to using the Dakota was that a helicopter gave them a better view of developments of the ground. However, helicopters were particularly vulnerable. Finally, it was decided that while overall command of an operation should be from the command Dakota, there should be backup by subordinate command personnel, who would fly in either a helicopter or a Lynx.

CHAPTER 44

Attack on Grand Reef

The Selous Scouts had planned an operation code-named Virile, which was designed to destroy bridges in Mozambique, effectively cutting the road and railway link between Espungabera and Dombe. The operation was originally planned to commence on 20th November 1977 but at the last minute it had to be postponed because Combined Operations feared that it might conflict with Operation Dingo—the attacks on Chimoio and Tembué. Operation Virile finally got under way on 26th November when the Scouts' column left Hot Springs heading for Chipinga and the border, which was crossed at dusk.

The Scouts spent four days in Mozambique and achieved everything they had set out to do. Espungabera was effectively cut off from Chimoio and so the garrison was denied any support. Added to which the Scouts liberated some very valuable equipment. Taking part in this operation was Air Lieutenant Chris Tucker:

> *I was flying out of Chipinga in support of a Scouts group and with me in the Lynx was Captain Athol (Gissepie) Gillespie who was in charge of the recce team on the ground. The guys had gone in to remove road-repairing equipment and to disrupt the flow of supplies to the terrs. I was also tasked to mark for the Hunters should they have to be used on strikes on road transport across the border. However, because of bad weather, the Hunters were unable to get into the target area, so Gissepie and I simply carried out our own little war and we ended up taking the enemy trucks out by ourselves. This also included a strike in support of a Scout column, which was waylaid by Frelimo and ZANLA on their way out of Mozambique, again ending up by our doing the jet boys' job! There were apparently up to 1,000 terrs in the area. I think we got through three or four full rearms that day. The outcome was that we were both to be court martialled for misuse of equipment and disobeying orders but I think the circumstances were on our side and we were treated leniently. Gissepie had to see the commander, Frank Mussell, for misuse of air force property, and I was warned. We then got our MFCs. We did however celebrate by trying to mow the carpets at the Chipinga Country Club.*

The citation read: "For five days Air Lieutenant Tucker was the sole war effort on a particular operation. He delivered numerous air strikes with little or no covering fire and played a major part in destroying equipment and neutralizing enemy positions. His highly effective participation materially assisted the ground forces in achieving their objective."

Maximum range uplift, 7th December 1977

Eight SAS led by Grahame Wilson had been dropped deep into Mozambique about ten days previously to ambush one of the main supply routes. Mission accomplished, they called for an uplift and two choppers from Mabalauta were tasked to pick them up. The choppers were to fly in at low level with a Lynx acting not only as top cover but also to ensure that they did not overfly any villages that might house unfriendly forces. Because of the vast distance, fuel would be required to be parachuted in by Dakota each time the choppers ran dry.

The operation began badly with Ian Rodwell's Dakota hitting a tree on final approach into Mabalauta and damaging the port wing tip. The metal was badly bent and in order to make it more aerodynamic, it was decided to cut off the offending protrusions with a hacksaw blade. This exercise took the best part of two hours and the gaping bite was masked over with helicopter blade tape. Nigel Lamb and Bill Sykes attended the briefing while the technicians filled up with fuel to the maximum.

Bill Sykes continues the story:

Navigation in the south-east of Mozambique was always different—the terrain was very flat and there were literally no landmarks. One had to fly by instinct. A compass was useless as there were metal deposits that slewed the instrument by anything up to 17 degrees. On a previous task, my compass was revolving at 35 rpm! As you crossed the Cabora Bassa power lines, you set the direction indicator to zero and simply flew a heading. The most vulnerable places en route were the refuelling stops and the power lines. The crews we had relieved had been shot at every time they crossed over the pylons, either by small arms or RPG-7s so we flew under them. With the prevailing south-east wind on our noses, there was some doubt that we would make it in one hop. As it happened we hit the pickup point 'on the nose' after more than three hours flying and uplifted the troops with three minutes fuel remaining, just enough to get us away from the pickup point and to an open area to refuel. The Dak meanwhile was ready with the first fuel drop. We kept the engines running while the techs filled up with one drum each. It is testimony to the designers that an Alouette can get airborne with four SAS plus equipment and fuel, although its progress is slow. On the second refuelling stop nearly an hour later, we also kept the engines running, but on the third stop we decided to shut down—five hours strapped to an armoured seat wearing a flak jacket and a survival jerkin had taken its toll. Having flown all that time in enemy territory without being molested and being in an unpopulated area, we were perhaps overconfident. Both aircraft starters had been performing well so we felt fairly safe in closing down. However, 'Murphy' was flying with us that day, and as per his law, one aircraft refused to start. We called the Dak and asked it to return to Chiredzi to fetch spares and tools. We were all a bit peckish at this stage so Graham shot a steenbok that was unlucky enough to pop its head up from behind a bush and we settled down for a braai followed by a sleep in the shade of the choppers. We thought little about the people at FAF 7 and Mabalauta who were undoubtedly worried stiff about us! Two hours later, the drone of engines could be heard and the Dak came in low to drop the tools. There was no parachute but their aim could not have been more accurate—so accurate in fact that the package missed the front blade by two feet, the chopper by three feet and my head by four. The possible consequences of these near misses were unthinkable. The two techs, in typical air force style, had the engine running in no time. Four and a half hours after stopping, we got airborne again and crossed the border just to the north of Malvernia. This taunted the enemy into putting on a magnificent 'fireworks' display for us, the tracer arcing their way into the night sky but falling a good distance short of us. We landed at Hooters (Mabalauta) well after dark. (Bill Sykes and Nigel Lamb)

Attack on Grand Reef

By December 1977, forward airfields, such as Grand Reef had been equipped with bomb pens. These bunkers had pig wire stretched around and over a network of five-metre gum poles, and were designed to catch or stop mortar bombs and RPG-7 rockets. Empty fuel drums were also piled to a height of four metres and filled with rubble to absorb the impact of rockets and shells. Helicopters and light aircraft deployed to more remote airfields would return at night to the larger bases that offered this protection.

Security at Grand Reef was a particular problem because it was so close to the Mozambique border. It was also a very busy forward airfield, which meant that army and air force personnel were moving in and out all the time. The area was protected by a perimeter fence with earth walls on the western flank, and regular army patrols were carried out in the area surrounding the airfield, but there was always the chance that the enemy would mount an attack. If they were to penetrate the perimeter defence, it could have spelt disaster. Most of the air force personnel were armed but they were not experienced in hand-to-hand combat and there was no army reaction stick within the cantonment. Robin Watson who was camp commandant at FAF 8, on Saturday 17th December 1977, says:

The army personnel were watching the 'Bless 'em All Show' on TV so there were no patrols deployed. Squadron Leader Rob McGregor was the FAF commander, Phil Clarke the SWO, and John Reeves my clerk/assistant. The OC had received a signal from Air HQ warning of a possible attack. Apparently a detailed map of Grand Reef, probably made by a casual worker, had been captured. The brown job colonel refused to believe that a military complex such as FAF 8 would be attacked. The day had been hot and it seemed that a thunderstorm was brewing when I went to my room-cum-office at the lower end of the camp. It was about 22h00.

Sergeant Phil Clarke remembers that:

Saturday 17th December had passed like most other days and as the sun set the personnel finished off their various tasks and headed for the pub, grub or showers. Security was of the utmost importance and, as on every other evening, we checked comms with all the armoured fighting vehicles (AFVs). Land-lines to the gun-pits were tested and duty members were briefed on the events of the day. Communications with the army were established from the air force command bunker. After a nice hot shower and a cup of coffee I lay on top of my bed, covered with a towel, dozing in the cool night air. It was nearly 23h00.

At about 23h00 Robin was awakened by what sounded like thunder, and hailstones drumming on the roofs of buildings. When he looked outside, he discovered that the hailstones were aglow. In fact, it was a stream of tracer passing overhead. The thunder was the tattoo of mortar bombs and rockets landing, for the most part, on the army camp.

At the very start of the attack, Phil had a narrow escape when a rifle grenade exploded on the sandbag parapet outside his room:

Suddenly there were two extremely loud bangs and my body and the bed were covered with sand. There was the sound of glass breaking, a dull thud and the rat-tat-tat of light and heavy machine gun fire. Propelled off my bed by the sudden charge of adrenaline, towel in one hand, rifle in the other, I scrambled for the door. My towel! Where's my bloody towel? Caught on the door handle! No time to go back for it. Another 'krump' and a volley of rat-tat-tats propelled me headlong into the safety of sandbag protection. "Hell, SWO!" said a voice from the darkness, "We're being revved!" It was Squadron Leader Rob McGregor, who did not scare easily, but the sight of a stark bollock naked man standing beside him in a mortar pit galvanized him into action. "Come on SWO, let's get comms with the army and find out what's going on!" We established comms with the AFVs and our air force gunpits. Pit 1 reported heavy fire coming from the opposite side of the runway, as did the car positioned closest to them. Pit 1 engaged the enemy, reporting movement close to the runway and in the tree line. They soon reported that ammunition was getting low, and that a re-supply was urgent. Flight Lieutenant Robin Watson appeared on the scene, immaculately dressed as always. "Good show chaps!" he said. (I'm not kidding.) "There must be a war on!" Then he noticed that among the sweaty bodies in the bunker there was one that was totally unclad. He suggested that as everyone was now awake, a pair of shorts would be a good idea. (Phil Clarke)

Phil Clarke and a TF member volunteered to cross the open space of the aircraft parking area to fetch ammunition for Pit 1.

First I made a quick detour for some shorts and the keys for the bomb dump. By this stage, we had established that most of the firing was coming from the tree line opposite the army positions and because it was unlikely that our troops would be on the runway, I advised Gun-pit 1 to continue firing into the enemy. They were also advised that persons running like hell towards the bomb dump were friendly. The gun-pit continued firing and we made it across the open ground taking as much cover from the aircraft revetments as we could. We got into the ammo store and grabbed a couple of boxes of 7.62 and made it safely to Gun-pit 1. (Phil Clarke)

Clarke and the TF member remained in the pit to assist the TF gunner in reloading and changing the overheated barrels on the MAG. The young gunner, Aircraftman Anstee showed remarkable coolness, and his fire into the enemy's flank undoubtedly helped to stop any advance across the runway. Both AFVs left the comparative safety of the revetments in order to take part in the fight, but were forced to pull back when rockets were fired directly at them.

In the middle of the battle, a very frightened young caterer reported to the bunker without a rifle or magazine. Corporal Reeves sent him back to fetch them. The young man was back very quickly carrying a rifle but still minus a magazine. Reeves looked at the white face and said, "Forget about the war. Make some coffee and sandwiches for the entire camp!" The caterer set to it and soon forgot all about the battle raging outside. When the firing had died down the bar was raided for a bottle of brandy to lace the coffee, which helped bolster the morale of all concerned. According to Clarke, that coffee was a blend to beat all blends.

Once the firing had ceased completely there was a chance to take stock of the situation. The attack had been well-planned and about 85 insurgents were involved. They were armed with automatic weapons, machine guns, mortars and RPG-7s. The men with the machine guns were positioned on the fence line to the south-east of the runway that ran between them and the camp. The men with the mortars were positioned further back. Their first target was the army camp. The whole assault could have been a disaster for the security forces had it not been for one vital error on the part of the attackers—a mortar has to be correctly bedded in order to strike the target each time. If not, every bomb that is fired beds the tube down further and alters the trajectory, bringing subsequent shells closer to the point of fire.

The first bombs fired landed squarely on their target—the army camp. One, hitting the branch of a tree, exploded onto the tent immediately below, killing a member of the RAR. His body was not found until the following morning because he had fallen off his camp bed and rolled beneath it. The next salvo fell short, the third salvo landed on the runway. The fourth fell between the runway and the fence and the fifth landed right on the fence line killing two members of the attacking force. The enemy machine gunners could not understand what was happening. They panicked and pulled out, leaving their dead and dragging their wounded, only one of whom had been hit by Rhodesian fire.

Two members of the volunteer reserve, Acting Sergeant P.R. Clarke and Corporal T.A. Case, distinguished themselves by continuing to ferry ammunition to a defensive gun position throughout the attack. In all, this attack resulted in a great deal of sound and fury with red and green tracer decorating the December sky but little damage was caused. One member of the security forces was killed and two soldiers in the army and police camp suffered severe abdominal or leg wounds. Fortunately there was one helicopter at the FAF, the others being away on operations.

Squadron Leader Rob McGregor was current on choppers and he volunteered to fly the injured men to Umtali.

> *It was very dark and the guti was rolling in. It would have been ideal to take the casualties into Umtali by road but there was the possibility that the road had been mined. I had no technician as the fireforce was away so an army medic volunteered to come with me. We did not know where the gooks were, so I took off from inside the revetments without using lights, while everyone gave me covering fire in case the enemy was still around. The flight was pretty hairy because there was no visible horizon and I had to fly on instruments. I tried to follow the railway track because I knew that it would lead me between the hills. You won't believe the relief I felt when I saw the lights of Umtali. I think it was about 04h30 when I landed.*

Commenting on the attack Rob McGregor says:

> *On that day, 17th December, the fireforce had been deployed to Mtoko along with all our aircraft except for one helicopter. Had we been without an army presence, the attack might have had a completely different outcome. We could well have been overrun. The support commando under Major Freddie Watts had arrived in camp that afternoon and no troops had been deployed. They were fantastic. They had their mortars operational in no time—and the upshot was that the attack was beaten off.*

Summing up for the year 1977, No 4 Squadron Diary commented:

> *This year has had a lot of black marks for the squadron, with another one this month. Donald Northcroft, an ex-air force pilot who did call-ups on 4 Squadron, was murdered by a group of terrorists on his farm on 19th December. Don was a member of No 19 Course and deservedly won the Sword of Honour. He was a talented sportsman who played 1st XV rugby for Thornhill and excelled at squash. Alf Wilde, on call this month, luckily escaped without injury when he hit a culvert on landing on the new runway at Rushinga, while carrying out a night casevac. Yet another poorly laid flarepath—fault of the browns! This re-emphasizes the care needed before landing at these strips.*

Situation Reports (Sitreps) and Squadron Diary entries usually give only very bald, factual comments on operational activities. For more detailed and dramatic accounts one has to turn to newspaper reports which may not always be accurate but often leave the reader with a better idea of what it was actually like to be involved in a contact.

For January 1978, we have the story of a typical contact, which was repeated hundreds of times during the Bush War. In the first contact, ten terrorists died, and eight were accounted for in the second. One of those killed was a woman wearing a green uniform with webbing strapped across her bosom. Nine insurgents died on the third day. This is the story:

> *The terrorist is 'visual'. He is wearing green trousers and a blue shirt and is carrying an AK assault rifle. He moves slowly, casually, across the complex of huts. Smoke from the cooking fires drifts lazily upwards towards the grey skies. A small child chases a thin uncared-for dog.*

Cooking pots are washed in an old oil drum containing water. Another terrorist steps out from one of the huts. He pauses, looks upwards to the gomo, his AK slung over his shoulder. He turns and re-enters the hut. The young section leader with the police support unit puts down his binoculars and gets on the radio. It is only minutes later that at the Grand Reef military base many, many kilometres away, a siren sounds and fighting men converge on the operations room at the double. Telephones are ringing and messages are shouted out in staccato tones. The fireforce commander pores over a map. He is a tall young man and mature beyond his years. He stabs the map with a finger tracing the outline of the hill feature. "We will drop sticks in here and here, sir," He says. The base commander nods his head in agreement. "Send it!" he says. There is a tremor in his voice. Within seconds, the helicopters are hovering over the small groups of young soldiers standing beside the runway. They drop and the men run forward, their heads low to avoid the rotor blades. The helicopters nose forward and are airborne. As they sweep away to the nearby gomos, the troopies give the thumbs up. This is a full fireforce operation. Young men of the 'second wave', their arms, legs and faces covered in thick camouflage grease, clamber aboard trucks. The rain is coming down in torrents; the men don't smile. There is a fixed grim look on their faces as they drive off into the unknown. Across at the air force section, the fireforce paras have donned their gear and are huddled together beneath plastic sheets seeking shelter from the rain. They don't know whether they are going to be dropped. They sit and wait, staring straight ahead. They don't talk. Then there is the command, 'Paras into the Dak'. Five sticks run forward through the pools of mud towards the Dakota. They are in and the ageing giant roars down the runway, then she's up, up and away. The men still say very little. Their thoughts are on the unknown. They don't know the type of scene they will be dropping into. The helicopters, spanned out across the sky, surge forward skimming the tops of the gum trees and scattering cattle in the fields below. The police station comes into view. The helicopter pilot banks sharply to the left and drops for a soft landing in a field. The rotor blades splutter to a halt, and other helicopters land throwing up a smokescreen of dirt, leaves and grass. This is the first rendezvous point. At a briefing, the police tell the fireforce commander that 12 terrorists have been 'visual'. They are all in and around the kraal complex. Maps are studied. If the terrorists run, in which direction will they head? The huts are fairly isolated but there is a thickly-wooded hill feature on one side and open ground and a river on the other. There is also a mealie field and a thick crop of bananas. The fireforce commander decides where he will place his stop groups, the men on the trucks, and where he will drop his paras. "There are twelve visual," he tells his men as he emerges from the briefing. There is a murmur of approval. The fireforce is out to beat its record kill for a bush camp and this number will go a considerable way towards meeting the objective. Tensions have relaxed all round—there is now an eager desire to get stuck in. The helicopters are four minutes away from the scene. As they approach, the support unit call sign radios to say the terrorists have started to break. "They are going in all directions," he yells. "Don't panic!" the fireforce commander replies with the calm of a veteran. He has the kraal located and hovers (sic) while the troops are landed. The terrorists let fire two RPG-7 rockets. They are both way-off direction. "Cheeky!" says the fireforce commander. Then he is lifting (sic) to start directing the operations from the air. The Dakota is almost overhead. The commander is in radio contact with the pilot. He wants the scattering terrorists.

"How many sticks?"

"All five!"

The men are gone within seconds, immediately cutting off one escape route. The weather has cleared considerably by now but there is a crosswind and the men tend to drift. One hurts his ankle against a rock as he lands; another damages his neck—two minor casualties. Two terrorists running for the river come face to face with the paradrop, stop and head back towards the kraal. They run straight into FN fire and drop instantly like two stones without so much as a *whimper. The security forces have the kraal virtually surrounded. Most of the terrorists make for the shelter of the banana trees. On the hill feature, security forces are firing at those terrorists still seeking shelter among the huts. One has placed a blanket around his shoulders and surrounded himself with small children, pretending to be a village woman. He is shot from 100 metres and the AK falls out of the folds of the blanket. The children scatter, terrified. Without warning, a terrorist pops up from behind a rock a few metres in front of the security forces' position on the hill feature. He doesn't live long enough to pop down again. The main battle concentration has moved to the banana trees; it provides thick cover and in all, the fight goes on for more than five hours. In this time, one terrorist surrenders waving a white flag. "I have never seen that before," says the fireforce commander. The fireforce sweeps forward, three men move in single file to search a rock feature. A terrorist emerges from the shadows unseen. He aims his AK but it has jammed and he is captured. In come the helicopters, first to evacuate the civilians injured in crossfire, then to carry away captured terrorists. The captured men are stripped of all clothing except their trousers and blindfolded. They are met at the second rendezvous point by special branch. Civilians suspected of actively assisting the terrorists are taken to the same rendezvous point. There is initial questioning and one old man is immediately released. The others climb into the back of a truck and are driven away. The helicopters fly out the bodies, captured equipment and personal belongings. The troopies at the rendezvous point search the bodies and strip them of webbing. Tucked inside a magazine is a letter from a girlfriend. They carry cigarettes, charm beads to protect them from death, and spare clothing. This particular battle is over. The men are being flown back to the rendezvous point for the long ride back to base. Their parachutes are being collected. They look like a line of dead bodies—there is no comment. They have been out here for five hours and their faces record the strain. Then someone reads an entry on one of the captured documents—'We were never told about the power of fireforce on the other side', the terrorist had written. The troopies laugh.* (Rhodesia Herald)

Incident at Mtoko

During a major contact with insurgents on 12th January 1978, the airborne army commander was wounded and unable to continue to control the battle. Flight Lieutenant Gerrit Francois du Toit, flying an Alouette III took over command of all the army stop groups and deployed them to surround and cut off the terrorists. For the remainder of the day-long battle, during which he flew for six and a half hours, Flight Lieutenant du Toit continued to command the operation. He later received the Military Forces Commendation (Operational).

Norman Maasdorp was the pilot of one of the G-Cars:

On 12th January 1978 I was part of the Mtoko fireforce cleaning up after a lemon to the west of Mtoko when the K-Car with Chas Goatley and Ian Fleming was ambushed as they went through the Nyadiri River gap just west of the base. We heard that 'Flamo' Fleming had been hit and the rest of us packed up and moved out asap to carry out a follow-up. We returned to Mtoko where Henry Jarvie and I refuelled, picked up a fresh RAR stick and returned to the area where Flamo had been shot. Chas, who was back running the scene as K-Car pilot guided me to an LZ, and as soon as I had it visual he broke away to attend to something else. As I entered the LZ there was instant pandemonium and we came under heavy RPD fire. I can remember the bullets striking, sounding like a myriad of strange loud cracking noises—nothing like one hears on the movies. Henry slumped over onto the middle of the floor and the troopies just froze, not knowing what to do. The instrument panel seemed to vibrate and vanish as all the radios and instruments were shot to pieces. My legs also seemed to feel a bit funny and there was a sting going up both of them. The collective lever immediately became very heavy owing to the loss of hydraulics, so with maximum effort I just pulled like heck and flew out and tried to get away as far as possible. I was unable to get hold of anybody as the radio was out. I was concerned that there might be possible structural failure and even fuel leakage, so I put down in an LZ that I hoped would be safe from attack. Once on the ground I found that the stick commander had been shot through both his leg and hand, so I took over command of his stick and placed them in a defensive circle to guard us. I was unable to walk and was not sure why, so I crawled around the chopper to check on Henry but when I got to him I could see he was dead. Under the chopper was a loud gushing noise, and looking underneath I could see the fuel pouring out at quite a rate as there was a large hole in one corner of the fuel tank. I was relieved that I had landed and not kept going. I then crawled back to the stick commander to see if I could help him. I gave him first aid and painkillers and then took his radio to call for help. The shock had by this time set in and I could barely make a coherent transmission. Eventually I was able to speak, and the other K-Car tasked Al Thorogood to casevac us out of there. I nearly got left behind as nobody realized I could not walk and I had to call him back to fetch me. It turned out there was shrapnel in my legs and heel. According to the techs who examined the aircraft afterwards, they were amazed that I had received such light injuries considering the extent of bullet damage around the pedal area. (Norman Maasdorp)

Flight Sergeant Alexander Ian Fleming, flying as a technician/gunner for Air Lieutenant Chas Goatley was killed by fire from the ground about two minutes' flying time west of Mtoko.

Mini-golf bomb

The deaths of Henry Jarvie and 'Flamo' Fleming affected Peter Petter-Bowyer considerably and he immediately flew to Mtoko to discuss the problem of flushing out the enemy when they were hiding in dense bush. What was needed was a small bomb with a sizeable punch that could be dropped by the Lynx during the initial phase of a contact. Project Juliet was born. The result was an ugly tailless bomb designed to be dropped at low level. A parachute was used to pitch the bomb vertically and an electric switch housed in an alpha bomb sphere was released from the nose. This dangled 15 feet below the bomb and on impact with the ground detonated the main charge causing a high airburst, which sent shock waves down into any depressions. A pentolite booster was installed in the tail producing a downward propagation of the explosive wave with a wide swathe of dense shrapnel over 70 metres in diameter.

In bush trials it was found that one man who had been on the edge of the effective range and had been screened by trees told how he had been suddenly overcome by a need to sleep. He had not heard the explosion. But the ground troops who had been within 100 metres of the bang reported that they had been totally devastated by the huge blast and the shock wave. This shock effect paid off. The Air Strike Reports recorded that after the bomb had been dropped, the enemy tended to remain where they were and ground fire either ceased or was substantially reduced. The mini-golf bomb as it became affectionately known was particularly effective in slowing down large enemy forces that were in pursuit of security forces.

On 17th January, FAF 7 was involved in a contact, as recorded in the FAF Diary: "The boss went up as a telstar for a police stick following tracks from a store breaking, picked up tracks and flushed a group of terrs and civvies. The only people available were cooks and bottle-washers who did a sterling job in the initial contact until experienced troops were found and brought in. Final total was 16 all told and four casualties. Fireforce was dispatched from Shabani eventually to clean up."

During the rest of the month, FAF 7 airmen were again prominent with early starts and late finishes as they flew in support of the SAS and Selous Scouts.

I was at FAF 7 from 11th January to 25th. The whole time there I was working with the SAS and the Scouts who had men deep in Mozambique, near Barragem, and around the Mapai area. I had the army commanders up most of the day with me doing telstar and top cover. Then at night I would act as telstar for the ground call signs and liase with their resupply using the Daks. I was putting in a fair amount of flying some days—up to eight or nine hours. Chris Tucker relieved me on that bush tour, and he had to come a day early as we could not cover the tasks with a single Lynx. On 25th January I had done six hours top cover prior to flying back to Thornhill in a Trojan. (Martin Hatfield)

I flew 13 hours on 24th/25th January in support of the SAS/SS recce. I also flew 45 hours in a period of five days, and then 95 hours in the ensuing 17 days. The FAF commander was Rob McGregor and he wisely grounded me after the first five days owing to fatigue, but then I had to fly straight away again as one of the call signs had lost contact. I returned nine hours later. My tech was Ken Turner who managed to keep me awake! (Chris Tucker)

And on 26th January comes this entry:

Early morning start with the Dak and Lynx airborne at 03h45. ComOps are working today to sort out a few admin and ops problems with the introduction of the new fireforce concept. The night operations planned for tonight were cancelled owing to crew fatigue!

At 18h00 on 28th January, Nigel Lamb and André Senekal, with Chris Tucker flying top cover in the Lynx were called out to an SAS call sign south of Mabalauta, near the railway line. The SAS men reported that they could cope with the opposition but needed a casevac for a trooper, who had been injured. Lamb and Senekal approached from the east while Tucker was overhead talking to the SAS. It is very flat near Mapai and the smoke marker was clearly visible from a distance. The landing zone was presumed secure but as the choppers approached, they came under persistent small arms, heavy machine gun and mortar fire.

Tucker attempted to draw fire by attacking the area but the choppers were forced to withdraw. However, he was able to pinpoint the source of the fire near a village. Evening was drawing in and there was no time to waste. The stick attempted to move to a more secure landing zone, but they were being constantly harried by ZANLA and Frelimo troops. Tucker and Lamb assessed the situation and decided to make a final attempt at rescue as the sun was setting. Lamb would go in with the sun at his back, making it difficult for the men on the ground to spot him. Meanwhile Senekal would stay a few kilometres to the east. When Lamb was a couple of minutes out, Tucker mounted a sustained attack on the enemy position. Lamb held off until Tucker made his guns and rocket attack. The enemy's attention was diverted as they blazed away with small arms, mortars and RPG, while Lamb dropped in and performed the uplift. The whole stick were hot extracted to safety. Tucker said later, "Neither Nigel nor I had any weapons or ammo left on return to Hooters [Mabalauta]. But the appreciation that the SAS gave the pilots was something special."

FAF 7 Daily Diary, 31st January 1978

Great jubilation from pilots and ops staff—no night-flying or early wake-ups. The first day for at least 14—what a pleasure!

In order to alleviate the situation on No 4 Squadron, increasing use was made of reserve pilots. Among the men who flew for the squadron during January were Group Captain John Mussell, Wing Commander Rob Gaunt, Air Lieutenant Ian Bond and Flight Lieutenant R.E.

(Dicky) Dives. No 7 Squadron pilots were also stretched to breaking point. During January, they flew a total of 1,494 hours. Squadron aircraft were deployed to FAFs 1, 5, 7, 8, Dorowa, Shabani, ADR (Air Det Repulse), Beitbridge, Karoi, Malapati and Deka. The Parachute Training School aircraft were also working flat out.

18	Dakota 3708	Ward	No 80 Basic night descent. Not too good
24	Dakota 3708	Ward	Last descent for 80 Basic 2 lifts a bad course
25	Dakota VIP	Ward	Move to FAF 7
25	Dakota 7031	Armstrong	1 x 8 Para visitors Op
26	Dakota 7031	Armstrong	1 x 12 Para visitors Op
27	Dakota 7031	Sheffield	Free-fall rehearsal
27	Dakota 7031	Armstrong	Op cancelled cloud
28	Dakota 7031	Armstrong	1 x 3 S/S Martin K.W + Denis deep
29	Dakota 7031	Armstrong	1 x 8 SAS in deep
30	Dakota 7031	Armstrong	Fireforce call out. Lemon
30	Dakota 7031	Armstrong	1 x 16 SAS in deep. Lovely game park
31	Dakota 7031	Armstrong	Return from Op

Commenting on this diary, Charlie Buchan says:

'In deep' meant we were dropping free-fall paratroops deep into Mozambique or Zambia. Game Park referred to drops in the Mapai and Sao Jorge do Limpopo areas when the Dakotas flew to the south-eastern corner of Rhodesia and then made their way along the edge of the Kruger Park before turning left into Mozambique. The South Africans got quite upset at times. The 'visitors' mentioned were SA recce commandos who were sometimes dropped in by Dakota. Frequently operations proved to be non-productive or a 'lemon', which resulted in wasted time and energy on the part of all concerned.

Changeover day

It was changeover day, 15th February 1978. The fireforce members were eagerly awaiting their rest and recuperation. They heard the pilot of the changeover Dakota calling to say that he was just ten minutes out. Then—the unbelievable happened. The hooter went for a call-out. There had been a sighting to the south of Bikita almost as far as a chopper could go on one tank of fuel. Norman Maasdorp, one of the pilots involved, says: "So we scrambled, refuelled en route at Bikita and ended up having a contact. This took most of the day and as we were about to leave there was a second contact, so the whole thing carried on with para drops—the works—and it took us until evening to clean up."

By the time the fireforce arrived back at Dorowa, the changeover Dakota had long since gone. However, New Sarum had dispatched an Islander to carry out the pickup. But then came a second problem. The technicians who had arrived in the Dakota had discovered cracks on the main blades of the spare G-Car, so the Islander had been turned back to Salisbury to collect a new set of blades. The result was that the Islander arrived well after dark and with no seats. Mark Vernon, Al Thorogood, John Jameson and Norman Maasdorp climbed aboard and as Maasdorp, was the senior man he sat in the front right-hand seat next to the Air Rhodesia pilot, Flight Lieutenant Bernie van Huyssteen, who was doing his first call-up. The rest of the men piled into the back of the Islander and made themselves as comfortable as they could on top of a load of parachutes. Sitting in the front seat, Maasdorp, had a perfect view of what happened next:

It was really dark and there was a storm brewing. We started our take-off roll. The Islander seemed slow on acceleration and after what seemed an eternity the pilot started to rotate. I certainly had the feeling that we were far too slow but he kept rotating and eventually we got airborne but almost immediately the big red 'stall warning' light right in front of me began flashing. This really scared the heck out of me. I can remember instinctively going for the controls to try to pull up because I knew that there were a set of electricity cables off the end of the extended runway. Next there was a great big bang and lurch as the Islander struck the cables. The aircraft slewed to the right, crashed into a mealie field and came to a very abrupt halt. Fortunately, we were not going too fast. The guys in the back were out and running. I couldn't move as the pilot was going through his checks and seemed to take an age doing it. I guess he was just being professional. Fortunately, nobody was seriously hurt although Mark Vernon got quite a nasty gash on his leg when one of the cables flicked in through the side of the aircraft. Once the dust had settled, it suddenly dawned on us that we were unarmed and in the middle of gook country. JJ went back to the Islander for his FN. Then we felt better until we noticed that the rifle barrel was noticeably bent! All we could do was laugh. The second humorous moment came when we heard the armoured car from base roaring around in the bush looking for us. I had a bunch of flares so I decided to put my survival training to good use—first I pulled out a 2-Star Red and activated it. Nothing happened. It was seriously time-expired. Not to be discouraged I pulled out a day/night flare—but I couldn't remember which side was which. I took a guess and we were enveloped in a huge cloud of smoke. In panic I dropped the flare—and lost it in the dark. Fortunately, I still had a packet of mini-flares—but the trigger was missing from the barrel, and it had been sealed! Fortunately the armoured car found us without assistance, and about one in the morning the para-Dak took us to New Sarum for our R&R. Mind you the R&R was totally messed up because we had to appear as witnesses at the Board of Inquiry.

Search and rescue

On 23rd February 1978, Norman Maasdorp was back at Dorowa:

Strange to be back so soon after the Islander crash. Anyway, this had been a long boring day and we tried to keep occupied with cribbage or backgammon. I had done a bit of trooping in the morning and was hanging around the ops room listening to the chatter on the SSB. It sounded as though a Police Reserve Air Wing (PRAW) had gone missing en route from Salisbury to Chiredzi but no search and rescue was being organized. Most of the south-east was covered in a heavy guti so a search from the air would be difficult if not impossible but the lack of response incensed Kevin Peinke. He asked for someone to go with him and I volunteered. There was no OC at Dorowa at that time and no authority was granted to us. We made a quick plan of the route from information we got from Fort Victoria, fuelled our choppers with maximum fuel and set course for Fort Vic. The guti was so low that the tops of the gomos were obscured and we could only scurry along the valleys. Once we had crossed the Fort Vic/Birchenough Bridge road we started landing at villages—asking if anybody had seen or heard anything. One of us would land—the other would orbit at 100 feet while the poor tech ran to the nearest hut. I can remember thinking, 'This is crazy!' We were in terr-infested country, unsure of our position. At last fading light forced us to quit. Fortunately, we had reached Renco Mine where we spent the night. Boy, this place was really like the Wild West. There were some Selous Scouts there and between them and the mine management we got the choppers secured, had some grub and a sleep. Just before we reached the mine, one of the techs reported that a villager had heard an aircraft so we had every hope that we would be successful in the morning. Next day we resumed the search with the weather still very bad. Both Kev and I now had a stick of Selous Scouts on board to help, so we felt a bit more secure. A short while out of the mine we were flying down a valley with a very steep gomo on the right, when the guy behind me pointed up to our right. It was impossible to see the top, and the tree line stopped where the gomo turned into a cliff face. There was something shining on the side of the rock face. It looked like a small waterfall or water seepage. I told Kev I was going to have a closer look. The silver streak was wreckage. The aircraft had flown straight into the hillside and was stuck there. It was a terrible feeling and we felt for the people involved. Apparently the pilot [Angelos Stam] was flying to Chiredzi with two women whose husbands had been injured in land-mine incidents. One of the women was pregnant, I believe. There was no way of dropping the troops anywhere near the wreckage so we picked an LZ below. Then they climbed up to search for survivors. While this was happening there was a call from Renco Mine to attend to an accident in which a railway wagon had broken away and crashed into a crowd of workers. There were deaths and injuries, so I flew off to attend to that scene. I carried out the casevac from Renco to Fort Vic while Kevin had the unenviable job of lifting down the bodies from the plane crash. (Norman Maasdorp)

Operation Turmoil

Mention had been made during 1976 of a ZIPRA camp on the Zambezi River close to the village of Kavalamanja in Zambia. The name of the camp, which was said to contain Chinese instructors, was given as Feira Base. During August and September 1977, the name cropped up again. Air reconnaissance was carried out but nothing unusual could be found on the photographs. Towards the end of June 1977, an SAS team was sent in. These men reported a large Zambian army presence but no guerrillas. However, radio intercepts kept coming up with references to freedom fighters in the area. These reports seemed to indicate a small camp and as other areas were more urgent, Feira Base was ignored. Then on 6th February 1978, a radio intercept relayed some startling information that owing to a shortage of food at Feira Base offensive exercises have been suspended. Suddenly Feira Base became top priority. Army personnel were placed on the Rhodesian bank of the Zambezi opposite Kavalamanja to keep watch and they confirmed the presence of ZIPRA cadres.

A platoon scouting the Rhodesian bank further upstream surprised a group of ZIPRA crossing the river. The security forces opened fire. The dead ZIPRA men together with some survivors floated downstream in their inflatable boats and as they drifted past the observation post the troops manning the post opened fire. This was unfortunate because it revealed the presence of security forces in the area. Fire was returned by the ZIPRA forces at Kavalamanja, and soon a battle was in full swing with mortars and machine guns hammering away across the river. A Hawker Hunter was called in and the enemy ceased firing. The question now was, knowing that there was a security force presence in the area, would the ZIPRA forces pull out of Feira Base?

No aerial reconnaissance could be carried out because of unfavourable weather, so on 1st March, Chris Schulenberg and Sergeant Chibanda were dropped by helicopter into the mountains west of Kavalamanja. By the following night they were in position overlooking the camp. Their task was to ascertain the type and quantity of any defensive weapons particularly anti-aircraft guns, to identify the various sections of the camp and estimate the number and status of the occupants. They had to act with caution because the Zambian army base was only about ten kilometres away. The two men passed their information back to the Scouts at headquarters and plans were developed for an attack.

Two commandos of the Rhodesian Light Infantry, one company RAR, and members of the SAS were chosen for the task. The plan was that the SAS would drop in to the north, carrying anti-tank weapons to block the road, and guard against an attack from the Zambian army.

Operation Turmoil as it was code-named was scheduled for 08h00 on Sunday 6th March 1978, but it had to be delayed for two hours because of low cloud and heavy rain.

Hawker Hunters went in first to neutralize the anti-aircraft positions. The Canberras followed. Coming in at low level from the south-west along the course of the Zambezi, they unloaded their alpha bombs. Behind the Canberras came the paratroop Dakotas, together with the troop-carrying helicopters. The heli-borne troops were put down on the western side of the complex, while the paratroopers were dropped in on the north-east. The army commanders were aloft in fixed wing aircraft to direct strikes onto any stubborn pockets of resistance.

The attack went exactly to plan. Once the troops were on the ground, they began sweeping from the perimeter towards the centre of the camp. However, their advance was delayed by heavy rain and thick bush so that most of the enemy were able to escape into the surrounding scrub. In fact, it was late afternoon before the security forces reached the ZIPRA base area. When darkness fell, the sweep had to be abandoned until the following morning, by which time any ZIPRA cadres still in the area had had time to make their getaway. Only 42 bodies were found although a large quantity of ammunition was destroyed.

During this airstrike at least one strela was fired at the Hunters. Tony Oakley comments:

With regard to strela, we simply accepted that we could not reduce our heat signature on the Hunter. Instead we relied on our speed and the lack of skill of the operators. We certainly had our fair share of strelas fired at us without success—except one. We actually saw the strela launch as an opportunity to pinpoint the b......s. Then we could stomp them nicely with the cannon. You simply followed the white smoke trail to the point of launch. One such occasion was at Kavalamanja when a strela team launched a couple at Vic Wightman and me from a vehicle. There is something very satisfying about having a vehicle in your gun sights. They found themselves on the receiving end of a large number of 30mm shells.

Schulenberg and Chibanda remained to observe for two further days but they only spotted two ZIPRA men who sneaked out of the bush to recce the abandoned camp. On 9th March, a party of Zambian soldiers appeared on foot, foraged around and then left. On 10th March, the SAS men were uplifted by helicopter and flown home.

Rhodesia's first black air force officers

Since August 1977, talks had been in progress between Rhodesia's internal black leaders and the government. On 3rd March 1978, the Internal Constitutional Agreement was signed by Bishop Abel Muzorewa for the United African National Council, Mr Ian Smith for the Rhodesian government, Senator Chief Chirau for the Zimbabwe United People's Organization, and the Reverend Ndabaningi Sithole for the African National Council. Under this agreement, majority rule was promised by 31st December 1978. By 21st March 1978, the transitional government had been established and shortly after this, internal nationalist ministers were appointed to share the tasks of government with their white counterparts. Under this agreement, General Walls was still to be in overall command of the war effort. In this context, it is interesting to note that nine days earlier, on 12th March, the first two black air force officers, Air Lieutenant J.D. Ncube and Air Lieutenant P.S. (Peter) Ngulu had their passing-out parade. Changes were happening fast but as far as the external nationalist groups were concerned, there was no letup in the onslaught.

The Rhodesian war machine, miniscule by world standards, was by the beginning of 1978 stretched to its full limit and although Combined Operations headquarters was getting good information about enemy activity, there was little that could be done. To fight the insurgents effectively, whether internally or externally, more air power was needed, particularly in the form of helicopters. Owing to the small numbers of fighting men Rhodesia possessed, any major cross-border attack meant that the internal scene was denuded, and consequently fireforce activities had to be suspended for periods of up to ten days at a time. Without the fireforce, the kill rate dropped back to zero and the infiltrators had a chance to regroup and assert their authority in rural areas. An additional burden was experienced when external targets were being checked out by the SAS or Selous Scouts and a hot extraction facility had to be provided.

FAF 7 Daily Diary, 7th March 1978

The Lynx was used last night to uplift a casevac to FAF 7. The casevac, with two bullet wounds in the leg, was suffering from shock and loss of blood. The weather was suspect and the pilot did a good job in getting him out at midnight. It is doubtful that the casevac would have lived otherwise. Trooping, top cover and telstar carried out by two G-Cars and the Lynx.

10th March

During the late afternoon, we were asked by the army to uplift one stick of troops to the Renco road to help guard a car that had broken down. At about ten minutes to seven, reacting to information from the browns, Hornet 9 (a Lynx) was positioned overhead to provide top cover for a farmhouse that was being revved. The attack was broken off fairly soon, however, and Hornet 9 found himself in low cloud and was ordered to return.

20th March

Busy day—30 hours flown—14 by helicopters. On 21st March 1978, an army patrol made contact with a large group of security forces, who were pinned down by the enemy fire and were in danger of being overrun. Air Lieutenant Martin Hatfield, of No 4 Squadron flying a support aircraft, was called in to assist the ground forces. He made several attacks on the enemy positions coming under heavy and accurate fire on each attack. His aircraft was hit five times but he only withdrew after he ran out of ammunition. The enemy position was so strongly held that subsequently a heavy air strike had to be put in. Martin Hatfield showed extreme courage and determination and in the opinion of the commander on the spot prevented the army position from being overrun.

22nd March

No rain. A heavy day for casevacs. Three land-mines accounted for five. Gunshots for two more. All evacuated by helicopter. No aggressive sorties.

29th March

The helicopters and Lynx got off at 06h00 for a task, as did the PRAW by 06h45. The whole lowveld was covered in what appeared to be ground mist but turned out to be low stratus. We had five aeroplanes stranded above the clouds and were a bit anxious for a while. Bruce Smith flew a Dak load of SS in at 22h30 tonight and on landing it hit a Sable antelope and is unserviceable at this time waiting for an airframe fitter to check it out.

30th March

After an abortive early start owing to heavy ground fog, we finally got Black Section up at 09h00 for their trooping task. They remained down at 'Hooters' (Mabalauta) until 14h00 setting up a relay for tomorrow's operation.

2nd April

The Dak is becoming a night flyer. He took fuel and rations into Grootvlei at last light and then uplifted 25 Selous Scouts to Inkomo.

5th April

Today was a madhouse. At one time we had five Dakotas standing on the hardstand. One belonged to the SAAF.

Flight Sergeant Benji

While the war effort continued, the *Bateleur* in April, carried more about that very special member of the air force–Benji. By this stage in the war, Flight Sergeant Benji, a security guard at FAF 5, held the title of longest-serving member in the Hurricane area. Benji had joined the air force at Eureka in 1973 and despite numerous efforts to repatriate him, kept returning to the FAF. Eventually his owner, Mrs Bezuidenhout agreed that the air force could keep him. He subsequently served at Centenary and Mount Darwin. The *Bateleur* article continued:

> *He earned rapid promotion to corporal for killing snakes, and to sergeant for a massacre of rats in a gun-pit. Eventually he was promoted to flight sergeant on the grounds that he was more intelligent than the average sergeant. He was, however, reduced to the rank of aircraftman in 1977 when he was found guilty of Conduct Prejudicial (urinating on the CO's carpet) and of cowardice in the face of the enemy (failing to engage in procreation with an obviously eager bitch in the presence of 14 witnesses). Undeterred by his fall from grace, Benji continued to perform his duties in cheerful and work-dog-like manner, reports our FAF 5 correspondent. He brings comfort and solace to security personnel in the lonely watches of the night and keeps them all awake by barking at shadows. He was fully reinstated in rank after a further notable snake battle and was brought onto ration strength at the rate of eight bones per week, two on Sundays. During his last posting, January of this year, Benji was airlifted in full uniform carrying his docs (rabies certificate etc.) in his back pocket. Since his arrival at FAF 5, he has assumed control of all security operations and is also heavily-involved as a culinary consultant as well.* (Bateleur)

Early in May, the new Joint Minister of Defence, the Honourable J. Kadzwite, toured the main bases at New Sarum and Thornhill in his first familiarization introduction to the air force. During the Thornhill visit, the minister was briefed on individual squadron aircraft, weapons and roles, and met many of the air and ground crews involved. He was also shown something of the immense technology of the backup services and spent a major part of his visit touring the Technical Wing. He attended an official luncheon at the officers' mess together with his host Air Vice-Marshal Chris Dams and the Ministry escort Mr Page. Later in the month, it was New Sarum's turn to play host. It was also during this month, May 1978, that No 8 Helicopter Squadron was formed.

Running repairs at Lake Alexander

Meanwhile No 7 Squadron had been carrying out on-going operations in the Chimoio circle, flying from a base at Lake Alexander. Peter McCabe was one of the technicians involved when one of the choppers took a number of hits. Recalling the incident, Peter says:

> *I was flying with Air Lieutenant Ray Bolton and we arrived at one of the satellite refuelling dumps in Mozambique, which was guarded by the brown jobs. When we landed, Beaver [Gordon] Shaw, the other tech, had the covers off his aircraft and was looking very shaken. I took a look at the damage and pulled out the control rods—all three had been pierced by rounds. Added to which the fuel tank looked like a colander. I cut some pieces of aluminum from the inspection hatch of the Mk 1 strela shroud on Beaver's aircraft while Alan Aird cut twigs from the trees to stick in the fuel tank. Using five minute Araldite, pop rivets and jubilee clips from*

my trusty toolbox, I repaired all three rods. The least damaged one I swapped with one from my aircraft, along with a good one. After a hover test, we flew very gently back to Lake Alexander.

Sergeant George Jansen was part of a team assigned to Lake Alexander as backup for the trans-border operation. The choppers started coming back again about 15h30. We were told to prepare for an aircraft recovery. We were told that one of choppers had a damaged connector angle box. We thought it must have landed on a tree stump.

Some time later we saw these two Alouettes coming in, one flying high, the other low. The damaged aircraft hadn't landed on a stump. It had been doing a sweep and as it went over a riverbed the gooks opened up on it. They had shot the living daylights out of the chopper. They managed to swap the connector rods and cut a few twigs off a tree and stuffed them in the holes in the fuel tank, so that it looked like a porcupine. So there we were with this helicopter. What were we going to do? The army guys said we are pulling out at 6 o'clock. They said there was no way we could stay after dark. There were too few of us. Anyway, they helped us load the fuel onto two trucks and they all set off. The techs did not want to chance the temporary repair lasting back to base so Pete McCabe volunteered to fly to Grand Reef. Meanwhile they had contacted the lads in Umtali to strip one of the helicopters for spares. Once Pete got back—I've never seen guys work so fast to get one connector box in. It was about 19h00 by the time we pulled out. We had three trucks with all the spares, ammunition and so on. The chopper flew with us a fair way but once we were in the mountains, he had to push off. We eventually got back to Grand Reef at about 21h30. Peter McCabe had arrived ahead of us. The barman wanted to shut the pub but he said, "My boys are still out there. The pub doesn't shut till they get back." Needless to say we had a roaring party. (George Jansen)

News from other areas

Air force Sergeant Boet Lamprecht was chaired off the rifle range in June when, for the third year running, he was the overall winner of the Rhodesia National Service Rifle Association shoot. Over a two-day period, firing FN rifles over ranges of between 100 and 600 metres, he scored a total of 487 points, three better than his nearest rival.

Also in June, on 22nd, Air Lieutenant Charlie Buchan (of the Parachute School) was a passenger in a helicopter that hit power lines and crashed into Henry Hallam Dam. The helicopter turned over. Charlie Buchan assisted the pilot to release his seat belt and when the pilot experienced further difficulties in the water, helped him to safety. Charlie's cool-headed courage undoubtedly saved the pilot's life.

The following day one of the worst atrocities of the war was carried out at the Elim Mission in the Vumba Mountains. Eight white missionaries and four of their children were hacked and beaten to death with axes and knobkerries. One lone survivor died later in hospital. Two of the 21 terrorists responsible for the massacre died in a contact with security forces on 10th August.

On 30th June 1978, Acting Sergeant Carlos Gomes of the Parachute Training School undertook the 50,000th training jump. In a ceremony, the officer commanding Parachute Training School, Squadron Leader Derek de Kock asked the Dakota captain Flight Lieutenant Al Bruce to accept a bottle of champagne as a gesture of thanks to No 3 Squadron from the jumping instructors (PJIs). Without the expertise and cooperation of the Dakota crews we could never do the job at all.

FAF 7* Daily Diary, 5th July 1978
At first light the two G-Cars and the Lynx took off on a task. All was quiet until about 10h00

★ 28th July Squadron Leader Briscoe was replaced by Squadron Leader Geldenhuys.

just after Squadron Leader Rob McGregor had taken off for Umtali. Thereafter life was pretty hectic until about 20h00. There was a contact just south of the Lundi, which we reacted to. At the same time, Vila Salazar was stomped and the Hunters were tasked to take out Malvernia. Then finally at 19h20 a Mateke Hills farmer's homestead was attacked 60km south-east of Rutenga.

21st July (Friday)

A quiet day flying-wise from here. However, the armoured cars got involved in a punch-up with a group of terrs exiting the country. The Lynx was deployed from Rutenga and he put in a bomb strike that seemed to quieten things down. Soon afterwards, they started to take strain so the Hunters were called in and dropped their bombs on target. Silencing that pain. The count of dead terrs at this stage—37 dead. A great show all round.

Hot extraction at Mount Darwin

On 27th July 1978, Francois du Toit with his technician Kevin Nelson and Nigel Lamb with technician Chris Saint were on hot extraction stand-by at Mount Darwin in support of the Selous Scouts. Nigel Lamb remembers that:

Both Francois and I had been awarded the MFC (Op) earlier that day. I am not sure what Francois got his for, but mine came as a big surprise as it was for the sort of operation everyone on No 7 Squadron was doing regularly. Pride was mixed with embarrassment. Late in the day, we were tasked to uplift a call sign north-east of Chioco in Mozambique. Neil Kriel was not best pleased to see 'his' two helicopters disappear. It was a long way and there were only four soldiers to bring out, so we took lots of fuel and planned a pickup of two soldiers each at last light. Our fuel load would preclude lifting the normal four in one helicopter. It was supposed to be a hot extraction. Little did I realize at that time the implications that the extra fuel would have. We planned our route carefully using all the latest intelligence on the areas we should avoid. This required lots of turning points. Flight Lieutenant Chris Abram was airborne in the Lynx and we established comms with the call sign without any problems. Francois was leading and I was formatting on him in a wide echelon starboard. Running in about two minutes out, our routine flight suddenly became a nightmare—there was a ferocious eruption of ground fire, mostly to our left. Within seconds, I saw Francois' G-Car descend rapidly into the trees. No fireball, no call on the radio. Chris Saint was blasting away and I was calling urgently to Chris Abram in the Lynx. We had overflown an unmarked camp containing about 300 terrorists. We must have crossed the edge of the camp because our helicopter came under reasonably intense fire but Francois went right into the middle of it. Our own troops were just a few miles away, so the obvious plan was to uplift two of them at a time and drop them as close as possible to the downed helicopter in an attempt to secure the area. Of course, at that time we had no idea how many insurgents we were up against but the almost constant firing was a clear indication that the opposition was huge. The light was not going to last but we had lots of fuel—far too much to pick up four troopies. I called for two soldiers to prepare for uplift. Having heard all the firing and probably seen the tracers, they were understandably apprehensive. I doubt their fear was greater than mine. Desperately hoping that the enemy would be just as frightened, I planned my approach from the position we had been in when Francois went down. It seemed logical to assume that the terrorists would not know how much opposition they had and were likely to be escaping to the east, away from the helicopter noise. By this time, Chris Abram was giving us maximum support and I distinctly remember looking up and seeing his Lynx surrounded by 'flak'. I guess they were popping off every RPG-7 and SAM-7 they had. Grateful for the heat he was drawing, we tried to stay hidden in the trees. We managed to overfly Francois' chopper at about 15 feet. It looked very flat—obviously a high rate of descent impact. The chance of survival seemed unlikely but we had to get the troops to confirm. The ground fire seemed to be continuous but I don't recall taking many hits—maybe they were firing blind—or aiming at the Lynx. We went back for the next two soldiers. As we were approaching for the second drop the call sign at the downed chopper began screeching. They were pinned down by heavy opposition, being overwhelmed and could not reach the crash site even though we had dropped them only 50 metres away. Now we had a real problem on our hands: fading light, two troops needing extraction, two on board and too much fuel to lift four men out. Plus of course the fact that we did not want to leave the downed crew. The troops on the ground were sounding more and more desperate. Chris Saint and I made a plan. We would lurk behind a ridge to the west and dump everything possible overboard. This would reduce our weight and allow time for the situation to change. Maybe the troops would be able to get through. The thought of leaving our colleagues was horrendous. I told the call sign to stand by with a white phosphorous grenade. On our run-in, Chris Abram would make a series of attacks in the Lynx. I would call for white phos, overfly their position and land at the next available clearing. This called for two prayers: one for a landing area before the main enemy concentration and one for a healthy engine and gearbox for the overweight take-off. As we flew up and down behind the ridge in relative security, there was time to ponder. Pondering was not good—my legs were on the verge of uncontrollable shakes and my mouth was bone dry and speaking had become less than natural. I felt pretty sure we would not make it. It's amazing how cool they seem in the movies! After about ten minutes, with fading light and the situation on the ground not improving, we had to accept the inevitable. My memories of the uplift are a blur: running in with Chris attacking in the Lynx, desperate shouting on the radio, Chris Saint firing our Brownings, the white phos, a frantic search for a clearing, and finally landing amongst the trees in very long grass. Then the eternal wait for the two desperate troopies. They scrambled on board and we hauled ourselves out from amongst the trees, guns firing, gearbox screaming, and away to the west and temporary refuge. I hardly dared look at the 'collective' gauge. It's a wonderful machine the Alouette. Then the trip home in the dark with not enough fuel for our original destination—planning for an alternative safe haven and having to leave the safe inbound track. After a long tense sortie, we landed at Marymount Mission, where I found that the senior army officer was Rudd, a prefect from school when I was a junior. I remembered having to clean his shoes and carry his books. It was good to see him. Having completed our 'sitrep' and sent it to base, Rudd provided some very welcome brandy. The next day Chris Saint and I were airborne before dawn. Our G-Car was fine—some holes but no serious damage. We were amazed to be tasked to return to Mt Darwin on hot extraction duties for Major Kriel rather than proceed with the rescue mission. Perhaps Air HQ thought our nerves were shot. Maybe they were right. Flight Lieutenant Francois du Toit and Sergeant Kevin Nelson were both found dead from gunshot wounds. For the last 22 years, I have found it more comfortable to believe that these were inflicted before impact. (Nigel Lamb)

In another unrelated incident, Flight Lieutenant Chris Abram was in a Lynx flying telstar for a fireforce operation in the Chikwakwa Tribal Trust Land, when he was subjected to accurate ground fire. The aircraft was so badly damaged that it had to return to base at New Sarum where the pilot made an emergency landing without the use of brakes or flaps. The hydraulics had been shot away. Flight Lieutenant Abram was awarded the Military Forces Commendation (Operational).

Operation Mascot—the second attack on Tembué in July/August 1978

Operation Dingo, the first attack on the Tembué complex, north of Cabora Bassa, which took place during November 1977 had been relatively unproductive. Since that time, aircraft on photographic reconnaissance had maintained a careful watch on the Tembué complex.

Towards the middle of 1978, the Joint Services Photographic Interpretation Staff (JSPIS) identified a series of camps forming a new complex close to the original one, which had been attacked in November 1977. This new camp was designated Tembué 2. From an evaluation of the path patterns, it was concluded that there could be 3,000 ZANLA soldiers living in a series of dispersed camps around the complex.

The Selous Scouts were asked to reconnoitre the area but they were told that a strike would be put in six days after their drop whether they came up with any further information or not. This meant that the Selous Scouts would have to be dropped close to the target area. Any error in navigation would mean that the Scouts would not reach their target in time to send useful information back. The moonlight on the night chosen for the drop was not sufficient for the pilots to navigate with pinpoint accuracy so a free-fall drop was ruled out. A low-level static line drop at last light was agreed upon.

After the drop, the Scouts would move into the pre-selected vantage points and set up observation posts. Seven camps dispersed over a wide area had been located so even with two teams operating, the task would be difficult to complete in the allotted time. The deployment was carried out late in the afternoon of 10th July 1978. Everything went according to plan and by 12th July, both teams were in position overlooking the camps. First reports indicated only about 500 ZANLA men in one camp and about 50 in another. In fact, the camp was not really a camp at all, just a series of grass shelters under the trees.

Then on 19th July, a member of one of the recce teams was spotted and drew fire from the enemy. He got away from the area safely but the operation was compromised. If the ZANLA cadres knew that security force members were in the area they would surely move out. Schulenberg kept watch for two more days and reported that all had returned to normal at the Tembué 2 camp. ComOps were surprised that ZANLA men should apparently still be in the area after a contact with a security force member, but they agreed to a strike taking place. The attack went in as planned at 08h00 on Sunday 30th July. Unfortunately, the paratroops dropped into the wrong area and the ZANLA forces managed to escape to the west. All in all, it was another 'lemon'.

Chopper crash

The Police Reserve Air Wing had one of their big camps in the area east of Bindura. A mini fireforce, one K-Car (Ted Lunt), two G-Cars (Ray Bolton and Geoff Oborne) and a Lynx were positioned at Bindura in support of the PRAW exercise. The army contingent was a few RAR sticks. On 28th August 1978, at about noon, Ray Bolton was tasked to do a resupply mission. This left the K-Car and just one G-Car. Shortly after this, a call came in that an insurgent camp had been spotted. Ted Lunt carried out the briefing. The K-Car and the G-Car got airborne and routed via the airfield to wait for the Lynx to join them. The balance of the RAR troops boarded their trucks and made off down the road to a point south of the suspected camp. Geoff Oborne continues:

The K-Car pulled up and I went into an orbit round the area. After about a minute Ted said that the K-Car had them visual and was opening fire. I could hear the 20mm cannon going wild in the background. On my second orbit Brian Booth my tech, said he had seen a gook running up the side of the hill in the open. We staggered over to the area (we were very heavy) and opened fire with our Brownings. The terr, realizing he was caught in the open, just stood there and fired back at us. After what seemed an eternity and a lot of .303 rounds he eventually dropped. By now Ted wanted my troops put on the ground. He directed me to an LZ amongst the trees. I landed and deployed the RAR stick. Then I went to the road to pick up another stick. I returned to the contact area where I could see the Lynx putting in a frantan strike. As we came into orbit again, we were shocked to see that the terr we thought we had killed had gone. This was a tactic we were to take note of for future contacts. Ted told me to drop my stick where the frantan strike had gone in. I was quite happy as I thought if there were any terrorists around they would either be dead or very sorry. I came into the hover and as I was about a metre from touchdown, I saw two terrs stand up behind the bushes about 30 metres away in the two o'clock position (on the opposite side to the Brownings). They brought up their AKs and opened fire. I pulled the collective lever up to the stop and we leapt into the air again. I pushed full right pedal to bring the guns to bear and also to place my armoured seat between me and the terrs. The clatter of gunfire was really loud and as we got to treetop level in a 30 degree bank, the engine suddenly stopped. I shouted over the radio. "I'm crashing." (No time for a formal Mayday). I managed to level the chopper as we hit the ground. The blades hit a tree off to the left and burnt grass and dust covered the chopper. Then it all went quiet. I looked behind to see if Brian and the troopies had survived the crash but they were nowhere to be seen. I unstrapped, jumped out and turned to grab my rifle. It was missing. I ran in the opposite direction from the gooks and lay down behind a tree about 50 metres away. Above me the K-Car was orbiting. I was wearing a green flying suit so I prayed that Ted and his gunner wouldn't mistake me for a terr. It also dawned on me that an immediate rescue was out of the question as the other G-Car was away. I looked around for friendly faces but all I could see was a dead body dressed in blue lying on the other side of the stream. After five minutes I saw the RAR stick, with Brian in the middle advancing towards the chopper. I whistled and they came over. Brian had my AK-47, which I promptly repossessed. We all moved further away from the crash site, taking shelter in the stream bed. The RAR stick leader informed us that we were to carry out a sweep of the gook camp. Cursing Ray Bolton for being away so long with the rescue chopper we began to move through the camp looking for terrs—not something we had been trained for. As blue jobs we had to walk behind the sweep line—probably because we would have been a liability if there had been a scene. We hadn't quite reached the camp area when we heard the sound of Ray's chopper. Three hours later we were in a PRAW aircraft on our way to New Sarum. The next day I phoned the squadron and was told that there was a spare chopper available and that I was needed back at the sharp end. So off I went back to the bush. Oh! Well, that's war! (Geoff Oborne)

CHAPTER 45

The Hunyani goes down & Green Leader takes revenge

Towards the middle of August 1978, Ian Smith travelled to Lusaka for talks with Joshua Nkomo. The plan was that ZIPRA would work together with the Rhodesian security forces against Robert Mugabe's ZANLA. It was hoped that a government that included Nkomo would be recognized by Zambia and Angola. It seemed that these talks might at last provide the breakthrough that everyone had been hoping for, but then an event occurred that put an end to any possible rapprochement between Smith and Nkomo.

The *Hunyani*

The Air Rhodesia four-engine Viscount *Hunyani* took off from Kariba Airport at 17h10 on 3rd September 1978 carrying 58 passengers and crew, most of them holidaymakers.

The aircraft gained altitude and crossed the lake heading towards Salisbury. As it flew high above the Urungwe Tribal Trust Land, five minutes out from Kariba the No Smoking lights went out and at that moment there was a loud explosion and the inner starboard engine burst into flames. The pilot immediately put out a Mayday call. The aircraft had been hit by a SAM-7 heat-seeking missile that put both starboard engines out of action. The Viscount went into a shallow dive and the pilot, Captain John Hood, fought for control. Seeing what appeared to be open ground ahead, he brought the aircraft in, scraping the fuselage against the treetops and executing a perfect emergency landing. It seemed that a miracle had happened and that all would be well, but what the pilot had not seen was a deep ditch running across the middle of the field. The undercarriage hit the ditch and the aircraft cartwheeled and exploded. Only 18 people in the tail section survived, some of whom were badly injured.

The immediate reaction in Salisbury was that the plane had been brought down by enemy action and the air force began a grid pattern search of the probable area of the crash. If the Viscount had been hit by a strela, there would be a fire at the crash site. However, the particular area of search was so full of the lights of small fires where the local people were cooking meals or merely keeping warm that it was impossible to identify any burning wreckage.

The aerial search continued into the following day, 4th September, with the Dakotas flying at 1,000 feet. Then at last came the sight that everyone expected, but dreaded finding, the still-smouldering wreckage of the *Hunyani*. The Dakota 3713 piloted by Flight Lieutenant Nick Mehmel, a reserve pilot, circled the area, and the paratroopers waiting to jump saw a group of bodies lying under the trees. The SAS men descended and as they dropped, they could clearly see the bodies: a woman, an old man, an air hostess and a small boy. These people had obviously not died in the crash.

Quickly the troopers secured the area and began a search. Then they saw a hand wave. Three people were still alive. They told a sickening story. Eighteen people, including an air hostess, had survived the crash. Five of these had left the scene to search for water and help.

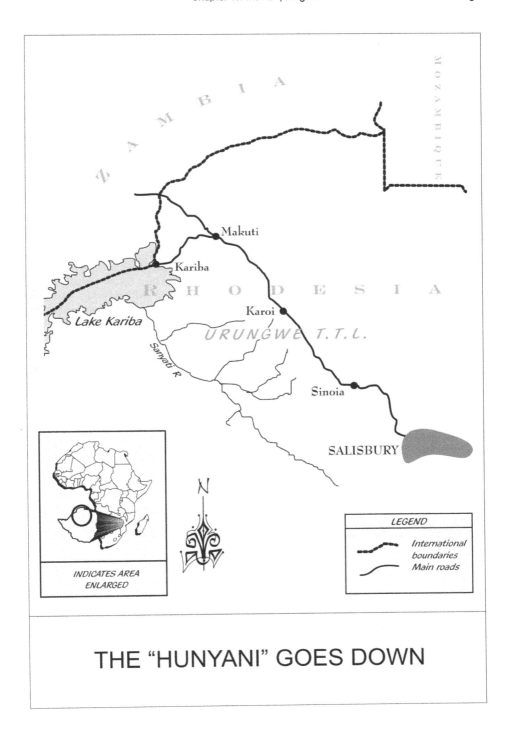

THE "HUNYANI" GOES DOWN

Shortly afterwards, a ZIPRA group had arrived at the crash site. At first, the survivors thought the ZIPRA men were going to help them but then the terrorists opened fire killing ten men, women and children. Three passengers managed to escape and hide. Hearing the gunfire, the group that had gone for help remained hidden. Of the 58 people aboard the *Hunyani*, ten had escaped the crash only to be massacred by the ZIPRA men. Only eight people survived the crash and the following massacre.

News that the aircraft had been brought down by a surface-to-air missile was not at first released but then Joshua Nkomo was interviewed on radio. He claimed that ZIPRA forces had shot down the plane but denied that his men had murdered the survivors. His voice crowed with satisfaction as he boasted of the incident. This attitude caused deep anger within Rhodesia and it meant that any deal between Ian Smith and Nkomo was out of the question. There were calls for a massive retaliation against ZIPRA.

Operation Snoopy—September 1978

However, the first external target after the shooting down of the Viscount was not, as had been expected, Zambia. On 20th September, another major attack was mounted on Chimoio. According to intelligence reports, four white abductees were being held at this camp. Few enemy were found but as the troops prepared to pull out, a Lynx on a reconnaissance flight about 35 kilometres away to the south, was shot at. Further aircraft were sent to check this area and they too came under fire. Security force members from the main camp who were speedily choppered into the new area met strong resistance on the ground, while reconnaissance aircraft reported a large network of trenches and small camps.

The new target was of considerable size, roughly 30 kilometres by 40 kilometres comprising dozens of small camps, with anti-aircraft gun positions manned by very determined men. Because this encampment was so dispersed, it was difficult to strike it effectively from the air. The pilots had a problem pinpointing suitable targets and, as is usual in September, there was a thick ground haze, which grew heavier as fires started to burn.

The second day of the attack was even more chaotic, with Canberras flying in one way, Hunters attacking another and Lynx circling, while the helicopters dodged in and out at ground height. Dave Bourhill describes the confusion that ensued:

J.R. Blythe-Wood was Blue Leader, I was Blue 2 and Brian Gordon was Blue 3. We had been tasked to suppress AA and cause general mayhem on the ground. The attack was to commence at the magic hour of 08h00 as this was when the gooks would be lined up on parade for roll call. Officer commanding No 1 Squadron, Vic Wightman, and Alf Wilde were leading sections of Hunters tasked to bomb from the high dive profile. As it was the end of the dry season, the haze was a thick dirty yellow below 12,000 feet. Vic identified his target, turned in and dropped his two golf bombs, but unfortunately it was the wrong hill and an SAS call sign, Trooper Steve Donnelly, was fatally injured. So a 'Stop Stop Stop' went out and the attack was called off. At this stage, we were in a descent. JR went into a lazy left turn with the two of us in tow. There was the normal chatter and bullshit going on over the R/T. During the turn, still descending, Blue Section was called in. Switches checked, I had positioned myself on JR for the run-in to the target when there was an almighty bang. All sorts of things whizzed through my mind, first and foremost of which was our position, deep in Mozambique (which meant a long walk home.) A quick scan of the instruments—everything was OK—no fire warning light, aircraft still flying, legs shaking uncontrollably. I did an external check. The first place I looked was where I had felt the bang and I noticed my starboard frantan was missing and that there was a gaping hole in the wing. Fortunately, I could not see the damage to the underside of the wing. Well, best let JR know:

Me: Blue leader 2.

JR: Go.

Me: I've been hit.

JR: So?

Me: Well, I've got a big hole in my wing.

JR: Well, what are you going to do, carry on?

Me: No. I think I'll go home.

By now my legs had stopped their little dance, and I levelled off at 30,000 feet heading in the general direction of Salisbury. I was still flying, no problem, so I sent out a 'Pan Pan Pan' call which was picked up by a Lufthansa 747 and relayed to Salisbury. This is when the training and discipline paid off: no baling out (too scared); no bleating over the R/T (didn't want to sound scared); just do the checks. Slow handling check—slight vibration, no flames or smoke (nothing left to burn). So into a wide circuit, undercarriage down, three greens, turn finals 06, keep the speed up, touch down lightly. After rolling to a stop at the high speed turn-off, shut down, seat pins in, I casually climbed out and walked away from aircraft. A CMED gang is working on the runway. Well, the old Whitey in charge of the gang walks up and says in his best Slopie/ Rhodie accent, "Are you the one who brought this back? Well done, well done! Yassus but what a mess," and then nearly pumps my right arm off at the shoulder. The aircraft was a mess. The strela had missed the tailpipe and hit the starboard aileron, skidded along the wing surface and then detonated downwards. The whole wing was distorted and cracked. The missile had blown the starboard frantan and carrier right off, and a section of the underwing from the outboard hard point to the wing tank attachment point. A large piece was still hanging on and blowing in the breeze. Seeing the extent of the damage, I was pleased I had been flying an FGA 9. It had certainly taken some punishment, and had flown on without a problem. (Dave Bourhill)

Operation Snoopy was proving hectic. The technicians were being kept very busy repairing holes in the aircraft as well as arming and de-arming. Somehow, the ground crews kept the aircraft flying. Another pilot who took part in the operation was Glen Pretorius:

When my navigator Paul Perioli and I arrived at our Canberra, Tony Cobbett, chief tech No 5 Squadron, jokingly said that we were please to look after his aircraft, and that for every hole that they might have to repair I would have to buy him a beer. The first run in to the target was at 300 feet. Only half of our load was to be dropped. The second run was to be at the same height but from a different direction, dropping the rest of the load. SAM-7 sightings had been frequent that morning and we were very much aware of them. These areas had been marked on our maps as no overfly areas, or 'spoil your day' places. The cloud was quite low, and this made us feel a little less vulnerable to the SAM-7s, but nevertheless, still respectful of the dangers. We dropped the remaining load, kept as low as possible and accelerated, once the bomb doors were closed. My idea was to zoom climb when we had passed over the danger area. This was no problem because the Canberra had plenty of power available, especially now that we were so light. Yes, well ... Paul was still lying in the nose, hanging onto his bombsight, when I pulled the nose up. Thrust was increased to maximum climb power. The rate of climb was very impressive. And we entered the cloud. Safe ... Then the whole plan went pear-shaped ... There was a huge bang, the aircraft yawed, and the port engine 'fire warning' light illuminated. I saw a supersonic navigator pass by me heading back towards his ejection seat. I don't know if it was feet first or head first—I don't think Paul remembers either. (Glen Pretorius)

Normally the time needed to strap in to the ejection in the rear of the Canberra cockpit seat would be about two minutes. Well, after we had completed the bombing run, we went vertical in order to get out of the SAM-7 range as fast as possible. I was hanging on to the bombsight in order to stop myself from falling back past the pilot, when the explosion occurred. I needed to get back to the ejection seat fast. I could achieve this by just letting go. The rest happened in a flash—I would guess about ten seconds. I remember having this huge wave of relief that I was safely strapped in—then it hit me. I had neglected to put on my leg restrainers! These are the first things you attach when strapping in and they are designed to keep your knees together on ejection, so preventing serious injury. I had a dilemma—should I unstrap, and take the chance that I might have to eject at that critical moment, or should I take the chance of walking like John Wayne for the rest of my life. I chose John Wayne. Fortunately, Glen had everything under control. (Paul Perioli)

The engine was shut down, the fire went out and I pointed for home. Fortunately, the Can flies very well on one engine. A Hunter was nearby, flown by the OC Vic Wightman and he managed to locate us. He came into formation and gave us a pretty good description of the damage. The missile had entered the rear of the port engine and had split open the jet pipe. There was fuel pouring out of the fuselage. This could have been serious as the fuel tanks, three of them, are located in the fuselage above the bomb bay. It was our number two tank that had been holed. So we isolated it. We had enough fuel in the other tanks to get home. We would not be able to use flap for landing but this was not a problem. We landed, but owing to the asymmetry with only one engine, we just managed to clear the runway but were unable to taxi in to the dispersal. At this point, Paul and I had had enough so we shut down and were out of the aircraft speedily. The fire department arrived and we walked back to the crew room. Tony, the chief tech, arrived with a huge order of beers—we began to relax. Then came the call from the fire department. They had smothered the Canberra in foam—but—they couldn't find the crew! Asked afterwards how we had felt at the time of the missile strike and the interminable flight back to base, I could only recall a comment made by a friend: 'Scared—never; terrified—often'. And we had to buy Tony Cobbett only one beer! (Glen Pretorius)

During the second night, several tanks arrived, blundered around for a bit and then left the area. On the following day, three Russian-built armoured personnel carriers were destroyed by the Hunters. No white prisoners were found but records were discovered which proved beyond doubt that these people were being held by ZANLA. As a result, representations were made to Amnesty International and the abductees were subsequently handed over and returned home. For the abductees, therefore, the operation was a success. On day three, the Rhodesian forces withdrew having experienced the heaviest anti-aircraft fire to date with a large number of aircraft hit by small arms and missile fire. The Rhodesians simply did not have the resources to maintain this action or the manpower to subdue such a vast area.

Four-legged hazards
Fighting a war in the bush sometimes meant watching out for four-legged hazards as well as the two-legged enemies as the following two episodes demonstrate.

FAF 7 Daily Diary, 3rd September 1978
A very quiet day only—one point of interest when A. Davies (PRAW) was coming in to land at 18h25 and ran into a herd of Impala. Killed two and sustained damage to his starboard wing. Will fly to Salisbury in the morning for repairs.

25th September. Whilst a runway was being cleared, a large wild pig made a savage attack on the patrol's Land Rover. The pig died gallantly for a lost cause.

On 9th October, Air Lieutenant Terence McCormick was piloting the lead helicopter in an action against terrorists when the army officer in his aircraft was wounded. McCormick took over control of the action, deploying the troops and coordinating the air strikes to maintain the momentum of the sweep lines. Despite heavy fire from the ground, he remained low over the area. He only handed over to another aircraft once the initiative was firmly with the security forces. He then evacuated the wounded army officer to safety, after which he resumed his aggressive role in the battle. He was later awarded the MFC (Op).

Also during October, Flight Lieutenant Rich Beaver, flying a fixed-wing aircraft, carried out hazardous air-to-ground attacks on terrorist positions at night by the light of flares which he had dropped. These attacks allowed the ground forces to withdraw from an untenable position. Later, over dangerous terrain in the Zambezi River Gorge, he successfully attacked terrorists who were attempting to cross the river by boat, after which he controlled a strike by jet aircraft on terrorist positions adjacent to the crossing point.He was later awarded the MFC (Op).

In October, the Zambian government reopened the Rhodesian border that had been closed since 1973. By 12th October, the first official wagons had rolled across the bridge at Victoria Falls—unofficially, trains loaded with copper had been crossing the bridge continually.

A new set of Rhodesian postage stamps issued on 18th October had been designed by Flight Lieutenant Cedric Herbert of the Rhodesian Air Force Photographic Section. The stamps were issued to commemorate the 75th anniversary of the first powered flight in 1903. Cedric Herbert who joined the air force in 1954 as a photographer was also involved in the redesign of buttons, badges and insignia in 1970.

The golf bomb

This was a project developed by Peter Petter-Bowyer to make a fuel/air explosive (FAE). The Americans had developed the concept using ethylene oxide which when ignited produced gas volumes many times greater than explosives such as TNT. It was claimed that FAE had a near nuclear performance and it was used by the Americans to clear pathways through minefields. Peter produced some spectacular fireballs and two terrific detonations, one of which blew out windows 500 metres away. The ground was pulverized to a powder and all vegetation, even substantial trees, was flattened for a distance of 45 metres. The sound was very distinctive in that, unlike the sharp bang from TNT, it was more of a deep kerump. However, ethylene oxide was dangerous to handle, difficult to obtain and made the weapon complicated to deliver.

Another substance had to be found. The answer was Anfo, a simple mixture of ammonium nitrate (fertilizer) and diesel, both of which were available in large quantities and could be mixed by hand using a shovel and a wheelbarrow. Later the process became more sophisticated when the team borrowed a concrete mixer.

Tests were carried out at Kutanga Range. Twenty kilograms of Anfo were placed in a hole one cubic metre in size and covered with rocks. The team retired to a distance of 1,000 metres and the charge was ignited. The rocks could be clearly seen passing 1,000 feet and then nothing. The team watched and waited but nothing was heard or seen. Then as the members of the team walked back to their cars, a strange sound was heard. Everyone dived for cover as the rocks came crashing down all round.

The golf bomb had been born. Steel canisters 1.5 metres in length and 450mm in diameter, the shape of liquid-gas cylinders, were filled with Anfo. A one metre-long proboscis was fitted on the front of each cylinder. This allowed detonation to take place above ground. An initiator charge such as pentolite generated a huge explosion with large amounts of high-pressure gas being forced outwards. The gas cooled immediately and returned at supersonic

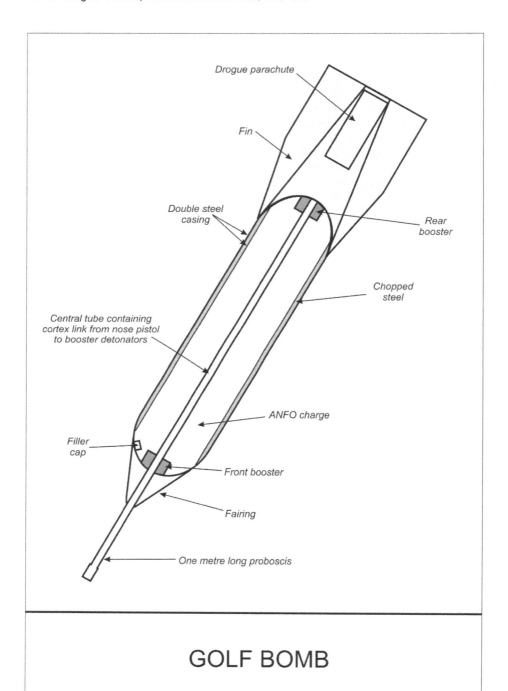

Drogue parachute

Fin

Double steel casing

Rear booster

Chopped steel

Central tube containing cortex link from nose pistol to booster detonators

ANFO charge

Filler cap

Front booster

Fairing

One metre long proboscis

GOLF BOMB

speed into the void causing an implosion—a double dose of no good. Initially the bomb produced a large crater which was energy wasted. So booster charges were placed in both the nose and the tail producing a squeezing effect, which flattened everything around the point of detonation. The tailpieces were usually found at the centre of detonation indicating that no energy had been lost skyward either.

The delivery profile from the Hunter was from a 60-degree dive. Two bombs were dropped simultaneously, one of which was fitted with paddles to retard it slightly so that it fell short, producing a bush-flattening area of 135 metres long by 90 metres wide. These rather crude efforts were soon discarded and replaced with small parachutes. In order to increase the effectiveness of the bomb, a double cylinder was made and the gap filled with thousands of pieces of chopped 10-millimetre steel bar, which gave it a lethal zone way beyond the over-pressure boundaries. The golf bomb officially named 450kg GP Bomb. Tony Oakley says:

The golf bombs had to be dropped as near to a vertical impact as possible and we had endless trouble getting the sighting picture right. You dropped into a dive and throttled back at the same time, doing your best to get the sight under control. It really was a very difficult sighting job especially if you drifted off the target because then you had to do a roll and pull manoeuvre to get the sight back. The release point was impossible to judge by looking through the sight— especially with the ground rushing up at you, so we released when a light came on indicating that we were at the correct height—this was pre-set on a spare altimeter. Once the bomb had gone you pulled for all you were worth in order to make a safe height. The other important aspect was to ensure you were not under any kind of 'g' loading, or sideslip at the time of release because this could put hundreds of metres on the accuracy of the bomb. Tactics with this weapon varied considerably. It depended not only on whether we were bombing in conjunction with the Canberras but also on how well the target was defended. When we dropped the golf bombs with the Canberras, we always ran in to the target in formation at very low level. At a point some kilometres from the target the lead Can would call 'go' and we would apply full power, accelerate away and zoom climb to the 'perch' position. It was imperative to turn in at exactly the right moment as our strikes were often used by the Cans for a last minute line-up. More especially, any delay in dropping meant that there was a risk of dropping the golfs on the Cans which would be running in over the target 20 seconds later. This proved to be a very successful combination and many strikes were done this way. The more strategic targets, buildings, radar sites, hangars, warehouses etc. were usually in well-defended areas, so the element of surprise was very important. In this case, we used to fly in at high level at 350 knots or so and then throttle back to idle as far from the target as possible and glide down to perch position—roll in and drop. Sounds easy, but 'Oh boy!'

Operation Gatling, October 1978

The targets for Operation Gatling were Joshua Nkomo's main training/holding camps in Zambia. Previously these camps had been considered safe by ZIPRA forces because they were deep in Zambian territory, the main camp Chikumbi, or Freedom Camp, at Westlands Farm being only 20 kilometres north of the Lusaka city centre. Aerial reconnaissance had pinpointed the area and it had been estimated that there were some 4,500 ZIPRA members undergoing training. This camp would be attacked by air only. The Hunters were to go in first carrying a cargo of Golf and 1,000-pound bombs. This attack was followed by Canberras using Alpha bombs, after which Alouette K-Cars would strafe the area with their 20mm cannon and finally a pair of Hunters armed with frantan would ensure the destruction of the communication centre.

The second attack was to be on Mboroma, also known as Old Mkushi, 160 kilometres

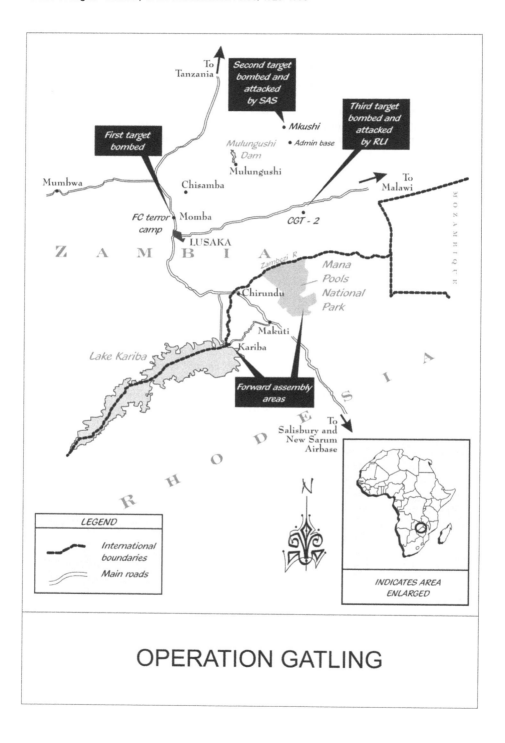

OPERATION GATLING

north-east of Lusaka. This target would be attacked by Canberras, Hunters, Vampires, Lynxes and K-Cars and vertically enveloped by troops of the SAS. The third attack of the day was on the four camps 130 kilometres north-east of Lusaka known as the CGT complex, which was thought to house another 5,000 men. The main camp, CGT2, was to be vertically enveloped by troops of the RLI after initial airstrikes while the remaining three camps would be attacked by air only.

Because of the distances, forward air bases were used at Kariba airport and Mana Pools airfield and an admin base was planned in the Muchinga Hills, about 22 kilometres from Mkushi camp, where the helicopters could rearm and refuel. The forward admin base for the CGT attack was about ten kilometres south-west of the CGT camps. The troops manning the refuelling areas in Zambia would be dropped in at the same time that the air force was carrying out its first attacks.

The Rhodesian Air Force had no wish to engage the Zambian Air Force, which was reported to have MiG 17 and MiG 19 aircraft based at Mumbwa, the main Zambian Air Force base, 124 kilometres west of Lusaka. There was also the possibility that the Rapier air-to-air missile system and Strelas could be used against the Rhodesian aircraft. However, two Hunters of Red Section patrolled the air above Mumbwa (armed with 30mm and 68mm rockets) to prevent any attempt to get ZAF into the air during the Freedom Camp attack only.

At dawn on 19th October 1978, the attack force assembled. Every member of the SAS was to take part. General Walls and Group Captain Norman Walsh climbed aboard the command Dakota, call sign Dolphin 3. In the morning light, two Hunters, four Canberras and four K-Cars entered Zambian airspace heading north. Tension in the air heightened. Tony Oakley remembers the adrenalin rush as he approached the target:

Target acquisition was a very serious problem and sometimes strikes would have to be postponed because of bad weather. Even when there was little or no cloud cover, the haze and the smoke made it difficult to identify targets in the bush. We were usually armed with a photograph that was the wrong size to manage in the cockpit and seemed to bear little resemblance to the view we had of the ground. Since our strikes were often the precursor to bigger air strikes followed by a ground assault, the timing was critical. I can still recall the tension that ran through my body as I got close to the target area and nothing seemed to fit the photo—then just as that sick feeling started rising in my throat—there it was. The elation was unbelievable and the photo got stuffed in next to the seat while you got your wits about you for the long almost vertical dive. Then you had to remind yourself to keep calm and make the right switch selections so you didn't bring your bombs home again! I often wondered what the pulse rate got up to at times like this.

Green Leader

This particular raid was recorded in the cockpit of the pilot leading the Canberras. This is an edited transcript of this tape recording. Most of the conversation takes place between Green Leader (Chris Dixon) and his navigator/bomb-aimer (Mike Ronne). Parts of this tape were released to the Rhodesia Broadcasting Corporation and the Press immediately after the raid. The strike force consisted of Green Section (Canberras), Red, White and Blue Sections (Hunters) and a number of K-Car helicopter gunships. As the aircraft approached the border, they began their descent from 4,500 feet to 1,600 feet to come in under the Zambian radar.

Nav: Start descending from this road.
GL: Okay. Do you want me to maintain the same speed or do you want me to reduce to 50?
Nav: No, maintain the speed. We'll have to increase it to maintain 300.
GL: Okay.

GL (to formation): Green descending.
Nav: Go right four degrees...
GL: (altimeter setting QNH) 1019 is set now, 4,500 feet, 310 knots.
Nav: Zero-zero-five.
GL: Zero-zero-five. Ya.
GL (to formation): Right, let's tighten it up a bit now.
Nav: Coming up to one minute out. We're on track and we're on time. Get your speed up.
Blue Sec: Green, what's your level?
GL: Roger, we're at 1,600 feet.
GL: 290 knots coming up.
Nav: 290 knots.
Blue Sec: Got you visual.

The Hunters come into loose formation with the Canberras.

GL: Okay. We're coming up to the stream now (Zambezi).
Nav: Zero-zero-six.
GL: Zero-zero-six we've got. We're crossing the stream now.
Blue Lead: Check.
GL: Well done JR (leading the Hunters).
Nav: Turn left now.
GL: Onto?
Nav: Now, three-zero-four.
GL: Three-zero-four.
Nav: We're going to have to climb a bit.
GL: Ya. One bird! Three-zero-four. Rolling out now. How's our speed? We're holding about 290.
Nav: No it's fine. Just check on these rivers. Go left—about two degrees.
GL: Three-zero-two. Roger.

The Canberras and Hunters are now heading on a course west-north-west towards their target—Joshua Nkomo's Chikumbi (Freedom) Camp at Westlands Farm.

Nav: We're a bit starboard of track.
GL: Roger. We didn't get round that turn as fast as I wanted.
Nav: Speed back 15 knots. On track. On time...
GL: Dead right.
GL: (Looking at the Hunters flying in formation with them): These Hunters with this bloody golf bomb here, or something. It's all painted bloody red. Quite f...ing weird!
Nav: Go two degrees left.
GL: Roger, that makes us three-zero-zero. I was on three-zero-two.
Nav: Steer three-zero-two.
GL: Three-zero-two. I was on three-zero-two.

The Canberra at low level is very susceptible to the turbulence and flying can be extremely uncomfortable. The pilot and the navigator can be heard trying to breathe normally, but the air is forced out of their lungs as they hit each bump. There had been a case of structural failure in the air force Canberras.

GL: Oh shit! I hope the f...ing wings don't fall off!

Nav: What's your speed?
GL: 275—which is the 15 you wanted off. Do you want me to get down?
Nav: Yes. You can go down a bit.
Nav: OK. We're on track, on time.
GL: Dead right—it's about a minute and a half before the Hunters leave us.
Nav: Two starboard onto three-zero-four.
GL: Two starboard.
Nav: No, make it three-zero-five
GL: Three-zero-five. OK.
Nav: Make it three-zero-six.
GL: Three-zero-six. OK, you've got it.
GL: There's not a peep out of tower so that's going to be superb. We won't have to talk to him.

The aircraft were listening in on the Lusaka tower frequency to see if they had been picked up on Zambian radar. It was almost time for the Hunters to accelerate ahead for their attack.

Nav: The Hunters will be going in about 50 seconds.
GL: Roger.
Nav: Go right another two degrees.
GL: Three-zero-eight?
Nav: Ya.

The voices of Lusaka tower are heard talking to a Kenya Airways flight.

GL: That's the bloody tower.
Nav: OK, just stand by sir, we're coming up to…

A second Canberra pilot offers advice.

2nd Canberra: I think we passed it—I think that rise on the right, is the one. That should have been our turning point.
GL (to 2nd Canberra): Oh! Shut up, man.
Nav (to GL): OK. Go Hunters go!
GL (to Hunters): Blue Section Go. Blue Section Go.

Blue Section, John Blythe-Wood, Tony Oakley and 'Baldy' Baldwin, leaves to carry out its mission.

Nav: OK. They were spot on time.
GL: That's OK. Roger—270 knots. You've got it now. Shit, they only accelerated bloody quickly.

It was now just before 08h30 and the ZIPRA forces were all on parade as the Hunters prepared to dive down on them with their cargoes of golf bombs.

Nav: Heading now two-eight-one, sir.
GL: Two-eight-one. Roger.
Nav: When I give you 'doors', can you switch on at the same time?
GL: Will do.
Nav: OK! We're coming up to 40 seconds to turn, sir.

GL: Roger.
Nav: We passed a river on our left here. We'll see the bridge fairly shortly.
GL: We've passed two-eight-one. Shall I turn back on it now?
Nav: Yes, back to two-eight-one.
GL: Two-eight-one we've got.
Nav: Can you bring the speed back—240?
GL: Steering two-eight-one.
Nav: Two-eight-zero.
GL: Two-eight-zero.

Green Section is now heading on a westerly course, which will take them over the camp.

Nav: Everything is set up and ready.
GL: There's a school coming up. Roger, I have 310 knots, two-eight-zero, QNH 1019.
GL: There's nothing from tower and I'm not going to call them. OK?
Nav: Okey doke.
GL: It's going to be perfect.
Nav: Little dam coming up. We're drifting port. Go to the right. Two-eight-three. Two-eight-four.
GL: Two-eight-four? Or two-eight-five?
Nav: I want to do a kink, sir, to get it spot on.
GL: Tell me when to roll out.
Nav: Go left. Two-eight-two.
GL: Roger, coming up to two minutes to run. Two-eight-two. Got two minutes to run. Perfect.
Nav: Go left a bit. Steady.
GL: Two-seven-eight?
Nav: Two-eight-two!
GL: A school coming up—acceleration point. Two-eight-two is the heading.
Nav: OK. We should start accelerating now.
GL: Roger. Shall I go?
Nav: Just leave it in case they (the Hunters) are going to be a bit late— to the minute.
GL: OK.
Nav: Accelerate!
GL: Roger.

At this stage, the tension becomes very apparent. The voices of both the pilot and navigator go up an octave and they begin to speak more quickly, using short phrases.

Nav: You want to get your doors open.
GL: Yes, as soon as I've got my speed.
Nav: Go left a bit. Go left.
GL: More?
Nav: No. OK. Flatten out on two-eight-two. Quickly. Carry on. Flatten out. Quickly. Carry on.
GL: Roger.
Nav: Up there—target!
GL: Ah! Beautiful. Yes! Switches. Speed up, or is it OK?
Nav: Speed's fine. Go left. Steady. Steady. Two-seven-eight.
GL: Roger.
Nav: Steady. Steady. Left a touch.
GL: Beautiful!

Nav: Steady. Steady. Left a touch. Steady. Steady. Steady. Can I switch the doors open?
GL: Yes. Switch your doors.

The adrenalin is now flowing as the excitement reaches fever pitch. Both the pilot and the navigator are shouting. They realize that the strike is going to be right on target. They can see the enemy running.

Nav: Right. I'm going to put them into the field.
GL: Yes!
Nav: Steady. I'm going to get them. Steady.
GL: YES! F...ing beautiful!
Nav: Steady. Steady. NOW! Bombs gone...They're running...
GL: Beautiful! Jeez! You want to see all those bastards. The f...ing bombs are beautiful!

The tension in the crew's almost breathless voices eases slightly, but the euphoria carries on for a long time. The fact that they have another duty to perform in getting the message to Lusaka tower reduces the elation for a moment, but it will soon come flooding back.

GL: Roger, just let me get onto the f...ing tower and give them our bloody message. Where's this f...ing piece of shit? (the message).
Nav: Things will be better when you've climbed up, sir. (Radio communication with the tower).
GL: Yes, I know. I'm just trying to get the thing ready...
Nav: That was lovely! F...ing hundreds of the bastards. It worked out better than we could have...they ran straight into the bombs.
GL: Those f...ing bastards.
Nav: Look out for aircraft, sir.
GL: There's the bloody city. There.

The K-Cars can then be heard over the target, with their cannons firing.

Nav: Are we putting in K-Cars here?
GL: Yes, they've got K-Cars there. They'll have a beautiful time. They are like f...ing ants running around there. Jeez. That was marvellous. Shit!
Nav: Straight ahead for one more minute.
GL: OK.
Nav: Keep an eye open, sir.
GL: Yes, I was going to say—a big pylon.
GL: Just check the tape recorder while you're there. Otherwise just leave it.
Nav: OK. Still turning.
GL: Roger. OK. Let me try and get this spiel off.
GL: Lusaka tower, this is Green Leader. How do you read? (No answer). Lusaka tower, this is Green Leader.
Lusaka tower: Station calling tower?
GL: Lusaka tower this is Green Leader. This is a message for the station commander at Mumbwa from the Rhodesian Air Force. We are attacking the terrorist base at Westlands Farm. This attack is against Rhodesian dissidents and not against Zambia. Rhodesia has no quarrel, repeat, no quarrel with Zambia or her security forces. We therefore ask you not to intervene or oppose our attack. However, we are orbiting your airfield now and are under orders to shoot down any Zambian Air Force aircraft, which does not comply with this request and attempts to take off. Did you copy all that?

Lusaka tower: Copied.
GL: Roger, thanks. Cheers.
GL: Jeez, you should have seen the bombs raining down from the other aircraft here. F…ing unreal.
Nav: I hope the K-Cars get those bastards. I was so tempted to drop short.
GL: But the other ones (alpha bombs from the other Canberras) were going onto them.
Nav: They were running that way.
Nav: It couldn't have worked out better— they ran straight into the bombs. I couldn't believe it.

The Canberras are now setting course for base, and Green Leader has to deal with the air traffic problems that have arisen at Lusaka.

Lusaka tower: Rhodesian Air Force, 118.1.
GL: Go ahead.
Tower: Can you confirm we can let our civil aircraft take-off from here? You have no objection?
GL: Roger. We have no objection there, but I advise you for the moment to stand-by on that. I request that you hang on for a short while—half an hour or so.
Tower: I copy. Can you please keep a listening watch on this frequency so we can ask you what we want to ask?
GL: Roger will do.
Tower: What do I call you?
GL: Green Leader!

Having dropped their golf bombs, Blue Section has completed their task, the Canberras are heading for home and it is now up to the K-Cars and White Section (John Blythe-Wood and Dave Bourhill) to mop up. The K-Car cannons can be heard in the background of the pilot interchanges. Meanwhile Red Section (Alf Wilde and Jim Stagman) is still orbiting Mumbwa to deal with any possible threat from the Zambian Air Force.

K-Car Lead: How does it look?
K-Car 1: Beautiful. (Bursts of machine gun fire).
White Lead: What would you like us to take out?
K-Car Lead: White Section—I think that building you are going for was taken out completely but you might like to have a re-go at it just to make absolutely certain.
White Lead: Roger. White 2, White Leader. Sir, if you would like to watch my strikes and then re-strike after us.
White 2: Roger.
White Lead: I think if you could take out the radio shack down there if you know which one it is.
White 2: Affirmative.
White Lead: Roger, sir—if you take out that one I'll put my frans on the headquarters. I'll be attacking from south to north.

The Kenya Airways aircraft, which has been denied landing permission, is becoming more and more frustrated with Lusaka tower. But the tower has other immediate concerns.

Kenya Airways: Lusaka tower this is Kenya 432.
Tower: 432 stand by.

The command Dakota, Dolphin 3, with Air Commodore Norman Walsh on board has kept a listening watch but has not heard the result of the Canberra attack.

Dolphin 3: We've heard nothing from Green Section. Confirm they did go through?
K-Car Lead: Affirmative. Right on target.
Dolphin 3: OK. Thanks very much.
GL: Dolphin 3 from Green Leader.
Dolphin 3: Green Leader, this is Dolphin 3, go ahead.
GL: Roger. Shortly I'm going to ask you to take over.
Tower: Green Leader, Lusaka.
GL: Go ahead.
Tower: How much longer is this operation?
GL: Roger. If you'll hang fire, I'll advise you shortly.
Tower: I have one to take off to the north and if you have no objection one to take off to the south. Civilian, you know.
GL: Request you hold them for another ten minutes.
Tower: Roger. Will do.
GL: Lusaka, this is Green Leader. Would you now contact Dolphin 3. He'll be taking over my transmissions.
Tower: Roger. Dolphin 3, Lusaka.
Dolphin 3: Lusaka, this is Dolphin 3, do you read me?
GL (interjecting): Dolphin 3, this is Green Leader. I have advised Lusaka to hold their civilian traffic for another ten minutes. We're going out of range shortly.
Dolphin 3: Roger. Lusaka, this is Dolphin 3. Just a message that you are to keep your air traffic on the ground for another ten minutes. Did you copy, over?
Tower: Copied, thank you. I have a civilian aircraft coming in from the north to land in about one-zero minutes. Any objection to him coming in to land?
Dolphin 3: Roger, there is no problem with that. You can let him come in and land. The main thing is that if there is any air force, repeat air force traffic, they are to remain on the ground. You can let that civilian traffic land—there's no hassle on that.
GL (to his nav): The Hunters are f...ing squalling back like scalded cats up there making little trails of white shit in the sky.

The captain of the Kenya Airways jet asks who has priority. Lusaka tower replies in all truth: "I think the Rhodesians do!" Meanwhile Green Section Canberras have moved out of range and Green Leader is checking with Salisbury radar. And so comes his final transmission:

GL: Salisbury radar, this is Green Section.
Salisbury: Green Section, radar.
GL: Flight level 250. We'll be top of descent at 58, the field at 08 and request priority landing for all our aircraft.
Salisbury: Report top of 'D'.

As the Alouettes pulled out there was one unfortunate incident. It's described by Nigel Lamb, the pilot of an Alouette III:

I was flying the 'Alpha Fit' (Dalmation) K-Car with Finch Bellringer as gunner. Hydraulically-operated, the 4 x .303 machine gun was designed to have a fantastic saturation killing ability. Actually, it was distinctly unpopular with some crews. Because of frequent stoppages, it could not compete with the 20mm cannon. Finch and I were tasked to join three other K-Cars [Mark Dawson, Chas Goatley and Ian Peacocke] to take out a very troublesome anti-aircraft gun position. A Vampire and Lynx attacked the target on our run-in and, almost immediately,

Cocky Benecke retired with a holed fuel tank in the Lynx. As we went in with the K-Cars, it immediately became apparent that we were in serious trouble—this place was heavily defended. With our guns firing and our collective lever somewhat higher than the designer intended, Finch and I joined the others in a maximum rate climb. Huge, easily visible shells arched lazily upwards, then seemed to accelerate past us. At 2,500 feet, three times higher than our normal firing orbit, the effectiveness of our machine guns was pitiful. Yet the shiny shells seemed unaffected in size and number. We were almost stationary and in perfect range. Mark called that he had taken some high explosive hits in the cockpit. He'd lost all his instruments and was wounded in the leg. I can't remember who was leader but his decision to make a dignified tactical withdrawal was a good one. Four K-Cars was not an effective force against that sort of opposition. So, with tail rotors firmly between our legs, we dived for the safety among the trees and split into pairs, one going each side of a ridge at very low level. Mark called for Chas to give him a visual inspection as he was having some directional control problems. Ian and I could not see them because they were behind the ridge. Moments later, we heard a shout from Chas. "Your tail rotor is slowing! It's stopped!" Mark was about 100 feet above the carpet of trees. Decelerating to 60 knots he was spinning violently, rotating once every two seconds. Following a lazy arc, the helicopter disappeared into the trees. Within seconds we were overhead. There was a clearing about 50 metres away. With Ian and Chas providing top cover, Finch and I went for it. Even before we landed, Finch was away, sprinting through the trees. Retarding the fuel flow, I stopped the rotors, climbed out and followed. Roelf Oelofse, the gunner was lying in the bush about 20 feet from the wreckage—alive but almost motionless with a back injury. He had been punched through the side door on impact. The trees had cushioned the Alouette's fall so the cockpit area was reasonably intact. Head hunched onto his right shoulder, Mark was slumped in his seat, alive but obviously unable to breathe. He looked blue. There was no time to lose. We'd taken a few minutes to reach him and, he was running the risk of oxygen starvation. Ripping his mask off, we slung him across my back and headed for the chopper with Finch supporting his head. The fact that there was no firing from the orbiting K-Cars was a good sign that we were in no physical danger. Mark was snoring heavily as we ran through the undergrowth. We lay him in the back of the chopper, wound up the blades and headed off for the medics at Mana Pools. Chas and Mike Smith went in to land and pick up Roelf.

Both Mark Dawson and Roelf Oelofse made complete recoveries. The Alouette III was destroyed by SAS. Remarking on this incident Bill Sykes says:

One outcome was a change in the design to the armoured seat. When the original seat had been designed, the back of the seat was only up to the pilot's shoulders, and the guide for the shoulder straps was positioned at the level of the pilot's shoulder blades. In Mark's case, he had slumped forward because the shoulder straps were ineffective in holding his body in the upright position. As a result, his neck was hard against the top of his flak jacket, cutting off the air supply. When the seat back was redesigned with additional protection for the pilot's head, the strap guide had remained in the same position. A simple modification was carried out so that the shoulder strap guide was cut at the height of the pilot's neck. This ensured that the pilot's shoulders were now held firmly back, with no chance of injury from the flak jacket even in the case of a high velocity vertical impact.

As the helicopters pulled out of Westlands Farm, a pall of smoke hung over the Zambian capital, and the scream of ambulance sirens sounded in the streets for many hours.

As soon as the command centre in Salisbury received news of the successful attack, the next phase was started. The troops boarded the six Dakotas that were to carry them to Mkushi

Camp. Once over Lake Cabora Bassa, the Dakotas dropped to treetop level under the radar cover. It was a bumpy ride and many of the troopers suffered airsickness.

Mkushi Base consisted of a main base with eight surrounding satellite camps. Although detailed intelligence on Mkushi was sketchy, the air force had carried out a thorough reconnaissance and the photographs showed about 500 uniformed ZIPRA on parade and undergoing weapons training.

The 120 SAS paratroops were to fly from New Sarum to Mkushi, while the heliborne SAS men would take off from Mana Pools. For the attack on the communist guerrilla-training camp complex, the RLI paratroopers would take off from Kariba and the heliborne RLI from Mana Pools. Because of the great distances, forward air bases were used; one each at Kariba and Mana Pools, and another, Rufunsa, inside Zambia, about five minutes' flying time from Mkushi Base where the helicopters could rearm and refuel.

The attack on Mkushi began badly with only one pair of Canberras dropping their bombs on target, but the Hunter strike was good and at 11h45 the Dakotas carrying the SAS arrived over Mkushi. The paratroops could see the results of the Hunter strikes—the craters, the columns of smoke and the fires. On the ground the panic was total. In the air the men stood ready, one hand on the containers that were to be dropped with them, one hand on the static lines. Within minutes of hitting the ground, the administration staff were out of their harnesses and at work, ready to accept the first fuel drop for the thirsty helicopters.

Meanwhile the SAS troopers had been dropped around Mkushi. Three sticks of six hit ground 1,500 metres from their target area while others landed too close for comfort. Contacts occurred before a proper sweep line could be established. A bush fire had been started and the thick smoke was blowing towards the SAS men. The commanders cleared the men away but many of the parachutes could not be salvaged. One member of the SAS was killed in a contact. The K-Cars with their machine guns and 20mm cannons flew ahead of the stop lines clearing the ground. No one had said anything about there being women soldiers, and the troops were a bit dismayed to find that their enemies were women but they were all in camouflage and many carried AKs. The ground was littered with foxholes. At the heart of the complex the troops found a parade ground, library, kitchen and an underground armoury. Then a Zambian Air Force MiG flew over—and the troops scattered for cover but it zoomed off into the smoke while the Hunters kept watch over the battleground.

The final target for the day was CGT-2 (communist guerilla training) Camp which was thought to house another 4,000 men. Once again an air strike by a Vampire, Lynx and four helicopter K-Cars was followed by an attack by heliborne troops of the RLI whose task was to surround and destroy the camp. However, this attack was a 'lemon' because the inhabitants had been warned by the earlier strikes and the camp was practically empty.

By 16h00 Mkushi Camp had been secured and the SAS settled down for the night. Next day the mopping up began. A woman prisoner was interviewed. She confirmed that there had been two separate camps containing an overall strength of about 2,000 combatants.

By the following day, half the attackers had already been choppered out when a large party of Zambian troops and ZIPRA members arrived. These men were engaged by the security forces and a number of prisoners were taken. Among them was Mountain Gutu, a ZIPRA officer. He gave the special branch valuable information which led, on 2nd November, to an attack on a logistics base near Lusaka. Further raids by Nos 1 and 4 Squadrons were carried out on 3rd and 5th November. These attacks caused panic in Zambia and for some time after this, any low flying plane that passed over the ZIPRA camps was liable to be targeted. Several domestic flights were hit by small-arms fire.

CHAPTER 46

Enter the Bells

Rhodesia's ability to fight the Bush War successfully depended largely on the availability of helicopters. The Rhodesian Air Force possessed a number of Alouette III machines but these could only transport four combat troops, fewer if the aircraft had to carry additional fuel. By 1978, it had become top priority to obtain more and larger helicopters. The aircraft chosen was the Agusta-Bell AB 205A. One of the men who played a role in negotiating the Agusta-Bell deal was Keith Thurman.

Originally, we wanted to obtain 'new' aircraft. We knew that these machines were being manufactured in Italy so we approached the Italian company but they were under licence to the Huey Company in the USA and were not able to supply any aircraft to us because of the political situation. However, we were given the name of a company in the United States, which had a marketing agreement for a number of aircraft. This company told us that that Israel had 40 Bell 205s surplus to their requirement. The aircraft were not airworthy but we were promised that they would be made serviceable. Another problem was that they were military aircraft, and had provision for armament. This meant that under USA regulations the State Department would have to sanction the sale and approve both the customer and the country. The American company agreed to obtain certification that the aircraft were for a commercial venture. The military status could then be downgraded and the deal could be handled by the department of 'end user' certificates for the sale. First we had to decide how many aircraft we needed, then the condition of the aircraft had to be checked and finally we had to negotiate a price. We assembled a team to visit Europe. They included Group Captain Alec Thomson, Group Captain Harry Watson, Air Commodore Dicky Bradshaw, Mr Norman Brandt (finance), our civilian agent and me. We met the Chicago-based representative and travelled to Paris, Brussels and Zürich. We were anxious to examine the aircraft but because of the political situation could not send our own people to Israel to carry out our own technical assessment. We had to rely on the American company, who agreed to send an engineer to Israel. Meanwhile we had received written reports on the aircraft that were made available and from this report Group Captain Watson decided on the aircraft that would interest us. The price was set and we agreed on a quantity. We still had one problem. We needed an 'end user's' certificate that would be acceptable to the Americans. An Italian contact put us in touch with the Vatican. They sent two cardinals to meet us and we paid for their upkeep for weeks at five star expense. The 'end users' they came up with were ridiculous—Cyprus being one. The price they required was also exorbitant. Needless to say, we sent them packing. Eventually we found a Singapore aviation company that was prepared to supply an 'end user' certificate. The story was that the aircraft were to be used for logging work in northern Malaysia. Meanwhile the American company had managed to get a certificate issued by the Department of Commerce. So a contract was signed and the details of shipment agreed upon. However, there were very few spares available

and no extra engines or blades so we had to try to buy spares to be sent with the consignment. I was positioned in Europe for a period of nine months to arrange the purchase of spares from Norway, Switzerland, France, Finland, Canada and so on and arrange for them to be delivered to Israel. At length everything was ready. Firstly, the aircraft had to be moved from the army stores to an Israeli government facility for stripping and packing. The next hurdle was to find a ship to carry the aircraft from Israel to Singapore via a SA port and then we needed the cooperation of the SA authorities to off-load and transit SA. Our civilian rep was most useful in arranging for an appropriate ship to transport the 'goods'. SA Defence Force was also most helpful. The ship docked one night in Durban. The cargo was miraculously removed and at dawn the next day, it left port again bound for Singapore. The helicopters were placed on railway trucks and transported to the SAAF base in Pietersburg. The consignment from Pietersburg was arranged with the help of both the SA CSI and the Rhodesian prime minister's special custom office, ram-rodded by Equipment Branch's wing commander, Tommy Quirk and team, with techs supplementing the movement. We had our own large trucks and we borrowed others from the army. When we finally got the aircraft into New Sarum and did our own evaluation, we were frankly appalled. We begged the air branch not to use them until they had been stripped and fully rebuilt. However, we were overruled because of operational necessity and there was one unfortunate incident. Eventually, with the help of an American based in Salisbury, we managed to get an ex-Bell engineer to come on a short contract and help us with rebuilding and training. It is interesting to note that on stripping the aircraft, we found evidence that they had been used in Vietnam and had many more flying hours than the documents showed. The Israelis had purchased them for a one-off operation and then discarded them. However, considering the sanctions position we got the best aircraft we could.
(Keith Thuman)

The eleven Agusta-Bell 205 Huey helicopters arrived in Durban in October 1978. George Jansen was one of the road pilots who took part in this particular ferry.

The OC of our unit, Air Lieutenant Alan Campbell, called me and said, "I want you to get hold of some horses and low-loaders and some chain. We need to rig nine crates at a time." He gave me the dimensions. I did a mental calculation. We needed about two and a half miles of chain. So I said, "What the hell are we chaining down?" He said, "That doesn't matter." I said, "What sort of weight?" He said, "Fairly heavy." So I scrounged around and eventually managed to locate what I needed. We had to work out our timetable so that we would reach the border at last light, refuel, then drive the three hours to the SAAF base at Pietersburg and load. About 05h30 next morning, we would be back at the border. At this stage, road convoys were running between Beitbridge and Fort Victoria and the civilian cars would be lined up ready to go through the border as soon as it opened. They would look at our air escort—two helicopters, a G-Car and a K-Car and a Lynx and a Genet—and wonder what was going on. I usually drove the breakdown vehicle, a Unimog loaded with tyres, drums of fuel, which sat right at the back of the convoy in case any of the vehicles broke down. We normally arrived back in Salisbury at about 18h30 and drove the trucks into what we called the 'smersh' hangar, an old tobacco shed. There was a Healey 22-ton forklift, which off-loaded the crates inside the hangar. Then the motor transport guys would spend the night checking the vehicles and sorting out the chains while we grabbed some sleep. At 05h00 we would be off again. For about two weeks we got only about four or five hours' sleep a night. Backwards and forwards. Added to all the other problems we had to pump the diesel fuel by hand. We carried our own diesel because the low-loaders couldn't get into a normal filling station; they were too big, and we didn't have time to unhitch the trailer and take the horse into a garage. So we would be right outside the Fort Victoria Hotel, topping up the tanks with hand pumps—putting in enough fuel to get to Beitbridge. We all took turns driving. There was no distinction between officers and men. You drove until you were knackered then you handed over. (George Jansen)

Rhodesia had acquired the vitally needed helicopters but they were in very poor mechanical condition when they arrived. The desert terrain over which they had operated with its sandstorms and dust had caused considerable damage to the engines. One Bell literally fell out of the sky on its first test flight on 9th February 1979 owing to the failure of the tail rotor drive shaft caused by the wear of sand in the tail rotor. The rest were stripped completely and rebuilt, bolt by bolt and it was not until May 1979 that the first Bells were used operationally.

When they at last entered service, much later than had been planned, they gave the Rhodesian Air Force a machine that could transport large numbers of men and equipment over much greater distances than the Alouette, without refuelling. Added to this they had a much greater carrying capacity. This made cross-border raids logistically easier. The rivalry between No 7 Squadron (Alouettes) and No 8 Squadron (Bells) was friendly but intense. A stencilled message on the battery inspection hatch at the front of one Bell read, "I eat Alouettes." The Alouette squadron was quick to retaliate—on the Bell hardstanding at FAF 8 they painted in large letters 'Matambanadzo Bus Service'.

Harvey the hornbill

As well as air force personnel, the various FAFs had acquired inhabitants of the furred and feathered variety. Among these was Harvey the hornbill whose story is told by Ian Dixon:

No visitor to Wankie FAF 1 could be unaware of the most important member of its establishment. Native born and Rhodesian, he actually came from the surrounding area. Discovered as a helpless orphan by a national parks game ranger, his arrival at the FAF was a pure fluke. The ranger displayed him to a group of TF security guards telling them sadly that he was probably too small to survive. The TFs begged the ranger to let them try to save him. The ranger, convinced that the orphan chick would be dead in a week, was persuaded to let the air force have a go. As soon as the ranger drove off, the orphan was placed in the guardroom in an empty grass-filled carton. Although there was little to commend FAF 1 to the average international traveller, it did have a massive and varied supply of insect life. Soon everybody on the station was engaged in insect hunts. Being blessed with a classical education, I discovered that by placing fire buckets full of water under the security lights at night, we were daily rewarded with a prodigious supply of bedraggled insects. This bounty was fed to our orphan who ate every single thing put before him. Far from being dead in a week, our tame Ground Hornbill grew rapidly to maturity. A name had to be found for him—so we named him Harvey. Harvey soon started demonstrating his amazing personality. A real nosey parker he trusted everybody on camp—with a few notable exceptions, one of which was the cook. It hadn't taken Harvey long to discover the attraction of sugar, which he knew could be found in containers on the mess hall tables. Periodically he would make a sugar raid. His technique was to knock the bowls over with his large powerful beak, and ingest the sugar in the manner of a flamingo gathering algae. The state of the room after one of his sorties had to be seen to be believed! The cook didn't like it and took anti-Harvey precautions. Harvey responded by extending his operational area into the kitchen proper where he found new supplies of sugar and other goodies. An impasse eventually was to be the only solution. Harvey allowed most people to handle him, but only on his own terms. He had some particular favourites amongst the TFs and the techs, following them around like any normal pet. He strongly disliked dogs and cats, seeing both off with great elan. It was seriously painful to be pecked by that massive beak, so few challenged him. Harvey wandered wherever the whim took him, be it into the Ops room, or the living quarters. He was also fond of a quiet kip in the guardroom, or in parked vehicles, much to the chagrin of visitors. I remember a meeting in the camp bar, with the fuzz (police), and the army breaking up in disorder after Harvey had soundlessly insinuated himself under the table. He could have stayed there undetected all day, but, unfortunately, he discovered a packet of liquorice allsorts in a policeman's briefcase, with devastating results. Nobody could call Harvey handsome, but he did have a very memorable face, with scarlet wattles, and expressive eyes with seductive lashes. He was frighteningly intelligent, a living lesson for the human world not to underrate wild animals. One stinking hot afternoon, exhausted after a busy week, I fell asleep. I was awakened by a furtive noise emanating from my locker. Very carefully and quietly, I rose from my bed to see the rear end of Harvey jutting out of my cupboard. He was busy inside looking for something edible. To assert command of the situation, I yelled, "Voetsek, you nosey bugger!" Showing no alarm at all, Harvey withdrew from the locker, and stared into my eyes. He then turned his head on one side, taking another long level stare at me before trotting over to the open door. In the doorway, he paused for another look. As he exited, I would not have been surprised to hear him say, "Same to you! You daft twit!" Harvey enjoyed helping the techs working on aircraft on the hardstanding. His assistance took the form of stealing the assorted spanners, wrenches, screwdrivers etc. and walking off to hide them in the surrounding veld. He had a great affection for the helicopters, and would perch, in contemplative mode, on their rotors for hours. His grip was tenacious, and he would stay on a rotor blade even when it began to rotate for start-up. Often the rotor blades were spinning at a fair speed before Harvey was projected from them like a rocket! Squawking like hell, he would break into flight, and after landing in the veld, trot back to the hardstanding in search of another helicopter to perch on. Conversely he detested Dakotas, and as they taxied in after landing, Harvey would trot out to mix it with them, wings outstretched, screeching defiance! These attacks were quite fearless, and we were convinced that he would meet his end chopped up by a propeller. Frequent miracles preserved him, despite some very close shaves. He never stopped showing antagonism towards the Daks. His agitation began when the Dakotas were on finals to landing, and he would remain stroppy until they departed! His attitude to other aircraft types was ambivalent. I watched him once, perched on the wing of a Trojan, as it taxied for take-off. Harvey stayed firmly put all the time the aircraft was taxiing down the runway. Then as the Trojan turned into the wind and began its take-off, Harvey was parted from his high perch with a great squawk! Harvey contributed greatly to the morale prevailing at FAF 1. It was my opinion that he qualified for a medal, and I accordingly put in an application to Air HQ. It was never acknowledged, nor acted upon. Which was a poor state of affairs. (Ian Dixon)

In October 1978, the *Bateleur* continued the story:

Harvey the hornbill, FAF 1's long-time man about the tarmac, is due for a posting and will shortly be leaving the air force altogether. Nothing political about the move, we are assured. It's more of a security matter, for Harvey is increasingly AWOL, explained Squadron Leader Tudor Thomas. "Whilst he's here there is no problem but he keeps on wandering away and he trusts humans so completely that he will just get himself run over or eaten very soon. We obviously can't keep chasing after him. There are occasions when we spend more time looking for Harvey than for the terrs, so a new home has been arranged at the Chipengali Wild Life Orphanage where Viv Wilson will arrange for Harvey to live to a ripe old age. The link with FAF 1 (Wankie) will not be broken completely, however, for the Bar Fund will pay for Harvey's keep." Not so much a punishment posting then; more of an honourable retirement on pension.

A Get-Harvey-Back campaign was waged unsuccessfully in January 1979 but by then Harvey had taken to civilian life like a duck to water. Viv Wilson reported that he had been given his freedom and was able to wander into the bush whenever it pleased him but he could still return to Chipengali for food and a bit of love and attention from humans when he needed it. Apparently, he was spending most of his time at a nearby dam. Obviously a story with a happy ending—for Harvey.

Benji—the end of the story

Then there was Benji of the ongoing saga. It appeared that he was also on the move again. Having been attested into the force at Centenary and been attached to FAF 4 and FAF 5 in turn, Benji had now been posted to FAF 8 because of his known abilities of leadership and specialized knowledge of the north-eastern operational area. In planning the move consideration was given to his rank, seniority and possible personality clashes with other members of his trade group. The posting became necessary because of a temporary mothballing of his former base. Benji's officer commanding signalled: Bearing in mind his affinity for bush life and his complete disregard for service protocol it is thought unlikely that he would accept a posting to Air HQ, Sarum or Thornhill.

Benji flew into FAF 8 on a resupply run on 15th November 1978 having been listed on the manifest as a VID, Very Important Dog. His arrival prompted the following signal: "Flight Sergeant Benji met by reception committee, including members of the local Press to whom he showed disrespect by relieving himself against the aircraft main wheel. Disciplinary action was attempted but disregarded by Benji who set off on an immediate clearance patrol ahead of his section. So Benji now patrols the spacious acres of FAF 8 protecting his countless air force friends from snakes, bullfrogs, displaced brown jobs and other terrors of the night."

When the war ended, FAF 8 was abandoned except for the caretakers and Benji. His posting to New Sarum had been arranged by Air headquarters and a team of dog handlers motored down to FAF 8 to effect his transfer. Benji could not be found. Sensing that he was going to be uprooted once more, he had gone to ground under a bed in one of the billets. He showed considerable reluctance to leave his beloved FAF 8 where he had spent so many happy years with his air force fellows. In fact, he had to be carried to the waiting Land Rover. Once in the vehicle he lay down on his bed in the back and slept throughout the whole journey. On arrival at New Sarum Benji was found to be dead. His friends believed that he had died of a broken heart.

On a happier note, there was a sort of Noah's Ark operation in reverse when No 3 Squadron assisted Chipengali boss Viv Wilson to return a troop of monkeys to the bush. Mostly ex-pets, the 20 vervets had been acquired over a period of time and this had prompted Viv to think about releasing them as a group. Gradually he changed their diet to the natural food they would find in the area and then identified a suitable island in Kariba, which could become their new home. The monkeys were crated and flown from Bulawayo in two hops by air force aircraft. Commenting on the operation one No 3 Squadron pilot said: "They ponged a bit but no more so than some of our other passengers and they were less hairy than most. In fact by the standards of some people we transport they were really quite cultured!"

Operation Vodka—December 1978

Mboroma was a ZIPRA camp in Zambia, situated 140 kilometres north of the Rhodesian border. Information had been received that it was a prison and detention camp, which housed captured Rhodesian security force personnel and a number of ZIPRA dissidents. Photographic surveys had been carried out from the air and on 28th November, two members of the Selous Scouts were dropped into an area about 25 kilometres from the camp. It was the middle of the rainy season and most days the sky was covered with seven-eighths (broken) cloud while the rain bucketed down. The watchers spotted the prisoners, counted the number of guards and saw what appeared to be emplacements for 14.5mm anti-aircraft guns. The ZIPRA guards were jumpy and opened fire on any aircraft that approached the camp. On 16th December, the Scouts withdrew and were lifted out.

A model of the camp was constructed so that the ground forces could familiarize themselves with the layout and probable position of the prisoners. D-Day was set for 22nd December.

The paratroopers took off from a forward airfield on the northern border and headed north into Zambia. Taking off later but synchronized to arrive over the target area just before they did were the Hunters. The air strike on the ZIPRA barracks went in at 08h30 followed by the No 3 Squadron static line drop of Selous Scouts. No 4 Squadron also played a major part in this operation. ZIPRA resistance was less than anticipated and out of the nearly 60 men guarding the prisoners only 18 were killed. It had been estimated that over 100 prisoners were in the camp but only 32 were found, many of whom had been in the underground detention cells for anything up to four months. Some of them had to have their eyes covered so that the daylight would not cause damage. They were bewildered and completely unable to comprehend what was happening. The Scouts had to explain that their ordeal was over and that they had been liberated. Many more prisoners could have been liberated but they were out of the camp on working parties when the attack took place. Dakotas uplifted the Scouts and the liberated prisoners and the following day the men who had been released were flown to the André Rabie Barracks where they were interviewed by the Press.

Operation Pygmy—November/December 1978

Meanwhile aerial photographs had confirmed the presence of a large group of men at Mulungushi, an old Federal army camp on the western shores of Mulungushi Dam 100 kilometres from Lusaka. According to information received, the Zambians had allowed ZIPRA to use the camp as a training centre for their conventional armed forces and it was rapidly being improved with Russian assistance. The centre made an attractive target for an airborne attack because the defenders could be hemmed in against the waters of the dam.

On 19th November, Schulenberg and Chibanda were flown in by helicopter and dropped 40 kilometres to the south. They reached the target on 26th November and settled down to observe the routine. They estimated that there were about 200 ZIPRA in the camp. There appeared to be a large amount of trenching going on and ComOps did not want to invite heavy casualties by attacking entrenched positions. It was decided, therefore, that an air-only attack should be launched against the camp. The Canberra strike was timed to coincide with the raid on Mboroma, on 22nd December. According to Zambian army intercepts, the camp had contained 270 conventionally trained ZIPRA members, 33 of whom were killed and many others wounded. Schulenberg and Chibanda took four days to get back to their pick-up point from where they were uplifted by helicopter.

On 12th December, Clive Style based at FAF 7 was tasked by the RLI to carry out a recce of the Sengwe area. At 14h55, tower received a Mayday call from him saying he had no aileron control and was going to try to put down at Ranch Louis. There was no further contact so another aircraft was sent out on a search and rescue mission. An hour later, this second aircraft reported that Style's aircraft had been spotted upside down on Ranch Louis but that the three passengers were OK. Style's plane had been shot at and one round had broken the cable shackle to the ailerons. A helicopter was detached from Rutenga and the guards lifted to the downed plan. The three passengers returned to Mabalauta from where they were flown back to FAF 7.

Salisbury fuel depot fire

Meanwhile on 11th December 1978, a ZANLA cadre parked their vehicle on the road that ran past Salisbury's hastily enlarged fuel depot. Only a railway line ran between them and the petrol, diesel and gas tanks which were closely grouped. They fired a heavy calibre weapon into a diesel tank and then used tracer to ignite the pool of diesel on the ground. The burning diesel soon reached the first petrol tank. Within minutes, jets of flame were shooting high into the stormy December sky. Rhodesia's precious fuel stocks were going up in smoke. Firemen, policemen and the army were all involved in fighting the blaze, and so was the air force. The equipment personnel from New Sarum played a key role early in the disaster, rushing vitally needed emergency supplies of foam and fire-fighting equipment to the scene of the fire. Led by Warrant Officers John Whiddett and Derek O'Toole, the air force team comprising trainees from No 1 Ground Training School, manhandled heavy drums of foam up ramps, over hoses and railway lines to the fire fighters. During the nine days that followed, virtually all the trainees worked non-stop sharing the risks experienced by the professional fire fighters. Despite all efforts to extinguish the fire, it continued to burn until 19th December.

Mid-air collision

At the beginning of January 1979, Ray Bolton was on temporary assignment from No 8 Squadron to No 7 Squadron owing to a dire shortage of experienced K-Car pilots. Based at a fireforce camp near Gwelo, he had been assigned to assist in the conversion of three new pilots, Kerry Fynn, Colyn James and Rob Parsons. These men were part of an experimental programme to recruit pilots with previous flying experience. Part of the pre-qualification requisites for this programme was a minimum of 1,000 flying hours. The pilots then underwent a mini Wings course of about six months. Once they received their Wings, they joined No 7 Squadron, flying the Alouette IIIs. Part of their operational training consisted of being assigned to a fireforce. Bolton continues the story:

> We had been up in Wankie for a week or so and on 2nd January, shortly after moving to this particular base, we were called out by an OP who had some CTs visual. The time to target was 10 to 15 minutes by helicopter. It was in the Selukwe area not too far from Ian Smith's farm. We made contact with the CTs but lost sight of them in thick bush. The OP still had them visual and I asked him to direct me overhead the target. As Kerry Fynn was an ex-game ranger, he had good 'bush' eyes and I called him up into orbit to see if he could spot them. We were both at about 300 to 400 feet. The OP told us to turn left, which we both did. He then told us to roll out. At that instant Kerry made visual contact with CTs and with the adrenaline flowing, he must have got caught up in the moment. He continued the turn and commenced firing. With his attention firmly focused on the target below, he obviously did not see me. I was going straight, slightly in front and to the right of him when his main rotor blades contacted my right wheel. The resulting debris flew up into my main rotor blades creating an uncontrollable imbalance in my main rotor. One of my blades then dipped and chopped my tail boom off, pulling the main transmission out and inverting my helicopter. By the grace of God, I ended up upside down wedged in a ditch that was the exact width of my armoured seat, so that my head was protected in the ditch. Brian Cutmore and Captain Doug Havnar, the army commander, who were with me, did not survive. Kerry's helicopter blades having made contact with my rear wheel were severely damaged and some of the debris flew into his tail rotor. Without this vital control, his helicopter went into a spin (anti-torque failure) and crashed, killing both Kerry and Tony Turner. I ended up with a mild concussion, five fractured vertebrae, a shattered elbow, a broken jaw and various lacerations and bruises. These injuries were caused by the eight-kilogram flak vest when I landed upside down. Colyn James who I had sent to refuel and fetch more troops, was just coming back into the area when the accident occurred. He dropped some men off at both of the accident sites and it was these army guys who heard me calling for help. They dug me out and I was flown to Gwelo where I spent a night in

the local hospital before being sent to Andrew Fleming Hospital in Salisbury. My memory of the accident is absolutely non-existent. All I know is what I was told later.

On the night of 14th January, a farmhouse came under attack. Air Lieutenant Trevor Arthur Jew of No 4 Squadron reacted although poor weather conditions and the terrain made navigation difficult. Reaching the farmhouse, Air Lieutenant Jew fired on the terrorist positions but the terrorists continued the assault. Jew delivered several more attacks and eventually the terrorists retreated. For this incident and for a previous action, Air Lieutenant Jew was later awarded the Military Forces Commendation (Operational).

No 1 Squadron Diary, January 1979:
We started off the New Year by providing top cover for some Cheetahs [Agusta-Bell 205s]. Baldy (Baldwin) came straight from a party to do his sortie. In the words of Squadron Leader Mike Saunders 'If you can't drink and fly you shouldn't be in the air force'. On 3rd January, Wing Commander Hugh Slatter had his last ride in a Hunter before taking up his new post as director of operations. We did some gunnery trials this month to sort out our exploding ammunition. We think we have isolated the problem and sorted it out as well. The work continues unabated and once again we have been golfing (i.e. dropping golf bombs). The Boss (Vic Wightman) and Tony went on a guns-only sortie to find a supply truck that was stuck in the mud. They found the truck the other side of old Tembué and it is stuck permanently now.

No 4 Squadron Diary, January:
Our squadron Walter Mitty has done it again. Carl Wilms, man of many war stories and of much experience was putting in a strike on a large number of terrs when he was shot. Unfortunately, the round hit his pipe and ricocheted off it and struck his finger, almost severing it. The damage to his finger has led to an amputation in hospital. Luckily it was not his social finger—if it was we'd never believe this war story!

The *Umniati* crash
Air Rhodesia Viscount *Umniati* took off from Kariba early on the evening of 11th February 1979. Only a few minutes out, there was a sickening explosion and a ball of flame appeared in the sky. *Umniati* had been hit by a SAM-7 missile. This time there was no chance for anyone aboard. The aircraft crashed killing all 54 passengers and 5 crew. Fifteen minutes later, a second Viscount took off with General Walls among its passengers. There were rumours that he had been the target. A No 3 Squadron Dakota was one of the first aircraft on the scene and dropped paratroops into the area to search for the group responsible for the attack. The captain of the aircraft, Jan André du Plessis, and the first officer, Michael Thomas Moolman, had both served with No 3 Squadron as reserve pilots. André du Plessis' son Leon had been killed while flying with No 4 Squadron on 2nd September 1977. No 4 Squadron took part in recces over the Urungwe area trying to locate the group responsible for the attack.

Following this second attack on a civilian airliner, No 1 Squadron carried out several retaliatory strikes. The first attacks on 15th and 16th February were against ZIPRA holding camps in the Livingstone area. Three days later, on 18th February, the area of combat moved east again as Rhodesian aircraft hit ZANLA buildings within the confines of a Frelimo camp at Mutarara near Chimoio. On 23rd February, the security forces struck again hitting two bases in Zambia.

The Canberras hit Angola
Then on 26th February 1979, came the most daring cross-border air attack so far. The target was a base that was being used as a training camp for ZIPRA soldiers at Boma near Vila Luso,

a regional capital in eastern Angola close to the Benguela railway line. The camp was believed to house about 3,000 ZIPRA soldiers. To reach Boma the Canberras had to fly a distance of over 2,000 kilometres there and back. Not only was the target at the extreme end of the Canberra's range but it was also known that Soviet MiG-17s, and MiG-21s flown by Cuban pilots of Fapa (Angolan air force) were based at Henrique de Carvalho only 300 kilometres from the base. Added to which the Angolans had a radar system supplied and operated by the Russians.

The Hunters armed with sidewinder missiles and carrying maximum fuel were ordered to penetrate as deeply as possible into Angola and to provide top cover at high altitude, while keeping radio silence unless an emergency arose. Three Canberras carried full loads of alpha bombs and the fourth had 6 x 1,000-pound general-purpose bombs fitted with fairly long-delay fuses. Talking about this raid Peter Petter-Bowyer remarked:

Four Canberras from No 5 Squadron were tasked with the raid. Three Dakotas from No 3 Squadron were not only engaged in the search and rescue stand-by role but also supplied the command aircraft. The Canberras took off from Vic Falls in western Rhodesia. Chris Dixon should have led the raid but at the last moment his aircraft had radio failure. Ted Brent was called on to lead the Canberras. Once the formation was airborne, news came that Chris was on his way and would be joining them. By then, the rest of the aircraft were already in Zambian air space.

It had been decided to fly to Kazungula, a border post on the Zambezi River in the Caprivi Strip and then head north-west over Zambia to Mongu on the Zambezi maintaining a height of 39,000 feet in order to conserve fuel. The Hunters were high above the cloud but at one point the crew of the Dakota saw an enormous explosion in the sky. This was probably an inaccurate SAM-7 missile.

It was over Mongu that Chris Dixon caught up with the formation and the control tower at this civil airfield requested identification but the request was ignored. As it left Mongu, the formation ran into cloud, with a layer of cirri-stratus above and another below. There was no chance of map reading. The success of the mission would depend on the skill of the lead navigator and an accurate compass course.

The Canberras' next turning point was on the Benguela railway line, a few kilometres west of Luso. The ZIPRA encampment was close to the town but to the east. The plan was to locate the railway and then turn east to the target, to deceive those on the ground into thinking that they were aircraft of the Angolan air force arriving from their bases on the west coast.

When his navigator estimated that they were nearing the turning point on the Benguela railway, Ted Brent led the formation down through the cloud and broke through at about 2,000 feet above ground level. Ted and his navigator began to scan their maps and the ground. They descended to treetop height to bring them in under the radar screen. Ted Brent picks up the story:

We saw the railway line and met it at an acute angle. We were only half a minute behind the DR [dead reckoning] time and two nautical miles west of our DR track. All the time we had been using met—meteorological forecast—winds with no chance of checking them. Our met people were really good. We turned east towards the target via the north, thus coming in from a deceptive direction, as planned. But then we got a real shock. Between Luso and us it was raining buckets. Visibility was down to six hundred feet. We were flying at treetop height, as we had been since dropping through the cloud. The storm was directly on our track so we had no choice but to go

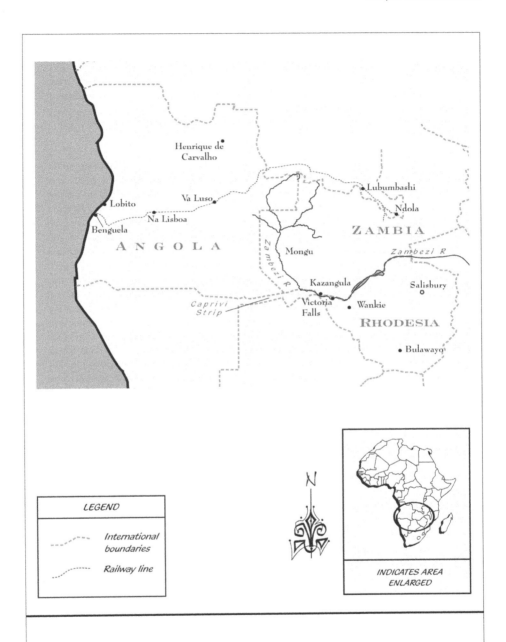

LEGEND

- - - - International boundaries
- - - - - Railway line

INDICATES AREA ENLARGED

CANBERRA STRIKE ON ANGOLA

straight through it. Fortunately, our briefing had been superb and our intelligence people had excelled themselves. We knew exactly where the target was in relation to Luso. We were five minutes from the strike and we climbed to bombing height, exactly three hundred feet. Two minutes from the strike we could just see Luso through the storm, so we knew where we were. I called for bomb doors, although I still could not see the target. Then, as happens sometimes in Africa, the storm ended in a clean-cut edge. From the navigator in the nose came:
"Target clear!"
"Left, left."
"Steady."
The rest of the formation was now in line abreast. Thirty seconds later the bombs were on the ground, exactly on target. Once clear of the target we went back to treetop height. It was very reassuring to know that the Hunters were up there at 30,000 feet, although we heard nothing from them. But they were constantly monitoring us and also monitoring Zambian and Angolan frequencies. Later we learnt that they had detected no enemy activity at all. To this day I am convinced we caught them completely napping. After the strike, we turned due south for five minutes, just to cause confusion. Then we headed direct for Vic Falls. We climbed to 41,000 feet to conserve fuel, although this took us well into trail height—the height at which vapour trails form—which we normally avoided like the plague. We kept our fingers crossed—but there was plenty of cloud about so perhaps they could not see us. As soon as the Hunters knew all was well, they headed for home too. We never saw anything of them at all. We arrived back at Vic Falls with fuel for seven to ten minutes low-level flying in our tanks but still the drama was not over. The Canberra, which carried the 1,000 G pound bombs, had a mishap. One of the bombs, already fused, had lodged in the bomb bay doors. Nothing the pilot could do in the air would dislodge it. So he just had to carry it home and make the most perfect landing of his life, which he did. With the aircraft safely on the ground and parked well away from the others, we scrounged and commandeered mattresses and palliasses, mostly from the BSAP. With these, we built an enormous cushion under the faulty door. Then we used a crowbar to prise the door slightly further open, so that an armourer could put his hand inside and try to make the bomb safe. This was done, but not really convinced that it was safe, we manhandled the bomb onto the mattress mountain. Fear I knew not—but terror—yes! (Ted Brent)

Estimates of the casualties varied widely but Angolan authorities admitted to a figure of 192 dead and 987 injured, many of them seriously.

No 4 Squadron Diary for February remarks on the external strikes and goes on to report the experiences of some of the pilots during the month. Mike Guinness and Jerry Skeeles had their elevator cable shot up leaving only one of seven strands. David 'Brick' Bryson and Jon Ludgater were in a Lynx when they were called in to provide top cover for two helicopters that had sustained damage from enemy small-arms fire. They found themselves amongst 100 – 150 insurgents and were hit twice with small-arms fire. Bryson discovered the value of the armoured seat. Ludgater had his ailerons shot away and did a magnificent job bringing the aircraft back safely. The Diary concludes: "Shows Hornets [Lynxes] mustn't joust with anything more than ten."

The attack on New Sarum—March 1979
For some time, in fact ever since the Bush War had begun in earnest, the air force had been concerned about a possible attack on New Sarum.

We had been receiving intelligence that an attack was pending since 1972. When the first real threat came, they had us patrolling night and day for weeks in our newly acquired Elands.

There were too few drivers for the cars, so the turret crews could afford the luxury of sleep but the driver could only sleep when the car halted, or between gear changes! I still remember the booming voice of Ken Salter in my headphones, awakening me from my slumbers with, "You can wake up now Paul!" He never panicked even when I fell asleep at the wheel seven times on the ring road round New Sarum. As soon as we parked at the camp, I was off again. Sergeant Pete Horsborough (later air lieutenant) switched off the car electrics for me, I am told. Things improved when we were able to get about four hours' sleep a night. It had been costly, however— accidents started to happen. I ended up with a permanent back injury because of a tired and inattentive turret crew directing me into a hole in the long grass at dusk. The view from an Eland driver's hatch is poor, to put it mildly. When the attack of New Sarum finally came it was a damp squib. The gooks popped off about a dozen mortar bombs at random into the area and we replied in the general direction from whence they came, which was somewhere in the mealie fields on the opposite side of the Ring Road. And that was it. A draw—Air Force 0, Gooks 0. In conversation with ZIPRA officers after the change of government, it became apparent that they considered the air force to be a hard target despite our aircraft being so tempting. In retrospect, this was quite pleasing to hear. (Paul Hill)

I was director of studies on a Senior Admin Course and minutes before the attack I had decided not to sleep at New Sarum but to go home. I drove right past the spot where the attackers were, on the Kutsaga Tobacco Research Station. When I got in to work next morning there was a lot of excitement. The students had all been standing on the verandah watching the attack. Here again the attackers had found that the base plates were too heavy to carry so they had fired the 82mm mortars without base plates—so the bombs ended up going straight across the road and none landed anywhere near a vital installation. But because it was an attack on Salisbury Airport it became a sensitive political issue so the air force was tasked with defending its own areas. This meant not only securing our own perimeter but also defending a much greater area, about ten kilometres in radius, which gives you 72 kilometres circumference. The text books will tell you that one battalion can hold an extended front of eight kilometres so we needed something like nine battalions per airfield! Which was obviously out of the question so what we attempted to do was deny the area to the enemy by using observation posts, carrying out patrols and instituting a curfew. We set up mortar positions on predetermined arcs of fire so that if we got a report from an observation post that there were intruders we could put down fire in that sector and then send a reaction force out with whatever weapons we had. The reaction force consisted of armoured cars, Unimogs with heavy weapons mounted, and so on. Then of course there was the question of air defence. By this time, we were hitting Mozambique and Zambia on a regular basis. And we knew that they had MiGs. There was the chance that they might retaliate so we planned gun sites around the airfield. We had half a dozen .5 Brownings and four 40mm Bofors guns; those were the heaviest armaments we had at the start. Later we deployed the guns we had captured but we never used any of them in anger. (Bruce Harrison)

Operation Neutron

Once again, the Chimoio area was causing concern. The SAS had located the camp at Vanduzi 15 kilometres from Chimoio Town. This camp contained a unique early warning system—two baboons, Janet and John, shell-shocked from previous raids who would go berserk at the sound of approaching aircraft. An SAS team consisting of two men, Rich Stannard and J.A. 'Jungle' Jordan, was dropped into the area by helicopter. A reconnaissance was carried out and it was estimated that about 400 ZANLA men were based in the area. A combined ground and air force operation was suggested but at this stage in the war, men were needed inside the country to combat the increased onslaught. It was, therefore, decided to put in an air-only strike.

The attack came at dawn on Saturday 17th March 1979. The Hunters struck first; then came the Canberras followed by the K-Cars, G-Cars and fixed wing aircraft. The surprise was complete— even Janet and John were caught napping as the two Hunters screamed in to the attack. Pandemonium reigned but then as the choppers came in a 14.5mm and two 12.7mm heavy machine guns opened up accompanied by small-arms fire. The pilots had flown right into trouble. The two SAS men had been aware of only a small part of the camp. Instead of being on the outer edge, as they believed, the SAS were in the centre of a well-concealed fortification containing possibly more than 1,000 men. One fixed wing aircraft took a hit and had to turn for home.

After their first strike, the planes returned to base to rearm, ready to strike again but the weather closed in and the plan had to be scrapped. However, Stannard and Jungle Jordan remained in position. During the day, Frelimo soldiers cautiously returned and began searching for any land-mines that might have been laid. They later withdrew but the following day they returned bringing with them an armoured personnel carrier and a truck. Then Stannard called for a Hunter strike.

What the security forces did not know was that the insurgents had positioned a strela on top of a rise in a perfect position for just such an attack. As the first Hunter completed its strike a missile homed in on it. The pilot of the second Hunter spotted the flash and shouted a warning. The first Hunter headed for the sun in order to get the missile to lock on to the stronger heat source. Both aircraft then turned back to attack the two-man strela team. They then dealt with the truck and the personnel carrier.

By now Frelimo had realized that there must be observers in the area. The team, exhausted, filthy and more than a little upset by the way things had gone began to move towards a position from which they could be choppered out. Dawn came as they reached a road and looking back, they saw two ZANLA soldiers watching them. Obviously, these men were not sure whether the SAS were friend or foe. But then the ZANLA men became suspicious, raised their RPDs and opened fire—Jungle Jordan was hit below the knee. There was no cover. Stannard, helping Jungle as best he could, began to run back down the road, calling for a hot extraction.

Norman Maasdorp was the helicopter pilot:

On 20th March 1979, I took part in a fireforce action with 1 Commando RLI in the Rusape area when I was reassigned to another task along with Dave Shirley. We returned to Grand Reef post haste. On arriving, we were briefed that the SAS had a requirement for a hot extraction in Mozambique where a two-man patrol had been compromised. We routed to Mozambique via Stapleford and Lake Alexander to the area of a huge gomo to the north-east of Umtali. The trees in the area were very tall, probably well over 30 metres in height and I can remember the bush being very thick. There were no LZs anywhere so Rich talked us overhead until my tech was able to sight them down through the foliage. There was a breeze coming in from the east, plus there was a steep slope, necessitating hovering downwind and well out of ground effect. Dave Shirley was in the orbit giving me top cover. We were advised that Jungle Jordan had been shot through the leg close to the knee, which added to the complications. Once I was in position, the tech dropped out the hot extraction harness for the guys to climb onto. Because of the proximity of the terrs, they just grabbed onto the harness instead of attaching themselves securely to it. Then the tech said "okay," and I thought that was the signal to lift them out and move into forward flight. What actually happened was that as I was given the okay, the tech had moved to the other side of the aircraft to check for obstructions and his mic/tel lead had come unplugged so I did not hear the rest of his instructions. I had lost contact with him at a crucial stage of the extraction and thinking that all was well began to move forward. I thought Rich and Jungle were well clear of the trees but they were in fact being dragged through the branches, and eventually were separated from the harness. Rich ended up back on the ground but Jungle was stuck in the upper branches of the tree. By now, comms between the tech and me had been re-established and he told me about the chaos going on underneath. To understand the problem we now had I must explain the design of the hot extraction unit. A rope about 25 metres in length is tethered to the underside of the chopper. At the bottom of the rope is a bar that can seat four. Above the bar are four clips which allow each extractee to secure himself by means of a strap worn around the chest and which is carried by him on external ops for that purpose. On arriving overhead, the tech throws the bar and rope out of the cabin of the chopper. Once out, it cannot be retrieved for a second try, so the pilot must climb to height and then lower the bar through the trees, an extremely difficult task under normal circumstances but impossible when under fire. In effect, the crew have only one chance. As the gear was so long and cumbersome I was unable to climb out and come in again, plus we did not have much time. So with the tech guiding me, I hovered backwards towards where Jungle was stuck and literally pushed the chopper down into the trees until the port wheel was near the stranded Jungle. Slowly he was able to manhandle himself, shot leg and all, along the exterior of the aircraft until the tech was able to grab hold of him. He was eventually pulled on board between the bulkhead and the Browning machine guns and unceremoniously dumped on the floor. I can remember seeing branches and leaves right up the front windscreen and sides of the chopper. While all these shenanigans were going on in the treetops, Rich, who was not going to miss out on the second uplift, made sure he was securely tied to the harness which he had scrambled to on the ground. Once Jungle Jordan was on board we concentrated on Rich and on this occasion, with better comms, were able to haul him right out and fly to a suitable LZ where we landed and put him aboard. We then returned to Grand Reef. I felt terribly embarrassed by this whole experience and when I saw Rich later, with his face all cut up, I did not feel any better. However, he put me at ease explaining that he was so grateful just to be out of there, that nothing else mattered.

No 3 Ground Training School

March saw the inauguration of No 3 Ground Training School at New Sarum under the command of Squadron Leader Maldwyn Griffiths. The new GTS took over responsibility for the basic training of all recruits. The complement was an officer commanding, two flight commanders, four PTI/DIs and seven academic instructors. The school's first intake was No 39 Local Airmen Recruit Course. These technicians would undergo two months' basic general service training before rescreening and posting to the Technical Training School for trade tuition.

No 3 Squadron Diary, March 1979:

Again a very busy month. George Sole and Spike [Norman] Marie were shot up going into Nyamaropa, and a week later Ian Armstrong and Tom Phillips picked up one round in the wing doing the same sort of task. Omega trials continue without too much success and a large number of teething problems have still to be overcome.

It had been announced that a general election would be held between 17th and 21st April. The Patriotic Front vowed that they would disrupt these elections. Added to the insurgents within the country, Special Branch believed that Joshua Nkomo's ZIPRA forces might try a conventional attack across the border in the region of the Victoria Falls. Obviously there would be increased insurgent activity during that period so all security forces were put on alert, leave was cancelled and there was a 30-day call-up for all reservists. The air force went into action with constant harassing attacks to disrupt the enemy.

Operation Liquid—April 1979

On 10th April 1979, No 1 Squadron attacked ZIPRA military headquarters west of Lusaka and then in conjunction with the Canberras later in the day, Mulungushi was attacked by the Hunters and the Canberras. Air photography and been maintained on Mulungushi Camp which had been attacked from the air in December, and it became obvious that ZIPRA had not vacated the camp but that it had in fact increased in size quite substantially. A Selous Scouts team consisting of Schulenberg and Chibanda went in on 9th April to carry out reconnaissance of the area. The plan was that if there were a large number of ZIPRA men in the camp they would set up flares for an air raid to be carried out on the following day. However, the numbers within the camp were disappointing and Schulenberg suggested that the raid be postponed until the following night. Obviously, from a security point of view no one operating from enemy territory should stay on air longer than necessary so the Scouts signed off presuming that his suggestion would be followed.

However, it was decided that the air attack should go in as planned. No contact was possible with Schulenberg and so no flares were set. The Canberra pilots thinking Schulenberg was expecting them, arrived over the target and attempted to call him but of course received no reply. The navigators searched the area for the flares that were supposed to have been set, but there was nothing but darkness. The aircraft overflew the camp. The squadron leader gave the order to bomb anyway so the Canberras turned in a full circle and by a miracle succeeded in the impossible manœuvre with no lights. They lined up again—by now the air was bright with small-arms fire. They commenced their run in. Schulenberg and Chibanda below took what cover they could. The ZIPRA anti-aircraft gunners opened up and continued to bombard the sky long after the Canberras had left.

ComOps ordered the Canberras in again early the next morning hoping to catch the ZIPRA men as they were assessing the damage. This was the first occasion on which a camp had been bombed on two days running and it was hoped that the air force might catch them off guard.

On 13th April, Lusaka was attacked. This was the first time that targets within the city had been hit. Nkomo's house in the suburb of Woodlands, close to the centre of the city was hit and burnt to the ground, while two Hunters based at Fylde flew patrols to Kariba to intercept any possible intruders. The following afternoon it was once again the turn of Mulungushi.

The Patriotic Front was also stepping up its attacks and on 16th April insurgents hit the fuel depot at Fort Victoria. Combined Operations called on the air force at Thornhill for help.

The response was immediate and a fire tender with Warrant Officer I.N. (Neville) Swanepoel in command left Thornhill at 01h30. About 70 kilometres out from Fort Victoria, a glow could be seen on the horizon. Soon afterwards, a giant ball of flame rose high into the night sky. The crew arrived at 04h00 to find that they were the only fire-fighting team combating the blaze. Two tanks had already blown and others were in danger of exploding. The fire-fighting team assessed the situation and set to work to contain the inferno. They were joined by fire fighters from the Salisbury City Council and Fort Victoria and the fire was finally extinguished at 05h30. Four thousand litres of foam were used together with a good few litres of sweat as well. A signal from JOC Repulse reads: "Thank you for all the willing assistance you provided for our fuel dump fire. Without your help we would have lost all. Your efforts greatly appreciated by the JOC and people of Fort Victoria."

During the election period, from 17th to 21st April 1979, the air force played a major role.

No 4 Squadron had 12 aircraft deployed at one time. This was the highest deployment to date. No 3 Squadron was kept busy transporting international observers all over the country. During the election period itself, two extra South African Defence Force teams lent a hand and four Cessna 185s were deployed. The elections were a success in more ways than one.

The Patriotic Front's vow to disrupt the polling came to nothing. Only 18 of the 932 polling stations were attacked and none was put out of action. There were some ambushing and land-mine incidents but there was a 63.9 per-cent poll. The result was a victory for the UANC with Bishop Muzorewa as the new prime minister designate. Following the excitement of the election, May settled back into the old routine. No 4 Squadron reported that:

The highlight of the month occurred when Carl Wilms ran out of fuel 20kms short of Thornhill and force-landed a Lynx damaging a main undercarriage leg and wing tip. Carl had no injuries; however the tech had a slight injury to his back. Alf Wilde narrowly escaped death while putting in an attack on a gook and pulled out a bit low, hitting the top of a tree with his starboard wing. The squadron is slowly settling down to a more steady deployment with Op Grapple stand-by counting as a bush deployment.

And as far as No 3 Squadron was concerned it was business as usual:

The squadron was quite busy this month with two Dakotas and an Islander deployed operationally. There were quite a few incidents to report with Will Smith and Ian Rodwell both having flat tyres on landing, but luckily nobody was hurt and no serious damage to either aircraft occurred. In addition to these Flight Lieutenant R.A. Jordan had a near miss in a Cessna 185 on the way to Grand Reef.

A new weapon—the flechette

At this stage in the war, a further weapon came into use. The French had produced an anti-personnel weapon consisting of thousands of tiny darts known as flechettes. These were banned internationally because they tumbled after hitting the body causing a nasty exit wound. In fact, an ordinary AK bullet caused more damage but that was considered acceptable. Peter Petter-Bowyer had carried out trials from a Provost during 1964, using a tear-gas canister loaded with six-inch nails that were released at 240 knots in a power dive. The effect was devastating but although the nails embedded themselves deeply into the hardwood trees, the flat heads of the nails did not give the required stability. Trials using a Vampire drop tank as the dispenser at 450 knots gave greater density and accuracy, so a bomb was designed for the Hunter: six-inch nails with plastic flights. The canister was manufactured in four hinged sections that were held together with an explosive bolt. When the device was dropped from a Hunter, its forward movement was the speed of the aircraft, that is about 400 knots. As the canister split open the flechettes, which twisted in flight, cut a swathe through the air, penetrating anything that was in their path. This weapon was used once in Mozambique and once within the borders of Rhodesia against a ZANLA gathering when 16 of the 26 men present were killed. Petter-Bowyer remarks that when he went to look at the area after the attack, the flechettes had penetrated everything even the trunks of the mopane trees.

No 7 Squadron receives its Standard

No 7 Squadron celebrated a very special day on 18th May 1979 when it received its Standard from Air Marshal F.W. Mussell. To qualify for the award of the Standard, a squadron had to satisfy one of two criteria. It must either have given 25 years' service, as in the case of Nos 1 and 3 Squadrons, or it must have earned the special appreciation of the commander in chief, the president of Rhodesia for outstanding operational performance. No 7 Squadron was officially born on 28th February 1962 so in 1979 it was eight years short of the number of years needed to qualify. The Standard was, therefore, being awarded for special services. The No 7 Squadron motto was 'Fight Anywhere and Everywhere', which was highly appropriate.

CHAPTER 47

The final chapter

The 26th June 1979 was to be a historic day. The country, now called Zimbabwe-Rhodesia, was celebrating the opening of a new parliament by President Gumede, the first under a black majority government. It was an occasion of great pomp and ceremony with a mounted police escort, a guard of honour, a 21-gun salute and a flypast by nine Hunters of No 1 Squadron.

To appreciate this incredible achievement, it must be remembered that 12 Hunters were originally ordered and flown out from the United Kingdom in 1962. They all arrived safely despite dire predictions by the Royal Air Force. During the following 17 years, three Hunters had been lost. The first on 28th October 1970 when a fuel pipe broke, the engine flamed out, and the pilot had to eject just two miles short of Bulawayo runway. The second on 10th June 1976, when a single bullet sheared the hydraulic lines in the wheel bay during an airstrike on Espungabera. The pilot could not get the main undercarriage legs to lock down and he ejected safely near Thornhill. The third Hunter crashed and the pilot was killed during an external raid into Mozambique on 4th October 1979.

All aircraft have a servicing cycle that is mandatory. A major service can deprive the squadron of an aircraft for a considerable period, and when that aircraft becomes serviceable, the next one is taken. Seldom does a squadron have all its aircraft at base at any one time, and rarely are all those aircraft all serviceable. It is a lasting tribute to the air force technicians and those at airwork that they were able to perform such miracles. With only nine Hunters remaining, each with 17 years of service and 14 years of sanctions, the chance of getting all nine into the air simultaneously was remote, but it was achieved.

And what few among the 10,000 crowd of spectators knew was that these aircraft had earlier in the day, been flying escort to an armada of Bell helicopters carrying members of the SAS on yet another raid into the heart of the Zambian capital, Lusaka. They had simply refuelled and got airborne again for the flypast.

Operation Carpet

26th June 1979: The target was a four-bedroom house known as The Vatican. It stood on a one-acre plot and was ringed with outbuildings that housed Joshua Nkomo's Department of National Security and Order, NSO for short. The NSO was modelled on the Russian intelligence service and headed by Dumiso Dabengwa who was second in command to Nkomo; the assistant director of Intelligence was Victor Mlambo. The ZIPRA intelligence headquarters was surrounded by a high wall, manned by Russian- and Cuban-trained guards.

The plan, devised by the SAS commanding officer, Garth Barrett, was for five Bell 205 helicopters to ferry troops and explosives, putting them down right next to the security fence.

Squadron Leader Ted Lunt was asked whether it was feasible to land troops with total surprise in a suburb of Lusaka. He agreed it was possible but doubted whether ComOps, let alone the commander of the air force would sanction a raid in which a large number of aircraft could be lost. The plan received the blessing of the hierarchy—but a total security ban was placed on the plan because it was believed that there was a leak in ComOps.

Aerial photographs were taken by high-flying Canberras and rehearsals were conducted in an isolated area of Darwendale. The pilots practised the run-in while the soldiers rehearsed deplaning as the helicopters came in to land. Ted had to plan his fuel requirements with great care because the maximum load of men and equipment had to be carried in the Bells.

D-Day had been set for 26th June. The task force positioned at Makuti on D minus one and the troops slept underneath the helicopters.

It was a cold dark winter morning when the Bells took off. Air Commodore Norman Walsh and SAS Major Grahame Wilson who would be in overall command of the operation, climbed aboard the command Dakota at New Sarum. They were to fly directly to the target. At Thornhill Air Base, four Hunters were starting up for the diversionary airstrike on the Zambian FC camp. Two Hunters were detailed to drop golf bombs while the second pair armed with South African Sidewinder air-to-air missiles acted as top cover to the Bells. These missiles were mounted on the wing tips and were intended as protection against the MiG 19s, which could carry the Russian atoll missiles.

The route was from Makuti, across the Zambezi, east of Lusaka to a point about 50 kilometres north-east of the city, then west across the railway line and on to the target. The plan was for the Bells to arrive at 06h15 but there were navigation problems and it was 06h38 when they reached the Lusaka suburb of Roma; despite the delay the operation went ahead. As they came within sight of The Vatican they noticed with alarm that changes had been made to the defences since the aerial photographs had been taken. Machine guns had been mounted on the outside walls.

However, it had been a cold night and the guards were taken completely by surprise and fortunately did not open fire at once. The Bells were committed to landing among these soldiers and when the guards realized what was happening, a hail of bullets met the descending choppers. The Rhodesians returned fire. The choppers were at just the right angle to give a perfect field of fire and the guards began dropping before the helicopters landed.

As the command helicopter touched down, a round fired by a lone guard positioned on an anthill outside the building, smashed the perspex alongside the pilot's head. The guard fired again but his weapon jammed and the Bell landed virtually on top of him. Garth Barrett leapt out and shot the man. Having dropped their loads the choppers lifted off to wait in the bush about seven minutes' flying time away where they could refuel from the drums that had been brought in. To save fuel, the pilots shut down their rotors while they waited.

The inhabitants of the normally quiet suburb were rudely awakened by the spatter of machine-gun fire and the sound of explosions. Leaflets fluttered down from circling helicopters assuring the people of Lusaka that the attack was not aimed against them. The Hunters screamed past towards the diversionary target at Mkushi, a ZAPU training centre about 125 kilometres north-east of the city.

The SAS blew their way inside the headquarters, losing Martin Pearse in the process. They cleared the houses, looking for VIPs. They discovered an underground bunker but there was no time to make a careful search. Meanwhile the eavesdroppers in the command Dakota had intercepted Zambian reaction and called in the helicopters two minutes earlier than planned. The choppers touched down and the troops rushed out with bulging sacks of captured papers. As they left, they encountered a man who said he was a gardener. The SAS took him along. At 07h30, the Bells staggered into the air leaving a shambles behind them. The two No 1 Squadron Hunters circled high above providing top cover during the withdrawal phase.

On the return trip, in order to save fuel, the choppers flew straight over the city of Lusaka instead of diverting round it. And when confirmation was received that there were MiGs in the area, the pilots asked their passengers to keep a sharp lookout while they flew low taking advantage of the terrain to protect them against any attack. In fact, during the raid the MiGs had been scrambled, but did not approach the Rhodesian aircraft.

Once across the border the Bells set down to refuel. Captain Frank Martin Pearse, holder of the Silver Cross of Rhodesia and the Military Forces Commendation, had been killed. His body and one wounded corporal were placed in the fifth Bell for transport to Salisbury. The Hunters which had taken part in the diversionary attack, hastily returned to Thornhill to prepare for the flypast that was to be part of the ceremonial opening of parliament.

An agency report put the death toll at 22 but according to eyewitnesses, ambulances with sirens wailing spent the day ferrying the dead and wounded to hospitals in the area. One considerable bonus was that the gardener turned out to be Alexander Brisk Vusa, the Russian-trained deputy head of intelligence. As a result, security forces discovered the location of a huge weapons cache 25 kilometres west of Lusaka.

On 1st July, this arms cache received attention from the SAS. Once again, they travelled in the Bell helicopters of No 8 Squadron, refuelling at Bumi Hills on the south bank of Lake Kariba. The Canberras and Hunters provided the airstrike force while the helicopters touched down. Once again, according to reports, the MiGs were scrambled, came to investigate and flew away. In fact, there does not seem to have been a single occasion during the whole Bush War when the Zambian or Mozambican air force actually engaged in combat or even threatened to engage Rhodesian aircraft. Zambian troops, however, did fire at the Bells as they were taking off. None of the helicopters were hit although one did have a slight collision with a tree but returned to base safely.

A change of government in the UK
Earlier in the year, on 3rd May 1979, the British electorate had gone to the polls and the Conservatives had triumphed. Mrs Margaret Thatcher, the Iron Lady, had become prime minister of the United Kingdom. Rhodesians were jubilant. They believed that they would get a better deal from the Conservatives than from the Labour party. In their election manifesto, the Conservative Party had promised to return Rhodesia to a state of legality. However, there were ominous mentions later of the necessity for detailed discussions with our European and American allies and the Commonwealth. Following her victory at the polls, Mrs Thatcher had announced that her new foreign secretary was to be Lord Carrington. The new prime minister of Zimbabwe-Rhodesia, Bishop Muzorewa, needed to deliver. In order to do that he needed to gain international recognition and bring about an end to the conflict. Meanwhile Carrington had consulted members of the Commonwealth and in July, the British government undertook to draw up a new constitution and convene an all-party conference. The aim of the conference was to come to an agreement with regards to a cease-fire and new elections.

The Provost flies again
Just two and a half years after the last Provost trainer aircraft made its final flight and was dispatched to No 1 Ground Training School New Sarum for instructional purposes, that same aircraft took to the skies again at New Sarum on 13th July 1979. The resurrection of the Provost that had served as the main piston-engine trainer for 25 years, was largely due to Warrant Officer Bill (Spike) Owens (No 6 Squadron) and his team of technicians. Major engine and airframe refits were carried out at New Sarum with spares being begged, borrowed and devised so as to make the aircraft fully airworthy. Its new livery was polished aluminium. Wing Commander Harold Griffiths who took the Provost through its paces

remarked afterwards, "It's a pleasure to fly a decent aircraft again!"

July was quite a busy month for No 3 Squadron.

There were two incidents during the month that were out of the ordinary. On 13th (not a Friday) Pat Forbes and Terry [Thierry] Ernst had trouble with their brakes at Mabalauta. During the final stages of the landing run, they lost one of their brakes and the aircraft did a ground loop at the bottom of the runway. Luckily, no one was hurt and the aircraft did not sustain any damage. On 26th, Alan Bradnick's aircraft 'blew apart' but again there were no major problems and the aircraft landed safely. (No 3 Squadron Diary)

A world first?

It was on 10th August that the Rhodesian Air Force claimed a world first. A successful raid had been carried out in a remote area 50 kilometres south-east of Francistown, Botswana, and about four kilometres from the Zimbabwe-Rhodesian border. As the Rhodesian helicopters came in to extract this force, a Britten-Norman Defender of the Botswana Defence force, possibly piloted by President Seretse Khama's son, carried out an attack. A No 7 Squadron Alouette III, tasked with providing cover and backup for the Rhodesian forces spotted the aircraft, and emerging from cover behind a hill, went in to the attack using its 20mm cannon. The Defender was forced down. This appears to be the only recorded occasion on which a helicopter has downed a fixed wing aircraft.

On 21st August, jets once again hit ZIPRA installations at Mulungushi. And on the following day, they were back on the job again. Working in the same area in conjunction with ground troops, the aircraft struck six ZIPRA targets, among which was one known as Moscow.

No 1 Squadron Diary carried the comment: "We were intercepted by two MiG 19s when we were about four minutes from the target. Fortunately, it seems, they were as clueless as we were, stooging around doing nothing. Consequently, we dropped our bombs and re-positioned." Two days later, No 1 Squadron was again on the job attacking six ZIPRA bases. These raids were a reminder to the insurgents that there was to be no letup in the war despite the government's amnesty campaign.

Enemy anti-aircraft weapons

At the beginning of the Bush War, the Rhodesian Air Force encountered only light resistance during their attacks on enemy camps. This changed drastically towards the end of the campaign.

Anti-aircraft weapons became an increasingly serious threat as the war progressed, and 12.7 and 14.5mm weapons gave way to 20mm, 23mm, 37mm and 57mm guns and eventually the ZSU 23-4s. It was imperative to hit this weaponry first during a strike on a big target. A number of Hunters would be given one or even two AAA sites. Other aircraft would be dedicated to the target for the day. How we did not lose more aircraft to ground fire, I will never know. Since the objective was to nail the target we simply went flying in—to even the most lethal areas—and just took our chances. When the RAF Monitoring Force team arrived at Thornhill in 1980, they could not believe how casually we treated the weapons. There were, however, some simple tactics that individuals followed depending on the nature of the target, and they will probably seem highly irresponsible now. One tactic, that I'm sure everyone will admit to having used, was practised on heavily defended targets. The trick was not to pull out after the attack, but rather turn away from the target with as many 'gees' as you could muster and keep heading for the deck. Very few weapons were good enough to get you at 20 feet and 500 knots. (Tony Oakley)

No 1 Squadron took time off from the war on 2nd September to carry out a flypast over Rufaro Stadium to honour the raising of the new Zimbabwe-Rhodesia flag. The following day, Ginger Baldwin destroyed a train north of Mapai. Unfortunately, the train had been dead since 1976!

Operation Uric, September 1979

Intelligence reports confirmed that a heavy build-up of weapons and equipment was taking place along the main road and rail links from the port of Maputo towards the Rhodesian border. It seemed that a ZANLA/Frelimo offensive could be in preparation. It was, therefore, decided to destroy strategic bridges in the Gaza province and so disrupt the flow of arms and equipment, and simultaneously eliminate Mapai as a terrorist base. This plan would take security forces nearly 350 kilometres into Mozambique and within 140 kilometres of the capital city Maputo. Every available aircraft was to be deployed—eight Hunters, 12 Dakotas, six Canberras, six Lynxes, and 28 helicopters including the Bells.

D-Day was scheduled for Sunday 2nd September but the weather was bad and the choppers could not take off from Chipinda Pools. In fact, the operation had to be delayed for three days while the anxious planners waited for the weather to clear.

The first targets were the bridges at Barragem. Early on the morning of Wednesday 5th September, four Hunters of No 1 Squadron flew down the valley in their strike pattern. A strong defence was mounted but there were no losses and the Hunters scored a number of direct hits. Following the air attack, 48 SAS helicopter-borne troops were dropped about one kilometre from Barragem and they dealt with the enemy machine guns that were still in action. One captured 23mm anti-aircraft gun was used to good effect against its original owners. The helicopters meanwhile had lifted off to hold the area. One security force member who had been shot in the leg was choppered out.

In the confusion of the fighting, a communications error occurred and a No 8 Squadron helicopter flew over an enemy position. As the Bell came in to land, an enemy RPG-7 rocket was fired, hit the rear cabin area and the helicopter plummeted to earth and burst into flames. Senior Aircraftman Alexander Wesson was killed on impact, but Flight Lieutenant Dick Paxton, the pilot, was pulled clear by an SAS sergeant, and only suffered a broken elbow, lacerations and shock. The helicopter was destroyed.

Meanwhile the SAS had placed explosives on the bridges and detonations had been carried out doing considerable damage. The other teams met no resistance and successfully mined the bridges at Chicacatem, Folgares, Canicado and Mezinchopes. By 14h30, the operation was complete.

On Day 2, the target was Mapai. Early in the morning, the Canberras and Hunters attacked with alpha and golf bombs respectively, hitting the communications centre, bunkers and armoury.

Returning briefly to Thornhill to refuel and rearm, the Hunters were soon back taking out a fuel storage tank and radar installations. The defenders fought back with great heroism putting up a ferocious anti-aircraft barrage.

Now it was time for the ground attack. The heavily laden helicopters lumbered towards their target. Then came a second tragedy. By pure chance, the helicopter carrying the main demolition team passed over a small enemy position. Although it was some distance from Mapai, the previous day's activity had alerted the defenders and they opened fire with RPG-7s. One of the rockets struck SAAF Puma 194 which rolled sideways and plunged to the ground, killing everyone on board. This was one of the worst disasters of the war in military terms. The Rhodesian dead included Captain Johannes du Plooy, Captain Charles Small, Second Lieutenant Bruce Burns, Sergeant Michael Jones, Corporal LeRoy Duberly, Lance

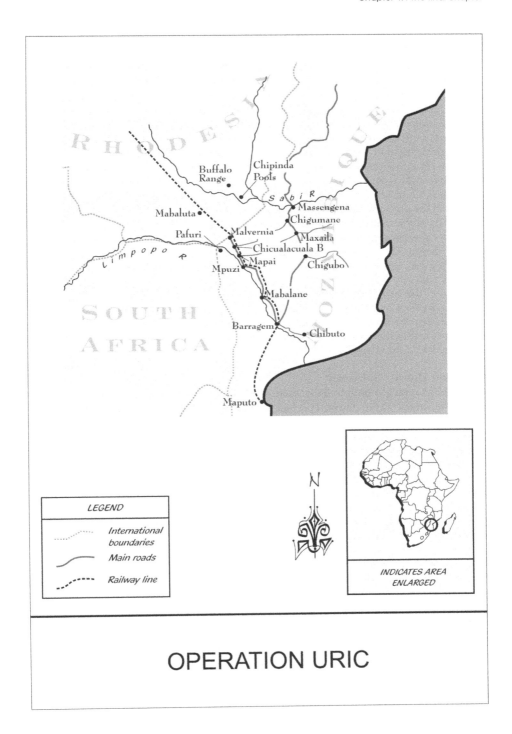

OPERATION URIC

Corporal Peter Fox, Corporal Gordon Fry, Troopers Jacobus Briel, Aidan Colman, Jeremy Crow, Brian Enslin, Stephen King, Colin Neasham and David Prosser, as well as the South African aircrew, Captain Paul Velleman, Lieutenant Nigel Osborne and Segeant Dirk Retief.

Meanwhile the main onslaught against Mapai was continuing and the ground forces were meeting stubborn resistance. Airstrikes were called in and the Canberras and Hunters flew back and forth delivering their cargoes of death and returning to base to rearm and refuel. The fastest turn-round time still left the ground forces unsupported for up to three hours. With the few aircraft that the air force had available it was not possible to maintain a cab-rank system. And once over the target, the aircraft were greeted by a hail of accurate and efficient fire from the anti-aircraft weapons massed around the ZANLA base. The Canberras were forced to restrike from 21,000 feet because it was just not safe to fly any lower. As they flew over Mapai, all the heavy weapons opened up on them. On the ground, the advance had been halted and the decision was taken to withdraw. In fact, the ground forces had to make their way out from the target area on foot. Rhodesia could not afford to lose another helicopter. There was now a race against time to pull the men out before dark. Late in the afternoon, the choppers began arriving to uplift the weary troops. As the helicopters made their way back to safety, they were continually subjected to ground fire, a frightening experience for passengers and crew alike.

This was the first occasion that the Rhodesian forces had failed to achieve their aim. However, massive quantities of supplies had been captured, communications and transport links had been disrupted, roads had been mined and various headquarters had been destroyed. In fact, because of this attack, the Russian advisers pulled out of Mapai. All in all, the enemy had been dealt a shattering blow.

Lancaster House Conference

Bishop Muzorewa had promised that there would be a run-down in the terrorist war once a black government was in power. This had not materialized. The incidence of terrorism had increased. During the Commonwealth leaders' conference held in Lusaka during August 1979 the decision was made that an all-party conference should be held in an attempt to resolve the Rhodesian problem. It was to be held in London under the auspices of Lord Carrington, British Foreign Secretary. On 12th August, Britain issued a set of proposals and invited the Prime Minister of Zimbabwe-Rhodesia, Bishop Abel Muzorewa, and the Patriotic Front Alliance of Joshua Nkomo and Robert Mugabe. Both parties were to send delegations of up to 12 members. The United Kingdom government published an eleven-point plan to end UDI. Both delegations accepted the invitations and the conference began at Lancaster House, in London on 10th September 1979.

Operation Norah, September 1979

Since the early 1970s, the Rhodesian security forces had been receiving information from an anti-Frelimo group, the Mozambique National Resistance (MNR). While being given support from Rhodesia and South Africa, the members of the movement had been encouraged to do their own thing and the undoubted success of the MNR demonstrated that in many areas Frelimo lacked popular support.

The SAS working together with the Mozambique National Resistance had carried out a series of operations. One such took place in September 1979, when 32 heavily laden men were dropped into Mozambique. Their target was a relay station at Monte Xilvuo, a vital part of the sophisticated communications link inside Mozambique. Local people provided guides, and the group, in conjunction with the MNR, made a successful attack on the communications centre.

However, the operation stirred a hornet's nest and Frelimo retaliated, making it impossible for the attackers to reach the rendezvous point with the choppers that were to extract them.

There was deep concern at ComOps when the situation became clear. A Lynx was dispatched to the area and the Hunters were placed on stand-by. Meanwhile the SAS men were in a tight spot. They could hear military vehicles and Frelimo troops being deployed all round them. Desperately they called for air support. The Lynx arrived overhead and the Hunters soon joined the fray, diving in to the attack. But all too soon the aircraft had to leave the scene. The Lynx needed to refuel and the Hunters to rearm. During the lull in air activity, the ring around the SAS men tightened and three of their number had gone missing.

A long hour passed before the Lynx arrived back overhead and then the men on the ground heard an even more welcome sound—the thump-thump of helicopter rotors. Soon a Bell appeared. The men scrambled aboard but the helicopter was so overladen that it was unable to climb out. Hastily equipment was ditched and the chopper clawed its way into the air. Most of the group were safe but two SAS men and a member of the MNR were still unaccounted for—possibly dead or wounded.

As it happened, the three men were alive but their situation was critical. They were deep in enemy territory and as they had been responsible for an attack on a major Frelimo installation, they could count on severe retaliation. They reached the Beira/Umtali road, which ran east-west. They could hear heavy vehicles moving. They quickly crossed the road and headed north. They walked until dawn and reached a river, which gave them a chance to refill their water bottles. Their plan was to continue walking north and attempt to reach the MNR-stronghold in the Gorongoza Mountains. By now they had covered about 12 kilometres since leaving the target area.

Then came that most welcome sound in the world—helicopter rotor blades. Hastily they released their green smoke grenades but the pilot failed to spot the smoke, and the sound of the chopper faded away. The three men were on their own again. Their position was desperate. In the distance, they could see the Frelimo sweep lines closing in on them. Yet another chopper flew over—and again the pilot failed to see them.

Then they saw a Bell. The huge machine passed over them, hovered and then settled down behind the trees—it seemed almost within touching distance. It was about half a kilometre away. The Bell had landed to refuel from the drums it was carrying. They were saved! The three men set off at a gallop towards the trees but the bush was thick and the going was hard. They were still 100 metres away when the great bird lifted back into the sky, banked and flew away to the north.

Now what? The SAS men were in an impossible situation. If they signalled to a passing aircraft the chances were that the Frelimo men would see them. If they remained hidden they had no chance of being rescued. Carefully they moved to higher ground, covering their tracks as they went. Eventually they found a spot that would give them cover from the enemy and stopped to rest. The sun was high in the sky and they were exhausted. Then, just after midday, two Lynx appeared. The aircraft circled the general area for about 20 minutes gradually drawing closer. The men on the ground had no more smoke grenades, so they tried attracting the pilots' attention by using their heliograph. Again the pilots did not spot them and eventually flew away.

Another two hours passed. A Lynx appeared again and circled in their general area. This time they tried lighting a fire—but it went out. Still the Lynx circled while they made desperate attempts to attract the pilot's attention. The aircraft dipped its wings, right and then left. They had been seen! Suddenly there was hope!

Meanwhile the Lynx pilot had called in a helicopter. But when he circled to pinpoint the men on the ground he could not find them. The pilot and his passenger peered through the evening light. Had they been mistaken? Perhaps it was just a cooking fire—or perhaps it had been lit to lure a helicopter into danger. Perhaps they should send the chopper back while there was still time. Then Sergeant Major Karl Lutz, the passenger in the chopper, spotted the light again, and beside it the figures of three men. The helicopter came in. The landing zone was tight and the Bell had to hover but the three men scrambled safely aboard and were whisked away over the heads of their enemies to safety.

Operation Miracle, September 1979

Repeated attacks had been made on ZANLA camps in what had become known as the Chimoio Circle. But information was now coming through that indicated a new large base with three others surrounding it. Captured documents revealed that New Chimoio was the most important camp in Mozambique. New Chimoio was known to be somewhere on the east side of the Chimoio/Tete road and it was believed to house about 2,000 combatants.

An SAS team was choppered in to carry out a recce of the area. Unfortunately, the area into which they were dropped was just about five kilometres from the main ZANLA camp. Armed ZANLA soldiers were all round them. The team carried out one ambush and then called for a hot extraction. As they withdrew towards the border, they were involved in running battles with their pursuers and the team came under increasingly heavy fire. A Lynx, with SAS commander Rob Johnstone, arrived overhead and the firing eased. He reported that four helicopters were on their way. But there were 16 men to rescue and it was going to be difficult with the fight still in progress. The choppers descended and before they touched ground, the men were climbing aboard. The helicopters struggled to lift off and the men jettisoned their gear. Suddenly a technician spotted a group of ZANLA. The choppers opened up with their Brownings while the troopers fired through the open doors. Smoke hung in the air as the helicopters—nose down to get speed—flew for the border. It had been a close thing and the team was lucky to have sustained no casualties. The next attempt at reconnaissance was a two-man Selous Scouts team that went in on foot. They were also compromised and there had to be another hot extraction.

So eventually, ComOps tasked the air force to execute a photographic reconnaissance despite the fact that this might alert the enemy to an attack. A Canberra run was made and the resultant photographs revealed a huge complex, apparently consisting of five separate camps, each very heavily defended with anti-aircraft weapons hewn into the rock on top of high ground. The most prominent feature was a bald koppie, which was to become known as Monte Cassino, after the famous battle in Italy during World War II. These high points were manned by well-trained ZANLA men who lived in a series of fortified bunkers roofed with logs and earth, which had been constructed under the supervision of Soviet and East German advisers.

The task of these men was to protect the camps beneath from raids by the aircraft of Nos 5 and 1 Squadrons. The defeat of the ZANLA forces on the top of the Monte Cassino outcrop would be vital to the success of the operation. In all, more than 1,000 people together with at least five Russian advisers, were believed to be permanently resident in the five camps. The new Chimoio complex was obviously not going to be an easy target. The plan was basically the same as on previous occasions—to send in an aerial strike force followed by a heavily-armed mobile column comprised of detachments from the Selous Scouts, the RLI and the Rhodesian Armoured Car Regiment. The force was mounted on Unimog vehicles with machine guns. The shock force of 100 men on ten of these highly mobile trucks was escorted by a troop of Eland armoured cars.

The convoy left the Selous Scouts Camp at Inkomo Barracks in Salisbury under cover of darkness on 26th September 1979. That night they reached Ruda Base Camp, one kilometre from the Mozambique border. Their route forward meant crossing the Gaerezi River, north of Ruda, in the Honde valley. The banks of the river were steep and had to be bulldozed down and a mat of logs put in place to enable the heavy vehicles to cross. From this point on the problems grew worse. The column should have traversed the river by first light, reaching the base code-named Madison Square, close to the target area, by 07h00 when the airstrike was due to take place. Unfortunately, however, the Canberras were still striking the target, while the column struggled across the river. It only reached Madison Square, which consisted of a deserted run-down bush store, some time after 14h00, seven hours after the airstrike.

From Madison Square, the column struck the road leading to the base and headed north. Meanwhile the 100 RLI, parachuted into a landing zone ten kilometres from the guerrilla base, had taken up ambush positions around the camp. When the security force vehicles reached the foot of Monte Cassino it was dark, and the troops had to find what cover they could for the night. During the hours of darkness, they came under heavy fire from RPG-7s and 75mm recoilless rifles emanating from the koppie. In addition, accurate fire was directed at the Rhodesians from an 82mm mortar on a nearby hill, Hill 805. Two helicopters coming in to land were fired on.

As day dawned it became obvious that the gunfire was being directed by lookouts on the top of Monte Cassino. At about 08h30, cloud descended and obscured the view and the Rhodesian armoured cars moved up to give supporting cover to the Selous Scouts. It was now clear that this was going to be a long drawn-out fight and so the Hunters were called in to reduce the morale of the defenders and if possible to take out the gun emplacements on the koppie. Unknown to the air force, a nearby hill, known as Hill 761, had been heavily armed with anti-aircraft guns and missiles. This became known as ack-ack hill.

At 13h00 a Lynx recce aircraft appeared, followed by the Hunters. They flew into an incredibly dense curtain of anti-aircraft fire thrown up from Hill 761. The Hunters dropped 16 golf bombs onto the enemy positions, and a well-defended high feature, Hill 774, flanking Monte Cassino, was finally captured by the Rhodesians.

At first light on Saturday, the third day, after consolidating Hill 774, work was started clearing the heavy weapons and then the attackers moved straight down the ridge. The Hunters struck again sending dust and smoke hundreds of metres into the air as they hit each high point in turn, before the infantry moved in. The enemy kept up a heavy fire. Subsequently Hill 761 was stormed but proved to be deserted. The defenders had fought well. Many of them had been killed and their bunkers destroyed in the bombing. The summit of Monte Cassino itself was now also empty, the enemy having withdrawn on D-Day plus 2 in the face of the devastating air bombardment.

At about 01h30 on Sunday 30th six T-34 tanks manned by Frelimo troops approached the Rhodesian positions in the camp complex and opened fire wildly. They made a lot of noise but hit nothing and there were no injuries. Fire was directed at the tanks and they withdrew. By now the ZANLA forces had pulled out and the Rhodesians were in command of the almost inconceivable 64 square kilometre camp with its sophisticated trench systems.

Obviously, an operation such as this was extremely expensive in both weapons and security force losses, and just as obviously the area, which was part of a foreign country, could not be held indefinitely. So on Sunday 30th the security forces pulled back across the border.

As part of Operation Miracle a mock fireforce mission was carried out in the Makoni Tribal Trust land, in order to give some explanation for the increased troop activity in the area. Unfortunately, an Alouette K-Car being used in this operation flew into a power line killing the officer commanding 3 Commando Rhodesian Light Infantry, Major Bruce Snelgar, as well as the pilot, Air Lieutenant Paddy Bate and Flight Sergeant Gary Carter, the technician.

After the main column pulled back, monitoring groups remained in the Operation Miracle area. Several days later one of these groups reported that a large Frelimo column, heavily armed and well equipped with Soviet-supplied 23mm anti-aircraft weapons had appeared. The column bombarded the long-vacated Monte Cassino with extreme accuracy. This column later moved on to the village of Christo Mento to the north. ComOps believed that this column intended to launch a reprisal raid on Ruda Security Force Base just over the border in Rhodesia. The air force was tasked with the destruction of the column. These airstrikes proved extremely costly. During the first strike, a Canberra bomber crewed by Air Lieutenants Kevin Peinke and J.J. Strydom was seriously damaged by ground fire and crashed after flying 20 kilometres back towards the border. Both the pilot and the navigator were killed. In a later strike a Hunter was hit by ground fire, and crashed killing the pilot, Air Lieutenant Brian Gordon. Tony Oakley, talking about the Hunter crash, says:

> *The conditions were atrocious, hazy and smoky. We will never be sure exactly what happened because no one actually saw the impact of the aircraft. We can assume, therefore, that it was some distance from the target. We know the wreckage was found by the enemy, because some of it was displayed in Maputo. Brian had been piloting the lead aircraft in a pair. Siggy [Michel Seegmuller] was No 2. We would not normally have had two such junior pilots on a strike of this nature, but four pairs were either en route or returning home and another pair had been called out to another operational area. This particular convoy was very long and extremely heavily armed, which meant that the attacking aircraft were highly vulnerable. Target acquisition was extremely difficult and Brian told Siggy to remain at altitude while he went down to try to pick it out. He was never heard from again. The absence of a radio call means that he might have been shot—or he could simply have gone into the ground. To lose Kevin on the same day rattled us all to our boots.*

During September, No 3 Squadron took part in an operation code named Disco Scene. This was an attempt to persuade insurgents to accept the proffered amnesty terms. Captured ex-combatants would be placed in a Dakota and flown over a contact area. Using a sky shout, they would endeavour to persuade their comrades in the bush to surrender.

Operation Cheese, October 1979

The Tanzam Railway built by the Chinese connected the Zambian railway system with the Tanzanian port of Dar es Salaam. This railway had become vital to Zambia's economy since the closing of the line through Rhodesia. The line-up to the Tanzanian border had been extensively photographed by the Canberras and in 1979 it was decided to carry out an attack on it. Early in September the go-ahead was given for a strike on the Chambesi rail bridge, which crossed the Chambeshi River in north-eastern Zambia. The rail bridge, one of the longest in the world, and the road bridge lay side by side. These two targets were 500 kilometres from the Rhodesian border. The plan was for a free-fall team of four SAS men to carry out a reconnaissance of the area. Another 12 men would do a static-line drop carrying all the equipment needed for the attack. The first problem was to find a suitable landing zone away from human habitation, close to the river, upstream from the bridges and at a point where there was a recognizable feature. One of the pilots in this operation was Jack Malloch flying his DC-7, which had been taken over by No 3 Squadron for paratrooping. Often ground haze made it virtually impossible to pinpoint features on the ground and finding suitable landing zones sometimes meant hours of dangerous and tedious searching. In fact, it was only on the second attempt that a suitable point was found but it was 40 kilometres downstream. The next major problem was uplifting the men after the attack. The helicopters could not fly that far without refuelling so it was decided that the SAS men should hijack a suitable vehicle and drive to a point from which they could be uplifted.

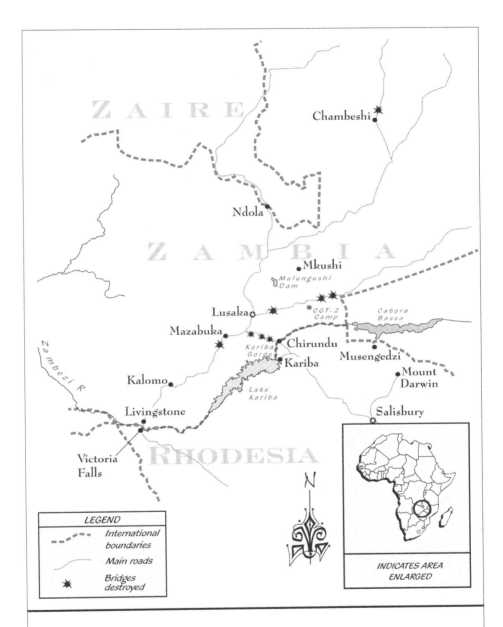

OPERATION CHEESE
BRIDGES DESTROYED - ZAMBIA

D-Day was set for 12th September but there was too much haze and the pilot was unable to locate the dropping zone. The next suitable night was 3rd October. Once again, the free-fall team climbed aboard the DC-7 and took off. Again, Jack Malloch and dispatcher Frank Hales had problems with the ground haze. After 20 minutes of peering through the gloom, the decision was made to call the operation off once again. Then Malloch spotted a recognizable feature. The green light flashed and the free-fallers were on their way.

On 8th October, the rest of the team made a successful static line drop. Three days later, they placed their explosives on the bridges, commandeered suitable vehicles and set off towards the Rhodesian border. By the following day, they were within 200 kilometres of safety but it was too late in the day for a pickup. They were told that the helicopters would uplift them at 08h00 next morning, 13th October. They spent the evening clearing a landing zone. Meanwhile the choppers flew from New Sarum to Mount Darwin, and on to Musengedzi Mission where they refuelled. They also carried additional drums of fuel from which they refuelled while in flight. The helicopters crossed the border, settled down in the landing zone and the grateful SAS men climbed aboard. Soon they were back at Musengedzi Mission having achieved their main objective of severing Zambia's lifeline to the east coast. This was one of the most successful operations of the war. Ten thousand tons of copper was stranded inside Zambia, unable to reach the coast for export causing the loss of much-needed foreign currency. A further 18,000 tons of imports, much of which was perishable, were left sitting on the docks at Dar es Salaam.

Operation Tepid, 18th October 1979

For some time it had been suspected that there was a strongly held ZIPRA position located some 60 kilometres south-west of Chirundu and north of Siavonga close to the main road from Kariba to Lusaka. Photographic reconnaissance of the area had proved unsuccessful although the photo-interpreter did identify what appeared to be well-camouflaged trenches and signs that the enemy were in battalion strength. The go ahead was given for a short sharp operation which it was hoped would persuade the enemy to abandon the camp.

On 18th October 1979, Hunters from Thornhill and Canberras from New Sarum led the paratroopers in. The SAS had positioned at FAF 2, Kariba, and the Dakotas followed the jet strikes into the target area. The troops were dropped on either side of the ridge bisecting the target area. After the airstrike a Dakota circled the area, then flew up one ridge and down another dropping incendiaries. The incendiaries were pushed out of the cargo door from 200 feet in the hope of starting a bush fire that would burn the place out. Although the Dakota pilot reported seeing the trenches, he could not see anyone in them. Not a shot was fired at the jets or the Dakota. Because of this lack of reaction, a third Hunter strike was called off.

The top cover Lynx piloted by Trevor Jew with SAS captain, Robert C. (Bob) MacKenzie on board, reported a lemon believing the camp had been vacated or abandoned. The troops on the ground were instructed to remain overnight and await helicopter uplift the next day. However, later in the day, a 20-man enemy sweep line came up against the main Rhodesian ambush group. In the following contact, one ZIPRA was killed and the remainder dispersed into the bush.

During the night, as one of the SAS groups moved cautiously up to the crest of a hill, it came under fire, and Lance Corporal John McLauren was seriously wounded in the stomach.

A night casevac was requested but it was impossible to bring a helicopter in and McLauren died of his wound. The following morning the corporal's body was choppered out along with another trooper who was suffering from heat fatigue. Meanwhile the SAS groups had been sweeping the top of the ridge and had come under heavy fire from AK-47s, recoilless rifles, mortars, 12.7 and 14.5mm heavy weapons. Lieutenant Phil Brooke and his corporal were both injured. The Hunters scrambled at Thornhill. Meanwhile Bob MacKenzie flying in a Lynx piloted by Trevor Jew crossed the Zambezi heading for the target area to act as top cover and FAC for the Hunters. The ZIPRA members, holed up in a labyrinth of trenches, began firing at the aircraft overhead. Jew dived to the attack through concentrated fire from 12.7mm and 14.5mm anti-aircraft guns and a hail of bullets from the automatic rifles of the men in the trenches. Jew aborted his strike without firing and turned away—seeking safety. As he did so, an armour-piercing incendiary tracer from a 14.5mm weapon smashed into the control panel between the pilot and his passenger and ricocheted off into the front engine. The cockpit filled with smoke. It was impossible to see a thing. Shrapnel hit Jew's legs and other pieces struck the plane. Flames licked towards the two men. They knew that at any moment the fuel could ignite or the bomb load explode blowing the aircraft and its occupants to kingdom come. Jew jettisoned his weapon load, called Mayday and instructed Bob MacKenzie to stand by to bale out. Bob MacKenzie shook his head, Negative was his reply and he managed to get his window open. As the smoke cleared it became obvious that the cockpit was not on fire but Jew also realized that his parachute was not fastened. Bob MacKenzie took over the controls while Jew fixed his parachute. Neither of the two men could see whether the aircraft was on fire outside. Could they get the Lynx back to base?

The pilot did a check and found that the automatic hydraulic controls were out of action. They tried to work the hand crank but all that happened was a spray of hot hydraulic fluid into the cockpit. That meant a wheels-up landing. Flying as gently as possible, Jew nursed the stricken plane back across the border, alerting Kariba Airport that he would be making an emergency landing. Just before they started crossing the lake the front engine packed up, leaving them to limp slowly across the water with only the rear engine functioning

Meanwhile at Kariba, crash crews, ambulance and fire engine were standing by. As Jew orbited the runway, he offered Bob MacKenzie another chance to bale out. Gently Jew lowered the Lynx onto the tarmac while Bob MacKenzie held the door open. The fire engine hurtled down the runway behind them as the Lynx hit belly down and slid along the tarmac sending sparks flying. As the plane skidded to a halt, its two occupants hit the tarmac running and sprinted as fast as possible away from the plane. By the time they realized that there was not going to be an explosion and turned round to look, the Lynx was hidden in a cocoon of foam. In fact, the aircraft had not been badly damaged and the two men got away unscathed.

Obviously the complex was much larger than had been reckoned and the ZIPRA men well disciplined. At 10h00 on Saturday 20th October, the Canberras carried out a bombing run on the main ridge. It was however largely ineffective. At 11h00 the choppers flew in to drop the RLI and SAS mortar teams a short way from the target. Unfortunately, the enemy had correctly identified the possible landing zone and had zeroed their mortars. The Rhodesians came under heavy and effective bombardment and a number of RPG-7 rockets were launched at them.

Three men were spotted sitting under a rocky outcrop. Two were shot, the third was captured and he turned out to be the camp logistics officer. He was immediately flown back to Rhodesia and handed over to the eager arms of the special branch officers. Further interrogation revealed that the captured man was part of the first battalion of ZIPRA's first brigade and that they had moved into the area five weeks earlier from Mulungushi. This was to serve as their forward base for a strike, in force, across the border into Rhodesia. At this juncture, there were 244 combatants in the camp, and another 100 men were expected soon. These men were well trained and disciplined and, following orders, had held their fire during the initial airstrikes, hoping that the Rhodesians would conclude that the camp had been abandoned.

An elaborate command and control organization existed with radio communications to the regional commander who was based in nearby Lusoto, and the commander had direct contact with Lusaka. Armed with this hot intelligence, ComOps decided to launch a full-scale assault employing two RLI commandos in support of the SAS. The commandos were flown to FAF 2 while the Hunters and Canberras were being bombed up. Because the RLI outnumbered the SAS, Lieutenant Colonel Ian Bate was placed in overall command, with Lieutenant Colonel Garth Barrett of the SAS providing the alternative command function. Both men were to command from a No 4 Squadron Lynx. Two Hunters were allocated to support the ground troops for the duration of the operation. Canberras were to be employed for specific bombing missions, and Squadron Leader Ted Lunt and his five Bell helicopters were to be used for trooping and casevac.

On Saturday 20th October, 'C' Squadron SAS were pre-positioned by air, and early on the following morning 21st October, despite rain-delayed timings, the five Bells ferried the remaining troops across Lake Kariba. Nine waves or lifts were required to carry the 72 men across and drop them three kilometres from their target.

At 10h00, two Canberras carried out a bombing run but the enemy was so well entrenched that the strike was largely ineffectual. At 11h00, the RLI and SAS mortar teams were dropped in by helicopter. Their landing zone was not ideal and ZIPRA forces put down an effective RPG-7, 75mm and mortar bombardment amongst them. The Rhodesians were pinned down by the fierce resistance and Major Pete Hean, OC 2 Commando RLI, called in the Hunters. Once again, the strike was no help in neutralizing the enemy fire and a further Hunter strike was ordered. However, the camouflage on the gun emplacements was so effective that it was difficult for the pilots to identify the guns and most of the strikes were off-target.

Pete Hean tried a flanking manœuvre along a little gully but eight of his men were slightly wounded. A helicopter brought in a 14.5mm gun from Kariba for the lightly armed ground troops. And a casevac chopper flown by Squadron Leader Ted Lunt came in for the injured troopies. Unfortunately, the troop commander mistook Ted's machine for another Bell and talked him straight over the enemy positions. The ZIPRA men stared in amazement at the lone Bell flying low overhead. Then they reacted and a trail of angry tracer sped after Ted as he made for the safety of the ridge. While the injured troopies were being loaded, yet another pair of Hunters had a go at the 14.5mm gun positions. The sun was just setting as Pete Hean desperately tried to indicate the exact gun positions to the pilots.

"Hang on," said Red Leader, "I'll send Red Two in first: watch the tracer coming up and follow him in. Red Two will strike where we think it is. I'll see exactly where the fire is coming from and strike on that." As number two turned in—and before he was halfway down in his attack—the 14.5s on both ridges opened up. Red Leader delayed his dive, holding back about 15 seconds, and then came in from a different angle. "Okay! I've got the bugger," he said. It was a pinpoint airstrike. Dust and stones flew everywhere and the weapon was momentarily silenced. "But then the cheeky bugger shook his head, grabbed hold of the 14.5 and swung it round, firing up at the Hunter as it pulled out of its dive!" Red tracer followed the hunter into the sunset. The ZIPRA gunner was so well protected, that short of getting him between the eyes, he was safe. It was clear that the Rhodesians were not going to take the position that day, and the RLI men pulled back for the night. The score? Day one: round one to ZIPRA for a sterling resistance.

However, unbeknown to the Rhodesians, the ZIPRA commander was a worried man. The camp had been under attack for hours, and what was more, he did not know when he would receive a resupply of ammunition. He made a plan. At midnight, ZIPRA mounted a heavy bombardment on the Rhodesian positions—and under cover of this attack, the ZIPRA forces carried out an orderly withdrawal. In the morning, a careful sweep revealed nothing but empty gun chests and ammunition boxes, endless kilometres of telephone wire linking the different posts, steel helmets and 14.5mm guns which had been rendered useless because the breech blocks had been removed.

Victoria Falls—ZIPRA contact

In October 1979, Martin Hatfield was based at FAF 1 (Wankie Town) in the Lynx. Also at FAF 1 there was a K-Car and a G-Car. On 19th October, reports came in that about 60 communist terrorists were in the Victoria Falls area and the Grey's Scouts were deployed to pick up tracks. Martin flew a recce over a possible ZIPRA camp and carried out top cover during the tracking. A big operation was taking place to the south so the only men at Kariba were cooks and camp administration staff who were determined but not very experienced. When, therefore, a contact was made late in the day, they pulled back. The following day, they picked up the tracks again. This time they had some PATU and RR with them. Then on 21st October, fresh tracks were found. Martin Hatfield picks up the story:

I positioned at Sprayview early in the morning, and the choppers went to Vic Falls Main. The Greys were now hot on the heels of the terrs. We were just about to be briefed when the contact occurred—so close that we could hear the shooting from the apron of the airport. An SAA Boeing 727 had just landed and the passengers were disembarking—there were some worried-looking faces on that apron. (Martin Hatfield)

Another pilot who played a role in this operation was Cocky Benecke:

We were told to position at Vic Falls Airport on stand-by. Within minutes of our having completed refuelling the call came that the Greys were pinned down just to the west of the airport—so we scrambled and headed west. As soon as we came over their position, we were met with a hail of bullets. Bruce Jameson my tech was lying over the cannon trying to protect himself from the fire, yelling expletives at me to get the hell out of it. Like all helicopter pilots under heavy fire, I pulled my feet up and tried to sink my head into my neck like a tortoise. It took about two minutes to get the Scouts visual. We still hadn't seen any terrs even though we were under constant fire. Suddenly we spotted first one and then the whole group. From the air, it was obvious that they were using the classic Matabele 'head and horns' method of ambush, with the main body in the centre and the two horns out on either side and swinging in. The Grey's Scouts were almost surrounded. It was a while before Bruce opened fire because he was having trouble seeing the enemy and he was nervous about the amount of fire we were attracting, but once he opened up his confidence surged. The amazing thing was that the gooks showed no sign of running—they were determined to stay and fight it out—and we were now the centre of their focus. Good news for the Scouts—bad news for us. But now Bruce had the bit between his teeth. He kept firing and they kept falling. (Cocky Benecke)

Meanwhile Martin Hatfield had got airborne:

And as I turned crosswind, the K-Car was already in contact. I had hardly retracted my gear when Cocky gave me a sitrep. The contact was in the Kalisosa Vlei area only three kilometres from the airport. As I turned in there was a fair amount of tracer. Cocky was having fun picking out targets because each time I pulled out, the terrs exposed themselves to take a shot at me. Their fire was accurate and concentrated and my aircraft was hit on each attack. On my third or fourth attack, they hit my rear engine and I had to shut it down because it had lost oil pressure. I could not stay in the area so I returned to the airport where I found that I had been hit about five times--one of the rounds had taken out the sump and another a cylinder on the rear engine. (Martin Hatfield)

Colyn James in the G-Car was orbiting the area at low level but as there were no troops available, there wasn't much he could do. Bruce continued to have successes until we ran out of ammunition and had to return to the airport to rearm. Colyn came into high orbit to keep the gooks' heads down and gave as much support with his .303s as he could until we returned. The Scouts were still in the position in which they had been ambushed because it would have been suicide for them to move. Just before we went to rearm, they came up with a strange request— they asked us to shoot some of their horses, which had been wounded, in the early ambush. They wanted us to put them out of their misery. It was an incredible request considering that here were a bunch of guys in imminent danger of being killed and they showed such concern. After rearming and refuelling and getting some temporary repairs to the chopper that had been hit several times, we returned to the contact area. We were amazed to find that the gooks had not fled, despite having taken some heavy punishment—we had killed about 30. Bruce was now going like a steam train and was totally oblivious of the fire directed at us. As more ZIPRA were killed or wounded, the fire grew less intense. But it was beginning to get dark and we were running out of ammunition again. There was no opportunity to go and rearm, so Bruce started firing his FN through the open chopper door at the few gooks who were now pulling back. The Grey's Scouts who had displayed immense courage, were keen to follow the fleeing enemy and wanted to sweep the area. But the light was getting bad and I suggested it would be a pity to lose a life now. It would have been a bonus to have lifted them out but it was too dangerous and there was no suitable landing zone in the immediate vicinity. Two things stand out in my mind about this contact. The Grey's Scouts who, facing almost certain death, showed such coolness and concern for their horses, and Bruce who overcame his initial fear and went on to fight a three-hour battle, displaying great courage under constant fire. (Cocky Benecke)

Kabanga Mission, 2nd November 1979

At the beginning of November, the target was a camp in the Kabanga Mission area south of Kalomo in Zambia. The target was a fairly densely inhabited area populated by Zambian tribesmen. There was a business centre with the normal kraals nearby, close to watering points. The whole area constituted a headquarters for ZIPRA deployed in that part of the country. The raid began on Friday morning 2nd November, with a wave of airstrikes, followed by ground troops. The airstrikes were planned to avoid the civilians in the villages and they were right on target. Initially there was little resistance but after the ZIPRA forces had recovered from the shock of the bombardment, they rallied to provide a spirited defence. Two ZIPRA members hid in a village complex and although called on to surrender, carried on fighting. This was when three local Zambians were killed. All security force members were back by Saturday afternoon. ZIPRA members were captured and taken back to Rhodesia for interrogation. Two days later, the ZIPRA bases came under attack again.

Operation Dice, 16th–20th November 1979

Just after the middle of November came the last major operation outside the borders of Rhodesia. Rhodesian intelligence sources were concerned about the possibility of a conventional cross-border invasion being launched from Zambia. It seemed that the ZIPRA plan was to cross the border with large numbers of infantry and armoured vehicles. This column would punch its way through any opposition and seize the airfields at Wankie and Kariba. Backup forces would then be airlifted in using Libyan transport aircraft. Air support would be provided by Soviet MiG fighters piloted by ZIPRA pilots. The plan hinged on the attacking force reaching and capturing the city of Salisbury within 24 hours. In fact, although the transport aircraft had arrived, they had not been uncrated at this stage and the invasion was never launched.

It was decided that to counteract this threat, major bridges on main roads inside Zambia should be destroyed. The routes to be attacked included the road from Lusaka to Kafue, the main road south from Lusaka to Chirundu and the road from Lusaka to Livingstone.

Operation Dice was planned for 16th – 20th November. The SAS were tasked with not only blowing the bridges but also with mounting ambushes on the border approach roads. Air support took the form of Hunters, and Bell helicopters were used for transport together with Dakotas for parachuting and supply drops. The targets had been photo-reconnoitred before the operation. Teams were carried in Bells to points as close to the bridges as possible, in some cases the helicopters even landing on the bridge itself. Roadblocks were then set up to prevent civilians being injured. Charges were placed, bridges blown and the team was then choppered out. As a result of practice, the time taken from landing to take-off was reduced to 15 minutes.

A dangerous casevac

Ray Haakonsen of No 4 Squadron carried out a nerve-racking casevac in November when he transported a badly wounded African policeman to Andrew Fleming Hospital. The man had a massive wound in his lower back and a piece of metal was protruding. X-ray photographs confirmed that it was part of the tail fin of an RPG-7. Fearing that the metal might contain an explosive charge, doctors ordered that a section of Salisbury's Andrew Fleming Hospital be cleared. However, army bomb experts confirmed that there was no explosive in the wound and the tail fin was removed in a three-hour operation.

Cross-border action halted

Meanwhile the bargaining at Lancaster House was continuing and on 22nd November 1979, all cross-border action was halted. The remaining disagreements between the Zimbabwe-Rhodesia government and the Patriotic Front revolved around the removal of the white blocking mechanism, and the control of military, judicial and administrative power. The final sticking point was the technicality of the cease-fire. By 26th November 1979, Bishop Muzorewa had agreed to the creation of 14 assembly points for the Patriotic Front guerrillas and to the withdrawal of the Rhodesian army to barracks once a cease-fire came into operation.

The Patriotic Front held out until 5th December but then they too agreed to the terms offered. Finally, the monitoring force was increased to 1,300 men and the number of assembly points to 16. The plan was that a British appointed governor, Lord Soames, with both executive and legislative powers should rule the country during the period running up to a general election. The existing civil service and police force would be used to maintain law and order, while the Patriotic Front insurgents were to be confined to the 16 assembly points.

On 12th December, the British Governor Lord Soames arrived in Salisbury, and Rhodesia came under direct British rule for the first time in its history. The agreement on the new constitution had been signed but despite this, attacks on the white population intensified. The cease-fire was signed in London on 21st December and was due to come into effect on 28th December. Under the cease-fire terms, various assembly points were set up and the guerrillas were told to make their way to these points. One of these assembly points was situated in the Chiduku Tribal Trust Lands.

The final operation, 28th December 1979

For years, guerrillas operating in the Chiduku Tribal Trust Lands 150 kilometres east of Salisbury had used a large mountain called Ruombwe as a base. Because of its prominence, it was an ideal rendezvous point for insurgents infiltrating from Mozambique. The mountain,

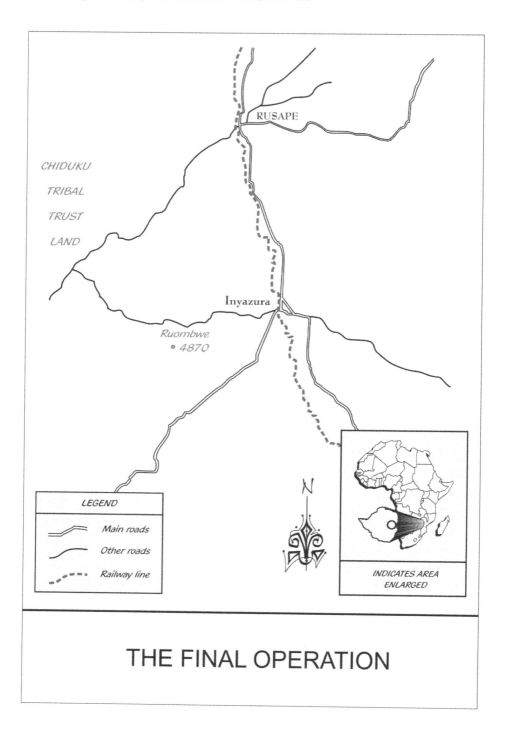

THE FINAL OPERATION

4,800 feet in height, lies eight kilometres from the Salisbury/Umtali road and provides an excellent view of the surrounding countryside. From Ruombwe the guerrillas could move into the European farmland around Inyazura. It was estimated that by 1978, about 500 insurgents fighting in the region were using this camp intermittently.

Late in December 1979, an African herder on a European farm bordering the Chiduku Tribal Trust Land, spotted a group of men moving across the farm and reported this to his employer. During the next four days, insurgent tracks were found on the farm, running west. It was obvious that there was large-scale movement taking place from Makoni Tribal Trust Land to Chiduku Tribal Trust Land. The farmer and a handful of his Africans sprang an ambush on a guerrilla group moving across the farm on 27th December, the night before the cease-fire was due to come into effect. The next morning, two Alouette III helicopters carried out an aerial search of Ruombwe but found nothing. Two counter-insurgency sticks from the police station at Rusape were dropped to the north of the mountain by chopper and carried out a sweep along its western face. They picked up the tracks of a large number of men leading up the steep south-western side of the mountain.

Early in the afternoon of 28th December, one of the police patrols came under fire and a fireforce was called in from Grand Reef. It comprised two K-Cars, one armed with 20mm cannon and the other with the Dalmation (alpha fit), a multiple .303 Browning mount, two Bell troop-carrying helicopters, a ground-strike Lynx and a Trojan with sky shout. When the fireforce arrived over the target at 14h45, the police patrol threw phosphorus grenades to mark its position.

The Lynx carried out two strikes with frantan. Then the K-Cars went in attacking across a wide front because the enemy were spread out. The insurgents returned fire with machine guns. While the duel between the Alouettes and the terrorists raged, the Bells deployed 30 RLI troops at the extreme northern tip of the mountain and these troops began to sweep the flank of the guerrilla line. One insurgent, nestled in a tree, pinned down an RLI stick with his machine gun. A fierce fight developed and the police patrol pulled back to the safety of a deserted kraal, from where it was uplifted by a Bell. The ground support Lynx returned from Grand Reef at sunset and once again revved the insurgents' positions with front gun, and dropped frantan. Despite this, the insurgents still kept up their fire, even putting in a mortar attack on an Alouette.

Two Hunters were unable to attack because the RLI sweep groups were too close to the enemy. They made a dummy run but called off the strike. At sunset the RLI sticks were uplifted back to Grand Reef. At midnight, the cease-fire came into effect.

At 02h00, two hours after the cease-fire, a company of 8th Battalion Rhodesia Regiment were deployed into the zone to cordon off the area. Early in the morning, a fireforce was dropped onto the mountain and swept it. One wounded guerrilla put up resistance. The rest had escaped in the dark and had made their way to St Anne's Mission. One of the interesting points about this engagement is that despite the intensity of the action, only 15 guerrillas were killed. This demonstrates very clearly the point that in broken country where there are rocky outcrops offering good cover to the men on the ground, aerial bombardment is largely ineffective. The guerrillas were in fact assembling their forces on Ruombwe before moving on to St Anne's Mission to the east and then to one of the Commonwealth forces assembly points for the cease-fire.

Cease-fire, 28th December 1979

With the coming into force of the cease-fire at midnight on 28th December 1979, the Rhodesian Air Force was grounded for three weeks. The final entry in No 4 Squadron Diary:

December 1979

Lynx: 545h05 Trojan: 17h05. Quiet month. Farewell Wing Commander John Bennie, Squadron Leader Alf Wilde, Carl Wilms, Rob Griffiths and Ken Turner.

The job of ensuring security was now up to the 1,300 men of the Commonwealth Cease-fire Monitoring Force. It was a task that they could not hope to perform and terrorism continued unabated. On Sunday, 13th January, Joshua Nkomo was greeted by a vast crowd of supporters when he flew into Salisbury. Two weeks later it was the turn of Robert Mugabe to receive songs of welcome from a huge crowd at Highfield Stadium. During the two-month period before the general election, intimidation was rife and discipline among ZANLA and ZIPRA members was practically non-existent.

Once again there was a complete mobilization and a 30-day call-up for all police personnel during the run-up to the general election which was held over three days: 27th, 28th, 29th February. The result was supposed to remain secret until it was announced to the public at 09h00 on Tuesday 4th March. In fact, the BBC began broadcasting the result soon after midnight local time. When confirmation came next morning, the BBC were only one seat out: ZANU (PF): 57; PF: 20; UANC: three. This, even with the 20 reserved white seats, gave ZANU (PF) an overall majority of 14.

One of the last events celebrated by the Rhodesian Air Force was the coming-of-age of No 5 Squadron and its durable Canberra bombers on 30th March 1980. Although the original squadron of 16 aircraft had shrunk to five, there was as yet no sign of the aircraft being retired. In fact, to celebrate the occasion, two Canberras made a 35-minute flight from New Sarum to Chiredzi, No 5 Squadron's affiliated town. It was the Canberras' first visit to their adopted home since 1975 and town officials welcomed the crews with a special lunch. By a happy chance, Squadron Leader Ted Brent, Officer Commanding No 5 Squadron had been one of the pilots who flew the Canberras from Britain in March 1959. Then a flight lieutenant, he didn't dream he would still be flying them in 1980. Dave Mew at 21, the squadron's youngest navigator had not been born when Squadron Leader Brent made that first flight. Of the eleven aircraft that were no longer in service, two were lost in action, two crashed because of mechanical failure and one went down as a result of bad weather. The rest simply became unserviceable.

At midnight on 17th April 1980, the new state of Zimbabwe came into being at a ceremony held in Rufaro Stadium and presided over by Prince Charles. Once again the air force changed its name. For the first time in more than 40 years, the word Rhodesia did not figure in the title. The name that was decided upon was the Air Force of Zimbabwe. Some air force members resigned immediately; others stayed on perhaps because they felt they had too much to lose or because they believed that they could influence the new regime. Until mid-1982, the air force remained a unit officered and controlled by Whites.

Then on 16th July 1982 came the attack on Thornhill Air Station with the resulting destruction of Zimbabwe's airstrike force. This event was followed by the arrest, torture, and detention without trial, for more than a year, of six white air force officers: Air Vice-Marshal Hugh Slatter, Air Commodore Phillip Pile, Wing Commander Peter Briscoe, Wing Commander John Cox, and Air Lieutenants Neville Weir and Barry Lloyd.* These men were subsequently found not guilty of any charge and released, having been deprived of any pension rights and their citizenship. These events signalled the end of the air force as an elite unit and the end of a proud history that spanned over 50 years.

---

* The full story of the arrest and torture of the air force officers can be found in *Sabotage and Torture* as told to Barbara Cole, and published by Three Knights Publishing, Amanzimtoti, RSA.

The remains of a Vampire FB 9 after it crashed at Kutanga Range following a weapons attack. The pilot Flt Lt Roy Hulley was killed. The cause of the accident was never established.

An Alouette III deploys a police detail with tracker dogs. These first exercises with dogs were done long before the war hotted up, as neither dustfilters nor anti-strela shrouds are fitted.

PRAW pilot Wally Barton and his wife Erica inspect the damage to the outside wall of their bedroom after a farm attack, an occurrence that had by then become commonplace. Wally was a prominent PRAW pilot who flew Mosquitoes during WWII. The onlookers are 'Brightlights' (farm security).

Note the damage to the nose of this Genet. The under wing stores are integral gun pods each of which houses a .762 machine gun.

The military version of the SF 260 Genet. The white tip tanks are in contradiction to the camouflage, but fuel evaporation was thought to be the cause of some engine failures. The paint kept the fuel at a lower temperature.

The early morning mist lends an eerie quality to the start of the day at a forward airfield. A Trojan, two Alouettes and a Lynx await what the day will bring.

On a narrow, wet, slippery bush airstrip it is well nigh impossible to keep one's direction. An Islander has a temporary unscheduled delay on its air task.

A hooded Warrior escapes the harmful sun at a forward airfield in the south-east. It was used as top cover for the convoys of civilian vehicles plying the route daily between Fort Victoria and Beit Bridge.

Wet airstrips are not easy in light aircraft, but in a Dakota there are added problems, although the Dak's balloon tyres keep it out of much of the trouble. Jerry Lynch lands on a road airstrip in the lowveld.

Lt-Col Peter Rich of the RLI, in his usual arms akimbo pose, listens intently, along with Sqn Ldr Steve Kesby, to Cocky Benecke's brief on a recent contact. The missing styrofoam cone of one of the rocket pods indicates that the weapon has been fired.

A re-supply by chopper to troops on ops or relays was always a pleasure for both parties. Honde View in the Eastern Highlands, overlooking Mozambique was one of the easier mountain LZs for an Alouette III.

Affretair's DC-7 in camouflage is hardly recognizable as the same aeroplane. The paint is just plain old PVA splashed on with brooms, and with no particular design in mind.

Affretair's sanction-busting DC-7 in normal livery with its sea horse logo on the tail.

The beautiful Spitfire F 22, gate guardian at New Sarum for many years, was taken down in the late '70s to be refurbished at Thornhill.

At Thornhill, the Spitfire was given pride of place on the Hunter hardstand. 1978. The war precluded Thornhill from doing the rebuild so the aircraft was dismantled and sent back to the Affretair hangar in Salisbury where Jack Malloch agreed to restore her to flying condition.

An informal gathering after the medals investiture conducted by President Wrathall, 16th February 1977. The relevant awards are in brackets. From left: Peter Cooke (DMM), Peter Simmonds (BCR), George Bavistock (DMM), Mike Borlace (SCR), The Hon John Wrathall, Mike Upton (BCR), Bill Jelley (DMM), Brian Smith (DMM), Eddy Wilkinson (DMM) and Cocky Benecke (SCR).

On 29th March 1980, Jack Malloch took to the air in the restored Spitfire PK350. Present were three air marshals, one Air Vice-Marshal, one air commodore and three group captains. From left: Charlie Paxton, Chris Dams, Johnny Deall, Dave Harvey, Frank Mussell, Jack Malloch, Archie Wilson, Mick McLaren, Des Anderson, Ossie Penton and John Mussell. All were Spitfire pilots. The Spitfire crashed on 26th March 1982 killing Jack Malloch the pilot.

Forty Alouette III helicopters of No 7 Squadron gather at lake Alexander in preparation for the biggest and most successful raid ever launched into enemy territory. As a result of the Chimoio raid, ZANLA had serious thoughts about capitulating.

Having struck power lines, the Dakota plunged onto the bank of the Lundi River south of Chiredzi. Squadron Leader Peter Barnett, Flt Lt Dave Mallett (ex-RAF) and Cpl Bradley (army) were killed. The others survived.

The remains of the original SR25 at Mapai airfield in Mozambique. The Dakota had just become airborne when it was hit by an RPG-7. The copilot, Bruce Collocott was killed; the captain, Jerry Lynch, the technician, Russell Wantenaar, and the passengers survived.

A 12.7mm machine gun and a B10 recoilless rifle are among a selection of weaponry seen here before they were taken back for use by the security forces.

One fewer anti-aircraft gun to worry about. Captured weapons were put to good use in airfield defence.

Left: Nine Hunters flying over Cecil Square on 22nd June 1977 for the opening of parliament.

Above: A public relations photograph features a GSU handler with his dog with a Provost aircraft taxiing past.

A normal day's work for the paraDak in the operational area. The dispatcher proceeds down the aisle of the Dakota checking the hook-up, before the green light to jump.

Aircraft taking off and landing were always vulnerable. An armoured car protects a Lynx getting airborne at Old Rutenga.

Security Training School, April 1977. From left, standing: AC Maheve, Sgt Gordon Drake, FS Paul Hill, FS André van der Walt, AC/W Rosie Kavanagh, Sgt Bob Jordaan. Seated: Cpl Solomon, Air Lt Ken Salter, (The Mouse), WO II Chimp Webster, FS Sake. Front: Sgt Don Junner, Sgt (TF) Chris Talbot, FS (TF) Howie Parker, Sgt (TF) Al McCrudden.

Best of the guard force versus the instructors at *Falling Plates* at the end of the day's instruction on the rifle range.

A new recruit is corrected by the GSU warrant officer. Their annual Inter-Station Drill Competition was an event not to be missed.

The first airwomen's intake, August 1977.

Sgt Gordon Pringle and Caesar II board an Alouette III for a familiarization flight.

The correct way to do it—the troops should already be on the runway waiting for the choppers. The choppers would then do a reduced power, dust-free, rolling take-off.

Ft Lt Ian Harvey is congratulated by OC Flying Wg Cdr Randy du Rand on the attainment of 3,000 hours on helicopters.

The choppers would take off from the revetment area and position opposite the army camp from where the troopies would emplane.

Over the vast open stretch of the lake one had to use the chopper ahead as a horizontal reference. The technician/gunner's view of his pilot and the lead aircraft.

The forward administration area was 225 kilometres inside Mozambique and just ten minutes from Tembué. The admin area with choppers on the ground can be seen on the left.

Supply drops of fuel and ammunition were a regular feature of the Tembué Raid.

Ample shade is provided by just one wing of the Dakota for the fully kitted-up troops on fireforce stand-by.

The Lynx overtakes the Dakotas in the Zambezi valley, in its eagerness to get to Tembué.

The Dakotas with full troops descend onto Lake Cabora Bassa on their final run-in to the target.

There were 14 choppers in Pink Section. Forty flew the 15 minutes across Lake Cabora Bassa on at least four occasions during the two-day raid. An aircraft with an engine failure must be able to reach land, thus a single-engine aircraft can't fly over water. In war, rules must be broken.

Flying back across the lake after the successful raid. Could that be the island that one of the helicopters had to land on to refuel?

With nose down and tail high, an Alouette III follows the rail line from Salisbury to Umtali.

The Dakota's task was to drop fuel to two Alouette IIIs on a max range uplift of SAS deep in Mozambique. Unfortunately, the Dakota wing tip hit a tree on coming in to land at Mabalauta. The bite out of the wing was temporarily repaired with blade tape and the fuel drums were dispatched successfully throughout the day. The formation made it back across the border fence well after dark. Ian Rodwell looks up.

An armed Lynx taxies out of FAF 8, Grand Reef, in support of a fireforce operation. The Dakota revetment wall is just about adequate at a height of five drums.

Rolling take-offs should be attempted on smooth surfaces only. Danny Svoboda holds the nose oleo after ripping it off on the rough Rutenga runway. Note the bent aerials and the mattresses under the fuselage. He smiles because he has just got himself a night stop in Salisbury to effect repairs.

Heavily laden the Islander didn't quite make it over the power lines, all onboard survived.

A photographic study of the robust undercarriage and wheel bay of the Dakota. The balloon tyres retract into the engine nacelles. The technician is working on the engine.

Another heavy landing—*If this continues I'll only be two feet tall at the end of the course.* Charlie Buchan smiles having completed the school's 5,000th jump.

Even though the war was a priority, there was always time for compassion. This mercy flight translocated a rhino that was undoubtedly saved from being killed for its valuable horn.

Henry Jarvie was killed instantly when this helicopter was crippled by gunfire north of FAF 5 (Mtoko). Norman Maasdorp the pilot whose feet were badly injured in the incident managed to put the chopper down safely. A heavy landing is invariably followed by the main rotor blades dipping down and removing the tail rotor drive shaft cover.

The two high points of the day at the old Rutenga airfield were the convoy on its way to Beit Bridge in the morning ...

... and the convoy on its way back in the afternoon. The machine gunner in the convoy comes under the usual ritual humiliation from the troops.

The convoy would have passed the burnt out shells of two vehicles attacked by terrorists the previous night south of Rutenga.

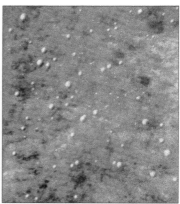

Ian Harvey and technician Sgt Thompson make it only 50 metres on a call-out at Grand Reef. The engine failed immediately after take-off causing superficial damage. Note how one of the blades has dipped down and removed the tail rotor drive shaft cover. The drums are to be used for a Dakota revetment.

Photographed from inside the bomb bay of a Canberra, 300 alpha bombs rain down onto the target on an actual cross-border raid. The bombs were designed to bounce back up to a height of about 15 feet before exploding.

The rising sun splashes off the port wing of a Dakota and the tension mounts as the attack force flies east. It will take just under an hour to cross the border into Mozambique and disgorge the paratroops to surround an enemy camp.

A Vampire T 11 is met by a team of technicians to refuel and re-arm. The 60-lb squashhead rockets were a pilot's dream as the explosion would thump the bottom of the aircraft on pull-out. A Belt Feed Mechanism (BFM) for the 20mm cannons lies on the tarmac near the rockets.

An engine change in the bush was done in a professional manner with the proper equipment. The Alouette III is designed for such eventualities. Technicians Paul Braun, Finch Bellringer and Frank Tyrrell complete their task at Bikita.

The Genet training aircraft was painted in a red and white colour scheme that not even a student pilot could mistake while flying in the training area.

A Dakota over Cabora Bassa on the way to Tembué.

The Hunter had a unique sound in a low level beat-up – a real morale booster for the troops at FAF 8.

The Hunter had a formidable array of weaponry: from back left: 130-pound concrete Cockle Shell, 1,000-pound GP bomb, (100 gallon drop tank), Golf Bomb with the 1m proboscis. Front left: 250-pound GP bomb, 68mm rocket pod, Frantan, belts of Aden 30mm cannon rounds and 68mm rockets. The 30mm Gun pack is central.

Safe in its revetment, the Lynx only has to be rolled forward a few feet to start up and taxi out for operations.

The 'Dalmatian' was the name given to the Alpha Fit, the South African designed hydraulically operated four Browning machine guns. The crews had mixed feelings about its effectiveness, and stoppages were a major problem. Many preferred the 20mm cannon.

Above right: Although there were other contributory factors to this Alouette III accident, the dangers of flying at night are only too apparent. The helicopter went in on its back seconds after taking off from FAF 4, at night and in poor weather. The pilot, André Senekal, was killed instantly.

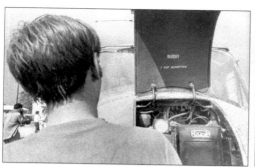

I eat Alouettes reads the comment on the Bell battery hatch. No 7 Squadron were quick to retaliate. They painted in large letters on the Bell landing pad at Grand Reef: *Matambanadzo Bus Service*

Flt Sgt Benji, master rat and snake catcher, herder of brown jobs and defender of the FAFs.

Harvey the Hornbill on the stabilizer of a chopper, one of his favourite perches at FAF 1 (Wankie Town). It was his eyes that haunted you.

Were they really that young?

The Salisbury fuel depot was attacked by terrorists, causing a fire that raged for days.

Heavy lifter, fighter, trainer—the full complement of helicopters over Henry Hallam Dam.

The Sidewinder missiles can be seen under the wings of one of the Hunters. They were never used in anger although on more than one occasion the opportunity did present itself.

The VIP Dakota takes off on runway 24 at New Sarum. There are no markings but the exhaust shrouds are clearly visible.

The *Hunyani* and *Umniati* Viscount incidents were a grim reminder that in modern warfare there are no civilians.

An Alouette III taxies out from Kariba Airport to fly to the *Umniati* crash, 11th February 1979. It is configured for hoisting.

The commander, Air Marshal F.W. Mussell stands upon the dais while the three army chaplains, Norman Woods, unknown, and Val Rajah bless and dedicate the No 7 Squadron Standard on 18th May 1979.

Not a soul for miles around—total tranquillity on a cool mountaintop in the Eastern Highlands.

The Canberra bomb bay is about to be filled with 300 deadly alpha bombs ...

... or six 1,000-pound general-purpose bombs.

Above: A Bell is hit by a bullet just below the pilot's windscreen. A little more to the right and things could have been different.

Below: The South African Air Force played a significant role in the April 1979 elections. A Puma picks up newsmen in a remote area of Rhodesia.

Jerry Lynch's shrapnel-spattered map was probably the result of the explosion of the hydraulic reservoir.

The Dakota engine was put on display in a park in Maputo.

Rhodesian troops cover the ground in the extended Operation Miracle. The air force played a large part in the destruction of this vast camp in Mozambique.

Opportunity photo—An RAF Puma has little difficulty in keeping up with a slow-flying Hercules C130 during the Monitoring Force visit.

A South African Puma helicopter comes in to land during the Monitoring Force exercise. The Rhodesian Air Force Dakota is waiting to uplift.

The Eland 90 is put to good use guarding the Zimbabwe-Rhodesia Broadcasting Studios. Note the initials on the building.

A tail rotor assembly gets attention.

At FAF 5 the endless servicing was carried out day or night, working until the job was done. Between call-outs the techs always had something to do.

Members of No 1 Squadron who took part in the second Mulungushi raid. From left: Brian Gordon, Varkie Varkevisser, Guy Dixon, Siggy Seegmuller, Dave Bourhill, Steve Kesby, Vic Wightman (OC), Ginger Baldwin and Tony Oakley.

The polished aluminium 'Silver Provost', with smoke generator, was a real crowd-pleaser in its many displays as a vintage aircraft.

Paradak painting – Artist: André du Plessis.

Between the first and second ranges of the four ranges of the Chimanimani mountains, two minutes by helicopter but four hours on foot, lies the beautiful Martin's Falls in Mozambique. This secluded Eden, close to the Arab traders' route, was frequented by No 7 Squadron in more peaceful times. Hugh Slatter is flying and Graham Cronshaw is not—but wishing he were ....

Selected bibliography

Cole, B. *The Elite: The Story of the Rhodesian Special Air Service. Amanzintoti*: Three Knights Publishing, 1984.

Flower, K. *Serving Secretly*. Galago Publishing (Pty) Ltd, 1987.

Ford, Brian. *German Secret Weapons: Blueprint for Mars*. Pan Books Ltd, 1972.

Frederikse, Julie. *None but Ourselves*. Braamfontein: Ravan Press (Pty) Ltd, 1982.

Hamence, M and Brent, W. *The Canberra in Southern Africa Service*. Nelspruit: Free World Publications, 1998.

History of the Second World War. Vols 2, 4, 5. Purnell.

Lovett, J. *Contact*. Galaxie Press, 1977.

Maule, Henry. *Great Battles of World War Two*. Hamlyn, 1972.

Macdonald, J F. *The War History of Southern Rhodesia 1939–1945*. Vols 1 and 2. Published by authority of the Government of Southern Rhodesia. Salisbury: Rhodesiana Reprint Library, 1947.

Moorcraft, P L. *Contact 1 & Contact 2*. Johannesburg: Sygma Books, 1981.

Phillips, N V. *Bush Horizons: The Story of Aviation in Southern Rhodesia 1896–1940*. Harare: Conlon Printers (Pty) Ltd, 1998.

Reid-Daly, R. *Selous Scouts: Top Secret War*, Alberton: Galago, 1983.

Verrier, Anthony. *The Bomber Offensive*. Revised ed. London: Pan Books Ltd, 1974.

Rhodesia Herald, later *The Herald*.

Bulawayo Chronicle

Bateleur.

Flight.

Ndege.

Index

PHOTOGRAPHS
Some photographs appear on pages of the text, but most
are grouped together.
Group A (photo pages A-1 to A-32) is between text
pages 176 and 177.
Group B (photo pages B-1 to B-16) is between text
pages 324 and 324.
Group C (photo pages C-1 to C-16) is between text
pages 438 and 439.
Group D (photo pages D-1 to D-16) is between text
pages 574 and 575.
Group E (photo pages E-1 to E-16) is between text
pages 698 and 699.

NOTES TO INDEX
1. For information on individual schools set up under
EATS/RATG, see under the names of the stations.
2. Where a person's rank is given, that is the rank
he held at the time when he is first mentioned.
Subsequent promotions are not necessarily indexed.
3. Aircraft types are listed under the names of the
manufacturers.
4. Names beginning with "Mac" or "Mc" are listed as
though they begin "Mac..."
5. If abbreviations are used, the entry appears where it
would if the word(s) were spelled out in full.
6. References to the Royal Rhodesian Air Force before
the "Royal" prefix was dropped will be found under
"Rhodesian Air Force".

The late **Beryl Salt** was born in London in 1931. She immigrated to Southern Rhodesia in 1952 to get married in Salisbury, where her two sons were born. In 1953 she joined the Southern Rhodesian Broadcasting Services (later the Rhodesian Broadcasting Corporation, the RBC). With a love of history she wanted to find out as much as she could about her new country. This interest led to radio dramas and feature programmes, followed by several books: *School History Text Book*, *The Encyclopaedia of Rhodesia* and *The Valiant Years*, a history of the country as seen through the newspapers. She also produced a dramatized radio series about the Rhodesian Air Force. In 1965 she left the RBC and spent three years with the Ministry of Information, following which she was a freelance writer/broadcaster involved in a wide variety of projects until 1980 when she moved to Cape Town. She died in England in November 2001.

Lightning Source UK Ltd.
Milton Keynes UK
UKHW02f1449150818
327295UK00005B/112/P